International Equity Markets –
The Art of the Deal

International Equity Markets –
The Art of the Deal

Robert Lilja

Published by Euromoney Books

Published by
Euromoney Publications PLC
Nestor House, Playhouse Yard
London EC4V 5EX

Telephone: +44 (171) 779 8888

Typeset by Julie Foster
Printed in England by BPC Wheatons Ltd.

About the author

Born in Stockholm, Sweden in 1956, Mr John Robert Lilja left his home country in 1976 and has since lived in Germany, Switzerland, South Africa, the United States and the UK. Following business studies at the St Gallen business school in Switzerland, Mr Lilja joined the Anglo American Corporation in Johannesburg, where he worked for three years in the Gold and Finance divisions. In 1985 Mr Lilja took up his investment banking career with Credit Suisse First Boston. After having spent six months in the New York office, Mr Lilja relocated to the London office, where he spent more than eight years in the corporate finance department. During this time, Mr Lilja assisted multinational corporations with the full range of corporate financings and strategic transactions such as acquisitions, divestitures etc., however, he spent the majority of his time advising corporations on how to tap the international equity market. Mr Lilja was promoted to Director-Investment Banking in 1991 and resigned in May 1994 to write this book.

Contents

Preface   **xi**

Acknowledgements   **xiii**

Chapter 1 **Introduction**   **1**

Definition of a successful equity offering   1
How the book is structured   2
Potential readers   2
How the research was carried out   2

Chapter 2 **Market development**   **3**

Chapter 3 **The case studies**   **9**

I **Akzo**   11
    ■ FEATURE TOPIC: The pros and cons of a managed rights offer and a bookbuilt issue   19
    ■ FEATURE TOPIC: How to do a bought deal   21

II **Argentaria**   27
    ■ FEATURE TOPIC: Getting a global deal done   37
    ■ FEATURE TOPIC: Deal economics   38

III **BNP**   42
    ■ FEATURE TOPIC: The formation of a core shareholder group in French privatisations   53
    ■ FEATURE TOPIC: Institutional investor views on privatisation   54

IV **Bulgari**   58
    ■ FEATURE TOPIC: The role of the 'due diligence' process for a medium-sized company IPO –   69
    the perspectives of the company and the lead sponsor

V **China Steel**   71

VI **Daimler-Benz**   84
    ■ FEATURE TOPIC: The significance of the discount in a rights issue   99

VII **Société Nationale Elf Aquitaine**   102
    ■ FEATURE TOPIC: Targeting the US investor base   118

VIII **Empresa Nacional de Electricidad**   121

IX **ENI**   132

X   **KPN**   147
■ FEATURE TOPIC: The role and usefulness of an independent adviser   159

XI   **Mayr-Melnhof Karton**   162
■ FEATURE TOPIC: Lessons from Mayr-Melnhof's profit warning   175

XII   **Nokia**   180
■ FEATURE TOPIC: Hitting the Big Board – Lessons from Nokia's listing on the NYSE   193

XIII   **Pharmacia**   196
■ FEATURE TOPIC: The tortuous prelude to the Pharmacia privatisation   211
■ FEATURE TOPIC: How to maximise retail demand in connection with a privatisation   215

XIV   **Railtrack**   217
■ FEATURE TOPIC: The role of the marketing adviser: an interview with Cary Martin, CEO of Dewe Rogerson   238
■ FEATURE TOPIC: Key facts of the Tory privatisation programme   241

XV   **Repsol**   243
■ FEATURE TOPIC: Recapturing the European retail investor – three major innovations in retail offering technology in the 1995 Repsol offering   255

XVI   **Roche**   259
■ FEATURE TOPIC: The US listing decision for non-US companies – IAS versus US GAAP   270

XVII   **Shandong Huaneng Power Development Corporation**   272
■ FEATURE TOPIC: The re-emergence of the Chinese securities market   287

XVIII   **Singapore Telecommunications**   291

XIX   **Tele Danmark**   305
■ FEATURE TOPIC: The role of the equity research analyst in a global equity offer – the approach adopted by Robert Morris of Goldman Sachs   319
■ FEATURE TOPIC: Tele Danmark's investor relations – an interview with the head of IR   322

XX   **Telecom Corporation of New Zealand**   324
■ FEATURE TOPIC: Pursuing a dual-track strategy   337

XXI   **USX - Marathon Group**   339
■ FEATURE TOPIC: Introduction to targeted stock   349

XXII   **Wellcome**   357
■ FEATURE TOPIC: Short selling in connection with global equity offers. What does it mean? When does it occur? Should it be stopped and how can it be prevented?   369
■ FEATURE TOPIC: The 1995 sale by the Wellcome Trust of its remaining 39.5 per cent interest in Wellcome plc to Glaxo, and Glaxo's subsequent full bid for Wellcome plc   371

XXIII   **YPF**   375

XXIV   **Zeneca**   390

Chapter 4   **The top banks**   **411**
International issuance by region and over time   412
Truly international banks   413
Market concentration   413
The leading houses in each region in 1996   414
Global equity research capability   415

Interviews with the European heads of ECM of the five leading houses during 1991–96
- Credit Suisse First Boston 415
- Goldman Sachs 419
- Merrill Lynch 422
- Morgan Stanley Dean Witter Discover 426
- SBC Warburg Dillon Read 428
The performance in the global equity new issue market of the top five houses 431

Chapter 5 The investor perspective 435
The investors 435
What companies should know about the institutions 438
Institutional investor views on the new issue process 438
The role of the new issue market in institutional investment 450
Lessons for company executives 451

Chapter 6 Getting the offering process right – the Art of the Deal 453
Preparation of assets for sale and appointment of parties 453
Preparation of the offer 456
Pricing and underwriting methods 457
Other preparatory steps 458
Execution of the offer 459
Immediate after-market/ongoing secondary market 460

Chapter 7 Conclusion 463
Supply and demand factors in market development 463
The core considerations: a word to the vendor 465

Glossary 467

Appendices 481
Non-US companies listed on the New York Stock Exchange 481
List of interviewees 487

Preface

Having spent almost 9 years in an environment where all I thought about was 'the deal', either the deal I was just competing for, the one I just missed, the deal my bosses wanted me to get but I didn't think that important, the deal I badly wanted to win myself, the one I had just done, the deal I was just doing , the many deals I hoped to do next year, the deal my competitors messed up and that we would have done a lot better, the deal I lost and therefore claimed I didn't want anyway, or the deal that shouldn't have been done, it seemed sensible to step back, pause for a while, reflect and again regain a healthy perspective on the investment banking business.

At the time, it seemed to me that a large amount had been written about bonds, foreign exchange etc. but nothing much about the global distribution of equity. Many books had been written on privatisations but, to the best of my knowledge, nobody had attempted the task of writing about how these deals are actually done.

I doubted this would be an easy task. First, these deals are more of an art than a science (hence the title of the book) and, second, unless I was going to get sufficient access to a broad range of people, this book was never going to add significant value. I am consequently very grateful to all those who gave their time and energy to present me with the information that I needed and I hope that the book manages to capture some of the artistry and flair that it takes to bring these transactions to a successful conclusion.

Aside from the fact that it had not been done before, the most important reason for embarking on this particular project was the fact that there appeared to me to be so much time and energy lost, so much mistrust between banker and client and so much misdirected thought going on in this particular market segment of investment banking.

Bankers simply did just about anything, or were pushed to do anything, to get a mandate, whilst the buyers of these services who listened to investment banking presentations did not believe half of what they heard. Intelligent people spent an inordinate amount of time preparing to make a presentation or a pitch with relatively low odds of winning and the audience was highly suspicious of the advice given.

I therefore hope that this book will contribute to a somewhat deeper understanding among potential users of the global equity market and help clients see through the bias of the presenting banks. If that is so, I will feel that my efforts have been worthwhile. If potential vendors become more educated buyers of this type of service, then they will only ask those banks to present their credentials that clearly have the capacity to do a good job. In essence, what I am saying is that a more intelligent acquisition of this type of service can lead to a much better end result for the client. Excessive competition among investment banks leads to unrealistic expectations on the part of the client in terms of what can be done in the market and this, in turn, can have highly adverse effects for individual transactions and entire privatisation programmes. I am for less competition, but more intelligent competition. It is my hope that a broad group of potential users will find this book a helpful tool for gaining a better understanding of this subject matter and a better end result. It is also my hope that the investor community will gain valuable insights into the offering process.

Robert Lilja

Acknowledgements

I want to thank H-J. Rudloff, former Chairman of CSFB in Europe and grand man of the Euromarkets for giving me an opportunity to work in the securities industry. I want to thank my dear friend and mentor Wolfgang Schürer for putting me in touch with the Euromoney organisation and Neil Osborn, the publisher of Euromoney magazine for introducing me to the book publishing unit of Euromoney Publications.

My sincere thanks go to all the companies, governments and other vendors from New Zealand, Taiwan and China in the East to the US, Chile and Argentina in the West that are represented as case studies, for taking such a keen interest in the project, for trusting me with confidential and sensitive information and for working with me in ensuring a very high degree of quality control of the case study materials. Special thanks go to all parties who were interviewed for the non-published case studies.

I owe sincere gratitude to the heads of equity capital markets of the banks that I have worked most closely with, namely Credit Suisse First Boston, Goldman Sachs, Merrill Lynch, Morgan Stanley Dean Witter Discover and SBC Warburg Dillon Read. These bankers in particular offered their very real support to this project over a period of almost three years – thank you very much for your patience and tremendous goodwill. I would also like to thank all other bank representatives who kindly made themselves available for interviews and consultation. I must thank especially all the younger bankers, all other assisting personnel, all secretaries and all library personnel who tirelessly helped me realise my dream project by locating all the documents, facts and figures required to underpin the analysis. You have done most of the hard work whilst getting the least direct exposure in the book. For that reason alone, I am particularly grateful.

Special acknowledgement goes to all institutional investors, who have kindly provided their perspectives on individual new issues and on the new issue process overall. This dialogue has played an important role in providing the reader with a complete picture of the new issue process. If the readers will be able to benefit only to the extent of a small fraction of what I have learnt from our discussions, my ambition will have been more than fulfilled.

I also want to thank all my friends in the securities industry and my personal friends who have helped me and encouraged me, be it in the context of interviews, through the provision of insights, perspectives, facts or 'war stories' about the industry and how it really works or for reading and commenting on the manuscript. I want to thank in particular Olof Clausson, David Englefield, Verne Grinstead and Håkan Strängh for making highly significant contributions.

I am most grateful to my sub-editors Will Goodhart and Robert Bentley for their considerable efforts to restructure and clarify the manuscript. I also want to thank the entire team at Euromoney Books for their hard work of getting this very comprehensive manuscript into shape.

I want to thank my parents for supporting me and encouraging me to finish this ambitious project and generally always being there for me. The fact that I have never doubted that you are fully behind me, no matter what, has given me a sense of security to finish the task at hand. I want to thank my wife Mari for believing in me and for giving me the confidence to complete this project. You have on endless occasions – be it on hot summer days or during public holidays – strengthened my resolve. You have encouraged me to believe that it was worthwhile to sacrifice so much for the completion of the book. Being a stockbroker, you have also given me invaluable feed-back on the materials produced and generally helped enhance the quality of the book. I love you and adore you for all that you have done.

A list of the people interviewed and those who have made substantial direct contributions to the manuscript are included in the Appendices.

Introduction

This book is intended to provide a number of useful lessons as to how to structure and execute a successful international equity transaction, as well as pointing out what was wrong with those deals that failed to meet their objective. It is therefore important to try to reach a definition of what exactly constitutes a 'successful' equity issue.

Definition of a successful equity offer

Share price performance

For the investor community, share price performance is the major indicator of success. While investors want the best possible performance, the best outcome for all parties is a moderate and stable share price appreciation following the pricing of the issue, as the vendor does not want to sell at too low a price. It may be of considerable value to the company to be seen to be generous on pricing. Too rapid a share price appreciation may induce investors to take immediate profits, adding only limited value to the offer. Ideally the share price should outperform the local market and comparable companies.

If the offer is one of shares that are already being traded, then the share price should not decline between announcement and pricing. The share price should experience a modest rise and should not underperform the local index or comparable companies.

Investment banks are under particular pressure during the first three days after the pricing of the issue to be seen to be in control of the offer in terms of the required share price performance and remain under pressure for the entire stabilisation period, ie, the first 30 days of trading. Pressure is then slowly transferred to the company, although the bank will retain a degree of responsibility for the performance of the offer during a period of up to 12 months. Some bankers argue that they feel responsible for the share price performance for even longer.

Transaction size

From the company's or the vendor's point of view, the transaction size is of significant importance. It is a clear sign of a successful transaction if the offer size can be increased and the greenshoe exercised without a negative impact on the share price performance, (bankers' enthusiasm for increasing deal size and exercising greenshoe options can often have negative implications for after-market share price performance).

Trading volume

While it is important to establish a liquid trading market in the securities offered, a very high turnover in the immediate after-market of an offer is normally a sign that something has gone wrong – the quality of placement was not good enough, the allocation was of sub-optimal quality or the share price performed too well or too badly. Although trading volumes in the immediate after-market vary significantly from market to market, a turnover during the first three days following the pricing of an issue which exceeds 15–25 per cent of the shares offered is considered relatively high.

Distribution

It is important that the distribution is sufficiently wide without being too wide: key institutions must be allocated enough shares to be in a position to establish a core holding and there must be a good geographical spread to avoid too high a percentage of the shares being placed within a single investment centre, as this can lead to considerable share price volatility. In privatisations it is politically important to place offers with the maximum number of retail investors possible. It is typically an indication of success if the proportion of the offer placed with retail customers is increased between the time of announcement and the final sizing and pricing. As it increases, confidence grows among institutional investors that the whole offer will be a success. It is, however, important that this is not done at the expense of institutional allocations to such an extent that institutions sell in the immediate after-market and fail to support the next privatisation. The relevant benchmark for success is typically set by prior offers from the same country. In the case of privatisations another sign of success is if a high proportion of an issue has been placed with company employees.

Timing

It is a sign of considerable success if the offer is seen to have been well timed in terms of offering the right shares (in terms of industry sector), from the right national market, with the right structure and at the right price. That notwithstanding, timing can often be more luck than skill, due to the long lead time of international equity offers.

This book seeks to highlight the factors that led to the success, or failure, of a number of the major international equity issues of recent years. The lessons that can be learned from the case studies encompass both technical issues and problems arising from human nature.

How the book is structured

Following this introductory chapter, Chapter 2 aims to give the reader an insight into the development of the overall global equity new issue market, which will make it possible to see the case studies in perspective.

The core section of this book, Chapter 3, is made up of the case studies and opens with a brief explanation of the means of their selection. All the case studies are identically structured to facilitate selective reading and many include a 'feature topic'. The feature topics were chosen on the grounds that they represented an important feature of that particular transaction and illustrated a point of more general interest, but could not be covered fully in the case study. For example, short selling in connection with secondary offers was chosen as a special feature topic for the 1992 Wellcome offer as it was a major issue at the time and continues to be of concern to many potential vendors.

Chapters 4 and 5 offer the bank and investor perspectives respectively; chapters 6 and 7 summarise and draw conclusions.

Potential readers

Corporate CEOs and CFOs

This book is primarily targeted at CEOs and CFOs of companies which are considering tapping the global equity market, whether in the context of raising new capital or being sold by somebody else, be it in connection with a privatisation or otherwise. It is as relevant for CEOs or CFOs of large companies as it is for those of medium-sized or smaller ones. The book considers the key issues relevant to state-owned companies as well as those owned by institutional investors or families. Making the right decisions when selling equity privately or publicly is one of the most crucial strategic tasks that senior company executives have to face, regardless of who owns the company. It is the author's experience that CEOs and CFOs without prior experience in this market grossly underestimate the complexity, sensitivity and time requirements of selling equity successfully in public markets. This is most often the case when bankers do not stress in their marketing the time commitment required from senior management.

Privatisation ministry officials

Experienced officials in the most active privatisation ministries around the world are among the most knowledgeable market participants both because they may have undertaken a significant number of offers themselves and because they are extensively briefed by the banking community. It is the author's belief that this book goes deeper than many of the briefings offered by the banking community as those briefings tend to focus primarily on distribution and major structural issues at the expense of other important aspects. The truth is that banks do not generally want to talk about problem areas in their own offers and those banks that were not involved in a particular offer simply do not know what the real issues were.

The banking and advisory communities

Whereas it was not originally my intention to address bankers, brokers, lawyers, accountants and other professional advisers involved in these offers, I now believe that this book represents a highly relevant work also for them. New recruits entering the advisory or investment banking business will learn a lot about new equity issues in particular and investment banking in general. Senior advisers will, I hope, enjoy reading about their own and other peoples' transactions. I trust that in particular the 'Investor Perspective' chapter should be of considerable interest to the equity research and equity sales communities.

Institutional investors

Although the equity new issue market represents a relatively small part of the business of most institutional investors, the case studies in this book offer a valuable insight into the workings of the new issue market.

As well as examining the way in which investors view the new issue market, how they can be more successful in it and how they can avoid some of its pitfalls, the book also discusses the assessment criteria that experienced institutional investors apply to cross-border equity investment.

Students of finance

Business school students wishing to embark on a career in investment banking in general, and the capital markets in particular, will find the book a valuable source of background material. It should give such students a very good understanding of the international equity market and the players involved.

How the research was carried out

All of the principal parties involved in each transaction – the vendors, the senior company management and the principal bankers involved – have been consulted about each case study, and extensive follow-up with all interviewees has been carried out, ensuring a high level of quality and accuracy. It was important to talk to all these parties in order to achieve impartiality.

A good deal of persistence, the fact that I had a good understanding of investment banking and the corporate world, and my undertaking to respect what was discussed both on and off the record, were the key elements of my methodology. The response exceeded all expectations: not one vendor, company or bank declined to be interviewed. No single party central to any of the particular case studies declined to talk and there were only two cases in which I did not visit the companies and the domestic bankers. In those cases I either interviewed the relevant people over the telephone or met them in London. The interviews were thus, with very few exceptions, conducted in one-on-one meetings in offices around the world. The author's air miles programme has benefited hugely.

Market development

The overall growth of the global market for cross-border equity issuance has been spectacular throughout the 1990s – far exceeding world economic growth. Over the six years to 1996 the annual average growth in international equity issuance – the sale of shares outside the domestic market – has amounted to 26.5 per cent. This was achieved despite a tightening of US monetary policy between 1994 and 1995 which led to a small reduction in world-wide issuance in 1995 (see Exhibit 2.1).

Compounded growth in the cross-border market as a whole (including the domestic tranches of global cross-border offers) over the past four years was a healthy 12.2 per cent per year (see Exhibit 2.2).

This tremendous growth is a result both of increased breadth, in terms of a broader variety of issuers from a larger number of countries and increased depth, in terms of the size of offer that can be achieved. The latter is illustrated by the number of transactions launched that were larger than US$1 billion. Whereas in 1991 there were only six transactions larger than US$1 billion, the equivalent figure was 29 in 1996. The fact that the number of corporate jumbo issues has increased faster than the number of large privatisation issues underscores the increasing maturity of the market (see Exhibit 2.3).

In terms of the origin of the issuers, the growth in international issuance over the six years to 1996 has been most spectacular in Europe, Africa and the Middle East, and Australasia and Japan. Growth in the international issuance of US companies was healthy but unspectacular while Latin American issuance was actually lower in 1996 than in 1991. Although the Latin American markets were effectively closed in 1995, there was a strong recovery in 1996 and it is likely that the pattern of strong underlying growth will continue in 1997 (see Exhibit 2.4).

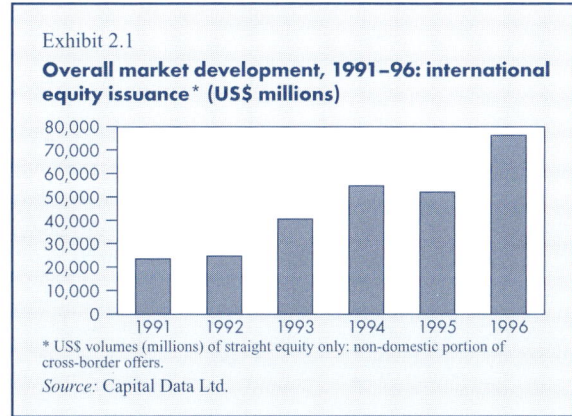

Exhibit 2.1

Overall market development, 1991–96: international equity issuance* (US$ millions)

* US$ volumes (millions) of straight equity only: non-domestic portion of cross-border offers.

Source: Capital Data Ltd.

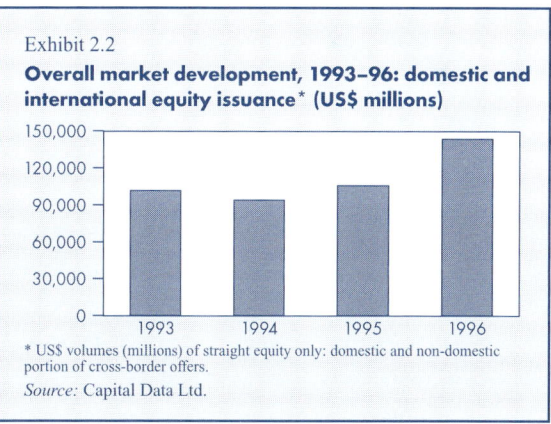

Exhibit 2.2

Overall market development, 1993–96: domestic and international equity issuance* (US$ millions)

* US$ volumes (millions) of straight equity only: domestic and non-domestic portion of cross-border offers.

Source: Capital Data Ltd.

Exhibit 2.3

Number of US$1 billion plus deals, 1991–96*

	1991	1992	1993	1994	1995	1996	Total
Privatisations	4	4	8	11	12	12	51
Corporate transactions	2	6	9	4	8	17	46
Total	**6**	**10**	**17**	**15**	**20**	**29**	**97**

* Privatisations involving the sale of more than one company simultaneously (e.g. the UK electricity generating companies) have been counted as one transaction. The figure includes one bought deal and three rights issues.

Exhibit 2.4
Geographic diversity, 1991–96: international equity issuance*

	1991	1992	1993	1994	1995	1996	Total
North America	6,594	8,534	13,179	6,064	11,771	10,801	56,943
Europe/Africa/Middle East	11,013	8,839	15,426	31,409	30,754	48,077	145,518
Australasia (including Japan)	2,079	3,396	5,965	12,672	8,973	13,855	46,940
Latin America	3,891	3,964	6,077	4,671	636	3,563	22,802
Total market	**23,577**	**24,733**	**40,647**	**54,816**	**52,134**	**76,296**	**272,203**

* US$ volumes (million) of straight equity only, non-domestic portion of cross-border offers.

Source: Capital Data Ltd.

Exhibit 2.5
Geographic diversity, 1993–96: domestic and international equity issuance*

	1993	1994	1995	1996	Total
North America	52,672	27,518	44,001	48,711	172,902
Europe/Africa/Middle East	30,784	44,292	46,952	69,706	191,734
Australasia (including Japan)	10,347	16,139	13,775	20,482	60,743
Latin America	7,826	6,013	1,023	4,603	19,465
Total market	**101,629**	**93,962**	**105,751**	**143,502**	**444,844**

* US$ volumes (million) of straight equity only, domestic and non-domestic portion of cross-border offers.

Source: Capital Data Ltd.

Exhibit 2.6
The importance of the privatisation business, 1991–96: international equity issuance*

	1991	1992	1993	1994	1995	1996	Total
Privatisations	5,665	4,649	12,009	22,291	16,449	22,548	83,611
% of total market	24%	19%	30%	41%	32%	30%	31%
Total market	**23,577**	**24,733**	**40,647**	**54,816**	**52,134**	**76,296**	**272,203**

* US$ volumes (million) of straight equity only; non-domestic portion of cross-border offers.

Source: Capital Data Ltd.

Exhibit 2.7
IPOs versus non-IPOs, 1991–96: international equity issuance*

	1991	1992	1993	1994	1995	1996
IPOs	10,216	7,345	17,151	23,633	25,912	30,174
% of total market	43%	30%	42%	43%	50%	40%
Total market	**23,577**	**24,733**	**40,647**	**54,816**	**52,134**	**76,295**

* US$ volumes (million) of straight equity only; non-domestic portion of cross-border offers.

Source: Capital Data Ltd.

European issuers accounted for 47 per cent of the total international market in 1991, and 63 per cent in 1996. Australasia (including Japan) accounted for 9 per cent and 18 per cent in the same years.

Taking the domestic tranches of cross-border offers into account, we see that while US and Latin American issuance fell between 1993 and 1996, in Europe it more than doubled, and in Asia it very nearly doubled (see Exhibit 2.5).

Between 1991 and 1996, the proportion of the total market accounted for by privatisations increased from 24–30 per cent. In 1994 privatisations accounted for no less than 41 per cent of the total market (see Exhibit 2.6).

A further sign that the market is broadening is the fact that in terms of international equity issuance, the proportion of the total market accounted for by IPOs – new companies coming to the market – increased steadily over the four years to 1995, before falling back in 1996 (see Exhibit 2.7).

There has been spectacular growth in the European IPO market, with issuance increasing from US$8.9 billion in 1993, to US$34.4 billion in 1996, when the European market for

Exhibit 2.8

Geographic distribution of IPOs, 1993–96: domestic and international equity issuance*

	1993	1994	1995	1996
North America	24,187	13,162	17,788	20,422
Europe/Middle East/Africa	8,891	20,846	24,748	34,421
Asia-Pacific/Japan	7,598	7,944	8,089	6,638
Latin America	5,165	1,913	222	1,785
Total IPO market	**45,841**	**43,865**	**50,847**	**63,266**

* US$ volumes (million) of straight equity only; domestic and non-domestic portion of cross-border offers.

Source: Capital Data Ltd.

Exhibit 2.9

Geographic distribution of corporate and privatisation IPOs, 1993–96: domestic and international equity issuance* (%)

	1993	1994	1995	1996
North American corporate issues	100	100	91	100
North American privatisations	–	–	9	–
European corporate issues	42	33	51	51
European privatisations	58	67	49	49
Asia-Pacific corporate issues	62	47	45	82
Asia-Pacific privatisations	38	53	55	18
Latin American corporate issues	37	66	100	43
Latin American privatisations	63	34	–	58

* Domestic and non-domestic portion of cross-border offers, straight equity only.

Source: Capital Data Ltd.

---

cross-border IPOs was actually 69 per cent larger than in the US (see Exhibit 2.8).

As far as Europe is concerned, privatisations no longer dominate the IPO market, as corporate IPOs now represent as large a portion of the total European IPO market as do privatisation IPOs. Nobody can dispute the role of privatisations in the development of the continental European IPO market, where historically they have dominated the new issue calendar in terms of volume, as well as making an important contribution to the overall development of the market by encouraging corporate IPO activity. Privatisations help expand the total size and liquidity of the market and develop the sophistication of local banks and investors.

The Asian IPO market has been dominated by the corporate sector and privatisations have played only a minor role. Asian governments have not been under much pressure to sell state assets and have been able to wait for favourable terms (see Exhibit 2.9).

Another way of analysing the market is to look at what proportion of the total new issue volume is represented by companies raising new money as opposed to restructuring by way of a sale of outstanding shares.

Exhibit 2.10 suggests that the rate of growth in restructurings (secondary issues) has now overtaken new money raising (primary issues). In recent years companies worldwide have felt shareholder pressure to realise value for shareholders by means of the sale of minority and majority stakes. Concentration on the core businesses and the maximisation of shareholder value have become key business themes.

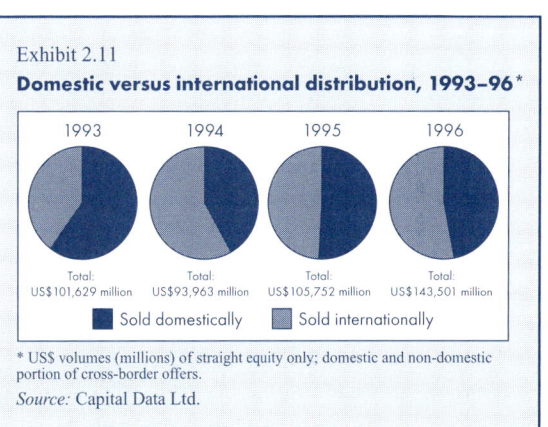

Exhibit 2.10

Primary versus secondary issuance, 1993–96: domestic and international issuance*

1993   1994   1995   1996

Total: US$101,629 million   Total: US$93,963 million   Total: US$105,752 million   Total: US$143,501 million

■ Primary issues   ■ Secondary issues   ■ Primary/secondary

* US$ volumes (millions) of straight equity only; domestic and non-domestic portion of cross-border offers.

Source: Capital Data Ltd.

Exhibit 2.11

Domestic versus international distribution, 1993–96*

1993   1994   1995   1996

Total: US$101,629 million   Total: US$93,963 million   Total: US$105,752 million   Total: US$143,501 million

■ Sold domestically   ■ Sold internationally

* US$ volumes (millions) of straight equity only; domestic and non-domestic portion of cross-border offers.

Source: Capital Data Ltd.

Over the four years to 1996 half of the total global cross-border issue volume has been sold domestically and half has been sold internationally. This global average obviously masks some very important variations: in the US 20 per cent of cross-border corporate equity offers are typically sold internationally, as in French and UK privatisations; in less developed continental European markets such as Italy and Spain, the equivalent figure in recent years has been closer to 50 per cent; in smaller countries such as Denmark and Austria, it has not been uncommon for up to 80 per cent of cross-border offers to be sold in the international market (see Exhibit 2.11).

The lion's share of privatisations has taken place in telecommunications, oil and gas, and bank/financial services; three industries which alone accounted for as much as one third of the total cross-border equity market during the four years to 1996 (see Exhibit 2.12).

The most important issuing counties are the US (by a wide margin), followed by the UK, France, Germany, the Netherlands and Italy. Whereas in the US the issue volume is wholly accounted for by the corporate sector, in the UK and other large European countries, privatisations have played a much bigger role. In Germany one privatisation alone – Deutsche Telekom – accounted for more than US$11 billion out of the

---

Exhibit 2.12

Domestic and international equity issuance by industry, 1993–96* (US$ million)

1	Telecoms/communications	69,288
2	Oil/coal/gas	41,293
3	Bank/financial services	36,058
4	Retailing/consumer goods	29,685
5	Insurance	28,436
6	Automotive	17,833
7	Electronics/electricals	17,728
8	Healthcare/pharmaceuticals	19,678
9	Energy/utility	17,377
10	Computer/software	15,116
	Total market	**444,844**

* These figures include the domestic and non-domestic portions of cross-border straight equity offers.

Source: Capital Data Ltd.

Exhibit 2.13

Country of issuer: domestic and international issuance, 1993-96* (US$ volumes)

1	US	159,764
2	UK	34,539
3	France	29,707
4	Germany	26,343
5	Netherlands	23,294
6	Italy	20,684
7	Sweden	12,361
8	Spain	11,683
9	Canada	8,532
10	Australia	8,199
	Total market	**444,844**

* These figures include the domestic and non-domestic portions of cross-border straight equity offers.

Source: Capital Data Ltd.

Exhibit 2.14

Compression of gross spreads, 1993–96 (%) *

	1993	1994	1995	1996
Privatisation IPOs	3.51	3.28	3.09	2.46
Privatisation non-IPOs	2.50	3.24	2.38	2.92
Corporate IPOs	5.18	4.70	4.54	4.43
Corporate non-IPOs	3.54	3.57	3.23	3.43
Total market	**3.88**	**3.65**	**3.53**	**3.51**

* Calculated on straight cross-border equity offers over US$100 million where fees were disclosed. The average gross spreads are calculated on a weighted basis.

Source: Capital Data Ltd.

Exhibit 2.15

Level of concentration in the international equity market, 1991–96: international equity issuance*

	1991	1992	1993	1994	1995	1996	Total
% of market accounted for by the 5 most active houses in each individual year	60%	59%	51%	46%	51%	46%	50%
% of market accounted for by the 10 most active houses in each individual year	77%	76%	72%	69%	74%	66%	71%

* US$ volumes of straight equity only; non-domestic portion of cross-border offers.

Source: Capital Data Ltd.

total new issue volume of US$26 billion. No less than 38 countries accounted for more than US$1 billion of cross-border offers during the four-year period (see Exhibit 2.13).

Governments and corporations have seen the cost of issuance fall significantly in recent years. The most marked development has taken place in the privatisation IPO sector, where average fees have fallen from 3.51 per cent in 1993 to 2.46 per cent in 1996 (see Exhibit 2.14).

With the development of the market, an increasing number of banks have claimed a share of the overall fee pool and the share of the total international market held by the five most active houses in each and every year has fallen from 60 per cent in 1991, to 46 per cent in 1996. Over the six years, the five most active houses in each year accounted for around 50 per cent of the market while the top 10 in each year accounted for an average of 71 per cent (see Exhibit 2.15).

The case studies

Selecting the case studies

The case studies were selected on the basis of a number of different criteria, the principal one being that of 'lessons learned'. In order to include a variety of these 'lessons', transactions with varying structures were chosen according to the criteria listed below. The majority of the transactions are landmark transactions from the period 1992 to 1996.

Privatisations/corporate issues

Given that privatisations represented 31 per cent by volume of international equity issuance during 1991–96, and that many of them were landmark transactions, the decision was made that at least half of the case studies should be of privatisations, defined broadly as transactions in which the government reduces its percentage ownership via means of an equity offer. These deals can be seen in Exhibit 3.1.

IPOs/non-IPOs

IPOs represented 42 per cent by volume of international equity issuance during 1991–96. It was felt to be appropriate to have an equivalent split of IPO and non-IPOs in the case studies. A breakdown of the 24 case studies is shown in Exhibit 3.2.

Primary/secondary issues

Given that primary issuance (ie, where companies are raising new capital for their balance sheets) represented roughly 45 per cent by volume of the new issuance in the international market during 1991–96, 10 of the 24 case studies are primary issues. The balance are secondary issues, (ie, where existing shares are sold by a shareholder or group of shareholders).

The 10 primary transactions are given in Exhibit 3.3.

Geographic diversity

The international equity market – the distribution of equities outside the home market – is becoming increasingly global, both in terms of those that issue and how the issues are distributed. This project covers issues from Europe (17 offers), Latin America (2 offers), North America (1 offer) and Asia-Pacific (4 offers).

In terms of global new issuance, the US is obviously heavily underweighted in this book: the principal reason being

Exhibit 3.1
Case study breakdown: the privatisations

1992	China Steel
1993	Argentaria
	YPF
	BNP
	Singapore Telecom
1994	Elf
	Tele Danmark
	KNP
	Pharmacia
	Shandong Huaneng
1995	Repsol
	ENI
1996	Railtrack

Exhibit 3.2
Case study breakdown: IPOs versus non-IPOs

1991	TCNZ	IPO
1992	USX - Marathon	Non-IPO
	China Steel	Non-IPO
	Wellcome	Non-IPO
	Roche Holding Ltd	Non-IPO
1993	Argentaria	IPO
	Zeneca	IPO
	YPF	IPO
	BNP	IPO
	Singapore Telecom	IPO
	Akzo	Non-IPO
1994	Mayr-Melnhof	IPO
	Tele Danmark	IPO
	KPN	IPO
	Shandong Huaneng	IPO
	Elf	Non-IPO
	Daimler-Benz	Non-IPO
	Pharmacia	Non-IPO
	Nokia	Non-IPO
	Endesa	Non-IPO
1995	Bulgari	IPO
	ENI	IPO
	Repsol	Non-IPO
1996	Railtrack	IPO

Exhibit 3.3

Case study breakdown: the primary offers

1992	USX-Marathon
1993	Zeneca
	Akzo
1994	Tele Danmark
	Daimler
	Nokia
	Endesa
	Shandong Huaneng
	Mayr-Melnhof
1995	Bulgari

that the new equity issue business in the US is substantially standardised in terms of offer structure, pricing and underwriting methodology. In addition, there is no privatisation programme in the US. No Japanese issues have been included since there has been very limited cross-border equity issuance by Japanese companies over the specified period. There are no eastern European issues included as this region only began to develop seriously after the case studies in this book had been chosen.

Concentration on certain industries

While every effort has been made to ensure a representative spread of industrial sectors – including automotive, banking, chemicals, forestry products, luxury goods, oil and gas, pharmaceuticals, steel, transportation and telecoms – there is a clear weighting in favour of those sectors in which the state has previously chosen to participate. Energy and telecommunications companies therefore make up a large proportion of the privatisation stocks.

In addition to these selection criteria, the author was concerned to ensure that all different types of pricing and underwriting structures were represented among the case studies. These include: pre-emptive and non pre-emptive fixed price offers, a Dutch auction, a bought deal and open-priced book-built offers, as well as various permutations of these basic structures. One offer (Zeneca) was combined with a demerger and USX - Marathon Group was selected to introduce the reader to targeted stock.

Akzo

This 'bought deal' placement of new Akzo shares represented a pre-funding of the cash alternative offered to Nobel minority shareholders, as a component of a share-for-share US$3 billion merger between Akzo of the Netherlands and Nobel Industries of Sweden. The merger – in truth, more of a takeover by the Dutch company – between Akzo and Nobel, announced in the morning of Monday, 8 November, 1993, represented one of the most important European mergers of 1993, and one of the most important chemicals industry mergers of the last decade. The share sale was also the largest non-privatisation offer from a Dutch company and represented the first time that a cross border merger was effected with a Swedish company where a foreign company offered foreign stock to Swedish investors.

This acquisition financing provided Akzo with the assurance of the pre-financing they required. Given Nobel's high indebtedness and existing goodwill, an all-equity financing was required to maintain Akzo's equity/net debt ratio. Akzo paid approximately Dfl4 billion (US$2.1 billion) for the equity and assumed Dfl1.8 billion of Nobel net debt, making the total purchase price Dfl5.8 billion (US$3 billion). Out of the total consideration, Dfl3.1 billion represented goodwill and was charged directly against Akzo's equity capital.

The equity was sourced from a bought deal placement of new shares, something that is highly unusual. Having sold the shares to SG Warburg and ABN AMRO before the merger (which was subject to shareholder approval) was announced, it is clear that Akzo would have kept the money even without the merger going ahead. The structure was even more unusual in that the shares were resold to the market with an open price range as a quasi-bookbuilding exercise, with SG Warburg and ABN AMRO as vendors. Notwithstanding the fact that Akzo was already quoted on Nasdaq, and that this issue was not SEC registered, SG Warburg was able to sell to US qualified institutional buyers (QIBs).

Nobel had been rescued by the Swedish banks in the early 1990s, most prominently by Nordbanken, which had had the largest outstandings to the business empire of Erik Penser, former majority owner of Nobel. As the Swedish financial crisis escalated in 1992, the government had to rescue Nordbanken itself, following which Nobel, along with some US$8 billion of Nordbanken non-performing (mostly property) loans, was put in a 'bad bank' vehicle, called Securum. It was Securum and Akzo who, between them, structured what was referred to as 'the perfect merger'. In the process Securum exchanged its 73 per cent holding in Nobel for a 20 per cent stake in Akzo Nobel and became the largest shareholder in the company.

The timing of this equity sale was driven primarily by the timing of the merger. Discussions began in the middle of 1992 with various cooperation agreements being proposed and by the summer of 1993 there was an agreement in principle to exchange certain businesses, including Akzo's paper chemicals business. During the summer and autumn these discussions were expanded and intensified to include a wider cooperation including a full merger, at which point Securum, as Nobel's largest shareholder, got involved.

Exhibit 1
Transaction summary

Issuer name: Akzo N.V. (Akzo Nobel following merger with Nobel Industries of Sweden) (The Netherlands)	*Global coordinator:* SG Warburg & Co.
Pricing date: 8 November, 1993 (CBS GEN: 266.7)	*Pricing/underwriting structure:* Bought deal
Vendor: Company	*Primary or secondary:* Primary
% of company sold: 14.6% of expanded share capital	*Privatisation or corporate:* Corporate
IPO or non-IPO: Non-IPO	*Industry:* Chemicals
Type of shares: Ordinary shares	*Offer price range:* Dfl180–187 *Offer price:* Dfl180
Total issue size: US$745 million	*US listing/SEC registration:* Although Akzo is quoted on Nasdaq, this was a non-registered private placement

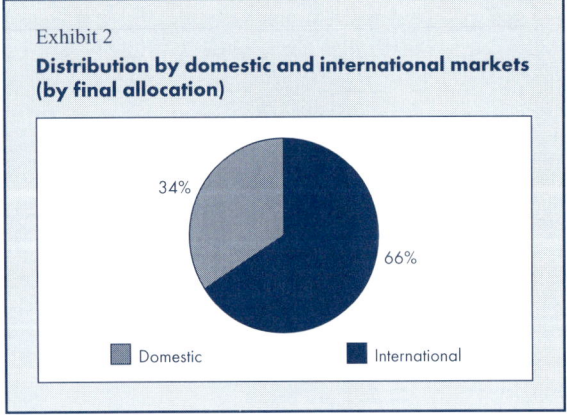

Exhibit 2
Distribution by domestic and international markets (by final allocation)

34%

66%

■ Domestic   ■ International

From Akzo's point of view, this was a fabulous opportunity as, unlike many of its peers in the chemical sector, the company had maintained a high level of profitability during the recession and was now able to capitalise on the opportunity. It effectively took over a company which had taken on far too much financial risk, and which eventually reached the point of insolvency as a result of highly-geared real estate investments. The full price paid by Akzo for Nobel must be seen against a background of Akzo's expectation of a sharply improving environment in the chemicals industry. This fact, and a generally strong new issue market, were the reasons that this placement was successfully completed despite minimal preparation.

Major challenges

The nature of the transaction presented the vendors with several specific challenges:

- SG Warburg was the only company in possession of all the relevant information concerning both the merger and the equity placement. This had to be distributed to the market within 15 hours, in order to sell US$745 million worth of shares;
- There was little time to fully explain the rationale for the merger;
- SG Warburg and ABN AMRO had no marketing material for the equity offer except for the press release regarding the merger; and
- Given the number of parties involved, keeping strict confidentiality with regard to both the acquisition and the placement was a considerable challenge. While news of the acquisition leaked prematurely, news of the placement did not.

Rationale and objectives

Why did the offer take place?

Given the considerable indebtedness of Nobel and the goodwill associated with its assets, the financing of the merger was, Akzo decided, to be achieved entirely by way of equity. Because of the drawn-out timetable, the transaction was

structured with a cash alternative for Nobel minority shareholders. It was important for financial, tax and political reasons to obtain full acceptance of the equity offer by Nobel minority shareholders. Such an acceptance would help to control cash and allow for tax consolidation.

Nobel minorities were offered two Akzo shares for every 57 Nobel shares held, or Skr26.50 of cash for each Nobel share. The question was whether they would take shares or cash. The answer was to depend on two things, both of which represented specific risks to Akzo:

- The risk of a fall in the Akzo share price expressed in Swedish krona between the announcement and approval of the transaction. If between the 5 November, when the exchange ratio was fixed, and the date of payment, either the Akzo share price fell by more than a given percentage, or the Dutch guilder fell against the krona, then Nobel minority shareholders would take the cash offer. The total amount that Akzo would have to pay the minority shareholders and holders of preference shares amounted to a potential Skr5.5 billion. Akzo being a prudently managed company wanted to have this cash available, hence the equity financing; and
- The second risk was also related to the Akzo share price and the exchange rate between the guilder and the krona. Assuming that Akzo would have to pay Skr26.50 of cash per share, there was a risk that the Swedish currency would appreciate and that the cash portion would become increasingly expensive. This risk was hedged by buying krona call options. In case there was no cash portion to be paid, the options would either expire worthless, or be exercised to realise a currency gain, depending on the movement of the exchange rate between the two currencies.

The importance of financing the entire merger by way of equity was substantially related to the Dfl3.1 billion of goodwill associated with the acquisition of the Nobel shares. As far as the accounting impact on Akzo was concerned, goodwill was a problem: it is Akzo's policy to write off goodwill directly against equity, as allowed under Dutch accounting standards. Additional equity of Dfl1.3 billion was required in order to maintain the company's pre-merger equity/net debt ratio of 0.66 at the end of September 1993. Depending on the portion of the Nobel minorities that would accept the cash alternative, the pro-forma equity/net debt ratio would be 0.55-0.65 at that date. Akzo also reports under US GAAP, and in keeping with treatment of goodwill under these accounting standards, goodwill is generally written off over 40 years.

Share capital and ownership

See Exhibit 3.

Akzo was and is a truly global stock. Prior to the offer 60 per cent of Akzo was held by foreign investors, with 22 per cent held in the US alone. Before the merger, Akzo was quoted on 12 European stock exchanges, including Amsterdam and London, and traded OTC on Nasdaq. It had also been a reporting company with the SEC since 1989. Syb Bergsma,

Exhibit 3
Share capital and ownership

Type of shares offered	Ordinary shares in bearer form of Dfl20, each carrying one vote. No person may cast more than 3,000 votes on his own behalf nor may he cast more than 3,000 additional votes as a proxy.
Share capital before offer	Ordinary shares (Dfl20) 46,088,000 Priority stock (Dfl1,000) 48 The priority stock is held by 'AKZOSTICHTING' (Akzo Foundation) which is controlled by the members of the supervisory board and the board of management. The meeting of holders of priority stock has the right to nominate candidates (in the form of a binding list) for the supervisory board and the board of management. Amendments of the articles of association are subject to the approval of this meeting.
Listings/quotations	Amsterdam and London among other exchanges since the formation of Akzo in 1969 and Nasdaq since 1989.
Market capitalisation at offer price (Dfl1.9024/US$) based on an expanded share capital of 54 million shares	US$5.1 billion
Free float before offer	100%
Liquidity – during January – October 1993 on Amsterdam, London and Nasdaq. (expressed per market as the number of shares traded on an annualised basis and as a percentage of the total number of ordinary shares outstanding before the bought deal)	Amsterdam 56% London 30% Nasdaq 8% Total liquidity 94%
Ownership by region before and after offer and merger	April 1993 April 1994 Netherlands 40% 26% USA 22% 20% ROW 38% 54%* * Including the 20% holding by Securum

Akzo's CFO says: 'All these foreign listings were actually done by my predecessor and, as far as I am concerned, they are, with the exceptions of London and Nasdaq, of only limited use today as they hardly, if at all, stimulate additional trading in our shares.'

Akzo Nobel applied for a listing on the Stockholm Stock Exchange and was admitted in February 1994.

Transaction components

Offer structure and syndicate
The offer was structured as a single tranche global placement of 7,878,788 shares representing 17.1 per cent of Akzo's outstanding capital prior to the offer. Authorisation for these shares had already been obtained, as required to allow the transaction to go ahead.

SG Warburg bought the shares from Akzo at a substantial discount to the Amsterdam market closing price of Dfl197.20 on the afternoon of 5 November. Over the weekend ABN AMRO, on the initiative of Akzo, joined SG Warburg in the placement and the risk was assumed on a 75/25 basis, with the Dutch bank making the smaller commitment. If the merger agreement had not been reached over the weekend, the purchase of Akzo shares by SG Warburg and ABN AMRO would still have gone ahead and Akzo would have kept the proceeds for other purposes.

SG Warburg and ABN AMRO, as the new owners of the shares, decided that the sale would best be structured as an 'express bookbuilding', whereby the placement was launched on Monday morning at an open price range of Dfl180-Dfl187 per share. Alfred Berg, the Swedish investment bank, was brought in on Sunday 7 November to place shares in Sweden. The placement was priced at Dfl180 at 7 pm New York time on Monday night, only 15 hours after announcement at 9 am in London. Selling in the US was restricted to QIBs as there was no time to register the offer with the SEC (see Exhibit 4).

Because Securum was not perceived as a long term holder of Akzo Nobel, given that its charter called for it to recover Nordbanken's non-performing loans rather than to participate in a global chemical company, the issue of lockup was particularly important. In accordance with the final outcome of the negotiations, Securum made the following undertakings, among others, with regard to its shareholding in the new Akzo Nobel:

Exhibit 4
Banks in bought deal placement

SG Warburg Securities	Bookrunner
ABN AMRO Bank	Joint lead manager
Alfred Berg	Co-lead manager
Merger advisers	
Adviser to Securum	Goldman Sachs
Adviser to Akzo	SG Warburg, Alfred Berg
Adviser to Nobel Industries	Morgan Stanley

Exhibit 5
The timetable for the merger and bought deal offer

Weekend, 30–31 October, 1993	• Merger discussions progressing.
Monday , 1 November	• The Akzo negotiating team reports to Akzo board meeting that a merger might be possible subject to a few open issues, not least the number of Akzo shares to be offered to Nobel shareholders. There was still a substantial discrepancy between what Akzo was willing to pay and what Securum was asking. Discussions were to continue on 3 November.
Wednesday, 3 November	• Akzo announces six-months results and share price rises from Dfl180 to Dfl200, a rise which certainly assisted the final discussions over the weekend 6/7 November as the exchange ratio now looked more attractive to Securum. News of the merger discussions leaked and was reported on Swedish television evening news.
Thursday, 4 November	• The Stockholm Stock Exchange suspended trading in Nobel shares and demanded a statement from the parties on the morning of Monday 8 November as to whether a merger would be concluded. This action put further pressure on the parties to reach agreement or otherwise abort discussions. The Amsterdam Stock Exchange did not want to suspend Akzo, as the company was listed on 13 stock exchanges world-wide which were certainly not going to close at such short notice. The share price did not react negatively to the news of the merger; • SG Warburg makes equity financing proposal to Akzo following indications earlier in the week. Several different financing proposals were still under consideration. Akzo invites ABN AMRO to a Friday morning meeting to discuss the equity financing and to get a second opinion on the proposed structure and terms of the placement.
Friday, 5 November	• At 9am Akzo meets with ABN AMRO in Arnhem to discuss the equity placement; • At 2pm SG Warburg joins the discussions with Akzo and ABN AMRO; • At 4pm SG Warburg buys 7,878,788 shares from Akzo and hedges a portion of the total risk through a variety of structures.
Weekend, 6–7 November	• Over the weekend, Akzo suggests, and SG Warburg agrees, that ABN AMRO take on 25% of the risk. This gives Akzo better terms than otherwise would have been available from SG Warburg alone. The inclusion of ABN AMRO was important from the point of view of augmenting the placement power in the Netherlands and because, from a regulatory point of view, the Dutch central bank requires a Dutch bank to be included in the syndicate in a management capacity. It was not certain that SG Warburg's local bank would have qualified.
Monday, 8 November	• At 4.30am, although a few details of the merger still remained unresolved, Cees van Lede, vice chairman and chairman elect of the board of management, left London for Stockholm by private jet in order to be able to participate in a Stockholm press conference, in case agreement would be reached; • At 5am the parties reached agreement at SG Warburg's offices. Immediately afterwards, Arnout Loudon, Akzo's chairman, left by private jet for an Amsterdam press conference; • At 8am the SG Warburg and ABN AMRO salesforces were invited to noon London and Amsterdam investor presentations; • At 9am London time, simultaneous press conferences in London, Stockholm and Amsterdam begin, during which the merger and equity placement were announced; • At 9.30am, immediately following those press conferences, SG Warburg and ABN AMRO launched the equity placement at an open price range of Dfl180–187. • Akzo CFO, Syb Bergsma departs on Concorde to New York for meetings with QIBs in New York and Boston; • At noon London time, 100 institutional investors attend a London investor presentation hosted by SG Warburg at the same time as 50 institutional investors attend an Amsterdam investor presentation hosted by ABN AMRO; • At 7pm US EST, on the basis of the book built during the day, the bought deal was priced at Dfl180, at the bottom of the indicated range. This price represented a 2.3% discount to the Nasdaq closing price of US$48.75/ADR. The Amsterdam closing price was Dfl185.10.
Tuesday, 9 November	• Allocation of the 7.9 million shares takes place.
20 December	• Alfred Berg and SG Warburg publish an offer document to Nobel shareholders.
27 January 1994	• Akzo's EGM unanimously approves the issuance of up to 17 million Akzo ordinary shares to be offered to Nobel ordinary and preference shareholders as part of the share exchange.
7 February 1994	• The last day for Nobel shareholders to register their acceptance of the merger. Less than 1% of Nobel's shareholders did not accept the Akzo offer, and more than 90% of the minorities elected to take the share rather than cash offer.

• To retain the entire holding for the 12 months to 7 November 1994;
• To reduce the holding to no less than 10 per cent of the total number of Akzo shares then outstanding during the 12 months to 7 November 1995. Securum was to have only one opportunity to reduce its holding during this period and any sale could go ahead only after reasonable consultation with Akzo Nobel; and

• Before and after 7 November 1995 to adhere to orderly market restrictions. Should Securum elect to sell a block of shares in Akzo Nobel, no further sales could take place for a period of 12 months following the date of such sale.

Exhibit 6
The costs of the bought deal

Closing price (5 November)	Offer price (Fixed on 8 November)	Discount 1	Discount 2 (estimated)	Total 'effective cost'
Dfl197.20	Dfl180	8.7%	3–5%	11.7–13.7%

These restrictions notwithstanding, Securum was allowed to sell up to 2 per cent of the then outstanding shares of Akzo Nobel during any one quarter.

The costs of the transaction

This was a bought deal placement, whereby SG Warburg and ABN AMRO bought the shares from Akzo at an undisclosed price which was fixed on Friday 5 November. The cost to Akzo can therefore only be estimated.

Technically, the 'total effective cost' to Akzo is quite simply calculated as the difference between the price at which they sold the shares to the banks (which has not been publicly disclosed) and the closing market price of Dfl197.20 on 5 November. This cost can theoretically be broken down in to two distinct discounts.

Discount 1 can be calculated as the difference between the Amsterdam market closing price on Friday 5 November, ie, Dfl197.20 and the price at which the banks sold the shares in the market in connection with the placement, ie, Dfl180. Discount 2 is the difference between the offer price of Dfl180 and the price at which the shares were sold to SG Warburg and ABN AMRO by the company. The latter was not disclosed but is estimated by the author to be at least 3–5 per cent below Dfl180.

That second discount is a real number to the banks and represents their total gross profit, before any expenses – including the cost of finance during the few days that they owned the shares and any discount offered to investors on the Dfl180 offer price. However SG Warburg did hedge a portion of its long position in Akzo and may therefore have made some money. (See Exhibit 6.)

The 'total effective cost' must be seen in the context of the considerable risks taken by SG Warburg and ABN AMRO:

- *Market risk:* The risk that the general stock market environment may deteriorate as it did for example in October 1987. Although the US market, measured by Dow Jones was up by 18 points on Friday, 5 November, the index actually fluctuated by 78 points in intra-day trading and SG Warburg were concerned that Monday could be a very bad day in the markets. Aside from any general fall in the market, the potential fall in Akzo would have been that much more dramatic given the additional supply from this placement and the added uncertainty created by the merger. In such a scenario a fall in the Akzo share price in excess of 13.7 per cent would by no means have been unthinkable;
- *Event risk:* To the impact of the general market risk must be added the specific risk that the market would not like the terms of the merger. In the opinion of one prominent

equity research analyst following Akzo, the company 'overpaid' by an amount of Dfl1.4 billion or Dfl30 per Akzo share, probably more than the discount at which SG Warburg and ABN AMRO bought the shares. This view was obviously one key reason for the fall in the Akzo share price on the Monday and if the market had experienced a major fall at the same time it is not inconceivable that the Akzo share price could have fallen below SG Warburg and ABN AMRO's acquisition cost; and

- *Financial risk:* A position of US$555 million worth of one security (representing 75 per cent of the total placement) financed by debt represented a huge additional financial risk, equivalent to more than 33 per cent of SG Warburg's total equity capital of £865 million at the end of March 1993.

Deal structure

Given the high goodwill and indebtedness of Nobel, Akzo's equity/net debt ratio would have fallen to 0.55 from 0.66 regardless of the effects of this equity placement, if all the Nobel minority shareholders had elected to take cash instead of shares. If they had all taken shares, as indeed they very nearly did, the equity/net debt ratio would have remained virtually unchanged at 0.65 despite the placement. If the equity placement had not taken place and all the minorities had elected to take cash, then the equity/net debt ratio would have fallen to 40 per cent. Akzo cannot be faulted for having a conservative balance sheet policy and wanting to maintain its balance sheet strength, especially when it is buying a company in another country, with all the associated risks, particularly when the company is operating in a highly cyclical industry.

There is still reason to question whether or not it would not have been in Akzo's best interest to wait and carry out the equity financing following the close of the merger. In retrospect, given the share price development and the economic recovery, that may have been the right thing to do. It is possible that the share price would have developed better because the issue would certainly have been better placed.

However, without the benefit of hindsight, the question is hard to answer. If SG Warburg and Akzo had believed in the benefits of the merger, and given an improving outlook for the European chemicals sector then, perhaps, they should have delayed the issue. The bottom line has to be that it would only have been right to wait if Akzo had been comfortable with the strategy of improving its equity/net debt ratio from internally generated cash flow to the targeted level within a reasonable period of time (without substantially having to curtail capital expenditure). The reason for this view is that you can never be sure that the equity market will be available when you want to tap it.

The other question to consider when looking at the structure of the deal is whether or not it was in Akzo's best interest to sell the 7.9 million shares to SG Warburg at a heavily discounted price to the market closing price on 5 November.

During the weeks leading up to the announcement of the merger, SG Warburg particularly recommended three different financing structures to Akzo:

- A 'bought deal' placement with the shares sold by Akzo before announcement, as was finally executed. Under this arrangement, Akzo would sell the shares on the Friday afternoon with the risk passing to the underwriters. The banks would then launch the offer on an open price basis following announcement of the merger first thing on Monday morning;
- A 'bought deal' placement with the timing of the sale of the shares by Akzo falling after the announcement of the merger. The idea in this case was to announce the merger on Monday morning, let the market react to the news and then sell the shares to SG Warburg and ABN AMRO on Monday night, with those banks pricing the offer immediately thereafter; and
- An international bookbuilt issue, following the closing of the merger in February 1994

When ABN AMRO got involved in discussions concerning the equity placement on Thursday 4 November, they strongly recommended the second alternative, whereas SG Warburg, with its understanding of Akzo's limited appetite for risk, continued to recommend the first structure. The third option was rejected at an early stage. It was deemed to leave Akzo with too much market risk – an offer including SEC registration could not have been achieved until April/May 1994.

SG Warburg believed that their choice was best because it recognised that Akzo was, and is, a company with prudent financial policies. It was also the case that the market environment was uncertain as there were concerns about interest rate hikes and the US market was clearly unsettled on Friday 5 November. SG Warburg perceived that there was a risk that the Dow Jones Industrial Average might fall by up to 50 points on the Monday.

By selling the shares to SG Warburg and ABN AMRO on the Friday night, Akzo eliminated its exposure to market risk and the impact on share prices of a negative market reaction to the merger. The sale gave the vendor, Securum, the reassurance that Akzo's financing was in place and made it easier for the underwriters to hedge their risk before the financing was announced.

Akzo was asked to pay a high 'total effective cost' estimated at up to 13.7 per cent, in the form of a discount to the Friday closing price and there was a risk that the market would frown upon the fact that it wanted to lock in the price before announcing the terms of the merger to the market.

ABN AMRO's adoption of the idea of selling the shares to the banks after the merger was announced hinged on their belief that the market would react positively to the merger, despite the dilution in year one. As the market would already have reacted to the merger terms during Monday trading, the risk that the banks would have to assume would also be correspondingly smaller and accordingly a lower discount would be required. Although the salesforces of both SG Warburg and ABN AMRO, as well the investors, would have had more time to study the merger consequences and the impact of the issue, the danger was that the ABN AMRO structure would expose Akzo to a worst case scenario, where the company might have to cope with a dramatically falling share price on the Monday.

The management of Akzo debated long and hard, in the little time they had, but ultimately decided on the structure suggested by SG Warburg. As a result of ABN AMRO's involvement the price at which Akzo sold the shares on Friday was (according to Akzo) considerably higher than that which had originally been proposed by SG Warburg.

Marketing

The entire marketing of the issue was conducted during 15 hours on Monday 8 November. There was:

- No documentation or marketing material other than one press release;
- Limited time to educate the salesforces; and
- Limited time to get to, let alone convince investors about the merits of the merger.

Rather than being able to compare Akzo against its industry peers, investors had to take a view on the Akzo management, the rationale of the merger and the size of the issue compared to the size of the discount. Investors also needed to have an element of trust in SG Warburg and ABN AMRO, as they had neither the time, nor the information to do a proper analysis.

Akzo was the right stock at the right time. The high price of the acquisition was compensated for by the attractive discount at which shares were now available. Furthermore:

- The chemical sector was in favour with investors;
- Akzo was considered a high quality company, one of the few in the sector that had remained profitable throughout the recession;
- Management had a good track record;
- The merged Akzo Nobel became the largest coatings manufacturer in the world;
- The strategic fit between the two companies was deemed almost perfect, particularly since Securum undertook to buy certain non-core assets out of Nobel;
- Through an all equity financing, the new Akzo Nobel maintained a strong financial position;
- Although slightly dilutive in the first year, the merger was expected to enhance earnings per share in the second year; and
- Investors were able to buy a highly liquid stock at a discount of more than Dfl20 compared to the price just a few days earlier.

Exhibit 7
Demand by country/region

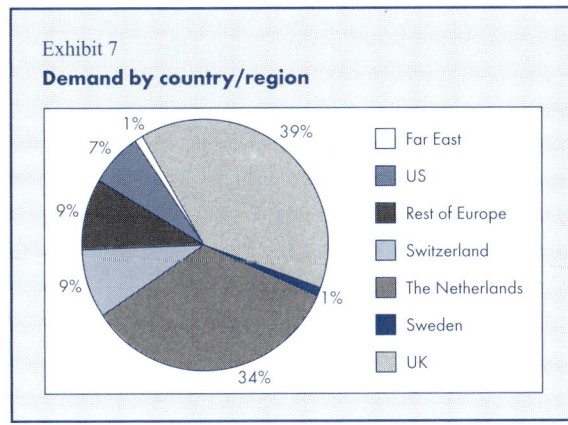

- Far East — 39%
- US
- Rest of Europe
- Switzerland
- The Netherlands
- Sweden
- UK

But there were also drawbacks. There was little time to study the merger consequences. Many analysts concluded that Akzo had overpaid for Nobel. The structure and timetable of the equity issue made it difficult for investors to subscribe. In the US, investments of this kind often require policy decisions, for example, which need significant time.

Results

Placement

The offer was placed with 246 institutions from the countries/regions shown in Exhibit 7.

It must be recognised that there is not typically the same high quality of placement with a bought deal as in a bookbuilt transaction. This discrepancy is related to the fact that the first and foremost consideration for the banks involved is to get the stock 'off the books' and therefore the quality of investor matters less. It would not be fair on the banks involved to expect as strong an after-market price performance as there might have been in the case of a bookbuilt, marketing-driven offer.

Share price performance

See Exhibit 8.

Before pricing

- Akzo's share price had only moved above Dfl180 one month before the pricing of the issue. The day before the announcement of the strong interim results on 3 November, the price was still only Dfl181. It closed at Dfl194.20 on 3rd November and then peaked at Dfl199.50 on 4 November before closing at Dfl197.20 on Friday before the announcement. It is noteworthy that the price did not fall on the rumours of a merger between Akzo and Nobel. It was only upon the simultaneous announcement of the merger terms and the 'bought deal' placement on 8 November that the price fell sharply, reflecting the expected dilution; and

- During the 6 months before pricing the price had increased from Dfl149.90 to Dfl197.20, outperforming the Dutch market (as measured by the CBS General Index) by 9.7 per cent reflecting in part a growing belief in the likely improved profit performance of the chemical sector.

Exhibit 8
Share price performance

Pricing date	8 November 1993
Offer price	Dfl180
Last trade	Dfl185.10
Relative index position	101.9%
Historic 52 week high/low	
High (4 November 1993)	Dfl199.50
Low (24 November 1992)	Dfl128.20

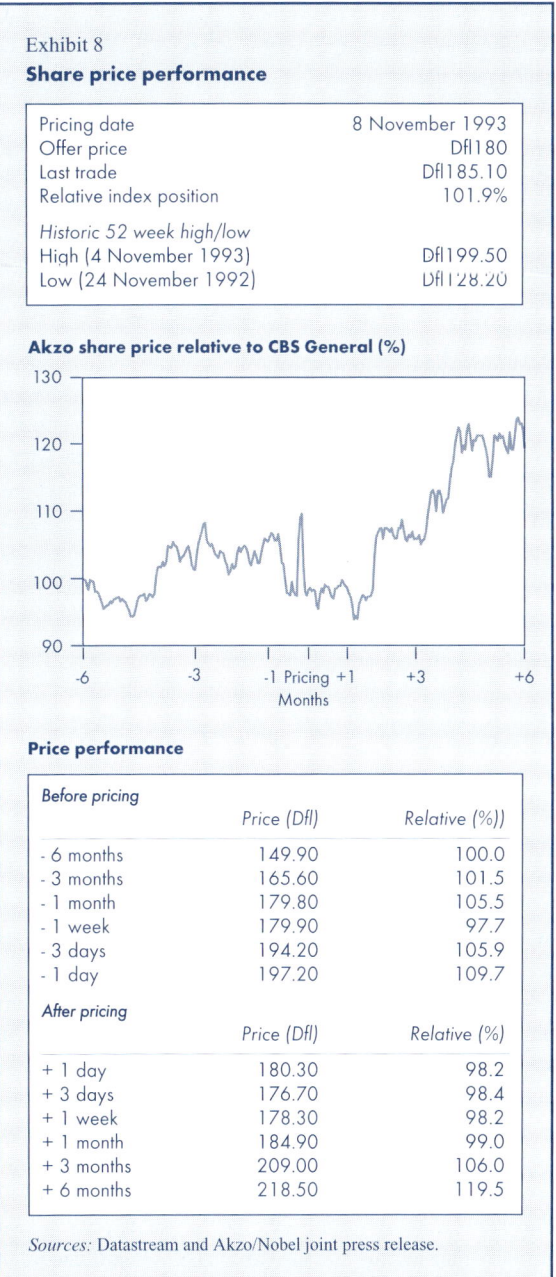

Akzo share price relative to CBS General (%)

Price performance

Before pricing	Price (Dfl)	Relative (%)
- 6 months	149.90	100.0
- 3 months	165.60	101.5
- 1 month	179.80	105.5
- 1 week	179.90	97.7
- 3 days	194.20	105.9
- 1 day	197.20	109.7

After pricing	Price (Dfl)	Relative (%)
+ 1 day	180.30	98.2
+ 3 days	176.70	98.4
+ 1 week	178.30	98.2
+ 1 month	184.90	99.0
+ 3 months	209.00	106.0
+ 6 months	218.50	119.5

Sources: Datastream and Akzo/Nobel joint press release.

After pricing

- On Tuesday 9 November, the price closed at Dfl180.30 in Amsterdam to then fall below Dfl180 where it traded for 17 consecutive trading days until 3 December. There were rumours that the issue had not been completely sold by Monday night/Tuesday morning and that SG Warburg was not supporting the price in the secondary market;

- The price only recovered to above the pre-announcement level on 5 January, 1994 and then continued to perform strongly, reaching a 1994 peak of Dfl228.20 on 15 March; and

- In the immediate after-market, while the absolute share price was below issue price, Akzo Nobel actually performed more or less in line with a weaker Dutch stock market. During the 6 months following the placement, Akzo Nobel outperformed the CBS General index by 17.6 per cent.

Exhibit 9
Percentage of total issue traded* (%)

	Day 1	Day 2	Day 3 (11 Nov.)	Total
Amsterdam	16.5	7.7	5.6	29.8
Nasdaq	2.1	9.5	0.8	12.4

* Based on the issue of 7,878,788 shares.

After-market trading volume

Whereas the volumes in Exhibit 9 appear high in comparison to other issues, they must be seen in the context of the merger which, in and of itself, would lead to much higher trading volumes. High trading volumes were already recorded both in Amsterdam and on Nasdaq during the three trading days before the announcement of the merger and the issue, as a result of the strong profit report and the leak concerning the merger.

The performance of the main parties

SG Warburg had been working with Akzo since 1992 on various acquisition structures in relation to Nobel, initially involving the purchase by Akzo of the coatings and/or paper chemicals divisions of Nobel, and in so doing had certainly been highly instrumental in getting the parties together. SG Warburg was therefore very close to the merger discussions and was hired as the merger adviser in the summer of 1993. Discussions on the financing of the merger were already under way by this point, but the decision to raise equity was not formally taken by the Akzo board until 4 November. Accordingly the equity financing mandate was not awarded until 5 November, as the precise structure was still not decided until then.

During the weeks leading up to the weekend of 6–7 November, Akzo and SG Warburg were still discussing several different equity financing structures. The most important considerations included whether or not the offer would be underwritten, when the price risk would pass to SG Warburg and at what price. The discussions on price are understood to have been very tough.

Akzo had initially decided not to involve its domestic house bank, ABN AMRO, as they were not aware of the merger discussions. SG Warburg had a great reputation, outstanding placement power and did a good job advising on the acquisition. But, given the size of the equity placement, the importance of placement in the Netherlands and the considerable discount at which SG Warburg was proposing to buy the shares, on 4 November Akzo began to seriously consider involving ABN AMRO. Consequently Akzo met ABN AMRO on the morning of 5 November, with SG Warburg joining the discussions in the afternoon.

ABN AMRO was not prepared to take on 100 per cent of the risk under the structure that it was recommending, and as Akzo ultimately felt more comfortable with the structure that

Warburgs were recommending, Akzo reached a verbal agreement with SG Warburg later that Friday afternoon.

Bergsma consider two criteria particularly important in the selection of a global coordinator: the long-standing track record of the firm and the firm's market share in the trading of the company's stock. SG Warburg ranked highly according to both criteria.

Key lessons learnt

One lesson that can be learnt from the deal is that in a good market it is possible for the right company to do a placement of this kind. There are not, however, very many companies of this kind: Akzo is an extraordinarily international name and, as such, can gain access to international investors at shorter notice than many other companies.

The timing was also crucial: Akzo had just reported strong third quarter results and the outlook for the chemicals sector was very positive.

It is also true that an offer for a stock as liquid as Akzo becomes self-pricing. The feasibility of the offer became more a question of the size of discount than the impact of the merger or the valuation against comparable companies.

Although having the same adviser for both the acquisition and the equity financing has many advantages, including confidentiality and the coordination of information, it may in fact be preferable to have a separate adviser for the equity placement, in order that it would have sufficient attention focused on it. The company is certainly of the opinion that it should have involved its house bank at an earlier stage.

An equity issue of this size, particularly against a background of a complex acquisition, would normally take months of hard work to prepare. Given that the successful conclusion of the merger negotiations was so much at the centre of everybody's thoughts during the days leading up to agreement on the merger terms, it may be that both Akzo and its advisers didn't give the equity placement the attention it deserved.

Given the challenge involved for both the company and its bankers in tackling a complex merger such as this and a major equity financing simultaneously, it may be advisable for companies to bridge finance with debt in order to tap the equity market on a fully prepared basis.

Conclusion

Akzo can hardly be faulted for having chosen to pursue a prudent approach with respect to the financing of the take-over of Nobel, ie, for wanting to equity finance the whole transaction, including the possible cash portion of the offer to Nobel shareholders.

The conservative all-equity financing structure chosen must be seen in the context of the merger itself, which was structured to avoid major risks and criticism from the many constituencies concerned. The take-over was 'agreed', with Securum delivering 73 per cent of Nobel and cleaning the company up for Akzo by buying the non-core assets out of Nobel. Nobel minorities were given the fairest possible treatment by Securum and Akzo. Securum and Nobel management were given operational responsibilities on the board of the new Akzo Nobel. This gentle approach was important in order not to embarrass the Swedish Government, which had rescued Nobel from bankruptcy. It was also important for the highly respected Lars Thunell, who, as CEO of Securum (and former CFO of engineering company ABB) had been given responsibility to maximise Nordbanken's investment in Nobel. Assisted by Goldman Sachs, he did so with flying colours.

The placement in 15 hours of US$745 million of new shares, representing 14.6 per cent of the expanded share capital, for a company that is undertaking a large and complex acquisition, without the benefit of any documentation or marketing material and with only one day of marketing/selling must be considered a considerable achievement. SG Warburg demonstrated outstanding organisation and placement power in the international market, while ABN AMRO showed its strength in distributing stock in the domestic market. It is also worth repeating that Akzo achieved the desired pre-funding and protected its equity/net debt ratio.

The execution was impressive, if not impeccable, as the price declined in Amsterdam from Dfl197.20 on Friday night to Dfl185.10 on Monday, 8 November. The issue was priced at Dfl180 per share. On Tuesday, 9 November, the price closed at Dfl180.30 in Amsterdam to then fall below Dfl180 where it stayed until 3 December. The price only recovered to above the pre-announcement level on 5 January, 1994. Once the issue had been fully digested by the market and the substantial synergies between Akzo and Nobel appreciated by investors, Akzo Nobel shares started outperforming.

Nevertheless, it is open to debate as to whether or not Akzo chose the optimal offer structure. If Akzo firmly believed in the benefits of this merger and was comfortable with the price paid, then perhaps given that the chemical cycle and Akzo's share price were trending up, it would have been reasonable to bridge finance the cash portion with debt and refinance in the global equity market after the completion of the merger in February/March 1994. At this point, it would also have been easier to determine the exact requirement for equity capital.

Even if the need to limit Akzo's exposure to market risk by doing the equity placement upfront is accepted, Akzo might have followed ABN AMRO's advice to sell the 7.9 million shares to SG Warburg and ABN AMRO only after the close of the market on Monday, allowing the market at least a full business day to adjust to the merger. This would have reduced the risk for the underwriters and allowed for a lower discount.

The quick timetable and lack of consultation with the major shareholders upset some important investors in the domestic market. If the shares had been sold to SG Warburg and ABN AMRO on Monday night and the issue priced to investors on Tuesday, a little more time could have been spent on convincing sceptical shareholders and new investors.

Securum did well on its investment in Akzo Nobel. In March 1997 the government-owned 'bad bank' vehicle sold its remaining 13 per cent stake in a US$1 billion placement through ABN AMRO Rothschild and a small syndicate of banks including SBC Warburg. The majority of the shares were sold to Dutch and international institutions at a price of Dfl279.20 via an accelerated non-prospectus bookbuilding exercise.

Feature topic: *The pros and cons of a managed rights offer and a bookbuilt issue*

During the weeks and days leading up to the announcement of the merger, Akzo considered a number of alternatives to the 'bought deal' structures proposed by both SG Warburg and ABN AMRO respectively. Two options in particular were closely analysed. They were a managed rights issue and a global bookbuilt deal. Both of these structures would have been dependent on the acceptance of the Akzo offer by Nobel's shareholders.

A managed rights issue

Despite the fact that Akzo had an authorisation from its shareholders to issue up to 10 million shares, if ever there was an occasion to go to shareholders for money, this would have been it. A rights issue would have allowed the owners a good chance to study the merits of the merger and then help finance it. Where existing shareholders did not take up their rights, a small syndicate of banks coordinated by SG

Warburg could have recirculated the rights and sold them to new investors through a global bookbuilding exercise.

The funding of the possible cash payment to Nobel minorities could easily have been arranged through a debt bridge financing, repayable with the proceeds from this offer, using up to four of Akzo's principal relationship banks.

Such an approach would have had a number of advantages over the bought deal placement that was actually executed:

- The size would more accurately have reflected the real need for equity depending on the amount of cash paid to Nobel minorities;
- A discount of 25–30 per cent to the prevailing market price at the end of February 1994, once the effects of the merger had been fully discounted, would probably have sufficed to ensure certainty of proceeds to Akzo without the banks having to underwrite the rights issue.

Underwriting fees would not have been necessary and Akzo could instead have paid an attractive management and placement fee to incentivise the entire syndicate to market the issue;

- This structure would have allowed a high quality prospectus to have been written, highlighting the strategic benefits and financial consequences of the merger. Existing shareholders and new investors alike would have had an opportunity to study the investment merits of the new group. There would have been sufficient time for the analyst community to study the merger consequences and update their estimates for the new Akzo Nobel. A comprehensive roadshow could have been arranged; and

- Because the merger would have been fully completed, Akzo's management and SG Warburg would have been able to devote themselves fully to the equity issue.

There would also have been some disadvantages:

- Akzo would have taken a very considerable market risk over a period of some four months;

- Given that the period up until 20 December was fully devoted to the writing of an offer document for the benefit of Nobel minority shareholders and that the process of converting the accounts of the new group to US GAAP and producing an appropriate registration statement for the SEC would most likely have taken at least four months, a February/March rights issue could not have included a public distribution in the US market. Akzo would certainly not have been prepared to delay the launch of any equity financing beyond February/March;

- The rights issue structure is not generally deemed to be the optimal way of tapping international demand for Dutch companies, regardless of the complication of having to exclude the US market (other than for QIBs);

- The rights issue would possibly have had to be done at an even lower price than the price at which Akzo sold shares to SG Warburg and ABN AMRO. Akzo's management belongs to the school of thought that considers deep discount rights issues to be negative in terms of dilution with the higher cost of financing as a consequence;

- The rights issue structure is especially attractive to retail shareholders, but since the retail portion of Akzo's shareholder had declined steadily in recent years, there was less reason to select this structure than might have been the case a few years ago. Furthermore, says Syb Bergsma, the CFO of AKZO: 'I am emotionally against giving a tax free distribution to retail shareholders unwilling to subscribe'; and

- A rights issue might have complicated the merger discussions between Akzo and Securum, both with regard to the setting of the exchange ratio (due to the discount

element) and the subsequent treatment of Securum as a shareholder.

This structure, although perhaps philosophically the logical one would have been associated with a number of technical difficulties even if Akzo could have been convinced to delay the equity financing until after the merger had been completed.

A global bookbuilt issue

The rationale is much the same to that outlined above except that in the interest of achieving the highest possible price for its shares, Akzo would do a non pre-emptive offer 'at market,' instead of a rights issue. The old authorisation actually used in the 'bought deal' would still have been available.

This structure not only shares the advantages of the managed rights issue, but has additional ones:

- This approach might have been preferable to Securum, although the issue of dilution in voting and economic interest would still have been valid. It is not certain that they could have agreed to a structure, such as a managed rights issue, whereby they would have had to put money into the new Akzo Nobel;

- Bookbuilding is considered to maximise investor demand by creating tension between investors in all markets and between existing shareholders and new investors alike;

- With bookbuilding selling pressure from domestic retail investors guided primarily by a relatively unsophisticated Dutch press would have been less influential; and

- The structure and timetable of a bookbuilt issue is more flexible than for a rights issue, enabling Akzo to be as sensitive as possible to market conditions. Both size and price would be set by the market.

This structure also shares the disadvantages of the managed rights issue, and would have been the least certain to guarantee proceeds to Akzo, as the company would have been exposed to market risk until the last day of marketing, which most likely would have been several weeks after the terms of a rights issue had been set.

This is the financing alternative that most observers not involved in the transaction would have recommended, but it is still associated with considerable disadvantages and risks. If Securum's consent had been available, and with the benefit of hindsight concerning the positive market development for chemical stocks and Akzo in particular, this structure might have yielded the best results. To those at the company at the time – the ones who had to make the hard decision – it seemed an uncertain route and taking it was reckoned irresponsible.

Feature topic: *How to do a bought deal*

Given all the demands and risks of bookbuilding (the long lead times, the substantial due diligence needed, the preparation of a prospectus and a roadshow), it is clear why certain vendors in certain situations prefer to employ alternative pricing and underwriting methods. One such alternative pricing and underwriting structure is the 'bought deal' in which the reputational risk is arguably lower than for a bookbuilt issue.

When we talk about bought deal transactions we tend to think of secondary transactions, ie, the sale by Shareholder A of shares in Company B. However there are situations where a bought deal may also make sense as a primary issue, such as Company A issuing new shares in connection with an acquisition such as in the case of the issue by Akzo of new shares to finance the potential cash portion of the acquisition of Nobel in Sweden to form Akzo Nobel.

Bought deals represent a relatively limited proportion of the overall global market for international distribution of equities (below 10 per cent), although it is becoming increasingly used as a method of sale not only by corporate vendors but also by governments, as evidenced by the UK Government's sale of shares in BP, BAA and British Energy, the French Government's sale of shares in Total and Elf and the Italian Government's sale of shares in IMI, all of which took place in 1996/1997. Bought deals are popular at times of strong market conditions and when there is strong competition for mandates among banks. Some bought deals come about as a result of large banks wanting to advertise their market presence and their strong capital position. Banks such as BZW, ABN AMRO Rothschild, DMG, DKB and SBC Warburg, which are the result of mergers between capital strong commercial banks and formerly not so strong investment banks, were particularly active in the bought deal market during 1995–97.

To examine the product in greater depth, we have selected some of the bought deals executed by BZW between 1991 and 1994, a period during which this method of sale

Exhibit 10

Bought deal transactions executed by BZW from February 1991 to November 1994

Company	Allied Lyons	Telecom NZ	Enso-Gutzeit	Avesta-Sheffield	SSAB	Skandia	Whitbread Brewery Stocks (7 diff. stocks*)	Enterprise Oil
Nationality of company	UK	New Zealand	Finland	Sweden	Sweden	Sweden	UK	UK
Vendor	Olympia & York	Bell Atlantic	Ahlström	NCC	LKAB	Uni-Stor./ Hafnia	Whitbread	Elf Acquitaine
Nationality of vendor	Canadian	USA	Finland	Sweden	Sweden	Norway/ Denmark	UK	France
Pricing date	16-Feb-95	12-Mar-97	2-Sep-97	14-Sep-98	11-May-98	9-Jun-97	11-Mar-98	4-Nov-98
Proceeds (US$ million equiv.)	804	149	275	302	170	439	376	300
% of company sold	9.8%	4.6%	17.5%	22.6%	13.0%	39.5%	Various	10.3%
Type of shares sold	Ordinary	Ordinary	R (Lim.Vot.)	Ordinary	1.625 m A 2.5 m B	Ordinary	Ord.+ Greenalls7% Conv	Ordinary
Market capitalisation (US$ million equiv.)	8,479	3,404	1,668	1,377	1,348	1,248	Various	3,072
Free float of company	N/A	32%	25%	10%	55%	40%	N/A	65%
Proceeds/daily liquidity	56 days	20 days	365 days	80 days	52 days	256 days	N/A	80 days
Total number of banks involved	3	3	3	3	3	3	4	3
% placed by BZW	100%	100%	95%	63%	78%	N/A	99%	47%
Issue price	497.5 p	NZ$2.60	FIM37.50	SEK64	SEK317 (4:6A/B)	SEK105	286 p*	369p
Market price (D-1 Close)	513.9 p	NZ$2.73	FIM39.80	SEK66	SEK327	SEK118	295p*	387p
Discount	3.2%	4.8%	5.8%	3.0%	3.0%	11.0%	5.9%*	4.7%
Name recognition/ international liquidity	High	High	Low	Low	Low	Average/ Low	Low	Average

Sources: BZW and Datastream.

started to become an increasingly feasible alternative for a variety of issuers.

BZW demonstrated the considerable diversity and depth of its bought deal executions during the period under review. Exhibit 10 shows BZW's publicly announced bought deal transactions. These demonstrate a considerable diversity in terms of the types of transactions that can be done with this execution structure.

The structure

- Bought deals are typically substantial 'secondary sales' of shares, whereby one company is selling already outstanding and publicly traded shares in another company. There are, however, some exceptions to this general rule, as mentioned above;
- Bought deals are underwritten transactions as opposed to transactions sold on a 'best efforts' basis as is the case with bookbuilt transactions. In the case of a bought deal, the lead bank underwrites at a fixed price and for a fixed number of shares before the deal is announced to the market: ie, it buys the shares from the vendor, hence the name 'bought deal'. Whether or not the lead bank sells the shares directly or maintains a certain position on its trading book is of little direct consequence to the vendor;
- The bought deal structure implies that the distribution of a block of shares bought by the lead bank takes place by way of distribution to a large number of investors. A sale of shares to one or only a few buyers would not be considered a bought deal;
- A classic bought deal does not include a situation in which a fund manager sells a block of shares in a company in his stock portfolio via a broker as part of his day-to-day business. Such transactions are rarely publicly disclosed and are often merely a question of adjusting the weighting of a particular stock in the fund manager's portfolio. There is typically more than one bank involved in a bought deal;
- There are no fees in the case of bought deal. The relevant 'issue price' is typically the prevailing market price less a discount of 3–5 per cent, however for very large placements of highly illiquid stocks the discount may be much greater. For high profile bought deals of well-known and highly liquid stocks which have been subject to competitive bidding, the discount can be significantly smaller than 3–5 per cent. The level of the discount does not indicate the exact price at which the shares were bought from the vendor. The lead bank would expect to earn between one and three per cent in terms of the difference between the issue price and the price at which they bought the shares. In the case of the US$745 million placement by SG Warburg and ABN AMRO of new shares in Akzo, corresponding to a 17.1 per cent capital increase, the discount is thought

to have been much greater because of the circumstances of the transaction;

- As a rule, no due diligence is carried out in connection with a bought deal nor is a prospectus published and these facts are clearly stated to investors. Accordingly, the lead bank's legal liability is limited as it is not responsible for any information on the company. In the context of bought deals, no due diligence is preferable to some due diligence, as this may lead to confusion and mislead investors;
- A bought deal involves a very simple underwriting agreement between the lead bank(s) and the vendor(s). In the case of the sale by Uni Storebrand and Hafnia of shares in Skandia, the 'share purchase agreement' between the vendors and BZW was only a few lines on a piece of paper. Typically there are no other agreements involved, although there are exceptions to this rule. In the case of the sale by Elf Acquitaine of shares in Enterprise Oil, the joint venture agreement between Elf and Enterprise had to be renegotiated prior to the execution of the sale and so the documentation was more complex; and
- Typically, the involvement of the management of the company subject to the bought deal, is minimal. However in special situations such as the dissolution of the ownership stalemate in Skandia, the Swedish insurance company, the Skandia management had already made certain unrelated presentations to institutional investors some time before the announcement of the transaction.

The advantages of a bought deal
- The risk is typically well defined from the point of view of the vendor as the price is known upfront (there is no 'Wellcome effect', where the vendor announced the sale when the market price was £11.25 and the sale was executed almost four and-a-half months later at a price of £8.00);
- The vendor typically has considerable flexibility to pick the best time for the sale. The vendor and the lead bank(s) can, to a very significant degree, avoid adverse market conditions, the announcement of economic/ financial data to which the market may react negatively or extraordinary events such as wars etc;
- There is minimal documentation and as a consequence limited legal liability for the vendor and the bank(s);
- Limited management involvement on the part of the vendor and the company subject to the sale;
- Avoidance of difficult negotiations between vendor and company regarding the company's full support as in the case of a 'prospectus offer'; and
- No public debate about the merits of the transaction until the transaction has been completed.

Why bought deals are not more common
- The vendor may not wish to upset the company management by executing an offer not fully coordinated

with it, particularly if he intends to retain a sizeable stake. The management often have strong views about how, and to whom, its shares are being sold and therefore want to be in control of the process: in addition, company managements may have other financing plans with which the bought deal would be in conflict;

- Some shares may not be sufficiently liquid, known or attractive in terms of the 'stock story' to be sold without considerable marketing, except in very strong market conditions;

- The quality of placement and/or the perception thereof is not as high as that of a 'prospectus offer'. These transactions are often done in the spirit of the 'first' rather than the 'best bid', although the lead bank obviously has to be mindful of who it is placing the shares with to ensure that is does not place the same shares twice during a 1–2 day placing exercise;

- Relatively few investment banks are equipped to handle this type of business in other than the strongest of market conditions. Yet fewer consider the risk/reward ratio of this structure to be appropriate;

- Although the risk to reputation is much smaller than in the case of a 'prospectus offer', there is still some risk to the lead bank should the placement fail or be of low quality as reflected by a poor after-market performance.

- Bought deals have traditionally been considered less appropriate in privatisations because transparency, and therefore accountability, is reduced; and

- Bought deal transactions are often relatively high profile and the market therefore will be aware of the price at which the vendor sold. This exposes it to potential adverse publicity should the stock price rise significantly following the placement. Many vendors may prefer to sell discreetly through one or more brokers in order not to draw attention to the sale, or simply to average out the price by not selling in a single block.

The execution of a bought deal

The execution of a bought deal is relatively straightforward. There is a short preparation phase followed by an equally short execution phase.

Preparation phase

Discussions between the vendor and the lead bank about the placement of a particular block of shares may start at any time between two weeks and 12 hours before the lead bank provides the vendor with a firm bid that is accepted. The approach may come from either party but usually comes from the lead bank. During this time, the lead bank decides whether to proceed with the bid.

In the case of BZW, this decision is taken by a committee made up of representatives from every major division of the bank, including the fixed income, equities and corporate finance divisions. Part of this decision is the risk management strategy to be employed, ie, how the bank will protect itself against the various risks involved. During this time it may also consider whether or not to bring in one or two other banks which will share the risk and assist with the placement. It will also prepare the necessary documentation and forward it to the vendor for review.

The vendor must confirm that it owns the stock and that it can deliver in the days following acceptance. It needs to review the documentation, which is typically made up of a 'Share Purchase Agreement' of anything between a few lines and several pages. If the proportion of the company to be sold exceeds 10 per cent of the outstanding share capital and if the vendor has had any representation in the board of directors or management of the company it may be necessary to include additional information for a 144A US private placement option. The vendor may or may not enter into negotiations with the company about how the sale will be executed and the nature of such discussions depends on the relationship between the vendor and the company, and the circumstances involved. In many cases the company is only informed by the vendor a few hours before the beginning of the placement.

Once the vendor is ready, it agrees a timetable with the lead bank which sets the exact time that the firm offer will be made and accepted. In redent years, not least because of many failed prospectus offers, governments have been increasingly attracted to this structure.

Execution phase

Once the offer has been accepted, the lead bank owns the stock at a price which is typically 3–5 per cent below the prevailing market price, and at this point the placement exercise begins. Depending on the size of the placement, the stock 'story', the liquidity of the stock and the prevailing market conditions, this exercise may take anything from a limited number of hours to a few days. To limit the exposure to market risk, these placements generally take place during the middle of the week. If the aim is for global placement involving several time horizons, one would expect to begin in the south-east Asian market, continue in Europe and finish in the US market, in order to place during as many 'open market' hours as possible. Once the placement is completed, there is often an announcement to the effect that the placement has taken place and the price at which it was done.

The risks

BZW considers two principal risks involved in a bought deal:

- *'Market risk':* the risk that the price of the company's shares falls before the placement is completed (specific price risk) and the fact that a general deterioration in the stock market environment may reduce the appetite to buy and therefore prevent the lead bank selling its entire position (general market risk). These are weighed and reviewed in the context of the cost of funding an unsold position and the period over which it must be held, the cost of carry, and the risk that this may increase during an enforced holding period (financial risk and interest rate risk respectively); and

- *'Demand risk':* the risk of not reading investor interest correctly. This can be broken down into the risks of reading investor interest incorrectly for the country, the sector and the particular company. A positive long-term view of the company concerned does not matter as much as what investors want to do over the days that the placement is to take place.

The required risk management capability

For a bank to be consistently successful in the bought deal segment of the market, the following capabilities are required:

- *Strong distribution capacity:* A large and/or high quality sales force with recognised overall strength, country strength and/or sector strength;
- *A good understanding of the stock:* To undertake an efficient transaction, a bank should understand the investment flows of the particular shares and have an appreciation of the fundamentals of its investment case. It has been suggested that the lead bank does not necessarily have to have a high opinion of the shares if they are very liquid, as it may just be a question of setting the discount at an appropriate level;
- *Capital:* It is obviously a great help if the lead bank has a substantial market-making operation in equities as the size of the particular bought deal in terms of its capital requirement will then be seen in an overall 'equity risk' context. An important presence in the relevant national market or industry sector would give the decision-makers the necessary comfort that the position is easily monetisable;
- *Risk management techniques:* Whether as a matter of policy or practice, bought deals are rarely fully and perfectly hedged. If they were easily hedgeable, anyone with the necessary expertise could enter this segment of the equity market. The specific risk must be seen in a much broader risk management context, ie, the overall capital of the firm and the overall size of the market-making operation. Nevertheless, the lead bank may try to do several things to limit the overall risk: buy market put options or short market futures, hedge the sector risk by shorting a basket of liquid stocks in the same industry sector and/or buy/put options on the particular stock. The employment of one or several of these hedging techniques would rarely if ever amount to a perfect hedge and would also be very costly. The degree to which attempts to hedge will be made usually depends on the general market conditions, the strength of the research view, the absolute and relative capital requirement and the liquidity of the particular stock; and
- *Credibility and track record:* Credibility in this segment of the market is important for several reasons: to obtain the mandate in the first place; for the internal

decision-making process (which sometimes has to be very fast); and with regard to the market once placement begins, because institutions may be reluctant to buy if they think they will be able to do so more cheaply following an unsuccessful placement.

Situations that lend themselves to bought deals

When a bought deal makes sense

The vendor's point of view:

- A block of shares or a stake has been acquired by 'accident', eg, indirectly in connection with the acquisition of a company that happened to own this block;
- He needs to or wants to sell quickly or has a firm view on the right price. Increasingly, state vendors have seen this as a useful tool to realise targeted proceeds within a particular budget year. In terms of a privatisation programme, bought deals make particular sense, when the state sells its small remaining stake, following earlier prospectus offers;
- If the company is located in a country with a small and cyclical stock market where it might not be advisable to take the risk of waiting for the completion of a 'prospectus offer'; or
- The vendor has already procured the support or blessing of the company management or is indifferent to such support because he does not have or need to have a relationship with the company.

The lead bank's point of view:

- When the general stock market environment is highly favourable and the market is specifically interested in buying the particular stock subject to the placement. In the examples used in this section, BZW managed to time the sales in such a way that six out of seven stocks had outperformed their respective local markets during the week before announcement of the bought deals;
- When the equity research view is very strong; or
- When a bank already has a few lead investors interested in a large proportion of the block.

Examples of bought deals

Examining some of the publicly announced bought deals executed by BZW in four different stock markets – the UK, New Zealand, Sweden and Finland – from February 1991 to November 1994, we can see the diverse range of the transactions (see Exhibit 10).

The absolute size

The absolute size of bought deals can vary considerably and can be significantly smaller than the smallest of BZW's placements tabled above, as in the US$149 million placement of shares in TCNZ and significantly bigger than the US$804 million placement for Allied Lyons.

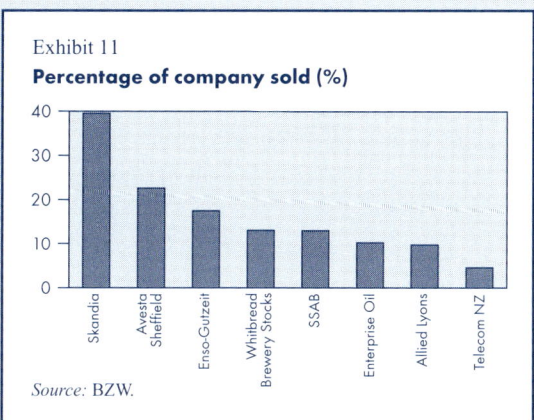

Exhibit 11
Percentage of company sold (%)

Source: BZW.

The proportion of the company that can be sold

The percentage of the company sold varies from 4.6 per cent in the case of TCNZ to almost 40 per cent in the case of Skandia, however considerably smaller percentages are possible if the market capitalisation of the company is sufficiently large to warrant a classic bought deal transaction (see Exhibit 11).

The market capitalisation required

If we discount some of the individual Whitbread companies, the smallest company for which BZW executed this type of transaction was Skandia, which had a market capitalisation of US$1,248 million. There is no formal minimum market capitalisation requirement. If a particular share is sufficiently liquid, bought deals for companies below US$500 million are not inconceivable (as was the case with a number of the companies involved in the disposals by Whitbread).

The minimum amount of secondary market liquidity required

The degree of secondary market liquidity is very important when assessing the feasibility of a bought deal. Nevertheless, as the experience of BZW shows, in a strong market, transactions that are large when seen in the context of the particular share's secondary market liquidity can still be executed successfully. In the case of Enso-Gutzeit for example the size of the bought deal corresponded to the equivalent of 365 days of secondary market trading volume, but it was purchased by BZW off the back of a very strong research view. Such a transaction amounts to an ambitious exercise compared to a bought deal where the size of the transaction seen in the context of its secondary market liquidity only amounts to 20 days, as in the case of Telecom Corporation New Zealand.

The banks

In all cases there were at least three banks involved, although on two occasions, BZW accounted for 100 per cent of the placement.

Discounts

The discount varied from a relatively modest 3 per cent in the case of SSAB – a relatively small transaction in the

context of the deals under discussion – to 11 per cent for Skandia, as the size of the placement represented 40 per cent of the company and 256 days equivalent of trading on the Stockholm Stock Exchange. The size of the discount is a matter of negotiation between the vendor and the bank, and depends on the respective negotiating positions of the two parties.

The companies

In two cases, Allied Lyons and TCNZ, the companies had a high international name recognition in the international equity market. In the four other cases, the companies were little known and not actively traded internationally.

The market reaction to bought deals

In the short term, without the benefit of the demand created by a prospectus, a research report or a roadshow, the market would typically be expected to react negatively to a sudden supply of shares. However, in the case of BZW's bought deals, investors who bought at the issue price saw the market close higher on the day of placement in four out of the seven cases (see Exhibit 12).

As there is a considerable difference between issue price and market price at the time of pricing, corresponding to the size of the discount, we should also look at how the market as a whole reacted over the day. Not entirely surprisingly, we find that the market as a whole did not fare as well (see Exhibit 13).

Exhibit 12
How did investors do over the same day?

	Issue price	Same day close	Gain/loss same day (%)
Telecom NZ	2.6	2.72	4.62
Enso Gutzeit	37.5	39.8	6.13
Skandia	105	111	5.71
Avesta Sheffield	64	64.5	0.78
Allied Lyons	498	496	-0.40
Enterprise Oil	387	385	-0.52
SSAB	327	322	-1.53

Source: Datastream.

Exhibit 13
How did the market react over the first day?

	Previous day's close	Same day close	Gain/loss day 1 (%)
Enterprise Oil	386	385	-0.26
Telecom NZ	2.73	2.72	-0.37
Skandia	112	111	-0.89
SSAB	327	322	-1.53
Allied Lyons	507	496	-2.15
Avesta Sheffield	66	64.50	-2.27
Enso Gutzeit	41.80	39.80	-4.78

Source: Datastream.

Exhibit 14

How did the market react over the first week?

	Market close on pricing day	Market price 1 week later	Gain/loss day 1 (%)
Skandia	111	118	6.30
Telecom NZ	2.72	2.84	4.41
Allied Lyons	496	510	2.82
SSAB	322	329	2.17
Enterprise Oil	385	380	-1.30
Avesta Sheffield	64.50	63	-2.33
Enso Gutzeit	39.80	38.5	-3.27

Source: Datastream.

Exhibit 15

What about the relative performance over the first 3 months? (%)

	IP/index on pricing date	Market price/ index + 3 months	Relative performance
Skandia	100	121	21
Telecom NZ	100	140	40
Allied Lyons	100	103	3
SSAB	100	111	11
Enterprise Oil	100	112	12
Avesta Sheffield	100	111	11
Enso Gutzeit	100	95	-5

Source: Datastream.

This underperformance of the market price on the day of pricing is related to the additional supply, and the fact that it typically adjusts some way towards the issue price. What is important is how quickly it recovers over the following days. This indicates a slightly better picture, with only three of the stocks being in negative territory (see Exhibit 14).

Over the first month the picture is the same as over the first week, with the same three stocks being in negative territory. Three months after pricing only Enso-Gutzeit was in negative territory, and then only marginally as it had again increased to FIM39.

The most important measure in the long term lies in the relative performance of these shares which would indicate that BZW not only picked them very astutely but also placed them well (see Exhibit 15).

Conclusion

The bought deal structure is a viable option for vendors of shares in another company, and has many distinct advantages when compared to the more rigorous bookbuilt prospectus offer, if handled by a bank with the appropriate capabilities.

To summarise, bought deals:

- Offer superior timing flexibility;
- Require a minimum of preparation;
- Are executed with a minimum time requirement on the part of the vendor;
- Conflict only to a limited degree, if at all, with the equity strategy of the company concerned if executed in a strong market and if appropriately coordinated with the management of the company concerned; and
- Are relatively inexpensive.

As we have seen from the sample of bought deals executed by BZW from 1991–94, the structure can be applied, in the right market environment, to almost any size of transaction. They are most suited to companies that are well known and highly liquid but can also be considered under less favourable circumstances. Out of BZW's bought deal transactions, only one, Enso-Gutzeit, performed below expectations following pricing. The likely reason was that the offer was too big in relation to its international liquidity.

Argentaria

Argentaria, one of the three largest banking groups in Spain, was formed in 1991 as part of the Spanish government's campaign to restructure and privatise the state's banking interests.

With the deregulation of the Spanish banking sector, the state-owned banks had ceased to be of strategic value to the state and the government took the view that it was going to achieve a higher value for its banking interests if they were merged, as a larger bank would make a more significant contribution towards a competitive Spanish banking sector. Recognising that Banco Bilbao Vizcaya had gone through the merger process a few years earlier, the socialist government of Felipe González appointed a BBV man, Francisco Luzón López, as Argentaria's first chairman.

The government set about privatising 25 per cent of Argentaria in May 1993. Against an initial expectation of relatively limited retail and institutional interest, Argentaria was a blow-out. Argentaria 2, through which the government sold off a further 23 per cent followed sooner than expected, in November 1993. This was also oversubscribed but fared substantially less well in the secondary market.

Luzón was keen that the government should continue to sell its stake down as soon as possible but during 1994 and 1995 market conditions militated against a further sale, as did the bank's own performance. Following hard on the heels on the fifth Repsol offer in March 1996, the Government privatised a further 25 per cent of Argentaria despite diffi-cult market conditions, occasioned by an inconclusive election result.

The first of these sales of Argentaria stock was the first continental European privatisation/IPO distributed to both retail and institutional investors using a US style bookbuilding method to determine demand at various prices across all tranches.

It was, however, still considered essential for marketing reasons to run a fixed price offer for Spanish retail investors, the implication of which was a 13-day hard underwriting period at the full offer price. The domestic retail subscription period was eight days, at the time the shortest ever in Spain for such a large offer, and Argentaria 1 was the first time that the concept of 'pre-registration' was adopted in Spain. This is a system whereby retail investors can indicate their interest prior to the retail subscription period, thereby earning a priority in the allocation process. The offer was, at the time, the largest Spanish IPO ever.

Major challenges

The deal faced a number of hurdles that had to be cleared for the offer to succeed:

- Previous Spanish and other European bank offers had not been successful in the US, nor had they been enthusiastically taken up elsewhere; and

---

Exhibit 1
Transaction summary

Issuer name: Corporation Bancaria de Espana S.A., Argentaria (Spain)	Global coordinator: Morgan Stanley Co global coordinator: Argentaria Bolsa
Pricing date: 23 April 1993 (Madrid SE Index 247.03)	Pricing/underwriting structure: Bookbuilding, followed by hard underwriting period for 2 weeks
Vendor: Sociedad Estatal de Patrimonio I, SA	Primary or secondary: Secondary
	Retail structure: –
% of company sold: 24.99%	Privatisation or corporate: Privatisation
IPO or non-IPO: IPO	Industry: Banking
Type of shares: Ordinary shares and ADRs (1 ADR = 2 ordinary shares)	Pricing range: Pta3500–3950 Offer price: Pta3800 & US$16.07/ADR
Total issue size: US$ 1,008 million	US listing/144 A: NYSE listing

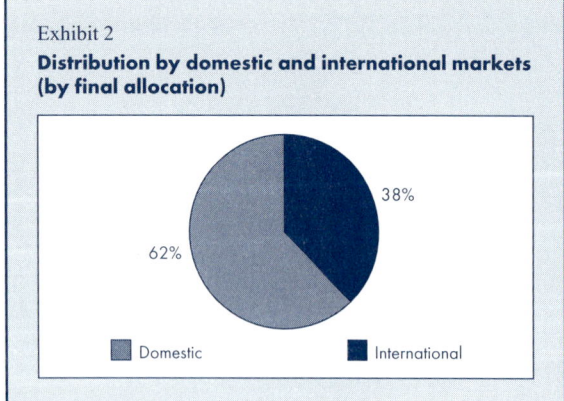

Exhibit 2

Distribution by domestic and international markets (by final allocation)

38%

62%

■ Domestic   ■ International

- High retail penetration was necessary, but the bank could not be sure of the cooperation and motivation of its competitors in distributing shares through their branch networks.
- Argentaria's management faced the challenge of harmonising the domestic retail and international offer practices. The bank would, for example, have to minimise the long hard underwriting period (23 April–12 May) traditionally associated with Spanish IPOs in order to ensure that trading could begin as quickly as possible after the issue had been priced.

Rationale and objectives

The creation of Argentaria was initiated by a government that wanted to introduce more competition and efficiency into the Spanish banking sector. The assets that now make up Argentaria were grouped with a view to privatisation.

The Spanish government, through the wholly-owned Patrimonio (the holding company for state-owned assets) and Argentaria, articulated the following offer objectives:

- Maximisation of proceeds, consistent with a successful IPO. A first day premium of 10–15 per cent was needed for this to qualify as a success;
- Creation of a wide, stable and happy domestic shareholder base;

- Creation of a stable institutional shareholder group – domestic and international;
- Market approval of the Argentaria project and the 'federation of banks' concept; and
- Flotation by way of a transparent process.

The Argentaria management, having mostly come from BBV, was keen to prove that they could achieve the same valuation as their competitors, and they were keen to develop a sense of independence from the state. Argentaria therefore wanted to find as many private shareholders as possible while achieving a healthy balance between retail and institutional shareholders. There was some political sensitivity regarding the balance between domestic and foreign participation in the float, with the desired limit on foreign participation being in the region of 50 per cent.

Share capital and ownership

See Exhibit 3.

Transaction components

Offer structure and syndicate

The initial offer was of 28 million already outstanding shares comprised of: the Spanish offer (representing 61 per cent of the combined offers) divided into a retail tranche and an institutional tranche; a US offer of ADRs, initially representing 14.3 per cent of the combined offers; and an international offer representing the remainder and made up of three separate tranches in the UK, continental Europe and rest of the world (RoW), as shown in Exhibit 4.

In addition to the lead managers, co-lead managers and the co-managers/underwriters, any financial institution in Spain was free to sell the shares. These 'placing agents' received a 'placement fee' from Argentaria, and were among more than 70 financial institutions which sold the Argentaria 1 offer in Spain.

The combined offer was marketed on an open-priced basis to international and domestic institutions allowing a book to

Exhibit 3

Share capital and ownership

Type of shares offered	Ordinary shares of Pta500. Twenty-five shares required for one vote.
Ownership restrictions	No specific restrictions on foreign portfolio investment. Person(s) acquiring more than 5% are subject to reporting requirements. Bank of Spain approval needed to buy more than 15%.
Share capital before and after offer	125,500,000 ordinary shares.
Listings	Listed on Madrid and other Spanish exchanges and on the New York Stock Exchange in connection with the offer.
Market capitalisation at offer price (Pta118.20/US$)	US$4.03 billion
Major shareholder before offer	The government owned 100% before the offer.
Most relevant stock exchange index/weighting	IBEX/4.3% weighting, taking 100% of Argentaria's share capital into account.

Exhibit 4
Offer structure

Target markets	Indicated tranche sizes**	Regional bookrunning lead managers	Co-lead managers
Spanish offer*	60.7%	Argentaria Bolsa	BBV, Banco Central, Banco Santander
US offer	14.3%	Morgan Stanley	Goldman, Merrill Lynch, SG Warburg
International offer			
UK and Ireland	12.5%	SG Warburg, Banco Santander	Morgan Stanley Intl UBS
Continental Europe	8.9%	UBS	Morgan Stanley Intl, Banco Santander, SG Warburg
RoW	3.6%	Merrill Lynch	Morgan Stanley Intl, Nikko Europe
Total combined offers (shares)	**28,000,000**		

* The syndicate was identical for both the retail and institutional tranches of the Spanish sale.
** Percentage of the initially indicated combined offer as announced on 12 April 1993.

Source: Capital Data Ltd.

Exhibit 5
Development of the offer size

Initially indicated number of shares to be sold (12 April)	28,000,000 + 1,650,000 greenshoe
Offer size after increase of offer size (6 May)	29,712,450 + 1,650,000 greenshoe
Greenshoe fully exercised (week of 12 May)	1,650,000
Final number of shares sold	31 362 450

Exhibit 6
Principal advisers

Financial adviser to the company	Morgan Stanley
Spanish legal adviser to the company and the vendor	J&A Garrigues
US legal adviser to the company and the vendor	Davis Polk & Wardwell
US legal adviser to the underwriters	Sullivan & Cromwell
Auditors	Arthur Andersen
Marketing advisers to the company	Dewe Rogerson, Bassat Ogilvy & Mather, Leader Mix (Argentaria Group)

be built, after which the offer price was fixed in pesetas. Once the price was fixed, an eight-day formal subscription period for domestic retail investors followed during which there was a clawback to the Spanish retail offer of 8 per cent from the US and International tranches.

The US and International tranches were structured with a greenshoe of 1.65 million shares, equivalent to 15 per cent of the non-Spanish portion of the combined offer. There was no general discount for retail, nor were bonus shares offered although Argentaria employees were offered a 7.5 per cent discount to the offer price. The shares were listed in Spain and on the NYSE.

The offer was first increased by 1.7 million shares on 6 May, due to strong demand and on 11 May, concurrent with the final allocations, the clawback was fully exercised in favour of the retail tranche. The greenshoe was exercised during the first week of trading, bringing

Exhibit 7
Distribution of gross spread (%)

Management	Underwriting	Selling concession	Gross spread
0.7	0.7	2.1	3.5

Source: Morgan Stanley.

the total number of shares offered to 31.4 million (see Exhibit 5).

Principal advisers
See Exhibit 6.

Transaction fee distribution
See Exhibit 7.

Management fee

Morgan Stanley and Argentaria Bolsa shared 25 per cent of the total management fee as the global coordinators'

praecipium, calculated on the gross proceeds of the combined offer. Outside the US, the lead and co-lead managers shared a further 25 per cent of the total management fee as the lead and co-lead managers' praecipium (see Exhibit 8).

In the US the management fees were allocated on the basis of underwriting commitment for the managers only, with the exception of the deduction of the global coordinators' praecipium. Syndicate members in the US do not participate in the management fee.

The underwriting fee was split pro rata to underwriting amounts across the whole syndicate including the managers.

Selling concession

Orders in the US fall into two categories – 'institutional pot' and 'free retention' (also known as retail demand). Institutional orders are subject to an 'economic arrangement' whereby there is a 'pre-split' or a fixed and guaranteed component of 30 per cent, calculated on the basis of underwriting commitments of all the managers and a competitive portion (or 'jump ball') subject to performance. Orders outside the 'pot' (retail orders) are not subject to the pre-split on economics and are 100 per cent competitive or 'jump ball' (see Exhibit 9).

In Europe the selling concession was paid in full to whomever the order was given (ie, 100 per cent jump-ball).

Exhibit 8

Distribution of management fee outside the US (%)

Total management fee	0.7
Of which: Global coordinators' praecipium	25
Of which: Lead/co-lead managers' praecipium split among all leads/co-leads	25
Of which: Management fees split among all managers	50

Source: Morgan Stanley.

Exhibit 9

Distribution of selling concession in the US (%)

Total selling concession in the US	2.1
Of which: Pre-agreed or fixed portion regardless of sales generated (available to managers only)	30
Of which: Paid pro-rata according to sales designated by investors	70

Source: Morgan Stanley.

Exhibit 10

The timetable

1st week of February 1993	• Morgan Stanley and Argentaria Bolsa appointed global coordinators.
2–10 February	• Keith Brown, Morgan Stanley's banking analyst, conducts awareness meetings throughout Europe.
4 March	• Announcement of the syndicate structure; global coordinator and regional lead manager appointments.
22 March	• Announcement of indicative transaction size, relative tranche sizes and price range.
24 March	• Registration period for retail investors begins.
29 March	• Public filing of Pink Herring with the US SEC; • Formal pre-marketing begins.
7 April	• Filing of prospectus with CNMV (Spanish 'SEC').
12 April	• Filing of Red Herring; • Roadshow starts; • Bookbuilding begins.
23 April	• Bookbuilding ends; • Peseta offer price fixed; • Primary underwriting agreement signed; • Registration period ends.
26 April	• Domestic offer subscription period begins.
5 May	• Domestic offer subscription period closes.
6 May	• Announcement of increase of offer size by 1.7 million shares.
10 May	• Allocation to domestic retail investors.
11 May	• Fixing of ADR offer price in US$; • Secondary underwriting agreement signed; • Allocation to institutional investors.
12 May	• Trading begins in Madrid and on the NYSE.
Week of 12 May	• Greenshoe exercised.

Deal structure

Prior to Argentaria 1, fixed price offers with a 30-day subscription period had been the norm in Spain. There was no competition between retail and institutional tranches and no flexibility with regard to the size of the different tranches.

For Argentaria this structure was replaced by a combination of institutional bookbuilding followed by an eight-day fixed price offer for retail investors. Thanks to the introduction of 'pre-registration', a process whereby these investors register their interest prior to the beginning of the OPV (*oferta pública de venta*) against the promise of priority in the allocation process, the managers and institutional investors had an indication of the level of interest before the beginning of the bookbuilding period. There was, therefore, simultaneous competition between the retail and institutional tranches. The offer price was only set after bookbuilding, which meant that pricing took place after crucial market information had been gathered from both retail and institutional investors.

The 'registration system' allowed Argentaria to maintain control over the offer and to increase the pressure directly on investors and the branch managers of both Argentaria's own branches, and more importantly, those of their competitors. Francisco Roldán, then general manager and CFO – now CEO said: 'We incorporated registration for two reasons: to retain control over our own offer by going directly to investors, and to be able to exercise some control over our competitors.'

To further motivate its domestic competitors to sell their shares, Argentaria included them not only in the domestic syndicate, but also as co-leads or joint leads in the international tranches. This was the first time Spanish banks had been invited in a senior capacity into the foreign tranches of a major privatisation.

Argentaria was well prepared for this offer. The bank had worked on its strategy formulation for some 18 months and had then gone through a period of consultation with international investment banks such as Morgan Stanley to decide whether or not to sell shares in the holding company or the individual operating units. (Morgan Stanley had a mandate in 1992 to offer shares in the already quoted Banco Exterior.) The decision was taken to go for the higher profile alternative of selling shares in the larger entity comprising all the operating units and the preparation for the IPO of Argentaria started in October 1992. The timing was excellent from the point of view of macroeconomic conditions and the company's readiness but there was a big question mark over the likely interest of the domestic retail investor.

Marketing

Retail

The marketing of Argentaria shares to retail investors in Spain was innovative, highly aggressive and ultimately very successful. It was perhaps this success, more than anything else, that paved the way for the strong interest among international institutions. The secret of the retail success lay, in particular, in the marketing campaigns, the system of registration

and the way Argentaria managed to get its competitors to cooperate with the sale of the shares.

There were three distinctly different retail marketing campaigns:

- The corporate awareness campaign: this campaign started in early 1991, and continued until one month before the beginning of 'pre-registration'. The objective was to raise the general awareness of Argentaria as a new force in Spanish banking;
- Corporate image campaign: this campaign built on the corporate awareness campaign and highlighted Argentaria's strengths as a competitor in Spain. The corporate image campaign ran for one month immediately before the beginning of the registration period; and
- Selling campaign: this campaign began at the same time as bookbuilding, on 12 April, and continued until the end of the retail subscription period on 5 May. The campaign initially focused on how to subscribe and once the price had been set on 23 April, on why it was financially astute to subscribe. The selling campaign was run both on television and in the press.

Retail interest in straight equity offers had been weak over the two years prior to the Argentaria offer. Limited retail demand had been one of the reasons Repsol decided to opt for an exchangeable bond offer to domestic retail investors in the summer of 1992, and had then gone for a purely institutional offer in early 1993. No previous privatisations had been based on a strategy of mass marketing to a retail audience.

For this strategy to work, it was vital not only for Argentaria to promote itself exceptionally well and to manage the offer very professionally, but also for the other major banks to participate willingly in the transaction. The strategy adopted was to ensure that participation was one that used both a 'carrot' and a 'stick'.

As far as the 'carrot' was concerned, the idea was to afford all the banks equal status in the Spanish offer and to pay them generously. There was an increased selling fee for those banks in the retail syndicate who placed a certain amount of shares in relation to their underwriting commitment.

The 'stick' was twofold, putting pressure on retail investors to apply for shares and on the branch managers of Argentaria's competitors to compete for that business. As Jose Sainz, CEO of Argentaria Bolsa, the investment banking arm of Argentaria explains: 'Through TV advertising, we asked people to contact the Share Information and Registration Office by telephone to request a reservation form. We handed the initiative to the investors and encouraged them to go to the bank branches to 'reserve' shares or 'register for the offer' during the two-week period prior to the beginning of the OPV period, rather than relying on the banks themselves to sell the offer.'

Because the Share Information and Registration Office operated by Argentaria would obtain the contact details of competitors' clients, the banks worked harder than they otherwise would have to be ready to receive investors coming into the branches as they wanted to ensure that they did not lose client business to Argentaria's branches.

The real secret was to get the customers to come into the branches. This strategy was achieved in four principal steps:

Step 1   Advertising campaign to encourage investor telephone calls to the Share Information and Registration Office;

Step 2   Investors request registration forms by telephone;

Step 3   Dispatch of registration forms by Argentaria to investors; and

Step 4   Retail investors visit their bank branches to discuss the Argentaria privatisation and to 'register' before the beginning of the OPV.

Roldán of Argentaria said: 'We were also very aggressive with our own branches and our own customers. In addition, we were in regular communication with the market stressing the scarcity of shares. We also gave regular progress reports in terms of people who had already registered or subscribed, to underpin the momentum.'

Exhibit 11

The Roadshow

Spanish Roadshow (3 working days)
- Madrid
- Bilbao
- Barcelona
- Valencia

US and Canada Roadshow (5 working days)
- Los Angeles
- Phoenix
- Philadelphia
- San Francisco
- Portland
- Boston
- Chicago
- Houston
- New York
- Denver
- Ft Lauderdale
- Toronto

European Roadshow (5 working days)
- London
- Zurich
- The Hague
- Glasgow
- Geneva
- Amsterdam
- Edinburgh
- Milan
- Frankfurt
- Paris

Institutional

In mid-April Argentaria embarked on a 10-day roadshow (see Exhibit 11) using two management teams. The emphasis of this and the specific destinations should be seen in the context of the plan to sell 60 per cent of the offer in Spain, 14 per cent in the US, 13 per cent in the UK, 9 per cent in continental Europe and 4 per cent in the rest of the world (RoW).

Argentaria was presented as a restructuring story with cost rationalisation, reduction of non-performing loans and increased cross selling as major themes. This was credible for two reasons: first, the Spanish economy was in a deep recession in 1992–93, and secondly, Argentaria was a recently established entity. The latter was responsible for a belief that, even without a full merger taking place, there would be considerable synergies both on the cost and revenue sides. Morgan Stanley sold Argentaria on the basis of the selling points shown in Exhibit 12.

Argentaria was attractively priced in terms of its price/book value (see Exhibit 13) and was also attractively valued in terms of its P/E ratio (see Exhibit 14).

Reasons for not buying

- Official government policy was to remain within the ERM bands, a policy which had required high interest rates and which had deepened the recession in 1992–93;
- The increasing threat of devaluation was viewed negatively by certain investors. When devaluation occurred on 13 May, it was, however, viewed positively by the equity market;
- The Spanish economy was in recession, but was expected to recover to manage GDP growth of 1.5 per cent in 1994, assuming currency devaluation;
- An election was due by December 1993 at the latest. In the event, a general election was called on April 12 for 6 June 1993;

Exhibit 12

Principal sales points

Market positions in Spain	• No 2 by assets • No 1 by loans • No 3 by deposits • No 3 by net income.
Growth	Above average growth relative to bank stocks and the market: • Potential to produce above average profit performance, due to synergies and cross-selling, recovery of written off loans, stable to improving margins and fee income potential (20% of '95 income was expected to come from fees) and rationalisation of cost base (staff to be reduced from 18,400 to 15,000 over 3–4 years, cost/income to improve from 58% in 92 to 48% in 1995). • 5-year compound earnings per share growth of 18.7% was expected.
Macro environment	• Recovering economy; • Falling interest rates; • Attractively valued equity market for investors.
Strong capital base	Total BIS ratio of 13.1% and Tier 1 capital ratio of 12%.
Asset quality	• Exceptional provisions made as part of clean-up, 50% coverage (loan loss reserve as a% of NPLs) of non-LDC loans and 76% coverage of LDC loans
Valuation	• Within Europe, the Spanish market had a low relative valuation, within the Spanish market, the banking sector provided attractive valuation and high sensitivity to lower interest rates and within the Spanish banking sector, Argentaria provided unique recovery prospects.

Sources: Morgan Stanley and Prospectus.

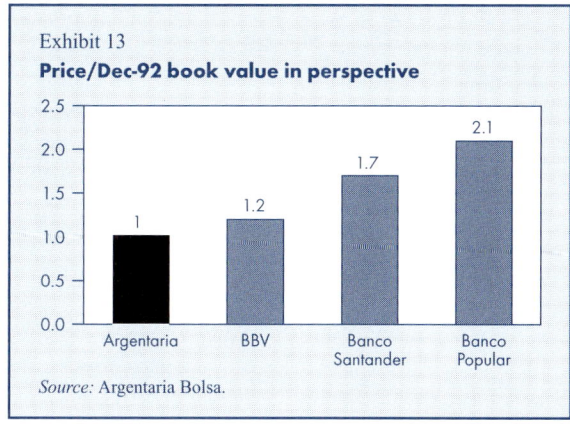

Exhibit 13
Price/Dec-92 book value in perspective

Source: Argentaria Bolsa.

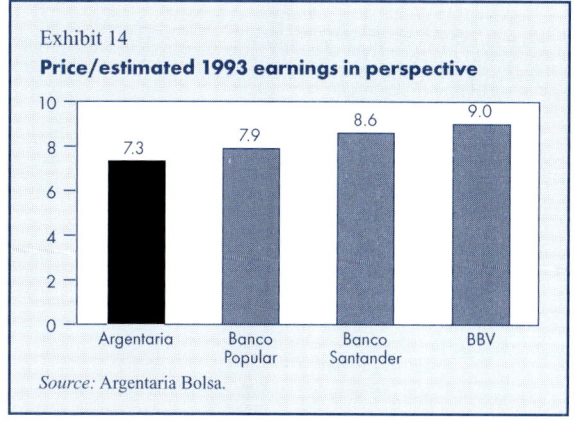

Exhibit 14
Price/estimated 1993 earnings in perspective

Source: Argentaria Bolsa.

Exhibit 15
Underwriting, demand and allocation (%)

	Initial underwriting (April 12)	Underwriting post increase and clawback (May 11)*	Demand	Allocation**
Spanish retail*	51.8	57.6	25.9	54.4
Spanish institutions	8.9	8.4	10.7	8.0
Total Spanish	60.7	66.0	36.6	62.4
United States	14.3	12.5	24.6	13.7
United Kingdom	12.5	10.8	22.8	12.4
Continental Europe	8.9	7.7	12.0	7.6
RoW	3.6	3.0	4.0	3.8
Total US and international offers	39.3	34.0	63.4	37.6
Total combined offers (shares)	**28,000,000**	**29,712,450**	**202,000,000**	**31,362,450**

* Including distribution to employees and pensioners.   ** Including the full greenshoe.

Sources: Argentaria and Morgan Stanley.

- The stockmarket had performed reasonably well in 1993, but a delay in the reduction of interest rates would stall the equity market's performance, despite the Spanish market's 'under-valuation';
- Although asset quality was a general concern for the entire Spanish banking sector, Argentaria had performed a clean-up. Initial indications were that non-performing loans would not increase in 1993; and
- There was increasing competition and margin pressure, particularly for deposits and mutual funds.

Results

Placement

The book built rapidly from the start of the bookbuilding period with the entire US and International offers oversubscribed by the second day. The big orders from the US and UK came in four days before the end of the subscription period (see Exhibit 15.)

On 6 May the decision was taken to increase the combined offer by 1.7 million shares, with the entire increase being allocated to the retail tranche. In addition, it was decided to exercise the full 8 per cent clawback provision, thereby increasing the Spanish retail tranche by a further 880,000

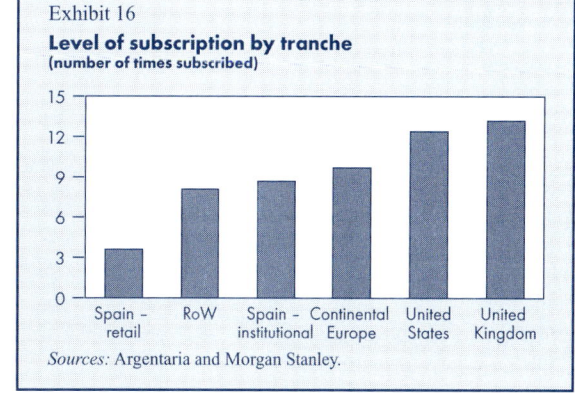

Exhibit 16
Level of subscription by tranche
(number of times subscribed)

Sources: Argentaria and Morgan Stanley.

shares and decreasing the US and International offers correspondingly.

The strongest demand came from the UK and US where practically all core accounts placed substantial orders. The combined offer was 7.2 times subscribed, with all the individual tranches being substantially oversubscribed as can be seen in Exhibit 16.

Investor concentration

- The top 10 orders accounted for total demand per tranche as follows: 59.2 per cent of the RoW tranche, 48.3 per cent

Exhibit 17
International investor concentration

	By demand	By allocation
Percentage of international institutional portion of total issue accounted for by the 10 largest international investors (by total size of institutional demand and allocation respectively)	22%	13%
Number of investors making up 80% of the international institutional portion of the issue (by total size of institutional demand and allocation respectively)	53	45
The 3 largest investors by size	US$ 60 million US$ 43 million US$ 30 million	US$ 50 million US$ 30 million US$ 30 million
Total number of international institutions	837*	516**

* Of which 355 from continental Europe, 210 from UK, 117 from US and 67 from the ROW.
** Of which 217 from continental Europe, 170 from UK, 129 from US and 66 from the ROW. These numbers do not add up due to the fact that there are multiple orders from the same institutions to different managers in Europe, UK and ROW.

of the US tranche, 35.6 per cent of the UK tranche and 22.0 per cent of the continental European tranche;
- The top 50 orders accounted for total demand per tranche as follows: 96.1 per cent for the RoW tranche, 90.7 per cent for the US tranche, 69.9 per cent of the UK tranche and 60.5 per cent for the continental European tranche; and
- There were 323,531 domestic retail subscribers, including 11,869 Argentaria employees.

(See Exhibit 17.)

The buyers
The main types of buyers were:

- Spain funds and Iberia funds;
- International funds;
- Pan-European funds;
- Those investors considering the bank a devaluation play; and
- Financial buyers and bank buyers.

Index buyers were not allocated shares as they were expected to come into the transaction in the after-market, thereby supporting the after-market trading. In the US, demand predominantly came from 'international accounts' but there was also some interest from 'domestic accounts', due to the NYSE listing. There were no privatisation funds in existence at the time.

After-market price performance
- Argentaria was priced at Pta3,800, towards the top end of the pricing range and at the higher end of market expectations. (See Exhibit 18.);
- On the first day of trading (12 May), the market price closed at a premium of 11.3 per cent to the offer price set on 23 April, inside the targeted premium on the first day of 10 per cent–15 per cent. Over the same period, the Spanish market had fallen by 2.1 per cent. Argentaria effectively out-performed the Madrid Stock Exchange Index

Exhibit 18
After-market price performance

Pricing date	23 April 1993
Filing range	Pta3,500–3,950
Offer price	Pta3,800

First year high/low	
High (4 Feb 1994)	Pta6,690
Low (11 May 1993)	Pta3,800

Argentaria share price relative to Madrid Stock Exchange (%)

Absolute and relative share price performance

	Price (Pta)	Relative* (%)
+ 1 day (12 May 1993)	4,230	113.4
+ 3 days	4,430	116.8
+ 5 days	4,445	113.0
+ 1 month	4,700	119.1
+ 3 months	5,950	143.9
+ 6 months	6,000	136.4
+ 9 months	6,460	130.0
+ 12 months (12 May 1994)	6,020	126.0

* Relative to the Madrid Stock Exchange index.

Sources: Datastream and offer circular.

by 13.4 per cent over this period;
- On the second trading day, the peseta was devalued by 8 per cent within the ERM. The Spanish equity market reacted positively and rose by 4 per cent, the banking

Exhibit 19
Percentage of total issue traded* (%)

	Day 1	Day 2	Day 3	Total: Day 1-3
Madrid	8.3	10.8	3.8	22.9
New York	5.1	2.9	0.9	8.9

* Based on the issue of 31.4 million shares.

Source: Datastream.

Exhibit 20
Development of the ownership of Argentaria's free float (%)

	Retail ownership	US ownership	Total foreign ownership
Following Argentaria 1	55	20	40
Spring 1994	45	20	45
November 1995	47	20	46
April 1996 (Following Argentaria 3)	40	16	44

Source: Argentaria.

sector rose by 5 per cent and Argentaria rose by 6.6 per cent;

- Top tier international accounts continued to purchase the stock and on the fifth trading day Argentaria closed at Pta4,445, up 17 per cent from the offer price;
- By 16 November 1993, the pricing date for Argentaria 2, the market price had risen to Pta6,410 allowing Argentaria 2 to be priced at Pta6,050, (equivalent to a discount of 5.6 per cent to the market price), 59 per cent above the offer price for Argentaria 1;
- During the first year of trading, Argentaria outperformed the Spanish market by 26 per cent and closed at Pta6,020, up by 58 per cent, a spectacular performance for a European privatisation; and
- Purchasers of Argentaria 2 had a less happy experience and saw their shares fall in value by 17 per cent from the offer price of Pta6,050 over the first year of trading. Over this period, Argentaria underperformed the Spanish market by 37 per cent and its failure to live up to the bullish forecasts for 1994 and 1995 – Morgan Stanley forecast that net profitability would hit Pta73 billion in 1994 and pass Pta83 billion in 1995; actual profitability was just Pta66.4 billion and Pta74.2 billion, respectively. This undoubtedly hurt Argentaria's credibility (and, to a certain extent, Morgan Stanley's as well) and made subsequent share sales more difficult.

After-market trading volume

See Exhibit 19.

- It was estimated that after some six weeks of trading approximately 80 per cent of retail investors still owned their shares; and

- The overall ownership of Argentaria's free float is thought to have developed approximately as described in Exhibit 20. It is notable that following the third Argentaria transaction which was executed in March 1996, retail ownership had fallen markedly as a percentage of the total free float, whereas the total foreign ownership had increased somewhat, notwithstanding a decline in the proportion owned by US institutions.

The performance of the main parties

The vendor

Patrimonio played a relatively low-key role in this offer, having given a written mandate to Argentaria's management to manage the offer process. This was an astute decision and probably led to a better overall result than would have otherwise been the case, for the simple reason that the people who were actually selling the shares felt highly motivated to do so.

The principal criticism of the vendor in this case is that selling in too many offers creates a constant overhang in the market. Perhaps it would have been appropriate to react to what the bookbuilding was saying, ie, that demand was seven times greater than what was offered. Although that figure would have been substantially inflated, it was certainly an indication that more could have been sold. If 30–35 per cent of the bank had been sold in Argentaria 1, then a second tranche could have brought the holding down to well under 50 per cent, perhaps even as low as 30 per cent. In November 1995 analysts at Carnegie Espana estimated that Argentaria was trading at a 15–20 per cent discount to book, primarily as a result of the overhang.

The company

The Argentaria management deserves credit for the planning and execution of this equity transaction. Specifically, it did the following well:

- It started preparations early – in October 1992;
- Together with McKinsey, the bank developed a strategy for the new Argentaria. Subsequently, with Morgan Stanley, it crafted a strong 'stock story' for the equity markets;
- The 'story' was convincingly delivered on the roadshow;
- The relationships with the vendor, the global coordinator and the regional lead managers were well managed; Argentaria understood the need to motivate the senior banks in the syndicate as well as the need to balance the power of the global coordinator by keeping in close touch with the regional lead managers; and
- Argentaria introduced the method of 'pre-registration' to the Spanish domestic market and subsequently pursued the retail offer aggressively and successfully.

Argentaria's share price performed strongly in the aftermarket, particularly for the first six to nine months. It is rare in European privatisations to see a 26 per cent relative out-performance over the first year. Argentaria 2 was less successful.

The global coordinators

The principal competitors for this mandate were Morgan Stanley, SG Warburg, Goldman Sachs, Merrill Lynch and UBS. The decision to appoint Morgan Stanley was taken by the Ministry of Finance together with Patrimonio on the recommendation of Argentaria's management. Argentaria's Roldán says: 'Morgan Stanley won the mandate because we felt that this was going to be a very important transaction for them, as their first major privatisation transaction in Europe, and, accordingly, they were prepared to put their very best people on the transaction. I guess it was an example of where commitment triumphed over experience because they had not done much in Spain compared to, say, Goldman Sachs who had done transactions for Telefónica, Endesa and Repsol. Of course, we also knew that Morgan Stanley was a top international equity house and that their bank analyst Keith Brown was among the most highly ranked in the industry. In the beauty contest all the competitors were pretty much the same on structure, value, distribution and fees. We really could not have taken a decision on the beauty contest alone.'

Morgan Stanley studied all the significant European privatisations and made a major contribution to the marketing strategy and campaigns both in Spain and internationally. The global coordinator achieved high marks for cooperation with the syndicate.

Over a period of twelve months Morgan Stanley had been involved in advising on the creation of Argentaria and the potential sale of shares in Banco Exterior. The investment bank was thoroughly familiar with the assets and the Argentaria staff which facilitated a speedy execution of the offer. Once Morgan Stanley was publicly appointed, it only needed 54 days to take the issue to filing.

Morgan Stanley was asked to arbitrate in an argument over the sensitive issue of relative valuation between Argentaria, who supported a higher valuation, and Argentaria's competitors, whose support was essential and who argued for a lower valuation. Morgan Stanley managed to bring the parties together, but it would appear as if Argentaria's competitors gained more ground in this negotiation than did Argentaria, judging from the strong after-market performance.

Argentaria's management is most complimentary about Morgan Stanley and have reappointed them twice, for both Argentaria 2 and Argentaria 3. Roldán said: 'Morgan Stanley showed a high level of commitment, mobilised all the resources necessary and had good people. Furthermore, they are less confrontational than some investment banks and were more worried about the success of the transaction than about their own economics.'

William Kneisel, then head of global equity capital markets at Morgan Stanley put it this way: 'We recognised early on, right from our chairman Dick Fischer down, that Argentaria's privatisation offered a superb opportunity for Morgan Stanley to showcase our particular skills in managing large and complex equity distributions. Together with the strength of our European banking franchise, this furnished us with the conviction that Morgan Stanley could add significant value to this landmark transaction.'

Argentaria acquired more than 365,000 Spanish retail share-

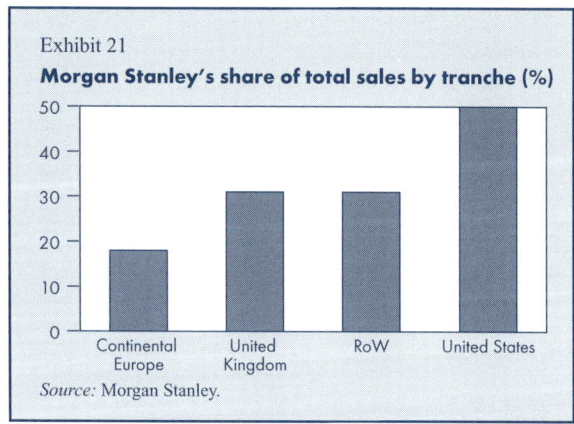

Exhibit 21

Morgan Stanley's share of total sales by tranche (%)

Source: Morgan Stanley.

holders. One key issue that Morgan Stanley had to cope with was allocation. Jerker Johansson, then officer responsible for the Spanish equity capital markets, and subsequently head of the equity capital markets group in Europe said: 'You would be astounded at how much time went into the allocation process.' Johansson and his colleagues spent hours poring over a fully transparent international book of demand, ultimately numbering more than 800 institutional accounts, in order to ensure an equitable distribution. Only 516 received an allocation.

Morgan Stanley also did well on the selling side and accounted for a very meaningful proportion of the overall sales in all four international tranches, as illustrated in Exhibit 21.

Argentaria Bolsa deserves considerable credit for spearheading the domestic retail tranche and for motivating Argentaria's competitors to support the offer.

Key lessons learnt

According to Roldán, the importance of the management's commitment to this transaction should not be underestimated: 'If the management had not been so dedicated to the task, the government most certainly would have achieved a lower price. It was a very profitable decision by the government to let us get on with it.' Even in a privatisation it is unusual for a management not selling new shares of the company to try so hard to achieve a good price for the vendor, but in this case it became a matter of pride and prestige for the management to achieve the same valuation as that of BBV. Adjusting for a customary IPO discount, Argentaria did achieve almost the same price/book value as their closest banking competitor.

This was Morgan Stanley's first major European privatisation as a global coordinator and they discovered that completing one of these transactions well is seriously hard work. The execution required tremendous cooperation and coordination with the client, within Morgan Stanley and with the syndicate at large. Roldán said: 'It worked very well having only one global coordinator; Morgan Stanley. To appoint multiple global coordinators, which has become increasingly frequent, typically indicates vendor weakness, which normally ends up costing something'.

The Argentaria issue was among the first of the Spanish privatisations to highlight the importance of retail demand. Jose Sainz of Argentaria Bolsa said: 'The retail tranche is always of paramount importance in these offers, particularly if, through the registration system, a strong retail interest can act as a catalyst to fuel institutional interest. It is like an insurance policy.'

Argentaria's management understood how to maximise the effort from the entire syndicate. Roldán said: ' the investment banks are very good and we were very happy with Morgan Stanley but you still have to handle the transaction yourself. You have to speak to at least all the regional lead managers directly on a regular basis. There is no substitute for a full commitment from the company itself.'

Conclusion

This transaction was ground breaking in that it was structurally innovative and creatively marketed. It reopened both the Spanish and European markets for large privatisations requiring retail involvement.

Everything went according to plan. The overall market environment was strong both domestically and internationally, the sector was in favour, Argentaria was a new and exciting name, the management was considered dynamic and the government was pragmatic concerning both the process and the offer price. The clawback option was fully exercised and the full over-allotment option of 15 per cent of the international tranches was fully exercised.

The key to the success of Argentaria 1 was the successful reception among retail investors. As news of this filtered through to international investors, they became convinced that the combined offer would be a success.

The only blemish on the transaction resulted from its very success. There was, as is typical for a heavily over-subscribed transaction, considerable dissatisfaction among major institutions that they had been given too small an allocation, thereby reducing the incentive to build a core holding in the share. The alternative would have been to not allocate to certain investors, or to increase the size of the offer.

Jerker Johansson, head of equity capital markets at Morgan Stanley in Europe concluded: 'The Argentaria IPO was a good example of an offer that most of us thought was going to be tough to execute, and, as a result, turned out to be a great success. The reason was that we prepared in the most thorough way possible with early building of name awareness, comprehensive market research, a highly ambitious domestic retail strategy, extensive global roadshow and three prospectuses, pink, red and final.'

Feature topic: *Getting a global deal done*

The Argentaria IPO of May 1993, illustrates the very significant workload undertaken both by a company and its advisers in preparing for a privatisation. Argentaria was only established in 1991 and the bank was therefore unknown to both Spanish and international investors. Considerable work was required to promote Argentaria to investors and to determine the key selling points which would be used to sell the bank's shares.

Even before this stage, a team from Morgan Stanley had been working with the management of what was originally Banco Exterior, advising them on a merger with another state-owned bank, Banco de Credito Industrial. After this Morgan Stanley had been giving advice regarding the appropriate vehicle to be floated in the equity markets. In fact, the decision about whether or not to offer more shares of Banco Exterior or to float the new, combined entity was not taken until the autumn of 1992.

The core Morgan Stanley team that managed the Argentaria offer was made up of representatives from the investment banking and research departments of the firm. Within investment banking, one managing director, based in London, had overall responsibility for the coordination of the project team.

A vice president, usually based in New York, who migrated to Spain for some six months, together with one Spanish associate in London and an analyst, were responsible for the collection of all the data and information required to help establish a value for Argentaria and to aid in the preparation of the prospectus.

Two senior coverage officers – one responsible for Morgan Stanley's relationships in Spain, the other for those with banks throughout Europe – spent a significant portion of their time assisting in the advisory function and ensuring that all the appropriate resources at Morgan Stanley were made available to Argentaria and the Spanish government.

Two firms of US lawyers, Davis Polk & Wardwell for the bank, and Sullivan & Cromwell for the underwriters, were also involved in the preparatory stages, as the proposed offer was to be registered with the Securities & Exchange Commission and listed on the New York Stock Exchange. The decision to list in New York added to the workload, requiring a pro-forma reconciliation of Argentaria's accounts to US GAAP going back three years.

Keith Brown, Morgan Stanley's highly respected research analyst for European banks was integrally involved in the preparation process. It was Brown, together with Argentaria and Dewe Rogerson (who were appointed to advise on the public relations aspects of the privatisation) who was to determine the key selling points which would make up the 'Argentaria story', as it would be marketed to equity investors from around the world.

These key selling points had to be determined relatively early on in the preparatory phase as they would later need to be used in an extensive domestic TV and newspaper campaign, as well as forming the basis for the prospectus, roadshow presentation and research publications which would accompany the offer.

Morgan Stanley's equity capital markets team was also involved at this stage, in providing both additional input on the marketing themes, as well as in determining some of the initial decisions relating to the offer structure. The core ECM team included the head of global equity capital markets based in New York, the officer responsible for Spanish equity capital markets and the European syndicate manager.

For reasons of political transparency, a 'beauty contest' for the global coordination mandate was held in early 1993. It was gratifying for the Morgan Stanley team to win the sought-after mandate, having already invested so much time and effort in the preparation of the offer.

After this work began in earnest: a timetable was determined and weekly steering committee meetings were held to discuss significant issues and evaluate work in progress. As the date for the offer approached, a significant portion of the time of the European ECM team was spent working with Argentaria Bolsa, the securities arm of Argentaria which had been appointed co-global coordinator.

The public announcement of the intention to float was accompanied by a flurry of preliminary research reports from the banks in the syndicate. The reports were based on meetings with Argentaria and an extensive briefing by Keith Brown. After this, Keith Brown and his colleagues from the other members of the syndicate engaged in an extensive pre-marketing campaign lasting two weeks. This involved canvassing opinion and delivering market positioning themes to leading investors expected to form the core demand for the offer.

Coincident with the announcement of the 1992 results, Argentaria made a number of investor presentations in continental Europe and the UK which served as an initial introduction to investors and a warm-up for the forthcoming roadshows. Throughout this period, Morgan Stanley was in constant dialogue with the other regional lead managers for the offer – SG Warburg and Banco Santander in the United Kingdom, UBS in continental Europe and Merrill Lynch in the RoW – as well as with BBV, Banco Central Hispano Americano, Banesto and Banco Santander in the Spanish offer. Jerker Johansson, the senior ECM officer based in Europe found himself spending at least one day a week in Spain, and towards the end of the offer, as much as four days of each week.

As the offer moved towards its climax, the roadshow and bookbuilding process got under way. In Spain, a vigorous marketing campaign, including for the first time the use of a pre-registration office, had captured the imagination of the banks depositors, employees and other retail investors. Senior Argentaria management, and representatives of the Spanish Ministry of Finance, together with members of the Morgan Stanley team, travelled around the world in search of pockets of demand in all of the major investment centres. Morgan Stanley's global salesforce was mobilised to identify and educate such investors as well as to compete with the salesforces of the other firms involved in the offer for orders.

In the end the international offer was 10 times subscribed and there were more than 365,000 Spanish retail shareholders. The next task was to allocate the transaction in a fair and equitable manner.

The period from the reception of the mandate early in 1993, to the pricing of the offer, represented four months of intense work. Advisory work commenced in 1991 and ran for the best part of 1992, which gives a strong impression of the significant work involved in a privatisation, even if the regulatory environment is not a significant structuring issue.

In total more than 400 people at Morgan Stanley were involved in the preparation and execution of the offer, including the Morgan Stanley global equity salesforce. If the Argentaria representatives, the lawyers, accountants, sales people and other representatives of the rest of the management group, including the personnel of the branch offices of the domestic retail banks, the marketing advisers and the representatives of the Bolsa de Madrid and the New York Stock Exchange are included, the number increases dramatically. All of these people were directly or indirectly under the management and control of the global coordinator. Does the syndicate deserve the 3 per cent typically paid for privatisations? If the job is well done, the answer is definitely yes.

Feature topic: *Deal economics*

The level, structure and equitable distribution of commissions between the banks involved in an offer are of critical importance in an international equity offer. The secret lies in optimising the balance between economic reward for the firms involved in the offer and the desire to incentivise participants to maximise their level of commitment, no matter what their seniority in the transaction.

It is important that the global coordinator or bookrunning lead managers are sufficiently incentivised to mobilise all the required resources and to make the particular offer a major priority for the firm. But it is also important to ensure that it is not only the global coordinator who works hard to achieve the offer objectives of the vendor. Where exactly to strike the balance depends on a number of factors, including the type of offer, the underwriting and pricing methodology, the size of the offer, the general prestige associated with the particular offer and the particular banks involved.

Increasingly, the total economics of international equity offers have tended to be concentrated in the hands of the global coordinators and regional lead managers. This,

Exhibit 22

Typical breakdown of the gross spread of an international equity offer

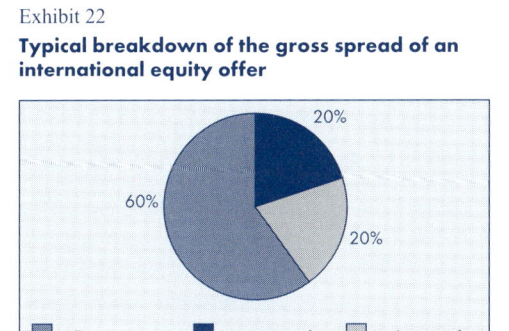

- Selling concession
- Management fee
- Underwriting fee

Exhibit 23

Typical split of management fee (%)

Outside the US	
Total management fee	100
Of which: Global coordinator's praecipium[1]	25
Of which: Lead/co-lead managers' praecipium split among all leads/co-Leads[2]	25
Of which: Management fees split among all syndicate members[3]	50
In the US	
Total management fee	100
Of which: Global coordinator's praecipium[1]	25
Of which: Paid to all managers (but not other syndicate members)[4]	75

[1] This praecipium is calculated on the total value of the offer and is payable to the global coordinator
[2] This praecipium is shared between the leads and the co-leads, usually calculated on notional underwriting amounts
[3] This portion of the management fee is usually calculated based on notional underwriting amounts
[4] This portion of the management fee is usually calculated based on notional underwriting amounts and is not payable to underwriters below manager level.

Source: Morgan Stanley.

of a 'level playing field' no matter what their level of seniority in the syndicate.

Before looking at how the economics were distributed across the syndicate members in Argentaria, let us first look at the basics of the economics in an international equity offer.

The fee structure is typically comprised of three parts: a management fee, an underwriting fee and a selling concession (see Exhibit 22).

The management fee, typically representing 20 per cent of the gross spread, is paid to compensate the banks for the work involved in managing the preparation and execution of an offer. This includes the structuring of the offer, the syndication of the transaction and the preparation of documentation and marketing materials. The management fee is split according to underwriting commitment, recognising that the higher the underwriting commitment, the more work is generally carried out by a particular institution. In order to pay the global coordinator (and in the case of non-US offers, the other lead and co-lead managers) in a way that reflects the disproportionate amount of work involved, there is a global coordinators' praecipium and a lead and co-lead managers praecipium (outside the US only). The different ways that the management fee is split outside and within the US are shown in Exhibit 23.

The underwriting fee, typically representing 20 per cent of the gross spread, is shared between all syndicate members, calculated on notional underwriting amounts. This fee is paid to compensate the syndicate members for the underwriting risk associated with an equity offer and is used to absorb both stabilisation expenses and any expense overruns which are not covered by the underwriters' expense reimbursement.

The selling concession, typically representing 60 per cent of the gross spread, is in principle paid in relation to the amount of stock sold by a particular syndicate member. The amount of the selling concession actually received by a particular bank depends to a large extent on the amount of stock allocated to either the syndicate member, or more commonly to the particular institutional clients of a syndicate member.

The largest portion of the gross spread is therefore distributed to a high degree at the discretion of the global coordinator or the bookrunning lead managers. Due to the inherent conflicts of interest associated with this system, the experienced vendor or issuer of shares is becoming increasingly involved in the allocation process in order to ensure fairness in both the allocation to investors and the remuneration of the individual syndicate banks. The selling concession is shared differently among syndicate members inside and outside the US, although US practice is becoming more widespread internationally.

In most offers outside the US (and in the non-US tranches of US transactions), the selling concession is traditionally paid to all syndicate members according to actual sales made, unless a pot or exempt list operates, in which case

at least according to the big houses, rightly reflects the nature of the offer process, in particular the preparation required of the global coordinators both prior to the offer, during the marketing process and following the pricing of the transaction. It also reflects the reality that given the large number of transactions in the market, most of the major firms really only have the capacity to focus on their own deals.

There is a tremendous 'franchise risk' undertaken by firms who are charged with the responsibility of 'making an offer happen'. The credit or blame for the success or failure of a major equity transaction is increasingly ascribed only to the most senior banks in a transaction and therefore, the argument goes, a co-lead manager of a regional tranche is not likely to try very hard. Accordingly, it is not seen as productive to give them too great a share of the cake. At the same time, issuers and vendors are increasingly trying to ensure that all participants feel that there is some sense

similar procedures to those described for the US are employed. In the US, there is a distinction between retail retention (the 'Retail Pot') and the 'Institutional Pot', with the institutional pot typically accounting for 75–80 per cent of the selling concession of a registered transaction.

The retail portion of the selling concession is paid based on a 'free retention' system, whereby firms are paid according to the quantity and quality of the non-institutional demand they generate. Retail retention fees are only paid to the extent demand is deemed to exist by the US lead manager.

The institutional pot is a portion of the selling concession (typically 30 per cent) which is guaranteed among the managers, and allocated pro rata according to their underwriting amounts, irrespective of the actual sales made. The remainder (70 per cent) is allocated to the banks according to designations received from investors.

The idea behind these designations is to avoid individual institutional investors giving split orders to different banks, allowing them to deal through a single bank. At the same time it rewards those houses involved in an offer in proportion to the amount of value added to that client.

This system does remove some of the discretionary power enjoyed by the global coordinator/bookrunning lead manager although an institutional investor will only designate selling concession on the amount of stock that he has been allocated. In practice a global coordinator/bookrunning lead manager may try to give higher allocations to investors who are likely to treat them well in the designation process.

The allocation should ensure that the shares are allocated to the highest quality investors, ie, those that are least likely to sell and most likely to buy more in the after-market,

rather than those that will maximise the profits of the global coordinator/bookrunning lead manager (see Exhibit 24).

Distribution of the economics in Argentaria 1

In the Argentaria 1 transaction Morgan Stanley was aiming to achieve a fair distribution of the economics. In the international offers, (the European, UK and RoW tranches), it was a specific point in the 'Terms of Reference' of the syndicate briefings that firms would be rewarded for their efforts in the marketing and distribution of the offer through an equitable allocation system which evaluated the quality of the orders on an even-handed basis. At the same time Morgan Stanley worked hard to ensure that the co-lead managers in each of the international tranches had a meaningful role in the marketing of the transaction including access to some one-on-one meetings.

In the end, the economics of the transaction were unusually fairly distributed and, despite the huge levels of over-subscription, all the firms involved were reported to be content with their overall economic reward. Exhibit 25 summarises the distribution of the economics in each international tranche.

In contrast to a big privatisation such as Argentaria, where a single global coordinator typically takes 30–50 per cent of the total fees, in most US style corporate book-built transactions, the lead manager takes 60–80 per cent of the total.

There are several reasons for this difference. Privatisations are typically large transactions so even a small percentage figure becomes a meaningful fee in dollar terms. Banks are prepared to work hard without requiring as high a proportion of the total economics as they would in a corporate transaction, in order to position themselves for subsequent privatisation mandates.

In a corporate transaction, the CFO typically has a close relationship with a single bank, and that bank has greater influence on how the economics of the deal should be allocated. As such transactions are normally one-off events, banks outside of the top positions in the syndicate will probably not feel the same need to try their hardest in order

Exhibit 24

Typical US split of selling concession (%)

Total selling concession	100
Of which: Pre-agreed or fixed portion regardless of sales generated	30
Of which: Paid pro-rata according to sales designated by investors	70

Exhibit 25

Distribution of total fees in Argentaria 1

Tranche	MS role	MS - % of fees	Tranche bookrunner % of fees	Co-lead managers * % of fees	Co-managers % of fees *
UK	Co-lead	31	35	29	5
Continental Europe	Co-lead	21	34	38	7
US	Lead	41	41	49	10
RoW	Co-lead	26	43	6	23

* Excludes Morgan Stanley if Morgan Stanley was a co-lead and includes joint lead managers who were not bookrunners.

Source: Morgan Stanley.

to be in position to win subsequent mandates and the bookrunner and lead managers will probably have to do the bulk of the work.

In order to maximise the motivation of the entire syndicate and avoid rewarding banks which add limited value to a transaction, it is important that the global coordinators do not receive a disproportionate percentage of the fees. Experienced vendors/issuers, such as privatisation units charged with the responsibility of executing large privatisation programmes, include measures to ensure that syndicate members who work hard are fairly compensated. These can include:

- Ensuring minimum remuneration for certain categories of syndicate members;
- Capping the global coordinator's portion of the selling concession: in the ENI 1 offer of November 1995, the fees payable to CSFB were capped at 40 per cent for each order; the entire amount of the selling concession was distributed by way of designations (ie, there was no fixed portion) thus there was no selling concession for those syndicate members that did not perform; and
- Ensuring fairness in the designations: for the system of designations to work the way it is intended to, institutional investors have to believe that their allocations will not be influenced by the amount of designations going to the global coordinator. In order to offset the pressure from senior syndicate members to get the institutions to designate them, vendors might openly declare to the institutional investors that what they do on designations will not affect their allocations. In the case of the Railtrack IPO, the designations were handled by SBC Warburg's corporate finance department rather than by equity capital markets, so that allocations were not affected by designations but rather by the quality of the order. The bookbuilding and allocation processes were then audited by UK accounting firm Coopers & Lybrand.

BNP

The privatisation of Banque National de Paris was the first to take place under the Balladur administration elected in March 1993. François Mitterand had, as a newly elected president, been responsible for the bank's nationalisation in 1982, but was now supporting the privatisation proposed by the conservative government led by prime minister Edouard Balladur.

Balladur's privatisation programme was made up of 21 companies valued at up to Ffr400 billion, including virtually all the major state-owned companies operating in competitive sectors. BNP was considered the ideal lead candidate because the bank was well-prepared, and knowledgeable about the privatisation process. BNP was well-known among French retail investors and the financial sector was in demand by the market: it was therefore deemed to stand a greater chance of success than even Elf Aquitaine and Rhône-Poulenc, both of which were already quoted on the New York Stock Exchange.

This first privatisation had to be a clear success in order to create the necessary momentum for the overall programme. To achieve success it was essential that the French retail investor be lured back to the equity market in general, and privatisations in particular. For these reasons the privatisation was structured to appeal primarily to the domestic retail investor, though steps were also taken to make the offer attractive to French and international institutions.

The work of building a core shareholder group for BNP was not made any easier by the fact that the bank already had strategic alliances with UAP, the largest French insurance company and Dresdner Bank, the second largest German bank.

The former had already been manifested by the creation of a substantial cross-holding, whilst the latter was only expected to be cemented by a cross-holding at a future date.

The privatisation of BNP was highly successful, but it clearly demonstrates the challenge facing the French government, which, in the absence of political support for the privatisation of the utilities, had to offer primarily cyclical industries at the beginning of the programme. This stands in sharp contrast to the UK, where the government was in a position to offer its utilities for sale much earlier in the programme.

Although Certificats d'Investissement ('CIs' – non-voting securities issued by state-owned entities) in BNP had traded since 1986, this sale was considered an IPO, as the trading level of the CIs was only taken as a partial indicator for the pricing of the voting shares that were offered.

This was at the time the largest ever privatisation to have taken place in terms of upfront cash proceeds, and the largest offer in France. It was one of the last major European privatisations to be structured as a fixed price offer for both retail and institutional investors, although the price was only fixed following a two-week pre-marketing period, during which time retail investors had the right to subscribe by way of giving banks 'purchase mandates' to buy shares.

The decision to fix the price at the end of the pre-marketing period rather than offer a price-range was taken because this issue was, as the first Balladur privatisation, likely to be attractively priced, and publishing a price range might for practical reasons have reduced the pricing flexibility.

Exhibit 1
Transaction summary

Issuer: Banque National de Paris ('BNP') (France)	*Global coordinator: BNP*
Pricing date: 4 October 1993 (CAC 40: 2,129)	*Pricing/underwriting structure: Fixed price offer with hard underwriting*
Vendor: Republic of France	*Primary or secondary: Secondary and primary*
	Retail structure: Bonus shares
% of company sold in the market offer: 40.5% (considering only the combined offer in relation to fully diluted capital)	*Privatisation or corporate: Privatisation*
IPO or non-IPO: IPO of ordinary shares (non-voting certificates had traded since 1986)	*Industry: Banking*
Type of shares: Ordinary shares and ADRs	*Offer price: Ffr240*
Total size of combined offer: US$3,209 million	*US listing/144 A: 144A tranche*

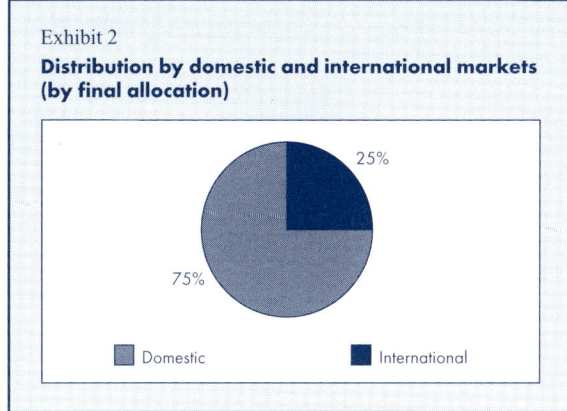

Exhibit 2
Distribution by domestic and international markets (by final allocation)

25%

75%

■ Domestic   ■ International

In its capacity as banker to its own privatisation, BNP invented the purchase mandates concept, an innovative subscription and payment structure for retail investors which improved retail participation and allowed the lead managers to get an early reading on the progress of the retail tranche. This structure has since been used consistently in French privatisations and also exported to other countries, such as Spain, where it was successfully introduced in the 1995 Repsol transaction.

The BNP privatisation marked the first time that global underwriting and global institutional bookbuilding were used in the French privatisation programme. This approach encouraged transparency and objectivity in bookbuilding and allocation and subsequent French privatisations were to represent evolutions from this structure.

The BNP privatisation was the first to be partially paid for through conversion of Balladur Bonds which had been issued by the Republic of France to raise money for the state and to encourage retail investors to take the first step towards committing money to the privatisation programme. Holders of these bonds, of which Ffr110 billion had been bought by retail investors, were given priority in the allocation process.

Major challenges

The BNP offer faced a number of difficulties. The first Balladur privatisation had to be a success. BNP's 1993/94 earnings were under pressure, falling 60 per cent in the first six months of 1993. There were worries over the capacity of the French retail market to absorb such a large placement, and privatisation rules prevented the use of 'price talk' prior to the official price setting date.

BNP met these challenges through careful planning, the selection of the best advisers and attractive pricing as well as emphasising its future earnings potential and the leadership strength of new chairman Michel Pébereau. To generate additional retail capacity there was extensive preparation of the BNP branch network and a concerted targeting of investors in Balladur bonds. To overcome the problem of not being able to warm the market up with price talk, the bank organised domestic and international investor roadshows to develop strong investor interest and held extensive meetings with international equity research analysts.

Other difficulties that had to be faced included the need to stimulate a high level of French institutional demand for the offer, the requirement for the syndicate banks to hold an 11-day underwriting position during retail marketing and the complications thrown up by the strategic stakes that UAP and Dresdner held in the bank.

Rationale and objectives

BNP was on the list to be privatised in 1986–87, but fell victim to the 1987 stock market crash. In 1993 it was seen by the Balladur Government to be the ideal candidate to launch the new privatisation programme as it was well-prepared, knowledgeable about the privatisation process and well-known among retail investors due to its 1,900 bank branches throughout France. In addition, the banking sector was in favour with investors.

The rationale behind the privatisation programme itself was the following:

- To refocus the state's role on the essential prerogatives of government;
- To develop the French financial market and re-channel savings into the productive sector; and
- To finance the deficit on the French fiscal budget.

The Government's specific offer objectives were:

- To have a very public success;
- To motivate French and international institutions to support the French privatisation programme;
- To meet the general privatisation objectives; and
- To reduce the Republic's direct and indirect interests in BNP to zero, except for shares to be retained for the purposes of the bonus share scheme.

BNP was keen to join the private sector as its competitor, Société Générale, had in 1987. Although government ownership had not been much of a constraint for the bank, there was still a perception in the international market that the bank acted as a state-owned bank. A move to the private sector would give it more flexibility with regard to acquisitions and strategic alliances as well as to financing.

In order to achieve a clear separation from the government with regard to the holding in UAP, the bank needed to raise money to finance the acquisition of the shares that it did not already own in Financière BNP, the holding company which owned a 20 per cent stake in UAP and which was previously 50.01/49.99 per cent owned by BNP and the government respectively. Immediately following the sale of the government's shares in BNP, the bank raised Ffr7.3 billion through the exercise of share warrants and investment certificate warrants to finance the purchase from the government of its 49.99 per cent in Financière BNP.

Share capital and ownership

See Exhibit 3.

Exhibit 3
Share capital and ownership

Type of shares offered	Ordinary or voting shares ('Shares') of Ffr25 nominal value and ADR (1 ADR representing one voting share).
Ownership restrictions	Several restrictions limit the building of a 'controlling' stake in BNP: • French banking law requires authorisation to acquire 10%, 20%, 33.3% or more in a French credit institution; • French privatisation law requires that the state cannot sell to non-EC persons more than 20% of the share capital of BNP in anyone transaction; • Under French foreign direct investment regulations, a prior authorisation of the French Ministry of the Economy is required for the acquisition of a 20% stake in BNP by a non-EC resident. In addition, it is arguable that the 15% cross-holding between BNP and UAP served the purpose of a major 'poison pill', or anti-takeover device.
Share capital before and after offer	Ordinary shares 117,278,886 CIs and old warrants* 36,300,000 Total capital 153,578,886 * The old warrants were exercisable into 9,382,064 CIs before 31 October 1993 New warrants (October 1993)** 30,716,108 Fully diluted capital 184,294,994 ** Exercisable into 23,455,777 shares at a price of Ffr240 and 7,260,000 CIs at a price of Ffr235 from 15 October to 22 November.
Listing/trading	The investment certificates had been listed in Paris and traded on Seaq International since 1986. The same was to apply to the ordinary shares from October 1993.
Market capitalisation at offer price (Ffr5.69/US$)	US$7.7 billion (based on fully diluted capital).
Major shareholder(s) before offer	% of capital Republic of France 71.5 Public (only CIs) 18.7 UAP (since April 1990) 9.8 (Including both the ordinary shares and the investment certificates, the state controlled approximately 90% of the voting rights of BNP before the offer as all the voting certificates, as separated from the CIs, were held by the government.)
Shareholder(s) immediately after offer	% French public 49.9 UAP 14.6 Core shareholders 13.5 International investors 9.8 French institutions 5.3 BNP employees 4.5 Republic of France 2.4
Foreign ownership following offer	Portfolio investment 10.0% Foreign core shareholders 4.5% Total foreign shareholdings 14.5%
Free float before offer	18.7% (representing the 26.9 million CIs).
Liquidity	1993 Average monthly trading volume of CIs 1 Q 1,947.684 2 Q 3,165,354 3 Q 5,749,245
Relevant stock exchange index/weighting	CAC 40/ 3.5% (17 November 1993).

Transaction components

Offer structure and syndicate

The privatisation of BNP consisted of three distinct offers, the relative sizes of which were (after considering clawback and certain other adjustments) as shown in Exhibit 4.

The combined offer consisted of a retail offer, the 'OPV', a French institutional offer and an international institutional sale. The international issue was a globally underwritten offer with three ring-fenced regional placement syndicates in the UK, the US and the rest of the world. There was no link between

Exhibit 4
Development of the offer size

	Before clawback	After clawback	% of capital*
Combined offer	72,129,786	74,617,764	42.7%
Employee offer	8,014,421	8,290,863	4.7%
Offer to stable shareholders	27,644,200	24,879,780	14.2%
Total number of shares sold by Republic	107,788,407	117,809,234**	67.4%**

* Assuming all warrants exercised and CIs converted to ordinary shares.
** These totals also include the sale of shares to UAP, which was not included under the sale to stable shareholders.

Exhibit 5
Offer structure

Target markets	% of total underwriting of combined offer*	Bookrunning lead managers/ Joint lead manager	Co-lead managers
French public offer (OPV)	52.0%	BNP (Bookrunner) Lazards (Joint lead manager)	Crédit Agricole, CDC, Crédit Lyonnais, Société Générale
French institutional offer	16.8%	BNP (Bookrunner) Lazards (Joint lead manager)	Indosuez, Paribas, Crédit Lyonnais, Société Générale, CCF, CDC, Crédit Agricole
International offer International placement	N/A	BNP (Bookrunner) Lazards (Joint lead manager)	Senior co-leads: Dresdner, CSFB Co-lead managers: 5 banks
UK placement	N/A	BNP (Bookrunner) Lazards (Joint lead manager)	Indosuez, BZW, CSFB, Kleinwort Benson, NM Rothschild/Smith New Court, S.G.Warburg
US placement	N/A	Merrill Lynch (Bookrunner)	Lazard Frères, Goldman Sachs, JP Morgan
Total international offer	**31.2%**		
Total combined offers (shares)	**72,129,786**		

* As announced on 4 October 1993.

the global underwriting commitment, the placement effort and the final allocations. In principle 100 per cent of the international issue could have been allocated to UK investors. There was an employee offer representing 10 per cent of the combined offer, as stipulated by French privatisation law, and an offer to stable shareholders 'Groupe d'Actionnaires Stables' (GAS), which used to be referred to as 'Noyaux Durs'. As in previous and subsequent privatisations where there were CIs outstanding, there was also an exchange offer to allow all holders of CIs to exchange them for voting shares.

In addition, there was a sale of just over 10 million new BNP shares (representing 5.4 per cent of BNP's capital) to UAP to cement the cross-holding between the two companies. For legal reasons this capital increase was structured as a distribution of short life warrants to CI holders and shareholders, rather than a straight issue of new shares. There was a clawback to the French retail offer of 20 per cent from the French institutional and international offers and 10 per cent from the offer to core shareholders which was exercised in full.

As far as the syndicate structure (see Exhibit 5) was concerned the following points should be noted:

- Unlike subsequent French privatisations, there was a sep-

arate tranche for French institutions. The introduction of bookbuilding was deemed a big enough step for the French banks to cope with without also exposing them to competition on equal terms with the foreign banks;

- The composition of the syndicate was complicated by the fact that because of its banking relationships, BNP had a large number of banks to satisfy and wanted to hand out more positions than would have been the case for a non-bank issuer. Although there were no regionally underwritten tranches within the international offer, BNP felt compelled to create positions of importance for certain foreign banks, giving rise to the three distinct placement syndicates; and

- With regard to BNP's own dominant position in all tranches, it must be appreciated that the bank wanted to minimise other banks' involvement in the bookbuilding process, so as not to be dependent on other banks for information on investor behaviour. Only in the US did BNP concede a bookbuilding role (to Merrill Lynch) as this was an important opportunity for BNP to establish its privatisation credentials in order to win a meaningful market share in the French privatisation programme.

Exhibit 6
Principal advisers

Financial adviser to the French state	Lazard Frères
French legal adviser to the French and international underwriters	Giroux, Buhagiar et Associés
US legal adviser to BNP	Cleary, Gottlieb, Steen & Hamilton
US legal adviser to the US placement agents	Shearman & Sterling
Auditors	Guy Barbier et Autres/ Arthur Andersen and Guérard-Viala

Exhibit 7
The timetable

Beginning September	• Trésor announces that the sale of BNP shares will take place within three months.
10 September	• Opening of the application period to become part of the 'GAS'; • BNP image campaign begins.
17 September	• Announcement of the offer; • Publication of preliminary prospectus.
20 September	• Beginning of the 'mandate period'; • Institutional marketing begins; • Roadshow begins.
27 September	• Deadline to submit offer to become part of the 'GAS.'
29 September	• Suspension of trading in investment certificates and the 1990 warrants on the Paris Bourse at a price of Ffr277.
1 October	• Marketing ends; • Roadshow ends.
Monday, 4 October	• Mandate period ends; • Selection of investors for the 'GAS'; • Signing of the underwriting agreement and certain other agreements; • Pricing takes place after the close of the Paris market.
5 October	• Start of the OPV period; • French institutional and international offers begin; • Employee offer opens; • Trading in CIs is resumed.
6 October	• French institutional and international offers close prematurely.
12 October	• End of OPV period.
15 October	• Publication of OPV results; • The Trésor announces that the clawback will be fully exercised; • Allocation of shares to investors; • End of the placement with employees.
Monday, 18 October	• Trading begins on the Paris Bourse; • Opening of the exchange offer period for CIs.
22 October	• Closing and payment.
23 November	• End of exchange offer period, whereby CIs were exchanged for voting shares.

The offer price was fixed on 4 October following a two-week pre-marketing period, after which the subscription period for both retail and institutional investors commenced. Investors' allocations were decided on 15 October and in the US, shares were sold to 'qualified institutional buyers' under Rule 144A. There was no greenshoe.

The French state did not retain a 'golden share' in BNP as it would in the case of Elf Aquitaine a few months later. The retail offer was structured with bonus shares entitling individuals receive one additional share for every 10 shares purchased and held for 18 months, up to a maximum value of Ffr30,000. There was no retail discount.

Principal advisers
See Exhibit 6.

Transaction fee distribution
The spread in the retail offer was close to 6 per cent; the institutional fees were 3 per cent (See Exhibit 8).

Management fee
BNP received 0.02 per cent of the total management fee as the 'global coordinators praecipium', calculated on the gross proceeds of the combined offer. Outside the US, the management fee had a further three components, calculated in the

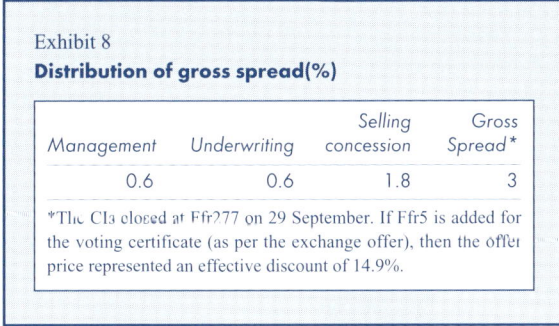

Exhibit 8
Distribution of gross spread(%)

Management	Underwriting	Selling concession	Gross Spread*
0.6	0.6	1.8	3

*The CIP closed at Ffr277 on 29 September. If Ffr5 is added for the voting certificate (as per the exchange offer), then the offer price represented an effective discount of 14.9%.

Exhibit 9
Management fee distribution outside the US (%)

Total management fee	0.6
Of which: Global coordinator's praecipium	0.02
Of which: Lead and joint lead managers praecipium split among leads and joint leads	0.13
Of which: Co-lead managers' praecipium split among all co-leads	0.15
Of which: Management fees split among all managers	0.30

Source: BNP.

Exhibit 10
Selling fee distribution in the US (%)

Total selling concession	1.8
Of which: Pre-agreed or fixed portion regardless of sales booked	30
Of which: Paid pro-rata according to sales designated by investors	70

Source: BNP.

same way. (See Exhibit 9.) In the US, the management fee (after deduction of the global coordinators praecipium) was distributed to the lead manager and co-managers based on the size of their underwriting commitments.

Selling concession

In the US, the selling concession had one fixed and one variable component: the fixed component of 30 per cent was calculated on the basis of underwriting commitments while the variable portion was subject to performance and designated by investors (see Exhibit 10).

In Europe, the selling concession was paid in full to whoever the order was given to.

Deal structure

The decision to go for a fixed price offer for both French institutions and retail customers was taken on the grounds that it was simpler and better understood among both retail and French institutional investors. It was also felt to be politically problematic to structure transactions with open pricing in

order to maximise the retail price: furthermore, had the open pricing structure been used in France, the OPV regulation would have had to be changed.

Two weeks of pre-marketing to retail and institutional investors was followed by pricing on 4 October after which the OPV and the institutional offer were meant to be open for six business days until Friday 12 October. However, the institutional offer closed heavily oversubscribed after only two days although allocation only took place on Monday, 15 October, thereby requiring an 11-day 'hard' underwriting period. While this is a relatively long underwriting period, the French *force majeure* clause is unusually strong and highly favourable to the banks. Any serious market disruption, be it for economic or political reasons, before the settlement of the issue would most likely have led to its cancellation.

The fact that the offer price was uniform was considered attractive to institutions, as they felt that they were getting the implied 'retail discount'. Although this transaction did not use a classic bookbuilding structure from a pricing and underwriting point of view, there was centralised bookbuilding with full transparency for all institutional orders larger than Ffr1 million. This was the first time in a French privatisation that the French banks were asked to name the investors behind their orders, a significant innovation which is never easy to introduce in a new market but which BNP, as global coordinator, handled well.

In previous privatisations French institutions had been lumped together with French retail investors and had typically fared badly in the allocation process. By structuring a separate institutional tranche, the institutions could be confident of more favourable treatment and the banks were not, as in subsequent privatisations, fully exposed to foreign competition. The creation of three sub-tranches in the international offer, in a placement if not in an underwriting sense, meant more foreign banks could be included in meaningful positions.

The BNP syndicate was a 'middle-way' structure, balanced between a heavily regionalised and ring-fenced structure such as that used in the Wellcome offer of July 1992 and the global syndicate structure employed in BT3 in July 1993. BNP decided against the BT3 structure, eventually declining a role in the transaction when it was offered a position in the ranks, below the 11 'global managers'. Paribas was the only French bank among the chosen 11.

The purchase mandate, available between the announcement of the offer on 20 September, and its pricing on 4 October, allowed retail investors to give any 'receiving bank' a 'mandate' to spend a certain amount of money on his or her behalf. This mandate could be withdrawn at any time until the penultimate day of the OPV period, failing which the mandates would be automatically converted into orders.

This structure had been developed because of the size of the retail offer and to comply with the French legal requirement that in an OPV, the price must be made known to investors. In addition, it was deemed impossible for the bank branches to process three million orders during the traditional six to seven day OPV period. As retail investors were not obligated to buy under the purchase mandate structure, but could cancel orders during the subsequent OPV period when the price became known, the legal challenge had been elegantly overcome.

The use of mandates gave the global coordinator an early reading on the likely success of the OPV, which in itself created further momentum for the institutional tranches. Out of the 2.8 million retail orders, one million came from the purchase mandate mechanism, with BNP itself accounting for 600,000 mandates. The mandate structure was considered a brilliant commercial idea and positioned BNP as the Trésor's favourite retail bank. Nicolas Berryer, corporate finance executive at BNP said: 'The key to the success of the purchase mandate structure was that it gave us enough time to really prepare the branch network and educate all our personnel in all aspects of the privatisation.' (See also Repsol and ENI case studies where purchase mandates were involved.)

Marketing

The Trésor and BNP wanted to reach 3 million retail shareholders and in order to do so both the vendor and the bank pursued an extensive radio and TV marketing campaign, during which Ffr80 million was spent on advertising, and incentives such as bonus shares and purchase mandates.

BNP was seen as a 'recovery play' and a core holding in any French portfolio as the country's flagship bank. The key sales points were:

- The market knew that it was the vendor's intention to make this privatisation a success, as it was the first of a comprehensive programme;
- The appointment of Pébereau as president was of great importance to the perception of the bank's future direction given his excellent track-record as he had successfully privatised CCF in May 1987;
- BNP was considered to have exercised a prudent level of provisioning and a conservative credit policy. It had avoided excessive expansion into the real estate sector and had a high quality corporate lending book; and
- BNP would benefit from lower interest rates and cost savings. The new management was expected to cut costs significantly.

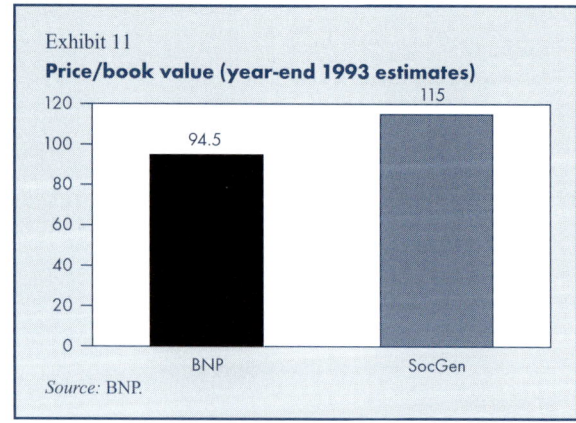

Exhibit 11
Price/book value (year-end 1993 estimates)
Source: BNP.

The primary valuation drivers were book value and to a lesser extent the price-earnings ratio on the basis of 1994 and 1995 earnings. At Ffr240, BNP was thought to be attractively valued at a discount to estimated year-end 1993 book value of 5.5 per cent. The equivalent figure for Société Générale was a premium of 15 per cent (see Exhibit 11).

Due to the depressed earnings level at BNP the issue was priced at a high P/E ratio of 25.1 times 1994 earnings. The equivalent figure for Société Générale was 11.6 times.

Results

See Exhibit 12.

The offer was 9.3 times subscribed overall, with the French retail offer being the least over-subscribed and the international tranche of the international offer being the most over-subscribed, (although there was no specific underwriting within the international offer, the appendix to the global underwriting contract listed the rough amounts expected to be placed in each tranche – see Exhibit 13.)

As a result of the clawback being exercised to the full 20 per cent, the international (UK, US and rest of the world tranches) and the French institutional offers were substantially reduced. In terms of the final allocation, they represented only 25 per cent and 13 per cent, respectively. The retail offer was further boosted by the full 10 per cent clawback from the GAS.

Exhibit 12
Underwriting, demand and allocation

Target markets	Indicative underwriting amounts	Demand	Allocation
French offer			
France retail (OPV)	52.0%	28%	62%
France institutional	16.8%	23%	13%
Total French	**68.8%**	**51%**	**75%**
International offer			
International	N/A	33%	16%
UK	N/A	11%	6%
US	N/A	5%	3%
Total international offer	**31.2%**	**49%**	**25%**
Total comined offers (shares)	**72,129,786**	**676,941,964**	**74,617,764***

* The size was increased as a result of the clawback from the offer to core shareholders which was allocated to the retail offer.

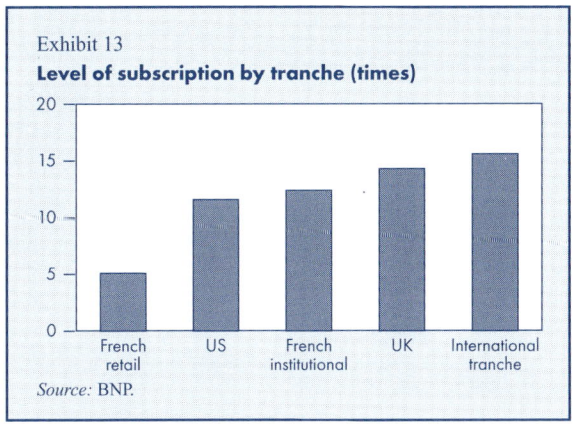

Exhibit 13
Level of subscription by tranche (times)

Source: BNP.

Investor concentration

See Exhibit 14.

Approximately 2.8 million French retail investors – some 4.8 per cent of the French population – participated in the BNP privatisation when the objective had been to reach 3 million. At the time there were 4.5 million individual shareholders in France, owning approximately a third of the market capitalisation of the French stock market (see Exhibit 15):

- In the case of BNP, in addition to the retail investors, 63,000 employees subscribed in the employee offer, corresponding to 68 per cent of the present and former employees of BNP entitled to subscribe;

- Following the offer to 15 core shareholders and the increase of the stake owned by UAP, 16 long-term shareholders owned 28.1 per cent of BNP; and

- In the US, Merrill Lynch targeted 300–400 QIBs, of which 90 institutions were allotted a total of US$103 million. Merrill Lynch accounted for over 50 per cent of the final allocations in the US tranche.

After-market price performance

The privatisation was announced on 17 September, 1993 after the CAC-40 had broken through the 2,000 level on 26 July, and while there was a strong expectation of falling interest rates. General market conditions were favourable and the financial sector was perceived as particularly attractive. The CI market price was thought to be too high to serve as a basis for the pricing of the offer, although the CI price provided a valuation reference. There had been considerable speculation in CIs and the price had risen from a low of Ffr210 in the first quarter of 1993 to Ffr277, having peaked at Ffr302 in August (see Exhibit 16):

- During the six months to pricing, the CIs outperformed the CAC-40 by more than 7 per cent as investors bought in expectation of an imminent BNP privatisation. Investors expected that, as in previous French privatisations, the government would offer to exchange CIs for ordinary shares on terms attractive to holders.

Exhibit 14
Investor concentration

	By demand	By allocation
Percentage of institutional portion of issue accounted for by the 10 largest investors (by total size of demand and allocation respectively)	10.1%	8.6%
Number of investors making up 80% of the institutional portion of issue (by total size of demand and allocation respectively)	1,042	3,046
The 3 largest investors by size	US$322 million US$298 million US$268 million	US$17.2 million US$10.7 million US$10.3 million
Total number of institutions globally	4,176	4,088

Source: BNP.

Exhibit 15
BNP retail penetration in perspective

Company	Date	Total size (US$million)	Proportion initially offered to retail* (%)	Retail subscription	No of retail investors (million)
BNP	October 1993	3,209	52	5.2 x	2.8
Rhône-Poulenc	November 1993	2,105	60	4.5 x	2.9
Elf	January 1994	4,195	55	3.0 x	3.1
UAP	April 1994	2,631	34	2.5 x	1.9
Renault 1	November 1994	2,048	60	1.4 x	1.1
Seita	February 1995	1,100	50	3.9 x	1.0
Usinor-Sacilor	June 1995	3,060	20	2.1 x	0.8
Pechiney	November 1995	929	33	1.4 x	0.5
AGF	May 1996	1,423	25	3.2 x	0.8

* The size of the retail tranche was, subject to demand further increased by clawing back up to 20% of the institutional offer, eg in the case of BNP, retail investors were allocated 62% of the total offer.

Sources: Offer circulars, the Trésor.

Exhibit 16
Past performance of BNP's CIs

	High (Ffr)	Low (Ffr)	Period -end (Ffr)	Average monthly trading volume (million CIs)
1991	172.5	155	159.5	1.9
1992	220.5	150	209.5	1.2
1993 – First quarter	259.5	210	264	1.9
1993 – Second quarter	283	249.5	268	3.2
1993 – Third quarter*	302	274	277	5.7

* Through 29 September.

Source: Offer circular. All figures are after 2:1 stock split, which became effective on 17 September 1993.

Exhibit 17
After-market price performance

Pricing date	4 October 1993
Offer price)	Ffr240
First year high/low	
High(17 November 1993)	Ffr294
Low (1 July 1994)	Ffr227

BNP share price relative to CAC-40 (%)

Absolute and relative share price performance

	Price (Ffr)	Relative to CAC-40 from 4 October (%)
+ 1 day	284	117.5
+ 3 days	279	115.2
+ 1 week	290	116
+ 1 month	289	119.3
+ 3 months	275	108.8
+ 6 months	251	103.1
+ 9 months	244	106.3
+ 12 months	251	103.1

Sources: Datastream and offer circular.

See Exhibit 17.

- On the first day of trading, the shares leapt 18.3 per cent, opening at Ffr270.20;
- Ten days after the BNP issue closed, the Bundesbank cut the discount rate to 5.75 per cent and the CAC-40 immediately gained 2.3 per cent, creating further momentum in the after-market;

Exhibit 18
Percentage of total issue traded* (%)

	Day 1	Day 2	Day 3	Total: Day 1 – 3
Paris	5.3	2.9	2.0	10.2

* Based on the issue of 76.1 million shares.

Source: Datastream.

- The BNP share price out-performed the French market over both the short and medium term. After one month, the relative out-performance was almost 20 per cent. After a year, however, BNP's share price had fallen to Ffr251, and the relative out-performance was only 3.1 per cent; and
- On the second anniversary of the BNP closing, the bank's market price stood Ffr55 below the offer price. At that time, BNP had underperformed the CAC–40 by just under 5 per cent. At the end of 1996, the share price was around Ffr200, which suggests that the fundamental value of BNP was much lower than the market was led to believe at the time of the privatisation.

After-market trading volume
See Exhibit 18.

The after-market trading volumes were relatively low, indicating that retail investors were not rushing to sell, although they increased somewhat on days four and five. During the first five trading days, 16.1 per cent of the offer changed hands.

The performance of the main parties

The vendor
The Trésor deserves credit for picking the ideal market timing for the BNP privatisation. They probably also took the right decision in letting BNP be the global coordinator of its own privatisation. Everyone in the market knew that the Trésor wanted this offer to be a success and the pricing was generous enough to ensure that this was the flying start that the Balladur privatisation programme required. The objectives

were easily met, although the number of retail investors fell just short of the targeted three million.

Although the pricing and underwriting structure was straightforward, the combination of CIs, voting shares, old and 1993 warrants, and an exchange offer might have confused some investors. But as one BNP official said: 'If anything, I am surprised that more investors were not confused. However, having created the CIs, we had little choice but to do an exchange offer. In addition, since it was important from a corporate governance point of view to sever the link with the government regarding BNP's holding in UAP, and since it was legally much more straightforward to raise capital by way of short life warrants than by a capital increase, we had limited structuring flexibility.'

Despite the euphoria surrounding the transaction at the time, BNP has since been a disappointment for the investor community. Although it appeared fairly priced, or even cheap, at the time, the 'real book value' was obviously much lower. International investors have been left with the impression that the French government was more interested in maximising value in the short-term than in selling a clean bank to the public. Although it would have been difficult to sell BNP at a lower price it may have been wiser for the government to have waited until it was satisfied as to the quality of the loan book. Needless to say, no banker suggesting such a course of action would have been asked to assist with this privatisation.

BNP as issuer

Market sentiment was very strong at the time of the privatisation, but BNP's chairman expressed caution about the bank's future prospects. Pébereau talked about achieving a return on equity of 3–4 per cent over the risk free rate in the medium term, indicating a net profit of approximately Ffr4 billion. He also warned that improvements in the bank's results would not come quickly: he was right. The bank's profit performance was clearly disappointing in 1994 and 1995 (see Exhibit 19).

BNP undoubtedly did the right thing in trying to stem overoptimistic expectations at the the time of the privatisation and, consistent with its cautious position, the bank managed to convince the vendor to sell at a price which was considerably lower than the market had expected – Ffr240 as against Ffr260–270.

Adviser and global coordinator

The Trésor invited 92 banks to solicit the mandate to become the adviser to the French State on BNP, of which 57 banks responded with a presentation. The Trésor shortlisted 10 banks,

who were asked to present orally in front of the Privatisation Commission in July 1993, each candidate having one hour. Lazards was appointed in the beginning of August 1993. With regard to this appointment, Michel Laffitte of the Trésor said: 'We would like to work with a small group of trusted domestic and foreign banks who are committed to understanding our needs and to providing good advice at the moment that we need it.'

One of the important considerations was that it was deemed to be difficult to appoint one of BNP's direct domestic competitors either in the capacity of the government's adviser or the global coordinator as they would, in connection with the due diligence, get access to too much sensitive information on the bank. As BNP was very keen to be the global coordinator for its own privatisation and as Lazards was probably not ideal for the role due to its relative lack of distribution capacity, the combination of Lazards as adviser to the government and BNP as global coordinator was deemed sensible. To have chosen a foreign bank as either global coordinator or government adviser for the first major privatisation under Balladur would have sent a strange signal to the French banking community, particularly when this privatisation was structured and priced primarily to sell to domestic retail investors. Many foreign investment banks commented on the minimal role both in terms of syndicate representation and size of the foreign tranches, which were further reduced as a result of the clawback and the absence of a greenshoe. 'Altogether, this was looking very much like a very French affair which, if continued with future privatisations, could earn the French privatisation programme a nationalistic image', said one senior London-based investment banker. This did indeed happen although, starting with the privatisation of Pechiney, the government included a foreign investment bank among the group of its financial advisers.

BNP was highly innovative in structuring the retail tranche with purchase mandates, and did a good job of maximising demand from its own and other banks' retail networks. The 'mandate structure' was subsequently adopted for all future French privatisations. BNP and the Trésor were praised by the market for having executed a fair allocation, a significant achievement considering how heavily subscribed the offer was. In terms of its sales effort, BNP did very well indeed (see Exhibit 20).

The decision to appoint Merrill Lynch as the US lead manager was taken jointly by Trésor, BNP and Lazards. The French government had historically worked primarily with Merrill Lynch, Morgan Stanley and Goldman Sachs for this role and the Trésor is thought to have pencilled in Goldman Sachs for Elf Aquitaine, Morgan Stanley for Rhône Poulenc and Merrill Lynch for BNP. The competition for the mandate was primarily between Merrill Lynch and Goldman Sachs.

Merrill's gameplan was to solicit both the Trésor and BNP. Regular meetings were held with the Trésor during the summer of 1993 to discuss the order in which privatisation candidates might come to the market. Merrill Lynch were then able to meet each of the candidates to propose possible solutions. Though the US bank was not on the steering committee that

---

Exhibit 19

Company post-issue profit performance

	Net profit (Ffr billions)	Return on equity (%)
1993	1.0	2
1994	1.7	3.5
1995	1.8	3.7

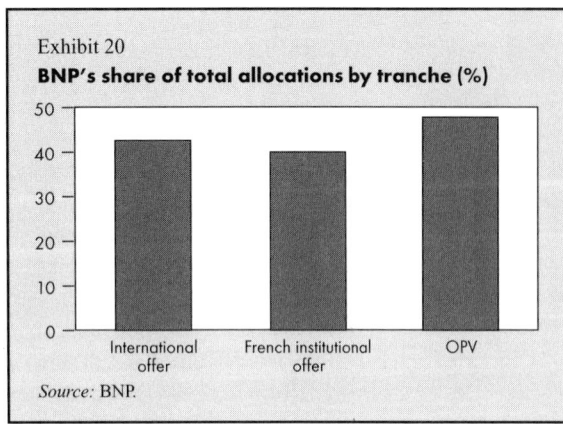

Exhibit 20

BNP's share of total allocations by tranche (%)

Source: BNP.

decided on the privatisation programme, it was able to get an inside track through its work on this, the first of the Balladur privatisations.

Although the final allocation to US investors was very small, at just US$100 million (3 per cent of the combined offers), Merrill Lynch's efforts were recognised and repaid with a much more lucrative task in the subsequent Elf Aquitaine privatisation.

Key lessons learnt

BNP became a benchmark for future privatisations as Tanguy Le Gouvello, partner at Lazard Frères pointed out: 'With BNP, we introduced a new spirit for global offers in France, namely one of transparency and allocation according to fair and pre-determined criteria. The change in transparency can be likened to when you order in a restaurant. Previously, we just ordered from the menu, now we go into the kitchen.'

Retail mandates work by generating higher retail subscriptions and allow for an early reading of the level of interest in the offer. Michel Laffitte of the Trésor said: 'The French public was not ready to buy shares without knowing the price.'

There were also specific lessons to be learned about what it is like for a bank to handle its own privatisation: syndication is more complex and sensitive; if the bank's staff is fully behind the privatisation the result is likely to be better than if it is handled by an outside party and, as the bank is both issuer, lead manager and global coordinator, certain conflicts of interest do arise which can, however, be successfully handled. One area of conflict may be due diligence and disclosure where subsequent to the offer the bank and the vendor have come under pressure from institutional investors for not revealing the relatively poor state of the loan book. Poor initial disclosure may also lead to poor research coverage in the secondary market.

The BNP privatisation illustrates the advantages and disadvantages of bank privatisation. It is relatively easy to sell in a good market environment but once the cycle turns down so does the share price.

Conclusion

The privatisation of BNP was as close to a genuine privatisation as there will ever be in France. The French Government retained only 2.4 per cent in order to satisfy bonus share commitments. There was no 'golden share' and the government was not to have any board representation. The only way in which the government could continue to exercise an indirect power in BNP was through UAP, itself a privatisation candidate, and through the core shareholder group, many of the members of which were still headed by political appointments.

By picking BNP as the first candidate, the Trésor and its advisers demonstrated a remarkable ability to pick what the market wanted.

BNP did a good job as issuer and global coordinator and was active in shaping its privatisation, demonstrating a high level of readiness and sophistication. The BNP share price performed well in the after-market for the first few months, particularly when measured against the market and its peer group.

The initial unqualified success of the offer greatly increased the attraction of future privatisations to the public and gave the Ffr300–400 billion privatisation programme a dream start. However, due to a disappointing business development, including higher than expected credit losses, BNP subsequently underperformed the market, a factor which has not helped the image of the French privatisation programme.

BNP's placement with 2.8 million retail investors (5.2 times subscribed), accounting for 62 per cent of the combined offers, represented a major success.

The offer to French and foreign institutions was closed after only two days of the official subscription period and international demand was left largely unfilled in order to satisfy domestic retail demand. This might have been a good approach in the first privatisation under the new programme, but the government continued this distribution policy in subsequent privatisations, resulting in declining institutional support. This, combined with a weak stock market performance for much of 1994 and 1995, led to growing apathy among French retail investors.

Bookbuilding, global underwriting and full transparency were successfully introduced into the French privatisation programme and BNP handled these innovations without generating much criticism.

This sale is a good example of how to privatise a bank: BNP was given an important say in all matters, both as issuer and as global coordinator, and fulfilled those roles substantially without criticism, despite the inherent conflicts of interest. The bank was innovative in the structuring of the offer and did an outstanding job in educating and motivating its branches to achieve a successful privatisation. Criticism of the bank only occurred once it became clear that the recovery in the bank's profitability would take much longer than expected.

Feature topic: *The formation of a core shareholder group in French privatisations (Groupe d'Actionnaires Stables or 'GAS')*

In order to ensure initial stability in the ownership structure of privatised companies – in other words, to discourage takeovers – and because there are no private pension funds in France, market offers have generally been supplemented by placements of a limited amount of stock, typically 10–20 per cent, with investors wishing to invest large sums of money in privatised companies for a period of at least 18–24 months. These investors have been collectively referred to as a 'Groupe d'Actionnaires Stables' (GAS for short, previously labelled Noyaux Durs or 'hard nuts'). The GAS may be made up of both French and foreign investors.

The relatively long minimum holding period is intended to enable a privatised company to gradually develop a 'natural' group of shareholders. It should be noted that these stable shareholders are not subject to any clauses governing their voting rights and should not necessarily be seen as tame shareholders, nor does membership of a core shareholder group entail representation on the board of directors.

The official selection process for the GAS takes place by invitation to tender. In practice, the CEO of the company concerned suggests a list to the minister of the economy on the basis of company contacts. The minister then makes a proposal, based on that list, to the privatisation committee, which then reviews it. The privatisation committee and the minister must then agree on the list of companies and the percentages involved. The privatisation committee has an effective veto on the selection of the GAS.

The decision on who becomes part of the GAS is more a question of politics than allocation, as the relationship between the CEO of the company being sold and that of the company buying in, in combination with political considerations, are more important than if a potential investor has a strong appetite to invest at a certain price. The members of the GAS typically pay a premium of 2–4 per cent above the institutional offer price. Officially only public information, such as the preliminary prospectus, is made available for the GAS: no special information is made available to them and there is no due diligence. Unofficially, there are many informal contacts.

A prominent privatisation banker in Paris said that there are two principal reasons for companies participating in this system: 'Either you consider it a nice way of getting a good allocation, or you consider it a bit of a favour to the company concerned on the basis that you scratch my back and I scratch yours'.

Sometimes, it is claimed, there is an industrial logic. Elf invested Ffr1 billion in Renault to become part of the car manufacturer's GAS in 1994, and claimed that there was just such a logic. But in 1995 Elf had to cut back its capital expenditure programme: most independent analysts failed to see any logic in this investment.

Typically the offer to the members of the GAS takes three weeks to complete and precedes the public offer, so that these stable shareholders can be included in the prospectus. Banks very often have corporate clients as members of the GAS, whereas industrial corporations include banks in their groups.

Critics maintain that the GAS are simply there to protect the interests of the political establishment and that they add no value. If the companies are efficiently run, the argument goes, there will be plenty of investors coming forward to buy. On the issue of the GAS being a necessary counterbalance to the absence of pension funds, a London based international investor reflected: 'If there was no institutional money in France to support the privatisation programme, then they should have carried out pension reform first, and only then privatised. There is little doubt in my mind that professional investment managers would add more value to these companies than the members of the GAS.'

In the case of BNP the particular considerations as to the GAS were:

- That the total percentage to be offered to stable shareholders should be approximately 15 per cent, subject to a 10 per cent clawback in favour of the French retail offer;
- With respect to UAP's increased investment in BNP (from 10 per cent to 15 per cent), the decision was taken to handle it outside the GAS because it was much larger and different in both purpose and scope. Taken together, the UAP holding and the GAS represented a 28 per cent ownership in BNP. The bank was thus virtually certain to be proof against take-overs;
- With respect to the strategic alliance with Dresdner Bank, approved by the respective shareholders in May 1993, but still subject to European Commission approval, the intention at the time of the privatisation was that Dresdner should take a stake at a later date, when BNP would buy an equivalent stake in Dresdner. Nevertheless, Dresdner participated in the GAS to the tune of 0.9 per cent;
- The size of the stakes to be offered to each individual stable shareholder would be relatively small, at between 0.5 per cent and 2.5 per cent of the total capital of BNP. Given that UAP became a 15 per cent shareholder in connection with the privatisation and that an equity swap with Dresdner Bank was also foreseen, it was not thought likely that any stable shareholder would want a larger stake. The total number of stable shareholders therefore was relatively large at 16. In addition to UAP and Dresdner, the group primarily included industrial companies with strong relations with BNP, the majority of which were former French state-owned companies (see Exhibit 21);

Exhibit 21
Total BNP stable shareholdings, post clawback (%)

UAP	14.6	Kuwait Investment Authority	0.9
Elf Acquitaine	1.9	PIFSS (Kuwait Social Security)	0.9
Saint Gobain	1.6	Pechiney	0.7
Marcel Daussault	1.0	Roche Finance S.A.	0.7
Rhône-Poulenc	1.0	General Electric Pension Fund	0.7
Peugeot Group	0.9	Compagnie Generale des Eaux	0.5
Renault	0.9	Saint -Louis	0.5
Dresdner	0.9	BAT Industries	0.5
Kuwait Investment Authority	0.9	**Total**	**28.1**

Exhibit 22
Retention of government control

	Date of privatisation	Size of GAS	Retained by government†	Golden share
BNP	October 1993	*28.1	2.4	No
Rhône-Poulenc	November 1993	**21.1	0	No
Elf	February 1994	8.6	13	Yes
UAP	May 1994	10.8	0	No
Renault 1	November 1994	5	53	No
Seita	February 1995	25	10	No
Usinor-Sacilor	June 1995	15	***11	No
Pechiney	November 1995	–	10.7	No
AGF	May 1996	–	2.0	No

† Prior to the sale of small stakes in these companies through the course of 1996.
* Including a 14.6% stake by UAP.
**Including a 7.4% holding by Crédit Lyonnais and a 7.7% holding by AGF.
** *Including a 3% held by state-owned Crédit Lyonnais.

Sources: Offer cirulars, the Trésor.

- The price to stable shareholders was 104 per cent of the public offer price, ie, Ffr249.60; and
- As far as the lock-up period for stable shareholders was concerned, nothing could be sold for the first three months, and 80 per cent had to be kept for a further 21 months, beginning 4 January 1994. Following the expiration of the first two years, any further sales of shares would be subject to the right of first refusal in favour of the existing core shareholders.

Critics still maintain that through political appointments, the GAS, the stakes retained by the government and the Golden Share, the French government retains a strong control over privatised companies. Judging by the facts contained in Exhibit 22, this criticism seems only partly justified. Furthermore, the French government reacted to the criticism of the GAS by structuring the Pechiney and AGF privatisations without 'stable shareholders'.

Feature topic: *Institutional investor views on privatisation*

Given that wholly or partly privatised companies account for a large portion of the market capitalisation of their respective markets and that they account for a large portion of the annual new issuance in Europe and many emerging markets, many investors can hardly afford to not look at the privatisation stocks. But how does the investment community look at these stocks? Do fund managers differentiate between privatisations and corporate issues? As always, the answer varies a great deal, depending on who you ask. Some fund managers expect privatisations to perform better in the short term but not necessarily in the long term. Others see no pattern. Some expect them to outperform in the longer term due to the customary considerable cost-cutting potential.

Patricia Maxwell-Arnot, managing director and head of European equities of Credit Suisse Asset Management: 'Generally we do not make a distinction between privatisations and corporate issues with regard to the new issue business as such. Having said that, we have learnt to hold a certain prejudice against privatisations due to the lack of history and track record of the management group. There are of course exceptions such as the Italian oil giant Eni where there had been an impressive programme of restructuring between 1992 and the time of the IPO in 1995. It has been carried out by a good management which was also the same as the one at the time of the IPO. We identified this situation as unique in a European context and tried to buy as much as we could. The appropriateness of our scepticism vis-à-vis privatisations was again confirmed when the new Spanish government in 1996, replaced, on a wholesale basis, the management of all the state-owned companies, despite only being minority shareholders. To replace bad management is one thing, but to replace somebody as successful as Oscar Fanjul, the former CEO of Repsol, is highly unfortunate and results in institutional investors commanding a risk premium for privatisations.'

When looking at privatisations, some institutions, such as Putnam Investments of the US, stress that they look at whether management control is being passed to the private sector in connection with a privatisation. If it is, then they would buy, other things being equal, if not, they will not. This area is for example one where the French privatisation programme has come under fire, as it is widely believed that the French state retains a high degree of influence in many of the partially or wholly privatised companies. On the other hand, these large institutions are big boys and should be able to handle the politics. In many cases, it simply becomes a question of demanding a risk premium for the political risk.

Huw Jones of Prudential Portfolio Managers: 'Investors expect privatisations to perform better in the short term, for two principal reasons; firstly privatisations, certainly in the UK, have been built on the perception of cheapness and this has worked and secondly, privatisations are driven by different value considerations and motivations than corporate issues that tend to come to the market at a time which may be fortuitous to the vendor.'

Another indisputable fact about privatisations and a considerable advantage is of course the fact that in some cases, it has added a whole new sector to a national equity market such as the utility sector in the UK and the telecoms sector in countries such as Denmark, the Netherlands and Germany

Dr. Sandy Nairn, of Templeton Worldwide: 'We are value investors and look for undervalued stocks on a fundamental basis and across the world. We often find that privatisations can be undervalued as a result of the fact that the timing of a privatisation is often not driven by the same timing considerations as are corporate issues. Whereas a corporate issuer would typically only sell stock at the 'right' time of the cycle, ie, when the price is high in an historic context, privatisations are often driven by budgetary and political considerations which may represent a considerable buying opportunity. We would require a risk premium commensurate with the level of uncertainty in the particular country.'

A senior UK- based fund manager commented on some of the individual programmes: 'We always require a risk premium for political risks and for the lack of historical information. You have to look at each country separately. We have for example had bad experience in France, Spain and Italy. We became a core shareholder in BNP based on an optimistic picture of rationalisation and restructuring, but we have been very disappointed with the performance and the high degree of politics involved. Whereas Peberau did a good job at CCF, things have been much more difficult at BNP. Moreover in France, many of the state's industrial holdings simply have not been managed well at all. In Austria the picture is mixed. Austrian privatisation proves the point that it does matter very much which the particular vendor is. The Austrian state industrial holding company OIAG has generally been applauded for the way it has prepared for sale a number of its privatisation sales including Böhler Uddeholm and VA Technologie whereas the shareholders in Vienna Airport – the City of Vienna and the provincial government of Lower Austria – have not done an equally commendable job. Italy is a very political market – I got an ENEL research report on my desk more than two years ago and the privatisation still hasn't happened. There are manic spikes of interest such as at the time of the BCI privatisation in the spring of 1994. The banks should not have been allowed to be privatised at the time. Furthermore, how can you take a market seriously where one or two banks have such a major influence on things and the minorities such a minor say. Finland hasn't done too badly, but we find that the companies simply have not been managed aggressively enough – I guess this is partly a cultural thing.'

Rudolf M. Staehelin of Capital International in Geneva: 'We do look differently at companies that have previously been in the state-owned sector. Whereas we do not expect a recycled LBO that is coming back to the stock market to carry a lot of extra fat, formerly state-owned companies often carry considerable extra fat and can indeed become interesting cost-cutting stories so long as they are allowed to cut without political interference. We also try to ascertain how state-owned companies will cope in a competitive environment.'

One UK fund manager commented: 'Of course we look at privatisations differently. We look at the track record of earlier privatisations. What do we find? The French have been bad with only two exceptions, Austria has been bad with only a few exceptions, however Spain has in general been good. Portugal has been successful and they are learning fast. Italy unfortunately has also had mixed results. The Nordic countries have handled their privatisation reasonably well, with the Swedes being the best of the four countries.'

One fund manager points out that the practice of giving retail discounts in privatisations is very unfair – incentives should rather be given in the form of fiscal incentives. What governments should do is to flag to the nation that privatisations are going to be attractively priced and let everyone participate at the same price. What many governments forget is that mutual fund managers ultimately represent retail investors and indirectly so do pension funds.

Thomas Madsen of JP Morgan Investment Management: 'The thing with privatisation is that over the long term, the investment returns are effectively capped as, if the privatised company does too well in terms of return on equity, the rules are typically changed, ie, regulation is tightened. If for example, a utility in one country would for any length of time show returns considerably higher than in an international context, then there would be strong pressure from consumers to reduce prices and therefore returns. An example of this is the UK, where the regulators under the Tory government changed the pricing formulas with the effect of putting downward pressure on the returns to shareholders. The new Labour government is taking this one step further by the introduction of the windfall tax on utilities.'

Elisabeth Weisenhorn of DWS: 'In general terms, we don't expect privatisations to perform either better or worse than other companies. Having said that, we are mindful of the added dimension of political risk in privatisations. With the emergence of the German retail investor, there is a strong temptation among politicians to price privatisations with attractive dividend yields for the benefit of retail investors. This can lead to inflated offer prices.' Although the Deutsche Telekom issue was thought at the time to have been aggressively priced off the back of retail demand, the valuation appears to be underpinned also by institutional investors. This however does not necessarily apply in the case of the more recent privatisation of the trade union-owned bank BHV. The pricing of privatisations based on retail demand at times of strong market conditions is a risky strategy, which can easily backfire and become highly inopportune for both the company and the government involved.

What is becoming increasingly clear is that because most governments around have a dismal track-record as owners of companies, they are increasingly going to have to demonstrate to the investment community that they are serious about severing the links to the companies that they are trying to sell. In order to privatise successfully governments also need to demonstrate that they truly recognise the validity of capitalism.

The French case stands out for political interference. The major difference compared to most other European countries is that the centre of the power elite is still found in the public sector and it has had a major impact on the running of the French state-owned companies. The system is highly centralist and privatisation therefore represents a challenge to the power elite. They have been clinging on to power as best they can with government-appointed chairmen and the concept of GAS (or core shareholders). There is indeed an ongoing dichotomy between the reluctance of the French political establishment to cede control over public services, and the need to privatise for budgetary reasons. Basically, there is a question as to whether

or not the French truly believe in the efficiency of capitalism, that is a system where the shareholders decide on who should be running the companies. There is too little evidence of people being appointed to run the French privatised companies who truly have the qualifications to run the companies as globally competitive businesses. It is probably also fair to say that before privatisation, most of these companies had not been run in the interest of the shareholders, ie, the French taxpayers.

It is notable that out of the 10 chairmen of the privatised companies listed in Exhibit 23, seven were educated at the famous Ena (Ecole nationale d'administration), the elite school for French public servants. In most cases, those that received an Ena degree, had previously received a political education at IEP (Institut d'études politiques de Paris), however some had received an engineering degree at Polytechnique. In no cases had any of these people received an accounting degree or an MBA and in only one case (Fourtou) had they not spent a considerable amount of time as civil servants. Therefore it is staightforward to conclude that practically without exception, the privatised companies are still being led by men forming part of the political establishment. Progress to rationalise and take unpopular decisions is therefore slowed by having to take into account too many political considerations rather than to create shareholder value.

Bertrand Le Pan de Ligny, investment manager and founder partner at Silchester International Investors, a private investment company managing money for US institutions and families: 'As bottom-up international value investors, we don't need to invest in any company where we don't see fundamental value, ie, we don't need to buy a particular company for asset allocation purposes, that is because it happens to represent a large portion of a particular national or international index. For that reason, we have not bought much in the French privatisation programme. We consider that the French are too interested in extracting maximum value and not enough interested in having the companies run efficiently by qualified people and to truly create popular capitalism in the sense of having the French public invited to invest in those companies at a decent valuation. After all the bad experiences in France, it is hardly surprising that the French public is getting increasingly reluctant to buy privatisations. First, they indirectly have to subsidise the companies through a heavy burden of taxation while they are still publicly owned, then they have to pay for them a second time by buying them from the people who have mismanaged them and thirdly they are asked time and time again to swallow loss of capital because the companies in many cases continue to be run with below average returns. Whereas in the UK, it seems that there has been a fundamental belief that privatisation would lead to higher efficiency through a process of making the board of directors and the management accountable to their shareholders, in France we are not sure that the political establishment

Exhibit 23

Political appointments and french privatisation

	Date of privatisation	Chairman at time of privatisation	Date appointed	Internal/ external appointment	Still in service (November 1996)	Background
BNP	October 1993	Pébereau	May 1993	External	Yes	Educated at Polytechnique/Ena (inspecteur des finances); previously chairman CCF, the bank privatised in 1987.
Rhône-Poulenc	November 1993	Fourtou	1986	External	Yes	Educated at Polytechnique, formerly senior partner at Bossard, the consulting firm
Elf	February 1994	Jaffré	August 1993	External	Yes	Educated at IEP/Ena (inspecteur des finances), former CEO Crédit Agricole and former deputy director of the Trésor. No prior industry experience.
UAP	May 1994	Friedman	November 1993	External	No	Educated at IEP/Ena (inspecteur des finances); former chairman CGM & Air France; known to have good contacts with Chirac & Balladur. No prior insurance experience; Friedman was 'promoted up' as chairman of the Supervisory Board following merger with AXA.
Renault 1	November 1994	Schweitzer	May 1992	Internal	Yes	Educated at IEP/Ena (inspecteur des finances); chef du cabinet under Fabius. Long number two at Renault.
Seita	February 1995	Comolli	1993	External	Yes	Educated at IEP/Ena. Formerly top civil servant with French customs organisation. No prior industry experience.
Usinor-Sacilor	June 1995	Mer	1986	Internal	Yes	Educated at Polytechnique (Ing. du corps des Mines). Former chairman, Pont à Mousson.
Pechiney	November 1995	Rodier	July 1994	External	Yes	Educated at Polytechnique (Ing. du corps des Mines); former chairman, Union Minière (controlled by SGB of Belgium).
AGF	May 1996	Jeancourt-Galignani	January 1994	External	Yes	Educated at Ena, former chairman and CEO, Banque Indosuez, where he was for some 20 years.
France Télécom	October 1997	Bon	February 1995	External	Yes	Educated at IEP/Ena (inspecteur des finances), former civil servant at ANPE (national employment agency), former CEO of Crédit Agricole and former chairman of Carrefour. No prior telecom experience.

really and truly believes in the beauty of private ownership and that market forces will bring about the most efficient allocation of resources. Looked at it slightly differently, even after the French state-owned companies have been privatised, there still seems to be some confusion as to whether it is the state or the private sector that actually owns the assets. This philosophy is well illustrated by an experience which we had with the CFO of a French blue chip industrial group which has been priva-

tised for some time. When asked if he ever listened to his shareholders, this CFO simply answered: 'I give investor presentations twice a year in London and New York.' Ultimately, it is our view that French privatisation is more about tapping the market in order to raise the maximum amount of cash in the sense of a bond auction or an auction at Sotheby's rather than to inject efficiency in French business life.'

Bulgari

In the absence of a credible Italian equity market – in spite of the high Italian savings ratio – medium-sized, family-owned companies such as Bulgari SpA, which form the backbone of the Italian economy, have had great difficulty in raising equity capital and have instead had to rely on internally generated cashflow and bank debt.

It is in this context that Bulgari's showcase IPO, one of the largest private sector Italian IPOs of the last decade, should be seen. Not only was it a remarkable success for the company and its investors, but it also helped to create a dedicated luxury goods sector, which, through repeated flotations and reratings, grew from five companies with a market capitalisation of US$28 billion to 14 companies valued at US$47 billion, in little over a year following Bulgari's offer.

Bulgari and Morgan Stanley were very much aware of the need for the deal to succeed as a less than successful transaction would tarnish the company's image. Equally, if the offer objective of providing both the company and its principal shareholders with liquidity was to be fulfilled, the stock would have to trade well in the secondary market, and as an international company, Bulgari was anxious to achieve a balanced investor base.

A New York Stock Exchange listing and dual listings in New York and Milan were considered, but ultimately rejected. Other Italian companies with a strong international presence, such as Fila, Natuzzi, Luxottica and Pirelli Tyre, had decided to list their shares exclusively on foreign stock exchanges. Bulgari decided to list its shares in Milan, but to do so in connection with an offer which was as much directed at the international market as at the domestic one.

The Bulgari transaction is also noteworthy as it was only the second truly bookbuilt corporate IPO in Italy, and Morgan Stanley, assisted by BCI, managed to overcome the constraint of the Consiglio di Borsa valuation. This convention represents an effective maximum IPO valuation as recommended by a department of the Milan Stock Exchange and is derived from a theoretical valuation approach. Bulgari was also able to take advantage of a tax ruling (the 'Tremonti Law') that allowed companies which went public in 1995 to pay reduced state taxes (21 per cent as opposed to 37 per cent) until 1998.

At the time of the IPO, Bulgari was, in terms of sales, the third largest fine jeweller after Cartier and Tiffany, and the fifth largest fine watchmaker after such names as Rolex, Baume & Mercier, Cartier and Ebel. In 1993, it entered the perfume business, where it competes most directly with other jewellers who produce perfume such as Boucheron, Cartier and Van Cleef, as well as designer brands. At the end of 1994, the company operated 25 owned and 11 franchised stores, and also sold its watches and perfumes through independent retailers. In 1994 jewellery accounted for 50 per cent of sales, watches for 43 per cent, perfumes for 5 per cent and other products for 2 per cent.

The Bulgari family, originally from Greece, opened its first shop in Rome in 1884. Following the flotation, just over 59 per cent of the company's shares were owned by Paolo and Nicola Bulgari, two brothers from the third generation of the family, while their nephew, Francesco Trapani, who

---

Exhibit 1
Transaction summary

Issuer name: Bulgari SpA (Italy)	*Global coordinator:* Morgan Stanley
Pricing date: 30 June 1995 (Mibtel 30 Index: 14,415)	*Pricing/underwriting structure:* International bookbuilding followed by a domestic fixed price offer for retail investors.
Vendors: Company and the selling shareholders, ie, Paolo Bulgari, Nicola Bulgari, Credit Suisse investment funds and Schroder Investment Management	*Primary or secondary:* 20 million shares primary / 6 million shares secondary
% of company sold: 36.2% of expanded share capital	*Privatisation or corporate:* Corporate
IPO or non-IPO: IPO	*Industry:* Retailing/luxury goods
Type of shares: Ordinary shares and ADRs (1 ordinary share = 1 ADR)	Pricing range: L7,800–8,600 per ordinary share / Offer price: L8,600 and US$5.32/ADR
Total issue size: US$138 million	*US listing/144 A:* 144 A

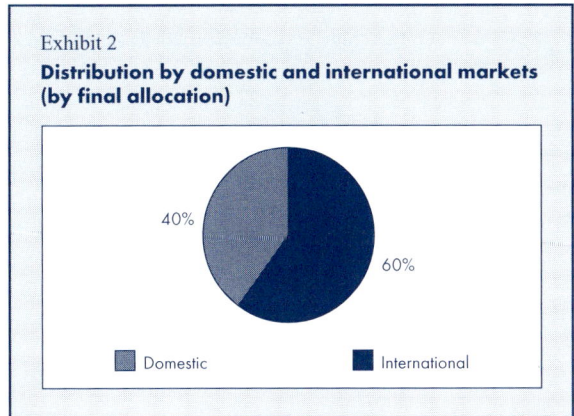

Exhibit 2
Distribution by domestic and international markets (by final allocation)

40%

60%

■ Domestic   ■ International

became CEO in 1984, owned 4.6 per cent. In 1992, Mr. Trapani and his highly rated management team embarked on a strategy of internationalisation and controlled diversification to broaden the appeal of the underexploited Bulgari brand name.

For the purposes of the IPO, the company, with only 17 per cent of 1994 sales in Italy, was positioned with investors as an international 'luxury goods company' rather than as an Italian or international retailer. As such, it was expected to have better growth prospects than the retail sector at large. At the time of the IPO, Morgan Stanley was expecting net profit growth of 30 per cent in 1995, and 17 per cent growth per year in the medium term.

At the time of the offer Bulgari was valued at US$382 million and in late November 1996 it was valued at almost US$1.4 billion. This value increase is attributable to both higher than expected profits growth and a substantial re-rating. Priced at 13.1 times 1996 earnings in June 1995, 17 months later, Bulgari was trading at 25 times 1997 earnings.

The Bulgari IPO was the first new issue for over four years by any company from what is now considered the 'luxury goods sector'. The fact that it was successful at a time of disappointing market conditions eased the way for the much bigger Gucci transaction which was globally coordinated by Morgan Stanley in October 1995. That offer also met its objectives and, within a year of the Bulgari IPO, Morgan Stanley had managed a second Gucci offer and IPOs for Harvey Nichols and Donna Karan.

Major challenges

Prior to the spate of offers in 1995, the luxury goods sector was not recognised as a dedicated industry sector for the purposes of equity research and asset allocation. Quoted companies such as Hermes, Vendôme, LVMH, Tiffany and Christian Dior had been grouped with other retail companies and were, therefore, covered by general retail analysts. There were few established relationships between fund managers and analysts who thought alike with respect to the pace of growth and value of the branded goods sector. The absence of a dedicated analyst community is important as fund managers take investment decisions primarily based on the recommendations of a trusted analyst rather than because of their faith in the investment bank sponsoring the issue, even if, as

in this case, the investment bank is a reputable one.

Following the Gulf War and the associated reduction in international travel, luxury goods consumers had become more value conscious when making a purchase. Claire Kent, Morgan Stanley's equity research analyst for the retail and luxury goods sector said: 'The luxury goods sector no longer had the froth of the eighties and it was, therefore, a considerable challenge to judge whether or not in mid-1995 an offer for a 'luxury goods company' could be successfully sold.'

To ensure that the IPO was successful, (which was of critical importance to the company's future as a listed company and to Morgan Stanley's European equity franchise), Morgan Stanley imposed a rigorous internal consensus-seeking process on itself, whereby the wisdom of bringing a luxury goods company to the market at that point in the cycle was evaluated, along with as to whether or not Bulgari was the right name and whether its prospects were realistic. The company was subjected to a comprehensive, US-style, due diligence process, which represented the single biggest challenge for the company. Francesco Trapani said: 'The due diligence process was very tough for us – a lot of questions came up that we had never been forced to think about in such detail before. All our processes, procedures and systems were challenged and often compared to those of our competitors. We had to explain why we were doing certain things and why we were not doing others. As an example, Morgan Stanley came to Rome for two days with a team of three people specifically to look into how fluctuations in exchange rates would impact our business.'

Pre-marketing the IPO was tricky due to the fact that there was no specific 'use of proceeds' strategy. The company management talked about its plans to acquire a company within the luxury goods sector but had no specific target in mind. The Bulgari management, although they had an excellent general track record, had no track record at all with respect to acquisitions. The roadshow was also a major challenge for the company: Trapani recalled that he gave 55 presentations in just over nine days. But he said: 'Although challenging, it was perhaps a little easier for us because our 'story' was truly a success story.'

Another major challenge was to price the offer in such a way that the company's excellent prospects were taken into account, which in practice meant that the offer price had to be higher than the L8,000 valuation recommended by the Consiglia di Borsa. Morgan Stanley were also having to price the IPO into an equity market which was highly volatile during the marketing period: the Italian market was down 3.3 per cent in the week before pricing. The poor performance of similar quoted companies did nothing to improve the primary market environment, while Vendôme, LVMH and Tiffany all issued profit warnings during this period.

Last but not least, the company and its global coordinator had to cope with the Italian factor : political turbulence, a high inflation rate, persistent budget deficits, the weakness of the lira, poor corporate governance standards and the fact that there had been few successful Italian equity transactions remained a worry throughout the preparation phase. In addition, the lack of depth and stability in the Italian equity market gave cause for concern. John Hyman, executive director, equity capital markets, at Morgan Stanley said: 'The Italian retail investor does

Exhibit 3
Share capital and ownership

Type of shares offered	Ordinary shares of L500 and ADRs, whereby 1 ordinary share = 1 ADR
Ownership restrictions	–
Share capital before and after offer	52 million/72 million
Listings/quotations	Milan Stock Exchange in connection with the offer, and Seaq International
Market capitalisation at offer price (L1,620//US$)	US$382 million (based on expanded share capital)
Major shareholder(s) before/after the offer and exercise of greenshoe	Paolo Bulgari 43.5/29.6% Nicola Bulgari 43.5/29.6% Francesco Trapani 6.4/4.6% Credit Suisse (funds) 4.0/0% Schroders Investment Management 2.6 0%
Free float after offer	36.2%
Foreign ownership after offer	21.7%
Most relevant stock exchange index/weighting	Mibtel index/0.315%

not trust the equity market and has historically sold as soon as an IPO has appreciated by 10 per cent.'

Rationale and objectives

There were three principal reasons for the IPO:

- To finance future organic growth, and potential growth by acquisition, in order to pursue a strategy of product diversification and an expansion of distribution channels;
- To monetise the portion of the Bulgari brothers' investment in the company that was not required to keep control of the business; and
- To 'institutionalise' the company, ie, to increase the pressure to perform. The owners and the management were conscious of the need to strike a better balance between the realisation of the company's long-term strategy and its short-term profit performance.

The company's objectives were:

- To carry out an international offer in order to avoid being dependent on the vagaries of the domestic market;
- To achieve a successful offer so as not to harm the company's excellent image and favourable brand recognition; and
- To achieve the highest price possible, consistent with the other objectives.

There were three principal uses of proceeds:

- To make investments in one or more luxury goods companies with recognised brand names;
- To fund the opening of new shops and increase marketing activities; and
- Depending on the timing of the above mentioned investments, to repay outstanding indebtedness.

Share capital and ownership

See Exhibit 3.

Schroders Investment Management and certain investment funds managed by Credit Suisse had been shareholders in Bulgari since 1989 and 1991 respectively, and were now given the opportunity to exit their investments at a considerable capital gain. Whereas these institutions were able to realise sizeable capital gains in connection with the IPO, the fact that they were prepared to sell was also welcomed by Morgan Stanley, as this made it possible to increase the free float, which was otherwise restricted by the wish on the part of the Bulgari brothers not to sell too much of their holding.

Transaction components

The offer structure

This offer of 20 million new shares and 3.1 million existing shares was comprised of two tranches: an institutional tranche initially representing 65 per cent of the total offer (of which 50 per cent was earmarked for sale internationally and 15 per cent to domestic institutions) and a domestic retail tranche (the OPV), initially representing 35 per cent of the total offer. The IPO was marketed on an open-priced basis to both international and domestic institutional investors, allowing a book to be built, after which the offer price was fixed. Once this was done, a mandatory formal subscription period (of a maximum of five days) for domestic retail investors followed: this retail offer was to close after just two days. There was a further seven-day period between the pricing and allocation to investors and another 10 day wait before trading commenced.

The institutional tranche included an option to sell shares in the US under Rule 144 A, and also allowed for a greenshoe of an additional 2.9 million secondary shares to be sold by the selling shareholders. The institutional and retail tranches also included an offer to all Bulgari employees (see Exhibits 4 and 5).

Exhibit 4
Development of the offer size (number of shares)

Indicated number of shares to be sold	23,100,000 + 2,933,564 greenshoe
Amount of greenshoe exercised	2,933,564
Final number of shares sold	26,033,564

Exhibit 5
Offer structure

Target markets	Indicated tranche sizes*	Bookrunning lead managers	Co-lead managers
Institutional tranche	65%	Morgan Stanley	BCI, Schroders, Paribas, UBS, Commerzbank
• of which earmarked internationally	50%		
• of which earmarked to Italy	15%		
Retail tranche	35%	BCI	Credito Italiano, IMI, San Paolo, Cassa di Risparmio di Trieste, Banca di Roma, Popolare Di Bergamo, Cariplo, Deutsche Bank
Total combined offers (shares)	**23,100,000**		

* percentage of indicated total offer, as published in the Red Herring, on 19 June 1995.

Sources: Offer circular and Morgan Stanley.

Exhibit 6
Distribution of gross spread (%)

Management fee	Underwriting fee	Selling concession	Gross spread
1	1	3	5

Exhibit 7
Distribution of management fee (%)

Allocation of the total management fee in the institutional tranche	1
Of which: Global coordinator's praecipium	0.375
Of which: Management fee split among all the managers	0.62

Exhibit 8
Distribution of selling concession (%)

Allocation of the total selling concession in the institutional tranche	3
Of which: Pre-agreed portion	0
Of which: Paid to whom ever received the order	100

Transaction fee distribution

The company paid an advisory fee of 0.75 per cent to Morgan Stanley, calculated on the aggregate purchase price of the shares in the international offer. In the retail tranche there was a lead managers' praecipium of 1.375 per cent, split among all the lead managers (see Exhibits 6,7 and 8).

Principal advisers

See Exhibit 9.

Exhibit 9
Principal advisers

Financial adviser to the company	Morgan Stanley
Italian legal adviser to the company	Pavia, Ansaldo e Verusio, Studio Legale
Italian legal adviser to the managers	Chiomenti e Associati
US legal adviser to the international managers	Davis Polk & Wardwell
Auditors	Arthur Andersen & Co

Exhibit 10
The timetable

End of February, 1995	• The company decides to go ahead with the IPO, following extensive valuation work in December and January.
Early March	• Morgan Stanley is formally mandated.
4 May	• Formal decision to proceed with the offer and first press announcement.
31 May	• Publication of research report.
6–12 June	• Pre-marketing.
8 June	• Publication of L8,000 price by 'Consiglio di Borsa'.
9 June	• Preliminary prospectus/red herring published; and • Indicated price range is announced.
19 June	• European roadshow commences. • Bookbuilding begins.
27 June	• US roadshow begins.
29 June	• Bookbuilding ends.
30 June	• Pricing of the offer; and • Signing of international and Italian subscription agreements.
3 July	• Italian OPV commences (maximum 5 days)
4 July	• Italian OPV closes early.
7 July	• Allocation to investors.
10 July	• Grey market trading begins.
17 July	• Official trading opens on the Milan Stock Exchange.
19 July	• Offer closes.
26 July	• Greenshoe exercised.

Deal structure

Listing strategy

One of the items that the company had to decide upon early in the proceedings was where its stock should be listed: in both Milan and New York, New York alone or Milan alone. The merits and drawbacks of the different options are discussed in Exhibit 11.

Ultimately, Bulgari decided that the most natural 'home market' for the company was in Italy and that there was no compelling reason to incur the expense and extra time commitment required to list in New York.

Valuation considerations

On top of the normal challenges associated with the valuation of international IPOs, whereby the domestic and international markets often have slightly different approaches to the valuation, in this case Morgan Stanley faced a constraint which had as much to do with market convention as with the particular valuation methodology.

In Italy IPO pricing has traditionally been based on the value that the 'Consiglia di Borsa', a department of the stock exchange, considers fair value for the company. This value is based primarily on a theoretical discounted cash flow calculation. Once calculated, this number is announced by the Consiglio di Borsa and must by law be included in the prospectus. This valuation reassures retail investors and also serves as a guide to the equity research community.

In practice, this valuation has come to be viewed as a max-imum price for an Italian IPO pricing and in fact, on only a single occasion prior to this had an IPO been priced above this valuation.

The fault inherent in the Italian approach to IPO pricing lies in the fact that while the members of the Consiglio di Borsa are very competent professionals, and have access to some equity research and due diligence information, they do not have access to the market, ie, to investors. Consequently, they are not in a position to judge what investors consider the company to be worth and what they are prepared to pay, an assessment which serves as the principal basis for international pricing, and which represents the very essence of book-building. It is also important to recognise that the members of the Consiglio di Borsa are short staffed and generally lack the incentive to come up with a fuller valuation. For the department there is only a downside to pushing for a higher valuation, as if the share price should slip below their valuation early in its trading history, the department would be criticised by the press and public.

On this occasion, instead of pushing the Consiglio di Borsa members for a full valuation, Morgan Stanley decided to work with them: the committee members were given full access to the due diligence information, comparable companies' trading information, research reports, access to analysts and perhaps most importantly, access to preliminary investor feedback.

It was also important for Morgan Stanley to bring BCI on board concerning the proposed valuation, as it was higher than the Consiglio di Borsa's valuation and, by implication, higher than that with which BCI would typically have been comfortable.

Exhibit 11
Bulgari listing strategy

	Advantages	Disadvantages
Milan and NYSE dual listings	• The US investment community had begun to invest increasingly in non-US stocks to improve returns and many non-US companies were beginning to take advantage of this trend by listing on a US stock exchange; • A dual listing might have generated stronger US institutional investor interest; • The transaction would have a higher international profile; and • The company would clearly have been perceived as having met the toughest disclosure and due diligence standards.	• To have had to cater to two major markets, more liquidity should ideally have been available. Given the intended size of the offer, there would be a significant risk of frustrating major institutional investors; • There were several Italian equity transactions in the pipeline and there was already some resistance among the Italian banks to the transaction due to conflict of interest considerations and the lack of depth of the Italian market. The banks would probably have felt even less compelled to support the IPO had there also been a NYSE listing; and • A NYSE listing would have required a very significant commitment from the company.
NYSE only	In addition to the advantages of listing in both New York and Milan as mentioned above, there was one further aspect to consider for Bulgari as an Italian based company: • A number of successful Italian IPOs had been done with a NYSE listing only, including Fila, Natuzzi and Luxottica; and • Compared to a dual listing, a single NYSE listing would have had the advantage of concentrating liquidity in one place. It would have made apparent, which the market of last resort would have been.	• The Bulgari name is still very much linked to the Italian image of style and Bulgari's presence in the US (20% of 1994 sales) was still not so strong as to justify the lack of a listing in the domestic market. It is questionable as to whether or not investors would have supported New York as the true 'home market'; • The lack of an Italian listing would have distracted the natural interest and after-market support from Italian institutions; and • Of the comparable companies, only Tiffany was listed in New York.
Milan only	• The image and nature of Bulgari's business is strongly associated with Italy, although only 17% of the its1994 sales were derived from the Italian market. The Milan listing would support this image and strengthen both the business and investors' comfort level; and • Most comparable companies are European (Vendôme, Hermes, Asprey and LVMH).	• The Italian stock market is volatile and generally considered relatively unsophisticated. Italian retail investors don't trust the equity market and typically sell as soon as the stock has appreciated in value by 5%–10%. There is limited buying power among Italian institutions.

Morgan Stanley had earlier had a negative experience in the pricing of an Austrian equity offer (the Mayr Melnhof IPO) where they had not agreed on pricing with their Austrian partner, Creditanstalt Bankverein. To coordinate valuation and pricing with the universal banks of continental Europe is a challenge at the best of times and it is essential to recognise that most European universal banks are inherently risk averse when it comes to the pricing of equity transactions. At senior management level there is insufficient interest in the underwriting of equity deals to warrant close attention as the bulk of profits are made on the lending side.

Because of the lack of senior support and the absence of performance-related compensation, there is limited interest in pushing for higher valuations. In addition, equity research analysts in continental Europe have not traditionally enjoyed the same high status as they do in the US or the UK. Representatives of the underwriting and equity research departments are only likely to hear from senior management if something goes wrong so there was no reason for BCI to push for a higher valuation than that recommended by the Consiglio di Borsa. Nevertheless, in the Bulgari IPO, Morgan Stanley successfully managed to overcome both of the above constraints on the pricing process, which was without a doubt a contributing factor to the success of the offer.

Marketing the offer

• The positioning of the company as an international luxury goods player, rather than as an Italian retailer, was understood and accepted by institutional investors; and
• Although Bulgari had a slightly erratic track record and there was a lack of true comparables, investors were convinced about the potential to further exploit the Bulgari brand.

Bulgari was predominantly marketed as a 'growth play', however, it was also a management story in so far as Bulgari's young and dynamic management had already proven its turnaround capability and had introduced modern management methods into an industry that had been slow to move away from more traditional practices (see Exhibits 12, 13, 14 and 15).

Results

Placement
See Exhibit 16.

The transaction was 6.5 times subscribed overall, and was particularly well received in the international market – the

Exhibit 12

Principal sales points

Brand name	• Bulgari is a well known brand name in Italy, Europe, the US and throughout Asia (including Japan). As a niche luxury goods company, Bulgari stands for prestige and focus. Contrary to more generalist luxury goods companies such as Gucci and Hermes, Bulgari was focused primarily on three segments of the industry, namely jewellery, watches and perfume; • Bulgari is committed to the preservation of its brand name by ensuring that all products are of a high quality, tightly controlling its distribution channels, avoiding discounting, focusing on key customer groups and extensive staff training; and • Bulgari's management team was intent on, and believed it would succeed in, broadening the appeal of the Bulgari brand name without at the same time diluting its prestige. This was to be achieved by entering a limited number of new segments within the luxury goods market, by developing a broader product portfolio within existing segments, by launching new creative product lines including more affordable ones, and by expanding its distribution network.
Management	• Bulgari had an impressive management team of dynamic and relatively young executives. The average age of the seven strong executive management team, including the CEO, was just over 38 at the time of the offer. The CEO, Francesco Trapani, is the nephew of Paolo and Nicola Bulgari, the two largest owners and the chairman and vice chairman of the Board respectively. Most of Trapani's management team had been hired from outside and brought with them experience from management consultancy at McKinsey and Bain, and from marketing-driven companies such as Procter & Gamble, IBM, American Express, Gucci, and Hewlett Packard; • The Bulgari management had already established an impressive track record having, grown the business from four shops in 1985 to 36 shops in 1994. Sales and profits had grown by a compound annual growth rate of 38.4% and 144.3%, between 1992 and 1994 respectively. Over the same period, the average number of days of inventory had dropped by 33% (from 732 days to 489 days) as a result of the introduction of a new on-line order and inventory system for jewellery and watches. In addition, the working capital requirements had been reduced as the proportion of the total turnover accounted for by watches and perfumes had increased.
Growth potential	• Bulgari's goal was to become a leader in luxury goods by the year 2000, through aggressive organic growth and by acquisition. At the time of the offer, Morgan Stanley expected earnings growth of 30% in 1995, and 17% annually in the medium term; • At the end of 1994, Bulgari had 36 stores (11 of which were franchised). The company was expecting to have 68 stores by the end of 1997 (23 franchised). This would still only represent half the number that Cartier had at the end of 1994. Bulgari believes that the longer term potential is 150 stores;. • Bulgari was also planning to expand the number of its outlets for its watches from 120 at the end of 1994, to 300 by 1998 (which would still be far fewer than its competitors); and • In perfumes, the company was planning to expand the number of distributors from 2,513 in 1994, to 8,000 by 1998.
Balanced geographical presence	• Bulgari has a geographically balanced customer base and has, to a large extent, managed to match the currencies in which it receives revenues and incurs its costs. Bulgari thus has relatively limited transaction exposure.
Close integration with suppliers	• Over many years Bulgari has established long-standing and tight relationships with its main suppliers for jewellery. This has allowed for the optimisation of the production schedule and very tight control over the quality of its production; and • In 1989 Bulgari entered into a joint venture with Girard-Perregaux, a company with a very strong reputation for quality and reliability in the manufacture of watch movements.
Valuation	• Bulgari was attractively valued in P/E terms – 14. 6 times 1995 and 13.1 times 1996 earnings – due to its strong projected growth. The company was valued in line with its two main competitors in terms of 'aggregate value' to 1994 sales (aggregate value equals equity market value plus preferred stock, minority interests and net debt).

Sources: Morgan Stanley and offer circular.

international portion of the institutional tranche was 10 times subscribed. The total institutional tranche, including the Italian placement, was nine times subscribed, reflecting the fact that the Italian institutional placement effort was slightly less successful (being 'only' 5.2 times subscribed) compared to initial expectations than was the international portion of the institutional tranche. Almost 25,000 retail investors participated in the domestic retail offer, which was 2.2 times subscribed, a considerable achievement given the poor market conditions at the time.

The most important countries in terms of the institutional placement were the UK, the US and Italy, followed by Switzerland (see Exhibit 17).

The issue was relatively broadly distributed with as many

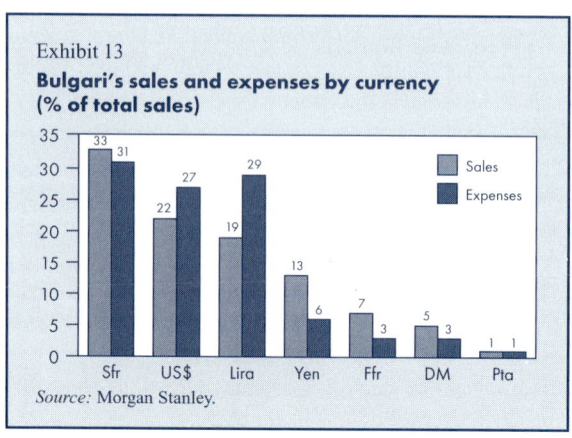

Exhibit 13

Bulgari's sales and expenses by currency (% of total sales)

Source: Morgan Stanley.

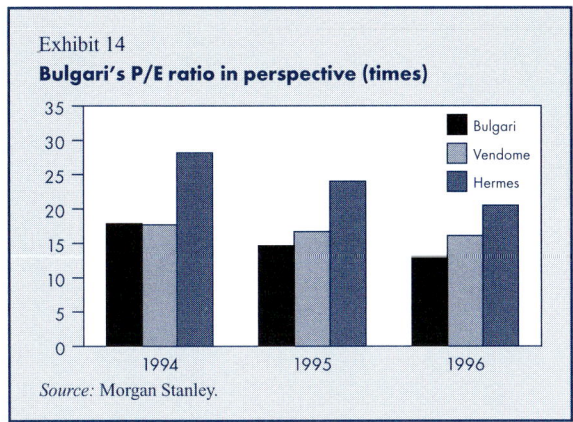

Exhibit 14
Bulgari's P/E ratio in perspective (times)

Source: Morgan Stanley.

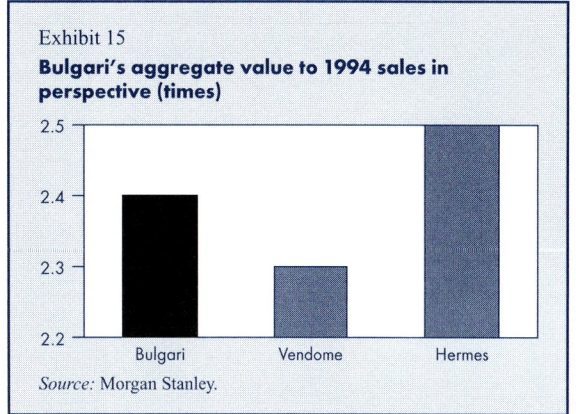

Exhibit 15
Bulgari's aggregate value to 1994 sales in perspective (times)

Source: Morgan Stanley.

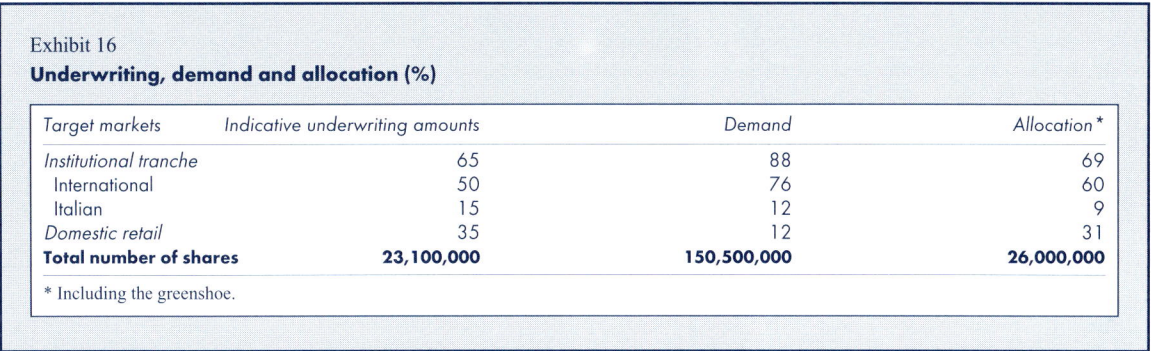

Exhibit 16
Underwriting, demand and allocation (%)

Target markets	Indicative underwriting amounts	Demand	Allocation*
Institutional tranche	65	88	69
International	50	76	60
Italian	15	12	9
Domestic retail	35	12	31
Total number of shares	**23,100,000**	**150,500,000**	**26,000,000**

* Including the greenshoe.

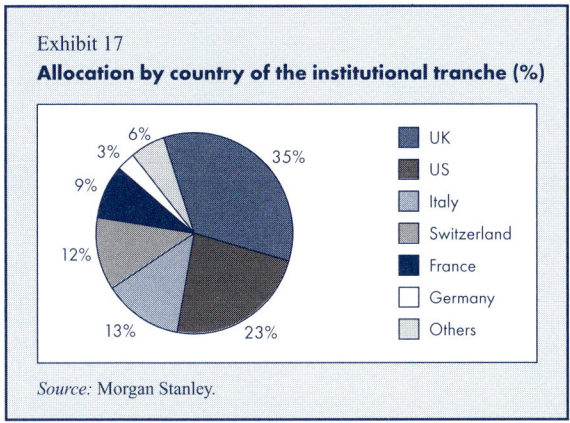

Exhibit 17
Allocation by country of the institutional tranche (%)

UK	35%
US	23%
Italy	13%
Switzerland	12%
France	9%
Germany	3%
Others	6%

Source: Morgan Stanley.

as 50 institutions accounting for 80 per cent of the total offer. In total 271 institutions were allocated in the institutional tranche. Given the relatively modest size of the offer

and the huge demand, there were many institutions, even some high quality ones, which did not receive any shares, despite the fact that the largest single allocation represented just over 1 per cent of the total institutional tranche (see Exhibit 18).

There were several different types of buyers, with nine categories making up the lion's share of the international portion. Of the non-domestic institutions, the dominant buyers were European and International Small Cap Funds and European and International Growth Funds (see Exhibit 19).

After-market price performance
See Exhibit 20.
- Although Bulgari closed trading on the first day up 5.7 per cent, showing an outperformance of 1.7 per cent since the pricing on 30 June. The trading performance in the immediate after-market was somewhat hesitant, with

Exhibit 18
Investor concentration

	By demand	By allocation
Percentage of issue accounted for by the 10 largest investors (by total size of demand and allocation respectively)	25%	30%
Number of investors making up 80% of the issue (by total size of demand and allocation respectively)	60	50
The 3 largest investors by size	US$6.6 million US$3.0 million US$2.9 million	US$1.0 million US$0.5 million US$0.5 million
Total number of institutions	**411**	**271**

Source: Morgan Stanley.

Exhibit 19

Types of buyers

	Small cap funds	Growth funds	Retail buyers
Italian buyers	Small	Small	Small
European funds	Big	Big	Medium
International	Big	Big	Medium

Bulgari showing an underperformance against the local market of almost 1 per cent by 25 July. The all time low of L8,860 was set on 20 July;

- Although up by 9.3 per cent in absolute terms, Bulgari only performed in line with the market over the first month of trading. In late August, its shares began to rise sharply off the back of strong interim results due to the fact that Morgan Stanley was no longer restricted from commenting on the stock as the overhang from selling retail shareholders was removed and as the luxury goods sector was generally strong. On 4 September, the shares had appreciated by 25 per cent in absolute terms and had outperformed the local market by 21 per cent. The outperformance had risen to 52 per cent after three months, and to 67.2 per cent after six months; and

- By late February 1996, Bulgari had more than doubled in price and had outperformed the market by more than 100 per cent. The first year high of L25,750 was reached on 3 July 1996, after which the price came back to stand at L22,000 on the first anniversary of trading, at which time the outperformance was 154 per cent, a truly spectacular result. Over the first year of trading, Bulgari had outperformed the Morgan Stanley luxury goods sector with a spectacular 82%.

After-market trading volume

As evidenced by the turnover figures on the Milan Stock Exchange during the first three trading days, the turnover in the immediate after-market was relatively modest by most standards. This is noteworthy given the small size of the allocations, which often leads to selling in the immediate after-market. The absence of such selling obviously confirms investors' confidence in Bulgari's prospects.

Italian retail investors are thought to have sold meaningful amounts in the immediate after-market. 'They will have sold approximately 50 per cent of their initial allocations during the first two to three months of trading,' said John Hyman of Morgan Stanley (see Exhibit 21).

The performance of the main parties

The company

The company deserves considerable credit in a number of respects: they were astute enough to pick an international bank as the sole global coordinator with overall responsibility for the offer, which meant that Morgan Stanley was in a position to pick BCI itself. This move immediately established a constructive working relationship between the two banks.

Exhibit 20

After-market price performance

Pricing date	30 June
Filing range	L7,800–8,600
Offer price	L8,600
First year high/low	
High (3 July 1996)	L25,750
Low (20 July 1995)	L8,860

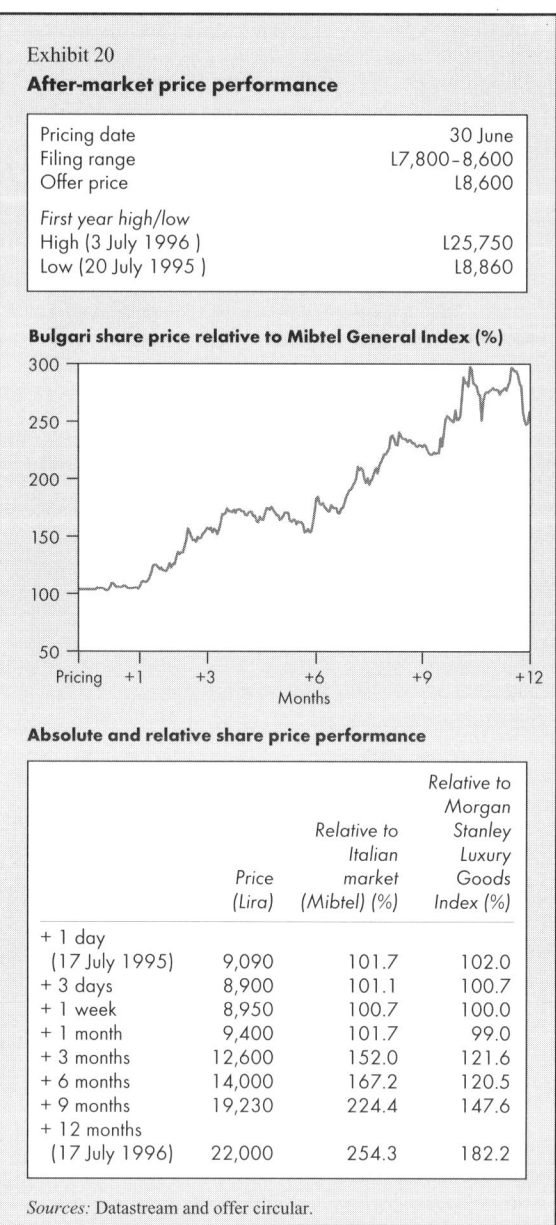

Bulgari share price relative to Mibtel General Index (%)

Absolute and relative share price performance

	Price (Lira)	Relative to Italian market (Mibtel) (%)	Relative to Morgan Stanley Luxury Goods Index (%)
+ 1 day (17 July 1995)	9,090	101.7	102.0
+ 3 days	8,900	101.1	100.7
+ 1 week	8,950	100.7	100.0
+ 1 month	9,400	101.7	99.0
+ 3 months	12,600	152.0	121.6
+ 6 months	14,000	167.2	120.5
+ 9 months	19,230	224.4	147.6
+ 12 months (17 July 1996)	22,000	254.3	182.2

Sources: Datastream and offer circular.

Exhibit 21

Percentage of total issue traded * (%)

	Day 1 (17 July)	Day 2 (18 July)	Day 3 (19 July)	Total Day 1–3
Milan	5.3	2.5	2.3	10.1

* Based on the issue of 23.1 million shares.

Source: Bloomberg.

The company also decided to go to the market when the prospects were excellent instead of waiting for a higher price at a later stage when the risk of a disappointing after-market performance might have been higher.

Another key factor was that the company agreed to subject itself to the highest due diligence standards and it also did an excellent job in communicating the 'Bulgari story' on the roadshow. Finally, Bulgari took a very long-term approach

Exhibit 22
Company profit performance (Lira billions)

	1994 actual	1995 forecast	1995 actual
Sales	283. 4	343.1	385.3
Net profit	25.1	32.5	39.5

Source: Offer circular and Morgan Stanley.

to becoming a public company. Taking the time to get to know the Morgan Stanley team over the years prior to the IPO enabled both sides to build up mutual trust. Claire Kent of Morgan Stanley said: 'We had a high level of confidence in the company by the time Bulgari went public. We could see that the company was successfully carrying out the strategy it had detailed several years earlier.'

After the IPO Bulgari surpassed even the ambitious projections in terms of sales and profit growth on which the offer was sold (see Exhibit 22). For the first six months of 1996, sales and net profit increased by 21 per cent and 207 per cent respectively, confirming the trend of better than expected performance by the company.

The global coordinator

Bulgari and Morgan Stanley started preliminary discussions about a possible flotation before the Gulf War in 1990. Discussions were resumed in 1992, but Morgan Stanley recommended that the company wait for a few years until there was more of a track record. Discussions were resumed again in late 1994, on the back of a solid 1993 and the prospect of an even better 1994.

There was considerable debate as to whether to launch the IPO on the back of a relatively short track record (really only 1993 and 1994), but with a promising outlook (at least for 1995–97), or to wait for six months to a year until a slightly longer track record had been built up, though the wait might come at the expense of a slightly more modest outlook in terms of future growth.

The reckoning was that as long as investors were truly convinced about the quality of the Bulgari management, a high multiple could be achieved based on the high growth expectations, even without a long track record.

Claudio Sposito, Morgan Stanley's executive director and head of the bank's Italian business, enjoyed a close relationship with Bulgari's CEO. Other representatives of Morgan Stanley, including the bank's equity research analyst for the retail sector, Claire Kent, had known the company management for a number of years. Morgan Stanley had unofficially advised Bulgari on both strategy and possible acquisitions, and in the process, the company's IPO had been discussed on a regular basis. Consequently, Bulgari decided to mandate Morgan Stanley without giving serious consideration to any other investment banks.

Morgan Stanley was given overall charge of the transaction and hence was instrumental in selecting BCI, the 'market leader' in the domestic distribution of shares to retail investors.

Morgan Stanley undoubtedly deserves a lot of credit for the professional preparation and execution of this IPO, it was the first investment bank to realise that market sentiment had moved in favour of luxury goods. The due diligence with the company was very thorough indeed and the bank interacted well with both the domestic lead manager, BCI, and the Italian regulators including the Consiglia di Borsa.

In its research on the company Morgan Stanley adopted a conservative approach with respect to achievable growth, assuming, for example, a slightly slower pace of store openings than did the company.

The pricing was clearly right – although it was L600 higher than the valuation recommended by the Milan Stock Exchange. It could certainly not have been much higher, and Morgan Stanley was lucky that the Italian market moved up by 4 per cent between pricing and the first day of trading.

In terms of placement, Morgan Stanley outsold the syndicate banks by an unusually high margin, accounting for 87 per cent of the non-US allocation. It also did very well with the Italian institutions, outselling BCI in both quality and quantity with allocations 3.2 times those achieved by BCI. The company's CEO, Francesco Trapani is full of praise for Morgan Stanley: 'They were outstanding – not only did they demonstrate impressive placement power, but we all liked the Morgan Stanley team members a lot. We were extremely pleased.'

With the benefit of hindsight, the only possible criticism of Morgan Stanley is that the bank might have advised Bulgari to have waited another year to do the deal, as it might have realised a much higher price. In many respects this is a bad argument as no-one could have predicted just how well the company's business was going to develop and that the equity markets would remain strong. If a company such as Bulgari is growing strongly year after year, then in theory the price will always be higher some time in the future and the financing might never be done. In fairness to Morgan Stanley, the bank did advise Bulgari in 1992 to wait before going for the IPO.

Key lessons learnt

Implications of going public

Francesco Trapani said: 'If you ask me today what advice I can pass on to other companies that are considering an IPO such as the one we did last year, I would say that in order to be successful as a quoted company, you have to have a clear strategy, you have to match and preferably exceed the market's expectations and you constantly need to explain what it is that you are doing – you need to operate with a much higher level of transparency that you have been used to as a private company.'

He added: 'What we learnt from the IPO is that as a public company you need to broaden your horizons – you need to focus much more on the external environment, for example in terms of what is happening in the industry, what your competitors are doing and generally what all the business opportunities are. We can't sit back and self-indulge – we now take nothing for granted. For a private company, the pressure is simply not the same.

Bulgari is a good example of the importance of the IPO process in bringing about the change of culture required in order to make the transformation from a traditional family-owned company to a more modern, larger international company. Exposure to bankers, lawyers and investors creates pressure and represents a significant learning opportunity for most managements. Ernesto Greco, CFO of Bulgari said: 'The due diligence process was so deep and detailed that even I myself had the chance to better understand certain activity flows relating to our operations and to clarify some important business issues.'

The Bulgari IPO is also a good example of how a strong relationship between a banker and a company can result in advice that is truly valuable to the company. The dynamics are very different from those which would prevail without the long-standing banking relationship, as there is a very competitive environment and the advice provided, particularly before the mandate is awarded, is often substantially tainted by any one bank's strategy to win the mandate and maximise its economic take in the process.

Cooperation between international and domestic banks in an international IPO

It is of crucial importance to involve the domestic banks, earn their respect and work closely with them. Without the full support of the domestic bank/domestic lead manager, the after-market will not be properly supported. International banks and their domestic partners should listen to each other in the discussions over price, total size and tranche size recommendations, timing and all other crucial decisions. For this to occur, the representative of the global coordinator should act with a little humility and flexibility. The attitude of the global coordinator is likely to be more accommodating if it has selected the domestic lead manager itself.

Market timing

Despite its spectacular after-market performance over the first year, the Bulgari IPO, as executed in 1995, could certainly not have been priced much higher. The offer clearly benefited from the fact that the Italian market rose by 4 per cent between pricing and trading, whereas it had fallen by 3 per cent during the week before pricing.

If the reverse had happened, the IPO might have got off to a rough start and the overall impression could well have been considerably less favourable. This demonstrates two things: that the pricing of one of these offers is very finely balanced and that luck can play a significant role, particularly when there is a delay between pricing and trading.

The importance of preparation

The preparations were rigorous to say the least. There was a highly comprehensive due diligence process. Morgan Stanley also undertook comprehensive valuation work including close coordination with the domestic market. The story was well packaged and articulated.

The fact that Morgan Stanley representatives, including equity research analyst Claire Kent, had known the Bulgari management for several years before the IPO, and discussed both the company's strategy and a possible IPO, helped both parties establish a highly productive working relationship with one another. Claudio Sposito of Morgan Stanley said: 'We advised the company over a period of five years to ensure that all the strategic decisions were consistent with the ultimate objective of going public.'

A strong company story

The company's CEO and his colleagues were convincing on the roadshow and there were no major questions from investors. Claire Kent of Morgan Stanley said: 'Bulgari is a marketing oriented company used to selling themselves. I believe selling the product to customers and selling the company's shares to investors go very much hand in hand.'

The Bulgari story was unquestionably very strong. The company was perceived as slightly less cyclical than the industry at large due to a very strong brand name, a young and dynamic management (not necessarily commonplace for this sector) and a growth oriented strategy. Investors believed that this management was going to be successful in transforming Bulgari from a medium-sized family company to one with a much broader brand recognition world-wide without diluting the image of the brand name. Francesco Trapani said: 'Ultimately investors believed, as we did, that the Bulgari brand name was underexploited and that there was a tremendous opportunity to expose it more broadly – so long as it was done properly, ie, that the products are creative and of the highest quality and that we are highly selective with our distribution channels. Not just the strategy but also the execution has to be right.'

He continues: 'Both during the preparation phase and during the roadshow we were significantly assisted by the fact that our strategy was not new. We had decided on the strategy already in 1992 and we therefore had two years of track-record, thus enabling investors to take a view on the next three years of more of the same strategy.'

Conclusion

The institutional marketing programme was very successful, with 64 per cent of the total deal being bought by roadshow attendees. At L8,600, the IPO was priced at the top of the range, 7.5 per cent above the L8,000 Consiglio di Borsa valuation, corresponding to an estimated 1995 P/E of 14.6x, in line with international comparable companies and at a small premium to the Italian market. The offer was 6.5 times subscribed with the international portion of the institutional tranche being 10 times subscribed.

During its first year as a public company, Bulgari significantly exceeded the financial projections on which the IPO was sold. As a result, the company's shares increased in value by 156 per cent over the first 12 months of trading, while the Italian market only moved sideways, making Bulgari one of the most successful international IPOs in Europe in recent years.

At the end of November 1996 Bulgari was trading at a P/E ratio of around 25 times based on projected earnings for 1997, having been substantially re-rated since the IPO. Investors have rewarded not only a high rate of growth but also the fact that there is a management at Bulgari that they trust. Ernesto Greco, CFO of Bulgari recalled the period just after the flotation: 'The company's decision to establish open and efficient communication channels was a key point in creating a positive feeling within the financial community. The result of this activity was so positive that we decided to implement a formal investor relations programme.' Bulgari has built trust by being prepared to come to the market at a time when the company clearly had a good future and by being prudent about the way it talks about its prospects. This type of credibility is difficult to establish and credit should go to Morgan Stanley for successfully guiding the company through the IPO and in the secondary market. In the event it was partly as a result of this success that Morgan Stanley was awarded the Gucci mandate which was successfully executed in the autumn of 1995. In fact Bulgari and Morgan Stanley can claim significant credit for establishing the highly vibrant luxury goods sector (for research and investment purposes) which in late 1996 was valued at about US$50 billion.

It was against this highly positive background that Nicola Bulgari, the Deputy Chairman was able in October 1996, to place 2 per cent of the company at a price of L27,650, corresponding to a 2.64 per cent discount to the prevailing market price, through a block trade via Morgan Stanley. With this sale, Nicola Bulgari reduced his stake in the company to 27.6 per cent leaving the three principal shareholders with a total ownership of 61.9 per cent.

Francesco Trapani concluded: 'I was in favour of doing the IPO at the time, but now I am 10 times more in favour. The IPO has given us three main advantages:

First, to be a public company and having to account to professional investors has instilled a healthy pressure to the way we run the business. We are now much more anxious to look at good business opportunities in order to realise the growth that the market is expecting us to deliver. It is in that spirit that we have decided to enter into the silk scarf, leather goods and eyewear businesses. This pressure has also helped us to achieve a better balance between long term strategy and short term performance.

Second, the success of the IPO and subsequent performance has improved the image of the company. We are now more widely known as a dynamic company which helps us not only with our customers but also with our suppliers, our banks, and the press, and in attracting the highest quality of staff.

Third, our balance sheet has obviously been significantly improved which means that we now have the means to expand the business and if we find the right company, make an acquisition. Although we have not yet found the right company at the right price, we are taken more seriously as an acquirer.'

Feature topic: *The role of the 'due diligence' process for a medium-sized company IPO – the perspectives of the company and the lead sponsor*

An initial public offer for a small to medium sized private company is not a short-term transaction for either the sponsoring bank or the company itself. It requires a huge amount of mutual trust on both sides to have a successful transaction for both the issuer and investors.

At the outset there is a natural tension between the sponsor's franchise risk and the company's reluctance to open up. The bankers need to be sure that they can trust the management's intentions and the implementation of the plans in hand. The management, typically lacking experience of what it means to go public, needs to be able to believe that the sponsors know what they are doing in terms of structuring, marketing and pricing the transaction.

In this case both parties were reassured by the fact that Morgan Stanley's officer responsible for Italy, Claudio Sposito, and Bulgari's CEO had known each other for some 10 years and had a good working relationship. In addition Claire Kent, the analyst who, at the time of the Bulgari offer, initiated equity research coverage for the luxury goods sector, had followed the company informally for several years. This made it easier for the company to open up to the Morgan Stanley/Davis Polk due diligence team.

If defined in the broadest context, due diligence comprises not only the actual management due diligence including the development of financial projections and legal due diligence; but also the work associated with the preparation of the prospectus and the equity research report, as well as the refinement and articulation of the company's strategy for purposes of the investor presentation – which is ultimately what sells the transaction. The key steps were:

- *Management due diligence* – Morgan Stanley corporate finance and equity research staff met with key company operational personnel, ie, the head of marketing and the finance director, to have in-depth discussions about the business and its prospects. The process was structured as a semi-formal question and answer session with the aim of giving Morgan Stanley confidence in the management team and to help establish an earnings model, which was critical in valuing the company. Morgan Stanley also visited manufacturing plants to gain further insight into the company;
- *Legal due diligence* – Davis Polk, Morgan Stanley's counsel, undertook a thorough review of the company's legal situation. This process included review of board minutes, key company contracts, licenses, trademarks and any litigation that the company might be involved in. As a result of the legal due diligence and

the work with the prospectus, Davis Polk gave a so-called '10-b-5 opinion', a US legal opinion which implies a level of satisfaction about the state of the company and the accuracy of the prospects;

- *Drafting of prospectus* – Once the initial due diligence work was completed and the lawyers and the bankers had a reasonable understanding of the business, the work of drafting the prospectus could commence. Although Bulgari's shares were only listed in Italy, the English language document was more akin to a US style prospectus. Notable items not usually included in an Italian prospectus included a risk factors section highlighting potential concerns and a so-called 'MD&A' (management's discussion and analysis of financial condition and results of operations), which is a review of the company's recent financial performance. The prospectus was written by the lawyers with major input from the company and the bankers. As a prospectus is a company document for which the board of directors has to take responsibility, the issuing company gets increasingly involved in each draft, particularly as it affects the technical detail of the company's operations and strategy. It is often only at this point that companies are really challenged to define their true strategy. The process of writing the prospectus is often underestimated, and usually ends up taking a lot more management time than expected. In this case, Bulgari had clarified their strategy in 1992 and it had therefore been in place for over two years;

- *Production of research* – Claire Kent produced a 40-page study on the company which included a detailed earnings model with a two year forecast and a thorough review of the company's key businesses – fine jewellery, fine watches and perfumes. Although this is not strictly a company document, the company provides feed-back on the report and, most importantly, on the projections, so as to make sure that the offer is not sold on overly optimistic assumptions. Morgan Stanley's bankers also reviewed the research report to ensure that it did not over-estimate the prospects of the company. The research was published one month before the offer, following which Claire Kent went on the road to pre-market the company to investors. This pre-marketing is typically undertaken one or two weeks prior to the company roadshow;

- *Dedicated exchange rate exposure discussion* – In order to ensure that both Morgan Stanley and the company would accurately represent the impact on the compa-

ny's balance sheet and profit and loss account of fluctuations in exchange rates to investors, Morgan Stanley sent a three-man delegation to Rome in order to study this important question;

- *Compliance with Italian regulatory requirements* – In addition to the English language prospectus, it was also necessary to produce an Italian prospectus, which involved Italian lawyers and the Italian lead manager BCI as well as the company; and

- *Preparation of the investor presentation* – A significant amount of time was spent on writing the investor presentation to be given by the CEO and CFO on the roadshow. The work of preparing the investor presentation usually starts once the prospectus work has gathered momentum and the strategy formulation has been clarified. The essence of the roadshow presentation is to articulate the company's strategy and how it will be realised. The roadshow presentation needs to be rehearsed and the company also has to prepare itself for any questions that might arise. Despite thorough preparation, during which the bankers coach and prompt company management, the presentation must not appear to be too rehearsed or dictated by what the bankers want the company to say. As part of the preparation for any IPO roadshow there needs to be an educative process informing the company management about the requirements of institutional investors, including who the investors are, how they think and what in particular they may want to know.

Conclusion

Although due diligence work is very time-consuming, its quality will always have a major impact on the execution of the offer. If the corporate finance team of the investment bank has done a good job with the due diligence, this creates confidence within the equity capital markets and syndicate departments. This confidence transmits to the salesforce and, ultimately, to investors. Senior management often underestimates the effort required. Francesco Trapani of Bulgari says: 'This work is all very productive and we learnt a lot, but it is absolutely essential that you as a company get organised in advance. You need to know what your strategy is and you need to field a team of people dedicated to the project so as not to disrupt the operating management of the company.'

China Steel

The privatisation of China Steel was the first international privatisation by way of a public sale of shares by a Taiwanese company, and the first Taiwanese GDR offer. The US$782 million transaction is still the largest ever GDR offer from Taiwan and was the most important Asian equity mandate of 1991–92.

China Steel Corporation was regarded as the best-managed state-owned enterprise in Taiwan and had consistently been one of the most profitable steel companies in the world.

The Taiwanese privatisation programme began in 1988 driven primarily by fiscal considerations, with the proceeds earmarked to finance a six-year US$300 billion infrastructure investment plan, and opened with a number of domestic transactions. The programme was accelerated in 1990 with the appointment of CY Wang to the post of secretary general of the Commission of National Corporations (CNC), the unit within the Ministry of Economic Affairs (MOEA) charged with privatisation. Wang had joined China Steel in 1972, and had risen up the ladder to executive vice president by the time he was called to the MOEA.

Wang was charged with administering the privatisation, by way of public sale, of 10 of the largest manufacturing companies in Taiwan. As the estimated market value of these companies was about four times greater than the entire market capitalisation of the Taiwanese Stock Exchange, it was clear that a significant portion of the proceeds was going to have to come from the international market. The CNC hired Shearson Global Financial Services, a locally-based joint ven-

ture in which Shearson Lehman (now Lehman Brothers) was the foreign partner, as an adviser. In addition to China Steel, the companies on the CNC list were:

- China Petroleum
- China Petrochemical
- Taiwan Sugar
- Taiwan Petroleum
- BES
- Taiwan Machinery
- China Shipbuilding
- Taiwan Salt
- Taiwan Fertiliser

Wang, now back as chairman of China Steel said: 'There were no laws and regulations in place to go ahead with these privatisations and the liberalisation of the capital market was very slow.'

China Steel was to be the first privatisation candidate. It was a relatively well managed company with a private-sector track record and a good international reputation. It also had a strong balance sheet and, last but not least, Wang knew the company well. China Steel became a test case and the vehicle to push through the necessary rules and regulations resulting in the GDR legislation which allowed Taiwanese companies to raise money abroad. While this was an important step forward, the legislation ended up being less than

---

Exhibit 1
Transaction summary

Issuer name: China Steel Corporation (Taiwan, Republic of China)	*Global coordinator:* Goldman Sachs & Co. *Co-global coordinator:* China Trust Company
Pricing date: 21 May 1992 (TSE Index: 4563.7)	*Pricing/underwriting structure:* International bookbuilding followed by fixed price domestic offer
Vendor: The Ministry of Economic Affairs	*Primary or secondary:* Secondary
	Retail structure: Retail discount and bonus shares
% of company sold: 12.6%	*Privatisation or corporate:* Privatisation
IPO or non-IPO: Non-IPO	*Industry:* Steel
Type of shares: Common shares & ADR/GDR (1 ADR/GDR = 20 common shares)	*Domestic offer price:* NT$21.14 *International offer price:* US$18.20 per GDR/ADR
Total issue size: US$782 million	*US listing/144A:* 144A

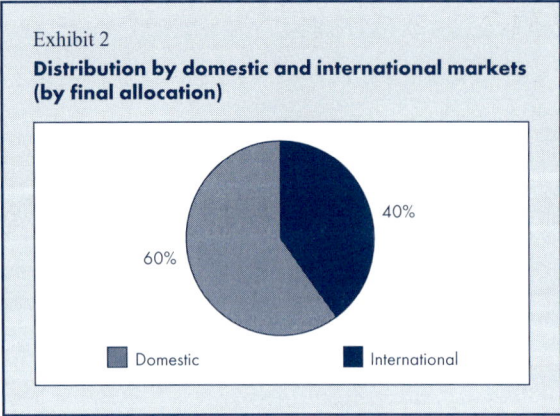

Exhibit 2

Distribution by domestic and international markets (by final allocation)

40%

60%

■ Domestic ■ International

optimal for the purposes of a global offer, as it did not allow for the necessary fungibility and flexibility between the domestic and international tranches of a global offer.

Major challenges

This was not a political transaction, other than that there was supposedly a difficult relationship between the Ministry of Finance and the central bank concerning foreign exchange restrictions. The frosty relationship was partly due to a personal conflict between a young, dynamic, Harvard Business School-educated finance minister and a more traditional central bank governor. The conflict meant that the participants received little help in solving the many technical challenges of achieving a high level of synchronisation between the offer mechanics in the domestic and international offers. Such synchronisation was necessary to generate an acceptable level of fungibility between China Steel's domestic and international equity securities. The markets lost a significant degree of confidence in the government's commitment to achieving a successful transaction.

Many rules and regulations existed in Taiwan which significantly hampered foreign investment in the country's stock market. These existed for a number of reasons: they were inherited from mainland Chinese practices; they were the product of Taiwanese fear of the Chinese buying up Taiwanese assets; and they were a reaction to the threat to the export industry of an appreciating NT$.

The rules gave rise to a long fixed-price underwriting period and a completely outdated domestic allocation system and process of payment mechanics. The domestic and international offers were treated as separate offers. They were sized independently and there was no possibility of moving shares between the domestic and international tranches. It was only possible for GDR holders to sell the GDRs into Taiwan 90 days after the offer closed. It was however not possible for the depositary to increase the number of GDRs in circulation by buying shares in the domestic market.

Investors in the domestic offer were allocated by way of lottery but had no obligation to pay for the shares. The public subscription period closed two weeks after the pricing of the GDR offer, after which domestic investors had a further two weeks to decide whether or not to pay for their subscriptions.

Because of the lottery allocation system and the impossibility of shifting shares between the domestic and international offers, demand in both markets remained untapped. This case study underscores the importance of harmonisation between the domestic and international tranches of a global equity offer and the significance of home-market leadership.

Structural faults did not provide the only challenge: it was also to be difficult to convince international investors to commit to buying a steel company at a time when many investors believed that steel prices were still on a downward trend. In May 1992 many people were still sceptical as to whether the bottom of the cycle had been reached and when the upswing was going to come. Despite representations to the contrary, the company lowered steel prices shortly after the offer.

The bookrunner's lack of local experience may also have contributed to the deal's difficulties: this was Goldman Sachs' first Taiwanese equity offer and a more thorough understanding of the local market on its part might have helped the offer. From the bankers' point of view, the principal challenge was to try to improve the flexibility of the offer structure and to achieve fungibility. Goldman Sachs was unable to meet this challenge as the vendor refused to listen to its advice. Perhaps the government might have been more inclined to listen if Goldman Sachs had had an historic presence in the local market. One Goldman Sachs employee said: 'There were things we might have asked for that might have improved the possibility of influencing the regulations.'

Nor, indeed, was the company's stock in great shape. Prior to the May 1992 offer, approximately 6.8 per cent of the capital stock of China Steel had been sold by the Taiwanese government to domestic investors in two separate offers, which generated proceeds of NT$15.2 billion (US$609 million). Since then both China Steel's share price and liquidity had fallen sharply.

The share price had come down substantially from its highs of 1989 and 1990 (see Exhibit 3) and its liquidity had been falling over recent quarters (see Exhibit 4).

Prevailing market conditions also militated against an offer between the beginning of 1992 and the pricing date as the Taiwanese market had fallen by approximately 11 per cent and was not in a particularly good shape. Christopher Yuan, research manager at Peregrine Securities (Taiwan) Limited said: 'Whereas the China Steel offer initially had a good reception internationally, the underlying Taiwanese market was not in good condition.'

International market conditions were basically good, but this transaction was far too big at this early stage of development of investor interest in the emerging markets. In addition, there was hardly any domestic institutional investment support for the Taiwanese market, as ownership was, and is, dominated by Taiwanese private individuals (see Exhibit 5).

In terms of stock market trading, the retail market is even more dominant. Domestic institutions accounted for less than 4 per cent of trading volume on the Taiwanese stock exchange in 1992 while foreign institutions claimed a 0.25 per cent share. Taiwanese institutions still only account for some 10 per cent of the stock market ownership (see Exhibit 6).

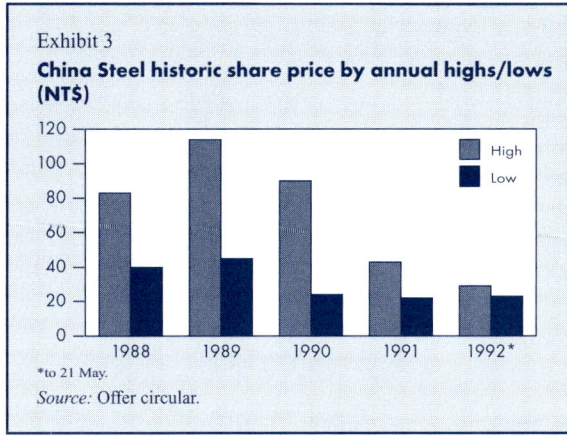

Exhibit 3

China Steel historic share price by annual highs/lows (NT$)

*to 21 May.

Source: Offer circular.

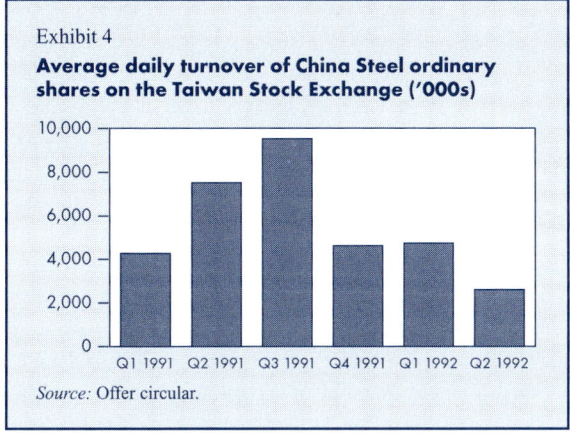

Exhibit 4

Average daily turnover of China Steel ordinary shares on the Taiwan Stock Exchange ('000s)

Source: Offer circular.

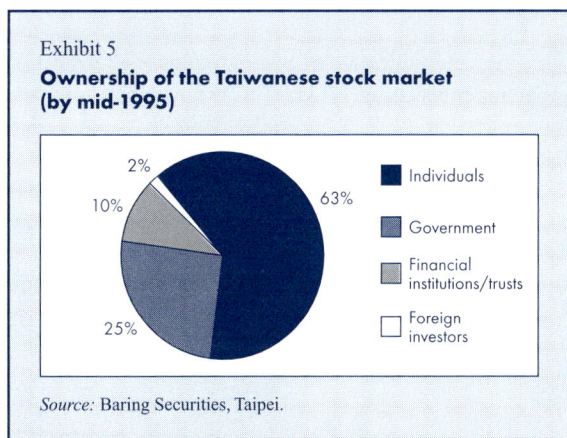

Exhibit 5

Ownership of the Taiwanese stock market (by mid-1995)

- Individuals 63%
- Government 25%
- Financial institutions/trusts 10%
- Foreign investors 2%

Source: Baring Securities, Taipei.

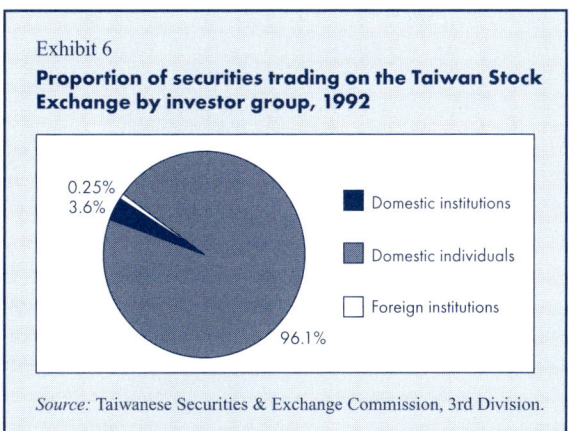

Exhibit 6

Proportion of securities trading on the Taiwan Stock Exchange by investor group, 1992

- Domestic institutions 3.6%
- Domestic individuals 96.1%
- Foreign institutions 0.25%

Source: Taiwanese Securities & Exchange Commission, 3rd Division.

Rationale and objectives

The rationale behind the Taiwanese privatisation programme was threefold:

- To raise finance for the six-year infrastructure investment plan. The fiscal budget was expected to be in deficit due to planned infrastructure investments of US$300 billion;
- To further the long-term strategic interests of the state-owned entities by providing a higher degree of flexibility to invest, by improving the corporate work ethic and by reducing corruption and the power of the unions; and
- To absorb surplus money. According to CY Wang of China Steel: 'There was too much 'hot' money in the system, which had been brought about by many years of very high economic growth. Privatisation was an elegant way of reducing the liquidity in the system.'

The CNC Privatisation Committee had articulated an objective of achieving at least a 5 per cent premium for the GDRs over the domestic offer price, and a broad distribution of the GDRs.

Share capital and ownership

See Exhibit 7.

Transaction components

This offer, initially of 1.04 billion outstanding shares (equivalent to 52 million GDRs), was comprised of three tranches: a tranche of ordinary shares to domestic retail and institutional investors, initially representing 49 per cent of the combined offer and known as 'the domestic offer'; an international tranche of GDRs comprised of six separately managed sub-tranches, initially representing 20.2 per cent of the combined offer and a US tranche of ADRs, initially representing 14.4 per cent of the combined offer. The US and international tranches are together referred to as the 'international offer'. In addition, there was a non-underwritten employee offer, initially representing 16.4 per cent of the combined offer (see Exhibit 8).

The international offer was marketed on an open-priced basis allowing a book to be built, after which the international and domestic offer prices were fixed. The domestic offer price was fixed at a 14.1 per cent discount to the market closing price of NT$24.60 on 21 May, and the international offer price was fixed at US$18.20/ADR, equivalent to a 7.4 per cent premium to the domestic offer price. Nine days later, the five business-day fixed-price domestic offer commenced.

The US offer was limited to qualified institutional buyers under Rule 144A. The international offer allowed for a green-shoe of 3.5 million GDRs/ADRs, equivalent to just under 20 per cent of the initial size of the international offer, to be sold by the global coordinator.

Exhibit 7
Share capital and ownership

Type of shares offered in the international market	GDRs and ADRs representing common stock. The ADRs and GDRs have no voting rights.
Foreign ownership restrictions	The Taiwanese stock market was, and remains, highly regulated. Foreign investors are restricted in a number of ways and, as a consequence, foreign investors owned less than 4% of the market capitalisation of the Taiwan Stock Exchange as at September 1996.
Share capital before and after offer (in May 1992 following the issue of stock dividends)	Common stock: 7,058,572,625 Preferred: 64,023,360 Total: 7,122,595 985 All shares have a par value of NT$10 and 1 vote per share.
Listings/quotations	The shares were listed on the Taiwan Stock Exchange in December, 1974. There were no other listings or quotations. In connection with the offer, the shares began trading over the counter on Seaq International and on Portal.
Market capitalisation at domestic offer price (NT$24.96/US$)	US$6 billion
Major shareholder(s) before the offer (as per 31 March 1992)	MOEA 91.30%
Free float before/after offer	7.5%/20.1%
Liquidity – 11 months to May 1992 (expressed as number of shares traded on an annualised basis as a percentage of the total number of shares outstanding)	20% on the Taiwan Stock Exchange. China Steel only ranked among the top 10 most liquid stocks on the TSE during two of the 12 months preceding the offer.
Foreign ownership before offer	Approx. 2% (owned by qualified foreign institutional investors and international funds).
Most relevant stock exchange index/China Steel weighting	Taiwan Stock Exchange Weighted Index/5.1% (at the time of pricing).

Exhibit 8
Offer structure

Target markets	Indicated* tranche sizes	Bookrunning lead managers	Co-leads/ co-managers
ROC public offer	49.0%	China Trust Corporation	–
Employee offer**	16.4%	China Trust Corporation	–
International offer			
US tranche	14.4%	Goldman Sachs	Lehman Brothers
International tranche			
UK and rest of Europe	6.7%	Goldman Sachs	BZW, Barings, SG Warburg
France and Monaco	1.9%	Indosuez	Goldman Sachs, Paribas
Germany	1.9%	Dresdner	Goldman Sachs, WestLB
Switzerland and Liechtenstein	1.9%	UBS	CSFB, Goldman Sachs, SBC
Hong Kong, Singapore and rest of South East Asia	4.8%	Jardine Fleming	Barings, Goldman Sachs, Lehman
Rest of the world	2.9%	Lehman Brothers	Daiwa, Goldman Sachs, Morgan Stanley International
Total international offer	34.6%		
Total combined offers (total number of GDRs)	**52,000,000**		

* % of indicated total offer on 20 April 1992.
** This tranche was not underwritten.

There was also a bonus share scheme for investors in the domestic and employee offers. Each Taiwanese investor who purchased shares in the domestic offer and continued to hold such shares on each of the first and second anniversaries of such purchase was entitled to purchase one new share for every four shares held, at a price of NT$10 per share. The bonus share scheme in effect enhanced the initial domestic discount from 14.1 per cent to 23.1 per cent, if calculated over the first year only, and to 29.2 per cent if calculated over two years.

As the employee offer was only 15.7 per cent subscribed, and due to the fact that the greenshoe was not exercised, the final number of shares sold by the company was reduced to 896 million, equivalent to just under 45 million GDRs (see Exhibit 9).

Exhibit 9
Development of the offer size (GDR equivalent)

Indicated number of shares and GDRs to be sold	52 million + 3.5 million greenshoe
Less shares not taken up in employee offer	(7,186,575)
Amount of greenshoe exercised	–
Final number of shares and GDRs sold	44,813,425

Exhibit 10
Principal advisers

Financial advisers to CNC and MOEA	Shearson – Global Financial Services, China Development Corporation
International legal adviser to MOEA and China Steel	Davis Polk & Wardwell
Domestic legal adviser to MOEA and China Steel	Lee & Li
International legal adviser to the underwriters	Sullivan & Cromwell
Domestic legal adviser to the underwriters	Tsar & Tsai
Auditors	TN Soong & Co. (a member of Arthur Andersen & Co
Depositary bank	Citibank NA

Exhibit 11
Distribution of gross spread (%)

Management fee	Underwriting fee	Selling concession	Gross spread	Discount	Total 'effective cost'
0.7143	0.7527	2.0330	3.50	7.68	11.18

Source: Goldman Sachs & Co.

Principal advisers

See Exhibit 10.

Transaction fee distribution

See Exhibit 11.

The ADR/GDR offer price in US$ was equivalent to NT$22.71 against a closing price on the Taiwan Stock Exchange of NT$24.60, equivalent to a discount of 7.7.per cent. There was a 14.1 per cent discount in the domestic offer. The exchange rate at the pricing date was NT$24.96/US$1.

Management fee

Goldman Sachs was paid a 'global coordinator's praecipium' of 30 per cent of the total management fee calculated on the gross proceeds of the total international offer.

In the US, the remainder of the management fee was shared between Goldman Sachs and Lehman Brothers on a 55/45 per cent basis. Outside the US the lead and co-lead managers shared a further 20 per cent of the total management fee as the lead and co-lead managers' praecipium calculated on the size of the underwriting commitments in the non-US portion of the international offer. The remainder of the management fee in the non-US portion of the international offer was split

Exhibit 12
Distribution of management fee in the non-US portion of the international offer (%)

Total management fee	0.7143
Of which: Global coordinators' praecipium	30
Of which: Lead/co-lead managers' praecipium split among the non-US leads/co-leads	20
Of which: Management fees split among all the managers	50

Source: Goldman Sachs & Co.

Exhibit 13
Distribution of selling concession in the US offer (%)

Total selling concession	2.0330
Of which: Pre-agreed or fixed portion regardless of sales booked	30
Of which: Paid pro-rata according to sales designated by investors	70

Source: Goldman Sachs & Co.

among the managers in proportion to their underwriting commitments, as shown in Exhibit 12.

Selling concession

In the US the selling concession had one fixed and one variable component. The fixed component of 30 per cent was split between Goldman Sachs and Lehman Brothers on a 55 /45 per cent basis while the variable proportion was subject to performance and designated by investors (see Exhibit 13).

In Europe the selling concession was paid in full to whomever the order was given.

Deal structure

Pricing

The Taiwanese market is largely driven by retail investors who are highly speculative by nature and don't invest on fundamentals. Considerable discounts are therefore required to get an offer off the ground: domestic secondary offers have typically been priced at discounts of 40–50 per cent. As China Steel's share price was close to its all-time low, and given the belief among domestic retail investors that foreign investor participation would render the offer more exciting (despite the fact that international investors could not buy in the domestic market), the domestic offer was priced at the unusually small discount of 14.1 per cent (though the true discount was larger as a result of the bonus share scheme).

The level of the domestic discount was also the product of concern about creating too great a differential between the domestic and international offer prices as this might have made it difficult to sell the deal to international investors. On the other hand, it was not politically feasible to offer the shares to foreign investors at too great a discount to the domestic market price. Given the prevailing market conditions, the 14.1 per cent discount at which the domestic offer was priced was to prove too small to attract substantial domestic interest.

The domestic offer price was arrived at by applying a 20 per cent discount to the average of the price 60-days, 30-days and 10-days prior to the pricing date. This formula translated into a 14.1 per cent discount to the domestic market closing price on 21 May. This formula was designed to take into account the volatility of the market, market convention (including domestic retail investors' expectation of a substantial discount) and the long (four-week) period between pricing and payment by domestic investors. The international offer was priced at a premium of 7.4 per cent to the domestic offer price, against an objective on the part of the CNC of at least a 5 per cent premium, but still at a 7 per cent discount to the domestic market closing price on 21 May.

From the international investor perspective the timetable had the following major shortcomings (see Exhibit 14):

- The subscription period in the domestic offer started eight days after the pricing on 21 May, and the international offer had to be priced without any meaningful feed-back from the domestic offer;
- Although the international offer started trading the day after its pricing, the after-market was naturally tentative due to the protracted timetable of the domestic sale. International investors were given some feedback on 15 June, when the result of the domestic offer was announced – 12 days after the end of the domestic subscription period. However, as there was no obligation to pay for subscriptions, the information that the domestic offer was 6.5 times subscribed was of limited use; and
- Not until one month after the international offer had started trading did the true result of the domestic offer become

---

Exhibit 14

The timetable

Early January 1992	• Goldman Sachs appointed global coordinator.
20 April	• Announcement of the offer.
27 April	• International roadshow commences.
15 May	• International roadshow ends.
21 May	• Pricing of the domestic and international offers after the Taiwan market close; • Domestic and international underwriting agreements executed; and • US and international allocations confirmed by the European and US openings.
22 May	• Trading in GDRs and ADRs commences simultaneously in London and New York.
26 May	• China Steel announces unexpected reductions in steel prices.
28 May	• Payment and closing of the international offer; and • Announcement of the domestic offer price.
29 May	• Subscription period for the domestic public offer commences.
3 June	• Subscription period for the domestic public offer ends.
15 June	• Result of the domestic public offer is announced. The domestic offer was 6.5 times subscribed.
23 June	• Last day for payment in the domestic offer.
24 June	• The payment rate in the domestic offer was announced to be an estimated 37%.
7 July	• China Steel announces its preliminary results for the fiscal year ended 30 June, with a higher-than-expected effective tax rate and, therefore, lower earnings.

clear, although it had started to become apparent that, as the share price had fallen to NT$22.45, reducing the effective discount from an initial 14.1 per cent to a mere 5.8 per cent, demand was likely to be limited. Only 37 per cent of domestic investors decided to pay for their shares.

Tom Tuft, Goldman Sachs' equity capital markets partner in charge of the offer said: 'This was a situation where the international investors were used as a stalking horse for domestic investors. It was not possible to create the competitive tension that is so important in these transactions. If anything, in this case, negative tension was created.'

Domestic allocation system

After the three-week public offer period, the domestic offer was almost seven times subscribed and a computer-aided lottery system was used to allocate shares. This system was also applied to institutional investors in the domestic sale as there was no distinction by type of investor. Six investors out of every seven were eliminated, with the seventh investor allocated to the extent of 100 per cent. After the allocation there was a two-week period before investors had to pay. Since the China Steel offer, a pro-rata system has been introduced in the Taiwanese market as an alternative to the lottery system so that vendors and underwriters can choose between two different allocation systems.

- *Allocation by lottery:* The inevitable consequence of this allocation method is that the entire demand from those investors that do not succeed in the lottery is lost for the purposes of the offer, as retail investors rarely buy significant amounts of shares in the after-market. In addition, those investors that do have shares allocated are probably more inclined to sell in the after-market than if they have been scaled back on a pro rata system.
- *Pro rata allocation:* This is more like a continental European system where all investors get a proportion of their total orders. With this system, however, no discount is allowed and the offer price has to be the market price. The offer period is only 12 days and because all investors are scaled back the after-market sales pressure from retail investors is likely to be lower than under the lottery system.

Because, according to local SEC regulations, a discount cannot be employed in the pro rata system, most issuers and underwriters have continued to employ the lottery system.

The depositary agreement

The lack of fungibility between the common shares, as traded in the domestic market, and the GDRs, as traded internationally, is not unique in GDR offers. The problem in this case, however, was the lack of fungibility in combination with the fact that there were almost simultaneous (although not quite simultaneous enough) domestic and international offers. Because of the lack of fungibility, there was no chance to move shares between the domestic and international offers. The specific structural deficiencies with respect to fungibility were the following:

- The global coordinator, on behalf of the foreign syndicate banks, could neither move GDRs to the domestic offer before pricing nor sell them in the domestic market following pricing;
- The only way for international investors to sell their allocation was to either sell to another foreign investor who wished to own GDRs, or ask the depositary bank to sell the securities in Taiwan for cash. However, no sales for cash were permitted in the first 90 days after the offer;
- The global coordinator could not stabilise the underlying share price by buying in the local market;
- International investors wishing to increase their exposure to China Steel could not buy ordinary shares in Taiwan, nor could they cause the depositary to buy ordinary shares in Taiwan against which they would issue depositary receipts; and
- The only way for international investors to increase their exposure to China Steel in the secondary market was to buy further GDRs from other holders of GDRs.

The initial GDR/ADR outstandings of US$328 million could, therefore, never increase, but could either stay constant or fall. The inevitable consequence was a gradual fall in the liquidity of China Steel's international equity securities.

The lack of fungibility and the rigorous foreign ownership restrictions that were at play in Taiwan severely hampered the sale. Doug Howland, with Goldman Sachs in London at the time of the offer said: 'The central bank wanted total security and control over the foreign exchange situation and were completely unprepared to consider alternatives that would have enhanced the chances of doing a successful offer.'

Chung-Dar Paul Lei, senior economist at the department of foreign exchange, Central Bank of China, retorted: 'It may be true that foreign investors only account for 1–2 per cent of the ownership of the market capitalisation but they have a very big impact on what local retail investors do. We are a small nation and cannot afford to have our currency destabilised as a result of excessive short-term capital flows.'

Marketing

This was going to be 'the deal of the year' in Asia and was considered 'hot' before marketing began: it was one of the world's most profitable steel companies, it was the first international privatisation from a country that had a lot of state assets to sell (and was, therefore, assumed to require a successful offer), it was a direct 'bet' on the six-year infrastructure investment plan and it was a proxy for the Taiwanese market to which access otherwise remained highly restricted for foreign investors. In a three-week, 13-city global roadshow attended by 432 institutions, Goldman Sachs marketed China Steel as 'the world's most profitable steel company in the most attractive steel market' (see Exhibits 15, 16, 17 and 18).

Exhibit 15
Principal sales points

Dominant market position	China Steel was the only integrated steel producer in Taiwan and the dominant force in the domestic steel market with market shares of 35%–70% in most product segments. The company was protected by significant barriers of trade.
The Taiwan story	Taiwan is one of the world's leading economic success stories. Economic growth had averaged 9% a year over the 10 years to 1991, and inflation had averaged only 1.5% over the previous five years. The country's strong export performance had led to the accumulation of foreign exchange reserves that amounted to US$82.6 billion at the end of 1991. The NT$ had appreciated by more than 25% against the US$ since year-end 1987. S&P, the US rating agency rated Taiwan AA+.
Profitability	China Steel was the most profitable steel company in the world in terms of most measures, eg, gross margin, operating margin, pre-tax margin, return on equity, etc.
High growth potential	Goldman Sachs was predicting considerable earnings growth primarily for the following reasons: • Near term: improvements in product mix to higher value added products; • Intermediate term: recovery in world steel prices; and • Long term: increase in capacity from approximately 6 million to 8 million tons by January 1997, when Phase Four of China Steel's capacity expansion plan was to come on stream.
Rock solid balance sheet	The company had no net debt. Only British Steel and Nucor of the US were in a similarly strong financial position.
Attractive valuation	China Steel was trading at a reasonable 14.1 times estimated fiscal 1993 earnings and at a discount of 31.4% and 31.1% to the 1992 and 1993 estimated Taiwanese market multiples, respectively.

Source: Goldman Sachs & Co.

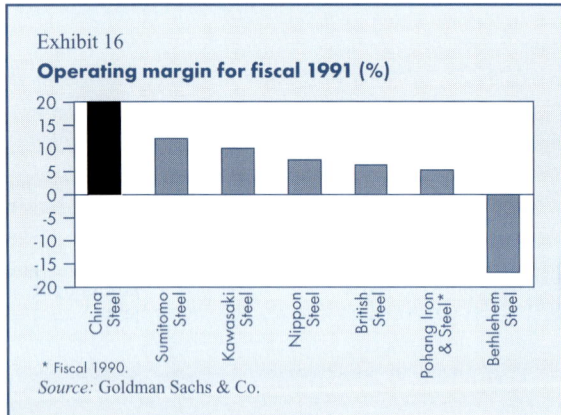

Exhibit 16
Operating margin for fiscal 1991 (%)

* Fiscal 1990.
Source: Goldman Sachs & Co.

Exhibit 17
Goldman Sachs' China Steel earnings per share forecast (NT$)

Source: Goldman Sachs & Co.

Results

Placement

The international offer was three times subscribed overall. The US market failed to deliver any sizeable orders and represented the weakest link in the international offer (see Exhibit 19).

The issue is thought to have been sold to too many investors who did not want it, in the absence of sufficient demand from high quality investors. One senior Goldman Sachs equity capital markets expert said: 'There was a fair amount of speculation among investors, not least because of the novelty factor and, consequently, the offer attracted more than the usual amount of hot money which disappeared as soon as there was bad news coming through from the domestic market. Also, a number of international investors were sceptical about the domestic reception, although of course formally the domestic subscription period only started after the pricing of the offer.'

Another senior Goldman Sachs equity capital markets professional said: 'We had a relatively good book with some first-

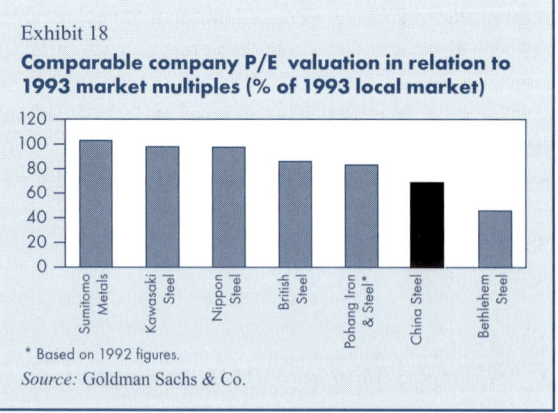

Exhibit 18
Comparable company P/E valuation in relation to 1993 market multiples (% of 1993 local market)

* Based on 1992 figures.
Source: Goldman Sachs & Co.

class names in there with sizeable orders, but it was by no means a stellar book. At the end of the roadshow, some investors were concerned about Taiwan. Others were concerned about the valuation relative to international steel companies and felt that China Steel's valuation was based on optimistic earnings projections – which of course never materialised.'

Exhibit 19
Underwriting, demand and allocation (%)

Target markets	Indicated* tranche sizes	Demand	Allocation‡
ROC public offer	49.0	**14.8	52.7
Employee offer†	16.4	†2.1	2.8
Total domestic offer	65.4	16.9	55.5
US tranche	14.4	††23.5	11.6
International tranche			
UK and rest of Europe	6.7	23.3	13.1
France and Monaco	1.9	4.4	2.5
Germany	1.9	4.1	2.5
Switzerland and Liechtenstein	1.9	7.0	3.0
Hong Kong, Singapore and rest of South East Asia	4.8	12.6	7.7
Rest of the world (including Japan)	2.9	8.2	4.1
Total international tranches	20.2	59.6	32.9
Total international and US tranches	34.6	83.1	44.5
Total combined offers (GDS equivalent)	**52,000,000**	**63,809,533**	**48,313,425**

* As indicated on 20 April 1992.
** Although the domestic offer was 6.5 times subscribed, it was only 37% paid for.
† The employee offer was not underwritten and only 15.7% subscribed.
†† The US tranche was approximately two times subscribed.
‡ Including certain overallotments in the international tranche.

Source: Goldman Sachs & Co and China Steel.

Investor concentration

Because there was only limited transparency in this offer – bookbuilding had yet to be adopted in many markets and Goldman Sachs would have allocated to regional lead managers, rather than to specific accounts – it is difficult to be precise about investor concentration. The single biggest order in the international offer was a US$57 million order from a UK institution, which was allocated to the extent of 52 per cent. Elsewhere in the UK, there were three orders between US$9 million and US$14 million. These three institutions were allocated to the extent of between 35 per cent and 53 per cent. In the US, order sizes were considerably smaller. Goldman Sachs' top three orders only amounted to US$23 million in total and the top 10 orders to US$51 million, corresponding to 27.4 per cent of Goldman Sachs' total US demand. There was a US$13 million order in Japan and a few large orders out of South-East Asia.

The principal buyers were, in order of declining importance: international funds, Asia funds, Taiwan funds, 'story' buyers (ie, hedge funds) and buyers of steel companies.

Share price performance

See Exhibit 20.

Before pricing

• The domestic offer price of NT$21.14 was 6 per cent below the lowest price during the 12 months to the pricing date and 41 per cent below the highest price during the same period. The domestic offer price was 81.5 per cent below the all-time high set in 1989; and
• China Steel's share price had outperformed the domestic market by 2 per cent during the six months prior to the pricing of the offer.

Exhibit 20
Share price performance

Pricing date	21 May 1992
International offer price in US$	US$18.20
International offer price in NT$	NT$22.71
Domestic offer price	NT$21.14
Last trade	NT$24.60
Relative index position	102.1%
Historic 52-week high/low	
High (23 May 1991)	NT$35.97
Low (13 April 1992)	NT$22.50

China Steel share price relative to IFC Taiwan Index (%)

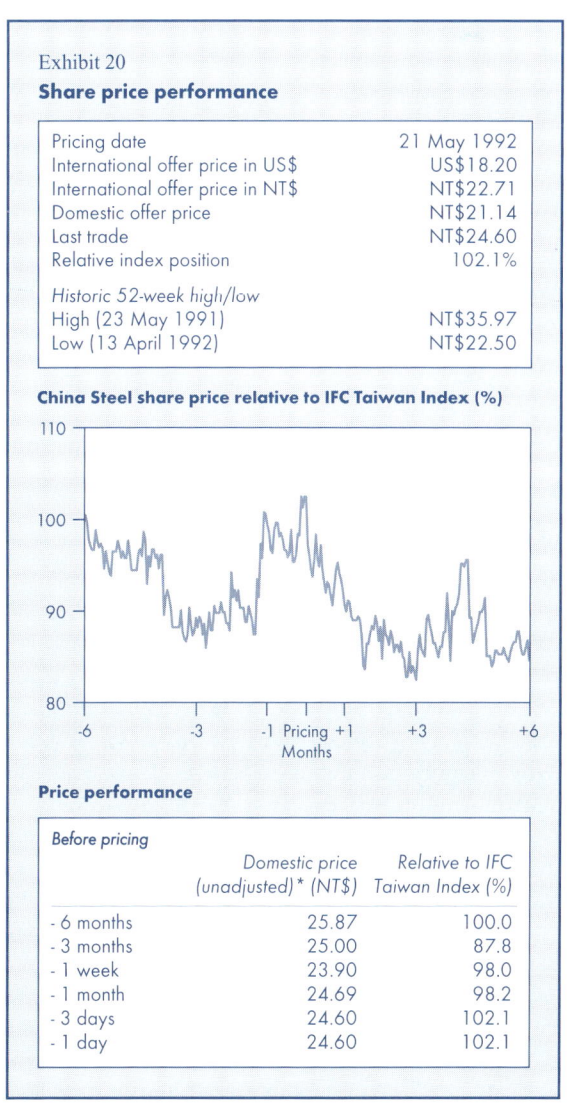

Price performance

Before pricing	Domestic price (unadjusted)* (NT$)	Relative to IFC Taiwan Index (%)
- 6 months	25.87	100.0
- 3 months	25.00	87.8
- 1 week	23.90	98.0
- 1 month	24.69	98.2
- 3 days	24.60	102.1
- 1 day	24.60	102.1

Exhibit 20 *continued*

Share price performance *continued*

Price performance continued

After pricing

	Domestic price (unadjusted)* (NT$)	Relative to IFC Taiwan Index (%)
+ 1 day (22 May)	24.50	96.8
+ 3 days (26 May)	23.79	94.0
+ 1 week (28 May)	24.10	95.2
+ 2 weeks (3 June)	23.79	96.7
15 June (Ann. of result of domestic offer)	23.40	92.1
+1 month (22 June)	22.90	91.8
24 June (Ann. of pay rate of domestic offer)	22.29	89.5
10 July (Ann. of prel. F92 Results on 7 July)	20.00	86.0
+ 3 months (21 August)	16.80	85.4
+ 6 months (20 November)	16.40	84.2

GDR performance

	GDR price (US$)	International/ domestic relative performance (%)
+ 1 day (22 May)	18.38	100.0
+ 3 days (26 May)	18.18	102.2
+ 1 week (28 May)	18.1	100.3
+ 2 weeks (3 June)	18	100.9
15 June (Ann. of result of domestic offer)	16.85	95.7
+1 month (22 June)	16.9	97.9
24 June (Ann. of pay rate of domestic offer)	15.85	94.8
10 July (Ann. of prel. F92 Results on 7 July)	12.8	87.1
+ 3 months (21 August)	12.43	99.8
+ 6 months (20 November)	11.97	99.6

* Unadjusted for the bonus/discount elements of certain subsequent offers.

Sources: Datastream and offer circular.

Exhibit 21

GDRs/ADRs outstanding during the 12 months after pricing

Source: Citibank.

After pricing

- China Steel's absolute share price in Taiwan fell gradually during the month after pricing. There had been no tangible signs that the transaction was going to go wrong at the time of pricing, although because of the structure, there

was always a considerable risk. It was only one day prior to payment for the domestic tranche that everyone knew that the payment rate was going to be low, and as a consequence the price fell from NT$22.90 at the close on 22 June to NT$22.29 on 24 June. This fall accelerated when it became clear that only 37 per cent of all those domestic investors who were allocated shares actually decided to apply for them. It was however not until 7 July, the day that China Steel came out with lower than expected preliminary results for fiscal 1992, that the share price fell below the domestic offer price of NT$21.14;

- The GDR price in US dollars traded down below the offer price already on the third trading day after pricing but did not fall below US$18 until 4 June. The announcement on 26 May that China Steel would reduce certain steel prices was not well received by the international market as this was contrary to what investors had understood during the roadshow. However, the GDR price outperformed the domestic price until the 16th trading day after pricing when international investors began to worry that the domestic investors were not going to pay for their shares. The GDR price fell to US$12.8 at the end of the week during which China Steel had published its preliminary results for 1992;

- Six months after pricing, the domestic price had fallen by 22.4 per cent from the domestic offer price and had underperformed the local market by over 15 per cent. The GDR price had recovered from its under-performance against the domestic price but was 34 per cent below the international offer price of US$18.20; and

- It was not until February 1993 that the price started to recover. WI Carr had put out a buy recommendation at the end of 1992, when the GDR price was trading around US$11–12. By June 1993 the price had gone up to US$16–17, but it was not until December 1993, that the US$ price again moved above the international offer price.

After 12 months, the total number of GDRs/ADRs outstanding had fallen by approximately 20 per cent, from 18 million to 14.4 million. The GDRs/ADRs outstandings developed as follows over the first 12 months after pricing (see Exhibit 21).

The performance of the main parties

The company

It was a big step for China Steel's management to go on a world-wide roadshow as they had only had minimal prior exposure of this kind. During the roadshow, the company was put in the uncomfortable position of having to comment on steel prices at a time when they were still soft.

Despite giving the impression that they would not lower steel prices, a reduction in some grades was announced already on 26 May, only five days after the pricing of the offer (but well before domestic investors had to commit to pay for their shares). On 7 July 1992 China Steel announced its preliminary results for the fiscal year ended 30 June 1992. The effective tax rate was higher than expected and earnings were there-

Sources: Goldman Sachs Equity Research.

Exhibit 22
Profit forecast versus actual profits, year-end June (NT$)

	1992	1993	1994	1995
EPS (Goldman Sachs Estimate, April 1992)	1.30 F	1.50 F	1.80 F	1.95 F
EPS (Goldman Sachs Estimate, November 1993)	1.12 A	0.74 F	1.05 F	1.50 F
Actuals	1.12 A	0.73 A	1.22 A	1.64 A

fore below expectations – NT$1.12 actual versus NT$1.30 forecast, a very significant difference as far as the international market was concerned. To announce lower than expected earnings on the first reporting occasion after an offer is most unfortunate at the best of times, when it happens only some six weeks after the pricing of an offer, investors have reason to be extremely upset.

Both 1992 and 1993 earnings were below Goldman Sachs' forecast at the time of the offer (see Exhibit 22) and their 1994 and 1995 forecasts also proved highly optimistic.

One banker involved in the transaction said: 'This is a very good company, but the management was not yet sophisticated enough in terms of its handling of the international investment community. How could they possibly have been sophisticated without any prior international experience and having only experienced very limited pressure from domestic institutions? The company should have had their own adviser to guide them through the process. Instead, China Steel felt abandoned by both the vendor and the global coordinator. Another banker involved with the company said: 'The China Steel management has come a very long way since 1992.'

The vendor

The MOEA and the CNC acting on behalf of the Taiwanese government in connection with its first major privatisation were forceful decision makers, but took a number of unfortunate decisions, in particular concerning the sizing of the transaction and its structuring with respect to the subscription and allocation system. While it must be recognised that the preparations were hindered by a large number of domestic rules and regulations that could not be altered, it is fair to say that the government did not appear to try nearly hard enough to get the central bank and the Ministry of Finance to work together in the best interests of the transaction. It is also the case that the CNC made the mistake of treating the domestic and international offers separately and were apparently uninterested in Goldman Sachs' advice as to the structuring of the domestic transaction.

The global coordinator

This was a highly frustrating assignment for Goldman Sachs. The bank claims to have had its advice on size rejected and maintains that the Taiwanese forced a decision on the deal size. It is probably equally true that Goldman Sachs slightly overestimated demand from high quality international institutions.

The structure was fundamentally flawed as the domestic and international offers were treated as separate offers and were not harmonised. The domestic offer timetable amounted to

what can be described as 'bull-market underwriting', ie, a structure that only works in a rising market, where the share price goes up between pricing and payment. On the other hand, it fails miserably when the share price is going down.

Goldman Sachs recommended synchronised timetables for the domestic and international offers and total fungibility between both sets of securities. As the bank's advice was ignored the most appropriate thing for Goldman Sachs to have done would have been to resign from the transaction.

China Steel felt let down in terms of after-market support, but Goldman Sachs claims to have taken a position of US$40 million in China Steel GDRs following the retail payment date when the offer started to crumble and feels that this demonstrated its commitment.

Because the company was inexperienced and unsophisticated in this area, it would have needed considerable handholding by Goldman Sachs. Instead, Goldman Sachs was too aggressive with the company while giving full priority to serving its client – CNC – rather than the company. Goldman Sachs had strongly recommended a NYSE listing but, whereas this might have had certain advantages, experience with the company suggests that the management would not have been well placed to service a US listing. On balance, this appears to have been the wrong advice.

The company remains upset that the GDR price underperformed the domestic price from 12 June – the time when foreign investors began to realise that the domestic offer might not be successful – and holds Goldman Sachs substantially responsible for this. But China Steel demonstrated its naiveté of international capital markets practices by calling for bookrunners to ensure that issues trade at a premium in the after-market. China Steel's Chung said: 'In future offers, I would like to see a provision in the underwriting agreement whereby the global coordinators undertake to maintain a market in the stock in such a way as to be of more real support in the after-market. As far as Taiwan is concerned, perhaps they should even have to undertake that the international GDR price would not fall below the domestic price.' Such a suggestion is wholly unrealistic, particularly in this case since there was no fungibility between the domestic and international offers and since it was primarily due to the failure of the domestic offer that the international offer crumbled. Having said that, global coordinators should be expected to play a major role in the stock following pricing and have more at stake in the case of weak performance than mere reputational exposure.

Goldman Sachs underwrote approximately 25 per cent of the international offer and 50 per cent of the US offer. Goldman Sachs sale performance was unspectacular (see Exhibit 23).

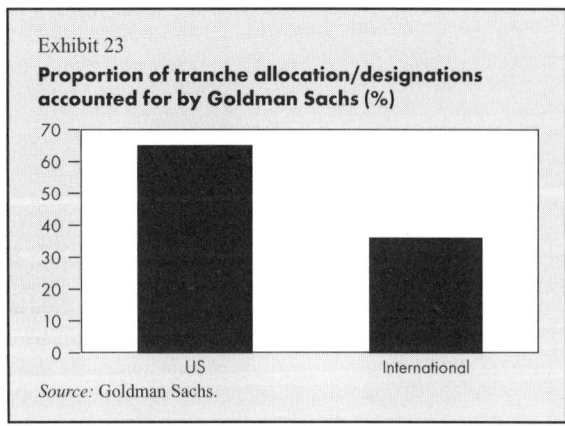

Exhibit 23

Proportion of tranche allocation/designations accounted for by Goldman Sachs (%)

Source: Goldman Sachs.

Key lessons learnt

Fungibility and subscription and payment mechanics

The offer mechanics and timetable are critical to a deal's success. Given the lack of fungibility this offer was effectively structured as two separate, uncoordinated sales. They crumbled individually and then brought each other down further.

Doug Howland said: 'You can't bypass the domestic market in a global equity offer as the Taiwanese seem to have believed, particularly not when there is also a domestic offer. You must either completely separate or completely integrate the domestic and international offers of a global transaction. Furthermore, when you do decide to do simultaneous domestic and international offers, particularly for companies that are unknown, untried and untested in the international market, it should be the domestic market that sets the pace. In this offer, however, there was a classic case of the 'tail wagging the dog' as it was the international offer which was asked to be the stalking horse.'

The time period between pricing and payment in the domestic tranche was far too long and the domestic allocation system illogical. The lottery system excluded six-sevenths of domestic demand on an entirely arbitrary basis. If only 15 per cent of this demand had been available at the time of payment for the domestic offer, it might have been a success. Voluntary payment creates a snowball effect in a weak market. As a result of these structural impediments, there was no bridge between the two offers and thus no shock absorbers.

Appoint bankers in good time

Goldman Sachs was appointed at a time when the preparations concerning the GDR legislation had gone too far. This is probably the principal reason why the CNC did not listen to Goldman Sachs' ideas on how to improve the offer structure. But why then did they not listened to Lehman Brothers? Another reason might be that the CNC wrongly believed that the two transactions were separate and that Goldman Sachs ought simply to concentrate on placing shares internationally.

Get the size and the timing right

At this early stage of development of the emerging markets the transaction was too large for the international market. 'There were not a lot of international funds dedicated to invest-

ment in Taiwan at the time and many investors were not familiar with the country and the market. This meant that the quality of the book was perhaps not what we would expect in a more mature market,' said one senior Goldman Sachs official. It was also too large for the domestic market given the relatively poor market conditions.

The Taipei-based head of equity research for one of the leading foreign houses in Taiwan said: 'What surprised me was the timing of the issue. It was apparent at the time that the steel market was still going down. It appeared that the government and the leading underwriters either didn't understand the importance of market timing, or didn't have any chance of influencing it. We had a 'sell recommendation' on the stock until late 1992.' Sunny Chen of WI Carr adds: 'If they had waited six months, this may well have been a highly successful offer.' Another Taiwan-based banker adds: 'Unfortunately, the CNC Committee had no idea about the correct timing, in fact they had very little idea about anything.'

Keep control of the offer

The syndicate was too large and there was less transparency than might have been hoped for. Tom Tuft of Goldman Sachs said: 'As is so often the case, the vendor and the company wanted to reward a lot of people who did not get the global coordinator role.' Goldman Sachs lost control of the international offer once bad news started to emerge from the domestic market. The loss of control was accentuated by the size of the offer, the size of the syndicate and the lack of familiarity among investors about investment in Taiwan.

Be flexible

The CNC was not interested in taking the advice of its advisers: it had passed a law making it possible for foreigners to buy GDRs in Taiwanese companies and that was it. It hadn't listened to its financial advisers while drafting the law and it was certainly not going to listen once the law was passed. Shortly after this, Goldman Sachs were effectively told by Lehman Brothers that they agreed with everything Goldman Sachs were recommending but that Goldman Sachs were certainly not going to be successful in convincing the Taiwanese. The Taiwanese had a 'take it or leave it' attitude. It is most unfortunate when inexperienced vendors are completely unprepared to listen to professional advice, especially on technical matters such as these.

Clear commitment from vendor and company

A former head of one of the largest securities firms in Taiwan said: 'The problem is that there was no real policy on privatisation. There was only a general notion that they ought to give to the people and that they ought to maximise the proceeds.' He continues: 'The problem is that the local SEC and the central bank don't really understand the global equity market. There is for example a notion that only domestic investors should be allowed to buy the good companies.'

The perception in the market of political and personal conflicts between the Minister of Finance and the governor of the central bank created uncertainty as to the government's commitment to a successful privatisation.

After tremendous turbulence, and having again come up against the same offer mechanics in a 1994 offer, as in 1992, although without attempting a simultaneous international offer, China Steel in 1995 finally ceased to be majority-owned by the state. This was the third offer of shares after the 1992 offer. Then in February 1997, the government's stake was further reduced in connection with a GDR offer through Merrill Lynch – the first sale of shares internationally since 1992. This offer was again not an unqualified success with the pricing having been delayed and the offer size cut. Whereas the Taiwanese demonstrated that they had learnt some lessons, including the complete de-linking of domestic and international offers and the introduction of sizing flexibility, bad timing and pricing inflexibility made this a very tough transaction. Moreover, the problem of a major overhang in China Steel shares remains as the market is expecting many more smaller offers. To solve that problem, via a jumbo global and fully integrated offer, fundamental securities reform is needed.

Conclusion

Global equity transactions are a lot more complex than most people initially assume. By the time they appreciate this fact, it is often too late and inexperienced people, as important as they may be, should realise that this is a technical and highly specialised field and be prepared to listen to the advice for which they pay dearly, even if it sometimes comes from overly aggressive bankers.

Effective communication between the vendor and the company on the one hand, and between the global coordinator and the company on the other is crucial to ensure a smooth transaction and after-market performance, and can not necessarily be taken for granted. Only people who are effective communicators and negotiators should be asked to play leading roles in complex processes of this kind. Whereas in the real estate business only three things matter: location, location,

location; in the equity business the mantra must be 'flexibility, flexibility and flexibility.'

Companies wishing to build up a good name in the equity market should to everything in their power to avoid embarrassing bankers, analysts and salesmen by producing lower than expected profits on the first reporting occasion following an offer. Whereas it is always important, it is particularly important over the first 6–12 months following an offer.

LM Chung, CFO of China Steel said: 'Although the vendor will suffer from a failure of this kind in terms of its chances of coming back to the market, it is really the company which suffers most. Therefore, in our opinion the company should by contractual obligation or by law have a more important role in these offers. Perhaps the company should even set the price, subject to approval by the government. Furthermore it is now evident to us that the company ought to have their own independent adviser in a situation like this, to assist with decisions such as timing, structure and pricing.'

It is difficult to legislate to prevent an owner from deciding how to dispose of its shares as this would violate basic property rights. But vendors will almost always get a better deal if the company is fully involved in the sale process. Although China Steel performed below expectations in terms of earnings per share at the crucial first reporting occasion six weeks after pricing, the lack of success was primarily attributable to arcane domestic issuing procedures and the Taiwanese central bank's fixation with managing the Taiwanese currency.

Given Goldman Sachs' inability to convince the Taiwanese of the structural shortcomings of the offer, the biggest service to the deregulation of the Asian capital markets that Goldman Sachs, as one of the market leaders in the global equity new issue business, could have performed, would have been to resign from this assignment.

Daimler-Benz AG

The Dm3 billion (US$1.8 billion) global SEC registered managed rights offer for transport conglomerate Daimler-Benz in June 1994 was the largest-ever rights offer in Germany and the first of its kind. Its structure combined important elements of a traditional German rights issue with international bookbuilding practice, enabling non-subscribing shareholders to achieve good value for rights sold to new investors. Daimler had been the first German company to register with the SEC and list its shares in the US, and was therefore also the first SEC registered rights issue by a German company. It was the first time that US shareholders could subscribe to a German equity financing, and also the first time that a Daimler equity financing syndicate included non-German banks.

This rights offer was the third major step within nine months of a new strategy to internationalise Daimler's equity and ensure improved access to the global equity capital market. The first step was a listing on the New York Stock Exchange in October 1993 and the second was a secondary offer in January 1994, through which Deutsche Bank reduced its holding to 24.4 per cent from 28.3 per cent. These three steps began a process intended to transform Daimler from a largely domestically owned and traded company to one whose ownership and status in the global financial markets would more accurately reflect the status of the company, the third largest in Europe on 1993 sales.

This case study also serves to illustrate that the three major sponsors of this strategy, Deutsche Bank, Daimler's largest

shareholder, as well as Goldman Sachs and Merrill Lynch and their US lawyers Cleary, Gottlieb, Steen & Hamilton got the due diligence wrong. Forecasts prior to the offers suggested that a net profit under German GAAP of at least Dm1.5 billion was expected for 1995: instead, the company booked a loss of Dm5.7 billion, the largest ever in German corporate history.

Historic perspective

The process of turning Daimler into a public company began in 1975 when the Flick family sold 29 per cent of the company to Deutsche Bank, which placed 3.9 per cent in the market and put 25.1 per cent into Mercedes Automobil Holding (MAH). In 1985 the family placed a further 10 per cent on the market at a price of Dm112, equivalent to almost four times the price achieved in 1975. The Quandt family had sold its holding to the Emirate of Kuwait in 1974.

Daimler had been profitable for years and had no need of further equity capital. During the five years before its diversification strategy its pre-tax return on equity had averaged 59 per cent. It was primarily a car producer, with foreign sales in excess of 60 per cent, although most production was based in Germany. In the mid-1980s it embarked on an ambitious diversification programme and in 1989 a new corporate structure was introduced with a holding company and

---

Exhibit 1
Transaction summary

Issuer name: Daimler-Benz AG (Germany)	Global coordinator: Deutsche Bank
Pricing date: 8 June 1994 (DAX: 2,145)	Pricing/underwriting structure: Global SEC registered managed rights issue
Vendor: Company	Primary or secondary: Primary
% of company sold: 10% (1:10 rights issue)	Privatisation or corporate: Corporate
IPO or non-IPO: Non-IPO	Industry: Transportation
Type of shares: Ordinary shares and ADRs 1 ADR = 1 ordinary share	Subscription price: DM64*/share, US$40.22/ADR
Total issue size: US$1,789 million	US listing/144A: NYSE listing

* Effective 1 July 1996, Daimler did a 10:1 stock split, whereby the nominal value of Daimler's ordinary shares was reduced from DM50 to DM5. Accordingly, the number of shares and all Daimler share prices in this case study have been adjusted by a factor of ten.

four corporate units: Mercedes-Benz (cars and trucks), Deutsche Aerospace (aerospace), AEG Daimler Industrie (electro-engineering) and Debis (information technology and financial services).

To finance its diversification, Daimler was forced in 1989 to raise Dm1.95 billion of new equity capital via a traditional 1:10 rights issue. This was the first Daimler equity financing for a long time where the overriding objective was to actually raise money. Before this it had raised only Dm1.2 billion from the market since World War II – all by way of deeply discounted rights issues, principally to give shareholders a more tax efficient return on investment than available via dividends.

The diversification backfired and profitability and market value declined. In 1986 the turnover was Dm65.5 billion, the pre-tax profit more than Dm3 billion and the market capitalisation at an all-time high of Dm52 billion. On the day of pricing of the global rights offer, market capitalisation was Dm37 billion (having hit a low of Dm24 billion in fourth-quarter 1992) and the turnover around Dm100 billion. The company made its first ever loss, under US GAAP, in 1993. The fall in market value by Dm15 billion gives an indication of the total cost of the diversification programme.

NYSE listing (step 1)

In the late 1980s, CFO Gerhard Liener realised that Daimler could no longer afford to rely solely on the domestic equity market, and a programme of foreign listings began including Tokyo and London in 1990, and Vienna and Paris in 1991. An NYSE listing was also considered but was thought too ambitious at this early stage. In March 1991 Liener and the CFOs of other German companies met with the then chairman of the US SEC, Richard Breeden, to discuss US registration and NYSE listing. The German approach was to try to extract concessions on the basis of reciprocity, arguing that as the Frankfurt Stock Exchange was open to US companies without requiring adjustments to US accounting standards, German companies should not have to adopt US GAAP to list in the US. This approach was rejected by the SEC.

Two years later, Daimler's operating performance had deteriorated further due to the diversification programme, severe recession and loss of market share in the car market resulting from an overly technocratic approach to production. This lack of competitiveness was exacerbated by a strong Deutschmark. Financial markets in Germany had come under pressure through increasing financial needs from the private and the public sectors, and at the same time the German investment community had become disillusioned with Daimler and was in any event beginning to invest a higher proportion of total assets outside Germany. Liener realised that Daimler needed access to the US capital market and therefore approached the SEC again, this time alone.

Liener's thinking on how to approach a US listing had matured. He had become convinced that as a global player, Daimler had to be comparable to its peers, at least in terms of its accounting standards, in order to be considered seriously as an investment. Eric Dobkin, Goldman Sach's global head of ECM explained the choice: 'Does Daimler want to be in the goldfish bowl of the domestic market or the shark pool of the international market?' In order to compete for global capital, Daimler had to go for the shark pool. To meet the comparability test, this time it did not try to achieve a compromise on accounting standards as this would have defeated the purpose of the exercise. Although there was talk – perhaps primarily for political reasons – of the SEC having given Daimler certain concessions, these were of no real significance. Daimler had therefore to open up to the investor community, which would inevitably be painful given current performance.

The decision to list on the NYSE was controversial within Daimler itself, elsewhere in Germany and in the board rooms of many continental European companies. Critics focused on the fact that while Daimler's adviser, Goldman Sachs, forecast a 1993 profit of Dm805 million under German GAAP, a loss of Dm1.63 billion was expected under US GAAP. In addition, Daimler had supposedly weakened the negotiating power of continental European companies lobbying the SEC to accept IAS. Deutsche Bank initially opposed the project and was not happy that Liener determinedly pursued the NYSE listing with the help of Goldman Sachs. However, Deutsche Bank subsequently came around to the idea, perhaps because it could be seen as a dry run for the expected listing of Deutsche Telekom. On the day Liener's contract was terminated by Hilmar Kopper, Ronaldo Schmitz of Deutsche Bank had apparently congratulated Liener and his team on the rights offer, saying: 'Deutsche Bank has learnt a lot from this global rights offer.'

Prior to the listing, 2–3 per cent of Daimler was owned by 26 US institutions – a much lower US ownership than other German companies such as Schering, Bayer and Veba which had estimated US ownership of 15–30 per cent. Except for the Kuwait stake, which had been held for about 20 years, less than 15 per cent of Daimler was owned from abroad. There were two principal reasons that US investors had not shown greater interest in Daimler: firstly they were obviously thoroughly unimpressed with a string of unsuccessful acquisitions such as Dornier, MTU, AEG, MBB (including Deutsche Airbus), Fokker; and secondly German GAAP was not understood or trusted by US investors, who felt that the only predictable figure in a German P&L account was the net income figure, as a result of the seemingly infinite flexibility of smoothing out the operating performance of the company by dissolving reserves in bad years and creating reserves in good years. Gerhard Liener felt that high-quality disclosure and transparency would help to compensate for Daimler's disastrous performance.

On 5 October 1993, Daimler started trading on the NYSE following a US roadshow involving five investor presentations and 19 one-on-one meetings in six cities. This roadshow culminated in the New York presentation at the Waldorf Astoria, attended by 900 people. During the roadshow Daimler met with a total of 200 institutions, and it could now claim to have achieved proper access to the US capital market.

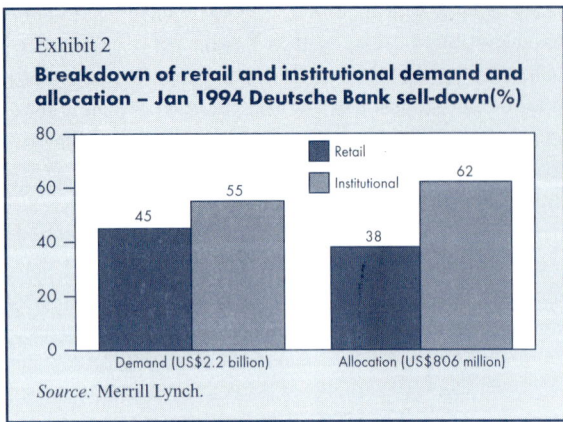

Exhibit 2

Breakdown of retail and institutional demand and allocation – Jan 1994 Deutsche Bank sell-down(%)

Source: Merrill Lynch.

Deutsche Bank sell-down (step 2)

Deutsche Bank's reduction of its stake in Daimler to below 25 per cent in an SEC registered secondary offer in January 1994 was consistent with the bank's long-term strategy of reducing its portfolio of industrial holdings. It created liquidity in the US market and avoided the risk of Daimler being deemed, under the US Bank Holding Company Act, to be controlled by Deutsche Bank, which would have rendered the rights offer infinitely more complex for both parties. The purpose of the offer was to:

- Follow Daimler's NYSE listing with a public offer targeted solely at US investors;
- Make sufficient shares available to satisfy long-term, high-quality investor demand;
- Focus the attention of investors on Daimler's strategy and recent corporate restructuring;
- Create a broad investor base to improve the likelihood of a successful 1994 rights offer; and
- Support Daimler's US business (eg, C-class launch).

On 27 January 1994 CJ Lawrence/Deutsche Bank, Merrill Lynch, Goldman Sachs and others sold ADRs representing 17.25 million Daimler shares (including the greenshoe which was exercised in full within two days of the pricing) at a US dollar price equivalent to Dm81 per share. The offer was placed entirely in the US and raised US$806 million for Deutsche Bank. Through this reduction Deutsche lost its blocking minority power at Daimler general meetings.

To promote the shares the management went on a two-week roadshow to 21 cities, holding 55 one-on-one meetings and 12 group presentations.

Total institutional demand was US$1.2 billion from 136 institutional investors and US$1.0 billion from retail investors. In the end, 62 per cent of the offer was allocated to 105 institutions and 38 per cent to 9,497 retail investors. The 10 largest investors accounted for 56 per cent of the institutional placement (see Exhibit 2).

Rights offer (step 3)

Although the three steps could have been combined in a glob-al registered bookbuilt offer with both Deutsche Bank and Daimler selling shares, for both technical and practical reasons, this did not happen. With the benefit of hindsight, this was probably beneficial as it meant that there were three due diligence sessions, three roadshow presentations and three prospectuses, a considerable learning experience for Daimler.

The timing of the rights issue coincided with improved sentiment for automotive stocks, though the German and world stock markets were generally weak, particularly during the first week of the subscription period. On 20 June, the DAX 30 (consisting of the most-traded blue chips on the German equities market) fell 4.0 per cent off the back of rising US dollar interest rates. For Daimler the timing was more fortunate, as the low point in its cyclical and structural downturn was thought to have been reached in the third quarter of 1993, since when there had been a considerable improvement in operating earnings. Comments from the AGM on the first quarter 1994 results indicated a slow recovery in revenues coupled with a rapid decline in costs, of which the head-count reduction was the most important component. There had been a sharp improvement in operating profits from the last quarter of 1993 and this had continued into 1994. At the time of the offer, there was a notion that Daimler was a '1995 story' though this was to prove hopelessly optimistic, principally as a result of a stronger than expected Deutschmark and much worse than expected results at Deutsche Aerospace.

Major challenges (rights offer)

The biggest challenge in the rights offer was to convince investors that Daimler was on a steady road to recovery, engineered by a fundamental restructuring and rationalisation programme.

The valuation was not made any easier by the fact that the company was a conglomerate and there were no comparable companies against which to establish its relative value.

A key challenge was to realise the full theoretical value of rights sold to new investors on behalf of selling shareholders. This was achieved by active marketing of subscription rights to new investors worldwide. In traditional rights issues there is a considerable supply of rights from non-subscribing shareholders, but only limited efforts are made to generate demand for them, forcing them to trade below theoretical value.

It was difficult to assess exactly how many shares the syndicate had to sell, a problem invariably thrown up by rights issues. Although the three largest shareholders had declared their intention to subscribe in full or in part, the intentions of other shareholders were not known. Consequently, the large syndicate designed to market Daimler shares could not tell target investors how much stock might become available.

US investors are not particularly familiar or comfortable with rights issues. In an attempt to overcome this, a special report prepared by Deutsche Bank: 'Rights Issues: A capital increase with pre-emptive rights (the German model)' was distributed to clients.

Those trying to place the new unsubscribed shares with US investors had to do so against the background of a recent sale of US$806 million worth of Daimler shares by a syndicate led by Deutsche Bank.

Taken together, these three steps (listing, secondary offer and this rights issue) marked the beginning of a new disclosure and communication policy with the investor community. Would reluctant Daimler executives, unfamiliar with having to account to investors, really be prepared to or be capable of doing so in a professional and reliable manner? As the events of 1995 would show, the answer was no.

Rationale and objectives

The rationale for raising Dm3 billion of equity was to repair the balance sheet after the costly diversification strategy begun in 1985 under the leadership of Edzard Reuter, and to continue internationalising Daimler's ownership. The latter move was designed to ensure access to large amounts of capital at a time when there was increasing competition for capital in the domestic market, to expand the investor base, to create stronger long-term demand for Daimler's shares and ultimately to reduce the cost of capital. According to Gerhard Liener, the rationale was as follows: 'We are aiming for an increased global presence in order to cut our capital costs.'

Exhibit 3
Daimler targeted ownership by the year 2000 (%)

Legend: Actual early 1995 / Target year 2000

	Actual early 1995	Target year 2000
Large holders	51	51
Europe	38	25
US	8	15
Asia	3	9

Source: Daimler-Benz.

Exhibit 4
Share capital and ownership

Type of shares offered	Ordinary shares in bearer form of Dm5 (also available as ADRs and Singapore Depositary Shares in each case representing 1 ordinary share).
Ownership restrictions	None. After the reduction in Deutsche's stake to below 25% and the abolition, through merger, of MAH (the holding company whose sole purpose was to protect Daimler against a hostile take-over) in March 1994, Daimler had further weakened its defences.
Share capital before/after offer	465,927,600/512,520,360 ordinary shares.
Listings	Basle, Zürich, Geneva (1977), Tokyo and London (1990), Vienna and Paris (1991), New York (October 1993), Singapore (May 1994).
Market capitalisation	US$22 billion (Based on the market price on the last day of the subscription period of Dm71.50 and an exchange rate of Dm1.666/US$, calculated on the expanded share capital).
Major shareholder(s) before offer	A Daimler extraordinary general meeting in December 1993 and a Mercedes (MAH) annual general meeting resolved to merge the two companies. Subsequently, MAH shares were exchanged one-for-one for those of Daimler. MAH held a 25.1% blocking minority in Daimler. After the merger with MAH and Daimler's January 1994 secondary issue the major shareholders were: Deutsche Bank 24.4% Emirate of Kuwait 14.0% Stella* 12.6% * Stella is effectively a syndicate of German institutional investors organised to take advantage of the tax holiday for shareholdings larger than 10%. Syndicate members include: Allianz, Dresdner Bank, Commerzbank, Baden Würtembergische Bank, Baden Würtembergische Versicherung, JM Voith.
Number of shareholders before offer	Daimler estimated that as of 31 May 1994 it had some 400,000 shareholders and that some 60% of its shares were owned by institutions and 40% by retail.
Free float before offer	Approximately 50%.
Liquidity – 1994 (expressed as number of shares traded per market on an annualised basis as a percentage of the total number of shares outstanding)	191% in Frankfurt/7.4% on NYSE and 15% on Seaq International. In terms of shares traded, Daimler was the second most liquid stock on the Frankfurt Stock Exchange in 1994 and the second largest by market capitalisation at the end of 1994.
Most relevant stock exchange index/weighting	DAX (comprising 30 German blue-chip companies)/ 8%–9% (June 1994).

The objectives

These were to:

- Raise Dm3 billion to strengthen finances and improve the equity-to-assets ratio;
- Complete the offer during the first six months of 1994;
- Ensure success without the full participation of certain large shareholders by doing a global managed rights offer;
- Cement the perception of a repositioned Daimler; and
- Increase foreign ownership and liquidity of Daimler shares, in particular to increase US ownership to 10 per cent.

Liener was of the view that the financial side of a global player should reflect the operational side. The long-term target was therefore to further globalise the Daimler share to better reflect the scope of foreign operations (see Exhibit 3).

The proceeds were to be used to finance growth in group operations, in particular product development and the vehicle-leasing business, with an appropriate level of equity and to sustain the group's solid financial structure.

Share capital and ownership

See Exhibit 4.

Trading is concentrated in Frankfurt and the other German stock exchanges with London the second most active market.

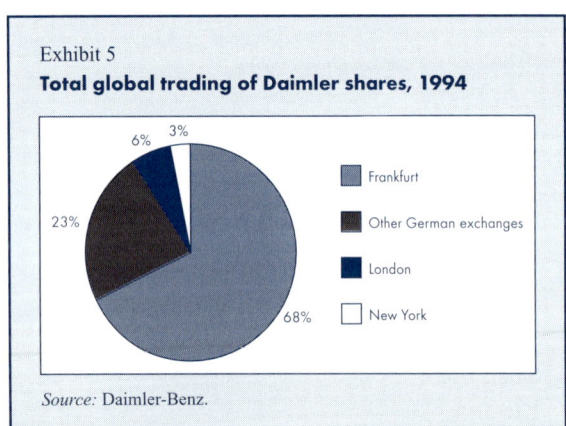

Exhibit 5
Total global trading of Daimler shares, 1994

- Frankfurt — 68%
- Other German exchanges — 23%
- London — 6%
- New York — 3%

Source: Daimler-Benz.

Other foreign markets account for negligible trading volumes (see Exhibit 5).

Transaction components

This was a global managed SEC-registered rights issue, an infinitely more complex affair than earlier Daimler rights issues. The syndicate was much larger than previous Daimler underwriting syndicates which had consisted of Deutsche Bank, Dresdner Bank and Commerzbank.

To effectively recirculate rights not taken up by existing shareholders, two separate marketing syndicates were superimposed on the underwriting syndicate. The emphasis on the US market justified the inclusion of a strong contingent of US banks (see Exhibit 6).

Both Daimler as client and Deutsche Bank as global coordinator were anxious that the four main banks – Dresdner, Commerzbank, Goldman Sachs and Merrill Lynch – be treated equally in all respects other than marketing in the US, where Goldman Sachs was the senior bank under Deutsche Bank. This was Daimler's way of thanking Goldman Sachs for its extensive advisory work on the NYSE listing, and it also was the most experienced investment bank in global SEC registered rights offers.

Deal structure

Due to a strong culture of pre-emptive rights offers in Germany, the fact that the major shareholders wanted to participate and because there had been a non pre-emptive secondary offer in January 1994 enabling distribution to new shareholders, a rights issue structure was deemed to be the most logical, despite its significant shortcomings, which included:

- A high degree of complexity;
- A lack of transparency as to whether shareholders intend to subscribe. Nobody knows in advance how many rights are available for placement through the syndicate;

Exhibit 6
Principal parties in the Daimler rights issue

Global coordinator and book-running lead manager	Deutsche Bank
Underwriting group (with underwriting commitments in %)	Deutsche 40% Dresdner 25% Commerzbank 10% Goldman Sachs 5% Merrill Lynch 2.75% and eight German and five foreign banks taking 1–1.75%
International marketing coordinators	Deutsche Bank, Goldman Sachs
International selling group	Deutsche, Goldman Sachs, Dresdner and nine German and 17 foreign banks
United States selling group	CJ Lawrence/Deutsche, Goldman Sachs, Dresdner and one German and eight foreign banks

Exhibit 7
The timetable

	Step 1
5 October 1993	• Daimler begins trading on the NYSE.
	Step 2
27 January 1994	• Deutsche Bank sells a 3.9% stake of Daimler in an SEC-registered secondary offer.
March 1994	• Merger of Daimler and Mercedes Aktiengesellschaft Holding (MAH) closed.
	Step 3
7 April	• Dividend for fiscal 1993 and the intention to do rights offer announced.
6 May	• Daimler's supervisory board approves 10% share capital increase.
17 May	• Preliminary F-1 registration statement filed with SEC.
18 May	• Daimler annual general meeting.
1 June	• Global roadshow begins in Europe.
8 June	• Daimler management board sets subscription price; • Underwriting at Dm64 effective.
9 June	• Publication of 'red herring'.
13 June	• Roadshow continues in the US; • Bookbuilding starts.
17 June	• SEC declares F-1 registration statement effective; • F-1 distributed to all ADR holders; • International prospectus issued; • Record date for ADR holders (last day for participation in rights offer).
20 June	• Subscription and rights trading period begins.
21 June	• Global roadshow ends in Vienna.
1 July	• Rights trading period and bookbuilding end.
5 July	• Subscription period ends; • Underwriting period lapses.

- A lack of access by the syndicate to all rights sold by shareholders;
- Inefficient marketing of the rights resulting in a trading discount of the rights compared to theoretical value;
- A relatively limited incentive on the part of the company to market its shares after the price has been fixed;
- An unfamiliarity on the part of US investors with the structure; and
- The difficulty of analysing post-mortem who subscribed and who did not.

Some of these shortcomings were countered in the Daimler structure: the incorporation of a global marketing and bookbuilding syndicate, and the NYSE listing reflected a desire to create maximum demand for the rights not taken up by existing shareholders, thus ensuring a strong price performance throughout the offer. The advantage of adding a bookbuilding process to a conventional rights issue is that demand from new investors is identified before the beginning of the subscription period. In this case, bookbuilding started on 13 June and the subscription period on 20 June. By separating the underwriting, bookbuilding and selling efforts, the allocation of shares to new shareholders was based on the quality of orders from individual selling group members. In traditional rights issues, no proper account is taken of the investors interested in buying rights from non-subscribing shareholders.

Exhibit 8 shows the main structural characteristics of the Daimler rights offer. To put this structure in context, there follows in Exhibit 9 a crude overview of three different types of rights offers and a number of the parameters that determine the precise structure of a rights issue:

1. Traditional rights issue with domestic banks only;
2. Traditional rights issue with participation of one or a few foreign banks; and
3. Global managed rights issue with substantial number of domestic and foreign banks.

Marketing

Investor presentations by Daimler took place in six cities world-wide and the company had one-on-one meetings with 30 institutions. Deutsche Bank hosted the German and international investor presentations and co-hosted the US presentations together with Goldman Sachs.

This offer benefited from the two earlier roadshows in connection with the NYSE listing and the secondary offer. These roadshows were the first time that Daimler had sold itself aggressively to investors. Exhibit 10 summarises Daimler's US marketing efforts during the nine months to June 1994.

Exhibit 8

The main structural characteristics of the Daimler rights offer

Terms	• This was a 1:10 rights issue (each holder of 10 shares received the right to buy 1 new share) with the effect of increasing the total number of shares outstanding by 46,592,760 shares. The subscription price was Dm64, representing a discount of 20.4% to the market closing price on the day of pricing.
SEC registration	• The rights offer was registered with the SEC, thereby making it possible for Daimler's existing and potential new US investors to subscribe.
Underwriting	• The issue was underwritten by the underwriting syndicate at the fixed price of Dm64 from 8 June to 5 July, which was the last day of the subscription period.
Acquisition of rights by syndicate	• Major shareholder Stella Automobil-Beteiligungsgesellschaft GmbH had in advance indicated it would exercise its rights only to the extent of 73.8%, thereby diluting its shareholding from 12.6% to 12.3%. Deutsche Bank on behalf of the selling syndicates coordinated the process of acquiring rights directly from Stella. In so doing, Deutsche Bank talked to Allianz as the leader of the Stella syndicate and Allianz in turn coordinated further with the syndicate members. Deutsche Bank and the Emirate of Kuwait had indicated that they would subscribe in full. No other Daimler shareholder communicated its intentions in advance (they had until 17 May to do so). In total therefore, 47.7% of the rights offer was pre-committed by the three largest shareholders. • Deutsche Bank in its capacity as global bookrunner also coordinated, on behalf of the selling syndicates, open market purchases of rights from around the world. All these transactions took place over the relevant stock exchanges.
Marketing/bookbuilding	• Two dedicated syndicates were responsible for marketing and bookbuilding in the US and international markets respectively. The purpose was to generate demand before the rights trading period began. Marketing and bookbuilding took place independently of the underwriting and the acquisition of rights. • There were both preliminary (red herring) and final US prospectuses on Form F-1. These prospectuses, meeting the highest disclosure standards, were available globally. In addition there were less comprehensive prospectuses in German, French and English to comply with local listing requirements.
Recirculation	• The international marketing coordinators and the two dedicated selling groups exercised the Stella rights as well as the rights/ADR rights bought in the market and placed the resulting new shares/new ADRs with investors world-wide (with priority focus on the US and Asia). • The purchase orders generated by individual syndicate members, forming the book for the day, were filled by the global bookrunner based on the perceived quality and geographic origin of the order, recognising that the first priority was the US market, the second priority the Asian markets and the third priority the European market. No syndicate member was guaranteed a minimum allocation of shares either in absolute terms or in relation to the size of demand generated. • This recirculation process required exemption from SEC's Rule 10 B 6, which stipulates that no underwriters involved in any part of an offer are allowed to trade during the offer period in order not to 'condition' the market.
Pricing mechanism for the pre-agreed sales and recirculated rights	• Of the rights not taken up by Stella, 20% were sold to new investors each day of the first week of the subscription period. These and other rights acquired in the open market each day before the Frankfurt Stock Exchange fixing (at noon) formed the 'book' for the day. The price was the daily 'fixing' price. Allocation took place immediately after fixing. Stella therefore received the average Frankfurt fixing price during this week and the underwriters/selling group members were not exposed to price risk on these shares. However the underwriters remained exposed to their underwriting at Dm64 until 5 July.
Commissions	• The underwriters received commissions calculated on the basis of a complex formula as follows: 4% of the nominal value of Dm5 per share; plus 4% of the amount by which the subscription price of Dm64 exceeded 55% of Dm71.80 (being the cum price on the last trading day before the beginning of the subscription period, save that only underwriting commissions of 1% were paid on the portion of the rights offer pre-committed by the three largest shareholders and on the portion that Stella had agreed to sell upfront). On this basis, the total underwriting commissions paid by the company were estimated to have been approximately Dm28.1 million, corresponding to 0.94% of the total amount of money raised. The underwriting was distinctly separate from the marketing and selling effort. There was no sub-underwriting. • The members of the two marketing syndicates received a 2% selling concession for shares/ADRs placed with new investors, calculated on the full market price of the shares/ADRs. These selling commissions were paid by Daimler with respect to the rights purchased in the market and by Stella with respect to the rights sold by Stella. • Deutsche Bank as the global coordinator was paid a praecipium of 20%, calculated on the total amount of commissions paid to the syndicate.

The Daimler-Benz story

In terms of 1993 sales, Daimler was the largest industrial group in Germany, the third largest in Europe and the 12th largest in the world. 1993 sales of Dm98 billion were distributed over the four operating divisions as shown in Exhibit 11.

In 1993 three of Daimler's four operating divisions incurred massive losses. The 1993 operating result per division (German GAAP) can be seen in Exhibit 12.

Exhibit 9
Different types of rights issues

	Traditional	Traditional with foreign banks	Global managed
Underwritten/non-underwritten	Either	Either	Either
Sub-underwritten	Either	Either	Either
Low/high discount	Either	Either	Either
Separate roles (merchant bank, broker and sub-underwriting institutions) or integrated	Either	Either	Either
SEC registration	No	No	Yes
Strength of marketing effort Number of banks Dedicated sales syndicates Sales incentives	Low	Medium	Highest standard of marketing
Market activity during subscription period 1. Passive market-making in rights 2. Active recirculation 3. Pre-agreed sales by existing shareholders	1	2 only, or 2 and 3	2 and 3
Price fixing for pre-committed sales of rights 1. In advance of subscription period 2. According to formula during subscription period 3. At the end of subscription period	1, 2 or 3	2 or 3	2 or 3

Exhibit 10
Daimler's US marketing in 1993–94

	Cities visited	Group presentations	One-on-ones
September 1993	6	5	19
January 1994	21	12	55
June 1994	6	6	30
Total	**33**	**23**	**104**

Source: Daimler–Benz.

Exhibit 11
Daimler-Benz sales by division, 1993

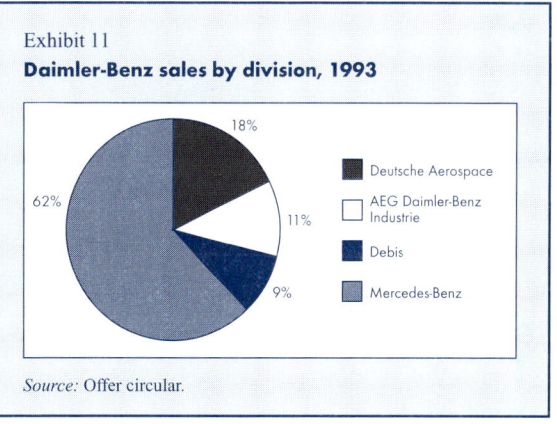

Source: Offer circular.

Exhibit 12
Divisional operating performance, 1993 (Dm millions)

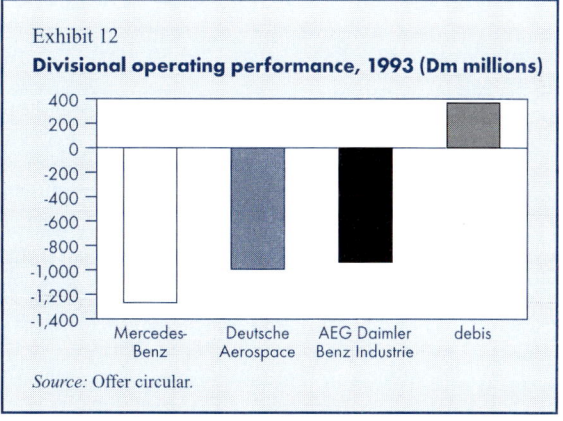

Source: Offer circular.

For the global rights offer, the strategy was to use Daimler's top quality name – considered one of the best brand names in the world through its passenger cars – and emphasise a radical turnaround story. First quarter 1994 sales were up almost 20 per cent and there was a feeling at the company that the corner had been turned. However investors would need to be convinced of a genuine turnaround in business and in management philosophy. Daimler admitted to past mistakes and investors therefore considered brokers' forecasts more credible than would otherwise have been the case. These forecasts (see below) suggested that after returning a loss in 1993 under US GAAP, Daimler would show much improved results in 1994 and 1995 (see Exhibit 13).

In May 1994 Goldman Sachs forecast that Daimler would make another loss in 1994 under US GAAP, and then achieve earnings per share of Dm2.70 and Dm5.40 in 1995 and 1996 respectively (see Exhibit 14).

Investor concerns

Investors had several significant concerns about buying Daimler shares including:

• Daimler's highly unfortunate diversification programme,

which led to the first ever loss in 1993 (under US GAAP);

• Lack of confidence in management's ability to turn Daimler around and therefore a belief that the forecast was unrealistic;

• Lack of cooperation from trade unions and employees to cut jobs;

Exhibit 13
Principal sales points

Restructuring	• There was a plan to reduce the workforce by 19% or 75,000 jobs of which 68,000 were on target to be cut by the end of 1994. Plant closures were to take place and non-core businesses to be sold. The NYSE listing with higher disclosure and transparency was seen as an indication of the turnaround in management philosophy. The following business steps were taken: • Cars: The objective was to improve market position while maintaining the highest quality. Growth was to come from new car lines (C and E models), revamped pricing strategies and a dramatically improved cost position. Capital was to be committed more economically and competitively. • Commercial vehicles: Daimler is the world's largest producer of trucks over six tons and production is strategically located in many countries. The Freightliner Corporation in the US was one of Daimler's successful acquisitions. Nevertheless the cost position had to be improved. • Aerospace: The plan was to attack the uncompetitive and fragmented structure by closing a number of plants acquired as a result of (mostly unsuccessful) acquisitions begun in 1985 including Dornier, MTU, Deutsche Airbus and Fokker. • AEG: Daimler planned to dispose of, or put into joint venture, some businesses in AEG.
Leasing	• Daimler's car leasing business, long underdeveloped, was now in a phase of profitable growth. This business was one of the soundest in the group and supported the overall car business.
Strong financials	• Daimler was rated AA (negative outlook) and Aa3 by S&P's and Moody's respectively.
Earnings momentum	• Goldman Sachs believed its earnings estimates (see below) were supported by progress on jobs cuts, general cost reduction measures and the recent disposals at AEG. Earnings were expected to gain momentum in 1996 and also in 1997 and 1998 when the truck and commercial aircraft demand-cycles were expected to peak. In 1995, Daimler would benefit from the new E-class car, the anticipated break-even at AEG and Deutsche Aerospace.
Valuation	• The 1996 earnings multiple reflects close to a 20% discount to the German 1996 market multiple although, in contrast to most of the market cyclicals which should peak in 1997, Goldman Sachs did not see Mercedes' commercial vehicle margins peaking before 1998 and DASA's margins before 1999 or 2000.

Exhibit 14
Earnings expectations at the time of issue

3 May 1994 (Dm80.75)	1991A	1992A	1993A	1994E	1995E	1996E
German GAAP						
Net income (Dm millions)	1,942	1,451	615	1,120	1,850	3,950
EPS (Dm)	4.02	3.05	1.29	2.34	3.61	7.71
P/E ratio (times)	–	–	–	34.5	22.4	10.5
US GAAP						
Net income (Dm millions)	1,886	1,350	(1,839)	n/a	n/a	n/a
EPS (Dm)	4.05	2.90	(3.95)	(0.5)	2.70	5.40
P/E ratio (times)	–	–	–	–	29.9	14.9

Source: Goldman Sachs Equity Research.

• Overall lack of competitiveness of Daimler and German manufacturing, particularly due to high cost levels, inflexible labour markets and a strong Deutschmark;

• Certain domestic (primarily retail) investors considered the subscription price too high; and

• Poor market conditions.

Results

The three largest shareholders who together owned 51 per cent of Daimler before the offer, undertook in advance to subscribe for 47.7 per cent of the offer. Deutsche Bank and the Emirate of Kuwait subscribed in full, while the Stella consortium subscribed to the extent of 73.8 per cent, reducing its holding from 12.6 per cent before the offer to 12.3 per cent after it.

Deutsche Bank and the other syndicate members placed (laid off) 11.7 per cent of the total rights issue, ie, 5,439,220 shares, with new investors around the world (see Exhibit 15).

The remainder of the rights issue, or 40.6 per cent, was subscribed for by other existing shareholders or by new investors who bought the rights on world stock exchanges. The fact that the Deutsche Bank syndicate did not gain access to this volume illustrates one of the general problems with rights issues, which occurs because each shareholder can elect at any time during the subscription period to sell his rights to any bank or broker.

Of the 5,439,220 shares laid off by the Deutsche syndicate, rights exercisable into 1,537,560 shares were purchased directly from Stella. The remainder, ie, rights exercisable into 3,901,660 shares, were purchased by Deutsche Bank on German and other stock exchanges from shareholders not wishing to subscribe in part or in full (see Exhibit 16).

Exhibit 15

Subscriptions in the Daimler rights issue

	No of shares	% of rights issue
Pre-committed subscriptions by the three largest shareholders	22,224,750	47.7%
Shares laid off by Deutsche Bank syndicate	5,439,220	11.7%
Shares otherwise subscribed by old or new shareholders outside the control of the Deutsche Bank syndicate	18,928,790	40.6%
Total size of rights offer	**46,592,760**	**100.0%**

Source: Deutsche Bank.

Exhibit 16

Acquisition of rights by Deutsche Consortium
(rights exercisable into 5,439,220 new Daimler shares valued at Dm391 million)

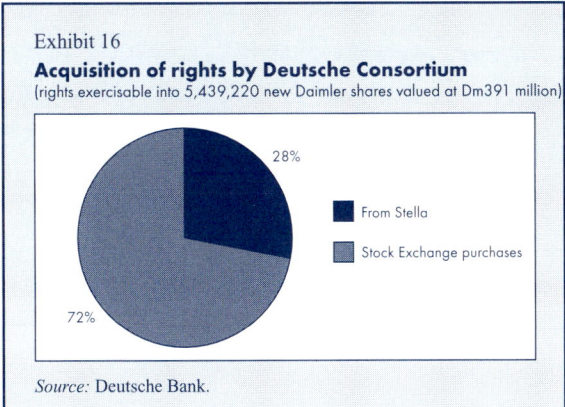

28%

■ From Stella
■ Stock Exchange purchases

72%

Source: Deutsche Bank.

Exhibit 17

The syndicate's access to subscription rights on international and US stock exchanges was limited (%)

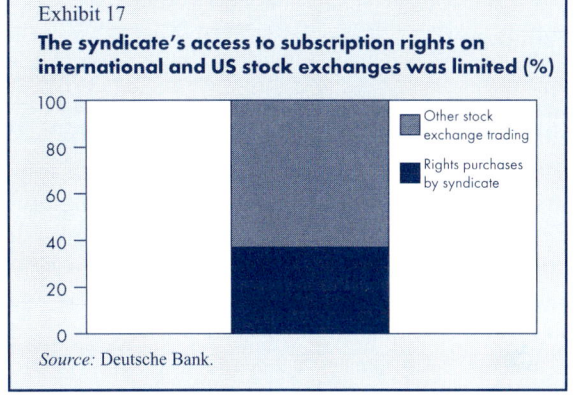

■ Other stock exchange trading
■ Rights purchases by syndicate

Source: Deutsche Bank.

No one knows in advance how many subscription rights existing shareholders will dispose of and how many the syndicate has available to sell unless some very large shareholders declare upfront their intention to sell, as Stella did on this occasion. Furthermore, even if the syndicate does know about certain shareholders intending to sell their rights, to the extent that those shareholders elect to sell through other banks or brokers on the German or other stock exchanges where Daimler is listed, the consortium does not gain access to such subscription rights.

Turnover statistics show that a total of 105.8 million rights, exercisable into 10.58 million new Daimler shares, traded on German and other stock exchanges. While 3,901,660 shares were acquired in the market by Deutsche Bank on behalf of the two selling syndicates – equivalent to 37 per cent of all subscription rights changing hands on stock exchanges, the remainder, rights exercisable into 6,678,340 shares, representing 63 per cent of total trading volume, were traded away from the Deutsche Bank syndicate (see Exhibit 17).

The banks involved have relatively limited control over the supply to the market in a rights issue. In the case of a bookbuilt offer, however, the selling consortium has control over 100 per cent of the supply.

Because the market price was above the subscription price, almost 100 per cent of the offer was subscribed, either by old shareholders or new investors. As the Deutsche Bank syndicate laid off only 11.7 per cent, it might appear as if 88.3 per cent of the offer was taken up by existing shareholders, but this figure does not take into account the fact that many existing shareholders sold their rights to others than the Deutsche Bank syndicate member. The actual take-up rate among existing shareholders is somewhere between 88.3 per cent (count-

Exhibit 18

Take-up rates at different assumptions (%)

	Based on whole offer	Based on non-pre-committed portion
Counting only Deutsche Bank 'lay-offs'	88.3	77.7
Considering all stock exchange trading volume as placed with new investors	74.0	50.3

ing only the Deutsche Bank lay-offs) and 74.0 per cent (assuming all of Stella rights sold to Deutsche Bank and all the 105.8 million rights traded on stock exchanges were sold to new investors).

If we consider that 47.7 per cent of the rights offer was firmly committed by the three largest shareholders, the take-up rate among remaining shareholders was obviously correspondingly lower, in fact between 77.7 per cent and 50.3 per cent. Exhibit 18 shows that the real take-up rate was therefore anywhere between 50.3 per cent and 88.3 per cent.

The geographic distribution of the 5,439,220 shares laid off by the Deutsche Bank syndicate (equivalent to approximately Dm390 million based on the market price on the last day of cum trading on 17 June 1994) was as shown in Exhibit 19.

As a result of the take-up from US shareholders and active recirculation into the US, the US shareholding increased from between 6 and 7 per cent to approximately 8 per cent, of which some 3 per cent was held by way of ADRs and the balance by ordinary shares.

Exhibit 19

Geographic distribution of syndicate's lay-offs

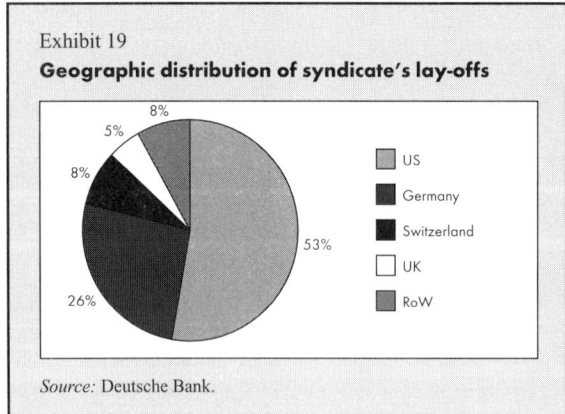

8%
5%
8%
26%
53%

- US
- Germany
- Switzerland
- UK
- RoW

Source: Deutsche Bank.

Buyers by type

Among US institutional investors, the offer was bought by both US domestic funds which buy predominantly US dollar-denominated and US-listed securities (including those of non-US companies) and international funds, which focus on buying securities of non-US companies. There was only limited interest among US funds dedicated to car companies given that Daimler was considered a conglomerate. Nor was there much interest among index buyers, those that would have to own Daimler because it is a major constituent of German and more broadly based European indices.

Share price performance

See Exhibit 20.

Before pricing

- On an adjusted basis, Daimler's share price rose from Dm74.30 six months before pricing to Dm79.50 on the day of pricing, an increase of 7 per cent. During this period, it had outperformed the German market by 7 per cent. The market price on the pricing date was only Dm0.3 below the adjusted offer price for the secondary offer in January 1994.

After pricing

- Both the German market and Daimler shares were in steady decline from the pricing date on 8 June until and including the first trading day on 20 June, when Daimler hit a low of Dm69.40, putting the price 23 per cent below its 1994 peak of Dm90.10 (adjusted for bonus element of rights issue) set on 2 May. From pricing to 20 June, Daimler underperformed the market by 5 per cent;
- On the first trading day, the adjusted share price fell by Dm2.40, off the back of weak US and German equity markets. The German stock market was off 4 per cent, mainly because of US interest rate increases and a weakening US dollar which negatively affected the earnings of German exporters. On that day, Daimler outperformed DAX 30 by 0.6 per cent;
- After the initial fall, the German market and Daimler performed strongly. From 20 June to the second last trading day on 30 June, the share price increased from Dm69.40 to Dm72.50, outperforming the market by 1.5 per cent over the period. The subscription rights traded close to their theoretical value during the subscription period – not

Exhibit 20

Share price performance

Pricing date	8 June 1994
Subscription price	Dm64
Terms of rights issue	1:10
Rights issue discount	20.4%
Adjusted price on day of pricing	Dm79.50
Relative index position on pricing date	107%
Historic 52-week high/low	
(Adjusted for bonus element)	
High (2 May 1994)	Dm90.10
Low (10 June 1993)	Dm57.30

Daimler share price relative to DAX (%)

Price performance

Before pricing (adjusted prices)

	Price (Dm)	Relative to DAX (%)
- 6 months	74.30	100
- 3 months	80.10	109
- 1 month	86.80	114
- 3 weeks	87.90	113
– 2 weeks	82.40	110
- 1 week	79.70	108
4 days	79.70	108
- 2 days	80.50	108
- 1 day (7 June)	79.20	107

After pricing (adjusted prices)

	Price (Dm)	Relative to DAX (%)
+ 1 day (9 June)	77.30	105
+2 days	76.60	104
Start of bookbuilding	73.80	101
Last day of cum trading	71.80	101
First day of rights trading	69.40	102
Last day of rights trading	71.80	102
+ 1 month	72.90	103
+ 3 months	83.30	111
+ 6 months	74.90	106

Sources: Datastream and offer circular.

usually the case with earlier German rights issues. On the last subscription day, Daimler's share fell back to Dm71.80 while the German market increased by 0.6 per cent;

- Daimler's share price in absolute terms was strong during the first three months after pricing, followed by a long period of weakness. Daimler performed in line with the market during the first six months after the pricing;
- In the spring of 1995 when it became clear that the year

was going to be worse than expected, and there was going to be a severe loss despite the fact that the outgoing chairman had only recently talked about an excellent 1995 – the share price almost broke through the Dm60 level. Over the 12 months since pricing, Daimler's shares depreciated by 13 per cent in a flat German market.

The performance of the main parties

The company

Under the late Gerhard Liener, Daimler's former CFO, some major steps were taken to improve the marketability of Daimler's shares. These substantially increased the free float and liquidity, improved transparency and disclosure standards and reduced Deutsche Bank's power in the general meeting. The steps were:

- *The NYSE listing.* The fact that Daimler was prepared to report a huge loss under US GAAP (while German GAAP showed a profit) provided the strongest indication that the company intended to adopt a more shareholder friendly policy. It realised that if it were to successfully raise equity capital, then it had to offer something attractive such as listed ADRs based on US GAAP accounting. As the head of investor relations at Daimler, Georg Bruns says: 'We need more customer orientation within Daimler.' Before Daimler's NYSE listing, six German companies were listed in Tokyo but not a single one in New York. Companies which listed in Tokyo did so because they could have the flexibility to present themselves as they wished. The fact that the Japanese invested very little money in foreign companies compared to US investors does not appear to have been an important factor;

- *The reduction of Deutsche Bank's stake to below 25 per cent in January 1994.* This was an important step to inject liquidity into the US market following the October 1993 listing. This offer increased US ownership from some 3 per cent to between 6 and 7 per cent. By going down to 24.4 per cent, Deutsche Bank also gave up its blocking minority power;

- *Merger with MAH.* By merging MAH into Daimler through a share swap, the company increased its financing flexibility, increased the free float and removed the blocking minority of MAH. The MAH structure had been a major constraint for Daimler as MAH shares had traded at a sub-

stantial discount to Daimler shares, making it inefficient to raise money in MAH in order to subscribe to Daimler rights issues. It limited Daimler on each equity financing occasion to conducting the offer during a specific period of only a few weeks in the fourth quarter;

- *Introduction of an active investor relations programme.* Since 1990 Daimler has carried out an active investor relations programme with regular presentations in all the major cities where it has listed. It has two experienced IR people in Stuttgart and one based in the US, dedicated to the US investment community. The IR effort is centralised so that only the CEO, CFO and the IR department talk to investors. This is to maintain control and to avoid any insider problems. Insider trading has been a criminal offence in Germany since August 1994;

- *Exposure to international due diligence standards.* Daimler was exposed to three rounds of American-style due diligence in only nine months. In addition, equity research analysts increasingly asked more detailed questions of the management. These exercises are thought to have substantially changed Daimler's culture, making it more open and understanding of the investor perspective. Obtaining ratings from Standard & Poor's and Moody's also helped. The rating process was pursued simultaneously with the listing project in the summer of 1993. Given the disastrous loss incurred in 1995, it must be asked what good these due diligence sessions did the investment community – the audience for whom they are intended; and

- *New dividend policy.* After the 1994 rights issue, Daimler indicated it was likely to begin paying dividends more closely linked to group earnings rather than just a fixed percentage of the nominal value of the shares, which had previously been the case.

These steps would have had a radically positive impact on Daimler shares had they been carried out in tandem with a successful business strategy and a reliable controlling and forecasting effort. As Exhibit 21 shows, Daimler delivered a 1994 net profit according to German GAAP, 20 per cent lower than forecast by Goldman Sachs just before the rights offer in May 1994. This is a severe shortfall from a forecast by a lead bank for the year in which an offer is conducted. Goldman Sachs was expecting a profit of Dm1.1 billion for 1995, prior to the 28 June 1995 profit warning – 42 per cent lower than forecast at the time of the offer. By August 1995 Goldman Sachs was expecting a loss of Dm456 million, Daimler's first

---

Exhibit 21
Actual profit performance (US forecast)

	1993	1994	1995	1996
German GAAP (Dm millions)				
Net income (forecast May 1994)	615A	1,120F	1,850F	3,950F
Net income (forecast prior to 1995 profit warning)	615A	895A	1,074F	3,345F
Net income (forecast August 1995)	615A	895A	(456)F	2,085F
Net income (actuals)	615A	895 A	(5,700) A	2,800 A

Source: Goldman Sachs Equity Research.

ever loss under German GAAP. Instead it became a loss of Deutschmark 5.7 billion, the biggest in German corporate history. This can be partly explained by currency movements as Daimler was badly affected by the strong Deutschmark when translating into Deutschmark all its non-Dm revenues. However, the deviation was symptomatic of severe structural problems in Deutsche Aerospace and AEG and Daimler's sub-standard controlling function.

Not only was the negative deviation in 1994 and 1995 business performance a grave embarrassment for all concerned, but it also reflected poorly on the quality of communication between Daimler and its banking sponsors during 1993–94, including Deutsche Bank. It appears that the management did not know what was going on in the company. If it did, it should have communicated its concerns in the due diligence. The analyst community continued to forecast incorrectly throughout 1994 and 1995.

The banks

On a technical level, Deutsche Bank, as global coordinator and sole bookrunner, did well in completing this transaction, which was far more ambitious than anything previously attempted in Germany in terms of size, number of parties involved, marketing effort and complexity. It helped Deutsche Bank that Goldman Sachs was closely involved as Goldman Sachs had been involved in several similarly structured rights issues, including Norsk Hydro (Norway), Novo-Nordisk (Denmark) and Zeneca (UK).

Deutsche Bank also performed well in terms of distribution, accounting for 75 per cent of total lay-offs in the international markets (including Germany) and 76 per cent in the US. Deutsche Bank has a major advantage in that it manages a huge amount of money via German brokerage accounts and therefore has something of a captive market. Somewhat surprisingly, Merrill Lynch outsold Goldman Sachs in the international market, however the situation was reversed in the US. Globally, the picture was as shown in Exhibit 22.

In the light of the development of the business following the offer, most notably in connection with the disastrous loss in 1995, the question arises as to whether or not Deutsche Bank and Goldman Sachs could not have done a better job in the due diligence process. Although the banks got Daimler to open up more than it ever had in the past, they obviously did not get to the bottom of the development of the business as

regards the inherent business risks. This is particularly remarkable given that this was the third set of due diligence meetings within nine months. The bankers and lawyers will have encountered numerous difficulties trying to understand a business as diverse as Daimler Benz's, but to the investment community, this looks like little more than guesswork. It severely dented investor confidence in both the company and the banks. Some large investors were sincerely trying to understand whether the bankers were biased or incompetent, or whether the management had been dishonest or simply did not know what was going on. Few investors are prepared to see unexpectedly large losses simply as a matter of coincidence.

Given Deutsche Bank's ownership and supervisory board influence at Daimler, the mandate as global coordinator was not subject to competition: the fact that any foreign banks were involved was seen as a big enough step. However, there was substantial competition for the role of the most senior foreign bank behind Deutsche Bank, in particular between Merrill Lynch and Goldman Sachs. Other competitors are thought to have included SG Warburg, CSFB and JP Morgan. Liener, who took the decision, considered 'Goldman to be the champion for the institutional market and Merrill Lynch to be the equivalent for the retail market'. Whereas Merrill Lynch had done a very good job in connection with the secondary offer in January 1994 (except perhaps with respect to due diligence), this was really Deutsche Bank's transaction and accordingly Merrill Lynch had been mandated by Deutsche Bank. The global rights offer presented Liener with an opportunity to thank Goldman Sachs for its hard work on the NYSE listing and registration process. Goldman Sachs had begun discussions with Daimler on the subject in late 1992: Daimler decided on the listing in February 1993 and two months later mandated Goldman Sachs, who had worked hard for almost a year without significant compensation and in so doing impressed Daimler. Once again, Goldman Sachs was awarded a highly significant mandate that it had prioritised and pursued.

Key lessons learnt

The NYSE listing and rating projects represented important internal processes at Daimler as they helped key executives understand the demands and interests of the financial markets. These processes also promote an understanding of shareholder value, a concept virtually unknown in Germany five years ago and still practiced by few. According to the late Gerhard Liener: 'We don't pay attention to shareholder value just because it is necessary but because it is our duty. As the customer is the king so are the shareholders. The capital market is always the winner.'

A global managed rights offer is the closest one can come to a bookbuilt issue while still honouring shareholders' pre-emptive rights. Having a number of banks with a global reach to buy rights from shareholders and sell them on to new investors allows shareholders to realise the theoretical value of their rights. The structure is much more effective when a few of the large shareholders commit upfront to selling a substantial portion of their rights, as the banks and investors then

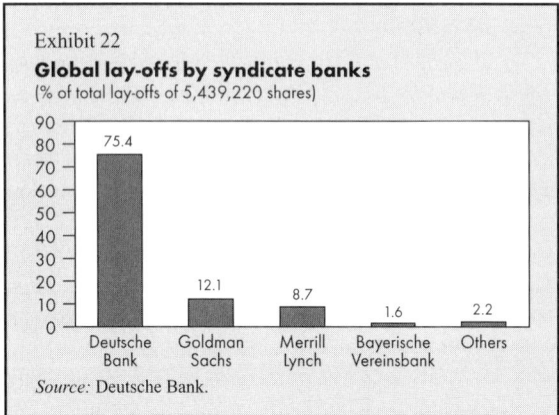

Exhibit 22
Global lay-offs by syndicate banks
(% of total lay-offs of 5,439,220 shares)

Source: Deutsche Bank.

know that there is a minimum number of shares available, creating a higher level of motivation for all parties concerned.

The dynamics between the investment bank and the market are very different for a rights issue and a bookbuilding. In a bookbuilding, the investment bank has complete control over the supply of shares. In a rights offer, the lead bank does not know (unless some large shareholders have pre-committed to selling a portion of their rights) how many shares will become available from non-subscribing shareholders wishing to sell their rights. These shareholders typically sell their rights through a significant number of banks or brokers, whether or not they are actually part of the rights offer syndicate. This makes the process of selling shares to new shareholders much less efficient, and means that the lead bank has both supply and demand to worry about. The market, on the other hand, gets a lot of information on turnover and prices of both rights and shares as traded during the subscription period, of which sophisticated investors can take advantage. In a bookbuilding, the bookrunner controls most of the information on investor behaviour and is therefore in a relatively advantageous situation.

The pricing mechanism for the pre-agreed sales of Stella rights was not optimal. Exactly 20 per cent of the total number of rights not taken up were sold each day of the first week of the subscription period, an inflexible structure which did not take fluctuating demand into account. The first 20 per cent had to be sold on the first day of the subscription period, the day when the German market fell by 4 per cent.

The lesson to be learned from the challenges encountered by the management in the running of Daimler–Benz and from the difficulties experienced in getting the due diligence and the analysts' estimates right, is that conglomerates deserve to trade at considerable discounts to net asset value or to what the peers of the constituent parts suggest the group should be theoretically trading at. Building multi-industry empires, as done by Edzard Reuter, is rarely conducive to the creation of shareholder value.

It now seems clear that the loss in the 1970s and 1980s of the Flick and Quant families – two prominent German industrial families – as shareholders and supervisory board members was more significant than was thought at the time. Certainly Deutsche Bank could have benefited from the help of strong industrial shareholders during the 10 years leading up to the offer. This case proves yet again that banks are not ideal shareholders of complex industrial conglomerates. It certainly demonstrates that banks and insurance companies in conjunction with passive institutional investors (those buying as an index stock) neither support nor sufficiently discipline the management to ensure that it does a competent job. There were few active international institutional investors (those buying based on fundamental analysis) putting pressure on the company to perform, because disclosure and German accounting standards were deemed too much of a hindrance for active portfolio managers. If there had been, then perhaps some of the disasters at Daimler may not have happened or at least may have come into the open at an earlier stage.

According to Daimler–Benz, the apparent disadvantage of reporting two sets of accounts actually proved to be less of

an issue with investors than perhaps first assumed. Still, Daimler is pleased to have been able to begin to report to investors solely according to US GAAP as it did from 1996. Accounts according to German standards are still produced for statutory purposes.

Conclusion

NYSE listing

While Daimler's decision to report under US GAAP, and the timing thereof, was criticised by other European companies and from within Daimler, the move was welcomed by the analyst and investor communities. The impact of US GAAP on Daimler's financials was to increase the equity capital dramatically and give a fairer reflection of current trading conditions. As a result, 1993 accounts under US GAAP showed a big loss – the first ever in the company's history – while under German GAAP Daimler continued to show a profit. Daimler was effectively undressed at a time when its weaknesses were evident. Liener judged that strategically Daimler could no longer rely soley on the German equity market, and that he had little choice with the timing of the listing as a return to profitability was not immediately in sight. It was a courageous decision as he was, as CFO, not entirely without blame for the losses.

In 1992 and 1993 the majority of Daimler's senior managers appeared unaware of the full consequences of the diversification strategy. Liener recognised that Daimler had to be managed in the interests of all shareholders rather than in a technocratic way and judged that a radical cultural revolution was needed within the company. In light of the losses incurred in 1995, it may seem that instigating a more effective equity and investor relations strategy was an inadequate response. However, the author is of the view that Liener's attempts to open up the company and fully expose the mistakes of the past via the disciplines of the financial market, acted as an important catalyst for change.

The discipline imposed by the due diligence teams, sophisticated institutional investors and equity research analysts was instrumental in raising self-awareness among corporate and divisional management as to how outsiders judged Daimler's strategy. Had this pressure not been applied at the beginning of 1993, then perhaps the full realisation of the severity of the problems might have been delayed because the company would have been able to continue to report profits under German GAAP.

In a broader German context, Daimler's US listing was not an immediate and unqualified success – US liquidity did not increase to the extent intended and for almost three years, no other German company followed in its footsteps. It can be argued that this had more to do with the business developments at Daimler and the tragic death of Liener. 'No German CFO wanted to be the second Liener and list on the NYSE,' says one London investment banker close to Daimler. Other reasons why German companies were reluctant to register with the SEC included:

- The fact that under US GAAP, total book equity capital increases substantially and return on equity falls;

- The possibility that the german authorities, which tax on the basis of reported earnings, may become more fully aware of excessively conservative depreciation by certain German companies;
- The lack of need for equity capital by German companies that had done well over recent years; and
- The hope that the US SEC would allow foreign companies to list in the US on the basis of IAS. Several important German companies including Deutsche Bank, Veba, Lufthansa and Bayer started reporting under IAS.

By August 1997 a further five companies had listed on the NYSE including Deutsche Telekom, which began trading on the NYSE in connection with its US$11 billion IPO in November 1996. This should act as a catalyst for other companies to do the same thing. By mid-year 1997 further German companies, including blue chips Hoechst and Veba had publicly announced their intention to begin reporting to the SEC with a view to listing on the NYSE.

Deutsche Bank sell-down

The NYSE listing paved the way for the January 1994 reduction of Deutsche Bank's stake in the company. Deutsche Bank and Merrill Lynch did an excellent job of placing US$806 million of shares in the US, some three-and-a-half-times as much as would subsequently be placed with new investors by the rights issue syndicate. At the time, it was one of the largest corporate offers in the US market by a non-US issuer. The offer was substantially oversubscribed and priced at market despite an increase in the market price of 2.7 per cent on the day of pricing. The split between retail (38 per cent) and institutional (62 per cent) allocations was excellent. The shares performed strongly in the after-market due to unfilled US demand and the greenshoe was exercised in full within two days. In the quarter following the offer the NYSE average daily trading volume was US$19.8 million representing 4.3 per cent of Frankfurt trading volume (compared to US$2.2 million and 0.5 per cent pre-offer).

According to Merrill Lynch, the performance of the syndicate in terms of institutional designations was as follows: CJ Lawrence/Deutsche Bank accounted for 43 per cent, Merrill Lynch for 31 per cent, Goldman Sachs for 16 per cent and the rest of the syndicate for 10 per cent. Of the US $305 million sold to retail investors, Merrill Lynch accounted for US$210 million or 69 per cent.

As Deutsche Bank had not been ready to sell shares in October 1993, the NYSE listing had taken place in isolation. While arranging a listing without a simultaneous offer is generally considered ineffective, Daimler took advantage of the opportunity to present to investors on three separate occasions as this gave it experience and assisted investors to better understand the group before the rights offer.

Global rights offer

Daimler's rights issue raised Dm3 billion and improved the equity-to-total-assets ratio (under German GAAP) from 20 per cent to 23 per cent. Although under US GAAP, the equity-to-assets ratio was almost 27 per cent before the offer, Daimler's long-term debt ratings were uncomfortably close to sliding into single-A territory. One can hardly criticise a company for wanting to protect a double-A rating, even though only Toyota, among car companies, had such strong debt ratings. The inclusion of a marketing and bookbuilding syndicate allowed the company to set the subscription price at a record small discount.

Given that only 11.7 per cent of the global rights offer, equivalent to Dm390 million at market prices, was placed by the two selling groups, the value of this complex structure is questionable. It was excessive to involve 28 banks in the offer, as the presence of such a large group can be counter-productive as regards the smooth execution of the transaction, but the syndicate size was dictated by a wish to look after certain banking relationships.

The pricing of the rights issue at a discount of 20.4 per cent was criticised by some German investors, as Daimler had traditionally set the terms of its rights issues in such a way that the subscription price was lower and the subscription rights worth more. Some investors were of the opinion that the offer had been too aggressively priced and the market price fell some Dm2 on the first trading day after the announcement of the subscription price. The tight pricing and the negative market reaction at one stage threatened to leave the whole issue with the underwriters. From the day of pricing on 8 June to the last day of trading of the rights on 1 July, the share price fell by just under 10 per cent. The average price achieved by selling shareholders was equivalent to a market price of approximately Dm71.35, the average market price for the first week of the subscription period. This was approximately 10 per cent lower (adjusted for the bonus element of the rights offer) than that achieved by Deutsche Bank in the secondary offer.

The syndicate structure and process of the global rights offer was complex, and a global bookbuilt issue would have had many advantages. However, there is a strong culture of rights issues in Germany, as they have important tax advantages – the value of rights received are tax-free whereas dividends are not. In 1995 a change in the legal framework was to make it easier to disapply the pre-emptive rights to the extent of up to 10 per cent a year of a company's share capital. In late 1995, Commerzbank was the first German company to take advantage of this by selling US$730 million of new shares in a non-registered global equity offer.

At the outset the objective had been to place shares firstly in the US, secondly in Asia and thirdly in Europe. The amount finally placed in Germany thus appears high while only 1 per cent was placed in Asia. Total US shareholding increased by no more than 1–2 per cent to a total of 8 per cent compared with the target of 10 per cent.

The offer was successful in the sense that subscription rights traded close to theoretical value, and except for the first and the last days of the subscription period, the Daimler ex-rights price outperformed DAX 30 during the two-week subscription period. In addition to the fact that the success of the January 1994 issue had created a positive feeling among investors and that market sentiment was turning positive during the subscription period, the major success factors included:

- The process of 'breaking with the past', whereby Daimler

admitted to the failures of the past and created a perception that it was committed to taking tough action to address the problems at hand and to communicate openly and candidly about the company's strengths and weaknesses;

- The fact that through a bookbuilding process, demand was generated from new investors before the beginning of the subscription period. As a result, there was strong demand for the subscription rights sold by existing shareholders during the subscription period;

- The fact that there was still considerable unsaturated demand in the US for the shares for which many shareholders in Germany and elsewhere didn't wish to subscribe. This also had a stabilising effect on the price. In this regard, the fact that Daimler did three sets of roadshows in the US, ie in September 1993, January 1994 and June 1994 was clearly helpful.

Prior to the repeated profit warnings in 1995 and the large loss in the same year, the rights offer temporarily helped to achieve investor perception of Daimler as a repositioned company, primarily as a result of an atypical openness of past mistakes. Many international investors clearly took comfort from Daimler also reporting its financials under US GAAP, which was seen as indicating a change in attitude toward the investor community. However reporting under US GAAP itself is obviously not sufficient to make shareholders happy. The next step is to have a proper controlling function so that the company can let shareholders know how the business is developing with at least a minimum degree of accuracy. This did not appear to have been the case under Reuter, particularly during the later years, when communications to the stock market appeared rather to be based on wishful thinking. The third step is to restore an appropriate level of profitability.

This work has begun under new chairman Jürgen Schrempp. Profits for 1996 were much better than expected, perhaps partly because of generous provisioning in 1995. Schrempp has clearly demonstrated his willingness to take action by restructuring and downsizing the group to bring it back to its automotive roots. He appears to be guided rather by the creation of profits and shareholder value than by the creation of a corporate empire. He realises that earnings per share growth is more important than sales growth. The stock market has given him the benefit of the doubt – the companies shares doubled in 1996 and have continued to perform strongly also in 1997. Investors who bought shares on the day that the rights offer was priced had seen their shares underperform the DAX 30 by 18 per cent by mid-August 1997.

There is therefore a lot more to be done. Serious fund managers will not be impressed if Daimler simply achieves a return on capital of 12 per cent (as Schrempp has set out to do), a figure which is probably calculated on the basis of substantially undervalued assets. What Jürgen Schrempp should be judged on is his ability to make Daimler beat its cost of capital on the basis of the real value of its assets. Only then does it make sense to be in business.

Feature topic: *The significance of the discount in a rights issue*

There is continuing argument about the relevance of the size of the discount in a rights issue, and a heated debate exists between the proponents of bookbuilt offers and those that argue that rights offers with a sizeable discount make more sense for shareholders. The former argue that the discount (including fees) is smaller in a bookbuilt offer. The latter argue that the size of the discount in a rights issue is irrelevant but that the total discount in bookbuilt offers is typically too large.

The size of the discount in connection with a rights issue does not matter in principle to the owners of the company as shown in the example below.

Basic assumptions and examples

Niven Limited has 1,000 shares outstanding, each with a nominal value of Dm100, trading at Dm1,000 each. The company is therefore valued at Dm1 million. Niven wishes to raise new capital of Dm200,000. Consider the position of Mr. Zorn, who is a 10 per cent shareholder in Niven under two scenarios, either he subscribes or does not subscribe. Exhibit 23 unequivocally demonstrates that regardless of whether shareholders subscribe or not, they are equally well off in either of the three hypothetical examples using three different discounts.

There are a number of reasons why people are still concerned with the size of the discount in a rights issue, which are more or less rational:

- The size of the discount is to a large extent a matter of prestige: a small discount is more prestigious than a large one because it indicates that the company is raising money on finer terms. In Germany it is traditional to price rights issues at discounts of 20–30 per cent. Daimler was right at the edge and priced at a 20.4 per cent discount. The cynical observer would say that these discounts are just small enough to require a syndicate of banks to underwrite the rights issue against a fee, and big enough to leave the underwriting banks sleeping comfortably at night for the three- to four-week underwriting period;

- It may be difficult for companies to cut the absolute size of dividend: if the discount is sufficiently large, the company would have to adjust historic earnings and dividend share numbers as well as the absolute level of dividends going forward. Take, the ultimate deep discount rights issue where the discount is close to 100 per

Exhibit 23

The economic irrelevance of the size of the discount in a rights issue

	Example 1	Example 2	Example 3
Size of discount	0%*	20%	60%
Subscription price	Dm1,000	Dm800	Dm400
Terms of the rights issue	1 new for 5 old	1 new for 4 old	1 new for 2 old
Number of new shares Issued	200	250	500
Total shares outstanding after new issue	1,200	1,250	1,500
Value of 1 subscription right	Dm0	Dm40	Dm200
Ex-rights price (adjusted market price)	Dm1,000	Dm960	Dm800
Expanded market capitalisation of company	Dm1,200,000	Dm1,200,000	Dm1,200,000
Scenario 1 – Zorn subscribes in full			
Zorn buys 20/25/50 new shares at			
Dm1,000/800/400 each respectively	Dm20,000	Dm20,000	Dm20,000
Total number of shares owned by Zorn	120	125	150
Total value of Zorn's investment in Company A	Dm120,000	Dm120,000	Dm120,000
Scenario 2 – Zorn does not subscribe			
Value of Zorn's original 100 shares	Dm100,000	Dm96,000	Dm80,000
Number of subscription rights posted to Zorn	100	100	200
Value of 1 subscription right	Dm0	Dm40	Dm100
Proceeds from sale of rights in the market	Dm0	Dm4,000	Dm20,000
Total value of cash received and shares owned	Dm100,000	Dm100,000	Dm100,000

* For illustrative purposes only. A discount of 0% is not allowed in Germany.

cent, and the company in reality does a stock split of two new shares for one old share. In this case, the company would have to halve the dividend. Using the above example, if Niven has been trading at a 6 per cent dividend yield, then as a result of a 2:1 stock split (or a 100 per cent discounted rights issue), Niven would have to adjust the absolute dividend from Dm60 to Dm30. Following the stock split, Niven would now have 2,000 shares outstanding, the shares would be trading at Dm500 instead of Dm1000 and the dividend of Dm30 would still amount to a dividend yield of 6 per cent. In certain countries, mainly among retail shareholders, tradition is such that retail investors may not see the connection between a discounted rights issue and a cut dividend, unless it is a 100 per cent discount and is called a stock split. In some countries, including Germany, dividends are traditionally paid in terms of a fixed percentage of the nominal capital. Shareholders are remunerated on top of this fixed dividend by receiving distributions such as bonus shares and subscription rights which can be sold on the market. This system works as long as the discount is not too large in relation to the earnings growth. If the number of shares is increased faster than earnings grow and dividends are kept constant in nominal capital terms, then the company effectively increases its pay-out ratio and cost of capital;

- Institutions find discounted rights issues with a maintained absolute dividend attractive, as the dividend yield on the new shares is higher than on the old ones. This is of particular relevance to income funds trying to maximise the income of the portfolio;
- Dilution of voting control for those shareholders who do not subscribe, as the larger the discount, the larger

the number of new shares that must be issued to raise a given amount of capital. If a large shareholder does not subscribe, his voting interest in the company will be correspondingly more diluted with a higher-discount rights issue;

- The banks would like a small enough discount for the company to require an underwriting and a big enough discount not to have to carry too much risk. Against a given fee, underwriting banks would like to take as small a risk as possible and therefore will try to keep the discount high. However, if the company proposed a deep discount structure without any underwriting, the bankers lose the opportunity of earning an underwriting fee, and they would earn only management and selling fees. This approach is found, for example, in Sweden. In August 1995, LM Ericsson announced a SEK 7.8 billion (US$1.1 billion) 1:10 rights issue with a 45 per cent discount. No underwriting was deemed necessary;
- The size of the discount may be determined by the decision-making process to issue new shares. If the board of directors (or supervisory board) has authorisation from the general meeting to issue a certain number of new shares and feels that it would be difficult to obtain a new authorisation, then clearly it will want to issue the shares at as high a price as possible to raise the targeted amount of capital; and
- The discount may matter because of the amount of cash a company wishes to distribute to its shareholders. In certain continental European countries, companies will conduct rights issues at a certain discount to give retail shareholders an attractive payment in the form of tradable subscription rights. Retail shareholders will view this as a form of distribution (along with dividend pay-

ments) while the company does not expect them to exercise their rights. In Germany subscription rights are tax free both for retail and institutional shareholders and this is a good reason for structuring an issue with a sizeable discount instead of doing a market-price issue. In a market-price issue, the company distributes cash to shareholders only in the form of taxable dividends

The above reasoning should make it clear that economically, ie, before considering certain legal, regulatory, market practice and technical considerations, the size of the discount of a rights issue does not matter. A higher discount does in itself not lead to higher dilution in earnings per share and does not put existing shareholders in a worse position.

Rights issues versus bookbuilt offers

The discount argument is, as illustrated above, generally not a valid reason to decide against a rights issue structure. However, the size of the discount matters, if the company is offering shares to new investors, as in a bookbuilt offer.

Existing shareholders are diluted if shares are sold to new investors at a discount. To sell 10 per cent of a company at a deep discount to new investors is to give away value – contrary to the case of rights issues where existing shareholders give up value only to themselves.

Many institutional shareholders oppose bookbuilt issues as a matter of principle. The logic in their opposition is two-fold: first, they feel that such issues cost too much, as the total discount including fees and marketing expenses is typically higher than the fees in a rights issue. The second part of the logic implied in this opposition to bookbuilt offers is that institutional shareholders would not hold the shares if they did not consider them undervalued. They therefore see the sale of shares to new investors even at a

fine discount as selling shares at a significant discount to the real value.

The other school of thought – that it is in the shareholders' interest to do bookbuilt offers – is represented primarily by the international investment banking community. The logic of this argument is that before the marketing process the market price does reflect the true worth of the company. Let us assume that a company is worth Dm100 per share: if by way of active marketing in connection with a bookbuilt offer, the shares can be driven up to Dm105 per share, then existing shareholders will benefit from anti-dilution. Since investment banks are in the business of marketing shares to new investors, they have to believe that their marketing makes a difference and accordingly that they act in shareholders' best interests. The problem, of course, is that the parties involved rarely agree on the validity of a company's market valuation.

In conclusion, in a bookbuilt issue a company should try to minimise the discount, whereas in a rights issue, the size of discount does not matter. It is probably fair to argue that if a company's shares are clearly undervalued, a rights issue would be more in the interest of existing shareholders than a bookbuilt issue. Equally, if a company is thought to be overvalued, then a sale of shares to new investors has to be in the interests of existing shareholders.

As there are two schools of thought on this subject, it is difficult to say whether one particular structure is better or worse. What is clear is that there are many vested interests in this debate and that arguments are often coloured. Company executives should be familiar with both schools of thought, should understand how particular parties (including different banks promoting different structures and certain shareholders) are biased and should then make up their minds based on the specifics of the situation. The best legal framework is one where companies have the flexibility to choose the most appropriate structure for the particular circumstances.

(See also the Zeneca case study.)

Société Nationale Elf Aquitaine

Circumstances seemed auspicious for the sale of Société Nationale Elf Aquitaine the flagship of French state holdings and the most valuable on the list of companies to be privatised, in early 1994. The privatisation programme launched by prime minister Edouard Balladur in the autumn of 1993 had started well, with the successful sell-offs of Banque Nationale de Paris and chemicals and pharmaceuticals company Rhône-Poulenc. Market conditions were good despite the fact that the US Federal Reserve had begun a tightening programme. In addition investors were looking to buy restructuring plays and high-yielding stocks such as Elf.

However, due to Elf's unique history, this sell-off was particularly sensitive politically. Elf had been created by the French government in the 1940s to produce and distribute natural gas in France. In the 1950s, French engineers were sent to prospect for oil in North and West Africa, a move which paid handsome dividends and laid the foundation for Elf's position as the third largest publicly traded oil and gas company in Europe and the eighth largest in the world at the end of 1993. At the time, 72 per cent of the company's proven crude oil reserves were located in Africa and the French government had come to use Elf as an instrument of foreign policy there. From the formation of Elf's predecessor in the early 1940s, the state had directly or indirectly owned more than 50 per cent. In 1976, when the government merged all its oil and gas assets to create Société Nationale Elf Aquitaine, its stake was as high as 70 per cent. The decision to privatise

the company was therefore a difficult one for President Mitterrand to accept, particularly as he had categorically opposed all privatisation as recently as 1991. He was worried that Elf might be sold too cheaply and be threatened by a foreign takeover.

Although Elf was a familiar name with global investors – the company had been listed on the NYSE since 1991 – the investment community had not been impressed by the company's management and had been concerned about political meddling. Consequently, Elf was a long way behind other international oil companies in its degree of US ownership and it therefore became important both for the company and the Trésor (the French Treasury) to broaden the US investor base. This could only be done if institutional investors became convinced that the new management, under Philippe Jaffré would be in a position to realise the company's considerable restructuring potential. The banks involved in the offer positioned Elf as the next British Petroleum (BP) and claimed that in early 1994, Elf was considered to be where BP had been in September 1992, before its restructuring began to benefit shareholders. Merrill Lynch had picked up on these themes in its presentations to Elf and the treasury and had convincingly demonstrated how it would reposition the company with US investors and how, as a consequence, US ownership would be significantly broadened and deepened. This was one of the reasons that it won the highly contested mandate to act as US lead manager ahead of Goldman Sachs.

Exhibit 1
Transaction summary

Company: Société Nationale Elf Aquitaine (France) (Name changed after offer to Elf Aquitaine)	Global coordinator: Paribas Co-global c-ordinator: Crédit Lyonnais
Pricing date: 2 February 1994 – retail offer 14 February – Institutional offer (CAC–40: 2,243)	Pricing/underwriting structure: Fixed price retail offer and institutional bookbuilding
Vendor: Entreprise de Recherches et d'Activités Pétrolières (ERAP)	Primary or secondary: Secondary
% of company sold in market offer: 24.3%	Privatisation or corporate: Privatisation
	Retail structure: Retail discount and bonus shares
IPO or non-IPO: Non-IPO	Industry: Oil and gas
Type of shares: Ordinary shares and ADRs (1 ADR = 1/2 share)	Offer price: Retail Ffr385 Institutional Ffr403 and US$34.35/ADR
Total size of market offer: US$4,178 million	US listing/144 A: NYSE

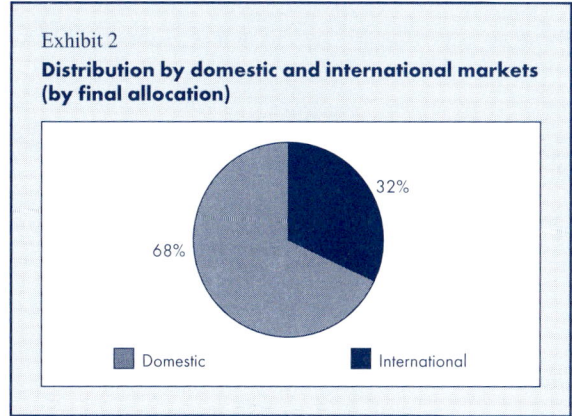

Exhibit 2

Distribution by domestic and international markets (by final allocation)

32%

68%

■ Domestic   ■ International

The offer raised US$4,178 million, at the time the highest-ever paid-up proceeds from a European privatisation. By mid-1997, it remained the third largest secondary privatisation offer behind ENI 2 in 1996 and ENI 3 in 1997. This sale was to be the third and last privatisation under Balladur where the French retail investor still expected to make a quick profit. This expectation was due to the strong performance of earlier sales, where the share price performed strongly in the months after the privatisation. No less than three million people within France subscribed to the issue, the second highest participation by French retail investors after the flotation of Banque Paribas, which attracted 3.8 million individual subscribers in 1986.

The Elf transaction employed several innovations: it combined global underwriting with regional selling syndicates – a sensible refinement of the innovative BT 3 structure. In addition, Paribas claims to have pioneered the concept of assigning specific 'warm-up' responsibilities to syndicate members, in this offer, a practice which is now widely used in most large privatisations. This approach was a response to the need for an unprecedented amount of pre-marketing, which in turn required unparalleled focus and transparency.

The retention by the Trésor of a 13 per cent stake was widely criticised in the market, particularly when combined with a golden share and a group of core shareholders holding 10 per cent of the company. The market therefore applauded the Trésor's sale in November 1996 of the bulk of its remaining 9.85 per cent stake. Approximately 4.6 per cent was sold via a successful US$1 billion bought deal at a price of Ffr417.50 – according to Paribas and SBC Warburg who executed the sale – at this time the largest ever bought deal involving a government vendor. A further 4.5 per cent was

placed with an Elf subsidiary. The history of the French state's disposal of shares in Elf, which began with the partial sale in 1986 – the first company to be partially sold under the Mitterand/Chirac regime of 1986/88, although not formally part of the actual privatisation programme – is as shown in Exhibit 3.

Major challenges

Given that Elf was still an important national asset when the 1994 secondary offer was mooted, the challenge lay in finding a structure that would enable the government to maintain a certain amount of influence while offering corporate governance standards acceptable to institutional investors. After much political debate it was decided that a 'golden share' would be used – the first time in eight years such a structure had been employed in a French privatisation – with the intention of protecting Elf against a foreign takeover. In addition, there would be a residual state ownership (planned at 13 per cent) and core shareholders (the GAS – see Glossary). For the sale to be successful, investor perception that Elf would remain a state company had to be changed.

Under French privatisation law, 10 per cent of the total number of shares sold in the market offer have to be reserved for the employee offer. As Elf was a large offer, the employee offer therefore became a major challenge.

Elf's size also meant that the investment required by the GAS was large (a 2.5 per cent stake in the company was valued at US$500 million). In the absence of any one natural partner for Elf, this made the offer to core shareholders rather tough. Elf also represented a very large offer at a time when most French institutions were fully weighted in Elf shares and the oil price was at a five-year low.

Elf had suffered from uncontrolled growth, perhaps not surprising given that politicians and engineers had been in charge. Gearing had become uncomfortably high, and profits had fallen for three consecutive years – by 82 per cent in 1993. In August that year Philippe Jaffré took charge of the company. Jaffré had no experience in the oil industry nor had he run a publicly quoted company but he had a reputation as a successful cost-cutter. He was a political appointee and a former deputy director of the Trésor.

While the real story was one of restructuring and rationalisation, Jaffré had to tread carefully during the roadshow as he had to cater for two audiences. On the one hand he want-

Exhibit 3

Evolution of the French Government stake in Elf Aquitaine

Date	Events	Government ownership
1976	Creation of Société Nationale Elf Aquitaine through merger	70.0%
1986	ERAP sold shares to employees and public – first Balladur privatisation	55.8%
1991	Capital increase and NYSE listing	53.9%
1992	Public sale of shares by ERAP	51.6%
1994	ERAP sale in global offer	13.0%
1996	The Trésor placed 4.6% with institutional investors and 4.5% with an Elf subsidiary	0.8%

ed to tell international institutions about planned radical restructuring but on the other he had domestic political and trade union considerations to worry about. Some US investors remained sceptical because he was unable to articulate publicly the scope of his restructuring plans.

The oil price was at a five-year low and the sector was not generally considered to be in favour.

Rationale and objectives

This sale represented a core part of the Balladur privatisation programme: both the government and the company had a high degree of motivation for the sale – the government needed the proceeds and Elf wanted to shed its image as a state-owned corporation. However, President Mitterand was anxious to ensure that Elf could not be taken over by a foreign company.

The government's overriding objectives were therefore to maximise proceeds and to successfully privatise Elf while maintaining a certain amount of state influence.

For Elf, to achieve a true privatisation, thereby allowing itself greater flexibility in its decision-making processes was a key consideration. The opportunity to achieve more financial flexibility and to improve the global equity market's perception of the company, especially in the US, following a rapid expansion programme, falling profits and management changes were also important. Elf's objectives in negotiations with the government were:

1. To achieve a stable shareholder base (GAS) of approximately 30 per cent (including the remaining stake held by the government);
2. To be released from legislation relating to state-controlled companies;
3. To structure a golden share to protect the company from a hostile takeover without limiting the flexibility of management to manage the business on a day-to-day basis;

4. To limit the size of the French public offer to 44 per cent of the total 'market offer', so as to ensure healthy institutional allocations (against the 60 per cent suggested by the government);
5. To structure the offer as a partly-paid sale only if absolutely necessary;
6. To ensure that the state make all possible benefits available for the employee offer; and
7. To have the chairman elected by the board of directors rather than appointed by the government.

In addition, Elf wanted to increase the number of US institutional shareholders to 150 (see Feature topic: *Targeting the US investor base*).

Sale proceeds of Ffr36 billion, all for the government, were significant in absolute terms and also in the context of projected budget deficits of Ffr300 billion in 1994 and Ffr275 billion in 1995.

Share capital and ownership

See Exhibits 4 and 5.

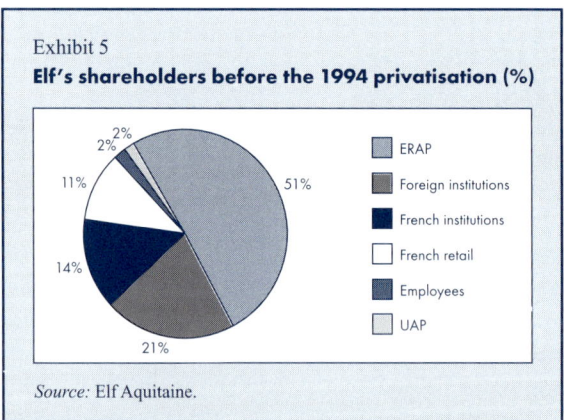

Exhibit 5

Elf's shareholders before the 1994 privatisation (%)

- ERAP — 51%
- Foreign institutions — 21%
- French institutions — 14%
- French retail — 11%
- Employees — 2%
- UAP — 2%

Source: Elf Aquitaine.

Exhibit 4
Share capital and ownership

Type of shares offered	Ordinary shares of Ffr50 and ADRs (1/2 ordinary share per ADR).
Ownership restrictions	Approval of French authorities is required for the acquisition of a controlling interest by any non-European Union party or group of non-EU parties acting in concert.
Share capital before and after offer	257,471,851 ordinary shares, held in either bearer or registered form.
Listings/quotations	Paris (1976) and New York (1991). (SNPA, the predecessor company to Elf, was listed in Paris before the 1976 merger.) Elf today is listed on seven other European stock exchanges.
Market capitalisation at international offer price (Ffr5.866/US$1)	US$17.7 billion.
Number of shareholders before offer	Approximately 300,000.
Free float before offer	49.2%.
Liquidity 38% in Paris (shares traded per market during the 12 months prior to the offer as a percentage of the total number of shares outstanding)	8.3% on NYSE. Seventh most liquid stock on the Paris Stock Exchange (in terms of total turnover) during the six months to pricing and the largest by market capitalisation on 14 February 1994.
Most relevant stock exchange index/weighting	CAC 40/6.9% (31 December 1993).

Transaction components

This offer of 60.4 million secondary shares (the market offer) comprised a French public offer (the OPV) and an offer to institutional shareholders in France and internationally (the international offer). The international offer was divided into five regional selling groups: France, the rest of Europe (RoE), the US, Japan and the rest of the world (RoW). However, to maintain the greatest flexibility in placing stock, banks in the international offer participated in a single global underwriting syndicate regardless of their role in the regional selling syndicates. There was no pre-determined split of shares between geographic areas reflected in the underwriting. (See Exhibit 6.)

After the pre-marketing, the retail offer price was fixed and the OPV and institutional bookbuilding began. The international offer was priced 12 calendar days after the pricing of the OPV. There was a 20 per cent clawback mechanism from the international offer to the OPV which also included a 1:10

bonus share scheme whereby retail investors who held their shares for a minimum period of 18 months received additional shares. The international offer included a 10 per cent greenshoe, calculated on the number of shares after exercise of the clawback. The concept of purchase mandates, pioneered in the BNP privatisation, was also deployed in Elf.

There were 13 underwriters globally each underwriting more than a million shares (1.7 per cent of the total market offer), of which 11 were French banks. The largest foreign underwriter was Merrill Lynch with a 2.6 per cent global underwriting commitment (see Exhibit 7).

In addition to the market offer, there was an employee offer and an offer to core shareholders. There was also an exchange offer whereby holders of ERAP Petroleum Certificates could exchange one certificate and Ffr40 cash for one Elf ordinary share. The certificates were non-voting shares which carried the normal Elf dividend, issued by ERAP as holder of Elf ordinary shares, much like a depositary (see Exhibit 8).

Exhibit 6
Offer structure

Selling syndicates/target markets	Indicated offer sizes	Bookrunner/joint lead	Co-lead managers
French public offer	55.0%	BNP/ Crédit Lyonnais	Crédit Agricole, Rothschild & Cie, CDC, Paribas, Société Générale
International offer	45.0%		
France	n/a	Paribas/Crédit Lyonnais	Indosuez, BNP, CCF, CDC, CNCA/Rothschild, Lazards, Société Générale
Rest of Europe	n/a	Paribas/Crédit Lyonnais	Indosuez, BNP, BZW, CNCA/ Rothschild, Deutsche, JP Morgan, Merrill Lynch, Société Générale, UBS, SG Warburg
Japan	n/a	Daiwa	Paribas, Crédit Lyonnais, Indosuez, Nomura
US	n/a	Merrill Lynch	Paribas, Crédit Lyonnais, Donaldson, Lufkin and Jenrette, Goldman Sachs, Morgan Stanley
Rest of world	n/a	Paribas/Crédit Lyonnais	Indosuez, Daiwa, Merrill Lynch, RBC Dominion, UBS
Total combined offers (shares)	**60,377,236**		

Exhibit 7
Initial global underwriting commitments (pre-clawback) (million shares)

Underwriters	OPV	International offer	Total market offer
Crédit Lyonnais	5.03	3.80	8.83 (14.6%)
Paribas	2.85	5.84	8.69 (14.4%)
BNP	7.21	1.41	8.62 (14.3%)
Crédit Agricole/Rothschild	3.52	0.68	4.20 (7.0%)
CDC	3.02	0.75	3.77 (6.2%)
Société Générale	2.68	0.79	3.47 (5.8%)
Banque Indosuez	1.18	1.41	2.59 (4.3%)
CCF	1.34	0.79	2.13 (3.5%)
CCBP	1.34	0.70	2.04 (3.4%)
CIC/Schroders	1.34	0.49	1.83 (3.0%)
Merrill Lynch	–	1.58	1.58 (2.6%)
UBS	–	1.41	1.41 (2.3%)
Crédit Mutuel	1.34	–	1.34 (2.2%)
Other underwriters	2.36	7.52	9.88 (16.4%)
Total number of shares underwritten	**33.21**	**27.17**	**60.38 (100%)**

Exhibit 8
The market offer and the other components of the Elf privatisation

	Initial size (Shares millions)	*Final size (after clawback and greenshoe) (Shares millions)	Final size (US$ million)	Final size % of Elf share capital
French public offer	33.2	38.6	2,536	15.0%
International offer	27.2	*23.9	1,642	9.3%
Total market offer	**60.4**	**62.5**	**4,178**	**24.3%**
Employee offer	6.7	6.9	365	2.7%
Offer to core shareholders	22.0	22.0	1542	8.5%
Exchange offer for petroleum certificates	5.8	5.8	**39	2.3%
Total offer	**94.9**	**97.2**	**6,124**	**37.8%**

* The international offer was reduced by the full amount of the clawback (5,433,959 shares) and increased by the full number of shares available under the greenshoe (2,173,584).
** Considering the cash proceeds of the exchange offer only.

Exhibit 9
Principal advisers

Financial adviser to the Republic of France	Crédit Lyonnais
Financial advisers to Elf	BNP and Paribas
US legal adviser to Elf and ERAP	Sullivan & Cromwell
French legal adviser to Elf	Internal Counsel
US legal adviser to international underwriters	Davis Polk & Wardwell
French legal adviser to the underwriters	Linklaters & Paines
Auditors	Ernst & Young

Market conditions

Stock markets were strong in November/December 1993 when the decision to proceed was taken and remained so until after the pricing of the issue, although the first in a series of interest rate increases by the US Federal Reserve Board during 1994 had taken place only a few days before pricing. At this stage, the equity market had not yet realised that this first increase was part of a major tightening programme which would continue over several months and lead to the deterioration of the global equity new-issue market during the remainder of 1994.

Despite the secondary market remaining static at around 2,200 on the CAC–40 index because of high short-term interest rates, the new-issue market in France was exceptionally strong with many issues coming to market. In addition to the privatisations of BNP in October and Rhône-Poulenc in November, several French issuers had come to market with offers of over US$200 million during the four months prior to the Elf offer: Lafarge Coppée, the cement company; Schneider, the electrical and electronics company; UAF, the insurance spin-off from Crédit Lyonnais; Saint-Gobain, the glassmaker and Générale des Eaux, the water company.

The oil-company sector was not considered to be in favour with investors although some houses, including Merrill Lynch, were bullish. At the time, Merrill Lynch was recommending oil and gas, cyclicals, and companies with restructuring potential and high dividend yields. Elf was rated A217 by Merrill

Lynch, indicating that it was both a short- and long-term buy, and that the dividend yield was on the increase.

Principal advisers

See Exhibit 9.

Transaction fee distribution

The institutional fee structure was as shown in Exhibit 11.

Underwriting commission

Underwriting fees were paid on global underwriting commitments, based on the OPV price and the institutional price respectively depending on the capacity in which a particular bank participated in the offer.

Management fee

Of the total management fee, half was paid out as a praecipium to the global coordinators and the lead and co-lead managers. The remainder of the management fee was paid on the basis of underwriting commitments (see Exhibit 12).

Selling concession

In the US the selling concession had one fixed and one variable component. The fixed portion was split equally among the top six selling syndicate members. The variable portion was paid to the respective syndicate banks based on investor designations (see Exhibit 13).

Exhibit 10
The timetable

21 July 1993	• Decree announces that Elf is to be privatised.
15 September	• The Trésor invites banks to bid for the role of government adviser.
11 October	• Paribas and BNP appointed advisers to Elf.
22 October	• Crédit Lyonnals appointed advisor to the Trésor.
December 1993	• Decision taken to proceed.
8 January 1994	• Application period to become core shareholder begins.
18 January 1994	• Elf announces preliminary results for 1993.
19 January	• Offer launched and global syndicate members invited; and • Filing with the SEC.
20 January	• Publication of preliminary prospectus and Red Herring; • Institutional pre-marketing (warm-ups) begin. From this date, institutions are invited to give indicative expressions of interest; • French roadshow begins; and • Purchase mandate period begins.
Mon 24 January	• European roadshow begins.
27 January	• US roadshow begins.
28 January	• Warm-up meetings end.
Mon 31 January	• Close of application period to become core shareholder.
1 February	• Purchase mandate period ends.
2 February	• Privatisation Commission sets minimum institutional offer price of Ffr377; • Composition of core shareholder group announced; • OPV price of Ffr385 announced; • Underwriting agreements signed; and • US roadshow ends.
3 February	• OPV, employee offer and institutional bookbuilding begin.
4 February	• Roadshow ends with further one-on-ones in Europe.
10 February	• OPV ends.
11 February	• Institutional bookbuilding ends.
Mon 14 February	• Clawback exercised; • Employee offer ends; • Institutional offer price set at Ffr403 following New York close; and • SEC registration statement declared effective.
15 February	• Allocation to investors; and • Trading of offered shares begin.
22 February	• Closing.
10 March	• Greenshoe exercised in full.

Exhibit 11
Distribution of gross spread (%)

Management	Underwriting	Selling concession	Gross spread	*Discount	**Total effective cost
0.60	0.60	1.80	***3.00	2.9	5.9

* This represented the discount for the international offer only. The Ffr385 retail offer price, set on 2 February, represented a discount of 9.1% to the Ffr424 market closing price on that day.
** In addition, the company and the Trésor paid financial advisory fees creditable against the gross spread.
*** The gross spread for the retail offer was also 3% although the split was different. The underwriting commissions were 1.7%, selling concession 1% and the management fee 0.3%.

In Europe the selling concession was paid in full to whomever received the order.

Co-lead managers received on average US$520,000 in management and underwriting fees, which can be seen in part as compensation for the commitment of their analysts to the transaction.

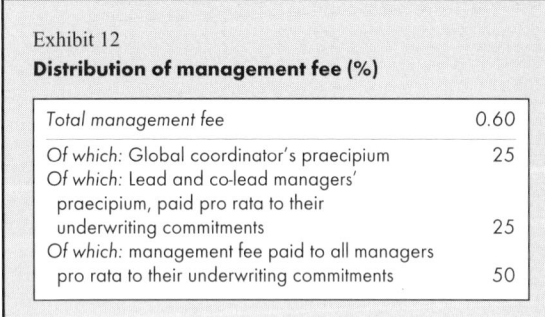

Exhibit 12

Distribution of management fee (%)

Total management fee	0.60
Of which: Global coordinator's praecipium	25
Of which: Lead and co-lead managers' praecipium, paid pro rata to their underwriting commitments	25
Of which: management fee paid to all managers pro rata to their underwriting commitments	50

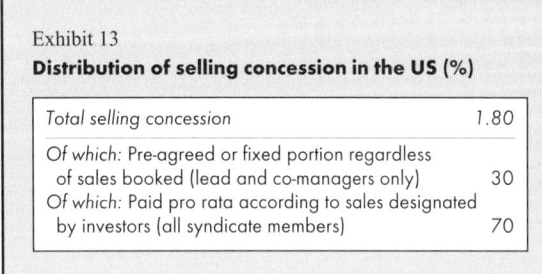

Exhibit 13

Distribution of selling concession in the US (%)

Total selling concession	1.80
Of which: Pre-agreed or fixed portion regardless of sales booked (lead and co-managers only)	30
Of which: Paid pro rata according to sales designated by investors (all syndicate members)	70

Deal structure

Pricing and underwriting

Unlike the privatisation of BNP which was a fixed price offer for both retail and institutional investors, both Rhône-Poulenc and Elf were structured with a six-day fixed price retail offer (the OPV) and an open-price bookbuilding for institutional investors.

Before the 3 February start of the OPV, there was a nine-day purchase-mandate period in which retail investors could give firm orders to buy shares which could be withdrawn before the end of the OPV period. Investors giving purchase mandates were afforded priority in the allocation process. Informal institutional bookbuilding had begun on 20 January in tandem with the pre-marketing and roadshow so that by the time of the OPV pricing on 2 February the advisers and the lead managers would have a good idea of the quality of the institutional book.

The OPV and the international offer were underwritten separately. The OPV was underwritten on 2 February, its pricing date, at the offer price of Ffr385, representing a 9.2 per cent discount to the market price on that day. The international offer was initially underwritten from 2 February at the minimum offer price of Ffr377, representing an 11 per cent discount on that day. Following the institutional pricing on 14 February, the international offer was underwritten until closing at the offer price of Ffr403, equivalent to a 2.9 per cent discount to the market price on 14 February. These underwriting arrangements meant that from 2 February, the French state was guaranteed a minimum amount of proceeds, whilst it maintained the full upside on the institutional portion of the market offer until 14 February.

Offer structure and syndicate

There were no 'management amounts', ie, the five regional tranches of the international offer were not sized, nor did individual selling group members have an underwriting commitment related to their particular selling syndicate. Instead individual banks had global underwriting commitments. Although most banks, particularly in the US, prefer to have an indication of the amount of stock they are expected to sell, the absence of such indicated amounts did not have any real effect on the transaction. On the other hand, some embarrassment was avoided as the demand generated in a particular tranche or by a particular bank was not measured against an underwritten (or expected) amount per tranche and per bank. No individual tranches of the international offer were therefore over or undersubscribed. All banks, however, knew what their global underwriting commitments were.

'Contrary to the BT 3 structure where all but Warburgs were somewhat disincentivised, in the case of Elf, the Trésor and Paribas were able to motivate all the regional leads,' explained Michel Fleuriet, president of Merrill Lynch France. He continued: 'The BT 3 structure was the first attempt at devising a truly global structure, however we felt that it needed to be adjusted for Elf's purposes in order to achieve broad global placement.'

Françoise Leroy, head of capital markets and financing at Elf, put it differently: 'There were a lot of good ideas behind the BT 3 structure but it was a rough structure. We wanted to design a mature product – call it a refinement of BT 3. We were grateful not to be the first company to attempt a global structure as we were able to learn from BT 3.'

Remy Caillaux, director and head of French investment banking at Paribas, the only French bank among the 11 global managers in BT 3, explained: 'We carefully analysed the criticism of the BT 3 structure and then tried to design the offer structure and syndicate to take advantage of the strengths of BT 3 whilst addressing the disadvantages.' Exhibit 14 shows the results of this analysis.

In the Elf offer, allotments to banks were not determined by their underwriting commitments. Syndicate members who performed badly received nothing while others received as much as 7.5 times their original global underwriting commitment. This offer was based on actual demand rather than informed guesswork.

Structure of the employee offer

Given the size of this transaction, US$418 million had to be raised from Elf employees. This required protracted negotiations with the government on terms and conditions, Elf being eager to procure the best possible terms for its employees. It also required a tremendous communication effort internally, as many of the 90,000 employees world-wide required a one-on-one explanation of the merits of each of the four purchase options (the employee options), representing different combinations of purchase price, payment terms and restrictions on share resales. In addition to the finance and communications departments, the personnel department was involved as administrator of the scheme. An external company was engaged to administer the actual employee offer. There was also the issue of who would be eligible to subscribe. The four employee options represent-

Exhibit 14

Analysis of the BT3 structure and implications for the Elf offer

BT 3 Critique	Implication for Elf
SG Warburg was appointed financial adviser, global co-ordinator and lead UK broker	SG Warburg was seen as getting too big a slice of the power and economics of the transaction, in that it was in charge of both retail and institutional offers in addition to its role as adviser to the UK Treasury. This criticism is, however, only partly fair, because SG Warburg actually did take a much smaller slice of the total economics than generally believed. Of the 11 global managers, five were UK houses. For the Elf transaction , a more balanced role split was devised: • Crédit Lyonnais was adviser to the Trésor and joint lead of the OPV and the French, RoE and RoW tranches of the international offer; • Paribas was adviser to Elf, global coordinator and joint lead and bookrunner of the French, RoE and RoW tranches; • BNP was in charge of the OPV; and • Merrill Lynch was the lead manager of the US tranche.
Tiering of managers – 11 'global managers' + members of four regional syndicates	The BT 3 structure was offensive to those banks not among the 11 global managers as they felt that they had been relegated to the second division. As a result, several banks invited only below the level of global manager declined to participate. In BT 3, very few of the regional syndicate banks were included in more than one regional syndicate. In the Elf international offer, there were: • Five regional ring-fenced selling syndicates with nine banks participating as lead or co-lead in more than one syndicate. Six of the banks were French, one US, one Swiss and one Japanese at the co-lead or higher level; • Of the nine, five participated in only two regional selling syndicates. Only Paribas and Crédit Lyonnais participated in all regions. Although it can be argued that at a senior level this syndicate was more French-dominated than BT 3 was UK-dominated, it was certainly a more subtle structure; and • Overall, half the syndicate members participated in more than one region.
Global exempt list	A list of the top 500 institutions around the world, as determined by the UK Treasury and SG Warburg, could be contacted only by the 11 global managers, the effect being that several local and regional banks were not allowed to talk to their best investment clients. Many of the investment institutions who did not make it on to the exempt list were insulted by this tiering. In Elf, there was no exempt list.
Competition among global managers not maximised to pre-marketing restrictions	In BT 3, pre-marketing was organised on a regional basis, which substantially restricted many of the global managers from global placement. This led to demotivation and frustration even among the global managers. Tony Alt, head of international business at Rothschild and a long-standing adviser to BT noted: 'The BT 3 transaction was the only truly non-global global deal I have seen.' Merrill Lynch's Michel Fleuriet explained: 'Although we were one of the global managers, we felt like a co-manager in BT 3. To really perform, you almost need to feel that your reputation is at stake.' In Elf: Syndicate members in all five regions had 'warm-up' responsibilities. Paribas designed a plan whereby each equity research analyst was responsible for pre-marketing to 40 investment institutions wherever these were located. The regional ring-fencing with cross-participation provided focused marketing and the opportunity to capitalise on the individual strengths of many banks to place shares outside their home markets. There was carefully organised but competitive pre-marketing and thereafter open competition within regions. By contrast, in BT 3 the pre-marketing and marketing were organised rigidly, reducing the level of competition between the banks.
Rigid market-monitoring	To prevent the BT share price from falling during the marketing period, the UK Treasury and SG Warburg tried to prevent institutional investors from selling short. This included requesting from the London Stock Exchange that they report to the vendor those institutions which did sell short. Further, shortsellers were penalised in the allocation process. This approach was widely criticised by institutional investors. In Elf, a more subtle approach was adopted to shortselling. The emphasis was on convincing institutions that they would have to buy back more expensively to cover any short sales and that they would be less well treated in the allocation process.

ed different combinations of one or more of the following preferential terms:

1. A 20 per cent discount to the retail offer price, subject to a minimum holding period;
2. Free shares (subject to a maximum number) based on the total number of shares purchased by an employee and held for a specified minimum period;
3. Delayed payment terms;
4. The possibility to borrow money through the company (the loan was provided by Crédit Commercial de France); and
5. A hedging scheme whereby employees were protected on the downside against receiving reduced dividends and on the upside through less participation (this was

arranged through a derivative structure designed by Elf and Bankers Trust).

According to one well-placed source, a few, if not all, the employee offers of French privatisations have cost the government almost as much in incentives as it has received in proceeds. In the case of Elf, when all costs were taken into account (including such items as discounts and future delivery of bonus shares) the employee offer was extremely expensive for the government. The total cost of the deal, translated to a total discount is thought to have been approximately 40 per cent: this is the price for the political goal of achieving employee participation, ie, trying to turn employees into capitalists.

The golden share

The challenge with the golden share lay in finding a balance between continued state influence and shareholder influence. The final structure had to be politically acceptable given Elf's importance as a strategic national asset. From the government's perspective, the purpose was purely and simply to make Elf sufficiently takeover proof. At the same time, it had to be acceptable to international institutional investors concerned about state influence and poor corporate governance standards in France. The following provisions were agreed after negotiations involving President Mitterrand:

- Approval from the French economy minister before any shareholder can cross the ownership thresholds of 10 per cent, 20 per cent and 33 per cent;
- Appointment of two state representatives without voting rights to attend board meetings;
- Possibility of the state to veto the sale of majority ownership of the capital of four specified subsidiaries of the group involved in upstream and downstream oil and gas activities; and
- The 1993 Privatisation Act had abolished the five-year maturity of the golden-share language of earlier privatisation legislation. The Elf golden share therefore had no maturity.

It was felt that this solution did not significantly limit Elf's flexibility to manage its core business and to restructure the group in the best interests of shareholders.

How effective the golden share will be is uncertain as it is unclear how the thresholds can be enforced, how much power is held by the two state representatives, and, given that Elf can sell the underlying assets of the subsidiaries, what this provision actually means. The good point about this structure, from Elf's point of view, is that it will deter hostile parties while providing management and board with ample flexibility. It was sensible not to introduce a maturity as heavy speculation often occurs around that time. 'Rather surprisingly, we did not get a lot of questions on the golden share on the roadshow,' remarked Remy Caillaux of Paribas.

Core shareholders

The task of arranging the core shareholders (GAS) involved

determining who had the money, who had good relationships with Elf and, especially, who chairman Philippe Jaffré knew. Having been at Crédit Agricole for many years and having previously served as deputy director of the treasury, Jaffré was naturally able to count on a significant number of business friends. Brigitte Molkhou, chef du bureau at the Trésor explained: 'Jaffré knew all the right people.' Given Elf's size, it was nevertheless still going to be a challenge to put together a group of core shareholders prepared to buy 10 per cent of the company. In the event, Union des Assurances de Paris raised its existing 1.5 per cent stake to 2.9 per cent and Elf and the Trésor were able to bring in eight other core shareholders to satisfy the 10 per cent requirement. These investors paid 102 per cent of the institutional offer price, ie, Ffr411.

Marketing

The most notable feature of the marketing strategy for the Elf offer was the approach to pre-marketing. 'The warm-up programme was the foundation for a highly successful marketing campaign,' commented Tony Bourne, head of global equity capital markets at Paribas. 'It was essential to make the syndicate banks partners in this process. Hence the high degree of consultation in drawing up warm-up lists, a procedure which has since become the industry standard.'

Pre-marketing

Paribas convinced the Trésor of the importance of pre-marketing. Before the Elf offer, the Trésor had been against comprehensive pre-marketing due to the notion that the share price falls during marketing. The perceived wisdom had been that the shorter the total marketing period, the shorter the period of exposure to market risk and therefore the higher the offer price.

Although there were no exempt lists, Paribas set out to strike a balance between a sufficient level of organisation of the warm-up programme and a healthy degree of competition among all syndicate members to solicit orders from institutional clients within a given region. The global coordinator had identified 450 'warm-up clients', based on: size of non-domestic European equity holdings, holdings in other European oil companies, investment behaviour in other European privatisations and their long-term investment horizon. These institutions were to be guaranteed comprehensive coverage in the warm-ups. The global coordinator, lead managers and co-lead managers conducted a total of 621 warm-ups world-wide, ie, an average of 1.38 warm-up meetings for each priority account. Twenty banks organised, on average, 31 warm-up meetings each during the pre-marketing (see Exhibit 15).

The roadshow

While 450 priority accounts were warmed up, 150 'leadership investors' were singled out for one-on-one meetings. The Elf roadshow was conducted by three dedicated management teams and Elf representatives were thoroughly briefed on the institutions to be visited in the one-on-ones, including information on their holdings of Elf shares, recent activity in Elf

Exhibit 15
Warm-up philosophy

- Warm-up responsibilities for lead and co-lead managers' analysts in the five regional selling syndicates were carefully planned and specifically assigned by Paribas. The specific institutional investors that the analysts of each lead and co-lead manager were to warm up were selected by Paribas to reflect lead and co-lead managers' own preferences, the reputation of the individual analysts, the placing power of the respective banks in a particular geographic region and logistical criteria, including the need to ensure a minimum coverage of each of the 450 target clients. On average, the 450 key investors were each offered two analyst warm-up meetings;
- Some institutional investors had only one syndicate bank formally responsible for a warm-up; larger institutions had several. Syndicate banks did not know who else, if anyone, was responsible for warming up a particular institution. This was intended to increase competition. To avoid demotivation of junior members, all syndicate members were allowed to warm up non-designated institutions because they had access to all investors in their selling region;
- Paribas as global coordinator collated investor feedback from written reports on all warm-ups. Institutions were asked to fill in questionnaires stating client name, fund manager/ buying fund, current holdings of Elf Aquitaine, recent activity in the stock, appetite to buy, potential order size, reasons for any lack of appetite, price-sensitivity and any required follow-up. This investor feed-back allowed for patterns of investor response to be identified and, if necessary, addressed by further/revised marketing. Subsequently, orders taken were compared with responses to the warm-ups to assess the quality of the order; and
- Paribas managed to satisfy 96% of co-lead managers' requests for clients they wanted to warm-up. A high 'satisfaction rate' was crucial to motivate co-leads to carry out their warm-up responsibilities enthusiastically. On average, 69% of the 450 clients who were offered warm-ups accepted and 55% of those warmed up placed an order larger than 100,000 shares (US$7 million).

Exhibit 16
Roadshow 'hit-ratio'

	Number of events	Number of investors	Demand generated
One-on-one meetings			
France	56	56	US$3.1 billion
Rest of Europe	29	29	US$1.4 billion
United States	*46	*46	US$1.6 billion
Rest of world	19	19	US$0.5 billion
Total	150	150	US$6.6 billion
Public presentations			
Europe (including France)	9	429	US$6.8 billion
United States	9	106	US 1.5 billion
Rest of world	5	94	US$0.8 billion
Total	23	629	US$9.1 billion

* Of which 39 were potential new investors.

shares and the holdings of comparable companies. In total, the US$15.9 billion of institutional demand was generated from investors participating in the roadshow (see Exhibit 16).

Retail marketing

Success with retail investors depends to a large extent on name recognition, the quality of the advertising campaign, whether or not investors made money on earlier privatisations and the amount and nature of retail incentives. All these factors worked in favour of the Elf offer, including the retail incentives which were generous:

- A 9.1 per cent discount to the market price prevailing at the time of pricing of the retail offer; and
- A bonus share scheme whereby holders receive one new share for every 10 held for a period of at least 18 months.

In addition, holders of Balladur bonds were able to pay by converting them into Elf shares and in so doing received preferential allocation. Retail investors were further encouraged by the fact that the offer structure included a 20 per cent clawback mechanism. Those who ordered during the

mandate period were also given preferential allocation treatment.

There was no marketing to US retail investors. US retail brokers need to know some two weeks ahead of pricing that they will receive stock but the French government, like others, was not prepared to make such a pre-allocation commitment.

The Elf story

Elf, it was said, would benefit from a turnaround in European economies, and from aggressive cost-cutting and divestiture of non-core assets. It was just beginning a major rationalisation programme, typically a good time to buy if management enjoys credibility with investors. Elf was therefore primarily positioned as a 'restructuring story' with its principal pillars as shown in Exhibit 17.

In the US market, Merrill Lynch tried to reposition Elf as a global integrated oil company and a true international oil major which compares favourably with BP, Chevron, Mobil and Texaco, rather than as a French oil company. Elf's increased focus on profitability was to improve results in the long term. Exhibit 18 shows the important factors in the sale of Elf.

Exhibit 17
Elf's restructuring objectives

Disposals	• Disposal of a major part of the company's financial assets, amounting in total to Ffr10.8 billion; • Divestiture of non-core operating assets to the extent of Ffr5 billion per annum; • Refocus on specialty chemicals; and • Merrill Lynch expected that assets worth up to Ffr20 billion could be disposed of over a two-year period.
Cost reduction	• A significant reduction in the cost base of each division. Merrill Lynch was projecting 15–20% staff cuts over two to three years.
Debt reduction	• Debt was to be stabilised by end-1994 and reduced thereafter.
Cash flow	• Elf was to generate free cash flow by 1996.
Profitability	• Jaffré articulated that Elf should achieve a return on equity of 10–12% by 1996.
Dividend growth	• Dividend growth was to be resumed as early as possible.

Sources: Merrill Lynch and Paribas.

Exhibit 18
Principal sales points

Market position	Of Elf's total net assets, 43.5% were in France, 30.5% in the Rest of Europe, 11.5% in the US and 14.5% in Africa and the Rest of the World. Elf was: • The world's eighth largest quoted international oil and gas company; and • The seventh largest refiner in Europe and the largest refiner in France.
Reserve life	• Higher than most international oil majors (12 years against 11 years for a broadly based composite of major oil companies*).
Production profile	• Elf was the only major international oil company with a rapidly growing production profile.
Production cost	• Well below the average (US$4.03 against US$5.13 for composite). In addition, due to planned staff-cuts, Elf was perceived as having a growing ability to compete in a low-oil-price environment.
Reserve replacement	• Significantly higher than most comparable international majors (149% against 102% for composite).
Management	• The change of chairman was communicated as a clear sign of a switch in strategy and a serious effort to increase earnings in a low-oil-price environment. Privatisation could provide a greater opportunity to tackle the cost base in the way enjoyed by most other large oil companies. Elf's new management was committed to improving shareholder returns.
Valuation	• The principal valuation drivers were the price/cash flow ratios for 1994 and 1995. On all measures other than earnings, Elf traded at a discount of 20–45% against its peer group. At 4.7%, Elf's dividend yield was high compared to its competitors.

* Composite comprised BP, Chevron, Mobil, Texaco, Royal Dutch/Shell, Exxon and Amoco.

Sources: Merrill Lynch and Paribas.

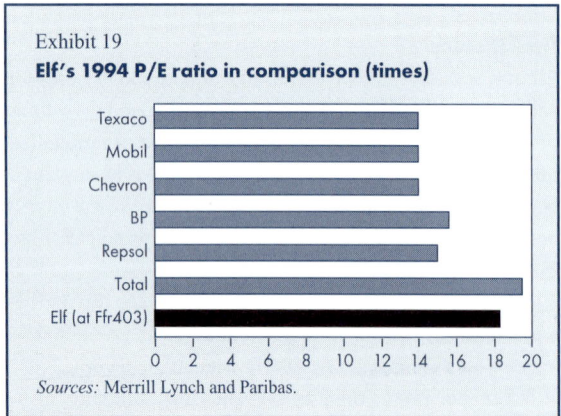

Exhibit 19
Elf's 1994 P/E ratio in comparison (times)

Sources: Merrill Lynch and Paribas.

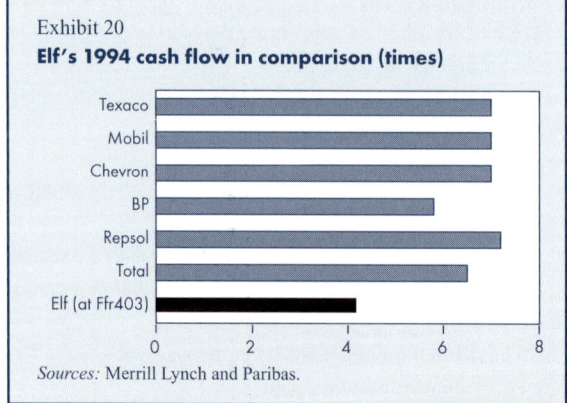

Exhibit 20
Elf's 1994 cash flow in comparison (times)

Sources: Merrill Lynch and Paribas.

Elf looked relatively expensive on the basis of 1994 earnings as the benefits of the restructuring programme were not yet visible (see Exhibit 19). On a cash-flow basis, however, Elf looked more attractively valued than its peers (see Exhibit 20.)

Reasons for not buying

There were three reasons in particular given by those investors who declined to participate in the international offer:

- Certain investors did not trust Jaffré's cost-cutting promises. There were also those who did not believe they went far enough;
- There was a feeling among some investors that the French state would not relinquish its influence over Elf; and
- Many investors were already fully weighted in Elf due to the fact that it had a substantial free float and was already included to the extent of 100 per cent of its capital in the CAC–40.

Results

Core shareholders

After the offer to stable shareholders and the increase of UAP's stake to 2.9 per cent from 1.5 per cent, nine long-term shareholders came to own just over 10 per cent of Elf (see Exhibit 21).

Market offer

The total market offer was almost six times subscribed. The international offer was particularly well received (see Exhibit 22).

The Elf OPV was three times subscribed. Following successful privatisations for BNP and Rhône-Poulenc, with 3.1 million, Elf set a record for the number of participating retail investors. Approximately 7 per cent of the retail offer was paid for by the Balladur bonds. Individuals were allocated a maximum of 13 shares each, with 12 additional shares for holders of Balladur bonds. The clawback was exercised to the full extent of 20 per cent, increasing the size of the OPV by 5,433,959 shares.

The number of Elf retail investors compares favourably with the US$11.3 billion Deutsche Telekom issue in 1996 where two million Germans subscribed, and the 1997 US$4.4 billion issue for Telefónica de Espana where 1.4 million Spaniards subscribed. With the exception of the 1986 Paribas privatisation (with 3.8 million subscribers) only British Gas and the Regional Electricity Companies privatisations in the UK attracted a higher number of retail investors – 4.6 million and 12.8 million respectively.

The international offer was almost 10 times subscribed, when seen in relation to the initial size, ie, before the exercise of the clawback. Demand was particularly strong in the RoE tranche, which included the UK institutional market. The further away from France, the less price-sensitive the institutions were, with US investors being the least price-sensitive. Ultimately, some 71 per cent of the international offer was allocated to European investors, with 27 per cent going to French institutions. As with BNP and Rhône-Poulenc, there was disappointment among international institutional investors, not least because such a high proportion of the offer had been allocated to retail investors. Allocations were agreed jointly by the Trésor, Paribas and Elf. The international offer was increased by the full exercise of the 10 per cent greenshoe.

Employee offer

In addition to the three million retail investors, 63,720 Elf employees (68 per cent of total group staff) applied for 12 million shares against the 6.7 million shares available in the employee offer.

Investor concentration

Paribas recorded 6,150 orders in the global book of which it recognised 4,500 as valid. In terms of number of institutions the situation naturally is a little different, as many institutions put in multiple orders through different offices (see Exhibit 23).

Exhibit 21

Core shareholders

UAP	2.90%
BNP	1.40%
Suez	1.40%
Renault	0.97%
AXA	0.96%
Paribas	0.96%
Crédit Agricole	0.49%
Albert Frères	0.49%
UBS	0.49%
Total	**10.06%**

Exhibit 22

Underwriting, demand and allocation

Target markets	Underwriting	Demand	Allocation*
French Public offer	55.0%	27.1%	61.2%
International offer			
France	N/A	18.6%	10.3%
Rest of Europe	N/A	32.3%	17.2%
Rest of World	N/A	6.1%	2.0%
Japan	N/A	1.2%	0.6%
US	N/A	14.7%	8.7%
Total international offer	45.0%	72.9%	38.8%
Total combined offers			
(shares)	**60.4 million**	**357.6 million**	**63.1 million**

* Including the greenshoe and a naked short.

Source: Paribas.

Exhibit 23

Investor concentration

	By demand	By allocation
% of international offer accounted for by the 10 largest buyers (by total size of demand and allocation respectively)	10.7%	8.7%
Number of buyers making up 80% of the international offer (by total size of demand and allocation respectively)	534	360
The three largest investors by size	US$408 million US$290 million US$239 million	N/A N/A N/A
Total number of institutional buyers	2,641	1,858

Buyers by type

In Europe and the US both country and sector buyers bought the issue:

- In the US, Elf was purchased primarily by international accounts running French and European funds but there was also considerable buying from US domestic oil and gas investors;
- In Europe buying followed primarily traditional continental European patterns in which portfolios are organised along country lines, however sector considerations are taken into account if and when money is available to invest in a given country;
- In France, there was considerable activity from 'momentum buyers' who felt that Elf was going to benefit from being freed from public control; and
- Index buyers, particularly in France, were fully weighted in Elf and consequently were not significant buyers. In the US, index considerations were not a significant source of demand either.

Share price performance

See Exhibit 24.

Before pricing

- In anticipation of the international offer being priced at a discount (the offer price was expected to be Ffr400) and on the assumption that it would be possible to subscribe for shares in the international offer or buy them in the after-market at a lower price, many institutions sold in advance of the offer, thereby depressing the price from the fourth-quarter 1993 high point of Ffr469; and
- During the six months to pricing, Elf therefore underperformed the French stock market by approximately 11 per cent.

After pricing

- On 15 February the share price opened at Ffr411 on the Paris Bourse and then declined in European trading before rebounding when the NYSE opened on strong US institutional after-market purchases. The ADRs closed at US$36.75 equivalent to around Ffr432 per share, up 5 per cent compared to the Paris Bourse low on the first day of trading;
- The Elf share price broke through the Ffr403 internation-

Exhibit 24

Share price performance

Pricing date (institutional)	14 February 1994
Institutional offer price	Ffr403
Retail offer price	Ffr385
Last trade on pricing date	Ffr415
Relative index position on pricing date	88.8%
Historic 52-week high/low	
High (22 October 1993)	Ffr469
Low (16 February 1993)	Ffr347

Elf share price relative to CAC-40 (%)

Price performance

Before pricing		
	Price (Ffr)	Relative to CAC-40 (%)
- 6 months	44.5	100
- 3 months	435	99.2
- 1 month	408	86.3
- 1 week	420	87.9
- 3 days	431	89.6
- 1 day	417	87.8
After pricing		
	Price (Ffr)	Relative to CAC-40 (%)
+ 1 day	424	90.2
+ 3 days	420	88.1
+ 1 week	415	90.1
+ 1 month	413	89.7
+ 3 months	427	94.1
+ 6 months	411	99.0

Sources: Datastream and offer circular.

al offer price on 22 August 1994 and the retail offer price on 28 September 1994. The 1994 low was set on 21 October at Ffr359; and

- Over the first three months of trading Elf outperformed a weak CAC–40 by 5.3 per cent. During the first six months it outperformed the same index by approximately 10.2 per cent.

One year after pricing, Elf's shares had fallen by 4.2 per cent from the international offer price, however at that stage Elf had performed exactly in line with the French market. Patient investors were not rewarded until 1996–97. By 21 August 1997, Elf had traded up to Ffr723, an increase of 79.4 per cent compared to the international offer price, representing an out-performance against the CAC–40 of more than 47 per cent.

After-market trading volume

In the after-market, large buy and sell orders came from the US as reflected in the comparatively high trading volumes on the NYSE compared to the Paris market (see Exhibit 25).

Nine months after the offer French retail had sold approximately 6 per cent of the company, which had been bought by foreign institutions. Of these net foreign institutional purchases, US institutions are thought to have accounted for well over 50 per cent (see Exhibit 26).

Following considerable foreign buying, fuelled by encouraging interim results announced in September 1996 and the realisation, in connection with the reduction of the Trésor's stake in Elf to 0.75 per cent on 12 November, that the gov-

ernment is at last letting go of Elf, some 43 per cent of the company's shares are thought to have been in foreign hands. This is unusually high for a large French company.

The performance of the main parties

The vendor

The Trésor involved Elf in several important decisions in a manner unusual for most privatisation ministries. Elf representatives participated in a meaningful way in decisions involving details of the offer structure, syndicate appointments, retail/institutional split, terms of the employee offer, core shareholders and institutional allocation and was full of praise for the Trésor.

The Trésor and its bankers improved on the BT 3 global offer structure which – although in many ways respected for what it tried to achieve – had been widely criticised by most market participants. Elf's structure, in contrast, received widespread approval. Global underwriting with regional selling syndicates has been adopted in every subsequent French privatisation as well as several non-French transactions, including transactions for Lufthansa and Adidas. One reason that this structure works well in France is that it gives the impression that the French banks have more influence than they actually do. Whereas it appears that the French banks are in charge of the offers, any bank which does a good selling job can take a substantial part of the overall economics of the transaction. If regional tranches had been sized, less would have been allocated to international institutions than is now the case through a truly global structure.

The company

Although some investors were concerned that the company did not spell out its restructuring plans sufficiently clearly, it did as well as expected on the roadshow. There was a considerable amount of straight talk about future cost cuts, particularly in the one-on-ones, and the management appeared to be sincere about its restructuring plans. However, the pace of restructuring was initially slower than expected. Interim results for the six months

---

Exhibit 25

Percentage of total offer traded * (%)

	Day 1 (15/2)	Day 2 (16/2)	Day 3 (17/2)	Total Day 1–3
Paris	4.6	3.1	2.3	10.0
New York	3.7	1.1	1.4	6.2

* Based on the issue of 62.5 million ordinary shares in the market offer.

Exhibit 26

Development of Elf ownership

	Pre-privatisation (31 January 1992)	Post-privatisation (March 1994)	*31 December 1994
ERAP	50.8	13	13
Foreign institutions	20.8	27.5	**34
French institutions	12.8	16.5	***17
French retail	10.8	28	22
Core shareholders	3.2	10	10
Employees	1.6	5	4
Total	100	100	100

* Between the end of 1994 and the end of 1995, ERAP reduced its holding to 10% from 13%, French retail holdings increased to 24% from 22%, and those of foreign institutions rose to 35% from 34%.
** Of which approx. 13% were owned by UK institutions and 11% by US institutions.
*** Including shares held in treasury.

Source: Elf.

Exhibit 27
Profit forecast compared to actual profitability

	1993	1994	1995
US GAAP *(Ffr billions)			
Recurring net profit (Paribas forecast, February 1994)	3,618 F	3,522 F	4,897 F
Recurring net profit (Paribas forecast, September 1994)	3,073 A	3,498 F	5,405 F
Recurring net profit (Paribas forecast October 1995)	3,073 A	3,300 A	5,535 F
Recurring net profit – actual profit performance	3,073 A	3,300 A	5,300 A
Exceptional items	(2,003) A	(8,739) A	(300) A
Stated net income	1,070 A	(5,439) A	5,000 A

* Elf produces its accounts solely under US GAAP.

Source: Paribas.

to June 1994 – the first reporting occasion after the offer – were below expectations and the shares traded down by 7.5 per cent during the three weeks following the announcement.

Elf did more restructuring than it had promised for the full-year 1994: more assets were sold (net sales of Ffr6 billion versus Ffr5 billion expected) and more debt was retired (net debt reduced by Ffr8 billion against an objective merely to stabilise it by the end of 1994). In addition, Elf achieved a positive free cash flow in 1994, two years earlier than planned. The 1994 net profits before restructuring charges were Ffr3.3 billion compared to Ffr3.1 billion in 1993, the first increase since 1990. This figure was more than Ffr200 million below the forecast at the time of the offer. However, Elf's board made a brave decision to take a Ffr8.7 billion non-recurring restructuring charge in 1994, which, although a sad indication of the mismanagement of the past, indicated to the stock market that the company was serious about restructuring and that the board had gained independence from the government. The actual net profit before restructuring charges, compared to the Paribas forecast at the time of the privatisation, developed as shown in Exhibit 27.

On the negative side, only 9 per cent staff cuts were achieved, against Merrill Lynch's expectations of 15–20 per cent over two years. The company did not achieve its 10–12 per cent RoE objective by 1996 as articulated at the time of the issue: the target subsequently became 10 per cent by 1998. Fleuriet of Merrill Lynch said: 'We believe that Elf has delivered everything that it promised to do at the time of privatisation. The reasons for the result being worse than expected are related to a falling oil price and weak refining margins. Nonetheless, the company has not communicated its achievement as well as it perhaps could have, which is one of the reasons for a relatively disappointing after-market share price performance.'

The banks

Paribas earned praise from competitors for its handling of the offer, although there was some criticism of the allocation, which was fiercely rejected by the bank. Besides raising the highest-ever proceeds from a continental European privatisation, the deal had a high degree of complexity which Paribas and its co-advisers overcame without too much difficulty. Paribas did reasonably well in terms of its selling effort, particularly in the RoE and RoW tranches, as illustrated in Exhibit 28.

Paribas was appointed adviser to Elf on 11 October 1993 and Elf's head of capital markets and financing, Françoise Leroy, commented: 'Paribas is perhaps the only French bank which can handle a global offer.' Paribas is Elf's main investment bank and had also been global coordinator with Goldman Sachs in the 1991 capital increase when Elf was listed in the US. In the 1994 offer, Paribas was responsible for the handling of the international offer, including documentation and advice on the golden share. With only 26 bank branches in France (not counting the 570 branches belonging to subsidiary Crédit du Nord) Paribas does not claim to have nationwide retail placement power.

Crédit Lyonnais was formally appointed by the Trésor on 22 October 1993. Notwithstanding its disastrous recent corporate history, Crédit Lyonnais has strong capabilities in equities and is recognised as one of the most successful fund management organisations in France. This has clearly been recognised by the Trésor, as evidenced in Exhibit 29.

BNP, traditionally Elf's main retail bank, was appointed by the company on 19 October 1993, and had special responsibilities for Elf's valuation and the retail and employee offers. BNP, had advised Elf on previous privatisation issues and had long been close to the company. The bank had proved itself creatively and in terms of retail placement power – achieved through 2,600 branches – not least during its own privatisation in 1993. It had also become an increasingly recognised force for institutional placement.

Merrill Lynch won the strongly contested US lead manager mandate, although Goldman Sachs was widely tipped to take this role. Goldman Sachs had acted as joint global coor-

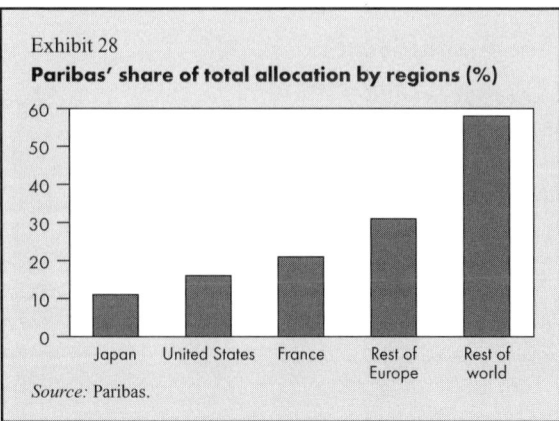

Exhibit 28
Paribas' share of total allocation by regions (%)

Source: Paribas.

Exhibit 29
Advisers and global coordinators since the beginning of the Balladur Privatisation Programme

Company/privatisation	Date	Government adviser	Company adviser	Global coordinator
BNP	October 1993	Lazard Brothers	N/A	BNP
Rhône-Poulenc	November 1993	Indosuez	Soc Gén	Indosuez/Soc Gén
Elf	January 1994	Crédit Lyonnais	BNP/Paribas	Paribas/Crédit Lyonnais
UAP	April 1994	Paribas	BNP/Lazards/Worms	BNP/Paribas
Renault 1	November 1994	CNCA/Rothschild	BNP/Lazards	BNP/CNCA
Seita	February 1995	Crédit Lyonnais	CCF/Soc Gén	Crédit Lyonnais/CCF
Usinor-Sacilor	June 1995	Paribas	Crédit Lyonnais/SGW	Paribas
Pechiney	November 1995	SocGén/Goldman Sachs	BNP/Lazards	BNP/Soc Gén
AGF	May 1996	CCF/JP Morgan	Soc Gén	CCF/Soc Gén
France Télécom	Expected 1997/98	Paribas/DMG	BNP/Lazards/Merrill Lynch	Paribas/BNP

dinator in Elf's registered and NYSE listed capital increase in 1991. Further, it was highly unusual for Goldman Sachs to lose mandates to competitors where they already had a strong relationship with a client. Merrill Lynch won on the strength of a very good presentation, a strong performance in the BNP privatisation and personal chemistry between Elf's representatives and Merrill Lynch's Elf team. The decision to appoint Merrill Lynch was taken by Elf and supported by the Trésor.

The following were also of importance in Merrill Lynch's appointment:

- It had a long-standing relationship with Elf, for which it had carried out many successful capital markets transactions;
- It was able to argue that, according to independent sources, it had broader access to the medium-sized US institutions (ie, targeted investors, particularly in the US$1–10 billion range) than any other investment bank. It was not hired for its US retail distribution capacity because US retail placement is deemed ineffective in privatisations where pre-allocation is not possible;
- Merrill Lynch's equity research analysts for the oil sector were highly ranked. Sue Graham in Europe was ranked No. 2 by *Extel* and Constantine Fliakos in the US was ranked No. 3 by *Institutional Investor*. It was also among the most active traders of Elf ordinary shares and ADRs; and
- The bank had made a strong commitment to France and was a major player in French stocks overall. It regularly accounted for 4–10 per cent of trading volumes on the Paris bourse.

Key lessons learnt

It takes a large offer to reposition a company with investors as a substantial percentage of existing and potential shareholders has to be convinced that the company should be regarded in a different light.

An offer such as Elf's requires a tremendous effort and focus by the leading banks' equity capital markets and equity sales departments. Even Merrill Lynch confessed that, at the time, it could not easily have handled another issue of such size and complexity.

The greatest challenge for Elf was to conduct the employee offer, which, given the widespread geographi-

cal distribution of employees, required a huge amount of information and administration.

The fact that there was a good working relationship between the Trésor and the company, significantly contributed to the success of the offer. This fact was attributable both to the Trésor's policy of involving the company and to the personalities involved.

It was disappointing that after a lot of work was put into trying to sell shares in Japan, little positive response was obtained.

The fact that Elf had already gone through the US SEC registration process and NYSE listing in 1991 proved helpful in completing the privatisation.

A partly paid structure proved unnecessary, even for this large transaction although the final decision was not taken until January 1994 and preliminary prospectuses were prepared for both structures. Whereas a partly paid share would generate considerable leverage on the annual dividend payment and therefore might generate higher demand, the final view was that it was complicated and undesirable to have two quotations in the market. Furthermore, US investors are not particularly keen on the partly paid structure, and Merrill Lynch thought it would attract more arbitrageurs and fewer fundamental buyers to the secondary market trading than if only one security was traded in the US.

A further reason not to do a partly paid structure – although this was played down by the Trésor – might have been that it would have been politically inopportune if the market declined between the first and second installments (as it did), because the second installment would have come shortly before the 1995 presidential election. As strong signals were coming back from the OPV syndicate indicating that three million retail investors might subscribe, the need for a partly paid structure was not seen as pressing. Philippe Allouche, adjoint chef du bureau at the Trésor explained: 'The major reasons for not doing it was that it was very complicated and in the end we judged that we didn't need it.'

Conclusion

The privatisation of Elf was a huge success at the time. 'This was a good deal for both the vendor and the company, the state got a lot of money and the company got its freedom,' commented Brigitte Molkhou of the Trésor. The transaction was substantially oversubscribed and initial after-market performance was as strong as could be expected for an already traded share. Following largely flat or negative share price performance for two to two-and-a-half years after the privatisation, patient investors have at last been rewarded as the company's restructuring begins to have an impact on the bottom line and as chairman Philippe Jaffré is increasingly perceived as being shareholder-friendly.

The fact that the privatisations of both BNP and Rhône-Poulenc had been successful and still traded above issue price, was of key importance for the public interest in Elf. It is a global stock and the equity research emphasising a 'restructuring and recovery story' was favourable – Elf's CEO convincingly talked about cost cutting on the roadshow and the company was attractively valued on the basis of price/cash flow, particularly against its US peer group. The dividend yield was attractive, particularly when compared to US dollar interest rates, all the key banks in the syndicate are thought to have done a good job which is evidence that the offer and syndicate structures achieved the desired level of motivation. It was the broadest ever marketing campaign in the US and included a full week's roadshow with two Elf teams targeting more than 1,000 accounts. There was very good organisation, and a great deal of hard work was put in by the working team.

Elf's objectives were almost fully met except that the retail offer represented a slightly larger proportion than the company desired and the fact that less than 30 per cent of the company came to be owned by the GAS and the Trésor after the offer. Its positioning in the US improved and Elf now is regarded as a major oil company comparing favourably with BP, Chevron, Mobil and Texaco. Management convinced investors that its focus on profitability would improve long-term results. A total of 110 new institutions in the US were allocated US$280 million in Elf stock, thus achieving the goal of broadening the US shareholder base by between 100 and 150 new investors. Seventeen existing US shareholders were allocated shares worth US$70 million.

Paribas and the other advisers did a good job in structuring the issue on the lines of BT 3. Placement was based not on location but on quality of investors, and banks competed more keenly than in BT 3 as stock was not allocated in advance to any particular region. Paribas pioneered a highly organised warm-up programme and the overall marketing appeared well organised, not least because Paribas had managed to motivate and incentivise a large number of the syndicate members.

However, the syndicate was too large, mainly a result of the many relationships developed by the Trésor. Pascal Jaubert, at the time director and head of primary markets at Crédit

Lyonnais noted: 'Clearly, it is important for the Trésor to encourage foreign banks at the time when Paris has considerable ambitions to become a major financial centre.' Yet many of the banks will not have added much value to the transaction – rather they will have diluted the motivation of others. It might have been useful to have had a foreign bank in a more senior position in the syndicate for what was the largest-ever French equity offer. This may have added further clout to the international offer and enhanced the international sponsorship, and therefore the perception of the transaction among international institutions.

There were complaints from some syndicate members and investors who felt that they had not been fairly treated in the allocations. Paribas was criticised for honouring early orders from small institutions rather than giving blue-chip institutions allocations big enough to hold long-term. Yet hugely subscribed offers invariably attract such complaints. Tony Bourne of Paribas explained: 'We merely stuck to the allocation criteria agreed, which stipulated that for the same quality order, the earlier one should be allocated.'

The continued state holding has puzzled some. 'The fact that ERAP retained a 13 per cent holding in Elf does not make much sense to me,' a senior banker involved in the privatisation commented. 'With the golden share, the core shareholders and the employee ownership, the company is sufficiently protected. The retention of this stake by the Trésor only depresses the share price.' Another senior Paris banker pointed out that the 13 per cent carries the Mitterrand hallmark.

The policy of maximising retail placement at the expense of not satisfying institutional allocations to a higher degree, as politically attractive as it might be in the short term, was haunting France's privatisation programme for some considerable time following this offer. Although, given the generally poor after-market performance, the small institutional allocations in the first few privatisations turned out to be a blessing in disguise for the institutions, it will have done little to obtain the support of international institutions for the more difficult part of the privatisation programme. Many institutions were also critical of having to pay a considerably higher price than retail investors, as the retail discount was at the upper end of expectations and the institutional discount at the lower end.

After the Elf offer *World Equity* wrote about the upcoming UAP sale: 'for institutional investors frustrated in the Elf privatisation, the upcoming sale of French insurer UAP will elicit feelings of *déja vu*. It will be cheap, more or less unavailable and probably run by Paribas.'

Feature topic: *Targeting the US investor base*

Merrill Lynch won the strongly contested US lead manager's mandate – the first time that a US bank had been given back-to-back assignments by the Trésor. It won the mandate primarily on the grounds of its argument, – tailor-made to defeat Goldman Sachs – that Elf was too narrowly held in the US and that they, better than any other house, could deliver a broad institutional shareholder base. It also

offered the view that the positioning of Elf in the US had not been optimal, as it had previously been sold as a French company, whereas now it was going to be repositioned to be an oil major based in France.

The reasons for a large and broadly based US tranche in the Elf privatisation were threefold:

- A low proportion of Elf's equity was held in the US compared to other major oil companies – only 5 per cent (although it represented 10 per cent of the free float);
- A major offer would be required to achieve a repositioning of the company; and
- Most of Elf's current US institutional holders were overweight in Elf (see Exhibit 30).

Elf's shareholder base was less balanced between institutions and retail investors than those of its peers. Only some 10 per cent of its total US shareholdings were held by retail compared to more than 25 per cent for Repsol. In addition, Elf's shares were narrowly held among a small number of US institutions, mainly such US investors as

are dedicated to international investment. Only 21 institutions accounted for 80 per cent of Elf's total US holdings; the remaining 20 per cent was held by 53 institutions. The potential therefore lay mainly with the domestic accounts (see Exhibit 31). Moreover, the medium-sized institutions (US$1–10 billion) represented a smaller part of Elf's shareholder base (see Exhibit 32).

US tranche objectives

Following its analysis of the US ownership of Elf, Merrill Lynch articulated the following objectives for Elf's US offer:

- To increase the number of US holders from the current 74 by introducing 100–150 new shareholders, whereby 40–50 institutions should represent 80 per cent of US institutional holdings; and
- Position company as another BP where a huge turnaround was to be expected, and as a global oil major along with BP, Chevron, Mobil, Texaco and Amoco, rather than primarily as a French company.

Marketing

The US marketing programme was one of the most comprehensive ever for a non-US company:

- No less than 250 institutions were warmed up, of which 130 were contacted directly by Merrill Lynch's own analysts;
- Elf management presented to the salesforces and sell-side analysts of all the US managers;
- Distribution of marketing document to 1,500 Merrill Lynch salesmen; and
- Over a period of one week, there were nine public presentations and 46 one-on-ones.

US allocation policy

Merrill Lynch had firm ideas about the allocation process. Allocation must:

- Be enough to represent initial holdings; and
- Encourage after-market buying by institutions with unfilled demand.

Inflated orders should be identified in the context of average holdings and investor behaviour in other offers to avoid over-allocation and immediate selling in the after-market.

Merrill's allocation proposal was as follows:

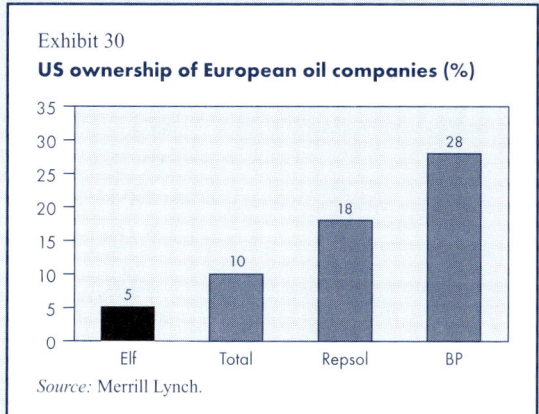

Exhibit 30
US ownership of European oil companies (%)

Source: Merrill Lynch.

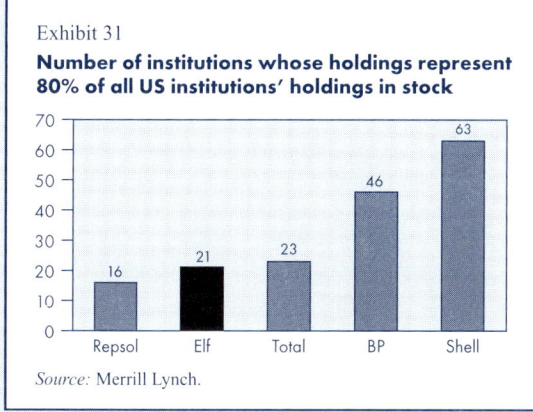

Exhibit 31
Number of institutions whose holdings represent 80% of all US institutions' holdings in stock

Source: Merrill Lynch.

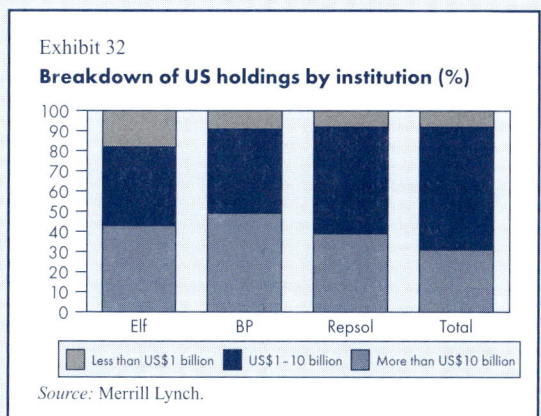

Exhibit 32
Breakdown of US holdings by institution (%)

Source: Merrill Lynch.

- It would do the allocation on a one-by-one bottom-up approach;
- Allocations would be based on in-depth discussions with institutions;
- It had to be done in such a way as to create strong after-market demand; and
- In order to accomplish the overall US offer goals, Merrill Lynch required the Trésor and the global coordinator to allocate a certain minimum number of shares to the US tranche.

Results of the US offer

The results of the US offer were in line with what Merrill Lynch had set out to do:

Roadshow success

- The one-on-one meetings were successful – 76 per cent of all institutions that attended a one-on-one meeting introduced an order; and
- One-on-one/roadshow attendees accounted for 71 per cent of the total demand.

Demand

- The Merrill Lynch-led US distribution effort yielded impressive results. Of the 189 institutions that came in with total orders worth US$3.6 billion (equivalent to 53 million shares), 171 came from institutional shareholders that had not previously owned Elf shares; 18 came from existing US shareholders (see Exhibit 33);
- US demand was not inflated (unlike European demand). A US$1.5 billion offer would have been feasible in the US;
- Average demand size (US$17.7 million) was similar to the January 1994 Daimler placement (US$15.2 million) and the 1993 privatisation of YPF (US $16.6 million);
- Demand was in line with BP, Mobil, Texaco, and Chevron holdings; and
- Merrill Lynch accounted for an impressive proportion of US designations while the French banks did well compared to the other US banks (see Exhibit 34).

Allocation

- A total of 127 of 189 institutions who put in orders received an allocation. The 110 new shareholders were primarily US 'domestic' accounts. This was within the target of 100–150 new institutional investors;
- No less than 56 accounts represented 80 per cent of the US offer. Consequently, the number of US institutions holding over 80 per cent of Elf in the US was significantly increased (see Exhibit 35);
- Total US allocations amounted to US$351 million or 5.1 million shares (pre-greenshoe);
- Average allocation per institution was only US$2.8 million;
- Average allocation was lower than comparable deals (Daimler, YPF) due to limited US placement size;
- The need to give critical mass of stock to certain institutions meant that a greater number than average (61) of potential new US institutional investors did not receive any allocations;
- Institutions that participated in roadshows or one-on-ones were favoured (12.0 per cent allocation versus 6.7 per cent for others); and
- This was an institutional transaction: only 9 per cent was placed with US retail investors.

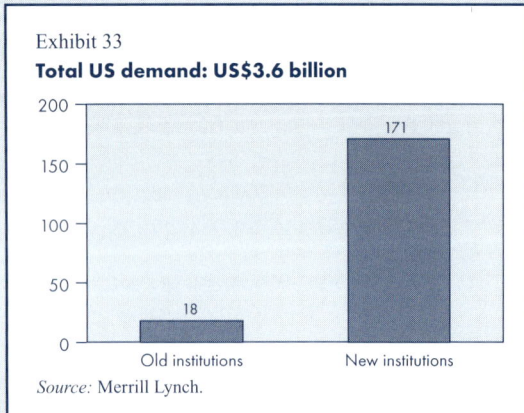

Exhibit 33
Total US demand: US$3.6 billion

Source: Merrill Lynch.

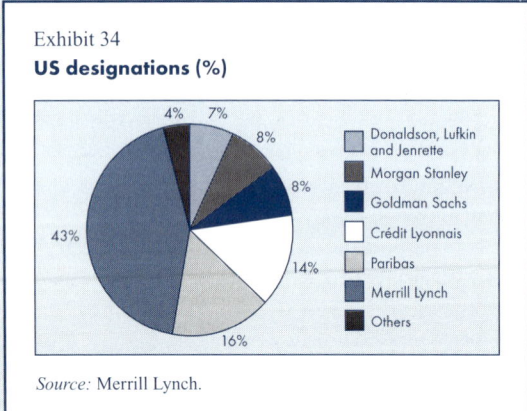

Exhibit 34
US designations (%)

Donaldson, Lufkin and Jenrette
Morgan Stanley
Goldman Sachs
Crédit Lyonnais
Paribas
Merrill Lynch
Others

Source: Merrill Lynch.

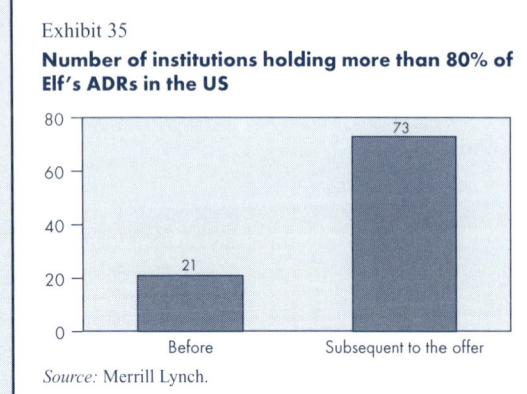

Exhibit 35
Number of institutions holding more than 80% of Elf's ADRs in the US

Source: Merrill Lynch.

Empresa Nacional de Electricidad

The US$57 million ADR issue for leading Chilean electricity utility Endesa represents a prime example of how local laws and regulations in an emerging market can frustrate the raising of equity capital in the international market, contributing to a higher cost of capital.

As one of the leading blue chips in Latin America and a world class utility, capitalised at US$6 billion, Endesa had strategic motives for this financing. Despite a rock solid balance sheet, it wanted to do a very small international offer off the back of a domestic pre-emptive rights offer in order to qualify for a NYSE listed ADR programme. This was deemed important in case there was a need to raise substantial funds in the future.

The problem for Endesa and other Chilean companies is that shareholders have pre-emptive rights to purchase enough shares to maintain existing ownership percentages before new shares can be offered to third parties. These pre-emptive rights cannot be waived, making the legislation highly inflexible, and shares offered to new holders cannot be sold for less than the maximum subscription price in the rights offer. Chilean central bank regulations also dictate that companies need at least US$50 million-worth of shares to sell internationally to qualify for a NYSE listing. This meant that if the existing shareholders had decided to take up a large part of their rights, leaving less than US$50 million-worth of shares unsubscribed, then Endesa would not have been able to go ahead with an international issue. In such a case, three months of hard work at great expense to the company would have been in vain,

and Endesa would have remained largely inaccessible to international investors.

In this rights offer, the subscription price was set 'at market' to discourage existing shareholders from subscribing in full. As the objective was not to tap the Chilean shareholder base, all the marketing efforts were directed toward the ADR issue though all domestic legal requirements were met, including advertising in the local press. Six other Chilean companies had already tapped the ADR market in 1994 so Endesa was keen to get there as soon as possible.

The result of this was a bizarre spectacle whereby Endesa had to do a US$143 million rights issue despite not actually needing additional equity capital. Moreover, the rights issue was designed not to succeed with existing shareholders. At the same time, Endesa embarked on a major overseas road-show not knowing whether there would be an international offer if existing shareholders subscribed at too high a level or if the minimum international offer price developed to too much of a premium over the domestic market price. The laws and regulations were clearly inappropriate for a company of this size and stature, and following this deal the central bank went some way toward recognising this by halving the US$50 million threshold requirement.

Endesa differed in a number of respects from the more usual emerging market investment in the 1990s: it had been wholly privatised in 1989, was an asset-rich utility rather than the more typical consumer goods 'play' and had a dividend policy of paying out 100 per cent of annual earnings. Without

---

Exhibit 1
Transaction summary

Issuer name: Empresa Nacional de Electricidad – Endesa (Chile)	Bookrunning lead manager: CS First Boston
Pricing date: 26 July 1994 (IPSA Gen: 81.20)	Pricing/underwriting structure: Domestic rights issue followed by international bookbuilding of unsubscribed rights.
Vendor: The company	Primary or secondary: Primary
% increase in share capital: 2. 5%	Privatisation or corporate: Corporate
IPO or non-IPO: Non-IPO	Industry: Electric utility
Type of shares: Ordinary shares in the rights offer and ADRs (1 ADR=30 shares) in the international issue.	Offer price: US$22.30 per ADR
Total issue size: US$142 million (of which US$57 million was offered in the ADR issue)	US listing/144 A: NYSE listing

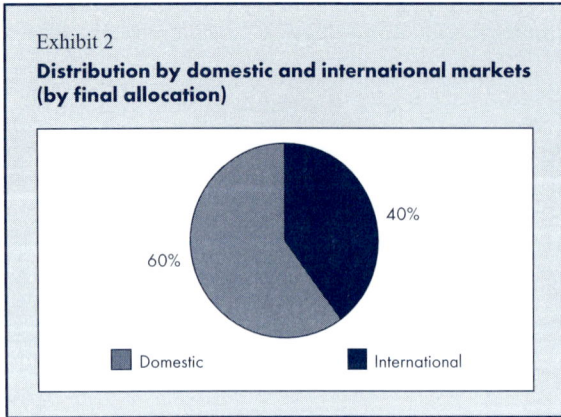

Exhibit 2
Distribution by domestic and international markets (by final allocation)

40%

60%

Domestic   International

the constraint of Chile's triple-B country rating, the company would probably have been rated at least as a strong single-A by the US rating agencies.

Despite the frustrations caused by the laws and regulations constraining this offer, Chile is one of the most prominent success stories among emerging market economies. One notable feature of the foresight of Chilean policy makers – heavily influenced by the Chicago school of monetarists – was the country's private pension fund system which was created in 1981 and soon became the envy of many countries around the world. By early 1996 these pension funds had some US$25 billion under management and controlled more than a third of the market capitalisation of the Chilean stock market, while foreign holdings accounted for only 7 per cent (as at 30 March 1995). These domestic institutional investors were responsible for stabilising the local stock market in the aftershocks of the Mexican financial crisis of 1995. Uniquely among emerging capital markets, Chile was relatively independent of foreign short-term portfolio investment. Whereas this stood the country in good stead in 1995, a price had to be paid in terms of domestic institutional shareholders being too powerful, and inflexible, conservative laws and regulations making it difficult for companies such as Endesa to internationalise its shareholder base.

Major challenges

While significantly constrained by domestic pre-emptive rights legislation and central bank regulations as mentioned, Endesa was trying to conduct the ADR offer, including first-time registration with the US SEC and the NYSE listing, in record time. The company worked on a timetable of 90 days, whereas other Chilean companies who had gone down the same route had taken six to eight months.

Given that the size of the international offer was small, that there was more than a fair chance that there would not be any international offer at all and that the shares might have to be sold at a premium to the domestic market price, few international fund managers found the motivation to study the Endesa story properly.

Endesa's P/E multiple at first appeared very high to many international investors as earnings per share had grown at 27

per cent a year from 1990–93 but bookrunning lead manager CSFB's analyst was projecting four-year compounded earnings per share growth of 'only' 18 per cent a year for 1994–97. Growth prospects were therefore below what most investors had come to expect from a typical emerging market investment.

Endesa's main, but much smaller, domestic competitor Chilgener had completed a rights offer in September 1993 and succeeded with difficulty in accessing the ADR market by pricing a US$68 million offer only eight days before Endesa was priced. Chilgener's market price had declined by 6 per cent during its marketing period and a discount of 2.9 per cent had been required, a fact which did not help the marketing of Endesa.

Rationale and objectives

The rationale behind the offer was to prepare for the future through an internationalisation of the share register. The company was increasingly investing outside Chile and if the right acquisition opportunity arose in, for example, the Brazilian power sector, it probably would cost more than US$1 billion. The equity capital required for such an investment would not be available domestically as Chilean pension funds, though large, are in most cases fully weighted in Endesa and have recently been put under pressure to diversify their holdings internationally.

Specific offer objectives included:

- To ensure that at least US$50 million of equity became available from the rights offer for sale in the ADR offer;
- To create some international liquidity, two-thirds of which would be in the US and one-third in Europe; and
- To complete the offer ahead of the Chilgener offer and before the August holidays.

Proceeds were expected to be used to fund the construction of Endesa's Pangue hydro-electric facility, for working capital and for general corporate purposes.

Share capital and ownership

See Exhibit 3.

Transaction components

The international offer was a one-tranche sale of ADRs directed at US and European institutional investors. As the sole purpose of the rights offer was to facilitate the ADR offer, it was sized on the expected appetite of domestic pension funds with the aim of leaving at least US$50 million-worth of shares unsubscribed to comply with central bank regulations on the minimum size for an ADR offer. Endesa had no way of knowing that this minimum requirement would be met until the end of the subscription period: of the 200 million shares (one new share for every 40 old shares held) in

Exhibit 3
Share capital and ownership

Share capital before offer	8,001,754,580 shares without nominal (par) value and with one vote each.
Ownership restrictions	No person may own directly or through related parties more than 26% of the company's capital stock.
Listings	Santiago in 1982 and the NYSE in connection with this offer.
Expanded market capitalisation at offer price (Ch$422/US$1)	US$6.1 billion
Shareholders before offer	Enersis (holding company) 16% Luksic 7% Chilean pension funds 31% Chilean private individuals 27% Other 19%
Number of shareholders before offer	Approximately 50,000
Free float before offer	77%
Historic liquidity (trading volume over the 12 months prior to the offer in relation to the total number of shares outstanding)	13% on the Santiago Exchange
Foreign ownership before offer	Before the offer only some 4% of Endesa was owned by foreign investors.
Most important stock exchange index/Endesa's weighting	IPSA/11.3% (June 1994)

Exhibit 4
Integrated rights offer and international offer

Rights offer	
Total size	200,000,000 ordinary shares
of which taken up by shareholders	116,861,682 ordinary shares
of which available for ADR offer	83,138,318 ordinary shares
International offer	
Indicated number of ADRs to be sold	2,450,000 + 180,000 greenshoe
Number of ADRs after increase	2,550,000 + 180,000 greenshoe
Amount of greenshoe exercised	–
Final number of ADRs sold	2,550,000 (representing 76,500,000 shares)
Both offers	
Total number of shares sold	193,361,682 shares

the rights offer only 116.9 million were subscribed for by shareholders. This meant that the international offer could proceed. The international offer was filed at 2.45 million ADRs (representing 73,500,000 ordinary shares) and was increased to 2.55 million ADRs when it became clear that there would be enough shares available. There was a green-shoe option which was not exercised due to the requirement that international shares be sold at a premium to the domestic market price (see Exhibit 4).

Unlike rights offers in most European countries, which usually are structured with a single subscription price, Chilean law allows either a fixed price or formula pricing. In this case, there was a formula whereby the subscription price per share was the higher of Ch$242.38 (representing the minimum price for the rights offer) and the moving weighted average of the trading prices of shares on the Santiago Stock Exchange during the five trading days immediately preceding the date of exercise of the related subscription

right. The average subscription price for the whole rights offer was Ch$311.33 per share, while the highest was Ch$313. The ADR offer could not therefore be priced below Ch$313, which at the time was equivalent to US$22.30 per ADR. As the domestic market price was trading below the minimum price at the time of pricing of the international issue, the ADRs were sold at a premium to the domestic market price.

Principal advisers

The international offer was done on a three-handed basis between CSFB, Goldman Sachs and Merrill Lynch, which all had the same underwriting commitments (see Exhibit 6). The rights offer was handled by the company, and no local bank was involved.

Transaction fee distribution

See Exhibit 7.

Exhibit 5

The timetable

Mid-April 1994	• Decision taken to proceed with an ADR offer and an NYSE listing.
21 April	• Endesa EGM approves 1: 40 rights issue (6,666,667 ADRs equivalent).
Late April	• CSFB appointed global coordinator (share price was Ch$250–260).
18 June	• Rights offer subscription period begins.
12 July	• Announcement of international offer and filing of F-1 registration statement.
14 July	• Global roadshow begins in Europe.
17 July	• Rights issue subscription period ends; • Minimum international offer price determined; and • Unsubscribed shares applied to ADR offer.
26 July	• Global roadshow ends in the US; and • Pricing and allocation of international offer.
27 July	• Trading of ADRs commences on the NYSE.

Exhibit 6

Principal advisers

Managing underwriters	CSFB (Books) Goldman Sachs & Co Merrill Lynch & Co
Adviser to the bookrunning lead manager	Excel (Chile)
International legal adviser to Endesa	Cleary, Gottlieb, Steen & Hamilton
Domestic legal adviser to Endesa	Carlos Parada Arce, General Counsel of Endesa
International legal adviser to the underwriters	Shearman & Sterling
Special Chilean transaction counsel	Guerrero, Olivos, Novoa y Errazuriz
Depository	Citibank NA
Auditors	Price Waterhouse

Exhibit 7

Distribution of gross spread(%)

Management	Underwriting	Selling concession	Gross spread *
0.67	0.81	1.79	3.27

* The offer price of US$22.30 represented a premium of 1.50% over the domestic market price. The effective cost to the company when measured against the domestic market price was therefore lower than 3.27%.

The selling concession was divided between a fixed portion of 30 per cent, to be split equally between the three managers, and a variable portion of 70 per cent paid to the managers on the basis of designations from investors (ie, jumpball).

Deal structure

Chile's pre-emptive rights laws coupled with the central bank's US$50 million minimum requirement for ADR issues created a situation whereby, unless major shareholders decided that they would not subscribe to the rights offer, the ADR offer could not go ahead. This almost happened to Endesa, despite the fact that Enersis, with 16 per cent of the shares, Luksic, with 7 per cent, and the Endesa Employee Pension Fund, which owned 4–5 per cent of the capital, decided not to exercise their rights.

Endesa's desire to internationalise its share register led the board to set the subscription price formula in such a way that existing shareholders had to subscribe 'at market' rather than at a discount, in the hope that this would discourage them. This was remarkable in itself, but created another complication in that it set a high minimum price for the international offer. As the market price fell after the end of the rights issue subscription period, ie, during the marketing period for the ADR issue, the likely offer price for the ADR offer increasingly represented a premium over the market price. A few days before the intended pricing date, the market price had fallen to Ch$307 indicating a premium of 2 per cent. The domestic market price had however risen by the end of the marketing period, so that at pricing the offer price represented a 1.5 per cent premium to the market price.

The timetable for the international offer was drawn out because the rights issue had to be completed first, leaving the company with a high degree of market exposure. In addition, by not being able to generate competitive tension between existing shareholders and new investors in order to maximise demand for the total number of shares on offer – as would have been the case if the two offers had been executed simultaneously – Endesa was not able to act in the best long-term interests of all its shareholders. If more shareholders had explicitly indicated at the outset that they would not exercise their right to subscribe, then the ADR issue could have been effected first, with the rights issue subscription price set at or below the ADR offer price. Although Enersis, Luksic and Endesa's Employee Pension Fund decided to do this, shareholders representing more than 70 per cent of the votes did not, and effectively prevented a simultaneous structure.

Endesa was therefore forced to set the highest possible subscription price in the rights issue as although a lower subscription price would have meant more pricing flexibility for the international offer, the flip-side would probably have been that less than US$50 million would have been unsubscribed, making the ADR offer and NYSE listing impossible.

An additional drawback of Chilean pre-emptive rights legislation is that as these rights cannot be waived, companies cannot use payment by shares to acquire another company.

Marketing

It was decided to do a 14-city roadshow which, under normal circumstances would appear highly ambitious for a US$57 million offer, but Endesa was almost unknown among international equity investors and the price was initially seen as prohibitive. It was therefore vital to emphasise Endesa's growth prospects and its near-monopoly position in Chile – it controlled 53 per cent of total installed capacity and most of the lines and substations connected to SIC, the main transmission system covering 92 per cent of the population. There was a comprehensive pre-marketing campaign, as described by CSFB equity research analyst Stephen Graham: 'We adopted an aggressive pre-marketing approach as far as number of calls and overall effort was concerned, whilst using conservative assumptions because we felt that the company's strengths and past performance would become fully transparent during the company roadshow.'

The Endesa story

Endesa was incorporated in 1943 by Corfo, a corporation owned by the state, to develop a national electricity development plan. Before its privatisation, the company was broken up and the part continuing as Endesa was given 45 per cent of the generation market as well as the main transmission system, but no distribution capacity to regulated customers. Privatised entirely through public share sales in the domestic market from 1986 to 1989, Endesa's equity had been available to foreign investors only through international country or regional funds investing in Chile or through domestically registered money (FICE accounts) which require investments in Chile to be kept for at least one year.

Endesa was the crown jewel in president Augusto Pinochet's privatisation programme, which began in 1974, five years before arch-privatiser Margaret Thatcher was elect-ed UK prime minister and 10 years before the first major UK public share sale, that of British Telecom. The programme was a key element in a wider plan of economic development that included pension reform, development of a domestic capital market, trade liberalisation and promotion of the export sector, deregulation and the introduction of competition, tight monetary and fiscal policies, and the encouragement of long-term foreign direct investment rather than short-term portfolio investment. The plan has given Chile an outstanding economic record, with average annual GDP growth of 5.7 per cent over the 10 years to 1993, while unemployment stayed low.

General Pinochet had been anxious to privatise Endesa while still in power, and many consider that he sold it far too cheaply. It was a major political issue and Pinochet was more concerned with getting the deal done than maximising proceeds. The privatisation was executed in several tranches, the first of which was directed at employees, whilst subsequent tranches included offers to the public and to domestic pension funds. The government made dividends income-tax-free for small investors, and provided financing for the public to buy shares with a high dividend yield in order to make debt servicing affordable. The emphasis was on wide distribution and following the final privatisation sale in 1989, Endesa had acquired around 60,000 shareholders.

Endesa has the highest-quality generation and transmission assets in the country, and its operating costs were at a record low because a large portion of its generating capacity comes from hydro-power, allowing it to pay out 100 per cent of earnings while still expanding and maintaining a very solid balance sheet. Endesa was unique as an investment opportunity as it combined the low risk of an electricity utility with both double-digit earnings growth and a comparatively high dividend yield (see Exhibit 8).

The Chilean economy represented a tremendous success story: rapid economic growth was achieved while the economy remained in a healthy balance. This was particularly impressive when compared to Argentina and Mexico. (See Exhibits 9 and 10.) Although weaker in 1994, economic growth recovered strongly in 1995 and 1996 and Chile was much less affected by the Mexican peso crisis than most of the other Latin American countries, not least because of a high domestic savings ratio and a lesser dependence on short term foreign capital flows than most of its peers.

Reasons for not buying

- The minimum international offer price, equivalent to US$22.30, was a considerable hurdle during the marketing period as it was significantly above the domestic market price, at one time by 2 per cent;
- Endesa was being sold at a high P/E multiple compared to electricity utilities in the US and most European countries. The combination of small issue size and high multiple meant that not necessarily all the major fund managers took a good look at Endesa; and
- Future earnings per share growth was at the time expected to be lower than in the recent past and at 15 per cent was lower than most other emerging-market stocks.

Exhibit 8
Principal sales points

Leading Latin American blue chip	• With a market capitalisation of US$6.1 billion and a market float of 77%, Endesa is the largest company in Chile and its leading blue chip. Endesa was perhaps also the leading blue chip in all of Latin America. Endesa's senior debt was rated BBB+ by S&P, the highest rating of any Latin American corporation.
Dominant market position	• Together with the 93%-owned Penhuenche, Endesa holds 63% of Chile's generating capacity and 80% of the transmission lines making it the dominant player in Latin America's most attractive power sector; • The next closest competitor was Chilgener, with less than half the installed capacity of Endesa; • Endesa's largest shareholder Enersis, a Chilean holding company also quoted on the NYSE, controls the majority of Chilectra, the largest distributor of electricity in the country; • Endesa also operates 2,600MW of installed capacity in Argentina, accounting for 20% of that country's total capacity; and. • Over the 3 years to 1993, demand in the SIC transmission system serving 92% of the population had increased on average by 8.8% p.a.. Prices had increased by a similar percentage over the past few years and were expected to continue to rise at a similar rate. Enormous growth potential remained as per capita electricity consumption was still 36% lower than in Argentina.
Hydro power creates unique cost advantage	• Of Endesa's installed Chilean generation capacity of 2,500MW, 87% was hydro-power which made it the system's low-cost producer with unmatched profitability.

Unparalleled combination of high earnings growth and exceptional cash flow	• Endesa had a tremendous earnings record over the previous four years. Earnings per share had increased by 27% a year on average between 1990 and 1993. CS First Boston expected growth in operating income to be 18% a year over the next four years and begin to accelerate when new capacity was added.
	• Endesa has multiple avenues of growth. It is expected to benefit from price increases, capacity additions through capital expenditure and continuation of a highly successful acquisition programme. Endesa has exceptional cash flow and despite paying out 100% of earnings is expected to be able to self-finance the planned growth. Potential plans to invest in Brazil, however, might represent an exception to this scenario:
	  – From 1994 to 2002, Endesa is expected to invest US$1.3 billion in Chile, to increase generating capacity by 42%;
	  – Competitors had been blocked from competing in hydro-power by Endesa's control of Chile's awarded yet unexploited prime water rights; and
	  – Endesa had successfully acquired operating control of 18% of the generating capacity in Argentina's national grid.
	• Following successful foreign investments in Argentina, Endesa was considering investments in Peru, Ecuador and Brazil where there is substantial hydro-power potential. All three are likely to adopt Chile's regulatory system but with changes.

High asset backing and unprecedented payout	• Whereas most emerging market stocks are in the consumer goods industry, Endesa is large and asset rich. Because Endesa's generating capacity is predominantly hydro-power it has limited variable costs and consequently a highly favourable cash-flow which allows it to pay out 100% of annual profits. This is unique for an emerging-market stock.

Favourable regulatory regime	• Regulations governing the Chilean electricity sector are highly favourable for Endesa as a low-cost hydro producer. Chile's national grid system operates on a merit order basis, i.e. it dispatches each hour the lowest-cost electricity. Endesa's 12 hydro-power stations are therefore dispatching constantly to the grid while prices are set high enough to cover the much-higher-cost thermal power. Further advantages of the Chilean regulatory model are:
	  – It rewards efficiency. Prices for power are set nationally at roughly the same level for all generating companies. Those generators with the lowest costs make the highest profits;
	  – It generates stable prices and stable revenues, particularly for the low cost producers, as long-term demand and supply are taken into account to calculate 'four-year average marginal cost prices';
	  – Planning of new power capacity is done in a fashion that optimises the system overall and therefore is of maximum benefit to the country as a whole;
	  – There is considerable competition in the Chilean electricity market with only partially regulated prices. Furthermore, regulated prices are adjusted closer to market prices if they are more than 10% apart. The four-year calculated theoretical marginal cost is based on the operating cost of the most advanced technology in the world. This fact forces the Chilean generators to be on the cutting edge of efficiency;
	  – Chilean electricity generating companies are not subject to periodic discretionary and arbitrary regulatory overhauls of rate regimes that can hurt share prices; and
	  – Consumers and producers share the benefits when productivity is increased at existing plants and the pricing system provides a market incentive for investment in the most efficient new capacity, thus avoiding public debate about how to share the profitability between shareholders and consumers.

Valuation (8 July 1994 with Endesa at Ch$313)	• Endesa's P/E ratio was in line with the sector and the cash-flow multiple was at a discount to Endesa's Chilean comparables. Endesa has the highest dividend yield of any comparable Latin American utility; and • In market capitalisation terms, it was more than double the size of Enersis and approximately four times that of Chilgener and Chilectra.

Sources: CSFB and Prospectus.

Exhibit 9

Chile's economic performance in perspective – prior to offer (Average over 1992–93)

	Chile	Argentina	Mexico
Real GDP (% change YoY)	8.7	8.3	2.2
Unemployment rate (%)	6.6	8.3	3.3
Producer price index (% change YoY)	7.8	1.7	7.6
Gross domestic savings (% of GDP)	23.7	14.9	12.5
Government debt (% of GDP)	23.0	30.0	19.2
Gross external debt (% of GDP)	42.4	30.9	30.0
Foreign exchange reserves, ex gold (US$ billions)	9.4	11.9	18.6
Long bond yield (%)	6.9	N/A	15.8

Source: ING Barings.

Exhibit 10

Chile's economic performance in perspective – following offer (Average over 1994–96)

	Chile	Argentina	Mexico
Real GDP (% change YoY)	6.6	2.7	1.1
Unemployment rate (%)	7.2	15.4	5.1
Producer price index (% change YoY)	6.4	4.6	28.1
Gross domestic savings (% of GDP)	24.4	17.3	14.1
Government debt (% of GDP)	12.7	29.3	26.5
Gross external debt (% of GDP)	35	34.8	46.4
Foreign exchange reserves, ex gold (US$ billions)	14.0	15.6	12.5
Long bond yield (%)	6.3	N/A	24.4

Source: ING Barings.

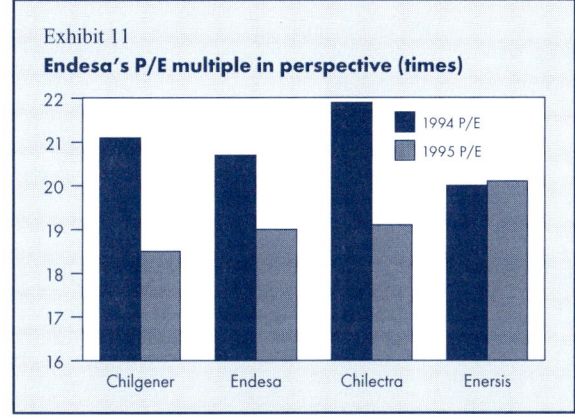

Exhibit 11

Endesa's P/E multiple in perspective (times)

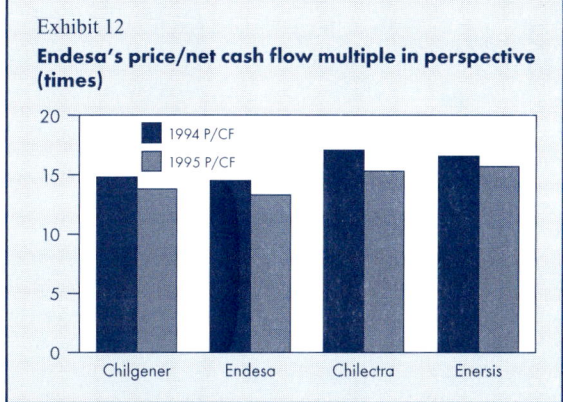

Exhibit 12

Endesa's price/net cash flow multiple in perspective (times)

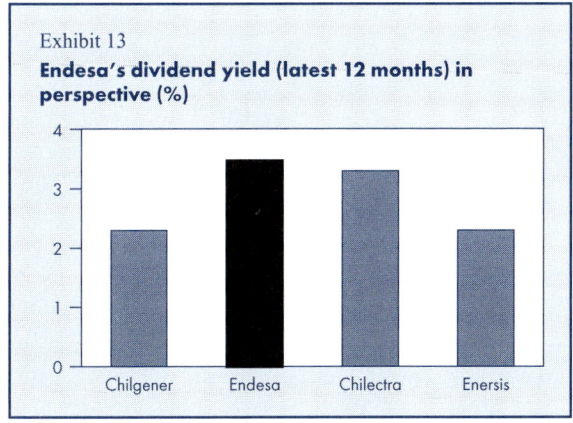

Exhibit 13

Endesa's dividend yield (latest 12 months) in perspective (%)

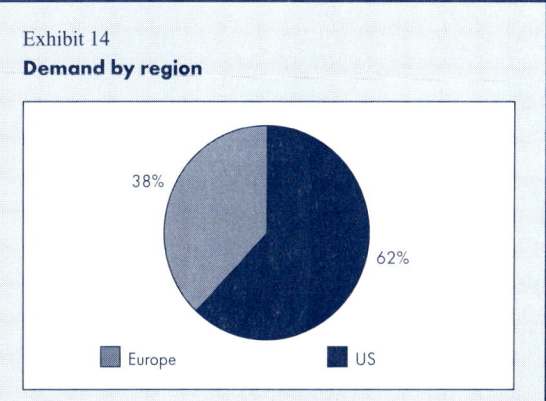

Exhibit 14

Demand by region

Exhibit 15
Investor concentration

	By demand	By allocation
% of issue accounted for by the 10 largest investors (by total size of demand and allocation respectively)	49%	54%
Number of investors making up 80% of the ADR issue (by total size of demand and allocation respectively)	18	36
The three largest investors by size of order	US$5.4 million US$5.0 million US$4.5 million	US$5.4 million US$4.5 million US$4.5 million
Total number of institutions	51	50

Results

The ADR offer was distributed in the US and in Europe, as indicated in Exhibit 14.

Investor concentration

The ADR offer was only just fully subscribed and distributed to 50 international institutional investors (see Exhibit 15.) The most important buyer categories were emerging-market funds followed by growth buyers and utility funds.

Share price performance

See Exhibit 16.

Before pricing

- As in many earlier Chilean ADR issues, there had been a considerable increase in the domestic market price ahead of the offer due to expectation of a company revaluation after establishment of the ADR facility. This was based largely on the fact that following the establishment of an ADR programme, there is no limitation on the conversion of domestically traded shares to ADRs.

After pricing

- According to David Hurd, senior analyst at Smith New Court Chile (now part of Merrill Lynch): 'The run-up in the absolute share price following the issue was related to the fact that many foreign funds were only beginning to realise that Endesa was likely to be able to continue to grow as it had for many years in the past.' Domestic investors, already bullish on the electricity sector, were further encouraged by the success of the ADR offer which in turn created momentum for international funds to buy more; and
- Endesa either slightly under-performed or performed in line with the market for the first three months. Over the first six months, however, the stock underperformed the domestic market by more than 20 per cent. Mario Valdivia, executive director of Excel Chile says: 'At the end of 1994 and beginning of 1995, the Santiago Stock Exchange was affected by the 'Tequila Effect', which hit those companies with substantial investments in Argentina, such as Endesa, much harder than those companies less exposed to the rest of Latin America'.

Exhibit 16
Share price performance

Pricing date	26 July 1994
Offer price	US$22.30
Last trade	Ch$310
Relative index position	142.1%
Historic 52 week high/low	
High (7 June 1994)	Ch$319
Low (19 August 1993)	Ch$152

Endesa share price relative to IGPA General Index (%)

Price performance

Before pricing

	Price (Ch$)	Relative (%)	
- 6 months	226	100	
- 3 months	268	124.8	
- 1 month	310	138.5	
- 1 week	318	143.3	
- 3 days	314	142.7	
- 1 day	309	141.4	

After pricing

	Price (Ch$)	Relative (%)	Price (US$)
+ 1 day (27 July)	310	141.9	22.125
+ 3 days	310	141.0	22.125
+ 1 week	314	140.9	23.5
+ 1 month	325	137.4	23.375
+ 3 months	365	138.4	27.75
+ 6 months	317	118.8	22.875

Source: Datastream and offer circular.

After-market trading volume

After an active first day of trading on the NYSE, liquidity

Exhibit 17
Percentage of total issue traded * (%)

	Day 1	Day 2	Day 3	Total Day 1-3
Santiago (ordinary shares)	4.1	2.5	1.8	8.4
New York (ADRs)	10.1	0.3	0.4	10.8

* Based on the total number of shares issued in the rights and ADR offers, ie,193,361,682 shares.

was significantly reduced reflecting the small size of the ADR offer and the fact that the majority of those investors who had subscribed wanted to own Endesa long-term (see Exhibit 17)

The performance of the main parties

The company

The ADR offer was executed in a much shorter time than had been the case for other Chilean companies, in part because its management had a high level of sophistication due to extensive domestic reporting requirements and in part because of its considerable international financing experience. The domestic securities regulatory body, SVS, was modelled on the US Securities and Exchange Commission and Endesa had reported four times a year for many years. It had also gone through the process of rating its debt with Standard & Poor's and had significant borrowings from international banks.

The company and its advisers did well in structuring the rights issue to have at least US$50 million available for the ADR issue despite the constraints of Chilean law. On the roadshow the management came across as sophisticated and highly professional, confirming Endesa's reputation with international investors as one of the leading blue-chip companies in Latin America. It performed better than expected in terms of 1994 earnings, overshooting CSFB's estimate by 17 per cent.

The bookrunning lead manager

CSFB, working closely with the bank's local partner Excel, earned praise from Endesa for doing a good job. It orchestrated a 14-city roadshow (five in Europe) and, despite the structural impediments with the offer, arranged 28 one-on-one meetings, seven of them in Europe. CSFB equity research analyst Stephen Graham's conservative approach towards Endesa projections in the pre-marketing phase gave institutional investors confidence in the numbers. CSFB, unsurprisingly for an offer of this kind, accounted for the lion's share of allocations and then did a good job generating further momentum for the shares in the after-market. The after-market performance was assisted by the fact that analysts realised that there was more potential for earnings growth than had been assumed at the time of the offer.

CSFB, as can be expected of the bookrunner, was the most active trader in ADRs post-offer. Its market share increased from 29 per cent during the first six months after the offer to

40 per cent over the first year. This trading effort was supported by a regular and high-quality research effort. Goldman Sachs and Merrill Lynch were not active in the stock and Goldman Sachs was criticised for weak follow-up on the research side. (See Exhibit 18.) Not least because of its strong trading and research performance, CSFB was given the responsibility to arrange a non-deal roadshow for Endesa in mid 1995.

How did CSFB get the bookrunning mandate? Endesa, at the time without prior experience in the area of international equity issuance, invited CSFB, Merrill Lynch and Goldman Sachs to compete for this mandate on equal terms. 'We wanted to be objective and fair in this process and accordingly we set up some very clear evaluation criteria,' says Endesa's CFO Jorge Lesser. Those are understood to have included:

- Relevant experience (ADR offers generally, offers for electricity utilities and local presence);
- Knowledge of Chile; and
- Competitiveness in terms of fee structure, etc.

By the time the Endesa mandate was awarded, only Goldman Sachs among the three contenders, had actually completed an ADR issue for a Chilean company although CSFB was to be the co-lead behind Morgan Stanley on the Banco O'Higgins offer and run the books of the Embottelladora Andina issue, the soft drink producer and Coca-Cola distributor, before Endesa was priced. Whilst Goldman Sachs was considered to have one of the strongest equity research analysts for the US utility sector, CSFB had in Excel a strong and well connected local partner which knew Endesa and Enersis, Endesa's largest shareholder. Excel had introduced CSFB to Endesa. Moreover, CSFB had worked successfully with Endesa on a syndicated loan transaction in 1993, had acquired experience in the Latin American electricity utility sector through the privatisation of the Argentine electricity industry and had in Stephen Graham the only equity research analyst dedicated to the Latin American utility sector among the three contenders. CSFB also gave a strong presentation and offered a competitive fee of 3.27 per cent. Morgan Stanley, highly regarded in Chile, had a conflict of interest as it was mandated to do an ADR issue for Chilgener, one of Endesa's principal competitors. Goldman Sachs had done two less than completely successful deals in Chile and many market participants were questioning its commitment to the region.

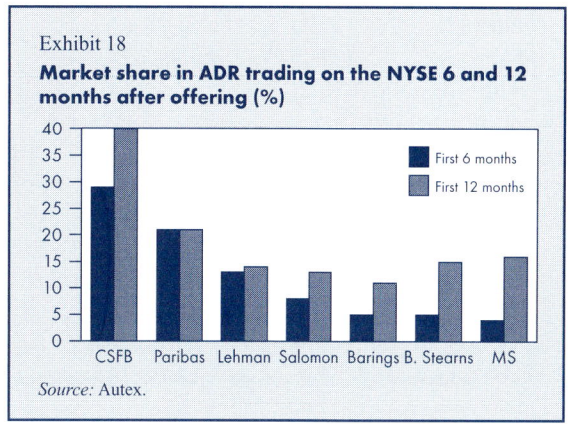

Exhibit 18
Market share in ADR trading on the NYSE 6 and 12 months after offering (%)

Source: Autex.

Key lessons learnt

Despite considerable structural impediments, it was possible to price the offer at a premium to the local market. This worked for two principal reasons: first, because of the small offer size and second, because it was argued that the minimum offer price of US$22.30 (as set by the rights issue) represented good value on a fundamental basis. In addition, the valid argument was made that institutional investors are used to paying premiums in emerging markets.

This offer illustrates the power of adopting a conservative approach to the estimation of future earnings, as if investors are given the impression that the company and its bankers are being conservative, they are often prepared to pay a higher price than if they feel that the earnings estimate is being aggressively marketed by the bookrunner. This does not appear to be widely understood by bankers and companies as they most often overstate likely earnings prospects.

Endesa learned that it is easy to underestimate the process of carrying out an ADR offer, and that it is of key importance to choose the right bookrunning lead manager. The investment bank adds value in particular in the crafting of the company story and in connection with the marketing and distribution of the shares. However, the company found the lawyers every bit as important as the bankers according to company CFO Jorge Lesser: 'Although we were very happy with our choice of bankers we realise now that the lawyers are of critical importance, not only because they do a lot of the work but also because in the final analysis they are the ones that really protect the company.'

The company felt that involving all three of the managing underwriters in due diligence and prospectus drafting work was time consuming and cumbersome, despite the fact that this is standard practice in the US. Endesa would have preferred to have involved only the bookrunning lead manager in these processes. Ernesto Cruz, managing director of equity capital markets at CSFB, counters this argument: 'While the burden of due diligence and documentation can be safely placed on the bookrunner, it is important that the other managers have an opportunity to be involved in the due diligence process so as to be in a better position to assist the bookrunner with the distribution of the shares.' The company also realised that it would have been advantageous to have a smaller in-house group involved in the exercise.

Endesa has found that reporting according to US GAAP and listing on the NYSE carries prestige which helps in international borrowings and business negotiations throughout the world.

Conclusion

Investors were attracted to Endesa's assets, cost structure, market position and prospects for growth. It had also demonstrated that it could invest successfully outside Chile, most notably in Argentina. Management did well on the roadshow and was highly rated by international investors, while Chile was regarded as a well managed and fast-growing economy.

It was ironic that Endesa had to increase its equity capital, when it did not need additional equity, in order to obtain a NYSE listing. A structure should have been found in which the company and a sufficient number of its shareholders worked together to package US$50 million-worth of already outstanding shares in an ADR offer. Alternatively, Endesa should have been able to take the required number of shares into treasury in order to then offer them to international investors. Achieving the NYSE listing without an offer would have been even more straightforward, if it had been allowed to do so by the Chilean central bank. However, this is not generally considered an effective way of attracting new investors as fund managers are not challenged to take a buy/non-buy decision.

The fact that Endesa raised equity that it did not need does not appear to have caused concern to the market given the company's aggressive growth strategy focusing on new power projects or privatisations of existing power companies in Peru, Argentina and Brazil. It is also part of a consortium building a gas pipeline from Argentina to Chile and it is investing in several domestic power projects. As a result, Endesa's leverage has increased since the offer.

Although the ADRs opened slightly below the offer price, they soon began to perform strongly, in line with the Chilean market. This was an impressive performance considering that they had outperformed the Chilean market by 41 per cent during the six months before pricing. Endesa was slightly more affected by the Mexican crisis than some other Chilean companies and consequently underperformed the domestic market around year-end 1994/95 after which its strong performance resumed.

The offer acted as a catalyst for the internationalisation of Endesa's shares. Following the establishment of the ADR facility there is no limitation on the amount of Endesa equity that can be acquired through this mechanism. The approach adopted allows for a gradual balancing of domestic and foreign ownership, as foreign institutions simply buy the ordinary shares locally and deposit them with Citibank, which then issues the equivalent number of ADRs.

Endesa is now the bellwether stock for many Latin American funds. The NYSE accounted for 26 per cent and Santiago for 74 per cent of total domestic and US trading volume during 1995, while it's aggregate foreign ownership increased from 4 per cent at the time of the offer to 8 per cent by early 1996. Of this, ADRs accounted for 4.5 per cent, the balance being owned via restricted FICE accounts and domestically registered Chile or Latin American country funds.

Before the offer few non-Chile-based analysts followed Endesa, but by 1996, there were at least 15 such analysts in the US and London writing high-quality research on the company.

The Chilean economic model·has been very successful, as evidenced by the country's resilience against the 'Tequila Effect' in late 1994 and early 1995 – the Chilean stock market fell by only 5 per cent between December 1994 and February 1995 versus around 40 per cent in the case of Mexico and Argentina.

At a time when capital markets are becoming increasingly global, the regulatory and legal constraints put on a world class company such as Endesa seem out of date. More should be done to provide the largest Chilean companies with increased flexibility to finance themselves on terms equal to those of their international peers. This could be done by gradually opening the capital account of the balance of payments, although any relaxation of the rules on capital inflow would have to be offset by encouraging domestic pension funds and financial institutions to lend and invest abroad in order to ensure that Chile's successful model of being relatively independent of foreign portfolio investment continues.

Chilean pre-emptive rights legislation should be updated to facilitate the disapplication of such rights to a certain extent and under certain conditions. The idea is not to compromise fundamental shareholder rights, but to afford companies the flexibility to choose the most appropriate way of issuing equity. It is likely that legislators in an increasing number of countries will go down this route in order to achieve a capital cost competitive with that of US companies, where open-priced non-pre-emptive offers are the norm. As Endesa continues to expand internationally and its need for equity grows, the company should not again be put in a position of having to combine rights offers with international ones.

ENI

The sale of a minority stake in ENI SpA in November 1995 was the Italian government's first public offer of shares in an industrial company, and the largest ever European single company IPO by initial cash proceeds until the US$11.3 billion IPO of Deutsche Telekom in November 1996.

The process of change at ENI began in 1992, with the passage of the Amato Law which provided for the corporatisation and eventual privatisation of a number of state-owned entities. The Ministry of the Treasury became the sole owner of ENI as the Ministry of State Participations was disbanded.

By 1992 ENI had, over a 30-year period, grown to become the world's eighth largest publicly quoted oil and gas group on the basis of 1994 sales. In the process, it had become progressively over-diversified, highly geared, bureaucratic and politicised. Although the company had a strong technological base and very good oil and gas assets, it was subject to state participation and political meddling, and suffered the concomitant constraints. The Ministry of State Participations had to approve major decisions and the executive board consisted of representatives of the main political parties. Decision-making was time-consuming and had to take into account the political objectives of the main parties. Moreover, political interference had transformed the company into a conglomerate, by imposing the acquisition of a number of economically unproductive activities (such as textiles, textile machinery and mechanical engineering) in order to maintain employment levels. By the late 1980s, ENI had, in certain regions of the country at least, become a fiefdom of the Italian political parties.

In 1992, the Treasury appointed Franco Bernabè, head of the company's strategic planning department, as CEO of ENI:

by 1994, he had transformed the company from a loss-maker into a highly profitable international oil major. ENI's workforce was cut by a third and, in May 1995, the company declared its first dividend for 23 years. The restructuring process was assisted by the fact that political interference ceased following the breaking of a series of corruption scandals – many of which involved the previous management – and a move to clean up the political system.

Due to government instability in the early 1990s, following the revelations of deep-seated political corruption, the different plans to privatise ENI or to sell shares in the operating subsidiaries were never realised. It was only in August 1995 when it became clear that a sale of shares in ENI must be executed before the end of the year to meet the Treasury's budgetary objectives, that a final decision was taken.

By the time of the IPO, ENI had been radically restructured and was a fully integrated oil and gas company engaged in all aspects of the petroleum business. ENI had leading operations in the exploration, development and production of oil and natural gas; the supply, transmission and distribution of natural gas; the refining and marketing of oil and petroleum products; the production and sale of petrochemicals, and oilfield services contracting and engineering. With 1994 consolidated sales of US$31 billion, ENI was the largest oil and gas company in Italy and, following its IPO, the fifth largest publicly traded oil and gas company located in Europe and the eighth in the world.

Following the poor performance of previous Italian privatisations and given the ambitious future programme of state sales, the success of this offer was crucial. Italy's internation-

---

Exhibit 1

Transaction summary

Issuer name: ENI SpA (Italy)	Joint global coordinators: IMI & CSFB
Pricing date: 18 November 1995 (Mibtel 30: 13,663)	Pricing/underwriting structure: Bookbuilding followed by 10-day fixed price underwriting
Vendor: Ministry of the Treasury	Primary or secondary: Secondary
% of company sold: 15%	Privatisation or corporate: Privatisation
	Retail structure: Money-back guarantee
IPO or non-IPO: IPO	Industry: Oil and gas
Type of shares: Ordinary shares (1 ADR = 10 Shares)	Pricing range: L5,250–6,000 per ordinary share Offer price: L5,250 and US$32.88/ADR
Total issue size: US$3.95 billion	US listing/144A: NYSE listing

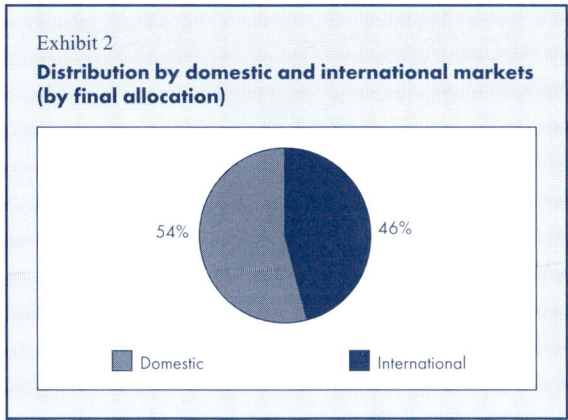

Exhibit 2

Distribution by domestic and international markets (by final allocation)

54%   46%

■ Domestic   ■ International

al credibility in the financial markets was at stake, and if this failed, the country's plans for future privatisations would have been substantially jeopardised. The ENI offer was hampered by a highly unstable political climate, and by the fact that both domestic and international bankers overestimated the likely demand for shares. Prevailing market conditions were very difficult as the Italian market had been the poorest performing continental European market in 1995, under-performing MSCI Europe by 25 per cent. Between the announcement on 10 August and the start of trading on 28 November, the Mibtel 30 fell by 15 per cent. Domestic and international investor sentiment towards Italy, already poor in early August, deteriorated further during the marketing period due to the worsening political situation (leading to a vote of no confidence on 26 October, which the Dini Government only just managed to survive), and the extreme volatility of the lira because of concerns over Italy's entry into EMU. By the beginning of the pre-marketing period on 16 October all the recent Italian privatisation offers were trading below issue price (see Exhibit 3).

To lure discouraged Italian retail investors into the ENI transaction two major structural innovations were introduced in the retail offer, both of which had worked exceptionally well in Spain's 1995 Repsol transaction.

First, the Treasury decided to insure retail investors against losses of up to 10 per cent by the first anniversary of the offer, provided they had retained their shares for the first year. Second, it decided to introduce revocable purchase mandates which the Italians rather confusingly chose to refer to as 'pre-registration', whereby retail investors could give their banks a mandate to purchase shares during the two weeks prior to

the OPV. These could be withdrawn during the first day of the OPV. The purpose of this structure was to increase retail subscriptions and afford momentum to the institutional offer.

Despite the merit of these structures, the Treasury had to settle for a more modest issue size and a lower offer price than originally planned.

In the end, the offer was successfully completed and after a hesitant start ENI began to perform strongly in the secondary market. Things appeared to be going well until the spring of 1996, when the government was allegedly put under strong political pressure to remove Bernabè from office. Although his re-appointment was delayed, he remained CEO. A strong after-market performance, an improved deal structure and a better stock market climate paved the way for the runaway success of the US$5.8 billion ENI 2 transaction in October 1996, at the time the largest ever European secondary offer since BP in 1987. A third successful ENI jumbo transaction – this time an amazing US$7.8 billion – was executed in July 1997, whereby the Treasury's stake was reduced from 69 per cent just over 50 per cent.

Major challenges

On 26 October, at the end of the crucial second week of pre-marketing, there was a vote of no confidence in the technocratic Dini Government: although the government narrowly survived this, it only did so on the basis that it would resign at year-end, which meant that there would be a period of considerable uncertainty leading up to a general election.

The Italian stock market was in a poor state and worsened during the marketing period. It was difficult to 'sell the Italian market' despite the fact that ENI was a very-high-quality company as many investors chose to focus on the country aspects rather than the company. There was also a general shift in investor focus away from the weaker to the stronger currency markets, which added to concerns about Italy. Because of the poor price performance of earlier Italian privatisations, there were justified concerns about the likely demand from Italian retail investors.

The credibility of European privatisations among European and US institutions was close to an all time low. There was a feeling that most privatisations were too finely priced in favour of governments. CSFB's global head of ECM Christopher Carter said: 'The gloss had started to come off some 18 months before ENI, as institutional investors took the view that governments had less of a political agenda with privatisations and more of an economic one. Institutional investors had expected good returns, but took a more negative view when the objective of maximising proceeds at the possible expense of a healthy secondary market appeared to become the priority.'

This was a large deal in the context of the poor state of the Italian equity market, as Bernabè pointed out: 'The problem of the very large size of the offer must be seen in the context of identity. ENI was not an American or a British company, but an Italian one, relatively unknown to the international markets, which were in any event suspicious about Italy. We did consider changing the name of the company to Agip for better name recognition, however this was difficult for inter-

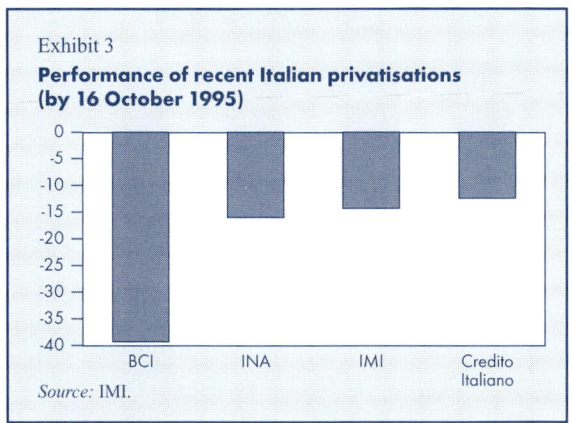

Exhibit 3

Performance of recent Italian privatisations (by 16 October 1995)

BCI   INA   IMI   Credito Italiano

Source: IMI.

nal reasons.' The ENI story was also a complex one given the diversity of the group.

The ENI transaction was subject to a tight timetable of just 13 weeks from mandate to pricing. James Leigh-Pemberton, head of European ECM at CSFB commented: 'One of the biggest challenges with this offer was to prepare it, from a corporate finance point of view, in a professional way given the tight timetable.' Bernabè added: 'The problem of timing was amplified by the novelty of the problems involved, such as the new legal procedures, a completely new kind of communication and reconciliation of the accounts to US GAAP.'

Rationale and objectives

Reasons for the offer

The rationale behind the privatisation programme was to reduce the size of the state sector, increase competition and efficiency in the economy, reduce state debt and lay the foundation for a more viable equity market. The most valuable contribution from a successful privatisation programme would come from an increased credibility of the Italian economy and, as a result, a reduction in interest rates. With total government debt of US$1.5 trillion by year-end 1995, equivalent to 124.9 per cent of GDP, it was estimated that a 1 per cent reduction in the annual cost of debt would save the Treasury about US$15 billion each year in interest expense.

ENI's role within the programme was of special importance as it was to lead to renewed support from Italian retail investors for the remainder of the privatisation programme.

The vendor's objectives were to:

- Accomplish the first step in the privatisation of ENI on terms which would maximise value and proceeds, consistent with a successful transaction;
- Put the country's privatisation programme back on track following delays and strong criticism of the price performance of earlier privatisations;

- Create a broadly based group of institutional shareholders and promote widespread share ownership of ENI amongst the Italian public;
- Complete the IPO prior to the end of the year;
- Successfully initiate the industrial phase of the privatisation programme, providing a platform for future sales of ENEL and Stet and further sales of ENI;
- Meet the government's 1995 budgeted privatisation receipts of L10,000 billion (US$6.3 billion); and
- Reduce Italian interest rates and the volatility of the Italian financial markets by repurchasing government bonds with the proceeds of the sale and by developing and enhancing the domestic and international credibility of the Italian equity market.

Christopher Carter of CSFB said: 'Once the decision to proceed was taken, the overriding objective was to complete the transaction before December 1995'. Vittorio Grilli, head of privatisation and debt management at the Ministry of the Treasury commented: 'With respect to the maximisation of value, we actually look at the pricing of the offer as a constraint rather than an objective. For a number of reasons we obviously have to achieve a reasonable price for the shares, corresponding to a fair valuation of the company. It can't be too high and it can't be too low as under both those scenarios, the other objectives would not be fulfilled.'

The company was positively disposed towards privatisation and there were no major conflicts between the vendor and the company. The company was keen to have at least 25 per cent of its stock floated in order to be included in the MSCI index, which was also thought to have been the objective of the Treasury, although this was not publicly announced.

The entire proceeds of the ENI sale were to be used to reduce Italy's public debt.

Share capital and ownership

See Exhibit 4.

Exhibit 4
Share capital and ownership

Type of shares offered	Ordinary shares of L1,000 and ADRs representing 10 shares each.
Ownership restrictions	Golden share and 3% ceiling on individual stakes. Provisions included protection against parties acting in concert. No discrimination against foreign shareholdings.
Share capital before and after offer	7,999,205,453 shares.
Listings/quotations	Telematico (Milan) and NYSE in connection with offer. ENI was also quoted on Seaq International from the time of the IPO.
Market capitalisation at offer price on 27 November 1995 (L1,597/US$1)	US$26.3 billion.
Major shareholder before offer	Ministry of the Treasury (100%).
Most relevant stock exchange index/weighting	Mibtel 30/19.3% (Included in mid-December 1995, reflecting 100% of ENI's share capital. At the offer price, ENI accounted for approximately 15% of the total market capitalisation of the Italian stock market.

Transaction components

This offer, for an initial 1.18–2.08 billion existing shares comprised a domestic offer to retail investors, the OPV, initially representing 0.4–1 billion shares, and an international offer to institutional investors in and outside Italy, initially representing 0.78–1.08 billion shares.

The international offer was structured with five regional tranches in order to achieve the widest possible placement. CSFB's Carter said: 'We chose a regional underwriting structure in order to achieve maximum breadth of placement, rather than a global underwriting structure that is typically more suited for achieving depth of placement in a secondary offer. We wanted to cast the net as widely as possible bearing in mind that many people only buy IPOs.' Until the time of pricing, these tranches were structured with ranged underwriting commitments to generate maximum competition between the regional syndicates.

A two-phased syndication process was used for the OPV to accommodate a pre-registration period in advance of the fixing of the offer price and size. The OPV syndicate accepted the indicative underwriting commitments before the price and size ranges were announced and the underwriters of the international offer accepted indicative underwriting commitments based on a percentage share of ranged tranche sizes at the outset of bookbuilding (see Exhibit 5).

The international offer included an SEC-registered tranche and ENI was listed on the NYSE in connection with the offer which was structured with a greenshoe of 15 per cent of the total offer.

The structure of the offer was to a significant degree determined by the experience of the privatisation of two commercial banks, Credito Italiano and Banca Commerciale Italiano, where Mediobanca, the Italian merchant bank, and its corporate allies had managed to gain effective control, much to the irritation of international investors. Although the Treasury did not contemplate selling more than a 25 per cent stake in ENI, concerted efforts were made to achieve a high level of transparency and avoid the undue influence of large shareholders. The ENI deal witnessed the introduction of the first golden share in Italy, a ceiling on individual stakes of 3 per cent, a provision against individual parties acting in concert and the reservation of some board seats for minority shareholders.

On 30 October the red herring was published with an indicated offer size of 1.18–2.08 billion shares, corresponding to between 14.8 and 26 per cent of the issued share capital. At the upper end of the price range, the total maximum offer size (excluding the greenshoe) was approximately US$7.6 billion. On 18 November, when the offer was sized, priced and underwritten, the total size was fixed at 1.2 billion shares, principally as a result of weaker than expected demand from retail investors (see Exhibit 6).

Principal advisers

See Exhibit 7.

Transaction fee distribution

Institutional economics

See Exhibits 9 and 10.

In order to achieve maximum motivation of the syndicate, the selling concession was earned entirely on a competitive basis both in Europe and the US. There was no pre-agreed portion of the selling concession, although CSFB's concession was capped in the US at 40 per cent of the regional total (see Exhibit 11).

Exhibit 5

Offer structure

Target markets	Indicated tranche sizes (million shares)*	Bookrunners/joint leads	Co-lead managers
Italian public offer	400–1,000	IMI (Books)	BCI, Banca di Roma, Banca Monte dei Paschi, BNL, Cariplo, Credito Italiano, Instituto Bancario San Paolo di Torino
International offer			
Italy	185–285	IMI (Books)	BCI, Banca di Roma, Banca Monte dei Paschi, BNL, Cariplo, Credito Italiano, Instituto Bancario San Paolo di Torino
US and Canada	270**	CSFB (Books)	Lehman Brothers, Merrill Lynch/NM Rothschild,
		Goldman Sachs (JLM)	JP Morgan, RBC Dominion, Smith Barney
UK and Ireland	170–240	SBC Warburg (Books)	CSFB, IMI, NM Rothschild/Merrill Lynch,
		Morgan Stanley (JLM)	Schroders
Continental Europe	100–170	Paribas (Books)	ABN AMRO Hoare Govett, CSFB, Deutsche Morgan Grenfell, Dresdner Kleinwort Benson, IMI, NM Rothschild, Merrill Lynch
RoW	55–115	Nomura (Books) Indosuez	CSFB, Robert Fleming, Banque
Total international offer	*780–1,080*		
Total combined offers	**1,180–2,080**		

* As reflected in the red herring published on 30 October 1995.
** Although this number was included in the Red Herring there was an understanding that this was a range of 270–340 million shares.

Exhibit 6
Development of the offer size

Indicated number of shares to be sold (30 October)	1.18 billion–2.08 billion + 15% greenshoe
Offer size as per final underwriting amounts (18 November)	1.2 billion + 180 million greenshoe
Proportion of greenshoe exercised	–
Final number of shares sold	1.2 billion

Exhibit 7
Principal advisers

Financial adviser to the Treasury	NM Rothschild & Eptaconsors
International legal adviser to the Treasury and ENI	Shearman & Sterling
Domestic legal adviser to the Treasury	Chiomenti e Associati
International legal adviser to the international and US underwriters	Sullivan & Cromwell
Domestic legal adviser to the international and US underwriters	Grimaldi e Associati
Auditors to ENI	Arthur Andersen & Co.
Marketing and PR consultants	Burson Marsteller

Exhibit 8
The timetable

10 May 1995	• Official decision, taken by governmental decree, to privatise ENI.
10 August	• CSFB and IMI appointed.
15 September	• Confidential filing with the SEC.
25/26 September	• Presentation to equity research analysts.
6 October	• Indicated valuation agreed.
12 October	• Italian Council of State, one of the country's highest judicial bodies, agrees that the Treasury can sell shares in ENI without having to wait for the establishment of a regulatory authority for the natural gas business of ENI, since the state intends to retain a majority of the shares.
16 October	• Public filing of pink herring with the SEC; and • Start of 10-day pre-marketing period.
26 October	• Government narrowly survives vote of no confidence; and • End of pre-marketing.
27 October	• Announcement of price range, overall size and tranche size ranges.
30 October	• Filing of red herring number one and publication of preliminary prospectus; • Preliminary underwriting of retail and international offers on the basis of size and price ranges becomes effective; and • Start of three-week roadshow and bookbuilding period.
6 November	• Start of revocable mandate period.
17 November	• Revocable mandate period ended; and • Roadshow and bookbuilding ended.
18 November	• Offer price of L5,250 announced; and • Filing of red herring number two. • Final underwriting commitments on the basis of fixed price become effective.
21 November	• Start of five-day OPV; and • Last day for cancellation of revocable mandates (as part of pre-registration).
22 November	• OPV closes early.
27 November	• Announcement of US dollar price for ADRs; • Allocation to investors; and • Publication of final prospectus.
28 November	• Start of trading.

Exhibit 9
Distribution of gross spread (%)

Management fee	Underwriting fee	Selling concession	Gross spread
0.56	0.56	1.68	2.80

Exhibit 10
Distribution of management fee outside the US

Total management fee	0.56
Of which: Global coordinators' praecipium	26.8
Of which: Lead/co-lead managers' praecipium split among all leads/co-leads	25.0
Of which: Management fees split among all managers/underwriters	48.2

Exhibit 11
Distribution of selling concession (%)

Total selling concession	1.68
Of which: Pre-agreed portion	0
Of which: Paid according to designations	100

Retail economics

Total fees for the retail offer were 2.7 per cent, although they were 2.9 per cent for orders received during the pre-registration period, of which 1.5–1.7 per cent represented selling concession, depending on when the order was booked. The balance of 1.2 per cent was to cover the praecipium, other management fees and the underwriting fees.

Deal structure

Given the disappointing after-market performance of prior Italian privatisations, it was clear that the retail offer was going to represent a major challenge for the overall success of this privatisation. Accordingly, the money-back guarantee

and the purchase mandate (known as pre-registration), were adopted for the first time in an Italian equity offer.

Money-back guarantee

Following two rounds of market research, the Treasury picked what it considered to be the most cost-effective retail incentive, the money-back guarantee. The Italian public feared losing money in another privatisation, so the Treasury decided to insure them against losses of up to 10 per cent by the first anniversary of the offer provided they had kept their shares for the first year. The reasoning that led to the selection of the money-back guarantee rather than any other incentive can be seen in Exhibit 12.

Unfortunately, this structure does not appear to have been well marketed and was, consequently, not really understood outside the 200,000–250,000 relatively sophisticated retail investors who have repeatedly invested in Italian privatisations, so the vendor did not manage to reach beyond this core retail group. Jürgen Dennert, head of ECM at IMI commented: 'Unfortunately this aspect of the transaction was clearly not well marketed and led to some confusion. Given the adverse market conditions, however, we still believe that under the circumstances, we made the right choice. After all, nobody knows what would have happened without it. Furthermore, the choice of retail incentive was underpinned by market research which consistently showed that the money-back guarantee was the preferred choice of investors.' But one of the equity research analysts involved in the offer noted: 'Notwithstanding what the market research might have shown, the fact that there were no tangible and easily understood retail incentives such as bonus shares or a retail discount made it more difficult to sell the offer to retail investors.'

Another reason for the lukewarm retail response to the money-back guarantee was scepticism about apparent government largesse, which may have translated into specific distrust of this highly complex guarantee. Many retail investors felt that there must have been something wrong with the company, as otherwise the government would not offer this incentive.

Pre-registration

It had become clear in the earlier INA privatisation that a normal two-day OPV was far too short for an offer with large numbers of orders. Jürgen Dennert explained: 'Before the final sizing decisions we used to be in the dark about actual

Exhibit 12
Analysis of alternative retail incentives

Type of incentive	Benefit	Cost to vendor
Money-back guarantee	Protection against a fall in ENI's share price for company-specific or market-related reasons.	Low/medium
Discount	Easily understood and of immediate attraction to retail investors.	Medium/high
Bonus share	Aimed at reducing selling pressure in the after-market and promoting a stable shareholder base.	Medium/high
Partly paid*	Increases the immediate dividend yield.	Medium/high

* Although this incentive formed part of the market research, there was no regulatory approval for such a structure at the time of ENI 1.

retail demand and needed feed-back. This type of revocable mandate, or pre-registration as we called it, is almost like bookbuilding for retail. It represents an indication of demand, which in most cases is then translated into final orders. While pre-registration fulfilled its primary objective, that is early demand assessment before the actual sizing and underwriting of the offer, it also turned out to have rather complex deal dynamics in a transaction which was not going particularly well.'

In order to encourage the banks to achieve as many revocable mandates as possible, the selling concession was higher on the orders received during the pre-registration period. Orders for approximately 330 million shares, or 84 per cent of all orders received during the OPV (including orders from employees) came during the two-week pre-registration period. Of those orders only 4.4 per cent (in terms of number of shares) were revoked.

Whereas pre-registration may well make sense in Italy, it did not work particularly well in this case, principally for the following reasons:

- *Mandate period:* The period during which pre-registration (or revocable mandates) could be received was generally considered too long. This is perhaps not surprising as Italians are used to an OPV of only a few days;
- *Market practice:* Many retail investors looked at the pre-registration period as an extension of the OPV period and expected this prolonged OPV period to be closed early as is typical in Italy. The fact that it was not closed early was interpreted as meaning that the issue was not successful, which discouraged investors;
- *Ineffective marketing:* The mandate structure was not well marketed or understood; and
- *Lack of momentum:* The Consob, the Italian securities regulator had prohibited the underwriters from communicating the progress of subscriptions during the pre-registration period. There was, therefore, no early communication to build initial momentum. On the other hand, while this regulatory constraint could probably have been overcome if the case had been made to the Consob at an early stage, the fact of the matter was that there was no good news to communicate to the market. Once regulatory clearance was received, the joint global coordinators did not know what to announce given the weak demand. International institutional investors often wait for positive signals from the domestic retail tranche before they show demand. In this case, there was complete silence from the domestic market.

Pre-registration works well when there is good retail demand and when tension is created between retail and institutional demand, but, without those positive demand signals, it can be a double-edged sword.

Motivation of syndicate

In order to maximise the motivation of the entire syndicate to try hard to sell shares, the Treasury structured the offer with the following features:

International offer

- The tranches were structured with ranged underwriting commitments. The proportion of the total offer underwritten in one particular region would only be fixed at the end of the bookbuilding period to create competition between tranches;
- The selling concession was to be paid entirely on the basis of designations around the world. There was no element of fixed economics;
- The economics of the joint global coordinators were capped at 40 per cent of the total selling concession for each of their respective bookrun tranches; and
- Morgan Stanley in the UK and Goldman Sachs in the US were elevated to the status of joint lead managers.

Retail offer

In addition to the innovations in the retail offer structure designed to encourage retail investors to subscribe, IMI introduced two further mechanisms to motivate the syndicate:

- To educate the salesforces of the eight senior OPV banks, about 2,000 branch salespeople participated in a video conference/presentation given by ENI's top management which was transmitted via satellite from the Milan Stock Exchange. In addition, ENI's management met individually with a further 13 medium-sized syndicate banks; and
- Retail banks were paid higher fees – 2.9 per cent vs 2.7 per cent – for orders received during the pre-registration period.

Marketing

Institutional marketing strategy

The strategy was to position ENI as a high-quality oil company and appeal to industry buyers. The Italian market was not in favour with investors and country buyers were not likely to commit large amounts. It was decided to cast the net as widely as possible and a three-week roadshow with two ENI management teams was deemed appropriate.

A 10-day pre-marketing campaign, during which 527 institutional investors in 20 countries outside Italy were contacted, was followed by a very comprehensive three-week company roadshow. The company's two teams travelled to

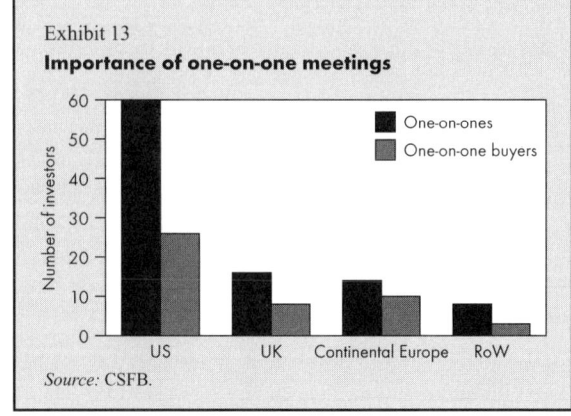

Exhibit 13
Importance of one-on-one meetings

Source: CSFB.

33 cities around the world, made 27 group presentations to almost 900 investors and held 96 one-on-one meetings. Half of the institutions met in one-on-ones bought stock. The number of one-on-ones and the number of buyers were distributed as shown in Exhibit 13.

Retail marketing

This was the first time that a proper roadshow had been carried out for the benefit of retail investors in Italy. A video conference/presentation was televised in all bank branches around the country, but bank branch personnel had become reluctant to recommend further privatisations to their clients due to the poor after-market performance of earlier deals.

The retail offer was launched with an unusually wide size range of 400 million–1 billion shares. This in itself undermined confidence as it gave the impression that there was an unlimited supply of shares. The joint global coordinators assumed that, because of the high quality of the company and with an effective marketing campaign, the targeted size could be achieved. However, they did not have access to adequate market research.

As a result of a poor marketing campaign and poor press management, the money-back guarantee was not well understood by the majority of potential investors and there was general confusion about pre-registration.

A senior representative of one of the banks involved in the offer says: 'The absence of an effective marketing and public relations effort in Italy jeopardised the OPV, due to the failure to direct press coverage and create a sufficiently high profile at an early stage. The absence of a clear and penetra-tive message delivered early and consistently to the broadest possible audience damaged both the image and progress of the transaction in Italy and, to some extent, abroad.'

The ENI story

ENI was positioned as a high-quality oil-major and as a turn-around story with above-average medium-term earnings growth. Operations were conducted through six principal subsidiaries, which contributed to the 1994 operating income of US$4.6 billion (see Exhibits 14 and 15). Profitability at the bottom line was also impressive despite a much higher debt burden than its peers (see Exhibit 16).

At L5,250, ENI was attractively valued in terms of estimated 1996 AMV/Adjusted EBITDAX (see Exhibit 17), as well as in terms of forecast 1996 price/cash flow (see Exhibit 18).

Exhibit 14
Operating income, 1994 (%)

	% of 1994 operating income
Agip (exploration and production)	46
Snam (natural gas supply, transmission and distribution)	38
AgipPetroli (refining and marketing)	8
ENIChem (petrochemicals)	5
Saipem and Snamprogetti (oilfield services, contracting and engineering)	3

Source: Offer circular.

Exhibit 15
Principal sales points

Market position	• With its IPO, ENI was to take its place among the oil majors as the Eighth Sister, based both on performance and scale of operations. ENI had a very high overall asset quality with solid upstream growth derived from Agip's African exposure, an unusually high downstream exposure to natural gas, high-quality refineries and considerable potential for margin expansion in the retail distribution of petrol.
Turnaround	• Since 1992 ENI's newly appointed management team had restructured and rationalised the company, achieving a strong turnaround performance. On a group level, ENI had realised US$3.4 billion from disposals. 50 plants and 140 subsidiaries had been closed and the number of employees reduced by 44,000 (33%); and • ENI's net debt to equity ratio had fallen from 160% in 1992 to 76% at 30 June 1995. CSFB forecast that the net debt to equity ratio would fall further, to 69%, by the end of 1996.
Natural gas business	• ENI's integrated natural gas operations (SNAM) provided stable earnings and significant growth potential.
Profitable upstream operations	• ENI's upstream operations (AGIP) had a proven track record of outstanding returns (1994: 18% ROA and US$3.58 net income per Boe).
Profitability	• Having turned a net loss in 1992, ENI, based on a high asset quality and following radical restructuring, became the third largest oil company in the world by operating profit in 1994.
Valuation	• The principal valuation drivers were 1996 AMV*/EBITDAX**, 1996 price/cash flow and 1996 P/E. Both European and US investors looked in particular at Repsol, Elf and Total as comparable companies. At L5,250, ENI was priced as follows: 1996 AMV/Adjusted EBITDAX: 3.9 times; 1996 price/cash flow: 3.4 times; and 1996 P/E (Italian GAAP): 8.6 times

* Adjusted market value = market value + net debt
** Earnings before interest, tax, depreciation, amortisation and exploration expenditure.

Sources: CSFB, prospectus and ENI.

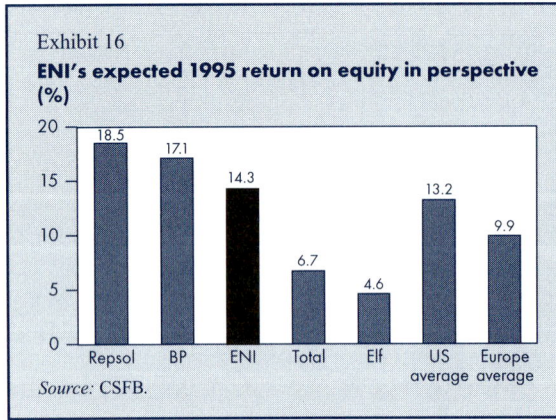

Exhibit 16

ENI's expected 1995 return on equity in perspective (%)

Source: CSFB.

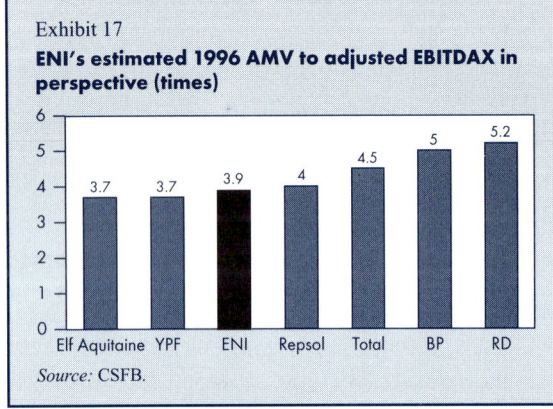

Exhibit 17

ENI's estimated 1996 AMV to adjusted EBITDAX in perspective (times)

Source: CSFB.

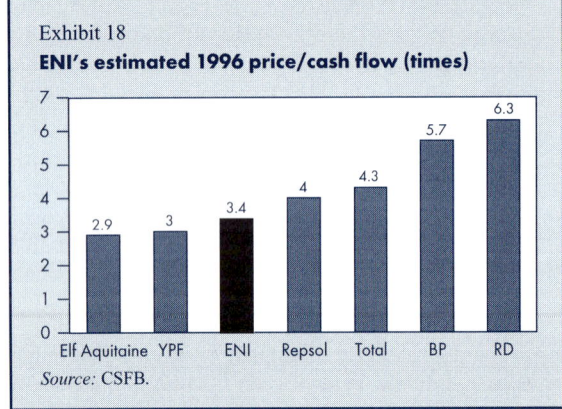

Exhibit 18

ENI's estimated 1996 price/cash flow (times)

Source: CSFB.

Reasons for not buying

- Concerns about the Italian political and economic situation;
- In the US there were a number of investors who declined to participate because they considered the valuation to have been on the high side, but this may have reflected concerns about Europe in general, and Italy in particular;
- ENI had a relatively high gearing compared to its peer group; and
- Some investors doubted that the government would be able to resist meddling in the company to the detriment of minority shareholders.

Results

Placement

See Exhibit 19.

The OPV was sized at 450 million shares, despite the fact that there was demand for only 400 million shares. Due to the under-subscription of the OPV, 50 million extra shares were allocated to the Italian institutional tranche which had been well oversubscribed. Italian retail participation was disappointing both compared to previous Italian privatisations and compared to initial expectations. Only 53 per cent of the demand targeted before the offer (L4 trillion or US$2.5 billion was expected to be raised from 400,000 subscribers taking an average of L10 million each) was achieved. Out of the total number of 194,357 applicants in the OPV, 29,979, or 15.4 per cent, were ENI employees (see Exhibit 20).

Institutional demand in each tranche exceeded the top end of the underwritten tranche sizes. In Italy, actual demand exceeded the allocable demand estimate by some 60 per cent. The Italian tranche was oversubscribed during the first week of book-building. The same was only true of the UK, Continental Europe and RoW tranches in their third weeks, but only during the last two days of bookbuilding in the case of the US tranche.

The joint global coordinators ranked the targeted investors in five quality categories, with category one being the highest quality. Approximately 75 per cent of the international offer was allocated with category one investors.

In total 1.4 billion shares were allocated to institutional and retail investors globally, generating an overall short posi-

Exhibit 19

Underwriting, demand and allocation (million shares)

Target markets	Indicated tranche sizes*	Final underwriting	Demand	Allocation
Italian public offer	400–1,000	450	401	401 (28.6%)
Institutional offer				
Italy	185–285	225	551	355 (25.3%)
US and Canada	270–340	200	365	295 (21.0%)
UK and Ireland	170–240	170	292	200 (14.2%)
Continental Europe	100–170	100	175	90 (6.4%)
Rest of world	55–115	55	117	63 (4.5%)
Total institutional offer	780–1,080	750	1,500	**1,003 (71.4%)
Total combined offers	**1,180–2,080**	**1,200**	**1,901**	**1,404 (100%)**

* As included in the red herring published on 30 October.
** Including greenshoe and naked short.

Sources: Prospectus, CSFB and IMI.

Exhibit 20

ENI 1 retail reception in perspective

	ENI (11/95)	Ina (6/94)	BCI (2/94)	IMI (1/94)	Credit (12/93)
Number of applications*	194,357	417,720	1,017,195	374,000	292,220
Total retail demand (US$ millions)	1,316	2,002	5,825	2,425	3,446
Retail offer size (US$ millions)	1,346	1,963	961	602	639
Retail as a % of total offer	33%	68%	51%	43%	62%
Average order size (US$)	6,771	4,792	5,726	6,484	11,792

* Including employees.

Source: IMI.

tion versus the 1.2 billion shares deal size of 204 million shares, comprising a 180 million share greenshoe and a naked short position beyond the greenshoe of 24 million shares. James Leigh-Pemberton explained: 'This allocation strategy meant that high-quality investors received 60–100 per cent of their demand, which constrained after-market orders. However, it was preferable to allocate in this way in order to create a short position which would provide certain after-market support rather than to under-allocate in the hope of generating after-market orders in a weak market.'

- *Italian tranche:* ENI generated broad participation from Italian institutions, generating an aggregate placement of close to US$1.2 billion, or 35 per cent of global institutional demand, the largest single component of the global institutional offer. Index investors, mutual funds and insurance companies contributed over 90 per cent of demand with 95 per cent of the Italian tranche coming from the highest-quality category of investors. Italian institutions represented the backbone of this offer. IMI's Dennert noted: 'The Italian institutional market is often underestimated by foreign bankers. The Italian institutional tranche in this offer is testimony to that fact;'
- *US and Canada tranche:* The US tranche was the weakest in relation to expectations and CSFB was forced to allocate some investors to the extent of 100 per cent of demand. Although there was only US institutional demand for 295 million shares, thanks to retail demand for another 70 million shares, it was possible to allocate to many US investors less than they had demanded. Approximately 49 per cent of US demand came from category one accounts;

- UK tranche: Approximately US$650 million-worth of ENI shares were placed with UK institutions, reflecting both the high levels of oil and gas industry expertise amongst the UK investor community as well as its relative familiarity with the Italian market. The quality of demand in this tranche was the highest among the international institutional tranches with 61 per cent of UK demand coming from category one investors. While the book as a whole comprised a broad spread of some 150 investors, only four of the top buyers took positions in excess of US$40 million;
- Continental European tranche: Only US$300 million-worth of ENI shares were placed with European investors. The average order size of the 500 investors allocated was just US$600,000 and only five investors bought more than US$10 million worth of stock. The quality of demand was the poorest overall in the international offer with only 34 per cent coming from the highest-quality investors; and
- RoW tranche: Only two key investors participated, together accounting for US$100 million, or 50 per cent, of the entire tranche. The majority of Japanese demand came from just three investors which took US$30 million. Only 35 per cent of demand in this tranche came from category one investors.

In light of the level, quality, price-sensitivity and regional break-down of institutional demand and the extent of domestic demand, the price and size of the ENI offer were both set at the low end of their respective ranges to provide a platform for a healthy after-market.

Exhibit 21

Investor concentration

	By demand	By allocation
Percentage of institutional offer accounted for by the 10 largest investors (by total size of demand and allocation respectively)	22%	25%
The three largest investors by size	US$150 million US$150 million US$110 million	US$125 million US$125 million US$96 million
Total number of institutions	1,500	1,284

Sources: CSFB and IMI.

Investor concentration

See Exhibit 21.

While order sizes from institutions were generally small relative to assets under management, a core of approximately 30 institutions in Italy and abroad each placed orders in excess of US$30 million. Four of the five largest orders worldwide came from Italian institutions.

After-market price performance

See Exhibit 22.

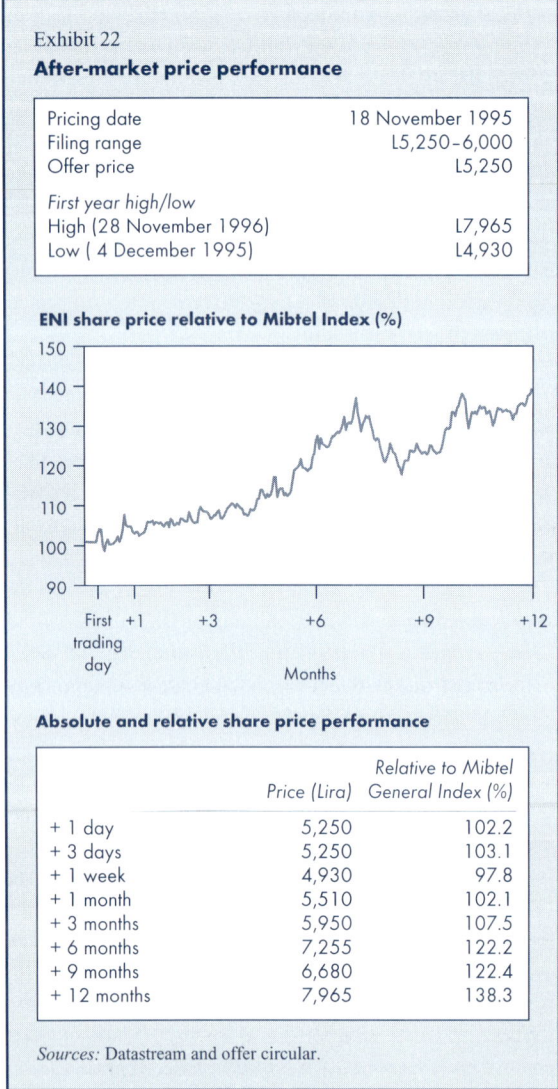

Exhibit 22

After-market price performance

Pricing date	18 November 1995
Filing range	L5,250–6,000
Offer price	L5,250
First year high/low	
High (28 November 1996)	L7,965
Low (4 December 1995)	L4,930

ENI share price relative to Mibtel Index (%)

Absolute and relative share price performance

	Price (Lira)	Relative to Mibtel General Index (%)
+ 1 day	5,250	102.2
+ 3 days	5,250	103.1
+ 1 week	4,930	97.8
+ 1 month	5,510	102.1
+ 3 months	5,950	107.5
+ 6 months	7,255	122.2
+ 9 months	6,680	122.4
+ 12 months	7,965	138.3

Sources: Datastream and offer circular.

Exhibit 23

Percentage of total issue traded * (%)

	Day 1	Day 2	Day 3	Total Day 1-3
Milan	3.8	1.5	2.7	8.0
New York	7.0	1.0	1.6	9.6

* Based on the issue of 1.2 billion shares.

- ENI failed to energise Milan's bourse in its trading debut and closed unchanged on its offer price. Despite a fall in the Mibtel index of 2.2 per cent between the pricing on 18 November and the close of the first trading day (28 November), and a further fall of almost 1 per cent during the subsequent two trading days, the global coordinators managed to hold the price. ENI had, therefore, outperformed the market by over 3 per cent during this period, though only by means of considerable stabilisation purchases;

- When stabilisation at the offer price proved ineffective due to strong selling pressure (not least from the US where 50 per cent of the US placement is thought to have flowed back in the immediate after-market, reflecting aggressive allocations) and a generally falling Italian market, the global coordinators were forced to let the shares trade to the level at which natural two-way business could develop. As a result, the price fell to L4,930 by the fifth trading day. After a week of trading, the absolute price had fallen by 6.1 per cent and ENI had under-performed the market by 2.2 per cent. This represented the all-time low of the stock, both in absolute and relative terms;

- When the share price stopped falling and some of the doubts disappeared, it bounced back strongly, and on 14 December 1995 broke through the offer price for the first time; and

- After 14 December ENI's share price never looked back. On 25 October 1996, CSFB and IMI priced ENI 2 at L7,161 (at the market), 36.4 per cent higher than the offer price for ENI 1. Between the two pricing dates, ENI had outperformed the Mibtel General Index by 29.1 per cent.

Trading volumes in the immediate after-market were relatively modest with only 10.8 per cent of the offer traded on the first day (against up to 30 per cent in many large offers), reflecting a relatively high average quality of placement and the fact that many investors were reluctant to sell at a loss when they were convinced about the medium-term potential for appreciation of the ENI share price. The initial buying was accounted for primarily by UK institutions. Subsequently, US institutions came in to top up their holdings (see Exhibit 23).

In the process of supporting the offer, the joint global coordinators bought 220 million shares in the first week of trading. These purchases covered the over-allotments, so the greenshoe was not exercised.

Over the first month of trading, 56 per cent of the total offer traded, with Telematico (Milan) accounting for 43 per cent, the NYSE 27 per cent and Seaq International 30 per cent of the total trading volumes. Since then Milan has become the dominant market with in excess of 75 per cent of total volume being traded there. The majority of the remainder has traded on the NYSE, with only minimal volumes being traded on Seaq International.

The performance of the main parties

The vendor

Although ENI's proposed privatisation had been bogged down in the corruption scandal and protracted political wranglings, once a clear mandate was given to Mario Draghi, director general of the Treasury, and Vittorio Grilli, head of privatisation and debt management, things started to happen with considerable speed. Leigh-Pemberton commented: 'Once the political negotiations were concluded and it was decided that ENI would be done before the end of 1995, the Italian Treasury was determined and decisive, which was crucial for the execution of the offer as we had little time to discuss matters.'

The Treasury also deserves credit for being market sensitive in agreeing to scale back the offer and price it at the bottom of the range, although strictly speaking, it had little choice. It realised that a successful offer was a necessary investment in the government's future privatisation programme. It was also important to appear generous given that the Treasury retained 85 per cent of the company and the achievement of good value for future sales would obviously be dependent on the positive development of the share price following the IPO.

Although this was an impressive transaction, a simpler retail structure, with a combination of discount and bonus shares for retail investors (as was introduced in ENI 2), might have been preferable given the short time available to explain these concepts. The choice of incentive is thought to have been substantially influenced by the cost to the Treasury, but given that it was the Treasury's intention to price this issue to do well in the secondary market, why look to save money on the retail incentives, a relatively modest cost in the overall context?

The Treasury deserves considerable credit for protecting the company from political interference. Bernabé commented: 'The Treasury acted very professionally as a shareholder – it effectively put up a barrier around the company.'

Former prime minister Amato also deserves credit for the successful privatisation of ENI as he laid the foundation for it by pushing through legislation, disbanding the Ministry of State Participations and doing away with political appointees. Franco Bernabè noted: 'He had the most difficult job because at that time the political parties were still strong.'

The company

Under Bernabé, the management had achieved an impressive restructuring of ENI which laid the foundation for a very strong stock story. Furthermore, the company had done a lot of preparatory work to facilitate a quick sale. Giorgio Anserini, head of Investor Relations at ENI explained: 'Notwithstanding the fact that it was difficult to motivate people to work on the privatisation before it had been explicitly decided, we did a lot of preparatory work over a period of two years, including work on the story and the US GAAP reconciliation. It was certainly difficult to motivate people to do the work but if we hadn't done it, I don't believe that it would have been possible to come to the market in 1995.'

The results for 1995 were in line with the forecast at the time of the IPO. While the operating income and net earnings were marginally lower than forecast by CSFB, the pace of debt reduction had been substantially faster than expected at the time of the transaction (see Exhibit 24).

The banks

In terms of sales, the joint global coordinators together account-

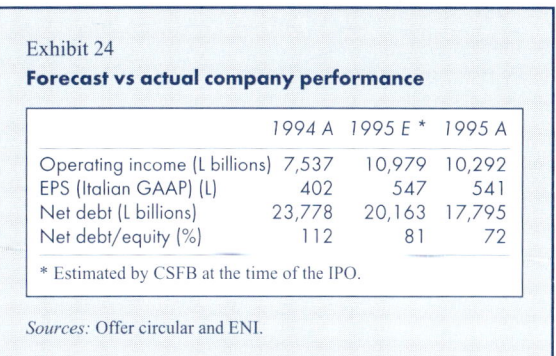

Exhibit 24
Forecast vs actual company performance

	1994 A	1995 E *	1995 A
Operating income (L billions)	7,537	10,979	10,292
EPS (Italian GAAP) (L)	402	547	541
Net debt (L billions)	23,778	20,163	17,795
Net debt/equity (%)	112	81	72

* Estimated by CSFB at the time of the IPO.

Sources: Offer circular and ENI.

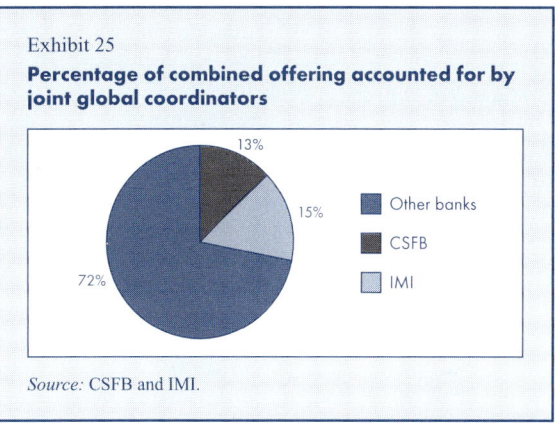

Exhibit 25
Percentage of combined offering accounted for by joint global coordinators

13% / 15% / 72% — Other banks, CSFB, IMI

Source: CSFB and IMI.

ed for 28.1 per cent of the total offer, with IMI placing 15.1 per cent and CSFB 13 per cent. The remaining 71.9 per cent was accounted for by the other 97 banks and 24 securities houses involved. Out of those, SBC Warburg did best, accounting for 5.3 per cent of total sales (see Exhibit 25).

The International offer
IMI accounted for 39 per cent of total sales in the Italian institutional tranche, with its closest competitor Instituto Bancario San Paolo di Torino accounting for only 15 per cent (see Exhibit 26).

CSFB outplaced its syndicate in all but the UK tranche. Its share of the allocations (designations in the US) of the four tranches of the international offer were as shown in Exhibit 27.

CSFB was particularly pleased with the cooperation from a few of the regional leads, notably Morgan Stanley and SBC Warburg, whereas Goldman Sachs and Paribas are thought to have disappointed it. Performances in ENI 1 and the quality of banks' secondary market research coverage were reflected in the ENI 2 syndicate. Morgan Stanley and SBC Warburg were upgraded and Paribas and Goldman Sachs downgraded.

The OPV
One close observer commented that the vendor and the bankers appeared to accept too easily what Consob told them. The most important issue was that Consob would not allow an increase in the size of the offer, resulting in the global coordinators announcing too wide a size range at the outset, which was a major inhibitor of positive momentum in the retail offer.

While it can be argued that IMI is more of an institutional house than a retail house, there is no tangible evidence that any of the commercial banks would have done a better job as

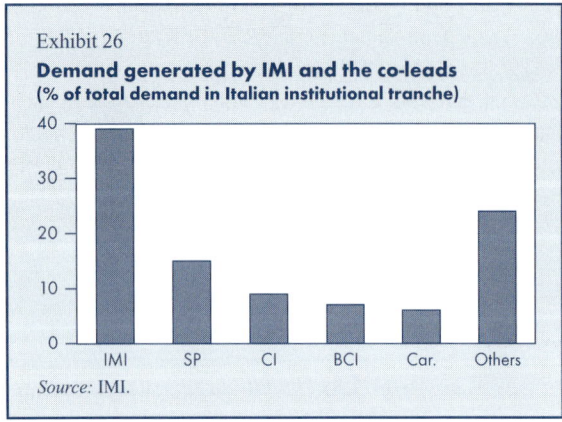

Exhibit 26

Demand generated by IMI and the co-leads
(% of total demand in Italian institutional tranche)

Source: IMI.

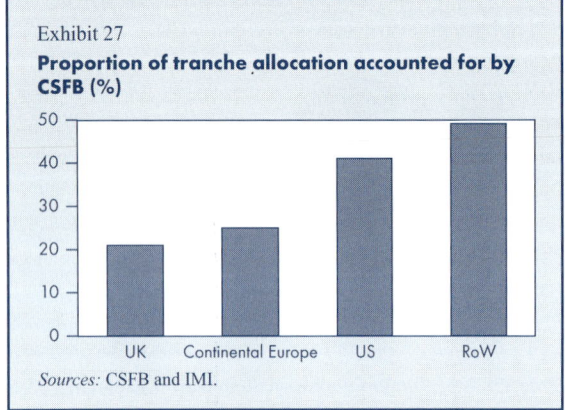

Exhibit 27

Proportion of tranche allocation accounted for by CSFB (%)

Sources: CSFB and IMI.

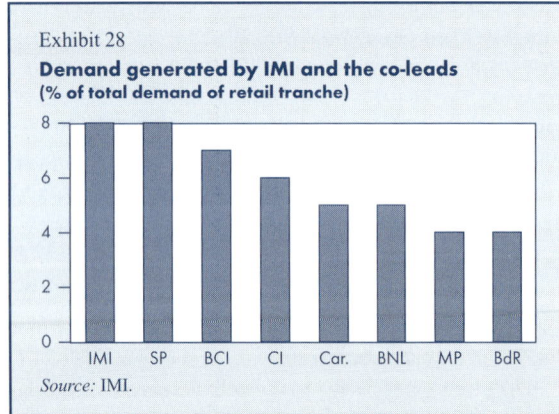

Exhibit 28

Demand generated by IMI and the co-leads
(% of total demand of retail tranche)

Source: IMI.

they do not possess the required expertise, structure or mechanisms to distribute shares. The outcome of the ENI retail offer begs the question as to whether or not IMI would have been more successful in reading demand and placing shares if it had direct access to a branch network. It was, after all, the failure to recognise the prevalent negative sentiment in bank branches across the country that led to the overestimation of retail demand, which in turn led to negative momentum in the retail offer.

In an international context, the proportion of the total demand accounted for by the bookrunning lead manager in the OPV is low: IMI and the seven co-leads together accounted for just 47 per cent of total demand, with the other 116 co-managers accounting for the remaining 53 per cent. The number of banks involved and their relatively even contribution to the total demand reflects the highly fragmented

nature of the banking industry in Italy, the fact that you can only subscribe from the bank where you have an account and the fact that no bank is very strong in the distribution of equities.

IMI was the best-qualified and most experienced bank in Italy at structuring and selling complex equity offers, but it had its hands full on this occasion because of the negative sentiment shared by retail investors and bank branch managers. IMI's Dennert commented: 'The profound impact of the negative performance of earlier privatisations had been grossly underestimated by the domestic banks, due partly to the fact that retail salesforces ignored internal selling recommendations and discouraged investors from buying ENI shares.' (See Exhibit 28.)

The PR, advertising and market research as coordinated by Burson Marsteller was clearly inadequate, and the poor market intelligence (eg, demand estimates) and less than effective communication to the market were major problems. This is something for which IMI, as joint global coordinator with specific responsibility for the OPV, has to take some responsibility, although Burson Marsteller was in fact accountable directly to the Treasury and its adviser, NM Rothschild. One source close to the transaction noted: 'It was of significant importance in this transaction, as in other major privatisations, that not only the bankers but also the PR and marketing consultants have a thorough understanding of privatisation in general and the Italian privatisation programme in particular.' This was clearly not the case.

Key lessons learnt

Preparation

The importance of adequate time to prepare was evident in this transaction and should never be underestimated.

To conclude successful negotiations with risk-averse regulators, such as Consob, sponsors need to be armed with precedents and well articulated arguments.

Structure and timetable

Retail markets differ from country to country due to political, economic and cultural factors. A structure that might work in one country, will not necessarily do so in another. The money-back guarantee worked in Spain but not in Italy.

Luis Mañas, deputy CFO of Repsol explained: 'Purchase mandates appear to have been introduced in the wrong way for Italian circumstances, which are clearly different to those in Spain. Instead of being able to say: "We are already subscribed", the headlines were "Nobody is queuing up for ENI" in Italy.'

Due to the regulatory constraints, the size of the offer could not be increased, and it was therefore seen as important to have sizing flexibility by announcing a wide size range for the OPV. What this offer however clearly demonstrates is that when size ranges are announced, and the final issue is then sized below the maximum, perception builds in the market that an offer is failing. This may become a self-fulfilling phenomenon.

Marketing and communication

The importance of marketing, particularly in big privatisations cannot be underestimated. This is illustrated by the fact that whereas only 200,000 retail investors subscribed for the world-class ENI, no less than 250,000 retail investors subscribed for the June 1996 offer for Italian media company Mediaset. This differential was not simply the product of improved market conditions, but can, to a large extent, be explained by the excellent media campaign in connection with Mediaset.

Franco Bernabè emphasised the importance of communication: 'You have to cope with analysts and experts who seem to know the company better than you do. They also know your markets and your competitors extremely well, and they ask questions on every element of your business. All of this has three consequences: first, you must have something attractive to sell, and this means that the process of restructuring and reorganisation must be well underway and the effects must be evident. Secondly, you must have a really clear vision of your business, ie, you must have clear objectives and you need to be clear about how you are going to get there. Lastly, and most importantly, you must be able to accomplish what you say you are going to do. Accountability becomes a must. The difference between the things you say and the things you do erodes your trustworthiness and that of your company.'

This offer demonstrated the importance of the domestic retail market, not only in order to account for a large portion of the offer, but also to send the right signals to international institutions.

Investor behaviour

Christopher Carter of CSFB commented: 'The ENI offer demonstrates yet again that, as far as the retail market is concerned, you may be only as good as your last deal. This one was, therefore, always going to be difficult given that previous privatisation issues traded well below their respective offer prices.'

Leigh-Pemberton added: 'This privatisation shows that international investors are still very focused on the country aspects of a cross-border equity investment as opposed to only the industry sector. When the country is out of favour, the country focus becomes even stronger.'

Other

The ENI offer powerfully demonstrates the danger of optimistic initial demand estimates from banks. To get an important mandate, investment banks are often prepared to tell clients what they want to hear. In this case, bullish demand estimates based on top-down estimates were given to the Treasury in the solicitation phase, the inevitable consequence of which was to create inflated expectations. This basic problem set up a negative momentum for the whole offer as those expectations led to the wide indicated issue size. Top-down estimates of demand can prove to be highly unreliable and cause tremendous damage. Grilli explained: 'We want more bottom-up-based information about investor intentions.'

The international investment banks are not experts on retail placement and don't pretend to be, while domestic banks, such as IMI, have no experience of retail distribution in other countries. There is limited communication between retail houses in different markets: IMI, for example, did not talk to BBV regarding that bank's experiences with the money-back guarantee and the revocable mandate structures, but relied on the international investment banks for feed-back. More direct cross-border contacts between retail banks in different countries might be useful.

Conclusion

To have completed a US$3.95 billion IPO within the indicated price range in less than four months, despite the fact that the Italian market lost 15 per cent and that the government almost fell at a crucial stage, is a commendable achievement by any standards. The ENI offer also enabled the government to exceed the budgeted privatisation proceeds for 1995, which was of considerable political significance. One of the principal reasons that this was not seen as a categoric success was the sheer ambition of the targeted size.

The most disappointing aspect of the ENI offer was the poor response from Italian retail investors. Having been sized towards the bottom of the indicated range, the OPV was undersubscribed by some 50 million shares. Although it was highly innovative in an Italian context, the likely market reaction to these innovations was inadequately researched and the innovations themselves were not communicated effectively to the market.

It is natural to compare the ENI offer with the 1995 Repsol offer, as they were both conducted under similar circumstances in their respective markets, and as the ENI offer incorporated two important structural innovations first used in the 1995 Repsol offer. While the Repsol offer was much more successful, it should be emphasised that Goldman Sachs and BBV had been working on it since 1993, and had the benefit of extensive market research. In addition, Repsol was a well known name among both retail and institutional investors. The ENI offer was more than twice the size of Repsol's and the political situation in Italy infinitely worse than it had been in Spain. ENI 1 was simply over-ambitious.

Although all tranches of the international offer, save for the US tranche, were covered at the top end of the size and price ranges by institutional orders, the total offer was probably too large by around 50–100 million shares. The US placement was disappointing as international funds focused on Italy's political and economic problems, rather than the fundamentals of ENI. Andrea Azzimondi, Italian equity strategist at CSFB explained: 'The further away from Italy that investors were based, the less the understanding was of the Italian political situation and the more difficult it was to attract demand.' Christopher Carter of CSFB noted: 'This transaction was bought by smart investors who realised that ENI is a high-quality company that they could buy at a discount because of concerns about Italy. They were right.'

After a poor start, ENI became a strong performer, so much so that 11 months later, ENI 2 could be priced 36.4 per cent above its predecessor's offer price. The Italian Treasury should be commended for having absorbed the lessons from ENI 1 and for having been flexible enough to push for and adopt the necessary changes in ENI 2 that enabled the runaway success of that offer in the autumn of 1996.

On 25 October 1996, the Italian Treasury sold a second tranche of ENI, thereby reducing its interest in the company from 85 per cent 69 per cent. NM Rothschild again advised the Treasury, and CSFB and IMI acted as joint global coordinators. ENI 2 was highly successful as the Italian Treasury and its advisers employed the lessons learnt in ENI 1 – the retail structure was simplified, retail marketing much improved and sizing flexibility was assured. However, the main reason for the success was the strong share price performance since the IPO. The share price came off by less than 3 per cent during the last 10 days of marketing and the offer was priced 'at market' rather than at a discount, was increased and traded very strongly in the immediate after-market (up some 11 per cent over the first month), with the greenshoe being exercised in full. In mid-1995, it would have been considered impossible to sell almost US$10 billion of ENI shares within a year, 60 per cent into Italy. Further proof of a revitalised Italian market and strong worldwide demand for ENI shares was given in the July 1997 ENI 3 offer which was again successful despite its unprecedented size (US$7.8 billion). After some difficult years, Italian privatisation now appeared to be going from strength to strength, due in part to the efforts of Draghi and Grilli.

One year after the IPO Franco Bernabè reflected on what the IPO has meant for the company: 'It has been a great opportunity, because it has permitted us to underpin and boost the culture of efficiency and value creation on which we have based ENI's revolution since 1992. The constant and pervasive relationship with investors and financial markets has become a permanent thermometer of our actions, and this, of course, represents a major spur to our aim of always being on the cutting edge and to always do a little bit better what we already do well. The biggest change between the old and the new culture is that we are now focused on value creation for shareholders, rather than simply creating the best industrial strategy there ever was. Our privatisation has also permitted us to save what I always refer to as ENI's genetic unity, ie, its nature as an integrated oil, gas, petrochemical and services company, so that we are able to exploit all the opportunities deriving from this integration.'

KPN

The privatisation by the Netherlands government of holding company Royal PTT Nederland NV (KPN) in June 1994 was the first major example of a large state postal organisation being included in a big telecom sell-off. PTT Post was contributing 30 per cent of total turnover to KPN at the time of the privatisation, the balance coming from PTT Telecom. By contrast, the postal operations of Singapore Telecom, which was privatised in 1993, for example, had accounted for just 8 per cent of total revenues.

KPN's flotation was the largest ever in the Netherlands – more than five times that of DSM in 1989. With 6 per cent of total Dutch market capitalisation, KPN became the third-largest stock in the Netherlands after Shell and Unilever.

Compared to other European countries, privatisation of the postal operations generated little in the way of domestic political debate – in the same way that there has never been a firm policy of nationalisation in the Netherlands there has been no dogmatic privatisation policy. According to KPN, the company's privatisation was a lesser development than its incorporation in 1989 following which, under Dutch company law, the government had only limited scope to interfere in management.

There were two main reasons for the five-year gap between incorporation and the IPO. The first was the law which allowed for the incorporation of KPN which included a clause stating that PTT was to be divided between 'the concession part of the business' and the 'non-concession part'. KPN opposed this from the outset, claiming that it would cause major inefficiencies. The debate as to whether this clause would be continued

post-flotation therefore had to be resolved to avoid complications during the legislative process required for the flotation. The second reason behind the delay was the need to reorganise the accounting system of KPN to achieve better transparency. The fine-tuning of the move to privatise was dictated by KPN's financial timetable and coordination with the privatisation of Tele Danmark, which immediately preceded it.

The decision to issue in the name of KPN rather than the well known Telecom/Post designations was taken only six months before the flotation. When it became apparent that recognition of the holding company's name was very limited there followed one of the largest corporate awareness advertising campaigns ever undertaken in the Netherlands. This was followed by an unusually long marketing period of five weeks.

There was strong resolve on the part of the government to motivate all the banks involved and remunerate those which did a good job, a resolve implemented through flexible tranche sizes and underwriting commitments and a clear allocation policy. 'This transaction was about clear objectives, mobilisation of resources, discipline, discipline, discipline and about making sure that the entire syndicate was part of the team,' said a senior representative of one of the regional lead managers. Henri van Heugten, head of state participations at the Ministry of Finance says: 'The idea was that everyone was going to be able to earn something and that the treatment was going to be the same across all tranches for the same quality of investors.' A hallmark of Dutch privatisations is the government's strict adherence to a separation of the advisory and selling roles to avoid conflicts of interest and to ensure that it gets truly independent advice.

Exhibit 1
Transaction summary

Company: KPN: (the Netherlands)	Global coordinator: ABN AMRO Bank
Pricing date: 6 June 1994 (CBS GEN: 275.2)	Pricing/underwriting structure: Bookbuilding followed by fixed-price retail offer
Vendor: State of the Netherlands	Primary or secondary: Secondary
% of company sold: 30%	Privatisation or corporate: Privatisation
	Retail structure: Retail discount
IPO or non-IPO: IPO	Industry: Telecommunications and post
Type of shares: Ordinary shares and ADRs (1 ADR = 1 ordinary share)	Pricing range: Dfl46–52 Offer price: Dfl49.75
Total issue size: US$3,681 million	US listing/144 A: 144 A

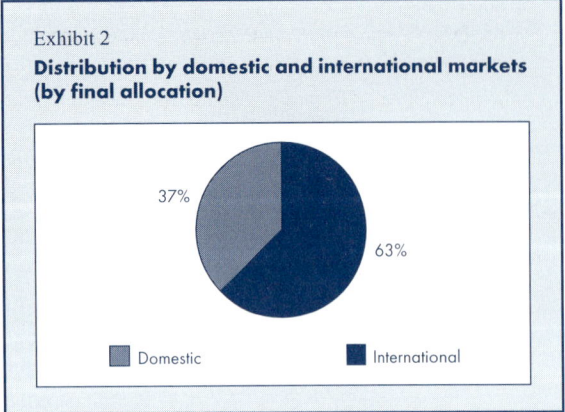

Exhibit 2

Distribution by domestic and international markets (by final allocation)

37%

63%

Domestic   International

For the first time in a Dutch privatisation, there was a discount for retail investors, and the US$3.7 billion IPO was also significant in that KPN was not listed on the NYSE, though in October 1995 the government returned to the market to sell a further US$4.1 billion-worth of KPN shares (KPN2) which were listed on the NYSE. This further sale reduced state ownership in KPN to 44.8 per cent. KPN2 was launched in to a very busy autumn new-issue market which included Telefónica of Spain and PT Telekom of Indonesia. The rationale behind this timing was to complete the transaction well ahead of the privatisation of Deutsche Telekom, expected in 1996, and several further European telecom offers.

Although the reception of the IPO by Dutch retail and institutional investors was a disappointment, the overall success of the 1994 offer was ensured through an outstanding performance in the international market.

Major challenges

One of the biggest challenges facing the flotation was the size of the offer, particularly when seen in the context of the domestic retail market.

The inclusion of PTT Post was seen as presenting a significant communications challenge leaving the government concerned about the chances of a successful offer. The question therefore arose as to how to best mobilise retail interest and persuade reluctant Dutch institutions to play a part in the book-building exercise.

A further complication was presented by adverse market conditions, which went from bad to worse. Both the local market and the other main markets of relevance performed poorly during the five-week marketing period (2 May to 6 June). Tele Danmark had traded down by 3 per cent over the period, although British Telecom had risen by 1.1 per cent.

Rationale and objectives

When KPN was incorporated on 1 January 1989, it was without any specific intention to privatise it and the possibility of selling shares in the future was included in the 1988 bill of incorporation only at the last minute. Privatisation took place not so much for ideological or fiscal reasons but mainly

because of a government report published in September 1985 which stated: 'Those companies where there is no specific and dominant reason for the state to own the majority of the shares should be transferred to the private sector.' KPN fitted into this category.

From 1989, KPN had become one of the most efficient national telecom operators in Europe and one of the most attractive employers in the Netherlands. Furthermore, over five years it had built the necessary track record to fulfil Amsterdam Stock Exchange listing requirements. The government also thought that if KPN were in the private sector it would be better prepared for the steadily increasing competition of a deregulated and liberalised European telecom market. Andre Betting, project coordinator of the flotation at the Ministry of Transport, summarises the reasons for flotation as:

- More freedom for KPN;
- Extra incentive for the company and its management;
- Exposure to capital markets, providing useful discipline;
- The possibility to enter into such activities as joint ventures; and
- KPN wanted to do it.

There was also a broad political consensus for the privatisation, but in the absence of a long list of further companies to sell, the government was not forced to price the transaction to generate a spectacular premium which would popularise privatisation with the Dutch public. Nevertheless, the government wanted a success to ensure that KPN 2, which at that time had been expected in 1996–97, would be feasible. 'Although the government was not a bad shareholder, the IPO gave us access to the equity capital market and the possibility to enter into strategic alliances,' says Cees Griffioen, KPN chief financial officer. 'We improved our international attractiveness.'

KPN agreed five important conditions with the government ahead of the IPO:

1. KPN should be a normal and independent company under Dutch law;
2. There should be no interference by politicians in KPN's day-to-day management;
3. There should be clear-cut separations between the government's role as regulator, as shareholder and as guardian of public interest;
4. The state should reduce its holding to under 50 per cent in due course; and
5. KPN should be protected against hostile takeover activity.

The offer objectives

The government's specific offer objectives were:

- To maximise the price per share, though there was no specified amount to be raised. There were three principal alternatives considered: 10–15 per cent, 20–30 per cent and 49–51 per cent. The first alternative would have meant many offers before the state had reduced its stake to the targeted 33 per cent leaving a continuous overhang in the market, while the third alternative was deemed too large an offer for the market without compromising on value. Therefore the decision was taken to do the largest size possible, consistent with achieving the highest price per share. The market capacity was deemed not to exceed 35 per cent and accordingly this is what the government asked parliament for in March 1994;

- To generate a successful offer, meaning that at least 50 per cent should be placed in the Netherlands; and
- To encourage wider share ownership, an aim that became more important as the deal progressed, in part because a general election was approaching. By the time of election few offer details had been made known – a situation which had less impact in the Netherlands than had been the case with telecom sell-offs in the UK and France.

Share capital and ownership

See Exhibit 3.

Exhibit 3
Share capital and ownership

Type of shares offered	Ordinary bearer shares of Dfl10 per share and ADRs representing one ordinary share each. The bearer shares can be converted to registered shares at any time.
Share capital before and after offer	*Authorised capital* 800,000,000 ordinary shares 1 special share 499,999,999 preference shares A 700,000,000 preference shares B *Issued capital* 460,273,810 ordinary shares 1 special share
Voting/ownership restrictions	There are no voting or ownership restrictions on the ordinary shares and all shares carry one vote each. That notwithstanding, certain rights pertaining to the ordinary shares are reflected in KPN's articles of association and in a separate agreement between the government and KPN: 1. KPN has extensive rights to issue new shares and in so doing also to disapply the pre-emptive rights, thereby diluting ordinary shareholders; 2. The state has an option to require KPN to issue to the state, under certain circumstances, Preference Shares A to increase the state's holding to 33% and 51% respectively to safeguard the 'general interest of the state', ie, the maintenance of an effective Dutch postal and communications system; 3. KPN and the 'Foundation for the Protection of KPN' (a legal structure common among Dutch public companies to protect them from unfriendly shareholder action that may threaten their continuity, independence or identity) have put and call options respectively to issue preference shares B to the Foundation, subject to the approval of the Supervisory Board and the government as holders of the special share. This is designed to protect the interests of KPN; and 4. To safeguard the 'general interest of the state', the latter has the right under the special share as reflected in the articles of association to approve important KPN resolutions concerning matters such as the issuance of shares, the disapplication of pre-emptive rights, mergers and acquisitions, capital expenditure above a certain size and under certain conditions, the change of the articles of association, etc.
Market capitalisation at offer price (Dfl1.866/US$)	US$12.3 billion
Major shareholder(s) before/after the offer	The state owned 100% of KPN before the offer, and, after it, 70% of the ordinary shares and 1 special share. At the time of the offer, the government announced that it intended to sell further shares in the company by 1996 or 1997, thereby reducing the state's ownership to below 50%. The state also declared its intention to retain at least 33% until 2004.
Most relevant stock exchange index/weighting/proportion of share capital included	CBS General Index/KPN included in June 1994 with a weighting of 6.7% taking 100% of KPN's share capital into account. KPN was also included in the AEX index of the 30 most traded shares, but only in February 1995 and based only on the free float. Following the February 1996 revision to the AEX index, KPN now accounts for 10%.

Exhibit 4
Offer structure

Target markets	Indicated tranche sizes*	Regional lead managers	Co-lead managers
Netherlands	45–55%	ABN AMRO	ING, Rabobank (joint leads)
RoW	15–25%	CSFB	ABN AMRO, Crédit Lyonnais, Dresdner, Kredietbank, Nomura, Swiss Bank Corporation
UK and Ireland	15–25%	SG Warburg	Hoare Govett** NatWest
US and Canada	10–15%	Morgan Stanley	Lehman, RBC Dominion
Total combined offers (shares)	**138,150,000**		

*% of Indicated total offer on 16 May 1994.
** Part of the ABN AMRO group.

Exhibit 5
Flexible underwriting commitments for the syndicate banks (% of total tranche sizes)

Lead manager	25–40
Co-lead manager	5–10
Senior co-manager	2.5–4.5
Co-manager	1–2

Transaction components

The offer of 138.15 million outstanding shares comprised four tranches: domestic (including separate retail and institutional offers); UK and Ireland; a US and Canada private placement; and the rest of the world (RoW). The indicated tranche sizes, based on best estimates or the desired breakdown of the global distribution can be seen in Exhibit 4.

At the beginning of the bookbuilding process on 16 May, only indicative underwriting ranges for individual tranches were announced. In addition, each syndicate member was given only a ranged underwriting commitment. The underwriting commitments by seniority of syndicate member were announced at the beginning of the bookbuilding period and are shown in Exhibit 5.

These flexible underwriting commitments were devised such that final underwriting amounts could reflect the relative performance of each of the four tranches and the performance of each individual syndicate bank during bookbuilding. This represented a considerable innovation and was one of the reasons behind the offer's success.

The offer was marketed on an open-priced basis to international and domestic investors allowing a book to be built,

after which the offer price was fixed. Once this was done, a three-and-a-half day formal subscription period for domestic retail investors followed, after which allocation to all investors took place. The syndicate therefore took a hard underwriting risk at a fixed price for seven calendar days. Dutch retail investors were given an advance guarantee of a 5 per cent discount to the institutional price on a maximum of 75 shares, and there was no official clawback for domestic retail investors. A five-month lock-up applied to KPN and a one-year lock-up to the state. The offer was structured with a 15 per cent greenshoe calculated on the total offer size.

Principal advisers
See Exhibit 7.

Transaction fee distribution
See Exhibit 9.

Management fee

ABN AMRO was paid a global coordinator's praecipium, corresponding to 25 per cent of the total management fee, which was itself calculated on the gross proceeds of the whole offer. The regional lead and co-lead managers outside the US were paid a lead managers' and co-lead managers' praecipium (see Exhibit 10).

Selling concession

In the US, the selling concession had one fixed and one variable component. The fixed component of 30 per cent was calculated on the basis of underwriting commitments. The variable portion was subject to performance and was designated by investors (see Exhibit 11).

In Europe the selling concession was in principle paid in

Exhibit 6
Development of the offer size

Indicated number of shares to be sold	138,150,000 + 20,715,000 greenshoe
Proportion of greenshoe exercised	–
Final number of shares sold	138,150,000

Exhibit 7
Principal advisers

Financial adviser to the state	NM Rothschild & Sons
Dutch legal adviser to the state	De Brauw Blackstone Westbroek
UK legal adviser to the state	Linklaters & Paines
US legal adviser to the state	Sullivan & Cromwell
Marketing adviser to the state	Dewe Rogerson Limited
Financial adviser to KPN	Goldman Sachs International
Dutch legal adviser to KPN	Loeff Claeys Verbeke
US legal adviser to KPN	Cravath, Swaine & Moore
Dutch legal adviser to the managers	Stibbe Simont Monahan Duhot
UK legal adviser to the managers	Allen & Overy
US legal adviser to the managers	Shearman & Sterling
Auditors to KPN	Coopers & Lybrand

Exhibit 8
The timetable

1 January 1989	• Incorporation of KPN.
1 July 1992	• Project Team Flotation (PTB) began preparation of government decision to float KPN. PTB included the Ministries of Transport and Finance as well as KPN. The principal tasks were legal, regulatory and organisational. This phase was completed at the end of 1993 whereafter the timetable for the flotation was agreed.
December 1992	• Goldman Sachs appointed adviser to KPN.
Late June 1993	• NM Rothschild & Sons appointed adviser to the ministries of finance and transport.
1 July 1993	• Joint Working Group (JWG) started advisory phase, ie, preparation of the offer. The JWG included the parties in PTB plus NM Rothschild, Goldman Sachs and, once appointed, ABN AMRO. The ministry of transport was quasi-representing the shareholder and the regulator. The ministry of finance was involved because under legislation on public accountability, the minister of finance is responsible for the sale of state participations; the ministry also had extensive privatisation experience. JWG dealt with all aspects of the flotation, including the appointment of parties, whether or not to list in the US, the entity to be floated, the positioning of KPN, the dividend policy, the employee participation scheme, the sizing of the first tranche, the marketing, the pricing and the allocation, etc. The KPN board of management, however, had final decision on which entity was to be floated, how KPN should be positioned with investors, whether or not to list in the US, the dividend policy and the extent to which KPN employees would be offered shares.
Mid-October 1993	• ABN AMRO Bank appointed global coordinator.
Early January 1994	• SG Warburg, Morgan Stanley and CSFB appointed regional lead managers.
14 February 1994	• Passage of the KPN Flotation Act.
27 April 1994	• US$3.0 billion IPO for Tele Danmark priced.
2 May 1994	• Pre-marketing begins.
16 May 1994	Official launch: • Preliminary prospectus distributed; • Overall issue size and indicative tranche size ranges announced; • Offer price range announced; and • Start of three-week bookbuilding period.
6 June 1994	Pricing: • Offer price announced and underwriting effective; • Tranche sizes fixed; • Size of underwriting commitment per bank fixed; • Publication of final prospectus; and • Application period for Dutch retail offer began.
9 June 1994	• Application period for Dutch retail offer period ended at 1 pm Dutch time.
13 June 1994	• Allocation to institutional and retail investors; and • Trading begins on the Amsterdam Stock Exchange

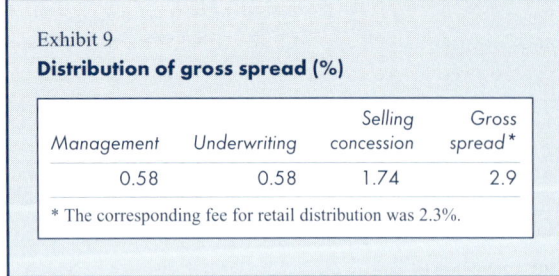

Exhibit 9

Distribution of gross spread (%)

Management	Underwriting	Selling concession	Gross spread*
0.58	0.58	1.74	2.9

* The corresponding fee for retail distribution was 2.3%.

Exhibit 10

Distribution of management fee outside the US (%)

Total management fee	0.58
Of which: Global coordinator's praecipium	25
Of which: Lead/co-lead managers' praecipium split among all leads/co-leads	25
Of which: Management fee split among all managers	50

Exhibit 11

Distribution of selling concession in the US (%)

Total selling concession	1.74
Of which: Pre-agreed or fixed portion regardless of sales booked	30
Of which: Paid pro rata according to sales designated by investors	70

full to whomever the order was given although institutions also had the choice of designating banks.

Deal structure

Size of issue

It seems as if the judgment on size was accurate, as to have done a smaller issue would have been unfortunate in the light of the government's wish to reduce its holding to one-third in the medium term. Given the relatively poor market conditions, the market would have had difficulty swallowing a larger offer: the domestic market – the weak link – would most probably have looked even more disproportionate. Perhaps expectations for domestic participation were a little too high to be realistic, but a 37 per cent domestic take-up is nothing to be ashamed of, particularly in such a large transaction.

Underwriting structure

The banks had to take seven calendar days underwriting risk at a fixed price, because the application period for retail investors started only when the offer was priced. This does not represent the latest state of development in terms of privatisation technology (compare, for example, the TCNZ issue in 1991, BT3 in 1993, YPF in 1993 and Pharmacia in 1994, all of which were structured with effectively open and simultaneous pricing for retail and institutional investors). This was the first major book-

built issue in the Netherlands and the domestic institutions were not willing participants. This initial reluctance to go along with bookbuilding is found in almost every market because it puts the domestic institutions under a lot of pressure and demands complete transparency. It is therefore of utmost importance to educate the institutions accordingly.

Corporate governance

Most large publicly traded Dutch companies are almost completely takeover-proof and controlled by a management board. Considerable effort was spent in the KPN IPO on ensuring that the state retained sufficient power to look after the best interests of the country as a whole, in terms of a functioning telephone and postal system. This was ensured through the special share, and the ability to issue Preference Shares A and B was put in place to protect the interests of the state and KPN respectively against hostile activity.

Marketing

Retail

There were three campaigns covering the principal media – television, newspapers and magazines – over 12 weeks starting 3 March 1994. The first was a corporate awareness campaign explaining about KPN which increased the level of awareness of the company from 3–4 per cent at Christmas 1993 to 90 per cent by the time of the IPO. Second came an offer campaign to explain what the offer was and why it should be subscribed to, and third was a subscription campaign to explain the process.

According to some analysts, the offer campaign, the biggest ever in the Netherlands, reached only 70 per cent of all households as opposed to the 90 per cent targeted. Part of the problem, they say, is that it was delayed by the corporate awareness campaign running late. All in all the two campaigns lost some of their effectiveness, and their lack of success may also have something to do with the fact that the Dutch are not used to these types of campaigns. Accordingly, the issue did not result in a significant widening of private shareholding in the Netherlands.

There was a discount for retail investors for the first time in the Netherlands, which amounted to 5 per cent (Dfl2.50) of the institutional offer price for up to 75 shares. A loyalty bonus was considered too difficult to implement due to the fact that bearer shares were being issued. A partly paid offer was never seriously considered, while discounts on telephone bills were considered but were found to be against Dutch law.

The outcome of the retail marketing was clearly disappointing. Only 188,000 individuals (including 31,000 KPN employees) bought shares, against 120,000 in connection with the much smaller DSM offer in 1989. There are said to be up to a million high net worth individuals in Holland. ABN AMRO never believed in mass retail, but in those high net worth individuals, and according to the bank's director of corporate finance, Charles van Schelle: 'Whereas the number of investors was below expectations, the amount raised from Dutch retail was more or less on target. There was some discrepancy between numbers of investors and amount.'

Institutional

Two factors are particularly interesting in the marketing of KPN: the pre-marketing and bookbuilding campaigns were organised with military discipline and the government managed to obtain a high level of motivation from a large number of the syndicate banks. Whereas many of the 'rules of engagement' which applied are fairly standard for most issues, it was the discipline with which they were imposed that was unusual and ultimately made a difference to the

outcome of the offer. The rules included: how to handle equity research and the press, when and where each bank was allowed to pre-market and sell, the need for complete transparency with regard to disclosure in detail of all orders above Dfl100,000, and instructions about trading during the stabilisation period.

The 'military operation' nevertheless had a considerable amount of flexibility. The global coordinator targeted 450 institutions world-wide and two major roadshows were conducted – an analysts' pre-marketing effort followed by the KPN roadshow (over 10 working days going to 24 cities around the world of which 12 were in the US). KPN had a total of 80 one-on-one meetings with investors (see Exhibit 12).

During the two-week pre-marketing period, organisational discipline was reinforced by a daily feedback procedure to each syndicate member. Pre-marketing had two main aims: the first was 'prospecting the terrain', through which the regional lead managers, the global coordinator, Rothschild and the state sought to receive high-quality information concerning investor intentions. This included the key factors most likely to determine the final interest by high-quality institutions and the principal reservations against buying. The most important feedback, however, was on how the inclusion of PTT

Exhibit 12

Pre-marketing and marketing (number of one-on-ones)

	Pre-marketing roadshow*	Company roadshow
Netherlands	50	15
UK	45	20
US	45	20
RoW	120	25

* In the Netherlands the number includes only meetings arranged by ABN AMRO and ING. Elsewhere, the numbers include those by the global coordinator, the regional lead managers and the joint lead managers.

Exhibit 13

Principal sales points

Earnings growth	• Low-risk, high-quality earnings growth averaging 7–8% over the next 5 years, derived from revenue growth of 5% and operating cost rationalisation and interest expense reduction of 2–3% a year.
Dividend growth	• Progressive dividend policy with dividends per ordinary share to grow at least in line with the growth of net income. At the time of the IPO, KPN's board of management expected that over the coming years, there would be a prudent increase in the dividend payout ratio. Analysts believed that the payout ratio would grow from 50% to 60% over the medium term. The progressive dividend policy was supported by a strong balance sheet.
Value added from PTT Post	• The postal business adds value to the KPN story and will drive earnings growth faster than pure, mature telecom peers. PTT Post is one of the few postal organisations in the world that is competitively positioned against providers of competing new technologies such as facsimile transmission and mobile communications. PTT Post contributes 30% of KPN's turnover and 15% of its operating profits. Whereas it operates with a lower operating margin than PTT Telecom, it has a higher return on capital employed.
Low industry and company risk	• The usual telecom investment risks – competition and regulation – although increasing are relatively low in this case, due to KPN's competitive prices and a favourable regulatory regime with regulated prices effectively allowed to track inflation. Only approximately 15% of PTT Telecom's 1993 sales were derived from activities exposed to competition. The equivalent number for PTT Post was 55%.
Low country risk	• Excellent macro-economic environment in the Netherlands – hard currency, economic recovery, low inflation, international focus and topographical benefits.
Quality of management	• Senior management has the marketing/commercial expertise (ex-Unilever/ex-Alcatel) needed to leverage up bottom-line growth in a mature telecom company, although none of the members of the senior management had prior experience running a publicly listed company.
Valuation (at Dfl49.75)	• KPN is attractively valued: On the assumption of estimated 1994 EPS of Dfl4.12 and a payout ratio of 52%: 1. *Total return (Dividend yield + 5-year compounded growth rate)*: Premium of 5.5% over the 10-year Dutch government bond yield against 4.1% for BT and 4.6% for the US regional telephone companies (Tele Danmark, however, was at a premium of nearly 10%); 2. *Dividend yield*: Premium of 0.8% to the Dutch market (yielding 3.5%); 3. *Price/earnings ratio*: KPN was priced at 12.1 times while BT was trading at 13.1 times and Tele Danmark at 17 times. KPN was priced at a reasonable P/E of 83% to the Dutch market; and 4. *Debt-adjusted price to cash-flow multiple*: Discount to most of the similarly mature telecom companies.

Sources: Prospectus, CSFB and ABN AMRO.

Exhibit 14

Valuation of KPN in perspective

Company	Price	94 P/E	P/E rel	P/ADJ CF	DY	DY rel	Payout	Adj. MV/Line
KPN	49.75	12.1x	83%	4.0x	4.3%	123%	52%	US$1,517
BT	393	13.1x	105%	4.9x	5.6%	121%	59%	US$1,450
Tele Danmark	310	16.8x	108%	5.5x	3.9%	298%	65%	US$1,975
Bells (average)	n/a	13.3x	86%	5.4x	5.5%	163%	74%	US$1,781
Tel NZ	5.12	16.3x	116%	8.4x	4.2%	110%	79%	US$3,976

Sources: CSFB and Goldman Sachs (Tele Danmark).

Post would be perceived, and the basis on which the institutions looked at the value of KPN.

The second major purpose of the pre-marketing phase was to determine where the artillery should be aimed during the marketing and bookbuilding phase: most important was to determine which institutions should be targeted through the crucial one-on-one meetings. Experience shows that in most offers, those institutions that are granted one-on-one meetings typically account for between 50 and 80 per cent of the total institutional book. It is thus of key importance to select the right institutions and not waste time on those unlikely to want to buy in large volumes.

A bottom-up strategy was employed – only tangible evidence from institutions was going to dictate tranche sizing, underwriting commitments and allocation. This principle led to a high degree of transparency and a higher degree of fairness.

The KPN story

At the time of the IPO, KPN was the sole provider of fixed-line national, international and mobile telecoms, and traditional postal services in the Netherlands. It represented a low-risk investment with an attractive yield which was expected to grow at a rate higher than that of the company's earnings: this made KPN an 'income play'. As a Dutch stock with a high yield, KPN had tremendous defensive characteristics (see Exhibits 13 and 14).

Major reasons for not buying

The reasons given by those who did not buy were related mainly to price in the case of Dutch institutions, and general market conditions elsewhere (see Exhibit 15).

Over the six months to the launch of the offer, BT had fall-

en steadily against the FT-SE 100 Index and over the past year it had under-performed the same index by 20 per cent, mainly because of concerns that it would have to give up increasing portions of its 90 per cent share of the UK domestic telephony market. At the beginning of 1994 however, foreign investors had kept their faith in the Dutch equity market while abandoning their holdings in many other European markets. International equity offers from the Netherlands, including KLM, VNU and Hoogovens, had generally been well received.

On the day of pricing the Dutch market actually rose by 1.1 per cent. The sector, despite Tele Danmark's poor performance, was still in favour with investors and KPN's outstanding story enabled the offer to be completed.

Results

Placement

At the offer price, which was slightly higher than many analysts had expected, the offer was 2.8 times subscribed. UK and US institutions demonstrated price leadership, continental European investors were not particularly price-sensitive, while domestic institutions were trying to talk down the price. This picture is not atypical in the case of a major international IPO where in general UK and US institutions have a clearer view on value (see Exhibit 16).

- Dutch institutional and retail demand was disappointing and there was considerable price sensitivity from domestic institutions which supposedly pushed hard for a price of around Dfl48 and insisted that they would not pay more than Dfl50. 'This shows yet again that the domestic institutions, like everywhere, don't want to pay up,' noted Matthew Westerman, director of NM Rothschild. Despite an eventual willingness to pay, Dutch institutions did not receive allocations to as high a degree as institutions elsewhere and accordingly they participated substantially in the after-market. Simon Barnasconi, vice president of ECM at ABN AMRO explained: 'The Dutch institutions counted on being favourably treated but they were not, although some of them increased their bids, many of which were still not honoured.' Despite a very disappointing domestic tranche, the global coordinator backed by the government and NM Rothschild fixed the Dutch underwriting amount at 47.5 per cent to maintain the impression that the Dutch tranche was successful. It was important to gen-

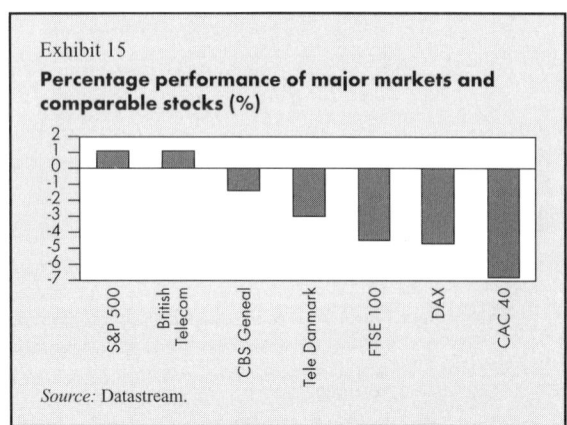

Exhibit 15

Percentage performance of major markets and comparable stocks (%)

Source: Datastream.

Exhibit 16
Underwriting, demand and allocation (%)

Target markets	Underwriting range fixed (16 May 1994)	Demand (6 June 1994)	Underwriting effective* (6 June 1994)	Allocation (13 June 1994)
Netherlands	45–55	26	47.5	37**
UK and Ireland	15–25	23	20	23
US and Canada	10–15	14	15	14
RoW	15–25	37	17.5	26
Total combined offers (shares)	**138 million**	**390 million**	**138 million**	**168 million**

* The underwriting commitments were fixed only at the end of the bookbuilding period.
** Of which approximately 20% was allocated to Dutch retail and 17% to Dutch institutions.

Source: ABN AMRO

Exhibit 17
Investor concentration

	By demand	By allocation
Percentage of issue accounted for by the 10 largest investors (by total size of demand and allocation respectively)	11%	14%
Number of investors making up 80% of the issue (by total size of demand and allocation respectively)	125–150	100–125
The three largest investors by size	US$173 million US$141 million US$120 million	US$95 million US$77 million US$68 million
Total number of institutions	2,500	2,500

Source: ABN AMRO.

erate as much momentum as possible during the four-day retail subscription period and to calm the overall syndicate, underwriting for seven calendar days. This decision also benefited the global coordinator economically;

• The RoW tranche was the most successful and was six times subscribed, based on the effective underwriting commitment. However, the government sent a signal to the RoW regional lead manager that the overall offer was more successful than it really was by giving it an underwriting commitment at the lower end of the range. The strategy was to convince CSFB and RoW syndicate members that the transaction was hugely successful in the UK and US, typically the 'leadership markets' for this type of offer. This was obviously hard medicine to swallow for CSFB. The government team maintained that the quality of RoW demand was not as high as that of institutional demand elsewhere. This might often be true but CSFB claimed that there was not a sufficient understanding of these institutions by the government team. The most important markets for the RoW tranche were Switzerland (33 per cent), Asia Pacific (14 per cent) and Scandinavia (12 per cent). The defensive characteristics of KPN made this an ideal stock for conservative European continental investors;

• Among the foreign tranches, the UK market was the most price-sensitive, ie, investor interest was dramatically lower above Dfl48; and

• US demand came in more or less on target but was relatively modest considering that half of the roadshow was devot-

ed to the US and Canada. This percentage is also dramatically lower than in the case of Tele Danmark where 38 per cent of the total issue was placed in the US. Price leadership still came mainly from the US market. Clearly, the fact that Tele Danmark had a US global coordinator and a NYSE listing made a big difference. This notwithstanding, the KPN 144A tranche was one of the biggest such offers ever.

The majority of institutional buyers belonged to one of three types: income, index or telecom. In continental Europe, there were many investors who bought KPN as a high-yielding defensive play from a sound country.

Investor concentration
See Exhibit 17.

The total of 188,000 Dutch retail investors was below expectations and a lower number than the Dutch banks had expected. The net number represents 1 per cent of the Dutch population whereas 2.5–5 per cent is the norm throughout Europe.

After-market price performance
See Exhibit 18.

• Menno de Jager, ABN AMRO senior vice-president, equity capital markets commented: 'Although on 13 June, the day the issue started trading, Dutch government bond yields shot up by 25–35 basis points depending on the maturity

Exhibit 18
After-market price performance

Pricing date	6 June 1994
Filing range	Dfl46–52
Offer price	Dfl49.75
First year high/low	
High (21 December 1994)	Dfl59.20
Low (20 June 1994)	Dfl47.70

KPN share price relative to CBS GEN Index (%)

Absolute and relative share price performance

	Price (Dfl)	Relative to CBS Gen (%)
First trading day (13 June 1994)	50.20	102.1
+ 3 days	50.10	101.9
+ 1 week	47.70	101.1
+ 1 month	48.40	102.5
+ 3 months	54.20	108.4
+ 6 months	54.80	111.2
+ 9 months	56.90	117.3
+ 12 months (13 June 1995)	54.80	105.3

Sources: Datastream and offer circular.

Exhibit 19
Percentage of total issue traded * (%)

	Day 1	Day 2	Day 3	Total Day 1–3
Amsterdam	5.8	5.5	3.0	14.3

* Based on the issue of 138,150,000 shares.

and the fact that the Dutch equity market had fallen by 1.2 per cent since pricing on 6 June, KPN closed at Dfl50.20, 0.9 per cent up from the offer price. There was therefore a relative outperformance of 2.1 per cent by the end of trading on the first day';

- During the first three days of trading, the KPN share price, in absolute terms, stayed above the offer price, only to fall below Dfl49.75 on the fourth day. It then stayed below the offer price until 27 June;
- At all times during these first two weeks of trading KPN outperformed the market (ie, the relative performance

index stayed above 100 per cent). During this period, the Amsterdam market fell by over 5 per cent, resulting in a relative market outperformance of just under 5 per cent;

- One year after the start of trading KPN shares were at Dfl54.80 and had outperformed the Dutch market by 5 per cent. During this first year, the highest level reached in the absolute price was Dfl59.20 on 21 December 1994. In relative terms, the outperformance peaked on 21 March 1995, when it reached 20 per cent. After this, KPN experienced a period of under-performance due in particular, to an expectation of additional supplies of telecom shares from Telefónica, Stet, Deutsche Telekom and the over-hang from the expected second tranche of KPN itself; and
- During the first year's trading, KPN outperformed BT and Tele Danmark in terms of relative performance against their local indices. BT under-performed the FT-SE 100 by 7 per cent and Tele Danmark under-performed the Danish KFX index by 0.1 per cent.

After-market trading volume
See Exhibit 19.

- On the first day of trading in Amsterdam, some 8 million shares changed hands and over a day-and-a-half approximately 10 per cent of the total issue had traded against a rule of thumb that 10 per cent of a new issue typically trades during the first three days. According to Simon Barnasconi: 'Retail investors initially didn't sell to any significant degree and still held some 90 per cent of what they had bought three months after the offer.' Jose Tijssen, IR manager at KPN, pointed out: 'When, however, KPN published better-than-expected half-year results at the end of August, a large number of retail investors sold at a profit of over Dfl7 and by May 1995, Dutch retail ownership had fallen to 11 per cent of the free float, ie, approximately half of what was sold at the time of the IPO'; and
- The flow-back from the US was more significant than from other tranches. In particular, ADR outstandings declined dramatically. 'The unlisted sponsored ADR programme didn't really work,' says Tijssen. 'As a percentage of the original placement, only 36 per cent elected to take delivery in the form of ADRs and after a few months not even 25 per cent of the originally issued ADRs were still outstanding.' (See Exhibit 20).

Given that its main original US shareholders kept their ADRs or exchanged them for ordinary shares in the secondary market, US ownership remained stable at around 15 per cent from the time of the original IPO to the end of 1995 (see Exhibit 21).

Despite the fact that KPN was listed on the NYSE in connection with KPN2, US ownership did not increase markedly. Also, secondary market trading volumes on the NYSE are relatively modest, and most such trading takes place in Amsterdam (see Exhibit 22).

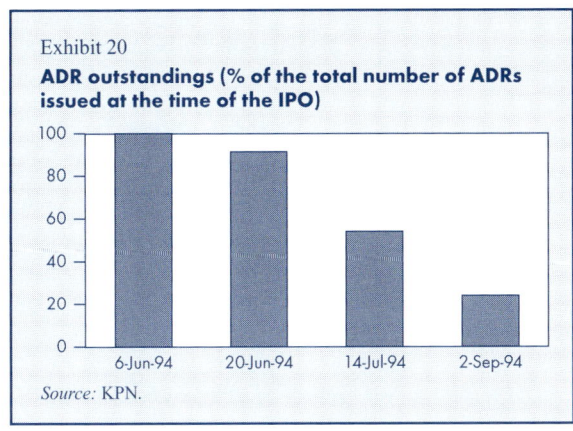

Exhibit 20

ADR outstandings (% of the total number of ADRs issued at the time of the IPO)

Source: KPN.

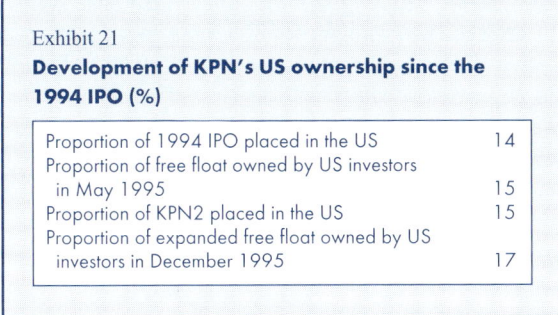

Exhibit 21

Development of KPN's US ownership since the 1994 IPO (%)

Proportion of 1994 IPO placed in the US	14
Proportion of free float owned by US investors in May 1995	15
Proportion of KPN2 placed in the US	15
Proportion of expanded free float owned by US investors in December 1995	17

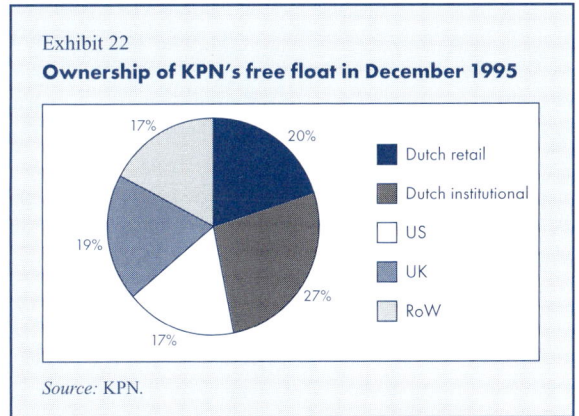

Exhibit 22

Ownership of KPN's free float in December 1995

Source: KPN.

The performance of the main parties

The vendor

There was a close and productive working relationship between the ministries of transport and finance and their joint adviser, NM Rothschild. The fact that two ministries were involved obviously had the potential to complicate matters but they worked well together. Both ministries were pragmatic, though some observers thought them over-sensitive about the competition from Tele Danmark whose flotation immediately preceded the issue – the ministries decided not to include in a senior capacity any banks that were actively involved in Tele Danmark. On analysis, it seems to the author that the ministries were justified in being concerned about their syndicate banks not giving their undivided attention to this privatisation. When the mystique of these large offers is removed, it comes down to focus, discipline and hard work, and few banks, if any, have the capacity to give

the necessary attention to too many offers at any one time. By way of example, pre-marketing tasks require analysts to fly all over the world to see investors prior to a company roadshow. Moreover, it stretches the credibility of a bank if one week it is describing Tele Danmark as the best buy among European telecom companies and two weeks later it is praising KPN.

The company

KPN's managers had demonstrated their professionalism in the five years since incorporation and this became evident in the roadshow. This proved that it makes sense to appoint management at a sufficiently early stage to enable it to build a track record. This strategy had two major implications:

1. The management demonstrated its credibility in the road-show and impressed investors; and
2. The Dutch state realised a much higher value for its KPN shares than if all the rationalisation had still to be done.

KPN fully delivered on the earnings forecast for 1994: net profit and earnings per share were 5–6 per cent better than ABN AMRO forecast at the time of the offer. However, the market sold off on the announcement because its expectations had increased since the privatisation. For the first six months of 1995, KPN delivered on what was expected at the time of the offer.

The independent adviser

NM Rothschild did a great job in this role. The bank and the government were the key architects behind the offer structure, the military manner of its execution and the motivation of the syndicate. In addition, they were of considerable support to ABN AMRO which at the time did not have much experience of this type of offer. If there was any criticism of NM Rothschild, it was that, because it does not lead-manage many transactions it was not as up to speed on all the institutional investors as it might have been for the purposes of the allocation process. It must be acknowledged that all the major houses would make this criticism, firstly because they are never completely happy with allocations in substantially over-subscribed transactions and secondly because regional lead managers do lose out in flexibility and ultimately profitability when an independent adviser is used.

NM Rothschild won the advisory role against competition from Schroders, JP Morgan, Lehman and Mees Pierson, who had been shortlisted from a initial group of 11 banks. The appointment of a foreign bank as independent adviser underscores the Dutch government's reputation for openness and impartiality in its privatisation programme. NM Rothschild drew on its experience both in the telecom sector and with privatisations in general both in the UK and internationally. The bank had advised BT in connection with BT2 and BT3, in the latter acting as a global manager, and had further advised BT on its US$4.3 billion link-up with MCI. It had been the initial adviser on the privatisation of OTE and adviser to the Hungarian government on the privatisation of Matav.

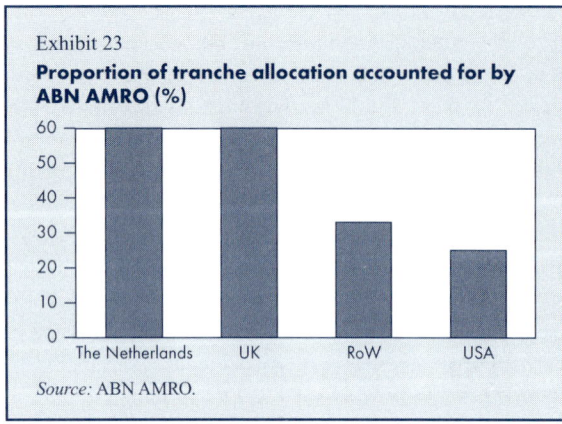

Exhibit 23

Proportion of tranche allocation accounted for by ABN AMRO (%)

Source: ABN AMRO.

The global coordinator

ABN AMRO added value on the selling side in particular, where it placed approximately 49 per cent of the total issue, broken down over the four tranches as shown in Exhibit 23.

Despite this very impressive performance there was criticism from the regional leads that ABN AMRO had been front-running, ie, had begun to sell before it was supposed to and had told or implied to many institutional investors that they ought to designate ABN AMRO if they wanted to be well treated in the allocation process. The proportion of total sales accounted for by the global coordinator should be compared to the proportion of the total transaction underwritten by ABN AMRO (34 per cent). ABN AMRO will have ended up with 35–40 per cent of the total economics of the transaction. Furthermore, a senior representative of one of the regional lead managers found that ABN AMRO played its cards close to its chest – nobody had an inkling of the weakness of the Dutch tranche, the assumed success of which was of the utmost importance to maintain confidence in the offer. The bank also earned significant praise for its after-market stabilisation efforts.

ABN AMRO beat off competition from eight foreign and domestic banks (including ING and Rabobank) to secure the role of global coordinator. The government was thought to favour having a single global coordinator, based on advice from Anthony Alt, director of NM Rothschild, who was of the opinion that execution would thereby be considerably smoother. Henri van Heugten of the Ministry of Finance explained: 'We were mindful of avoiding too many cooks and too much coordination.'

The bank's foremost qualification for the job was its leadership in the global distribution of Dutch shares. If it had a weakness, it was its US distribution capacity. However, this turned out to be less of an issue, given that it was decided not to list the IPO in the US. Although both the Dutch government and NM Rothschild were in favour of a NYSE listing, KPN resisted this and Goldman Sachs is thought to have been non-committal on the matter.

Other parties

CSFB, through its syndicate, clearly managed to generate the highest level of demand, even higher than the Dutch market. The RoW syndicate generated demand in excess of the total size of the offer, although, as is normal, not all of this was allocable (ie,

real) demand. Total demand is usually divided by two to arrive at the allocable demand. Moreover, the RoW tranche offered considerable price flexibility which was a significant plus point for the pricing of the offer. Goldman Sachs is thought to have done a good job as financial adviser to KPN. KPN CFO Cees Griffioen commented: 'Goldman Sachs was very quick in understanding our business and a terrific sparring partner in the process of articulating and refining our strategy.'

Key lessons learnt

The KPN IPO proved yet again that the success of these large offers often comes down to planning, organisation and hard work. 'To us, the most important criteria was whether or not you can work well with somebody under pressure,' explained Cees Griffioen. 'What we experienced is that an IPO is not just an exercise for the finance department but a process that is of strategic importance and highly relevant for the whole board. It is also a process from which there is an opportunity to derive maximum benefit in terms of managerial cohesion and it is fun too. What helped us tremendously through the process both in terms of our own thinking and in terms of negotiations with the government was the principle that we, as the management, acted as if we were shareholders of the company.'

The IPO also showed that the development of a 'level playing field' can destroy the myth that only US banks can sell to US institutions and that investors buy only from the lead manager. On a slightly more negative note, 'there should have been more two-way communication with the press, rather than just issuance of bulletins from the Ministry of Transport', according to the ministry's project coordinator, Andre Betting, although Charles van Schelle observed: 'The Dutch press do not ever write complimentary things about Dutch companies – period.'

Betting suggests: 'More time should have been allowed for the process of allocation; in particular we should have had more time to discuss the allocation with the regional lead managers.' The allocation process is a unique opportunity for a company to acquaint itself with its future shareholders, to whom it will increasingly talk directly. It therefore makes sense to include the company in these discussions although the final say clearly lies with the vendor.

Other criticisms are that the syndicate was unnecessarily big and that the bookbuilding probably should have taken two rather than three weeks, thereby reducing the total amount of time the offer was exposed to the market.

Conclusion

KPN was seen as one of the most efficient telecom companies in Europe with a favourable regulatory regime based in a good country. One person who listened to the roadshow said: 'This is a company with a crystal-clear strategy and a unified management who can convey that strategy with great enthusiasm.'

While initially the inclusion of PTT Post was seen by many analysts as a hindrance to the transaction, it turned out to be a very important bonus. Although PTT Post was an unusually efficient postal organisation, there clearly was considerable potential for further rationalisation.

The fact that the Netherlands had a strong standing with investors also assisted the offer, particularly as it was sold in the rest of the world as having a secure and growing dividend yield (ie, like a bond with an attractive total return).

There was a very disciplined two-week pre-marketing period from which the syndicate obtained a lot of feedback (importantly on the postal business) and which generated very substantial investor interest. High-quality research also was actively put to use, as Menno de Jager of ABN AMRO explained: 'The research really represents the engine room of an offer of this kind and is extraordinarily important.' CSFB, for example, sent its research report to 900 investors during pre-marketing.

Adoption of the bottom-up approach, according to Tony Alt of NM Rothschild: 'enables the vendor to take timely high-quality decisions concerning size of offer, tranche sizes and price ranges. At the time that the various decisions need to be taken, the facts are there and the final decision will depend on how the trade-off between greed and risk is tackled.' The pricing, at just under Dfl50, was seen as fair by most investor groups other than the domestic institutions.

The non-political, flexible and pragmatic approach by the government made it possible to think about the best interests of KPN, and the government's strong incentivisation of the syndicate was well received. It tried various measures to prevent freeloaders making money and to reward only those that worked hard: a high-performing co-lead manager of one of the regional tranches could make up to US$3 million. However, one senior equity capital market figure at a regional lead manager pointed out that they would have wanted to see a statement from the government saying to the institutional investors: 'What you do on designations will not affect your allocation,' to offset the pressure from the global coordinator and one or two other regional leads to get the institutions to designate them.

The offer was almost three times subscribed, which represented a considerable success, given its size and the generally adverse market conditions, although at 37 per cent of the total, Dutch participation was disappointing, especially from the retail side to which the government had allowed a 5 per cent discount. This lack of success was thought by some to have been related to too much political interference, volatile market conditions, low awareness of the KPN name and a less than completely successful corporate advertising campaign followed immediately by the offer campaign. Dutch institutions did not like bookbuilding.

The greenshoe was not exercised as KPN did not trade sufficiently strongly in the immediate after-market. However, in a year of mostly disappointing privatisations, KPN stood out as a well executed and successful one. Scottish Widows fund manager Albert Morillo commented (Reuters, 5 September 1995): 'Against the Financial Times sterling-based index to the end of 1994, there were only three outperforms European-wide – KPN, Lufthansa and Outokumpu.'

Some syndicate members said that although they were in favour of flexible tranche sizes, they were not in favour of flexible underwriting commitments because taken together the quantification of the risk became too difficult. In the event of a disaster, there was a huge spread between maximum and minimum loss. This uncertainty was perhaps felt particularly by the junior syndicate members who did not focus on the transaction in the same way as the senior syndicate members: even if you do not sign the underwriting agreement until much later, you are morally on the hook much earlier. Risk quantification is a considerable concern when you underwrite at a 'non-discounted' fixed price for seven days.

Some also criticised the Bloomberg automatic bookbuilding system, which broke down during a vital stage of the bookbuilding but which, the critics claimed, also took away an essential 'feel' generated by discussions of each individual order. By dividing institutions into eight categories, there was a danger of fixed percentages being applied without distinguishing between good and bad orders from the same institution.

Feature topic: *The role and usefulness of an independent adviser*

The Dutch government is unique in its firm belief in and application of the principle that neither its own adviser nor that of the company (in this case KPN) may participate in an underwriting or distribution capacity. Both the UK and Dutch governments had been influenced to that effect by what happened in the 1987 BP offer. Whereas the UK Treasury gave up this principle in connection with the BT2 offer in 1991, the Dutch government has kept religiously to this policy. The BP milestone was reached as set out below.

Sale of UK government's remaining 31.5 per cent stake in BP

On 14 October 1987, in a meeting at the UK Treasury, the then chancellor, Nigel Lawson, and Michael Richardson, the head of corporate finance at NM Rothschild, signed the underwriting agreement for the £7.25 billion fixed-price sale of shares in BP. The sale combined the disposal of the government's remaining 31.5 per cent stake and a £1.5 billion capital increase for BP itself.

NM Rothschild was adviser to the government and the lead underwriter of the offer: in that capacity it was on the one hand advising the UK Treasury of its best interests and on the other representing the global underwriting syndicate, ie, it represented both parties to the underwriting agreement. This was an accepted practice in the City of London and would have worked well for the BP offer had the largest share sale ever undertaken not also coincided with one of the biggest stock market crashes in history.

The issue was underwritten at a price of £3.30, the amount to be paid under the first instalment being £1.20. On 20 October, the fully paid price had fallen to £2.85.

Discussions immediately started as to whether or not the issue should go ahead or be pulled. Whereas the UK portion of the total issue had been sub-underwritten in the normal fashion, NM Rothschild and SG Warburg (acting as BP's adviser) had decided to take on considerable primary underwriting commitments. The banks stood to lose up to £10 million each if the BP issue went ahead as originally planned. The US underwriters led by Goldman Sachs, were unfamiliar with the concept of sub-underwriting, and as a group stood to lose up to £330 million. These amounts were enormous both in absolute terms and in relation to many of the banks' total available capital resources.

The losses to be realised by all the members of the syndicate and the potential £10 million loss for NM Rothschild itself caused the latter to recommend to the UK Treasury that the *force majeure* clause be invoked and the issue be cancelled. These pleas were added to by the secretary to the US Treasury, Jim Baker, his assistant secretary David Mulford and their counterparts in Canada. The Japanese government also wrote to NM Rothschild, and even the Bank of England recommended that the issue be postponed.

Lawson, in his memoirs, *The View from No. 11*, explained how, at the time, he 'took a firm line with all these pleas for mercy, pointing out that they were inviting him to abandon the right to claim on an insurance policy'. Noting that he could not recall a time when he was under heavier pressure, he writes: 'Rothschilds, although still nominally advisers to the government, were now acting on behalf of the underwriters. Indeed, it was soon pretty clear that Rothschilds had in effect changed sides. The document they had asked Freshfields, the solicitors, to prepare for the Friday meeting of the underwriting group was apparently heavily slanted in favour of postponing the issue. These developments caused some reconsideration in subsequent privatisation issues, both of the terms of the *force majeure* clause and the practice of appointing the advisers to the government as the lead underwriters to the issue.' It was this experience more than any other factor that led the UK government and others around the world to appoint separate financial advisers so as to avoid such conflicts of interest.

In the event, on 29 October Lawson announced his decision, fully backed by the prime minister, Margaret Thatcher, to go ahead with the issue, with the Bank of England undertaking to buy shares in the market at the market closing partly paid price on 28 October of £0.70 (against an issue price of £1.20) for a period of two months. On the following day, the partly paid price closed at £0.85.

Starting with the BT2 offer in 1991, the UK Treasury decided effectively to retain the underwriting risk itself by adopting the bookbuilding approach. Additionally, it is thought to have felt that it had accumulated sufficient experience and thus had less need for a dedicated financial adviser. Therefore, in BT2 the UK Treasury hired SG Warburg effectively as a distribution network, and while preparing for the offer the bank was also pro-forma advising the Treasury.

Today, the Italian government probably is the closest to the Dutch approach in terms of philosophy on independent advisers. It does not allow its adviser to be the global coordinator but rather encourages it to be involved in the syndicate in a less senior capacity. The thinking behind this is that the adviser should also be able to sell at the price it recommends that the global coordinator proceeds on.

The Dutch government's reasoning behind its use of independent advisers is set out below.

The case for an independent adviser

The Dutch government wishes to have an adviser which categorically looks after only its interest and does not have a conflict of interest on, for example, underwriting, pricing, sizing and allocation.

There is no question that in general, global coordinators have their own agenda. A senior equity capital markets professional at one of the regional lead managers, while not commenting specifically on the KPN issue noted: 'Once the success of the offer is assured, the global coordinator typically starts to optimise his own position – and often even before that happens too.' There are many ways in which the global coordinator, particularly in the case of a less sophisticated client, could optimise his position, including:

- Negotiating an unreasonably high total commission, global coordinator's praecipium and/or global coordinator's advisory fee;
- Recommending an offer structure that suits the particular profile of the bank, eg, a US bank would more often than not recommend a US listing, sometimes when it may not be in the company's best interest to do so, whereas a UK bank would perhaps recommend against it when it may well be advisable;
- Paying back favours in connection with syndicate appointments or creating IOUs rather than recommending the particular bank that is best qualified for the particular job at hand;
- Proposing 'exempt lists' which unduly favour the global coordinator;
- Taking an unreasonably large portion of the management and underwriting commissions within each tranche;
- Monopolising company management for internal sales briefings rather than making management more broadly available;
- Scheduling the roadshow, including one-on-one meetings to optimise the bank's own sales effort;
- Allocating in favour of itself rather than others. In a highly successful offer, institutions are put under pressure to order shares from the lead manager/global coor-

dinator rather than co-leads or co-managers, against a promise of better treatment in the allocation process;

- The return of favours and creation of IOUs may also apply in the relationships between the investment banks and investment institutions. In other words, the global coordinator may allocate a lower-quality investor for its own purposes rather than in the best interest of the transaction itself; and
- Charging a full fee for the greenshoe option when this may not be fair.

The duties

In the case of KPN, the Dutch government appointed NM Rothschild to advise on all aspects of the IPO and charged the bank with numerous responsibilities, including:

- Formulation of objectives for the IPO;
- Analysis and recommendations on the following items:
  – Valuation;
  – Offer structure and the appropriate marketing strategy for both the retail and the institutional markets;
  – Choice of global coordinator;
  – Syndicate structure and individual appointments;
  – Selection of other advisers such as lawyers, PR advisers, IR advisers, etc;
  – Size of the IPO, respective tranche sizes and individual underwriting commitments;
  – Allocation policy; and
  – Utilisation of the greenshoe and stabilisation policy;
- Due diligence;
- Review of regulatory environment (KPN had been incorporated in 1989 and the regulatory framework, including price regulation, was already in place; one of NM Rothschild's tasks was clearly to advise the government on the further development of a competitive environment);
- Determination of fee levels for the IPO, both with respect to the retail and institutional markets; and
- The decision whether or not to proceed with the offer.

In the case of KPN, the ministries of finance and transport appointed NM Rothschild at the beginning of July 1993, ie, 11 months before the pricing of the offer.

Sometimes, an independent adviser can help the global coordinator convince the issuer or vendor of a particular idea which the latter may at first not perceive as being in its best interest. This can be achieved by a non-confrontational private discussion between the issuer/vendor and the independent adviser. The issuer/vendor is more likely to listen when it is convinced that the advice comes from a party that represents only its best interests.

According to Anthony Northrop, a former partner of Lazard Brothers who started his own partnership, Touchstone Securities in mid-1995, advising on equity offers: 'An independent adviser can give the issuer a much

better feel for the negotiation with the global coordinator, in terms of where it can give and where not, and offer to the issuer/vendor a better understanding of the downside of certain decisions, recognising that unanimity is rare and that the process of completing a large equity offer is not a precise science.'

Luis Ruigomez, deputy general manager of BBV Interactivos, commented: 'Sometimes it is important for an independent adviser to simply be there as there are many tricks the lead manager(s) don't try if there is a credible adviser at the opposite side of the table.'

The expertise

An independent privatisation adviser should have:

- First and foremost, experience with the industry in question, in this case telecommunications;
- Experience in privatisations;
- Experience with large equity offers; and
- Experience of local markets.

The case against

Those who are against independent advisers typically criticise the concept on various grounds:

- The top houses say that it isn't necessary, because they are, in any event, very focused on the client. Why pay the extra money?
- The big banks are nervous about their competitors. A company such as Merrill Lynch, for example, would not be delighted to have Goldman Sachs look over its shoulder because there is always too much history: for every issue that is being discussed there are other transactions where something was done that was not deemed by the other party to be in the client's best interest or where it was to the detriment of the less senior party in the transaction. When two of the big boys are forced to work together, they often find it difficult to concentrate only on what is good in that particular situation;
- The large investment banks allege that those houses less active in distribution, such as Rothschilds and Lazards, cannot advise on allocation because they do not have as much knowledge of these accounts – only the big players who are constantly in the market talking to institutions can advise appropriately;
- As already indicated, there are many ways for a global coordinator to optimise its own situation. 'No global coordinator wants an educated customer,' says one senior investment banker; and
- There is no such thing as an independent adviser, meaning that the firms who specialise in giving advice are to a degree dependent on the big houses giving them a favourable review.

Mayr-Melnhof Karton AG

A tragic death in the sixth generation of the great Austrian industrial dynasty Mayr-Melnhof was to speed up the flotation of the family business which began by revolutionising domestic steel-making in the 1860s and is now the world leader in recycled cartonboard for packaging. Yet even before Franz Mayr-Melnhof IV died in a car crash in Italy in June 1993, it had become increasingly clear to the controlling family that the largely self-financing Mayr-Melnhof Karton Aktiengesellschaft, one of the largest industrial companies in Austria, needed an injection of capital to finance growth. Given that the Austrian equity market is underdeveloped and unsophisticated, in the absence of significant institutional investors, the raising of up to US$250 million was going to be anything but straightforward. In the event, this was to become the largest-ever equity offer by an Austrian private company and a good example of a transaction that was completed despite most observers thinking it too big – and despite the shortcomings of the domestic market.

In order to avoid giving the impression that the family was cashing in, global coordinator Morgan Stanley and the vendor structured the transaction in such a way that the family would sell shares if and only if those sold by the company generated sufficient demand to guarantee a successful offer, as proved to be the case. The issue was deemed sufficiently successful following bookbuilding to allow the family to raise US$48 million from an increase in the deal size and exercise of the greenshoe. A combination of bad luck, bad company management, an unconstructive domestic house bank and a somewhat aggressive international investment bank, meant that after the initial success of the IPO, Mayr-Melnhof was subsequently to be severely damaged by the international investment and analyst communities.

Despite being a good company with highly experienced operating management, which hired some of the best advisers available, for more than three years since the IPO the shares have traded well below the price at which the company went public. Matters began to go wrong soon after the IPO had been completed: an apparently unforeseeable event – dramatically rising prices for waste paper, the company's main raw material – triggered a profit warning and substantial downward pressure on the stock price within three months of the offer. Some clever damage-control by Morgan Stanley led to many investors continuing to give the benefit of the doubt to the management, which had impressed on its roadshow. The bank's action underscored two significant aspects of a flotation such as this: the importance of timely and comprehensive education by the lead sponsors as to how company management should conduct itself in the secondary market, and the vital importance of the two parties continuing to maintain a very close relationship after an issue is completed. Unfortunately, Mayr-Melnhof has disappointed on more than one occasion with the result that many of the original investors have sold and moved on to fresher stories.

This case study highlights the overnight change in culture associated with going public – from being a cosy, family-owned company to one where management becomes exposed to the shark pool of the global equity market. It highlights in particular the dramatic difference in disclosure and commu-

---

Exhibit 1
Transaction summary

Issuer name: Mayr-Melnhof Karton AG (Austria)	Global coordinator: Morgan Stanley International
Pricing date: 15 April 1994 (ATX Index: 1,070)	Pricing/underwriting structure: International bookbuilding and fixed price domestic offer
Vendor: Company and Mayr-Melnhof family	Primary or secondary: 4.0 million primary, 0.8 million secondary
% of company sold: 40% of expanded share capital	Privatisation or corporate: Corporate
IPO or non-IPO: IPO	Industry: Paper and packaging
Type of shares: Ordinary shares and ADRs (4 ordinary shares per ADR)	Pricing range: ASch: 690–750/ordinary share Offer price: ASch: 720; US$15.07/ADR
Total issue size: US$288 million	US listing/144 A: 144A placement

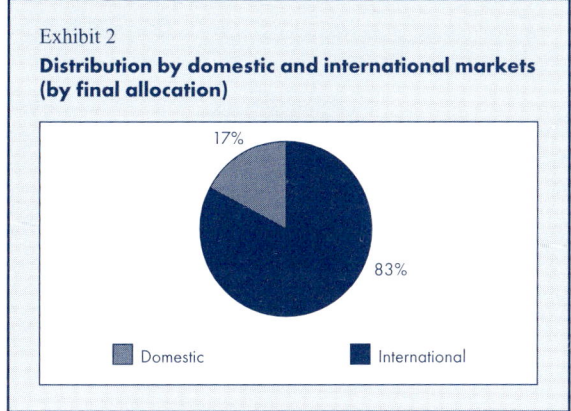

Exhibit 2
Distribution by domestic and international markets (by final allocation)

17%

83%

■ Domestic   ■ International

nication standards required from a company owned by international institutions and a traditional non-quoted family business in Austria, a country which is not, at the best of times, at the forefront of disclosure standards. It should prompt any family-owned company, big or small, to think twice before taking the plunge, and serve to encourage proper preparation for such an undertaking.

Major challenges

This was a very large offer given that the Austrian market is underdeveloped, that market conditions generally were weak, that the management was untested in running a publicly quoted company and that a specific acquisition target had not been identified as a use for the proceeds. However, Mayr-Melnhof's managers did have a clearly articulated strategy to acquire companies in the folding-carton segment of the packaging business. The offer therefore had to be sold to an unusually large extent on the basis of trust in the management's ability to pay the right price for the right future acquisition. This in turn meant that the management had to be particularly convincing when talking to investors about its acquisition track record.

The lack of institutional investors in Austria meant that the offer had to be priced and sold almost entirely in the international market, and this, coupled with the large issue size, lack of name recognition and difficult market conditions meant that the marketing campaign required a lot of work.

A significant challenge was presented by the radically different approach to valuation in the domestic and international markets. The domestic lead manager focused on low reported earnings while Morgan Stanley argued that the company should be valued on the basis of its strong cash flow. In the end, international institutions decided the offer price in the bookbuilding process.

It was necessary to find a structure acceptable to domestic and international markets whereby the family would have sufficient flexibility to move shares between family members or sell a certain amount to third-party investors, without losing control of the company.

From the company's point of view, the cultural change from being a very private company to operating in a highly exposed environment was to prove tough for the management in the months following the offer.

Rationale and objectives

Rationale and timing

Historically, Mayr-Melnhof had expanded primarily by use of internally generated cash flow, even if that meant exposing the family to a certain amount of financial stress. Although operationally and financially the best interests of the company had always been paramount, accounting profits had been kept low to minimise both corporate and wealth tax for the family. Now, however, the company needed to move on to the next stage of development, which was to expand the converting side of the business. There was no specific acquisition target in sight but the management saw many opportunities and wanted to put the funding in place. Although part of the family also had substantial assets in the form of forest land, these had always been kept separate and could not be used to finance the growth of the company. Therefore going public was a question of when rather than if: two events occurred in close succession which dictated the timing of the IPO: the death of Franz Mayr-Melnhof and a change in Austria's tax regime.

Franz Mayr-Melnhof Sarau had only taken over as supervisory board chairman a few years earlier from his father Carl Anton Goess-Sarau who had run the business for 36 years. On his death, Franz owned 40 per cent of Mayr-Melnhof and had he lived it is possible that he would have acquired an additional 20 per cent from other family members to gain full control before going public, thus delaying the sale. He might have had the opportunity to buy at a relatively low price from some members of the family and then sell out at a higher price to the stock market. As it was, Franz's 40 per cent was split between six children, which complicated matters significantly as this meant that for the first time, no one member of the family had overall control: Franz's eldest son was only 16 years old at this time. With the ownership now more broadly distributed among many family members, the view was taken that by going public, the valuation of the company would become more transparent in that there would at all times be a market price for the shares. In addition, there would be the opportunity, within limits, for family members to realise cash by selling shares. Carl Anton Goess-Sarau, who resumed the chairmanship of the supervisory board after the death of his son said: 'As head of the Mayr-Melnhof family, I also had an informal fiduciary duty towards my family and felt a little uncomfortable having all our eggs in one basket. This was a further reason for establishing a market value for the company.'

The new tax regime in Austria, effective from January 1994, cut corporate tax from 50 per cent to 30 per cent, cut dividend tax from 62 per cent to 22 per cent and abolished the 1 per cent wealth tax. The wealth tax had been a deciding factor in not going for the IPO earlier and its scrapping now made it possible for the family to publicise for the first time the real value of the company. The decision to proceed with the IPO was taken in the autumn of 1993. Once internal reorganisation was complete and bankers hired, the earliest possible time to do the offer was in the spring of 1994.

Although the paper and packaging sector was in favour with investors along with other cyclical stocks, the overall new issue market internationally was less than ideal as the

US Federal Reserve had begun to tighten monetary policy in February 1994. Other IPOs for European companies executed in early 1994 had opened at only modest premiums or even discounts. In Austria the new issue market was still strong, although the secondary market was beginning to look a little shaky. The company and its advisers took a bold step: Mayr-Melnhof would be the first Austrian company to come to the market in 1994. The timing – just a few weeks before the privatisation of engineering company VA Technologie – raised controversy in many quarters, although as it turned out, the Mayr-Melnhof offer probably put the market in a positive mood for the VA Technologie offer.

Offer objectives

The management – which traditionally has not contained significant shareholders – and the controlling family were united in their objectives:

- To raise US$250 million for future acquisitions and investments;
- To achieve at least a minimum price per share, under which the family would not sell;
- To enhance Mayr-Melnhof's blue-chip image as a leading company in the global packaging industry; and
- To avoid in the future undue dilution of the existing shareholders' economic interest in the company, ie, to enable

the family to sell a certain number of shares without the shareholding being diluted from 59.3 per cent following the IPO, to below 50 per cent.

Use of proceeds

The proceeds were designated for forward integration in the carton-conversion business through selected acquisitions and investments by way of capital expenditure in maintenance and machinery. Although there was no major specific acquisition under consideration, Mayr-Melnhof wanted to raise the money before spending.

Share capital and ownership

See Exhibit 3.

Transaction components

This offer of four million new shares comprised a domestic tranche initially representing 25 per cent of the total offer and an international tranche initially representing 75 per cent of the total. The international tranche included an option to sell shares in the US under Rule 144 A. The offer allowed for an increase of 400,000 shares and a greenshoe of 400,000 shares

Exhibit 3
Share capital and ownership

Type of shares offered	Ordinary bearer shares of ASch100 with 1 vote per share. There are no voting restrictions.
Share capital after offer	12,000,000.
Listings/quotations	First listed in Vienna and quoted on Seaq International in connection with this offer.
Market capitalisation at offer price (ASch12.03/US$1)	US$718 million.
Major shareholder(s) before/after the offer	The family owned 100% before and 59.3% post offer (following the increase and the excercise of the greenshoe). The family cannot be diluted to less than 51% until at least 2009.
Free float after offer	40.0%.
Liquidity (Number of shares traded during 1994 expressed on an annualised basis and as a percentage of the total number of shares outstanding)	37% on the Vienna Stock Exchange. 7th most liquid stock on the Vienna Stock Exchange in 1994 and the 4th largest industrial company by market capitalisation on 22 April 1994.
Foreign ownership after offer	Approx. 85% of the free float was owned from abroad by the end of 1994.
Relevant stock exchange index/weighting	ATX index/3.9% (22 April 1994).

Exhibit 4
Development of the offer size

Indicated number of shares to be sold	4,000,000 + 400,000 greenshoe
Offer size after increase of offer size	4,400,000 + 400,000 greenshoe
Amount of greenshoe exercised	400,000
Final number of shares sold	4,800,000

to be sold by the controlling family if the company's initial sale of four million new shares proved to be a success.

Following a successful roadshow, the offer was initially increased by 400,000 secondary shares. Two weeks after the pricing, the vendor and Morgan Stanley decided to exercise the greenshoe which allowed the controlling family to sell an additional 400,000 shares (see Exhibit 4).

The offer was marketed on an open-priced basis to international and domestic investors, allowing a book to be built. The offer price was then fixed, following which there was a two-day formal subscription period for domestic investors, and a seven-day delay between pricing and the start of trading on the Vienna Stock Exchange. During this time a fixed price underwriting at the offer price was required from the syndicate.

Exhibit 5
Offer structure

Target markets	Indicated tranche sizes*	Bookrunners	Co-lead managers
Austria	25%	Creditanstalt Bankverein	Die Erste Österreichische Sparkasse, Girocredit Bank der Sparkassen, Raiffeisen Zentralbank Österreich Bank Austria Investment Bank
International	75%	Morgan Stanley International	Creditanstalt Bankverein Kleinwort Benson
Total combined offers (shares)	**4,000,000**		

*% of indicated total offer on 22 March 1994.

Exhibit 6
Principal advisers

Financial adviser to Mayr-Melnhof	Lazard Brothers
Austrian legal adviser to the company and international managers	Weiss-Tessbach Rechtsanwälte OEG
US legal advisers to the international managers	Davis Polk & Wardwell

---

Exhibit 7
The timetable

June 1993	• Death of Franz Mayr-Melnhof Sarau.
Autumn 1993	• Decision in principle by family to take company public.
Early January 1994	• Lazard Brothers appointed financial adviser to the company; and • Morgan Stanley appointed global coordinator.
16 February 1994	• Decision to go ahead with the offer and first press announcement.
1 March 1994	• Publication of company research.
7 March 1994	• Pre-marketing commenced.
21 March 1994	• Preliminary filing with Vienna Stock Exchange.
22 March 1994	• Public announcement of the offer; • Publication of preliminary prospectus; and • Briefing of Morgan Stanley's salesforce.
30 March 1994	• Offer price range set; and • Bookbuilding commenced.
5 April 1994	• European roadshow commenced.
13 April 1994	• US roadshow commenced.
Friday 15 April 1994	• Roadshow ended; • Pricing of offer; • Signing of underwriting agreement; and • Final prospectus distributed.
19/20 April 1994	• Allotment to international investors; and • Austrian public offer commenced and closed.
Friday 22 April 1994	• Trading started on Vienna Stock Exchange; and
Friday 29 April 1994	• Greenshoe exercised.

Exhibit 8
Distribution of gross spread (%)

Management fee	Underwriting fee	Selling concession	Gross spread
0.85	0.85	2.55	4.25

Exhibit 9
Distribution of management fee (%)

Total management fee	0.85
Of which: Global coordinator's praecipium	25
Of which: Lead/co-lead managers' praecipium split among all leads/co-leads	25
Of which: Management fees split among all the managers	50

Exhibit 10
Distribution of selling concession (%)

Total selling concession	2.55
Of which: Pre-agreed portion	0
Of which: Paid according to designations by institutions (US/UK) and elsewhere to whomever received the order	100

The offer was essentially designed to be done on a two-handed basis by Morgan Stanley and Creditanstalt Bankverein, however four Austrian banks were included as co-lead managers in the domestic tranche while Creditanstalt was one of two co-leads in the international tranche. In its capacity as global coordinator, Morgan Stanley was responsible for the whole offer (see Exhibit 5).

Principal advisers

Mayr-Melnhof engaged Lazard Brothers in London to assist with the appointment of the global coordinator and to act as a sounding board on structural issues (see Exhibit 6).

Transaction fee distribution

The total gross spread of 4.25 per cent was distributed as shown in Exhibit 8.

Management fee

The management fee was split in the same way everywhere as each bank had a global underwriting commitment (see Exhibit 9).

Selling concession

A pot system was operated for orders out of the US and the UK. In order to maximise competition among the syndicate banks and reward those that did well, there was no fixed or pre-agreed portion of the selling concession (see Exhibit 10).

Deal structure

The Mayr-Melnhof IPO was structured to meet three principal objectives:

- To raise a substantial amount of money ahead of the company pinpointing a potential acquisition. This strategy was chosen in favour of first identifying an acquisition target and then beginning the process of raising the finance as the Austrian market lacks depth and market access would by no means be guaranteed at the time when a potential acquisition was on the cards. It was a question of taking advantage of good market conditions;
- To price the offer in line with international valuation methods for packaging companies – in particular cash flow – and to sell mainly to international investors; and
- To have all the 'targeted' proceeds from the sale of four million shares go to the company. Only once this financing was successful would the opportunity arise for the family to sell outstanding shares, firstly through an increase of the underwritten offer size and secondly through the exercise of the greenshoe. The intention behind this structure was to demonstrate clearly to the market that the family was not cashing in.

Marketing

To sell almost US$300 million-worth of equity in a largely unknown company based in a country which is not itself popular among international investors posed particular challenges. Morgan Stanley identified a number of key marketing issues and developed strategies to cope with them (see Exhibit 11). Once the strategy had been developed, a detailed marketing plan was put into effect (see Exhibit 12).

In addition to the implementation of this plan, Morgan Stanley's equity capital markets department and global equity salesforce were continuously developing and defining the investor universe for this issue. In so doing, the bank's European and US salesforces initially approached its 1,000 institutional clients for preliminary discussions. From the initial feedback obtained, an investor target list was drawn up which was organised as shown in Exhibit 13.

Having approached those on the target list, the emphasis was then on trying to secure some 10 'elephant orders' – large orders from high-quality investors to serve as the foundation of the investor book. Other investors are often attracted into transactions if the big names are thought likely to participate. It is also important to determine the extent to which indicated demand reflects true demand. For that purpose, a 'shadow book' of institutions that were likely to come into the transaction was maintained.

To prepare for the allocation process and to secure the strongest possible after-market, it is essential to classify the investor universe before the close of bookbuilding so as to be able to allocate a higher percentage of indicated demand to the highest-quality investors – those who are sophisticated, who know the particular industry and who have a record of long-term holding in that industry. The different quality categories

Exhibit 11
Key marketing issues

Marketing issues	Marketing strategies
1. Limited size of Austrian equity market (only US$23 billion market capitalisation)	• Small domestic tranche; and • Broad international marketing campaign.
2. Limited prior investor awareness	• Early pre-marketing; and • Comprehensive step-by-step marketing plan.
3. Low reported earnings despite high underlying profitability	• Education of salesforce and investors as to the reasons for the relatively low historic earnings, ie, reported earnings for accounting and tax purposes kept to a minimum to minimise the family's tax liability; and • Marketing of the issue emphasising price/cash flow valuation rather than P/E.
4. Focus by Austrian market on P/E ratios	• Substantial education of Austrian banks and key domestic investors on how international peer group is valued, i.e. price/cash flow basis; • Small size of domestic tranche to try to engineer real scarcity in the home market; and • Size and price the issue so as to be able to rely on substantial after-market buy orders from international investors in order not to put too much pressure on the domestic market before investor confidence is established in the domestic market.
5. Business at cyclical low in 1993	• Stress that Mayr-Melnhof was one of only few companies in the industry that remained profitable in 1993; and • Sell on 1994 and 1995 expected performance.
6. Substantial new issue backlog	• Target pricing date of issue for as early as possible within spring new-issue season; and • Target pricing of issue before major Austrian privatisation (VA Technologie).

Exhibit 12
The marketing plan

Step 1	February	• Company included as special topic in Morgan Stanley monthly paper and pulp equity research bulletin distributed to investors.
Step 2	February	• Mayr-Melnhof's CEO invited as keynote speaker at Oslo paper & pulp investor conference arranged by Morgan Stanley.
Step 3	March	• Mayr-Melnhof dedicated equity research report published and sent to investors; and • Pre-marketing campaign by equity research analysts in Europe and US – 30 one-on-one meetings with institutional investors.
Step 4	March	• First briefing of Morgan Stanley salesforce by equity capital markets and equity research; • Thereafter continuous education of salesforce by equity research; and • Continuous review of 'shadow book' of orders.
Step 5	5–15 April	• Company roadshow in Europe and US; and • Active bookbuilding begins.
Step 6	5–15 April	• Sales campaign. Equity research makes approximately 100 sales calls to investors; and • Marketing campaign by equity research analysts in Europe and US. The analysts will follow up with the most important investors after the company has visited; 15 one-on-one meetings and two investor conference calls.

Exhibit 13
Investor targeting

Categories of targeted investors	Investor names					
1. Expressions of preliminary interest						
2. Holders of paper and packaging stocks						
3. Holders of Austrian stocks						
4. Holders of Austrian funds						
5. Buyers of previous paper and packaging new issues						
6. Buyers of Austrian new issues						
7. Buyers of previous IPOs						

might be, for example: *excellent, high, good, average* and *below average*. Of the institutions who bought Mayr-Melnhof, more than 80 per cent were classified according to these criteria.

According to Jerker Johansson, head of European equity capital markets at Morgan Stanley, the philosophy when marketing a new name to investors is always the same:

- Capture the attention of investors on the overall story; then
- Get people interested by providing only limited information; then
- Consolidate interest by providing more information; then
- Convince the investors that the price is right.

The most important part of the entire marketing and sales effort is the roadshow, in particular the one-on-one meetings between Mayr-Melnhof's management and those institutional investors most likely to come in with big high-quality orders.

In this case, 32 one-on-one meetings were arranged with investors who bought 61 per cent of the offer. An additional 15 per cent of demand was generated from investors who attended the more public investor presentations (see Exhibit 14).

The Mayr-Melnhof story

Mayr-Melnhof is one of the largest and most successful European paper-based packaging companies and the only company with a capacity to operate on a 100 per cent recycled basis. Mayr Melnhof's primary strength is in transforming low-quality waste paper to high-quality cartonboard used for packaging in the consumer goods industry. Morgan Stanley sold the offer on the basis of the sales points shown in Exhibit 15.

Whereas Mayr-Melnhof was priced at 21.4 times forecast 1994 and 13.1 times forecast 1995 earnings, which was very clearly expensive against the sector, on a cash-flow basis, the situation looked quite different (see Exhibit 16).

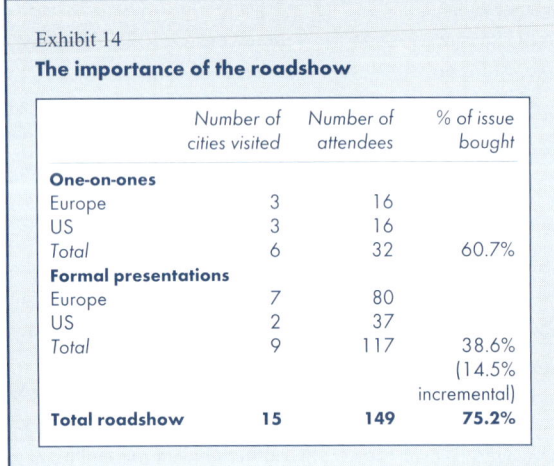

Exhibit 14

The importance of the roadshow

	Number of cities visited	Number of attendees	% of issue bought
One-on-ones			
Europe	3	16	
US	3	16	
Total	6	32	60.7%
Formal presentations			
Europe	7	80	
US	2	37	
Total	9	117	38.6% (14.5% incremental)
Total roadshow	**15**	**149**	**75.2%**

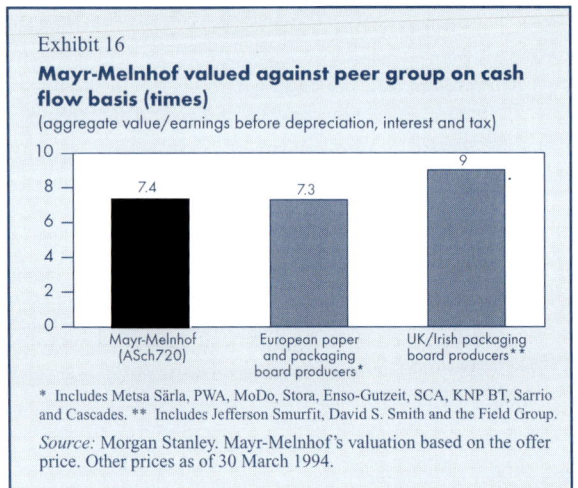

Exhibit 16

Mayr-Melnhof valued against peer group on cash flow basis (times)

(aggregate value/earnings before depreciation, interest and tax)

Mayr-Melnhof (ASch720): 7.4
European paper and packaging board producers*: 7.3
UK/Irish packaging board producers**: 9

* Includes Metsa Särla, PWA, MoDo, Stora, Enso-Gutzeit, SCA, KNP BT, Sarrio and Cascades. ** Includes Jefferson Smurfit, David S. Smith and the Field Group.

Source: Morgan Stanley. Mayr-Melnhof's valuation based on the offer price. Other prices as of 30 March 1994.

Exhibit 15

Principal sales points

Market position	• The world leader in recycled cartonboard and a major European carton converter; and • Mayr-Melnhof is the leading folding-carton-board producer in Europe with eight mills in: Austria, Germany, Switzerland, the Netherlands and England.
Raw material supply	• A major European waste-paper recycler ensuring long-term supply of raw material.
Technological leadership	• The company's technological leadership enables it to produce high-quality cartonboard from low-cost waste paper.
High efficiency	• The highest efficiency per employee in the industry.
Cyclical recovery	• The industry experienced its cyclical trough in 1993 and board prices were expected to start to increase in 1994.
Secular growth in converting	• The converting industry was expected to experience significant growth; this was the activity on which Mayr-Melnhof was expected to focus for its acquisitions.
High depreciation	• Highest depreciation levels in the industry. This high level of depreciation had depressed Mayr-Melnhof's historic earnings by more than ASch0.5 billion over the three years to 1993.
Experienced management	• Mayr-Melnhof has a highly experienced management team: Michael Gröller, the CEO, responsible for the cartonboard and waste-paper divisions and Alfred Fogarassy, responsible for the folding-carton division, have each been with the company for 28 years.
Valuation	• The above positioning of Mayr-Melnhof allowed for a valuation of the company based mainly on cash flow against the European packaging sector rather than on an earnings basis against other packaging stocks or against the Austrian market, which trades mainly on earnings.

Sources: Morgan Stanley and offer circular.

Principal reasons for not buying

Those investors who declined to buy voiced the following concerns:

- The decline in the demand for cartonboard in recent years was partly seen as structural, and therefore long-term in nature, as the weight of packaging per unit of packaged goods was being minimised;
- There was over-capacity in European cartonboard production with 25 per cent of total production going to export markets. At the same time, capacity was expanding in the Far East and in North America. This could have negative long-term consequences for cartonboard prices;
- With one quarter of the European industry output exported, exposure to exchange rate movements was high;
- Investors were worried about the EC cartel case against the European cartonboard producers with maximum fines of 10 per cent of annual sales; however Mayr-Melnhof was thought to be well provisioned against possible fines;
- The possibility that the company would put the proceeds in the bank at a low return rather than make prudent acquisitions in the converting business;
- The threat of German waste-paper collectors burning the waste paper. This could limit supply and increase waste-paper prices; and
- There was a feeling that the company was too far ahead in the paper and packaging cycle and that therefore other companies which were lagging behind Mayr-Melnhof in the cycle might be more undervalued.

Results

Placement

The international tranche was more than twice subscribed and accounted for 83 per cent of total allocations. The domestic tranche was relatively poorly subscribed and received only 17 per cent of final allocations (see Exhibit 17).

As is often the case, the international book came together only during the last three days. This is to a large extent because US investors rarely make a decision before they have met with the company management on the roadshow which they like to do just before pricing. Given the power of the large US institutions, US investment banks tend to accom-

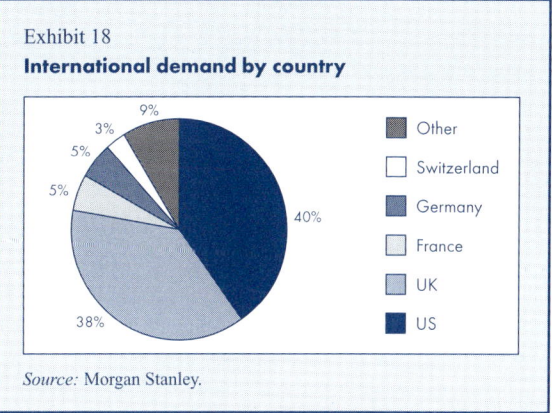

Exhibit 18
International demand by country

Source: Morgan Stanley.

modate them by scheduling the US roadshow for the week immediately preceding pricing.

As expected, the US and UK markets were by far the most important in terms of international institutional demand. The balance of demand was spread widely but mostly in continental Europe, where France, Germany and Switzerland were the most important markets (see Exhibit 18).

On this occasion UK institutions were given higher average allocations than their US counterparts because of their perceived higher average quality. As a result, they accounted for 45.8 per cent of total international allocations against 35.1 per cent for the US institutions. The extent of placement in the US was highly impressive considering that prior to this issue there had been very limited US ownership of Austrian stocks, and that this issue was done under Rule 144 A rather than as an SEC registered offer.

Most domestic demand came from retail investors as there are no pension funds in Austria, and as the insurance companies rarely invest in equities although they are technically allowed to do so. Mayr-Melnhof, a very old and established name in Austria, and the largest privately owned company in the country, traditionally had a very good image with people who could be categorised as substantial retail investors. Even so, the Austrian demand was disappointing given the considerable effort made by the domestic syndicate to educate the domestic investor base about cash-flow valuation as a basis for pricing.

In terms of the type of funds (or buyers) that bought the issue, international demand was split between paper and packaging buyers, European funds and cyclical buyers. Paper and packaging buyers accounted for some 50–70 per cent of total

Exhibit 17
Underwriting, demand and allocation (million shares)

Target markets	Indicative underwriting amounts (after increase)	Demand	Allocation *
Austria	1.0	N/A	0.8
International	3.4	7.3	4.0
of which: US	–	2.9	1.4
of which: RoW excluding Austria	–	4.4	2.6
Total combined offers	**4.4**	**N/A**	**4.8**

* In addition to the underwritten size, Morgan Stanley also allocated the full greenshoe of 400,000 shares.

Exhibit 19

Investor concentration

	By demand	By allocation
Percentage of issue accounted for by the 10 largest investors (by total size of demand and allocation respectively)	50%	43%
Number of institutional investors making up 80% of the issue (by total size of demand and allocation respectively)	47	41
The three largest investors by size	US$39.3 million US$24.7 million US$20.0 million	US$20.6 million US$17.9 million US$14.5 million
Total number of institutions (all international)	176	175

Source: Morgan Stanley.

demand, while most of the cyclical money came out of the US. Due to the fact that the Austrian market is small and underdeveloped, there were only very few dedicated Austrian buyers among international institutions as not many investors felt compelled to buy an Austrian stock simply to gain exposure to the Austrian market, although there was some investment by international funds dedicated to European emerging markets. In terms of the type of organisations that bought the issue, over 70 per cent of the offer was allocated to investment managers, 10 per cent to insurance companies, 6 per cent to banks (for their own accounts) and 4 per cent to mutual funds.

Investor concentration

A relatively small number of institutions accounted for a large portion of demand and allocation. The 10 largest investors accounted for 50 per cent of the total demand. There were several large leadership orders from top-rated US and UK institutions. The largest order accounted for 17 per cent of the total deal size (at the offer price and before the increase of the offer) as shown in Exhibit 19.

After-market price performance

See Exhibit 20.

On 22 April 1994, the first day of trading on the Vienna Stock Exchange, Mayr-Melnhof closed at ASch737. Trading volume was normal, with approximately 12.3 per cent of the 4.4 million shares sold in the offer changing hands. Of this volume, approximately 90 per cent was traded on Seaq International and the balance in Vienna. The greenshoe was exercised on 29 April by which time the price had increased to ASch742. On the following day it reached ASch744 where it stayed for one week. On 10 May it fell below the offer price for the first time.

Although investors had understood from the company that it would not be affected by higher waste-paper prices, the share price reacted gradually to the accelerating increases in the monthly average price of mixed sorted waste-paper in Germany – by Dm10/ton in April and by Dm43/ton in May. By 24 June the share price was ASch700. It then began to fall more quickly following the spontaneous 30 June statement by the company's CEO that it would not be able to live up to Morgan Stanley's 'optimistic' forecast issued at the time of

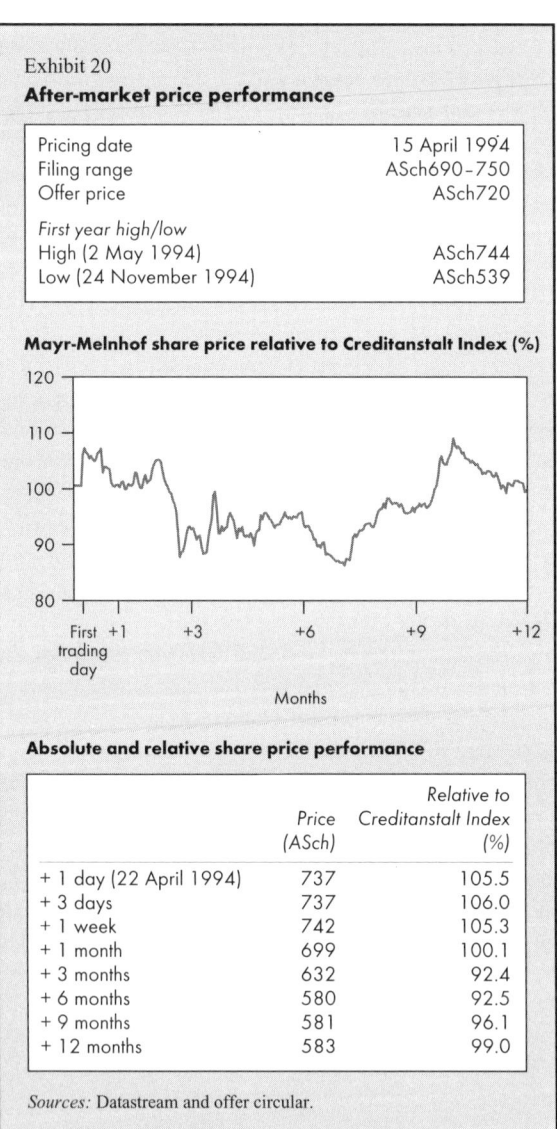

Exhibit 20

After-market price performance

Pricing date	15 April 1994
Filing range	ASch690–750
Offer price	ASch720
First year high/low	
High (2 May 1994)	ASch744
Low (24 November 1994)	ASch539

Mayr-Melnhof share price relative to Creditanstalt Index (%)

Absolute and relative share price performance

	Price (ASch)	Relative to Creditanstalt Index (%)
+ 1 day (22 April 1994)	737	105.5
+ 3 days	737	106.0
+ 1 week	742	105.3
+ 1 month	699	100.1
+ 3 months	632	92.4
+ 6 months	580	92.5
+ 9 months	581	96.1
+ 12 months	583	99.0

Sources: Datastream and offer circular.

the IPO. This statement led to considerable confusion in view of an allegedly repeated assurance by the company that Mayr-Melnhof would not suffer as a result of higher waste-paper prices. The company denies having made such reassurances.

These adverse developments were particularly disappointing as they occurred at a time when most companies in the sector, including fully integrated virgin-fibre-based companies, achieved better than expected results. Morgan Stanley became involved and a profits warning was issued, indicating that the 1994 numbers would be below expectations.

Over the first 12 months of trading, Mayr-Melnhof fell by 19 per cent from its offer price, but performed more or less in line with a weak Austrian market. More significant was the fact that over the first 12 months of trading, Mayr-Melnhof under-performed a broadly based Morgan Stanley index of the 10 major European paper companies by 26 per cent.

The performance of the main parties

The company

Mayr-Melnhof's management had tremendous operating experience and a good track record of running the business as a privately owned company. Together with the controlling shareholder, it was decisive and efficient in preparing for the offer. The management hired Lazard Brothers as adviser when faced with inconclusive and at times confusing advice from the investment banks soliciting for the mandate. Together with its team of bankers and advisers, it took many bold decisions, including those on timing, sizing and structure of the issue. The decision on timing looks particularly good in retrospect, when seen in relation to the performance of the domestic market. Over the 12 months prior to pricing, the Austrian market was up 31 per cent, and the transaction was announced only two weeks after the Austrian market peaked on 2 February 1994 (at which time it was up 40 per cent compared to mid-April 1993). In the 12 months after pricing, the Austrian market fell by 17 per cent.

Together with Morgan Stanley, the management prepared a first-class investor presentation which was convincingly delivered on the roadshow. Anthony Northrop, at that time Lazard partner advising the Mayr-Melnhof management and now managing director of Touchstone Securities, gave the management credit for being extremely independent and clear-thinking: 'The management deeply entrenched themselves and exercised a high level of control over the process. They were a small team and wanted to get on with the flotation. They acted as owners in their own right representing the family, which is a professional approach to take. Once they had a full understanding of a particular issue they were very pragmatic in reaching appropriate compromises and finding suitable alternatives. On the roadshow the company was open and forthright, which was much appreciated by investors.'

However, the company does not get full marks for disclosure, as the management could have placed more emphasis in the prospectus, during the roadshow and during the various conference calls with investors and analysts, on the potentially negative impact on profits from a rise in the price of waste-paper, the company's main raw material. This resulted from the fact that the company had six- to nine-month sales contracts with cartonboard customers whereas most waste-paper purchases are effectively priced on a spot basis. The market was clearly under the impression that rising waste-paper prices were not going to harm the company's profitability. This widely held belief was evidenced by a strong share price, which by 25 June 1994 still stood at ASch700. Even Morgan Stanley appeared to be in the dark on this issue, as evidenced by its research report dated 8 June.

The fact that the company publicly denied that there would be a negative impact from rising waste-paper prices did not help the management's credibility. When first asked by an Austrian business magazine on 30 June 1994 Mayr-Melnhof CEO Michael Gröller was quoted as denying that rising waste-paper prices would lead to lower profits for 1994 but acknowledged that the company might not be able to live up to Morgan Stanley's 'optimistic forecast'. The share price plummeted. Mayr-Melnhof is blamed for not communicating earlier to its lead sponsor that there might be a problem with the 1994 profit forecast issued at the time of the IPO. The company argues that, given the time lag between when prices are actually charged by the waste-paper vendors and when they are subsequently known to the market at large, they had not seen any unusual price movements in the period leading up to the forecast. For the uninitiated investor, this is difficult to understand, particularly since Mayr-Melnhof's own waste-paper division is a major player in the collection, sorting and trading of waste-paper. Perhaps the company should have been more aggressively educated by its advisers: regardless of who was to blame, the market gained the impression that the issuer and the lead sponsor were substantially uncoordinated and suspected that Morgan Stanley had been over-aggressive in its original marketing.

Mayr-Melnhof had not been prepared for the magazine interview and 11 days elapsed before it was able to make a statement. But its 11 July press release did not quantify the impact of rising waste-paper prices, and left the market expecting the worst until the following day when Creditanstalt came out with a forecast pointing to a near halving of the expected net profits for fiscal 1994, though not of cash flow. Following its initial profit warning in July 1994 the management did everything possible to communicate with investors. The company's revised forecast issued on 17 August was conservative, as evidenced by the fact that the actual result for 1994 substantially exceeded it.

Actual cash earnings achieved for 1994 were only 12 per cent lower than Morgan Stanley's forecast at the time of the offer. At the end of April 1995, Morgan Stanley was forecasting 1995 cash flow only 10 per cent lower than forecast at the time of the IPO. Mayr-Melnhof has also made a number of acquisitions and on average paid considerably less for those assets than the valuation at they were trading. Through bad luck and an understandable lack of experience of running a public company, the management has learnt a number of lessons which, although expensive, will hopefully serve it well in the future.

Mayr-Melnhof has not quite achieved its business development objective as articulated at the time of the IPO. 'The company has increased the folding-carton capacity by 120 per cent over a period of two-and-a-half years,' noted Mads Asprem, Morgan Stanley's equity research analyst for the sector. 'However, the objective at the time of the offer was to increase the capacity by 200 per cent over three years. Unless a significant acquisition is announced soon, they will only have achieved a little more than 50 per cent of their growth objective within the folding-carton business.'

Morgan Stanley

Morgan Stanley devised a good marketing plan which would have allowed for the placement of the whole issue outside Austria. Given the lack of depth in the Austrian market and its traditional approach to the valuation and pricing of new issues, this was probably the right strategy. Having said that, it was important that at least 17 per cent of the offer was placed domestically in order to obtain some domestic trading liquidity and a measure of sponsorship by the domestic equity community. Morgan Stanley organised a first-class roadshow which represented the most important part of the marketing plan. Investors taking part in the one-on-one meetings bought 61 per cent of the issue. The bank underwrote 50 per cent of the international tranche and placed more than 85 per cent of it, which is impressive, if not entirely unusual for an issue of this kind. It positioned the company with international investors as a European packaging company, which allowed the pricing to be based on cash flow rather than earnings. The bank also worked hard to obtain Creditanstalt's support for valuation and pricing based on cash flow, but this effort did not achieve the desired result. With international demand dominating the book, it was the international institutions who provided price leadership and enabled the offer price to be fixed at a level pleasing to the vendor. The share price performance in the immediate after-market was strong if not spectacular.

All this good work notwithstanding, Morgan Stanley has to share in the responsibility for poor disclosure in the prospectus. It appears not to have identified the mismatch in the contract terms between the purchase of waste-paper and sale of cartonboard during the due diligence process, and as a consequence the prospectus did not focus sufficiently on the risk of rising raw material prices (although it vaguely alluded to it) and the associated potential negative impact on Mayr-Melnhof's profitability. Historically, waste-paper prices had fluctuated substantially – from Dm65/ton in April 1988 to Dm120/ton in July 1988. Equally, during the five months leading up to the issue, prices increased by Dm35 from negative Dm50 to negative Dm15. Although a price increase in itself would not necessarily have had a negative impact on profitability if the company had been in a position to pass it on to customers immediately, given these substantial historic movements in the price of waste-paper, one might have expected Morgan Stanley to look into the issue in much more detail. If the mismatch was indeed uncovered in the due diligence process, it should have been disclosed in the prospectus.

After the stabilisation period, the communication between Morgan Stanley and Mayr-Melnhof appears to have tailed off somewhat, if not in regularity then perhaps in substance, as otherwise the bank might have learnt earlier about the impact of the dramatic but unpredictable rises in the price of waste-paper on the company.

Once Morgan Stanley was aware that Mayr-Melnhof was unlikely to achieve the forecast as published at the time of the issue, it took drastic action and following substantial due diligence and forecasting, quickly organised a mini-roadshow to London and New York to see the major investors. A formal quantified profits warning was issued by Mayr-Melnhof in August together with the interim results. This effort was well received by investors and selling pressure abated. There was not much selling but prices were marked down on relatively low volumes. Ideally the profit warning should have happened earlier, on the initiative of Mayr-Melnhof, advised by Morgan Stanley. It is always better if the company takes the initiative to communicate bad news to the market.

Morgan Stanley's earnings and cash-flow forecasts were by far the most optimistic in the market (the earnings forecast was almost 40 per cent higher than that of Creditanstalt although the difference in cash flow was much smaller) which, given the events that transpired, did not look too good. Yet with stable waste-paper prices, Mayr-Melnhof might have achieved this forecast. Mads Asprem acknowledged that he misread the market for waste-paper prices: 'I upgraded the Mayr-Melnhof forecast off the back of very good first-quarter 1994 results, but I assumed a lower EBIT (earnings before interest and tax) margin than at the time of the peak in the earlier cycle. However, I clearly misjudged the waste-paper market.'

Morgan Stanley's main competitor for the Mayr-Melnhof mandate had been Kleinwort Benson. 'Compared to the other banks we felt that our strong card was knowledge of the paper sector and overall placement power,' explained Jerker Johansson. 'We perceived Kleinwort Benson as the Austrian experts.'

According to Mayr-Melnhof's chief financial officer Wilhelm Hörmanseder: 'Both candidates were strong and recommended a more or less similar structure with placement heavily concentrated in the UK and the US. We felt perhaps that Morgan Stanley had a somewhat deeper and broader placement power than Kleinwort Benson but the deciding factor was Morgan Stanley's views on pricing. They were less concerned about the Austrian approach to valuation, which was basically earnings-based, and more in tune with international cash-flow valuation. Morgan Stanley's valuation range was wider and they seemed more prepared to try to get us the best possible price.'

Creditanstalt Bankverein

Creditanstalt Bankverein, obviously disappointed at seeing one of its oldest clients going public on advice coming mainly from a foreign investment bank, had a very difficult time convincing its fellow Austrian syndicate banks and their own investors about the pricing methodology and therefore the absolute offer price. These problems were related to the lack of sophistication in the Austrian market as a whole rather than to Mayr-Melnhof specifically, but they were accentuated because of the unusually large difference in earnings and cash flow. Although the domestic tranche supposedly closed oversubscribed after only one day, the overall quality of Austrian demand was low, due to the absence of domestic institutional participation. This was evident in the secondary market when the problems set in, as retail behaviour is easily influenced by the news media.

Creditanstalt deserves credit for taking Mayr-Melnhof's side in the contentious issue of whether or not to launch the offer before the privatisation of VA Technologie. This was a politically courageous decision on the part of Creditanstalt and also a good market call as, if anything, the Mayr-Melnhof offer had a positive effect on the VA Technologie privatisation. However, Creditanstalt appeared unconstructive in the eyes of the vendor with respect to some of the crucial decisions including tranche sizing, valuation and pricing. There were allegedly also instances of public criticism of the approach adopted by the global coordinator, and the working relationship between Creditanstalt and Morgan Stanley is thought to have been anything but good. Many of the problems with the domestic tranche can be explained by an absence of large institutional investors in Austria and a relative lack of sophistication on the part of the Austrian banking and investment communities. Whereas Creditanstalt might have done better in terms of promoting valuation on the basis of cash flow and sales to investors, it was never going to achieve a complete change in the way equities are valued in Austria. Given what happened in the after-market, Morgan Stanley and Mayr-Melnhof would have done well to price the issue more centrally between the valuations indicated by the domestic and international valuation methodologies respectively.

Although the Austrian bank had traditionally been Mayr-Melnhof's house bank, it was never seriously considered for the role of global coordinator. It had helped to rescue the company from bankruptcy in the 1930s, and Carl Anton Goess-Sarau, chairman of Mayr-Melnhof's supervisory board, was the vice chairman of the bank. The decision not to give Creditanstalt senior, or even equal, status in the transaction is an indication of the business-like fashion with which the Mayr-Melnhof family ran its company.

Lazard Brothers

Lazard Brothers added value to the issuer primarily during the solicitation phase and in the early stages of structuring. Decisions made early in the process are very important and should not be underestimated in the overall context of completing a successful transaction. Later in the process, Lazards acted primarily as a sounding board for the management on a range of issues. The role of an independent adviser is to stand in the background and provide advice when called upon.

Early advice provided by Lazards covered a wide range of issues including the terms and conditions of the contract with the global coordinator, the practicality of the family's and the company's objectives, how much should be sold internationally and domestically, how to handle a pending cartel case and how to structure the shareholders' agreement – including considerations such as how to restrict family members from selling shares to the market in an uncoordinated fashion.

Lazards put a lot of pressure on Morgan Stanley over pricing, ensuring that the latter would understand the importance of achieving the highest possible price that still allowed for a successful transaction right from the start. With the benefit of hindsight, it would perhaps have been better for Mayr-Melnhof if less effort had been spent on this. Lazards advised the management, as representatives of the vendor, not to disclose the minimum price at which the family would agree to sell. This is particularly important in the case of an IPO as the range of possible valuations is often very high and interpretation of the available information is an art rather than a science. By not disclosing the target price, the vendor will motivate the global coordinator to work harder. It is important for all vendors to realise that the investment bank (at least the syndication, sales trading and research arm thereof, if not the corporate finance department) has a vested interest in a lower issue price. Although the bank does not want too quick a price appreciation following the start of trading, it will feel more exposed if the price falls in absolute terms or substantially under-performs the market.

Lazards also tried hard to prepare the management for the cruel world of public ownership and the market's disclosure requirements. In light of what transpired, it appears that it could have been more successful in this area.

Mayr-Melnhof had not initially considered a separate adviser, but once the solicitation process had started it became clear to the company that it was receiving conflicting advice from the contenders, that the process of conducting an offer was more complex and time-consuming than anticipated. It therefore made sense to have a truly independent adviser.

Key lessons learnt

From the successful IPO

A powerful investment bank such as Morgan Stanley can generate very substantial investor demand for an unknown name such as Mayr-Melnhof in a relatively short time through intensive and skilful marketing. By positioning the company against the right peer group, the investment bank can significantly influence the basis of valuation.

Provided that the bank has prepared the ground during the pre-marketing phase of an offer, it is the management that sells the stock in the one-on-one meetings. In the case of this US$288 million IPO, 32 one-on-one meetings were arranged with investors who bought 61 per cent of the offer.

The valuation of Mayr-Melnhof by the international investment community was dramatically different from that of the domestic market. 'Proof of the pudding' is often thought to be found in the bookbuilding process as all investors compete on equal terms. However aggressive marketing by the global coordinator can have a substantial influence on investors' perception of value. That notwithstanding, the truth is only revealed once the stock has become seasoned.

Even if the offer was more than two times subscribed at the midpoint/top of the pricing range and even if the company decided not to take advantage of the possibility of setting the offer price at an even higher level, it may, judging from the price performance after the stabilisation period, have been overambitious to increase the total offer size by 800,000 shares. Demand is not always what it seems.

The timing – just a few weeks before the major privatisation of VA Technologie – raised controversy in many quarters due to the risk of oversupply. But Marko Musulin, head of capital markets at Creditanstalt, who supported the fast-track solution, explained: 'We felt that, in fact, VA Technologie – as essentially an engineering company – and Mayr-Melnhof were sufficiently different. As it turned out, the Mayr-Melnhof offer probably gave the market a positive tone for the VA

Technologie offer.' This is an example of supply creating demand rather than exhausting the limited existing demand.

From subsequent events

The transition from very private to very public company with sophisticated international shareholders can be dramatic. Carl Anton Goess-Sarau commented: 'When you run a private company you are pessimistic and keep a low profile in order to maintain good relations with employees, trade unions and the tax authorities. When you are a public company you constantly need to talk about how well you are doing and in so doing you obviously raise the expectations of employees and get problems with the trade unions. I saw the mentality of the management change overnight.'

The Mayr-Melnhof IPO also demonstrates the importance of cohesion within the management group. Open and public dissent between the two lead sponsors on issues such as pricing will undermine confidence among investors and inevitably lead to a lesser result. The difference in company culture and the different levels of sophistication between the Morgan Stanley and Creditanstalt teams appear to have been the main problems on this occasion. On top of the more tangible qualifications, humility, subtlety and patience are important qualities for an international investment bank wanting to do a really good job in an unsophisticated market. Since the chemistry between the domestic and international bookrunners is crucial, it may in some cases make sense for the senior party to be involved in the appointment of the less senior one, so that the team starts off knowing who is in charge and with a good team spirit. This would have meant involving Morgan Stanley in the selection of the domestic lead-manger. The specific circumstances will dictate whether such an approach is practical and feasible.

The importance of thorough due diligence conducted by bankers and lawyers with appropriate industry sector experience cannot be stressed enough. If the mismatch in Mayr-Melnhof's contract terms between the purchase of waste-paper and sales of cartonboard had been identified in the due diligence and disclosed in the prospectus, its shares may well have been trading considerably higher today.

It is possible to price and distribute an IPO successfully away from the domestic market: if and when things go wrong, however, the impact on the share price is likely to be accentuated without the appropriate support in the home market. The market of last resort is always going to be the domestic market, and the importance of strong long-term sponsorship in this market should not be underestimated.

During the preparation and execution phases of an offer such as this, the lead sponsors and the company typically work closely with one another: this offer highlights the importance of that close relationship being maintained for a considerable period after the offer, particularly in the case of an IPO. For such an ongoing relationship to be fully productive, there must be mutual trust and openness between the company and the bankers. The traditional UK approach, whereby an investment bank is formally appointed on an ongoing basis can have many advantages over a more transaction-based approach, particularly for companies which have limited experience in the capital markets.

It is not easy for a corporate management, regardless of how experienced it may be in terms of managing a business, to be humble enough regarding the challenges of running a publicly quoted company without prior experience, particularly if the shareholders include the largest institutional investors in the world. It is therefore important to put full trust in, and take the advice of, the bankers as to how to prepare for life during and after the IPO. Often it makes sense to appoint to the executive management a person with prior experience of running a public company.

It is paramount that the company and the lead sponsor fully synchronise their views on the prospects of the company and that the lead sponsor then expresses this in a profit forecast with which the company is comfortable. It is crucial for the company's credibility with investors that it lives up to this forecast. Should there appear to be disagreement between the company and bankers about the forecast, the market will punish the stock as both parties lose credibility. Credibility is difficult to build and maintain but easy to lose.

Conclusion

The successful completion of this transaction was undoubtedly a considerable achievement. The offer was large in absolute terms for an unknown company, and also relative to the size of both Mayr-Melnhof and the Austrian market. Morgan Stanley applied international valuation methods and the price achieved was substantially above what the domestic banks recommended. Accordingly, approximately 83 per cent of the offer was placed in the international market. The issue was increased by 10 per cent and was more than two times subscribed, and the greenshoe was exercised in the two weeks following pricing. The quality of placement was high with the list of international shareholders reading like a 'Who's Who' of global fund managers. The high level of placement in the US, which catapulted Mayr-Melnhof to the position of the most US-owned Austrian company, was particularly impressive. The timing was highly opportune for the company but was criticised in Austria, as it was only one month before the VA Technologie privatisation. It was also opportune for the vendor as it was close to the peak of the Austrian market. The issue initially traded well in the after-market.

As everyone relaxed after a job well done, serious trouble was around the corner in the form of sharply rising waste-paper prices. Although the extent of these price rises could not easily have been foreseen, they had started rising several months before the offer. Investors were clearly concerned about the matter prior to the completion of the offer but were supposedly reassured by the Mayr-Melnhof management that there would not be a negative impact on 1994 profitability, as the company was in a position to increase the price of cartonboard in pace with the rising cost of raw material. When it became clear that the company was going to be affected by these price rises, due to the unexpected pace of increases and an undisclosed mismatch in the contract terms between the buying of waste-paper and the selling of cartonboard, the market sold off dramatically. Investors might have expected a higher degree of disclosure in the prospectus to alert them to the risk of a margin squeeze in the event of rising waste-paper prices. The fall in the share price was accentuated by an increasing belief among investors that Mayr-Melnhof and Morgan Stanley were not fully synchronised on forecast earnings.

Once Morgan Stanley became fully aware of the problem – albeit much later than should have been the case – comprehensive due diligence was conducted on the effects of the price rises. On 11 July the company admitted for the first time that the rise in the cost of raw material would have an impact on 1994 profitability. Shortly afterwards, Morgan Stanley took Mayr-Melnhof on a mini-roadshow which helped to calm the shareholders' nerves. A quantified profit warning was issued with the publication of the six-months' results on 17 August.

The sudden rise in waste-paper prices for this high-quality company – still 59 per cent-owned by one of Europe's great industrial families – was truly unfortunate. However, the management had been warned by its advisers that the first year as a public company would be challenging, although it was clearly shaken by these events. Once the problem of the temporary margin squeeze was duly recognised, appropriate action was taken by the company. Furthermore, Mayr-Melnhof's management has spent the proceeds from the issue prudently to expand the converting business in accordance with its strategy, and has also increased waste-paper collection capacity. No irreparable damage has been done among serious investors, although it is indisputable that Mayr-Melnhof's credibility has suffered and placed the company on the defensive in the international equity market.

Feature topic: *Lessons from Mayr-Melnhof's profit warning*

Following an intensive marketing period the Mayr-Melnhof share offer was successfully sold and priced. Two weeks later, the greenshoe was exercised and the intensity of the relationship between the global coordinator and the company began to ease. It was just at this time that things started to go wrong for Mayr-Melnhof, as waste-paper prices began a dramatic rise. What happened during the crucial 12 months following the issue can been seen in Exhibit 21. These events were unfortunate, in that they followed on so quickly from the completion of the IPO. They pose a number of questions for Mayr-Melnhof's management, bankers and financial advisers and demonstrate to others the type of questions they will face if they run the risk of putting themselves in a similar situation:

- Did the company and its bankers warn investors sufficiently of the impact of rising waste-paper prices in the prospectus dated 15 April 1994, particularly given the fact that historically prices had been much higher, that the price level had already increased by Dm35/ton over the six months preceding publication of the prospectus and that there was a mismatch between short-term contracts for the purchase of waste-paper and longer-term contracts for the sale of cartonboard? (See Exhibit 22.)

- When did the company begin to suspect that it might have a problem with the 1994 profit forecast, and did the company immediately communicate its concerns to the lead sponsors? (See Exhibit 23.)

- When did the company finally realise that the 1994 forecast could not be reached, ie, when was management convinced that waste-paper prices would stay high and that the increase in final product prices would not fully compensate for increased raw material prices due to the mismatch between short-term purchase contracts and fixed-sales contracts expiring in September 1994 for a proportion of the carton board production? If only in late June/July why was this so?

- Was the above-mentioned mismatch in the contract terms identified in the due diligence? If it was, why did the market not know about it? Should this mismatch not have been disclosed in the prospectus? Was it not deemed material at the time? If Morgan Stanley had known, should it not have insisted upon an earlier profit warning?

- When did Morgan Stanley, whose equity research department follows waste-paper prices on a regular basis (particularly having been the lead sponsor of this transaction), challenge the company as to the achievability of the 1994 forecast? Did this only happen following the 30 June article in Wirtschaftswoche, and if so was this because Morgan Stanley and the remainder of the market were unaware of the mismatch in the contract terms and therefore thought that increasing waste-paper prices were either neutral or positive for the company?

- Did the lead sponsors of the issue sufficiently educate the company concerning its obligations to investors following completion of the issue and was the company aware that it ought to issue a profit warning as soon as the management became concerned that the company would not make the forecast?

- At the time of the issue was the company comfortable with Morgan Stanley's original forecast or was the management put under pressure to put its name to the forecast so as to facilitate the sale? Had the management put itself in this situation by insisting on a high offer price which would be achievable only with an upbeat forecast?

These questions illustrate some of the complex issues that a public company has to contend with and underscore some of the challenges facing a company making the transition from a private to a public company. It is impossible to answer the above questions without very detailed research, which is beyond the scope of this book.

Exhibit 21

Chronology of events leading up to and following the profit warning

Date		Share price (ASch)
15 April-94	• At the time of the issue, Mayr-Melnhof's management was thought to have smoothed over investors' concerns that the group would be negatively affected by rising waste-paper prices. Raw material price increases were supposedly to be easily controlled both by the group's own waste-paper collection activities and because it would have advance knowledge of cost increases and hence could pass them on by increasing cartonboard prices. The issue was sold on Morgan Stanley's 1994–1995 EPS forecast of ASch34/56 and CFPS of ASch113/139. Morgan Stanley's 1994 earnings and cash-flow estimates are significantly higher than those of Creditanstalt.	720
29 April	• Full 400,000 shares greenshoe was exercised.	742
2 May	• All-time high in the share price was reached. The pace of increase of waste-paper prices was escalating but the company claimed not to have seen this movement due to a time lag effect.	744
15 May	• End of 30-day stabilisation period. Market price only just held at offer price level.	720
8 June	• Morgan Stanley publishes research report reiterating positive outlook communicated at time of offer. Higher waste-paper prices are not thought to have a negative impact on Mayr-Melnhof's profits.	686
15 June	• Company issued press release advising of price increase for cartonboard by mid-year as a result of strong demand and high capacity utilisation. Although this clearly flagged the issue of rising waste-paper prices, the tone was, if anything, positive, giving no indication that the net impact on the company would be negative. Many investors interpreted this as confirmation of Morgan Stanley's forecast. The share price fell only ASch6 on the day. Off the back of this news, Morgan Stanley upgraded its 1995 CFPS forecast to ASch150 from ASch139. The market still had no idea that the 1994 results could be negatively affected by higher waste-paper prices.	703
30 June	• Article in Wirtschaftswoche featuring interview with CEO Gröller. He denied that there would be a negative impact on 1994 profitability from increases in waste-paper prices. However, Gröller also said that it was unlikely that the company would achieve Morgan Stanley's 'optimistic forecast' for 1994. Share price fell by ASch6 on the day and continued to fall every day until 12 July.	689
11 July	• Company issued press release acknowledging for the first time that there would be a negative impact on the 1994 figures (this effectively amounted to a profit warning) as a result of dramatic increases in waste-paper prices which continued into July. Company admitted to having a problem with fixed price contracts for cartonboard. Now company had to reduce cartonboard contract delivery periods to be able to pass on the price increases to end-customers more quickly. A 10% price increase to become effective in July 1994. The impact on the results for the first six months would be limited, there would be substantial impact on the third quarter and by fourth quarter the company would have the necessary flexibility to pass on price increases to end-customers hence eliminating any profit impact as a result of the increasing waste-paper prices. The impact on 1994 earnings as a whole not quantified and the profit outlook for 1995 remained unchanged. Share price fell by ASch29.	620
12 July	• Creditanstalt profit downgrade published whereby 1994 projected profits were reduced from ASch260 million to ASch140 million (ASch23 per share to ASch12 per share). Morgan Stanley downgraded its 1994–1995 EPS forecast from ASch34/56 to ASch13/44. CFPS for 1994–1995 downgraded to ASch86/126 from ASch113/150. Shares hit temporary low of ASch586.	586
13 July	• On Wednesday evening Brussels anti-trust verdict announced – company to pay ASch283 million. This is already provided against and accordingly the market does not sell off further.	592
18–21 July	• Mini- roadshow – investor meetings in London and New York to discuss the impact of waste-paper price rises and the outlook. This effort was well received by investors. During this week, the share price increases from ASch619 to ASch632.	632
15 August	• MS upgrades 1994 EPS from ASch13 to ASch15 and 1994 CFPS from ASch86 to ASch89.	630
17 August	• Company announced six-months' results up sharply over 1993: net income of ASch105 million and cash earnings of ASch511 million. For the first time the company issued a specific forecast for 1994 of ASch140 million net income and ASch920 million cash earnings, in line with Creditanstalt's forecast of 12 July, but slightly lower than Morgan Stanley's cash forecast for 1994.	640
25 November	• Company upgraded 1994 net profit forecast from ASch140 million to ASch160 million and cash earnings to ASch940 million. Share price began a steady increase from ASch539 the day before this announcement to ASch641 on the last trading day of the year. Price increases for cartonboard of 10% in July were followed by another increase in October. A further 10% increase was to be announced for 1995.	550
23 February-95	• Company announced full 1994 results of ASch182 million net profit (EPS of ASch18) and ASch1.01 billion cash earnings (CFPS of ASch98).	679
22 April	• One year after the IPO, the share price stood at ASch583 or 19% below the offer price, which is broadly in line with performance of the Austrian market but a 26% under-performance against its European peers. At this time, Morgan Stanley expected 1995 EPS to amount to ASch45 and CFPS to ASch125, or 20% lower and 10% lower respectively than forecast at the time of the IPO. Unfortunately, Mayr-Melnhof was also to disappoint in terms of its 1995 performance.	569

Exhibit 22

Mixed sorted paper and board monthly averages for Germany (Dm/ton)

June 1987	20
July	35
October	48
April 1988	65
July	120
February– October 1993	minus prices
November	-50
December	-25
March 1994	-25
April	-15

Source: PPI This Week, Brussels.

Exhibit 23

Mixed sorted paper and board monthly averages for Germany (Dm/ton)

April 1994	-15
May	28
June	70
July	117
August	163
November	143
December	135
January 1995	120
February	148
March	175
April	220
May	300
June	310
July	295
August	280
September	225

Source: PPI This Week, Brussels.

The specialist viewpoint

At one stage or another every publicly traded company will have to face the problems of profit warnings. Here, leading international bankers answer the question of if and when a company should issue a profit warning.

Peter Wilmot Sitwell, former chairman of Warburg Securities:

'As soon as the board of directors decides that the company is not likely to be able to meet the market's expectations, which is something the company jolly well should know. If there is doubt as to whether or not the particular circumstances warrant a profit warning, it is clearly better to do one than not.'

Håkan Strängh, executive director, European equity sales, Goldman Sachs:

'As soon as possible when the company knows that it will not live up to consensus earnings, ie, if the company has reason to believe that the results to be reported will be out-side the range of analysts' forecasts. This is of course an Anglo-Saxon standard but one which ultimately should also be adopted in continental Europe and elsewhere. The need to issue a profit warning will to an extent also depend on whether the company itself has traditionally commented on its future earnings or whether it simply takes the view that it only comments in connection with the ordinary earnings releases. Not to make a profit warning when a company has already commented on analysts' forecasts and hence legitimised them would be worse than if you never comment on the market's expectations. As a salesman, you are naturally more likely to recommend a share to a client if you feel comfortable about the earnings forecast. This will clearly impact the performance of the share. Most likely you will find that out of two similar companies, *ceteris paribus*, the company that is open with the stock market and immediately informs when the circumstances change will trade at a lower-risk premium and a correspondingly higher valuation. Trust is highly valued by most investors.'

'How do you avoid making a profit warning? By firstly having an accounting system that allows the management to know where they are and secondly to continuously communicate with the market without having to reveal clearly price-sensitive information.'

Sten Lindholm, senior vice president, corporate communications, SCA:

'According to our listing contract with the Stockholm Stock Exchange, we are obliged to update our forecast as soon as we determine that we are likely to deviate from the previously announced forecast in a material way. By material we are talking plus/minus 10 per cent. Because of the frequency of our official reporting occasions, at which times we always update or confirm our forecast (we report quarterly and in the spring we publish the fourth-quarter and full-year results on a preliminary basis, then our annual report is published and thereafter comes the AGM), and because we always provide our forecast in terms of a range, we have so far not had to do a profit warning.'

John Woolland, executive director – corporate broking, SBC Warburg Dillon Reed:

'The practice of doing a public profit warning has developed to a large extent as a result of the introduction of insider legislation in many countries (which stipulates that you can't give price-sensitive information to one market participant without giving it to the entire market) and the steadily improving disclosure standards whereby companies ought to tell investors what is going on. The market does not like surprises. Therefore, as soon as a false market develops in the stock, you ought to do a profit warning.

'The way this subject is handled is different from sector to sector. UK retail companies, for example, have developed a practice of formally commenting on the state of trading in January, hence bridging the long gap between when the six-months' results are published in September and the full-year results are announced in March. The same problem does not arise in the spring because trading conditions are typically discussed in May each year in connection with the AGM. The advantage of commenting in January is also that a large portion of the annual trade in this sector is achieved during the period leading up to Christmas.

'A way often used to avoid a false market being created in a company's share and without making a formal profit warning is to refer to external events such as, for example, the general price situation in a company's raw materials or output prices. By pointing to what are perfectly transparent general market developments, a company can flag that this is perhaps a concern for the particular company as well. This would not represent insider information if these prices are generally considered as being in the public domain.'

Philip Bradley, director, corporate finance, Robert Fleming & Co:

'There shouldn't be a false market in the stock, ie, you as an issuer have an obligation not to mislead the market. Therefore, as soon as you know that you can't deliver what the market is expecting, then you should come out with a profit warning. In the case of an IPO, the onus is to a higher degree on the sponsor of the issue to ascertain that the company is living up to the market's expectation than in the case of an issue for an already seasoned stock where the management has more experience.'

A senior equity research analyst of a US bank, researching the insurance sector:

'In my sector, formal profit warnings are unusual due to inherent unpredictability as a result of claims. You tend to find profit warnings more often in small companies where a large claim would make a larger impact. Scrupulous compliance requirements notwithstanding, large companies tend to soften the market a little by telling people one by one to quell over-optimistic expectations. When doing that, management obviously has to be very careful indeed so as not to give obviously price-sensitive information to only one market participant but this is a bit of a grey area. In general terms it is my view that companies that do not properly manage the market's expectations are foolish in all but extraordinary circumstances. The important thing is to talk to a sufficiently large number of market participants on a sufficiently frequent basis in order not to have to say too much at any one time. If that is not done and a false market develops, then clearly you may have to make a profit warning.'

Johan Ewerlöf, executive director pan-European equity distribution, SBC Warburg Dillon Read:

'When there is a reasonable concern about the profit outlook, it being understood that the concern has to be material.'

Whereas the general answers seem straightforward enough, it is more difficult to determine whether or not a specific situation requires a profit warning. It is very difficult indeed to generalise and it is even more difficult to answer the question with regard to a specific situation without having full access to all the facts. Some of the factors to be taken into consideration when evaluating whether or not a specific set of circumstances warrants a profit warning might include:

- What the market is expecting (average and range of analysts' forecasts);
- What the company itself has said publicly with regard to the current year;
- The company's historic approach to communication with the stock market;

Exhibit 24

Six golden rules of successful investor relations

Initiative	The company must at all times maintain the initiative vis-à-vis the stock market. Specifically this means that adverse information should be communicated immediately by the company rather than giving the market an opportunity to assume that something negative has happened and challenge the company accordingly.
Focus	The company should report only on the most important and most relevant matters such that the market is not bombarded by too much information. The information should be of value to the recipient, ie, there is no point reporting something that the recipient will not appreciate knowing.
Consistency	The company should report on a consistent basis so as not to confuse the market, ie, it makes sense to report the same type of information at regular intervals and on a consistent basis.
Access	The market must have immediate access to the company's IR people, or otherwise the management should have the capacity to respond to most enquires within 24 hours. Investors want to talk to people who know and are authorised to talk.
Honesty	Every company is dependent on building up trust with the investor and analyst communities. This can only be achieved by reporting good and bad news on a completely honest basis.
Openness	Only by being open and by adhering to a high level of disclosure standards will true confidence and enthusiasm be established among investors. Those companies that tell investors what is going on should ultimately trade better than highly secretive companies.

- Whether or not the company itself knows with a reasonable degree of certainty where it stands with regard to the profit development in the current year;
- Whether or not the market already knows or should know (reason for deviation);
- What other companies in the sector do in this respect; and
- The particular time of year and proximity to the next ordinary earnings announcement.

Each case will be different. The most important step is for the CEO or CFO to discuss with the company's financial adviser the pros and cons of putting out a profit warning as soon as a problem is discovered. To issue a profit warning is a serious matter and often, but not always, represents a failure to communicate effectively in the ordinary course of events. When in doubt, it is generally better to issue a warning than not to.

Some general rules for communication with the stock market

When considering whether or not to issue a profit warning and when communicating with the stock market, the following general principles (see Exhibit 24), articulated by Sten Lindholm, senior vice president, corporate communications, of SCA of Sweden, might also be helpful.

Nokia Corporation

Nokia used a high profile US equity strategy as an integral part of its transformation from a heavily indebted Finnish conglomerate in the late 1980s to a world-class telecommunications equipment company and the favourite global growth stock among many fund managers. The two main pillars of this strategy were a NYSE listing and a global registered offer in July 1994 (Nokia 2).

In 1988 Nokia operated in 11 different business areas and the telecommunications related business accounted for only 11 per cent of total turnover. It was run by engineers and the corporate culture was one of measuring prestige in terms of numbers of employees and sales rather than in terms of return on capital employed and growth in earnings per share. The pre-tax profit margin of 5 per cent in 1988 declined sharply in the following years and in 1991 and 1992 Nokia turned in substantial losses. From a foundation in paper and rubber, Nokia had diversified into new areas (such as information technology and consumer electronics) which had turned sour. The consumer electronics business cost Nokia an estimated US$1.3 billion by the time it was finally sold in 1996. As recently as 1991–92 Nokia was financially stymied, with very limited access to the world's international capital markets.

Following considerable restructuring in 1990 and 1991, the new CEO Jorma Ollila announced in 1992 that the 'future lies in telecommunications'. He began to speed up the concentration on the telecommunications businesses which had

accounted for 33 per cent of group sales in 1991. During the first four months of 1993 Nokia climbed out of the red to turn in a small profit as the sales contribution from the telecommunications business headed towards 50 per cent.

With some confidence restored, Nokia cautiously approached the international equity market in June 1993, via CSFB, to raise a modest US$67 million (Nokia 1). The positive response to this offer among US investors took almost everyone by surprise as until this time the company had considered the European equity market the one to which any new equity raising activity would be targeted However Nokia's management reluctantly agreed to allocate two days of the roadshow to the US with a view to placing 40 per cent of the offer with US QIBs via the Rule 144A market. The main reason for including a US tranche was simply to raise more money. Nokia's scepticism was understandable given that, at the end of 1992, 80 per cent of its shares were owned by Finnish investors and no more than 5 per cent were owned in the US. By the time the offer was priced, Nokia had raised US$167 million following strong share price performance during the marketing period, an increase in the number of shares underwritten and the exercise of the greenshoe. Approximately 35 per cent of Nokia 1 was placed with 17 US institutions and a significant proportion of after-market orders had come from the US. The Nokia name had undoubtedly been very well received albeit, by a small segment of the market.

Exhibit 1
Transaction summary

Issuer name: Nokia Corporation (Finland)	Global coordinator: CSFB
Pricing date: 1 July 1994 (HEX:1,678)	Pricing/underwriting structure: Bookbuilding
Vendor: Company	Primary or secondary: Primary
% of company sold: 8.0% of expanded share capital	Privatisation or corporate: Corporate
IPO or non-IPO: Non-IPO	Industry: Telecommunications equipment
Type of shares: A shares and ADRs (1/2 A share per ADR)	Offer price: FIM108/A share* US$10 1/8 per ADR
Issue size: US$484 million (up to 10% of the offer was targeted to Finnish institutions)	US listing/144A: NYSE listing

* In April, 1995, Nokia did a 4:1 share split reducing the nominal value of the share from FIM20 to FIM5. All prices and numbers of shares in this case study have been recalculated accordingly. In April 1995, the shares here offered were renamed A shares, having previously been known as preferred shares.

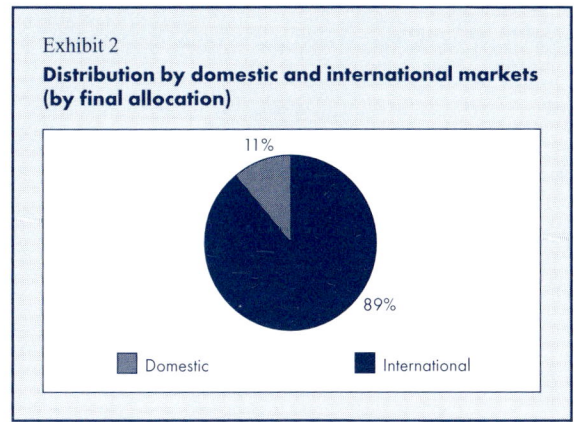

Exhibit 2

Distribution by domestic and international markets (by final allocation)

11%

89%

■ Domestic   ■ International

Impressed by the Nokia management and unhappy with their small allocations, US institutions continued to buy in the after-market, which resulted in a strongly appreciating share price (up by 81 per cent during the six months after the offer from an offer price of Fmk39.75). The love affair between Nokia and the US investment community had just begun. Following the offer, Ollila and his team continued to see US fund managers in connection with business trips to the US and became increasingly convinced of the depth of the US investor market and sophistication of US fund managers. It was this experience more than anything that ultimately contributed towards the decision to approach the US market on a more concerted basis by conducting a US listing and a largely US targeted offer in July 1994. Apart from having a need to finance its accelerating growth, Nokia's major consideration was very much one of targeting the US market on a strategic basis by simultaneously listing on the NYSE and offering shares.

With domestic and European investors largely fully weighted in Nokia, and with Nokia representing 15 per cent of the domestic index at the end of 1993, now was the time to find a new investor base. This need was judged increasingly important as Nokia was fast becoming a telecommunications equipment company, the valuation of which was foreign to the domestic investment community. Despite being widely known in Europe and despite the success of the 1993 offer, Nokia still lacked investor awareness in the US. This also contributed towards the conviction, no doubt encouraged by CSFB, that to break into the US market in earnest and to achieve a valuation more consistent with its peers, it needed to list on the NYSE. The rationale for a US listing appeared clear-cut, namely:

- To ensure long-term access to the US equity market, the largest capital market in the world;
- To enhance the perception of Nokia as a world-class company and an internationally traded stock, particularly among US investors;
- To reduce dependence on the Finnish equity market, a process begun with the 1993 offer;
- To underpin the company's valuation as an international telecommunications equipment company;
- To increase liquidity of Nokia's A shares;
- To support its business presence in the US; and

- To be, as a matter of prestige, the first Finnish company to list its shares on the NYSE.

The NYSE listing, which came into effect on 1 July 1994, was to be accompanied by a US$484 million global registered offer of new shares, 70 per cent of which was to be targeted towards the US market. This was at the time the largest ever international equity offer by a Finnish corporation. Highly successful, Nokia 2 was priced at Fmk108 and traded up to Fmk174.50 by the end of 1994. A little over one year after the second offer, on 14 September 1995, the shares reached a high of Fmk336, up 543 per cent over two years. Immediately following Nokia 2, some 25 per cent of Nokia's shares were owned by US investors – a year later this number had doubled to 50 per cent. Since January 1994, Nokia had outperformed the Helsinki HEX general index by 423 per cent, despite its heavy and growing weighting in that index. Throughout this period the company had constantly exceeded the market's profit expectations. But all good things come to an end – at least temporarily.

Nokia began to stumble during the second four months of 1995. On 19 October 1995 Nokia announced that pre-tax profits were up by only 58 per cent for the first eight months of 1995 due to slowing growth in mobile phone sales and intense competition in the US TV market. Within two business days the share price fell by 18 per cent to Fmk235. On 14 December 1995 the company warned that the mobile phones division would be below budget during the last four months of the year due to increased price competition in mobile telephones, component supply problems and other logistical difficulties. The company also warned that the consumer electronics division, one of the largest business activities, would have a significant loss in 1995. Investors reacted with brutal force and marked down Nokia's ADRs by nearly 30 per cent on that day, while the Helsinki price closed down 26 per cent to Fmk158. Just over two months later, Nokia announced its 1995 results (up 23 per cent on 1994) and issued its second profits warning: in the first six months of 1996, profits would be substantially below 1995 levels. The shares fell 7 per cent to Fmk157 in London trading: Nokia had become a victim of its own success and had to pay for the market's extremely high growth expectations of recent years.

Despite the fact that Nokia's problems were mainly of its own making, as the manufacturing side of the mobile phones division could not keep up with the growth in sales, the fall from grace was also symptomatic of the notoriously volatile high-tech industry. Indeed, the entire sector declined from September–October 1995 as aggressive growth-and-momentum investors began to shift their focus to other sectors.

Although Nokia's profits and share price recovered strongly in the second half of 1996 the negative developments in late 1995 and early 1996 tainted the successes of earlier years. However, three years after the Nokia 2 offer the company's shares rose above Fmk400 and the company seemed set to resume its impressive profit growth from the telecom business areas which accounted for some 90 per cent of 1996 group turnover.

The lessons learnt from Nokia's experience with the US market, both in good times and bad are of great relevance for all non-US companies considering a US equity strategy.

Major challenges

Nokia regarded the registration process with the US Securities and Exchange Commission as a major challenge and a concerted strategy was developed to cope with this. The NYSE listing would also require a strong and continuing investor relations commitment to the US market.

Through the offer, Nokia hoped to substantially expand its US investor base. The company had acquired only 17 US institutional shareholders through its 1993 Rule 144A placement and the medium-term target was to acquire 500.

Closer to home, Nokia had to convince European and domestic investors of the company's improving outlook for sales, market share and earnings growth. One problem was that many of these investors had a full index weighting of

Finnish stocks, including Nokia, whose share price they had seen rise by more than 160 per cent since the 1993 offer. Unlike the situation in the US, every significant European investor knew of, or had at some stage owned, Nokia stock.

The company also had to respond to concerns, expressed primarily by domestic and European investors, as to the use of proceeds and dilution in earnings per share as a result of the offer. On the announcement of the offer, the share price initially fell by more than 6 per cent.

Rationale and objectives

Reasons for the offer

- To raise money to finance Nokia's 30 per cent a year growth rate, particularly in the telecommunications and mobile phone businesses.

Offer objectives

- To broaden the shareholder base and widen name recog-

Exhibit 3
Share capital and ownership

Type of securities offered	A Shares and ADRs representing A shares (1/2 A share per ADR), with 1/10 of the voting right of K shares, entitled to a dividend of 10% of the nominal value of the shares before the K shares receive a dividend.
Share capital after offer	135,156,916 A shares 164,393,064 K shares 299,549,980 total number of shares In addition to the approval of this offer, the 23 June 1994 EGM also approved an amendment to Nokia's articles of association establishing the right for holders of K shares to convert their holdings on a one-for-one basis to A shares.
Ownership restrictions	None
Listings	Helsinki since 1915/London since 1987/New York since 1994 Nokia is also listed in Stockholm, Paris and Frankfurt.
Expanded market capitalisation at offer price (Fmk5.35/US$)	US$6.0 billion
Major shareholder(s) before offer	Fidelity (10%), Alliance Capital, Capital International, International Capital in Chicago, Kymmene, UBF Pension Fund and Pohjola Insurance.
Free float before offer	100%
Liquidity – A shares – first six months of 1994 (number of shares traded expressed on an annualised basis and as a percentage of the total number of shares outstanding).	22% in Helsinki. Most liquid stock on the Helsinki Stock Exchange during the 12 months to 30 June 1994 and the largest by market capitalisation by 30 June 1994.
Foreign ownership before offer 45%	
Most relevant stock exchange index/weighting	Helsinki Stock Exchange General Index/19.5% (30 June 1994)

Exhibit 4
Development of the offer size

Indicated number of A shares to be sold:	20 million + 3 million greenshoe
Offer size after increase	21 million + 3 million greenshoe
Amount of greenshoe exercised	3 million
Final number of shares sold	24 million

Exhibit 5
Offer structure

Target markets	% of initial underwriting*	Bookrunners	Co-managers
US	70%	CSFB	Goldman Sachs & Morgan Stanley
International	30%	CSFB	Enskilda & Mandatum
Total offer	**20,000,000**		

* As indicated on 2 June 1994.

Exhibit 6
Principal advisers

US legal adviser to Nokia	Shearman & Sterling
Finnish legal adviser to Nokia	Ursula Ranin (General Counsel)
US legal adviser to the underwriters	Cleary Gottlieb, Steen & Hamilton
Finnish legal adviser to the underwriters	Roshier-Holmberg & Waselius
Auditors	Coopers & Lybrand and KPMG Wideri

---

nition, particularly in the US. Nokia's medium-term objective was to acquire at least 500 institutional shareholders in the US;

- To sell approximately 70 per cent in the US, 20 per cent internationally and 10 per cent in Finland;
- To sell up to 24 million A shares at a price above Fmk100 without offering a discount to the market price (the 1993 offer had been priced at a 3.64 per cent discount); and
- To improve the balance sheet in view of the Fmk1.9 billion restructuring charge at the end of 1993, although balance sheet considerations were much more of an issue in connection with the 1993 issue.

Intended use of proceeds
- One third for working capital;
- One third for capital expenditure, primarily in the telecom business; and
- One third to repay Fmk694 million of debt maturing in December 1996.

Share capital and ownership

See Exhibit 3.

Transaction components

This was a two-tranche bookbuilt open-priced issue with a publicly registered offer of ADRs in the US and an international placement of A shares. There was provision in the international tranche for placement with Finnish institutional investors of up to 10 per cent of the total offer. The ADRs were listed on the NYSE and trading began immediately after pricing on 1 July 1994.

How the offer size changed

Launched as an offer of 28 million ADRs (representing 14 million A shares) and six million A shares with a three million greenshoe, the offer was subsequently increased by one million shares dedicated to the international tranche. The greenshoe was exercised one business day after pricing (see Exhibit 4).

There were no structural considerations out of the ordinary. The only other structure contemplated was a listing without an offer, but this was rejected on the grounds that it would have only a limited impact on investors (see Exhibit 5).

Principal advisers
See Exhibit 6.

Transaction fee distribution

The total gross spread of 3.23 per cent was distributed as shown in Exhibit 7.

Exhibit 7
Distribution of gross spread (%)

Management fee	Underwriting fee	Selling concession	Gross spread
0.8343	0.6019	1.794	3.23

Exhibit 8
Distribution of management fee outside the US (%)

Total management fee	0.8343
Of which: Global coordinator's praecipium	27.8
Of which: Lead manager's praecipium	36.1
Of which: Management fees split among all managers according to underwriting commitment.	36.1

Management fee

In the international tranche, CSFB picked up the lion's share of the management fee in its capacity as global coordinator, lead manager and the largest underwriter (see Exhibit 8).

In the US, the management fee, net of global coordinator's praecipium, was split among the three managers.

Selling concession

In the US the traditional pot system was employed, whereby the selling concession was partly fixed (ie, paid on the basis of underwriting commitments) and partly variable and paid according to designations by investors (see Exhibit 9).

CSFB ended up with an overwhelming majority of the US designations.

In Europe the selling concession was paid pro rata according to whomever received the order.

Underwriting fee

The underwriting fee of 0.6019 per cent was split according to the final underwriting commitments (see Exhibit 10).

Exhibit 9
Distribution of selling concession in the US (%)

Total selling concession	*1.794*
Of which: Pre-agreed portion	30
Of which: Paid pro rata according to sales	70

Exhibit 10
Final underwriting commitments (shares underwritten)

	International	US	International and US
CSFB	4,152,000	3,146,672	7,298,672 (34.8%)
Goldman Sachs	–	3,146,672	3,146,672 (15.0%)
Morgan Stanley	–	3,146,672	3,146,672 (15.0%)
Enskilda	816,000	–	816,000 (3.9%)
Mandatum	632,000	–	632,000 (3.0%)
+ further 5 firms	1,400,000	–	1,400,000 (6.7%)
+ further 27 firms	–	4,559,984	4,559,984 (21.7%)
Total	**7,000,000**	**14,000,000**	**21,000,000 (100.0%)**

Sources: International and US offer circulars.

Exhibit 11
The timetable

February	• Nokia commences work with internal accountants on US GAAP reconciliation.
1 March	• Nokia announces 1993 results and intention to list on NYSE.
Early April	• Nokia appoints CSFB global coordinator for SEC registered offer; • Documentation work commences (typical time requirement for F-1 is up to six weeks).
11 May	• Confidential SEC filing of F-1.
25 May	• Nokia calls EGM for 23 June and announces intention to sell up to 24 million shares (including greenshoe) by way of a global share offer to raise more than US$370 million.
End May	• Feed-back from SEC on non-public filing of 11 May.
2 June	• First public filing with SEC of F-1. Timing and size of offer not announced; and • Pre-marketing begins (without the interim report for four months to April 1994).
16 June	• Nokia announces strong results for first four months of 1994, confirming company's recovery and potential for future earnings growth.
Friday 17 June	• Roadshow begins with presentations in Helsinki and Stockholm.
Monday 20 June	• Amended F-1 filed with the SEC (including four months to April 1994 results); • Red herring printed; and • Roadshow continues in Europe and Asia (20–23 June); CEO team in Europe and CFO team in Tokyo and Europe.
23 June	• EGM authorises issue of up to 24 million A shares and amended articles of association to allow holders of K shares to convert to A shares. Purpose of conversion is to increase liquidity of A shares.
Friday 24 June	• Midsummer holiday in Finland.
Monday 27 June	• Roadshow continues with four-day 16-city US tour.
Friday 1 July	• Pricing of the transaction after the close in Helsinki and at the opening in New York to allow for one full trading day in New York before 4 July US holiday.
Monday 4 July	• US markets closed for Independence Day.
5 July	• Greenshoe fully exercised.

Timing of sale

At the time of the offer, Nokia's management appears to have underestimated its future earnings growth. In the spring of 1994, CSFB estimated 1994 earnings per share of about Fmk22. This rose steadily through the year, reaching Fmk39 after the release of the second tertial results in October. It could therefore be argued that it would have been better for the offer to have taken place in the autumn of 1994.

During the two to three years before the offer, telecommunications operators and telecommunications equipment manufacturers had been in vogue with investors. The global market for mobile phones was expected to grow by 40–80 per cent in 1994 and Nokia was ideally positioned to capitalise due to its strength in the fastest growing sector of this market – digital technology.

Only a few years ago it would have been inconceivable that Nokia, Motorola and Ericsson would be as successful as their Japanese competitors. Their success is best explained by the fact that, contrary to earlier expectations, the telecom and mobile phone businesses are not simply a manufacturing game but also a software and marketing game.

Marketing

Investor targeting

About 100 US investors and 112 international investors were specifically targeted by CSFB for the purposes of pre-marketing and marketing. These investors were divided into three distinct groups:

- The top 100 US institutional holders of Motorola and Ericsson;
- International investors in Ericsson and Nokia;
- Institutional buyers of Nokia's 1993 US$168 million offer (of which there were 17 in the US and 38 internationally).

Roadshow

Nokia's management held a comprehensive two-week roadshow with two teams, covering Europe, the US and Japan, visiting 25 cities. The US part spanned 16 cities over four full working days. In 1993, the management had spent just two days in the US visiting only the major accounts in Boston and New York.

- Globally, Nokia met 240 investors, of which 60 were seen on a one-on-one basis;
- In the US, they met 160 investors of which 49 were seen on a one-on-one basis; and
- The New York lunch alone was attended by 67 investors.

When comparing the 1993 and 1994 offers, the higher investor attendance and the much higher effectiveness of the US one-on-ones, as illustrated in the table below, stand out. This was a reflection of growing confidence among US investors and the much higher profile of Nokia 2 as a result of the NYSE listing. Of the 20 largest buyers in Nokia 2, 19 were from the US and all but two met Nokia's management in one-on-one meetings. The much lower effectiveness of the

European one-on-ones reflected the sharp appreciation in the share price and the fact that most European investors already had a full weighting in Nokia shares. (See Exhibit 12.)

Retail marketing

At the time of Nokia 2 the company was not seen as a name that would have a strong appeal to US retail investors. Priority was therefore focused on the US institutional market. A number of retail firms were, however, included in the US syndicate but received only small commitments. By late 1996, Nokia had acquired almost 70,000 US retail shareholders.

The Nokia story

In 1994 Nokia was both a telecommunications equipment story and a growth story. It was also to an extent a 'focus on core business' story.

With a market capitalisation of US$6 billion (post-offer) and 1993 sales of US$4.4 billion, Nokia was one of the world's leading international telecommunications equipment companies and the most profitable of its kind. It is Finland's largest publicly traded company, and in 1993 no less than 85 per cent of its sales were generated outside Finland. The telecommunications businesses accounted for approximately 52 per cent of 1993 turnover and Nokia was well positioned in some of the fastest-growing segments of the sector. The 1993 net sales and operating profit per business group are shown in Exhibit 13.

CSFB sold the offer on the basis of the sales points given in Exhibit 14.

Exhibit 12

Number of one-on-ones and their effectiveness in the 1993 and 1994 offers

	Nokia 1	Nokia 2
US tranche		
Number of investors	8	49
% of tranche bought by one-on-one attendees (by allocation)	25.0%	63.8%
European tranche		
Number of investors	6	11
% of tranche bought by one-on-one attendees (by allocation)	83.3%	28.6%

Source: CSFB.

Exhibit 13

1993 net sales and operating profit per business group (Fmk million)

	Sales	Operating profit
Telecommunications	4,578	983
Mobile phones	6,314	950
Consumer electronics	6,938	-747
Cables and machinery	4,933	261
Other operations	1,500	18
Eliminations	-566	–
Total	**23,697**	**1,465**

Source: Offer circular.

Exhibit 14
Principal sales points

Telecommunications	• Nokia has an extremely broadly based set of customers both geographically and by number in all three of its divisions: cellular systems, switching systems and transmission systems. Its NMT analogue systems and GSM digital systems, for example, were delivered to PTTs and private operators in 23 and 14 countries respectively; and • This major strength had been developed as a result of Nokia's small and unprotected home market which forced the company to compete internationally long before most of its competitors.
Mobile phones	• Nokia ranked No. 1 in Europe, No. 2 in the US and No. 2 in the world; • The global market share had increased from 10% in 1990 to 18% in 1994. CSFB estimated that this market would double by 1997 from a US$5 billion market in 1994 and that Nokia's share would increase to 23% by that time; and • Nokia had just started to compete on the Japanese market and analysts expected it to capture 20%–25% of this, the world's second-largest cellular market.
Consumer electronics	• Consumer electronics had undergone massive restructuring and was positioned to break-even. Cost-cutting measures, including a 46% staff reduction, and technological improvements, had been implemented since 1992 and culminated in an extraordinary restructuring charge of Fmk1.9 billion (US$347 million) in 1993.
Cable and machinery	• The business had been increasingly focused on the cables side; and • Promised operating margin improvements had been delivered.
Nokia was positioned for global growth	• Competition among PTTs and between PTTs and new operators, liberalisation and standardisation across the globe provide Nokia with steadily increasing business opportunities; • Given Nokia's strength in digital infrastructure and digital mobile phones, it is a primary beneficiary of the world-wide digital cellular revolution. Over 70% of Nokia's cellular infrastructure sales were in digital systems, compared to 50% for Ericsson and less than 25% for Northern Telecom, Motorola and AT&T; and • Over 85% of Nokia's telecommunications sales were in high-growth markets (ie markets growing at a rate of at least 15%).
Financial performance in 1993	• Net group sales increased by 30% to US$4.4 billion; • Telecommunications' sales increased by 43% and operating profit by 130%; and • Mobile phone sales grew by 73% and operating profit by 117%.
Corporate culture	• The organisational structure under Jorma Ollila was flat, unbureaucratic and emphasised cooperation and teamwork; • The average age of the management team was 44 years; and • Nokia is focused on meeting customer needs rather than developing technology for the sake of it.
Valuation (2 June 1994)	• Despite spectacular recent share price performance, Nokia's shares, at Fmk101, were valued at a substantial discount to its principal peers, in terms of the two most relevant measures of value: P/E (31% discount against Ericsson) and adjusted market value/operating cash flow (27% discount against Ericsson).

Source: CSFB.

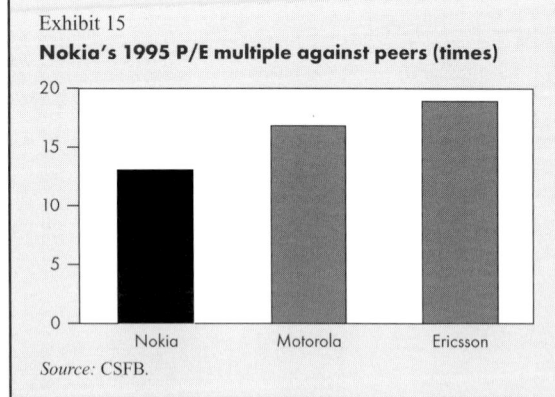

Exhibit 15
Nokia's 1995 P/E multiple against peers (times)

Source: CSFB.

Exhibit 16
Nokia's 1995 adjusted market value to operating cash flow against principal peers (times)

Source: CSFB.

Investor concerns

Those investors who declined to participate did so principally for the following reasons:

• Fear that the consumer electronics business would not break even in 1994 as expected;
• Margin pressure on mobile phones;
• Dilution and use of proceeds considerations;
• Strong historic share price performance; and
• Many European investors were fully weighted on Finland and in Nokia.

Market conditions

Unlike in Nokia 1, which was done at a time of an excep-

tionally strong new issue market, the general market conditions in 1994 were very difficult. The new issue market had been in steady decline since the US Federal Reserve started to raise short-term interest rates in February 1994, however due to the strength of its story, Nokia was relatively unaffected by general market conditions.

Results

Placement

The offer was three-and-a-half times subscribed before the increase in the offer size from 20 to 21 million shares. The US tranche was four times subscribed, and the international tranche was just over two times subscribed (see Exhibit 17).

By far the most important geographic markets in the international tranche, in terms of allocation, were the UK and Finland. The UK share was almost 60 per cent larger than that of Finland.

Investor concentration

With 27 institutions accounting for 80 per cent of total allocations, the placement was concentrated in relatively few hands (see Exhibit 18).

The largest order represented 40 per cent of the entire issue before the increase and the exercise of the greenshoe, but it was scaled back to represent 17 per cent of the total number of shares allocated. Of the top 10 buyers world-wide, six had not bought shares in the 1993 offer and of the 20 largest buyers, 19 were from the US.

Share price performance

See Exhibit 19.

Before pricing
- In absolute terms the shares had risen by 172 per cent since Nokia 1 and by 51 per cent over the six months leading up to the 1994 offer;
- Having reacted positively to the decision to list the shares in New York, the price fell by 6.4 per cent on the news of Nokia's intention to conduct the offer, as announced on 25 May 1994. Investors initially questioned the purpose of the offer and were concerned about dilution in earnings per share;
- The share price increased from Fmk105 at the time of filing on 2 June to Fmk108 on the pricing day; and
- Nokia's A shares had outperformed the Helsinki market by 46 per cent during the six months to pricing.

After pricing
- In the immediate after-market the share price rose strongly on several large US after-market orders and closed at a premium of 4.2 per cent to the offer price on the first day of trading;
- Nokia's share price continued to perform strongly in both absolute and relative terms, rising by 64 per cent in absolute terms and outperforming the Helsinki market by 84 per cent during the six months following pricing;
- The price of Nokia's A shares reached a peak on 14 September 1995 at Fmk336 and closed at Fmk175 at the end of 1995, following a profit warning in mid-December;
- Following a strong performance during the second half of 1996 and early 1997, by mid-1997 the shares were priced at Fmk400, due to a growing realisation that Nokia was back on its growth track.

Exhibit 17

Underwriting, demand and allocation

Target markets	Final underwriting	Demand	Allocation
US tranche	67%	80%	71%
International tranche	33%	20%	29%
Total number of A shares	**21,000,000**	**70,000,000**	**24,000,000**

Source: CSFB.

Exhibit 18

Investor concentration

	By demand	By allocation
Percentage of issue accounted for by the 10 largest investors (by total size of demand and allocation respectively)	35%	49%
Number of investors making up 80% of the issue (by total size of demand and allocation respectively)	50	27
The three largest investors by size	US$161 million US$81 million US$39 million	US$81 million US$36 million US$20 million
Total number of institutions	**205**	**155**

Source: CSFB.

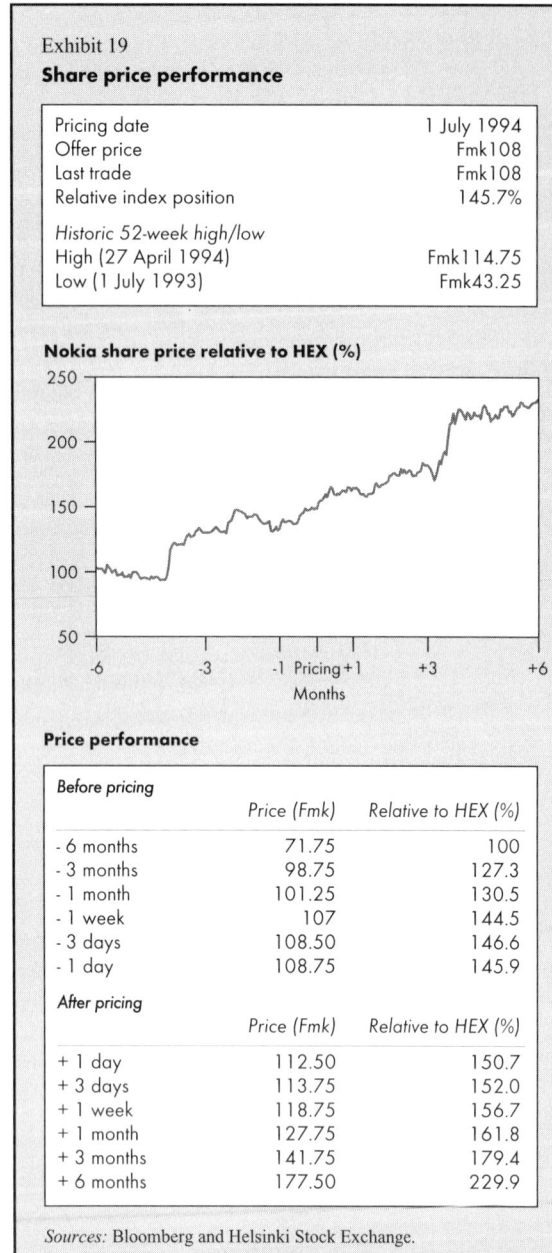

Exhibit 19

Share price performance

Pricing date	1 July 1994
Offer price	Fmk108
Last trade	Fmk108
Relative index position	145.7%

Historic 52-week high/low	
High (27 April 1994)	Fmk114.75
Low (1 July 1993)	Fmk43.25

Nokia share price relative to HEX (%)

Price performance

Before pricing

	Price (Fmk)	Relative to HEX (%)
- 6 months	71.75	100
- 3 months	98.75	127.3
- 1 month	101.25	130.5
- 1 week	107	144.5
- 3 days	108.50	146.6
- 1 day	108.75	145.9

After pricing

	Price (Fmk)	Relative to HEX (%)
+ 1 day	112.50	150.7
+ 3 days	113.75	152.0
+ 1 week	118.75	156.7
+ 1 month	127.75	161.8
+ 3 months	141.75	179.4
+ 6 months	177.50	229.9

Sources: Bloomberg and Helsinki Stock Exchange.

Exhibit 20

Percentage of total issue traded * (%)

	Day 1	Day 2	Day 3	Total Day 1 - Day 3
New York	9.0	Holiday	3.3	12.3
Helsinki	0.9	5.5	2.7	9.1

* Based on the issue of 21 million A shares.

Source: Bloomberg.

After-market trading volume

A relatively modest 12.3 per cent of the offer traded in New York over the first two trading days, reflecting investors' strong belief that Nokia would continue its strong performance (see Exhibit 20).

One of Nokia's major US shareholders increased its holding by over one million shares in the after-market, equivalent to more than 25 per cent of the original allocation. Other US institutions were even more aggressive in the secondary market compared to their original allocations. There were practically no sellers in the US. There was some minor selling in Finland reflecting the fact that Finnish investors were looking at Nokia's share price in an historic perspective rather than valuing the company on a fundamental basis. Most of the after-market selling is thought to have come from European institutions, which is consistent with the European tranche being less over-subscribed and the fact that the price leadership in the offer came from the US market. Following the offer, price leadership continued to come from the US – while the price was rising daily in New York, in Europe it was just catching up to the previous night's NYSE close.

The performance of the main parties

The company

The foundation for a successful listing project was already laid in Nokia's basic accounting, which was in very good shape, partly because the company had reported under IAS since 1987. The registration process was well planned and initiated at a sufficiently early stage, and Nokia had a very good internal working group of about ten people who struck up a good relationship with the SEC. Nokia worked without any financial advisers for this project, although a representative of CSFB participated in the first few meetings. The company produced an F-1 registration statement of the highest standard and received very few comments in return. It was comfortable with the registration process, while recognising that it was very time-consuming.

CEO Ollila and his team deserve a lot of credit for excellent investor presentations during the 1994 offer and, importantly, in the period between the 1993 and 1994 offers. 'Clearly Nokia is not just paying lip-service to an active IR strategy, they are actually also doing something,' commented one large US institutional investor. Adam Inselbuch, director – investment banking at CSFB, added: 'These guys were seen as extremely knowledgeable about the business, very honest and straightforward.' Despite this praise, there was to be considerable criticism of Nokia's IR effort in connection with the profit warning of 1995.

After the offer, the share price performed spectacularly, due to accelerating earnings growth and an expanding investor base. If the management is to be criticised, it is for being too conservative with its earnings forecast. 'They should have realised that the earnings growth was beginning to accelerate and therefore should have delayed the offer until after the publication of the eight-months' figures in late 1994,' commented one senior banker not involved in the transaction. But to have a reputation for being financially conservative can be a great asset as it is tremendously difficult to acquire such a reputation, but very easy to lose it, something that Nokia was to experience in late 1995 due to its temporary problems in the mobile phone business.

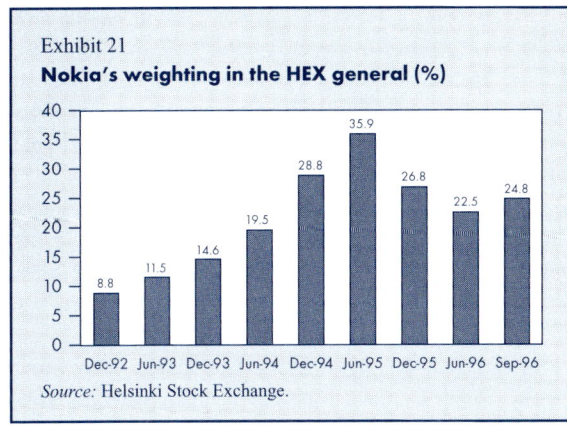

Exhibit 21
Nokia's weighting in the HEX general (%)

Source: Helsinki Stock Exchange.

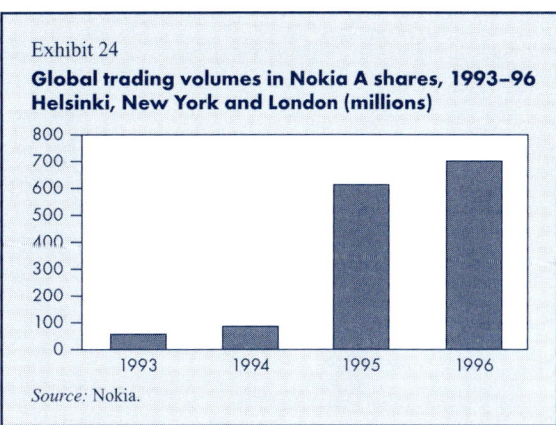

Exhibit 24
Global trading volumes in Nokia A shares, 1993–96 Helsinki, New York and London (millions)

Source: Nokia.

Exhibit 22
Nokia's ownership by region (%)

	Finland	US	RoW
End of 1992	80	5	15
August 1993 (after 1993 offer)	65	12	23
August 1994 (after 1994 offer)	50	25	25
August 1995	35	50	15
August 1996	31	56	13

Source: Company estimate. The geographical ownership is defined on the basis of the institution's physical location rather than the nationality of the parent company.

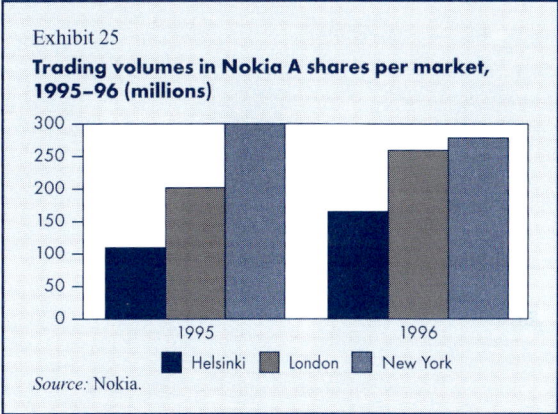

Exhibit 25
Trading volumes in Nokia A shares per market, 1995–96 (millions)

■ Helsinki ■ London ■ New York

Source: Nokia.

Exhibit 23
Nokia's ownership by region (number of institutional investors)

	Finland	US	RoW
End of 1992	2,419	–	40
August 1993 (after 1993 offer)	1,969	20	100
May/June 1994	1,523	50	100
August 1994 (after 1994 offer)	1,521	100	200
August 1995	1,353	400	250
December 1996	1,300– 1,400	1,500– 2,000*	350– 400

* Nokia had some 70,000 US shareholders in late 1996, of which 1,500–2,000 were institutional. The medium-term objective is to raise this to 200,000 US individual shareholders and 3,000 institutional shareholders.

Source: Company estimate.

This offer, together with the NYSE listing, represented part of an ongoing process of reducing the company's dependence on its high and increasing weighting in the local market (see Exhibit 21).

Whilst Nokia's weighting in the local index has increased dramatically in recent years, the proportion of its ownership accounted for by Finnish investors has declined and has been replaced by additional US ownership (see Exhibit 22).

Increased foreign ownership can also be measured in terms of the number of international institutional shareholders.

Nokia's medium-term objective in connection with the 1994 offer was to acquire at least 500 US institutional shareholders. This goal appeared optimistic at the time, but within two years it had been surpassed by a factor of between three and four. This was partly due to the fact that Nokia had become better known and partly because some large institutions had sold to smaller institutions and retail investors during Nokia's problems in late 1995 and 1996 (see Exhibit 23).

In tandem with the internationalisation of the share and its strong performance, the total turnover on domestic and foreign exchanges increased dramatically, fulfilling Nokia's objective of becoming a globally traded stock. In addition to the company's ongoing success and the NYSE listing in mid-1994, the explosive growth in the 1995 and 1996 trading volumes was contributed to by performance problems at the time, as some large holders decided to reduce their holdings (see Exhibit 24).

Nokia's shares had traded predominantly in Helsinki and London until 1995, when the NYSE became the largest single trading market in Nokia's A shares, hardly surprising considering the ownership situation. In 1996, the official Seaq International volumes were almost as large as those of the NYSE; however London volumes may be inflated as a result of a degree of double counting (see Exhibit 25).

The global coordinator

Although in early 1994 both Nokia and CSFB were somewhat nervous about the size of the offer because of the rise in the company's share price, the bank soon became convinced that Nokia could issue as many as 24 million shares. This proved possible thanks to accelerating earnings growth and a widespread belief that Nokia's management was of the highest quality. CSFB certainly did a good job in judging the markets and crafting the 1994 story, which differed from the 1993 story in that there was now less emphasis on the consumer electronics business. The market was confident that Nokia's management had sorted out this previously ailing division and CSFB had actively serviced the market with research coverage through Kevin Brau, CSFB's telecommunications equipment analyst, and trading in the secondary market.

CSFB also organised a global 25-city roadshow for Nokia's management, and investor attendance was impressive, reflecting both the company's performance and CSFB's secondary market coverage.

CSFB was well positioned for this mandate, following the highly successful 1993 transaction and faced no real competition. There were, however, tough negotiations on fees which were reduced to 3.23 per cent from 3.75 per cent in Nokia 1. In addition, Nokia insisted that the transaction be priced without a discount. Olli-Pekka Kallasvuo, Nokia's CFO explained: 'The mandate was essentially awarded on the basis of quality of research, long-term relationship and trust built over several years in connection with the 1993 equity issue and prior debt transactions.' Neither Goldman Sachs nor Morgan Stanley were in the 1993 transaction but were appointed in 1994, mainly on the basis of their research coverage and their US placement power. They did not stand a realistic chance of getting the global coordinator mandate.

This was a tremendously important mandate for CSFB, as it was the largest equity offer for a European issuer in which the bank had acted as both global coordinator and book-running lead manager for all parts of the transaction. It was also confirmation that CSFB had done a good job on Nokia 1. The real coup for the bank was to get the 1993 mandate with hardly any secondary market trading presence in Nokia shares, and an analyst who had earlier put out a hold recommendation because of problems within the consumer electronics business.

Key lessons learnt

The registration process presented fewer hurdles than expected. 'If your basic accounting is in good shape, the US GAAP reconciliation is time-consuming but otherwise straightforward,' explained Nokia CFO Kallasvuo, who was impressed by the professionalism of the SEC staff and came to regard the commission's representatives almost as members of the transaction team. The registration process was considered a positive experience from which Nokia learnt a great deal.

There is a clear advantage in combining a listing with an offer: the offer is good for the listing as it dramatically enhances the attention received from investors and the press, while the listing is good for the offer in that the universe of investors reached is much wider and the impact on investors is significantly stronger. 'To not do an issue in connection with a listing is like dancing with your mother,' commented Beau Mathieu, a managing director of CSFB responsible for the bank's relationship with Nokia.

It is necessary to promote actively a company story to potential investors as without such a forceful approach there is no guarantee that they will understand the importance of the issue. Although Nokia was very well known in Europe and the largest company in Finland, the US investor community, with a few notable exceptions, knew very little about it. Only by being listed in the US and offering stock did Nokia connect with its investors: a classic example of supply creating demand. The result speaks for itself: just before the 1994 offer Nokia had 50 US institutional shareholders – 14 months later the same figure was 400. The lesson is that the dissemination of information in the global equity market is by no means as perfect as many market participants may think.

It would be a mistake to underestimate the sophistication of the US institutional investor community, including smaller institutions outside the big financial centres. The depth of understanding of the global telecommunications business was far superior to that demonstrated in other parts of the world where Nokia had traditionally met with investors. 'It is of critical importance to realise that the US market is very different from European markets,' explained Martin Sandelin, Nokia's head of investor relations. He warned that to go to the US unprepared can be a mistake: 'Even at Nokia, we didn't really have enough information and understanding of the US investor universe and the way it works before our 1994 NYSE listing. We had to learn very quickly and we were perhaps lucky not to make too many serious mistakes.' He also makes the point that US investor relations cannot be conducted on a semi-committed basis. Nokia put Sandelin in charge of global investor relations and based him in the US, and he knows the telecommunications business well having spent 12 years as vice president for communications within Nokia's telecommunications businesses. He continued: 'One of the main challenges of doing this job (except for keeping up with what is happening internally and in the industry generally) is to try to understand what the financial community expects from the company, what the financial community is looking at as triggers (in terms of identifying the turns in the industry) and what investors' investment criteria are, which obviously varies from investor to investor.'

Many of the institutions Nokia has met have had limited experience of foreign investment and thus have taken great comfort from being able to buy listed US dollar-denominated ADRs and deal with market-makers on the NYSE with whom they are familiar and who work in the same time zone. 'You've got to be able to paint the car in the colour the customer wants – offering listed ADRs to small customers can make a big difference,' explained Harold Bogle, managing director and at the time head of equity capital markets at CSFB in Europe. Listed ADRs are also preferred by the US institutions, as evidenced by the fact that in Nokia 2, 87 per cent of the total US tranche size was requested in the form of ADRs. When restricted Rule 144A ADRs were offered in 1993, the equivalent figure was only 5 per cent.

The offer was unaffected by the generally weak market conditions prevailing at the time. As Bogle noted: 'High-growth companies are always financeable in any but the worst

Exhibit 26

Implications of Nokia's increased US and overall foreign ownership

Name recognition	Due to a unique combination of a highly successful NYSE listing and the 1994 offer, a spectacular share price performance since then and the continued success of Nokia's products in world markets, the company dramatically enhanced its standing among investors and customers. The fact that most major financial magazines and newspapers have featured Nokia has significantly accelerated this development.
Price leadership	Nokia's CFO Kallasvuo explained: 'Whereas our domestic shareholders are very big and represented on the board, they are price followers – our increased US ownership has meant that the price leadership has now been taken over, in particular, by the US investor community, that is to say it is now US investors who drive the price up or down, whereas Finnish investors to a much larger degree follow the trends.'
Valuation	Nokia's valuation is no longer significantly dependent on a comparison with other Finnish companies. The increased Americanisation of the ownership has led to Nokia's valuation being based on the relevant international peer group – most notably Ericsson and Motorola – and has led to a reduction in the trading discount against these companies from 25% at the end of 1993 to approximately 10% in August 1995. The discount widened in connection with Nokia's problems in 1995 and 1996 but should again begin to reduce given consistent performance from the company.
Volatility	Nokia has become less dependent on fluctuations in the Helsinki market and now trades much more according to fluctuations in the Ericsson and Motorola share prices. It is Nokia's experience that the US investor community reacts more swiftly to bad news. This was evidenced not only by the market's reaction to Nokia's 1995–96 problems but also to the New York market's reaction to Ericsson's nine-months' 1993 interim report when the results, although dramatically up, came in only slightly below expectations. Despite Ericsson's CEO reiterating the earlier positive forecast, the company's share price tumbled by 15% in just a few hours on 19 November. Ericsson felt that many analysts had substantially overreacted to an attempt to quell some overoptimistic forecasts that were way out of line. The increased risk level in the Nokia and Ericsson shares is obviously also related to the high growth rates and the high degree of global competition in the telecommunications equipment industry.
Commitment to investor relations	Nokia has committed to investor relations at the highest level of the organisation. Jorma Ollila, Nokia's CEO and former CFO, spends 10–15 days per annum on IR matters. The head of IR reports directly to the CEO. Nokia knows and talks to some 350–400 US and some 250–350 international institutions on a regular basis, albeit not necessarily on a one-on-one basis. In addition, Nokia speaks to a growing number of its near 70,000 US retail shareholders. Nokia meets 100–125 US institutions and 75–100 international institutions on a one-on-one basis for 1–3 hours each year. There is an ongoing programme of bigger investor presentations in the major financial centres and regular conference calls with investors in connection with interim and annual results. There are up to five analyst conferences each year, typically in Helsinki, London or New York. In addition, Nokia representatives typically participate in three to four telecommunications conferences per month, most often organised by financial institutions. Nokia IR staff spend 50% of their time talking to analysts (both buy- and sell-side analysts), 30% with fund managers and brokers and 20% on internal matters.
Increased analyst coverage	Some 50 analysts now follow Nokia more or less regularly – of which approximately 30 do so on a consistent basis. This compares favourably with only 10 analysts before the 1993 offer.
Quality of management	Nokia's Kallasvuo articulated well the new Nokia management's basic view of one major consequence of the increased foreign ownership when he said: 'The financial market is the ultimate judge of the quality of the management.' This represents the Anglo-Saxon perspective but has not been a commonly held view on the European continent. Sandelin emphasised the importance of IR from the point of view of receiving feed-back from the market: 'It would be a great mistake and a lost opportunity to think that this work is a one-way street. We derive substantial benefits from being able to talk to well informed analysts and investors, in terms of where the product markets are developing, what our end-customers are doing, how we are doing against competitors, etc. The more institutional shareholders we have, the more intelligence potentially available to us.' Feed-back of course can be both positive and negative as Nokia sadly had to discover in late 1995. By inviting more foreign ownership, Nokia's management not only automatically acquires a high-quality dialogue with sophisticated analysts and investors but also accepts a much higher exposure. If things start to go badly at Nokia, the first result will be a tumble in the share price and the second is that the analyst and investor community will become increasingly vocal.
Capital market access	Through increased international name recognition and ownership, Nokia's access to international capital has been dramatically broadened. Specifically, as a result of Nokia's decision to register with the SEC, the company's access to US equity and debt markets (both long-term and short-term debt) was dramatically improved.

market conditions.' Another senior London banker commented: 'To do a US$500 million deal in the current markets, you either have to be cheap or have a good story.' Both undoubtedly applied to Nokia: at the time of the first issue, favourable market conditions had been deemed essential to launch what was initially conceived as an offer smaller than US$100 million. In 1994, however, CSFB was confident about the success of completing a US$400–450 million offer in exceptionally poor market conditions.

When Nokia hit problems in late 1995, US institutional investors reacted more strongly than other international shareholders – some of the company's largest US shareholders sold out altogether. CSFB's Brau said: 'Based on the secondary market turnover that we saw, I believe that US institutional investors reacted more sharply to Nokia's problems in the mobile phones division than did institutional investors elsewhere. Interestingly, US institutional investors reacted more negatively to Nokia's temporary problems than they did to Motorola's structural problems. It is our experience that US investors will typically treat US and European companies equally so long as things go according to plan. When, however, problems occur and if US investors feel that they have been let down, then they will react more sharply to foreign companies. It is only natural that you trust less what is further away from home.'

The specific lessons that can be learnt from Nokia's strategy of internationalising its shares can be seen in Exhibit 26.

Conclusion

Following a successful Rule 144 A placement in 1993, Nokia's level of ambition and confidence had grown in tandem with spectacular profitability and share price performance over the 12 months between the two issues. In early 1994 Nokia had decided for long-term strategic purposes to list on the NYSE but not necessarily to conduct an issue. However, during the ensuing months, the company's growth had begun to accelerate and Nokia had accepted that conducting a listing without an issue was probably not going to achieve the initial impact and momentum in the US equity market that it wanted.

The NYSE listing and the offer were overwhelming successes, mainly due to Nokia having laid a solid foundation with the 1993 offer, an active investor relations effort between the two issues, the Nokia story being still more attractive in 1994 and the company's ability to sell itself.

Although it is hard to imagine that any competent investment bank would have failed with this offer, CSFB nevertheless deserves credit for having advised Nokia to do the right thing since before Nokia 1. Without the successful 1993 issue the company may not have been in a position to take the huge write-off at the end of 1993 that it did and may not have been able to finance the increase in capacity that took place. A long-standing relationship between company and bank made it easier for Nokia to follow CSFB's advice. This was relationship banking at its best.

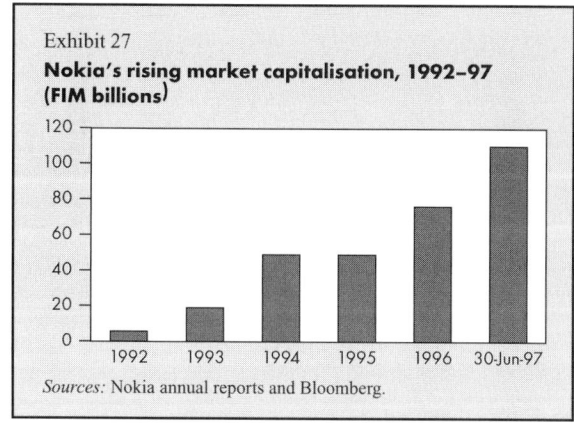

Exhibit 27

Nokia's rising market capitalisation, 1992–97 (FIM billions)

Sources: Nokia annual reports and Bloomberg.

Nokia's management can be accused of not recognising early enough the acceleration in earnings which led to a further revaluation of the company, as by waiting a little longer, Nokia would have achieved a much higher price. The alternative argument is that if you are in a cycle of accelerating growth you would in that case never conduct the financing until it is too late.

The result of this financing was that Nokia came to be more than 50 per cent owned from abroad, the hoped for revaluation took place, the US investor community provided price leadership and genuine liquidity was generated on the NYSE.

Despite the sharply negative reactions of US investors in late 1995 and early 1996, there is no question but that the company's US equity strategy has been a good one. Nokia is today a core holding among US fund managers and is one of only a few European companies that have a strong following among both European and US-based analysts. The company has learnt a lot from the US investor community and its long-term valuation has undoubtedly benefited from US ownership. However, Nokia's experience also shows that developing and maintaining a significant US investor base is a high stakes game. Unexpected under-performance can be met with brutal force. Asked if, with the benefit of hindsight, the company would have done anything differently in its international equity strategy, management replied: 'No'. That may very well be true for Nokia but a NYSE listing is not the recommended strategy for every company.

After serious temporary problems in 1995–96, the growth in earnings seems set to resume – certainly the market appears to believe so (see Exhibit 27).

A management which has created an amazing Fmk115 billion (US$22 billion) of additional market value between the end of 1992 and June 1997 clearly deserves more than the benefit of the doubt. So why in July 1997 does Nokia trade at a P/E discount of approximately 30 per cent against Ericsson? An important part of the explanation is that Nokia is to an extent still paying for past mistakes. It is not easy to build and maintain credibility in the global equity market.

Feature topic: *Hitting the Big Board – Lessons from Nokia's listing on the NYSE*

While listing on the NYSE is a big decision for most companies, it was perhaps not quite so daunting for Nokia, as the company had become highly change-orientated in recent years. What is significant is that the decision to list came first and it was only later that the company decided on a simultaneous offer. The decision to list was more a strategic decision and did not have the raising of capital as its immediate purpose. Nokia had several important reasons for seeking to join the NYSE:

- It wanted to ensure long-term access to the US capital market as the largest capital market in the world. For that to happen, a broad US investor base had to be built. In the medium term, it wanted to acquire 500 US institutional investors;
- It wanted to enhance investor and customer perceptions of Nokia as a world-class company with an internationally traded stock. While Nokia was very well known in Europe, it was not in the US – and those US institutions that had heard the name thought it was Japanese. As a relatively small private placement under Rule 144A, the 1993 offer had had little impact with US institutions. Nokia needed to reach the same status in the financial markets as its major competitors and an NYSE listing was the best way to do this, especially as all but one of it's competitors already were listed in the US (see Exhibit 28); and
- Nokia felt that it was important not to be valued or priced in Helsinki by investors who were traditionally less familiar with the global telecommunications industry, but rather to be compared with its international peer group and priced accordingly. The hope was that the discount at which Nokia was trading against Motorola and Ericsson would decline over time as the overlap of the three companies' investor bases increased. This appears to have happened to a significant degree, and Nokia's forward P/E ratio discount to Ericsson developed as shown in Exhibit 29.

By the end of August 1995, Nokia's future profits were valued almost as highly as those of Ericsson, as evidenced by the P/E discount to Ericsson shrinking to 10 per cent. Following the problems in Nokia Mobile Phones in late 1995 and early 1996, this discount widened dramatically as investors temporarily lost faith in the management. After the problems of late 1995, the discount stood at its widest in February 1996, at just over 40 per cent. As the market became increasingly convinced that Nokia's problems were temporary, the discount again began to narrow. By early December 1996 the Nokia versus Ericsson P/E discount based on CSFB analyst Kevin Brau's 1997 estimated earnings stood at 31 per cent. Brau commented: 'If Nokia continues to deliver high profit growth in line with the market's expectations this discount should narrow to no

more than 15 per cent, particularly since the two companies' technologies are more or less equivalent and as Nokia actually has a higher return on capital than Ericsson.'

- As a matter of prestige, Nokia wanted to be the first

Exhibit 28

Listing strategy of Nokia's peers

Company	Country	US Listing
AT&T	US	NYSE
Motorola	US	NYSE
Northern Telecom	Canada	NYSE
Alcatel Alsthom	France	NYSE
NEC	Japan	Nasdaq
Ericsson	Sweden	Nasdaq
Siemens	Germany	–

Sources: NYSE, Nasdaq, CSFB.

Exhibit 29

Nokia's declining P/E discount versus Ericsson (%)

	Nokia versus Ericsson discount
June 1993 (Just before 1993 equity offer) (1994 P/E)	43
June 1994 (Just before 1994 offer) (1995 P/E)	31
June 1995 (1996 P/E)	22

Source: CSFB.

Exhibit 30

Nordic companies listed on the NYSE (as of August 1997)

Company	Country	Date of Listing
Novo-Nordisk	Denmark	September 1981
Norsk Hydro	Norway	June 1986
Hafslund Nycomed	Norway	June 1992
Tele Danmark	Denmark	April 1994
Nokia	Finland	July 1994
ISS-International Service System	Denmark	October 1994
Rauma	Finland	June 1995
Saga Petroleum	Norway	April 1995
Scania	Sweden	April 1996
Astra	Sweden	May 1996
Valmet	Finland	May 1996
Nycomed	Norway	May 1996
Smedvig	Norway	November 1996
Petroleum Geo services	Norway	April 1997

Source: NYSE..

Finnish company to list its shares on the NYSE. Prior to this listing only four Nordic companies had listed on the NYSE; subsequently a further nine Nordic companies have listed on NYSE. The Nordic companies listed on the NYSE in August 1997 are as shown in Exhibit 30.

The strategy for a successful listing

Like most companies contemplating SEC registration and a NYSE listing, Nokia took this very seriously. A concerted effort was therefore made to develop a successful strategy to complete this project, the principal elements of which were:

- Early preparation. Nokia began its internal accounting work in February 1994, although the listing was not intended to become effective until four months later. At this stage Nokia did not plan to conduct an offer, so there was no pressure on that front;
- To present a good initial F-1 document, and once a listing with a simultaneous offer was planned, to minimise the risk of receiving substantial SEC comments on the confidential filing in May. This was important as there was a risk that substantial comments from the SEC on the first filing would lead to rigorous comments on the public filing of the F-1 in early June. If that happened, there would be a risk of delaying the timetable into the Finnish summer holidays in July. In the event, shortly after the public filing on 2 June, Nokia received an indi-

cation from the SEC that there would probably not be any substantial comments on either the public filing of the F-1 (which did not yet include the tertial numbers), nor on the subsequent filing of the F-1 including the tertial results and the red herring. This allowed CSFB to confirm the timetable and jump-start the pre-marketing during the second week of June. At this stage, the tertial numbers were not yet available and their incorporation in the final filing had to wait until they were publicly announced on 16 June. On 14–15 June, Nokia received final confirmation that the SEC would not have substantial comments on the red herring. CSFB was then able to include the tertial numbers in the red herring and publish it in time for the roadshow that started the day after the official publication of the tertial results;

- To establish a good and informal working relationship with the SEC. While Nokia may have expected a rigid and bureaucratic approach among the staff, they instead found an extremely professional, diligent and productive attitude, so much so that Nokia's CFO was able to accomplish much on the telephone – even over the weekend. Nokia was in a comparatively favourable position: since 1987 it had been reporting according to International Accounting Standards (IAS), which are much closer to US GAAP than are Finnish Accounting Standards (FAS).

The commitments

- To file an annual report on Form 20-F each year with the SEC. This should include financial statements pre-

Exhibit 31

Ten good reasons to consider a US listing

		Relevance for Nokia
1.	If the company, in connection with one or more offers, is dependent on raising substantial amounts of new equity capital from the international markets or if it is subject to a large secondary sale of shares as in the case of a privatisation.	Medium
2.	If the company is in an industry that is well understood in the US and if there are good equity research analysts that follow the sector and/or if the principal peers are US companies or listed in the US. Preferably US investors should already have shown some interest in the shares in connection with a US private placement or otherwise.	High
3.	If the company is obviously undervalued by its domestic market and against its US peer group.	High
4.	If the company's more traditional investor bases are fully weighted on either a country basis, on an industry sector basis or in terms of the specific company.	High
5.	If the company has a business presence in the US and if that presence is growing.	Medium
6.	If the management is prepared to make the time commitment required to maintain a US investor base.	High
7.	If the company can offer enough shares in the US to create a substantial domestic trading market in that country.	High
8.	If the company has sufficiently sophisticated staff who can communicate effectively with the US investor and analyst community.	High
9.	If the management sees the need to change the management culture within the company towards a more shareholder-conscious philosophy.	Low
10.	If the company's basic accounting is in good shape. It clearly helps if the company already is reporting under IAS.	High

sented under US GAAP or include an annual reconciliation between FAS and US GAAP or between IAS and US GAAP, quantifying as a minimum the differences in net income, earnings per share and shareholders' equity. Nokia provides full financial statements under FAS and IAS, as well as separate reconciliations between US GAAP and IAS, and between FAS and IAS.

- To file at least one interim report a year on Form 6-K as soon as relevant information is made public to non-US investors. The information filed on Form 6-K is not subject to SEC requirements: it merely consists of copies of information filed or made public in the domestic market. It is not necessary to report quarterly results, as many people believe. Nokia continued to report interim results after four and eight months until 1996 when it switched to quarterly reporting in order to improve global comparability.

The pros and cons of an NYSE listing

A US listing is not necessarily something that every company should consider: Exhibit 31 states the general criteria relevant to the listing decision. If several of these apply it may be worth considering seriously, but if none or only a few apply, then it may be premature or simply not a good idea. The fact that so many criteria actually applied to Nokia's situation made the case for a US listing very strong. The factors that specifically applied to Nokia to a larger or smaller degree are indicated to the right in Exhibit 31.

Pharmacia

The US$1.2 billion secondary offer of Swedish pharmaceutical company Pharmacia in June 1994 was the fourth public sale of assets by the government of Carl Bildt, which had come to power three years earlier toting an ambitious privatisation programme. It was the largest of the Swedish privatisations and the first in Europe to be structured with a truly open-priced offer to retail investors. The UK partly-paid privatisations, where the first instalment was known upfront, were the closest that Europe had previously come to such a structure.

At the time that Sweden's centre-right coalition took office, Pharmacia was one of two main business activities – the other was food-beverages-tobacco – of a company called Procordia. This was the government's leading candidate for privatisation, earmarked for early sale. But a bewildering series of corporate developments characterised by a public dispute between the government and Procordia's other major shareholder, the vehicle manufacturer Volvo, resulted in two postponements of the planned privatisation before it was rushed out, as Pharmacia, only three months before the Bildt government was defeated in the 1994 general election. Understanding the complexities of this Nordic saga is the key to understanding the challenges faced by the banks charged with moving Pharmacia successfully into the hands of the private investor.

An IPO of Procordia shares took place in 1987 when the then Social Democrat government allowed it to issue new shares, diluting the state's holding from 100 per cent to a voting stake of 84 per cent. The aim was to allow Procordia to raise new capital for expansion, and through a listing become exposed to the discipline of the financial markets. Procordia's shares remained tightly held, mostly by Swedish institutions, because of the limited free float and a perceived lack of need to market the company to new investors – it had a very strong cash flow from the tobacco business.

In late 1989, Volvo initiated the creation of a new and much larger Procordia by selling 100 per cent of its consumer products company Provendor and a 49.9 per cent voting interest in pharmaceuticals company Pharmacia (the old Pharmacia) to the old Procordia. Volvo received newly issued Procordia shares such that the state and Volvo now controlled 43 per cent each of the votes in the new company.

The new Procordia began to put more emphasis on the internationalisation of its ownership. It started to market its shares outside Sweden, mainly in London and Edinburgh. Given the relatively limited float, however, it was the summer of 1991 before Procordia became more exposed internationally. When it became increasingly probable that a coalition of centre-right parties with ambitious privatisation plans would win the September 1991 general election, foreign investment banks wishing to play a role in the privatisation programme initiated equity research coverage on Procordia.

Exhibit 1
Transaction summary

Issuer name: Pharmacia AB (of Sweden)	Joint global coordinators and international advisers: Goldman Sachs and SG Warburg Swedish adviser and Nordic coordinator: Enskilda
Pricing date: 16 June 1994 (Affärsvärlden General Index: 1,406)	Pricing/underwriting structure: Bookbuilding for institutions with fixed SEK10 discount for retail
Vendor: Ministry of Industry and Commerce of the Kingdom of Sweden	Primary or secondary: Secondary
	Retail structure: Retail discount
% of company sold: 31.3 per cent (46 per cent voting stake)	Privatisation or corporate: Privatisation
IPO or non-IPO: Non-IPO	Industry: Pharmaceuticals
Type of shares: Ordinary A shares and ADRs (1 A share = 1 ADR)	International offer price: SEK120(US$15.30/ADR) Retail offer price: SEK110
Total issue size: US$1,156 million	US listing/144 A: Nasdaq quotation

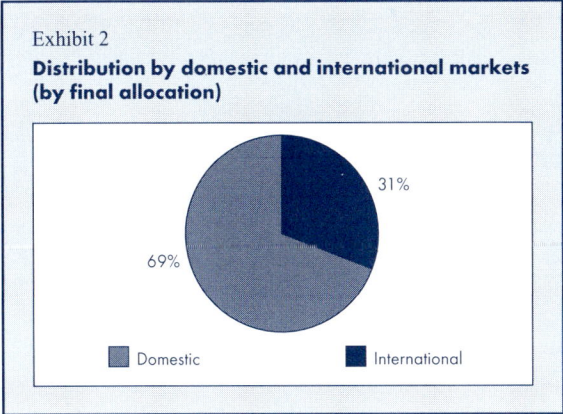

Exhibit 2
Distribution by domestic and international markets (by final allocation)

- 31% International
- 69% Domestic
- Domestic
- International

Once in office, the Bildt government moved swiftly and had a privatisation law on the statute books within three months of taking office. It announced its intention to sell a substantial portion of its Procordia shares to the public: however, Volvo had a radically different idea about what ought to happen to Procordia. A major power struggle between the two ensued, the basic conflict being that the government for ideological reasons wanted to create a 'people's share' out of Procordia while Volvo wanted to buy the whole company in order to lay its hands on the cash-flow, which it needed for the yet to be announced full merger with Renault.

These differences could only be resolved by breaking up the company, which was probably not a bad thing, as Procordia was a classic conglomerate which had limited appeal with international investors. It was eventually split into Pharmacia, a focused pharmaceuticals company, and Branded Consumer Products (BCP), a consumer goods business. The break-up was followed by a share swap between the government and Volvo, making the government the dominant holder in Pharmacia and Volvo the dominant holder in BCP. Thus the government had Pharmacia, which it could sell to the Swedish public and Volvo had BCP, from which it could derive cash-flow. However, a satisfactory settlement with Volvo was not the only challenge with which the government had to contend. An unprecedented financial crisis had erupted in Sweden and Procordia had an opportunity to buy into a major Italian pharmaceuticals company Farmitalia Carlo Erba, which would radically change the nature of the company to be privatised.

Following this challenging prelude to the sale, the offer itself proved to be a considerable success. The Pharmacia transaction was the first Swedish privatisation by way of a truly global equity offer and the first to include an SEC registered component. It was also only the second time (after the sale of Roussel-Uclaf of France) that a major equity offer for a pharmaceutical company had been done on the basis of a 'restructuring story' rather than as a growth or defensive-play story. Yet the incremental US demand vital to ensure the success of the offer materialised only during the last few hours of bookbuilding.

The resolution of the question of ownership between the two shareholders and a successful global sale of shares in Pharmacia paved the way for the company's merger with Upjohn of the US to form Pharmacia & Upjohn in November 1995, with Volvo (14 per cent) and the Swedish government (7 per cent) as its largest shareholders. From being a small part of Volvo and subsequently a bigger part of Procordia, the new Pharmacia

Exhibit 3
Milestones in the Pharmacia privatisation

December 1989	• Volvo and state become equal partners in Procordia, each with a 43% voting interest.
September 1991	• Carl Bildt forms coalition government with privatisation high on the policy agenda. Procordia is the top privatisation candidate.
January 1992	• Announcement of proposed merger of Procordia and Volvo – rejected by government. An early privatisation of Procordia is frustrated by the Volvo initiated hostility.
September 1992	• Central bank of Sweden forced to raise short-term interest rates to 500% in order to defend the krona. Procordia privatisation officially postponed. By November the financial crisis was to force the krona to float freely.
May 1992	• State and Volvo end open hostilities regarding Procordia.
March 1993	• Procordia announces US$395 million acquisition of a 51% interest in Farmitalia Carlo Erba ('FICE'), an Italian pharma company. Procordia privatisation officially postponed for the second time. The remainder of FICE is acquired for US$472 million in December 1993.
June 1993	• Procordia announces demerger of consumer products businesses out of Procordia to create two publicly listed entities, Pharmacia and BCP.
September 1993	• Volvo and Renault announce full merger subject to Volvo shareholder approval.
November 1993	• Shareholder opposition to Volvo/Renault merger forces Volvo chairman to withdraw merger proposal. Majority of Volvo board resigns.
April 1994	• Volvo announces the disposal of all non-core holdings, including Pharmacia, before the end of 1996.
June 1994	• Pharmacia global equity offer successfully completed.
November 1995	• Pharmacia and Upjohn of the US announce merger to form Pharmacia & Upjohn.
July 1996	• Volvo sells two thirds of its 14% cent stake in a US$2 billion global sale coordinated by Goldman Sachs and Merrill Lynch. The state with 7% and Volvo with 4% remain the largest shareholders.

had become an equal part of a major global pharmaceuticals company listed on the NYSE.

Major challenges

Offer structure

Pharmacia was the largest ever equity issue from Sweden and a large offer by absolute standards. It led to a doubling of Pharmacia's free float. This was also to be the first ever truly open-priced retail offer in Sweden (in fact anywhere in the world) at a time when close to 60 per cent of total demand was expected to come from Swedish retail investors. 'Convincing ourselves and our financial and media advisers than an open-price offer with a pre-determined Swedish krona discount to the institutional offer price would work was probably the single toughest challenge in this offer,' commented Jan Amethier, at the time special adviser at the Ministry of Industry and Commerce, and now a managing director at JP Morgan in London.

A new strategy by Volvo, articulated only weeks before the announcement of the privatisation, to sell its remaining holding in Pharmacia along with other non-core interests by the end of 1996 again highlighted the uncertainty surrounding Pharmacia's ownership and threatened to unsettle the privatisation. A significant challenge, therefore, lay in trying to reach agreement on sufficiently long lock-up periods for both major shareholders. This was a difficult issue for Volvo, given its weakened financial position and pressure from the rating agencies. The lock-up agreement was only concluded shortly before the publication of the preliminary prospectus.

Marketing

The domestic retail campaign and the roadshow needed to be of the highest quality, and Pharmacia's chief executive officer Jan Ekberg had only limited experience in running a public company, let alone marketing and presenting to highly sophisticated institutional investors worldwide.

There was also the problem of overcoming a residue of negative attitudes in the US toward Pharmacia which had developed from the unsuccessful trading history of the old Pharmacia on Nasdaq in the 1980s. It had been de-listed from Nasdaq at the end of the decade. This is closely linked to the problem of company identity. Much the same management that was trying to sell Pharmacia as a pure pharmaceutical play had been trying only two years earlier to sell Procordia as a diversified consumer products company.

Bookbuilding and pricing

The market environment was unfavourable. Most major markets had traded at best sideways since the beginning of the year, in sympathy with a weak bond market. Added to this, the healthcare sector had been out of favour with investors in the UK and the US since the Clintons' proposed US healthcare reform in late 1992. Companies selling prescription drugs were hit particularly hard, for example, Astra had fallen by 13 per cent since the beginning of the year. The new issue market was extremely busy in the second quarter of 1994 and the majori-

ty of privatisation issues had traded poorly in the after-market. Large European privatisations launched or priced during the Pharmacia marketing period included US$1.1 billion for Endesa of Spain, US$3.7 billion for KPN of the Netherlands and US$2.9 billion for INA of Italy. There were also two large corporate offers from Scandinavia: US$664 million for Norsk Hydro of Norway and US$631 million for Swedish automotive components company Autoliv. Several large European privatisations and corporate offers were postponed around this time, as US investor interest in non-US companies declined dramatically.

There was a need to minimise domestic institutional selling pressure during the pre-marketing and marketing of Pharmacia to protect the absolute level of the offer price. Although Swedish institutions could not be allowed to price the offer through price-sensitivity, their support as 'buyers of last resort' was important for the offer and for future secondary market trading.

Other

A further challenge was posed by the remarkable number of parties involved in the transaction– the Ministry of Industry and Commerce (the ministry), Volvo, Pharmacia management, Goldman Sachs and SG Warburg as joint global coordinators and international advisers, and Enskilda as Nordic coordinator and Swedish adviser. Reconciliation of their objectives and agendas was to take considerable skill.

This was the last and most high profile of the Swedish privatisations, and coming only three months before a general election, it naturally had political overtones. The opposition was critical of the privatisation programme and the government therefore considered it important to satisfy retail investors (soon to be voters) with a successful issue. On the other hand, too strong an after-market performance would have drawn further opposition critique for selling too cheaply.

Rationale and objectives

The reasons for the sale were:

* to reduce the government's stake after Pharmacia's restructuring;
* to fulfil Pharmacia's wish to expand the shareholder base;
* to enable Pharmacia to tap the international capital market; and
* to create a successful finale to the Bildt government's privatisation programme.

The offer objectives were:

* to achieve a good price, ie, to minimise the discount against the market price;
* to achieve broadly distributed retail and international offers with the help of an attractive retail discount (5–10 per cent) and extensive marketing; and
* to clarify as far as possible the ownership of Pharmacia.

'Since the early days of contemplating the privatisation

Exhibit 4
Share capital and ownership

Type of shares offered	A shares and ADRs evidencing A shares (1 share/1 ADR). Investors in the offer did not receive the 1993 dividend of SEK2.20 per share approved by the 1 June 1994 AGM.
Share capital before and after offer	Class of shares Number of shares A shares 164,724,715 B shares 88,916,068 253,640,783 Each share has a nominal value of SEK25 and equal economic rights but the A shares have 1 vote per share and the B shares have 1/10 vote per share.
Listings/quotations	The A and B shares have been listed in Stockholm since 1987. The B shares have been quoted on Seaq International since 1987. The A shares were first quoted on Nasdaq and Seaq International in connection with the offer.
Market capitalisation at offer price (SEK7.843/US$)	US$3.9 billion.
Major shareholders before (after) offer	Votes (% Capital (%) Government 58 (12) 45 (14) Volvo 28 (28) 28 (28)
Free float before/after offer	27/58%.
Liquidity-12 November 1993 to 16 June 1994	9.1% in Stockholm.
(expressed as number of A shares traded on an annualised basis as a percentage of the total number of A shares outstanding)	18th most liquid stock on the Stockholm Stock Exchange during the 6 months to June 1994 (by value of turnover of A & B shares) and the 6th largest Swedish company by market capitalisation on 30 June 1994.
Foreign ownership before/after offer	Before the offer, Pharmacia was 3–4% owned from abroad, of which less than 1% was held in the United States. After the offer, the foreign ownership had increased to 13–14%, of which some 5–6% was held in the US.
Most relevant stock exchange index/weighting	Affärsvärlden General/3.5% (taking 100% of Pharmacia's share capital into account).

of Procordia back in 1991, these objectives never changed', stated Per Tegnér of the ministry.

The government used the proceeds to fund the growing budget deficit.

Share capital and ownership

See Exhibit 4.

Transaction components

This offer comprised a retail offer of initially 40 million shares and an international offer of initially 32 million shares. A maximum 7.5 million shares could be clawed back from the international to the retail tranche should the latter create strong demand (see Exhibit 5).

There was cross-participation by the three lead banks to leverage research and maximise the marketing effort. Otherwise there was no sale outside the designated tranches. Only Enskilda, Alfred Berg and Sparbanken sold to Swedish institutions within the Nordic tranche. Goldman Sachs and SG Warburg were allowed to sell in all international tranches. In Japan, only Enskilda, Goldman Sachs, Nomura and SG Warburg were able to sell to 49 pre-identified institutions as

part of the Continental Europe and RoW tranche under the normal private placement rules.

The public offer to all Swedish residents was marketed on an open-priced basis, structured with a SEK10 pre-determined discount to the international offer price, subject to a maximum retail offer price of SEK140 and a maximum of 250 shares per applicant. The maximum retail offer price was included in the preliminary prospectus, published on 24 May and a marketing brochure was distributed to all Swedish households. Company employees had allocation priority to a maximum of 250 shares. Retail investors paid following confirmation of allocation between 20–27 June, and the last day for payment by retail investors was 1 July. The retail offer was not underwritten.

The international offer was a bookbuilt offer through four ring-fenced regional syndicates. The sale to Swedish institutions was included within the Nordic tranche. It included an SEC-registered portion and Pharmacia's A shares were quoted on Nasdaq immediately after the offer was priced. The international offer was structured with an unusually large greenshoe of 10.2 million shares representing 32 per cent of the pre-clawback international offer size, to ensure stable after-market trading. The international offer was priced at SEK120 per share and the underwriting was 'over-night' at the end of the international bookbuilding period. Institutional investors paid five days after allocation.

Given the relationship between the state and Volvo with

Exhibit 5
Offer structure

Target markets	Indicated tranche sizes *	Bookrunners	Co-lead managers
Retail offer	56%	Enskilda	Föreningsbanken, Handelsbanken, Nordbanken, Sparbanken, Swedish Post
International offer			
Continental Europe and rest of the world	7%	Goldman Sachs, SG Warburg	Dresdner, Enskilda, Nomura, Paribas, Swiss Bank Corporation, Wood Gundy
Nordic	10%	Enskilda	Alfred Berg, Goldman Sachs, Swedbank, SG Warburg
UK	13%	SG Warburg	Enskilda, Goldman Sachs
US	14%	Goldman Sachs	Morgan Stanley, Smith Barney, SG Warburg
Total combined offers (shares)	**72,000,000**		

* percentage of indicated total offer (excluding greenshoe) as announced on 24 May 1994.

Exhibit 6
Lock-up arrangements

Parties to lock-up agreement	Duration of lock-up
The Ministry of Industry and Commerce of the Kingdom of Sweden	July 1996 (25 months)
Volvo	December 1995 (18 months)
Pharmacia	April 1995 (10 months)

Exhibit 7
Development of the offer size

Indicated number of shares to be sold	72,000,000 + 10,200,000 greenshoe
Amount of greenshoe exercised	7,500,000
Final number of shares sold	79,500,000

Exhibit 8
Principal advisers

Joint global coordinators and international advisers	Goldman Sachs and SG Warburg
Swedish adviser and Nordic coordinator	Enskilda Corporate/Skandinaviska Enskilda Banken
Swedish legal adviser to Pharmacia	Internal Counsel
Swedish legal adviser to the underwriters	Enskilda Law
Swedish legal adviser to the state	Advokatfirman Vinge
Swedish marketing adviser	Askus
US legal adviser to the state	Cleary, Gottlieb, Steen & Hamilton
US legal adviser to Pharmacia	Shearman & Sterling
US legal adviser to the underwriters	Sullivan & Cromwell
Auditors	KPMG/Bohlins, Öhrlings Reveko/Coopers & Lybrand (Pharmacia) and Reconta/Ernst & Young (Erbamont)

regard to Pharmacia (previously Procordia), the lock-up agreement was important and became more so when Volvo announced it was to divest itself of all its non-core holdings by the end of 1996. There were three parties to this agreement (see Exhibit 6).

The 7.5 million-share clawback was exercised in full on

Exhibit 9
The timetable

November 1993	• Pharmacia's company campaign starts.
2 May1994	• The ministry's offer campaign starts.
6 May	Preliminary announcement: • Press briefing, including outline terms and timing; and • Pre-marketing begins for retail and international offers.
10 May	• Pharmacia announces better than expected results for 1Q 1994.
19 May	• Agreement of lock-up terms between underwriters, the ministry, Volvo and Pharmacia.
23 May	• TV advertising campaign commences.
24/25 May	*Formal launch of the offer:* • Preliminary prospectus published in Swedish and English, including maximum retail offer price, fixed SEK10 retail discount, indicated total offer size and tranche sizes; • Information brochure dispatched to all Swedish households; • Public filing with the SEC on Form F–1; and • European roadshow begins in Stockholm.
1 June	• Retail subscription period starts.
3 June	• Bookbuilding starts for international offer.
7 June	• European roadshow ends in Edinburgh.
8 June	• US roadshow begins.
10 June	• Retail subscription period ends.
15 June	• US roadshow ends.
16 June	*Pricing of international and retail offers:* • International bookbuilding closes; • Retail offer increased by 7.5 million shares through exercise of clawback provision; • Retail and international offers priced following close of Stockholm market; and • International offer underwritten.
17 June	• Trading commences on Nasdaq and Seaq International.
20–27 June	• Notification of retail allocation.
23 June	• Payment and closing of the international offer.
24 June	• Public holiday in Sweden.
1 July	• Last payment day for retail.
15 July	• Greenshoe exercised to the extent of 7,500,000 shares.

the pricing date and 7.5 million shares in the greenshoe were exercised at the end of the stabilisation period, thus compensating for the shares removed from the international to the retail offer as shown in Exhibit 7.

Principal advisers

See Exhibit 8.

The timetable

The retail offer closed six days before the close of the international offer in order to allow sufficient time to count the retail subscriptions. It also enabled the positive retail feedback to be used to build momentum for the international offer and for the retail clawback to be exercised before the closing of the international offer (see Exhibit 9).

Transaction fee distribution

The economics of the international offer were structured as shown in Exhibit 10.

The gross spread for the retail offer was substantially lower – partly reflecting the fact that it was not underwritten – based

more on direct cost and made up of a significant number of different components.

Management fee

Outside the US, the lead and co-lead managers shared 50 per cent of the total management fee as the lead and co-lead managers' praecipium calculated on the non-US portion of the combined offer (see Exhibit 11).

The management fee in the US was allocated on the basis of underwriting commitment only.

Selling concession

In the US, the selling concession had one fixed and one variable component. The pre-agreed portion of the pot was split equally among the four managers (7.5 per cent each). The variable portion was paid to the respective syndicate banks according to designations by investors (see Exhibit 12).

In Europe the selling concession was paid in full to whichever bank received the order.

Total compensation to the three senior banks was more or less equal when counting the institutional tranches only.

Exhibit 10
Distribution of gross spread (%)

Management	Underwriting	Selling concession	Gross spread	Coordinators advisory fee*	Discount**	Total effective cost
0.69	0.69	2.07	3.45	0.25	0.83	4.53

* In addition to the 3.45% gross spread, Goldman Sachs, SG Warburg and Enskilda shared equally in a 0.25% coordinators' praecipium on the gross proceeds of the total offer. This was treated as a separate advisory fee.

** This represented the discount for the international offer only. The SEK110 retail offer price represented a discount of 9.1% to the SEK121 market price prevailing at the close on the day of pricing.

Exhibit 11
Distribution of management fee outside the US (%)

Total management fee	0.69
Of which: Lead/co-lead managers' praecipium split among all leads/co-leads	50
Of which: Management fees split among all managers	50

Exhibit 12
Distribution of selling concession in the US (%)

Total selling concession	2.07
Of which: Pre-agreed or fixed portion regardless of sales booked	30
Of which: Paid pro-rata according to sales designated by investors	70

Deal structure

'Executing a large secondary offer is typically much more difficult than doing an IPO,' commented Tim Bunting, executive director in the ECM department of Goldman Sachs. The challenge lies in preventing outright selling or short-selling during the run-up to pricing by designing a competitive offer structure and creating demand and price tension. In this case, the foremost challenge was to convince the Swedish institutions, which together with Volvo and the state, had been the only significant shareholders in Pharmacia before the offer, that they were not going to get as much stock as they wanted and certainly not at any price. The first opportunity to send this signal came at the time that the total offer was split into indicative tranche sizes on 24 May. There was no dedicated Swedish institutional tranche as Sweden was included in the Nordic tranche. Having created a sense of competition through the offer structure and the syndicate, the Nordic tranche was sized smaller than had been expected by the Swedish institutions. These institutions were told during the bookbuilding process that because of the broad and deep interest in the offer, they were not going to get much stock unless they bid high. In the event, they indicated a large portion of their demand at less than the market price and did not receive as much stock as they would have liked.

Sizing was based on market conditions and assumed a moderately successful retail offer. The sizing was significantly helped by the high reliability of market research indicating the relationship between the size of the retail discount and retail demand.

If additional market capacity had been available, there is no reason why both Volvo and the government could not have sold their entire stakes, particularly as Volvo had declared its intention to sell all its non-core holdings by end-1996, which included its 28 per cent interest in Pharmacia. However, because of the two major shareholders' difficult past relationship, the government wanted to retain a blocking minority until Volvo reduced its stake, after which the state would also consider selling its remaining 14 per cent. Pharmacia's management thus had to continue under an uncertain ownership situation. The lock-up provisions were of limited comfort.

US listing

Pharmacia's management was initially against a US listing because of the time and expense required to maintain relations with US investors, and the belief that it would not bring sufficient benefits. The government, however, was pushing hard for such a listing on advice from its bankers that the US market would be needed to secure a successful sale and that a listing would help the selling effort in the US. The government prevailed and the decision now was whether the listing would be on the NYSE or whether the shares should be traded over-the-counter on Nasdaq. At the time, the arguments for Nasdaq were that liquidity was thought to be higher under normal trading conditions; that other Swedish companies reporting to the SEC were quoted on Nasdaq (subsequently Astra and Scania have listed on the NYSE); and that it is easier to de-list from Nasdaq. An NYSE-listing, on the other hand, offered a higher-profile and because of this, more shares were likely to be sold. It was decided to go for Nasdaq, which, according to Pharmacia CFO Jan Blomberg, has worked well.

Method of payment for retail investors

An interesting structural element of the transaction was how and when retail investors paid for the shares. Three models are predominantly used worldwide:

1. *Swedish model:* Retail investors instruct their banks to pay only when the final price is set and the allocation confirmed. The sequence of pricing, allocation and payment is therefore the same for both retail and institutional

investors. There is clearly some risk for the vendor if the share price falls between allocation and payment as some investors might be tempted not to pay despite their contractual obligation to do so (in Pharmacia, the retail portion of the offer was not underwritten so the syndicate banks were not at risk). The only practical leverage on such investors is moral suasion as the legal route is generally not considered worth the effort. However, this method of payment was crucial for the smooth execution of the retail offer. To have asked retail investors to pay before the price was fixed and the allocation known – particularly in connection with the first ever Swedish open price retail offer – would have been expensive to administer and legally complex;

2. *UK model:* In the UK the public has always written a cheque upfront for the number of shares subscribed for. In a partly-paid transaction, it is easy because the payment for the first instalment can always be fixed, even if the entire offer price is not determined until later. In a fixed-price fully-paid transaction, retail investors apply for a fixed number of shares and receive a refund if they are not fully allocated. In such fully-paid open-priced offers as BSKYB and Orange, investors applied for a fixed sum worth of shares and may or may not have received a refund;

3. *Australian model:* In Australia, where issues are typically not partly-paid, investors are asked to pay for the number of shares subscribed for, times the maximum price in the pricing range, with a refund covering adjustment in number of shares and price.

Marketing

The marketing benefits arising from Pharmacia's status as a near-pure pharmaceutical company after the demerger in July 1993 were largely offset by negative views about the pharma sector, which had underperformed since 1992. The marketing programme therefore was designed to distinguish Pharmacia from its peers, highlighting in particular its restructuring potential and the high proportion of its sales accounted for by the European hospital market, a market segment which was less affected by cuts in public expenditure on healthcare.

Retail marketing

The government intended to carry out a classic privatisation with strong retail participation. Pharmacia was in a position to benefit from the retail success in the privatisation of forest-products company Assi Domän in March 1994, though market conditions then had been better. It also helped that at the outset of Pharmacia's pre-marketing, the market price of Assi Domän was 23 per cent above its retail offer price. Almost 600,000 Swedes had applied for shares in Assi Domän.

Retail demand for Pharmacia reflected what had been projected and was clearly stimulated by the 9 per cent retail discount. A bonus share scheme had been considered but was deemed less effective than a discount because of the complexity of controlling the entitlement. Martin Brandt, associate director of Enskilda Corporate Finance explained: 'It is

difficult to control whether or not retail investors have owned the shares all the time or whether they have sold and then bought again before the applicable anniversary of the offer.' There was also a desire to keep the structure relatively simple. One problem created by a significant retail discount is that while good demand is generated, selling pressure increases in the immediate after-market. In Pharmacia, this problem was mitigated by retail investors receiving confirmation of their allocations and being able to start trading only a few days after the institutional allocations.

Pre-registration (as employed in UK privatisations) or purchase mandates (as widely employed in Spanish and French privatisations) were not seriously considered as they were not expected to add much value in a Swedish context. 'The Swedish retail investor is probably more sophisticated than in many other countries,' commented Brandt. 'He is going to want to evaluate all available information until virtually the end of the subscription period and he would therefore not want to commit early. Why should he be asked to commit before the institutions? Any readings of investor interest derived from pre-registration or purchase mandates would therefore not be reliable. In Sweden, monthly trackings of investor interest through market research also made pre-registration redundant. One of the purposes of pre-registration is of course to establish a reliable database of names for marketing purposes. In Sweden, however, there are in any event many different such databases available with all the necessary information to make a targeted retail marketing campaign possible.'

Institutional marketing

Comprehensive pre-marketing was deemed essential for the institutional offer. Equity research reports were circulated to between 3,000 and 4,000 investors across the syndicate and equity research analysts addressed more than 150 investors in Europe and more than 100 in the US.

Although fund managers and buy-side analysts are frequently sceptical of sell-side analysts – often considered glorified salesmen rather than objective analysts – these meetings are still useful to ensure that fund managers focus on the particular investment opportunity, to answer certain questions and to point out the particular profit drivers. To fund managers, the importance and effectiveness of these meetings depends entirely on the analyst's track-record. Those with credibility can add considerable value.

After the successful pre-marketing came a three-pronged approach:

- The company met one-on-one with 48 institutions (23 in the US) and addressed another 160 in group presentations and conference calls (84 in the US);
- Research analysts made follow-up calls or visited the institutions; and
- Salesmen made a final series of investor calls to argue the case for the company story and the accuracy of the valuation, and finally to ask for investors' orders.

The two most important aspects in an institutional sales

Exhibit 13
Principal sales points

Market position	• Pharmacia has critical mass: the 1993 acquisition of FICE gives it consolidated sales of US$3.2 billion. It becomes the number 10 drug company in Europe and Number 20 in the world with US$450–500 million p.a. available for R&D; and • Pharmacia relies on dominant positions in targeted niche markets where the competition from the drug giants is relatively limited. It is a European market leader in five specialities: cataract surgery, allergies, growth hormones, nutrition and smoking cessation.
Limited exposure to cuts in healthcare spending	• Because of the broad product portfolio, Pharmacia argues that it is less exposed to cuts in health-care spending in any one area. It also benefits by having a relatively high exposure to the hospital sector, rather than the retail market where many of the cuts have been focused.
Earnings growth	• The results for the first quarter of 1994 exceed expectations, eps increasing by 191%; • Extensive restructuring is expected to lead to significant margin expansion and earnings are expected to grow by 19%, 16% and 17% in 1994, 1995 and 1996; and • Cost-cutting is regarded as an easier way of achieving earnings growth than top-line growth.
Promising R&D pipeline	• Significant sales potential. R&D projects for coming years offer potential for long-term growth; Pharmacia has seven drugs in Phase III of clinical trials and six in Phase II with annual sales potential of some US$65 million each.
Politically important privatisation	• A successful Pharmacia privatisation is politically of key importance; and • Pharmacia should benefit from strong retail interest: Assi Domän attracted 600,000 subscribers.
Valuation (SEK126, 20 May)	• The P/E-to-growth multiple, at 88.2%, makes Pharmacia look attractively valued against its peer group.

Sources: Goldman Sachs and prospectus.

drive are the pre-marketing calls by the equity research analysts and the company roadshow. The advisers made Pharmacia management go everywhere in Europe and the US on the roadshow, which was tough on the company's representatives. But according to Goldman Sachs this contributed considerably to the success of the offer. Michael McNish executive director of equity corporate finance at SBC Warburg added: 'Pharmacia is in a global sector and consequently all the major financial centres needed to be covered.' The company travelled to 19 cities in Europe and the US over a period of 14 working days.

The Pharmacia story

Pharmacia was sold as a restructuring story with considerable short-term earnings momentum. Long-term growth in earnings through the product pipeline was seen as a secondary issue (see Exhibit 13).

Pharmacia was clearly trading at the bottom of the range in terms of its 1995 P/E ratio against its peers as shown in Exhibit 14.

When compared to its expected five-year growth rate, Pharmacia's undervaluation seemed even more apparent (see Exhibit 15).

Principal reasons for not buying

Despite a good story and an attractive valuation, investors had many reservations:

• Lack of significant top-line sales growth;
• A question mark over management's ability to deliver expected sales growth;
• Lack of 'blockbuster' products in the research pipeline and in clinical tests;
• Relatively low visibility of earnings drivers;

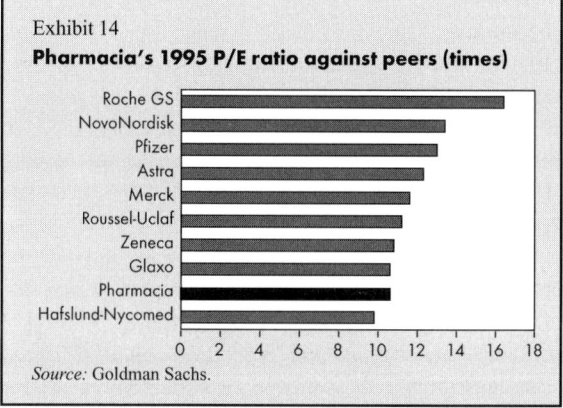

Exhibit 14
Pharmacia's 1995 P/E ratio against peers (times)

Source: Goldman Sachs.

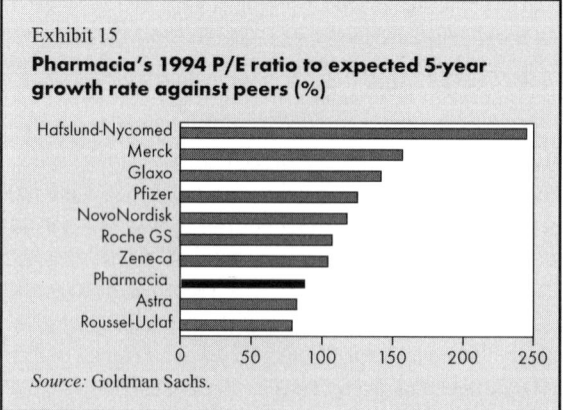

Exhibit 15
Pharmacia's 1994 P/E ratio to expected 5-year growth rate against peers (%)

Source: Goldman Sachs.

• FICE had been on the market for a long time and many investors did not rate it a good acquisition;
• Potential overhang in Pharmacia shares given Volvo's and the state's continued ownership;
• Market conditions were poor and drug companies were out of favour with investors;

Exhibit 16

Underwriting, demand and allocation (%)

Target markets	Indicative underwriting amounts	Demand	Allocation **
Retail offer *	56	58	56
International offer			
Continental Europe and rest of the world	7	7	6
Nordic	10	12	13
UK	13	9	9
US	14	15	16
Total combined offers (number of shares)	**72,000,000**	**125,200,000**	**85,200,000**

* The retail offer was not underwritten.

** Including over-allotment corresponding to the size of the greenshoe and a naked short.

- Pharmacia's CEO Jan Ekberg had, as recently as 1992, been urging investors to invest in Procordia, the consumer products conglomerate. Now he was talking about the benefits of being a 'pure play'; and
- Chequered trading history and reputation of the old Pharmacia in the US until its de-listing in 1990.

Results

Placement

The offer as a whole was 1.7 times subscribed, a relatively modest degree of over-subscription (see Exhibit 16).

Retail

'The retail demand came in more or less as expected but the late confirmation of this demand was clearly nerve-wrecking', commented Krister Sundling of Goldman Sachs' ECM department. However, according to Martin Brandt of Enskilda: 'This is normal. Typically we see 90 per cent of retail demand materialising during the last two days.' Applications were eventually received from more than 519,000 individuals, at 6 per cent, an unusually high proportion of the population in any country but down on the 600,000 Swedes who demanded shares in Assi Domän. The retail offer was 1.8 times subscribed so the maximum 7.5 million shares was clawed back from the international offer.

The 47.5 million shares allocated to 516,000 individuals in the retail tranche was equivalent to 19 per cent of the total share capital, raising retail ownership from 4 per cent before the offer to approximately 23 per cent. By year-end 1994 the number of Pharmacia shareholders had fallen to 444,000 and retail ownership of Pharmacia to just over 21 per cent, indicating that although quite a few very small shareholders had sold, the amount of retail ownership had actually not fallen very much in percentage terms. One part of the explanation appears to be that somewhat larger retail shareholders had increased their holdings between the time of the offer and year-end 1994. This is certainly an unusual occurrence and would tend to confirm the fact that Swedish retail investors are comparatively sophisticated compared to those in other countries. The retail ownership that Pharmacia had acquired in the sale process matched the company's long-term target of 20 per cent. A sizeable retail shareholder base, argued Pharmacia's management, should make bigger shareholders think twice before selling out to an industrial buyer, hence creating some stability in the share register. Of Pharmacia's 6,000 Swedish employees, 53 per cent applied for shares.

International

Demand in the US tranche was above expectations but came in very late. UK demand was below expectations. Demand in continental Europe and the RoW was more or less as expected though demand from Canada and Germany was above expectations. Nordic demand to an overwhelming degree came from Swedish institutions, many of which had sold in February and March 1994, in expectation of the offer. Although most of the big Swedish institutions in the end participated in the offer, their demand was relatively price-sensitive. As a result, certain Swedish institutions did not get as much stock as they may have expected. Given that the roadshow had started in Sweden, the Swedish institutions came in early thereby providing a basic foundation of demand for the offer. At the end of the stabilisation period, the joint global coordinators exercised the greenshoe option to the extent of 7.5 million shares, despite the fact that Pharmacia's A shares had traded below the offer price for most of the stabilisation period, thereby fully compensating for the shares that had been clawed back to the retail offer.

Although 144 non-Swedish institutions were allocated 28 million shares in the offer, equivalent to around 11 per cent ownership of Pharmacia, within nine months about 50 foreign institutions owned around 14 per cent, according to company estimates. Before the offer, they owned 3–4 per cent of the company. This would indicate that whereas total foreign ownership remained reasonably constant, the larger foreign institutions were significant buyers in the after-market.

Investor concentration

An unusually small number of investors carried the offer, with 31 institutions accounting for 80 per cent of the international allocations. Eight institutions demanded in excess of US$30 million worth of Pharmacia shares, of which two were UK institutions, three US institutions and three Swedish institutions. The largest order from the continental Europe and RoW tranche was US$14 million (see Exhibit 17).

Exhibit 17
Investor concentration

	By demand	By allocation
Percentage of international offer accounted for by the 10 largest buyers (by total size of demand and allocation respectively)	48%	51%
Number of buyers making up 80% of the international offer (by total size of demand and allocation respectively)	46	31
The three largest investors by size	US$53.5million US$47.4 million US$42.8 million	US$42.6 million US$36.7 million US$33.7 million
Total number of institutional buyers	223	212

Sources: Goldman Sachs and SBC Warburg.

Exhibit 18
Success of the Pharmacia one-on-ones

	Number of one-on-ones	'Hit ratio'	Demand from one-on-ones as % of initial total tranche size
Nordic	5	60%	72%
Continental Europe and rest of the world	11	73%	17%
UK	9	22%	38%
US	23	40%	125%
Total	**48**	**46%**	**70%**

Source: Goldman Sachs.

Buyers by type

Much of the UK demand came from the Nordic oriented country funds whereas in the US buying was generated from dedicated pharmaceutical funds. To the big US and UK institutions, index weighting was a small factor as the weighting of Sweden itself is relatively small. Interestingly, many of the US institutions had their own analysts (buy-side analysts) dedicated to European pharmaceutical stocks, indicating the increasingly global nature of the pharma sector. In continental Europe, Pharmacia was bought more as a Swedish share, indicating that these investors still tend to analyse and buy stocks on a geographic rather than industry sector basis.

Institutions participating in the 48 one-on-one meetings with Pharmacia management accounted for 70 per cent of total demand. There was a marked contrast between the success of the UK and US one-on-ones (see Exhibit 18).

Share price performance

See Exhibit 19.

Before pricing

Over the six months to pricing Pharmacia underperformed the local market by just over 20 per cent, due mainly to sector concerns and the overhang in the stock. Between the announcement of preliminary terms and timing of the transaction on 6 May, and the pricing date, the A shares traded in a SEK121–131 range with an average of SEK125–126. During the last four days before pricing, the price fell from SEK126 to SEK121 with a fall of SEK3 on the pricing day. As the price had already been driven down by the market, only a

minimal discount of SEK1 was required. Between 6 May and the pricing date, Pharmacia outperformed the local market by 5.6 per cent, indicating that the market supported the preliminary sizing decision.

After pricing

On the first day of trading, the joint global coordinators and Enskilda managed to hold the price at SEK121 but for the next 18 trading days shares traded below the issue price. On the 20th trading day, the second last day of the stabilisation period, the price recovered to SEK120 only to fall back again. This begs the question as to whether it was right to exercise the greenshoe.

In relative terms, Pharmacia managed to trade in line with or slightly outperform the market until 28 June. Thereafter it underperformed the market until 24 August 1994. In absolute terms it was not until the fourth week of August that the price started to perform strongly, hitting SEK137 on 15 September.

After three months Pharmacia had outperformed the local market by 11.6 per cent, supported by a strong six-months' report. However, six months after pricing, this positive trend was reversed to an under-performance of 7.3 per cent due to a disappointing nine-months' report which, against expectations, revealed a fall in sales growth. This unexpected fall begs the question as to whether the due diligence was of the high quality that it ought to have been.

The share price never fell below SEK114 during the six months after pricing, leaving a cushion of at least SEK4 for retail investors (who had paid SEK110). This represents a

Exhibit 19

Share price performance

Pricing date	16 June 1994
Offer price	SEK120
Last trade	SEK121
Relative index position on pricing date	79.2%

Historic high/low since November 1993 demerger
High (24 January 1994)	SEK155
Low (20 April 1994)	SEK111

Pharmacia share price relative to Attärsvärlden Index (%)

-6   -3   -1 Pricing +1   +3   +6
Months

Price performance

Before pricing

	Price (SEK)	Relative to Affärsvärlden General (%)
- 6 months	138	100.0
- 3 months	118	65.7
- 1 month	126	71.4
- 1 week	125	79.7
- 3 days	126	81.6
- 1 day	124	80.5

After pricing

+ 1 day	121	79.8
+ 3 days	116	79.7
+ 1 week	118	79.5
+ 1 month	120	77.4
+ 3 months	137	90.8
+ 6 months	118	71.9

Sources: Datastream and offer circular.

Exhibit 20

Percentage of total issue traded * (%)

	Day 1 (17 Jun)	Day 2 (20 Jun)	Day 3 (21 Jun)	Total Day 1-3
Stockholm	2.1	0.5	0.4	3.0
Nasdaq	3.6	0.4	0.4	4.4

* Based on the issue of 72 million A shares. The greenshoe was exercised only on 15 July. Swedish retail investors received confirmation of their allocations only between 20–27 June.

Sources: Bloomberg.

strong performance compared with most European privatisations in 1994.

During 1995 Pharmacia started to perform strongly and by the time of the completion of the merger with Upjohn in November 1995, its shares had almost doubled in value since the offer.

After-market trading volume

There was relatively limited selling in the immediate after-market (see Exhibit 20).

The performance of the main parties

The company

The entire management, and in particular the controllers' department of the old Procordia and Pharmacia (following the break-up of the company) had been under considerable pressure over the 12 months leading up to the privatisation. They had to prepare accounts for: the financial years ended December 1992, June 1993 (as changed specifically for the approval of the demerger of BCP) and December 1993; the acquisition of FICE in March 1993; the demerger of BCP announced in June 1993; and the privatisation, including US SEC registration of a radically new group in June 1994. They did an outstanding job to pull it all off. Management did well on the roadshow and Pharmacia's investor relations effort continued to impress, certainly until the merger with Upjohn. The initial challenge lay in effective communication with US dedicated pharmaceutical buyers. Pharmacia's management received an early taste of their power when the third-quarter 1994 interim report produced a sharply negative US investor reaction. Top-line growth was not quite what had been envisaged at the time of the privatisation although the bottom line was very much on target, as was the the full-year result for 1994.

The vendor

This was the last of four privatisations by public offer under the Westerberg regime at the Ministry of Industry and Commerce. Of the 34 companies on the original privatisation list, action was taken in 22 companies – by way of strategic sale, merger or broadly distributed equity transactions. The privatisations of Assi Domän and Pharmacia created 300,000 new Swedish shareholders. As many as 900,000 people bought either or both of these two issues. Of these, 85 per cent financed the purchase by taking money out of the bank rather than selling other securities, resulting in new money flowing in to the capital market. There are now 2.3 million Swedish shareholders (not including ownership through funds etc) which is 25 per cent of the population, one of the highest degrees of penetration in the world.

Against the background of false starts, adverse market conditions and a relatively hostile political environment, the ministry, with the help of its advisers, did well in deciding on the crucial elements of this offer, such as size, timing, marketing campaigns, retail discount and lock-up provisions. There is a small question mark over the decision to exercise the greenshoe on the last day of the stabilisation period, given the weak absolute share price performance since pricing.

The ministry deserves credit for hiring top quality people to execute the privatisation. Jan Amethier, a Scandinavian markets specialist previously with Goldman Sachs, was widely praised by all the parties concerned. Westerberg had also hired a sharp former McKinsey consultant, Hans Lundgren. In addition, Per Tegnér handled the delicate negotiations with Volvo and the relationship with the Pharmacia management with particular tact.

However, the vendors' decision to work with three advisers of equal status did not make the execution of this offer any easier. The ministry originally intended to appoint one international adviser, but because of the importance of the US market and the fact that there were two vendors Volvo suggested, and the ministry agreed that there be two international banks. Pharmacia's CFO Blomberg commented: 'If we were to do this again, we would like to more clearly separate the advisory phase and the execution and work with one international and one domestic bank during the preparation phase. Basically, the fewer advisers involved, the better. Perhaps having a separate adviser not involved in the transaction itself might also be a good idea. Subsequently we would need to consider how best to motivate the syndicate in a selling sense. Furthermore, it makes a lot of sense for the company to have its own adviser given that the interests of the company and the state as vendor are not always the same.'

The coordinators

Most of the offer was sold by Goldman Sachs, SG Warburg and Enskilda. Goldman Sachs and SG Warburg dominated the international offer as shown in Exhibit 21.

Enskilda performed strongly in the retail offer and the Nordic tranche of the international offer, accounting for 24 per cent and 65 per cent of the total allocations respectively. 'Enskilda delivered on its promises on placement in the Nordic markets and the bank's deep understanding of the dynamics of the domestic market was crucial to successfully harmonise the domestic and international offers,' noted Tegnér of the ministry.

The good personal relationship between the then heads of ECM in London for Goldman Sachs and SG Warburg, John Downing and Maurice Thompson and their respective colleagues Tim Bunting and James Sassoon, ensured a relatively smooth execution.

Solicitation for the mandate had started directly after the

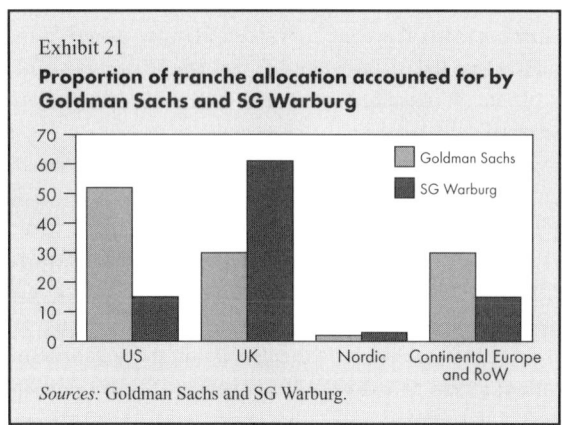

Exhibit 21

Proportion of tranche allocation accounted for by Goldman Sachs and SG Warburg

Sources: Goldman Sachs and SG Warburg.

September 1991 general election when a dozen or so foreign investment banks were invited to recommend how and when the 10 most likely candidates could be privatised. SG Warburg, Goldman Sachs and CSFB were shortlisted for the lead advisory role on Procordia. Initially the government was looking for one domestic bank and one foreign bank, and selected Enskilda as the strongest Swedish equity house and SG Warburg which had a close relationship with the government. SG Warburg had undoubtedly acquired the inside track by advising the ministry in connection with the Procordia bid on Volvo in January 1992. However, Goldman Sachs would not be left out of the most important equity transaction ever in Sweden without putting up a fight. After considerable arm-twisting and significant assistance from Volvo, Goldman Sachs managed to edge itself back into the transaction. Under the May 1992 agreement between the ministry and Volvo, which scotched the Procordia bid for Volvo, the government had to consult the auto-maker when selecting advisers for the privatisation. Volvo proposed a bank with a strong US presence and the ministry chose Goldman Sachs. The ministry had been concerned from the outset about a possible conflict of interest through Jan Amethier's appointment, however Volvo lent its support to the selection. SG Warburg was naturally less than pleased, as it now had to share its power not only with Enskilda but also with Goldman Sachs.

This team, selected in May 1992 for the privatisation proposed for the autumn of 1992, finally carried out the job in 1994, although the syndicate structure was much simplified by then. 'We decided to keep the same team, although in 1994 the transaction was focused much more on the domestic market,' explained Tegnér. 'It would have been a nightmare to renegotiate everyone's role.' The challenge for this team, common in large privatisation offers, was that none of the three banks was in overall charge, although Goldman Sachs was technically running the books.

Key lessons learnt

Structuring

This offer demonstrated, at least in a Swedish but perhaps even in a broader context, that it is not necessary to have a fixed price to successfully sell shares to retail investors.

According to Jan Blomberg of Pharmacia, the vendor drove the sale process and Pharmacia's management had only a limited say in most matters: 'The dynamics of a capital increase and a secondary privatisation are very different. What we really did was help a large shareholder sell its stake. Whilst we are obligated by Swedish law to do so and whilst it is important for the company to have a successful offer, the motivation for management, particularly since we had already been traded on the Stockholm Stock Exchange since 1987, was not the same as if we had sold shares to raise money for the company.'

Michael Orrgard, director of Enskilda Corporate Finance points out the danger of concentrating on how other big privatisations have been structured rather than focusing on what is consistent with the company's business and equity strategy: 'The emphasis on the US market for example, in terms of listing, length of roadshow and tranche size might have been handled differently. While the US market turned out to be highly important for the success of the offer it is not inconceivable that the after-market would have been just as strong if the European market had received the same emphasis during the marketing campaign. Most of the flowback after the offer actually came from the US.'

Pharmacia investor relations chief Jan Isoz countered: 'As the company was planning to grow its business in the US and as the occasion could be foreseen when Pharmacia might be advantaged by being able to offer shares rather than cash in the US, we were actually happy to have the US listing and offer. We had better access to the US capital market and we clearly benefited from the professionalism of the US equity research community.' The Upjohn transaction proved his point, but Orrgard's observation is still valid and of general relevance as the choice of bank(s) is key to the way an offer is structured and sold. In addition to what might be good for the particular company, two further factors always come into play; firstly, how the particular bookrunner judges that it can ensure the success of the execution (specifically in the short term) and secondly how it can maximise its own profitability from the transaction.

Marketing

Michael Orrgard of Enskilda stressed the importance of the media advisers: 'The fact that the retail offer was highly successful is much to the credit of the media advisers, Askus.' When market conditions are bad, the importance of targeting the right investors should not be underestimated. 'Proper research on which investors to target, and what those investors were looking for was key to a successful roadshow', added Blomberg.

The research warm-ups proved highly important in dispelling memories of the old Procordia story and setting the stage for the Pharmacia story. Paul Krikler of Goldman Sachs was widely praised for capable and diligent work during this important phase of the transaction. According to Blomberg: 'The research was well prepared and the investors were extremely well briefed by the time we saw them.'

When marketing a transaction such as Pharmacia, it is helpful to have around 10 leadership investors. Smaller institutions, which may not have the in-house research capability, will be reassured by the knowledge that a Capital Group or a Morgan Grenfell have studied the transaction in detail and have decided to buy.

Tim Bunting of Goldman Sachs stressed the importance of a comprehensive roadshow: 'Forcing the company to go everywhere on the roadshow was highly important as demand was patchy and not readily identifiable.'

'It is easy to underestimate the importance of articulating exactly what your strategy is,' stated Blomberg. 'During a 20 minute investor presentation, people want to know who we are, where we want to go and how we intend to get there.' He said that management also discovered that while investors in London and the US are open to investment in new companies, it takes a lot longer to acquire new investors in continental Europe.

Bookbuilding and pricing

A secondary transaction, ie, the sale of existing shares in an already traded company, can be more difficult than an IPO as many investors have already taken the decision not to buy, and there is not the flexibility of a size/price trade-off that exists in an IPO. SBC Warburg's managing director James Sassoon emphasised that a bigger Pharmacia transaction could not have been successfully completed.

Tim Bunting suggested that the best way to conquer short-selling: 'is to do it the other way around, ie, not trying to prevent it by laws and regulations but rather convince the institutions that the offer will be a success and that institutions will not get any stock. This is a rather obvious strategy as short-selling occurs when institutions believe that the offer is not likely to be a success.'

Enskilda took issue with the fact that the Swedish institutions were criticised by the ministry for speaking up about the right price for the Pharmacia privatisation. The institutions may well have subscribed less aggressively because of the ministry's comments, and ultimately were proved right because they were able to buy more cheaply in the secondary market to satisfy their real demand. Michael Orrgard argued: 'The institutions are the ones that have the money, they manage all our pensions and of course they should set the price. You can't just expect them to come up with the money regardless of price. It is time that we recognise that the balance of power is now shifting from the sellers of shares towards the buyers. The investors are getting stronger and they demand shareholder value.'

Jan Amethier commented: 'As you get closer to pricing you can really feel how your bankers' interests shift from maximising your selling price to ensuring that the investors who are the bread and butter clients of their equity franchises are also left with some upside. For a government that will be a recurring seller, dealing with this natural conflict of interest is a complex issue. We are quite happy with the balance struck by the SEK120 offer price, ie, a one krona discount, although our bankers would have liked to shave a krona or two off that.'

Other lessons

To do a transaction of this kind, with so many interested parties, is extremely challenging. Firstly, the government clearly had a political and fiscal agenda; secondly, Volvo had strong opinions on how the sale should be carried out; thirdly Pharmacia tried to protect its best interests and fourthly there were the multiple advisers, who did not speak with one voice.

Given the resources required to do such an offer and the importance of strategy articulation for the purposes of the prospectus and the roadshow presentation, the involvement by senior management is of key significance. The sooner this is realised, the smoother the whole process is likely to be. Pharmacia's Blomberg maintained that: 'a process such as this is only possible if there is absolute commitment from the top of the organisation.'

Amethier underscored the political sensitivity of the allocation process: 'It was very difficult for our bankers to grasp the political dynamite inherent in discretionary allocation.

Nothing is more politically sensitive than a process that could be construed as having favoured one group of investors over another.'

Tegnér said that although everybody made an important contribution, the use of three different advisers created added complexities. On a general note, he stated: 'the UK and US banks are very different. The US banks are so focused on all the legal risks. Although important, this becomes very tiresome.' He added: 'In total, we saw 80 banks in connection with our overall privatisation work and as far as we are concerned the most important thing is the quality of the working team. We have wasted a lot of time with senior vice presidents learning nothing new. To us, the quality of the back-up team and placement power are the other important criteria.'

Jan Blomberg said that while Pharmacia had nothing but praise for the way the state had handled its role as shareholder over recent years, the privatisation proved that it has much more difficulty in exercising its role during a change of ownership: 'This is due to the political decision-making process, which in many cases depends on the creation of a political consensus, which can be slow and difficult to anticipate.' Hans Lundgren, added: 'The Pharmacia privatisation and its long and complex prelude represents a typical example of the difficulties encountered when a government negotiates with a private organisation full of financially creative people. A state is typically a rather inflexible owner that operates under a number of constraints within a specifically articulated privatisation programme; it can typically only sell rather than buy; it can on many occasions only sell to certain types of buyers (most often a broad distribution to the public is required) and the timetable is most often inflexible due to political and other considerations. Notwithstanding the fact that governments typically operate within relatively narrow parameters, the politicians can not usually be pinned down to a specific alternative substantially in advance of the proposed execution. The fact that the end result on this occasion was a good one, was not only a matter of coincidence but also a result of the fact that the minister had a keen personal interest in, and commitment to, privatisation.'

Conclusion

After a complex and tiresome prelude, the sale itself proved a bit of a struggle. The book only came together satisfactorily during the final hours of the bookbuilding process, when a number of large US orders materialised, and the institutional book was only 1.7 times subscribed. Given that general market conditions were poor and that the pharma sector was still out of favour, it was a notable achievement to get the transaction done at all. The absolute share price performance in the immediate after-market was disappointing but at least it never fell below the retail offer price. The relative share price performance was acceptable, particularly when seen in the context of many other poorly performing European privatisations. Patient investors saw the price almost double by the time that the Pharmacia and Upjohn merger was concluded in November 1995.

This privatisation undoubtedly made a significant contribution to the broadening and deepening of popular capitalism in Sweden and the Swedish public accounted for 60 per cent of the total transaction. No less than 6 per cent of all Swedes, and more than half the company's employees participated in the offer. In addition, the Pharmacia offer clearly helped establish a good reputation for the Swedish privatisation programme. It was the last of four privatisations by public sale, and all performed well, an enviable record by any standards. Sweden clearly has a highly developed equity culture and the domestic offer and payment mechanics represent state of the art equity capital markets technology. The Swedes showed that it is possible to market shares to retail investors on an open-price basis.

The transaction ended a 30-month tug-of-war between Volvo and the government and left the management with a temporary peace of mind. The conflict between the state and Volvo – whilst unprecedented – produced a constructive result, and it is possible that the ministry would have struggled to sell the unfocused Procordia either just before or just after the summer of 1992. The after-market would certainly have suffered due to the Swedish financial crisis and the fact that the pharma sector was out of favour.

As a conglomerate, Procordia was not attractive to investors and its individual businesses were not strong enough on their own. Pharmacia therefore became a 'pure play', its ownership was internationalised and it subsequently found a partner in Upjohn. If it had still been part of Procordia, it might not have appeared attractive as a merger partner, and might therefore have been left out of the merger frenzy in the pharma sector, to the detriment of shareholders. As far as BCP was concerned, the individual pieces were sold off by Volvo in a way that made industrial sense. The fact that most of the food and beverage businesses of BCP are owned by the Orkla group of Norway, and Pharmacia is no longer controlled by Swedish interests is simply an inevitable result of the trend towards the globalisation of industry.

However, whereas Volvo did well financially out of its part of Procordia – it realised considerable value by breaking up BCP and by waiting to sell its holding in Pharmacia until it had merged with Upjohn and the pharma sector had recovered – the Bildt government appears to have paid a considerable price for the pursuit of its political agenda as it sold the majority portion of its stake in Pharmacia at what proved to be a low price. This represents a valuable lesson for investors: the reason that privatisations frequently offer excellent value is precisely that the timing is often driven by politics rather than financial considerations.

The privatisation itself did not conclusively solve the Pharmacia ownership situation, given that Volvo and the government retained substantial holdings in the company. The situation was, however, to be further clarified in connection with the November 1995 merger with Upjohn. The stock market at first reacted favourably to this merger of equals – investors in the privatisation had seen the value of their shares increase by more than 150 per cent by early 1996. Pharmacia & Upjohn, as the new company was to be called, would be one of the 10 largest drug companies in the world. There would be US$500 million worth of synergies and the geographic overlap was perfect.

In July 1996, just over two years after the privatisation, Volvo was able to sell two-thirds of its 14 per cent stake in Pharmacia & Upjohn at more than double the price at which Pharmacia was privatised. Volvo appeared to judge its timing well, as only months after the US$2 billion sale, Pharmacia & Upjohn made a profit warning – a considerable embarrassment to Goldman Sachs and Merrill Lynch who handled the sale. Within nine months, a further three profit warnings were to follow and investor confidence was severely shaken. The first CEO of the merged company was ousted in January 1997 and three months later the acting CEO, Jan Ekberg, had

to admit that the company had been too optimistic in its forecast: 'We sold too hard both the speed of the integration and its benefits.' There are reportedly substantial differences in culture between the two organisations, the reporting lines were unclear and the company's controlling function appeared to be of shocking quality. During the 21 months following the merger, Pharmacia & Upjohn underperformed the European markets (Eurotrack) by some 35 per cent.

The new CEO, Fred Hassan, appointed in May 1997 must complete the merger and restore management credibility. The market is waiting to find out if he can do this. Three years after the privatisation, the Swedish state and Volvo still owned 7 per cent and 3.9 per cent respectively of Pharmacia & Upjohn.

Feature topic: *The tortuous prelude to the Pharmacia privatisation*

The privatisation of Pharmacia was delayed by almost two years, primarily because of a tug-of-war between its two major shareholders. When two major shareholders fight for control, it is typically because both parties want to buy, but here Volvo wanted to buy and the state wanted to sell. The fundamental reason for the conflict was therefore that the newly elected Bildt government wanted to create a 'people's share' rather than selling to Volvo while Volvo needed access to Procordia's cash-flow for initially undisclosed reasons. Rarely have business and politics become so muddled.

January 1986: Volvo bought a 26 per cent voting stake in Pharmacia, a pharmaceuticals company.

December 1989: Volvo effectively created the modern Procordia, a pharmaceuticals and food processing group, by selling its interest in the old Pharmacia, and in Provendor, its wholly-owned consumer goods business, to the state-owned Procordia, the food processing group. Volvo and the Swedish State each acquired approximately 43 per cent of the voting rights in the new Procordia, although Volvo owned a slightly bigger portion of the equity capital than did the state (40 per cent vs. 34 per cent) and perhaps felt that of the two, it was the slightly senior partner. However, a former Procordia man points out that the initiative to create the new company came from Sören Gyll, the Procordia CEO, rather than Pehr Gyllenhammar, the Volvo chairman.

The public minorities of Pharmacia were bought out and the company was delisted from Nasdaq. Pehr Gyllenhammar became chairman of Procordia.

February 1990: Volvo and the French state-owned automotive company Renault announced their 'engagement', whereby Volvo became a 20 per cent shareholder in Renault, the parent company, and a 45 per cent shareholder in Renault Vehicles Industrielles. At the same time, Renault became a 25 per cent shareholder in Volvo Car and a 45 per cent shareholder in Volvo Truck. In addition, Renault declared its intention to buy up to 10 per cent of AB Volvo, the parent company.

January 1991: The Volvo/Renault alliance was finalised. Volvo paid Ffr6.8 billion to Renault, as the net difference in value between the various transactions, subject to an adjustment depending on the future profit development of the vehicle businesses.

September 1991: A centre-right coalition won the Swedish general election and Carl Bildt became the first 'conservative' prime minister since 1930. Radical privatisation was high on the agenda. Per Westerberg was appointed Minister of Industry and Commerce (the minister) in charge of privatisation. He got off to a flying start and within only three months the privatisation bill was passed by parliament. Procordia was the top early privatisation candidate, as it was already quoted, profitable and fully exposed to competition. Therefore the minister thought it would be the easiest to privatise.

End of 1991: Volvo and Renault conducted confidential negotiations concerning a full merger. The parties expected to reach an agreement and to receive the necessary approvals from the French government during the spring of 1992.

January 1992: On 25 January, 1992, Procordia launched a surprise share for share bid for Volvo in a reverse takeover that took the market by surprise. This bid threw the government's privatisation plans into disarray and was a major embarrassment for the minister. The merged company was to be called Volvo, and Gyllenhammar was to become its chairman. The minister soon declared himself sceptical of the bid and the recently appointed privatisation commission (the commission), a French style panel of independent experts made up of industrialists, bankers and other influential business people, set up on the initiative of the minister to sign off on the structure and valuation of each of the privatisations, soon rejected the bid. The equity market had difficulty in fully understanding the rationale for the merger, particularly since Volvo could not yet talk about its further plans for which it needed access to Procordia's cash flow, ie, a full merger with Renault.

Why did Volvo want Procordia? Firstly, AB Volvo had given up access to the cash-flow in its vehicle businesses through the Renault alliance. Secondly, Volvo already owned 43 per cent of the voting power in Procordia but did not control its cash flow. Volvo was in need of cash to service its debt at the holding company level. The need for cash would become more acute in case of a full merger with Renault.

Gyllenhammar's idea was for Volvo to have two principal businesses: a 35 per cent minority holding in an enlarged Renault/Volvo transportation group (Renault would own 65 per cent) and Procordia as a wholly-owned diversified pharmaceuticals and consumer products conglomerate, which would serve as a cash cow. The rationale for this transaction stemmed from the conviction that it made more sense to have a small interest in something that was bigger and viable than full control of something that wasn't viable in the long term (ie, Volvo's car business on its own). Procordia was thus going to be the most important part of the new Volvo.

Why did Procordia bid for Volvo and not the other way around? Because there were no operational synergies, Volvo could not afford to buy Procordia, as it could not justify to its shareholders the dilutive impact of amortising the substantial goodwill associated with such a purchase. Therefore Procordia had to buy Volvo.

Why did Volvo initiate the hostile Procordia bid on itself? Ideally the merger with Renault, and the merger with Procordia should have been announced at the same time. Volvo, however, had a timing problem, as the French were dragging their feet on the merger while the Swedish government was pressing ahead with making Procordia the 'people's share'. Volvo may have decided to engineer the reverse bid for either of two reasons:

- First, Volvo thought that the government had effectively given its support to the Procordia/Volvo merger. Sources within Volvo maintain that their wish to buy Procordia was well-known both to the government and the leader of the opposition. It is believed that Gyllenhammar had understood from discussions with Carl Bildt and Per Westerberg that the government was prepared to let Volvo take control of Procordia at the expense of not being able to launch the privatisation. This impression may have been reinforced by the fact that it was supposedly the financially creative Westerberg who had actually introduced the idea of a reverse take-over in the discussion with Gyllenhammar. Sources on the government side, however maintain that the government had reacted politely but inconclusively to Volvo's soundings. Following these initial discussions, Volvo had, however, followed up with a direct approach to the ministry and received an informal but clearly negative reaction.
- Second, Volvo had concluded that if the government did not want to negotiate a solution, then Volvo would

stand a better chance of winning control of Procordia by putting it under pressure via the equity markets. Having in the past had many successful negotiations with consecutive Social Democratic governments, Gyllenhammar now found in Westerberg a young and relatively inexperienced minister with whom it was more difficult to reach an agreement. It would be easier to let the market talk.

- Volvo is thought to have had information that the government was planning to launch the privatisation of Procordia without first having reached an agreement with it. This, however, does not make sense because no reputable lawyer would have signed off on a Procordia offer circular without having done proper due diligence on Volvo's future intentions vis-à-vis its Procordia holding.

Why was the bid rejected by the State? The commission rejected the bid on the grounds that:

- It was clearly dilutive to Procordia shareholders;
- The merger lacked industrial logic, a fact that nobody at either Procordia or Volvo denied;
- The merged company would trade at a 'conglomerate discount';
- Procordia's shareholders would not get a premium through the proposed merger, whereas Volvo's would (22 per cent on the day of the bid); and
- It would have been difficult for the government to privatise its stake in the new company. Were the Procordia/Volvo merger to go ahead, then the Swedish government would be put in a situation of being a significant shareholder in a merged Volvo/Procordia/Renault with the French state as the dominant shareholder. To coordinate a privatisation between two governments was never going to be easy, particularly as the French could not commit to a timetable for Renault's privatisation.

Volvo believed that the government was nervous of being perceived as the weak party in the battle for Procordia and that it might look to the Swedish electorate as if Gyllenhammar rather than Bildt was running the country. They also thought that the Stockholm business elite was afraid that Gyllenhammar was getting too strong in Gothenburg, the country's second largest city. Gyllenhammar blamed the commission, chaired by Curt Nicolin, a key Wallenberg sphere confidante, for blocking him for power reasons rather than for industrial or valuation reasons (Marcus Wallenberg, the previous head of the family, had once looked to Gyllenhammar to take over the empire rather than to his son Peter. Peter was not therefore likely to support Gyllenhammar's scheme). Gyllenhammar accused the commission of not being truly independent. There were many, even admirers of the minister, who maintain that for all his energy and enthusiasm he was far too dogmatic about wanting to privatise by way of a public share sale.

January–April 1992: As result of the government's rejection of the reverse bid, an unprecedented public row broke out between Gyllenhammar on the one hand and the prime minister and his minister of industry on the other. In this climate, Volvo and the government had to find a way to unlock the stalemate concerning the ownership of Procordia. The ministry hired SG Warburg and Carnegie as their financial advisers. Goldman Sachs acted as an unofficial speaking partner to Volvo. Several possibilities were considered, including:

- For Volvo to buy the whole of Procordia;
- Procordia 'targeted stock' (see USX case study). There would be one class of Procordia parent company stock attributable to the pharma business and another to the consumer products business whereby Volvo could own the majority of one class and the government the majority of the other;
- A demerger of one of the two principal business areas out of Procordia followed by a Volvo bid for the state's stake and the minority interests in the demerged company (similar to what happened in 1993); and
- An outright sale of one of the two business areas to Volvo.

All of these alternatives were rejected by at least one of the parties for either political or financial reasons, including the following:

- The minister urgently wanted to press ahead with a public sale of Procordia;
- The government would, for political reasons, not want to be seen to be proposing a 'break-up' of a major Swedish company;
- Any solution whereby Volvo would buy either of the two business areas of Procordia and that would involve a large amount of goodwill could not be justified to Volvo shareholders due to the absence of operational synergies; and
- Any solution whereby the state would forego a premium on the sale of its shares while other Procordia shareholders would realise a premium in connection with a bid by Volvo for either of the two business areas could not be justified.

Consequently, no solution could be found whereby Volvo would get control of even a portion of Procordia's overall cash flow, and the government could create a 'people's share' out of the remnant. A spring 1992 privatisation was clearly out of the question.

April 1992: The French government decided to postpone its approval of the proposed Volvo/Renault merger it would appear, primarily for political reasons.

May 1992: On 4 May, Volvo and the government reached an agreement regarding their respective holdings in Procordia under which: Volvo's support for a privatisation was obtained, the Procordia bid for Volvo withdrawn and an undertaking given by Volvo not to initiate a further bid involving Procordia. As a result of the agreement, Volvo was able to increase its voting interest from 42.7 per cent to 45 per cent through a limited share swap with the state (the state's voting interest was thereby reduced to 40.4 per cent) and obtain the right of first refusal on any block of shares larger than 5 per cent sold to any one single buyer or buyer group in connection with the privatisation or otherwise. Volvo was also free to buy Procordia shares in the market. Further, it was agreed that the state, Volvo and Procordia were to coordinate the planning and preparation of Procordia's privatisation. This agreement, however did not solve the basic conflict between the government's wish to privatise by way of a public share offer and Volvo's need for access to at least a part of Procordia's cash flow.

At the Procordia AGM on 13 May 1992, Gyllenhammar stepped down as chairman of Procordia and was succeeded by Gyll. Gyll stepped down as CEO of Procordia and instead became CEO of Volvo. The new CEO of Procordia became Jan Ekberg, who at the time had no experience of running a public company and no experience with public shareholders in the US. Gyll was to manage Volvo's investment in Procordia from Gothenburg. He was not supposed to run the Volvo vehicles businesses as those were to be turned into a financial investment within the framework of a merged Volvo/Renault.

August 1992: Procordia did a limited international roadshow to comment on the six months' report. At this stage a possible privatisation offer later in 1992 was still on the cards.

Discussions between Procordia and Montedison regarding a potential purchase by Procordia of Montedison-owned pharmaceuticals company Farmitialia Carlo Erba (FICE) were broken off. The Procordia board was divided as to whether it really was a good transaction, how it would affect the privatisation and how it would affect Volvo's chances of solving its cash flow problem. This would increase Procordia's exposure to the pharmaceutical sector. Volvo and the government's advisers were at this stage clearly against the acquisition, however discussions were restarted in January 1993 given the Procordia management's strong recommendation to buy.

Autumn 1992: The market for pharmaceutical stocks had deteriorated badly during the spring and hit rock bottom in mid July.

Sweden was going through a financial crisis of an unprecedented scale. In September 1992, the Swedish Central Bank had to increase short-term interest rates to 500 per cent in order to defend the krona, but by November the government was forced to let it float freely, resulting in an initial devaluation of some 14 per cent.

On 20 September the government reached an agreement with the opposition concerning a savings package to improve the fiscal situation in the country. The opposition insisted that the privatisation of Procordia be postponed: the official reason for the postponement was 'due to market conditions', ie, the Swedish financial crisis and the fact that pharmaceuticals sector was out of favour.

Although this was certainly not the stock market environment that Westerberg had contemplated for his first UK style privatisation, Volvo and the state had not yet reached an agreement on how to solve the dispute over Procordia.

December 1992 and Spring 1993: The small boutique of Maizels, Westerberg & Co, were hired by Volvo to unlock the situation that would ultimately solve its cash flow problem and allow the minister to proceed with the privatisation. The assignment at first led to nothing and the contract was terminated. The alternatives proposed had again failed to satisfy the concern of not being able to justify paying an acquisition premium for gaining access to a cash-flow stream. The government was adamant that the pharma business within Procordia should be allowed to grow as an independent company, reinvesting the cash generated in research and development rather than to serve as a cash-cow for Volvo. However the Maizels, Westerberg & Co contract was renewed shortly after, as they came back with what was to be the final solution, announced in June 1993.

March 1993: Procordia's discussions with the shareholders of FICE were taken up again in January, and by March Volvo had come round to supporting the acquisition. The principal reasons for Volvo's support are thought to have been: first, given the management's strong recommendation to buy FICE, for Volvo to have blocked the transaction only because it might complicate its chances of getting control of Procordia (or a part thereof), would not have been to act in the best interests of all the latter's shareholders. Second, Volvo could now see a solution to unlock the Procordia ownership situation (as announced a few months later). The government, whose privatisation plans were frustrated by the FICE acquisition, had to consider the same argument and support it. Consequently the acquisition was announced on 22 March.

As a result, the prospects for privatisation were complicated in several ways: first management became preoccupied with the acquisition, second the market initially considered the price too high, third FICE had been on the market for a long time and was therefore not considered a prime asset, and fourth the fact that FICE was very active within cancer research seemed to conflict with the Procordia's strategy which derived substantial cash flow from Swedish Tobacco. Before the acquisition, it used the cash flow from the tobacco business to fund the growth within the pharma and food and beverage businesses. This now became difficult to defend publicly due to FICE's substantial exposure to cancer research, particularly in connection with a mass privatisation. Morgan Stanley advised Procordia on the FICE acquisition, which was completed in early May 1993. The privatisation was postponed a second time, and the process was only to restart in November 1993.

June 1993: Having just closed the acquisition of FICE the decision to demerge the consumer products businesses out of Procordia to create two publicly listed entities, Pharmacia and BCP, was announced in early June. Holders of Procordia shares were to receive one new BCP share while Volvo and the state agreed to exchange shares such that Volvo received all the state's shares in BCP and the state became the majority owner of Pharmacia. This transaction unlocked the stand-off between Volvo and the government, as Volvo would now be able to buy out the minorities in BCP to shore up its cash-flow (in view of the proposed merger with Renault) and the state could get on with its privatisation. Both sides were able to save face. The key to this solution was that, unlike earlier proposals, both the state and Volvo now achieved control premiums in connection with the share exchange. In addition, the demerger of BCP created a pure pharmaceuticals play which would be easier to privatise.

Volvo's ulterior motive with the acquisition of BCP, ie, to shore up the cash-flow situation at AB Volvo, could still not be revealed as the plan to merge with Renault was still confidential.

One important reason that this did not happen in 1992 is that following the acquisition of FICE, Pharmacia was now big enough on its own, and following the acquisition by Procordia of Swedish Match (which also happened during the spring of 1993), BCP was considered big enough. The two parts of Procordia no longer needed each other.

September 1993: On 6 September Volvo and Renault announced that they were going to merge, subject to Volvo shareholder approval.

November 1993: An important group of Volvo institutional shareholders together with a group of Volvo executives publicly announced that they would not vote in favour of the merger at the Volvo EGM scheduled for 7 December. The principal reasons were:

- The perception of an unfavourable valuation for Volvo shareholders. The fact that Volvo was to give up control and only become a minority shareholder in its core businesses without achieving a control premium;
- The fact that no guarantees concerning Renault's eventual privatisation were available from the French government; and
- Volvo shareholders were unhappy about the way that Volvo's chairman had conducted the negotiations with the French government, in particular with respect to the Renault golden share which the Volvo board had only been informed about at a very late stage.

Gyllenhammar and the majority of Volvo's directors therefore decided not to recommend the merger and instead resigned as a direct consequence of the collapse of shareholder support for the merger. Volvo shareholders subsequently elected a new board but to Gyllenhammar's surprise and disappointment Sören Gyll stayed on as CEO of Volvo. Gyll was, so Gyllenhammar thought, on his side and supported the merger. He apparently justified the change of face with the fact that so many at Volvo had come to him to plead the case for not going through with it. At the time of the April 1994 AGM the new Volvo board was to announce a complete reversal of the strategy pursued by Gyllenhammar, whereby it would concentrate on its core vehicles operations and sell all its non core assets, including its remaining interest in Pharmacia, before the end of 1996.

March 1994: Pharmacia full year 1993 results were announced, however it was not yet ready to come to the

market – not least because the required US GAAP reconciliation was not available. However, as there were only six months to the next general election and Westerberg had not yet achieved a classic mass privatisation, it was decided that Assi Domän should become the first Swedish 'people's share'. The non-registered and predominantly domestic Assi Domän offer was a considerable success. It was six times subscribed and placed with almost 600,000 shareholders. Carnegie, the Swedish based investment bank, was the government's adviser and the sole global coordinator.

June 1994: Global offer of Pharmacia shares was successfully completed.

Feature topic: *How to maximise retail demand in connection with a privatisation*

How to maximise retail interest in connection with a privatisation depends very much on country-specific circumstances, including equity culture, prosperity of the population, tax legislation etc. In the case of Pharmacia, at least four thrusts contributed to the overall success of the sale. Those were:

1. Commitment from the highest political level;
2. Successful market research;
3. Sufficient and the right type of retail incentives;
4. Successful communication.

Let us now examine these thrusts a little closer:

Political commitment

Demonstrating commitment:

Investors, both retail and institutional need to know that the government is fully behind both the overall privatisation programme and the particular candidate. People need to understand the rationale for the programme and that the government truly wants to unleash market forces rather than simply cashing in on a one-off opportunity. In this case it was clear that privatisation was high on the political agenda and people understood the rationale behind the programme, as legislation was passed only three months after the Bildt government came to power. A number of important changes in the taxation of equity investment were introduced immediately. It also helped that the industry minister talked about creating a 'people's share' which was the case with Pharmacia, and clearly articulated the objective that 95 per cent of all Swedes should be aware of the privatisation programme, and that the strategy was to reach every Swedish household with the campaigns. By doing so he increased the political stakes and therefore the commitment to create a successful privatisation. To further underscore the government's commitment, the Swedish

government negotiated an agreement with the Swedish Post to deliver a 16-page mini prospectus to all Swedish households on either of three working days.

Creating momentum

These measures combined to make investment professionals enthusiastic. They then influenced the media, and eventually the man in the street caught on. The first privatisation in a programme must be a huge success, as everybody has to understand that it is quite possible to make money on privatisations. Following sales are then much easier. In Sweden it was clever to start the programme with an IPO such as Assi Domän, as the IPO structure gave pricing flexibility and people understood trees. Many investors bought Pharmacia because Assi Domän was a huge success. Prior to Assi Domän, two smaller privatisations had been executed, both of which were successful from an investor's point of view. These two, SSAB and Celsius, were however primarily targeted at institutional investors.

Market research

Selling shares is actually not that different from selling anything else: you have to know your customer and your product and the extent to which you can adjust your product to customers' needs. The market research in the case of Pharmacia was designed to answer three very simple questions:

1. What does the public think about privatisation in general terms?
2. What do people know about Pharmacia?
3. What interest is there in participation in the offer, with or without a discount?

The answers to these questions gave the ministry, Pharmacia and the advisers all the essential information they needed to know. Indirectly, the following questions were also answered: do we need to explain privatisation more; how shall we market the Pharmacia name and how big does the discount need to be to ensure the success of the public offer? In the case of Pharmacia, the market research enabled the marketing consultants to come up with a slogan for Pharmacia: 'to life – Pharmacia as a long-term insurance policy – to be had at a discount'.

Right type of retail incentives

The banks were tremendously innovative in this privatisation, as shares were being sold to the public at a completely open price for the first time in such a large privatisation. It was therefore decided that the retail incentive should be as simple as possible, and so a discount, rather than a bonus or partly-paid shares was used. The frequently used slogan 'KISS – Keep It Simple, Stupid' is particularly appropriate when attempting to reach a whole population.

Communication

The retail marketing effort

There were two separate campaigns. The corporate campaign was orchestrated by the company: following its name change from Procordia to Pharmacia in late 1993, Pharmacia launched its 'to life' campaign to explain who it was. The offer campaign was orchestrated by the government and was all about why and how to buy shares in Pharmacia.

Multi-media and repetition

Communication took place via TV, press, direct mailing to all households of a 16 page brochure and through practically every bank branch and post office in the country. All bank branches participating in the offer, as well as 4,500 post office branches were provided with a four page pamphlet for bank employees, allowing them to answer questions from investors.

Fair and transparent allocation policy

The government was concerned to ensure that everyone should receive at least 50 shares in the allocation and opted to communicate this clearly at the outset to motivate people to apply.

Railtrack Group PLC

The near US$3 billion IPO of Railtrack in May 1996 was a complex affair, intimately tied up with the privatisation of the £11 billion UK railway industry. That sell-off – of the former British Railways Board (BR) – had been widely regarded as one privatisation too many – one that not even Margaret Thatcher wanted to take on.

BR suffered from chronic under-investment and weak strategic planning. The provision of services was engineering-driven and based on annual cash availability from the government budget rather than customer requirements. Service standards were poor and prices rose well in excess of underlying inflation over long periods – in part a deliberate policy to reduce subsidies and in part a result of inefficiency. Commercialism was foreign to BR, as all of its services were provided internally. There was a long-standing inability to grow either the passenger or the freight businesses, and labour relations were poor. During the 10 years to March 1996 BR cost the British taxpayer £11.3 billion in annual subsidies.

The privatisation was overdue, but because of its complexity and unpopularity with the public it was delayed until the end of the governments privatisation programme. There were compelling reasons for pushing ahead:

- To secure private capital investment;
- To comply with EC rules on the separation of infrastructure and operations;
- To inject commercialism and efficiency into BR by breaking it up and creating responsibilities for different areas;
- To improve maintenance and upgrade track, rolling stock and stations;
- To reduce the annual subsidy ie, to get better value for the taxpayer; and
- To reduce fares in real terms.

The formal process of breaking-up and privatising BR began with the Railways Act of 1993. The command-and-control structure gave way to a contract-based structure between 100 newly created companies, each of which fell into one of several categories:

- One company owning and operating the entire railway infrastructure (Railtrack);
- 25 regional passenger-train operating companies (TOCs);
- Seven freight operating companies (FCs);
- Three companies which own and lease rolling stock to the TOCs (ROSCOs);
- Seven infrastructure maintenance companies (IMCs);
- Six track renewal companies (TRCs);
- Six heavy maintenance suppliers, which maintain the rolling stock (BRML).

The regulatory regime included the creation of a rail regulator who grants and enforces licenses and approves access

---

Exhibit 1

Transaction summary

Issuer name: Railtrack Group PLC (UK)	*Global coordinator:* SBC Warburg
Pricing date: 17 May, 1996 (FT 100: 3,789.6)	*Pricing/underwriting structure:* Open price bookbuilding
Vendor: The Secretary of State for Transport	*Primary or secondary:* Secondary
% of company sold: 100%*	*Privatisation or corporate:* Privatisation
	Retail structure: Retail discount and bonus shares
IPO or non-IPO: IPO	*Industry:* Transportation
Type of shares: Ordinary shares of 25p ADRs representing 10 ordinary shares	*Institutional price range:* 350–390p/share *Institutional offer price:* 390p/share; US$58.97/ADR *Retail offer price:* 380p/share
Total issue size: US$2,948 million	*US listing/rule 144A:* Rule 144A
* Including 1% of the company which was withheld by the Department of Transport to meet future bonus share commitments.	

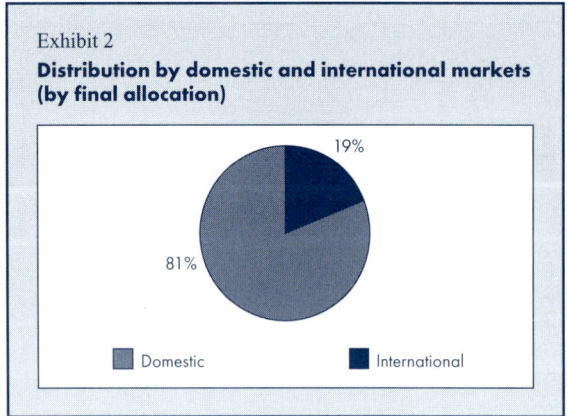

Exhibit 2
**Distribution by domestic and international markets
(by final allocation)**

19%

81%

■ Domestic   ■ International

agreements, and a franchising director who awards franchises and pays subsidies to the TOCs on behalf of the government (see Exhibit 3).

Railtrack

On 1 April 1994 almost all of BR's infrastructure, encompassing some 16,000 kilometres of track with associated signalling and electrical control equipment, around 40,000 bridges, viaducts and tunnels, some 2,500 stations, 90 light maintenance depots and over 9,000 level crossings together with approximately 11,000 employees were transferred to Railtrack.

This company now became the sole owner and operator of the rail network, providing access to that network for train operators and coordinating train movements. In November 1994, the government announced its intention to privatise Railtrack.

By the time of the flotation, almost 40 per cent by turnover of the former BR (excluding Railtrack) had been privatised. Five of the 25 TOCs had been transferred to the private sector and the franchising of two more was near completion. Four of the seven freight companies had been sold as had six of the seven IMCs, four of the six TRCs and all three of the ROSCOs. In total, some 54 former BR companies had been transferred to the private sector and total staff had been almost halved from a base of 121,000 at 1 April 1994. Several service businesses had also been sold. This provided evidence to the market that the process of franchising the regional passenger-train operating companies worked and that there was overall momentum in the break-up of BR.

Although perhaps the single most important part of the overall railway privatisation, the actual IPO of Railtrack (in the narrow sense of the term) was one of the least complex elements of the BR privatisation. It was the first substantial IPO by the state since the flotation of the electricity generating companies in 1991 and the first open-priced bookbuilt UK government IPO. It was unusual, in that, unlike private-sector sales and most other privatisations (with the exception of the electricity industry), the IPO was preceded by a radical

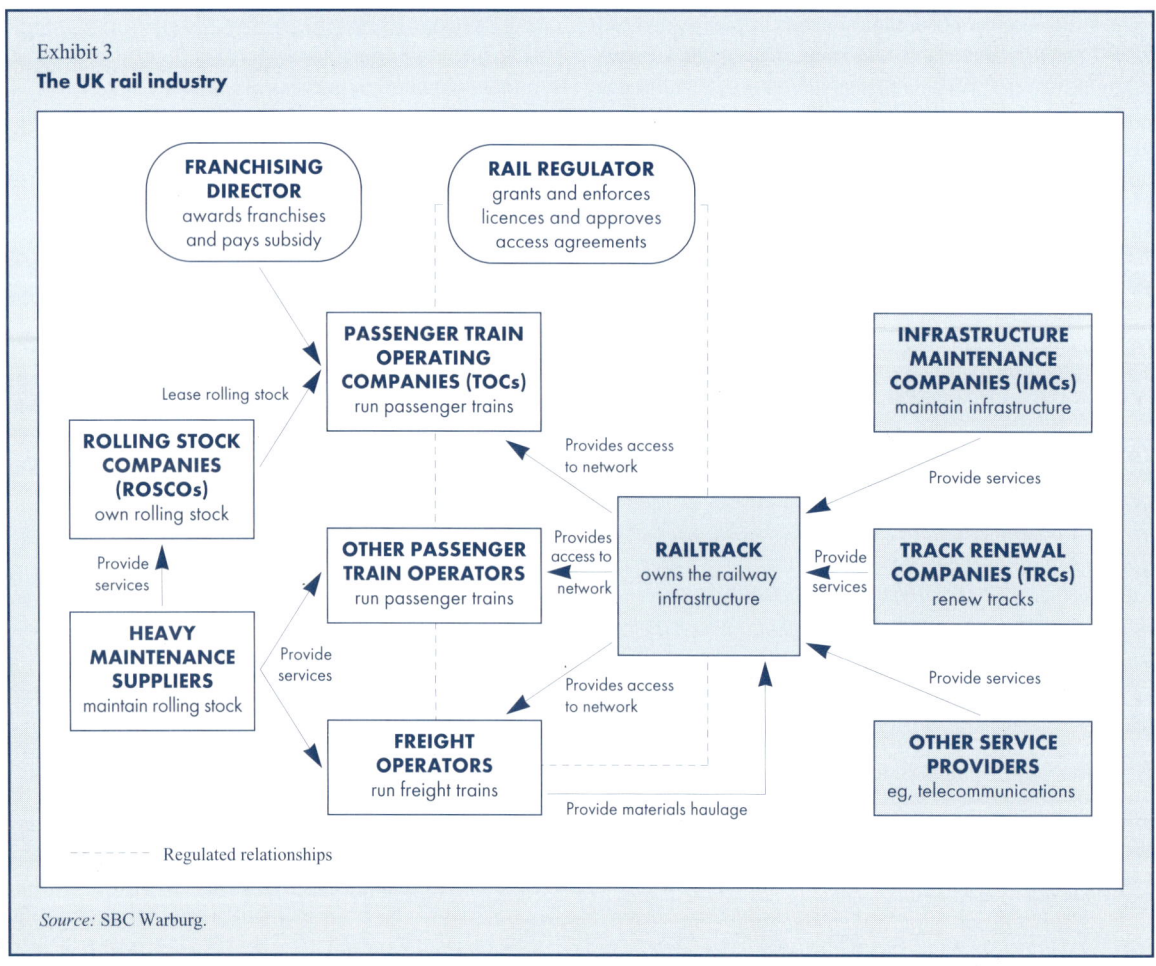

Exhibit 3
The UK rail industry

FRANCHISING DIRECTOR
awards franchises and pays subsidy

RAIL REGULATOR
grants and enforces licences and approves access agreements

PASSENGER TRAIN OPERATING COMPANIES (TOCs)
run passenger trains

INFRASTRUCTURE MAINTENANCE COMPANIES (IMCs)
maintain infrastructure

ROLLING STOCK COMPANIES (ROSCOs)
own rolling stock

Lease rolling stock

Provides access to network

Provide services

RAILTRACK
owns the railway infrastructure

TRACK RENEWAL COMPANIES (TRCs)
renew tracks

OTHER PASSENGER TRAIN OPERATORS
run passenger trains

Provides access to network

Provide services

Provide services

HEAVY MAINTENANCE SUPPLIERS
maintain rolling stock

Provide services

Provide services

Provides access to network

Provide services

FREIGHT OPERATORS
run freight trains

OTHER SERVICE PROVIDERS
eg, telecommunications

Provide materials haulage

- - - - - Regulated relationships

Source: SBC Warburg.

Exhibit 4
Milestones in the British railway industry

1948	• Nationalisation of the four main private UK railway companies.
1962	• BR established to integrate all railway services in Great Britain.
July 1992	• Proposals for regulatory regime detailed by government white paper entitled: *New Opportunities for the Railways – The Privatisation of British Rail.*
November 1993	• The Railways Act passed. It provides the legislative framework for the break-up of the UK railway industry; and • Offices of rail regulator and franchising director established.
December 1993	• John Swift, QC, appointed rail regulator.
April 1994	• Railtrack was vested out of BR.
November 1994	• Structure of track access charges for franchised passenger services determined; and • Government announced its intention to privatise Railtrack.
December 1994	• SBC Warburg appointed financial adviser and global coordinator.
January 1995	• Rail regulator issued policy statement providing for franchised passenger access charges to be adjusted annually by a 'retail price index minus X formula'. For the year to 31 March 1996, charges were rebased to achieve an overall reduction of 8% in real terms. By the time of the flotation, Railtrack had operated with sharply reduced access charges for one year. For each of the five subsequent years, the X factor was set at 2%.
July 1995	• Government announced intention to float Railtrack before end of current parliament (ie, before May 1997).
December 1995	• Performance regimes became operational. Only modest progress yet in overall BR privatisation.
January 1996	• Government announced Railtrack to be floated in May 1996.
March 1996	• Railtrack's balance sheet formalised: government wrote off £1,459 million of Railtrack debt and left £585 million of borrowings in the company.
May 1996	• Flotation of Railtrack. Companies – including Railtrack – making up approximately 61% of the former BR in terms of turnover, had now been privatised.
March 1997	• 100% of the old BR had been privatised.

restructuring of the entire industry. Furthermore, the privatisation of the railway system is the first in the UK of an industry that is unprofitable and therefore reliant on state subsidies.

Competition in the new UK railway set-up will be prohibited almost entirely until 1999 and then moderated by the rail regulator at least until 2001. Under the new structure, hundreds of thousands of contracts, described as a 'contractual matrix', have been drawn up between the newly established companies. Railtrack, has separate contracts with the TOCs and the FCs as its customers and the IMCs, TRCs and other service providers as its principal suppliers. Contracts are legally enforceable and therefore reduce the political risk associated with an investment in Railtrack.

A performance regime has also been introduced, whereby each party to the contracts has an incentive to deliver against certain performance standards. Punctuality of trains, for example, is measured against the timetable. The responsibility for any delays against agreed standards is attributed to one of the parties concerned so-called fault attribution) and compensation is paid accordingly. Railtrack receives its rewards and/or penalties in the form of lower or higher access charges.

The rail regulator was put in place two and a half years before the flotation to enable him to develop a comprehensive understanding of the industry well beforehand, an unprecedented approach among UK regulated utilities. As in prior UK utility privatisations, the regulator decided upon a price cap formula for Railtrack (Retail Price Index – X formula) designed to encourage efficiency and increase profitability by cutting costs as opposed to a cost-plus or explicit rate of return regulation, which would cap the return to investors (see Exhibit 4).

Major challenges

The general environment
Railways have accounted for a falling share of the transportation market, and in most countries are regarded as a poor bet for investment. Railtrack was perhaps the most controversial and unpopular privatisation ever in the UK: a year before the flotation UK daily newspaper *The Independent* wrote: 'The unpalatable truth for Railtrack ... is that almost no one in Britain yet believes that breaking up the network into more than 60 units and selling them individually will be anything other than a disaster for customers and very possibly for investors as well.'

The Conservative government was highly unpopular with the UK public; it was on the verge of losing its parliamentary majority before the end of parliament and a change of government was widely predicted at the upcoming general election. The opposition Labour Party was talking of major changes to the operating and regulatory environment if it came to power. The sale was unpopular for several reasons: the public at large felt that the railways ought to be a public service;

the widely publicised fat cat syndrome (referring to generous incentive schemes given to senior management of other privatised utilities) and a large portion of UK taxpayers felt they would have to finance dividend payments to Railtrack shareholders via the TOCs' access charges and annual state subsidies. Moreover, BR's bureaucracy was overtly and covertly opposing the privatisation, and the press was almost universally negative. Richard Aitken-Davies, at the time director of privatisation at Railtrack and now project director flotation for London & Continental Railways Limited commented: 'A joke at the time was that only 13 people in Britain were in favour of rail privatisation and by a huge coincidence they were all members of the John Major cabinet.'

Due to the electricity regulator announcing a regulatory review of the electricity distribution companies one day after pricing of the second sale of shares in the electricity generating companies (Gencos) in March 1995, the feeling among many investors (particularly in the US) was that regulatory risk in UK privatisation had increased. The government was therefore anxious to re-establish the credibility of the regulatory system. The fact that the gas regulator announced tougher than expected revisions to the regulatory framework for British Gas during Railtrack's marketing period did not help either.

The corporate finance perspective

The time pressure in the Railtrack flotation was intense, as there was only one realistic time slot – Spring 1996. To do it sooner was impossible as the franchising process was not sufficiently advanced and there was an unprecedented degree of complexity. The performance regime had to be put in place before the privatisation (it was installed by April 1995) but could not begin to function until the fault-attribution mechanism was activated, which did not happen until December 1995. Robert Jennings, executive director of SBC Warburg and the bank's main corporate finance executive on the Railtrack privatisation explained: 'As soon as we were appointed, we recognised that the performance regime and the fault attribution processes would be one of the largest challenges.' Indeed the performance regimes became the number one critical path issue during the preparation phase. However, to delay until the autumn would have brought this privatisation too close to the general election which had to take place by the following spring, and a flotation too close to an election could have undermined market sentiment. Even at a year's distance from the eventual election on 1 May 1997 the flotation was politically highly sensitive.

Those that drove the privatisation had set off without knowing whether or not it could actually be done and importantly whether or not it could be done in such a way that investors would be confident that it would not be reversible should the Labour Party get into power at the next election. The pressure was therefore enormous to succeed the first time. In order to gain credibility with the investor community contractual relationships were introduced between the parties concerned and the impression given to investors that it would be too expensive for a potential future Labour government to renationalise the company. The sale was highly political and all the arguments were widely communicated by and through the

media. The actual flotation process in a more technical sense, however, was relatively free of party politics. Jenny Williams, director of Railways at the Department of Transport (DoT) and the government's effective team leader on this privatisation commented: 'The overriding perspective was how we were going to get value for the taxpayer. In that sense, we acted like any other commercial vendor'.

The Railtrack flotation (in the broad sense of the term) was undoubtedly among the most complex privatisations ever undertaken. Robert Jennings of SBC Warburg noted: 'We spent a lot of time anticipating all possible problems that might arise between the various parties following the flotation. We were particularly concerned to ensure that there were no structural flaws in the way the industry would operate, with new elements of the arrangement being put in place only weeks before the pathfinder prospectus was published. Our task was to ensure that these arrangements were fair as between the parties, that they would operate in the interests of the industry and that the prospectus gave full and proper disclosure.' The fact that the industry was broken up into almost 100 companies to be sold in quick succession required a fine balancing act between these various interests.

One of the principal challenges was the lack of private-sector experience among most people within Railtrack below boardroom level. To establish the contractual matrix and sell it within the organisation was therefore a huge challenge. In light of this inexperience, it was an unprecedented challenge among UK privatised utilities (with the exception of the water companies) for Railtrack to handle its huge backlog of investment.

The regulator reduced Railtrack's access charges by 8 per cent in real terms for the financial year ended 31 March 1996, which halved its value given a fixed amount of debt in the company. However, according to Jenny Williams of the DoT: 'It really didn't matter because had the price regime as determined by the rail regulator been more lenient, we would have put in more debt in Railtrack. Ultimately, it was our task to maximise the amount of debt that we put in while ensuring that Railtrack's financial ratios such as interest cover, dividend cover and gearing would be strong enough to see it through several years of heavy investment. What mattered more to the company was the RPI-2 per cent price regime from 1996 until 2001, which, given that the potential for rationalisation within Railtrack is smaller than in many other privatised utilities since the labour-intensive infrastructure companies had been taken out, is perhaps tougher than it appears.'

Railtrack's management experienced difficulty in getting their message across to investors, a combination perhaps of the 'story' being unusually complex and investors being badly prepared. Railtrack's finance director Norman Broadhurst: 'Of the people who we presented to, 40 per cent were well prepared, had detailed questions and had done their homework, 30 per cent appeared to know the basics and 30 per cent appeared not to be well prepared at all, which in our minds begged the question of the effectiveness of the pre-marketing.' This company view might be valid, yet most institutions expect to hear a story in full and want to be convinced by management as to why they should invest; others set out to make life difficult for management by concealing what they know.

Rationale and objectives

The rationale for the Railtrack IPO is intertwined with that for the overall privatisation of BR. Railtrack was sold in a public sale because of the size of the business and the fact that it has many characteristics of a regulated monopoly utility with which the UK retail investor is familiar – other parts of BR were sold by way of trade sales or in the case of the TOCs, franchised. Furthermore, a trade sale of Railtrack might have been seen by the public as concentrating too much power in too few hands and would not have satisfied the government's objective of achieving wider share ownership. Still, according to Williams of the DoT: 'We never ruled out the option of a trade sale nor did we structure this privatisation with a 'golden share'. Most of the golden shares in the UK have been of limited duration, the only effect of which is that the government foregoes a potential control premium upon privatisation which is instead available to the shareholders at the time of the expiry of the golden share. Golden shares in perpetuity really only make sense when matters of national security are involved.'

Vendor's objectives

The vendor's principal objective, as formulated in early August 1995, was to secure, as soon as reasonably practicable, the flotation of Railtrack and in pursuing that objective to have regard to:

* Securing a good deal for the taxpayer by maximising net proceeds (equity and debt) in the context of the need to secure a successful franchising and privatisation programme;
* To continue to promote deeper and wider share ownership, subject to the constraints of the overall size of the offer; and
* To maintain the momentum of the privatisation programme by achieving a recognition that the sale had been a success.

Although not articulated as a formal objective, it was understood at an early stage that the objective was to sell the majority of Railtrack. It was only in early 1996 that a decision was taken to sell 100 per cent, although this was not publicly announced until 15 April.

As this was an IPO rather than a secondary issue – where all publicly announced information is reflected in the share price and where therefore there is less of an expectation of a premium – the DoT and SBC Warburg wanted to see a small but sustainable secondary market premium of 3–5 per cent at least during the first month or two of trading. A smaller or bigger premium would not have been categorised as a success. Julian Waldron, executive director of ECM at SBC Warburg explained: 'The key is a small and stable premium over the weeks following pricing. We also wanted a certain amount of liquidity so that people could buy and sell shares easily. It makes sense to look at a longer period than just the

first few days for several reasons: first, retail investors don't always get their share certificates immediately; second, some time is typically required for institutional investors to adjust their portfolios to what they really want to own as opposed to what they are allocated and third, there may be stabilisation in the immediate after-market.'

Railtrack's perspective

Railtrack was keen for:

* A 100 per cent sale – a partial sale would have created uncertainty;
* A flotation rather than a strategic sale;
* A big share register to guard against any shareholder unfriendly actions taken by a possible future Labour government;
* As strong a balance sheet as possible (preferably equivalent to a double-A credit rating);
* Reasonable benchmarks for the performance regimes;
* Some anti-take over provisions; and
* BR to be off its back: it wanted its customers and suppliers to be in the private sector.

The only really tough negotiating point between the DoT and Railtrack was the capital structure, however it manifested itself in several ways. First, the initial pricing regime of RPI- 8 per cent for the year ended March 1996, which the company saw as very demanding – on this point, the government was able to refer to the independent regulator; second, Railtrack's accounting policies; third, the benchmarks for the performance regimes; fourth, the investment in new infrastructure which Railtrack would undertake to fund; and fifth, the level of debt that was to be left in the company. Jennings noted: 'To secure maximum enterprise value for the government it was essential for us to leave debt in Railtrack even though the company's capital expenditure programme meant that it would be cash-flow-negative for several years. Understandably, the company felt differently about this.'

Use of proceeds

There were no proceeds to Railtrack.

The regulatory framework

Railtrack operates as a privatised company within a system of economic regulations similar to those imposed on other UK utilities.

The regulator's functions under the Railways Act include: the granting of licences to operate trains, networks, stations and light maintenance depots; monitoring and enforcing compliance with the licence terms; approving the terms, including price, on which access to track, stations and light maintenance depots is obtained; functions covering domestic competition law in relation to railway services; and taking decisions on the closure of passenger facilities and services.

The regulator must exercise his functions in accordance with his general duties under the Railways Act, which include protecting the interests of users, promoting the use and development of the network and promoting efficiency, economy and competition in the provision of railway services. He is also under a duty not to exercise his functions in a manner which will make it unduly difficult for holders of network licences, principally Railtrack, to finance their activities. He must also have regard to the financial position of the franchising director (ie, the total cost to the state of subsidising the railways).

The franchising director was charged with the franchising of the TOCs to the private sector and the provision of subsidies to them, as well as receiving payments from them in later years, as stipulated in the franchising agreements, when they start to make profits. Having completed the franchising process, his principal objective is to secure an overall improvement in the quality of passenger rail and station services.

The advantages of Railtrack's regulatory framework are several:

- Although not specifically appointed for the flotation of Railtrack, the fact that the regulator (John Swift) was in place by December 1993 was important. He was in part responsible for the original regulatory structure and he had already set Railtrack's price regime well before the flotation. The risk of material change of regulatory methodology or practice at an early stage in the post-privatisation period was therefore much reduced;
- John Swift had stated on several occasions that he would not meddle with access charges until April 2001, an action that had a calming influence on the market, particularly in view of the many regulatory interventions in the other UK privatised utilities. John Swift is a competition lawyer with relevant experience, as opposed to some UK regulators who mainly have academic backgrounds. Although he may impose stricter pricing regimes in recognition of the spectacular returns achieved by other privatised utilities, the expectation is that investors will know what to expect. There was therefore a feeling that there was more

regulatory stability for Railtrack than for the other utilities;

- There are in-built direct and indirect incentives for Railtrack to invest. First, access charges received from the TOCs will, via a clearly defined performance regime and benchmarks, vary according to the quality of service delivered. Second, by investing, maintenance expenditure can be reduced, and third there is an indirect incentive to invest, in that if service is improved and more passengers travel on more trains, transport volumes will go up long term and turnover will increase.

Norman Broadhurst of Railtrack underscored this point: 'There is an important difference in the regulation of Railtrack compared to other UK utilities and that is Section 4 of the Railways Act. It says: "The rail regulator shall not make it unduly difficult for Railtrack to finance its activities" ... Also, "the company's route for appeal is to judicial review rather than the Monopolies & Mergers Commission." This means that if the Labour government wants to substantially change the regime, then they have to pass a new Railways Act in parliament, which could take at least 18 months.'

Share capital and ownership

See Exhibit 5.

Transaction components

This offer of initially up to 434.8 million outstanding Railtrack shares comprised three tranches: a UK public offer representing at least 30 per cent of the combined offers, an international offer representing on an indicative basis 200 million shares (including the retail tender), and the free and matching offer for eligible Railtrack employees.

Exhibit 5
Share capital and ownership

Type of shares offered	Ordinary shares of 25p and ADRs representing 10 ordinary shares.
Ownership restrictions	The Secretary of State for Transport after consultation with the rail regulator (and under certain circumstances the franchising director), retains the right to terminate Railtrack's licences if and when a person obtains control (defined as over 30%) of Railtrack without the approval of the Secretary of State.
Share capital before and after offer	500 million ordinary shares.
Listing	London Stock Exchange.
Market capitalisation at offer price (US$1.51/£1)	US$2.9 billion.
Long-term senior debt ratings	A+ (Standard & Poor's), A2 (Moody's).
Major shareholder(s) before (after) offer	The Secretary of State for Transport owned 100% before the offer and retained 1% afterwards solely to meet share loyalty commitments. As per late 1996, Mutual Shares and Threadneedle Asset Management owned more than 3% of Railtrack.
Most relevant stock exchange index/weighting	Railtrack initially was included in the FT–SE 250 Index with a market capitalisation placing it in the top 120 companies. However, due to strong performance in the secondary market, Railtrack made it into the FT–SE 100 Index in July 1996.

The international offer comprised an institutional offer aimed at both UK and international institutions and a UK retail tender aimed primarily at UK investors with Personal Equity Plans (PEPs). The public offer was not underwritten and the international offer was underwritten only in a book-building sense, ie, the underwriting became binding only at the same time as allocations were made to investors.

Payment was structured with two roughly equal instalments falling in two tax years, with the 190p first instalment of the retail offer price published in the pathfinder prospectus dated 15 April. The 200p first instalment of the international offer and the pre-determined discount on the total retail offer price of 10p (fully reflected in the first instalment), were announced at the launch of the UK public offer on 1 May. This effectively enabled the public offer to be marketed on a fixed-priced basis. The second installment of both offers, and therefore the total offer prices, were fixed following book-building (see Exhibit 6).

The international offer included an option to sell shares to QIBs in the US and Canada under Rule 144A and there was a private placement with 49 authorised Japanese investors. The greenshoe of 65.2 million shares, equivalent to 15 per cent of the combined offers, was large by UK government standards but not unusual in the international market. The greenshoe was fully exercised two weeks after the offer had started trading.

In addition to the 10 pence retail discount on the first instalment, which was available to all retail investors, those who reg-istered with a share shop before 29 April 1996 were entitled to receive either one additional share for every 15 purchased and held for three years (subject to a maximum of 80 bonus shares per applicant) or an instalment discount of 15 pence per share on the second instalment on each of the first 800 shares purchased and held continuously until that instalment is paid.

As the privatisation took place shortly after the end of Railtrack's financial year, the DoT decided that Railtrack was to pay to investors a dividend for the full financial year ended 31 March 1996, thereby offering retail investors a first year gross retail return on the partly paid shares of approximately 19 per cent (25 per cent equivalent on an annualised basis).

Given its partly paid structure and the fact that the UK retail market accounted for such a large portion of the combined offers, the amount of cash that had to be raised from international institutions was therefore relatively small. This enabled the vendor to decide on an unusually small syndicate for such an important privatisation. Three global managers sold shares globally and the six co-managers sold in specific regions only (see Exhibit 7).

Principal advisers
See Exhibit 8.

NM Rothschild was appointed by Railtrack in November 1993 to advise on the flotation, although the appointment was formalised only when Railtrack Plc was vested out of BR in April 1994. Simmons & Simmons was appointed in mid-1993 following a beauty contest. They had no experience with UK government privatisation offers but are thought to have been competitive on price.

Transaction fee distribution
The institutional economics were calculated on the total proceeds and structured as shown in Exhibit 10.

As global coordinator SBC Warburg was guaranteed a financial advisory fee of 0.08 per cent, which was partly offset against the management fee and selling concession earned upon the successful completion of the offer.

Exhibit 6
Payment by installment

	1st Installment (May-96)	2nd Installment (June-97)	Total offer price
UK public offer	190p	190p	380p
International offer	200p	190p	390p

Exhibit 7
Offer structure

Target markets	Indicated tranche sizes*	Global managers	Co-managers
UK public offer	At least 30%, up to 54%	SBC Warburg	N/A
International offer			
Institutional offer			
UK	N/A	SBC Warburg (Books) Merrill Lynch, UBS	Nikko Securities**
US and Canada	N/A	SBC Warburg (Books) Merrill Lynch, UBS	Schroder Wertheim
Japan	N/A	SBC Warburg (Books) Merrill Lynch, UBS	Nikko Securities
RoW	N/A	SBC Warburg (Books) Merrill Lynch, UBS	Crédit Lyonnais, Robert Fleming, HSBC James Capel, Nikko Sec., Schroder Wertheim, WestLB
UK retail tender	N/A	SBC Warburg	N/A
Total international offer	No less than 200 million shares		
Total combined offers (shares)	**434,800,000**		

* % of indicated total offer on 1 May 1996.
** Nikko Securities was mandated to place shares with UK-based branches of Japanese fund managers.

Exhibit 8
Principal advisers

Financial adviser to HM Government and co-sponsor to the listing	SBC Warburg
Legal adviser to HM Government	Linklaters & Paines
Financial adviser to Railtrack and co-sponsor to the listing	NM Rothschild & Sons
Accounting adviser to HM Government	Ernst & Young
Retail advisers to HM Government	Solid Solutions Associates
Stockbroker to Railtrack	Merrill Lynch International
Legal adviser to Railtrack	Simmons & Simmons
Auditors to Railtrack	Deloitte & Touche
Legal adviser to SBC Warburg	Freshfields
Marketing advisers	Dewe Rogerson Limited
Registrars and receiving bankers	The Royal Bank of Scotland
ADR depositary bank	Morgan Guaranty Trust Co.

Exhibit 9
The timetable

December 1994	• SBC Warburg appointed government adviser and global coordinator.
26 March 1996	• Railtrack equity research reports published; • Retail marketing campaign launched with mail shots to five million households; and • First day for registration with share shops.
1 April	• Analysts' pre-marketing meetings with institutional investors start in the UK.
15 April	*Pathfinder prospectus published, containing:* • Intention to sell up to 100%; • Price of first instalment for retail offer; and • Retail incentives for registrants with a share shop.
17 April	• Roadshow begins with seven business days of UK one-on-ones and one day for London group meeting.
26 April	• Analysts' pre-marketing meetings with institutional investors ends in Asia.
29 April	• Last day for registration with share shops (ie, for entitlement to preferential allocation and certain retail incentives on the second instalment); and • Roadshow continues with six business days in the US.
1 May	• Launch of UK public offer; and • Publication of prospectus, including: first instalment amount of institutional offer (and therefore pre-determined retail discount on total institutional offer price) and price range for total offer price.
2 May	• Bookbuilding begins.
8 May	• Roadshow continues with four business days in Europe.
14–15 May	• Further UK one-on-ones and video-conference to Asian investors.
15 May	• Public offer closes at noon (last day for payment under this offer).
16 May	• DoT announces size of public offer to be increased.
Friday 17 May	• UK retail tender closes; • Bookbuilding closes.
Sun, 19 May	*Pricing and allocation of combined offers:* • Second instalment amount, UK public and international offer prices announced; and • Allocations to investors.
Monday 20 May	• Trading begins on London Stock Exchange.
6 June	• Greenshoe exercised in full.

Management fee

This was split globally, two-thirds to the global managers and one-third to the co-managers. Within each manager group, the fee was split on an equal basis. Each global manager received four times the commission received by each co-manager. This structure was designed to encourage maximum effort from all syndicate members by offering them a guaranteed minimum fixed fee (see Exhibit 11).

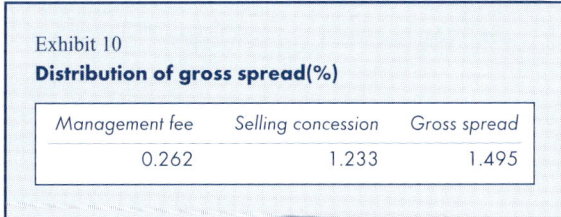

Exhibit 10
Distribution of gross spread(%)

Management fee	Selling concession	Gross spread
0.262	1.233	1.495

Exhibit 11
Distribution of management fee (%)

Total management fee	0.262
Of which: shared equally between the global managers	0.175
Of which: shared equally between the co-managers	0.087

The selling concession

The 1.233 per cent selling concession was shared among the managers in proportion to designated sales and there was no fixed element.

To achieve fairness, the designations were handled separately by the SBC Warburg corporate finance department, without involvement on the part of the bookrunning equity capital markets team, to ensure that allocations were not based on the likely investor designations but rather on the quality of the order. The bookbuilding and allocation processes were audited by Coopers & Lybrand.

Retail economics

Each share shop received selling commissions of 1 per cent on the first £9,000-worth of shares allocated to its clients and 0.5 per cent on the next £21,000, subject to a minimum payment of £12.50 per successful underlying applicant and subject to there being at least 15 applications per share shop.

Deal structure

Sizing of the transaction

The decision on how much to sell was kept open until a late stage for three main reasons:

1. An antagonistic stance by the Labour Party and widespread public opposition to the privatisation meant that initially it was politically more opportune to indicate only that 'at least 51 per cent' would be sold;
2. Because of public disquiet, retail demand was uncertain. Julian Waldron of SBC Warburg commented: 'Nobody knew how much retail demand there was going to be – still we needed to sell a minimum portion of the total transaction to UK retail investors both to meet DoT's overall objectives of wider and deeper share ownership and in order to draw institutional interest. Therefore it was prudent to work on the assumption initially that we were not going to be able to sell the whole company'; and
3. Railtrack was keen to be fully privatised so as to be inde-

pendent of any future Labour government. The DoT was able to use this to indicate to Railtrack management that unless it achieved a good offer price it might not be possible to sell the entire company. It thus became the DoT's bargaining chip in the sensitive and difficult negotiations on capital structure, benchmarks for the performance regime and earnings estimates.

For these reasons, and to create momentum during marketing, the vendor and global coordinator decided not to communicate too early the percentage of the company to be sold. Whereas the fact that at least 30 per cent of the combined offer was to be sold to retail investors was communicated on 3 January 1996, the fact that at least 51 per cent of the company was to be sold was only communicated on 26 March. This allowed considerable flexibility both in terms of the amount to be sold to retail and the total size of the offer. On 15 April it was announced that most of the company was to be sold. Jenny Williams added: 'We had to push hard to keep the sizing an open issue. The company only naturally pushed hard for the sale of 100 per cent. It was however not clear until a fairly late stage that the market was going to pay full value for the sale of the entire company'.

Richard Aitken-Davies commented: 'Experience suggests that governments will receive higher proceeds overall by selling in tranches rather than selling 100 per cent at the time of the IPO, as demonstrated here in the UK in the cases of BT and the Gencos. However, Railtrack was a smaller privatisation, there was no problem with market capacity and there were strong political and marketing reasons for a 100 per cent sale. I suspect that a partial sale of Railtrack was never a serious possibility. Selling less than 50 per cent of a public-sector organisation would leave the constant threat of meddling by the majority shareholder.'

Underwriting method

This was the first open-priced bookbuilt UK privatisation IPO. Bookbuilding was chosen because it was considered to be more likely to maximise proceeds than an underwritten structure – the precedent set by previous privatisations – despite the absence of a guarantee of success. Bookbuilt offers are often either huge successes or bad failures. In hot deals, investors tend to inflate their demand, so the bookrunner needs to consider carefully how the book develops, who the long-term investors are and where each investor is prepared to buy in the after-market.

Syndicate structure

There had been considerable evolution since BT 3, the first offer with a truly global syndicate, and SBC Warburg's last UK privatisation before Railtrack. 'The idea behind BT 3 was that the best way to market an offer of already traded shares was by reference to the secondary market, where institutions have generally formed a few established broking relationships in a given stock,' explained Waldron. 'The situation is different in an IPO where there is no secondary market in the stock prior to the offer. Therefore restrictions on marketing should be minimal as few such relationships exist.'

The most important differences between the two syndicate structures were:

- Size – nine banks in Railtrack against 31 in BT 3;
- There was no exempt list in Railtrack as in BT 3, ie, all managers selling in a particular region had complete access to all investors;
- There was much less ring-fencing in Railtrack. In BT 3, there was strong ring-fencing for pre-marketing and marketing. In Railtrack the number of banks selling in any one market was limited to the number of people who investors would wish to speak to, ie, two to four banks; and
- Railtrack's syndicate structure was a very clear one. The syndicate banks and investors had a good understanding of what was going on and who had responsibility for what.

Bookbuilding model

For the first time in a global equity offer, a real-time computerised bookbuilding system was employed. There were terminals in the offices of all the managers world-wide, enabling them to input their own orders. This had several advantages:

- The absolute timeliness of the information meant that the state of the global book was available at any time, improving management of the offer and decision-making based on a bottom-up approach. This was important to determine: how to refine the investment story during the roadshow; how to allocate the one-on-one meetings; how to adjust advertising expenditure, etc. This information was used to price, size and allocate the transaction. In previous offers, the state of the book could only be reported with a delay;
- Whereas a computer based system might be perceived to be anonymous, in this case there was also room for comments on the order forms, making it possible for the global coordinator and the vendor to get all the important qualitative feed-back without delay;
- The system was more transparent from the point of view of the co-managers in that all comments were available to the vendor in their original form without having been coloured by the global coordinator. In this way, the global coordinator's subjectivity in the allocation process was to an extent neutralised;
- It made it possible to do the first allocation on the Friday night after the close of the book, with more consultation and thinking over the week-end. The final allocations were decided on by Sunday afternoon following a high-quality dialogue over the weekend. Julian Waldron noted: 'Altogether, it made the allocation process much less of a nightmare than in previous bookbuilt secondary offers.'

Clearly the employment of this system was facilitated by the fact that the syndicate was of a much more manageable size than had traditionally been the case in large privatisations.

US registration/listing

Waldron commented: '... registration has become increasingly fashionable, so we considered it quite carefully before rejecting it.' The reasoning behind SBC Warburg's eventual rejection of SEC registration in this particular case was as follows:

Arguments for a US registration

- You can theoretically tap 100 per cent of the US market by having access to big institutions, smaller institutions and retail investors, high-net-worth individuals and domestically oriented funds/ institutions;
- Certain investors perceive registered offers to be sounder because the disclosure standards are higher and the due diligence is more comprehensive; and
- The company could have handled it because US disclosure requirements are not much more challenging than in the UK.

Arguments against a US registration

- US retail demand is relatively low-quality when it comes to non-US shares;
- The incremental institutional demand as a result of a registration is limited for two reasons: first the domestic funds who are entitled to buy foreign shares if they are registered with the SEC are managed by less sophisticated fund managers and given the specialist nature of the Railtrack story it was judged that the incremental demand would be small. Second, because the domestic funds need to beat the US S&P Index, they are unlikely to take very large bets on foreign stocks;
- Enough demand was likely to be generated from the more sophisticated US institutions entitled to buy non-registered securities;
- Taking everything into account, it was felt that 80–90 per cent of the quality demand potential could be accessed through a Rule 144A offer.

Julian Waldron reflected: 'Ultimately we decided on the Rule 144 A option and our hunch was correct. Some of the very biggest US institutions wanted ordinary shares and wanted to trade in London. Also, a number of institutions are of the opinion that 144A transactions are better handled from a due diligence standpoint, as it focuses more on business than legal matters, right through to the after-market which is frequently much more volatile in a registered offer. Experience increasingly shows that SEC registration is of much less importance than the scope and quality of the US marketing. In the end, we missed none of the big institutions and we had a number of US$200–300 million orders.'

Application in the UK public offer

There were two ways to apply for shares in the public offer. Either through a share shop or via public application forms. Retail investors wishing to secure larger allocations could also apply at the international offer price in the retail tender.

The share shop scheme

UK commercial banks had not traditionally distributed shares to the public, first because there was very little interest and second because they did not have permission to do so. The role of the commercial banks had largely been confined to acting as receiving banks, which is merely a processing job. Equity distribution to individuals had been the domain of private client stockbrokers where the minimum investment was far larger than what the average person could afford. Privatisation challenged these relationships and new methods of distribution were developed.

Prior to BT2, individuals were encouraged to register interest and apply for shares through specially constituted government run share information offices (SIOs). These arrangements generated demand in specific sales but did little to familiarise the public with share dealing. The SIOs were not equipped to handle secondary market sales orders and the government provided no infrastructure for secondary market dealing. In some of the privatisations, there were certain schemes put together whereby sell orders from retail clients could be executed by certain bank branches and brokers. A list of brokers who would execute retail orders at a fixed fee for a certain period of time following the offer was included in the British Gas prospectus, but there were only very few organisations that provided this service on an ongoing basis.

In the BT 2, offer the government sought to promote public knowledge and understanding of private-sector share dealing services by appointing eight share shops, mainly high street banks, to provide cheap and accessible buying and selling services for BT shares. Individuals had the opportunity to nominate a share shop when registering with the SIO. Those doing so received preference in allocation. The share shops were able to market their services, but not to market the offer or process applications for BT shares.

In BT 3, the Treasury replaced the previous arrangements and appointed some 150 share shops. The two key elements of these new arrangements were:

- That individuals could, for the first time, register and apply for shares through a share shop or through the SIO; and
- That all share shops were to be members of a self-regulatory organisation, authorised to carry on investment business, enabling them to market the public offer.

Individuals who registered and applied through a share shop were again given preference in allocation. The scheme was a success: share shops attracted nearly 59 per cent of all applicants and were more successful in converting registrations into applications than the SIO.

In Gencos 2 in 1995, the Treasury did not set up a SIO. Individuals could register an interest in the sale only with share shops. Although those who had not registered with a share shop could still apply for shares on public application forms, such applicants were not entitled to discounts on the second and third instalments or bonus shares, or to preference in allocation if the public offer was over-subscribed. In this sale, share shops accounted for 98 per cent of demand in the public offer. The rate of conversion from registrations to applications was marginally higher than in BT 3 (32 per cent for the SIO and share shops combined in BT 3 and 33 per cent in Gencos 2 US°.

In Railtrack, the share shop technology had been improved further and, as in Gencos2, all the retail marketing was carried out by the share shops:

- There were some 110 organisations acting as share shops in relation to the public offer, offering more than 10,000 outlets across the country. A list of share shops, including the telephone numbers which people could call to register, were published regularly in national newspapers;
- Share shops had an exclusive role in collecting registrations for the UK public offer. Registration took place between 26 March and 29 April;
- Share shops sent out a share shop application form and a copy of the share shop mini prospectus to all registrants;
- The share shops collected and processed the application forms and submitted bulk application forms on their behalf; and
- Those that registered with a share shop before 29 April became entitled to preferential allocation and loyalty retail incentives in the form of bonus shares or discount on the second instalment.

Over a number of years, the government had helped create a new distribution channel for privatisation shares to retail investors. Importantly, the development of the share shop has also served the purpose of developing, on an ongoing basis, share dealing services for UK retail investors, a development which certainly should improve the overall equity culture in the country and increase retail holdings in all shares. Today most high street banks and the biggest building societies are equipped with share dealing services and are capable of distributing new issues. In addition, the privatisation industry has also helped a number of dedicated retail brokers and telephone share dealing services such as Sharelink to become viable businesses.

Application via public application form

Individuals who were not registered with a share shop by 29 April 1996 but who wished to apply for shares in the UK public offer, had to apply on a public application form.

UK retail tender

The international offer included a retail tender through which investors could apply for additional shares or a larger number of shares than was possible in the public offer. The minimum investment was £3,000 for the first instalment, equivalent to 1,500 shares whereas in the public offer the minimum investment was 200 shares. Retail investors tendered through one of 100 designated retail brokers, most of which were also share shops. The aim was:

- To enable those retail investors who wished to buy a larger number of shares but who did not want to compete with the large institutions to achieve a decent allocation;
- To maximise proceeds by attracting additional retail demand at the institutional offer price;
- To stimulate investment in Personal Equity Plans (PEPs), a form of tax-effective retail investment; and
- To mobilise the full force of the private client stockbroker network.

Exhibit 12
Marketing challenges

Challenge	Solution	Presentation
Annual subsidy required	Contractual nature of income flow	SBC Warburg's financial model setting out projections for Railtrack published in January 1996.
Unpopular privatisation and a hostile press	Switch attention towards value; Retrospective dividend	Press briefings Dec 1995–Jan 1996 Dividend announcement May 1
Regulatory risk	Regulator establishes own regime	City seminar with regulators Jan 1996
Political opposition aims to subvert system	Contractual matrix undermines change	Press briefings emphasise progress March–April 1996

Exhibit 13
Creating momentum in the marketing

	Institutional marketing	Retail marketing
April 1995	Publication of 100-page rail privatisation report by SBC Warburg.	
3 January 1996	Retail announcement communicated to institutional investors.	Launch of share shop scheme and timetable.
29 January	Rail conference with all key players including Secretary of State for Transport, rail regulator, franchising director and Railtrack chairman.	
26 March	Retail announcement communicated to institutional investors.	Retail marketing campaign launched: • Offer structure announced; • Share shops opened for registrations; • Advertisements in press, TV and radio; and • Mailing to five million households.
1 April	Two-week pre-marketing begins (research analysts meet with investors).	
11 April		Announcement of retail incentives (available only for those who register with share shops).
15 April	*Pathfinder Prospectus Published:* First instalment amount for retail offer; Retail loyalty incentives; and Announcement that 910,000 people had registered.	
17 April	Four-week institutional roadshow begins (Company management meets with investors).	
April	Final SBC Warburg research update.	
29 April		Last day for registration with share shops.
1 May	*Publication of prospectus:* First instalment amount for institutional offer (and therefore retail discount); Offer price range announced; and Announcement that 1.9 million people had registered.	
1 May		Public offer opened.
2 May	Institutional bookbuilding begins.	
Week of 6 May		Mini-prospectus delivered to registrants.
15 May		Public offer closes with 665,000 applicants; Public offer increased from 'at least 30%' to 48.3% (excluding retail tender and greenshoe).
17 May	Close of institutional bookbuilding.	Close of retail tender.
20 May	Announcement of retail and institutional offer prices; and trading begins.	

Marketing

The marketing thrust in an IPO such as Railtrack is to build momentum in investor interest in three steps:

1. What does the company do?
2. Why invest in it?
3. What price to pay?

Whereas this might under normal circumstances be straightforward enough, in the case of Railtrack there were four major challenges that needed to be addressed in the marketing. The structural solutions to those challenges and the presentation thereof to the market took a number of forms (see Exhibit 12).

Altogether SBC Warburg published six research reports between April 1995 and April 1996, organised the City seminar and, towards the end, managed a comprehensive pre-marketing and marketing campaign together with the other syndicate banks. The marketing advisers and SBC Warburg made multiple press announcements with increasing amounts of information, conducted targeted advertising campaigns and on a subtle basis managed the financial press. The retail and institutional marketing campaigns were in the main separate although parallel and inter-linked (see Exhibit 13).

Retail marketing

At the outset it was clear that Railtrack was going to appeal to a financially more aware audience than some of the earlier privatisations. Given the substantial UK experience of who buys privatisations, it was possible to focus much more narrowly on key potential investor groups than was previously the case. The marketing advisers knew which radio programmes appealed to those who had bought before, enabling the government to cut back on expensive TV advertising.

The government-sponsored share offer marketing campaign started on 26 March. Advertisements ran in the press, on TV and on radio. Many of the share shops undertook their own marketing.

The government mailed five million UK households information which included a list of share shops, a leaflet on how to register and a reply paid card for registration with a share shop. This was a more targeted campaign than those of earlier privatisations – 20 million and 10 million households had been sent information in BT 3 and Gencos 2 respectively.

Institutional marketing

A key step in the institutional marketing was taken in January 1996, when SBC Warburg arranged a City seminar for institutional investors. The speakers included the key personali-

---

Exhibit 14
Principal sales points

Secure revenue stream	• Secure, non-cyclical, predictable and largely unaffected by state of economy. Revenue derived principally from access charges paid by passenger train operators (86%) and freight operators (8%) for access to network and stations.
Regulatory certainty	• Unparalleled regulatory certainty and stability for a UK privatisation. Track access charges contracted for next five years and subject to RPI -2% pricing formula. Vast majority (about 90%) is a fixed element. Rules established at the outset and clear understanding reached with the rail regulator.
Cost savings	• Efficiencies and cost savings will be the main near-term drivers to profit growth. SBC Warburg financial model assumed 3% a year cost savings until 2000 – very conservative in light of other utilities' experience. Great scope for using people and technology more effectively. The lion's share of cost savings is not going to come from cutting staff at Railtrack as it is generally understood that Bob Horton had taken only the people from BR that he really needed in Railtrack, but rather indirectly as Railtrack's service suppliers are rationalised.
Strong balance sheet	• Capital structure resolved. Balance sheet leaves significant headroom for investment. Borrowings of just £585 million after government write-off. Proforma gearing of 25%.
Enhancement programme	• Two major projects planned: West Coast Main Line linking London, West Midlands, the Northwest and Scotland and Thameslink 2000 linking north and south London and beyond; direct access to City of London; interchange with the Channel Tunnel Rail Link and seven underground stations.
Property portfolio and non-core revenue growth	• Railtrack owns 16,000 route kilometres, 2,500 stations, 90 light maintenance depots, 40,000 bridges, viaducts and tunnels and 9,000 level crossings. Net book value of land and buildings at 30 September 1995 was £1,416 million, investment properties accounting for £228 million. Scope to develop retail revenues at the 14 major stations (building on success of Liverpool Street and Victoria stations).
Management	• Mix of public company and lifetime rail experience. Bob Horton, 56 (chairman) is former chairman of BP. John Edmonds, 59 (chief executive) is a lifetime railman. Norman Broadhurst, 54 (finance director) is former joint-deputy chief executive and finance director of VSEL shipbuilders.
Valuation	• Predictable nature of revenue flows and focus on cost base together with other Railtrack characteristics (regulated monopoly supplier, infrastructure asset base, capex backlog, etc) draws comparisons with the UK's privatised utilities sector. The consensus is that such stocks are valued primarily on the basis of dividend yield. The National Grid Company and BT were deemed to be the two most comparable companies.

Sources: SBC Warburg and prospectus.

ties who would shape Railtrack's privatisation, most notably the regulators.

The approach to the roadshow was different from most European privatisations in two important ways:

- The UK roadshow was finished before the price range was fixed, allowing for a tighter and higher-quality range; and
- The US roadshow was scheduled directly after the price range was fixed. In the past, US issuing houses have insisted on doing European offers in such a way that the US roadshow came shortly before pricing, thereby giving US institutions all the leeway as to whether or not to enter the offer at the very end of the bookbuilding process. The approach in Railtrack gave the UK institutions the 'home advantage' of which they have regularly been deprived.

The US roadshow covered 11 cities. 'The days of seeing US investors in only Boston and New York are long gone, even if you only do a Rule 144A transaction,' noted Waldron. There were discussions with more than 270 investors in 21 countries during pre-marketing. Management addressed over 300 investors in 10 countries on the roadshow. There were 130 one-on-one meetings between management and institutional investors, mostly in the UK and the US.

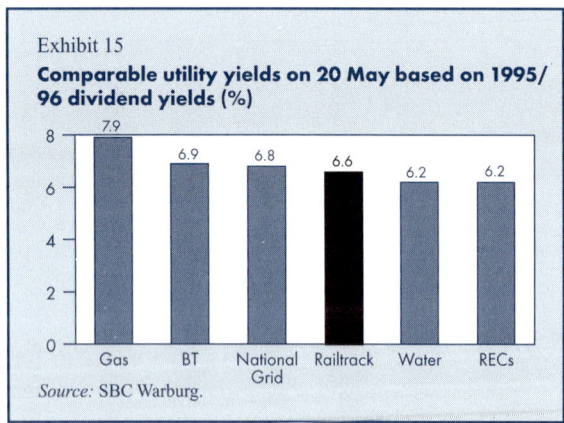

Exhibit 15

Comparable utility yields on 20 May based on 1995/96 dividend yields (%)

Gas 7.9, BT 6.9, National Grid 6.8, Railtrack 6.6, Water 6.2, RECs 6.2

Source: SBC Warburg.

The Railtrack story

SBC Warburg at first considered positioning Railtrack as a growth story but soon concluded that because the railway industry had experienced negative growth over the past 50–70 years and generally had a poor reputation among investors, Railtrack, despite considerable prospects for earnings growth, had to be sold as a yield story. (See Exhibit 14.)

At the institutional offer price of 390 pence, corresponding to an historic gross dividend yield of 6.6 per cent, Railtrack was priced inside both BT and the National Grid Company (see Exhibit 15).

Results

Placement

Based on the original offer size, the total offer was approximately seven times subscribed. There was surprisingly strong demand from the UK public and international institutions. The global coordinator received an early indication that US institutions were interested and the US market proved to be the most significant source of international demand (see Exhibit 16).

UK public offer

On 11 April, just over two weeks after the first day of registration, 910,000 UK retail investors had registered with share shops. By 19 April the number had increased to 1.4 million. By the close of registration on 29 April 1996 there was a total of 1.9 million registrations with share shops. These positive announcements encouraged further demand as applicants joined the bandwagon and helped create additional momentum in institutional demand and in the UK retail tender.

By the close of the public offer the 1.9 million registrations had been converted to 665,000 applications, corresponding to a conversion ratio of 35 per cent, in line with previous UK public offers. Of the 665,000 applications, 90 per cent had come via share shops, and most of the balance

Exhibit 16

Underwriting, demand and allocation

Target markets	*Indicated tranche sizes	Demand	Allocation**
UK public offer***	At least 30%, up to 54%	12.7%	42.0%
International offer			
Institutional offer			
UK	N/A	43.9%	30.5%
US and Canada	N/A	19.1%	10.9%
Japan	N/A	0.5%	0.3%
Rest of world	N/A	19.5%	7.4%
Total institutional offer	N/A	82.9%	49.1%
UK retail tender	N/A	****4.4%	8.9%
Total international offer	At least 200 million shares	87.3%	58.0%
Total combined offers (shares)	**434,800,000**	**3,083,000,000**	**500,000,000**

* Percentage of indicated total offer on 1 May
** Including over-allotments corresponding to the 65.2 million share greenshoe.
*** Including the employee free and matching offers, the employee discount and priority offer and the pensioner priority offer. The UK public offer was not underwritten
**** Of which 32.5 million shares represented 'PEP bids'.

Exhibit 17
Railtrack retail penetration in perspective

Date	Company/ privatisation	Total size (£ billions)	Proportion initially offered to retail*	Retail subscription	Final retail allocations*	Number of retail applications
Mar-91	Gencos 1	2.2	28%	5.0x	49%	1.9 million
Jun-91	Scottish Electr.	2.9	33%	3.2x	56%	2.0 million
December-91	BT 2	5.3	50%	2.6x	67%	2.8 million
Jul-93	BT 3	5.2	50%	1.7x	60%	1.7 million
Mar-95	Gencos 2	3.6	49%	2.1x	63%	1.1 million
May-96	Railtrack	1.9	At least 30%	3.0x	48%	0.7 million

* Final proportion of the total offer allocated to the public offer, before exercise of the greenshoe. This percentage does not include the shares sold in the retail tender, which are included in the international offer.

Exhibit 18
Allocations in the public offer

Number of shares applied for	Allocations to share shop applicants	Allocations to applicants on public application forms
200	200	200
300	300	200
400	315	200
500	330	200
600	360	Nil
700	390	Nil
800	420	Nil
900	450	Nil
1,000	480	Nil
1,500	495	Nil
2,000	510	Nil
2,500 +	Nil	Nil

from employee applications. Retail demand built very strongly despite an announcement of stricter regulation of British Gas which caused utilities prices to weaken by 5 per cent over the last three days of the public offer.

The public offer was approximately three times subscribed if total demand is set in relation to the minimum number of shares to be sold to retail investors. On 16 May, the day after the close of the public offer and one day before the close of bookbuilding, it was announced that the DoT intended to increase the size of the public offer as a proportion of the combined offers, sending a signal to institutional investors that shares would be in scarce supply. After the close of the combined offers on 17 May it was decided that the public offer should be increased to 48.3 per cent of shares sold (excluding over-allotments). Compared to initial expectations, the Railtrack public offer was one of the more successful of the UK privatisations (see Exhibit 17).

As indicated throughout the marketing period, those who registered and applied via share shops were substantially advantaged in the allocation process. Only those who had applied via share shops were allocated more than 200 shares (see Exhibit 18).

International offer

The international offer, comprising UK and international institutions and the UK retail tender, was strongly oversubscribed,

the total number of shares demanded being 13.4 times larger than the minimum 200 million shares initially dedicated to it.

The unusual approach, in the case of a non-US offer, to schedule the US market at the beginning of the roadshow led to constructive feed-back and strong early demand from US institutions. This in turn encouraged demand in Europe and elsewhere and thus had a beneficial impact on the overall bookbuilding process. Other notable features of the international offer included:

- UK institutions alone covered the book of the whole offer at the top of the price range on day one;
- There was a fair amount of price-sensitivity initially, but most investors moved to the top end of the price range by the 11th of the 12 bookbuilding days, the gas regulator announcement notwithstanding. This positive reaction coincided with strong signals from the public offer as announced on 16 May (day 11 of bookbuilding);
- An increase in demand at the top end of the price range was achieved over the last two days of bookbuilding; and
- Sophisticated retail investors understood that the allocation policy would favour PEP bids (bids under tax-exempt Personal Equity Plans). This encouraged demand in the UK retail tender: over 136 million shares were demanded of which 32.5 million represented PEP bids. A total of 44.4 million shares was allocated in the retail tender. All PEP bids were met in full; non-PEP bidders were allocated 1,000 shares each.

There were four main criteria determining the allocation:

1. *Price leadership:* bids at specified prices were preferred to bids at strike;
2. *Timeliness:* the prompt submission of a bid following any contact with management;
3. *Quality:* the government's independent assessment, based on SBC Warburg's recommendation, of an investor's likely short- and long-term after-market behaviour; and
4. *Involvement:* interest in the offer expressed by participation in pre-marketing, roadshow and one-on-one meetings.

Julian Waldron stated: 'The allocation criteria favoured earliness of demand in relation to participation in the roadshow, propensity to hold shares for the long-term and after-market interest. Whereas in BT 3 there was little difference in percentage allocations, we wanted a more concentrated approach in Railtrack, reflecting the fact that it was an IPO where we wanted to create a solid core shareholder base, and that it didn't fit into large specific industry sector funds such as for example the telecom funds in the case of BT 3.'

Most investors scored highly on price-leadership and time-liness as the book was well covered at the higher end of the price range on the first day of bookbuilding. Consequently, involvement and investor quality proved to be the differenti-ating factors at the allocation meetings. The targeted investors were ranked in six categories in advance of pre-marketing, 'A' representing the highest quality and 'F' the lowest. Exhibit 19 illustrates just how big an advantage the high-quality insti-tutions had in this allocation process.

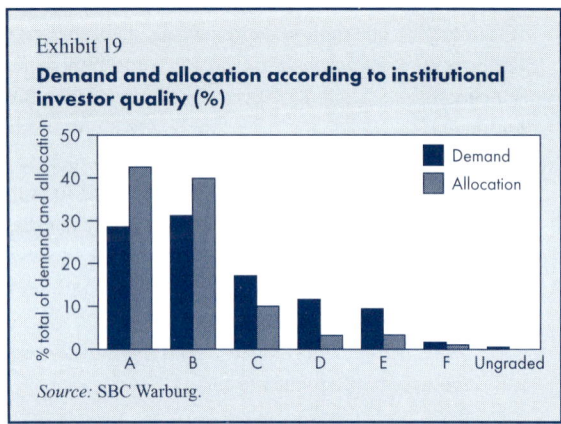

Exhibit 19

Demand and allocation according to institutional investor quality (%)

Source: SBC Warburg.

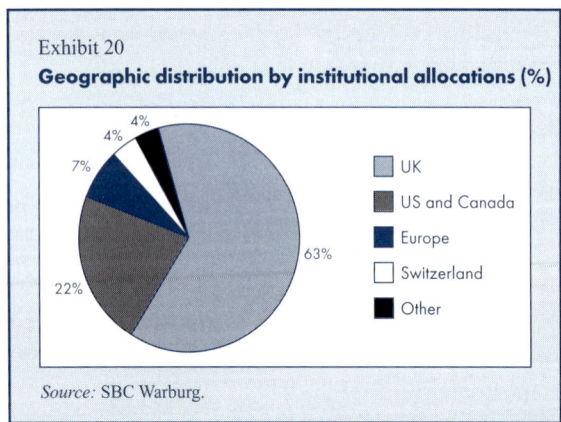

Exhibit 20

Geographic distribution by institutional allocations (%)

Source: SBC Warburg.

The UK accounted for 54.4 per cent of institutional demand and received 63.2 per cent of allocations. US institutions were allocated more or less in proportion to demand while European investors demanded 12.5 per cent of the total but received only 7.1 per cent of allocations (see Exhibit 20).

Investor concentration

Whereas demand was reasonably broad, allocations were more concentrated, which was consistent with the objective of cre-ating a solid core shareholder base for Railtrack. Even when considering order inflation, there were some astonishingly big orders (see Exhibit 21).

Buyers by type

Generalist country funds was the pre-dominant category of buyer. There was some buying by one or two UK income funds and considerable buying by utility funds. Transport funds were less important as there are relatively few. Given that during the marketing phase Railtrack was not thought likely to become a FT–SE100 Index stock, SBC Warburg did not emphasise indexation. As Railtrack was unlikely to rep-resent more than 0.25–0.5 per cent of a broad UK portfolio of stocks, no-one needed to own it for index purposes and there was only limited buying by index funds.

After-market price performance

See Exhibit 22.

* Priced at 390 pence (international offer) on a fully paid basis, the shares closed at 409.5 pence on the first day of trading, which was equivalent to a 5 per cent premium. Retail investors were looking at a first-day premium of 7.8 per cent on a fully paid basis. As the UK stock mar-ket (as measured by the FT–SE 100 Index) fell by 0.3 per cent on 20 May Railtrack outperformed the market by 5.3 per cent during its first trading day. The fully paid premi-um on the first day of trading was the second lowest of all the major UK government IPOs, as shown in Exhibit 23;

* The share price held steady over 400 pence for the first two months of trading only to drop to 399 pence on 16 July 1996. This temporary drop should be seen in the con-text of a slightly falling market. At the time of Railtrack's all-time low on 16 July 1996 it had still outperformed the market by 6.5 per cent. Thereafter it began to rise steadi-

Exhibit 21

Investor concentration

	By demand	By allocation
Percentage of issue accounted for by the 10 largest investors (by total size of demand and allocation respectively)	21%	25%
Number of investors making up 80% of the issue (by total size of demand and allocation respectively)	185	129
The three largest investors by size	US$643 million US$497 million US$292 million	US$67 million US$67 million US$41 million
Total number of institutions	1,055	719

Source: SBC Warburg.

Exhibit 22

After-market price performance

Pricing date	17 May 1996
Institutional price range	350–390p
Institutional offer price	390p
Retail offer price	380p
First year high/low	
High (10 March 1997)	681.5p
Low (16 July 1996)	399p

Railtrack share price relative to FTSE 100 (%)

Absolute and relative price performance after pricing

	Price(pence) (Fully paid)	Relative to FT-SE 100 (%)
+ 1 day (20 May)	409.5	105.3
+ 3 days	409	105.5
+ 1 week	406	105.1
+ 1 month	405	104.6
+ 3 months	448	112.7
+ 6 months	504.5	124.8
+ 9 months)	583.5	135.2
+12 months	616.5	135.5

Sources: Datastream and offer circular.

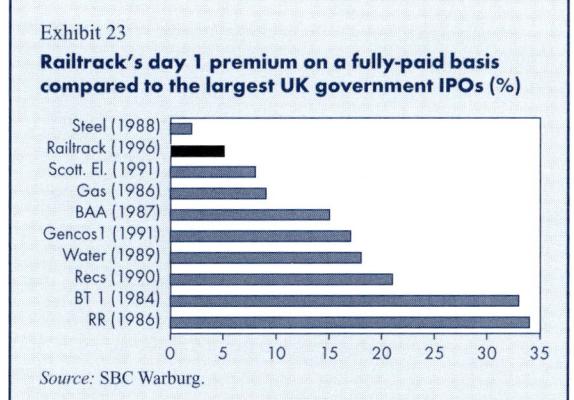

Exhibit 23

Railtrack's day 1 premium on a fully-paid basis compared to the largest UK government IPOs (%)

Source: SBC Warburg.

Exhibit 24

Percentage of total issue traded * (%)

	Day 1	Day 2	Day 3	Total: Day 1–3
London	38.4	4.5	5.8	48.7

* Based on the issue of 434.8 million shares.

Source: Datastream.

industry, the share price rose to 505 pence after six months, representing an increase of 29.5 per cent since privatisation and an outperformance of the FT–SE 100 of 25 per cent over the period; and

• After 12 months trading, and following a resounding success by the Labour Party in the general election, Railtrack stood at 617p, up 58 per cent since privatisation corresponding to a 35 per cent outperformance of a strong UK equity market. This performance was due to stronger than expected operating performance, reduced political uncertainty as the Labour party backtracked from its earlier policies 'to restore a publicly owned and publicly accountable UK railway industry'. There was, however considerable uncertainty as to the amount of windfall tax that Railtrack would have to pay. This tax, introduced by the Labour government, will be levied on those privatised utilities that are deemed to have achieved excess profits.

This after-market price performance is nothing short of spectacular – much better than had generally been expected either before or immediately after pricing.

After-market trading volume

Trading volume of 38.4 per cent of the total offer on the first day was large by most standards (see Exhibit 24).

There was considerable selling by retail investors in the immediate after-market, predictable selling by those institutions not allocated enough stock to build a core holding and the usual selling by speculative investors. After-market buyers included UK income funds which had not been satisfied in the allocation, UK institutions that had pre-committed to buying in the after-market and a few of the biggest US money managers. SBC Warburg accounted for around 46 per cent of first-day trading.

Over the first year, retail ownership fell to 34 per cent and UK institutional ownership increased from 27–53 per cent. US ownership had remained constant at approximately 9 per cent. Only two institutions had accumulated stakes larger than 3 per cent – Franklin Resources of the US owned 4 per cent and BAT Industries of the UK owned 3.3 per cent.

The performance of the main parties

The vendor

Although the DoT was responsible for the policy and implementation of this sale, the UK Treasury, responsible for gen-

ly in a generally strong equity market to reach 448 pence after three months, representing an outperformance of 13 per cent;

• Following the announcement of better than expected six-months' results, the fact that a further four franchises had been successfully transferred to the private sector (bringing the total to 17) and growing signs that the Labour Party appeared now to be less opposed to a privatised railway

eral privatisation policy, brought its extensive experience to bear, particularly on structuring. It remains responsible for secondary offers, whereas the various departments, as owners, handle government IPOs.

The DoT's negotiating team – a handful of civil servants under the leadership of Jenny Williams – did a commendable job in bringing such a complex privatisation to its conclusion on schedule. Although the pricing initially looked spot on, only six months after the float it began to look as if it would be added to the long list of underpriced UK Government IPOs. It is, however, difficult to see how Railtrack could have been priced at a much lower yield or how, given its heavy commitment to capital expenditure, it could have been given a weaker balance sheet. The DoT, together with its financial advisers, took the view at the time, that Railtrack could not be priced primarily on an earnings basis.

The appointment of Robert Horton, chairman of Railtrack, was a risky one given that his reputation was somewhat tainted as far as the City of London was concerned following his forced departure from BP under tumultuous circumstances. But it proved to be a government masterstroke as he was keen to succeed and in so doing restore his reputation. If this meant that he adopted a more reasonable negotiating position than might a traditional railway baron, this can hardly have been a bad thing. Industry barons always protected the integrity of their businesses and were opposed to any kind of break-up. Such an approach would obviously have rendered a Railtrack flotation impossible.

The overall BR privatisation was perhaps unnecessarily complex with 100 new companies and a separate lease for every station. Most of the parties needed their own lawyers to avoid conflicts of interest. 'In retrospect, we gave many of the contractual parties too much flexibility,' commented Williams. 'As a result, there were too many people playing shops, trying to substitute for the lack of market mechanism. We then began imposing strict deadlines for decisions and, if necessary, the decisions themselves. Ideally we would first have developed the master contracts and then got the parties to customise them, but there was not sufficient time so the processes had to proceed in parallel with, inevitably, some abortive effort.'

At ministerial level Sir George Young, transport secretary at the time of the float, made the Railtrack privatisation a reality. Richard Aitken-Davies explained: 'He created confidence about this privatisation; he was businesslike, there was no panic, he simply explained what had been done and what was going to happen and he reassured everyone that it would work. He was the Wakeham of the DoT.' This last comment refers to the crucial role that John Wakeham played in the electricity privatisation. Prime minister John Major deserves credit for his political courage in pushing through this highly controversial privatisation.

On a technical level the DoT deserves credit for deciding on a small syndicate, despite pressures to the contrary, which substantially facilitated the marketing and execution of the offer. The Treasury suggested putting in place a structure which allowed for an increase in the price range in case of strong momentum during bookbuilding. Although standard practice in corporate issues, this had never before been attempted in a major privatisation.

The company

Nobody within Railtrack had been through an exercise of this type before and management did not initially pull together as senior management was not uniformly enthusiastic about privatisation. The resolve of the top team was constantly challenged by a series of document leaks to the media. Only at a later stage when the objective was clearly in view did the team start to work coherently.

The members of senior management had complementary skills and did a good job on the roadshow. Bob Horton (knighted in the 1996 New Years honours list for services to the rail industry) had a strong drive and the vision to see Railtrack as a privatised company, extensive experience of running a public company and of doing business in the US. He was therefore effective in selling the Railtrack story to US fund managers. John Edmonds, CEO, was good at describing what was wrong with BR, what could be improved and how Railtrack could bring down its cost base. Finance director Norman Broadhurst made it credible that Railtrack would be run effectively as a publicly quoted company.

Management did not entirely achieve its objective on the capital structure, a reflection of its tough negotiations with the DoT. The result was a long-term single-A senior debt rating from the US rating agencies, below that of most of the other UK privatised utilities, with the exception of British Gas, which at the time was rated A3 by Moody's. Moody's justified its initial A2 rating of Railtrack in its June 1996 rating announcement as follows: 'The rating reflects the certainty and predictability of the company's revenue streams, Moody's expectations that the company will be able to manage its cost structure and a supportive regulatory environment. However, the rating also acknowledges the risks inherent in the enormity of the capital maintenance projects facing the company and the potential financial burdens that could ensue from the performance regimes, if the egregious condition of the rail infrastructure is not expeditiously improved. It also recognises the significant cultural shift that Railtrack personnel will have to undergo to adapt to the new structure of the sector and the political risks attendant upon its privatisation.'

The global coordinator

Jenny Williams of the DoT commented: 'SBC Warburg were very good at anticipating problems, both on our and their own behalf, which was most helpful as there was an unusually large number of things that could have gone wrong in this privatisation. Also, they got the pricing right, as evidenced by the small but very stable premium during the first month of secondary-market trading. This was achieved off the back of high-quality placement of the offer. SBC Warburg mastered the logistics and the internal communication of a very complex exercise.'

However, it is understood that there was not much love lost between the company and certain individuals within SBC Warburg. This might be a reflection of a number of things: first, SBC Warburg represented the seller, which was engaged in

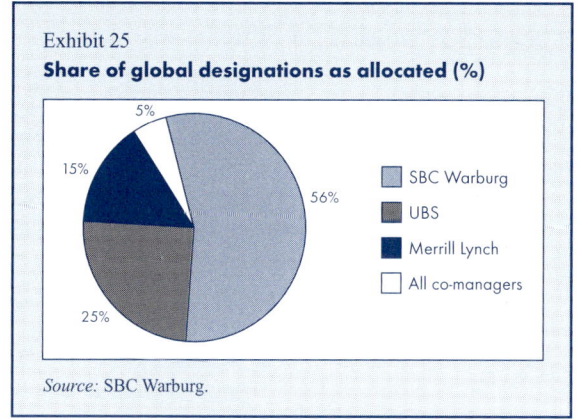

Exhibit 25
Share of global designations as allocated (%)

- SBC Warburg — 56%
- UBS — 25%
- Merrill Lynch — 15%
- All co-managers — 5%

Source: SBC Warburg.

tough negotiations with the company; second, the company management was initially ill-equipped to handle this type of complex exercise as it had not had similar experience in the past; third, some of the principal parties involved felt that there was a significant element of 'just-in-time management' on the part of SBC Warburg, although this is the way that much of the investment banking business works and it does put a lot of pressure on the parties involved; and fifth, this type of process is a tremendously tough one where all parties have to work extremely hard for a long period of time, and consequently there are bound to be some personality clashes.

SBC Warburg generated 70 per cent of total global institutional demand and accounted for 56 per cent of the designations (see Exhibit 25).

The fact that SBC Warburg accounted for 'only' 56 per cent of the designations shows that the system of taking orders and designating selling concessions works. Remarkably, it accounted for 90 per cent of total demand in the US. Julian Waldron noted: 'As evidenced by US designations, this offer demonstrated yet again that European firms do a better job selling European equities in the US than do US firms.' Having just bought Smith New Court, this was a chance for Merrill Lynch to prove its major strength in UK equities on an important privatisation. Yet it did not do so, as Michael Ryan, co-head of global ECM at Merrill Lynch explained: 'The concentration of allocations can sometimes result in aggregate numbers which, if not analysed further may be misleading in assessing the support and effort of syndicate members. The global institutional offer was, we understand, almost covered by the demand from two institutions with whom we might reasonably expect to be disadvantaged on designations. Within the US it is customary to see 90 per cent of orders go to the bookrunners. We understand that in this respect the US distribution of Railtrack was very much in line with precedent and expectations.'

Why was SBC Warburg hired as government adviser and global coordinator? It is an integrated house, with both advisory expertise and distribution skills; it had an impressive record in bookbuilt offers, on other privatisations in the UK and elsewhere, in the transportation industry and they made a good pitch. The selection criteria were many, but certainly included an assessment of the experience of the leading people on the team, their knowledge of the UK railway industry and how well the team acted together. The principal competition for

this mandate is thought to have come from Schroders/NatWest Markets, although there were several further credible pitches. Schroders was considered to have had particularly relevant experience as they handled the water privatisation, considered the most complex UK privatisation prior to BR.

Up to the time of SBC Warburg's appointment, Samuel Montagu had been the government's main rail privatisation adviser. Because of the close interaction between the various sale processes, the DoT held a competition with the mandate including, besides the Railtrack float, the role of advising on rail privatisation in general including other BR sales which SBC Warburg won. However, Christopher Clark of Samuel Montagu retained his role as personal adviser to the transport secretary and the bank continued to act as adviser to the franchising director.

The formal decision on the appointment of the financial adviser and global coordinator was taken by the transport minister, however he relied on the advice of a selection committee made up of officials from the DoT and the Treasury. The Treasury team was led by Steve Robson, director, Finance, Regulation and Industry at HM Treasury, who has extensive experience of the UK privatisation programme. The company was consulted about the government's choice of adviser but raised no objections.

Other parties

NM Rothschild made a positive contribution in educating Railtrack on the many issues involved. Richard Aitken-Davies commented: 'Rothschilds added intellectual fire-power to the Railtrack team in terms of how to respond to the government, in particular in the debate on the contractual matrix. They were also helpful in developing accounting standards, performance standards and generally in the process of setting up the company.' Norman Broadhurst of Railtrack added: 'There is no doubt that Rothschilds added very significant value to this privatisation.' There was however a question mark over NM Rothschild's definition of targets and deadlines, which tended to move with the flow of events and made timetable discipline more difficult.

Simmons and Simmons, Railtrack's legal adviser, had no relevant experience, which was a disadvantage given the extreme complexity of this privatisation, but they were able to deliver in the end.

Dewe Rogerson, the marketing and public relations consultants did an excellent job creating momentum in retail demand. This was achieved through market research, valuable input on the retail offer structure, targeted advertising campaigns and highly skilled management of the press. The financial press, which was unanimously sceptical six months before the float, ended by supporting the offer.

Key lessons learnt

Structural lessons

- Bookbuilding proved successful, as it helped the offer to be more tightly priced than would have been possible with a traditional fixed-price underwritten structure;

- In UK privatisations, unlike many UK corporate issues, all possible investor bases, including UK retail investors and institutional investors around the world, are tapped simultaneously creating demand tension. The Railtrack offer again proved the importance of the retail investor in privatisations: not only did UK retail investors (including those who participated in the retail tender) account for just over 50 per cent of the combined offer, but they also stimulated institutional investors around the world to participate because it became a virtual certainty during the course of the public offer that the overall offer would be a success;

- Richard Aitken-Davies noted: 'If you are going to restructure a major industry or bureaucracy it is important to break it up completely rather than leaving the old organisation around, as was the case with BR, since the remaining bureaucracy is likely to hinder rather than promote change';

- It might be thought that the owner and the management of a company would have the same interests in connection with an IPO but this is rarely the case. It is important to recognise this when appointing the board, management and advisers to the float and when structuring the flotation and the management incentive scheme. In most reward systems, management will benefit if the stock price rises from the flotation price. This means that management is likely to be cautious about prospects and will attempt to avoid a high offer price. Aitken-Davies stressed the importance of an incentive to management 'to try their hardest in terms of the quality of due diligence, a clear and well-written prospectus, a good investor presentation, and ultimately therefore the highest possible offer price'. He says: 'If the company itself is selling the shares or if there are incentives more directly linked to the offer price, then the interests of the vendor and the management will be more closely linked and the overall result better from the vendor's point of view';

- Non-US institutions are becoming used to the jump-ball system of compensating syndicate members in new issues. Under this system, the variable portion of the selling concession is designated to one or several of the banks/brokers who have marketed a particular stock to an institution, independently of the firm which takes the order and settles the trade. 'In Railtrack, we got 80–85 per cent of all the designation forms back from Europe, Japan and Asia, which proves that this system is beginning to be understood and appreciated by investors in these regions as much as in the US and in the UK,' said Waldron;

- Richard Aitken-Davies explained: 'Given how time-consuming a flotation project is, you do need a project organisation to handle most of the work, such that the line management can continue to run the business.'

Marketing lessons

- A stable and market-sensitive regulatory framework is needed in utility privatisations. On this occasion, the rail regulator was appointed well ahead of the float, giving two major advantages: first, it was possible to use him in the marketing, most notably in the case of the rail privatisation forum in January 1996, and second, it gave investors an opportunity to satisfy themselves about his approach to regulation. James Sassoon, managing director at SBC Warburg explained: 'Particularly following the experience of investors in the Gencos 2 sale, when the electricity regulator's actions led to an immediate fall in the after-market trading price of the shares, it was critical that investors were directly exposed to the rail regulator to get comfortable with his approach. The fact that investors heard from John Swift in this forum about his approach to rail regulation and derived considerable comfort from what they heard was critical to the success of the whole marketing campaign';

- A company without a long track record can be successfully floated, particularly if a reputable management is appointed. However, as the strong Railtrack after-market price performance has shown, this is not necessarily the best way of maximising the proceeds to the state;

- The right mixture of people in the management team is important for an IPO of any kind, and a major privatisation is no exception. The early appointment of the team is also of key significance, enabling them to get to know the business and build a track record. The former aspect was satisfactory in this case but the latter didn't work quite as well as it might have done;

- To build and maintain momentum in the marketing is paramount. One of the many ways in which SBC Warburg generated such momentum was to ensure that investors were entitled to the dividend in respect of the financial year ended March 1996, ie, attributable to an accounting period before the IPO. This was a clever marketing initiative that had only previously been used in the BT 3 secondary sale, where it did not have the same impact. Sassoon noted: 'The announcement of this dividend payment at the pathfinder prospectus launch, without any pre-publicity, caused a considerable stir. The beauty of it was that it got the final stage of the marketing off to a flying start without costing the government anything. The government got full value for the dividend as it was reflected in the yield calculations used by institutional investors in the book-building – yet the press, encouraged by politicians from the Labour Party, branded it a give-away';

- Skilful press management is critical, particularly in the UK, to the generation of retail investor interest in these privatisation offers. In what was perceived to be the UK's most difficult and controversial privatisation ever, the vendor and the advisers managed to reverse public opinion on the sale. Only six months before the IPO, few people believed that Railtrack would even be floated, let alone be a success;

- This case showed that a small syndicate can make the marketing much more effective and facilitate the education process both within the syndication and vis-à-vis the market. This is particularly important if, as in the case of Railtrack, the company story is complex; and

- Contrary to general belief prior to the flotation, it is possible to schedule the US roadshow early for non-US offers and achieve early US demand. Given the importance of the big US institutions, if early US demand is achieved, this can create tremendous momentum elsewhere.

Conclusion

Flotation of Railtrack

The flotation of Railtrack was a huge success for a number of reasons. The whole company was sold, rather than the 51 per cent initially indicated and it was sold on time, despite unprecedented complexities. The offer was broadly distributed: approximately 1.9 million retail investors registering against a target of 1.5 million. Some 665,000 retail investors applied, and eventually accounted for approximately 50 per cent of the total offer (including the retail tender, but before the exercise of the greenshoe). Approximately 90 per cent of Railtrack's employees became shareholders.

The total offer was seven times subscribed, priced at the top of the price range and at yields lower than those at which The National Grid Company and BT were trading. On the first day of trading, the shares closed at a premium of 5.3 per cent on a fully paid basis, making Railtrack the second most tightly priced of the top 10 UK government IPOs. For the first two to three months, Railtrack traded at only a small premium to the offer price.

The main factors contributing to the success of the IPO were: first, institutional investors believed in the robust nature of the new industry structure and Railtrack's future revenue base; second, the regulatory framework seemed relatively secure; third, the offer structure was flexible allowing momentum to be built and the syndicate was small; fourth, the management of Railtrack did a good job on the roadshow; fifth, SBC Warburg staged a highly comprehensive and successful marketing campaign; sixth, the marketing advisers managed to turn around the press which eventually supported the issue based on valuation and seventh; retail investors had done well on virtually all previous government IPOs. In addition, hard work and determination in many areas was of key significance. Railtrack's Broadhurst explained: 'Given how politically sensitive and generally unpopular this privatisation was at the outset, it was of paramount importance that our people believed that it would happen and pushed vigorously forward. But it was without a doubt the most mentally and physically draining process I have ever experienced.'

Over the first year of trading, Railtrack's fully paid shares increased by 58 per cent from the institutional offer price and in so doing outperformed a strong UK market by nearly 36 per cent. Despite having to pay the Labour government's windfall tax of £160 million over two years, equivalent to 47 per cent of the fiscal 1997 operating profit, by the end of July 1997 Railtrack's shares had traded above 800 pence – in just over 14 months, its market capitalisation had more than doubled.

The strong share price performance reflects an excellent operating performance for the year ended March 1997 (operating profits up 15 per cent on 1996 to £339 million on turnover of £2.4 billion). The operating performance was in fact slightly better than expected at the time of the flotation, not least because of bonuses earned under the performance regime which netted an extra £26 million. The strong share price also reflects a perception of reduced political and regulatory risk and an increasing realisation among institutional investors

that Railtrack is actually a growth stock, at least until 2001 when the regulator will adjust price regulation.

A further reason for the strong share price performance during the Spring and Summer of 1997 is that Railtrack and the regulator have settled their dispute over the amount of money that Railtrack will invest and Railtrack's network licence has been amended accordingly. It is committed to invest £16 billion over 10 years to maintain and upgrade its asset base and the regulator will have some powers to ensure that it delivers.

With the benefit of hindsight, it is hard to argue that the Railtrack IPO was not underpriced, however it is not obvious how SBC Warburg could have achieved a better price at the time. Perhaps some of the responsibility for conservative pricing lies with the Labour party. If the political and regulatory threat from Labour had been lower profile, then perhaps Railtrack could have been priced on an earnings rather than dividend yield basis and its excellent prospects could have been taken into account.

Although Railtrack has been heavily criticised for excessive profits and having fallen behind its investment plan, the new industry structure has worked better than expected. The performance regimes – including incentives and penalties, accountability to shareholders and regulator – have produced much better results than anyone had dared hope for. With respect to the criticism of slower than expected investments, Broadhurst explained: 'Under the old regime, the planning was so bad that there simply were not enough developed projects on which capital could be spent. This is perhaps mind-boggling given how huge the under-investment had been but represents best testimony to the way things used to be managed at BR.' Railtrack increased its investment by 29 per cent in the financial year ended 1997, which was more than it was committed to.

Given the odds for success and the unpopularity of this privatisation, the IPO was a remarkable achievement. Railtrack still has some way to go before it has become a truly market-oriented organisation – it would be wholly unreasonable to expect a formerly state-owned monopoly run by engineers and civil servants to adjust in a year.

Privatisation of BR

A year after Railtrack's flotation, almost 100 per cent of BR, including the 25 TOCs, had been sold to the private sector.

Critics have said that there was no mechanism to provide investment, the franchise period is too short (seven years), competition doesn't work, service is still bad, and safety will be compromised. The whole arrangement may have been unnecessarily complex and some companies may have been sold off far too cheaply, in particular the rolling stock leasing companies, but there is an increasing body of evidence that suggests that the BR privatisation will work out well:

- *Investment:* A simplified decision-making process is beginning to show results. Railtrack has embarked on a £10 billion capital expenditure programme – £8.3 billion will be spent on renewing existing infrastructure including stations, and £1.9 billion will be spent on major projects to enhance the network, most notably the West Coast Main Line and the Thameslink 2000 projects. The rail regulator has significant powers to enforce these commitments. The 25 TOCs have committed to spend a further £1.5 billion under their franchise agreements, principally on new rolling stock. Much of this investment activity is already under way;

- *Service quality:* Punctuality and reliability are increasing as Railtrack and the TOCs are subjected to the performance regimes. Delays fell by 30 per cent in 1997 and both Railtrack and the TOCs as a group earned bonuses as they improved compared with the performance standards. At the same time journey times have been cut, a trend which is expected to gather momentum with the delivery of new rolling stock. Despite continued complaints about services provided by the train enquiry bureaux and ticketing offices, passenger traffic is up sharply on a number of lines. Some operators, most notably in the south of England, have performed badly but corrective measures from the regulator have proven effective. Overall, passenger complaints fell by 40 per cent during the 1997 financial year, reversing a 13-year trend of an increasing number of complaints each year. Only the most dogmatic anti-privatisers will deny that standards are likely to improve when people as dynamic as Richard Branson, the British entrepreneur behind Virgin Atlantic Airways, are involved as franchisees;

- *Safety:* After four successive years of safety improvements, 1996–1997 maintained the trend. This is a considerable achievement, particularly as the whole railway industry has been radically restructured;

- *Competition:* There was intense competition for the 25 passenger franchises, a strong endorsement by private enterprise of the industry. Although the level of competition will be limited until 1999, thereafter competition is expected to increase as new operating licences are granted. There is already some direct competition on certain lines, indeed price wars between operators have broken out on several lines. The new railway entrepreneurs consider their competition to come from cars, coaches and air travel and there are signs that the railways will soon be in a position to take market share on inter-city routes; and

- *Cost to the state:* According to the office of the rail franchising director annual support from the taxpayer for the railways will fall over the six years to March 2003 from in excess of £2.1 billion to just over £900 million. This is due to keen competition for the 25 passenger franchises, where the bidders have competed on the basis of the annual subsidy required to take on operation of a particular service. Although the gross cost to the taxpayer increased prior to privatisation due to the need to pay dividends to

Railtrack shareholders (via the access charges paid by the TOCs), the cost of running privatised train services will be significantly lower than under BR. Given that the franchising contracts set out how much the state will pay per annum (as well as how much the franchisees will eventually pay to the state) until the end of the franchising period, there is a high level of predictability in the annual budget requirements.

Private owners have a long way to go before winning over public opinion, as decades of under-investment in a £11 billion business, poor punctuality and reliability cannot be reversed over night. Finding out when trains run and reserving seats remains difficult but this problem is being addressed. It is only by investing more to enhance service standards and safety, by improving customer orientation and cost awareness that the privatised railways will obtain the public's support and escape a much tougher regulatory regime under the new Labour government. The rail regulator and the franchising director will remain vigilant in the way that they monitor performance, and enforce licence conditions and franchising agreements. They have increasingly sophisticated computer systems to do so, and they have both the carrot and the stick needed to ensure effective regulation.

Unfortunately, if prior UK privatisations are anything to go by, even if a privatised railway proves to be both a financial success and service quality is drastically improved, it does not mean that it will turn out to be a political success. Despite privatisation proceeds of over £60 billion under the Tories, and the fact that annual subsidies to nationalised firms of £300 million during 1980–82 were reversed to annual proceeds from tax and dividends from the same firms from 1987–95 of £4.8 billion, and that gas and telecom prices to the consumer have fallen by 40–50 per cent in real terms since privatisation, privatisation in the UK is still not popular with the public (*Economist,* 22 February 1997). A 1995 MORI poll showed that only 20 per cent of the population wanted more privatisation compared to a third who wanted more nationalisation.

This unpopularity of privatisation among the public, often based on emotions and perceptions rather than hard facts, may disappear with the Tories out of government and as the real benefits become increasingly apparent. There is more than a fair chance that Labour will be able to take considerable credit if they do not meddle with the structures that are currently in place.

Feature topic: *The role of the marketing adviser: an interview with Cary Martin, CEO of Dewe Rogerson*

In large equity issues, particularly when there is an emphasis on retail placement, marketing and public relations consultants increasingly work side by side with the investment banks and other advisers.

The development of marketing and public relations consultancy in Europe is attributed in particular to two developments. First, the birth of 'popular capitalism' in the UK with the first sale of shares in British Telecom in

1984 and second, the emergence of the hostile takeover game in the mid- to late 1980s which meant that marketing advisers began to be recognised as potentially valued consultants to senior management, as directors of companies involved in contested takeovers came to realise that their stock price could be influenced by the media.

Dewe Rogerson is a consultancy which operates across the complete spectrum of marketing techniques, with emphasis on investor relations; media relations; public relations; market research; shareholder identification; financial and corporate advertising; annual report and literature design and employee communications. To date it has been employed as marketing and public relations advisers to about 90 per cent, by value, of the UK government's public share sales and from that base increasingly diversified internationally. To find out how such agencies add value in the world's privatisation programmes, the author met with Cary J. Martin, CEO of Dewe Rogerson.

JRL: How do you add value to your clients?

CJM: By researching in advance of the offers what the attitudes among the public are towards buying specific companies and then being able to advise the vendor on likely demand. With the outcome of the market research at hand, we can recommend offer structures and retail incentive schemes to maximise demand from retail investors and advise on the required campaign structure, timetable and marketing expenditure. As a successful retail offer is typically a prerequisite for a successful institutional tranche, we feel that we play a key role in these big offers.

If you take, for example, the UK, our expertise on the retail side is unique, as the merchant banks do not have access to retail clients (other than the numerically very small number of wealthy private clients) and the commercial banks have typically acted only as receiving banks, although their stockbroking arms are now becoming more active as share shops in some recent offers. This is where we come in: on the basis of our market research, we devise the appropriate marketing campaign and overall media strategy. Moreover, our expertise is based upon extensive international experience with global offers, particularly involving retail offers, and this is probably wider than that of any investment bank or any of the local domestic banks. In addition to our privatisation experience in the UK, we have been involved in the majority of the major European privatisation programmes. Experience is essential but we never pre-suppose that we can take a structure that worked in one country and automatically employ it in another country. We first have to test these ideas by extensive research in each individual market.

JRL: Is that what happened in the case of ENI 1 in Italy, with the retail indemnification scheme?

CJM: Yes that is precisely what happened. As Repsol was a huge success in Spain, it was assumed that the retail indemnification scheme would also work in Italy. But it didn't, due to the fact that the Italian retail market is very different from the Spanish one. Italian investors were mistrustful of something that looked too good to be true. Therefore, they became suspicious about the need for this indemnification scheme and felt that there had to be a trick. There was a view among some retail investors that the government had introduced the reimbursement scheme because it expected the share price to fall. It therefore had the effect of creating a loss of confidence in the offer rather than doing what it was supposed to do, ie, creating protection against stock market volatility. Accordingly the scheme was not used in the secondary offer in 1996, for which a new incentive structure was developed involving the issuance of bonus shares after 12 months (the first time that bonus shares had been issued within 12 months in any European offer) and a discount for retail investors (the first time this has been used in Italy). The offer was a great success. It was by far the largest Italian retail offer to date and the global offer raised US$5.9 billion.

JRL: What was your role in the early days of the UK privatisation programme?

CJM: Although we were first appointed by the UK government in connection with the 1981 privatisation by public share sale of Cable & Wireless, it was with the first sale of shares in British Telecom in 1984 that there was a major breakthrough in the marketing of privatisations. Kleinwort Benson had advised the government that its objective of selling 51 per cent of BT was not achievable if the shares were only marketed in the domestic institutional capital market. For political reasons, the government was not prepared to rely too heavily on the international market and a third market had therefore to be found: the UK retail market. Without the retail investor a £4 billion sale would not have been possible. But could the British public, who had not been significant investors in the equity market for decades, be galvanised into buying British Telecom shares? We devised a two-stage national marketing campaign with the focus on buying a part of British Telecom, not buying shares *per se*. This campaign was the result of comprehensive market research. Following our appointment in November 1983, we carried out a national poll through MORI, from which we learnt the important lesson that the British public was in general not interested in buying shares. Buying shares was 'not for us but rather for them' (ie, the affluent people who already had cosy client-broker relationships). This attitude was also evidenced by the statistics, which showed a steady decline in UK public share ownership. Before BT1 only some two million Britons (or 5 per cent of the adult population) owned shares. Our research, however, also showed that the British public might be interested in buying a part of British Telecom, an institution with which they came in daily contact. It was like buying a part of the national heritage. This revelation, perhaps more than any other, revolutionised the privatisation game. We were able to identify a core group or a target audience of the six million people most likely to buy a portion of their national telephone company. Before the marketing campaign, only some 16 per cent had an interest in buying BT shares. Following extensive corporate awareness and offer campaigns, at a total cost to the government of around £20 million (of which £10 million was spent on the corporate campaign and £10 million on the offer campaign), interest in BT shares soared to 27 per cent by November 1984. As a direct result of the marketing campaign, some two million people bought BT shares and in the process, the number of shareholders in the UK nearly doubled to four million.

JRL: What is your perspective on the Railtrack privatisation?

CJM: Railtrack was certainly one of the most challenging privatisations we have been involved in. The British public were very sentimental about the railways, but they loathed British Rail. They ought to have welcomed privatisation, because privatisation should lead to an improvement in quality and performance. The reality, however, was that they were not supportive, primarily because they did not believe that privatisation would lead to anything other than more closures and an even worse service. We decided upfront that to try and sell the case for privatisation was not going to work. The intellectual justification for rail privatisation had been lost and it was only going to be credible when it was completed and the public could see improved performance.

Consequently, we focused purely on the financial arguments. It was a long process as everyone's starting point was emotional, but once legislation was passed and it was accepted, albeit grudgingly, that privatisation was a reality, then commentators and investors were prepared to listen.

The success of the marketing was based on a number of factors, but three stand out. The first was the way in which the Department of Transport and its financial advisers had structured Railtrack's financials, which effec-

tively gave it a guaranteed income stream. The second was the selling effort put in by the Railtrack management, who particularly impressed investors with their presentations. The third was the decision to pay investors who bought in the offer the final dividend for 1995–1996, even though they only purchased the shares after the end of that financial year. The payment of this dividend in October 1996, and the fact that the issue was partly paid meant that investors received an effective first-year return of 25 per cent, making it a very attractive proposition. This combination of a well structured income stream, a strong management team and a clever piece of financial engineering resulted in one of the most successful privatisations of the 1990s.

JRL: What are the particular investment characteristics that attract retail investors?

CJM: You can only generalise to a certain extent, but the most important investment characteristics are:

- Perception of security (including a large size company and an apparently small risk of bankruptcy);
- Perceived profitability; and
- Awareness/understanding of the business and the investment case.

As far as the actual purchase decision is concerned, it varies from country to country, but the following are generally the most important:

- Perception of scarcity (the feeling that this is an investment that everyone else, whether they be professional investors, or family and friends, is also interested in);
- Recommendation by the relevant financial adviser (eg, the bank staff/financial advisers); and
- The opinion expressed by the financial media.

Feature topic: *Key facts of the Tory Privatisation Programme*

During consecutive Tory governments from 1979 to 1997, the UK government sold companies worth £61 billion, much more than in any other country. (See Exhibits 26, 27 and 28.)

Price performance of UK goverment IPOs

Exhibit 29 shows that of 11 major UK government IPOs, seven outperformed and four under-performed the UK market from the time of flotation to the end of 1996.

Exhibit 26

UK privatisations by public offers, 1981–1996

Company/privatisation	Date of offer	*Total size of privatisation (£ millions)	Type of offer	% sold	% retained by public sector
British Aerospace	February 1981	149	IPO	52	48
Cable & Wireless	October 1981	224	IPO	50	50
Amersham International	February 1982	71	IPO	100	0
Britoil	November 1982	549	IPO	51	49
Assoc. British Ports	February 1983	22	IPO	52	48
BP	September 1983	566	Secondary	7	32
Cable & Wireless	December 1983	275	Secondary	27	23
Assoc. British Ports	April 1984	52	Secondary	48	0
Enterprise Oil	June 1984	392	IPO	100	0
Jaguar	July 1984	297	IPO	99	1
BT 1	November 1984	3,916	IPO	51	49
British Aerospace	May 1985	551	Secondary	48	0
Britoil	August 1985	449	Secondary	49	0
Cable & Wireless	December 1985	933	Secondary	23	0
British Gas	December 1986	5,434	IPO	97	3
British Airways	February 1987	892	IPO	100	0
Rolls-Royce	May 1987	1,348	IPO	100	0
British Airports Authority	July 1987	1,225	IPO	96	0
BP	October 1987	6,906	Secondary	32	1.8
British Steel	December 1988	2,500	IPO	100	0
Water Companies	December 1989	5,113	IPO	100	0
Regional Electricity	December 1990	5,182	IPO	100	0
Electricity Generation 1	March 1991	2,228	IPO	60	40
Scottish Electricity	June 1991	2,918	IPO	100	0
BT 2	December 1991	5,403	Secondary	26	22
NI Electricity	June 1993	348	IPO	96	4
BT 3	July 1993	5,335	Secondary	22	0
Electricity Generation 2	March 1995	3,670	Secondary	40	0
BP	December 1995	514	Block Sale	1.8	0
BAA	January 1996	145	Block Sale	2.9	0
Railtrack	May 1996	1,930	IPO	100	0
British Energy	July 1996	1,408	IPO	88	12
AEA Technology	September 1996	215	IPO	100	0
British Energy	December 1996	118	Block Sale	12	0
Total proceeds		**61,278**			

*Note that before the BA privatisation in February 1987, the numbers were net proceeds. After and including the BA privatisation the amounts are gross amounts, ie, not net of costs.

Sources: HM Treasury, Capital Data Ltd and prospectuses.

Exhibit 27

Financial advisers and global coordinators of UK public offers (Dec 1991 – Sept 1996)

Company/privatisation	Date	Government financial adviser(s)	Company adviser(s)	Global coordinator(s)
BT 2	December 1991	SG Warburg	NM Rothschild	SG Warburg
NI Electricity	May 1992	NM Rothschild	BZW	Hoare Govett
BT 3	July 1993	SG Warburg	NM Rothschild	SG Warburg
Electricity Generation 2	March 1995	BZW Kleinwort Benson	Schroders (NP) SG Warburg (PG) Goldman Sachs (PG)	BZW Kleinwort Benson
Railtrack	May 1996	SBC Warburg	NM Rothschild	SBC Warburg
British Energy	July 1996	BZW	Lazard Brothers	BZW
AEA Techn.	September 1996	Schroders	Lazard Brothers	Cazenove

Sources: HM Treasury and prospectuses.

Exhibit 28

Financial advisers and lead brokers of UK public offers (February 1981 – June 1991)

Company/privatisation	Date	Financial adviser to the government and lead underwriter	Lead broker	Company adviser
British Aerospace	February 1981	Kleinwort Benson	Hoare Govett	Kleinwort Benson
Cable & Wireless	October 1981	Kleinwort Benson	Cazenove	Kleinwort Benson
Amersham	February 1982	NM Rothschild	Cazenove	Morgan Grenfell
Britoil	November 1982	SG Warburg	Rowe & Pitman	NM Rothschild
Assoc. British Ports	February 1983	Schroders	Greenwell	Kleinwort Benson
BP	September 1983	SG Warburg	Mullens	SG Warburg
Cable & Wireless	December 1983	SG Warburg	Mullens	SG Warburg
Assoc. British Ports	April 1984	Schroders	Greenwell	Kleinwort Benson
Enterprise Oil	June 1984	Kleinwort Benson	Cazenove	Lazard Brothers
BT	November 1984	Kleinwort Benson	Hoare Govett	SG Warburg
British Aerospace	May 1985	Lazard Brothers	Hoare Govett	Kleinwort Benson
Britoil	August 1985	Lazard Brothers	Hoare Govett	NM Rothschild
Cable & Wireless	December 1985	Schroders	Rowe & Pitman	Kleinwort Benson
British Gas	December 1986	NM Rothschild	Cazenove	Kleinwort Benson
British Airways	February 1987	Hill Samuel	Cazenove	Lazard Brothers
Rolls-Royce	May 1987	Samuel Montagu	James Capel	NM Rothschild
British Airports	July 1987	County NatWest	Cazenove	Schroders
BP	October 1987	NM Rothschild	Hoare Govett	SG Warburg
British Steel	December 1988	Samuel Montagu	Rowe & Pitman	BZW
Water Companies	December 1989	Schroders	Rowe & Pitman	NM Rothschild
Regional Electricity	December 1990	Kleinwort Benson	James Capel	NM Rothschild
Electricity Generation 1	March 1991	Kleinwort Benson	James Capel	Lazard Brothers (NP) SG Warburg (PG)
Scottish Electricity	June 1991	BZW	de Zoete & Bevan	Charterhouse (SE) Samuel Montagu and Noble Grossart (SP)

Sources: HM Treasury and prospectuses.

Exhibit 29

Price performance of principal UK privatisations (cumulative absolute and relative performance at year-end related to offer price) (%)

Privatisation	1984	1985	1986	1987	1988	1989	1990	1991	1992	1993	1994	1995	1996
BT (Nov-84)	43	78	66	71	97	138	118	153	210	263	190	172	197
Rel FT–SE 100	38	59	24	26	46	33	37	42	69	74	31	-40	-40
Gas (Dec-86)	N/A	N/A	11	21	17	76	67	96	116	153	133	88	62
Rel FT–SE 100	N/A	N/A	7	15	6	25	34	42	40	41	43	-40	-85
BA (Feb-87)	N/A	N/A	N/A	16	28	82	14	85	147	275	198	289	389
Rel FT–SE 100	N/A	N/A	N/A	25	32	53	1	52	95	293	135	192	276
Rolls-Royce (May-87)	N/A	N/A	N/A	-31	-22	8	-6	-26	-32	-2	8	14	43
Rel FT–SE 100	N/A	N/A	N/A	-8	-3	-2	-3	-38	-60	-56	-30	-53	-36
BAA (Jul-87)	N/A	N/A	N/A	-4	10	56	69	117	221	332	286	296	294
Rel FT–SE- 100	N/A	N/A	N/A	23	33	52	78	110	199	285	255	238	223
BSteel (Dec-88)	N/A	N/A	N/A	N/A	1	8	-6	-45	-54	1	23	30	34
Rel FT–SE- 100	N/A	N/A	N/A	N/A	-1	-29	-27	-86	-115	-93	-51	-79	-91
Water (Dec-89)	N/A	N/A	N/A	N/A	N/A	25	39	38	107	159	126	168	174
Rel FT–SE 100	N/A	N/A	N/A	N/A	N/A	21	48	32	87	113	96	111	104
Recs (Dec-90)	N/A	N/A	N/A	N/A	N/A	N/A	19	44	92	184	235	221	198
Rel FT–SE 100	N/A	N/A	N/A	N/A	N/A	N/A	21	30	62	128	195	152	115
Gencos (Mar-91)	N/A	N/A	N/A	N/A	N/A	N/A	N/A	29	63	194	193	181	189
Rel FT–SE 100	N/A	N/A	N/A	N/A	N/A	N/A	N/A	27	47	155	168	131	127
Railtrack (May-96)	N/A	N/A	N/A	N/A	N/A	N/A	N/A	N/A	N/A	N/A	N/A	N/A	38
Rel FT–SE 100	N/A	N/A	N/A	N/A	N/A	N/A	N/A	N/A	N/A	N/A	N/A	N/A	33
BE (Jun-96)	N/A	N/A	N/A	N/A	N/A	N/A	N/A	N/A	N/A	N/A	N/A	N/A	22
Rel FT–SE 100	N/A	N/A	N/A	N/A	N/A	N/A	N/A	N/A	N/A	N/A	N/A	N/A	16

Sources: Datastream and prospectuses .

Repsol

The secondary offer of Repsol shares by Spanish government agency Instituto Nacional Hidrocarburos in April 1995 was the largest privatisation ever to have taken place in Spain, and the largest equity issue in Spanish history. At the time, the deal represented the third largest equity offer from the European oil and gas industry.

This was Repsol's fourth privatisation offer (following the 1989 IPO, the 1992 domestic exchangeable bond offer and the 1993 institutional equity offer). It came in the wake of a string of unsuccessful European privatisations and was, by contrast, a huge success. A further highly successful fifth transaction for Repsol came to the market in early 1996 and a sixth and last privatisation sale was executed in 1997.

Repsol was the first company to be subjected to the new Spanish law of 1995 on golden shares, through which the government retains its power of decree on certain important decisions even when its ownership falls below 15 per cent. The decree was enacted in early 1996.

Of Repsol's 1995 offer, 63 per cent was placed domestically, more than any previous Spanish privatisation equity offer. The entire offer could easily have been absorbed by Spanish retail investors.

The transaction employed a number of ground-breaking techniques to stimulate retail investor demand including: purchase mandates, money-back guarantees and variable commissions.

Repsol is a relatively rare example of a company where the vendor has allowed the company management to play a major role in the offer process – a strategy which has undoubtedly paid handsome dividends.

The entire Repsol offer was fully underwritten at a fixed price, in that the vendor was guaranteed a minimum offer price. Ultimately, the vendor captured the full upside, using bookbuilding to set the final offer price. Bookbuilding had been introduced by Goldman Sachs in connection with the 1993 Repsol offer and was to be fully accepted in this instance although there had been some resistance to it in the earlier sale. Dante Roscini, managing director of Goldman Sachs, recalls that the head of equity capital markets at one of the Spanish banks was horrified when he was asked to disclose the names of its investors: 'He thought we asked only him to provide the names of his investors and he told me this was like asking him to go naked to a party. It was okay to do so if everyone else did, but not if he was the only one.'

The Repsol issue of 1995 was the first time that a Spanish bank had conducted a poll to ascertain the particular concerns felt most strongly by retail investors. Whereas the BBV sponsored campaign was designed primarily to address the structuring of the offer, Repsol itself also carried out extensive market research in order to tailor its company advertising campaign to specific investor concerns.

The Telefónica and ENI offers later in 1995 were almost carbon copies of the Repsol 1995 transaction, except for the significant structuring inconsistency in the Telefónica offer which prevented the clawback provision from being fully exercised.

Given the many innovations in this transaction, communication to the market about the rationale for the changes became an unusually significant issue: this is an area in which Repsol excels.

Exhibit 1

Transaction summary

Issuer name: Repsol SA (Spain)	*Global coordinators:* Goldman Sachs & BBV
Pricing date: 10 April 1995 (Madrid SE: 276.6)	*Pricing/underwriting structure:* Fixed price underwriting below market, combined open-price offer for retail and institutional bookbuilding
Vendor: Instituto Nacional Hidrocarburos	*Primary or secondary:* Secondary
	Retail structure: Retail discount, money-back guarantee
% of company sold: 19%	*Privatisation or corporate:* Privatisation
IPO or non-IPO: Non-IPO	*Industry:* Oil and gas
Type of shares: Ordinary shares and ADR (1 ADR = 1 ordinary share)	*Institutional offer price:* Pta3,620 and US$28.83/ADR *Retail offer price:* Pta3,448
Total issue size: US$1.67 billion	*US listing/144 A:* NYSE listing

Exhibit 2
Distribution by domestic and international markets (by final allocation)

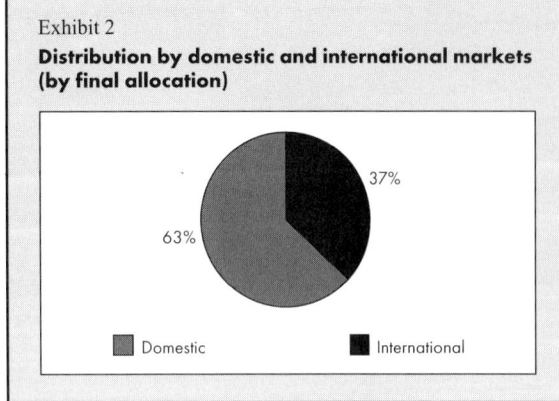

37%

63%

■ Domestic   ■ International

Major challenges

Equity and currency market conditions were extremely volatile at the time of the Repsol sale as the local equity market had been hit by rising interest rates and political troubles falling by 25 per cent from its peak in early 1993. Some international investors had relegated Spain to emerging-market status or withdrawn their investments altogether while the foreign exchange markets were highly volatile and the peseta was under pressure.

By the time Repsol decided to go ahead with its offer on 23 February 1995, the two most recent Spanish privatisation offers, for Endesa and Argentaria, were trading 12 per cent and 31 per cent below their respective offer prices. Confidence among Spanish retail investors was shattered and several major global offers were postponed or downsized during the Repsol marketing period. The majority of the large European privatisations traded substantially below issue price (eg, BCI 38 per cent, Rhone-Poulenc 20 per cent, UAP 17 per cent and the UK generators 11 per cent).

This offer had been postponed at least twice, creating an overhang in the equity market and depressing the Repsol share price. Oscar Fanjul, Repsol's chairman at the time of the sale noted: 'A secondary transaction is always a bit of a challenge because you are supposed to price the transaction 'at market'. You don't want the price to fall too much during the months and weeks leading up to the transaction and, consequently, you have to go out and create a lot of extra demand during the roadshow.'

Rationale and objectives

Why did the offer take place?

The privatisation of Repsol represents an important part of the Spanish privatisation programme. Not only did this Repsol offer net the Treasury Pta200billion (US$1.67billion) of valuable privatisation proceeds, it also revived the entire programme of asset sales. Furthermore, in a speech marking the launch of the transaction, Alfredo Pastor, minister for the economy in the socialist government, conceded that: 'State-control of industry was not the most efficient way of operating,' something that had hitherto not been officially stated by the Spanish government.

The principal objectives were:

- To cover the budgetary needs of the Spanish Treasury;
- To maximise the proceeds to INH;
- To reduce INH's holding in the company to 25 per cent;
- To reduce the overhang in Repsol shares and the associated valuation discount;
- To procure broad support for the offer from the domestic retail market;
- To broaden and deepen the international institutional shareholder base; and
- To achieve a highly successful offer to reaffirm Repsol as a world-class oil and gas company.

Share capital and ownership

See Exhibits 3 and 4.

Exhibit 3
Share capital and ownership

Type of shares offered	Ordinary bearer shares of Pta500 (capital stock)
Ownership restrictions	Although not applicable to this transaction, Repsol would be subject to new golden share legislation that enabled the government to decree the terms of certain transactions when the state's ownership fell below 15%.
Share capital before and after offer	300 million ordinary shares
Listings	First listed in Spain and New York in May 1989
Market capitalisation at offer price (Pta125.57/US$1)	US$8.65 billion
Number of shareholders before offer	Approximately 220,000
Liquidity (number of shares traded during the 12 months to pricing expressed per market as a percentage of the total number of shares outstanding)	53% in Madrid/25% on NYSE • 2nd most liquid stock on the Madrid Stock Exchange in 1994 (in absolute money terms); • 3rd largest by market capitalisation at the end of 1994.
Most relevant stock exchange index/weighting	IBEX 35 (35 most liquid stocks)/9.7% (early 1995)

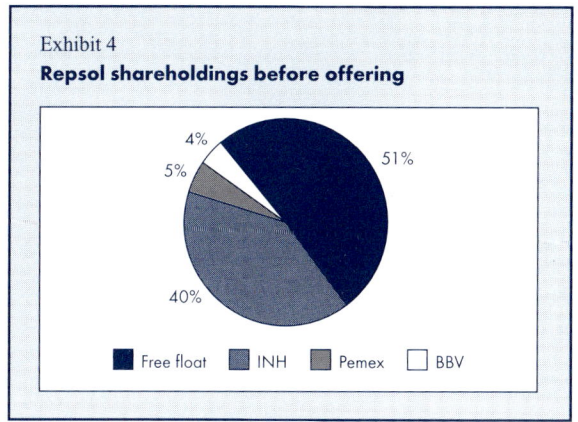

Exhibit 4
Repsol shareholdings before offering

51%
4%
5%
40%

■ Free float ■ INH ■ Pemex □ BBV

Transaction components

The offer, initially of 40.5 million outstanding shares, representing 13.5 per cent of Repsol's capital, comprised a domestic retail offer, a sale of shares to employees, a US SEC-registered offer, and an international institutional offer comprising separate tranches for the UK, continental Europe, Spain, and the rest of the world (see Exhibit 5).

The vendor granted the underwriters a greenshoe option of 4.5 million additional shares to be exercised by the joint global coordinators should demand warrant it. There was no formal clawback in favour of the retail offer, although the underwriters had the option to move stock freely between the international and retail offers.

The combined offer was fully underwritten at a fixed price, corresponding to a considerable discount to the market price on the day it became effective. The discount was set by quantifying the risk as 1 per cent per day for the eight-day period until the offer price was fixed. The vendor retained the full upside for the entire offer by employing bookbuilding.

In order to get the crucial early read on the progress of the retail offer, a so-called mandate period was introduced, a first for the Spanish market. During this period, open-price marketing to retail investors was to take place allowing them to place purchase mandates with their bank branches. Those retail investors which put in their purchase mandates during this period were given priority in the allocation. After the end of the period, a maximum retail offer price was fixed, whereafter the five-day subscription period, the *oferta pública de venta* (OPV) followed.

The institutional and retail offer prices were to be fixed on the same day, 10 April with the institutional offer price being fixed with reference to the market closing price on the pricing date. The retail offer price was to be set as the lowest of: the maximum retail price; the weighted average share price on the pricing date (less a 5 per cent discount): and the institutional offer price. Both the retail and international offers were thus marketed on an open-price basis.

Another significant incentive introduced in the Repsol share sale came in the form of a 10 per cent 'money-back guarantee' for retail investors. Under this indemnification scheme, INH undertook to reimburse retail investors who held the shares for a period of 12 months from the offer date if at that time Repsol's share price were lower than the retail offer price, subject to a maximum reimbursement of 10 per cent of that price. The reference price for reimbursement would be the weighted average price of Repsol shares during the last 20 trading days of the 12-month period after the issue.

In view of the volatile stock market environment, the initial sizing of the transaction was deliberately conservative. The success of the retail offer, established during the first few days of the mandate period, allowed the retail offer to be increased by 12 million shares. That increase, combined with the exercise of the 4.5 million greenshoe option (representing 22 per cent of the institutional portion of the combined offer as originally sized), meant that a total of 57 million shares were issued under the transaction.

Principal advisers
See Exhibit 7.

Transaction fee distribution
See Exhibit 8.

Exhibit 5
Offer structure

Target markets	Indicated tranche sizes*	Regional bookrunning lead managers	Co-lead managers
Retail offer	42.0%	Argentaria. Caja de Madrid, BBV, BCH, BSN	N/A
Employee offer	7.4%	N/A	N/A
US offer	21.0%	Goldman Sachs	CSFB, Merrill Lynch, Morgan Stanley, Howard Weil
International offer			
UK	12.3%	SG Warburg, BSN	BBV, Goldman Sachs, Kleinwort Benson
Continental Europe	7.4%	Paribas, Argentaria	BBV, Deutsche, Goldman Sachs, UBS
RoW	2.5%	CSFB	Daiwa, Goldman Sachs
Spain	7.4%	BCH	Argentaria, BBV, BSN, Caja de Madrid
Total combined offers (shares)	**40,500,000**		

* Percentage of indicated combined offer on 20 March 1995.

Exhibit 6
The timetable

23 February 1995	• Decision to go ahead with the offer.
20 March	• Filing with US SEC; and • European warm-ups (meetings between the equity research analysts of the lead manager and the most important institutional accounts) begin.
21 March	• Retail 'mandate period' begins.
24 March	• European warm-ups end.
25 March	• New privatisation law approved by parliament.
27 March	• European roadshow and US warm-ups begin; and • Bookbuilding begins.
31 March	• Government authorisation to increase the offer from 45 to a maximum of 57 million shares; • European roadshow and US warm-ups ended; and • Retail mandate period ends.
2 April	• Increase of the Spanish retail offer; and • Initial underwriting agreement signed fixing minimum price for the vendor.
3 April	• Maximum retail price fixed at Pta3,585 per share; • OPV begins; and • US roadshow begins.
5 April	• End of the cancellation period, until which date purchase mandates could be revoked.
7 April	• OPV closes; and • US roadshow ends.
8 April	• Initial allocation meeting between the vendor, the company, the global coordinators and the tranche lead managers at Goldman Sachs' offices.
10 April	• End of bookbuilding; • Institutional and the final retail offer prices fixed after NYSE closes; • Underwriting at offer price effective and final underwriting agreement signed; and • Allocation takes place overnight.
11 April	• Trading begins.
12 April	• Greenshoe is exercised.

Exhibit 7
Principal advisers

Financial adviser to INH and Repsol	Lazard Brothers
US legal adviser to INH and Repsol	Davis Polk & Wardwell
Spanish legal adviser to INH and Repsol	Uria & Menendez
US legal adviser to the underwriters	Sullivan & Cromwell
Auditors	Arthur Andersen

Exhibit 8
Distribution of gross spread (%)

Management fee	Underwriting fee	Selling concession	Gross spread	Discount	Total effective cost
0.60	0.60	1.80	3.0	0	3.0

Source: Offer circular.

Management fee

Goldman Sachs and BBV shared 25 per cent of the total management fee as the global coordinators' praecipium calculated on the gross proceeds of the combined offer. Outside the US, the lead and co-lead managers shared a further 25 per cent of this fee as the lead and co-lead managers' praecipium calculated on the non-US portion of the combined offer (see Exhibit 9).

In the US, the management and underwriting fees were allocated on the basis of underwriting commitment only.

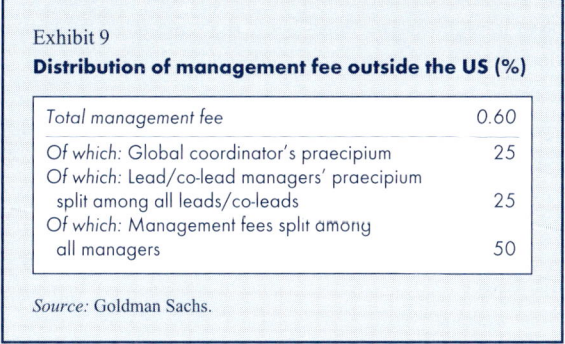

Exhibit 9

Distribution of management fee outside the US (%)

Total management fee	0.60
Of which: Global coordinator's praecipium	25
Of which: Lead/co-lead managers' praecipium split among all leads/co-leads	25
Of which: Management fees split among all managers	50

Source: Goldman Sachs.

Exhibit 10

Distribution of selling concession in the US (%)

Total selling concession	1.80
Of which: Pre-agreed or fixed portion regardless of sales booked	30
Of which: Paid pro rata according to sales designated by investors	70

Source: Goldman Sachs.

Selling concession

In the US the selling concession had one fixed and one variable component. The fixed component of 30 per cent was calculated on the basis of the underwriting commitments. The variable proportion was subject to performance and was designated by investors (see Exhibit 10).

In Europe the selling concession was paid in full to whomever executed the order. There were no designations; however in some cases large orders were split between two institutions.

Deal structure

Retail offer structure

The innovative structure of the Repsol retail offer contributed to an unprecedented level of domestic demand. Market research revealing a number of particular challenges

helped crystallise specific objectives for the retail offer (see Exhibit 11).

Whereas retail discounts are common, if not universally employed, there were several key features and innovations in the Repsol offer:

- Retail indemnification: the money-back guarantee of up to 10 per cent;
- Purchase mandates with retraction period;
- The use of variable (ie, progressive) commissions for retail placement;
- Full (so-called hard) underwriting of the offer at a substantial discount to the prevailing market price; and
- The decision not to use partly paid shares.

The decision to go for a fully underwritten offer was taken because the vendor was of the view that the banks should take on more of the risk given the fees that they were proposing. It was supported in its decision by the domestic securities regulator, the CNMV, which argued that the offer should be underwritten due to the fact that the purchase mandate structure effectively acted as a type of sub-underwriting by retail investors.

A partly paid structure had been suggested by Lazard Brothers, the advisers to INH and Repsol, but was rejected after much debate because the domestic bank branches did not like the idea. Their view was that it would not significantly increase demand and would add to share price volatility in the after-market. Their concern was supported by the fact that, given the leverage effect, the hypothetical losses of the two most recent privatisations, if structured with partly paid shares, would have been magnified – to 62 per cent for Argentaria and 24 per cent for Endesa on the basis of two installments.

The offer was structured taking full account of the context in which it was to take place: Spanish retail investors had experienced huge capital losses on previous issues and bank branches in Spain were against selling shares.

Previous attempts to structure retail offers that addressed the concerns of retail investors were not deemed credible. Institutional investors in Spain and elsewhere had lost confidence in the investment banking community's ability to bring

Exhibit 11

Design of the retail offer structure

Challenges	Design
1. Spanish retail investors don't buy shares.	1. Immediate discount of 5% and US$30 million advertising campaign.
2. Spanish retail investors are risk averse.	2. Indemnification of retail investors via a money-back guarantee of up to 10%.
3. Need to secure orders early in the process.	3. Purchase mandates with retraction period, preferential allocation and variable commissions.
4. Minimise retail selling in the after-market.	4. Short maturity of incentives: 12 months.
5. Bank branches are no longer attracted by traditional risk/reward ratio of selling privatisations.	5. Progressive incentivisation for retail placement by means of variable commissions.
6. Minimise cost of the structure to the selling shareholder.	6. Indemnification contingent on share price.
7. Attractive pricing.	7. Flexible pricing, subject to maximum retail offer price.

successful new issues, and particularly large privatisations, to the market.

A number of structural decisions were therefore taken: retail investors were to be indemnified against losses; the deal would be of limited initial size; the purchase mandate would be used to allow for early reading of retail interest and an adjustment of the offer size; and there was to be target-linked remuneration for the syndicate.

The offer structure was designed to generate success with retail investors which, when communicated to the institutional market, would drive the entire issue. The emphasis had to be on early communication, and the 'purchase mandate' was the tool that enabled that communication.

Marketing

Retail

The key reasons for the success of the retail offer were the carefully planned and tightly executed advertising campaign – which started three weeks before the placement and was carried out in five stages – and the incentivisation of the retail banks.

The domestic market research carried out prior to the beginning of the retail offer highlighted the importance of the bank branch as the focal point for the placement. The existence of other centres, such as a registry office (as was employed successfully in Argentaria 1, but less so in subsequent offers), was found to dilute the efforts of the bank branches. The marketing strategy accordingly emphasised the importance of the branch while Repsol's management made an important contribution towards the reinforcement of the role of the branches:

- Repsol's chairman gave presentations to each of the five banks involved in the domestic placement. These presentations were typically co-hosted by the chairmen of the respective banks;
- Repsol's chairman was repeatedly photographed together with the chairman of BBV and the other banks involved, in order to get the message across to the branch managers that this offer was taken seriously at the highest level of each of the banks; and
- Repsol provided marketing material for the bank branches.

Institutional

An intensive and targeted institutional marketing programme was executed in four distinct phases:

1. Extensive surveys of international institutional investors conducted by the Goldman Sachs salesforce before the announcement of the transaction;
2. Development of the new 'Repsol equity story';
3. Pre-marketing meetings held by the syndicate research analysts; and
4. Extensive roadshows by top management.

Institutional investor survey

The investor surveys were a fundamental marketing tool in developing the framework for the Repsol offer. Goldman

Sachs conducted two extensive surveys of the international institutional investor community which targeted investors chosen from among current and previous holders of Repsol, owners of European oil stocks and Spanish stocks and large investors in privatisations. The surveys proved to be invaluable in several respects as they facilitated:

- Evaluation of international investor demand;
- Identification of issues to be addressed during the roadshow;
- Tranche sizing decisions; and
- Precise targeting for one-on-one meetings.

More than 250 investors were surveyed in July 1994, and almost 100 of these were again surveyed in February 1995. The survey was conducted over the telephone by the Goldman Sachs European equity salesforce, following which investor survey forms had to be filled in for each targeted investor. The forms included questions on the following topics:

- Repsol share ownership;
- Potential order size;
- Purchasing fund;
- Attractions of Repsol;
- Concerns about Repsol;
- Attractions of Spain;
- Concerns about Spain; and
- Interest in taking part in a pre-marketing event.

The investor survey and the pre-marketing allowed the underwriters to get a clear picture of investors' concerns, which were as follows:

- at 25 per cent, there was a relatively low self-sufficiency in crude oil (not counting the Pemex delivery contract);
- the sustainability of refining and marketing margins;
- the decision to diversify into natural gas;
- chemicals profits might have peaked;
- the sustainability of earnings growth;
- the effectiveness of exploration and production operations;
- what effect political instability in key oil-producing countries might have;
- an overhang in Repsol's shares existed as a result of the step-by-step approach to privatisation; and
- there were poor market conditions generally and a poor new issue market in particular.

The new Repsol equity story

With expected annual earnings growth of 15 per cent a year, Repsol was principally a growth story. It was also a restructuring story, with new radical cost-reduction programmes to follow on those already successfully concluded. A restructuring story is only truly convincing with a convincing management and in that regard Repsol ranks at the very top. Its management had always delivered on previous undertakings and therefore enjoyed the highest credibility in the equity markets.

Former chairman Oscar Fanjul commented: 'Repsol had a very good name in two specific respects. First, we were well known among retail investors who had done well on Repsol's shares in the past, and secondly we had credibility with domestic and international institutions because we had delivered the earnings growth that we had promised. If you want to be successful in the equity market, you simply have to deliver on your forecast.' (See Exhibits 12, 13, 14 and 15.)

Repsol's strong reputation at home and abroad, the annual growth in net income of 14 per cent a year since 1987, and an increase in net profits of 21 per cent in 1994 meant that the company had a good story to tell. At 8.7 times 1995 earnings and 4.1 times 1995 cash flow, Repsol was also trading at very substantial discounts to its peer group.

Mark Giacopazzi, research analyst of Carnegie Espana said: 'Repsol is the only state-owned Spanish company which has cut costs aggressively. One-third of the 1994 pre-tax profit was due to cost-cutting. That notwithstanding, on a net basis, jobs have not been lost at Repsol. Naturally, Repsol has historically been helped a great deal by its monopolistic situation and they are still in a very strong position although in theory, they are now fully exposed to competition. We like the top and middle management a great deal.'

Pre-marketing meetings held by the syndicate research analysts
As a result of the intelligence gathered through the investor surveys, the pre-marketing was unusually effective.

- More than 250 institutions in Europe were visited ahead of the roadshow by syndicate members' analysts; and
- Research analysts contacted more than 160 accounts in the US.

Extensive roadshows by top management
To maximise the penetration of both top and second-tier accounts, Repsol fielded two teams of top managers who had

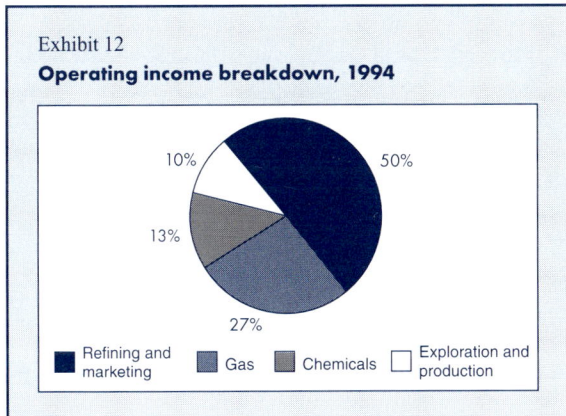

Exhibit 12
Operating income breakdown, 1994

- 50% — Refining and marketing
- 27% — Gas
- 13% — Chemicals
- 10% — Exploration and production

Exhibit 13
Principal sales points

Market position	Strong position in refining and marketing: • Repsol's five refineries account for 60% of Spanish crude refining capacity; • Market share of 58% in retail automotive marketing; and • Superior cost position which is continually strengthened. Dominant position in gas: • Market share of 80–90% in natural gas, depending on market segment; and • The only significant LPG distributor in Spain and the largest in Europe.
Earnings	Higher-quality earnings than peers: • Repsol is invested to a greater extent than its competitors (40% versus 10%) in businesses with low earnings volatility such as logistics, LPG and NG and to a lesser extent in exploration, production, refining, marketing and chemicals; and • Repsol had an established track record in cost-cutting and was planning further cuts of Pta50 billion each year by 2000, representing 28% of total 1994 operating income.
Higher prices	Future benefits from higher prices: • The Spanish price level for LPG has for regulatory reasons been 30%–50% lower than the European average. There is, therefore, room for price increases. If not, Repsol will continue to benefit from relatively modest competition.
Growth	High volume growth over the next 10 years: • Domestic oil products sales expected to increase by more than 4% a year; • Oil and gas production outside the Gulf to increase by more than 5% a year; and • Natural gas sales in Spain expected to increase by more than 10% a year. Goldman Sachs expected earnings to increase by 28% in 1995 and by 15% a year until 1997.
Attractive portfolio of investments	Repsol's planned investments of Pta1.2 trillion between 1995 and 1999, were expected to return 17% a year on a DCF basis.
Profitability	Repsol has consistently had among the highest ROE in the sector at 14%–18%.
Balance sheet	Net debt to total capital (net debt + equity) was 27% at the end of 1994. At the time of the offer, Repsol had long-term ratings of AA-/AA3 from Standard & Poor's and Moody's, respectively.
Valuation	Repsol was attractively valued in terms of both P/E and P/CF, although the undervaluation may appear exaggerated by Repsol's unusually high chemicals earnings in 1994 and 1995.

Sources: Goldman Sachs and offer circular.

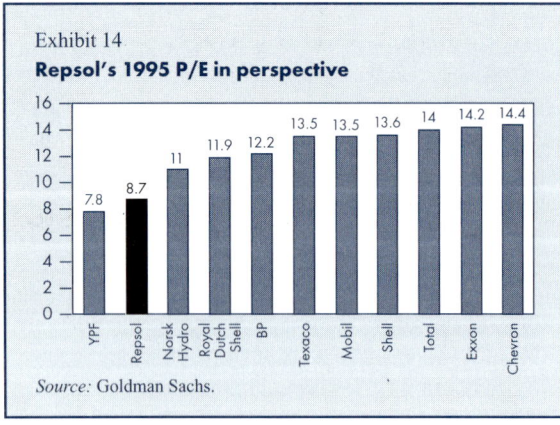

Exhibit 14

Repsol's 1995 P/E in perspective

Source: Goldman Sachs.

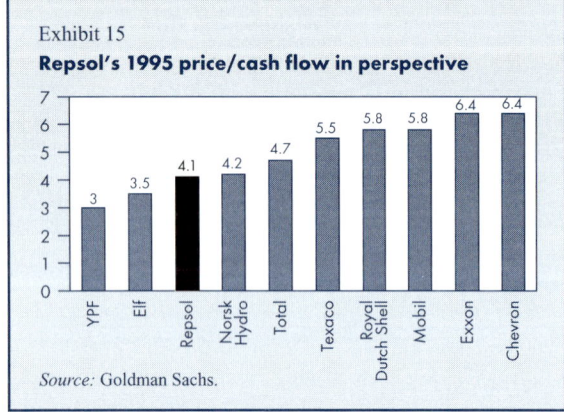

Exhibit 15

Repsol's 1995 price/cash flow in perspective

Source: Goldman Sachs.

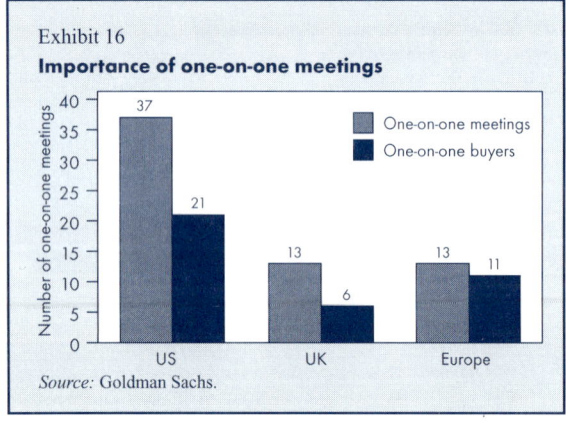

Exhibit 16

Importance of one-on-one meetings

Source: Goldman Sachs.

one-on-one meetings and presentations with investors in 24 different cities over the course of 10 days. Accurate targeting of the institutions visited was crucial to generating the transaction's leadership orders (see Exhibit 16).

- More than 500 investors attended the presentations given by the management during the roadshow;
- International investors visited in one-on-one meetings demanded 120 per cent of the shares offered outside Spain;
- Of the 63 institutions visited in one-on-one meetings, 38 placed orders. The meetings also helped to prevent the major shareholders from selling prior to the offer; and
- The average order size from those institutions that participated in one-on-one meetings was almost seven times the average size of all other institutional orders. Orders from UK institutions targeted were 10 times larger than the average UK institutional order.

Results

Placement

In terms of the retail tranche 355,000 retail investors subscribed, of whom 22,000 were employees. The average order size was Pta672,000 (US$5,375) and the pro rata allocation to retail investors favoured small investors: those with mandated purchases of up to Pta100,000-worth of shares received 100 per cent of their orders, while those with orders of the maximum of 10 million shares for retail orders received only 19 per cent. (See Exhibit 17.)

The decision to increase the retail tranche from 17 million to 29 million shares was taken as more than 300,000 Spanish retail investors had subscribed for the offer. By the end of the mandate period some 270,000 investors had given mandates to purchase. Luis Mañas, deputy finance director of Repsol commented: 'Everyone agreed that an increase was appropriate, as otherwise the allocations would have been ridiculously small. It has been our strategy in all our offers to start with a modest size – we call it the feasible size – and then increase subject to demand.'

Although the institutional tranches were more than covered by the beginning of the OPV period, as a result of the posi-

Exhibit 17

Underwriting, demand and allocation (%)

Target markets	Initial underwriting	Final underwriting	Demand	Allocation
Retail offer	42.0	55.2	44.1	49.8
Employee offer	7.4	5.7	3.6	6.3
US offer	21.0	16.2	19.5	18.4
International offer				
UK	12.3	9.5	15.1	11.4
Continental Europe	7.4	5.7	9.4	6.4
RoW	2.5	1.9	1.0	0.6
Spain	7.4	5.7	7.4	7.0
Total combined offers (shares)	**40,500,000**	**52,500,000**	**150,814,000**	**57,000,000**

Source: Goldman Sachs and BBV.

tive response to the purchase mandate concept, many institutional orders were still only placed on the last two days, because of the following:

- information on the evolution of the institutional book was not given to the rest of the syndicate to prevent the orders from being inflated;
- although orders were not binding before bookbuilding closed, many investors were hesitant due to the market volatility;
- many non-US investors were waiting to see what the US institutions were going to do. The US roadshow was, as is most often the case for non-US offers, at the end of the bookbuilding period;
- there were fears of shares being transferred from the institutional tranches to the retail tranche;
- some institutional investors were still not convinced that there was strong and genuine interest among retail investors; and
- there were expectations that the offer would be increased, hence increasing the supply to the market.

Of the individual tranches, the Paribas-led continental European tranche was the most oversubscribed and the CSFB-led RoW tranche the least oversubscribed (see Exhibit 18).

- To accommodate US accounts, the book was kept open for one extra day following late one-on-ones with certain investors. This was the source of one of the few complaints from the syndicate, with some maintaining that the book

was artificially skewed towards the US tranche. Luis Mañas replied: 'It is true that we had for logistical reasons to schedule a few conference calls on the Monday, after the roadshow had finished on the Friday. It is also true that the US tranche was allocated to a higher degree than some of the other institutional tranches, principally for the following reasons: first, it is our experience that US investors inflate less when indicating their demand during the bookbuilding period which is evidenced not least by their pattern of behaviour in the after-market; second, US investors do less 'flipping' in the immediate after-market as evidenced by the data on US institutional shareholdings, and instead tend to hold the stock for the long term; third, since the outstanding majority of the US demand comes from institutions which we see in the one-on-one meetings, we have a higher degree of confidence concerning the intentions of those institutions';

- Several orders came in sizes not seen since the heady days of 1993, with some individual requests for stock in excess of US$50 million; and
- No particular region is thought to have shown greater price-sensitivity than any other, although the Spanish buyers are said to have been first with their orders.

Investor concentration

The average order size for the top 10 orders (in terms of allocation) was US$16.8 million in the US and US$13.4 million in the UK. (See Exhibit 19.)

Whereas integrated oil companies are typically bought by 'value investors', Repsol was also purchased by many growth investors because of its double-digit growth. Repsol made it on to Paine Webber's Focus List, which is a list of 30 companies world-wide that the firm rates buy or attractive, using a selection criteria which emphasises growth and low risk. Index investors were less keen on the transaction as they were already fully weighted.

Share price performance
See Exhibit 20.

Before pricing
- Not only was the underlying Spanish market weak from the time that the deal was announced five weeks prior to pricing, but feeling throughout Europe was also negative.

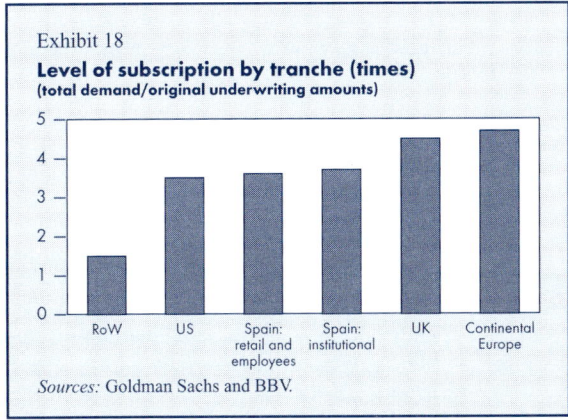

Exhibit 18
Level of subscription by tranche (times)
(total demand/original underwriting amounts)

Sources: Goldman Sachs and BBV.

Exhibit 19
Investor concentration

	By demand	By allocation
Percentage of institutional portion of the issue accounted for by the 10 largest investors	17%	24%
Number of investors making up 80% of the institutional portion of the issue	340	244
The three largest investors by size	US$58 million US$52 million US$52 million	US$25 million US$24 million US$23 million
Total number of institutions	772	643

Source: Goldman Sachs.

Exhibit 20

Share price performance

Pricing date	10 April 1995
Offer price	Pta3,620
Last trade	Pta3,620
Relative index position	97.7%
Historic 52-week high/low	
High (16 May 1994)	Pta4,670
Low (29 December 1994)	Pta3,475

Repsol share price relative to Madrid Stock Exchange (%)

Price performance

Before pricing

	Price (Pta)	Relative (%)
- 6 months	3,955	100
- 3 months	3,570	96.0
- 1 month	3,595	100.3
- 1 week	3,635	100.8
- 3 days	3,705	100.4
- 1 day	3,640	98.7

After pricing

	Price (Pta)	Relative (%)
+ 1 day	3,640	98.5
+ 3 days	3,735	100.7
+ 1 week	3,705	99.3
+ 1 month	4,060	100.7
+ 3 months	3,900	95.8
+ 6 months	3,725	94.0

Sources: Datastream and offer circular.

Exhibit 21

Percentage of total issue traded* (%)

	Day 1	Day 2	Day 3	Total: Day 1-3
Madrid	9.1	4.6	Closed	13.7
New York	7.1	2.4	0.4	9.9

* Based on the issue of 57 million shares.

Source: Datastream.

Numerous privatisation issues had been scaled back or cancelled before the Repsol pricing;

- Repsol's share price fell by only Pta20 between the filing on 20 March and the pricing day. It under-performed the market by 3.7 per cent over the period as investors sold shares in the hope of being allocated more in the offer; and

- The absolute price fell by Pta85 during the last three days of marketing. The share price fell by Pta20 on the pricing day to close at Pta3,620, 22.5 per cent below the 52-week high.

After pricing

- The institutional offer price was set at the lower of the Madrid and New York closing prices: the issue was therefore priced at the market in Madrid on 10 April;

- The retail offer price was set at a 5 per cent discount to a weighted average of prices on Monday's continuous market of Pta3,630;

- As is customary in all privatisations, there was some selling on the first trading day by both institutional and retail investors. Retail investors were attracted by the opportunity of making a quick profit from the 5 per cent retail discount although according to Repsol, retail selling was moderate. As at June 1995, 74 per cent of all retail investors who purchased in the offer still owned the stock and the majority of the after-market orders came from US investors, with some from UK institutions;

- BBV was seen to support the stock in the immediate after-market. One trader said: 'If it wasn't for the money BBV Interactivos was spending, the shares would be falling.' Goldman Sachs executed all its stabilisation orders through BBV;

- Repsol performed adequately in absolute and relative terms in the immediate after-market; and

- Despite achieving a positive absolute share price development over three and six months, Repsol substantially underperformed the strong Spanish market over the same period.

After-market trading volume

See Exhibit 21.

The performance of the main parties

The company

With Oscar Fanjul as chairman of both INH and Repsol, the relationship between the vendor and the company was sure to be a good one. Both deserve enormous credit for the way they handled this transaction as the structuring of the offer was particularly intelligent and resulted from hard work in terms of market research. Repsol's management enjoys a trust and credibility in the international equity market that is matched by few others: this is based on the development of an astute strategy and the fact that Repsol has always delivered on its cost-cutting programmes and its profit forecasts.

It also seems as if Repsol has perfected the art of presenting to the investor community. Luis Ruigómez, deputy general manager of BBV Interactivos commented: 'The Repsol roadshow team, lead by Oscar Fanjul, probably performs among the most professional investor presentations, not only in Spain but also internationally. They know the company extremely well. In addition to the 25–40 slides typically prepared for the formal presentation, they also have some 100 additional slides for questions. Mr Fanjul knows all the slides by number, which clearly impresses the audience. Their secondary market investor relations effort is also impressive. Investors get an immediate response to their questions. Retail investors have access 365 days a year to a shareholder information office. Therefore, all of Repsol's investors get very good coverage and treatment.'

Dante Roscini, managing director of Goldman Sachs added: 'Repsol's marketing and investor relations teams respectively, deserve considerable credit for the repeated successes of Repsol's equity offers. They are masters of both internal and external communication and they are completely dedicated to the highest standards of client and investor service alike.'

Repsol's finance staff (including in particular Carmelo de las Morenas López and Luis Mañas Antón, finance director and deputy finance director respectively) made a much bigger contribution to the structuring and the management of the issue than is normally the case. It was Luis Mañas rather than the investment bankers who came up with the retail indemnification and the purchase mandate structures.

Repsol managed to galvanise the whole Spanish banking system through a carefully crafted approach, which included: the creation of a meaningful position for all the domestic banks, not solely BBV; a fair remuneration system with proper incentives and presentations by the Repsol chairman to all five members of the retail syndicate; tight management of its banks and generation of a healthy sense of competition both on the retail side and on the institutional side. Furthermore Luis Mañas, the chief designer of the offer structure, requested daily progress reports from each of the banks in the retail syndicate and Repsol was electronically connected to the institutional book and could monitor every institutional order.

The only important point of criticism of the Repsol privatisation process is that there have been too many offers and not sufficient flexibility to increase issue sizes. The question has been asked as to why Repsol could not do a US$3 billion offer if YPF of Argentina could successfully do so. This constraint was imposed by the government, rather than the Repsol management team. Consequently, there has been a considerable overhang in Repsol shares which has led to a discounted valuation, estimated at 15–20 per cent in late November 1995. Oscar Fanjul noted: 'The step-by-step approach to privatisation has been very expensive for the government and very time-consuming for the management.'

Furthermore, the golden share legislation has not spelt out clearly enough and early enough exactly how much the government will interfere with Repsol. Although the idea of a golden share is not unique, particularly in the oil industry, to lay out the rules of the game after four offers does not help to remove uncertainty. It was only because the rest of the Repsol story had been so convincing that the market was relatively unconcerned about the golden share.

Goldman Sachs

Without a doubt Goldman Sachs earned its role as Repsol's premier international equity house when it first assisted the company with its NYSE listing and US offer in 1989. Although Repsol must be categorised as a dream client, with which it

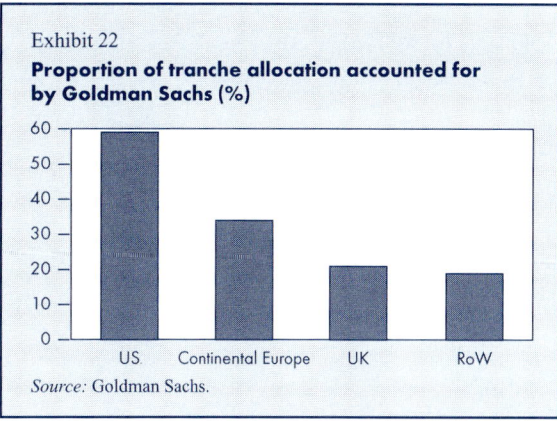

Exhibit 22
Proportion of tranche allocation accounted for by Goldman Sachs (%)

Source: Goldman Sachs.

would be rather difficult to fail, Goldman did an outstanding job of steering Repsol through very tough market conditions in 1993 and 1995 and read the market well in terms of offer structure, pricing and timing. The foundation for that work was laid in the 1994 and 1995 investor surveys among international institutions that helped to fine-tune the Repsol story.

Goldman Sachs accounted for a solid but unspectacular 36 per cent of the total institutional allocation, broken down over the four tranches in which it participated (see Exhibit 22).

Over the years Goldman Sachs has developed a unique knowledge of the Repsol investor base and by being active in sales, trading and research had demonstrated continued sponsorship of the Repsol name. They have become the reference bank for Repsol, as Luis Mañas explained: 'A key reason for having given Goldman Sachs repeat mandates is that we expect much more secondary market performance from them than from anybody else – perhaps they have a different culture from other houses. They appear to have more at stake in terms of the value of their franchise in this business. They certainly have a lot at stake vis-à-vis the investment community having placed such a large portion of our equity. The most crucial thing for us however is to know that we have a reliable partner in bad times, as that is when you need your friends – we believe Goldman Sachs will be there for us should we really have a need.'

De las Morenas commented: 'Goldman Sachs has a long-standing track record and credibility in Spain. They came to Spain in the 1970s. Sure there are other houses that could do a great job for us today but many of those were at best lukewarm on Spain as late as in the late 1980s. Before our IPO in 1989, Goldman Sachs had done Telefónica in 1987 and Endesa in 1988. That notwithstanding, we considered the choice very carefully indeed. In the end, perhaps the most important consideration that made us decide in favour of Goldman Sachs in 1989 was that they were the only house which was not ambiguous about the fact that they wanted to be the underwriter rather than the adviser. All the others didn't wish to commit themselves to either of the roles, despite the fact that we had clearly communicated that we wanted to distinguish the two roles. Having done a very good job for us, there was no point in replacing Goldman Sachs. Why change a winning team? Also, Goldman Sachs' position was if anything getting stronger through a commendable and consistent commitment both to Spain as a market and to Repsol

Exhibit 23

The Repsol retail offer in perspective

	Repsol (April 1995)	Endesa (June 1994)	Argentaria (November 1993)	Argentaria (May 1993)
Number of applications	355,000	199,000	440,000	365,000
Total retail demand (Pta billions)	235.3	140.0	198.0	167.9
Average order size (Pta)	672,000	700,000	450,000	460,000

Source: BBV.

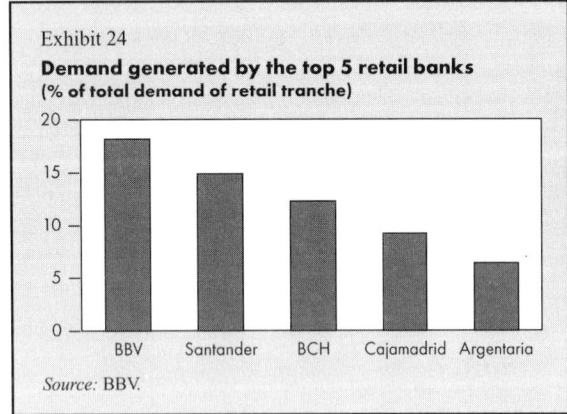

Exhibit 24

Demand generated by the top 5 retail banks
(% of total demand of retail tranche)

Source: BBV.

specifically. Undoubtedly, in connection with transactions of this type you do invest an extraordinary amount of time and commitment in one another. It is like a marriage – to break it up is associated with a great deal of cost. We can tell the other houses that they are very beautiful but that we already have five children with Goldman Sachs. You can't be married to more than one woman at a time.'

Goldman Sachs deserves credit for not having drawn criticism over the allocation of Repsol shares, a considerable achievement given the high level of oversubscription.

BBV

The retail offer was a remarkable success in absolute terms and in comparison to earlier privatisations, particularly given the poor stock market environment (see Exhibit 23).

The success can be attributed to the the strong company story, the retail indemnification structure, the purchase mandate system and the progressive incentivisation scheme.

The five houses making up the management group of the domestic offer covered the whole of the retail tranche. BBV outsold the other banks and Banco Santander also did well (see Exhibit 24).

BBV deserves credit for being at the forefront of domestic equity placement and for having developed a high level of expertise on how to transact global equity offers. It contributed substantially to the correct reading of the mood among retail investors, which triggered the innovative retail incentives, and also motivated the domestic syndicate. Overall BBV, together with the Repsol team, substantially raised the level of sophistication in Spanish retail placement by introducing certain methods which have been adopted in subsequent privatisations. Luis Mañas said: 'We have taken tremendous comfort from the fact that BBV has been there in the secondary mar-

ket. As a significant long-term holder, they don't mind supporting the share price at times of volatility.' As far as BBV is concerned, he continued: 'They have very clever people and they have, over the past few years, had opportunities to learn this business. They have earned the respect of others.'

Key lessons learnt

Structuring

Without the 10 per cent money-back guarantee, the offer would probably not have been a success and a lukewarm response from retail investors would have discouraged international investors from getting involved.

Luis Ruigómez of BBV explained: 'You have to build a transaction such as this the same way you build a house. You first need to build a solid foundation by designing the retail tranche in the appropriate way. If the foundation is solid the rest of the house will also be high quality. Institutional investors will buy if they are confident about the success of the retail tranche. In this case, the foundation turned out to be so strong that the whole transaction was covered by 'purchase mandates' even before the bookbuilding started.'

Luis Mañas has tried to dispel the notion that retail demand is more expensive than institutional demand due to retail incentives and publicity expenditure: 'The foreign investment banks always tell me how expensive it is to place shares with retail customers but we don't look at it that way. Retail demand tends to be relatively price insensitive and this can be of great value. It goes without saying that institutional demand follows a normal demand curve whereby the demand increases at lower prices. Retail demand allows you to cut off those institutions not willing to pay up and you can price the whole offer at a higher price. Effectively, you increase your bargaining power vis-à-vis the institutions which can be of great value.' But a senior equity capital markets specialist with one of the major US investment banks countered: 'That sounds fine in theory, but that is not the way it really works – it is not a mathematical calculation. You can't really afford to ignore the the pricing views of the big institutions because they will drive the market price in the after-market. You won't get any help from retail in the after-market.'

The number of structural innovations in this transaction is remarkable, given the bias against innovation in transactions. De las Morenas commented: 'One of the most difficult things in this market is what we call 'the struggle against market practice'. What this means is that if you have a creative idea, it is usually very difficult to implement it because all the investments banks will immediately give you all the reasons that it can't be done, particularly if there is a chance that their economics might be affected. It is even more difficult in connection with privatisations because governments are typically risk-averse and government officials are paranoid about being criticised if something goes wrong.'

Marketing

These offers clearly prove the importance of successful communication, either by way of advertising or by investor presentations. A successful track record alone is not enough: it has to be marketed successfully, which is something that Repsol has understood.

Repsol has taken time and care over the way it communicates its message to the market, but Fanjul was happy to admit that however much groundwork a company does, a really successful deal still needs a little luck: 'Getting the timing right for one of these big secondary transactions is to a large extent a matter of luck because you have no idea whether or not the market will be good over the four weeks following the announcement of an offer. At least in an IPO you don't have stock trading out there before pricing, which makes it slightly easier. Furthermore you really don't have much flexibility to pick the time as you can't do it too close to Christmas, you can't do it in the summer and certainly not when people pay taxes as that would have a negative impact on retail demand. On the subject of luck, you also need the right amount of luck after the pricing. If the price falls after the pricing you are criticised and if it goes up too much you are criticised too'.

Management

In addition to the basic structural elements of an offer it is important that communication with, and the incentivisation of, the entire syndicate is balanced and fair. The sooner the conflicts of interest inherent in any offer can be identified and dealt with, the better. This cannot always be left to the global coordinator who, in addition to working for the success of the overall deal, is also motivated by its own income from the transaction.

Repsol has strong views on the issue of conflicts of interest and deal economics: 'There are conflicts of interest at every step of the way during the process of preparing and executing a transaction of this kind. Whenever you believe there might be a conflict, you can be sure that there is one. We have learnt to deal with that in two ways. First, during our initial transactions we employed an independent adviser who told us what was reasonable and what was not, which was useful when negotiating with the global coordinator, although it is an illusion to believe that there is such a thing as a truly independent adviser. Secondly, we have learnt to deal with the very important subject of economics head on and upfront: we made it our business to understand the economics of the transaction down to the last detail and we were able to understand the economic implications of each decision at every step of the way. Since the banks were aware that we understood who gained or lost by each decision, no games were played and pointless discussions were avoided and, consequently, everybody rather behaved professionally and in the best interests of the transaction.'

Repsol has not only sought to understand but also to behave entirely equitably: 'It is extremely important to achieve fairness in the transaction. In order to do so, we let our co-leads know that they also have a say, ie, not all information is filtered through the global coordinator. When structuring an offer we start by looking at the regional syndicate structure and the approximate tranche sizes, we then structure the economics and only thereafter do we decide on which banks should do what in the syndicate. The last major decision is on allocation and there we favour an open discussion with all the regional leads concerning the quality of investors.'

Conclusion

Despite the many challenges encountered during the offer, including highly volatile equity, bond and foreign exchange markets, the issue was completed and took its place as the largest ever in the Spanish market.

The deal performed well almost immediately after its announcement. By using the innovative retail indemnification scheme, risk-averse domestic investors were lured back to the stock market: after only four days of the mandate period, ie, before the beginning of the OPV, the entire retail offer was covered. Only 2 per cent of the demand generated during of the mandate period was cancelled.

The momentum generated in the retail offer created a powerful follow-through demand from institutions which had been slow to respond to the offer due to macroeconomic worries about Spain, and the fact that many institutions were fully weighted in Repsol.

The transparency of the structure attracted institutional investors from around the world. Although the absolute share price performance had been disappointing during the marketing period, the institutional tranches were priced at market: Repsol achieved an immediate after-market premium.

The success of this transaction gave the European new-issue market a kick-start and its structure was closely copied in the subsequent privatisations of Telefónica and ENI.

Feature topic: *Recapturing the European retail investor – three major innovations in retail offer technology in the 1995 Repsol offer*

The secret to the success of the Repsol transaction lay in its success among retail investors, who had been badly affected by a weak equity market in general, and poor performance of the two most recent privatisations – the November 1993 sale of Argentaria and the June 1994 sale of Endesa – in particular (see Exhibit 25).

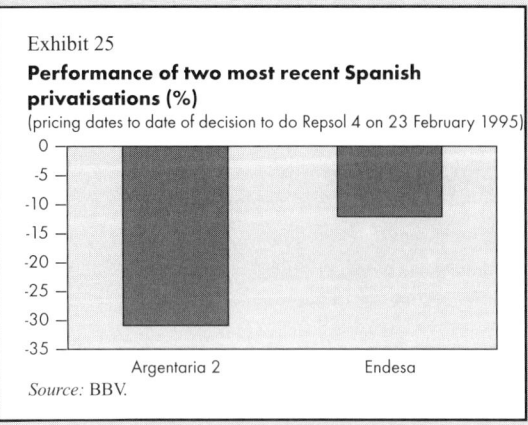

Exhibit 25

Performance of two most recent Spanish privatisations (%)

(pricing dates to date of decision to do Repsol 4 on 23 February 1995)

Source: BBV.

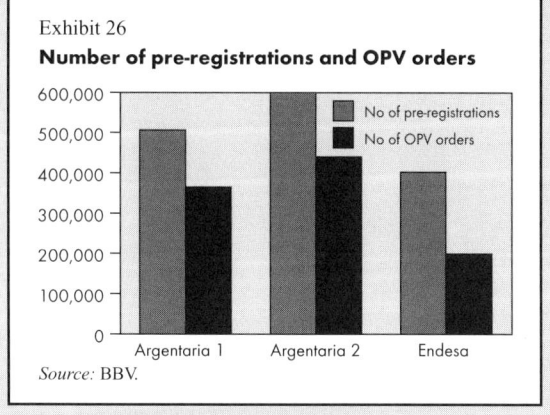

Exhibit 26

Number of pre-registrations and OPV orders

Source: BBV.

Investor survey

To understand the specific concerns among retail investors, BBV carried out a detailed investor survey, the conclusions of which would help shape the structure of the retail offer. Investors were asked a number of questions, including the following:

1. Would you buy another privatisation?
2. Under what conditions would you buy another privatisation?
3. What is your impression of Repsol?
4. How would you react to the following types of incentives: partly paid structure, retail discount and insurance policy against losses of principal on the investment.

The principal conclusion drawn from this survey was that few people were interested in equity and there was little or no confidence in the merchant banks. Those that were interested in the offer conceded that Repsol was among the top three companies in Spain and had a very good image. The survey revealed that their interest in buying would be dramatically enhanced by some sort of insurance policy against loss of capital.

To overcome this negative sentiment INH, Repsol and the bankers came up with a number of solutions using a combination of traditional methods to maximise retail interest. These included increased spending on publicity, increased pressure on bank branches to sell to clients, more flexibility in determining the size of the retail offer and a lengthening of the offer period. They also adopted certain new mechanisms to encourage retail participation. These were:

- Purchase mandates (including a preferential allocation for prompt subscription);
- Money-back guarantee (or retail indemnification); and
- Variable (and progressive) commissions.

Purchase mandate

Pre-registration, whilst a significant innovation in the May

1993 Argentaria offer, had subsequently become less effective and less reliable as an indicator of final demand. There had been many instances where the data provided by prospective investors over the telephone did not match the details on the subscription form, meaning that many investors did not initially receive an allocation. The conversion ratio (the number of pre-registrations converted to firm orders during the OPV) had fallen from 74 per cent in Argentaria 2 to only 49 per cent in the subsequent Endesa offer (see Exhibit 26).

Repsol and its advisers needed to come up with a method that would encourage early commitments, create momentum for the institutional offer and represent a more reliable indicator of final retail demand. Their answer was the purchase mandate, a concept that had first been employed in the 1993 privatisation of BNP, but had never before been tried in Spain. Luis Mañas of Repsol, the chief designer of the retail offer commented: 'We began to look seriously at different structures prior to the 1993 offer, when INH considered selling down to zero by doing a jumbo offer. We tried to change the shape of the demand curve from late to early orders, which are clearly more valuable. In our search for something that would make sense in Spain, we looked in particular at both the French and the Italian systems and our solution represents a combination of the two. In Italy, allocation is based on the first come, first served principle, which is a fair system for rewarding promptness. BNP in France had introduced purchase mandates for its privatisation in 1993, primarily in order to prolong the effective retail subscription period, however they did not specifically encourage early orders by offer preferential allocation to those that gave mandates. It was nevertheless of crucial importance to have found the precedent in a country such as France, with a similar legal system to our own, as regulators are notoriously risk averse.'

The idea behind the purchase mandate is for retail investors to give their bank a firm mandate to purchase shares (and debit their accounts to the extent of the value of the allocation) before the beginning of the OPV period. Investors have an option to cancel during the first few days of the OPV period, and after this the mandates are upgraded to firm orders. Purchase mandates submitted during the mandate period are given priority in the allocation process and the banks are rewarded for achieving early orders.

There are several advantages to the purchase mandate system:

- It allows for a more reliable reading of retail demand at an early stage;
- It allows for more direct demand tension between the institutional and retail offers;
- Investors only have to visit their bank once, unless they wish to cancel their orders, whereas pre-registration requires two visits;
- It may generate some additional demand as the purchase mandate effectively extends the OPV period; and
- Because of the reliability of demand information received early in the process, the vendor can adjust advertising expenditure.

The purchase mandate system places both the initiative and responsibility with the bank branches whereas pre-registration gathers some information on the progress of retail demand but the branches cannot tell whether early registration will be converted into firm orders. Payment takes place at the 'trade date' in both cases. Only once allocations are confirmed are accounts debited.

To encourage early orders, it was decided to give preferential allocation to those who gave purchase mandates during the mandate period rather than those who bought during the OPV. Those investors who had given mandates to purchase shares for the minimum amount of Pta100,000 were allocated shares for Pta99,992, while those who requested the same amount of shares during the OPV received only Pta55,168 worth of shares.

In contrast to the disappointing conversion ratio of 49 per cent for the Endesa transaction, only 1.5 per cent of the applications made during the mandate period were retracted during the cancellation period. Approximately 82 per cent of the applications were made during the mandate period: purchase mandates achieve early results in retail demand.

Retail indemnification

For the first time ever (although apparently considered in the British Gas privatisation) a privatisation offer included a scheme to protect retail investors against losses of up to 10 per cent, for a period of 12 months after the closure of the retail offer. It worked as shown in Exhibit 27.

The money-back guarantee (or retail indemnification) was only valid if the shares were not traded within 12 months following the close of the offer. The amount of cash compensation was based on the difference between Pta3,448 and the 20-day average prior to the anniversary of the close of the offer. This would represent a contingent reimbursement of up to Pta345.

Exhibit 27
Retail indemnification (%)

Percentage fall (from retail offer price of Pta3,448)	Cash compensation from INH
2	2
6	6
10	10
14	10

Investors hypothetically bought a put option (which INH wrote) at a strike price of Pta3,448 and wrote another put option (which INH bought) at a strike price of Pta3,103. The estimated maximum total cost of hedging for the vendor was approximately 2.5 per cent. In the event, the cost was nil because the Spanish Treasury did not hedge and on the first anniversary the share price was well above the offer price.

INH decided against hedging its additional long position at the time of the issue for three reasons:

- It created more confidence in the market if Repsol did not hedge;
- INH had always been long in Repsol and had never hedged; and
- Hedging can increase volatility and would have amounted to the creation of a short in the market to compensate for Repsol's small long position as a result of the guarantee provided.

The fact that INH did not hedge at the time of the offer does not mean that it could not have done so at a later stage if it had looked like the option would be in the money.

In Spain, as in most of continental Europe, it is the branch manager who, as the quasi portfolio adviser to a large number of retail clients, will determine the success or failure of a retail offer. Branch managers had been badly burned by the recent poor performance of equity issues in general, and privatisations in particular. The challenge lay in convincing them to support the offer: the 10 per cent money-back guarantee did this as branch managers judged that it would delay repercussions from unhappy clients.

Incentivisation – variable commissions

In order to achieve a successful retail placement, bank branches have to make an enormous effort to mobilise a large number of clients and convince them to buy shares. In order to persuade branch managers to give priority to the sale of Repsol shares, they were given increased remuneration for higher sales. Since the banks were already paid proportionally more to sell more, the incentive scheme had two additional aspects:

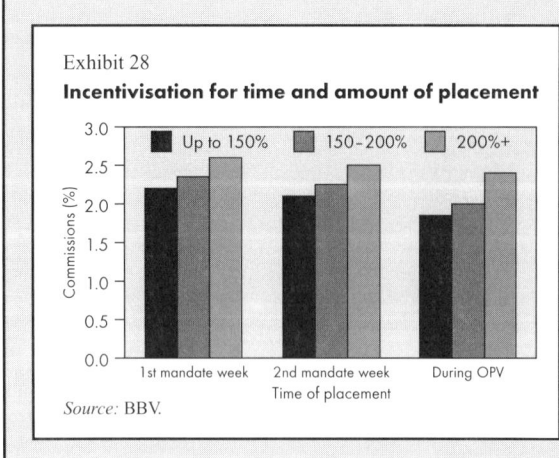

Exhibit 28

Incentivisation for time and amount of placement

Source: BBV.

- Higher remuneration for early orders; and
- Higher remuneration for achieving more than the original commitment (see Exhibit 28).

Managers in the retail offer were given a sliding scale of commissions based on early orders and the volume of demand. Placement in the first week of the mandate period generated a 2.2 per cent commission, falling to 1.85 per cent during the OPV. The commission for placement in the first week rose to 2.35 per cent if the demand registered was between 150 per cent and 200 per cent of the manager's commitment and to 2.6 per cent if it surpassed 200 per cent.

Roche Holding Ltd

It is hard to imagine that in the summer of 1992 US investors owned only 1 per cent of Swiss healthcare company Roche Holding, one of the outstanding European success stories of the past 10 years. The company was largely undiscovered, and certainly under-owned in the US. Although the big US institutions had been free to buy Roche equity securities in London and Zürich, they had shown very little interest. So when the company – the originator of Valium – accepted Merrill Lynch's proposal to do a targeted US placement of existing shares owned by a Roche subsidiary, it was with one aim in mind: to promote itself to US investors.

The offer of ADRs was placed under Rule 144A which meant that only qualified institutional buyers (QIBs) – those investors who have at least US$100 million under management – could purchase. This was the only type of equity security that Roche could offer in the US in the absence of an SEC registration and US listing. It was more than 75 per cent larger than the second-largest pure Rule 144A placement, and differed from previous large Rule 144A placements in that they had been part of attractively priced global privatisations or corporate IPOs. With the exception of two rights offers in 1989 and 1991, Roche had never before sold equity in any market and this offer also represented the first-ever equity issue in the US by a Swiss company.

Many US fund managers were hearing the Roche story for the first time and it attracted considerable interest: the company's total market value increased by 11 per cent (or US$2.3 billion) during the marketing period. For Roche, which raised US$275 million, it proved to be a successful first penetration of the US investor community. The company had been

unknown in the financial markets until the late 1980s and now, after some five years of redirection, management had taken it to the highest level of issuer quality – that rather indefinable mix of high credit quality, high name recognition and a reputation afforded to those relatively few issuers who do big and successful international capital markets transactions on which investors make money. During the two years prior to the offer, Roche's market value had more than doubled, and over the four-year period that followed it increased by more than 180 per cent. Those that invested when the new management was appointed in 1986 have made a profit of more than 10 times their original investment. Today, Roche ranks among the top three European companies in terms of market capitalisation.

The management's continuing US equity strategy assumes that the SEC, which currently requires non-US companies to report under US GAAP, will eventually decide to accept IAS for US listing purposes. Until this happens, Roche will remain without a US listing but will continue to attract US investor interest. The principal means of achieving this is through an active investor-relations programme in its Swiss franc denominated non-voting securities (Genussscheine), non-listed ADRs and equity-linked securities denominated in US dollars which over time convert to Genussscheine.

Major challenges

The transaction had to be big enough to attract attention but small enough to be viable given that Rule 144A ADRs are not the preferred type of security among investors. Those US

Exhibit 1

Transaction summary

Issuer name: Roche Holding Ltd (Switzerland)	*Bookrunning lead manager:* Merrill Lynch
Pricing date: 24 September 1992 (SPI:1,160)	*Pricing/underwriting structure:* Bookbuilding
Vendor: Company sold stock acquired in the market	*Primary or secondary:* Secondary
% of company sold: 1.2% of total capital	*Privatisation or corporate:* Corporate
IPO or non-IPO: Non-IPO	*Industry:* Healthcare
Type of shares: ADRs representing 1/100 of one non-voting equity security (Genussschein)	*Offer price:* US$27.50 per ADR (equivalent to Sfr3,590 per Genussschein)
Total issue size: US$275 million	*US listing/144 A:* This was a US-targeted Rule 144A placement. Roche is not listed in the US

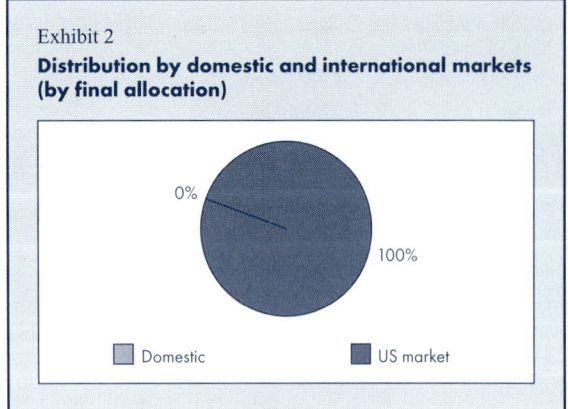

Exhibit 2

Distribution by domestic and international markets (by final allocation)

0%

100%

☐ Domestic   ■ US market

institutions targeted in the offer would have preferred to buy bearer shares or Genussscheine denominated in Swiss francs or listed ADRs, neither of which could be offered to US investors without an SEC registration. As there was only minimal prior US ownership of other classes of Roche stock, it was difficult to channel demand from such securities into the Rule 144A securities on offer.

While the universe of investors eligible to buy 144A securities is very large indeed, Merrill Lynch estimates that those who do buy them account for no more than 20 per cent of the total available pool of funds. The main reason that US investors prefer not to own 144A securities is that buyers can sell them only to other QIBs. 'We were aware that the type of security substantially dampened demand for this offer,' commented John Jensen, managing director of Merrill Lynch's ECM group. 'US investors were offered too many choices. In addition to considering the investment merits of Roche against other pharmaceutical companies, US investors also had the opportunity to buy several other classes Roche securities other than the 144A ADRs here on offer. Why buy restricted securities if you don't have to?'

Farley Bolwell, Merrill Lynch's ECM director, explained that once investors appreciated the strong fundamentals of the Roche story, the challenge became twofold: 'First, to convince investors to buy restricted Rule 144A securities rather than ordinary Genussscheine available in the open market and traded in Zürich and London, and second to convince investors to wait until the end of the marketing period to purchase the securities at the prevailing market price – an unattractive proposition given that the price was rising steadily throughout the marketing period.'

Another difficulty arose because the offer was targeted only at US investors, which meant that there was no flexibil-

ity to move shares to another market, as is usually the case with a global offer.

The offer required a high initial investment in management time for due diligence, prospectus drafting and investor presentations. This was a considerable challenge, not least because this was the first time that Roche's management had been exposed to this kind of work.

Rationale and objectives

There were three main reasons behind the issue:

- To expand Roche's international investor base;
- To establish a long-term relationship with US investors; and
- To use the financial markets to make money.

Roche's desire to internationalise its shareholder base was driven by financial and commercial considerations. The most important financial reason was that Roche, as a result of spectacular share price performance, was becoming too big for the Swiss market, which might constrain the valuation of the company's shares. Most Swiss portfolio managers were restricted from investing more than 10 per cent of their total portfolio in anyone company, even if that company represented more than 10 per cent of the relevant index. In order to reduce dependence on the Swiss equity market and to promote a more realistic market valuation, Roche therefore had to internationalise and diversify its shareholder base. Whereas this was an issue in 1992, internationalisation has become all the more important with the constantly increasing weighting of Roche in the Swiss market (see Exhibit 3).

The commercial reasons are down to the fact that the main customers of pharmaceutical companies are governments – which are invariably running substantial budget deficits and are trying to curb the cost of healthcare, which means that the pharmaceutical industry is politically highly exposed. It is the view of Roche's management that one strategy to counter this risk is to let the respective countries participate in any potential benefits by acquiring substantial local shareholders in such countries. In this way, the country's interests are in line with the company's and are shared by domestic investors. By being more of a local player in foreign markets, Roche would become a more effective lobbying force in those countries, and ultimately ownership should reflect sales and costs in those foreign markets.

Exhibit 3

Roche in relation to the size of the Swiss market

	1986	1988	1990	1992	1994	1996*
Roche year-end market value (Sfr billion)	9	11	18	38	62	96
Roche – % of Swiss Performance Index (%)	5	6	9	13	15	18

* By 25 November 1996.

Source: Roche.

With respect to the US market, Roche's objective was to increase US institutional investor awareness and ownership of shares without subjecting the company to the additional cost of SEC registration and continuous reporting under US GAAP. The medium-term objective was to reach a 10 per cent shareholding without a US listing and in the long term, with a listing, to achieve a much larger US shareholding, more in tune with the proportion of US sales. Roche also wanted to disassociate itself from the image of being a secretive Swiss company, without, however, excessively Americanising the corporate and financial culture, which it felt should remain international. This was deemed necessary given an increasing business presence in the US – biotech company Genentech had been acquired in 1990, and Syntex, a major pharmaceutical company, was acquired in 1994.

In terms of the objective of making money in the financial markets, the idea was to use the flexibility afforded by Swiss corporate law for companies to acquire their own shares in the market in order to resell them at a later date and at a higher price, most often in the form of repackaged securities. After this offer, Roche became ever more sophisticated in the way that it was taking advantage of its cash resources and strong credit standing by arbitraging in the financial markets. Several large transactions have been structured by applying Roche debt to increasingly marketable and highly valued Roche equity in the form of options. These equity-linked securities were then targeted and sold to certain specific investor bases to achieve well defined distribution objectives. For every transaction of this kind, Roche becomes better known in the global capital markets and as a result an increasing number of arbitrage opportunities will be shown to the company by the banking community.

Roche chief financial officer Henri B Meier put it bluntly: 'People miss out on hundreds of millions of dollars by not taking advantage of arbitrage opportunities in the market. You can't think that you are a good manager if you are only good

---

Exhibit 4
Share capital and ownership

Type of shares offered	ADRs evidencing ownership of 1/100 of a non-voting equity security (NES, Genussschein or 'GS').
Share capital before and after offer	Bearer shares (Sfr100 nominal value.) 1,600,000 Genussscheine (No nominal. value) 7,025,627 Each NES confers the same financial rights as any of the bearer shares of the company. However, they have no nominal value, no voting rights and are formally not part of the share capital under Swiss law.
Listings/quotations	Roche received a full listing on the Swiss Stock Exchanges in 1989. The stock was, however, traded before it was listed. The Genussscheine are also quoted on Seaq International.
Market capitalisation at offer price (Sfr1.3055/US$1) for the NES and the Zurich closing bid price on the pricing date for the bearer shares	Bearer shares (at Sfr5,400*): US$6.6 billion; Genussscheine (at Sfr3,590): US$19.3 billion; and Total market capitalisation: US$25.9 billion.
Major shareholder(s) before/after offer	In the absence of registered shares, limited information is available on the ownership of Roche. The Hoffmann and Oeri–Hoffmann families and Dr P Sacher, through a pool, control over 50% of the voting rights attached to the bearer shares. It is also believed that individual family members directly own shares and Genussscheine. Pharma Vision, effectively a closed-end investment fund (although not under Swiss law) dedicated to the healthcare sector and sponsored by the private Swiss bank BZ Bank, owned 216,000 shares or 13.5% of the total voting rights of Roche on 31 December 1994. It is understood that some major packages have been with the same owners for decades.
Free float of the bearer shares before offer	Estimated at 10%–30%. (As all classes of Roche's equity securities are bearer shares and therefore not registered in Switzerland, ownership cannot easily be accurately documented.)
Liquidity (Number of NESs traded during the first 8 months of 1992 expressed on an annualised basis and as a percentage of the total number of NES outstanding).	45% in Zurich. The most liquid stock (on the above measure) on the Zürich Stock Exchange in 1992 and the largest by market capitalisation.
Estimated foreign ownership (ie, managed outside Switzerland)	Before the offer (by June 1992) it was estimated that in total 30%–40% of the Genussscheine were owned from abroad, with US ownership accounting for approximately 1%. Just after the offer, it was estimated that up to 10% of the Genussscheine had been bought by US investors.
Relevant stock exchange index/weighting	Swiss Performance Index/10.6% in December 1992

* The 50% premium on bearer shares is not truly rational given that they carry the same financial rights as the Genussscheine, except for liquidation rights on the share capital paid in by shareholders (Sfr160 million). The explanation: scarcity value. 'The bearer share has become a collector's item,' says Max Gurtner, head of corporate communications and investor relations at Roche. 'Given the founding family's ownership of the majority of the bearer shares and the holdings of certain other long-term investors, the free float of the bearer share is very limited and people know that we are extremely reluctant to increase the number of bearer shares. It is a matter of great pride in Switzerland to own even one bearer share and be entitled to come to the AGM.' Note that bearer shares are not registered in Switzerland.

at producing drugs or machines, you also have to be good at hiring people and investing money. There is a simple basic rule: we compare everything against the return on the alternative investment, be it acquisitions of companies or financial assets. If the increased return compared to the return on cash is such that we deem the risk/return trade-off to be reasonable, then we go ahead. We don't invest in anything for the sake of our own ego. During 1994, we looked at 100 acquisition opportunities and bought only five companies. In 1989, we walked away from the acquisition of Sterling Drug of the US because it did not meet our investment criteria.'

As the securities sold represented stock previously acquired in the market by an indirect wholly owned subsidiary of Roche Holding, the only impact on the consolidated accounts is an accounting (and cash flow) gain resulting from the arbitrage of buying shares cheaply and selling them at a higher price. A specific gain on this transaction was not a defined objective and its size was not disclosed by the company.

Share capital and ownership

See Exhibit 4.

Transaction components

This was a straightforward one-tranche targeted Rule 144A secondary offer of 10 million ADRs, representing 100,000 Genussscheine. The offer was structured with a 15 per cent greenshoe which was not exercised (see Exhibit 5).

As this was a 144A private placement, there was no announcement of the offer. The big institutions began to find out about the placement only when they were invited to the US roadshow (see Exhibit 6).

Principal advisers
See Exhibit 7.

Exhibit 5

Offer structure

Managers	Underwriting commitment
Merrill Lynch (Books)	4,000,000
Donaldson, Lufkin and Jenrette	2,000,000
Goldman Sachs	2,000,000
JP Morgan	2,000,000
Total	**10,000,000**

Exhibit 6

The timetable

7 August 1992	• Merrill Lynch mandated to do the Rule 144A placement.
Early September	• Merrill Lynch invites QIBs to Roche's first-ever US roadshow.
9 September	• US roadshow begins with presentation by Roche management to Merrill Lynch salesforce in New York.
22 September	• US roadshow ends with luncheon presentations and one-on-one meetings in Boston.
24 September	• Pricing & underwriting of the issue.
25 September	• Limited trading in the Portal (OTC) market begins.

Exhibit 7

Principal advisers

US legal adviser to Roche	Davis Polk & Wardwell
Legal adviser to the managers	Brown & Wood
Swiss legal adviser to Roche	Dr Hans-Rudolf Widmer (Internal Counsel)
Auditors	Price Waterhouse

Exhibit 8

Distribution of gross spread (%)

Management commission	Underwriting commission	Selling concession	Gross spread	Discount	Total effective cost
0.62*	0.56*	1.82**	3.00	4.01***	7.01

* The management and underwriting commissions were split according to underwriting commitment.
** The selling concession was 50% pre-agreed among the underwriters and 50% subject to designation by investors.
*** The issue was priced at the equivalent of a discount of 4.01% to the closing bid price in Zürich of Sfr3,740 on 24 September 1992 but 10% above the price at the start of the offer on 9 September.

Transaction fee distribution

See Exhibit 8.

Deal structure

This offer represented a vehicle to get attention from US investors as Roche wanted to confront them with a buy/non-buy decision. In the absence of SEC registration and a US listing, Roche could not offer any equity securities other than 144A ADRs in the US.

Private placements under Rule 144A have several important shortcomings, including:

- Rule 144A ADRs can only be bought by QIBs, and according to Merrill Lynch, less than 20 per cent of these institutions are estimated to actually invest in 144A securities;
- There are substantial limitations in terms of how much any one QIB will buy of a particular Rule 144A placement. The main constraint is that each and every investment portfolio, irrespective of what is managed by any one single portfolio manager, cannot have more than a maximum of 5 per cent of restricted securities; and
- Once bought, Rule 144A ADRs can only be resold to other QIBs, resulting in poor liquidity.

Roche is only prepared to consider a US listing if it can be done under IAS. According to CFO Henri B Meier, Roche takes this position 'primarily for cost reasons'. Registering with the SEC and continuously reporting under two separate accounting standards involve substantial additional costs. Were Roche to need equity and were there no attractive financing opportunities available other than the US registered market, then the company would presumably reconsider.

The option of approaching the US market by way of a roadshow without an offer was rejected on the grounds of its probable ineffectiveness, as this would amount to little more than a corporate-awareness drive. Regular investor presentations are a must in terms of keeping existing shareholders informed about ongoing corporate developments and financial performance but a roadshow without an offer is not enough to motivate fund managers to look at a new name.

Marketing

The cornerstone of the marketing effort was an eight-day roadshow across the US (see Exhibit 9). Roche fielded a strong delegation:

- Fritz Gerber, chairman and CEO (in New York only);
- Henri B Meier, member of the board and executive committee, and CFO;
- Anne Kessler, head of international project management;
- William Burns, head of business operations in the pharmaceuticals division; and
- Max W Gurtner, head of investor relations and corporate communications.

Roche managers met some 250 investors representing 117 QIBs in nine cities. In addition, the salesforces of Merrill Lynch and the co-managers directly solicited an additional 250 or so QIBs to participate in the placement.

The Roche roadshow compared favourably with competitor Wellcome plc's July 1992 US roadshow which incorporated visits to 19 cities with almost 300 institutions attending group presentations and more than 40 institutions participating in one-on-one meetings. Wellcome was priced only two months before Roche and was listed on the NYSE. Of the total Wellcome offer, 23.5 per cent, corresponding to just over US$1 billion, was placed in the US.

Given that Roche was offering unlisted ADRs, that there was limited US-based research coverage and that the company did not have a US-based investor relations representative, it was hardly surprising that the majority of the institutions which bought the Rule 144A ADRs were large institutions which are not dependent on a US listing, US-based research analysts or a US dedicated company investor

---

Exhibit 9
US roadshow – September 1992

Date	City	Type of event	Attendance (Number of QIBs)
9 September 1992	New York	Presentation to salesforces of Merrill Lynch and co-managers	N/A
14 September	Minneapolis	Breakfast presentation	7
	Chicago	Lunch presentation and two one-on-one meetings	10
15 September	Los Angeles	Lunch presentation and three one-on-ones	10
16 September	San Francisco	Breakfast	9
	Portland	One-on-one	1
	Denver	Dinner one-on-one	1
17 September	Denver	Breakfast and two one-on-ones	6
	Kansas City	One-on-ones	2
18 September	New York	One-on-ones	4
21 September	New York	Lunch and four one-on-ones	48
22 September	Boston	Lunch and seven one-on-ones	19

Exhibit 10
Types of US investor

	Large institutions	Medium size institutions	Small institutions	Individuals
Assets under management	US$10 billion +	US$5–10 billion	US$0.1–5 billion	Various
Average equity holding	US$10–200 million	US$10–50 million	US$1–25 million	US$1,000–250,000
Number in US	100	250	3,500	25 million+
Preference for ADRs	Mixed	Mixed	High	Very high
Preference for NYSE listing	Medium	Medium	Very high	Very high
Preference for US-based research coverage	Medium	High	High	Very high
Preference for US-based company IR				
representative	Very high	Very high	Very high	Low
Internal sector analysis	Often	Mixed	Rare	Non-existent
Overseas representation	Often	Rare	Rare	Non-existent
Investment allocation by:				
Region	High	Medium	Medium	Low
Sector	High	High	High	Medium

Source: Merrill Lynch.

relations representative. John Jensen of Merrill Lynch explained: 'The success of this placement showed that major US institutions were starting to take a sectoral approach to companies, rather than a country view. In the major sectors, such as oil and gas, pharmaceuticals and chemicals, this is especially true'.

Exhibit 10 clearly illustrates that the type of securities offered were not suited to any but the largest institutions.

The Roche story

In 1986 Roche was in a difficult situation: it had brought no major new products to the market between 1965 and 1982 and the managers and shareholders lived in a sleepy coexistence. The fact that the last Valium patent (in the US) was going to come to an end in 1985 didn't seem to particularly bother anyone under the old management. Until then growth had been financed exclusively by operating cash flow and Roche had an awkward twin-share structure – a remnant from after World War I. The company was overstaffed and financially weakened, and the management information system did not indicate where profits and losses were made. At the same time Roche was confronted with the revolution in healthcare (meaning cost-cutting) in the developed world. Less than 10 per cent of the company's shares were thought to be owned outside Switzerland, and these were mainly in the UK. This fact was hardly surprising as the company had never given an investor presentation outside Basel, and even there by invitation only. A new direction was called for.

Fritz Gerber proved to be the right man at the right time, and he was to create a revolution within Roche. Gerber had transformed Zürich Insurance in the 1970s and in 1978 had been hired by the Hoffman-Sacher family to do the same at Roche with only one major caveat: he was not to issue voting shares and dilute the family's control. The group's expansion had to be funded primarily by operating cash flow and gains in the financial markets. In 1985 and 1986 Gerber hired a new management team, which included Henri B Meier as CFO. They began to build huge cash reserves to increase financing flexibility. In 1989 Roche raised Sfr451 million

from existing shareholders in connection with a reorganisation of the company's legal structure, whereby it also liberated itself from the old twin-share structure.

The new company, Roche Holding, listed its bearer shares and Genussscheine on the Swiss stock exchanges and gradually began to open up to the investor community. However, Roche still did not give a formal investor presentation outside Switzerland although an abortive bid for Sterling Drug in 1989 was to move Roche into the limelight. At this time Swiss and UK institutions were becoming fully weighted in Roche, despite the fact that only the major Swiss banks wrote equity research on the company. There was still only minimal interest from US investors.

Between the Sterling Drug bid and the Rule 144A placement in 1992, a number of further steps were taken to make Roche more investor friendly. A state-of-the-art MIS was introduced to facilitate internal decision-making and external reporting; sales figures were reported on a quarterly basis and in 1990 Roche, was one of the first companies in Europe to publish its accounts under IAS. In addition, in 1990, Roche bought 60 per cent of US biotechnology company Genentech for US$2 billion. All this activity had led to a dozen or so non-Swiss houses picking up research coverage of Roche and the market had now begun to take it very seriously. Needless to say, the constantly improving name in the capital market went hand in hand with a dramatically improving profitability, share price appreciation and an aggressive acquisition strategy.

The management was gaining a reputation for independent thinking – when most competitors were integrating vertically, Roche was integrating horizontally and in so doing could show an impressive record of not overpaying for acquisitions. With his insurance background, Gerber realised that by taking many smaller risks, a company could more easily afford to take some big ones – not every drug had to be a new Valium. He was among the first in the pharmaceutical industry to hire experienced people from competitors, to cooperate with other drug companies until Roche had developed its own special lines (such as in the case of the US distribution of Glaxo's Zantac ulcer drug), and to

Exhibit 11
Principal sales points

Market position	• No. 12 drug company in the world (1991 group sales of Sfr11.5 billion); • No. 2. world-wide in terms of drug deliveries to hospitals; • No. 4 in the European market for over-the-counter drugs; • No. 2 operator of medical testing laboratories in the US; • No. 2 world-wide producer of fragrances and flavours; and • A world leader in vitamins, carotenoids and some fine chemicals.
Strategic transition	• Since 1986 the group has concentrated on the healthcare industry, particularly those areas where it is strong internationally. Each division has focused on products and technologies where Roche can become a market leader. Consequently acquisitions of some US$3 billion during 1990–1992 were made in key areas: biotechnology, OTC products, diagnostics, testing laboratories, and fragrances and flavours. A total of 23 businesses had been acquired since 1986; and • Since 1996, 18 businesses had been divested, including electronics and instruments, plant protection, radiopharmaceutical and microbiology.
Increased focus	• The net effect of the strategic transition was that the pharmaceutical business, which in 1986 accounted for 41% of group sales, in the first half of 1991 accounted for 53% and most of the non-core businesses were sold.
R&D	• In 1991 pharmaceutical R&D accounted for 23% of pharmaceutical sales. The emphasis was on innovative and market-driven R&D in a limited number of areas where Roche was, or could become, the market leader. If the clients (ie, governments) are under pressure to cut costs, drugs that assist in this effort have to be developed. Roche is renowned for strong and innovative research project management.
Balanced product portfolio and markets	• Contrary to the late 1970s and early 1980s when Roche was a one-drug company off the back of the blockbuster Valium, the company in 1991 had a balanced portfolio of drugs. The company's number one drug Rocephin (injectable antibiotic) represented less than 19% of pharmaceutical sales. The top 14 drugs in the pharmaceuticals division made up only 67% of divisional sales; • Approximately 59% of pharmaceutical sales were patented at least until 1998 and Roche was one of only a few companies that did not face a major patent expiration before the end of the decade; • Roche was also building an important OTC business, with a view to extending the life of products that lose their patent. In 1991 this accounted for 13% of total pharmaceutical sales; and • Roche's sales were geographically diverse. In 1991, sales to Europe and North America accounted for 39% and 38% respectively. Asia accounted for 12%.
Growth	• Roche was expected to grow faster than any major US drug company and as fast as the fastest non-US drug companies, except Astra.
Profitability	• Roche's corporate operating margin of 12.1% was among the lowest of the major drug companies, creating expectations of divestitures and cost-cutting.
Management	• Roche's senior management unquestionably had a good track record both before joining Roche and since 1986 when the strategic reorientation started.
Financial strength	• At the end of 1991, Roche had Sfr11.1 billion of cash and marketable securities (valued conservatively at cost), total debt of Sfr5.4 billion and total equity of Sfr14.4 billion.
Stable ownership	• Despite more emphasis on selling shares in the US, Roche management is anxious not to be driven by short-termism. Roche thinks long term, which is easier if the ownership situation is stable. According to chairman Fritz Gerber: 'There is an iron-clad pooling arrangement among family members to maintain an outright majority of the voting shares well into the next century.'
Valuation	*The principal valuation drivers were:* • growth in Roche's fundamentals driven by an excellent R&D pipeline in several therapeutic areas and significant global patent protection on major drugs; and • a highly impressive liquidity as the number two or number three market-capitalisation stock in Europe and the most liquid stock in Switzerland. With an estimated five-year compounded growth rate in earnings per share of 25% and a P/E of only 14.3 times 1993 earnings, Roche was attractively valued compared to its expected growth in earnings per share.

Sources: Prospectus; Merrill Lynch.

improve profitability by cutting costs as well as by increasing sales.

In November 1991, Roche raised Sfr1 billion by way of a rights issue. The Rule 144A placement was therefore to be the first time that Roche actively promoted its equity outside Switzerland and it was timed to be done off the back of interim sales figures for the first six months of 1992, following the establishment of a sponsored Level 1 ADR programme for its Genussscheine which began trading on 22 July 1992.

Roche came to be regarded mainly as a growth and management play; however, the company also represented a restructuring story, while Merrill Lynch marketed the Roche placement on the basis of the sales points shown in Exhibit 11.

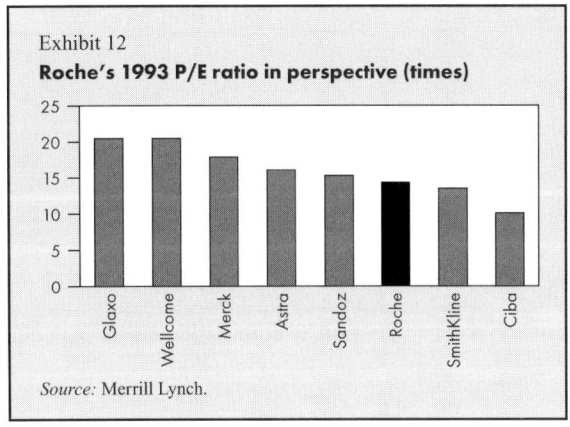

Exhibit 12

Roche's 1993 P/E ratio in perspective (times)

Source: Merrill Lynch.

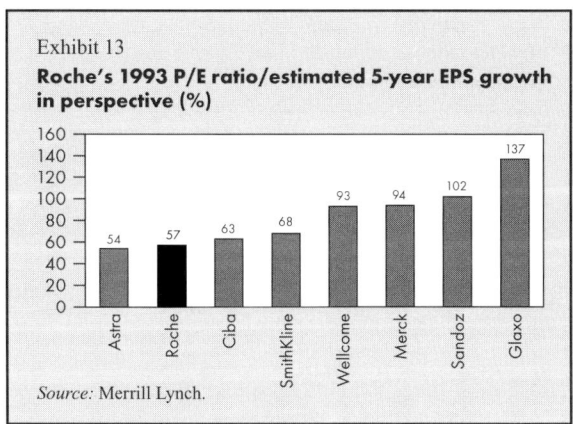

Exhibit 13

Roche's 1993 P/E ratio/estimated 5-year EPS growth in perspective (%)

Source: Merrill Lynch.

Whereas Roche was attractively valued in terms of its 1993 P/E ratio (see Exhibit 12), it was even more attractively valued when the 1993 P/E ratio was set in relation to its expected sustainable growth rate (see Exhibit 13).

The reasons for not buying

Those investors who declined to participate did so mainly for the following reasons:

- Concerns about US healthcare reform;
- World-wide pressure to reduce government expenditure on healthcare;
- Concern about the impact on Roche's earnings of exchange rate volatility;
- Volatility in financial income; in 1991 financial income accounted for 32 per cent of 1991 pre-tax income against 6 per cent for 1990;
- Pharmaceutical stocks were performing poorly; and
- Dislike for restricted and relatively illiquid 144A ADRs.

Market conditions

While the new issue market was generally strong during this period, the US drug sector was performing badly because of uncertainty about US healthcare reform as proposed by the Clintons during the presidential election campaign. By September 1992, it seemed likely that Bill Clinton would be elected, and given that healthcare reform implied lower total expenditure on pharmaceuticals, the markets reacted accordingly. However, Wellcome had performed well since its pricing in July 1992 which was encouraging for US institutions. The importance of the general market conditions for a name such as Roche is still relatively limited, as financings for companies with such strong track records are usually completed successfully even in bad market conditions.

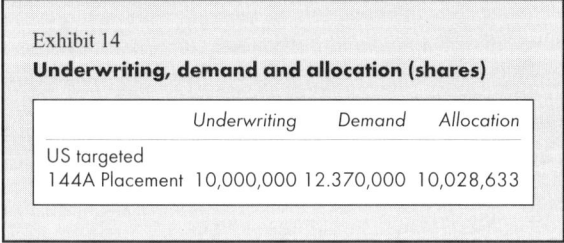

Exhibit 14

Underwriting, demand and allocation (shares)

	Underwriting	Demand	Allocation
US targeted 144A Placement	10,000,000	12.370,000	10,028,633

Results

It was a struggle to generate sufficient demand for this placement, but in the end demand slightly exceeded the underwritten amount (see Exhibit 14). Still awareness and ownership among US investors was overwhelmingly accomplished. Roche met with 117 QIBs and salesforces from Merrill Lynch and the co-managers solicited approximately 250 additional QIBs. A total of 29 institutions bought in the placement and as a result of the roadshow and the offer, US ownership increased to almost 10 per cent.

To reward those US investors who had supported the offer rather than merely buying the non-restricted securities in Europe, and in recognition of the 11 per cent price appreciation of the Genussscheine during the marketing period, the company, on Merrill Lynch's recommendation, decided to price the offer at a discount of just over 4 per cent. Merrill Lynch maintains that it could have priced at market but felt that it was in Roche's interest to concede a discount. The strong price showing during the marketing period was slightly tainted by the relatively disappointing after-market price performance, although this was only a temporary weakness in the share price.

The buyers included large and medium-sized institutions, all of which were based in the US. Approximately 70 per cent were institutional funds dedicated to international investment

Exhibit 15

The Roche US roadshow

	Number of QIBs whom Roche management met	% of QIBs met who participated in placement	% of placement bought
One-on-ones	27	48	57
Formal presentations	90	18	43
Total roadshow	**117**	**25**	**100**

Exhibit 16
Investor concentration

	By demand	By allocation
Percentage of issue accounted for by the 10 largest investors (by total size of demand and allocation respectively)	79%	82%
Number of investors making up 80% of the issue (by total size of demand and allocation respectively)	11	10
The three largest investors by size	US$41 million US$41 million US$28 million	US$41 million US$41 million US$28 million
Total number of institutions	**29**	**29**

Source: Merrill Lynch.

and 30 per cent were institutional funds dedicated to investment in US securities. Mutual funds were the biggest group of buyers (40 per cent), followed by pension funds (30 per cent), insurance companies (20 per cent) and others (10 per cent). Growth buyers accounted for 70 per cent of the offer and value investors for 30 per cent.

Ultimately, 48 per cent of the 27 QIBs who had one-on-one meetings with Roche management participated in the 144A placement, buying 57 per cent of the total ADRs sold. Taken as a whole, 100 per cent of the issue was purchased by QIBs who participated in the roadshow (see Exhibit 15).

No more than 10 investors accounted for 82 per cent of total allocations and in total only 29 institutions came into the transaction (see Exhibit 16).

Share price performance
See Exhibit 17.

Before pricing
- During the six months prior to the offer, Roche's share price had increased by almost 26 per cent, outperforming a flat Swiss market by almost the same percentage;
- Roche's market value increased by Sfr3 billion (US$2.3 billion) or 11 per cent during the two-and-a-half week marketing period, ie, between the time that Merrill Lynch started issuing invitations to the roadshow (3 September) and the pricing of the offer. Over this period, Roche outperformed the Swiss market by 8 per cent, the S&P 500 index by 12 per cent, a composite of comparable European drug companies by 11 per cent and the S&P Drug Index by 13 per cent; and
- As a result of the US roadshow and the sale of 144A ADRs in the US, the liquidity of the Genussscheine on the two most active exchanges for Roche shares in Europe (ie, Zürich and Seaq International) increased by 59 per cent and 177 per cent respectively during the same two-and-a-half week marketing period.

After pricing
- During the first day after the offer, the price of the Genussscheine in Zürich increased by Sfr20. Less than 1 per cent of the placement traded in spite of downward pressure on comparable European drug stocks (-3.2 per

Exhibit 17
Share price performance

Pricing date	24 September 1992
Offer price (US$27.50)	Sfr3,590
Last trade	Sfr3,740
Relative index position	123.5%
Historic 52-week high/low	
High (23 September 1992)	Sfr3,760
Low (30 September 1991)	Sfr2,462

Roche share price relative to Swiss Performance Index (%)

Price performance

Before pricing	Price (Sfr)	Relative to SPI (%)
- 6 months	2,980	100.0
- 3 months	3,320	108.8
- 1 month	3,290	115.2
- 1 week	3,610	119.2
- 3 days	3,680	121.9
- 1 day	3,760	123.6

After pricing	Price (Sfr)	Relative to SPI (%)
+ 1 day	3,760	123.6
+ 3 days	3,640	120.9
+ 1 week	3,580	119.0
+ 1 month	3,640	119.7
+ 3 months	4,140	130.0
+ 6 months	4,030	119.0

Sources: Datastream and offer circular.

cent) and the US market in general (-1.0 per cent for the S&P 500);

- After the first trading day, the Zürich Genussscheine price started to fall and dropped below the Swiss franc equivalent of the offer price on 1 October. By that time the entire cushion of the 4 per cent discount had been given up;

- The Genussscheine continued to fall until 5 October, by which time almost the entire price appreciation during the marketing period of 11 per cent had been given up. Over the period 3 September to 5 October, Roche outperformed the Swiss market by only 1 per cent. The reason for the 10.4 per cent fall during the seven trading days from 25 September to 5 October was primarily Roche's significant currency exposure to the US dollar (which weakened by 4 per cent during this period) and the weakness in drug stocks generally, as evidenced by a fall in the S&P Drug Index of 5 per cent during this period; and

- After this post-issue low, the price rallied strongly and increased by 8 per cent over the next four days. During the six months following the offer, the Genussscheine appreciated by 7.5 per cent but under-performed the Swiss market by 4.5 per cent.

The performance of the main parties

The company

Although Roche had done a US-style due diligence in connection with the aborted bid for Sterling Drug in 1989 and had a state-of-the-art management information system in place, an issue of this kind, particularly since it was the first ever equity issue for a Swiss company in the US market, was still a challenge. Roche and Merrill Lynch wrote a good prospectus, which established a solid foundation for many similar exercises over the coming years. The investor presentation was of the highest quality and delivered with great professionalism. This was the management that had built an entirely new company since 1986 and in so doing had raised the market value of Roche from approximately Sfr9 billion to some Sfr34 billion on the day of pricing, an average annual increase of 25 per cent.

Merrill Lynch

Merrill Lynch was undoubtedly clever in bringing this opportunity to Roche's attention and it did well in convincing the management to dedicate the necessary resources to the project, preparing the issue, organising the roadshow and placing US$275 million of Rule 144A securities against considerable competition in the form of Roche's Genussscheine and bearer shares as traded in Zürich and London. US investors preferred to buy the non-restricted securities and Merrill Lynch had to work hard to keep investors in the deal. The issue was modestly over-subscribed and the full 10 million ADRs were allocated, though the greenshoe was not exercised. Total demand for all of Roche's securities including the Rule 144A ADRs during the marketing period was almost 400 per cent of the size of the placement.

In the placing, because of the delicate task of promoting the restricted 144A ADRs relative to the underlying unrestricted Genussscheine, Merrill Lynch was left to generate almost 100 per cent of the demand (it received 97.7 per cent of all designations by investors). This is unusual, as the other houses had not been invited into the transaction to sell but rather to add research sponsorship to Roche's first US equity offer. Donaldson, Lufkin & Jenrette, for example, had been invited on the basis of an undertaking to initiate equity research on Roche, while both JP Morgan and Goldman Sachs had to commit to continue to provide research coverage.

'Merrill Lynch, which we regard highly and which has a very strong distribution network in the US, brought this opportunity to our attention in late July and we were able to take a relatively quick decision because we immediately liked the proposal,' commented Meier. 'This, of course, doesn't necessarily mean that they came up with an entirely new idea. We were seriously considering other similar proposals.

'Generally, we believe that in the investment banking community, the particular individuals make the real difference, something which in our view the managements of these banks don't generally appreciate to the full extent. For us, the most important criteria is a very high level of integrity, ie, that they don't in any way take advantage of Roche as an issuer. This we find more important than that the particular banker is brilliant. We want to work with people that we can trust.'

Judging from the banks that Roche repeatedly uses for large capital markets transactions and acquisition work, one can conclude that Henri Meier and his colleagues have identified such individuals at Merrill Lynch, JP Morgan and Swiss Bank Corporation.

Key lessons learnt

The fact that Merrill Lynch struggled to sell US$275 million-worth of Rule 144A ADRs but at the same time was responsible for generating additional demand of more than US$800 million-worth of other Roche securities, demonstrates forcefully that even large and sophisticated US investors by far prefer either ordinary shares or listed ADRs to Rule 144A securities. As investors have either sold or switched to non-restricted securities, outstandings of Rule 144A ADRs have long since fallen close to zero.

This placement also demonstrated the importance of marketing the story to investors which is bad news for those who argue that the market is perfect. In reality, because the choice of investment is so broad, each name in the market has to compete for the attention of fund managers.

It was also apparent that selling shares is not so different from selling other goods or services: it doesn't happen simply because the product is available on the shelf – it has to be actively promoted by forcing investors to consider the merits of buying or not buying. 'In the case of a stock such as Roche, you have to make it clear to investors that they are taking a risk by not going to the presentation,' commented Max W Gurtner, the company's head of investor relations and corporate communications.

The substantial increase in the outstandings of Roche's Level 1 ADR programme during the marketing period (from US$50 million to more than US$100 million) underscores the fact that establishing a sponsored ADR programme without an offer does not generate demand from investors.

The company derived lasting benefits from the due diligence process, prospectus work and investor presentations, not least by exposing divisional managers and functional heads to the demands of the investor community.

Although Roche has done an excellent job of promoting its shares within and outside Switzerland, a level of ownership in the US that more fully reflects the company's major business presence (some 35 per cent of sales) will only be attained with a full US listing. The company's US ownership has struggled to rise above 10–15 per cent despite the company doing everything possible except for a listing.

Conclusion

Merrill Lynch's proposal to Roche to do a secondary Rule 144A placement of already outstanding shares as an appetiser to tempt US investors to study the Roche story was obvious, straightforward and sound. However, the execution was to prove challenging. The overall results were even better than expected:

- More than US$1 billion of total estimated US investor purchases: in addition to the US$275 million Rule 144A placement, demand also developed for Roche equity in the two other forms available to US investors: (i) the underlying equity available in Europe and (ii) the unrestricted Level 1 (unlisted) ADRs in the US. During the marketing period, as reflected in the substantially higher trading volumes in Zürich and on Seaq International, it is estimated that approximately US$750million of Roche equity was purchased by US investors in the European markets. Over the same period, the unrestricted Level 1 ADR outstandings more than doubled; and
- Roche's market value increased by US$2.3 billion during the marketing period: between the launch date and the pricing date the price of the underlying shares increased by 11 per cent outperforming all relevant indices.

The Genussscheine underlying this placement were acquired before 30 June 1992 and although Roche did not disclose the book cost of these shares, it is reasonable to assume that the profit achieved on the sale was substantial, even before considering the 11 per cent appreciation in the market value of the company during the marketing period. After paying 3 per cent commission, a 4 per cent discount and no more than 1 per cent of total issuing expenses, Roche would still have made a direct net profit of around 3 per cent on the share price appreciation during that time. Importantly, all Roche shareholders will have benefited indirectly from the 11 per cent appreciation in the share price.

The after-market price performance was at first disappointing due to a strongly appreciating Swiss franc and a general weakness among US drug stocks. Thereafter the positive price trend in Roche's non-voting equity securities continued, as evidenced by a 41 per cent appreciation over the year to September 1993. This outperformance is partly attributable to the increased attention afforded to the stock by US investors. At the beginning of 1994, total US ownership of Roche's Genussscheine was estimated to be between 10 and 15 per cent.

The next major step in the internationalisation of Roche's equity could come in connection with a US listing, though this is only likely to happen as and when the SEC accepts IAS. According to the schedule agreed between the International Accounting Standards Committee (IASC) and the International Organisation of Securities Commissions (IOSCO) this will not happen before 1999 at the earliest, and may take a lot longer. According to Meier: 'We will not go to any market where national considerations prevail. That excludes for the time being a US listing. A uniform set of accounting standards world-wide is in the interest of everybody – in fact in the age of electronic trading this is a must'. This position is perhaps understandable coming from the CFO of one of the the three most valuable companies in Europe and which has a mountain of cash on the balance sheet. Most other companies must go to where the money is.

The question remains as to whether the Roche board is really maximising the value of the company for the benefit of all shareholders – as it has a fiduciary duty to do – if it is not listing in the US. The company management, one of the most respected in Europe, appears to argue that the answer is yes, while many other market participants are not so sure. Whereas many Europeans believe that the US will soon be in a position to accept listings by foreign companies under improved IAS, the American view is much more cautious.

Except for a US listing, since the Rule 144A placement in 1992 Roche appears to have done everything possible to promote its shares in the international market. In addition to posting steady earnings growth and being active on the acquisition trail – the company has financed three multi-billion dollar transactions (Genentech, Syntex and Boeringer Mannheim) in less than seven years without an increase of its share capital – Roche has become highly proactive in marketing its story around the world. It has also built up huge liquidity which it has used to make huge arbitrage profits in the capital markets, in particular by acquiring its own shares, repackaging and reselling them as equity-linked securities. In doing so it has used its good name to target specific investor groups on terms favourable to both the company and investors. In the process Henri Meier and his team dramatically increased foreign ownership, from some 10 per cent in 1986 to more than 50 per cent in 1997. Not only have these arbitrage activities yielded even higher returns than those generated in the core business but it is also likely that the track record and the more active marketing of this track record have improved the earnings multiple at which Roche securities are trading. Given the company's already high stock market value and earnings level, for every 1 per cent that the earnings multiple is increased, the market value of the company will have improved by somewhere in the region of 1 billion Swiss francs – a highly impressive achievement by any standards.

Feature topic: *The US listing decision for non-US companies – IAS versus US GAAP*

The Roche case underlines the continuing debate over whether to use IAS or US GAAP or both. The arguments put forward by major international companies such as Roche unwilling to conduct a US listing other than under IAS are the following:

1. To maintain several sets of accounts to conform to specific national preferences adds a substantial and unnecessary cost burden. There is usually no deeper wisdom in the various definitions of cost categories, of values or profits under US GAAP than under IAS. Roche, for example, is quite philosophical about whether goodwill is charged to past or future earnings, etc. What is important is that investors know the standards. Uniform standards world-wide would make the life of international companies easier and reduce costs dramatically – by tens of millions of dollars. Accounting standards should after all serve the needs of management and shareholders. Any bureaucracy – meaning the creation of data and paper nobody reads – should be avoided. So far IAS has found this careful balance between necessities and nice to haves;

2. The differences between US GAAP and IAS are getting very small and it should now be only a matter of time before the two standards are identical and the US SEC accepts IAS;

3. IAS will soon be accepted everywhere in the world except the US, Canada and Japan. Since a simple and uniform way of accounting is in everybody's interest, a world-wide standard should only be a question of time;

4. The SEC and the IASC (the International Accounting Standards Committee) have a common goal – global accounting standards – and it is only politics that prevents the two organisations from agreeing on standards;

5. Many European companies are coming round to the view that they should have only one set of accounting standards. Like Roche, they have given up their domestic standards for IAS and, having done so, are reluctant to add US GAAP as a second standard; and

6. US investors are becoming increasingly sophisticated about investment outside the US and therefore less and less dependent on buying US-listed ADRs under US GAAP.

In July 1995, IOSCO (the International Organisation of Securities Commissions), of which the US SEC is an important member and IASC (the International Accounting Standards Committee), the body responsible for developing IAS, reached agreement on a work plan whereby the remaining differences between IAS and US GAAP will be overcome by the end of 1999. According to this agreement, the IASC will develop a comprehensive set of core standards which will require endorsement from a unanimous IOSCO committee. Such an endorsement, when it comes,

would mean that the US SEC would allow foreign companies to list on US exchanges and offer securities in the US based on IAS. The earliest this is likely to happen is 1999.

The press release issued at the time of the 1995 agreement read: 'Both the IASC and IOSCO agree that there is a compelling need for high-quality, comprehensive IASs. The goal of both bodies is that financial statements prepared in accordance with IAS can be used world-wide in cross-border offers and listings as an alternative to the use of national accounting.'

The work plan will address three types of issues that need to be harmonised between IASC and IOSCO before the US, Canada and Japan, the three members of the IOSCO 14-member committee who currently have different standards, are in a position to accept global accounting standards based on IASs. Those are:

1. Areas where there are tangible differences between IAS and US GAAP, ie, if you follow one of the two standards, you do not follow the other. Two such areas are the treatment of development costs and goodwill. Development costs are expensed under US GAAP whereas they are capitalised and amortised as intangibles under IAS. Goodwill is amortised over a period of up to 40 years under US GAAP but over only 20 years under IAS;

2. US GAAP is a lot more detailed than IAS and enforced rigorously. If foreign companies are allowed to list and offer securities in the US based on less detailed standards, then US companies would want to do the same. If IOSCO can endorse IAS, is there still a need for US GAAP? If there isn't, all US companies would be subjected to less detailed reporting and the US Financial Accounting Standards Board (FASB) would become redundant. Some companies feel that it would not be to the advantage of US companies for these standards to become less detailed, while others feel that these details work only to the advantage of accountants and bureaucrats; and

3. The mechanism for interpretation. The IASC does not interpret its standards whereas the US FASB does, so a decision needs to be made as to whether the US SEC would need to interpret IAS.

The above initiatives notwithstanding, the position of the US SEC is that it does not feel bound by the position of IOSCO. It is understood that there is a long way to go before US GAAP and IAS are sufficiently close to warrant US listings of foreign companies under IAS. In April 1996, the US SEC issued this statement regarding international accounting standards:

'The commission is pleased that the IASC has undertaken a plan to accelerate its developmental efforts with a view towards completion of the requisite core set of standards by March 1998. The commission supports the IASC's objective to develop, as expeditiously as possible, accounting standards that could be used for preparing financial statements used in cross-border offers. From the commission's perspective, there are three key elements to this programme and the commission's acceptance of its results:

- The standards must include a core set of accounting pronouncements that constitutes a comprehensive, generally accepted basis of accounting;
- The standards must be of high quality – they must result in comparability and transparency, and they must provide for full disclosure; and
- The standards must be rigorously interpreted and applied.

The commission is committed to working with its securities regulatory colleagues, through IOSCO, and with the IASC to provide the necessary input to achieve the goal of establishing a comprehensive set of international accounting standards. As soon as the IASC accomplishes all of the noted key elements, it is the commission's intention to consider allowing the utilisation of the resulting standards by foreign issuers offer securities in the US.'

Whereas the spirit of cooperation might be there, this statement makes it perfectly clear that the US SEC does not appear inclined to compromise its own standards to accommodate foreign companies. Furthermore, there are no firm commitments – all that it is saying is that it 'intends to consider' the use of the resulting standards. The real issue is that this statement is such that whether or not the two standards become sufficiently close for the US SEC will be entirely a matter of interpretation. As those with strong vested interests will be arguing that the standards are still far apart, it is by no means certain that the stated common objective will be reached.

According to US investment bankers, it is most unlikely that the US SEC will allow foreign companies to list in the US on the basis of accounting standards that it considers inferior to US GAAP, generally regarded as the most rigorous in the world. John Jensen of Merrill Lynch explained: 'We must remember that the Securities Acts of 1933 and 1934 were passed to protect the small investor who had suffered the consequences of market manipulation by the big investors in connection with the 1929 crash. They will therefore not compromise on the standards required to protect the small investor. To my mind, it is inconceivable that there be two different accounting standards, one for US companies and one for foreign companies. Firstly, this would not offer the appropriate protection to US investors and secondly there will be an uproar among the thousands of US companies that have had to comply with US GAAP. It is likely therefore, that the US SEC will continue to require non-US registrants to reconcile their accounts to US GAAP. To the extent, however, that IAS effectively becomes equivalent to US GAAP, which is up to IASC, a reconciliation would be redundant.

'Having said that, the US SEC has been flexible in a number of ways to accommodate foreign companies, for example less frequent home-country reporting, confidential filing prior to the public filing to allow for a faster and more reliable timetable following public filing, at times a faster review period and in some cases no review at all following public filing if and when advised by the SEC within 24 hours of public filing.

'We typically recommend companies to list in the US even if they do not have an immediate financing need, if we believe that the company concerned will be positively revalued in the process. To register and list on that premise would be to maximise the value of the company for the benefit of all shareholders, something every management should want to do.'

In other words, although to register and list without actually conducting an offer does not typically generate maximum impact with investors, it should still be considered if it represents a means of improving the valuation of the company. It is likely that a company as formidable as Roche would stand a very good chance of being revalued following a US listing, given that it operates in an industry that is well understood in the US, that most of Roche's fellow peers in the sector are listed in the US (eg, Astra, Zeneca, Glaxo-Wellcome, SmithKline Beecham and Pharmacia and Upjohn) and the fact that Roche has the management capability to do very well in the US equity market. By way of an example, this revaluation effect was exactly what happened in the case of Astra, whose share price rose by 4.4 per cent on 21 February 1995, the day the company announced that it would seek a listing on the NYSE.

Jensen added: 'If you are, for example, a telecom company today, from a valuation point of view it is clearly a disadvantage not to be listed in the US as the overwhelming majority of all telecom companies are now listed there. Following KPN's and Deutsche Telekom's NYSE listings in 1995 and 1996 respectively, all the quoted European telecommunications operators, with the exception of OTE, are now listed in the US. Globally, only Malaysia Telekom and Singapore Telecom are not listed in the US.'

Whether or not non-US companies such as Roche will wait until IOSCO and the US SEC have agreed to accept IAS will depend on the following factors:

- Their need to raise money in the US equity market;
- Their assessment of the likely valuation impact of being able to tap 100 per cent of the available US investment capital rather than the much smaller pool available for investment in Rule 144A securities; and
- The view they take on the likelihood of a timely endorsement by IOSCO and the US SEC of the work by IASC to harmonise its standards to US GAAP, to the extent that this is significant.

Shandong Huaneng Power Development Corporation

China fever among international investors had long since waned when Shandong Huaneng Power Development Corporation ('SH'), came to the market in August 1994. Interest was nevertheless substantial in this IPO – the first mainland Chinese electric utility to be approved for foreign listing and the first of any category to do a direct primary listing on the NYSE. The issue raised US$333 million and on the first day of trading an unprecedented 60 per cent of shares changed hands, making SH the most-traded stock on the NYSE that day. Sadly the price was soon on a downward slide, in a story that came to illustrate the problems of doing a sole share listing a long way from home. This offer also illustrated how bureaucratic inexperience of capital markets and political string-pulling can exert a huge influence on company prospects in emerging markets.

The SH offer developed from China's need for huge investments in a power industry that was unable to meet demand generated by phenomenal economic growth. Supply was estimated to be lagging behind demand by up to 20 per cent at the end of 1993, a year in which GDP grew by more than 13 per cent and industrial output by more than 23 per cent. The government selected Shandong province, to lead the experiment in raising foreign equity capital for the power industry. In June 1994 the provincial authorities and the China Huaneng Group, one of 55 state-owned enterprises, with US$9 billion of assets at the end of 1994, created SH as the investment vehicle.

This IPO marked the culmination of a remarkable period of less than three-and-a-half years in the development of China's securities market: the Shenzhen and Shanghai stock exchanges had been opened; three foreign partners in Sino-foreign joint ventures had been listed on the NYSE; a dual Hong Kong/NYSE listing had been achieved; and 11 Chinese companies had been listed on the Hong Kong Stock Exchange. SH was to be the first Chinese company to file with the US SEC and have a primary listing on the NYSE.

The listing was significant in that the company was exempted by the SEC from the need to provide three years of audited financial information. Given the short time since its formation, it was permitted 'fresh start' accounting – with only one year of historical information. New York was the company's only listing venue. This situation was quickly repeated (but only once, with another power company), before the Chinese government realised that it would be better to do the primary listing in Hong Kong with its greater understanding of Chinese business, with a simultaneous secondary listing on the NYSE. The US$343 million Shanghai Petrochemical IPO, one of the largest offers by a Chinese company, had already been successfully completed in this way in July 1993. The reverse situation – a primary listing in New York and the secondary listing in Hong Kong – was impossible as the Hong Kong Stock Exchange refuses to be used for secondary listings.

The political dimension of this transaction and that of

Exhibit 1
Transaction summary

Issuer name: Shandong Huaneng Power Development Corporation (People's Republic of China)	*Global coordinator:* CSFB
Pricing date: 4 August 1994 (HSCEI: 1,299.7)	*Pricing/underwriting structure:* Bookbuilding
Vendor: Company	*Primary or secondary:* Primary
% of company sold: 27.15% of expanded share capital	*Privatisation or corporate:* Privatisation
IPO or non-IPO: IPO	*Industry:* Electricity generation
Type of shares: ADRs representing N shares (50 shares/ADR)	*Pricing range:* US$13–17/ADR *Offer price:* US$14.25/ADR
Total issue size: US$333 million	*US listing/144A:* NYSE listing

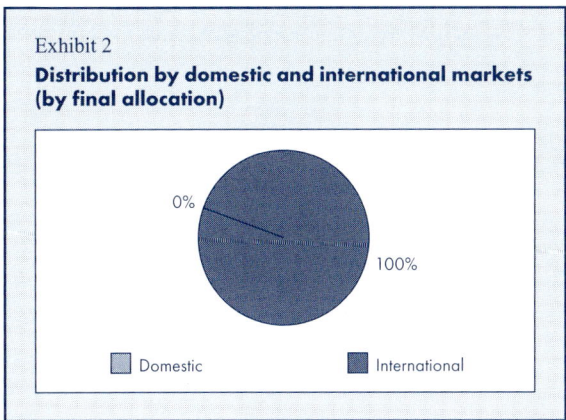

Exhibit 2

Distribution by domestic and international markets (by final allocation)

0%

100%

☐ Domestic   ■ International

Huaneng Power International (HPI), another subsidiary of the China Huaneng Group and the next Chinese company looking to raise capital in the international markets, is perhaps better appreciated when considering the fact that the son of the Chinese Premier Li Peng, Li Xiaopeng, is the vice president of HPI. Li Peng himself is a former Minister of Electric Power in Beijing. Li Xiaopeng wanted HPI to be the first Chinese power company to list on NYSE, but he was unsuccessful. Unfortunately for the long term success of the Chinese overseas listing programme, the US$675 million HPI offer was pre-marketed shortly after the pricing of the SH offer and priced only eight weeks after it. More than US$1 billion-worth of Chinese electric power generation shares were sold in the international market within only two months, at a time when the China fever among international investors was long gone.

Other factors with a strong bearing on the SH offer included its new market-orientated electricity tariff, a formula, approved by Chinese authorities, which called for tariffs to cover generating costs and taxes and provide a 15 per cent return on fixed assets. Unfortunately this became caught up in national deflationary policies, and the government did not permit the SH expansion programmes to go ahead as planned, which further adversely affected market sentiment.

At 18.8 times estimated 1994 earnings, at the time, SH's IPO price represented the highest earnings multiple ever obtained by a Chinese state-owned enterprise (SOE). It was also a substantial premium to prior H share offers (those of Chinese companies listed in Hong Kong) which had been priced at nine to 10 times estimated 1994 earnings.

Major challenges

While the trickiest task was to persuade the US SEC that one year of audited financial statements was sufficient for an unknown Chinese company in a hurry to get to market, undoubtedly the most arduous was the 16 months that it took to secure approvals for the listing from 26 national and provincial Chinese authorities.

The China factor – worries about an overheating economy, inflation and the possibility of currency devaluation – inevitably affected potential investors, so it was decided to try to position SH as a growing Asian utility rather than a typical China play. Although from a valuation point of view the most comparable companies might have been other Asian

utilities, this positioning was not entirely credible given that SH had no assets outside China and that the Chinese power sector is highly dependent on economic and political decision-making in Beijing. This latter factor also posed questions as to the permanence of the tariff structure.

The SH managers, ministries, senior government officials and the China Securities Regulatory Commission (CSRC) all needed to be educated about what makes a successful listing on the NYSE, a process which took 18 months.

SH had to maintain strong momentum to ensure that it became the first Chinese company to achieve the prestigious primary listing in New York, ahead of HPI, despite the latter's powerful connections in Beijing. The SH offer finally came eight weeks before that of its rival. This became a problem as HPI was marketed off the back of SH, cannibalising demand from SH in the process of marketing and triggering after-market sales of SH to buy HPI. But HPI was not the only other company scheduled to come to market and the SH deal had to be executed against the background of a heavy forward calendar for Chinese issuers.

The offer was made under difficult global market conditions, in the traditionally slower summer months.

Rationale and objectives

In China privatisation by way of the public sale of shares on domestic and foreign stock exchanges serve a dual purpose: firstly, to improve the managements and therefore over time the operating efficiencies of the SOEs and secondly to raise money for investment purposes.

In this case SH was formed to own and expand certain coal-fired electricity generating plants in Shandong province and to build, own and operate new power plants. Its incorporation was a central element in the government's reform movement which emphasises increasing foreign investment in the power industry. To the government the NYSE listing was an experiment, and a reaction to the courting of China by foreign investment banks in search of mandates. To Shandong Provincial Power Bureau, which controls one of SH's shareholders, it was a way to raise money to help with expansion. The bureau was interested in corporatising all its assets.

The company's objectives were to:

- Raise cash to fund its expansion plan;
- Sell up to 30 per cent of the company (the maximum percentage allowed by the government);
- Achieve a successful global public offer:
  - increase investor awareness of China's long-term infrastructure policies and development;
  - create stable international demand; and
  - ensure a favourable after-market performance, ie, have the shares appreciate by 5–10 per cent.
- Promote capital flows into China; and
- Set the stage for future Chinese offers.

'Although a prospective P/E ratio of 20 times had been discussed with CSFB and actually submitted to the govern-

Exhibit 3
Share capital and ownership

Type of shares offered	ADRs representing 50 ordinary new N (ie, NYSE-listed) shares.
Foreign ownership restrictions	Foreign investors can buy only N shares, Chinese citizens only A shares. Chinese authorities will not allow more than 30% foreign ownership.
Share capital after offer	A shares: 3,136,016,000 (72.85%) H shares: 1,168,700,000 (27,15%) A and N shares have one vote each.
Listing	NYSE, in connection with this offer.
Market capitalisation at offer price	US$1.23 billion.
Major shareholders after offer	Huaneng Power Generation Corporation 33.1% Shandong ITIC 19.9% Shandong Provincial Electric Power Co 19.9%
Free float after offer	27.2%
Foreign ownership after offer	27.2%
Most relevant stock exchange index/weighting	Initially SH was not included in any index. From Jan. 1995 SH featured in the newly established Credit Lyonnais China World Index comprising 14 H shares, 4 N shares, 8 Shanghai B shares, 2 Shenzhen B shares and 2 'Red Chips'*. On 8 July 1996, Shandong's weighting was 3.85% (HPI was 11.1%).

* Red Chips are companies headquartered and listed in Hong Kong but which derive substantial earnings from China and whose major shareholders are from the Chinese mainland.

ment, admittedly at a time when the China market was much hotter, we had no artificial target at which we wanted to sell but rather were concerned about a healthy after-market,' commented SH director Lu Dan.

The proceeds were to be used to repay principal and interest on outstanding shareholder loans and to finance the expansion of existing power plants.

Share capital and ownership

See Exhibit 3.

The shareholders

Huaneng Power Generation Corporation (HPGC), Shandong International Trust & Investment Corporation (SITIC) and Shandong Province Electric Power Company (Shandong Power) formally established Shandong Huaneng Power Development Corporation on 27 June 1994. In return for A shares in the new company, HPGC and SITIC contributed 50 per cent each of their shares in the Dezhou power station and 30 per cent each of Weihai power station while Shandong Power contributed 75 per cent of the Jining power station.

HPGC, a state-owned enterprise and the largest operating subsidiary of the China Huaneng Group (China Huaneng), was established in 1985 to convert oil-fired power plants to coal-fired ones, to construct new coal-fired plants, to operate and manage thermal power stations and to develop and import power generation technology. By the end of 1993, HPGC had participated in 32 power plant projects in 15 regions across China with a planned total installed capacity of 11,178 MW. The China Huaneng Group, itself only established in 1984, is one of the 55 large groups designated by the State Planning

Commission and the State Commission for the Restructuring of the Economic System to play leading roles in their industry, improve competitiveness, institute management reforms and increase the effectiveness of state macroeconomic management policies. The group has 12 subsidiaries including the Sino-foreign joint venture Huaneng International Power Development Corporation, which owns 40 per cent of HPI.

SITIC is a non-bank financial institution established in 1988 under the authority of the Shandong government and the People's Bank of China. It is responsible for raising domestic and international funding for major construction projects and for developing export-orientated industries in Shandong province. It has interests in 23 power generating plants in the province with an aggregate capacity of more than 5,000 MW.

Shandong Power is the largest fully integrated provincial power company in China and the operator of the Shandong provincial grid, which at end-1993 had installed capacity of 10,783 MW of which 8,786 MW were operated and managed by Shandong Power. The Ministry of Electric Power in Beijing exercises control over Shandong Power through the Shandong Power Bureau which oversees the provincial electricity industry.

Transaction components

This offer of 23,374,000 ADRs representing 1,168,700 new N shares comprised a US tranche initially representing 60 per cent of the offer, a European tranche (20 per cent) and an Asia-Pacific tranche (20 per cent). It was structured as a classic open-priced bookbuilt offer with US-style underwriting and included a greenshoe (unexercised) of 3,506,100 ADRs. There was a 180-day lock-up for SH and a five-year founders' lock-up under Chinese law (see Exhibit 4).

Exhibit 4
Offer structure

Target markets	Indicated tranche sizes*	Bookrunner	Co-lead managers
Europe	20%	CSFB	Merrill Lynch (Senior co-lead), ABN AMRO, Dresdner, SG Warburg
Asia-Pacific	20%	CSFB	Merrill Lynch, SG Warburg, Wardley
US	60%	CSFB	Merrill Lynch, McMahon Securities
Total combined offers (ADRs)	**23,374,000**		

*% of indicated total offer on 27 June 1994.

Exhibit 5
Principal advisers

Financial adviser to the company	CSFB
US legal adviser to the company	Sullivan & Cromwell (Hong Kong and New York)
Chinese legal adviser to the company	Haiwen & Partners, Beijing
US legal adviser to the underwriters	Paul, Weiss, Rifkind, Wharton & Garrison of Beijing, Hong Kong and New York
Chinese legal adviser to the underwriters	Commerce and Finance Law Office, Beijing
Auditors	Arthur Andersen

Exhibit 6
The timetable

January 1993	• CSFB gives first formal presentation to China Huaneng Group on international capital-raising strategy; • Chinese vice-premier Zhu Rongji lent his support to the proposal.
March	• First due diligence in Shandong province to investigate power plant assets.
April	• CSFB mandated.
May–August	• Shareholders begin analysis of assets and negotiations to form company.
September	• Initiation of preparations for SEC registration and NYSE listing.
December	• Chinese government approval received to proceed with NYSE capital-raising strategy.
January 1994	• Final on-site due diligence by CSFB, co-managers, Chinese and US counsel and discussions with provincial and Beijing authorities.
Weeks of 7 and 14 March	*Working group meetings in Beijing to prepare:* • Overseas listing proposal; • Company incorporation proposal; • Preparation of SEC Form F-1.
Week of 4 April	• Submission of listing and incorporation proposals to Chinese authorities.
Week of 25 April	• Confidential submission of Form F-1 to SEC and application for NYSE listing.
27 June	• Company's formation completed; • Public filing with SEC of Form F-1; • Pre-marketing begins.
13 July	*Presentation by SH management in New York to:* • CSFB's US, European and Asian salesforces; • Merrill Lynch's salesforce; • Salesforces of the other syndicate banks (by video conference); • Leadership investors in one-on-one meetings.
15 July	• The roadshow moves to Europe.
22 July	• The roadshow returns to US.
28 July	• Roadshow Team A stays in US while Team B travels to Asia.
3 August	• The roadshow concludes with one-on-one meetings in US.
4 August	• Pricing and underwriting. Pricing meeting in New York starts after the New York market close at 5pm and finishes early next morning New York time.

Exhibit 7
Most important approvals

January 1993	• China Huaneng CEO seeks support from Chinese vice-premier Zhu Rongji for project to sell shares internationally and list on the NYSE (although at this stage it was not clear that this was possible). Zhu approves and instructs the CSRC accordingly. At this point, there had been no foreign listings of mainland Chinese companies on foreign stock exchanges.
August	• The Ministry of Electric Power approves company restructuring.
December	• Formal approval by the State Council for China Huaneng to allow both SH and HPI to go to the US market as part of the second batch of 22 companies approved for overseas listing.
Late March/early April 1994	• A delegation including SH, CSRC and Arthur Andersen visits US SEC in Washington and receives approval to register on basis of one-year of audited historical financials only – a significant relaxation from the normal three-year rule. Accounts for past three years would be meaningless as SH had only operated as a profit-orientated enterprise for one year.
Week of 25 April	• Confidential filing of F-1 with SEC and listing application with NYSE.
30 May	• Amended F-1 filed on confidential basis. Pricing of issue scheduled for 23 June but timing successfully opposed by Li Xiaopeng, vice president of HPI.
13 Jun	• SH and CSFB attend Beijing hearing when CSRC, the State Planning Commission, State Commission for Economic Reform, the Ministry of Electric Power and the State Economic Trading Commission take decision that SH is to be first Chinese company to list directly on the NYSE.
24 June	• State Commission for Economic Reform approves establishment of the issuing company.
27 June	• Public filing of F-1 with SEC.
8 July	• Formal approval received by CSRC to proceed with the issue.

Principal advisers

See Exhibit 5.

The timetable

The initiative for this offer was taken in late 1992, when CSFB's Beijing office approached the China Huaneng Group (see Exhibit 6).

The offer was first scheduled for late 1993 but bureaucracy got in the way: the assets to be included in SH were still being discussed among the three shareholders in late 1993. The company was formally established in June 1994, the month when final approvals for the offer were obtained. CSFB Beijing representative Carl Walter explained: 'Contrary to what many people believe in the West, China is not a wholly autocratic society but rather a consensus society. That is why the approval process was what it was. Amazingly, some relatively junior official at one of the ministries could easily have derailed this project . . . We required approvals from 26 different authorities to go ahead with the offer. The real number of bureaucratic hurdles was, however, far larger than that given that there were also many internal approvals within each of those institutions.' (See Exhibit 7.)

Market conditions

Emerging markets in general, and China in particular, had performed poorly since the beginning of the year (see Exhibit 8). However, market sentiment started to turn more positive shortly before the SH pricing: the H share index for China's Hong Kong-listed companies appreciated by 25 per cent from 8 July, topped only by the Shanghai and Shenzhen markets which surged by some 60 per cent just a few days before pricing. Improving market sentiment towards China was triggered by increasing signs of a successful soft landing of the econ-

omy, a suspension of new A share listings and the announcement that foreign funds would be allowed to buy A shares, which until then had only been available to Chinese nationals, on a trial basis.

In the Hong Kong market there were three smaller issues for Chinese companies between mid-May and the end of June. Those for Tianjin Bohai Chemical and Luoyang Glass opened at discounts of 8 per cent and 20 per cent respectively compared with their issue prices, although they later stabilised at discounts of 7 and 8 per cent. Shanghai Haixing Shipping was pulled at the last minute. Dongfang Electric was 15 times subscribed and was trading at a premium of 32 per cent in early August. Qingling Motors, priced at nine times current earnings, closed 23 times subscribed only days before the pricing of SH and helped boost investor confidence.

The US IPO market had deteriorated substantially as US monetary policy was tightened in February (see Exhibit 9).

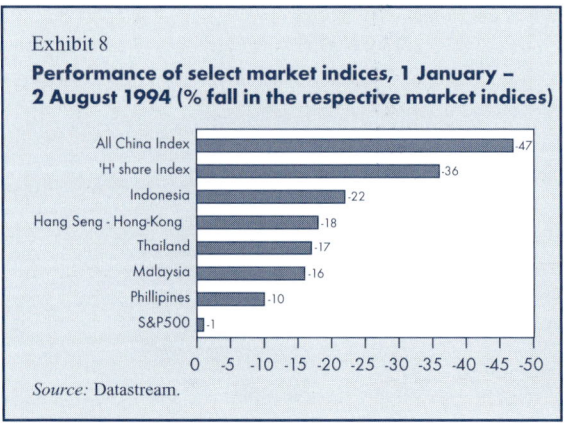

Exhibit 8

Performance of select market indices, 1 January – 2 August 1994 (% fall in the respective market indices)

Source: Datastream.

Exhibit 9

Performance of the US IPO market

	(Q 1) 1994	(Q 2) 1994	April to July 1994
Number of IPOs	81	85	104
Number priced below filing range	10	42	51
Average premium/(discount) to filing* (%)	3.9	(9.9)	(9.8)
Number of IPOs postponed/withdrawn	19	32	46

* Relates offer price to the mid-point of the filing range; Note: excludes reits, rights, funds and units, all deals greater than US$15 million.

Source: CSFB.

Exhibit 10

Distribution of gross spread (%)

Management fee	Underwriting fee	Selling concession	Gross spread
0.9825	1.1930	2.6667	4.8421

Exhibit 11

Distribution of management fee outside the US (%)

Total management fee	0.9825
Of which: Global coordinators' praecipium	25
Of which: Lead/co-lead managers' praecipium split among all leads/co-leads	25
Of which: Management fees split among all managers	50

Exhibit 12

Distribution of selling concession in the US (%)

Total selling concession	2.6667
Of which: Pre-agreed or fixed portion regardless of sales booked	30
Of which: Designated by investors	70

Transaction fee distribution

See Exhibit 10.

Management fee

CSFB received 25 per cent of the total management fee as the global coordinator's praecipium calculated on the gross proceeds of the combined offer. Outside the US, the lead and co-lead managers shared a further 25 per cent of the total management fee as the lead and co-lead managers' praecipium – calculated on the non-US portion of the combined offer (see Exhibit 11).

In the US the management fees were allocated among the managers on the basis of underwriting commitment only, with the exception of the deduction of the global coordinators' praecipium.

Selling concession

In the US the selling concession had one fixed and one variable component. The fixed component of 30 per cent was calculated on the basis of underwriting commitments. The variable portion was subject to performance and was designated by investors (see Exhibit 12).

In Europe and Asia the selling concession was paid in full to whomever the order was given.

Deal structure

Two decisions were vital to the structure: listing in New York and SH's new electricity tariff.

Listing strategy

On CSFB's recommendation in late 1992/early 1993, the China Huaneng group decided to apply for a listing on the NYSE. CSFB had just completed a successful US$80 million SEC-registered and NYSE-listed offer for Brilliance China Automotive, a Sino-foreign joint venture. A New York listing appeared much more attractive than one in Hong Kong, mainly because of a valuation differential. The NYSE was still able to offer higher valuations in August 1994 despite the fact that by then Hong Kong had become the main market for foreign listings of Chinese companies.

The main arguments for a US primary listing were:

- Higher valuation by US investors because they apply more sophisticated valuation techniques for companies such as SH (eg, discounted cash-flow valuation) than do investors in the more retail-driven Hong Kong market;
- The possibility of a larger offer in the US due to the perception that there would be more liquidity and transparency in New York. China Huaneng saw the NYSE as the only exchange that could absorb the substantial volumes of stock that it planned to sell in the SH and HPI offers;
- The Hong-Kong market did not recognise open-price book-building: issues were underwritten on a fixed-price basis;
- A lower IPO discount is required in the US market and therefore a higher pricing is achievable;
- There were few industrial companies listed in Hong Kong in early 1993 when China Huaneng decided to apply for a foreign listing. The Hong Kong market was dominated by property, trading, financial and shipping stocks; and
- A NYSE listing was considered more prestigious by the Chinese.

Exhibit 13
Listing strategy

	New York	Hong Kong
Retail participation	15–25%	40–50%
Pricing method	Open price	Fixed price
Underwriting method	Underwritten at the end of the marketing period	Hard underwriting at fixed price for a 2-week offer period
Expected secondary market premium	10–15%	25%
Typical deal size	Up to several billion US$	*Up to US$100 million

*There are several exceptions to the smaller offers in Hong Kong: CEPA with five power plants in China and the Philippines did a US$766 million issue in November 1993, Maanshan Iron & Steel a US$510 million issue and Shanghai Petrochemical a US$343 million issue. However, all these happened after SH had applied for a US listing.

The arguments for New York instead of Hong Kong seemed compelling (see Exhibit 13).

The new tariff agreement

SH is supposed to charge electricity tariffs at a rate sufficient to cover generating costs and taxes, and achieve a 15 per cent return on average net fixed assets. The thinking behind the formula is that profit growth should be linked to asset growth to stimulate new generating capacity. Operating assets provide a shrinking base (as they are depreciated) for the determination of the allowed return. Therefore, the addition of assets (either operating assets or work in progress) each year is vital to earnings growth. Although profits are directly linked to assets, it is still possible for the company to gain from efficiency in any one year. As costs are estimated at the beginning of the year to determine tariffs, keeping them below forecast will to a limited extent lead to returns in excess of the allowed minimum. Given the central role that assets play in determining profits, projecting capital expenditure is the key to determining profit growth.

Thus the advantages of the SH tariff formula and the governing regulatory structure were supposed to be:

- Fair and stable returns of 15 per cent. Although return on assets was capped, the return to investors could be higher if the asset growth is higher. This encourages growth, so the company has a profit incentive to institute expansion plans as expeditiously as possible;
- The return-on-assets approach retains future leverage benefits for shareholders. It allows SH to earn returns on future expansion financed by debt. The current conservative capital structure should enable it to finance its aggressive expansion programme without raising additional equity;
- SH is protected from future inflation impact. All major operating costs are considered in calculating the electricity tariff, including depreciation, fuel, water, labour, and taxes. This cost plus calculation means that any inflationary price increases will be passed through each year in the form of higher electricity prices; and
- SH is party to an equal treatment undertaking with the other generators on the Shandong Grid – Shandong Power Bureau and Shandong Power Company – covering tariff setting, on-grid output levels and participation in new construction and expansion projects.

The disadvantages were considered to include:

- Political dependency. The annual tariff increases and major capital expenditure projects are subject to approval by the regulator. The government may impose controls on industrial and consumer electricity prices or take other action which could inhibit economic activity in China, depressing demand for electricity and disrupting the planned expansion. This happened when price increases for 1995 and capital expenditure plans were not approved;
- Relatively low risk-adjusted return. Experienced China investors such as CEPA's Gordon Wu soon recognised that a 15 per cent return on average fixed assets is too low. Although with a higher asset growth rate, earnings growth can be correspondingly higher, the reality is that there are too many hurdles to be able to realise a higher rate of asset growth in a politically influenced industry;
- Delayed effect between rising costs and prices. Price rises are approved by the Shandong Power Bureau and the Shandong Province Price Control Bureau on an annual basis for the year ahead, so the company can recover unexpected cost increases only by raising tariffs in the following year; and
- Conflict of interest: SH's only customer is Shandong Power which is controlled by the Shandong Power Bureau which is also the provincial regulator. Shandong Power is also a competitor as an operator of the overwhelming majority of provincial power capacity. SH's other two shareholders also have significant power interests elsewhere and it is relatively uncertain which potential projects initiated by shareholders would be channelled to SH and which might go to other companies.

Marketing

The investment story was fundamentally sound but market conditions were not what had been hoped for when the project was initiated early in 1993, so CSFB had to give careful thought to the marketing programme. A tight timetable was chosen, a decision driven by the view of market conditions and the need to create momentum; as there were relatively few companies on the road, SH received a lot of

Exhibit 14

Roadshow 'hit ratio'

	Number of attendees	Number of orders
One-on-ones		
US	30	11
Asia	13	10
Europe	7	6
Total	50	27
Group functions		
US	74	22
Asia	70	20
Europe	109	35
Total	253	77
Analyst presentations	23	15
Conference calls		
US	7	3
Asia	-	-
Europe	2	1
Total	9	4
Total roadshow	**335**	**123**

Source: CSFB.

attention despite this being the summer season. Two road-show teams were used, to facilitate pricing in the first week of August.

In a difficult market, the focus must be on the right investors. Pre-marketing assisted the global coordinator to fine-tune the investment story and define the target market. The marketing was directed towards:

- Investors in Asian utilities; eg, CEPA, CL&P, HKE, KEPCO, Manila Electric and Tenaga;
- Investors in Chinese equities; and
- Open-end and closed-end mutual funds specialising in: privatisation, Asian power, infrastructure, China, emerging markets, Asia, growth, income, US utilities, international equity and global equity.

To add credibility to the China story, CSFB enlisted external China specialist David Lampton, president of the National Committee for US-China Relations and internal specialist Paul Schulte, Asian portfolio strategist of CSFB Hong Kong to brief its salesforce.

As part of the pre-marketing, and to create demand momentum, CSFB equity research analyst Michael Worms conducted an active programme of 'warm-ups' of key accounts to identify those investors who might commit large amounts at an early stage.

Senior representatives from the Beijing Ministry of Electric Power participated in the roadshow to explain China's policies on tariff structure and industry development. In all there were meetings with more than 300 institutions globally through 50 one-on-one meetings, 15 roadshow presentations and a series of conference calls. Following the roadshow Michael Worms saw several important investors who were seriously considering participating in the offer (see Exhibit 14).

The Shandong Huaneng Story

CSFB positioned SH as a high-growth Asian power company rather than primarily a China play. There was also emphasis on this being the first opportunity to invest in a Chinese power company, a sector of great strategic importance. While the US electricity-generating market is characterised by oversupply, the focus here was very much on supply shortages, estimated to have been 14 per cent of demand in Shandong province at the end of 1993. (See Exhibits 15, 16 and 17.)

SH was, at 12.9 times 1995 earnings, valued at a considerable discount to the Asian electric utility sector (compare in particular CEPA at 17.5x 1995 earnings and China Light & Power at 15.7x 1995 earnings). (See Exhibit 18.)

Asian utilities trade at a higher valuation than China plays traded in New York or Hong Kong. (See Exhibit 19.)

Investor concerns

There was increasing discussion of austerity measures triggered by the publication of the inflation figure for 1993, which was 20 per cent. The power industry was an obvious target – indeed the Chinese government had decided to cap the return on power projects at 15 per cent. Gordon Wu, the highly respected Hong Kong Chinese Chairman of CEPA, had reacted to this decision by ceasing all new investment in Chinese power projects. Intelligent portfolio investors followed his direction. Specific concerns included:

- Inflation leading to currency devaluation;
- Inflationary pressures on tariff structure affecting consumers' ability to bear the cost;

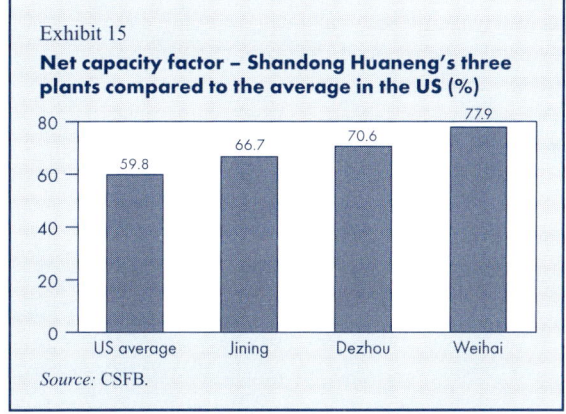

Exhibit 15

Net capacity factor – Shandong Huaneng's three plants compared to the average in the US (%)

Source: CSFB.

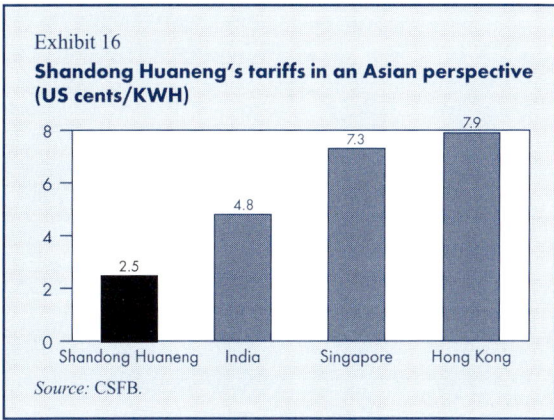

Exhibit 16

Shandong Huaneng's tariffs in an Asian perspective (US cents/KWH)

Source: CSFB.

Exhibit 17
Principal sales points

The Chinese power sector	China's electricity industry is an attractive high-growth sector: • Installed capacity of 181,000 MW places China fourth in the world in size but it is insufficient to meet the country's rapid economic development. National supply shortage estimated at 15–20%; • GNP has grown at average annual rate of over 9% since 1980 but average growth in power generation capacity has risen only by 8%; • For China to match Hong Kong's current per capita consumption 20 years from now, per capita electricity consumption would need to increase by 11% per annum; and • The government is sponsoring aggressive expansion plans. The current five-year plan seeks to maintain growth in electricity generation in excess of GNP growth which will require more new capacity each year than currently exists in Hong Kong.
Shandong province	Shandong province is at the forefront of Chinese economic development: • Straddling the Yellow River, Shandong is one of China's most important provincial economies. Its US$31 billion GDP is the second largest in the country. Over the past 15 years, Shandong's economy has grown at the second-fastest rate in China; • Shandong's power sector should continue to grow rapidly. The government's goal is to double the province's existing capacity by 2000; and • SH will benefit from the provincial government's aggressive expansion plan. Its share of the province's installed capacity was expected to grow from 13.7% in 1994 to 20% by 2000.
Strong shareholders	• SH is backed by three powerful, experienced and knowledgeable companies as founding share-holders.
The assets	SH has efficient and well operated power plants: • All three of its plants are in rapidly developing industrial centres; • Each plant is equipped with Chinese-manufactured generating equipment which enables SH to contract/develop new capacity for an approximate cost of US$300–400 per KW, equivalent to less than half the cost of foreign technology; and • The plants compare favourably in terms of net capacity factor, ie, the plant's total output divided by the maximum it could have generated had it experienced 100% availability and 100% load factor.
Company growth	The company has a well defined and aggressive expansion plan through 2000: • Total installed capacity is expected to grow from 1,325 MW in 1993 to 6,050 MW in 2000; • Growth is from existing plants and greenfield development: Dezhou will grow from 900 to 2,400 MW, Weihai from 125 to 850 MW and the new Rizhao greenfield plants will grow in three phases to 2,500 MW by 2000. Jining Plant will remain unchanged at 300 MW; • All near-term expansions were approved by the Ministry of Electric Power and the State Planning Commission; and • The plants had a track record of profitability.
Regulatory environment	• There is a favourable regulatory environment and contractual arrangements designed to promote profitable operations and rapid growth.
Tariffs	• SH's tariffs are low compared to other rates in the Asian region. These indicate that the company should enjoy significant flexibility to pass through additional price increases as its costs of operations rise.
Balance sheet	The strong balance sheet will support future leverage: • Post-offer, SH is virtually debt free; • Internal cash flow and IPO proceeds will cover expansion programme costs for at least two years; • Management has targeted a future debt/capitalisation rate of no more than 25–30% by 2000 and envisions future corporate borrowings via domestic and foreign markets. SH intends also to use project financing structures when feasible or desirable; and • Future leverage will benefit shareholders: RoA-based tariff provides for a 15% after-tax return. If a 10% pre-tax interest expense is assumed, debt costs would represent 6.60% after-tax cost of money. Therefore future asset growth will enhance return to shareholders.
Track record	• SH has a track record of finishing project construction ahead of schedule and exceeding planned output levels. For the past two years it has bettered its planned output for tariff-setting purposes by 2–3%.
Earnings	CSFB is forecasting significant earnings growth over the next five years. • Earnings per ADR were expected to grow from US$0.92 (pro forma) in 1994 to US$2.03 in 1998 fuelled by anticipated growth in fixed assets from US$518 million in 1994 to US$1,288 million by year-end 1998; and • Earnings are understated by adherence to national regulatory depreciation accounting (16 rather than 25 years depreciation).
Valuation (as of 29 June 1994)	• Asian utilities are used as the most direct comparables to obtain the highest potential valuation. Other benchmarks are NYSE-listed Chinese companies and Hong Kong-listed H shares.

Source: CSFB

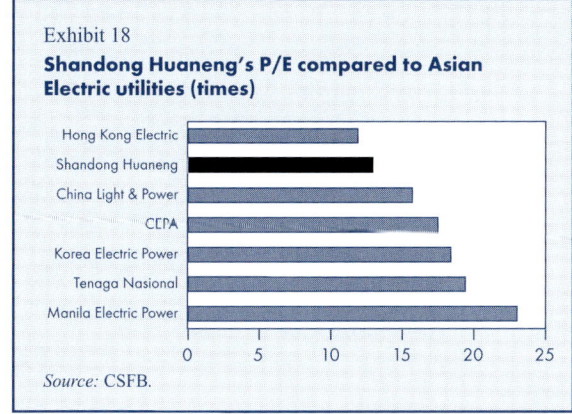

Exhibit 18

Shandong Huaneng's P/E compared to Asian Electric utilities (times)

Source: CSFB.

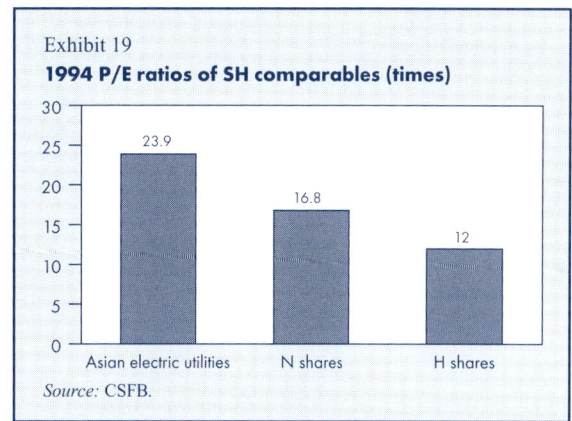

Exhibit 19

1994 P/E ratios of SH comparables (times)

Source: CSFB.

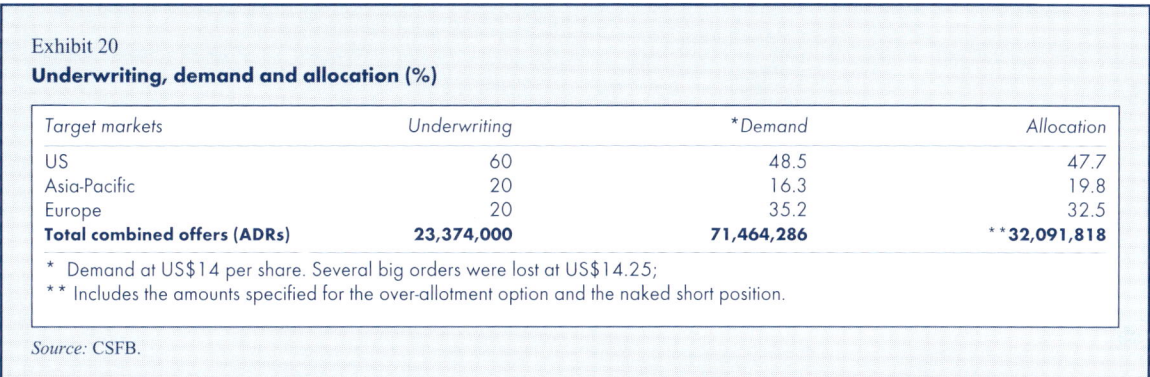

Exhibit 20

Underwriting, demand and allocation (%)

Target markets	Underwriting	*Demand	Allocation
US	60	48.5	47.7
Asia-Pacific	20	16.3	19.8
Europe	20	35.2	32.5
Total combined offers (ADRs)	**23,374,000**	**71,464,286**	** **32,091,818**

*   Demand at US$14 per share. Several big orders were lost at US$14.25;
** Includes the amounts specified for the over-allotment option and the naked short position.

Source: CSFB.

- SH's assets might not be revalued in pace with inflation for purposes of calculating RoA;
- The fact that the 15 per cent RoA tariff structure has no term and is subject to political influence;
- Competition from other Chinese or foreign power companies for future projects;
- Potential future dilution of shareholders due to need to raise further equity capital;
- SH ownership and potential conflict of interest between company and shareholders;
- Potential conflict of interest: SH wholly owns and operates only one plant. Both the Weihai and the Jining plants are operated by Shandong Electrical Power Bureau, a minority shareholder in SH;
- SH is much less likely to successfully complete power projects in other Chinese provinces because of an absence of strong political sponsorship nationwide. This leaves SH highly exposed to provincial politics; and
- Poor performance of other Chinese B and H share issues.

Results

Placement

The offer was approximately three times subscribed at a price of US$14. Of the total demand only 43 per cent (just over 30 million shares) was considered allocable demand at that price. Demand was very price-sensitive with price leadership coming mainly from the US market. As a result of final price negotiations driving up the offer price to US$14.25, two US$20 million orders were lost, making the offer only

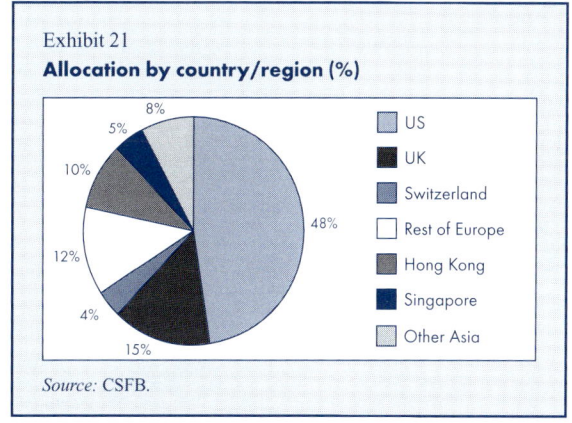

Exhibit 21

Allocation by country/region (%)

US 48%
UK 15%
Switzerland 4%
Rest of Europe 12%
Hong Kong 10%
Singapore 5%
Other Asia 8%

Source: CSFB.

modestly over-subscribed by high-quality investors (see Exhibit 20).

European demand had clearly been underestimated as there was interest from throughout Europe whereas US demand was disappointing (see Exhibit 21).

Investor concentration

The large number of institutions who subscribed but were not allocated shares indicates that the average quality of the book was not as high as had been hoped (see Exhibit 22). This was to be confirmed in the exceptionally high trading volumes in the immediate after-market.

China buyers were the single largest group of investors, contrasting with CSFB's strategy of positioning the company as a high-growth Asian power company rather than a 'China play' (see Exhibit 23).

Exhibit 22

Investor concentration

	By demand	By allocation
Percentage of issue accounted for by the 10 largest investors (by total size of demand and allocation respectively)	58.2%	24.0%
Number of investors making up 80% of the issue (by total size of demand and allocation respectively)	76	53
The three largest investors by size	US$30 million US$22.5 million US$20.1 million	US$17.5 million US$9.1 million US$8.4 million
Total number of institutions	174	92

Source: CSFB.

Exhibit 23

Buyers of Shandong Huaneng by type of investor (%)

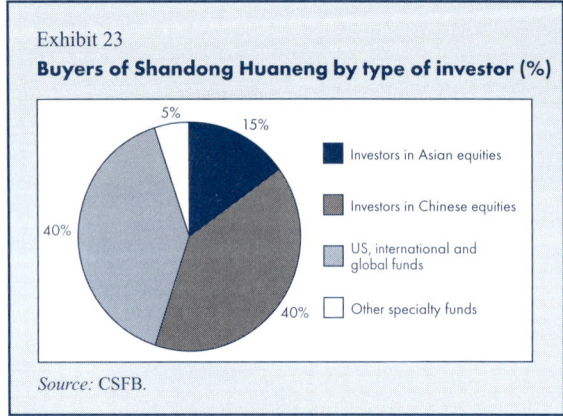

- Investors in Asian equities — 15%
- Investors in Chinese equities — 40%
- US, international and global funds — 40%
- Other specialty funds — 5%

Source: CSFB.

After-market price performance

See Exhibit 24.

On the first day of trading the closing price was held at the offer price in very high turnover, as a result of a below average investor quality and the fact that confidence was undermined by the delay in pricing and allocation. Having fallen to US$13.625 on the third day, despite substantial stabilisation efforts from CSFB, the issue traded to an all-time high of US$14.375 on 12 August 1994.

When initial trading did not yield a premium, the market started to look for reasons why SH was not a good investment. Assisted by the press, it picked up on the fact that SH was not an established company with a corresponding track record but rather three plants that had been put into one company to raise money from the market. In addition, SH only provided one year of historical audited financials. This argument was, perhaps, blown out of proportion by the press.

The decline that followed was to an extent caused by the prospective additional supply of Chinese power shares from the soon-to-follow HPI offer, although SH did not perform too badly during the first two weeks of HPI marketing.

On 15 September the SH price fell by US$0.75 on negative news: China's retail price inflation in the major cities had soared to 27.1 per cent on an annual basis; a newswire article compared SH unfavourably to HPI; and a newspaper reported that major Hong Kong group Hutchison Whampoa intended to take a large stake in HPI's IPO. HPI undoubtedly cannibalised demand from SH as many investors who had pur-

Exhibit 24

After-market price performance

Pricing date	4 August 1994
Filing range	US$13–17
Offer price	US$14.25

First year high/low	
High (12 August 1994)	US$14.375
Low (19 July 1995)	US$6.625

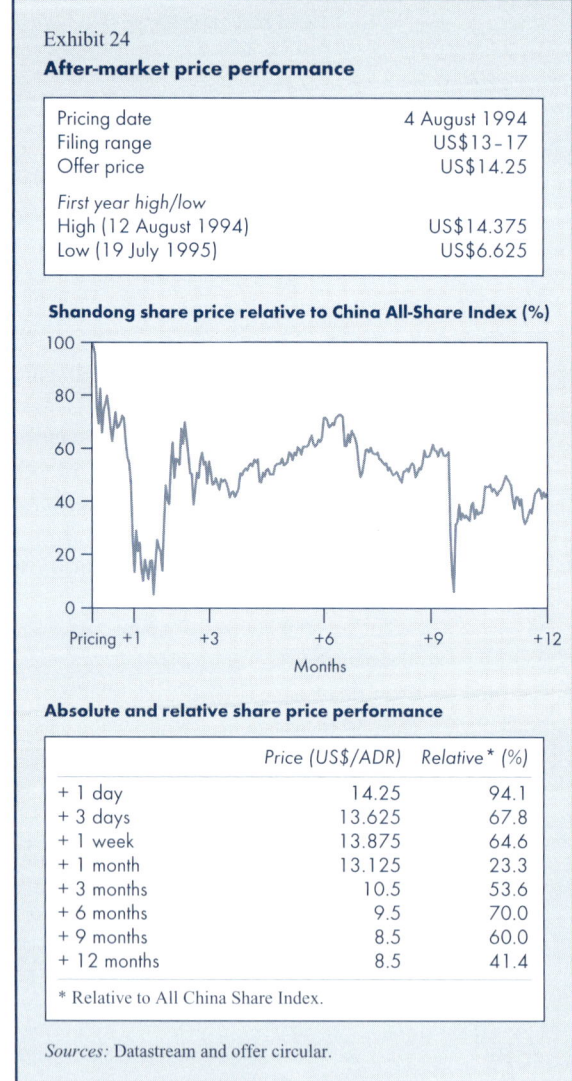

Shandong share price relative to China All-Share Index (%)

Absolute and relative share price performance

	Price (US$/ADR)	Relative* (%)
+ 1 day	14.25	94.1
+ 3 days	13.625	67.8
+ 1 week	13.875	64.6
+ 1 month	13.125	23.3
+ 3 months	10.5	53.6
+ 6 months	9.5	70.0
+ 9 months	8.5	60.0
+ 12 months	8.5	41.4

* Relative to All China Share Index.

Sources: Datastream and offer circular.

chased SH sold it and bought HPI. HPI was widely perceived as a stronger company because it used foreign technology, had geographically diverse generating assets, a larger number of power plants and three years of audited financials. By 5 October, the day HPI priced, SH had fallen to US$11.63, where it stayed until 17 October. By 26 October it was down to US$10.5.

SH's shares continued a steady decline and one year after

Exhibit 25
Percentage of total issue traded * (%)

	Day 1	Day 2	Day 3	Total Day 1-3
New York	60.2	11.9	2.1	74.2

* Based on the issue of 23.4 million ADRs.

panies as possible would do their IPOs and primary listings in Hong Kong. This strategy has paid off as most large Chinese offers now have their primary listing in Hong Kong even if they also list on overseas exchanges such as New York or London.

The performance of the main parties

The Chinese authorities
The offer represented a learning curve for authorities and investors alike, but it was clear that the Chinese did themselves no favours by allowing a prospectus as important as that of SH to be finalised, only to disregard its contents a few months later by not approving tariff increases and capital expenditure projects. In order to become a successful market-based economy, the Chinese administration would do well to rationalise its bureaucracy, although this is easier said than done. Flexibility with respect to timing, sizing, which markets to tap, etc. is the key to success in the capital markets. Instead, given the cumbersome decision-making processes in Beijing, the company and CSFB desperately needed to do everything to keep the original plan, provisionally agreed upon in early 1993. Any wavering on the part of CSFB and the project would have been killed immediately. No one involved in this project over the two years was prepared to suggest that, for example, the timing was not optimal.

pricing the market price had fallen by 40 per cent from the offer price, as the company's business was affected by macro-economic and political decisions. It was remarkable that the schedules for SH's capital expenditure projects as described in the prospectus were postponed only a few months after pricing. Over the first year, SH under-performed the highly volatile All China Share Index by 58.6 per cent.

After-market trading volume
See Exhibit 25.

An exceptionally high 14.1 million ADRs, or 60.2 per cent of the total issue, was traded on the first day, making SH the most actively traded security on the NYSE that day. Some analysts said the heavy trading reflected the large amount of speculative professional buying and the issue failing to match its considerable grey market premium, while some investors may have sold as a result of being scaled back (though the scale-back for high-quality investors was less than 50 per cent).

The disappointing trading performance soon had SH (and HPI) wondering if a subsequent secondary listing would be feasible. Out of the theoretically possible choices such as Hong Kong, Shanghai and Singapore, Hong Kong would make the most sense, however this was impossible as Hong Kong does not recognise the concept of secondary listings, whether at the time of an IPO or subsequently. For an additional Hong Kong listing to be feasible, SH would have to fully comply with Hong Kong listing requirements, issue a new prospectus and call it a primary listing. Such efforts, however, are hard to justify without raising further money. To undertake the work associated with a Hong Kong listing the company 'story' really ought to be an appealing one, and this was no longer the case given its poor after-market performance.

No doubt the decision on the part of the member firms of the Hong Kong Stock Exchange not to accommodate secondary listings was partly adopted to ensure that as many Chinese com-

SH's shareholders, including the China Huaneng Group, and the Beijing authorities would have been well advised not to have done the HPI offer so soon after that of SH. The problem of the timing of the HPI offer was compounded by its very large issue size. It is remarkable that SH's disappointing after-market performance did not lead to a reduction in HPI's offer size. 'Believe it or not', commented Walter, 'it was inconceivable that they should have reduced the size given that the transaction had been approved for a certain amount of money, particularly since the price had to be reduced twice. There simply was not that flexibility available. However, there was a considerable transfer of experience between the two issues as evidenced by the fact that what took us 18 months, took HPI only 7 months. The same thing was true with the pricing meeting – what took us 12 hours they did in only 15 minutes. Unlike the case of SH, it had not been set up as a negotiating session.'

The company
SH management gained credit for openness and profession-

Exhibit 26
Profit forecast versus actual profitability

	1993	1994	1995	1996
US GAAP (US$)				
EPADR (CSFB, 15 September 1994)	0.75A	*0.92F	1.17F	1.29F
EPADR (CSFB, 17 November, 1994)	0.75A	*0.92F	1.17F	1.29F
EPADR (CSFB, 20 September, 1995)	0.75A	0.74A	0.98F	1.06F
EPADR (CSFB, 14 May, 1996 1996)	0.75A	0.74A	0.92A	1.07F

* Pro-forma earnings on the basis that the new tariff formula had been in place for the entire year.

Source: CSFB.

alism on the roadshow and in the secondary market, and cannot be blamed for the effects of the government's failure to approve expansion plans on time (this is a highly tedious process in China) and the stipulated tariff increases for 1995. But together with the Ministry of Electric Power, the management can be blamed for driving a hard bargain on pricing, which led to weakness in the immediate after-market and an undermining of investor confidence.

Despite the fact that the offer price, at US$14.25, was below the middle of the pricing range (US$13–17), it was too aggressive given that demand was very price-sensitive. The pricing meeting, starting after close of business in New York at 5pm on 4 August (equivalent to 6am on 5 August in Hong Kong) took too long. Allocations in the Asian tranche were not done before the close of business on 5 August in Hong Kong and accordingly Asian confidence in the offer was undermined. This led to Asian selling in the immediate after-market, triggering selling elsewhere.

SH's earnings for 1994 and 1995 were substantially below CSFB's forecasts at the time of the offer in August 1994 (see Exhibit 26).

On-grid output and revenue were on target for 1994 but net profit was affected by higher fuel costs (coal prices increased by 15 per cent year-on-year). Profit was also affected by unrealised foreign exchange losses due to a currency translation loss on the US$-denominated cash balances (representing the issue proceeds) when the renmimbi appreciated against the dollar during the second half of 1994. The outlook was then clouded by the government keeping 1995 tariffs unchanged as part of its anti-inflationary measures.

Both SH and HPI performed more or less in line with the Hong Kong China Enterprises Index until the publication of the 1994 results, since when HPI has substantially outperformed SH, reflecting the former's 1995 tariff increases. The fact that HPI was permitted the new tariffs and SH was not was interpreted in the markets as indicating that HPI had better political connections. Whereas there may be some truth in that, the tariff arrangements are not strictly comparable. HPI at the outset negotiated a different tariff agreement with its regulators in which it would be allowed to increase tariffs only to achieve a RoA of 15 per cent over a period of several years (whereas SH was promised a 15 per cent RoA from the outset). There were delays in HPI's capital expenditure projects, though less severe than those at SH.

The global coordinator

CSFB got the offer done against very long odds. The bank has a first-rate team in Beijing, which is well plugged into the local market. SH was full of praise for the bank's efforts as Lu Dan stated: 'CSFB had a dedicated and a highly professional China team . . . They had the necessary courage, confidence, competence and determination to get the deal done, qualities which proved to be major assets during the 18 months of work between the initial discussions and the execution of the offer.'

The offer, well prepared and marketed, was three times subscribed at a price of US$14, the offer price that CSFB recommended to its client. The bank deserves some criticism for not sufficiently educating its client on the process of setting

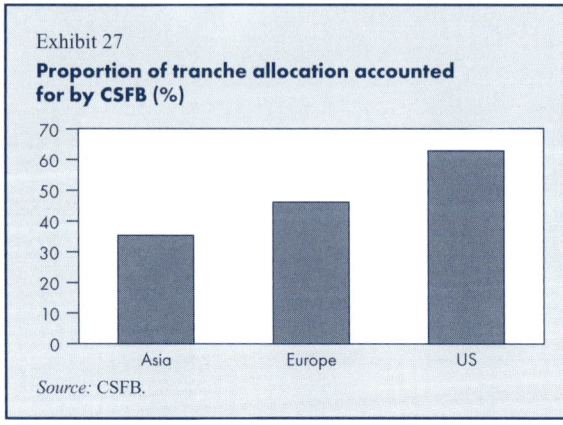

Exhibit 27

Proportion of tranche allocation accounted for by CSFB (%)

Source: CSFB.

the offer price, the consequence of which was that they were forced to agree to a more aggressive price than was ideal. The duration of the pricing meeting undermined investor confidence in the Asian tranche which is thought to have triggered the high turnover on the first day of trading. The global coordinator has to take direct blame for this – as even if they had managed to procure a lower offer price, much of the damage would have been done by not pricing and allocating before the close of business in Hong-Kong. Some very good work over two years was undone in a number of hours.

Hindsight shows that it would have been advisable to list SH (and HPI) both in Hong Kong and New York: yet if the offer price had been slightly lower SH might have traded well, at least until the arrival of adverse news in late 1994 and 1995.

CSFB underwrote 45 per cent of the offer globally and placed 52 per cent, perhaps on the low side of what might have been expected for an offer of this kind. It did relatively well in the US tranche and had the least impressive relative performance in the Asian tranche, as illustrated in Exhibit 27.

CSFB was the first of the large US investment banks in China to complete an international equity offer for a Chinese company (Brilliance China Automotive in October 1992) and the first to talk to the China Huaneng Group about foreign equity raising and listing strategies in December 1992. Lehman Brothers, as perhaps the closest competitor for the mandate, and others (such as Merrill Lynch and Goldman Sachs) only began their dialogues at a later stage. By the time of the beauty contest in March 1993 CSFB was already in a strong position. The decision to hire CSFB was taken jointly by China Huaneng Group and the operating management of SH.

CSFB's role as adviser to SH, for which the bank was not paid a separate advisory fee, included the following responsibilities:

- Advice on the optimal combination of assets necessary to appeal to investors;
- Assistance with negotiations between the company and its shareholders;
- Advice on likely investor reaction to proposed tariff structures;
- Assistance with negotiations on the tariff agreement; and
- Advice on capital structure, dividend policy and other financial matters.

Key lessons learnt

Listing strategy

The decision where to list may not always be clear cut but generally it would be beneficial to establish a home market for the stock, where there is optimal access to information, trading of comparable companies, specialist analysts and investors. For SH, that stock exchange would have been Hong Kong, as Colin Hermon, head of Asian ECM at Jardine Fleming explained: 'Because of the different time zones, there is very limited interest among Asian investors in buying Chinese companies listed on the NYSE only.' A senior Hong Kong fund manager commented: 'Overseas investors do understand China, but most of them are here in Hong Kong, not in New York.' Yet a US investment banker with considerable knowledge of the region says: 'Although it is different now, in 1992–93, Hong Kong based investors didn't really have that much of an edge in terms of China knowledge because there had not been any listed Chinese companies to invest in.'

A British banker based in Hong Kong added: 'I am not a believer in a primary listing outside the home market. The liquidity soon dries up because of a general lack of information and a lack of research coverage. SH and HPI should never have done NYSE listings only. They came about because the Chinese were attracted to the prestige associated with a NYSE listing and because the US investment banks lured the Chinese with highly attractive P/E ratios that of course proved not to be sustainable. I fail to see that just because a stock is listed on the NYSE, US investors would continue to pay a higher price for a stock than would investors closer to home.' This seems especially true since many of the largest US institutions base their Asia specialists in Hong-Kong. It is the availability of such temporary valuation discrepancies and the efforts by less sophisticated vendors and opportunistic bankers to exploit them that earn certain emerging markets and vendors a bad reputation.

Walter commented: 'The original price was of key importance when selecting the listing venue and this price was clearly a lot higher in New York than what could have been done in Hong Kong.' A Hong Kong based ECM specialist commented: 'The concept of doing a NYSE listing only is not necessarily flawed, although we prefer dual listings, but the first NYSE issue should have been the best possible company with the best possible management.' Steven Wisch, head of Asian ECM at Goldman Sachs supported, in principle, CSFB's choice of listing venue: 'We recommend a US listing when the offer is big and complex and when the methodology of valuation is primarily based on discounted cash flow rather than only earnings, as was the case here. However, we disagreed with the timing and the pricing. In our judgment, the market was simply not there.'

Carl Walter answered: 'It may well be correct that the timing was unfortunate but it was controlled by the government, not the company and not the underwriters. Had we not gone at that time, we would most likely never have done the offer, principally for political reasons.'

The single NYSE listings also came about because the Hong Kong market was not prepared to afford these two companies secondary listings at the time of their IPOs. 'With hindsight, the inability to achieve a secondary Hong Kong listing at the time of the IPO measurably impacted the potential demand for SH shares,' concedes CSFB ECM managing director Bob Cooney.

Jesse Wang, former chief accountant and director of international operations of the China Securities Regulatory Commission, noted: 'We realise now that to list in New York only is not a good idea. US investors are not as familiar with Chinese companies as investors in our region and our companies are simply not yet in a position to offer the same high disclosure as US companies.' Both the Chinese authorities and the investment banks now realise that a dual listing is probably the best strategy for a large offer. An increasing number of Chinese companies therefore now do a primary listing in Hong Kong and a simultaneous secondary one in New York.

It is important to bear in mind that one reason for the failure of many Chinese listings is that the listing candidates were selected by the Chinese authorities based on different criteria from those significant to investors. This process is changing and the sponsoring investment banks now have an increasing role in the selection process.

Pricing and allocation

It appears that the founding shareholders of SH listened to all the foreign bankers during the solicitation phase and in the process developed an inflated opinion of the price at which the transaction could be done. This opinion was the basis for the negotiating strategy of SH and its shareholders at the pricing meeting. The lesson here is that companies and vendors should disregard all promises made during the solicitation phase if they want to have successful transactions and build a good name in the market. The Chinese will not have appreciated, due to inexperience, that the equity market changes in such a way that what might be possible in a good market may not be feasible in a tougher market environment.

The difference between 'tight but right' and too aggressive pricing can be small, and have consequences beyond the imagination of an inexperienced person. CSFB's Cooney says: 'At US$14 we would not have had a great deal but one that would have worked.' A book which is two to three times subscribed does not guarantee healthy after-market performance.

A senior Hong Kong-based ECM banker specialising in China commented: ' The pricing was too aggressive but then it always is in China. The Chinese are definitely not helping themselves to secure long-term access to the international equity market on attractive terms. Virtually none of the Chinese deals listed overseas have traded well.' Vendors eager to achieve favourable terms on the basis of aggressive assumptions at the time of sale need to understand that this short-term strategy is doomed to fail in the long term. The global capital markets do not easily forget and there are many investment alternatives. Trust and credibility are difficult to establish and maintain but easy to lose.

SH provides clear evidence of the price to be paid for loss of credibility. In August 1994 Shandong's IPO was priced at 12.3x estimated 1995 earnings, a year later, at US$8/ADR, SH was trading at 7.5x CSFB's estimated 1996 earnings. Not only did investors react to the fact that projected 1996 earnings were 18 per cent lower one year out than at the time of the IPO, but they decided to substantially derate the shares. SH's share price development suggests that it is difficult to recover from such a loss of credibility. Three years later SH was still trading at a 14 per cent discount to its offer price, whereas HPI was trading at a premium of over 41 per cent.

The pricing and allocation process is highly sensitive and needs to be handled with utmost care. Because of the protracted pricing negotiations between CSFB and SH and the failure to allocate on time in Hong Kong, investor sentiment turned negative. This spread to Europe before the opening of the New York market: a basically sound offer had turned sour partly as a result of a too protracted pricing negotiation. 'Why didn't CSFB's New York syndicate realise that they were up against an important deadline as far as allocation to Asian investors was concerned?' asked an ECM specialist at a competing bank.

What the Chinese tried to do in the pricing meeting was to negotiate with the capital markets, a strategy which simply does not work. They should have listened to what the market was telling them and adopted a flexible approach. Flexibility is the key to success in the markets – on timing, sizing of transaction and tranches and most importantly on pricing.

Immediate after-market

A relatively healthy book and strong grey market trading is not a guarantee for a successful issue. If the syndicate is not seen as being in total control of the immediate after-market, the integrity of the offer is soon questioned by investors. As soon as a weakness is spotted, speculative investors will sell triggering further sales from those who had intended to hold the stock long term.

The importance of getting off to a good start in the immediate after-market cannot be overstated. This is especially true for emerging-market IPOs where there is no trading history, no real comparables and where creation of 'the right' impression is of key importance. It was the global coordinator who decided to position SH as an Asian growth utility rather than a China play, and judging from the order book the market at first probably believed in this positioning. The issue may have done better, at least in the short to medium term, if the immediate after-market trading had yielded a premium. This experience also shows that first transactions in emerging markets – in this case the first NYSE listing for a Chinese company – are either huge successes or huge failures.

Other

It is important to educate an inexperienced client about the processes involved in a global equity offer, especially on subjects like bookbuilding and the pricing process. These are very specialised fields and first time issuers need considerable coaching. 'The company didn't understand the pricing process,' acknowledges Lu Dan of SH. CSFB has accepted responsibility for this and has taken appropriate action.

In an emerging market where language can prove a barrier between company and investors – especially if the geo-

graphic distance between them is huge – successful communication becomes vital. Companies need to be accessible geographically and employ people with appropriate language and communication skills. The fact that SH's head office was located in the provincial capital Jinan will have prevented certain analysts and investors from allocating the necessary time to visit the company's management and research the company as might otherwise have been the case.

It is a regrettable reality that for bankers to remain in business, they will have to continue to recommend that issuers exploit more or less real valuation discrepancies such as the one temporarily available between Hong Kong and New York. Much of the responsibility lies with the issuers/vendors to see through the hidden agendas of the bankers – too few vendors will give a mandate to banks that come up with an assessment that is merely realistic. The Chinese are setting themselves up for continued failure as long as they refuse to hire and pay independent advisers for a qualified opinion on what they should do. CSFB can hardly be blamed for wanting to see the SH issue happen as it had worked for almost two years to achieve it. They knew, as did the company, that there would only be one chance to come to the market. To cut the issue size, move the listing venue or otherwise radically restructure the offer would have been sure dealbreakers.

It is an illusion that where a true pioneering effort is required, such as in the case of the first NYSE listing for a Chinese company, the investment bank can pick the optimal timing for the offer. 'When you are faced with having to break a bureaucratic deadlock, you need to seize the opportunity when it presents itself,' explained Walter. 'This is the Chinese mentality, it will not change easily.' The fact that CSFB was not paid an advisory fee also made it more difficult to recommend that the issue be postponed or restructured.

Conclusion

It was a tremendous pioneering achievement by SH and CSFB's Beijing office to navigate through the political, legal and regulatory minefield to get the offer done. CSFB had to educate the Chinese from a very low level of understanding, which took time. However, what appeared to be a reasonable proposition in 1992–1993 – to list on the NYSE only – became less and less appropriate.

Not only had the flow of funds from the US started to dry up but those Chinese companies that came to market in 1993 had started to report their 1993 results, which were almost universally below expectations. This reporting season also coincided with increasing discussion of austerity measures due to rising inflation. In addition, the shine had almost certainly gone out of the power sector.

This deal – of enormous importance to China's privatisation programme – was successfully marketed, but the pricing was too aggressive and the average quality of the book not what it should have been. Given the offer's size, lack of local comparable companies, and absence of a natural home market combined with the uncertainties associated with investment in China, confidence in the offer evaporated quickly. As 60 per cent of the issue traded on the first day, most market participants took the view that this was not going to be a successful issue. Even the highest quality institutions do not hang on to their allocations under such circumstances, particularly since there was an even larger Chinese power offer to be priced within weeks. The bankers should have stopped this from happening, but there was no flexibility in the system. The offer was clearly structured with very little regard for the secondary market, with respect to timing, valuation and a listing venue which precluded an active trading market in the company's time zone.

The offer was marketed on the basis of growth, a strong regulatory framework and an attractive return. Bryant Seaman, managing director of ECM at CSFB responsible for the offer, concluded the roadshow presentation with the following statement: 'Please remember, future growth is not based on letters of intent or MOUs – SH has major projects under construction at three sites in the Province of Shandong.' But, added Walter: 'The real problem is that what was said in the prospectus has not happened – the company has effectively lost a year.' The Chinese authorities were clearly irresponsible in supporting this landmark deal only a short while before they decided not to approve the company's expansion plans. The market had assumed that infrastructure investment was not going to be affected by austerity measures (although the prospectus referred to the requirement of final approval for capital expenditure programmes). Either the SH offer should have been postponed until the effects of the austerity package were clear or SH should have been shielded against such measures.

China's legal and regulatory framework has to be tightened but at the same time simplified, and the transparency of the markets improved to rekindle western investor interest. The regulators and state-owned companies have to adjust their optimistic expectations as to what is possible. Investor returns need to be uncapped or at least improved to attract funds for the capital-starved energy sector. And the Chinese authorities must begin to realise that they do not lose face by letting foreign investors make money on their privatisations. Hopefully, this offer taught the Chinese to be more market sensitive – indications are that it did, as the concept of primary listings without a simultaneous local or regional listing was killed.

Despite the setback with SH and many other companies, and a much reduced interest among international investors, vice-premier Zhu Rongji confirmed on a visit to Shanghai Stock Exchange in early 1996, that overseas IPOs would be continued and were no longer experimental. Carl Walter says: 'This may perhaps seem unimportant but it is not: we can expect the process – the learning process – to go on, with the listing venues to be diversified to include London, Singapore, Tokyo etc.'

Feature topic: *The re-emergence of the Chinese securities market*

International privatisations of Chinese state-owned enterprises

Domestic listings

In 1992 the first listings of B shares (technically restricted to foreign investors) took place on the two domestic stock exchanges, Shanghai and Shenzhen (see Exhibits 28 and 29).

By the end of 1996, there were 85 B-share companies, with a total market capitalisation of just over US$4 billion, trading on these two exchanges. In total, including A-share listings, there were 520 Chinese companies listed on domestic exchanges. The total number of Chinese shareholders was estimated at 21 million.

Exhibit 28

Trends in non-Japan Asian equity issuance (US$ millions)

* Companies that can be bought by foreign investors, i.e. this table does not include companies that were listed but could only be bought by domestic investors (A shares).

Source: CSFB.

Exhibit 29

Shanghai and Shenzhen B-share listings in an Asian perspective* (number of companies)

	1991	1992	1993	1994	1995
Chinese listings	0	6	16	16	7
Non-Japan Asian listings	15	18 28	92	48	

* Companies that can be bought by foreign investors, ie, this table does not include companies that were listed but could only be bought by domestic investors (ie, A shares).

Source: CSFB.

Exhibit 30

Highlights from the early years

1 December 1990	• Trading on Shenzhen Stock Exchange started as an experiment though the exchange is not officially opened until July 1991. There has not been an organised equity market in China since before the Communists took over in 1949.
19 December 1990	• Shanghai Stock Exchange opened. Both domestic stock exchanges are supervised by the People's Bank of China. The PBOC is responsible for the financial markets.
November 1991	• The first B share listing in China is Shanghai Vacuum on the Shanghai Stock Exchange. B shares are shares issued by Chinese companies that can only be owned by foreign investors, ie, foreign shares with domestic listing. B shares trade in US$ in Shanghai and US$ or HK$ in Shenzhen. All B shares are registered shares. To buy them investors need foreign resident status. However, estimates suggest that in late 1995/early 1996 approximately one-third of B shares were owned by local Chinese.
End of 1991	• There were only 14 A shares (shares that can be owned only by Chinese investors, ie, domestic shares with domestic listing) quoted on the two stock exchanges.
January 1992	• China's leader Mr. Deng Xiaoping travelled to Guandong province, where he got a first-hand impression of the workings of capitalism and stock exchange trading at the Shenzhen Stock Exchange. The 'listing experiment' gathered momentum and the idea of a foreign listing of a Sino-foreign joint venture was conceived. Brilliance China Automotive, the mini-van manufacturer, was to become the first case.
9 October 1992	• Brilliance China Automotive, through a Bermuda holding company, listed its shares on the NYSE in a hugely successful US$80 million offer through CSFB. Widely applauded as 'Asian Deal of the Year'. • Why overseas listings? In the early 1980s when China began to open up to foreign investment, the emphasis was on transfer of technology and not on portfolio investment. However, as Chinese control of some of these joint ventures was challenged, the Chinese began to emphasise portfolio investment as it allowed local managements to retain control while still raising overseas finance. In late 1991 it was increasingly argued that foreign investors should be let into China and that Chinese companies should be allowed to raise offshore money. It was, however, soon realised that the Chinese market was not yet ready to open up to foreign investors. There were too few quoted companies (ie, too few A shares), no domestic institutional investors, no national securities regulation, no laws and not enough trading facilities. • There was an increasing lobby among foreign banks and stock exchanges to have Chinese companies listed on foreign exchanges. This keen interest coincided with a general 'China fever', in particular during 1991–92. The Hong Kong stock market, the most natural foreign market for Chinese companies, was keen to welcome industrials into its list of stocks to balance the preponderance of conglomerates, property companies and financials. The US houses pushed for NYSE listings.
26 October 1992	• The China Securities Regulatory Commission (CSRC) was established as the operating body within the framework of a two-tier regulatory system. The CSRC answers to the State Council Securities Policy Committee (SCSPC) on which 14 vice ministers of relevant ministries are represented. The CSRC aims to strengthen regulation of the Chinese securities market which has not been sufficiently monitored by the People's Bank of China. The CSRC, modelled on the US SEC, was given the following terms of reference by the SCSPC: • Regulation of the Chinese stock markets; • Approval of new domestic B share and overseas listings; • Guidance and development of markets; and • Promotion of the stock markets.
28 June 1993	• Food and drinks company Tsingtao Brewery became the first of a batch of nine Chinese companies to list H shares on the HKSE in a US$99 million offer which was 111 times subscribed. The HKSE soon accounted for the largest number of foreign listings by Chinese companies but the market is relatively small and its capacity to absorb larger issues is questionable.
23 July 1993	• Shanghai Petrochemical was the first Chinese company to carry out simultaneous dual listings – a primary listing on the HKSE and a secondary listing on the NYSE.
13 December 1993	• The Hang Seng China Enterprises Index (measuring the performance of H-shares trading in Hong Kong) reaches a peak of 2,177.
January 1994	• Recognising the need to diversify capital sources, the Chinese government decided that of the second batch of 22 foreign listing candidates, five were to have their primary listings on the NYSE (secondary listings are not envisaged).
August 1994	• The CSRC suspended all new listings on Shanghai and Shenzhen stock exchanges (ie, both A and B shares). It also announced that it was considering allowing foreign funds (together with Chinese joint-venture partners) to invest in A shares hitherto reserved for Chinese investors. The A-share index rose by 155% in the four weeks following the announcement.
4 August 1994	• SH became the first direct Chinese primary listing on the NYSE. HPI followed two months later, after which the Chinese authorities ruled out further such listings. The lack of success with these two power offers and the austerity programme itself put an end to any further listings by Chinese power companies. It was not until March 1997 that the third of the four power companies included under the second batch of companies earmarked for foreign listings could get its offer and foreign listing completed (Datang Power, which listed on the HKSE and the LSE).
July 1995	• The Shanghai and Shenzhen stock exchanges lift the freeze on new A and B share listings.

Exhibit 31

Bermuda holding companies for Chinese joint ventures on the NYSE

Company	Date	Size offer (US$ millions)	Industry	Lead manager
Brilliance China Automotive	9 October 1992	80	Automotive	CSFB
Ek Chor China Motorcycle	28 June 1993	102	Automotive	Bear Stearns
China Tyre Holding	15 July 1993	104	Rubber/plastics	Morgan Stanley
China Yuchai International	15 December 1994	75	Engineering	Bear Stearns

Source: Capital Data Ltd.

Exhibit 32

Direct primary NYSE listing ('N' shares)

Company	Date	Size of offer (US$ millions)	Industry	Lead manager
Shandong Huaneng	4 August 1994	333	Power generation	CSFB
Huaneng Power International	5 October 1994	675	Power generation	Lehman Brothers

Source: Capital Data Ltd.

Exhibit 33

Primary listings on Hong Kong Stock Exchange ('H' shares), 1993–95

Company	Date	Size of offer (US$ millions)	Industry	Lead manager
First batch of 9 Chinese H share listings				
Tsingtao Brewery	28 June 1993	99	Food and drink	CDFC
Guangzhou Shipyard	21 July 1993	39	Transport and shipping	Peregrine Cap.
Beiren Printing Machinery	23 July 1993	27	Manufacturing	Standard Chartered
Shanghai Petrochemicals	23 July 1993	343	Chemicals	Merrill Lynch
Maanshan Iron & Steel*	19 October 1993	510	Iron and steel	Wardley
Kunming Machine Tools	23 November 1993	17	Manufacturing	Barings
Yizheng Chemical Fibre*	14 March 1994	308	Textiles and clothing	SG Warburg
Tianjin Bohai Chemicals	3 May 1994	53	Chemicals	CDFC
Dongfang Electrical Machinery	18 May 1994	62	Engineering	Nomura
Second batch of 22 companies to be listed abroad				
Luoyang Glass	16 June 1994	118	Glass and ceramics	Salomon/CDFC
Qingling Motors	25 July 1994	134	Automotive	Smith Barney
Shanghai Hai Xing Shipping	1 November 1994	204	Transport and shipping	Morgan Grenfell
Zhenhai Refining & Chemical	10 November 1994	185	Oil, coal and gas	Barings
Chengdu Telecom Cable	29 November 1994	58	Telecommunications and communications	Crédit Lyonnais
Harbin Power	30 November 1994	145	Engineering	SG Warburg
Jilin Chemicals	19 May 1995	200	Chemicals	Merrill Lynch
Northeast Electr. Transm. &Transf.	28 June 1995	60	Engineering	Daiwa Securities

* These companies have sponsored ADR programmes in the US without being listed.

Source: Capital Data Ltd.

Foreign listings

Brilliance China Automotive became the first Chinese company to list anywhere internationally, when in October 1992 it listed on the NYSE. In fact, what was listed was a Bermuda holding company, the foreign partner in a Sino-foreign joint venture. This provided investors with greater protection and transaction transparency (the accounts were presented according to US GAAP). No other structure was realistic, as a direct foreign listing of a Chinese company was unprecedented. At the time there was no Chinese securities regulator, therefore there were no rules and regulations concerning foreign listings and no memorandum of understanding with the NYSE/SEC. Brilliance China Automotive was completed shortly before the formation of the CSRC and the announcement of the first nine H share candidates. It was of enormous significance as it demon-

Exhibit 34

Dual Hong Kong & New York listings ('H' shares with a secondary NYSE listing), 1993–95

Company	Date	Size offer (US$ millions)	Industry	Lead manager
Shanghai Petrochemicals	23 July 1993	343	Chemicals	Merrill Lynch
Jilin Chemical	19 May 1995	200	Chemicals	Merrill Lynch

Source: Capital Data Ltd.

strated that a Chinese company, even if indirectly, could fulfil the requirements of the US SEC and the NYSE. Other NYSE listings on the same basis followed, and the same structure was copied with listings on other foreign stock exchanges including Hong Kong and Singapore. In each case, the majority of the foreign partner's shares was offered and the proceeds invested in the joint venture. The local partner usually matched this investment by contributing fixed assets (see Exhibit 31).

SH opened the market for direct listings (both the issuer and the underlying operations are Chinese) on the NYSE. It was the first of five companies destined for primary listings on the exchange: the others were Huaneng Power International, China Southern Airlines, China Eastern Airlines and Tianjin Steel Pipe Factory. Only SH and HPI, however, obtained primary NYSE listings before the authorities decided not to pursue this strategy further (see Exhibit 32).

The Hong Kong market has been the principal source of capital for Chinese issuers, either in the form of H-shares, which are shares issued by former mainland state-owned enterprises and listed in Hong Kong, or in the form of so called red chips, which are Hong Kong listed subsidiaries of mainland enterprises or government departments (see Exhibit 33).

In 1996 no more than a handful of further H-share listings took place, including the dual listing for Guangshen Railway (see below). By July 1997 a total of 33 H-shares had been listed in Hong Kong.

As H-shares began to fall out of favour with investors due to poor quality of management, misuse of proceeds, poor disclosure and corporate governance standards, and as a result of the fact that the credit squeeze was typically hitting these companies particularly hard, Chinese and Hong Kong entrepreneurs recognised that it would be easier to sell the market shares of Hong Kong registered, but mainland-backed, companies listed in Hong Kong. These red chips would typically employ higher quality management, would not operate in basic industries, which were most sus-

ceptible to the austerity measures still affecting the Chinese economy and would have important connections on the mainland. While H-share companies are typically single-industry enterprises, the red chips are often mini-conglomerates, with interests spanning property, retail and infrastructure. The red chip market began to take off in 1996. By mid-1997, the red chips accounted for 10–15 per cent of the total market capitalisation of the Hong-Kong stock exchange, making it the largest sector, by a wide margin, of China related stocks traded anywhere offshore.

Dual listings

See Exhibit 34.

Following the unsuccessful direct listings of the two power companies on the NYSE in 1994, the Chinese realised that a foreign listing in a different time zone should also be accompanied by a local listing in Shanghai, Hong Kong or Singapore. Seven months later when Jilin Chemical listed on the NYSE, it was a secondary listing with the primary listing in Hong Kong. Due to the depressed state of the market for Chinese equities, it was a further year, in May 1996, until the next Chinese company copied this formula. The US$473 million issue for Guangshen Railway was equally listed in Hong Kong and New York. During the first seven months of 1997 two Chinese airlines, China Eastern and China Southern, did their much delayed offers with Hong-Kong and NYSE listings. The US$631 million China Southern offer in July 1997 was the biggest ever by a mainland company. By August 1997 a total of seven Chinese companies had done SEC registered offers and listed on NYSE. In addition, some B-share companies have registered with the SEC and had their sponsored ADRs quoted on Nasdaq.

In March 1997 Datang (Beijing) Power listed in Hong Kong and London in connection with a US$466 million offer – the first ever London listing by a Chinese company and the first Chinese power offer since October 1994.

Singapore Telecommunications

The island state of Singapore, with a population of only three million, is one of the world's success stories. High growth, low inflation, fiscal and current-account surpluses, huge foreign reserves, a savings ratio of over 45 per cent of GDP in 1995, and an appreciating currency have all led to triple-A ratings from Standard & Poor's and Moody's. Add political stability, law and order, first-class public services and a national airline considered one of the best in the world and it is small wonder that the country is the envy of politicians everywhere.

It is no surprise, then, that Singapore Telecommunications (SingTel), a highly profitable and relatively efficient monopoly, was considered of such high quality that its shares, even if offered at a substantial premium to the domestic market and to its international peers, should virtually sell themselves. They did, in a US$2.67 billion three-tranche IPO in October 1993, in which the first two tranches were restricted to Singaporeans and the third was open both to domestic and international investors. Yet there has been large-scale disappointment in the international community at the overall execution of the deal and little surprise at the subsequent under-performance of the share price. It was almost three years after flotation that the share price climbed above the S$3.60 tender price in the IPO, a development which has made it difficult for the Singapore government to sell further shares.

Privatisation in Singapore is an integral part of a philosophy of not losing political control. The SingTel offer was not a headlong rush to gain money for state coffers; the government did not even need the cash. Rather, the move represented a significant step in the government's programme to encourage Singaporeans to become substantial shareholders in certain key companies, thereby taking a stake in their booming economy and ensuring continued support for the political leadership.

Prime minister Goh Chok Tong told parliament in the run-up to the flotation that he wanted Singaporeans to own a piece of the economy: 'They will have a direct stake in Singapore's success. Their shares will appreciate so long as the Singapore economy continues to grow.' One international banker close to the privatisation programme explained: 'Nowhere in the world has a government enfranchised the people like they did in the SingTel privatisation – to everyone and virtually without limit.'

It helps the understanding of this unique transaction to look at the government of Singapore as the management of a private corporation (Singapore Inc.) with SingTel as the telecommunications subsidiary, whereby what was here proposed was the partial demerger by Singapore Inc. of SingTel to its shareholders (ie, Singapore citizens) at a heavily discounted price combined with a sale at market to new investors. Another appropriate analogy might be to liken the transaction to a first distribution under an Employee Stock Ownership Plan whereby the employees of Singapore Inc. got an opportunity to buy shares in the telecommunications subsidiary at

---

Exhibit 1

Transaction summary

Issuer name: Singapore Telecom (Singapore)	*Bookrunning lead manager:* DBS Bank *International coordinator:* Goldman Sachs & Co.
Pricing date: 28 October 1993 (Straits Times Industrial Index: 2,102)	*Pricing/underwriting structure:* Non-underwritten fixed-price offer and tender offer
Vendor: Temasek Holdings (Private) Limited	*Primary or secondary:* Secondary
	Retail structure: –
% of company sold: 11.1 %	*Privatisation or corporate:* Privatisation
IPO or non-IPO: IPO	*Industry:* Telecommunications
Type of shares: Ordinary shares	*Offer prices:* S$1.90 for tranche A S$2.00 for tranche B S$3.60 for tranche C
Total issue size: US$2.67 billion	*US listing/144 A:* Rule 144A

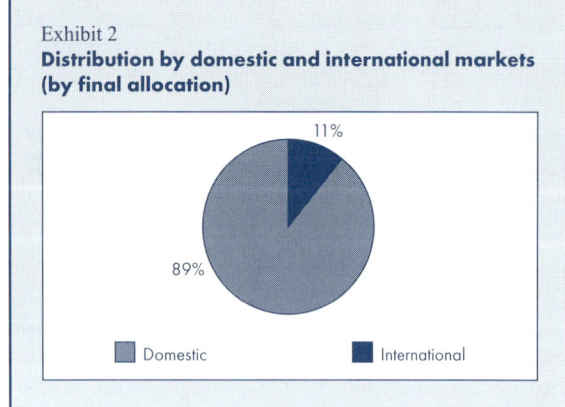

Exhibit 2
Distribution by domestic and international markets (by final allocation)

11%

89%

■ Domestic   ■ International

a heavily discounted price. So long as the employees continue to stay with Singapore Inc. (by holding on to their SingTel shares), they will get further free shares over a period of six years.

The Singapore government's attitude towards its citizens can be categorised as paternalistic, to say the least. It tells them what to do and what not to do but also looks after them well. As an example, a mandatory 20 per cent of each Singaporean's annual salary goes into a state pension fund, the Central Provident Fund. The government then offers citizens the opportunity to buy state flats with those savings: consequently, 88 per cent of Singaporeans now own their homes.

There is no doubt as to the success of the overall philosophy, achieved as a result of hard work, good planning and foresight on the part of the government – in particular that of Lee Kuan Yew, the country's first leader and now senior minister. Yet the political system is not among the most democratic in the world and the nation retains a sense of insecurity, squeezed as it is by competition from the much bigger Malaysia to the north and Indonesia to the south.

At the time of the SingTel issue, market conditions were strong, Asia in general was politically stable and considered hot for investment, and the telecom sector was in strong demand with US and European investors. Seen from an international perspective, the SingTel IPO was therefore expected to be one of the most significant deals in the history of the Asian equity capital markets. It was the first significant local company regarded as a proxy for the Singapore economy, and would be a core holding for international funds. Accordingly, the solicitation of the mandate among four of the world's top investment banks turned into one of the fiercest bidding battles ever seen, surpassed in its ferocity perhaps only by the Deutsche Telekom solicitation process. However the objectives of the Singapore government changed in favour of a more political and a more domestically structured transaction, thereby quashing the high expectations of the international banking and investment communities. Instead of a sizeable separate bookbuilt international tranche, the government opted for a traditional fixed price offer combined with a tender structure. Therefore, the SingTel IPO represented the first major telecommunications IPO to be conducted on a wholly non-underwritten basis.

This privatisation remains to date the largest ever IPO and the largest privatisation in Asia (excluding Japan). It was also the largest ever public offer on the Singapore stock market

and the world's first telecommunications privatisation to include a postal business, which at the time accounted for 8.3 per cent of SingTel group revenues.

The sale of SingTel was the first of a statutory board in the island state, and was delayed to enable Morgan Grenfell Singapore to complete a study which included advice on incorporation, the structure of the privatisation and the valuation of the company. Incorporation took place on 1 April 1992 and the flotation was arranged to give SingTel a minimum of one year's experience as a corporate entity.

Privatisation of other government monopolies such as Mass Rapid Transit Ltd, the Public Utilities Board (excluding the Water Department) and possibly the Port Authority of Singapore were to be considered after SingTel. None has taken place so far.

It was June 1996 before DBS Bank and SBC Warburg privately placed a further 100 million shares with domestic and international institutional investors at a price of S$3.68. This was a very low-key affair which followed the inclusion on 4 June 1996 of SingTel in the MSCI index. On 11 August 1996, by which time the price had fallen to S$3.58, the government announced that it would sell a further 400–450 million SingTel shares (2–3 per cent of the issued capital) over the next three years to boost the stock's trading volume and to move closer to the medium-term target of a 25 per cent free float, against an initial float from the IPO of only 11 per cent. Then in mid-September, the government proceeded to sell over 804 million shares (or 5.3 per cent of the capital) to domestic retail investors at a heavily discounted price of S$2.50.

Major challenges

As the first local statutory board to be privatised, SingTel created its own set of problems and uncertainty. Prior to the issue, the largest amount raised on the Singapore market had been S$500 million for Singapore International Airlines and in a normal year total new-issuance activity did not usually exceed S$2 billion. The SingTel IPO alone added 25 per cent to Singapore's stock market capitalisation.

The novelty of the operation together with its sheer scale was completely unprecedented in a Singapore context and presented significant logistical and administrative challenges. The public had to be educated on a wholesale basis on the intricacies of investing in equities, because for many Singaporeans this would be their first foray into the stock market, and the government wanted mass participation. Hundreds of thousands of new accounts had to be opened, numerous letters dispatched informing applicants of their allotment and a flood of enquiries from inexperienced investors had to be answered.

Fund managers at high-quality international institutions also needed persuading to participate in a meaningful way, not least because of the inflated valuation in tranche C – the strike price in the tender corresponded to a staggering 48.5 times forecast fiscal 1994 earnings. At that price, SingTel had the same market capitalisation as BT in the UK, with a population 20 times that of Singapore.

The fact that the fees were record low at 1 per cent and that international investors had to adjust to an entirely domestic offer structure did not help. At one stage international institutions were going to have to pay up front for the shares, ie, at the time of application and before they were advised of their allocations. To avoid this procedure, Goldman Sachs was forced to arrange a complicated bank loan from a Singapore bank.

Rationale and objectives

Reasons for the offer

The government hoped that its privatisation plan would improve the efficiency of state-owned companies and enable them to be more flexible and responsive to market forces. SingTel also had to be privatised to take full advantage of the global trend toward liberalisation of the telecommunications industry. The government stated that it intended, within five to seven years of the first offer, to sell up to 25 per cent. A second offer of the company's shares was expected within three years.

The offer objectives

The Singapore government had three principal objectives:

1. To maximise share ownership among Singaporeans. Singapore, run like a large corporation, is only 30 years old and in need of a national identity. The privatisation of SingTel afforded the government a first-rate opportunity to turn more than half of the population into shareholders overnight, helping to cement national loyalty. It was therefore politically important that SingTel shares be affordable and the sale be sufficiently attractive to encourage the public to purchase;
2. To maximise the tender price of tranche C. This objective was primarily of political significance. To charge over-

seas institutions a high price in the only tranche on offer to foreigners was always going to prove attractive to the local audience, even though this tranche was also open to domestic institutions; and
3. To give the local stock market more depth and breadth. The intention was to develop the market for the benefit of domestic rather than international investors.

'At the end of the day, the Singapore government's objectives were not that different from those of any other government: maximisation of proceeds and maximisation of retail placement,' says a senior international investment banker involved in the privatisation. 'The unusual thing was that they found a structure to optimise the two objectives individually rather than together.'

Share capital and ownership

See Exhibit 3.

Transaction components

The offer of a minimum 1.1 billion outstanding shares comprised three tranches: A and B were open only to Singapore citizens and tranche C was open both to Singaporean and international investors. Tranche C included an option to sell shares in the US under Rule 144 A. The offer was not underwritten (see Exhibit 4).

Tranche A: This comprised an offer of a minimum 350 million shares to Singaporeans who were members of the Central Provident Fund (government pension fund). Demand was to be satisfied in full, all of the 1.75 million CPF account holders who applied would receive a maximum of 600 shares each, which had to be paid for with funds from individual

---

Exhibit 3
Share capital and ownership

Type of shares offered	Ordinary shares of S$0.15 each.
Ownership restrictions	No person or related group of persons, other than vendor Temasek, to own more than 5% of SingTel's share capital. Total foreign shareholding limited to 40% of total share capital.
Share capital before and after offer	15,249,369,748 ordinary shares. In addition, the minister of finance owns one special share, which requires his approval of all company and board resolutions, amendment of articles, issue of shares, appointment of directors, disposal of material assets or any matter which in his opinion may affect the interests of public security or national defence or relations between Singapore and another government.
Listings/quotations	Stock Exchange of Singapore (SES) in connection with the offer.
Market capitalisation at S$3.60 (S$1.574/US$)	US$34.8 billion, the largest company on the SES.
Major shareholder before offer	Temasek Holdings (Private) Limited, an investment holding company wholly owned by the Ministry of Finance, owned 100% of the issued ordinary shares of SingTel before the offer.
Most relevant stock exchange index/weighting/ % of capital included	DBS 50/32.5%/100%

Exhibit 4

Offer structure

Tranches	Offer price (S$)	Indicated number of shares (millions)	Shares allocated (millions)
A: Discounted fixed price offer to members of the CPF	1.90	350	837
B: Fixed price domestic offer to Singaporean citizens	2.00	200	195
C: Domestic and international tender offer	Min. 2.00	550	650
			(180 internationally)
Total		**1,100**	**1,682**

Exhibit 5

Syndicate

	Lead manager (books)	Singapore lead managers*
Domestic market (Tranches A and B and domestic part of C)	DBS	• Keppel Bank of Singapore • Oversea-Chinese Banking Corp • Overseas Union Bank • Tat Lee Bank • United Overseas Bank Ltd – Singapore
	International market coordinator	*International marketing agents*
International market (Tranche C – international part)	Goldman Sachs & Co.	• CSFB • Daiwa • Lehman Brothers • SG Warburg

* In addition, Morgan Grenfell was a co-manager.

CPF accounts. To encourage CPF holders to retain their shares long term, tranche A included an ambitious loyalty share scheme. Under this, each purchaser of original tranche A shares would be entitled to receive without consideration on each of the first, second, fourth and sixth anniversaries, 10 per cent of the number of shares originally purchased and still held on each of those anniversaries. The discount available in tranche A was aggressively marketed as 45 per cent compared to tranche B, of which 5 per cent represented a cash discount and 40 per cent bonus shares amounting to 10 per cent a year for four years. In fact, the real discount (without even counting the time value of money) was 32 per cent. Compared to the offer price paid in tranche C, the real discount in tranche A was 62 per cent.

Tranche B: This was an offer of 200 million shares to Singapore citizens though approximately 41 million were reserved for directors, management and staff of SingTel. The thinking behind tranche B was to take care of any excess retail demand that could not be satisfied under tranche A. Each application under tranche B had to be for 1,000 shares only, the tranche would not be increased and there would be pro rata allocation in case of oversubscription. Applications under tranche B could be made using either cash or CPF funds, provided the applicant had a securities account with the Central Depository (Pte) Ltd.

Tranche C: This was an offer by tender to domestic and international investors of 550 million shares, subject to an increase by a maximum of 100 million shares. Tranche C was open to domestic retail and institutional investors and hence was designed to satisfy any overflow from tranche B, although it was also open to overseas institutions. Each investor could submit more than one application but no two from the same investor could contain identical tender prices. Should applications be received for more than all the Group C shares offered, such applications were to be accepted in descending order commencing with the highest price tendered. However, all successful bidders would pay the price of the lowest successful bid (the strike price) subject to the minimum tender price of S$2.00. Successful applications above the strike price were to be accepted in full whereas those at the strike price would be scaled down. Singapore citizens could make applications using cash or CPF funds provided they had a securities account with the Central Depository (Pte) Ltd. The aggregate number of shares applied for by any one applicant and/or related parties could not exceed 55 million, ie, 10 per cent of the original size of the tranche.

The shares sold in the three separate tranches were immediately fungible – there was only one market price once trading had begun. The vendor offered a one-year lock-up.

Syndicate

Given the size of the offer, the syndicate was of a manageable size as illustrated in Exhibit 5.

Principal advisers

See Exhibit 6.

Exhibit 6
Principal advisers*

Domestic legal adviser to Temasek and SingTel	Allen & Gledhill
International legal adviser to Temasek and SingTel	Sullivan & Cromwell
Domestic legal adviser to the international marketing agents and the Singapore managers	Lee & Lee
International legal adviser to the international marketing agents	Cleary, Gottlieb, Steen & Hamilton
Auditors	Price Waterhouse

* Morgan Grenfell had been the adviser for the incorporation of SingTel, ie, its creation out of Telecommunication Authority of Singapore.

Exhibit 7
The timetable

August 1992	• Prime minister Goh Chok Tong announced that SingTel would be privatised in 1993.
February 1993	• DBS Bank appointed domestic lead manager (as the senior bank among six domestic leads).
3 March	• Goldman Sachs appointed global coordinator (the role was subsequently changed to international marketing coordinator).
Early August	• The government launched an 'Invest Singapore' newspaper and television advertising campaign to encourage people to consider shares as an investment alternative to bank savings and property.
19 August	*Government announced structure of the transaction:* • Tranches A, B and C; • Indicative number of shares to be sold under each tranche; • Nature and scope of retail incentives; and • Pricing mechanism for tranche C.
Beginning September	• The government launched a two-month roadshow at some 25 community centres as part of a National Share Education Scheme to explain why and how to invest in shares.
Late September	• Pre-marketing began with International Marketing Agents making client presentations.
9 October	*Announcement of the offer:* • Publication of prospectus with offer prices for tranches A, B and minimum tender price for tranche C; • International marketing agents agreement signed; • International marketing commenced; • Subscription period for tranches A and B commenced; and • Tender period for tranche C commenced.
14 October	• International roadshow began with Hong Kong presentation.
21 October	• International roadshow ended with Boston presentation.
27 October	• Bids due to individual international marketing agents.
28 October	*Pricing and allocation* • All subscriptions due under tranches A and B before noon; and • All domestic bids to DBS and all international bids to Goldman Sachs under tender offer due by noon.
29 October	• Announcement of allocation formula for tranches A and B; • Announcement of the strike price in tranche C; and • Preliminary confirmation of allotment to clients under tranche C.
1 November	• Final confirmation of allotment under tranche C; and • When-issued trading commenced.

The timetable

The time between the first announcement and the execution represented a period of no less than 15 months, allowing for thorough preparation of the offer (see Exhibit 7).

Transaction fee distribution

The six domestic lead managers were paid 0.5 per cent for subscriptions under tranches A and B. In total, these banks were paid S$2 million.

For the tender, Temasek paid a brokerage commission of 1.0 per cent to the domestic lead managers and international marketing agents who intermediated successful bids (see Exhibit 8). The commissions were calculated on the number of shares times the strike price.

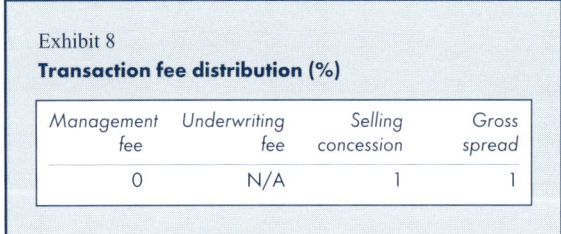

Exhibit 8
Transaction fee distribution (%)

Management fee	Underwriting fee	Selling concession	Gross spread
0	N/A	1	1

In addition, Goldman Sachs was paid an undisclosed advisory fee. The total cost of issuance was S$32 million (including marketing expenses, legal fees, commissions, etc.), representing 0.76 per cent of the total proceeds of the offer. This is a record low by any standards.

Deal structure

The deal structure changed significantly from solicitation to execution, much to the disappointment of Goldman Sachs and the international investment community. The notion of a separate foreign tranche was dropped (and therefore also that of a NYSE listing) and the total transaction became significantly smaller. Because of the tender mechanism in tranche C, the shares also became much more expensive for foreign investors. These were dramatic changes. One senior international investment banker involved commented: 'the Singapore government's objectives changed substantially during the preparation of this privatisation but then they almost always do.' The main differences between the structure as originally contemplated and the final structure were as set out in Exhibit 9.

Against recommendations from Goldman Sachs and all the foreign investment banks interviewed by the government for the role of global coordinator, the vendor decided to conduct the entire non-retail portion of the SingTel IPO as a tender rather than as a bookbuilt offer. The tender structure should be seen in context –as in Singapore tenders are part of the commercial culture – for example, Singaporeans wishing to buy a car have to tender for a Certificate of Entitlement before

they can actually buy the car. Brigadier-General Lee, the son of Lee Kuan Yew, apparently gave impetus to the idea of making this a wholly domestic offer, so as to avoid giving anything away to foreigners. In the event the structure adopted was the politically safest one – a very real consideration as the government was afraid of losing popularity.

Nevertheless, before deciding on the tender structure for the entire institutional portion of the offer, the merits of alternative pricing and underwriting structures were carefully considered:

Tender offer: In a tender (or auction) investors bid for a certain number of shares at any price they choose, though often subject to a minimum price such as in this case. The strike price, in the type of auction employed in the SingTel offer, is the highest tender price at which all shares are sold. Investors who have tendered above this price automatically receive their full allocation. A bidder determined to obtain a certain amount of stock will bid at a very high price knowing that he will never be held to it, as all successful bidders pay the strike price. This creates order inflation in the bidding process. The tender structure is completely price-based and is designed to generate the highest possible offer price. The vendor does not retain discretion about the quality of investor and thus has no influence over the number, type or geographic origin of investors.

Open-price bookbuilding: Under an open-price bookbuilding structure, the vendor gives price guidance by setting a price range at the beginning of the bookbuilding period. Investors typically subscribe within that range or without stipulating a price. The offer price is most often set below the highest price at which the issue is fully subscribed so as to save some demand for the after-market. The bookrunner and the vendor together retain the flexibility to pick and choose among the bids. Only very rarely is an investor allocated his full indicated demand. Would-be investors not deemed to be of high enough quality may not be allocated any shares. This structure is designed to generate a healthy after-market.

Fixed price offer: Whereas in the tender and the bookbuilding structures, the offer price is set at the end of the marketing period, in a fixed-price offer the price is set at the beginning. Fixed-price offers have been the tradition in most

Exhibit 9
Expected vs actual deal structure

	Expected in March 1993	Actual deal structure
% of company sold	15–25%	6–8% (subject to increase)
% of total offer to be sold in the international market	50%	15%
Registration/Rule 144 A	Registration and NYSE listing a distinct possibility	US placement under Rule 144 A
Pricing/underwriting	Fixed-price domestic offer and international bookbuilding	Fixed-price domestic offer (tranches A and B) Domestic non-underwritten tender with international participation (tranche C)
Syndicate structure	Global syndicate or regional tranches	Five international banks included in tranche C for international distribution
Valuation/pricing	S$1.50–2.00 per share	S$1.90/2.00/3.60 per share

Exhibit 10
Pros and cons of alternative pricing and underwriting structures

	Advantages	Disadvantages
Fixed price underwritten offer	• Full valuation and pricing transparency for investors from the beginning of the marketing period; and • The vendor achieves certainty of proceeds as he has transferred the market risk to the underwriter.	• Offer price fixed before the investment story has been fully digested by the market; • Does not usually optimise proceeds to the vendor; • Banks take underwriting risk and are more anxious to quickly lay off this risk than to place shares with high-quality investors; • Requires higher underwriting fees; and • With a long offer period, the offer may prove to be either grossly overpriced or far too cheap due to market fluctuation.
Tender offer	• Offer price set at the end of the marketing period, ie, with the market having digested all the selling points; • The most objective pricing structure as all investors have an equal chance to be allocated shares; • Typically optimises proceeds to the vendor.	• Proceeds not guaranteed. In some cases tenders can be underwritten at the minimum tender price; • Demand, and therefore the offer price, tend to be inflated, particularly in a bullish market; • After-market performance is generally weak as bidders above the strike price receive full allocation, thereby exhausting potential after-market demand. Substantial after-market demand only below strike price; • The vendor has no control over the quality of investors; and • Banks do not feel the same degree of responsibility for generating high-quality orders or for after-market performance.
Open price bookbuilding	• Offer price set at the end of the marketing period, ie, with the market having digested all the selling points; • The vendor has full transparency and control over development of the book; • Each order is analysed on the basis of quality and allocation is made accordingly; and • Allows the offer price to be fixed at a level that will guarantee substantial demand and strong price performance in the after-market.	• Certainty of proceeds not guaranteed as underwriting effective only at the end of the marketing period; and • Investors often complain about the allocation which per definition is made on a discretionary rather than on a pre-programmed basis.

markets, including the UK. For a long time, it was the received wisdom that a fixed offer price was required to achieve effective marketing, especially to retail investors. In recent years, however, this notion has been increasingly challenged, even in big privatisations. For example, in the case of Pharmacia, the offer was marketed to retail investors on the basis of a fixed discount to the institutional offer price, to be set at the end of the marketing period.

The respective advantages and disadvantages of these different structures can be summarised as shown in Exhibit 10.

The Singapore government decided on a tender structure for tranche C despite the expectation of a weak after-market performance because:

• Maximisation of proceeds from tranche C was one of the most important objectives. The vendor judged that it would

not be a significant problem if the secondary market price fell below the strike price so long as it did not decline to anywhere near the offer prices in the retail tranches (S\$1.90 and S\$2.00 respectively) and this risk was deemed to be small. It was politically the safest structure;

• It is market practice in Singapore to structure IPOs with one fixed-price tranche and one tender tranche. Since, for political reasons, this was going to be a very domestic offer, there was no point in adopting an international structure, and there was no domestic precedent for a bookbuilt offer. It had been noted that in April 1992 the Malaysian government had structured a US\$1.2 billion IPO for electricity utility Tenaga Nasional as a tender offer and in late 1991 and early 1992 the Republic of Argentina had privatised telecommunications companies Telefónica de Argentina and Telecom Argentina by way of separate tenders; and

- As Singapore is run like a private corporation, it was difficult to justify leaving anything on the table for any investors other than Singaporean citizens. Domestic and foreign institutions were considered capable of looking after themselves. After all, the risks were completely transparent as the tender structure represents the ultimate free market.

Marketing

In addition to the solid quality of the company and the favourable regulatory regime, one of the most striking aspects of the marketing of SingTel was the strong commitment shown by the government towards the success of the domestic retail tranches, in particular tranche A. This was demonstrated by:

- The National Share Education Programme, which was devised to enlighten the man in the street about the technical aspects of stock market investment;
- The Invest Singapore Campaign, a broad domestic marketing programme conceived to encourage stock market investment;
- The Share Ownership Top-Up Scheme, designed to assist lower-income groups to buy SingTel shares and other shares approved by the government. In this scheme the government gave each citizen a grant of S$200 in their CPF accounts provided a minimum deposit of S$500 was made between 1 March and 31 August 1993;
- A liberalisation from 1 October 1993 of the rules governing Singaporeans' use of their CPF savings, making at least S$31 billion eligible for investment in equities. This measure substantially enhanced local liquidity;

- A more generous and longer duration bonus share scheme than found in any other privatisation in the world; and
- The application procedures for tranche A shares were greatly simplified. Pre-printed forms were sent to would-be subscribers who had only to tick the number of shares required and add their signature. Singapore banks also launched an electronic share-application programme allowing investors to apply through automated teller machines. This eliminated a substantial amount of paperwork.

The marketing of the SingTel story was interesting in that it was significantly facilitated by geography. Singapore is less a country than a city, and this, together with the government's paternalistic relationship with its citizens and the fact that the media is tightly controlled, helped to get the SingTel story across.

The Singapore Telecom story

SingTel was a well managed, high-growth company substantially protected by a highly favourable regulatory regime (see Exhibit 11). There were two key points determining fair value for Singapore Telecom:

- The Singapore market was fairly valued at 23.5 times 1993 and 20.5 times 1994 earnings respectively (DBS 50 index including foreign board premiums and excluding Singapore International Airlines). At these levels, the market was trading almost exactly at the average multiple since 1988; and
- SingTel was expected to trade at a premium to this multiple because of its superior financial characteristics as shown in Exhibit 12.

Exhibit 11
Principal sales points

Operating environment	Political and economic stability, high economic growth, high per-capita GDP, low inflation, strong currency, focus on increasing labour productivity, budget surpluses and excellent infrastructure.
Regulatory environment	SingTel had a 15-year monopoly (until 2007) on local and overseas phone services and a five-year monopoly on mobile phone services. It also enjoyed an attractive pricing framework based on a weighted basket of prices for telecom operators throughout the region and the world. This framework was designed to keep SingTel competitive in global terms and also to help ensure that Singapore itself remained a competitive regional and global telecommunications centre. By not capping the company's returns or interfering with its overall operations, this approach allowed SingTel to retain a large portion of increased operating efficiencies and cost reductions.
Revenue growth	Significant revenue growth opportunities associated with strong unit growth: access-line growth, opportunities to expand value-added services, double-digit international call volume growth and investment in new growth areas.
Margin expansion	The opportunity to expand operating margins by taking full advantage of the company's strong technological leadership and by generating productivity improvements, cost control and reduction of traffic and staff costs.
Profitability	Return on capital employed averaged 22% a year during the three years to March 1992.
Earnings growth	Attractive double-digit earnings growth associated with growing revenues and expanding margins: EPS was expected to grow by 15% in 1994 and 14% in fiscal 1995.
Financial position	No net debt.
Singapore stock market	Attractive prospects for Singapore market, positive supply/demand outlook for Singapore stocks and a general observation that many state-owned enterprises trade at substantial premiums to their respective private-sector peers.

Sources: Prospectus and Goldman Sachs.

Although at S$2.00 SingTel appeared somewhat expensive against its peers on an absolute basis (see Exhibit 13) it looked fairly valued on a relative basis (see Exhibit 14).

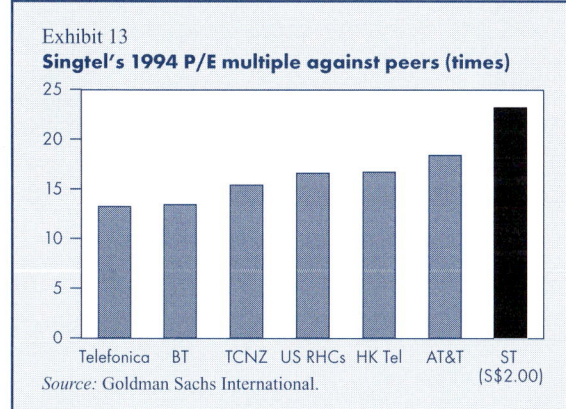

Exhibit 12

SingTel's superior financial characteristics (%)

	DBS 50	S&P 400	SingTel
Pre-tax margin	12.7	6.1	47.1
Return on average assets	4.3	3.9	19.5
Return on average equity	8.3	16.3	41.0
Long-term debt/equity	28.5	72.0	0.2
Expected long-term EPS growth	10.0	n/a	15.0

Source: Goldman Sachs International.

Exhibit 13

Singtel's 1994 P/E multiple against peers (times)

Source: Goldman Sachs International.

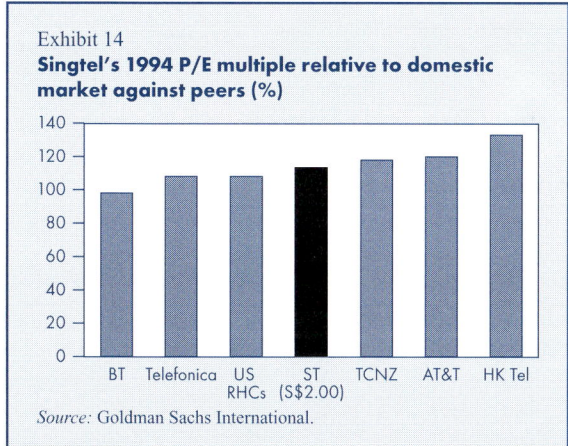

Exhibit 14

Singtel's 1994 P/E multiple relative to domestic market against peers (%)

Source: Goldman Sachs International.

Based on the above, Goldman Sachs estimated fair value for SingTel to be S$2.20–2.28, which corresponded to a premium of 25–30 per cent to the DBS 50. Goldman Sachs therefore advised investors to submit bids around these levels.

Reasons for not buying

Despite the strong SingTel story, investors had a number of concerns:

- The strong dependency of Singapore's economy on exports;
- The strong link to the Malaysian market and therefore economic dependency on its northern neighbour;
- Increasing competition in telecom services in the region;
- Possible inflationary pressures;
- The regulatory review of the pricing basket scheduled for 1995;
- Anticipated changes in telecom traffic mix were expected to put pressure on margins;
- The upcoming competition in mobile services and possible decline in average revenue per cellular subscriber; and
- Long pay-back period for some of the company's strategic investments.

Results

Placement

All the three tranches were substantially oversubscribed (see Exhibit 15).

Tranche A: Almost 1.4 million of the 1.75 million Singaporeans eligible to purchase the maximum of 600 shares per person with their CPF savings did so. This was almost 50 per cent of the total population. This tranche was therefore increased by 487 million shares to 837 million shares to satisfy demand. In addition, Temasek was committed to delivering a further 335 million shares maximum, equivalent to a 2.2 per cent interest in SingTel, through the Loyalty Share Scheme over the six years from the date of the offer.

Tranche B: Total demand in this tranche was 835 million shares (excluding reserved shares). A final allocation of 200 shares each was made to the 795,272 eligible Singaporeans who had applied for 1,000 shares per person.

Tranche C: Almost 63,000 investors (private citizens, institutional investors, etc.) tendered for 2.8 million shares

Exhibit 15

Level of interest by tranche

Tranches	Indicated number of shares (millions)	Total demand (millions)	Number of investors	Subscription rate (times)	Final number of shares (millions)
A: Fixed price offer	350	837	1,396,000	2.4	837
B: Fixed price offer	200	835	795,272	4.2	195
C: Tender offer					
domestic	N/A	1,645	N/A	N/A	470
international	N/A	1,155	N/A	N/A	180
total	550	2,800	62,931	5.1	650
Total combined offers	**1,100**	**4,472**		**4.1**	**1,682**

Exhibit 16
Tender bids

Tender prices (S$)	Number of applications	% of the total number of shares (2.8 million) applied for
4.00 and above	34,571	14.1
3.90–3.99	2,646	0.9
3.80–3.89	10,643	3.7
3.70–3.79	4,602	3.0
3.61–3.69	3,107	1.0
3.60	7,362	2.8
3.50–3.59	28,879	19.2
3.49 and below	70,682	55.3
Total	**162,492**	**100.0**

Source: Singapore Telecom.

Exhibit 17
Proceeds per tranche (total: US$2.67 billion)

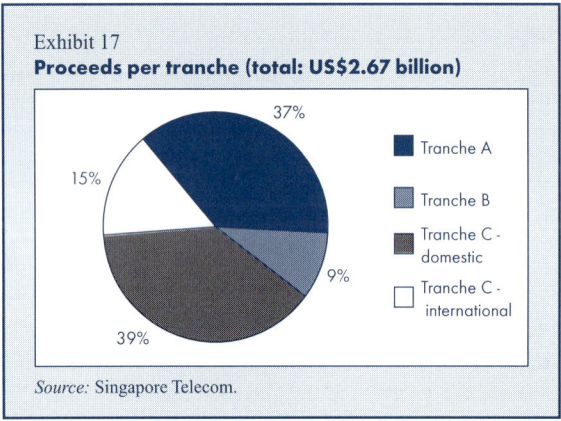

- Tranche A — 37%
- Tranche B — 9%
- Tranche C – domestic — 39%
- Tranche C – international — 15%

Source: Singapore Telecom.

Exhibit 18
After-market price performance

Pricing date	28 October 1993
Offer price – tranche C	S$3.60
First year high/low	
High (1 November 1993)	S$4.14
Low (25 October 1994)	S$3.18

Singtel share price relative to Straits Times Index (%)

Absolute and relative share price performance

	Price (S$)	Relative to Straits Times Index (%)
+ 1 day (1 November 1993)	4.14	116.05
+ 3 days	3.90	107.64
+ 1 week	3.82	110.90
+ 1 month	3.92	111.95
+ 3 months	3.72	92.63
+ 6 months	3.50	91.13
+ 9 months	3.48	88.42
+ 12 months	3.22	70.93

Sources: Datastream and offer circular.

and the government exercised its option to increase the tranche by a further 100 million shares. Bids over S$3.60 received 100 per cent allocation while bids at the strike price were scaled down to 20 per cent. Domestic investors bid more aggressively, evidenced by the fact that while international investors, who were more focused on fundamentals, accounted for 59 per cent of the total bids, they only accounted for 28 per cent of the successful bids, ie, those at or above the strike price of S$3.60. The highest international bid was S$5.33 compared to S$9.00 from the domestic market (see Exhibit 16).

Geographic distribution
Of the international bids, more than 80 per cent represented either Asia-based investors or Asia specialist investment managers. On average, Japanese investors bid at significantly higher prices than any other national group and while they accounted for only 7 per cent of international applicants they represented 15 per cent of those who were successful. In descending order of importance, regional demand in the international portion of tranche C came from Asia, Europe and the US.

Exhibit 17 illustrates distribution of the overall offer by proceeds but does not reflect as foreign demand those applications made by foreign investors through local banks.

Whereas in terms of number of shares, approximately 61.5 per cent of the total offer was allocated to tranches A and B as indicated earlier, the equivalent figure in terms of proceeds

was only 46 per cent, reflecting the different offer prices.

Investor concentration
At US$5–10 million, international orders were small compared to most offers of this size, reflecting the inflated valuation. Few of the major US and UK institutions tendered above the strike price. Those international investors who bid at S$3.60 or higher included:

- Momentum players; and
- Emotional buyers.

After-market price performance
See Exhibit 18.

- On 1 November, the first day of trading, the shares moved between S$3.80 and S$5.00 during the morning and closed at S$4.14, a 15 per cent premium to the strike price and a 117 per cent premium to the tranche A offer price of S$1.90. Japanese investors were said to have been a substantial factor in pushing the price above S$4.00. Indeed, one trader said the Japanese were the only significant international buyers during the first four days of trading. Others, however, believed that domestic investors had driven the

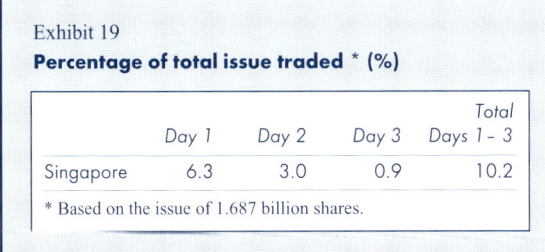

Exhibit 19
Percentage of total issue traded * (%)

	Day 1	Day 2	Day 3	Total Days 1 - 3
Singapore	6.3	3.0	0.9	10.2

* Based on the issue of 1.687 billion shares.

tender pricing, received most of the stock during the tender and purchased most of the stock available in the secondary market;

- After a week, the stock had fallen to S$3.82 and was expected to continue downward, though the S$3.60 strike price was expected to form a psychological floor price for some time to come;

- For the first three months, the shares traded above the S$3.60 strike price but then began to fall steadily. The market price was below the strike price after six, nine and 12 months;

- During the first 12 months of trading SingTel under-performed the Singapore market by 29 per cent, at a time when that market was reasonably strong and increased by 12.3 per cent; and

- The share price continued to fall during the second year of trading, at the end of which it stood at S$2.88, having under-performed the market by approximately 20 per cent over 24 months.

After-market trading volume
See Exhibit 19.

Trading volume on the first day was lighter than expected. SingTel accounted for only 16 per cent of total market volume when 106 million shares, representing 6.3 per cent of the total issue size, changed hands on the Stock Exchange of Singapore. On the second day, only 16 million shares traded, representing 3 per cent of the total issue size. Much of this activity has been described as profit-taking. The lower than expected level of activity led the SES to end on the Wednesday, two days earlier than planned, the 12-hour extended trading sessions that had been introduced in connection with the flotation. Singaporeans were holding on to their shares, because that is what the government wanted: the extensive bonus share scheme was an effective locking-in mechanism. The large US and UK institutions, typically the biggest after-market buyers in most offers, were not buying SingTel.

All trading in this world-class company takes place in Singapore. Goldman Sachs and the other international marketing coordinators had to execute orders through a member of the SES. Goldman Sachs initially had a Singapore page on Reuters which it discontinued through lack of trading activity.

The performance of the main parties

The vendor
The Singapore government was a sophisticated vendor albeit

with a fixed view of life. It gave priority to those offer objectives that served particular political purposes and found an ideal structure for them. From that point of view, the offer was a great success, at least in the short term. But from the perspective of the institutional investors, the deal was clearly not a success, as the share price performance has been highly disappointing. This poor showing has also had a negative effect on the 1.4 million retail investors who have seen a steadily declining share price, and has not helped to stimulate a genuine equity culture in Singapore. On the other hand, until 1997 the price has remained comfortably above the offer prices for tranches A and B. The major consequence of the structural decisions in the SingTel IPO was that the structuring and execution of further SingTel offers became much more difficult.

Credit is due to the government for the committed support it gave to the offer and to tranche A in particular. The economic price for this support, in terms of the opportunity cost of the large discounts in tranches A & B, was probably the highest ever paid in a privatisation. Singapore, however, was able to afford it and the government was correct in thinking that the big institutional investors could look after themselves, but it probably would have been in SingTel's best interest for the offer to have been a wholly domestic affair. Such a strategy would have paved the way for a better reception by international investors in connection with any future issues. As it turned out, due to the way that the offer was structured and the poor share price performance, the Singapore government is not likely to have made many friends in the international financial community. The international investment banking community for one remains highly critical of how it was initially led to believe that the SingTel IPO was going to be a truly global offer.

The Singapore government also supported the offer with a highly favourable regulatory regime. SingTel's licence provided for a monopoly on basic telephone services until 2007 (however this was since shortened to 2000 against compensation to the company to the tune of S$1.5 billion), mobile services until 1997 and mail services until 2007. Ms Chua, CFO of SingTel commented: 'The good thing about this regulatory regime is that the government does not mind if SingTel is very profitable, so long as the services are competitive in pricing and quality.'

The company
SingTel has done better in terms of earnings per share for fiscal 1994 and 1995 than was forecast at the time of the offer but it undertook only two international roadshows during those years. In 1994 presentations were held in London, Tokyo and Hong Kong and in 1995 the effort was limited to Tokyo. This level of activity is below best practice for a world-class company but consistent with the low priority that the international equity market has so far played in SingTel's fortunes – less than 2 per cent of the company is owned internationally.

The bookrunning lead manager
DBS Bank was hired in February 1993 on the basis of its experience with Singapore privatisations (Singapore Airlines and DBS Land, for example), its general equity credentials

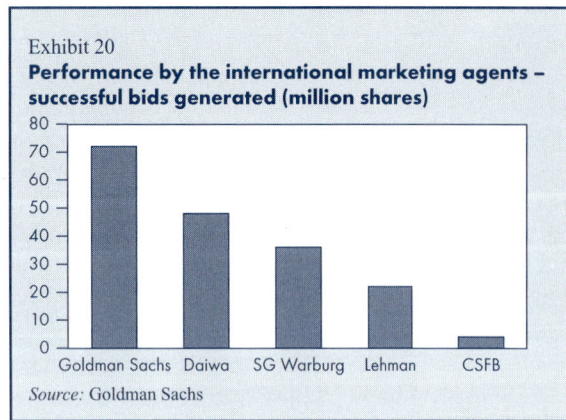

Exhibit 20
**Performance by the international marketing agents –
successful bids generated (million shares)**

Source: Goldman Sachs

and an infrastructure which enabled it to handle large numbers of retail clients. DBS was itself privatised in 1987 but the government retains a 47 per cent stake, a fact which presumably did not hurt the bank's chances of being hired for this deal. DBS's role became stronger as the transaction became increasingly political and domestic in its nature, however it appeared in the domestic retail syndicate on an equal basis with its five principal competitors.

The international marketing coordinator

Having worked extremely hard both before and after being hired in March 1993, having valued SingTel on the basis of its fundamentals at S$2.20–2.28 and having had almost all of its recommendations rejected, Goldman Sachs must have felt extremely frustrated to have to allocate, without any degree of discretion, only US$165 million-worth of shares at what was undoubtedly an inflated price. It was only a small consolation to Goldman Sachs that its clients accounted for a good portion of the international part of tranche C (see Exhibit 20).

The formal solicitation process for the global coordinator mandate had begun in August 1992. In early November, all the 21 banks which up to that time had made a significant effort were asked to present their credentials in writing. In December a shortlist of four banks was drawn up: Goldman Sachs, Lehman Brothers, CSFB and SG Warburg. It soon became clear that the two major contenders were Goldman Sachs and CSFB.

Goldman Sachs had held various discussions with the government over the preceding 18 months and Doug Howland, then with the bank and now head of ECM at Deutsche Morgan Grenfell in Asia, explained: 'It was our strategy to do a reverse roadshow – to give SingTel and the government a very high level of service concerning everything that was happening in the market and that might possibly be relevant to the privatisation.' The tactic clearly paid off in terms of getting the mandate – however probably not in terms of economic reward for a gigantic effort over more than a year.

The government's criteria for selection of the global coordinator are thought to have included experience with telecom IPOs, a strong research team, placement power and a good track record. Goldman Sachs' strengths included experience with Telmex and Telecom Corporation of New Zealand and the fact that it had, in Robert Morris, one of the most highly rated telecom analysts as consistently indicated by independent surveys such as Institutional Investor. Goldman Sachs also had experience, as did SG Warburg, of the earlier privatisations of Singapore's DBS Land and SIA. Goldman Sachs' weaknesses were that it did not have a major presence in Singapore and that its Asian track record was not among the best.

SG Warburg had valuable experience with BT (although the BT3 transaction of July 1993 might have created a conflict of interest with the SingTel deal) and the bank and its fund management subsidiary Mercury Asset Management (since spun off) were understood to have enjoyed excellent relations with the Singapore government. CSFB could point to a long-standing presence in Singapore and recent experience with the placement of shares in Malaysia Telekom and Philippine Long Distance Corporation. It is generally understood that in the final analysis, CSFB was the runner-up in this fierce bidding contest. Goldman Sachs allegedly quoted fees in the neighbourhood of 2 per cent against CSFB's 3 per cent. Goldman Sachs had been accused by disappointed competitors of winning the mandate on the basis of a low fee quote and an aggressive valuation of the company; however Chua of SingTel put the record straight: 'It is not accurate to say that Goldman Sachs quoted the lowest fee among the four shortlisted candidates.' On the question of valuation she added: 'Goldman Sachs' valuation was also not the highest among the shortlisted banks. The valuations were in fact very close...all were within a range of 5 to 10 per cent.'

The decision on the appointment was taken by a committee of high-level civil servants from several ministries. The chairman of the committee was Lim Siong Guan, permanent secretary at the Ministry of Defence. The decision-makers most certainly also included prime minister Goh and Brigadier-General Lee Hsien Loong, who subsequently became the deputy prime minister.

Seven months after its appointment as global coordinator, Goldman Sachs found itself coordinating only the international marketing of a largely domestic transaction and was given the new title of international marketing coordinator. The international part of the offer became a relatively simple execution job. The fee had been cut from approximately 2 per cent to 1 per cent by omitting the underwriting. Although arguably on par with the fees in BT3 (if calculated on the full proceeds of BT 3 as opposed to only the first installment), this was a record low fee and has not been repeated since. However, Goldman Sachs did receive a separate advisory fee as had SG Warburg in the case of BT3. Nevertheless, Goldman Sachs did an unprecedented amount of work in servicing the Singapore government both before and after its appointment.

Key lessons learnt

Objectives and special circumstances

'One of the most important things in a privatisation,' explained Chua, 'is that the government is very clear about its objectives, as everything else will soon fall into place.'

It is vital for all concerned to understand the political and economic objectives as well as the overall dynamics of a particular privatisation, as these will determine structure, pricing and after-market price performance. In this case, the government decided to cater mainly for the Singaporean CPF holder, who was destined to do well out of the investment.

Clearly the raising of Singapore's profile as a financial centre or increased foreign interest in the domestic stock market were not among the government's objectives. From this, institutional investors in tranche C ought to have realised that the possibility of making money was going to be small.

The government demonstrated how a clear understanding of its position, and confidence in its objectives as well as how to achieve them meant that it was able to stand up to the international investment banking community. Having said that, this stand was substantially facilitated by the fact that the vendor was operating from a position of strength as neither SingTel nor the state needed to raise money.

Privatisation philosophy

Privatisation can mean very different things from country to country. In Singapore, privatisation is not driven by fiscal considerations, nor is it driven by a powerful desire to transfer control of important companies to the private sector. It means primarily a stock market quotation and more focus on the bottom line. Most importantly, it is about building a more efficient and competitive nation.

The Singapore government, unlike most others with experience in the capital markets, does not appear to agree that a good deal is one that is good for all groups of investors. This is something that sophisticated institutional investors will remember for a long time.

Compensation of advisers and bankers

The domestic bankers, lawyers and accountants were paid either nothing or only nominal amounts for their hard work. Even the US lawyers were asked to work for a fixed nominal fee, while the foreign bankers were paid much less than they had expected. The various advisers were hired only after they had been providing free advice for some considerable time. 'It is very difficult to earn advisory fees in Asia but the Singaporeans perfected the art of acquiring top-quality advice free of charge,' explained a Hong Kong-based investment banker. 'In Asia you only make money by raising money.' In Singapore, the government demanded and got full cooperation from all parties involved – almost without compensation. One Singaporean involved in the privatisation commented: 'In Singapore, this was a national project and we were all asked to do national service.'

The government took full advantage of the fact that it was considered prestigious to be involved with the SingTel offer and it believed that despite mediocre compensation, people would still return to offer their services to the Singapore government. This might prove to have been misguided. 'After this experience it is clearly much more difficult to get the right level of support from our London and New York colleagues,' according to a senior Singapore-based foreign investment banker. 'We may get certain specialists to come here but they are not necessarily likely to be the best. The best people are needed to make money for the firm.' As a rep-

resentative of one of the shortlisted banks put it: 'We can't go on to finance their no-cost learning for ever. The Singaporeans and also other Asians are experts at intellectual hoovering.' Another senior banker involved in the transaction noted: 'If all foreign bankers were treated in this way, more and more of us would leave Singapore and Singaporean companies would have increasing difficulties raising money in the international market.'

The privatisation of SingTel, however, was a truly exceptional case which enabled the Singapore government to cut commissions to 1 per cent and many bankers say that this is unlikely to be repeated in the foreseeable future. The head of ECM at a major US investment bank says: 'As shares are sold, not bought, and as equity salesmen work on a bonus basis, they are much more likely to sell shares which carry 3 per cent commissions rather than those that carry only 1 per cent. Having said that, the UK Treasury also pays only 1 per cent.'

Structure of the offer

The structure was crafted with great ingenuity. The combination of a heavily discounted fixed-price offer and a substantially over-priced tender offer allowed the government to achieve maximum political leverage in the short term. Singaporean citizens benefited twice, first as subscribers from a highly generous discount package and second as taxpayers through a cunning maximisation of proceeds from institutional investors.

In a longer-term perspective, a bookbuilding structure with proper support from international institutions would have done more to maximise SingTel's valuation and the shares most probably would be trading higher today. There is currently limited liquidity for either institutional or retail block sizes, few if any international core shareholders and less than ideal prospects for a meaningful second tranche.

Pricing and secondary market valuation

The disappointing after-market price performance of tranche C was to be expected, particularly as the tender took place amid bullish market conditions. This will make the next tranche more difficult to structure as there will be investor scepticism and there is much less flexibility to offer large discounts in a secondary offer. What remains clear is that the structure chosen for SingTel 1 has not maximised the company's long-term valuation. This is perhaps a classic example of a vendor being short-term rather than long-term greedy, in terms of maximising its political and economic objectives.

Other

The privatisation of SingTel has supposedly allowed the company to react more quickly to the challenges of globalisation, technological change and increased competition. It has also required a change in the mindset of the company's employees. 'Having previously had a civil service mentality, the company is now more focused on bottom-line management,' says Chua. 'Every decision made has to enhance efficiency, productivity and shareholder value. Competition is a key word – we want to become even more efficient.' One Singapore-based investment banker with a British firm counters: 'It is important to keep in mind that it was corporatisation that led to SingTel becoming more efficient, not the sale of 11 per cent of the shares to the public. The sale of the shares was simply designed to deepen the stakeholder economy, or put differently, to increase the popularity of the government.'

Conclusion

The government clearly achieved its political aim of encouraging widespread share ownership as 1.4 million people or 82 per cent of eligible Singaporeans took up the offer. Three years later, 95 per cent of them still held their shares. Until the SingTel privatisation, there had been only 200,000 core shareholders in the island state. No doubt the offer also contributed to the simplification of Singapore's domestic share application procedures. All equity issues are now applied for through ATMs.

The government's generosity to CPF holders was unprecedented. The 1.4 million subscribers in tranche A paid S$1.42 billion less up front than if they had paid the full strike price of tranche C. If the bonus shares are valued at the strike price and applied to the calculation up front and if it is assumed that all subscribers received the S$200 benefit under the top-up scheme then the total discount in tranche A was S$2.9 billion or S$3.47 per share: an extraordinary 96.5 per cent.

Although it can be argued that until 1997 the market price has not been near to the S$1.90 offer price for tranche A, most Singaporeans soon discounted the windfall profit and began focusing on the day-to-day price development. The shares fell more or less consistently for the first 24 months, which is not conducive to the creation of public confidence in the stock market. Then, after an upswing in the company's fortunes in 1996 – a development quickly taken advantage of through two share sales – in 1997 things went from bad to worse as the shares tested the S$2.00 level for the first time. There was a growing realisation that, due to the loss of its monopoly in mobile telephony and pagers, SingTel was losing market share much more quickly than generally expected. This weak share price performance put those retail shareholders who bought shares at S$2.50 in September 1996 into the red.

Internationally, the issue did nothing to enhance the reputation of Singapore's capital markets, though this was not a stated objective. Foreigners owned a meagre 1.2 per cent of SingTel just after the offer and two years later the figure had risen to only 1.9 per cent. 'The balance between giving the local retail investors an effective 96.5 per cent discount on the strike price and then paying the banks only 1 per cent commissions in tranche C does not make much sense for a small country trying to sell itself as a regional financial cen-

tre,' commented a senior London-based investment banker. International shareholders feel discriminated against and are asking themselves whether or not the SingTel board will be allowed to exercise its fiduciary duty to treat all shareholders equally. Certainly, the September 1996 sale of 5.3 per cent of the company to domestic retail shareholders at a 25 per cent discount to the then market price will have done nothing to improve the image of the Singapore government or the local equity capital markets among international investors.

It appears that as a result of repeated give-aways of shares to retail shareholders and the increasing competition in the local market resulting in a steadily declining share price, the Singapore government has found a recipe for disaster. Retail shareholders will demand ever-growing discounts to persuade them to participate in further SingTel share sales. Not only will this development not have helped the government's popularity with the people, but clearly a major opportunity to maximise the value of a terrific asset was lost forever. It provides the best evidence that it was always going to be difficult to satisfy both the domestic political agenda and the longer-term aim of maximising the value of SingTel.

Clearly the best interests of the company were not served in this privatisation: limited liquidity in the shares, few if any international core shareholders and less than ideal prospects for the company's further privatisation. SingTel was used for political ends and an obvious opportunity was missed to position it among its most prestigious international peers, where it belongs. One major London-based institutional investor who bid below the strike price in the IPO had harsh words for the Singaporeans: 'Looking at what is now happening with SingTel, we can't help feeling some *Schadenfreude* – at the time of the privatisation in 1993, the Singaporeans were extraordinarily arrogant vis-à-vis the international investment community and now they really appear to be struggling – the company is hardly impressing the world with its international business strategy, they appear to be outsmarted by the competition in the domestic mobile telephony market, and given the very poor share price performance both the 1993 and 1996 share sales to domestic retail investors look like failures.'

Tele Danmark

Some deals seem to do themselves, while others throw up numerous complexities. The US$3 billion IPO for Danish telecommunications company Tele Danmark in April 1994 was one of the latter. Tele Danmark was created by the government in a cross-party agreement in November 1990 to serve as a holding company for the country's four regional telecommunications enterprises and Telecom A/S which handled international traffic. The aim was to underpin the competitiveness of the Danish telecommunications sector and, as a result, that of Danish industry as a whole. The agreement stipulated that the company should be 51 per cent owned by the state and 49 per cent by private shareholders: this was to be implemented at the earliest opportunity. An initial plan to privatise Tele Danmark in November 1992 failed when an attempt was made to sell shares with a redemption clause and dividend restrictions. To all intents and purposes, these securities resembled bonds rather than shares, and therefore did not give an indication of the real value of the company: most politicians did not know how valuable the company was, and based on fundamentals it was worth double what they assumed.

It was the legal complexities associated with the old capital structure that led many bankers to believe that the privatisation would never happen. Undoubtedly, Goldman Sachs and Den Danske Bank, the joint global coordinators appointed in October 1993 following a highly competitive solicitation process, were faced with an unusually complex execution. The IPO was huge and the size inflexible – exactly 48.3 per cent of this US$6 billion company had to be sold. Market conditions

were deteriorating during the final stages of the execution of but postponement was not an option.

For two reasons the privatisation of Tele Danmark became a primary offer, ie, an offer where the company sells the shares and collects the proceeds. First, a charge by the European Union of unlawful state subsidy relating to the outdated share capital structure meant that Tele Danmark had to redeem old A shares and then issue new B shares. Second, there was a threat of investors in the old restricted A shares suing the government. In addition, the pension fund was hugely underfunded and Tele Danmark therefore needed capital, although certainly not the full US$3 billion.

The Tele Danmark IPO represented the first privatisation of a northern European telecommunications company since BT in 1984. It was the largest ever Danish equity offer and, on a fully diluted basis, Tele Danmark became the nation's largest listed company. In terms of the amount raised, the equity offer was at the time also the largest ever outside a domestic market, the largest foreign offer in the UK and the second largest foreign offer in the US.

Major challenges

According to a political agreement made in 1990, Tele Danmark had to be 51 per cent-owned by the government, so the size of the offer was therefore an 'all or nothing' situation, making the issue extremely large for its domestic mar-

---

Exhibit 1
Transaction summary

Issuer name: Tele Danmark A/S (Denmark)	*Joint global coordinators:* Goldman Sachs and Den Danske Bank
Pricing date: 27 April 1994 (KFX 20: 109.28)	*Pricing/underwriting structure:* Global bookbuilding
Vendor: Company	*Primary or secondary:* Primary
	Retail structure: –
% of company sold: 48.3% of nominal capital post-issue	*Privatisation or corporate:* Privatisation
IPO or non-IPO: IPO	*Industry:* Telecommunications operator
Type of shares: Ordinary B shares and ADRs (1 ADR represents 0.5 class B shares)	*Filing range:* Dkr275–315 per share Offer price: Dkr310/share; or US$23.526/ADR
Total issue size: US$2.,975 billion	*US listing/144A:* NYSE listing

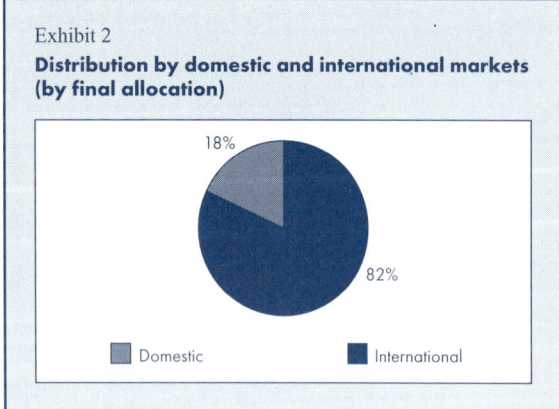

Exhibit 2

Distribution by domestic and international markets (by final allocation)

18%

82%

■ Domestic   ■ International

ket. There had never been a mass-marketed issue on this scale in Denmark so there was no reliable precedent as to the capacity of the domestic retail market. It was not known how the home market would stand up to potential selling pressure from international investors in the immediate after-market and on an ongoing basis.

There was a July 1994 deadline for completion of the capital restructuring and the offer. In addition, Tele Danmark was anxious to come to the market before KPN, the much larger Dutch telecom operator, which was scheduled for late spring of 1994. This timing conflict was a common theme and a major driving force throughout the execution of the offer.

Tele Danmark's share capital structure was outdated and resembled a bond with a redemption option every five years. To normalise the share capital, a necessary step in order to value the company and execute a successful privatisation, there had to be a complex capital restructuring which needed to comply with both Danish law and European Union subsidy legislation. This issue had represented a major challenge for several years, and furthermore, the bankers and the company were presented with a major communication challenge in explaining these complexities to investors.

The Danish regulatory regime for the telecoms industry was historically opaque and needed to be updated prior to the float. A new regulatory regime was established, which was seen by investors as unsatisfactory: under this new regime the government would act as both owner and regulator, leaving the market feeling that the price regime was subject to political influence.

Although there was a general political consensus on the Tele Danmark privatisation, many decisions had been compromises, such as the decision to create Tele Danmark by merging five companies without letting the new entity realise all synergies available from rationalisation. This meant that investors could not expect substantial rationalisation benefits to underpin the profit growth of the company in the foreseeable future.

A further challenge arose from deteriorating market conditions following a February 1994 decision by the Federal Reserve to increase short-term interest rates in the US. During the marketing period, all the principal markets relevant to the offer were off: Copenhagen by 2 per cent, the Goldman Sachs Telecom Index by 3.5 per cent, FT-SE 100 by 4.5 per cent and S&P 500 by 5.5 per cent.

Rationale and objectives

Reasons for the offer

The stated reasons for the creation of Tele Danmark and its privatisation under the 1990 legislation were:

- To strengthen the competitiveness of the Danish telecommunications sector;
- To improve Danish telecommunications research and development;
- With respect to concessionary services, to attempt to reduce tariffs in real terms while maintaining a high-quality service;
- With respect to liberalised services, to serve the interests of Danish users as much as possible in light of increased competition and internationalisation; and
- To separate the regulatory from the operational functions in accordance with EU requirements.

Offer objectives

The government's privatisation objectives were mainly:

- To ensure that Tele Danmark was ready and equipped for competition well before 1 January 1998 when the telecommunications sector within the EU is supposed to be fully liberalised; and
- To be seen to be among the first European countries to deregulate and privatise the telecom sector.

In addition, the government was committed to implementing the 1990 political agreement, resolving the A-share problem and, over time, realising value through conversion of its remaining A shares into B shares.

Tele Danmark had certain requirements, which were not necessarily in conflict with the government's objectives:

- To receive the proceeds from the offer to finance substantial deficits in the company's pension fund and to allow for a normalisation of Tele Danmark's capital structure;
- To be free from government interference in light of increasing competition, and to expand internationally to compensate for loss of revenue as a result of domestic competition;
- To run the company on a wholly commercial basis; and
- To streamline the five operating subsidiaries into one company.

Hans Munk Nielsen, Tele Danmark's CFO commented: 'It was perhaps not generally appreciated that we only had equity of Dkr6.5 billion in 1991, representing an equity-to-total-assets ratio of 24 per cent, whereas we had unfunded pension liabilities of Dkr7 billion and as such our equity could easily have been wiped out overnight. We also had a relatively low profit ratio as we had to pay, annually, contributions to the pension fund amounting to 20 per cent of total salaries. Therefore we had a strong need to normalise the share capital, allowing us the same financial flexibility afforded any other publicly traded enterprise. We also had a less official reason for wanting to normalise our share capital, which was that previously the A shareholders had no interest whatsoever in the performance of the company as they simply got the same Dkr10 dividend each year, regardless of the company's performance. Also, in the past, the company was a perfect playground for political intervention.'

Use of the proceeds

The net proceeds from the offer – approximately Dkr18.7 billion (US$2.8 billion) – were to be used to make payments in respect of the company's pension obligations (about Dkr7.0 billion) and to repay indebtedness to its pension funds (about Dkr3.3 billion). These repayments would significantly reduce annual pension costs from around 20 per cent to 6 per cent of pensionable salaries for the majority of employees. Interest charges were also reduced significantly in 1994 as the company was put into a net cash position due to the proceeds from

the issue. Some Dkr1.1 billion were used to purchase A shares in connection with the reorganisation of the share capital structure and the remaining proceeds of approximately Dkr7.3 billion were available for certain capital expenditures, to repay existing debt and to increase working capital.

Share capital and ownership

See Exhibit 3.

Timing of the sale

The intention was initially to privatise Tele Danmark by a straightforward sale of 43 per cent of the government's 94 per cent holding as soon as possible after the creation of the company. Investors were therefore buying the A shares in the hope that they would be converted to ordinary shares without the

---

Exhibit 3
Share capital and ownership

Type of shares offered	Class B limited voting (1 vote) registered shares of Dkr10 nominal value and ADRs representing 0.5 class B share.
Ownership restrictions	No investor except the state may hold more than 7.5% of the total nominal share capital, either in the form of B shares or ADRs. This provision was included in the articles of association for anti-takeover purposes and to prevent anyone from building a stake that would make Tele Danmark less attractive as a strategic partner.
Major shareholder(s) before offer	The state owned 89.9% of the nominal share capital and voting rights before the offer. Minority shareholders held the balance.

The post-offer ownership and capital structure of Tele Danmark

The company tendered for 49% of the outstanding state and privately held A shares and by the closing date on 8 March had received acceptances from holders of 48.3%. In the process, the government reduced its holding of the nominal capital and the voting rights from 89.9% to 51%. Private A shareholders retain a 0.7% interest in the company. Tele Danmark issued new B shares in the equivalent amount of nominal capital, ie, 48.3%. Post-offer, the state owns 51% of the nominal capital in the form of restricted A shares. Since the state's A shares will be converted into B shares in June 1998, it effectively also owns 51% of the economic rights of Tele Danmark, although until then the state will only receive A share dividends.

	Number of shares	Nominal value	Share capital (% of total nominal capital)
State held A shares (a)(c)	6,680,000	Dkr100	51.0%
Privately held A shares (b)(c)	97,023	Dkr100	0.7%
B shares	63,229,770	Dkr10	48.3%
Total			**100.0%**

(a) A shares are redeemable every five years at Dkr125 and dividends are restricted to Dkr10 per share.
(b) Privately held A shares remaining outstanding after the close of the tender offer.
(c) The remaining privately held A shares will be purchased by the government in 1997 at a fixed price of Dkr125. All the state's A shares will then be be converted into B shares in June 1998. Subsequently the government will then sell this 0.7% in the market so as to maintain an exact ownership of 51%.

Listings	The B shares were listed in Copenhagen and on the NYSE in April 1994. They also traded on Seaq International after the offer. (Tele Danmark's A shares were listed on the Copenhagen Stock Exchange from 1992 when the public holders of A shares in two of the four regional telecommunications companies, now forming part of the Tele Danmark group, exchanged their shares for shares in Tele Danmark.)
Market capitalisation at offer price (Dkr6.5885/US$)	US$6.2 billion (assuming that all A shares have been converted to B shares).
Most relevant stock exchange index/weighting	KFX Index of 20 most valuable stocks selected from the 25 shares with the highest turnover. Included since 2 December 1994 with 13.7% weighting.

dividend restriction and redemption clause. The first attempt to privatise was made by Unibank in November 1992 when a decision not to proceed was taken only one hour before a scheduled press conference to announce the terms of the sale. The official reason for the postponement was bad market conditions, although many observers thought that it was in fact due to the market's reluctance to buy the A shares. The real reason for the postponement was allegedly that Tele Danmark wanted the state to sell only 18 per cent to the public and reserve 25 per cent for a business partner with which it announced that it was in negotiations. Accordingly, Tele Danmark approached the government with a view to having the share sale reduced in

size, and the offer then had to be postponed in its entirety due to the uncertainty created by the partnership discussions. At this stage, the company was given six months to sort out the situation and a working group was formed to come up with a solution, including ways to normalise the A shares.

The problem with Tele Danmark's share capital structure was inherited from Copenhagen Telephone and Jutland Telephone, two of the regional telephone companies, as their shares had a dividend cap and a redemption clause. These had previously been sold by Danish equity salesmen to foreign investors (including Fidelity of the US) as KTAS and JTAS ordinary shares, allegedly without highlighting the restrictions on them. As a

---

Exhibit 4

How the delay in the offer developed

June 1990	• 1990 political agreement concerning the establishment and privatisation of Tele Danmark. In June 1993 and in February 1994, two supplements to the agreement were adopted that set out a plan for the reduction in the kingdom's shareholding and guidelines for the further liberalisation of the Danish telecommunications sector.
November	• Telecommunications Act of 1990 (the 1990 act) passed; and • Danish government founded Tele Danmark.
January–February 1991	• Tele Danmark acquired two regional telecom companies, Tele Soenderjylland and Fyns Telefon as well as Telecom, which was responsible for international traffic, and made a share exchange offer to KTAS and JTAS minority shareholders, which was 80% accepted. Tele Danmark's A shares were listed on the Copenhagen Stock Exchange.
March 1992	• Compulsory redemption of KTAS shares not already exchanged for Tele Danmark shares, whereby the state's ownership in Tele Danmark was increased from 74% to 94%.
November	• Offer, via Unibank, of 43% of Tele Danmark A shares postponed.
December	• Danish company law modified, with respect to the right of minority shareholders to be bought out at a fair price if the majority shareholder holds above 90% (reverse minority squeeze-out). New law became effective on 1 August 1993. This would give Fidelity, as an important owner of A shares, an opportunity to negotiate a settlement recognising more fully the real value of Tele Danmark, in which case, other minority shareholders who had already exchanged or redeemed at Dkr125 most probably would also have taken legal action.
June 1993	• The threat of the reverse minority squeeze-out led to a political agreement of 25 June 1993. The plan was that the state would place 5% of Tele Danmark in the market via Unibank, hence reducing ownership to 89.9%, and also make arrangements to sell back 39% to the company at Dkr170 (the price prevailing on the day of the political agreement). Private shareholders were also invited to sell to Tele Danmark at the same price. Tele Danmark would then issue B shares before July 1994 on the assumption that this did not infringe EU subsidy legislation.
August 1993	• The EU Commission was notified of this plan and negotiations started later in the autumn of 1993. The fact that Tele Danmark was going to buy A shares from the government at Dkr170 and then sell B shares in the market at a considerably higher price initially created suspicions at the commission that the Danish government was intending to subsidise Tele Danmark; and • The principal argument against the EU allegation of unlawful subsidy was that the buy-back by Tele Danmark was going to put the company in a worse situation than if it had not bought back the shares but simply issued new shares to dilute the government stake to 51%.
February 1994	• As the proposed structure implied that Tele Danmark would pay the same dividends on all shares after 1998, the allegations of unlawful subsidy could be successfully overcome. On this basis, it became possible to conduct the offer as executed in 1994.
March	• The Telecommunications Amendment Act of 1994 provided for a reorganisation of Tele Danmark's share capital structure, including (pursuant to the 1990 political agreement) a reduction in the kingdom's ownership of the company's nominal share capital and voting power to 51%. The Danish government would purchase, effective 1 March 1997, all privately held A shares then outstanding (0.733% of the nominal share capital and voting power) at Dkr125 per share. In June 1998, the kingdom's A shares were to be converted into B shares on a nominal value basis, ie, 10 B shares for each A share, and the A shares were to cease to exist; and • Tender offer to redeem A shares held by the government and the public.
April	• Although the Tele Danmark IPO was successfully completed, it can be argued that the transaction will not be fully executed until 1998 when Tele Danmark's share capital becomes fully normalised. Until then, the holders of the 63.2 million B shares sold in this offer are entitled to close to 100% of the cash flow of Tele Danmark as the remainder of the share capital (the A shares) is associated with a dividend cap.

Exhibit 5
Offer structure

Target markets	Indicated tranche sizes (% of indicated total offer on 18 March)	Regional lead managers	Co-lead managers
International offer			
Nordic	20%	Den Danske Bank	Carnegie, DnB, Goldman Sachs, Unibank
UK	16%	BZW	DDB, Goldman Sachs, Kleinwort Benson
Europe	14%	UBS	DDB, Deutsche, Goldman Sachs, Paribas
RoW	9%	Goldman Sachs	Daiwa, DDB, Robert Fleming, Wood Gundy
Total international offer	59%		
US offer	41%	Goldman Sachs	Merrill Lynch
Total combined offers (shares)	**63,229,770**		

Exhibit 6
Principal advisers

Independent financial adviser to Tele Danmark	Johansen & Co.
Financial adviser to the Kingdom of Denmark	Unibank and Price Waterhouse
US legal adviser to Tele Danmark	Debevoise & Plimpton
Danish legal adviser to Tele Danmark	Kromann & Muenter
US legal adviser to the underwriters	Cleary Gottlieb, Steen & Hamilton
Danish legal adviser to the underwriters	Reumert & Partners
US legal adviser to the Kingdom of Denmark	Sullivan & Cromwell
Danish legal adviser to the Crown	Kommersadvokaten

result, the price of these shares rose substantially above the intrinsic value, until it became clear to these investors that the shares had only a bond value and consequently the price started to fall. The redemption clause was originally designed to protect shareholders at a price which was at the time deemed attractive, while the Dkr10 dividend was to provide the share with a certain stability. The 1990 political agreement establishing Tele Danmark included a decision not to compensate for any losses arising from speculation in KTAS and JTAS shares on the government's abolition of the dividend restriction and the redemption clause (see Exhibit 4).

Transaction components

This IPO of 63.2 million new B shares comprised an international offer divided into four regions and a US publicly registered offer. The Nordic tranche of the international offer included sub-offers for domestic retail, domestic institutions, Tele Danmark employees and Nordic institutions outside Denmark.

The offer was marketed on an open-price basis to both international and domestic investors, allowing a book to be built, after which the offer price was fixed. There was complete transparency of demand, and although retail investors applying for shares did not form part of the formal book-building process, they were asked to indicate a price limit on their subscription forms. Retail investors were defined as orders up to an amount of US$300,000, or 7,000 shares. There were no retail incentives.

There was no greenshoe, and the state and Tele Danmark are both effectively subject to a lock-up until 1998 (see Exhibit 5).

Principal advisers

Neither Tele Danmark nor the government hired separate international financial advisers and the government's domestic advisers kept very much in the background. Given the short time available to prepare the offer, it would have been difficult had the government had separate international advisers. Tim Bunting of Goldman Sachs explained: 'The case for splitting the advisory roles is not clear for a primary issue.' Price Waterhouse, the company's auditor, was appointed financial adviser to the government (see Exhibit 6).

Transaction fee distribution

The institutional fees of 3.50 per cent were distributed as shown in Exhibit 8.

Management fee

The global coordinators received 25 per cent of the total management fee, calculated on the total proceeds of the offer.

In the international offer, a further 25 per cent of the management fee was paid to the lead and co-lead managers respectively, calculated on the basis of their underwriting commitments. The breakdown of the total management fee in the international offer is given in Exhibit 9.

In the US except for the deduction of the global coordinator's praecipium, management fees were allocated among the managers on the basis of underwriting commitment only.

Exhibit 7
The timetable

Preparation	
Beginning of October 1993	• Goldman Sachs and Den Danske Bank appointed joint global coordinators.
November	• Preparation of offer began.
November to mid-February 1994	• Capital restructuring.
November to end-February	• Development of regulatory framework.
December to early March	• US GAAP reconciliation and preparation of SEC registration statement.
December to mid-March	• Prospectus drafting.
December to April	• Valuation of the company.
February to mid-March	• Dividend policy formulation.
Execution	
31 January and 1 February 1994	• Equity research analyst meeting with company.
24 February	• Equity research published outside the US.
18 March	• Filing of the F-1 registration statement with the SEC.
21 March	• Distribution of prospectus and beginning of pre-marketing.
5 April	• Global roadshow began in Stockholm and with video conference for Asia; and • Institutional bookbuilding began.
11 April	• Danish retail subscription period began; and • Roadshow moved to European continent.
18 April	• Roadshow continued in the US.
22 April	• Danish retail subscription period ended.
26 April	• Roadshow ended in the US.
27 April	• Pricing and allocation.
28 April	• Trading began at 3.30pm in Copenhagen (trading was extended by two-and-a-half hours), 2.30pm on Seaq International and 9.30am in New York.

Exhibit 8
Distribution of gross spread (%)

Management	Underwriting	Selling concession	Gross spread
0.70	0.7032	2.0968	3.50

Exhibit 9
Distribution of management fee outside the US (%)

Total management fee	0.70
Of which: Global coordinator's praecipium	25
Of which: Lead/co-lead managers' praecipium split among all leads/co-leads	25
Of which: Management fees split among all managers	50

Exhibit 10
Distribution of selling concession in the US (%)

Total selling concession	2.0968
Of which: Pre-agreed or fixed portion	30
Of which: Paid pro rata according to sales designated by investors	70

Selling concession

In the US, the selling concession had one fixed and one variable component. The pre-agreed or fixed portion is split according to the underwriting amounts. The distribution of the selling concession in the US is given in Exhibit 10. Outside the US, the selling concession was paid in full to whomever the order was given.

Deal structure

Reasons for primary rather than secondary issue

Despite the fact that a secondary sale was foreseen in the 1990 agreement, there were several legal reasons why the government could not sell the shares and receive the proceeds from the sale, as is typical in most telecom privatisations:

• The 1990 agreement provided for a sale of A shares, ie, it did not provide for the sale of a normalised share at a full equity value;

• The government could probably not have redeemed the A

shares at Dkr170 (per Dkr100 nominal value) and then sold ordinary B shares at a price more than 18 times higher (Dkr310 per Dkr10 nominal value) as this would have been against the Danish telecommunications acts of 1915 and 1917 (referring to the redemption clause for JTAS and KTAS) which stipulated that the government could not redeem the shares to make a profit; and

- The decision by the state to sell back A shares to Tele Danmark did not put the state in a worse situation than if – as originally foreseen in the 1990 political agreement – it had simply sold the A shares in the market. It meant that the government became a 51 per cent shareholder in a company valued at US$6 billion, which was better for both parties, and was therefore a win-win situation.

Having decided on a primary offer, the government took the view that the flotation was going to be more successful if Tele Danmark's management could be fully motivated to achieve a successful offer, as this would give the government's remaining stake a higher long-term value. The way to achieve a high level of motivation was to let it manage the entire offer process with only minimal interference from the government. Munk Nielsen commented: 'We believe that who gets the proceeds in a privatisation like this makes an enormous difference. If the company gets the proceeds, the entire management is motivated to achieve the highest value. If the government gets the proceeds then the company is likely to adopt a much more conservative attitude to budgets, forecasts, competitive data, etc. If the government appears to give something up, then they will get it back by owning a more valuable company.'

Pricing/underwriting method

This was a classic bookbuilt offer, and according to Tim Bunting there were no real challenges in integrating the domestic and international tranches: 'My counterparty at Den Danske Bank did a great job in educating the Copenhagen Stock Exchange as to the requirements of the international market. Equally he was able to communicate to us the various constraints of the domestic market that we had to take into account when structuring the non-Danish part of the offer.'

Although there were no real challenges with the pricing and underwriting, domestic institutional investors did not appreciate the bookbuilding approach, as during the course of the process, they felt that they were put under considerable competitive pressure. They also did not like the fact that it was an open-ended commitment, with the price being fixed at the end of the process. This criticism from institutions is typical in countries where bookbuilding is not often used.

Syndicate structure

The rationale behind combining the retail and institutional tranches in Denmark and incorporating the Nordic markets outside Denmark into the same tranche was to avoid failure due to making any single component too transparent. If, for example, retail demand had been disappointing it would not necessarily have been apparent because institutional demand might have compensated for it.

Size

As a result of the 1990 agreement, the size of the offer was larger than Tele Danmark's capital requirement and probably too large for the domestic market.

Perhaps more interesting than the absolute size of the offer was the fact that at the time it was the largest equity offer ever undertaken in terms of the amount raised outside the domestic market (see Exhibit 11). Furthermore, at US$1.2 billion, Tele Danmark was at the time the second largest offer by a foreign company in the US after YPF (US$1.4 billion), and at US$565 million, it was the largest ever offer by a foreign company in the UK.

The reason for the offer being structured without a greenshoe was related to the requirement for the state to own exactly 51 per cent of the company. Although, technically, a solution was found involving the use of treasury shares specially created for the purpose, the added complexity and the risk that investor focus might have been deflected, together with the generally strong market conditions during the preparation phase, led to the decision not to include a greenshoe. According to Robert Morris, Goldman Sachs' acclaimed telecommunications analyst, the absence of a greenshoe may have had an influence on the pricing: 'It is possible that the offer might have been priced at the top of the price range had it been structured with a normal greenshoe.' Because of the state's require-

Exhibit 11
Largest offers by amount sold outside home market

	Issuer	Date	Total size (US$ million)	Sold internationally (%)	International size (US$ million)
1.	Tele Danmark	April 1994	2,952	82	2,445
2.	YPF	June 1993	3,040	75	2,280
3.	Wellcome	July 1992	4,419	48	2,123
4.	Telmex	May 1991	2,173	93	2,017
5.	BP	October 1987	4,571	39	1,804
6.	Telmex	June 1992	1,403	89	1,243
7.	RECs (UK)	December 1990	4,255	20	851
8.	Repsol	March 1993	947	89	846
9.	BNP	October 1993	3,043	25	759
10.	Grupo Televisa	October 1991	863	87	748

Exhibit 12
Global pre-marketing

City/country	Number of meetings/calls	City/country	Number of meetings/calls	City/country	Number of meetings/calls	City/country	Number of meetings/calls
London	45	Zurich	5	Dusseldorf	2	Chicago	24
Geneva	14	Singapore	4	Taiwan	1	Boston	20
Frankfurt	14	Dublin	3	New Zealand	1	Minneapolis	11
Scotland	11	Australia	3	Munich	1	New York	11
Hong Kong	9	Paris	3	Stuttgart	1	+ 13 further US cities	29
Tokyo	9	Italy	3	Abu Dhabi	1		
Stockholm	5	Spain	2				
				Total international	**137**	**Total US**	**95**

ment to own exactly 51 per cent, both the state and Tele Danmark are effectively subject to a lock-up until 1998, when this requirement falls away.

Marketing

Pre-marketing

From the beginning of March to 5 April (after 18 March in the US), Robert Morris and Stuart Birdt of Goldman Sachs' London-based telecommunications research team, met with or called a large number of institutions to get them sufficiently interested in the Tele Danmark story to decide to attend the company roadshow. Institutions were visited or called as shown in Exhibit 12.

Retail marketing

It was deemed of utmost importance that the transaction gain momentum through Danish retail subscriptions so as to generate enthusiasm among domestic and international institutions. Given that the retail market was unproven, as a large mass-marketed retail offer had never before been attempted in Denmark, an extensive sales campaign was needed to reach individuals. A successful campaign was all the more important, as at the time of the offer, the Tele Danmark name was new to the public.

'The campaign included advertising by Tele Danmark in daily newspapers and on television,' explained Jens Peter Toft, senior vice president of Den Danske Bank. 'Signs, posters and three-dimensional displays were used by the branches of the domestic syndicate banks. Den Danske Bank supported the marketing campaign by using direct mail and by arranging extensive internal marketing activities. While all these methods had been used individually in share marketing campaigns, no single prior campaign had used all methods at once.' There were also the following considerations to take into account:

- To offer a discount is not legal in Denmark and consequently this incentive could not be employed as it is in most retail offers around the world; and
- Bonus shares also could not be considered as there was no flexibility with respect to the number of shares sold

because of the 51 per cent post-offer government ownership requirement. On the other hand, employees were able to acquire up to 75 shares each at the deeply discounted price of Dkr100 per share.

The retail marketing strategy turned out much better than expected and was a real success. The advertising campaign reached 85 per cent of all targeted households and all branches of Den Danske Bank and Unibank were employed in the offer. The absence of retail incentives in no way affected demand in what was, at over US$300 million, the largest ever Danish retail offer. Den Danske Bank alone placed 60 per cent of this amount, and in the end demand from Danish retail investors was stronger in absolute terms than that from institutional investors.

Institutional marketing

The Tele Danmark management embarked on a full three-week roadshow, which should be seen in the context of the plan to sell 41 per cent of the issue in the US, 20 per cent in Denmark and the Nordic countries, and 39 per cent in the UK, Europe and the RoW(see Exhibit 13).

Comprehensive pre-marketing, and positive equity research available 30 days before the preliminary prospectus was published, meant that the whole book was full on day one of bookbuilding. Tele Danmark's management was thus in a relatively comfortable position during the roadshow.

Exhibit 13
The company roadshow

European Roadshow (5–15 April during 8 working days)*

- Stockholm
- Frankfurt
- Zurich
- Edinburgh
- Copenhagen
- Geneva
- Paris
- Amsterdam
- London
- Glasgow

US Roadshow (18–26 April during 7 working days)*

- New York
- Chicago
- San Francisco
- Madison
- Boston
- Denver
- Portland
- Kansas City
- Baltimore
- Los Angeles
- Minneapolis
- Philadelphia

* In addition there was a video conference for investors in Tokyo, Hong Kong and Singapore.

Exhibit 14
Principal sales points

Revenue growth	Tele Danmark was expecting revenue growth of 5–6% during the next few years, as a result of: • the growth in the Danish economy (estimated at 2.1% in 1994); • increased demand for multiple lines; • modest subscriber growth; • increased international traffic as the economy picks up in the rest of Europe; and • increased cellular penetration. The high operating leverage in the business results in much of this revenue growth flowing through to the bottom line.
Improving profitability	• *Headcount reductions:* The management expected to improve labour productivity and reduce headcount by around 2,700 by 1997, mainly through a gradual elimination of the duplicate functions which the regional structure had created and through the modernisation of the network; • *Cost reductions:* In addition to the reductions in pension costs, depreciation charges were expected to fall from 21% of revenues as capital expenditure declined and revenues grew. The concession fee was expected to fall by approximately Dkr115 million on an annual basis in 1994 alone. Further liberalisation was expected to lead to additional reductions in the concession fee; • *Margin expansion:* The ongoing reductions in costs and revenue growth were expected to lead to further improved margins. Excluding the step-up in base earnings associated with the reduction in the funding of pension liabilities, Goldman Sachs expected operating expenses to grow by only 4.3% in 1994 and 2.5% in 1995, and by 2%–3% beyond 1995; • *Earnings growth:* Excluding the benefits from reduced pension expense and interest on pension debt, earnings growth was estimated at 25% in 1994 and 22% in 1995. The five-year growth rate was estimated at 15%.
Scarcity of alternative investments	There were at the time only three publicly traded telecom companies in Europe: • BT; • Telefónica; and • Stet. Goldman Sachs believed that Tele Danmark offered more attractive earnings and dividend growth prospects than these others.
Tariff structure	Tele Danmark believed that the proposed price cap formula for tariffs on non-competitive businesses, of Danish inflation less 3%, to be introduced from January 1995, still allowed the company: • to pass benefits of productivity increases to shareholders; and • sufficient flexibility to adjust individual prices to respond to increased competition.
Cellular business	• Mobile penetration in Denmark had reached 7%, which, although high by international standards, is the lowest in the Nordic region.
Competition	• Around 33% of Tele Danmark's revenues were subject to competition. In reality, it had few competitors even in the fully liberalised areas. Tele Danmark's historically dominant position and well balanced tariff structure, and the dispersed small business nature of its customer base will mean that new entrants to the market will find it difficult to compete.
Valuation	The driving valuation parameters were: • *1994 P/E multiple:* Tele Danmark's premium to many of its peers was justified by the higher expected growth in earnings per share; and • *Dividend yield:* Tele Danmark had a policy of linking dividends to earnings indicating substantial dividend growth. The indicated dividend payout ratio for 1994 was approximately. 65%. The yield of 3.9% compared favourably in the domestic market; • *Cash flow multiples:* Tele Danmark's levered cash flow multiple of 6.7x for 1993 was attractive. In addition, the network will require only limited capital expenditure to go forward.

Source: Goldman Sachs International.

The Tele Danmark story

Tele Danmark is the principal provider of domestic and international telephone services in Denmark with over three million subscriber lines to residential and business customers. At the time of the offer it was the sole direct provider of leased lines and one of two operators of public mobile telephone services. It also provides other services, including cable television, and sells telecommunications equipment. In 1993 Tele Danmark had net revenues of US$2.4 billion and net income of US$230 million. The company was primarily a growth play and to a lesser extent a rationalisation play. At the time, Goldman Sachs' marketing included the points outlined in Exhibit 14.

Tele Danmark's 1994 P/E ratio was relatively high compared to its peer group (see Exhibit 15) but its expected earnings per share growth was much higher (see Exhibit 16).

Principal reasons for not buying

Those investors who declined to buy Tele Danmark shares gave the following reasons:

• Fear of increased competition and faster than expected liberalisation;
• Concern that the excess cash would not be spent in an optimal way post-issue;

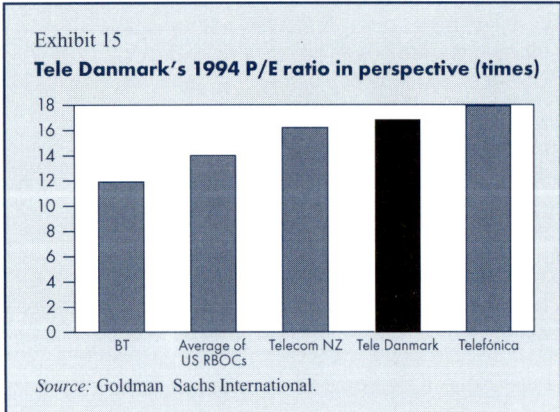

Exhibit 15

Tele Danmark's 1994 P/E ratio in perspective (times)

Source: Goldman Sachs International.

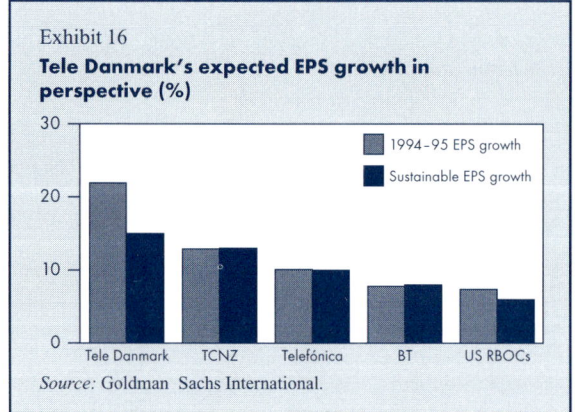

Exhibit 16

Tele Danmark's expected EPS growth in perspective (%)

1994–95 EPS growth

Sustainable EPS growth

Source: Goldman Sachs International.

- The management's relative lack of experience;
- The large and inflexible offer size; and
- The market conditions were deteriorating during the marketing period.

Results

Placement

The overall issue was four-and-a-half times subscribed due to substantially inflated orders: the US offer was five times subscribed, the UK tranche four times, the European tranche five times, the RoW tranche four times and the Nordic tranche two times. In total, this offer generated demand of more than US$12 billion. The allocations corresponded closely to the underwriting amounts per region with an increase in the UK and a minor decrease for the Nordic and RoW regions (see Exhibit 17).

UK institutions playing the privatisation game came in early and then waned: they were told by BZW, the regional lead manager for the UK tranche, that the earlier they indicated demand, the better their allocations would be. In the global book, the US came in as the UK institutional orders began to wane: they were also the most active in the after-market.

It is conceivable that Danish institutional demand would have been stronger if the institutions had been more familiar with bookbuilding or if the pricing/underwriting method had

been different, as they were clearly uncomfortable with bookbuilding. In any event, the support from domestic institutions, which is typically crucial in these offers, was on this occasion of limited significance given firstly that domestic retail demand was above expectations and secondly that Danish institutions collectively accounted for no more than 8 per cent of the total offer.

Danish retail, including employees, represented over 50 per cent of the Nordic tranche. Some 28,000 individuals (0.5 per cent of the Danish population) bought the issue, in addition to 10,500 Tele Danmark employees.

The issue price was clearly dictated by foreign investors and could probably have been Dkr315 had the offer been structured with a greenshoe. In the event, Robert Morris of Goldman Sachs fought hard against a Dkr315 issue price, and has been vindicated.

Type of buyers

Those international institutions that bought the issue included telecom buyers, value investors, growth utility or growth industry buyers, and yield investors. Hardly any international buyers were looking for Danish exposure as such, and index considerations were important mainly for Danish investors. As there were no large quoted telecom operators in the Nordic region, Nordic institutions were not familiar with the sector, and accordingly there were few large orders from Nordic institutions outside Denmark.

Exhibit 17

Underwriting, demand and allocation (%)

Target markets	Underwriting	Demand	Allocation
Danish retail	N/A	N/A	9
Danish Institutions	N/A	N/A	8
Employee (preferential terms)	N/A	N/A	1
Non-Danish Nordic institutions	N/A	N/A	1
Total Nordic	20	8	19
UK	16	25	19
Europe	14	23	14
RoW	9	7	7
Total international offer	59	63	59
US offer	41	37	41
Total combined offers (shares)	**63,229,770**	**255,000,000**	**63,229,700**

Sources: Goldman Sachs International and Den Danske Bank.

Exhibit 18
Investor concentration

	By demand	By allocation
Percentage of issue accounted for by the 10 largest investors (by total size of demand and allocation respectively)	16.3%	11.4%
Number of investors making up 80% of the issue (by total size of demand and allocation respectively)	632	466
The three largest investors by size	US$141 million US$129 million US$128 million	US$20 million US$20 million US$18 million
Total number of institutions	975	849

Source: Goldman Sachs International.

In the US, a large proportion of telecom buyers considered Tele Danmark to be a low-risk investment in a stable country. In Europe there was more emphasis on geography (eg, Fidelity's London-based Scandinavian Fund) and the growth aspects of Tele Danmark.

Investor concentration

As can be seen from Exhibit 18, the largest orders were scaled back by a factor of six to seven times.

After-market price performance

See Exhibit 19.

The stock traded up in the immediate after-market and closed at Dkr328 on Seaq International on the first day of trading, an appreciation in absolute terms of 5.7 per cent. The market price stayed above the offer price until 12 December 1994, when it closed at Dkr301. Although a weak performer in absolute terms over the first year of trading, Tele Danmark did outperform the domestic market by 6.3 per cent.

As is typical in any issue of this size, there is a first wave of restructuring of the shareholder base directly after trading begins: investors whose orders were not filled in the allocation process bought heavily in Copenhagen. The second wave of selling came during the first half of December 1994, when US investors sold in connection with an overall restructuring of their portfolios, whereby international holdings were reduced and fixed income investments increased. This process was escalated by the emerging currency crisis in Mexico. US investors had begun to look over their holdings of telecom stocks, which had begun to underperform as interest rates increased: most internationally traded telecom stocks declined by some 10–20 per cent during the second half of 1994.

More specifically, the reasons for Tele Danmark's relatively weak performance during its first year of trading as a public company included:

- Danish market conditions were depressed in the first half of 1994 and there was initially considerable selling pressure outside Denmark;
- The size of the Danish equity market was a factor, as its capacity to absorb foreign selling was limited;
- There was considerable concern among international

Exhibit 19
After-market price performance

Pricing date	27 April 1994
Filing range	Dkr275–315
Offer price	Dkr310
First-year high/low	
High (2 September 1994)	Dkr354
Low (8 March 1995)	Dkr278

Tele Danmark share price relative to KFX (%)

Absolute and relative share price performance

	Price (Dkr)	Relative to KFX (%)
+ 1 day	328	105.7
+ 3 days	333	107.9
+ 1 week	328	108.5
+ 1 month	323	111.3
+ 3 months	319	105.1
+ 6 months	340	123.4
+ 9 months	300	110.9
+ 12 months	287	106.3

Sources: Datastream and offer circular.

investors over the supply of shares from European telecommunications companies, with offers from Holland, Spain, Italy, Greece, Germany and France expected over the coming months and years. US investors had already begun to make room for Deutsche Telekom by selling certain other telecommunications stocks;

- There was a feeling that liberalisation and competition in Europe was gaining momentum, particularly towards the end of the year, which had a further depressing effect on the sector;

- Many investors were concerned about Tele Danmark's internationalisation strategy (it was clearly overcapitalised following the IPO);
- Tele Danmark's earnings pattern had not yet seasoned, ie, investors did not have a clear grasp of how earnings were likely to develop, particularly in relation to the effect of the huge cash proceeds, falling pension costs etc;
- According to Goldman Sachs, overall company performance was disappointing relative to analysts' expectations at the time of the IPO, principally for three reasons. First, although analysts' bottom-line earnings forecasts were met in the short term, it soon became clear that the top-line revenues (post–1994) were not accelerating in the way that the company and the analyst community had originally forecast. Second, in this lower-revenue growth environment, the company's ability to cut costs more dramatically than forecast was limited, due to the regional structure prevalent in its core domestic business. Third, competition in the mobile sector, which was expected to abate somewhat, has continued;
- US flowback and selling pressure became an issue in late 1994. One large US shareholder sold 70 per cent of his holding over a three-week period in late November and December 1994 and was instrumental in bringing the price down from Dkr340 to Dkr290. In connection with this second wave of selling, US shareholdings are estimated to have fallen from 41 to 35–38 per cent. A reduction in the ADR outstandings from 50 million to 40 million was not wholly counterbalanced by a corresponding increase in US holdings of ordinary shares. Munk Nielsen of Tele Danmark noted: 'The argument of large US flowback is exaggerated by those who try to deny the importance of the US market, most notably the European banks. To maintain that US shareholders are shorter-term holders than other institutional shareholders simply does not hold water. You can't stereotype.' Henning Rostung, senior vice president and head of investor relations at Tele Danmark added: 'US shareholders are more stable than generally believed. Furthermore, it is not that relevant to look at the nationality of some of the largest institutional investors, such as for example the Capital Group. We have contacts with them in Los Angeles, New York, London and Geneva. Including fund managers and telecom analysts, we have regular contact with 10 people within that organisation, wherever they may be. Furthermore their two different arms manage pension fund money and mutual funds respectively and have two entirely different investment philosophies and react differently'; and
- One year after the IPO, it was estimated that total foreign ownership of the free float remained at approximately 82 per cent, with US ownership having been slightly reduced and UK and continental European ownership correspondingly increased.

After-market trading volume

In the immediate after-market, most of the turnover happened on the NYSE, which is by no means unusual (see Exhibit 20).

Exhibit 20
Percentage of total issue traded * (%)

	Day 1 (28/4)	Day 2 (29/4)	Day 3 (2/5)	Total Day 1 - 3
New York	11.2	3.6	2.0	16.8
Copenhagen	3.2	–	1.2	4.4

* Based on the issue of 63,229,770 shares.

In the secondary market, a pattern has developed over time whereby Tele Danmark's B Shares are actively traded on the Copenhagen Stock Exchange and on Seaq International. A lot of volume is registered in Copenhagen, where it is typically the most traded share, but is actually generated internationally. The ADRs are actively traded on NYSE and Seaq International. The share price is not set in any of the three principal trading markets.

Due to the unusually high foreign ownership, Tele Danmark is among the more volatile shares in Copenhagen trading. Unlike the majority of the stocks on the Copenhagen Stock Exchange, there are a multitude of forces in New York and London determining the share price, many of which are unrelated to the company's prospects or of limited significance to the Danish market as a whole. The Danish krona/US dollar exchange rate, for example, is relatively insignificant for the company's profit development but of considerable significance for the foreign investor in Tele Danmark.

The performance of the main parties

The government

The former deputy permanent secretary of the Ministry of Research and at the time the government's senior civil servant involved with this privatisation, now a senior vice president of Tele Danmark, Jorgen Stig Andersen, was complimented by Goldman Sachs and others for his highly constructive approach and for guiding the transaction through the maze of EU subsidy legislation and Danish telecommunications law. He also procured backing for regulatory reform and new articles of association for Tele Danmark, which included such matters as provision for the election of directors and voting at general meetings. Stig Andersen's effectiveness was partly due to the positive political environment which followed the successful restructuring of Tele Danmark's share capital. The government's low-key approach was connected with the fact that it was preoccupied with the legal issues surrounding the company. Stig Andersen explained: 'We would simply not have had the resources to carry out the sale.'

A highly constructive working environment was maintained because the government kept its own advisers in the background and let the company and its advisers drive the process. It was Tele Danmark that appointed the global coordinator, which is consistent with the fact that it was the company that received the proceeds from the issue. It also helped that there was no strong political agenda relating to the placement of shares with the Danish retail sector.

It is conventional wisdom that a company tries harder in a primary issue than in a secondary issue. The Danish government recognised that it would be counterproductive to get too closely involved, even if this meant that it lost some control over the preparation process. Inevitably, the party responsible for the drafting of the prospectus has the upper hand in negotiations relating to issues such as the articles of association, the concession and the regulatory framework.

The company

Hans Würtzen, Tele Danmark's CEO, was exceptionally effective in dealing with the politicians. CFO Hans Munk Nielsen commented: 'We began to fully appreciate the value of the company in connection with all the bank presentations in September 1993. However, since the government was preoccupied with legal issues, it didn't necessarily know. To minimise the amount of government involvement during the preparation phase, it was our strategy to move as fast as possible to be always a couple of steps ahead. Since we were writing the prospectus, we were setting the agenda and by moving fast we were able to maintain our negotiating advantage. In the end, I believe that the government also benefited from this.'

Despite the fact that none of the company's senior managers had experience in running a publicly listed company, they adjusted well to the demands of highly sophisticated institutional investors. According to Bunting: 'Management were very quick learners. They did really well on the roadshow.' The management also deserves credit for realising the importance of a highly professional investor relations effort. It made decisions efficiently and managed the whole process well.

Tele Danmark delivered the earnings per share for 1994 that it set out to achieve at the time of the offer. On 17 March 1995 the company reported earnings per share of Dkr19.60, against Goldman Sachs' estimate at the time of the IPO of Dkr19.25. However, performance since then has disappointed the stock market in a number of respects.

The global coordinators

In June 1993 Lars Johansen was asked by Munk Nielsen if he would be available to advise Tele Danmark in the autumn. He said yes, and was formally hired in August to work closely with Munk Nielsen under a broad brief. Having been involved with equity new issuance in Denmark for many years, Johansen was one of the most experienced investment bankers in the country and Munk Nielsen wanted his help to pick the global coordinators and to act as a sounding board for the management on such matters as the offer objectives and the structure of the issue. As Munk Nielsen and Johansen recognised that the value of the company was probably double what most people thought and that the offer would therefore be a very large one, it was quickly established that the offer needed to include both a mass-marketed public offer in Denmark and a major offer globally, including, most probably, a US-registered offer. They therefore needed the strongest domestic bank and one of the international power-houses to work together as joint global coordinators.

Johansen and Munk Nielsen drew up a shortlist of six banks: Goldman Sachs, Merrill Lynch and Morgan Stanley as the strongest US houses, and SG Warburg and UBS as two of the strongest international houses. Den Danske Bank – with traditionally the best reputation in Denmark – had already held informal discussions with Tele Danmark about its privatisation by February 1993, and was the natural choice for a domestic bank. Though Den Danske Bank knew that it was the only Danish bank on the shortlist, it was not sure that this meant that it would necessarily be appointed.

On 1 September the shortlisted banks were sent a questionnaire requesting written and verbal presentations, the former due by 21 September. Goldman Sachs delivered by far the best written presentation, whereas Merrill Lynch gave a better verbal presentation, demonstrating great team spirit and cohesion. SG Warburg, perhaps one of the early favourites, failed to impress the management. Munk Nielsen said: 'Had we decided not to list in the US, then we probably would have given the mandate to UBS.' In the end Goldman Sachs won the mandate for some obvious and one not so obvious reason. The obvious reasons were that it had:

- The best experience at the time as global coordinator of large equity offers;
- The best track record for offers in the telecommunications industry, including: Telefónica of Spain, Hong Kong Telecom, Telmex, Cable & Wireless and Singapore Telecom. At the time it was also advising KPN;
- Robert Morris, one of the most highly ranked equity research analysts for the telecommunications sector;
- A good track record with Danish transactions, including a US-registered offer for Novo-Nordisk; and
- The best dedicated written Tele Danmark presentation, demonstrating that the bank was thoroughly informed and dedicated to the task of privatising Tele Danmark.

To these, according to Munk Nielsen, can be added 'perhaps the most important criteria of all – we considered Goldman Sachs to have a very good work ethic and a very hard-working attitude'.

Merrill Lynch lost only narrowly: Tele Danmark was exceptionally impressed with the bank's team spirit and the fact that it was extremely well prepared and coordinated for the verbal presentation. Merrill Lynch also had analyst Dan Rheingold, ranked second only to Morris.

Although KPN was scheduled to be executed after Tele Danmark, it had beaten the latter in the process of picking regional lead managers. Thus Tele Danmark lost SG Warburg as a regional lead manager for the UK tranche, as it had been appointed in this capacity for KPN. The Dutch government is renowned for its tough policy on conflicts of interest and would not have allowed SG Warburg to work on both offers.

As joint global coordinators, Goldman Sachs and Den Danske Bank did a great job in securing a transparent regulatory framework in line with what international investors are used to. The banks and Tele Danmark managed to ensure that a Danish version of the UK telecommunications watchdog Oftel was organised, although there are many who do not believe the Danish regulator to be politically independent and feel that it is wrong that the regulatory function falls under the jurisdiction of the Ministry of Research, which is also administering the shareholding in the company.

Goldman Sachs assisted Tele Danmark in its presentation to the EU Commission of the proposals on share capital restructuring. To Brussels, the issue was whether the introduction of a new class of shares represented an unlawful subsidy. Goldman Sachs successfully argued that the government was not putting money into Tele Danmark by selling A shares back to the company, and furthermore, that the government did not need to write down its investment in the company, which before and after the buyback was carried in the books at the same value.

Den Danske Bank did a good job in educating Goldman Sachs on the capital structure and the valuation of Tele Danmark, which was very complex. Den Danske Bank's valuation model was used by the joint global coordinators throughout the preparation and execution stages of the offer. It also performed well in the domestic and international placement of shares. 'We feel that Den Danske Bank was highly successful in creating demand, especially in the Nordic and Rest-of-Europe tranches,' commented the bank's executive vice president, Jens-Peter Toft. 'Outside the US, Den Danske Bank created almost 20 per cent of total demand.'

There were few contentious issues during the execution process: the political agreement of 1990 was too difficult to change, and everyone considered it as given and not worth bothering with. The main thrust during the execution was simply to get the deal done and to do everything required to accomplish that objective. Goldman Sachs introduced the notion that 'the state should view its holding in Tele Danmark in the same way that any other shareholder does', which was helpful when writing the articles of association, concession, etc, as it effectively separated the government's role as regulator from its role as shareholder. Munk Nielsen explained: 'Although this may sound nice, the global coordinators knew that this statement of philosophy was only of relative importance as it was not underpinned by a legal structure. The fear is that once the pressure is on the government, then they will say, if we can't do it as a regulator then we do it as a 51 per cent shareholder, which entitles us to elect 100 per cent of the board.'

Although Tele Danmark was happy with Goldman Sachs as global coordinator and subsequently in the after-market, Munk Nielsen says the company now needs to diversify its investment banking relationships as it requires the broadest possible research coverage. It would not be in the company's best interest to be seen to be too closely linked to Goldman Sachs.

Goldman Sachs and Den Danske Bank had a good working relationship based on mutual respect however, large banks such as Goldman Sachs are not generally comfortable with independent advisers such as Johansen working for the vendor. 'Nobody wants an educated customer,' noted one senior banker involved in the process. Munk Nielsen added: 'Lars Johansen was very helpful throughout. He had a broad brief and added value throughout the process, in particular in the beginning. He knew all the banks, he knew how to organise a beauty contest and he understood how to compare the banks. He certainly educated us as a customer in preparation for the negotiations with Goldman Sachs. Therefore, he may have added more value than was actually apparent at the time. It is my impression that Goldman Sachs and Den Danske Bank respected him but didn't want him involved. In the beginning, I thought that perhaps he would be able to manage the project but it soon became clear that it was necessary for me as a decision-maker to be present in many of the meetings.'

Key lessons learnt

This offer illustrated the importance of getting the company to issue equity and receive the proceeds rather than for the government to act as the vendor, as the management will try considerably harder if it gets the proceeds. In certain privatisations, it may be in the government's interest to either declare an extraordinary dividend pre-sale or to load the company with debt repayable to the state, and then let the company be the issuer.

Privatisations are often more successful when the management is given time to get the company ready for privatisation and to build a track record. Whereas a considerable amount had been done at Tele Danmark, politics had prevented the full integration of the regional companies.

Political decisions and privatisation go hand in hand and can never be separated; however, most privatisations would be more successful if political interference in the preparation and execution of the offers could be kept to a minimum. It is of key importance that the government is seen to be letting go of the control of the company. In the case of Tele Danmark, a few political decisions taken at an early stage substantially complicated the execution, most notably that exactly 48.3 per cent of the company had to be sold. On the other hand, part of the reason for the success was that the government let the company handle the execution phase.

The decision to appoint the right global coordinators is clearly a crucial one. Munk Nielsen emphasised: 'A lot of things could have gone wrong with another global coordinator.'

Once the advisers have been appointed, it is extremely important to be organised, with a detailed timetable and a close definition of the exact roles and responsibilities of everyone on the team so as to be able to report to the board, the government and all the other parties involved.

Although many offers have been badly executed as a result of insufficient preparation time, the case of Tele Danmark demonstrated that time pressure can be positive. A certain amount of time pressure combined with a small working team allowed for a smooth and effective execution of this offer.

The early decisions, such as the listing decision, are important in a process of this kind. Rostung commented: 'At the outset of this exercise, we realised that we were a small company in a small country. Accordingly, we have to grow faster and pay a higher dividend yield. We consider ourselves only Danish on the fringe.'

Conclusion

The completion of this offer was a very impressive achievement, in particular considering the many constraints resulting from the outdated share capital structure. Due to the small team and a sense of urgency, the execution ended up being surprisingly smooth. The fact that Tele Danmark received the proceeds was also helpful for the dynamics of the execution. This structure was not seen as being in conflict with the Danish government's objectives. The company's management worked harder, was more motivated and probably achieved a higher valuation than the state would have done as vendor.

However, the company ended up being too highly capitalised, even allowing for pension funding, the repayment of a loan to the pension fund and international acquisitions. 'We knew this,' explained Bunting. 'There was no way around it. It would have looked very odd to pay an extraordinary dividend.' The degree of over-capitalisation was officially recognised in September 1997, when Tele Danmark announced an agreement with the Danish government to buy back (from the government) approximately 30 per cent of its shares for around Dkr14 billion during the first half of 1998. It is expected that the state will then sell its remaining 25 per cent stake in the company.

Having been more than four times subscribed, the offer traded well in the immediate after-market; however, there has been substantial volatility during the first year of trading. This is understandable given that Tele Danmark has a small home market and a large portion of shares owned by international investors, while operating in a global industry. Accordingly, the management has accepted that it must be better than the competition both in terms of financial performance and communication with investors. The privatisation also had a major impact on the strategic direction pursued by the management. 'The IPO has been tremendously important in refocusing the mindset within the company that we are no longer an arm of the government,' according to Rostung.

This was also an important transaction for Goldman Sachs, as the bank wanted the league table credit and the overall credentials resulting from a successful Tele Danmark transaction to facilitate the successful pitch for 'the mother of all equity offers' – the privatisation of Deutsche Telekom. This transaction was an important contributory factor towards making Michael Evans and Scott Mead partners of Goldman Sachs at the end of 1994.

By the end of 1996, more than two-and-a-half years after the offer, Tele Danmark's market price was Dkr310, having traded down to below Dkr270 at one stage during 1996. Although, according to the international investment community, Tele Danmark has made a few mistakes, it is certainly a good company. Therefore, one can only conclude that the offer was overpriced.

Feature topic: *The role of the equity research analyst in a global equity offer – the approach adopted by Robert Morris of Goldman Sachs*

Most CEOs and privatisation officials who haven't been through at least one global equity offer are inclined to underestimate the role of the equity research analyst. During the solicitation process they will notice, however, that bankers stress how highly ranked their analysts are.

As Goldman Sachs' franchise within the telecommunications sector is among its strongest, the author met with Robert Morris to ask him how he does it. Since he has been one of the firm's strongest assets in securing these important telecom privatisation mandates and subsequently structuring and selling the transactions, it is interesting to know how he adds value to the process.

Morris, born in 1952, started his career as a fund manager with Wells Fargo Investment Advisors where he worked for five years. He then started his own consulting firm and focused on advising telecommunications companies, primarily on regulatory issues, before he joined Goldman Sachs as an equity research analyst in 1988. Initially he worked in San Francisco and he is now based in London.

Whereas he doesn't stress his role at the solicitation stage, during which offer structure, size, price and other recommendations are discussed and credentials presented, everyone within Goldman Sachs would confirm the importance of his participation in this process. Morris himself looks at his real role as being threefold:

* Preparing the company for meeting the public;
* Introducing the company to the underwriting group; and
* Introducing the company to the broader universe of investors, analysts, media, etc.

Preparing the company for meeting the public

This task implies very different things depending on the particular company concerned, the extent to which it has already been exposed to competition, whether or not it is an initial public offer, etc. Briefly summarised, however, what Morris does in preparing the company for going public is driven by what he understands the particular potential investor concerns to be. He advises either the company or the government (the latter is typically the firm's client in connection with telecom privatisations) or both parties together on regulatory and legal issues, company strategy, operating issues and capital structure. At this early stage of the appointment and if the firm has the latitude to bring about the necessary changes, Morris often works closely with the corporate finance and ECM departments of Goldman Sachs to bring the firm's full resources to bear. Morris's involvement in this respect is only possible if and when he is brought over the Chinese wall, the implication of which is that until the information he acquires is made public, he can not recommend the securities to investors.

The practical side of this, which helps to unfreeze the old company culture, is to sit down with the management and talk about how investors think, what their concerns are and how they make their investment decisions. This discussion works out what investors will perceive as the strengths and weaknesses of the company. As international investors always have plenty of alternative investment opportunities, the company has to compete for scarce capital just as it competes in the market for telecommunications services. Whereas the management may have had several years to adjust to this fact, the reality of having to sell the company to investors is completely new. The earlier Morris has these discussions with the management, the more time Goldman Sachs will have to ensure that the company is as attractive an investment opportunity as possible by the time it goes public. In order to reduce complexity, Morris analyses and ranks the company's attractiveness to investors relative to its peers with the help of nine simple criteria – the so-called key indicators of relative attractiveness (see Exhibit 21) and develops a total score.

These criteria and the total score should not be confused with whether or not a particular company is attractively valued but rather should provide an indication of how the particular company should be positioned relative

to its peers. The actual valuation and pricing of the issue is something that comes later in the process and depends on the success of this first phase of the preparation process – preparing the company for meeting the public.

In the case of Tele Danmark, the most important preparatory steps taken between appointment in October 1993 and pricing in April 1994 included the creation of a new regulatory framework and a new share capital structure, as well as the overall restructuring of the balance sheet.

Introducing the company to the underwriting group

Some six to eight weeks before the launch of a transaction, Morris arranges with the company for the equity research analysts of the most important syndicate members to visit the company for one to two full days of research due diligence. No investment bankers are present, and the analysts have unrestricted access to the management, together with the opportunity for a completely candid dialogue.

In the Telmex privatisation for example, Morris identified the country risk as a particular investor concern and accordingly he arranged for Professor Wayne A Cornelius of the University of California at San Diego, a former adviser on economic affairs to President Salinas of Mexico, to make a presentation. The evening before his presentation to the analysts, Cornelius had met with President Salinas and was therefore able to give the analysts direct assurance regarding the commitment of the Mexican Government to the privatisation of Telmex. This approach was very well received by all the analysts.

In the evening, a social programme is organised to allow the analysts to develop a rapport with and direct channels of communication to the management independently of Morris and Goldman Sachs. In the case of the Tele Danmark research due diligence, a dinner was organised in Louisiana,

---

Exhibit 21
Key indicators of relative attractiveness

	Company A	Company B	Company C	Company D
1. Motivation for privatisation				
2. Regulation				
3. Revenue growth				
4. Productivity opportunities				
5. State of technology				
6. Capital position				
7. Competitive environment				
8. Geographic location				
9. Growth				
Overall evaluation				

the famous Danish art museum, and during dinner the management circulated between tables in order to get to know all the analysts.

The programme typically ends with Morris conducting a summing-up session whereby he presents his projections for the company and discusses the risks and opportunities for the company as he sees them. He typically ends with a talk on the valuation of the company.

The research due diligence as a whole serves the following purposes:

1. It provides all the analysts of the senior members of the underwriting group with access to the management and high-quality information, thereby creating commitment and a certain consensus around the critical issues facing the company and its valuation;

2. Analysts are encouraged to ask questions. This gives the management valuable feedback, thereby reinforcing views that Goldman Sachs may have presented to the company. Instead of it always being Goldman Sachs suggesting and recommending, it becomes more of a market view; and

3. Because of the first-class treatment of all the analysts, considerable enthusiasm and commitment is created. Everyone is free to interpret the information as they please, hence ensuring the independence of each analyst's research view. Through the summing-up session, however, Morris provides leadership in terms of the valuation and positioning of the company.

The only possible drawback to this approach is that the company needs to be ready to present earlier than might otherwise have been required. It will, however, have major benefits in terms of the remainder of the preparatory work, as the writing of the sales points, the prospectus and the company's investor presentation will feed from the information generated from the research due diligence. In fact, in the case of Robert Morris, he and his team will assist in the writing of the bank's sales points memorandum and also assist the management in preparing the investor presentation. At the same time, Morris will start work on his own research report which should be published and distributed outside the US at least 30 days before filing.

Introducing the company to investors, analysts and media

Briefing sessions with Goldman Sachs' salesforce

After the filing and some two to three weeks before the beginning of the roadshow, Morris and his colleagues arrange for briefing sessions in London and New York where he briefs the entire salesforce. In the case of the 1991 Telmex offer, for example, he spent a whole day with Goldman Sachs' US salesforce in the New York office, and there was also a three to four hour briefing

session with the RoW salesforce in the London office. The same procedure was followed for Tele Danmark.

Pre-marketing – warm-ups

During the two weeks prior to the company roadshow, Morris travels around the world to see as many investors as possible in one-on-one meetings. He would typically spend one week in the US and one week in the rest of the world. During this period, investor conference calls are also organised for those investors with whom Morris and his colleagues could not meet. In these meetings and calls, Morris goes through the indicators of relative attractiveness, positions the company relative to its peers and discusses financials and valuation. At the same time, he gathers as much feedback as possible concerning investor perception of the company and its value. The proper recording of any particular concerns that investors may have is of great significance, allowing the management to respond to those concerns during the roadshow. This feedback represents valuable input to Goldman Sachs' ECM department in terms of the assessment of where demand is likely to come from, overall sizing, pricing and who the company management should see by way of one-on-one meetings during its roadshow.

In the case of Tele Danmark, Morris and his colleagues saw or talked to 95 institutions in the US and 137 institutions internationally in the pre-marketing phase.

Company roadshow

The company roadshow and the one-on-one meetings are absolutely crucial for the offer, as it is typically the management that sells the company. What Morris does during the warm-up is to create momentum and ensure that the management sees the right institutions and talks about the things that are most relevant and interesting to that particular institution rather than just going over the same script as in the formal presentations, which tend to be far too general to be of real interest to most investors.

During the company roadshow, Morris and his colleagues sweep in behind the management, this time by telephone, to receive feedback on how the meetings went, what any remaining concerns might be and what the price expectations are. Morris provides this information to the ECM department and the salesman responsible. In the case of the secondary sale by BT of AT&T shares in early 1995, Morris's close monitoring of how the management's message was received on the roadshow significantly aided the transaction. There were four separate AT&T management teams on the road but after the first day it was clear that the message was not getting across to investors. Accordingly, the Goldman Sachs team discussed with the AT&T management how the script could be changed to address the concerns of investors: the presentation was changed, following which the syndicate sold over US$2 billion of AT&T stock.

In the Tele Danmark privatisation, the feedback from

investors convinced him that it would be difficult to sell the issue if it were priced at the top end of the Dkr275–315 range, and he consequently pressed for, and achieved, a price of Dkr310.

The success formula

The most important reasons for Morris's success are his long experience with the telecommunications industry, his openness and communication skills, and the fact that he has a large and successful organisation behind him which allows him to be in the middle of these vast flows of telecommunication privatisations. All this notwithstanding, it is ultimately his integrity which is the most important factor. He is allowed to address the various components of attractiveness at an early stage, in such a way that the total package ultimately becomes attractive to investors. In the case of Tele Danmark, for example, Goldman Sachs substantially influenced the regulatory regime, simplified the capital structure and improved the company's corporate governance as seen from the perspective of the public shareholders.

Feature topic: *Tele Danmark's IR – an interview with the head of IR*

Tele Danmark's management recognised that it was a relatively small company from a small country and highly dependent on the foreign investment community. Accordingly, it decided that they had to be more professional in the area of investor relations. It hired Henning Rostung as senior vice president responsible for investor relations: prior to joining Tele Danmark, he had held various senior executive management positions and was the co-founder and chairman of the Danish Investor Relations Society. The author interviewed Rostung to learn about Tele Danmark's approach to investor relations.

JRL: What was your IR Strategy in connection with and immediately following the issue?
HR: To establish a broad contact basis very quickly. We wanted all the institutions in the issue to establish a Tele Danmark file and we did the same with the help of our IR Contact Management System. We also needed to establish trust with our shareholders by providing reliable information and to be accessible.

JRL: What is your information and disclosure policy?
HR: We disclose what we consider to be material to investors – that is, we disclose according to the principle that if an investor knows about it, he will appreciate knowing it, in the sense that it may impact his investment decision.

JRL: How do you release the information?
HR: With regard to the US market, we firstly inform the NYSE (who don't distribute the information further) and secondly we also send a copy to the so-called wire services. In Denmark, we send a facsimile to the Copenhagen Stock Exchange and follow up with a telephone call in order to confirm receipt, as only then is the information officially disclosed. The CSE then broadcasts this further via facsimile to the brokers and the media. We try to release the information while both the New York and Copenhagen markets are open for trading. This effectively limits us to between 2–3 pm Danish time and 8–9 am US Eastern Standard Time; however, this does not always succeed.

JRL: How is Tele Danmark's IR organised?
HR: I report directly to the CFO of Tele Danmark, Hans Munk Nielsen. Nobody other than me communicates with shareholders or analysts in the organisation. We made an exception for Goldman Sachs' analysts during the two months following the issue. Other exceptions obviously include roadshows, conference calls and a limited number of visits here in Denmark. The advantage of this is that the management can get on with the management of the company and everyone gets the same information. The disadvantages with this system are twofold: firstly that certain investors will not invest unless they meet the most senior management, and secondly the fact that this approach places a burden on me acquiring the relevant information within the company. The fact that I am a member of the senior management gives me a good idea of what is going on, which is obviously important. I also have a senior colleague in the IR department, an administrative person and a secretary. Press relations are handled separately.

JRL: What external advisers, if any, have you employed and for what purpose?
HR: We work with Taylor Rafferty, the US IR consultancy. They assist primarily in the dissemination of information through the wire services such as First Call, Bloomberg, etc. They also help us organise investor meetings. The single biggest service required, however, which is very difficult to get, is reliable information on the trading of our shares in the various financial centres.

JRL: Please describe how you have been able to handle dealings with institutional investors following the issue.
HR: We have, as I mentioned earlier, what we call an Investor Relations and Communication Contact Management System, in which we have details of some 1,800 people representing 1,300 organisations (be they brokers, fund managers or research analysts). In this system we record basic details, such as: full contact details,

a complete history of the communication with the particular organisation, broker estimates and recommendations, changes in holdings to the extent available, and much more.

JRL: Who do you consider to be the top five analysts of Tele Danmark world-wide?

HR: No fewer than 25 international and 17 Nordic houses write regular research on Tele Danmark, excluding those that only wrote in connection with the privatisation in 1994. It is difficult for us to be specific as to who the top analysts are as they all have different strengths and weaknesses which vary over time. It is our challenge to try to capitalise in the best possible way on the particular strengths of each institution.

JRL: Out of these analysts/houses, how many provide global research where a team of analysts based in different locations focuses on different aspects of investing in Tele Danmark and/or covers investors in different parts of the world?

HR: Although we are aware of certain companies being covered on a global basis, we don't feel that this has to date applied to Tele Danmark, probably because we are primarily a Danish company and secondarily a European one. Perhaps things would be different if we owned substantial assets in, for example, the US.

JRL: How do you allocate your time?

HR: As a rough estimate, I spend half of my time on internal matters and the other half on external matters. Of the time spent on external activities, very roughly I spend 75 per cent talking to sell-side analysts and 25 per cent talking to buy-side analysts and fund managers.

JRL: What is the ongoing programme for presentations?

HR: We go to the US six or seven times a year, spending one week at a time, and we go to the UK pretty much once a month. We also visit other European investment centres on a regular basis. In addition, we host a lot of meetings in Denmark. On average we see three to four fund managers or analysts here in Copenhagen every week.

JRL: What is the biggest challenge for you in running an IR department for a company such as Tele Danmark?

HR: Without a doubt, the biggest challenge is to keep fully updated on the company and industry-specific develop-

ments, and to pass on this information in an efficient and user-friendly way to a large, diverse group of people around the world.

JRL: What is in your view the most common mistake in the IR area generally?

HR: To believe that the principal and only role of the IR function is to increase the share price. It is our goal to provide investors with sufficient information to allow them to form their own opinion about what is going on. In the long term, we strongly believe that we are more credible, as this basic philosophy will drive the type of information we disclose and how we do it. Ultimately, we believe that if the company is well managed and the strategy is known and understood, the share price will reflect that. We often feel when we meet investors and analysts that we are expected to give a sales pitch, however we simply won't do it. Put differently, in our view, a higher share price should be the effect rather than the target of what a modern IR function should achieve.

JRL: How do you see the IR business developing in the future?

HR: I believe that, as concepts such as shareholder value and shareholder democracy become more important and as the investors become increasingly sophisticated, we will see more two-way communication via the IR department – that is to say that we as IR people will provide increasingly useful feedback to the managements of our companies as a result of our relationship with our owners and potential new shareholders. In other words, what is today primarily a function of one-way communication will in the future increasingly develop into two-way communication. We fundamentally believe that the owners are the masters and that their opinions should be taken into account by the management. We are already thinking in those terms at Tele Danmark. This, incidentally, is also true for the public relations function at Tele Danmark.

Telecom Corporation of New Zealand

The sale of 30.8 per cent of Telecom Corporation of New Zealand (TCNZ) which raised US$818 million for US owners Ameritech and Bell Atlantic was one of the largest global equity offers of 1991and the biggest ever IPO from NZ. Upon flotation, TCNZ represented approximately 20 per cent of the the total market capitalisation of the NZ stock exchange, a high figure by any standards. It became the first NZ company to be listed simultaneously on the domestic market and on a major foreign stock exchange, the NYSE, where it was also the first NZ listing. The transaction was one of the largest foreign company IPOs registered with the US SEC in 1991 and represented the first bookbuilt equity offer in an Australasian market. The final offer price for both institutional and retail investors was fixed after bookbuilding, the issue size was increased by 50 per cent and the greenshoe was exercised in full. However, the IPO was only one stage in the development of TCNZ and needs to be seen in the context of what came before and after.

One of the world's richest countries in the 1960s on the strength of its farming industry, NZ entered into a steady decline when the then EEC imposed phased tariffs on imports of NZ foodstuffs in 1971. Comprehensive social services (the so called 'cradle to grave' concept) could not be taken away overnight and the government's fiscal deficits therefore became an increasing burden on the economy. The country's indebtedness began to rise to unsustainable levels and in 1984 the Labour government with Roger Douglas as minister of finance embarked on a radical reform of the economy. Under a 1986 act, inefficient state-run activities were to become commercial entities managed as private companies. One of these was the Post and Telecommunications monopoly, generally recognised as one of the most inefficient providers of telecommunications services in the developed world. The telecom operations were demerged in April 1987 and incorporated as TCNZ, with total annual profits of only NZ$150,000. Progressive deregulation of the telecoms sector was set in motion, and a subsequent National Party (Conservative) government under Finance Minister Ruth Richardson continued the reforms, establishing a 'balance sheet' to account for the disposition of national resources as is done in private companies. It became increasingly clear that TCNZ was going to be privatised, despite opposition from the public.

In March 1989, Goldman Sachs/Rothschild and the small NZ merchant bank Jarden Morgan were hired by the NZ Treasury to evaluate TCNZ's readiness for privatisation, and the risk and rewards of the options available. This was known as the 'scoping study'. A central issue was to assess whether, in light of the monopoly attributes of some aspects of TCNZ,

---

Exhibit 1

Transaction summary

Issuer name: Telecom Corporation of New Zealand (of New Zealand)	*Joint global coordinators:* Goldman Sachs and Merrill Lynch
Pricing date: 16 July 1991 (NY and London time) 17 July (NZ time) (MSCI NZ:61.43)	*Pricing/underwriting structure:* Global institutional bookbuilding, retail offer marketed based on maximum offer price
Vendors: Ameritech & Bell Atlantic	*Primary or secondary:* Secondary
% of company sold: 30.8%	*Privatisation or corporate:* Corporate
	Retail structure: –
IPO or non-IPO: IPO	*Industry:* Telecommunications
Type of shares: Ordinary shares and ADRs (20 shares/ADR)	*Pricing range:* NZ$1.80–2.00/share Offer price: NZ$2.00/share and US$22.58/ADR
Total issue size: US$818 million	*US listing/144A:* NYSE listing

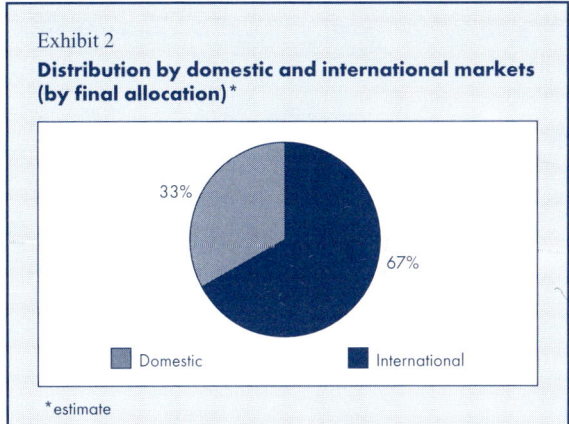

Exhibit 2

Distribution by domestic and international markets (by final allocation)*

- Domestic (33%)
- International (67%)

*estimate

a regulatory regime could be established which balanced the government's interest in promoting national welfare through a competitive telecommunications market with its desire to remove commercial risk from its balance sheet. After two months, the advisers recommended two options: the sale of 100 per cent to a strategic buyer or the sale of 100 per cent through an IPO. Then, in June 1989, CSFB and Buttle Wilson (owned by SG Warburg) were hired to advise on the formal privatisation, and in early 1990, the government announced that it would go ahead.

The NZ Treasury adopted a dual-track strategy whereby a strategic sale of 99.9 per cent of TCNZ and a strategic sale of 49.9 per cent combined with a soon-to-follow SEC-registered IPO of 49 per cent (with CSFB as the global coordinator) were pursued simultaneously. The government was uncomfortable taking market risk, and was therefore attracted to the first option, which had the potential to achieve a higher price than would be possible through a smaller strategic sale plus an IPO, as NZ stock market conditions were poor. The local market had come down by some 25 per cent since the third quarter of 1989, the country was in recession, and real interest rates were persistently high at around 7 per cent. Prospects for a large equity offer were not good. This fact was the principal reason behind the rejection of the Goldman Sachs/Rothschild/Jarden Morgan suggestion of an IPO of the entire amount in several tranches. The government thus decided on a strategic sale by auction though the plans for a 49 per cent IPO remained in force until the auction was completed. BZW was engaged to advise TCNZ.

The sale of 99.9 per cent of TCNZ to Ameritech and Bell Atlantic (the US Baby Bells, advised by Salomon Brothers) for approximately NZ$4.25 billion (US$2.46 billion), representing NZ$1.81 per share, was announced on 14 June 1990. The proceeds were NZ$500–750 million higher than most analysts' expectations. The government was delighted with the outcome and considered that it had made the right decision, particularly when on 1 August, the day that had been scheduled for pricing the now-abandoned IPO, Iraq invaded Kuwait, sparking the Gulf War and effectively closing the international equity new-issue market until May 1991. While price was a major factor, the decision to sell to the Baby Bells was thought to have been influenced by the simplicity of their bid and the participation (token at first, firmer later) of two NZ partners, Fay Richwhite Holdings Ltd and Freightways

Holdings Ltd. Fay Richwhite subsequently earned one of the biggest investment banking fees in NZ history off the back of the IPO.

CSFB and Buttle Wilson also did well, earning enormous investment banking fees, as the NZ Treasury had elected to incentivise its advisers to the maximum possible extent by not capping the success fee. Judging from the much higher than expected proceeds, the strategy appears to have worked: CSFB used its fee to acquire Jarden Morgan, the bank that had been involved with the scoping study. Ameritech and Bell Atlantic also had achieved a purchase of note: theirs was the first major foreign acquisition by any US Baby Bell and the forerunner of many such transactions worldwide. For the two regional companies to buy a foreign company that provided international telephone services to and from the US had required an exemption from anti-trust provisions put in place by US Judge Greene in connection with the break-up of AT&T in 1984.

'We decided to go ahead with this acquisition because we were comfortable with the technology of TCNZ following a considerable investment programme and we were also comfortable with the management of the company although we were of the opinion that they had not fully taken advantage of opportunities to improve labour productivity,' says William Albertini, Bell Atlantic's CFO. 'We also became comfortable with the regulatory framework. We knew our US partners Ameritech well, and in Fay Richwhite and Freightways we were able to link up with influential and highly regarded local partners.'

Many analysts were less convinced about the merits of the purchase, and on 15 June 1990 the Lex column of the London *Financial Times* wrote: 'Buying TCNZ, the communications company, will leave Bell Atlantic and Ameritech well placed to sell mobile telephones to penguins if the Antarctic market takes off. Other than that, it is hard to see why these two US local telephone companies wish to pay 16 times earnings for what looks like a heavily over-staffed network in a country with a population rather smaller than that of greater Chicago. Given the unpopularity in NZ of this privatisation, the new owners must tread carefully anyway in reshaping the business. Then there is the issue of finding buyers at this sort of price for the 40.1 per cent of the shares which the Ameritech/ Bell Atlantic consortium intends to sell on to the public. While the NZ Government deserves congratulations, the episode adds weight to arguments that Judge Greene, who oversaw the break-up of AT& T, should lose none of his powers over the Baby Bells, including Ameritech and Bell Atlantic. Why should US customers finance such foreign forays.' What the Lex column failed to recognise was in fact that TCNZ was an attractive asset because it was over staffed and that there were going to be opportunities to cut excessive fat above and beyond what was discounted in the price paid.

Ameritech's executive vice president for corporate strategy, Louis J Rutigliano says the purchase meant 'a chance for us to understand what it means to prepare this company for increasing competition'. Learning to operate in the much less structured environment of NZ could help Ameritech and Bell Atlantic prepare for the day when most of the US market will have looser, incentive-based regulation instead of the traditional rate-of-return limits to profitability.

The transaction with Ameritech and Bell Atlantic closed on 12 September 1990. NZ's Treasury kept a golden share (the Kiwi share) and a provision in the sale and purchase agreement meant that within three years (extendible by one year under certain circumstances) the Baby Bells had to reduce their combined ownership in TCNZ to not more than 49.9 per cent and make a public offer of at least NZ$500 million to the NZ public. On the same day, Ameritech and Bell Atlantic sold 0.5 per cent of their newly acquired stake to their local partners, Fay Richwhite and Freightways, and in November they agreed that this would be raised to 10 per cent at a later date. This duly occurred in September 1993 at the completion of the sell-down when the two NZ companies bought 9.5 per cent of TCNZ for NZ$1.81 per share plus financing cost. They were immediately able to sell on 6.6 per cent in the market for NZ$3.82 per share through BZW and Doyle Paterson Brown. The capital gain realised by Fay Richwhite represented a highly significant proportion of the bank's total capital base. Some analysts even claim that it is uncertain whether or not Fay Richwhite would have survived without the fees earned on the TCNZ transactions.

In October 1990, the Baby Bells appointed Goldman Sachs, Merrill Lynch and Fay Richwhite as bookrunning lead managers. Initially it was thought that the IPO could come in early 1991 but while the Gulf War continued this was impossible. As TCNZ had a March end of year it seemed logical to wait for the annual accounts but market uncertainties meant the timetable remained unfixed and Ameritech and Bell Atlantic retained the flexibility to call off the float at any time. They were naturally sceptical of being able to recover their purchase price given the poor market conditions which persisted until May 1991. Size and price indications early in the year were much different from what eventually transpired. Understandably, the vendors were keen not to be seen to be too anxiously putting the offer in the market and not getting a good price, yet waiting to do the sale(s) toward the end of the stipulated sell-down period would be an unwise move. Furthermore, Bell Atlantic was under financial pressure to sell (it had been put on credit watch for a possible downgrade as a direct consequence of the acquisition). Bell Atlantic would have preferred to buy only 49 per cent up front with its partner but had elected to bid for the whole company as the two were concerned about losing out in the auction to bidders prepared to take all of TCNZ. In addition, neither Ameritech nor Bell Atlantic was doing particularly well operationally so there was a clear attraction in getting on with the float.

The IPO of July 1991, which is the principal focus of this case study, was part of the government's stipulated sell-down. Throughout the run-up to the IPO, the government kept a low profile, content merely to watch that the terms of the 1990 sale and purchase agreement were met. Through the structure of that sale, the New Zealand government had cleverly passed on to Ameritech and Bell Atlantic the market risk on the portion of TCNZ to be sold to domestic and international investors.

Major challenges

The first challenge lay in positioning TCNZ as a global stock priced against comparable telephone companies such as Hong Kong Telecom, BT and Telefónica rather than against a depressed Australia/NZ market. 'This was the only way that we were going to recover our purchase price,' says Bell Atlantic executive director and corporate communications head Peter Crawford. This challenge was not made any easier by US and international investors believing that Bell Atlantic and Ameritech had substantially overpaid for TCNZ.

NZ was in deep recession, real interest rates were at a record high, the country had lost exports because of the crumbling Soviet Union and war in the Persian Gulf had created uncertainty in the world economy. World equity markets started to recover only in May 1991 but the NZ market was still relatively depressed, some 40 per cent off its peak in the third quarter of 1989. On the other hand, international institutions had increased their total holding in the NZ market from 10 per cent at the end of 1989 to approximately 20 per cent by mid-1991, though this amounted to a total foreign equity portfolio investment of only about US$2.3 billion. There were indications that interest rates were about to fall and the Barclays stock market index had increased by almost 30 per cent since the end of 1990.

The domestic new-issue calendar was heavy, particularly considering that the market was only just beginning to recover from its virtual shut-down during the Gulf War. NZ corporations had embarked on what some analysts termed a giant debt-equity swap, tapping the market for some NZ$2 billion of equity capital in the first six months of 1991. Partly as a result of this flurry of activity and in expectation of the TCNZ offer, NZ resources group Fletcher Challenge postponed an offer of shares in its natural gas subsidiary.

The changing market conditions meant that for months both the number and price of the shares to be sold were highly uncertain – the transaction was cancelled several times as the vendors could not be seen to be selling TCNZ shares at a book loss. While 49 per cent of TCNZ had been scheduled for sale in the planned but abandoned 1990 IPO, the 1991 offer envisaged a relatively modest sale of 18 per cent and the eventual size was 31 per cent.

Increasing competition meant that TCNZ could expect to lose market share. Since 1988, the NZ telecommunications market had been progressively deregulated and a second major operator, in the form of an international consortium, was already in place. Added to this, NZ was considered a small market for telecommunications and it was not an equity market with which many international investors were familiar.

Having paid a high price, including a control premium of some 25 per cent, to buy TCNZ in September 1990, Ameritech and Bell Atlantic were now – only nine months later – trying to recover that price through an IPO.

The chosen structure meant that bookbuilding was to be introduced for the first time in NZ and the fixed-price domestic offer for retail was combined with bookbuilding for institutions. The NZ institutions did not like the fact that though only 30.8 per cent of TCNZ was offered, domestic lead manager Fay Richwhite pushed to include 100 per cent of the capital in the Barclays Index (predecessor to the NZSE 40 Index). The NZ institutional market was expected to be a weak link in the deal, but the domestic retail market also proved weaker than expected.

Political manoeuverings also created uncertainty. In February 1990, while the government was preparing to sell at least 49.9 per cent of TCNZ to a foreign-dominated consortium, the right-wing opposition National Party threatened that if it came to power it would force divestment to bring foreign holdings to below 24 per cent. It did come to power later in 1990 but did not carry out its threat.

The majority of New Zealanders had been against privatisation in general and that of TCNZ in particular. Richard Shallcrass, director of commercial relations at the NZ Treasury said: 'While the debate was nothing if not lively, it was real, as on the one hand everyone had a phone, and therefore cared, and on the other, service under TCNZ was streets ahead of the old Post Office, and some people would be able to share in the excitement by buying shares. In practice, the terms of the Kiwi Share represented the public gesture needed for the sale to proceed.'

For TCNZ it was hard work in a short time to achieve a dual float with listings in NZ and on the NYSE. Complying with SEC regulations and doing US GAAP reconciliation was a major exercise despite TCNZ being relatively well prepared. Getting all the parties involved to work together successfully presented a huge challenge: they included TCNZ, two vendors, two joint global coordinators, domestic bankers, the company's financial adviser and multiple sets of lawyers operating in three time zones. Most of the bankers and lawyers had never before worked on anything similar.

Rationale and objectives

On 12 September 1990, a consortium led by Ameritech and Bell Atlantic purchased in a competitive trade sale 99.9 per cent of TCNZ's outstanding ordinary shares from the NZ government which needed to reduce its debt. The deal obligated the new owners to reduce their aggregate ownership in TCNZ to not more than 49.9 per cent of the then outstanding shares by 12 September 1993.

Through the subsequent IPO, Ameritech and Bell Atlantic sought to:

- recover their full original purchase price of NZ$1.90/share (including the cost of carry);
- lay off as quickly as possible the underwriting risk of the 50.1 per cent of TCNZ that Ameritech and Bell Atlantic were not going to own long term;
- secure a successful offer, which was important both for the vendors and the NZ government; and
- achieve a high degree of liquidity to prepare for subsequent offers.

The management of TCNZ did not have an opposing interest in the IPO although because of the nationalities and personalities involved, the process ended up being somewhat confrontational. TCNZ had been eager to get out of government

control and now with the introduction of public minorities through the IPO, it would be more independent of the Baby Bells. The management was also keen to participate in the TCNZ share option scheme offered to senior management of the Baby Bells.

TCNZ was not to receive any of the proceeds from the IPO.

Share capital and ownership

See Exhibit 3.

Transaction components

This offer of initially 420 million secondary shares comprised a domestic tranche, an international tranche and a US tranche, each representing 33 per cent each of the total offer. It was marketed to institutional investors globally on an open-priced basis allowing a book to be built, after which the offer price was fixed. The domestic tranche included a separate retail offer in which retail investors subscribed and paid at the upper end of the NZ$1.80–2.00 price range and would have received a rebate (or more shares) had the offer been priced below the top of the range. There was a 63 million-share greenshoe, representing 15% of the total size of the offer, and a clawback provision (see Exhibit 4).

According to John Jensen, managing director of equity capital markets at Merrill Lynch: 'Both Goldman Sachs and Merrill Lynch wanted to run the books on both the US and international tranches and I flipped a coin with Brian Hehir of Goldman Sachs in the offices of Fay Richwhite in Wellington as to who was going to lead which tranche.' Thus it was decided that Goldman Sachs would handle the international tranche and Merrill Lynch the US tranche. Brian Hehir, now co-head of global equity capital markets at Merrill Lynch, recalls: 'John and I also flipped coins about who was going to be in Wellington and who in New York at pricing. Since trades were still recorded on a blackboard in Wellington, we felt that in case stabilisation was necessary, a senior representative of the global coordinators ought to be present locally. In the event, John lost the bet but because the deal was in such good shape, stabilisation was not necessary and accordingly we could both be at Merrill's offices in New York at the time of the pricing.'

Development of offer size

The original 420 million share offer was increased by 50 per cent on the day of pricing and the full expanded greenshoe was subsequently exercised (see Exhibit 5).

Principal advisers

See Exhibit 7.

Transaction fee distribution

See Exhibit 8.

Management fee

Merrill Lynch and Goldman Sachs shared 25 per cent of the total management fee as the global coordinators' praecipium

Exhibit 3
Share capital and ownership

Type of shares offered	Ordinary shares of NZ$1.00 and ADRs, representing 20 shares
Share capital before/after offer	2.35 billion ordinary shares at the time of offer. One 'Kiwi share' (one convertible preference share owned by the NZ government) which can be owned only by the minister of finance on behalf of the NZ government, carrying certain rights. His rights included the rights to: • consent to certain changes in the articles of association; • consent to certain changes in ownership (see below); • require TCNZ to maintain certain services for residential customers at standard charges throughout the country; and • require TCNZ not to increase the standard residential rental charge by more than the increase in the NZ CPI. At an EGM on 19 November 1993, TCNZ shareholders passed a special resolution to cancel one ordinary share of NZ$1.00 each for every five in issue, and to pay shareholders the par value of NZ$1 per cancelled share, ie, holders of 1,000 shares were given 800 shares and NZ$200 in cash. The transaction was effective on 5 March 1994. As a result 472.4 million shares were cancelled and NZ$472.4 million repaid to shareholders. This was the reverse of a deeply discounted rights issue. Historic earnings per share and share prices were increased by dividing by a factor of 0.838207. At the time the unadjusted price was NZ$4.30 and the adjusted price became NZ$5.13. In this case study, the original unadjusted figures have been used throughout.
Ownership restrictions	• No single foreign buyer is allowed to own more than 49.9% without the prior approval of the holder of the Kiwi share; and • No person may own 10% or more without the prior written approval of the board and the holder of the Kiwi share.
Listings	The ADRs were listed on the NYSE and quoted on Seaq International and the ordinary shares were listed on the NZ Stock Exchanges. Application was also made to the Australian Stock Exchange though this did not happen due to insufficient liquidity in that market.
Market capitalisation at offer price (NZ$1.7715/US$)	US$2.65 billion: TCNZ became the second largest NZ company by market capitalisation after Fletcher Challenge, which it subsequently surpassed.
Major shareholder(s) before/after offer	Ameritech and Bell Atlantic owned 99% before the offer and 68.2% after. At the completion of the required sell-down on 29 September 1993, they owned 49.9%.
Most relevant stock exchange index/ weighting/% of share capital included	NZSE 40 Index/20%/100%.

Exhibit 4
Offer structure

Target markets	Indicated tranche sizes*	Bookrunning lead managers	Co-lead managers
New Zealand	33%	Fay Richwhite	Ord Minnett
International	33%	Goldman Sachs	Merrill Lynch, Salomon Brothers
US and Canada	33%	Merrill Lynch	Goldman Sachs, Salomon Brothers
Total combined offers (shares)	**420,000,000**		

*% of indicated total offer on 10 June 1991

Exhibit 5
Development of the offer size

Indicated number of shares to be sold	420 million + 63 million greenshoe
Offer size after increase (16 July)	630 million + 94.5 million greenshoe
Amount of greenshoe exercised	94.5 million
Final number of shares sold	724.5 million

calculated on the gross proceeds of the total offer. Outside the US, the lead and co-lead managers shared a further 25 per cent of the total management fee as the lead and co-lead managers' praecipium (see Exhibit 9).

Exhibit 6
The timetable

October 1990	• Joint global coordinators hired.
15 April 1991	• Confidential filing with the US SEC.
10 June	• Public SEC filing.
11 June	• Publication of preliminary domestic and international offer documents including offer price range; • Roadshow and bookbuilding begin; and • Domestic retail subscription period begins.
Friday 12 July	• Domestic retail subscription period ends; and • Roadshow ends in Toronto, Canada; • Close of bookbuilding.
16 July (NY time)	• Announcement of offer price and 50% increase in offer size; and • Signing of all underwriting agreements.
17 July (NY time)	• Trading of ADRs commences on NYSE and Seaq Int. simultaneously at 9.30am NY time and 2.30 pm London time. Trading of ordinary shares starts simultaneously in NZ, ie, at 1.30 am on 18 July.
24 July	• Greenshoe exercised.

Exhibit 7
Principal advisers

1991 IPO	
Financial adviser to Ameritech and Bell Atlantic	Salomon Brothers Inc.
Financial adviser to TCNZ	BZW*
International legal adviser to the company and vendors	Kirkland & Ellis
International legal adviser to the underwriters	Skadden Arps, Slate, Meagher & Flom
1990 strategic sale (dual-track; strategic sale/IPO)	
International financial adviser to the Baby Bells	Salomon Brothers Inc.
International legal adviser to the Baby Bells	Kirkland & Ellis
International legal adviser to the company	Davis, Polk & Wardwell
NZ advisers to Ameritech and Bell Atlantic	Fay Richwhite and Freightways Holdings. These companies also became local partners to the US companies in the purchase of TCNZ.
Financial adviser to the New Zealand Treasury	CSFB and Buttle Wilson (Warburg)
Financial adviser to TCNZ	BZW*

* BZW had been hired in 1988 to assist the TCNZ management in preparing for privatisation and negotiating with the government. BZW had been thoroughly involved in the strategic sale in 1990 and in the preparation for the proposed 1990 IPO but played a more low-key role in the 1991 IPO.

Exhibit 8
Distribution of gross spread (%)

Management	Underwriting	Selling concession	Gross spread
0.71	0.66	2.13	3.49

Exhibit 9
Distribution of management fee outside the US (%)

Total management fee	0.7086
Of which: Global coordinators' praecipium	25
Of which: Lead/co-lead managers' praecipium split among all leads/co-leads	25
Of which: Management fees split among all managers	50

In the US, the management fees were allocated on the basis of underwriting commitments for the managers only with the exception of the deduction of the global coordinators' praecipium. Syndicate members in the US do not participate in the management fee.

Selling concession

Orders in the US fell into two categories: institutional pot and free retention (also known as retail demand). Institutional orders are subject to an economic arrangement whereby there

Exhibit 10
Distribution of selling concession in the US (%)

Total selling concession	2.1258
Of which: Pre-agreed or fixed portion regardless of sales generated	30
Of which: Paid pro rata according to sales designated by investors	70

is a pre-split or a fixed and guaranteed component of 30 per cent, calculated on the basis of the underwriting commitments of all the managers and underwriters, and a competitive portion (or jump-ball) subject to performance. Orders outside the pot are not subject to the pre-split on economics and are 100 per cent competitive (see Exhibit 10).

In Europe the selling concession was paid in full to whomever the order was given to (ie, 100 per cent jump-ball).

Deal structure

Size

The initial float of 17.9 per cent (excluding a 15 per cent greenshoe) of TCNZ as announced on 10 June 1991 was smaller than contemplated earlier in the year, and significantly less than the 49 per cent officially planned for the proposed 1990 IPO under the dual-track strategy. At the lower end of the pricing range, this represented approximately US$427 million-worth of shares. As 10 per cent were to be sold to the NZ partners, this meant that a further 21.3 per cent had to be sold within the next two years. It was therefore good news when all three tranches were over-subscribed, heavily so in the US and internationally. In the end, 30.8 per cent of TCNZ was sold, including the 15 per cent greenshoe (calculated on the increased size) which was exercised in full, bringing the amount to US$818 million. This demonstrates the difficulty of estimating demand, particularly when a sale involves shares in a company coming to market for the first time and from a country unfamiliar to most investors.

Sell-down provisions and further sales

At the time of the IPO, a second global prospectus offer was on the cards (as part of the sell-down programme) with Merrill Lynch and Goldman Sachs again mandated. This had been pencilled in for August 1992, was then set back until July 1993 and then abandoned, as Bell Atlantic had broken ranks with Ameritech and decided to conduct a bought deal through BZW. Bell Atlantic saw this structure as having many advantages over a prospectus offer, particularly at a time when there were major management changes at TCNZ. The bought deal took place on 11 March 1993, not long before the second global bookbuilt offer was to have been filed with the SEC. Though Ameritech's management had initially participated in negotiations with Bell Atlantic to sell 2–3 per cent, it decided against this, believing that there was significant upside potential in the share price. This proved to be a good decision for Ameritech – four months later it sold a 4.6% stake at a substantially higher price to the Capital Group of Los Angeles. Ameritech paid Goldman Sachs and Merrill Lynch a fee for their efforts in preparing the second global prospectus offer. These sell-downs are set out in Exhibit 11.

Pricing and underwriting

One of the challenges of this IPO was combining the domestic fixed-price retail offer with international bookbuilding practice. The price and size of NZ offers had usually been set before the marketing period, but in this case investors were required to register for the deal, and told that the price would be between NZ$1.80 and NZ$2.00. The investors were required to pay NZ$2.00 for each share and were to be given a refund or receive more shares if the offer price was lower. While this approach was a satisfactory way of harmonising local and international offer methods, it made it impossible to increase the price range upwards though it did offer flexibility downwards. The domestic tranche was underwritten by Fay Richwhite and immediately sub-underwritten by NZ and Australian institutions.

This structure represented an innovation in that Ameritech and Bell Atlantic achieved a higher price on the retail offer than would have been the case with a traditional fixed-price

Exhibit 11
The Ameritech and Bell Atlantic sell-down programme

Vendor(s)	Date	Stake sold	Bell Atlantic and Ameritech aggregate holding	Price*	Comment
Ameritech/Bell Atlantic	12 Sept 1990	0.5%	99.5%	NZ$1.81	Sale to Fay Richwhite and Freightway Holdings
Ameritech/Bell Atlantic	16 July 1991	30.8%	68.7%	NZ$2.00	Global IPO through GS and ML
Bell Atlantic	11 Mar 1993	4.6%	64.1%	NZ$2.60	Bought deal placement via BZW
Ameritech	3 July 1993	4.6%	59.4%	NZ$2.90–3.00	Sale to Capital Group
Ameritech/Bell Atlantic	29 Sept 1993	9.5%	49.9%	NZ$1.81 + cost of carry	Sale to Fay Richwhite and Freightway Holdings as agreed at time of IPO.**

* Actual unadjusted prices. Divide by 0.8382 to convert to prices comparable with actual prices after the 5 March 1994 1: 5 stock repurchase.
** Of which approx. 6.6% was onsold on 20 September to institutional investors at NZ$3.82 through BZW and Doyle Paterson Brown, raising US$323 million for Fay Richwhite and Freightways.

offer, though it is evident that a more modern structure would have yielded still higher proceeds. Had it been possible to market the retail offer at a fixed discount to the institutional price, a more ambitious price range might have been attempted. In the event, this structure was not so different from a traditional fixed-price offer because an offer price below NZ$2.00 might have undermined confidence in the offer. As the range had to be fixed five weeks before pricing, all parties had to be confident about achieving an offer price of NZ$2.00. The purpose of the price range was to attract sceptical investors.

As Ameritech and Bell Atlantic had paid NZ$1.81 per share for TCNZ in September 1990, their break-even price, including financing cost, was approximately NZ$1.90. The offer price range thus implied that they would be prepared to sell at a loss. The combination of the modest initial offer size and what might have seemed a low offer price range indicates that this offer was not considered straightforward during its preparation.

Regulation and competition

The NZ telecommunications market is governed by the Commerce Act of 1986, the Telecommunications Act of 1987 and the Radiocommunications Act of 1989. There is no detailed regulation and no dedicated regulatory body. The Commerce Ministry is responsible for telecommunications policy and reports to the government on the emergence of competition. The issue of competition between TCNZ and new operators was therefore only dealt with in normal anti-competitive legislation. There was no maximum rate of return stipulated for TCNZ.

The government's regulatory role is defined by provisions in the Kiwi share (convertible preference stock) which form a part of TCNZ's articles of association, meaning the government would be a party to any proposed change to those articles. This is a very different approach to that in the UK, where in addition to five-yearly reviews, telecommunications regulator Oftel is involved in the fine print of BT's licence on a continuous basis. This has created uncertainty for BT shares and substantially complicated the second sale of BT shares in December 1991. The NZ government's light-handed approach to regulation seemingly was one of the factors that attracted the two Baby Bells to invest in TCNZ..

The flipside to NZ's lighter regulation nevertheless has meant that TCNZ is open to unlimited competition. Final statutory barriers to market entry were removed on 1 April 1989. These covered basic network services, the resale of capacity on leased lines and the supply of PABX systems. The government had begun, 18 months earlier, to allow companies other than TCNZ to enter the domestic telecommunications market, the initial relaxations affecting various items of CPE (customer premises equipment) and residential and business wiring. A potent competitor soon emerged in Clear Communications Limited, a consortium led by US long-distance operator MCI and including Bell Canada International Ltd, Todd Corp., and Television NZ Ltd. Clear could cherry-pick the areas where it wanted to compete because, unlike TCNZ, it was not under any obligation to offer services in sparsely populated areas. Within a limited period, Clear had taken substantial market share in the high-margin trunk-call segment of the market and had forced down prices.

Despite the government's largely hands-off approach, it has retained the ability to regulate certain policies on residential telephone services. For example, TCNZ must maintain a local free-calling option for all residential customers, it cannot increase the standard residential rental charge by more than the increase in NZ CPI and neither can it charge residential users in rural areas more for line rental than the standard residential charge. It also has to continue to make ordinary residential telephone services as widely available as was the case in September 1990 when TCNZ was bought by Ameritech and Bell Atlantic.

'The price provisions included in the Kiwi share represented a pledge by the company which it is legally entitled to dishonour should it so wish,' explained Shallcrass. There are no provisions for government recourse within the terms of the Kiwi share should TCNZ choose to dishonour the provisions. 'The fact that Telecom has decided to honour the obligations has more do with good public relations than a specific legal or regulatory framework,' continued Shallcrass. However, if TCNZ decided not to honour its pledge, then the government could initiate proceedings under the Fair Trading Act.

The Kiwi share did not stipulate the interconnection arrangements by which TCNZ was required to provide competitors access to the local network and this created a long dispute between the number two operator, Clear, and TCNZ which was finally settled in 1995. The settlement stipulates that in return for connection to the TCNZ network, Clear has to pay both the operating cost and TCNZ's opportunity cost of not being able to use the capacity taken up by Clear.

Marketing strategy

There were two TCNZ teams for the roadshow which spanned 22 working days and 24 cities worldwide. The CEO and CFO of TCNZ started in NZ on 11 June then went to Australia, Asia, California, US Mid-West, Scotland, London, continental Europe, New York, Boston, Baltimore and finished in Toronto on 12 July, the last day of bookbuilding.

As this was the first global offer from NZ, the country story had to be told in order to provide a background to the company story. It was also important to emphasise the absence of telecommunications regulation in NZ, and the fact that there was a lot of competition in the sector.

Retail marketing

The vendors concentrated promotional efforts on a heavy television advertising schedule, increasing awareness from 35 per cent in April 1991 to 92 per cent in July 1991. The marketing included mail shots to all NZ households. TCNZ hired a train to take management across the nation for the domestic roadshow. Overall, the retail campaign was thought to have been over the top and probably too American. The domestic campaign was primarily orchestrated by Fay Richwhite as the domestic lead manager but Merrill Lynch was also involved in the advertising campaign. Dewe Rogerson was hired to work with the underwriters.

As this was a corporate sale (as opposed to a privatisation), there were no retail incentives to stimulate demand. The only requirements from a political point of view were that Ameritech and Bell Atlantic had to reduce their joint ownership in the company to 49.9 per cent over a period of three years and that they had to offer at least NZ$500 million of shares to domestic investors in the sell-down process. Contrary to what Fay Richwhite had initially assumed, the NZSE insisted on a special mini -prospectus for the retail market. This was an additional burden on the underwriters and the management as it was another important document that had to be produced before marketing began. It had to fulfil the same disclosure standards as the US prospectus in addition to meeting all the local requirements.

The TCNZ story

TCNZ was one of the most modern and technologically advanced telecommunications companies in the world, having effectively skipped one generation of development as a result of pragmatic government policies, considerable investment, timely incorporation and the hiring of internationally experienced management. The absence of a heavy-handed regulatory approach, expected high growth in earnings and a comparatively high dividend yield made this investment attractive, despite the expectation of increasing competition. The offer was marketed to institutions with the help of the sales points outlined in Exhibit 12.

Reasons for not buying

In addition to the generally poor economic climate and weak market conditions, three reasons in particular were given by those investors who declined to participate:

- As regulatory barriers came down TCNZ faced increased competition. Clear Communications had begun to offer private network services, national call services and outgoing international call services in May 1991. Bellsouth had announced intentions to begin offer cellular services in 1992 and had opened negotiations to interconnect with TCNZ's network;
- Through its ownership of the Kiwi share, the government was effectively able to regulate certain TCNZ policies on residential telephone services. This represented a pledge by the company on advice from the politicians and was undertaken to facilitate the privatisation; and
- Ameritech and Bell Atlantic were obligated to reduce their aggregate ownership in TCNZ to not more than 49.9 per cent of the then outstanding shares by 12 September 1994 at the latest.

Results of the offer

Distribution

All three tranches were over-subscribed even after the increased deal size, and the book had started building strongly from the start.

The domestic placement was less over-subscribed than were the US and international tranches: total domestic demand was 375 million shares compared to the 140 million initially offered, indicating that before increase the domestic offer was 2.7 times subscribed. Approximately half of this demand came from retail investors and half from institutions who were relatively aggressive on price despite disliking the bookbuilding process. About 35,000 NZ retail investors (fewer than the 50,000 envisaged) applied for NZ$300 million-worth of shares, making it by far the most popular flotation in the country's history.

Foreign demand was undoubtedly stronger than expected, although the US market was less aggressive on price, in part because of the unfavourable press that had accompanied the price paid by Bell Atlantic and Ameritech to buy TCNZ in 1990. Of the total US tranche, 75 per cent was sold to institutions and 25 per cent to retail investors. As far as the international tranche was concerned, there was a lot of interest not only in the UK but also in continental Europe, particularly in Switzerland and Belgium. TCNZ was anxious to allocate more stock to European institutions because it had actively marketed its debt there, and it took the view that investor interest from these countries was of a high quality. It was not wholly successful in this, as the vendors and the bankers wanted more stock placed in the US. Although the vendors have the right to chose whom they sell to, the company has to live with its shareholders, and with those who complain about unfair allocation: a fair compromise is therefore a good idea.

The transaction was allocated in more or less the same way as it had been underwritten, a third of the transaction going to each tranche. Underwriters involved in the sale say demand came from a wide range of institutions, including Pacific-targeted funds and investors bullish on the global telecommunications industry, although there were few dedicated international telecom funds in existence at the time.

After-market share price performance
See Exhibit 13.

The shares opened strongly at NZ$2.27, trading up to NZ$2.38 before closing the first day at NZ$2.35. The issue opened at US$25.60 per ADR in New York. Within the first hour 100 million shares equivalent had changed hands.

Following a substantial increase during the first three to six months on the euphoria of a highly successful issue, the shares began to under-perform after six to nine months on the realisation that TCNZ was exposed to more competition than first assumed. A year after issue the market price was lower than the close on the first trading day. However, based on the offer price, it had still outperformed the local market by 18 per cent over the first year. TCNZ's strong track record led it to outperform the market at a later date.

After-market trading volume

There was heavy turnover in the immediate secondary market, with more than half the issue changing hands during the first three days of trading (see Exhibit 14).

Exhibit 12
Principal sales points

Market position	• More than 93% of all households and virtually all businesses in NZ were customers of TCNZ, though competition had developed for some of its services such as national calls.
Advanced network	• TCNZ had invested more than NZ$2.5 billion in capital assets during the previous four years. Approximately 50% of its network equipment was less than three years old and some 87% of its total number of lines were connected to digital exchanges.
New products	• TCNZ was a full-range communications provider with balanced revenues. Local phone services accounted for only 35% of fiscal 1991 revenues; • National toll services (calls that originate and terminate in different local calling areas in NZ) and international services, higher growth businesses, provided 42% of the total; and • About 23% of total revenue was derived from rapidly growing businesses such as cellular and directories. TCNZ began a cellular network in 1987 when it was the only such operator in NZ although future competition was expected as NZ had one of the fastest growing cellular connection rates in the world.
Favourable regulation	• TCNZ has no profit regulation. Since it became a separate government-owned utility in 1987, the NZ telecom industry had been substantially deregulated. TCNZ operated in a comparatively unregulated environment and was not required to appear before any regulatory authority to effect a change in prices. However, the company had made a pledge, as reflected in the Kiwi share, to maintain services to residential customers and to not increase certain prices in that market segment.
Continued productivity gains	• Although TCNZ had realised significant cost savings through redundancies there remained ample scope for generating additional cost savings. There were at the time 118 access lines per regional operating company employee at TCNZ compared with an average of 224 for the US Bell Regional Operating Companies (RBOCs), 167 for Telefónica of Spain and 120 for BT. Given the modern network, it seems reasonable to assume that TCNZ can approach similar productivity levels, although because different companies may sometimes use different data in calculating this ratio, such comparisons are not considered to be precise; and • The redundancies meant increased personnel productivity. The total number of employees (expressed as full-time equivalents) was cut from approximately 24,500 on 11 April 1987 to 14,925 by 31 March 1991. In addition, quality of service targets were established and monitored and, as a result, customer satisfaction had increased markedly.
Restructuring	• Beginning in 1988, TCNZ restructured its management organisation and adopted a new business philosophy. A new management was recruited and a new holding company structure was introduced reducing central management functions, decentralising decision-making and improving operating performance by making each business directly accountable for its own customer satisfaction and financial performance; and • Since November 1988, TCNZ has implemented a significant tariff rebalancing programme which was largely completed by the time of the offer. This restructured the prices charged for telephone services to remove cross-subsidies and to establish prices that more accurately reflect the underlying costs of those services through big reductions in long-distance rates and increases in local rates. TCNZ was therefore better positioned to respond to competition and identify opportunities for future capital spending. The significant reduction in international and domestic long-distance rates had masked double-digit volume growth.
Earnings growth	• Over the two fiscal years ended March 1991, earnings from operations grew by an average 19.9% a year This resulted from operating revenues growing by 6.1% a year and operating expenses increasing at a lower rate of 2.3% a year.
Strong balance sheet	• TCNZ had a debt-to-total-capitalisation ratio of around 37%. Its NZ$ debt was rated AAA while its non-NZ$ debt was rated Aa3 by Moody's and AA- by Standard & Poor's.
Ameritech and Bell Atlantic relationship	• These two companies considered themselves to be among the most efficient and technologically advanced RBOCs and had agreed to work jointly to make their telecommunications expertise, services and products available to TCNZ.
Valuation	• *Dividend yield:* TCNZ was priced at a gross prospective dividend yield of 6.5% (5.5% net of withholding tax). This compared with a 5.9% yield for the RBOCs and 3.9% for BT. The stated dividend policy was to pay out at least 70% of earnings; • *P/E ratio:* TCNZ was priced at 11.8x NZ GAAP forecast earnings. This compared favourably with the US RBOCs which traded at 12.6x calendar 1991 estimated earnings; and • *Total returns:* The combination of a dividend yield of 5.5% net to US investors and TCNZ's earnings growth objective of approx. 15% p.a. produces a total return of over 20%. This compares favourably with the dividend yield of 5.9% and annual growth of 5% for US RBOCs and a 3.9% dividend yield and 12%–15% growth rate for BT.

Source: Goldman Sachs & Co.

The performance of the main parties

The company

TCNZ's management had turned the company from being one of the world's most inefficient providers of telecommunications services into a highly successful and dynamic operation. In 1987, when TCNZ was formed, the company's assets generated profits of only NZ$150,000. Rationalisation and

Exhibit 13

After-market share price performance

Pricing date (US time)	16 July
Filing range	NZ$1.80–2.00
Offer price	NZ$2.00

First year high/low	
High (12 November 1991)	NZ$2.82
Low (1 May 1992)	NZ$2.05

New Zealand Telecom share price relative to MSNZ Index (%)

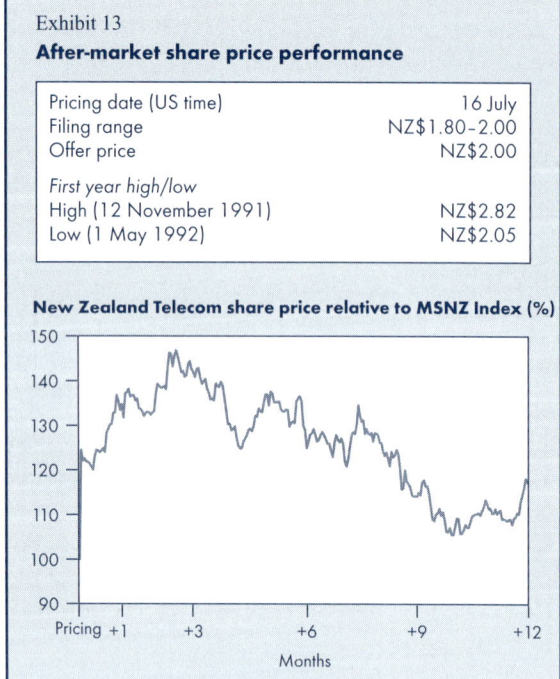

Absolute and relative price performance

	Price (unadjusted)* (NZ$)	Relative to MSNZ Index (%)
+ 1 day	2.35	124
+ 3 days	2.30	123
+ 1 week	2.27	122
+ 1 month	2.46	136
+ 3 months	2.62	143
+ 6 months	2.45	129
+ 9 months	2.02	114
+ 12 months	2.31	118

*Note the absolute prices above are unadjusted and therefore not comparable to prices following the capital repayment which was effective on 5 March 1994. To achieve comparability, the unadjusted prices should be divided by a factor of 0.838207. At the time the price was NZ$4.30 and the adjusted price became NZ$5.13. (See also to the section headed Share capital and ownership).

Sources: Datastream and offer circular.

Exhibit 14

Percentage of total issue traded* (%)

	Day 1	Day 2	Day 3	Total Day 1–3
New Zealand	11.1	1.9	1.4	14.4
New York	27.7	5.5	2.4	35.6
Globally	38.8	7.4	3.8	50.0

* Based on the issue of 724.5 million shares.

investment meant that for the financial year ended March 1991, annual net earnings had grown to NZ$332 million.

There were some tough negotiations between the vendors and the company management over what figures to use in the profit forecast and generally what information to disclose for purposes of the IPO. Management was thought to be too cautious and not very cooperative, while Ameritech and Bell Atlantic had difficulty in understanding that NZ insider legislation is even more stringent than its US equivalent. These difficulties arose because TCNZ had to give a forecast according to NZSE listing requirements but was nervous of doing so because of the risk of litigation in the US, where a quantified company forecast is unusual. In New Zealand, companies can undershoot the forecast by 20 per cent in the first year after an issue without causing uproar, while in the US, even a much smaller under-performance could lead to litigation. However, the vendors needed a sale price which was higher than their purchase price and there was therefore much discussion over the figures. At one point TCNZ's CFO Ross Campbell insisted he would release certain information only if a legal opinion to do so was obtained.

The management did well on the roadshow after some coaching. Peter Troughton, the CEO, was open and frank with investors, which was well received, although the roadshow was initially perceived as highly orchestrated and formal.

TCNZ delivered – just – on its NZ$401 million net earnings forecast for 1992 (NZ$405 million achieved) and slightly undershot on the NZ$2.7 billion revenue forecast (NZ$2.6 billion achieved). Over the three years after the float, it slightly exceeded its pledge to increase earnings per share by 15 per cent a year, achieving 17.2 per cent.

The vendors

Ameritech and Bell Atlantic took sound decisions on timing, sizing and pricing which resulted in a highly successful flotation. However, the appointment of joint global coordinators was the first of several decisions on which they found it difficult to act as one. The size of the original float was subject to considerable debate and did not make the job easier for the underwriters. The further sell-down was a difficult issue and one which created some friction between the two partners. The TCNZ management felt that the vendors had been heavy-handed in their approach to the company, a factor which certainly did not facilitate the smooth running of the sale. Ameritech and Bell Atlantic are, however, given credit for facilitating the float by substantially assisting TCNZ with such matters as initial investor targeting and crafting of the story. Their state-of-the-art investor relations functions were undoubtedly highly beneficial to the float.

The global coordinators

The success of the offer speaks for itself, but none of the international bankers and few if any of the international lawyers had prior experience with the NZ market. Equally, the domestic underwriters had no experience with the US registration process and many of the international bankers had only limited experience of global offers. The underwriters are thought to have had a problem with the NZSE, in that the international bankers were accused of drip-feeding the local exchange with various requirements and requests for waivers to make the deal work domestically and in the US. Even on the last day before the filing and announcement, there were many unresolved issues with the NZ exchange. The bankers reportedly had to eat a fair amount of humble pie before certain rules and regulations were overcome. On the other hand, the NZSE did not waive the requirement for a forecast and a domestic-style mini prospectus, although the forecast was in fact substantially hedged: the US approach is intended to offer investors sufficient guidance to give them a good idea of the situation.

TCNZ management was frustrated about the last-minute nature of the briefing they received from, in particular, the US underwriters, as to whom they were to meet on the roadshow, but such occurrences are often the case in these offers. The company also thought that Goldman Sachs did not have as big an impact on Australian investors as it did elsewhere in the world. Not enough shares were distributed in Australia and subsequent trading volumes were thus insufficient to warrant TCNZ's inclusion in the important Australian stock exchange index, which would have obliged institutions there to own the stock. The Australian listing project was consequently aborted.

The decision to include 100 per cent of TCNZ's share capital in the Barclays 40 index, although only 31 per cent of the company was on offer (only a portion of which was sold in NZ) led to controversy because TCNZ came to represent 20 per cent of the local index, making it virtually impossible for the local institutions to try to track the index's performance. This was due to two factors: first, there was not enough stock available, and second, many institutions had restrictions that prevented them from investing more than 10 per cent of their total portfolios in any one stock. Fay Richwhite argued for the 100 per cent decision so as to underpin the NZ offer but many domestic institutions felt that they had been pushed around and thus bought less than they otherwise might have done. This negativity was compounded by their unfamiliarity with bookbuilding, which could have been overcome if the global coordinators and domestic lead manager had spent more time educating them on the bookbuilding process. By 1995 the weighting of TCNZ had risen to 25 per cent: now, as soon as TCNZ sneezes, the market catches a cold.

The appointment of Goldman Sachs and Merrill Lynch was due to established relationships between the vendors and the banks. Ameritech was close to Goldman Sachs and Bell Atlantic was close to Merrill Lynch. However, according to Bell Atlantic's Crawford, his firm saw the benefits of the involvement in and endorsement of the transaction by Robert Morris, Goldman Sachs' highly respected telecommunications analyst. Although the two Baby Bells had not planned to engage two global coordinators, they saw advantages in engaging both firms. It was logical that the two US vendors should pick US firms to do the offer: Goldman Sachs and Merrill Lynch are among the best global distributors of equities and the former had worked on the scoping study, while Merrill Lynch had been TCNZ's rating adviser since April 1990. Despite its scoping study work, though, Goldman Sachs did not manage to convert that mandate into the privatisation advisory role, which went to CSFB and Buttle Wilson (SG Warburg). One of the key reasons for this is thought to have been the fact that Goldman Sachs did not have local representation.

To have lost out in the contest to become a global coordinator was a huge disappointment to Salomon Brothers, which had acted for Ameritech and Bell Atlantic in the 1990

purchase. It became the third most senior bank in the syndicate and adviser to the vendors on the IPO; however, they were thought not to have been paid a separate advisory fee.

Key lessons learnt

Strategic sale in June 1990

From the point of view of the state, it was clearly beneficial for three years to pass between TCNZ's incorporation and privatisation as this gave the management time to improve efficiency and build a track record.

Ross Campbell, TCNZ's first CFO said: 'Looking at what happened and given that the regulatory regime was clarified in 1988 but not fully introduced until substantially later, the TCNZ case confirms the view that the threat of competition is almost as effective as competition.'

According to Matthew Westerman, now a director of NM Rothschild, but at the time with CSFB which advised the NZ government on the 1990 sale of TCNZ: 'The dual-track strategy works. Until the day the NZ government signed the sale and purchase agreement with Bell Atlantic and Ameritech, we were fully prepared to launch a global IPO. As a result of the highly competitive environment created by the interest of the strategic buyers and the threat of the IPO, the NZ government is thought to have increased the proceeds by more than NZ$500 million.'

Although the sale price of NZ$4.25 billion was seen as attractive at the time – proceeds were higher than even the most optimistic observers expected – Campbell suggests that the NZ government might have achieved even greater proceeds had it sold TCNZ in tranches. However, the government had a clear policy on privatisation, was adverse to taking market risk and badly needed the money; it therefore acted accordingly.

IPO in July 1991

This sale proved that there was strong international demand for a telephone company from a small country (only BT, Telefónica and Telmex among non-US telephone companies were publicly traded at the time). Although this does not seem like a major revelation today, it was a significant discovery at the time. This offer laid the foundation for the globally distributed telecom offers that were to follow, including Singapore Telecom, Indosat, Tele Danmark and KPN.

'To me, the interesting lesson is that a lot of smart people were very conservative concerning the valuation of this company,' said Joe Dempsey, executive director of Goldman Sachs' telecommunications group, which worked on the original scoping study in 1989. He added: 'Nobody foresaw the very positive development that TCNZ has experienced since privatisation.'

Of the decision to appoint joint global coordinators, John Jensen of Merrill Lynch's ECM department said: 'Joint efforts, ie, two or more global coordinators, doesn't make sense. You end up doing four times as much work as otherwise required.'

It proved possible to combine a quasi-fixed-price offer for domestic retail with a global bookbuilding process for institutional investors, something done many times since, though innovative at the time.

This IPO also showed how a privatisation can achieve broad domestic public ownership and control of a prized national asset by first selling 100 per cent to foreign strategic buyers and only subsequently have those buyers offer shares to the local public, leaving the market risk with the strategic buyers.

Yet the complexity of a global offer with dual listings in New York and Wellington, with two vendors based in different time zones and three sets of bankers based in three time zones, should not be underestimated. Lisa Pawel, director of Cowen & Co (formerly with Goldman Sachs) said: 'Given the unusually challenging logistics of this transaction, we initiated a weekly conference call during the preparation phase between all the parties involved. This significantly assisted the execution.'

While the 1991 IPO and the further sell-down ultimately worked well, this offer underscores the challenge of having two owners/partners agree on a sell-down programme such as the one imposed by the NZ Treasury. Inevitably there will be differences of opinion on the right time to sell, how much, at what price and the method of sale. Bell Atlantic appeared more in a hurry than its partner to sell. This disunity created uncertainty which, under weaker market conditions, might have had a negative affect on the TCNZ share price.

Management would have done an even better job had it enjoyed a more direct stake in the success of the float. This could have been achieved by letting it participate in more of the decision-making about the float. However, according to Stewart Millman, now of NatWest Markets but then BZW adviser to TCNZ: 'This was simply not the way the Baby Bells managed their operating companies in the US. There was therefore no reason this was going to happen in the case of TCNZ.'

Former CFO Campbell said: 'A further mistake in the float was that the Kiwi share should have allowed for more rebalancing between local and national/international calls. As it now happened, competitors could not profitably finance their own network and offer local call services. Equally, due to the low local rates, TCNZ could not charge competitors for interconnection without actually subsidising such charges. As a result, new competitors such as Clear competed only on the profitable segments of the business, such as trunk calls.'

Conclusion

The sale of 99.9 per cent of TCNZ to Ameritech and Bell Atlantic was an impressive transaction and the result of a clear long-term policy and professional execution by the NZ Treasury. It formed an integral part of wide-ranging economic reforms through which the NZ economy has been opened to the rigours of international competition. A vital component of these reforms was the separation of the government's ownership and regulatory roles.

The sale was initally opposed by the public, however everyone knew that the country was in trouble. Therefore says Stewart Millman: 'The sale of the company was accepted as an unpleasant inevitability and the structure chosen with sell-down provisions, domestic partners and the inclusion of the Kiwi share made it possible. The high price achieved was also important in overcoming any remaining opposition.'

Soon after the purchase, Ameritech and Bell Atlantic met the US investor community at New York's Waldorf Astoria Hotel to explain why they'd bought TCNZ and to discuss its prospects, thereby effectively kicking off the pre-marketing of the IPO which was to follow. It was important to prepare the US market for this new name and counter initial market reaction that the two Baby Bells had overpaid. They also created name recognition for TCNZ before the IPO as part of their ongoing investor relations efforts. Both companies had successful IR teams and good shareholder relations, and were therefore able to give TCNZ's IR team a head start by leveraging off established investor contacts.

Ameritech and Bell Atlantic needed to recover their purchase price and, if possible, the full economic cost of the acquisition (including the cost of carry) of about NZ$1.90 through the IPO. This was achieved with an offer price of NZ$2.00 though with hindsight the vendors realised that they probably could have squeezed out a little more from the transaction. Compared to the price indications received earlier in 1991, this was, however, a highly satisfactory result. The success was also important to ensure that the market would be receptive for subsequent tranches.

The NZ offer was the weak link in the IPO, with the retail campaign considered to have been too American for local purposes. The targeted number of retail investors was not reached and domestic institutions were uncomfortable with the bookbuilding process, as well as with the decision to include 100 per cent of TCNZ's capital in the local index.

Australian distribution was a disappointment, and Goldman Sachs faced criticism for its efforts in this area. The country which had neither a quoted telecommunications company nor equity research analysts following the sector and institutions thus lacked appreciation of the opportunities. 'Instead of concentrating on the top Australian institutions, of which there are not much more than a handful, Goldman Sachs should rather have targeted the Australian affiliates of the foreign institutions,' says Millman. 'After all, the sector was not known in the UK before the 1984 privatisation of BT.'

Overall the issue was heavily over-subscribed, increased by 50 per cent and the greenshoe was exercised in full. It was priced at the top of the range and traded well in the after-market, allowing Ameritech and Bell Atlantic to sell further shares at substantially higher prices on subsequent occasions. The offer increased the size of the NZ stock market by some 20 per cent and gave it a bellwether stock. Many international investors discovered both the NZ stock market and the nation's impressive economic reform programme in connection with this offer.

TCNZ was not only one of the first telecommunications companies distributed globally, but was also one of the most successful privatisations anywhere. This was due in part to TCNZ being incorporated more than three years before privatisation, allowing time for development and preparation within a regulatory regime that increasingly allowed competition to develop. Peter Troughton, formerly with BT, had gathered a lot of talented people around him and this team had made substantial progress in cutting costs and updating technology. 'TCNZ had effectively skipped a generation,' noted Matthew Westerman. Peter Troughton personally deserves a lot of credit for this according to a former colleague. A further reason for the success, according to John Jensen of Merrill Lynch, 'was that the sponsors to the issue managed to convince domestic retail investors that the fundamentals of the business and the management strategy were sufficient to overcome the unknown risk of competition'.

No doubt Bell Atlantic's and Ameritech's investment in TCNZ has been one of the most successful cross-border strategic investments in the telecommunications industry. By late August 1997 – just over six years after the IPO – TCNZ was trading approximately 75 per cent higher in US-dollar terms – and in the meantime, had paid handsome dividends and bought back its own shares on two occasions. Over the same period, BT had only appreciated by 12.5 per cent in local currency terms.

Feature topic: *Pursuing a dual-track strategy*

A dual-track strategy sale is a process whereby a vendor selling an asset simultaneously pursues a strategic sale (ie, a private or negotiated sale) and a public sale of shares. In the case of TCNZ, the NZ Treasury specified that the following two main sale routes be pursued:

1. Strategic stake sale of 49.9 per cent of TCNZ to a domestic or foreign buyer(s) as soon as practically possible immediately followed by a global registered IPO of up to 49 per cent, in one or two tranches subject to market capacity, by August 1990; or

2. Sale of 99.9 per cent of TCNZ to one or several domestic or foreign strategic buyers, subject to a limitation on foreign ownership of 49.9 per cent, a public offer to domestic investors of NZ$500 million-worth of shares and certain provisions relating to telecommunication services to residential customers.

TCNZ's management appreciated that the strategic sale was chosen for several reasons. First, it was unlikely that the management would have been able to conduct an IPO in the little time available; second, the Gulf War would have prevented that offer from happening before the 1991 IPO actually happened; and third, were TCNZ not to be sold in 1990 it was uncertain that a later sale would have been politically possible, as the proposed but not realised electricity privatisation had proved.

The rationale

The rationale behind a dual-track strategy sale is to eliminate or reduce exposure to the public equity markets. By keeping an open mind as to the method of sale, more competition is injected in the process and in many cases this leads to maximisation of proceeds. Strategic buyers are put under competitive pressure and the vendor hedges against deteriorating equity market conditions. The beauty of this strategy is that the vendor does not pre-judge the sale process but lets the market arrive at the maximum valuation.

The main advantages of a dual-track strategy are:

* It means reduced exposure to volatile public markets;
* The process is subject to more competition;
* The vendor retains greater flexibility; and
* It should lead to a maximisation of proceeds.

The main disadvantages are:

* It is more challenging to administer. In the case of privatisations, pressurised civil servants have to do twice as much work;
* The sale process is more expensive; and
* Some strategic buyers may not be prepared to negotiate on this basis.

One senior M&A banker who is familiar with the TCNZ privatisation and who is a critic of the concept said: 'In general, you turn corporate buyers off without really threatening them. Dual-track strategy is more theory than practice.'

In the case of the sale of TCNZ, the NZ fiscal budget was heavily in deficit and it was considered essential to maximise proceeds. The government had two policies: one was to avoid commercial risk, meaning selling the asset as soon as it had been declared non-strategic; the other was to avoid market risk, implying an avoidance of a public sale. It was therefore clear that a strategic sale of 99.9 per cent of TCNZ was the preferred option. So why was a simultaneous IPO pursued?

'Firstly,' said Richard Shallcrass of the Treasury, 'it was generally recognised at an early stage that the most effective sale process in all likelihood entailed a combination of a strategic sale and an international public float. Secondly, it was our impression that the potential buyers found the threat of the government itself continuing to be involved in the company after the initial sale, through mounting an IPO, to be off-putting to say the least. The IPO threat was just one element of that overall competitive environment that we strove hard to create.'

When the strategy makes sense

The dual-track strategy generally makes sense when the vendor wants to hedge his bets. This may apply to a situation when there is concern about the public markets and where the valuations between public and private markets are uncertain and fluctuate over time. In a privatisation, it is important that there is political support for both methods of sale as otherwise a dual-track strategy is not fully credible. Were a 100 per cent sale to foreign strategic buyers to generate huge political opposition, there probably would be little merit in pursuing a dual-track strategy.

The advisers

It is important that the chosen adviser has credibility to execute both types of sale. Matthew Westerman, director of NM Rothschild said that if, for example, CSFB had not been believed capable of conducting an IPO by the strategic buyers, then the buyers may not have been as aware of the competition from the public markets and accordingly may not have been prepared to pay as high a price. 'In addition,' he continued 'it is also in the interest of the vendor to see to it that the bank advising it on the dual-track strategy does not have too strong an economic or institutional bias in pursuing one method of sale or another. If, for one reason or another, there might be a bias, then it also goes without saying that the vendor cannot and should not be completely comfortable that it is receiving the best possible advice. This could also undermine the credibility of the process and upset many of the interested parties.'

Handling the strategy

The vendor must be open about the fact that two different methods of sale are being pursued, otherwise competition in the sale process will suffer. There is also a risk of upsetting the strategic buyers if the process is not transparent. To keep maximum flexibility and generate maximum competition, it is essential to work on both alternatives to the end, otherwise credibility suffers. Shallcrass said: 'In the case of the IPO of TCNZ it was essential that the increasing reservations of the Treasury concerning the possibility of selling 49 per cent of the company in the public markets should not become apparent to the strategic buyers as this would have sent a signal that the IPO was unlikely to happen.'

The TCNZ strategic sale

The NZ Government decided to sell TCNZ through a strategic sale to Ameritech and Bell Atlantic for these main reasons:

- The government was not comfortable with the management of market risk of the kind associated with a public offer, ie, the pricing of a complex structure. It felt that it was better at raising revenue through taxation;
- Given its agonising experience with a privatised bank, DFC, which went bankrupt, the government felt uncomfortable about having to give warranties and indemnities – as is customary in a public sale – concerning the financial record of TCNZ;
- The price was attractive. Former CFO Ross Campbell said that TCNZ was valued at NZ$3.5–4.0 billion and the buyers ended up paying NZ$750 million more than they otherwise would have as a result of the overall competitive environment created by both the threat of the IPO and the numerous strategic buyers (officially only two or three, but in fact five did due diligence);
- A sale to two strategic buyers was considered much less uncertain than one through the stock market. Indeed, the NZ government has never privatised a company by way of a public sale via the stock market as it has been unwilling to take the market risk; and
- Ameritech and Bell Atlantic were prepared to undertake to sell-down to 49.9 per cent of TCNZ within a period of three years (four years under certain circumstances) and to offer at least NZ$500 million-worth of shares to the NZ public.

USX – Marathon Group

In 1982 US Steel (the first billion-dollar corporation in history) acquired Marathon Oil Company which was the 17th largest oil producer in the country, for US$6.2 billion. The acquisition was designed to reduce US Steel's dependence on the steel business and to smooth out earnings, as energy was typically up when steel was down and vice versa. Four years later this was followed by the US$3 billion purchase of Texas Oil & Gas, after which the company changed its name to USX. The debt market initially liked these acquisitions and the company's debt ratings were underpinned accordingly.

The equity market, which increasingly focused on pure plays was less enthusiastic. USX's share price started to underperform as investors often focused on whichever business was doing less well. The unit which was battling a market slump persistently blighted the accomplishments of the other. Alfred Kingsley, deputy to corporate raider Carl Icahn, observed in the March 1993 issue of CFO Magazine: 'USX as a corporation reflected the worst of whatever happened. If steel was trading at a low multiple, then the entire company would trade at a low multiple – and if oil was down, then it was the same thing.'

Energy buyers found that USX was too exposed to the steel industry and steel buyers found it too exposed to the energy industry. Analysts covering USX were either steel or oil analysts with only limited expertise in the other business. Most all-star industry sector analysts did not want to jeopardise their reputations by covering a company that was significantly exposed to an industry that they did not know well.

USX was therefore viewed as undervalued compared to publicly traded energy and steel companies. Carl Icahn was certainly of this opinion and acted on it by buying an initial 11.4 per cent stake in 1986. By 1989 he had accumulated a 13.3 per cent stake in USX and in May 1990 he proposed at the shareholders' meeting that USX spin off 80 per cent of the steel division as a separate company, hence obtaining separate quotations for Marathon and US Steel to allow the market to reflect the full value of Marathon.

The board objected for two reasons: first, financing and administrative costs would be higher to the extent of approximately US$115 million a year and secondly, the spin-off would most likely be a taxable event. Icahn's spin-off proposal received 43 per cent of the votes (19 per cent of which were from non-Icahn shareholders) and was defeated. There was, however, still pressure on the board, as there had been since 1986 when Icahn bought his initial stake and attempted a full take over. This hostility might well have been successful had insider trading scandals not led to a federal investigation of Drexel Burnham Lambert, Icahn's investment bank. Following his defeat at the 1990 annual meeting, Icahn stated publicly that he planned another proxy battle to gain a slate of seats on the board of directors at the 1991 shareholders' meeting.

He might well have succeeded, had USX's management, together with investment bank Lehman Brothers, not come up with an alternative, improved way of realising shareholder value, namely targeted stock.

As illustrated in Exhibit 3, USX was clearly undervalued before the announcement of the steel stock proposal. Stock

---

Exhibit 1
Transaction summary

Issuer name: USX – Marathon Group (USA)	Bookrunning lead manager: Lehman Brothers
Pricing date: 14 January 1992: (S&P 500: 420.4)	Pricing/underwriting structure: Bookbuilding
Vendor: The company	Primary or secondary: Primary
% of Marathon Group sold: 8.9% of expanded share capital	Privatisation or corporate: Corporate
IPO or non-IPO: Non-IPO	Industry: Oil and gas
Type of shares: USX-Marathon Group common stock (ie, targeted stock of USX designed to reflect the performance of USX's energy business).	Offer price: US$22.375
Total issue size: US$559 million	US listing/144A: NYSE listing

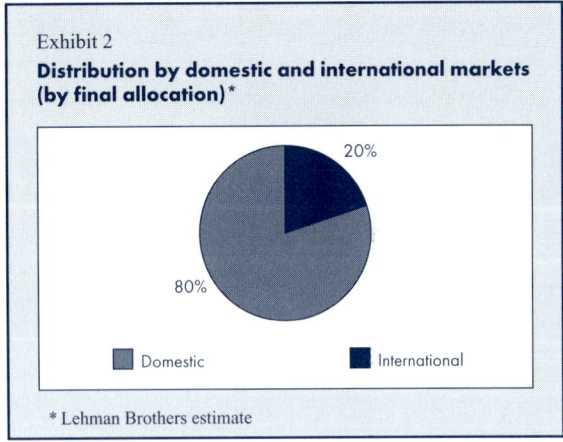

Exhibit 2

Distribution by domestic and international markets (by final allocation)*

20%

80%

Domestic ■ International

* Lehman Brothers estimate

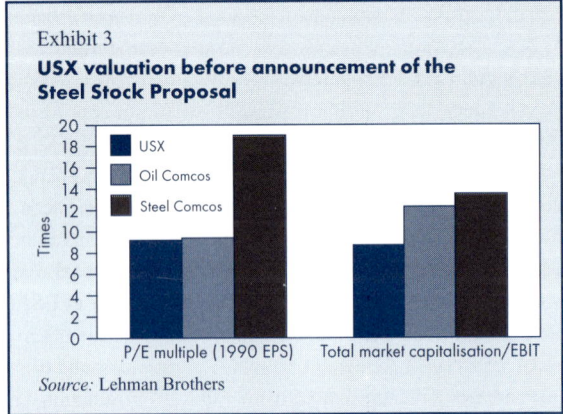

Exhibit 3

USX valuation before announcement of the Steel Stock Proposal

■ USX
■ Oil Comcos
■ Steel Comcos

P/E multiple (1990 EPS)   Total market capitalisation/EBIT

Source: Lehman Brothers

prices are as of 30 January 1991, the day before the proposal was announced; P/E multiples are based on 1990 reported earnings; other financial data is as of the 12 months ended September 1990.

The proposal, passed by 96 per cent of the votes at the 1991 annual meeting, was, like Icahn's proposed spin-off, focused on the creation of two separate common stocks designed to trade based on the performance of the steel division and the energy business respectively.

While Icahn's proposal would have created two separately traded corporations, the new proposal involved the creation of two separate classes of USX parent company stock called USX-US Steel common stock and USX-Marathon common stock. This structure allowed USX to retain the benefits of being a consolidated company while allowing the market to value energy and steel businesses separately. Although it was denied by the company, independent analysts viewed the proposal as serving takeover defence purposes. At this point no new money was raised from the market.

It was not until January 1992 that the concept was to be fully vindicated, when, despite a depressed market for energy stocks, USX accomplished a highly successful US$560 million offer of Marathon stock which was, at the time, one of the largest energy-related equity financings ever.

Targeted stock

Targeted stock had been invented as an acquisition currency

in 1984 in connection with General Motors' US$2.5 billion purchase of Ross Perot's EDS, when Perot did not want to be paid in GM common stock. It was used again by GM in 1985, in connection with the purchase of Hughes Aircraft.

By the end of 1996 no less than 33 targeted stock transactions, from the US, Canada and New Zealand, had either been issued, or announced. Since three had been shelved and six were pending, just 24 targeted stocks with a market value in excess of US$100 billion were trading in public markets. In addition to GM and USX, other companies which had successfully restructured their share capital into two or more classes of targeted stocks by the end of 1996 include: The Pittston Company, Genzyme Corporation, CMS Energy Corporation, American Health Properties, Tele Communications Inc. and US West.

RJR Nabisco obtained shareholder approval for a US$1.7 billion IPO based on Nabisco Food targeted stock which was cancelled for reasons primarily unrelated to the targeted stock concept. IBM was thought to have seriously considered the concept as part of its attempt to restructure itself and in August 1995 MCI Communications Corporation announced its intention to consider targeted stock to separate its long-distance business from its various ventures and investments. These plans were shelved following AT&T's announcement in late September 1995 that it wanted to split into three companies as MCI decided that the timing for a share capital restructuring was not optimal.

Outside the US, two companies, Fletcher Challenge of New Zealand and Inco Ltd of Canada, have structured their share capital with targeted stock. Several big UK companies are thought to have looked at the concept but decided not to go ahead, at least not yet. Targeted stock was studied in Sweden in connection with the stand-off between Volvo and the state concerning the privatisation of Procordia (eventually privatised as Pharmacia following a tax-free spin-off of the non-pharmaceutical assets).

The US Steel stock proposal

On 6 May 1991 96 per cent of USX shareholders voted for the US Steel stock proposal, which became effective on 7 May. Holders of one old USX common share received one-fifth of a US Steel share. Existing common stock changed into Marathon stock.

USX initially provided three separate sets of financial statements: one each for USX Corporation, Marathon and US Steel. This was increased to four following the creation of the Delhi Group (the natural gas interests that originally formed part of Marathon).

All corporate items including net interest expense and administrative expense were allocated to the business groups. Net interest expense was allocated on the basis of the portion of the total USX group debt outstanding which was allocated to each business group, plus changes in debt based on each business group's cash flow, and charged at a rate equal to USX's average financing cost.

Notwithstanding the fact that for financial reporting purposes preferred stock and debt was allocated to each group, there is no legal separation, so USX debt holders look to all assets and earnings of USX to service the debt. Corporate financial activities, including repayment and repurchase of short-term and long-term debt were reflected in the initial financial statements of the business groups based upon their respective cash flows after giving consideration to the historical debt and equity structure of the corporation. Historical financials were derived based on the established capital structure and historical cash flows of each business group. USX continued to access the capital markets on behalf of the business groups.

Contingent liabilities were allocated to business groups, but each group's debt cost is not isolated from the overhang of any other group. Capital expenditure within US Steel was to be financed over the long term from funds generated internally, including proceeds from asset sales. Inter-group transactions are conducted on an arm's length basis.

Dividends are primarily based on the long-term earnings and cash flow of each business group, as well as on the dividend policies of publicly traded energy and steel companies.

One of the reasons for the success of the proposal was that there was no retained interest (ie, where one class of targeted stock retains some ownership in another class) and, therefore, the Marathon and US Steel stocks were entirely pure plays.

Although negative corporate developments and a difficult business environment masked the benefits of the share capital restructuring, the introduction of targeted stock succeeded because it is a genuinely useful restructuring tool which in this case allowed the old USX shareholders and new investors alike to expose themselves to ownership of either, or both, of the two businesses.

USX's increased financing flexibility

The Marathon offer in January 1992 was the first offer of targeted stock to raise money, as opposed to a distribution to shareholders.

Given that there had not been any significant equity offers from energy companies for some time and as this was a large issue, it became a hotly contested mandate, as reflected by the relatively low fees.

Since Icahn appeared on the scene, USX had effectively been prevented from raising substantial amounts of equity as this would have diluted his holding and been seen as a hostile act. It was generally considered that July 1991 was the first opportunity in nearly 10 years for USX to raise common equity capital for the group as Icahn was no longer a threat.

From then until July 1995 USX made six common stock offers totalling US$1.65 billion (including the Marathon offer and subsequent offers of Marathon, US Steel and Delhi stocks). During this period it also launched a convertible preferred issue (convertible into steel stock) for proceeds of US$345 million.

Major challenges

The US Steel stock proposal

Although GM had introduced targeted stock in 1984, it was

still a largely untested concept with a relatively high degree of complexity. USX therefore had to spend a lot of time explaining targeted stock to investors and analysts.

Although Icahn had supported the US Steel stock proposal, on 14 May 1991 he sold his entire stake, valued at US$1.1 billion, through Lehman Brothers, Salomon Brothers and Goldman Sachs in what was (at the time) the second largest block trade ever. He realised a 25 per cent return over five years, half of what the US stock market had achieved over the same period. The block trade was only possible as a result of the extensive roadshow that USX had conducted just before the proposal became effective.

The effect of the block trade was to flood the market in Marathon and US Steel shares during the months following the sale and as a consequence the immediate valuation benefits of the proposal, which might otherwise have been reflected in outperformance against the respective comparable companies, were not apparent.

The Marathon offer

The market in USX and Marathon stock had been highly volatile during the year leading up to the offer as arbitrageurs had accumulated USX shares in 1990 in anticipation of a bid from Icahn. After the announcement of the US Steel stock proposal, but before it became effective, there was a high turnover in USX shares as certain institutions sold out altogether while others sold to buy back either Marathon or US Steel shares and others again bought to benefit from an expected revaluation of USX. Only one week after Marathon started trading as an independent stock, Icahn sold his entire stake disrupting the market at least until the beginning of July 1991.

USX first filed an offer of 20 million shares of Marathon stock on 5 November 1991 when the price was US$29.625. During the subsequent six weeks, oil prices declined by 20 per cent, further negative results concerning a Tunisian oil discovery became available, and a recommendation was delivered on 29 November by a court appointed magistrate that USX be held liable in an action relating to the original acquisition of Marathon (Pryor vs USX). Press reports alleged a US$400 million potential liability: as a result of the these adverse developments, the share price fell almost US$9 and on 16 December, Marathon decided to postpone the offer.

The offer was refiled on 6 January 1992 and was priced on 14 January. Lehman successfully met the challenge of keeping the book together from the December bookbuilding process and the cash strapped Marathon was then forced to accept an offer price of US$22.375 on 14 January, the same price as on the day the offer was postponed in December.

Rationale and objectives

The steel stock proposal

Following the rejection by shareholders of Icahn's proposal to spin-off the steel business, USX's board was under pressure to create shareholder value in recognition of the fact that the value of the oil and gas assets, representing roughly five times the value of the steel assets, was being hidden by the earnings-driven valuation of the overall company. In addition, USX was in need of substantial amounts of equity capital, as it had not been possible to raise it while Icahn was pursuing the company. The US Steel stock proposal was designed:

- to allow USX to retain the benefits of being a consolidated corporation, while providing for the separate equity market valuation of the energy and steel businesses;
- to create flexibility for the old USX shareholders to own either the energy business or the steel business, or both;
- to accomplish the tax-free recapitalisation of USX; and
- to allow continued flexibility for USX to pursue other strategic alternatives for the steel business including joint ventures or an outright sale.

Ron Gallatin, managing director of Lehman Brothers in New York said in the June 1995 issue of Euromoney *Corporate Finance*: 'When USX traded prior to the creation of targeted stock, it traded horribly. Why? Because if you wanted to buy an oil stock and you thought the price of oil was going higher, would you rather own an oil company or an oil company that's got a steel business which in a recession could cost you a million dollars a day.' He continued: 'Suppose you're coming out of a recession and you're convinced that Saddam Hussein is going to be allowed to pump oil. You want to own a steel stock but you don't want to be killed on an oil play because there's going to be an oil glut. For that reason nobody bought the stock.'

The sale of USX-Marathon stock

Marathon's production was declining and financing was required for the East Brae field in the UK's North Sea as well as for other ongoing capital expenditures. Because of the group's already high leverage, the financial management felt

that part of the heavy capital spending projected for the next few years should come from equity. The offer was the first opportunity to raise a substantial amount of equity for at least five years.

Objectives of the Marathon offer

- To finance Marathon's capital projects; and
- To achieve a successful offer in the domestic and international markets.

The proceeds of the offer were used to fund Marathon's capital projects world-wide and the proceeds of the offer were reflected in the financial statements of Marathon alone.

Share capital and ownership

See Exhibit 4.

The most important terms and conditions of USX's targeted stocks are:

- *Dividends:* The USX board undertook to declare and pay dividends on the Marathon stock based on the financial condition and results of operations of Marathon and the dividend policies of publicly traded energy companies. Dividends on the Marathon stock will be payable when, as and if declared by the board out of all the funds of the USX Corporation legally available for the purpose;
- *Voting power:* The holders of Marathon stock and US Steel stock vote together as a single class on all matters on which all common USX stockholders are entitled to vote. On such matters, each share of the Marathon stock has one vote and each share of US Steel stock has a fluctuating vote based upon the relative market capitalisation of the two classes, calculated during a specified

Exhibit 4
Share capital and ownership

Type of shares offered	USX-Marathon common stock of par value US$1.00 (Marathon stock is common stock of USX Corporation and has been designed to reflect the performance of USX's energy business).
USX Corporation share capital before the offer[1]	Marathon common stock 256,998,456 US Steel common stock 50,988,351 Adjustable preference. 2,099,970
Listings/quotations	The Marathon stock first started trading on the NYSE on 7 May 1991.
Market capitalisation at offer price after offer	US$6.4 billion (Marathon stock only).
Marathon free float before offer	100%.
Liquidity – six months to December 1991[2]	105%.
Foreign ownership before offer	There was virtually no foreign ownership of the old USX. There was an insignificant amount of foreign ownership of Marathon stock before the Marathon offer.
Most relevant stock exchange index/weighting?	S&P 500 / 0.27% at 11/91 (as part of Oil – Domestic Integrated: US Steel stock was included separately under the Steel section of the S&P 500).

[1] Shares outstanding are as of 30 September 1991.
[2] Expressed as number of shares traded on an annualised basis as a percentage of the total number of USX-Marathon shares outstanding.

Exhibit 5
Offer structure

Target markets	Indicated tranche sizes*	Bookrunner	Co-lead managers**
US	80%	Lehman Brothers	Goldman Sachs, Morgan Stanley
International	20%	Lehman Brothers	Goldman Sachs, Morgan Stanley
Total combined offers (shares)	**20 million**		

*Percentage of indicated total offer on 6 December 1991. **In the US co-lead managers are referred to as co-managers.

Exhibit 6
Development of the offer size

Indicated number of shares to be sold	20 million + 3 million greenshoe
Number of shares after increase of offer	22 million + 3 million greenshoe
Amount of greenshoe exercised	3 million
Final number of shares sold	25 million

period prior to the record date. Neither the increase or the decrease of the authorised amount of Marathon stock and US Steel stock requires a separate vote of either class. Certain matters, where the holders of Marathon stock may be adversely affected, require a 66.7 per cent qualified majority of Marathon stockholders as a separate class, including: (i) payment of dividends or any other distribution to US Steel stockholders if any such dividend, payment or distribution is to be made with proceeds from the disposition of assets from Marathon; (ii) the use of funds within US Steel that are proceeds from the disposition of assets from Marathon or (iii) the merger or consolidation of the corporation into or with any other corporation if such a merger or consolidation would adversely affect the power or special rights of Marathon stock. US Steel stockholders as a separate class have the equivalent voting rights;

- *Liquidation rights:* The rights of the holders of Marathon stock and US Steel stock upon the liquidation of USX would be based on their relative market capitalisation;

- *Attribution of assets:* Although the financial statements of Marathon and US Steel report separately the assets, liabilities (including contingent liabilities) and shareholders' equity of USX attributed to them, such attribution does not affect legal title to such assets or responsibility for such liabilities. Holders of both Marathon and US Steel stock are shareholders of USX, which continues to be responsible for all its liabilities;

- *Exchange and redemption:* At a future date, USX can exchange Marathon stock for shares of a wholly owned subsidiary, which holds all assets and liabilities of Marathon. In the event of the sale of all or substantially all of the assets (80 per cent) of US Steel, the corporation must, within 60 days, either: (i) pay a special dividend to the holders of US Steel shares equal to the net proceeds of such sale; (ii) redeem US Steel shares for an

amount equal to the net proceeds; or (iii) exchange each outstanding US Steel share for a number of Marathon shares equivalent to a 10 per cent premium on the price of Steel shares subsequent to the completion of the sale of US Steel;

- *Fiduciary duties of the board:* The board must act with due care and in the best interests of all shareholders, including the holders of Marathon and US Steel shares; and

- *Tax:* The USX Corporation is liable to pay tax rather than the individual business groups.

The original US Steel stock proposal did not include a call provision, ie, the terms for a reversal of US Steel stock into other USX group common stocks. Such a provision was later included in the case of the USX-Delhi stock, whereby Delhi stock can, at any time, be exchanged for Marathon stock (or US Steel stock if there are no Marathon shares outstanding), at a premium of 15 per cent.

Transaction components

The offer, initially of 20 million new Marathon shares, was comprised of two tranches, a domestic tranche representing 80 per cent of the total offer and an international tranche, representing 20 per cent of the total offer (see Exhibit 5). The offer was underwritten, distributed and priced by way of a classic US bookbuilding. The shares were marketed on an open-priced basis to both domestic and international investors, allowing a book to be built after which the offer price was fixed. The offer was structured with a greenshoe of three million shares.

Filed as a 20 million share offer, the offer was increased to 22 million by the pricing date. On the following day, the greenshoe was exercised in full, bringing the total number of shares issued to 25 million (see Exhibits 6 and 8).

Exhibit 7
Principal advisers

Financial adviser to USX on the steel stock proposal*	Lehman Brothers
US legal adviser to USX	Internal Counsel
US legal adviser to the underwriters	Simpson Thatcher & Bartlett
Auditors	Price Waterhouse

* Goldman Sachs and First Boston had advised USX in the defence against Icahn but did not advise on the US steel stock proposal.

Exhibit 8
The timetable

5 November 1991	• Filing of offer of 20 million shares.
2 December	• Roadshow begins (two teams with simultaneous presentations in the US and Europe).
13 December	• Roadshow ends.
16 December	• Offer postponed.
6 January 1992	• Re-filing of offer of 20 million shares.
14 January	• Offer increased to 22 million shares and priced after the NYSE closing.
15 January	• Trading of the new shares begin on the NYSE; and • The greenshoe of three million shares is exercised.

Exhibit 9
Distribution of gross spread (%)

Management fee	Underwriting fee	Selling concession	Gross spread	Discount	Total effective cost
0.6704	0.6704	1.8771	3.2179	0	3.2179

Principal advisers

See Exhibit 7.

Transaction fee distribution

See Exhibit 9.

Management fee

Lehman Brothers received 25 per cent of the international management fee as the bookrunning lead manager's praecipium calculated on the gross proceeds of the international tranche. The remainder of the management fee on the international portion was allocated to all the managers on the basis of underwriting commitments (see Exhibit 10).

In the US, lead and comanagers shared the management fee based on underwriting commitments.

Selling concession

In the US the selling concession had one fixed and one variable component. The fixed component of 30 per cent was calculated on the basis of underwriting commitments while the variable proportion was subject to performance and was designated by investors (see Exhibit 11).

In Europe the selling concession was paid in full to whomever was given the order.

Exhibit 10
Distribution of management fee outside the US (%)

Total management fee – split outside the US	0.6704
Of which: Bookrunning lead manager's praecipium	25
Of which: Management fee split among all managers	75

Exhibit 11
Distribution of selling concession in the US (%)

Total selling concession	1.8771
Of which: Pre-agreed or fixed portion regardless of sales booked	30
Of which: Paid pro rata according to sales designated by investors	70

Deal structure

For a detailed discussion of targeted stock, see Feature topic: Introduction to targeted stock.

Marketing

The marketing in this offer had three thrusts: first, investors needed to understand the operating fundamentals of Marathon; second, they needed to understand the concept of targeted stock; and third, they needed to understand the specific terms

of the USX–Marathon common stock including Marathon's relationship with the rest of USX (see Exhibit 12).

Marathon was considered a growth story on the basis of considerable exploration successes and a rising production profile. It was also a play on the recovery in the refining and marketing business (see Exhibit 13).

In late October, prior to the initial filing in early November, 1991 Marathon traded at US$28.875, a small premium to its comparables with respect to P/E ratios, reflecting high hopes about the Tunisian oil find.

During the weeks immediately following the 5 November 1991 filing, the posted price for WTI crude oil declined from US$23.50/barrel to US$21.50/barrel. The decline continued during December, reaching a level of US$19.50/barrel by the date of the postponement of the issue on 16 December. The posted price dropped to US$16.50/barrel by 8 January. Much of this decline can be traced to market fears that Iraq would soon be resuming oil exports.

During this time the market also received news that Marathon's highly anticipated Belli-2 and Belli-3 wells in Tunisia had flowed non-commercial quantities of hydrocar-

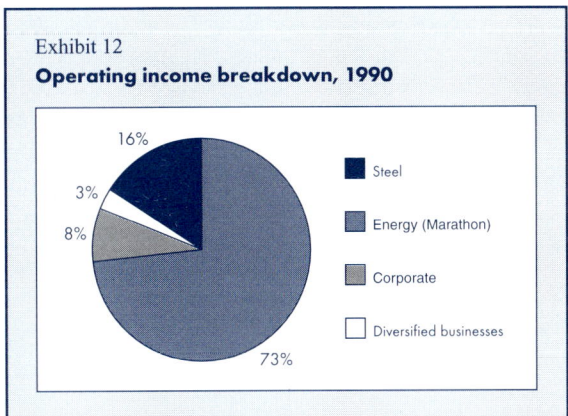

Exhibit 12
Operating income breakdown, 1990

- Steel
- Energy (Marathon)
- Corporate
- Diversified businesses

16%
3%
8%
73%

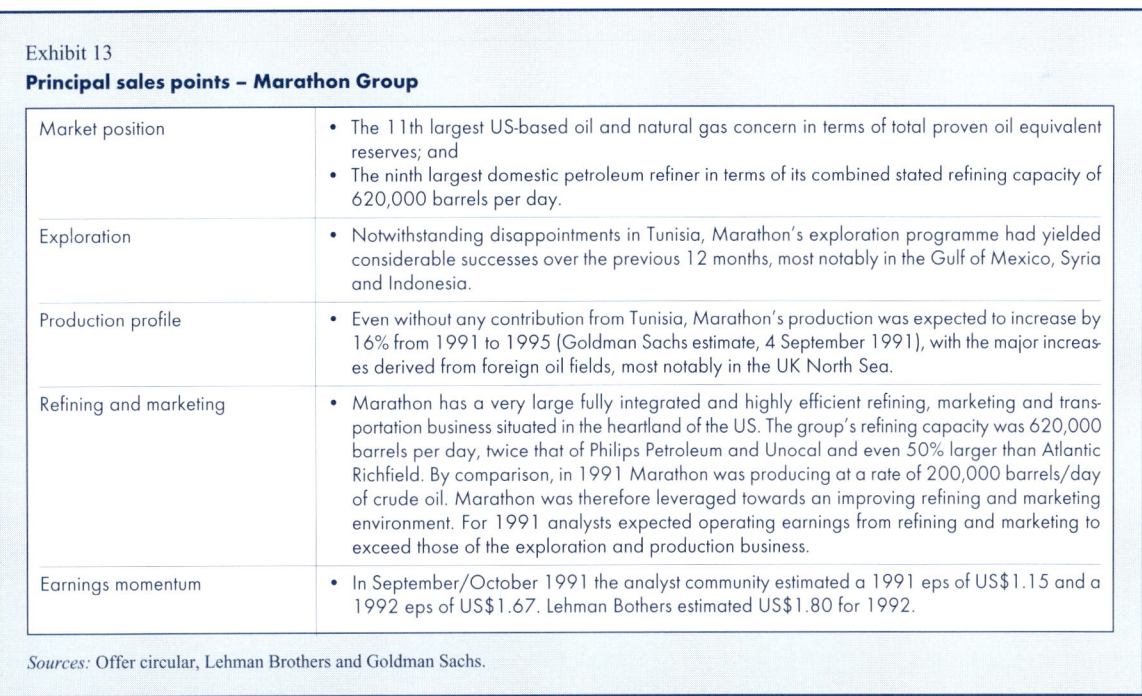

Exhibit 13
Principal sales points – Marathon Group

Market position	• The 11th largest US-based oil and natural gas concern in terms of total proven oil equivalent reserves; and • The ninth largest domestic petroleum refiner in terms of its combined stated refining capacity of 620,000 barrels per day.
Exploration	• Notwithstanding disappointments in Tunisia, Marathon's exploration programme had yielded considerable successes over the previous 12 months, most notably in the Gulf of Mexico, Syria and Indonesia.
Production profile	• Even without any contribution from Tunisia, Marathon's production was expected to increase by 16% from 1991 to 1995 (Goldman Sachs estimate, 4 September 1991), with the major increases derived from foreign oil fields, most notably in the UK North Sea.
Refining and marketing	• Marathon has a very large fully integrated and highly efficient refining, marketing and transportation business situated in the heartland of the US. The group's refining capacity was 620,000 barrels per day, twice that of Philips Petroleum and Unocal and even 50% larger than Atlantic Richfield. By comparison, in 1991 Marathon was producing at a rate of 200,000 barrels/day of crude oil. Marathon was therefore leveraged towards an improving refining and marketing environment. For 1991 analysts expected operating earnings from refining and marketing to exceed those of the exploration and production business.
Earnings momentum	• In September/October 1991 the analyst community estimated a 1991 eps of US$1.15 and a 1992 eps of US$1.67. Lehman Bothers estimated US$1.80 for 1992.

Sources: Offer circular, Lehman Brothers and Goldman Sachs.

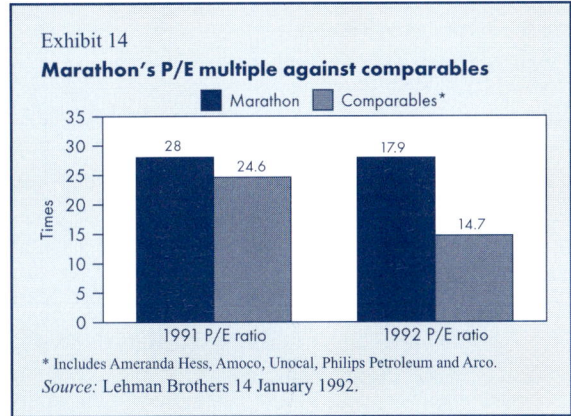

Exhibit 14
Marathon's P/E multiple against comparables

■ Marathon   ■ Comparables*

Times

	1991 P/E ratio	1992 P/E ratio
Marathon	28	17.9
Comparables*	24.6	14.7

* Includes Ameranda Hess, Amoco, Unocal, Philips Petroleum and Arco.
Source: Lehman Brothers 14 January 1992.

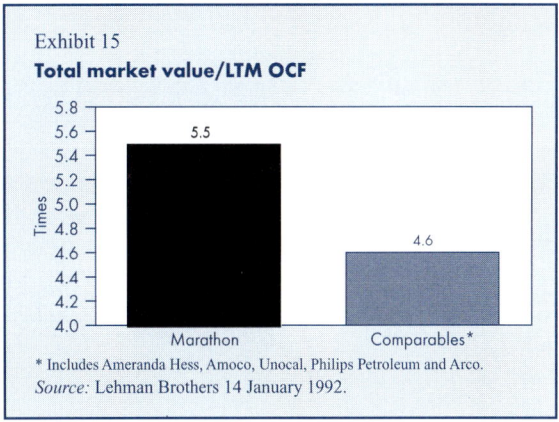

Exhibit 15
Total market value/LTM OCF

Times

Marathon	Comparables*
5.5	4.6

* Includes Ameranda Hess, Amoco, Unocal, Philips Petroleum and Arco.
Source: Lehman Brothers 14 January 1992.

bons, causing a pronounced negative reaction from a market which had built up unreasonable expectations for this project (reserve estimates of one to two billion barrels by some analysts, with the highest estimates in the range of five to six billion barrels).

The price of Marathon stock was also impacted by an unexpected recommendation on 29 November 1990, by a court-appointed magistrate, regarding long-standing litigation in which the press alleged a US$400 million liability to Marathon.

Despite a deterioration in the outlook for Marathon, and a decline in its share price during November and December, the offer was still priced at a premium to its comparables in terms of earnings and cash flow from operations (see Exhibits 14 and 15).

Results

Placement

The offer was substantially oversubscribed at the end of book-building, enabling the underwriters to increase its size from 20 milion to 22 million shares, and subsequently exercise the full greenshoe of three million shares.

The deal succeeded for a number of reasons:

- The Marathon stock was not issued as an IPO but rather represented seasoned stock, and therefore there was a trading record;
- The Marathon stock price had come down significantly from its highs and investors considered the shares to be highly attractive at the offer price; and
- The stock story was at the time considered very good, even though the Tunisian oil find (or lack thereof) turned out to be a big disappointment.

Of the US tranche, institutions took 80 per cent of the shares, whereas 20 per cent was sold to US retail investors. There was good demand in the international market, despite

a lesser familiarity with the targeted stock concept. Accordingly, international allocations corresponded approximately to the portion of the total transaction underwritten by international underwriters (see Exhibit 16).

Investor concentration

Of the 10 largest buyers, six were institutions that had owned either nothing or only very small holdings prior to the offer. Of the 30 largest buyers, the corresponding figure was nine investors. Although some of the largest buyers were new investors, the bulk of the offer was accounted for by existing investors: approximately 60 per cent of the total number of shares acquired by the 30 largest institutional investors were accounted for by these existing investors (see Exhibit 17).

Share price performance
See Exhibit 18.

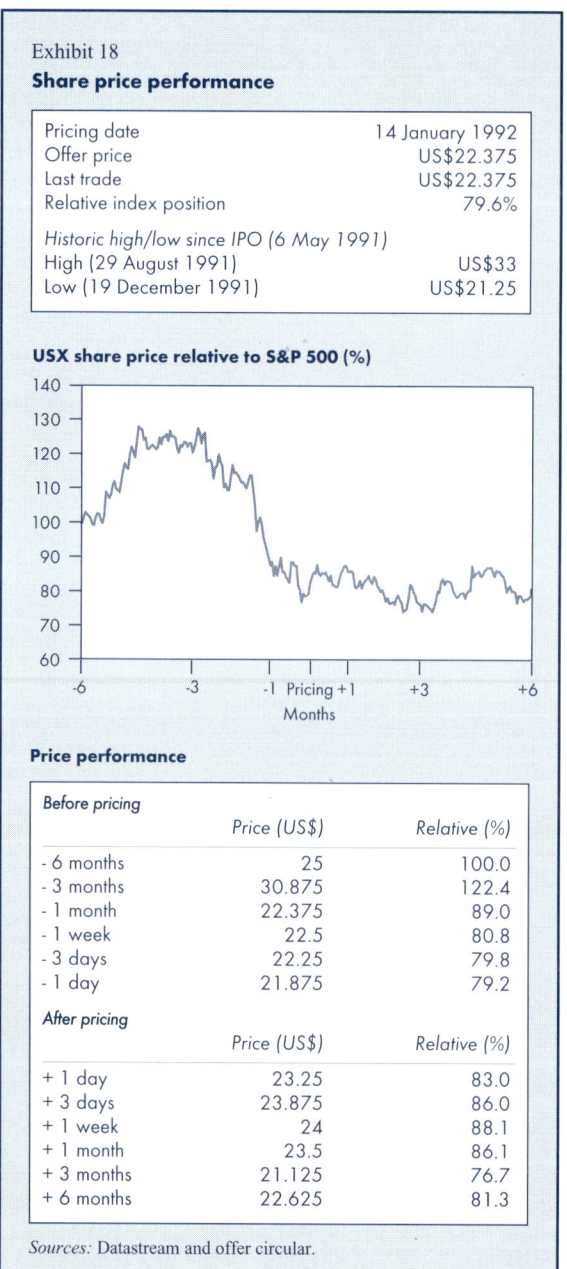

Exhibit 18

Share price performance

Pricing date	14 January 1992
Offer price	US$22.375
Last trade	US$22.375
Relative index position	79.6%
Historic high/low since IPO (6 May 1991)	
High (29 August 1991)	US$33
Low (19 December 1991)	US$21.25

USX share price relative to S&P 500 (%)

Price performance

Before pricing

	Price (US$)	Relative (%)
- 6 months	25	100.0
- 3 months	30.875	122.4
- 1 month	22.375	89.0
- 1 week	22.5	80.8
- 3 days	22.25	79.8
- 1 day	21.875	79.2

After pricing

	Price (US$)	Relative (%)
+ 1 day	23.25	83.0
+ 3 days	23.875	86.0
+ 1 week	24	88.1
+ 1 month	23.5	86.1
+ 3 months	21.125	76.7
+ 6 months	22.625	81.3

Sources: Datastream and offer circular.

Exhibit 16

Underwriting allocation

Target markets	Underwriting	Allocation*
US	80%	80%
International	20%	20%
Total	20 million	25 million

* Lehman Brothers' estimate.

Exhibit 17

Investor concentration

	By allocation
Percentage of issue accounted for by the:	
10 largest investors	33%
Total number of institutions allocated in the offer	237

Source: Lehman Brothers.

Before pricing

- Marathon began trading at US$28.125 on 7 May 1991 and fell by 7 per cent during the first week of trading. Following the placement of the Icahn stake on 14 May, the share price at first stabilised, only to begin a gradual decline during June. By 28 June the price had fallen to a temporary low of US$22.50;

- The initial performance had been negatively impacted for three reasons: first, because of the sale of the Icahn block which had not initially been fully placed with long-term investors; second, as a result of the investment community's learning curve with respect to targeted stock and, third, due to Marathon's new investment story;

- Once the Icahn overhang was fully removed, the Marathon share price increased from just over US$20 in early July to an all-time high of US$33 in late August 1991, fuelled in particular by analysts' speculation as to the ultimate size of Marathon's discoveries in Tunisia;

- USX had first filed an offer of 20 million shares on 5 November 1991 when the price was US$29.625. During the subsequent six weeks oil prices declined by 20 per cent, further negative results concerning the Tunisian oil discovery became available and Marathon was named in a summary judgment relating to the original acquisition of Marathon. For these reasons and the fact that an increasing number of investors were closing their books for the year, USX was forced to postpone the offer on 16 December;

- During the six months to pricing, Marathon under-performed the US equity market by just over 20 per cent. During the period between the initial filing on 5 November and pricing on 14 January, the underperformance was 37.3 per cent. This poor relative performance was primarily related to the initially very high and subsequently more realistic expectations concerning the Tunisian discovery rather than the concept of targeted stock or the size of the Marathon offer, which was increased from 20 to 22 million shares; and

- Between re-filing on 6 January and pricing on 14 January the absolute price fell from US$22.5 to US$22.375. In relative terms, this represented an under-performance of 2.6 per cent.

After pricing

- Despite the fact that the Marathon price increased by US$0.5 on the pricing day, Lehman Brothers managed to price the offer at market, ie, at no discount to the last sale. This was impressive given the large size of the offer. The immediate after-market performance was strong if not spectacular and shares closed the next day at a premium of US$0.875 and continued to rise to US$23.875 during the following two business days. During the first three business days, Marathon outperformed the US market by over six per cent; and

- Marathon common stock also outperformed over one week, one month and six months, although there was a small under-performance during the three months following the offer due to weak earnings projections by analysts, rumours of a dividend cut and an increase in oil prices with the effect of reducing refining margins.

Trading volume on the first day was high, if not exceptional (see Exhibit 19).

The performance of the main parties

The company

USX, which probably has more restructuring experience than any other company in the US, is highly sophisticated and was quick to pick up the concept of targeted stock. Robert Hernandez, vice chairman and CFO of USX, and his team marketed the concept well throughout 1991, and again in connection with the Marathon offer. Having filed in November, and having had to withdraw the offer in mid-December, the company did well in keeping its nerve until the offer was successfully completed.

Both the 1991 and 1992 results turned out much worse than the market had expected at the time of the offer. As far as 1991 was concerned, this was due primarily to a substantial negative earnings momentum (with negative earnings revisions almost every month), particularly in the fourth quarter of 1991 when crude prices were falling sharply. Lower production volumes, lower oil prices and lower refining and marketing margins were the principal reasons for the disappointing operating results in 1992, however, financial expenses were considerably lower in 1992 than in 1991, reflecting the sale of both Marathon and Delhi Stock, helping Marathon back to a net profit in 1992 (before the changes in accounting principles).

The bookrunning lead manager

Having helped USX restructure its share capital in May 1991, Lehman Brothers did well to complete this large offer so soon after a dramatic fall in the share price had forced it to be postponed. It was obviously right to postpone it in mid-December 1991, as the targeted offer size could not have been achieved and as the offer price (as fixed on 14 January) was the same as the price on the day of postponement, a fact which paved the way for an impressive after-market performance.

Lehman Brothers clearly deserves credit both for the successful introduction of targeted stock and the execution of the offer itself, which vindicated the concept of targeted stock as a successful financing vehicle. Hernandez of USX commented: 'To me, Lehman and our roadshow team deserve the credit. In December, the roadshow team set the stage by

Exhibit 19				
Percentage of total issue traded* (%)				
	Day 1	Day 2	Day 3	Total: Day 1-3
New York	31.6	9.5	7.1	48.2

* Based on the issue of 25 million shares.

showing the market what good prospects Marathon had. Lehman gave us the right advice and the right execution. Anyone can be successful when the market is going your way. However, this was not one of those deals. We received a negative recommendation in the Pryor case, drilled some dry holes, and oil prices – and therefore share prices – had been declining. It was becoming clear that the energy environment was going to be difficult for the next few years. On top of that, we were doing the first ever targeted stock sale. To have a successful deal in that situation is a testament to the quality of your story and your bankers. I'll just take the credit for having good nerves.'

Key lessons learnt

The US Steel stock proposal

This structure was initially confusing and USX had to market it extensively. Today, given the significant number of targeted stocks outstanding in the US market, investors are reasonably familiar with the concept and relatively limited explanation is required. Given that many US companies with targeted stock are owned from abroad to a significant extent, an increasing number of non-US institutions are now comfortable with this concept.

Despite disappointing underlying profit and share price development in both the Marathon and US Steel stocks, analysts generally agree that the targeted stock concept has helped USX. It has focused management attention on each business unit rather than on the combined business and has helped raise US$2.0 billion from the equity market – a considerable achievement that probably would not have been possible under the old conglomerate structure. Heidi Kunz, former treasurer of GM commented: 'With targeted stock you gain better flexibility to sell different stories to the equity market – you can sell an oil story when the oil environment is favourable, and a steel story when steel stocks are in demand.' Hernandez emphasised: 'USX has been to the equity market six times since we first introduced the targeted stock in May 1991. That could definitely not have been done in the name of the old USX.'

The separately audited accounts for the different classes of stock mean that more detailed disclosure is available than under the old capital structure. According to Gretchen Haggerty, treasurer of USX: 'The recapitalisation enabled us to have better analytical coverage and help our managers be better managers. We had tried to manage by focusing on operating income in the past but the senior management now has a much greater appreciation of our total financial performance, including the impact of debt, interest expense and dividends.' On the other hand, she continued: 'Whereas we have had good experience with targeted stock, it has clearly been a lot of work. We effectively manage three quoted vehicles at the cost of one. The USX board of directors has done well in coping with the three groups and has not really been faced with any material conflicts of interest because of the limited amount of business performed among the three groups.'

Marathon stock offer

It is better to introduce targeted stock as a distribution rather than as an IPO and then carry out financing once the targeted stock is fully seasoned. Tony Garcia, senior vice president of Lehman Brothers underscores the importance of allowing for a seasoning period when introducing targeted stocks: 'Explaining the businesses underlying the new securities during a roadshow for analysts and potential investors is an important part of the process, even if the company plans to issue the targeted stock through a stock distribution rather than an offer to raise capital. This enables research analysts to become familiar with the underlying businesses, to commence publication of research reports and to develop a following for the securities among the appropriate types of investors, all of which contribute to a more successful capital-raising effort.'

Judging by the fact that there were only a few questions concerning the losses on the steel side during the roadshow investors appeared to be confident that Marathon shares were trading solely on the basis of future profits and dividends.

The offer confirmed that it is better not to launch an issue late in the year, as many investors effectively close their books and are substantially more risk-averse than earlier in the year.

Conclusion

US Steel stock proposal

The stock market reacted favourably to the original announcement (up 8.2 per cent on 31 January 1991) of USX's steel stock proposal. Icahn had wanted two separately quoted stocks and this was what he got, although not in the way he had proposed.

USX would probably not have introduced targeted stock without the overhanging threat of Icahn: the US Steel stock proposal not only diminished his influence, but also facilitated his exit by way of the placement of his US$1.05 billion stake in USX. By the spring of 1991, the USX board would have pushed through the steel stock proposal regardless of Icahn's support, although in the end he too voted for it.

Many research houses had not previously followed USX, but the introduction of targeted stock led to much improved coverage (qualitatively and quantitatively) by industry sector analysts and has ensured that both US Steel stock and Marathon stock have traded as designed, ie, in line with their respective peer groups. Analysts quickly focused on the fundamentals of each business and have not been distracted by the targeted stock structure.

According to Hernandez, USX's different classes of targeted stock really do trade independently: 'We lost a hellacious lawsuit on the steel side of our business, which didn't impact the trading of Marathon stock at all.' Gallatin added to this in the June 1995 issue of Euromoney *Corporate Finance*: 'We have seen total consistency across the board that targeted stocks trade consistently, in cash flow or P/E multiple terms, to other companies in their industries. Sometimes they trade better than their peers and sometimes worse. Well, guess what? Some of them are better than their competitors and some are worse.'

The valuations of Marathon and US Steel are consistent

with those of their respective comparables. There has, therefore, been a revaluation of the two listed vehicles, although it is impossible to quantify, because there is no way of telling how USX stock would have traded today.

Hernandez pointed out: 'It is impossible to prove specifically that you have created value, because you'd have to go back and track what the old USX shares would have done. However, nobody will seriously dispute the fact that USX got a valuation boost due to the increased and much improved coverage by equity analysts. The number of analysts, both on the buy and on the sell side, increased by 100 per cent during the two years following the introduction of targeted stock.' Those who initiated research coverage of Marathon soon after it began trading as a separate vehicle included County NatWest, First Boston, Kidder Peabody, Morgan Stanley, Salomon Brothers, Smith Barney and UBS Securities. Whether or not a particular house had or had not covered the former USX, the significant event was that industry sector specialists, particularly the all-star analysts, picked up coverage. Gallatin added: 'Some people say that if you added up the pieces of USX today and compare it to where it was when it was done, the components add up to less, so it didn't work. That overlooks two things. First, when we did the targeted stock, Marathon had a dividend of US$1.40, which is now down to US$0.70. Second, when the original deal was proposed, Marathon had an oil find in Tunisia that the market thought was going to be bigger than Saudi Arabia. It wasn't.'

Substantial changes in ownership took place both before and after the steel stock proposal became effective. Most institutions on the Marathon side kept their positions constant or increased their ownership whereas on the US Steel side, some institutions apparently sold their shares and reinvested their funds in Marathon. Overall, institutional ownership increased substantially: whereas a total of 250 institutions owned 44.2 per cent of USX on 31 March 1991, 18 months later 450 institutions held Marathon stock and 325 institutions owned US Steel stock. After the Marathon offer, Marathon's institutional ownership was 50–55 per cent, while institutional ownership of US Steel increased to 65–75 per cent over the 18 months to September 1992. Marathon's institutional ownership has since increased to 65–70 per cent.

The only valid reservations against the concept are certain corporate governance issues – which most of the time can be handled successfully – substantially added complexity and a lot more work for the accounting and investor relations departments than if there is a single quoted stock to administer. Moreover, certain funds may elect not to purchase targeted stocks due to concern over their inability to calculate an asset liquidation value.

Marathon stock offer

The successful Marathon offer, perhaps more than any other transaction, vindicated the concept of targeted stock which is now considered a valid, and more cost-effective, form of IPO. It can be used to improve valuation or to gain better access to the equity market for companies with diverse businesses.

Despite the depressed market for energy stocks at the time and the fact that USX Corporation was to have one of its least profitable years in 1991, recording a loss of US$587 million, Marathon accomplished one of the largest energy equity financings to date, at a valuation which was at least on a par with its principal competitors. Targeted stock emerged as both an effective pure play concept and a powerful financing vehicle.

Feature topic: *Introduction to targeted stock*

Defining targeted stock

Targeted stock is a separate class of a company's common stock, designed to provide a return to equity investors linked to the performance of a distinct business unit. Targeted businesses may follow a company's legal structure or, alternatively, be defined by grouping assets without regard to the legal structure. It allows for different dividend policies for the different classes of stock and can act as an effective restructuring tool without many of the constraints associated with other restructuring options. Such versatility provides corporate management with unique strategic restructuring flexibility, while addressing the concerns of both equity and fixed income investors. Other names for similar types of stock include letter stock, alphabet stock and tracking stock.

Introducing targeted stock

Targeted stock is typically introduced for one of the following reasons:

- As acquisition currency in connection with an acquisition (eg, GM-E, GM-H , Genzyme Corporation and Inco Ltd);
- As an IPO in connection with a funding need (eg, USX–Delhi stock and the proposed IPO of Nabisco Foods); or
- As a straightforward recapitalisation to improve valuation, and therefore the cost of capital, and to improve access to the equity capital market (eg, USX–US Steel and Marathon stocks).

Exhibit 20
Overview of targeted stock financings (1991–96)

Date	Amount raised (US$million)	Issuer	Description of transaction
14 January 1992	560	USX	25 million shares of Marathon common.
11 February 1992	1,500	GM	GM preferred stock convertible into GM-E common.
3 June 1992	180	USX	8.05 million shares of US Steel common.
24 September 1992	144	USX	9 million share IPO of Delhi Group common.
15 October 1992	524	GM	29 million GM-H common shares (21.5 million shares sold on behalf of General Dynamics) in connection with the acquisition by Hughes Aircraft of General Dynamics' missile business.
11 February 1993	345	USX	6.9 million shares of USX preferred stock convertible into US Steel common.
22 July 93	326	USX	10 million shares of US Steel common.
24 January 1994	80.5	Pittston	161,000 shares of Pittston preferred stock convertible into Minerals Group common.
26 January 1994	185	USX	5 million shares of US Steel common.
April 1995	220	Fletcher Challenge	160 million Forest Division shares out of retained interest held by Ordinary Division.
28 April 1995	578	GM	15 million shares of GM-H common stock (sold by Hughes Medical Institute).
May 1995	75	Fletcher Challenge	54 million Forest Division shares out of retained interest held by Ordinary Division.
9 June 1995	1,540	GM	37 million shares of GM-E common stock (all secondary for GM pension plans)
21 July 1995	169	USX	5 million shares of US Steel common stock.
21 July 1995	124	CMS	7 million share IPO of Class G common stock of Consumers Gas Group
21 September 1995	45	Genzyme	3 million shares of Genzyme Tissue Repair Group common.
12 October 1995	128	Genzyme	2.87 million shares of Genzyme General Group common.
17 October 1995	53	American Health	2.5 million shares of American Health Properties Acute Care Group common.
9 January 1996	200	TCI	2 million shares of preferred stock exchangeable into TCI Group common.

The main benefits

Strategic

Targeted stock is a viable restructuring alternative that should be considered along with a spin-off, divestiture or IPO of a subsidiary. It has the significant advantage of allowing the group board to maintain full control of the targeted business and keeping the group together whilst at the same time achieving many of the advantages typically associated with a spin-off.

Targeted stock may deter hostile approaches, serving as a poison pill, as in most cases businesses would be more highly valued following the introduction of targeted stock. In addition, a hostile party would have to buy control of all the classes of targeted stock, particularly in the case of the floating vote concept (where the relative voting power of a particular class in relation to other classes of targeted stock fluctuates according to the market value of that particular class.), rather than just one, making a takeover sub-

stantially more complex. Take over defence was one important consideration for TCI, the US cable company, in going down the targeted stock route rather than spinning-off Liberty Media Group.

Targeted stock is a less radical form of a corporate break-up, and one that may less often lead to legal suits by creditors.

Financing tool

Targeted stock can allow broader, deeper and more flexible access to the equity market as different stories can be sold to the market at different times. A good example of this is the case of GM which was able to finance through GM-E and GM-H at a time when the car business was doing extremely badly and where an offer of GM automotive stock was virtually impossible.

Companies that have used targeted stock typically

enjoy a higher debt rating and lower debt cost than if they had separated by way of spin-off. USX, sometimes referred to as the most restructured corporation in the US, was extremely anxious to maintain its credibility with the bond market and prided itself on having virtually covenant-free bond and credit agreements and almost no secured debt. It was of utmost importance to maintain this situation, hence the attraction of targeted stock (see Exhibit 20).

Value enhancement

Targeted stock also promotes value enhancement, establishing a quasi-pure play and removing or reducing any conglomerate discount by ensuring that all parts of a group are efficiently valued. Gallatin commented: 'Targeted stock makes a lot of sense for any company where the sum of the parts is greater than the whole from an equity standpoint – but where for any number of reasons there aren't going to be multiple spin-offs.'

Groups using targeted stock enjoy better equity research coverage than they would have as conglomerates. With targeted stock, the disclosure of a group automatically increases, as more information is provided on each targeted business than is typical when a group is trading as a conglomerate. Moreover, the existence of separate equity securities enables the market to trade on this information in a manner which would be unlikely to occur with a single conglomerate stock.

There is substantial flexibility in the initial notional allocation of goodwill, purchase accounting adjustments, other intangibles and interest expense, which may substantially enhance overall group valuation. GM, for example, allocated over US$6 billion of goodwill/intangibles to its low P/E car company and away from the higher P/E GM-E and GM-H in order that the classes trading at the highest P/E multiples would show the biggest net profits. There is also increased dividend payment flexibility, as the board can set the dividend levels of each targeted stock to reflect the performance of its underlying targeted business relative to comparable companies.

Tax efficiency

Targeted stock can also be tax efficient as no capital gains tax exposure is generated because the distribution of targeted stock is not a taxable event. In the case of a spin-off this depends on the tax jurisdiction and the particular circumstances. There is no income tax to pay on the part of the shareholders as the creation of a new targeted stock typically represents a tax-free recapitalisation. A targeted stock structure typically generates a lower consolidated income tax bill than in the case of a spin-off, as net operating losses in one part of the business can be used to offset profits in another unit (as was the case for USX in 1991 when the steel losses shielded the energy profits). A single legal entity is maintained for administrative, tax and credit purposes, keeping overheads low.

The drawbacks

Some say that the structure allows directors to transfer resources from one targeted business to another at will, while lawyers maintain that there are numerous impediments to that sort of behaviour and that directors who did try something of the kind would lay themselves open to lawsuits. In the case of USX for example, this type of action is precluded by the company's charter.

Certain conflicts of interest may arise however, between the different classes of shares which either vote jointly or separately, despite the fact that the board of directors has a fiduciary responsibility to ensure that it acts in the best interests of all shareholders. Instances when divergent shareholder interests may occur include the declaration of dividends, cash acquisitions leading to higher indebtedness for the group, major dispositions, repurchasing of stock, intragroup pricing policy, etc. Both GM and USX have addressed this issue by setting up a committee of outside directors to handle divergent interests.

This problem does not really occur in the case of bankruptcy as there are no separate legal entities. It is only when there is a bankruptcy scenario in one part of the business that the trading pattern of a targeted stock would begin to be influenced by the financial performance of other parts of the legal entity. Lehman's Gallatin explained: 'If you own the side that is earning US$3 per share, you don't care if the other side earns US$2, US$1 or US$0.50, but you do care if they lose US$12, because if they lose all their money the next dollar they lose is yours.' When there is a serious risk of bankruptcy in one part of the business, the targeted stock concept does not work as designed and the trading price of the healthy business will be negatively affected by the bankruptcy risk in the other business.

Some people are concerned about the fact that investors only earn an income stream rather than directly own the underlying business. Brian Finn, managing director of CSFB disagrees: 'That concern is way overblown. If I buy a share in IBM, what does it really entitle me to? There is some myth that it entitles me to the assets, but what I'm really entitled to is a passive participation in the earnings stream of the company. I'm never going to be a big enough shareholder to control the company; I am never going to have any influence; and they're never going to liquidate and distribute the assets. I am relying principally on the board of directors that I elected to create value. And if it does go bust, I'll get nothing because the creditors will get to it before me. So tell me how targeted stock is different to that?'

Some observers feel that targeted stock is only a half-measure. A senior corporate financier with one of the bulge-bracket firms commented: 'If it's a good idea to split up the company, then it is a good idea to go all the way.'

Professor Carliss Baldwin of Harvard Business School reflected in the March 1993 issue of *CFO Magazine*: 'Targeted stock is most suitable as a temporary arrangement

Exhibit 21

Targeted stock deals to the end of 1996

Date	Company	Security/classes	Underlying business	Adviser(s)
September 1984	GM	• GM–E[1] • GM– US$1.66 common	• EDS • Automotive	Morgan Stanley/ Salomon
October 1985	GM	• GM–H	• Hughes Aircraft	Morgan Stanley/ CSFB
May 1991	USX	• USX-Steel • USX-Marathon •	• Steel Oil and gas	Lehman Brothers
September 1992	USX	• USX-Delhi	• Gas	Lehman Brothers
July 1993	The Pittston Company	• Pittston–Minerals • Pittston–Services[2]	• Coal • Air Express & Security Services	CSFB
July 1993	Ralston Purina	• Continental Baking[3] • Ralston Purina	• Fresh baked goods • Cereal, baby food, etc.	Lehman Brothers
November 1993	Fletcher Challenge	• Forest Division • Ordinary Division[4]	• Fast growing forests • Paper, pulp, etc.	CSFB
December 1994	Genzyme Corporation	• General Division • Tissue Repair •	• Surgical, therapeutic and diagnostic products Human tissue repair products	CSFB
July 1995	CMS Energy	• CMS Energy • Class G	• Electric utility and other operations • Consumer gas utility	Morgan Stanley/ Merrill Lynch
July 1995	American Health Properties	• Core Group • Psychiatric Group	• Acute care • Psychiatric care	Goldman Sachs
August 1995	Tele-Communications Inc.	• TCI Group • Liberty Media Group	• Cable operator • Cable programming	CSFB/ Lehman Brothers
October 1995	US West	• Media Group • Communications Group	• Multimedia • Telecom operator	Lehman Brothers/ Morgan Stanley
August 1996	Inco Ltd	• Class VBN Shares • Inco Ordinary	• Voisey's Bay mining project • Rest of Inco	Morgan Stanley/ Smith Barney/ CSFB
August 1996	Delmarva Power & Atlantic Energy[5]	• Class A common • Holding Company	• Atlantic Energy (regulated business) • Rest of merged group	Merrill Lynch/ Morgan Stanley
November 1996	Circuit City Stores[5]	• Carl Max Group • Circuit City Group	• Automobile retailing • Consumer appliance goods retailing	Morgan Stanley
November 1996	Epitope Inc[5]	• Agritope • Epitope Medical Products	• Agricultural business • Medical products	N/A

[1] Split off from GM as EDS Corporation in June 1996.

[2] Replaced by Pittston Brinks Group common stock and Pittston Burlington Group common stock in January 1996.

[3] Exchanged for Ralston Purina in May 1995.

[4] The ordinary division common stock was replaced by three new classes representing the paper, energy and building divisions in March 1996.

[5] Pending.

designed to preserve the existing corporate structure. It looks to me like a good interim structure – a way to get to something. But I don't see it as a likely long-term solution.' He added: 'The principal justification for this form, as opposed to a full-scale splitting apart, is interim issues such as tax shields. Issuing targeted stock is, in effect, a reversible experiment in splitting up.'

Parts of the US financial press have taken a negative attitude towards targeted stock, perhaps because they are confused about the concept and they have focused on the proposed targeted stocks for RJR Nabisco and K-mart Corporation, both of which never happened. In the case of the Nabisco IPO, shareholder approval was obtained for the offer, but because the offer price was not acceptable to the vendor, it did not go ahead. This was not primarily because there was something wrong with the targeted stock concept, but rather because the price of branded consumer products fell by 15 per cent during the marketing period, as a result of the highly publicised Marlboro price cut. In the case of K-mart, shareholders did not approve the restructuring proposed by K-mart's CEO, which had more to do with the lack of confidence in the management team rather than with a flaw with the targeted stock concept itself.

Targeted stock deals to date

As at the end of 1996 a total of 33 targeted stocks (including the GM US$1.66) had been either issued or announced. Of these, 24 stocks traded in the public market, three transactions had been pulled and six more targeted stock transactions were pending (see Exhibit 21).

Why do deals happen?

GM: GM-E and GM-H

GM-E stock was created as an acquisition currency in connection with GM's US$2.5 billion acquisition of EDS, because the seller, Ross Perot – the Texan entrepreneur and former presidential candidate – did not wish to be paid with ordinary GM stock. In addition, the managers of EDS were more easily compensated for their performance using GM-E stock than if they had simply been given GM stock.

GM-E initially worked well because EDS was already a well known and liquid stock before GM's acquisition. At the time of the creation of GM-E, some 71 per cent of EDS's revenues came from GM: however, as that proportion declined and as GM came to the view that it no longer needed to own assets of EDS to have access to its technology, the rationale for GM-E targeted stock ceased to be apparent. Furthermore it is thought that the two management teams could not get on and that EDS wanted more independence. The eventual reversal of the GM-E stock in May 1996 should be seen in the overall context of the restructuring of GM's balance sheet.

GM-H was created as part consideration for the acquisition by GM of Hughes Aircraft. Unlike EDS, Hughes Aircraft had not previously been a quoted stock. Lack of liquidity has clearly been an issue with GM-H stock, although as additional GM-H shares were sold in the market, the liquidity gradually improved, first in October 1992, when Hughes Aircraft bought the missile business of General Dynamics and paid with GM-H shares, and subsequently in April 1995, when GM sold already outstanding GM-H shares on behalf of the Hughes Medical Institute (from which GM had purchased the Hughes business in 1985).

The Pittston Company: Pittston–Minerals and Pittston–Services

Pittston initiated a share capital restructuring in 1993, to improve the valuation of the company. It estimated that the savings in corporate overheads, including taxes, interest expense and administrative cost, would be US$25 million a year compared to a spin-off structure.

At the beginning of 1996 the company replaced the services stock created in 1993 with Burlington stock and Brinks stock. The idea was to create a more pure play investment opportunity. Burlington stock represents the air-freight forwarding business, and the Brinks stock represents the residential electronic security and armoured car divisions. These stocks were distributed tax-free to holders of Pittston Services stock. Pittston's three targeted stocks had an aggregate market value of approximately US $1.7 billion in mid-1996.

Fletcher Challenge: Forest Division and Ordinary Division

The analysts that had traditionally covered New Zealand conglomerate Fletcher Challenge had little idea of how to value the fast-growing Forest Division and the company was anxious to maintain a strong link between this and the main pulp and paper businesses as they together represented a resource-to-market chain. The Ordinary Division initially kept 49.5 per cent of the Forest Division as retained interest, having initially distributed 50.5 per cent to the Ordinary Division shareholders however, this was eventually reduced to 0 per cent.

After creating Forest stock and Ordinary stock in 1993, Fletcher Challenge created Paper stock, Energy stock and Building stock to replace Ordinary stock in 1996. The objective remained to create more focused pure play investment opportunities. The new classes of stock were distributed tax-free to holders of Ordinary Division stock. Fletcher Challenge's four targeted stocks had a total market value of just under US$4 billion in mid-1996.

Inco Ltd: Class VBN Shares and Inco Ordinary

In April 1996 Inco Ltd of Canada made an agreed C$ 4.3 billion cash and securities offer for Diamond Fields Resources, also of Canada. Part of the total consideration to be paid by Inco to Diamond Fields shareholders was a newly created security, Inco Class VBN Shares, which was designed to reflect a 25 per cent interest in the financial performance of the Voisey's Bay mining project and all future discoveries in Labrador, as well as in its existing exploration properties in Norway and Greenland. By structuring Inco Class VBN Shares as a separate class of Inco parent company stock, Diamond Field's selling shareholders were able to retain a direct interest in the much coveted nickel-copper-cobalt project.

Tele Communications Inc: TCI and Liberty Media Group

The rationale behind this targeted stock was mainly the impossibility of a tax-free spin-off. In addition, there were strategic reasons to maintain a closer relationship than is possible contractually between the main cable business and Liberty's programming assets.

TCI-Liberty Media Group targeted stock was structured such that TCI would be able to dispose of Liberty Media without invoking the disposition provision which requires the targeted stockholders to be bought out. This was a development on previous targeted stocks, and was

Exhibit 22

Targeted stock versus spin-off

	Advantages	Disadvantages
Spin-off	• A clearer separation between businesses may lead to a higher motivation of management; • No danger of contamination of healthy business in case of a bankruptcy of spun-off business; • In a spin-off, the company, even if it is small, will get more attention from a dedicated and fully independent board; • If for a valid business purpose and if structured properly, it is not typically a taxable event – either at company or at shareholder level; • The US Internal Revenue Service has traditionally provided a tax ruling in advance of announcement.	• Substantial incremental cost of completely severing the companies; • If not structured properly and under certain circumstances, it may be subject to taxation, both at the company and shareholder levels; • Group tax consolidation not available; • Often involves complex discussion with creditors as to how to split the debt; • Lower debt rating and higher debt cost; • Difficult to reverse; • A relatively high risk of lawsuits from creditors.
Targeted stock	• If structured properly, it is typically not a taxable event – either at company or at shareholder level; • Under certain circumstances lower consolidated tax on an ongoing basis; • Only one board and corporate management; • Lower overall administration cost; • Higher rating and lower debt cost; • Relatively limited risk of lawsuits from creditors in connection with restructuring; • Relatively easy to reverse; • Can to a degree act as a deterrent to a hostile takeover; • Maintains corporate empire – more acceptable to a management which is reluctant to restructure; • Increases financing flexibility; • Creates additional acquisition currency.	• Higher reporting cost than with a single class of shares; • Higher degree of complexity; • Potential concerns regarding corporate governance; • A targeted stock, representing only a small portion of the total equity of a company, may not be given sufficient attention from a pre-occupied board; • IRS will not provide a ruling in advance as to the tax-free status of a proposed targeted stock structure; • The holders of targeted stock share in the liabilities of the other business groups – the concept does not work in a bankruptcy scenario.

designed to give TCI the flexibility to conduct a joint venture or subsidiary merger without triggering the redemption of the targeted stock.

The original version of the TCI targeted stock structure would have incorporated five individual targeted stocks, one each for four major business areas and one that would have held the retained interest in the other four. This structure was ultimately considered too complicated and was dropped in favour of only two targeted stocks.

Targeted stock compared to a spin-off

Targeted stock is a less far-reaching way of creating a pure play than a spin-off, ie, where the parent company stockholders receive a new share in an independent subsidiary. Targeted stock implies a much higher degree of corporate integration and control. Other restructuring alternatives, such as a full IPO, where a company sells shares for cash or a divestiture, are similar to a spin-off in severing corporate integration and control, while a partial IPO may be somewhere in between the spin-off and targeted stock in this regard (see Exhibit 22).

The principal structural variations

There is considerable structuring flexibility to take account of the particular circumstances of each targeted stock. Some of the more important issues to consider when structuring such stock include:

- *Fixed or floating voting rights:* Floating voting rights were introduced for the first time in connection with USX targeted stock, partly as a result of the case of GM, where the relative voting rights had been fixed and GM-E and GM-H shareholders felt that the automotive side had too much voting power compared to its declining market capitalisation. Many companies have since structured their targeted stocks with floating voting rights with the relative rights being recalculated once a year, not least for anti-takeover purposes. In the case of The Pittston Company, the calculation is performed only every two years;

- *Disposition rights:* In the case of a sale of the targeted business, the targeted shareholders can either participate fully, including a take over premium (as envisaged in USX), or have a limited participation in any premium paid (GM-E);

- *Unwind mechanism:* the terms of targeted stock can allow the parent company the right to exchange one class of targeted stock for stock of another group either at any time (as was the case in the proposed Nabisco Foods IPO) or only if certain conditions are met, eg, the sale of at least 80 per cent of the underlying assets of the business group, as is the case with USX. Some targeted stock structures provide the exact options open to the board in the case of a sale of a substantial proportion of the assets of a targeted business and others leave the treatment of proceeds to the complete discretion of the board; and

- *Dividend rights:* Whether or not the calculation of the available dividend amount from which dividends are paid on targeted stock, takes into account the effects of new accounting principles such as FAS 106 (accounting for post-retirement healthcare services) can be decisive, as it may determine whether or not dividends can actually be paid on a particular targeted stock (eg, USX-US Steel, where incorporation of FAS 106 in the dividend calculation would have hit very hard indeed). Whatever the alternative chosen, it must be disclosed in the original proxy materials.

When to use targeted stock

Any company considering a spin-off, a divestiture or an IPO of a subsidiary or a division should seriously consider targeted stock as a restructuring technique. It is particularly relevant if the activities underlying the targeted business are considered core in terms of the overall group strategy.

Other reasons to go down the targeted stock route include:

- When the investor community is prepared to put a higher value on pure plays than a conglomerate and when a full spin-off is not desirable. James Hartough, treasurer of Pittston explained: 'It's an example of how the efficient market theory doesn't work.' Before Pittston announced the targeted stock transaction in March 1993 the share price was US$15.625: at the end of 1993 the combined value of the two stocks was US$34. The market value of the group doubled without any management or operating changes, although it is difficult to argue that this increase was directly attributable to the introduction of targeted stock. Hartough adds: 'We gave the shareholders what they already had, but we gave it to them in two separate pieces';
- When the approaches to valuation are clearly different between the various business groups: if, for example, one business is valued on a price/cash flow basis whereas another one is valued on a price/earnings basis (eg, the proposed Nabisco Foods targeted stock IPO); if one business is growing fast and the other is not (Fletcher Challenge); or if one business is regulated and the other is not (US West);
- When there are strong synergies and, therefore, good reasons for a continued close relationship between the main company and a targeted business: this was one of the most important considerations behind Fletcher Challenge's decision to target its Forest Division in

November 1993, leaving the paper, pulp, energy and construction businesses under the Ordinary Division. Barry Akers, head of investor relations at Fletcher Challenge explained: 'We wanted to maintain the link because the forestry activity is an important one, not only for its own virtues but also because we have a resource-to-market chain as a company, and forestry is an important resource';

- In the case of an acquisition, when the buyer is not in a position to pay cash and the vendor not prepared to accept as consideration the shares of the buyer (eg, GM's acquisitions of EDS and Genzyme Corporation's acquisition of Biosurface); this way of paying selling shareholders may be particularly suitable when entrepreneurs who have created their businesses have been bought out;
- Many companies look at targeted stock from a financing point of view, as improved access to the equity market can evidently be gained through this structure (USX); and
- When a management or a board of directors is compelled to do something to enhance shareholder value, but is not prepared to give up control, targeted stock can provide a solution.

Reversal

A targeted business may be spun-off, sold in a public offer or divested; there is nothing about a targeted stock structure that is irreversible, affording full flexibility to fold the targeted stock businesses back into the parent company stock. So far there are only a limited number of cases of reversal, including Ralston Purina's Continental Baking targeted stock, structured in June 1993, and GM-E, first issued in 1984, in connection with GM's take over of EDS.

In the case of GM-E, a first attempt at reversal was made in 1993 when GM was on the verge of selling EDS to BT of the UK for a large premium. Because the GM-E stock provided that the GM-E shareholders be restricted in connection with the exchange to a 20 per cent premium to the average GM-E stock price during the 20-day period prior to the announcement, the sale did not go through. The structure of the stock was one of the principal reasons why this merger did not go through; similar problems were encountered in connection with a proposed merger between EDS and Sprint in early 1994. Targeted stocks announced subsequently have had much more flexible terms with respect to unwinding provisions.

In June 1996 all classes of GM common stock approved a spin-off, whereby the holders of GM-E stock, including GM's pension fund, would receive newly issued EDS stock on a 1:1 basis. In December 1995 GM had received a ruling from the US tax authorities that the spin-off would be tax-free, ie, that no capital gains tax would be payable by GM and no income tax would be payable by investors in

GM-E stock. GM said the spin-off was intended to accomplish three objectives for EDS: first, to enhance its ability to participate in strategic alliances; second, to enable it to obtain additional business from and establish relationships with companies that compete with GM or its subsidiaries; and third, to enhance its access to the capital necessary for growth.

Why so few companies use targeted stock

In the US there is some uncertainty concerning the tax treatment due to the absence of specific laws and the IRS does not issue rulings regarding targeted stock. In the case of spin-offs, however, most tax lawyers have historically agreed that the tax situation is relatively clear, ie, that tax-free spin-offs are permissible in the US.

In certain European countries it has been possible to conduct tax-free spin-offs (eg, the Zeneca demerger), which takes away one important advantage of targeted stock.

Further reasons for not going ahead, depending on the jurisdiction, include the fact that a qualified majority may be required to alter the articles of association (while only a simple majority is required in the US) and the issue of pre-emptive rights. A further obstacle to the adoption of the targeted stock concept in certain non-US jurisdictions is inalienable rights, which prevent a shareholder from agreeing to waive his rights with respect to certain aspects of the company (eg, the creation of a new class of shares with different dividend rights), as this might cause existing stock to forfeit certain of its existing rights.

Most importantly, however, it appears that nobody wants to be the first with all the work and exposure that goes with it, and the press has taken an unnecessarily negative attitude, perhaps due to a lack of understanding of the issues involved. Less than a handful of US investment banks, most notably Lehman Brothers, CSFB and Morgan Stanley, have experience in an advisory capacity, and this may be a good enough reason for other investment banks to recommend against it.

Wellcome

When Sir Henry Wellcome died in 1936, he left all the shares of what later became Wellcome plc to be held in charitable trusts, today collectively known as the Wellcome Trust. The trustees held 100 per cent of the Welcome Company until it went public in 1986. At the time when the Wellcome Company became Wellcome plc in February 1986, it was valued at £1 billion and interestingly enough rated on precisely the same price/earnings (P/E) ratio as Glaxo. With a portfolio valued at £10 billion (1 August 1997), the Wellcome Trust is the largest charitable trust in the world. Its object is to advance research in human and animal medicine 'for the benefit of mankind' and to support the study of the history of medicine.

The impressive performance of Wellcome plc, as evidenced by an increase in market capitalisation from £1 billion in February 1986 to £9.7 billion by March 1992, meant that the Trust's investment in the company had come to represent 95 per cent of its income-producing assets. Despite the expectation of continued strong performance, this concentration of assets in a single investment was deemed inappropriate. The decision was taken to reduce the Trust's stake in Wellcome plc from 73.5 per cent to below 50 per cent and possibly down to 25 per cent, subject to investor demand. The importance of asset diversification was not likely to be overlooked by Sir Roger Gibbs, the Trust's chairman since 1989. His father, a distinguished banker, battled unsuccessfully for many years in his capacity as chairman of the Nuffield Foundation between 1949 and 1972, to persuade Lord Nuffield to diversify out of shares in the ailing British Motor Corporation. Lord Nuffield had said: 'My foundation rises or

falls on the fortunes of my original bicycle shop'. It fell. Sir Roger was not likely to let the same thing happen to the Wellcome Trust.

Prior to the 1992 sale, the Wellcome Trust had divested a portion of its stake in the February 1986 IPO. Despite the fact that the Trust only managed to sell a further 33.5 per cent of Wellcome plc, at the time this was the largest ever private offer of a non-US company in the US market, and the first major UK non-privatisation to incorporate US-style bookbuilding.

The sale was completed under difficult market conditions and clearly demonstrated the effectiveness of bookbuilding in a falling market. The presence of short sellers in this offer and their impact on the price during the marketing period led to the London Stock Exchange initiating an intensive dialogue with its member firms on the impact of short selling in large equity offers. The key lessons of the offer include the critical importance of timetable and timing issues and the value of a good working relationship between the vendor and the company in a secondary sale of shares.

Sir Roger Gibbs started preparing for the sale in March 1991 in order to be ready when the right market opportunity presented itself. He recognised early on that, from the market's point of view, at least two things were necessary for a successful offer: a progressive dividend policy needed to be introduced, and the prospects for the company had to be excellent. In addition, the Charity Commissioners had to be convinced about the merits of further diversification of the Wellcome Trust's asset base to allow the Trust to reduce its holding to below 50 per cent.

Exhibit 1
Transaction summary

Issuer name: Wellcome Plc (United Kingdom)	Global coordinator: Robert Fleming & Co. Limited
Pricing date: 27 July 1992	Pricing/underwriting structure: Bookbuilding
Vendor: The Trustees of The Wellcome Trust	Primary or secondary: Secondary
	Retail structure: –
% of company sold: 33.5%	Privatisation or corporate: Corporate
IPO or non-IPO: Non-IPO	Industry: Pharmaceuticals
Type of shares: Ordinary shares and ADRs	Offer price: £8.00/Ordinary share and US$15.25/ADR
Total issue size: US$4,420 million	US listing/144 A: NYSE listing

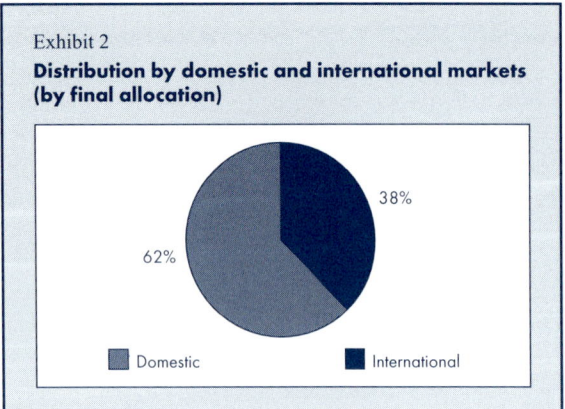

Exhibit 2

Distribution by domestic and international markets (by final allocation)

38%

62%

■ Domestic   ■ International

On 1 November 1991 the company's dividend for the year ending 31 August 1991 was increased from 6.5 pence to 10 pence, which meant that over a two-year period the dividend had been doubled and dividend cover (profits over dividends) reduced from four to three times. This decision significantly contributed to the increase in the share price from £7.50 in late October 1991, to £11.73 in early February 1992.

The change of dividend policy had been brought about by two particular developments. The first was the July 1990 arrival of a more commercially-minded senior management team in the form of Sir Alistair Frame (former chairman of Rio Tinto Zinc) as chairman, and John Robb (the former group managing director of Beecham) as chief executive. Second was the interest expressed by the Trust in a higher payout. The company was traditionally viewed as an academic research institution rather than a commercial enterprise and the change in its dividend policy, taken with the arrival of the dynamic new senior management, showed that it was taking a more commercial direction.

The higher payout ratio also created confidence in the company's prospects, which had never been better. It's two most important drugs, Zovirax (for use in the treatment of herpes, shingles and chicken pox) and Retrovir (used to combat AIDS and HIV), which together accounted for 44 per cent of 1991 group sales and had an average market share of 81 per cent, were expected to achieve sales growth of 18 and 20 per cent respectively.

In early 1992 the Trust decided that, on the basis of the company's excellent underlying trading projections and consciousness of the exposure to a single asset in the portfolio, the time was right to push ahead with further diversification of the portfolio through another sale of shares. The sale enabled the Trust to switch out of Wellcome plc shares, yielding 1.7 per cent, into a broad spread of equities yielding 5 per cent.

Major challenges

Timing the share sale presented a major challenge. This was because of the following factors:

- Scheduling an offer in light of the fact that the UK general election could take place any time before June 1992. The uncertainty associated with the general election would make it difficult to execute a share sale of this magnitude. The date of the general election was only fixed (at 9 April) in mid-March;

- It was necessary to petition the courts, which required a period of advance notice and, therefore, publicity;

- There were certain constraints as to the availability of the High Court and the final court hearing took place on 30th April. The ruling on whether or not the Trust would be allowed to sell below 50 per cent, as was finally decided, could not be taken for granted;

- A major AIDS conference was scheduled to take place in Amsterdam during the third week of July. It would have been difficult to go to the market too close to such a conference, as institutions would probably have held back their orders due to concerns that negative information on Retrovir might be about to come out. John Woolland, then a director of SG Warburg said: 'It would have been irresponsible to go before the conference, as institutions would clearly not have had the confidence to bid aggressively';

- There was also the question of which financials the offer was going to be based on as the interim results for the six months to 28 February were to be announced on 26 March. For US regulatory reasons, an offer cannot take place on the basis of stale accounts, ie, accounts that are more than six months old. This meant that the offer could take place up to the end of August: however as this is holiday season in Europe, it really meant that it had to be launched before the end of July at the latest, or else postponed until the announcement of the full year results, year ending 31 August, which was not expected until November; and

- The issue of the US presidential election also had to be taken into consideration. Because of the importance of the US market both to the company and to the offer, and even before considering the significance of the Clinton plans to reform the US healthcare system, the decision was taken that the sale had to be carried out well before the US Presidential election in November 1992.

The net effect of these considerations was that there was really only one weekend during which pricing and allocation of the offer was advisable.

Prevailing market conditions also presented a significant challenge to the sale of the 33.5 per cent stake. Initially strong stock markets in the UK and US deteriorated during the first half of 1992. Heavy supply hampered the new issue market, with IPOs typically being priced at, or below the lower end of their filing ranges during the second quarter. Many large issues, such as Irish aircraft leasing company GPA, US beverage company Dr.Pepper and cosmetics company Revlon, were either cancelled or postponed. Although a favourable US interest rate environment was underpinning the Dow Jones Index at high valuations, the reverse was true in Europe, with increasing talk of a hike in German interest rates. Towards the end of the marketing period the latest US economic statistics cast doubts on the strength of the recovery. During the final weeks before the pricing the press was full of headlines such as 'general investor fatigue', 'lack of liquidity' and 'significant uncertainty over the US economic recovery'.

Nor was it simply the UK political situation that complicated affairs. On 24 July, the last day of bookbuilding, James Baker, the US secretary of state, delivered an ultimatum to Iraqi leader Saddam Hussein to the effect that unless the United Nations was given permission to inspect Iraqi nuclear facilities, the US would be forced to consider further military action in Iraq. The FTSE 100 index immediately fell by 35 points. When asked about this Sir Roger admitted: 'This was the only fractionally unsettling moment of the six month's exercise'. If a United Nations supported attack had gone ahead, the sale would most probably have been postponed.

The Iraqi crisis probably slowed the final surge of demand out of the US, and generating international interest in the offer was another major challenge. Following the 1986 IPO, the company had achieved only limited international name recognition. There was little incentive for the company to concentrate on further promotion given the limited size of the free float. By mid-1991, only a few non-UK houses published regular equity research on the company and it had still not made any presentations to investors outside the UK. Market research carried out prior to the 1992 offer estimated that the Wellcome plc awareness factor was 70 per cent in the UK, 25 per cent in Continental Europe and 3 per cent in the US. Only 2 per cent of the company's shares were owned outside the UK.

A further challenge was presented by the company's high valuation at the time of the offer. In early 1992, the company was trading at a historically high P/E ratio of almost 40 with a dividend yield of just 1.5 per cent.

is a charitable trust charged with the promotion of medical research in a wide sense; as such it requires a growing and broadly spread source of income. 'Although we thought that prospects for the company remained excellent, the case for diversifying further seemed overwhelming', says Sir Roger. It was the Trust's objective to reduce its shareholding in Wellcome plc to below 50 per cent by way of a successful global offer and to maintain a long-term holding of at least 25 per cent.

This was the case that was presented to the Charity Commissioners and the High Court. The will of the late Sir Henry Wellcome provided that if any unforeseen circumstances should arise in the future which, in the opinion of the trustees, would represent an unavoidable reason for sale, then it would be legal for the trustees to sell, with the consent of the High Court. However, the Trustees were advised, prior to the flotation that it was doubtful whether any such power could validly be conferred by the Court and it was therefore necessary to rely on the general law if they wished to obtain a power to reduce their shareholding. It was in these circumstances that a power was sought from the Charity Commissioners. On 1 May 1992, the High Court and the Charity Commissioners ruled that the need to diversify fulfilled these criteria and that a sale of shares to bring the Wellcome Trust's stake to below 50 per cent would be legal.

The proceeds from the sale were received entirely by the Trust, enabling it to enlarge and broaden its income to meet the ever-increasing demands of medical research. As a result of the offer, the Wellcome Trust's income from investments doubled to £220 million, enabling it to continue as the largest grant-giving charity in the world.

Rationale and objectives

It made sense for the Wellcome Trust to diversify its investments, primarily to avoid and over-concentration of risk, but also in this case to increase its income. The Wellcome Trust

Share capital and ownership

See Exhibit 3.

Exhibit 3
Share capital and ownership

Share capital before and after offer	860,368,808 ordinary shares
Listings	London – February 1986/ New York – July 1992
Market capitalisation at offer price (US$1.9183)	US$13.2 billion
Major shareholder(s) before/after offer	Wellcome Trust 73.5%/40%
Number of shareholders before offer	Approximately 46,000
Free float before offer	26.5%
Liquidity	24% in London (Number of shares traded during the 12 months to 24 June, 1992, expressed as a percentage of the total number of shares outstanding) Fourth most liquid stock on the LSE during the 12 months to 24 June 1992, in terms of value traded, and the 15th largest by market capitalisation on 27 July 1992.
Foreign ownership before offer	Less than 2%
Most important stock exchange index/Wellcome's weighting	Wellcome was included in the FTSE 100 from 1986. In June 1992, Wellcome's weighting in the index was 2.01%. The weighting was not affected as a result of the offer.

Transaction components

At the time of the March 1992 announcement by the trustees of their intention to sell shares in Wellcome plc, the maximum size of the issue was estimated at about 417 million shares. On 25 June 1992 when the preliminary prospectus was published, the size of the offer had been reduced to 330 million shares, excluding the 15 per cent greenshoe option. However, due to the adverse market conditions prevailing towards the end of the bookbuilding period, it became clear that the Trust was only going to sell 270 million shares, excluding the greenshoe. (See Exhibit 4.)

The bookbuilding method used in pricing and underwriting the transaction involves setting the offer price at the end of the bookbuilding period, which provides flexibility in sizing. The offer is only underwritten after pricing.

The offer was structured as a single international offer, divided into eight regional selling syndicates and one retail syndicate which, for purposes of pricing and allocation, would form one global order book. Unlike most UK privatisations it was a fully-paid offer with no particular retail incentives. Sir Roger Gibbs said: 'We were not in the business of promoting wider share ownership in the UK, but rather maximising the price'. Up to £180 million of the offer was reserved for retail investors and there was priority allocation for existing shareholders at a value of up to £5,000.

The deal was structured with a 17-month lock-up period and there was an undertaking on the part of the Trust not to

---

Exhibit 4
Development of the offer size

Indicated number of shares to be sold	330 million + 50 million greenshoe
Offer size after decrease of offer size	270 million + 40.5 million greenshoe
Amount of greenshoe exercised	18 million
Final number of shares sold	288 million

Exhibit 5
Offer structure

Target markets	Indicated tranche sizes*	Bookrunning lead managers	Co-lead managers
UK **	62.6%	SG Warburg	Cazenove, Robert Fleming, James Capel, BZW, Hoare Govett, NM Rothschild & Smith New Court
UK public offer**	–	Robert Fleming	–
US	23.7%	Morgan Stanley	Lehman Brothers, Merrill Lynch, Robert Fleming Japan
	5.4%	Nikko Securities	Nomura Securities, Daiwa Securities, Yamaichi Securities, Baring Securities (Japan), Jardine Fleming Securities
International	3.4%	Robert Fleming	Kleinwort Benson, Wood Gundy
Switzerland	2.5%	Swiss Bank Corporation	CSFB, UBS P&D Securities, Robert Fleming
Germany	1.3%	Dresdner	Deutsche Bank, Robert Fleming
France	0.8%	Crédit Lyonnais	Banque Indosuez, Paribas Capital Markets, Robert Fleming
Far East	0.3%	Jardine Fleming	Buttle Wilson, Development Bank of Singapore, JB Were
Total combined offers (shares)	**330,000,000**		

* % of indicated total offer on 25 June 1992.
**£180 million-worth at the offer price was reserved for retail applicants

---

Exhibit 6
Principal advisers

Global coordinator	Robert Fleming & Co Limited
Financial adviser to the Wellcome Trust	Robert Fleming & Co Limited
Financial adviser to Wellcome plc	Baring Brothers & Co Limited
Legal adviser to the Wellcome Trust	Cameron Markby Hewitt
Legal adviser to Wellcome plc	Slaughter and May
Legal adviser to the managers	Linklaters & Paines

Exhibit 7
The timetable

2 March 1992	• The Trust announces intention to reduce its holding in Wellcome plc to below 50%.
4 June	• Announcement of structure (without regional sizing) and timing of offer, confidential filing with SEC on form F-3, publication of international preliminary prospectus and US 'Pink Herring'; and • International pre-marketing programme and retail marketing begin.
24 June	• Execution of international tender offer agreement.
25 June	• Announcement of provisional size – 330 million shares, 80 million to be placed in the US; • Publication of international offer circular and US 'Red Herring '; • First amendment to F-3 Registration statement; and • Timetable for tender offer announced.
26 June	• UK and international roadshow commences.
6 July	• Bookbuilding commences. US roadshow begins.
16 July	• US roadshow ends.
21 July	• Last day for retail applications.
23 July	• Second amendment to F-3. F-3 declared effective; and • Announcement of minimum price of £8.00
24 July	• Bookbuilding ends. Last day for institutional subscriptions.
25–26 July	• Analysis of 'book' and determination of tender price and allocation over week-end.
27 July	• Announcement of £8.00 offer price on Monday morning; • Allotment of shares to investors; • Underwriting effective; • London trading begins at 8.30am GMT; and • NYSE listing effective and New York trading begins.

Exhibit 8
Distribution of gross spread (%)

Management and underwriting combined	Selling concession	Gross spread	Discount	Total effective cost
1.4	2.1	3.5	3.15	6.65

sell any further shares prior to 1 January 1994. In any event the Trust intended to retain a long-term shareholding of at least 25 per cent. The issue was registered with the SEC in order to accommodate a public offer in the US and Wellcome plc's ADRs were listed on the New York Stock Exchange. (See Exhibit 5.)

Principal advisers

See Exhibit 6.

The timetable

See Exhibit 7.

Transaction fee distribution

Flemings was paid a global coordinators praecipium. There was also a lead and co-lead managers praecipium. The latter was split according to the size of the underwriting commitment; it came out of the total management and underwriting fee of 1.4 per cent. (See Exhibit 8.)

The selling concession of 2.1 per cent consisted of a fixed element, representing 50 per cent of the total, split among all banks according to underwriting commitments, and a vari-able element, representing the other 50 per cent of the total which, for the first time in the UK, was decided by the institutions on formal designation forms. A similar, but informal, process was used in the US.

Deal structure

Flemings recommended a global bookbuilding structure with the price being fixed at the end of the marketing period for both retail and institutional investors. There were no retail incentives such as bonus shares or discounts on the cash offer price, and the offer was fully paid.

As the share price was tumbling during the week before the close of the subscription period, the wisdom of selecting open-price bookbuilding was questioned. In a falling market few of the participants involved, other than the vendor itself, have a real interest in supporting the price, and the opportunity for the creation of price tension is lost.

But, it is obvious that US-style bookbuilding was the sensible and possibly the only structure available for the offer. It was estimated that a 10 per cent discount would have been required to get BT2, the December 1991 sale of the second tranche of UK telecoms company British Telecommunications, underwritten. Considering the much greater liquidity and name recognition of BT, it is conceivable that a discount of more than 20 per cent would have been required to get this offer underwritten, if indeed it would have been possible at all. Peter Wilmot-Sitwell, former chairman of Warburg Securities said: 'It is not inconceivable that an underwritten or non-underwritten cash placing with a discount of 5–10 per cent could have been done, however for a considerably smaller amount, which would probably not have enabled the Trust to achieve its objective of reducing its stake to below 50 per cent.' Given that Wellcome plc's reception in the US market was most probably going to make or break the transaction, it seemed particularly important to choose a structure with which US investors would be comfortable. US banks and investors had not forgotten the BP transaction which was underwritten only three business days before the 1987 stock market crash. During the beauty parade of potential lead managers, not one bank had recommended anything other than bookbuilding.

One of the principal benefits of bookbuilding is that it gives flexibility with respect to the offer size until the last moment. More than 400 million shares were potentially for sale, but after pre-marketing, the offer was launched on 25 June for330 million shares. The global coordinator estimated that, at an offer price of £8.00, a strong after-market could only be guaranteed with the sale of 270 million shares, plus a greenshoe option. After the pricing, it was possible, due to successful stabilisation and after-market marketing by the Trust, to sell a further 18 million shares as partial exercise of the greenshoe.

It is questionable whether, by generating more demand from UK retail investors, (albeit at a considerable cost), a larger sale could have been achieved at the same, or even a higher net price, ie, after taking the cost of retail incentives into account.

When you consider that in the case of Wellcome plc only £107 million of the issue was placed with UK retail investors, as against £3.5 billion (on a fully-paid basis) in the case of BT2, it is easy to assume that incurring the expense of some retail incentives might have been worthwhile. It is also conceivable that a partly-paid structure would have allowed a larger number to be sold at a higher price, since the company's low dividend yield was a constraint for attracting retail investors. A number of banks did recommend a partly-paid structure, but, because of the volatility of the stock, its limited liquidity and the enhanced profit opportunities for short sellers who would be able to cover their short positions with less than a full cash outlay, Flemings advised a fully-paid structure – a recommendation with which the Trust wholeheartedly agreed. Whereas a strategy involving more retail placement might possibly have seemed to be a reasonable idea at an early stage, it was probably fortunate, given the poor market conditions, that the offer was not expected to be underpinned by retail demand. If potential institutional investors had expected retail demand and that demand had not materialised, then the entire operation could have been destabilised.

Marketing

Given that Wellcome plc was hardly known outside the UK, that up to 48.5 per cent of the company was for sale and that this represented a potential issue size of US$8 billion at the time of announcement, this offer was almost akin to an international IPO and no effort was spared in marketing the company. In effect, marketing started on 2 March and continued until the offer closed on 24 July. This period was divided into several phases:

Phase 1 - Consultation (2 March - 10 May).
- Basic structure announced;
- All banks hoping to participate in the issue prepared for beauty parades;
- Beauty parades for lead manager positions; and
- The Wellcome Trust and Wellcome plc took the decision to leave County Natwest out of the syndicate to allow the investment community to have access to independent research.

Phase 2 - Education (11 May - 3 June).
- 700 'flagship' investors identified by the global coordinator in conjunction with the syndicate lead managers;
- Equity research published. Research should be published at least 30 days before the publication of the preliminary prospectus in order not to condition the market;
- Equity research analysts of US and European banks met with company management; and
- Regional syndicates constructed.

Phase 3 - Pre-marketing (4 June - 5 July).
- 'Pink Herring' published to provide for early US marketing;
- UK and US sales forces of lead managers briefed by Wellcome plc's management;
- Group of 25 salesmen from Japanese lead manager visited Wellcome plc's UK plants;
- 700 targeted investors visited by lead managers' analysts;
- Flemings' equity research analysts visited over 100 institutions world-wide before the company roadshow and in the UK Flemings, Warburgs and Cazenoves split a list of over 200 institutions for pre-marketing purposes;
- Preliminary prospectus and 'Red Herring' published on 25 June. Offer size indicated;
- UK and international roadshows began on 26 June; and
- Initial assessment of demand by regional syndicates.

Phase 4 - Selling and bookbuilding (6 July - 24 July).
- Regional syndicate tranche sizes indicated;
- company management visits a total of 29 cities on its roadshow, of which 16 were in the US;
- US roadshow began on 6 July and ended on 16 July; and
- 230 houses, including 75 retail brokers in the UK, involved in the selling effort.

Analysts have commented on the extremely long period between the announcement of the offer on 2 March and the first dealings on 27 July. Although there was a considerable need to educate investors, there is always a danger that momentum will be lost. Lawrence Banks, deputy chairman of Robert Fleming & Co, conceded that four weeks of formal pre-marketing and two and a half weeks of bookbuilding is too long, but argues that the length was determined by specific timetable challenges and international investors' lack of knowledge. Banks commented 'This offer underscores very well the importance of getting the timetable right. The general lesson has to be to give timetable considerations the attention they deserve at a sufficiently early stage and, in the end, to try to leave yourself with as much flexibility as possible, however this is not always possible, as Wellcome demonstrated.' Peter Wilmot-

Sitwell, former chairman of Warburg Securities said: 'This sale went on and on and on. People were struck by battle fatigue and the marketing lost a lot of momentum towards the end.'

Compared to its peers, the company was sold at a relatively high P/E multiple (see Exhibit 9) due to its excellent prospects at the time, as measured in terms of the expected five-year growth rate in earnings per share (eps), the company was considered attractively valued in comparison to its peer group (see Exhibit 10).

The reasons investors might have found not to participate in the offer were: an over-dependence on antiviral drugs; the lack of blockbuster drugs in the research pipeline; challenges to the Retrovir patent and concerns about various clinical trials; the upcoming patent expiry on Zovirax; the size of the issue and the prevailing market conditions; and the prospect of US healthcare reform following the presidential election.

Retail marketing

A relatively high percentage of the US tranche was taken up by retail investors. As it was possible to give 'protection' to those brokers targeting the US retail investor base by guaranteeing them a portion of their subscriptions, there was a significant incentive to retail firms to continue to solicit orders throughout the marketing period.

European privatisations rarely achieve significant placement with US retail investors. Because of the political significance of a high level of retail participation in the home market in connection with privatisations, safeguarded by clawback and allocation provisions, the uncertainty as to the availability of stock is too great for US retail brokers.

The fact that US retail investors accounted for 45 per cent of the total US placement proved that Wellcome had retail appeal, despite its relatively low dividend yield. To some

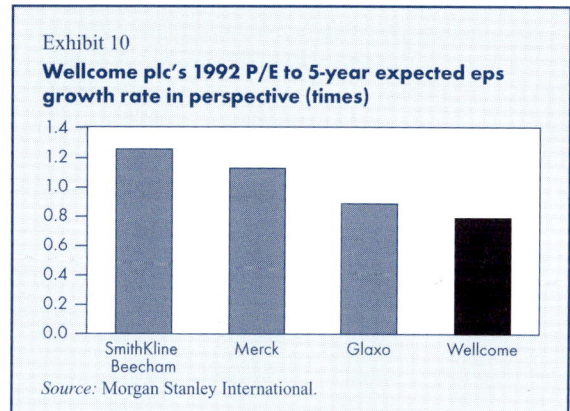

Exhibit 9

Wellcome plc's 1992 P/E ratio in perspective (times)

Source: Morgan Stanley International.

Exhibit 10

Wellcome plc's 1992 P/E to 5-year expected eps growth rate in perspective (times)

Source: Morgan Stanley International.

Exhibit 11

Principal sales points

Market position	• Wellcome Plc, established in 1880, was a major research-based pharmaceutical group, engaged in the research, development, manufacture and marketing of human healthcare products for sale in both the prescription medicine and OTC markets. With sales of £1.6 billion, Wellcome was the 23rd largest pharmaceutical company in the world in 1991, measured by sales. On 22 June 1992 Wellcome was, with a market capitalisation of £7.9 billion (US$15.1 billion), the 15th largest UK registered company quoted on the London Stock Exchange. Wellcome, at the time, had 17,000 employees of whom 31% worked in the UK and 27% in the US. • The company was successfully positioned as a top-tier global pharmaceutical company with among the highest growth rates in the industry. Wellcome had experienced a compounded annual sales growth of 15.8% over the previous five years.
Blockbuster drugs	• Wellcome had two particularly high profile anti-viral drugs, Zovirax and Retrovir. These drugs together represented 44% of 1991 sales and were deemed to have excellent growth prospects. Zovirax and Retrovir had average market shares in excess of 80% in Europe, US and Japan. The company's research and development capability was deemed a leader in antivirals and at the time, there were several projects in the pipeline.
Profitability	• Operating margins had expanded to almost 27% for the six months to 29 February 1992. This trend was expected to continue and to reach 31% in 1995. The equivalent figure had been below 16% in 1987.
Earnings record	• The earnings history is exceptionally impressive with five-year annual earnings per share growth of 27%. This rate of growth was expected to continue in 1992 and 1993. The anticipated five-year average annual growth rate was 20%.
Valuation (24 July 92)	• The issue was priced at more than 20 times calendar year 1992 forecast earnings. • Wellcome was valued at 0.79 times in terms of the relationship between its P/E ratio and expected future five-year earnings growth. A ratio of less than 1 is believed to imply an attractive valuation.

Sources: Offer circular, The Wellcome Trust, Morgan Stanley and Robert Fleming

extent, Morgan Stanley's decision to opt for retail placement in the US was due to the relative paucity of demand among high quality institutions.

The relatively high retail placement in the US does not mean that Flemings should have tried to achieve greater retail participation in the UK as this would not have been possible in the absence of significant retail incentives. As the Trust was not in the business of widening retail shareholdings for its own sake, and as such an approach would have involved considerable expense, this was not an option.

Results

Placement

As can be seen from Exhibit 12, more than 85 per cent of the issue was placed in the UK and US.

US institutional demand was below expectation and orders were slow in arriving. Very few of the top 10 institutions in the US participated. Tony Brooks, managing director and head of European equities at Lehman Brothers says: 'The size of the US institutional commitments, seen in relation to the size of the US offer and particularly when seen in the context of the global offer, was less than one would normally expect. The largest single US order was only 4.3 million shares, equiv-

alent to less than five per cent of the total US demand. The lack of endorsement from US institutional investors was attributable in particular to two factors: firstly, they had a sufficient number of alternative ways of gaining exposure to the global pharmaceutical sector, and secondly the valuation was not exactly compelling when seen in relation to the US drug sector.'

Approximately 53 per cent of the total offer was placed with existing shareholders. Retail investors world-wide accounted for 11.7 per cent. In the US, retail demand accounted for approximately 45 per cent of the total offer.

Because Wellcome plc had been weighted in the FTSE 100 index to the full extent of its market capitalisation, but had been under-owned because of the limited free float, UK institutions bought to increase their weighting. Other than index players, no major fund type dominated the order book.

When targeting US pharmaceutical equity buyers, Morgan Stanley looked at which stocks the top 40 holders owned. The institutions were divided into different categories of equity orientation: growth, index, value, income and asset allocation. The majority of US institutions were either growth or index investors.

Investor concentration
See Exhibit 13.

Exhibit 12
Underwriting, demand and allocation (%)

Target markets	Underwriting (%)*	Demand (%)	Allocation (%)**
UK institutional*** }	62.6	55.6	57.5
UK public offer*** }		4.1	4.6
US	23.7	24.9	23.5
Japan	5.4	5.4	5.3
International	3.4	3.3	3.4
Switzerland	2.5	2.9	2.5
Germany	1.3	1.4	1.3
France	0.8	0.7	0.7
Far East	0.3	1.7	1.2
Total combined offers (shares)	**330,000,000**	**355,000,000**	**310,000,000**

* % of indicated total offer on 25 June 1992. ** Including the greenshoe and 'naked short'. *** £180 million-worth of shares at the offer price was reserved for retail applicants.

Source: Robert Fleming & Co.

Exhibit 13
Investor concentration

	By demand	By allocation
Percentage of issue accounted for by the 10 largest investors (by total size of demand and allocation, respectively)	26%	37%
Number of investors making up 80% of the Issue (by total size of demand and allocation, respectively)	128	121
The three largest investors by size	US$179 million US$104 million US$76 million	US$176 million US$88 million US$72 million
Total number of institutions*	**1,137**	**1,119**

* Double counts institutions which made multiple bids either for different funds, or as part of a bidding strategy.

Exhibit 14
Share price performance

Pricing date*	24 July 1992
Offer price	800p
Last trade	826p
Relative index position	82%

Historic 52 week high/low	
High (3 February 1992)	1,173p
Low (20 August 1991)	703p

* The official pricing date was Monday, 27 July, as the price was announced early that morning, however, for the purposes of this table the real pricing date was Friday, 24 July, as the offer was priced off that day's London close.

Wellcome share price relative to FT 100 (%)

Price performance

Before pricing

	Price (pence)	Relative to FT 100 (%)
- 6 months	1,094	100
- 3 months	1,032	90
- 1 month	913	84
- 1 week	870	84
- 3 days	833	81
- 1 day (23 July 1992)	830	81

After pricing

	Price (pence)	Relative to FT 100 (%)
+ 1 day (27 July 1992)	800.5	81
+ 3 days	807	78
+ 1 week	802	79
+ 1 month	804	83
+ 3 months	1,009	87
+ 6 months	915	75

Source: Datastream and offer circular.

Share price performance

See Exhibit 14.

Before pricing

- The Wellcome plc share price hit its all-time peak of £11.73 on 3 February 1992 and at the time of the announcement of the share sale on 2 March, the price was £11.25. Between the announcement and the pricing, it fell by 27 per cent, while Glaxo fell by 22.3 per cent, and the UK market as a whole (FT All Share Index) fell by 7.2 per cent. During the period between the publication of the preliminary prospectus on 25 June, and 24 July, Wellcome's share price fell by

9.5 per cent whilst the UK market fell by 7.8 per cent and Glaxo by 0.3 per cent. Concern over US healthcare reform helped this fall, as did James Baker's threat on the last day of bookbuilding of a military strike against Iraq. Baker's threat was withdrawn on Sunday 26 July, one day before the pricing of the issue. Short selling also played a major role of the slide in the share price during the offer period; and

- The price exceeded £8.00 for the first time in November 1991. On the basis of the absolute historic P/E of 27.3 times 1991 earnings, a 1.7 per cent dividend yield and the various relative valuation benchmarks by which the offer price represented a premium to Glaxo's prospective multiple, £8.00 was a good price. In fact, Wellcome plc's share price only exceeded £8.00 for just over 18 months between the company going public in February 1986, and Glaxo's bid in January 1995.

Wellcome's share price was closely monitored by Flemings during the offer period and all market-makers connected with the offer were required by the terms of their engagement to reveal their dealing activities and the position of their market-makers' book to ensure that nothing was being done which would jeopardise the offer. Market-makers were contacted daily and this, together with the other contacts, acted as a vital source of intelligence. As a result of these and other enquiries, it soon became apparent that in the thin volumes prevailing during the offer period, a small number of market operators were deliberately driving the price of the stock down by selling stock they did not own in the expectation of buying it back more cheaply, perhaps in the offer (ie, short selling). Further probing and in-depth examination of the share register by Flemings flushed out these short sellers and their brokers.

Urgent action was required and it was agreed that the only course available was to issue notices under Section 212 of the UK Companies Act. These notices are designed for use by companies wishing to establish the identity of shareholders who remain on their register. The problem in this instance, however, was that by their very nature, short sellers do not own any shares. After some thought, Flemings together with its legal advisers constructed a Section 212 notice which was sent to the brokers concerned and which required disclosure by the broker of information about the identity of the client for whom he acted. Flemings argued that in purchasing stock a broker acquired 'an interest' (by virtue of the debt owed to him) which required disclosure. The broker was, in any event, required to disclose the name of the person to whom he sold shares. By establishing this 'interest', Flemings was able to pursue the brokers to disclose the names of those for whom they were acting. Once the names had been obtained, it was then possible to contact the short sellers directly and threaten them with the possibility of having their identities publicised and being barred from participating in the offer. Over the course of 10 days, a number of significant short sellers were identified and excluded from the offer. Whilst some sellers remained obdurate, it is clear that short selling effectively 'dried-up' and a number of those excluded from the offer purchased stock in the closing days of the tender offer to cover

Exhibit 15

Percentage of total issue traded*(%)

	Day 1	Day 2	Day 3	Total Day 1-3
London	8.3	0.8	1.5	10.6
New York	5.2	3.9	4.9	14.0
Globally	13.5	4.7	6.4	24.6

* Based on the issue of 270 million shares. London turnover figures include ADR trading in London, and New York figures include ordinary share trading in New York.

Source: Datastream and Flemings.

their short position. This exercise, known as 'bear hunting' undoubtedly played an important part in arresting the slide in the share price prior to the pricing date.

After pricing

- Having been priced at a modest discount to the Friday closing price, the after-market price performance was reasonable given the poor market conditions. With the help of stabilisation, Flemings managed to hold the market price above the offer price until 12 August. After this it fell below £8.00 and continued to fluctuate just under the £8.00 level until the beginning of September. It then began an impressive ascent and decisively broke through £10.00 in November/December before falling back in late December and January. Compared to the FTSE 100 index, Wellcome did well during the first three months after the sale, outperforming the market by some 6 per cent before beginning to under-perform in December 1992; and
- In 1993 and 1994, the price was much lower: in the first quarter of 1994 it briefly fell below £5.00.

After-market trading volume

See Exhibit 15.

The performance of the main parties

The Trust and the company

The management was not initially enthusiastic about the Trust selling its stake down to below 50 per cent. Although the merger mania in the pharmaceutical sector had not yet begun and there was no apparent threat of hostility, the management had enjoyed great stability from having a 73.5 per cent shareholder who didn't interfere in the running of the company.

In order to carry out the largest non-privatisation share sale ever undertaken, the Trust needed the management's full support, particularly in regard to the due diligence process and the roadshow. A Memorandum of Understanding ('MOU') was therefore signed by the Wellcome Trust and Wellcome plc, at the time of the announcement of the offer, in order to make Wellcome plc as resistant to take-over as possible or, from the management's point of view, at least create the illusion of the Trust being a stable long-term shareholder. The signing of the MOU, which was to become the subject of con-

siderable debate and the cause of rather sharp accusations in connection with the Glaxo take-over in 1995, represented the price that the Trust had to pay for the management's support. Wellcome plc chief executive, John Robb said: 'It is very unlikely that the company would have cooperated with the Trust without this MOU, after all what was in it for us?'. This amazing statement serves as a reminder that the importance of a good relationship between vendor and company in a secondary sale should not be underestimated.

The principal provisions of the MOU, which was not legally binding, were:

- The Trust intended to maintain a long-term holding of at least 25 per cent in Wellcome plc;
- The Trust would discuss and use all reasonable endeavours to agree with Wellcome plc any proposed sales of shares;
- The Trust would continue, for at least five years, not to solicit or encourage take-over offers for the company;
- The Trust undertook to consult with Wellcome plc before discussing with the Charity Commissioners any further scheme which would affect its obligation to retain 25 per cent of the company; and
- The Trust would continue to pay due regard to the views of the board of Wellcome plc on the best interests of the company in relation to any offer for its shareholding.

The MOU was subject to review if significant changes in circumstances should occur and if the trustees were advised that other actions were required to fulfil their fiduciary duties.

In addition, the Trust entered into a legally binding Deed of Covenant (the 'Deed') with the company, which provided that on a sale by the Trust within five years from 30 April 1992, it would endeavour to ensure that, as a result of such a sale, no person individually or acting in concert with it, would own more than 10 per cent of the company. The Deed, however, did not oblige the Trust to do, or omit to do, anything which the Trust considered would be contrary to its best interests. The MOU and the Deed motivated the management to provide its fullest support for the offer.

The due diligence was allegedly described by Flemings' lawyers as 'the most comprehensive ever undertaken in the UK'. About 3,500 man hours were spent by lawyers on the due diligence and verification process alone. The company also agreed to go through the SEC registration process to allow both a public offer in the US and a New York Stock Exchange listing, without which the important US offer would have had very much less favourable odds of succeeding. The management worked extremely hard throughout, prepared carefully for the three-week roadshow and performed exceptionally well in presenting Wellcome plc to investors in 29 cities around the world.

On the roadshow the Trust outlined their reasons for selling cogently and logically, which was important to encourage the market to have confidence in the company's prospects. There can be no doubt that the management honoured its side of the Memorandum of Understanding. Whether or not the Trust would do so was not to be tested until Glaxo came along in 1995.

Broadly speaking, the management delivered what it

promised to investors during the roadshow, at least with respect to the financial years ending August 1992 and 1993, during which sales grew by 17 per cent and 20 per cent respectively, and earnings grew on average by 28.5 per cent. The operating margin expanded to 30.9 per cent in 1993, a greater margin expansion than had been predicted. Zovirax's sales growth was faster than predicted, although sales of Retrovir grew much more slowly than originally forecast. The fact that expectations for compounded earnings growth came down from over 20 per cent at the time of the offer, to 6–7 per cent only two years later is to a large extent attributable to the changing industry environment, which the management could not have been expected to foresee.

To carry out a major sale of this kind the vendor needs nerve and decisiveness. In this respect Sir Roger Gibbs earned significant praise from many quarters: he certainly took some big decisions, some of which can hardly be described as conventional. By deciding to appoint Flemings as global coordinator and putting Cazenove on the 'left' in front of Warburgs in the UK tranche, although Warburgs had the books of the UK syndicate, Sir Roger indicated to the banking community who was in charge (himself), thereby facilitating a successful working environment among the banks involved. He was simply going to do what he thought was best for the offer and not get bogged down in convention: importantly, he opted for a bookbuilt offer which was an innovative move in the UK, and obtained the full cooperation of the management. Perhaps the boldest decision was to announce the day before the close of the offer that the Trust was not prepared to sell below £8.00 despite having worked on the sale for more than six months. He had the vision to see that £8.00 was a good price although the market price had been much higher earlier in the year. Sir Roger felt that a number of important lessons were learnt during this offer:

- It is paramount that the vendor keeps his nerve: 'it was our head on the chopping block and if anything had gone badly wrong, the Trust would have been blamed';
- High quality houses, if properly briefed and managed, can work very well together;
- Bookbuilding was a great advantage and gave management confidence about the quality of demand, which was crucial during the last two weeks before pricing. It allowed management publicly to announce that it was not going to sell below £8.00, which was important to check the activity of the short sellers; and
- It is important not to believe every word you hear, even from the banking community. 'You have to be so cynical' he says.

The global coordinator

This proposed international offer was a highly sought-after mandate and of tremendous importance to both the Wellcome Trust and Wellcome plc. Despite the strengths of the story, the offer was also a major challenge given its scale and the lack of name recognition outside the UK.

There was no formal solicitation process for the role of global coordinator and the natural choice was Flemings.

Lawrence Banks was originally appointed the Trust's principal merchant banker in 1984 by Sir David Steel, Sir Roger's predecessor. Flemings had continued to advise the Wellcome Trust since the original flotation in 1986. As Flemings had no direct relevant experience of international offers it would only get the mandate to be global coordinator if it could satisfy the Trust that it had the necessary syndicate and book-building expertise. At the time, Ian Hannam, previously head of Equity Syndicate UK and Europe at Salomon Brothers, was available and, accordingly, Banks proposed to engage him as a consultant to Flemings and charge him with the task of running the syndication and bookbuilding.

Flemings was successful in securing the role because of its longstanding relationship with the Trust, its successful work in connection with the 1986 IPO, an unprecedented knowledge and understanding of both the Trust and the company, as well as regular and deep coverage of the client. Sir Roger said: 'Flemings' after sales service had been superb. Perhaps another telling factor, however, was the feeling on the part of the Trust that this was going to be by far the most important transaction for Flemings, whereas at other major investment banks, the Trust was going to be one of many important clients.'

Flemings was formally appointed on 1 March 1992. Syndicate lead manager selection followed with Sir Roger and colleagues, along with representatives from Wellcome plc, Flemings and Barings as the company's advisers, interviewing 40 banks during six working days in March.

Flemings was widely praised for the professional handling of the issue by syndicate members, one banker even called their work an 'amazing achievement'. Their achievement was even more impressive when you consider that the syndicate and wider selling group included a total of 230 houses. Flemings participated in each of the regional syndicates to keep watch over local events.

The decision to hire Hannam as a consultant and charge him with the syndication and bookbuilding is not a decision Banks had reason to regret, as he was almost universally praised for his work, even by his peer group within the industry, a group of individuals not generally known for giving praise to competitors. Hannam also had the wisdom to strike up an harmonious working relationship with Warburgs and Cazenove, who provided high quality support for the whole offer, not least in connection with the tactical decision to announce that the Trust would not be selling below £8.00. Hannam was close to Maurice Thompson, then head of Warburg's ECM department and was not too proud to involve him substantially in the offer. Given that Flemings was widely praised for the way it handled this offer, it is perhaps surprising that the merchant bank has not been appointed as global coordinator in more UK and European offers.

Key lessons learnt

Structuring

Timing and timetable issues are often underestimated in these types of offers and should receive the fullest attention at an early stage. It is very difficult to fine-tune the timing of offers of this size and complexity.

Tony Brooks of Lehman Brothers' said, when commenting on the share price performance between announcement and pricing: 'The Wellcome offer demonstrated as clearly as can be that there is a different price for size. A very large offer which more than doubles the free float can not necessarily be done at a price based on modest volumes in the secondary market. This is perhaps particularly evident in a case such as Wellcome where the run-up in the share price before the announcement of the sale resulted in a market price above that at which such a large block could be distributed.'

Bookbuilding may be the only structure that really works in a negative market environment. However short selling can easily escalate price falls prior to pricing.

Management

The vendor of a large shareholding in a publicly traded company is extremely dependent on the cooperation of the company's management. The relationship between vendor and company is not usually straightforward and the success of a secondary offer of this type depends on delicate negotiation involving 'give and take' from both parties, legal rights notwithstanding.

It is important that the vendor shows decisiveness and leadership with regard to dealings with advisers and other banks.

Marketing

There were clearly too many regional syndicates and too many banks involved, which simply created extra administration and made overall control of the offer more challenging whilst being of limited benefit. The marketing period was far too long and as a result momentum was lost towards the end of the bookbuilding period.

There is a strong correlation between the number of retail incentives and placement achieved: successful retail placement in the US requires protection.

Conclusion

This was an historic offer and a remarkable achievement given that market conditions were clearly weak. The fact that the GPA offer was pulled had substantially undermined general investor confidence. It is a real tribute to the company's management at the time, the Trust, and its advisers that the offer could be so successfully completed.

The difficulty of policing short sellers in the UK, and penalising them, was a notable element in the closing stages of the bookbuilding process. The presence of significant short selling clearly cost the Wellcome Trust a substantial amount

in terms of proceeds. However, the fact that there was such widespread talk about short selling may in fact have underpinned the expectation of a bounce back in the share price following pricing, hence adding demand during the closing stages of the offer.

In these poor market conditions it was difficult to generate the type of price tension desirable towards the final stages of the bookbuilding process and competition between UK and US institutions failed to materialise to the desired degree, as US demand only came in at the last moment and failed to make a positive contribution towards building the required momentum for a higher offer price.

Although the formal objective was to reduce the Trust's stake to below 50 per cent, analysts knew that it could sell down to 25 per cent. As a consequence, the vendor was always on the defensive against the investor community, as both the price and the number of shares to be offered were falling during the weeks leading up to pricing. It would have been advantageous not to let the market know that the Trust was contemplating going down to 25 per cent but the court order and subsequent press release made that impossible.

The timing was fortunate from the Trust's point of view in that the proceeds could be reinvested in UK equities, at a time when the UK stock market was at a low ebb (the FTSE 100 was at 2,300). By the time the UK government announced that it was to take sterling out of the ERM on 15 September 1992 the Trust was 93 per cent reinvested. Given the subsequent strong performance of the UK equity market, the outcome was close to optimal. Sir Roger Gibbs commends Schroder Investment Management in particular for its advice on how to reinvest the issue proceeds.

The fact that the Trust only sold down to 40 per cent proved to be highly fortunate. In 1995 it was unexpectedly approached by UK pharmaceuticals company Glaxo to sell its remaining holding at £10.25, a price representing a 50 per cent premium to the market price just before the announcement of the bid.

The Trust was undoubtedly astute in launching an equity offer in 1992 when the company's prospects were the best they had ever been. The trustees demonstrated the same acumen in selling the balance to a single buyer in 1995, when a very high bid premium was available. In so doing, Sir Roger Gibbs undoubtedly demonstrated that he had carried out his fiduciary duty to the very highest standard. He put aside all personal wishes and feelings, however strongly held, in the best interests of the Wellcome Trust.

Feature topic: *Short selling in connection with global equity offers. What does it mean? When does it occur? Should it be stopped and how can it be prevented?*

Naked short selling' is the sale of securities by a party which does not own them. Ideally, no delivery of the underlying shares ever takes place. If the original selling position is carried beyond the due settlement date without being closed, then the stock is either borrowed to effect settlement, rolled over, or the vendor fails to settle. Short selling can occur in the course of ordinary secondary market trading or at the time of an equity offer. In the case of an equity offer, certain market participants might sell shares during the marketing period in the hope of being allocated shares in the offer at a lower price than the one at which they executed the short sale. Other sellers may believe that they can close out their short positions by buying at a lower price in the secondary market once official trading has begun. Another practice which is not strictly short selling, but which has the same impact, is for an investor 'to sell from inventory' during the lead up to an equity offer with a view to buying back at a lower price in connection with the equity offer.

The presence of short sellers, and those that sell from inventory during the marketing period with a view to buying back in the offer or at a later stage, combined with the absence of natural buying interest during the marketing period, often leads to a decline in the share price during the period leading up to the pricing of the offer. This represents one of the principal challenges to the vendors and arrangers of secondary offers (the sale of outstanding shares in a quoted company) and certain rights issues. The success of the marketing of a secondary offer should to a large extent be judged on the share price performance during the weeks and months leading up to pricing and not just afterwards.

In certain countries, such as the UK, market participants are not required to distinguish short sales from sales of existing holdings when reporting sales of shares; the securities of many companies are traded on several stock exchanges and over-the-counter markets around the world; and it is possible effectively 'to go short' in a company's shares through the derivatives markets. This can make it difficult to determine the extent to which short selling has actually taken place in a particular case. Despite this, the suspicion of short selling may arise when the market price falls sharply between the announcement and pricing of an equity offer only to rise following the pricing period.

Short selling as a problem

The occurrence of substantial short selling was suspected in several high profile UK bookbuilt offers and rights issues of the early 1990s. Despite the fact that the London Stock Exchange does not prohibit short selling, it decided to analyse the problem in connection with new issues and subsequently to develop some regulatory tools. A detailed investigation into alleged short selling in BT 2, Wellcome plc, BT3, Euro Disney and Eurotunnel was carried out and, in September 1994, the LSE published a consultation document named 'Regulation of short selling of UK equities and related securities during secondary offers'. This document set out, among other things, the principal conclusions from its investigation into the five equity offers mentioned above. The following is a summary of two of them

- *BT2:* On 1 October 1991 HM Treasury announced the structure of the sale of the second tranche of BT shares. Dealing commenced on 9 December with 1.575 billion shares being offered at a fully paid price of £3.50 for the international offer and £3.35 for the UK retail offer. Between the date of announcement and the date of the sale, there was extensive selling and the price of BT fell from 413 pence on 1 October, to 341.5 pence on the day preceding the pricing and allocation, representing a fall of 17.3 per cent. During the same period, the FTSE 100 Index fell by only 9.7 per cent. According to the London Stock Exchange: 'There was a strong belief by market practitioners that short selling by hedge and trading funds had contributed substantially to the fall in price.' HM Treasury's experience in BT2 was a strong reason for the treasury to attempt to protect itself from the negative effects of short selling on its secondary offers. In so doing, the Treasury, as an important market participant, acted as a catalyst in bringing about change; and
- *Wellcome plc:* On 2 March 1992 the Wellcome Trust announced its intention to reduce its holding in Wellcome plc from 73.5 per cent to a minimum of 25 per cent by selling up to 417 million shares. At the time of the announcement on 2 March the price was £11.25. By the time the offer was priced on 24 July, the Trust decided that the market was only receptive to an offer of 270 million shares at £8.00. From announcement to pricing, the share price fell by 27 per cent, while the UK market as a whole (FTSE 100 Index) fell by only 7.2 per cent. According to the London Stock Exchange: 'There was anecdotal evidence of short selling, in some cases significant, and although difficult to prove, it was widely perceived that this had had a major effect on the price of the security and the ultimate success of the issue.'

Judging from these and other examples it would appear that substantial short selling may occur under the following circumstances

- When an announcement of the sale of a large number of shares in a quoted company at a price to be determined at a future date occurs (ie, in the case of a bookbuilding structure or a pre-announced rights issue). The incentive to sell short is typically greater if the pricing of the offer only occurs at the end of the marketing period (as is the case of bookbuilding) because the sponsoring bank will have to take the market activity during the period leading up to the pricing into account when pricing the offer. In a rights issue, where the pricing and underwriting occurs at the beginning of the process, there is less incentive to drive the market price down below a certain level as the issue price has already been fixed;

- When the likelihood is high that the offer would go ahead even at a substantially lower price than the one at the time of announcement. This is often the case in privatisations, when offers have to be executed for political reasons or when a company is in a precarious financial position and in desperate need of equity;

- When there is an announcement that would indicate that the vendor would effectively be selling as many shares as possible;

- When there is a significant time period between announcement and pricing;

- When the markets are weak: when there is negative momentum in the particular stock, as was the case in BT prior to BT2, or when the lead manager does not appear to be in control of the offer, leading to a general perception in the market that the offer price and/or the market price following the offer, will be lower than at the time of the proposed short sale;

- When there is no regulation of short selling, no explicit way of identifying the short sellers and no way of exercising any leverage over them. If a short selling institution cannot be identified, there is no way to threaten them with exclusion from the sale. It is more difficult to police short sellers in countries with bearer rather than registered shares; and

- When the possibilities of stock borrowing are good and the sanctions for late delivery are mild or non-existent, or when clients are allowed to roll-over their short positions.

Reasons for preventing short selling

Although short selling is not illegal, it is plainly in the interests of the vendor to deter it. There are those who think that short selling must be stopped and those that disagree.

Representatives of the view that it should be stopped argue that short selling is an example of powerful market participants using their positions unfairly to secure an advantage by manipulating the market price to the detriment of the vendor, other existing shareholders and the sponsoring banks.

Adherents to the opposite view argue that this is no more than a common securities market practice of using generally available market information in combination with strong financial resources to achieve a competitive advantage. It is a useful tool for market-makers who have an obligation to make two-way prices to secure market liquidity. Sponsors of issues should take potential short selling activity into account when devising the marketing, pricing and allocation strategies.

Regulatory approaches

Different countries take widely different approaches to the practice of short selling. It is completely prohibited in certain countries (eg, Singapore, Malaysia and Japan) and largely unregulated in others (eg, the UK, until January 1995, France, Spain and South Korea). In most other countries, short selling is constrained in one way or the other. In the US, there are two principal ways by which short selling is regulated

- The scope for manipulation during offers is restricted under Rule 10b-21 of the Securities Exchange Act of 1934, by prohibiting all short sellers in the lead up to an offer from covering their sales with the shares being offered. This rule does not restrict sales from inventory; and

- The practice of short selling of exchange listed securities is constrained by Rule 10a-1 of the Securities Exchange Act of 1934, which allows short sales only where they have been carried out on an 'uptick', ie, where the short sale occurs at a price that is above the immediately preceding trade in the same security.

Ways of preventing short selling

The September 1994 consultation document published by the London Stock Exchange (LSE) sets out four different approaches to the regulation of short selling in connection with large equity offers, all of which have distinct advantages and disadvantages. Although it has to be recognised that the situation is different in every country, many of these measures are likely to be applicable in countries other than the UK

1. *Disclosure of the aggregate customer short interest to the market.* The regular publication of the aggregate short position would increase transparency and indicate to the market the extent to which the market price had been driven down, and the amount of stock that needs to be purchased by short sellers to close out their positions. The disadvantage of this approach is its lack of reliability. There is a danger that the published figure could misrepresent the actual situation due to trading on other exchanges, over-the-counter trading and trading in derivatives. The other shortcoming of this approach is that it presupposes that the short position

has to be covered on a certain date, which for a number of reasons need not be the case;

2. *Prohibition on covering a sale by subscribing for shares in the offer.* This approach would emulate the US regulatory approach which is currently in place, whereby the onus for controlling short selling would lie primarily with the regulator. Contrary to the case in the US, it could be applied to both naked short sales and sales from certain existing holdings (where settlement is to be made with borrowed stock). It would include market-makers' short positions that had not been derived in the course of ordinary market making. The LSE is of the view that this would be an effective way of protecting the issue price in connection with equity offers, particularly if it was possible to include both on- and off-exchange dealings;

3. *Issuer's/vendor's control of allocation policy.* This approach would include the issuer/vendor taking steps which might include one or more of the following: an allocation policy to reward loyal owners; undertakings from relevant market participants concerning the use of derivatives, and postponement of the issue in case

of excessive price falls. All measures to be employed in a particular offer would have to be disclosed in the prospectus and be subject to regulatory approval. This is a sensible approach and variations of the above measures are now included in most major offers as a matter of course. In certain instances, it could become very expensive and fall short of the objective of stopping shorting altogether, unless it could be combined with other measures. Although the onus would be on the vendor and its advisers, its success would also depend on the exchange's careful monitoring of market activity. This approach would be particularly relevant for bookbuilt offers, but less so for pre-emptive rights issues.

4. *The application of settlement based constraints.* There are two possible variations on this approach, namely 'dealing for cash settlement' and 'a progressive reduction of the settlement period and mandatory buying-in where transactions fail to settle on the due date'. Both variations would allow short selling practices to continue, but by penalising the seller who does not deliver on time, the potential financial reward of short selling would be reduced or removed.

Feature topic: *The 1995 sale by the Wellcome Trust of its remaining 39.5 per cent interest in Wellcome plc to Glaxo, and Glaxo's subsequent full bid for Wellcome plc*

On 23 January 1995 Glaxo announced a £9.1 billion bid valuing each Wellcome plc share at £10.25. The bid consisted of approximately 70 per cent cash and 30 per cent new Glaxo Wellcome shares. By the time the bid closed it was worth £10.60 to Wellcome plc shareholders as the Glaxo share price, having initially dipped, rallied from the time of announcement. As a result of the eventual sale by the Trust of its remaining stake in Wellcome plc, it became a 4.7 per cent shareholder in Glaxo Wellcome, a stake which represented some 17 per cent of the Trust's total asset base and approximately 25 per cent of its income.

The Wellcome Trust was categorically informed, both

verbally and in writing, that no offer for the shares would be forthcoming from Glaxo if the Trust contacted the company before executing an undertaking to sign an 'irrevocable' agreement to sell its shares in Wellcome plc to Glaxo. This placed the Trust in a most difficult and uncomfortable position and put it under an enormous amount of pressure as, under the 1992 Memorandum of Understanding, it had undertaken to consult with Wellcome plc prior to the sale of any further shares. For making such a commitment, the Trust had exposed itself to considerable criticism from a wide range of observers including the City and the press.

Sir Roger Gibbs, chairman of the Wellcome Trust was right to do what he did. The price received from Glaxo was a good one, and the decision to sell was very much in the best interests of the Trust and its beneficiaries. Eighteen months on, it is clear that the Trust made the right decision in early 1995, as sales of Zovirax and Retrovir were slightly down during calendar 1995, even allowing for the fact that the former Wellcome plc salesforce may have been unsettled during the year.

The best evidence of the quality of the decisions taken by the Trust since it first decided to float Wellcome plc in 1986, including the most recent decision to sell out to Glaxo, is provided by the considerable growth in net asset value (see Exhibit 16).

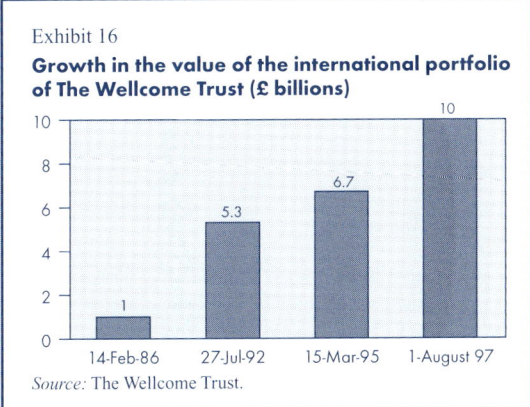

Exhibit 16

Growth in the value of the international portfolio of The Wellcome Trust (£ billions)

Source: The Wellcome Trust.

Exhibit 17

The timetable

10 January	• Sir Roger Gibbs and Sir Richard Sykes have lunch, following invitation by Sir Richard. This is a 'get to know' lunch, following which Sir Roger has no specific reason to expect an approach by Glaxo of the kind that transpired 10 days later.
20 January	• Glaxo makes formal approach to the Wellcome Trust with a view to making an offer for Wellcome plc, but strictly on the basis that no contact is made with the company until after the Glaxo offer is publicly announced.
22 January	• On Sunday night, the Trust gives an undertaking to Glaxo (the Undertaking) to enter into an irrevocable agreement, subject to being committed to consult with the company after the public announcement of the offer.
23 January	• Glaxo announces offer of £10.25 to all Wellcome shareholders.
26 January	• Wellcome plc declared that Glaxo's bid undervalues the company. John Robb, chairman and chief executive of Wellcome plc said: 'I soon realised that the days of independence were over, but who was to say that somebody else was not to pay more.'
27 January	• The Wellcome Trust, having consulted with Wellcome plc through Flemings and taken financial advice from Flemings and legal advice from Cameron Markby Hewitt, decides to enter into the irrevocable agreement with Glaxo (the Agreement), subject to court approval and there being no higher offer.
7 February	• Glaxo, advised by Lazard Brothers, publishes an offer document. Glaxo has 21 days to gain acceptances from more than 50% of Wellcome plc shareholders. They already had a commitment of 39.5% from the Trust, subject to no higher offer being made by another bidder.
15 February	• Wellcome plc, advised by Barings and Morgan Stanley, publishes a defence document with better than expected sales projections.
17 February	• High Court gives approval to the Wellcome Trust's entering into the Agreement, subject to certain modifications following two days of court hearings.
6 March	• Two days before the expiry of the offer period, the Wellcome plc board recommends the Glaxo offer after it becomes clear that none of the potential white knights, including Roche of Switzerland, Zeneca of the UK and Pfizer of the US was prepared to launch a counter-bid. On this day, the Glaxo offer is worth £10.60 to Wellcome shareholders due to an appreciation in the Glaxo share price since the bid was made on 23 January.

Rationale

The underlying rationale behind the Trust's decision to sell its stake to Glaxo was the same as it had been in the share sales of 1986 and 1992 – asset diversification. The first two were meticulously prepared for by the Trust, but Glaxo's approach in 1995 was completely unsolicited. Sir Roger Gibbs had never met Sir Richard Sykes, Glaxo's chief executive, before they had lunch on 10 January 1995. Furthermore, in 1992, Sir Roger firmly believed that the Trust would retain a 40 per cent shareholding in Wellcome plc for at least five years.

In early 1995 40 per cent of the Wellcome Trust's assets were invested in Wellcome plc and 60 per cent in a portfolio of 1,200 stocks. Following the stake sale, the Trust now has 20 per cent of its total assets invested in Glaxo Wellcome and 80 per cent in 2,200 stocks around the world. The Trust's annual income increased from £224 million to over £300 million as a result of the transaction, and total assets increased from £5.3 to £6.8 billion. These were very powerful arguments to bring to the UK courts, which had the final say in whether or not the sale could go ahead.

Glaxo's offer to The Wellcome Trust

On Friday 20 January, before the public announcement of the bid on the following Monday morning, Glaxo wrote to The Wellcome Trust with a view to making a full bid for Wellcome plc, subject to:

1. The Trust signing an undertaking to give an irrevocable agreement to sell its 39.5 per cent interest in Wellcome plc to Glaxo; and
2. The Trust agreeing not to talk to Wellcome plc under any circumstances about the Glaxo bid. If no such agreement was forthcoming Glaxo would not proceed with its offer.

The Wellcome Trust, after exhaustive discussions with its financial and legal advisers reluctantly agreed to these conditions and signed the undertaking to enter into the irrevocable agreement on the Sunday night before the public announcement early on the Monday morning. The Wellcome Trust's financial advisers had advised the Trust that it would be contrary to its best interests not to sign. The Trust has been criticised for having been able to agree so quickly, but Sir Roger, his colleagues, and his team of advisers had prepared themselves in great depth to deal with all foreseeable possibilities some time earlier. How could he not have thought carefully about the Trust's investment in Wellcome plc, then valued at £2.2 billion, and representing 40 per cent of the its entire asset base?

The undertaking and the irrevocable agreement

Glaxo was categorical that it was not prepared to launch a public bid without having first secured some form of undertaking over the Trust's 39.5 per cent stake. The way to do this was to attack the Trust's fiduciary duty and put it in a position whereby it would find it impossible to ignore the opportunity.

Glaxo insisted on the Trust signing an undertaking to give an irrevocable agreement to accept Glaxo's offer, before Glaxo would announce its offer for the company. The undertaking had attached the form of the irrevocable agreement which the Trust agreed to sign.

This undertaking was subject to the Trust having the right to withdraw from its obligation to give Glaxo the irrevocable commitment if, no later than 27 January it was advised by Flemings (after taking into account the views of the board of the company) that Flemings were no longer of the opinion that it was in the best interests of the Trust to give the irrevocable opinion.

The undertaking to give the irrevocable agreement was also subject to:

1. High court approval;
2. The Trust having the right to accept a higher offer from a third party.

The Trust could not, however, give the third party bidder an irrevocable undertaking prior to that bidder publicly announcing a bid.

On reflection, this seems to represent a successful negotiating result on the part of the Trust and its team of advisers as the first provision, at least to some extent, makes up for the fact that it was absolutely forbidden to talk to Wellcome plc before the announcement of the bid. The fact that an 'irrevocable' agreement was negotiated that was in fact revocable should a higher bid materialise, was in the interest of the Trust, and all the company's shareholders.

The controversy

The company management criticised the Trust on three grounds:

1. The Trust had failed, as undertaken in 1992, to consult with Wellcome plc following the approach by Glaxo;
2. There was not enough time to find counterbidders as a result of the tight timetable; and
3. By giving Glaxo the irrevocable agreement, which prevented the Trust giving such an agreement to any higher bidder prior to the public announcement of any such bid, the Trust had not facilitated higher offers from other

potentially interested bidders and, therefore, prevented the board of Wellcome plc from obtaining a more attractive bid in the interests of all its shareholders.

Following the recommendation of the Glaxo bid, John Robb of Wellcome plc said: 'I have nothing but admiration for Glaxo...but I can't say the same for our major shareholder. To have sold its interest in the company without talking to the management is something many employees in the company will never forgive the Trust for.' He added: 'The Trust should have called Glaxo's bluff and asked them to make a full bid for the company, following which the Trust would seriously consider its position.' When asked if he would have done the same thing if he had been in Glaxo's shoes, he admitted that Glaxo and Lazards were 'very clever'. The situation was obviously very delicate, because although it is not inconceivable that Glaxo may ultimately have accepted that the Trust would talk to Wellcome plc, Glaxo had been preparing for the bid since May 1994, and it was not a gamble that it would have been reasonable to expect the Trust to take. What if, as John Robb suggested, the Trust had endeavoured to call Glaxo's bluff without success? The result could have been a £1.2 billion mistake – the difference between the market value of the Trust's stake before the bid and the £10.25 value of the bid when it was announced – and the way the fiduciary duty had been carried out would most certainly have been queried and challenged.

Be that as it may, one can clearly understand John Robb's bitterness, on behalf of the board and the employees. John Robb was offered the role of non-executive deputy chairman of Glaxo Wellcome but he did not to accept the offer and put up a strong fight against very poor odds.

If John Robb had not insisted on the Memorandum of Understanding in 1992 it is possible that Glaxo would have offered less. It is argued that Glaxo was very much aware of the MOU and how reluctant Sir Roger would be to break that agreement. Whereas he would not break it for a bid that was not of exceptional interest, there was a chance that he would do so if the bid was spectacular, which in the event it undoubtedly was. The company's shareholders should recognise the value in that bitter irony, and give Robb credit for it, on top of the credit he deserves for his successful running of the company.

With regard to the understanding between the Wellcome Trust and Wellcome plc, the reader is reminded of the provisions of the 1992 MOU and the Deed of Covenant which essentially provided that the Trust should not solicit take-over offers, nor sell further shares without first consulting the company, and not facilitate any one investor or group of investors to buy a 10 per cent stake in Wellcome plc.

While it was John Robb's duty, as the chairman of Wellcome plc, to procure the best possible offer for all his shareholders, he is not justified in attacking the Wellcome Trust. First, the 1992 MOU was not legally binding. Second, neither the MOU nor the Deed of Covenant could result in the trustees having to do, or omit to do, anything which they considered to be contrary to the best interests of the Trust. This language is clearly included in the 1992 prospectus.

Russell Denoon Duncan, a former senior partner of Cameron Markby Hewitt, who has been involved with the Wellcome Trust's affairs since well before the 1986 flotation says: 'The reason why it was agreed that the Memorandum of Understanding would not be legally binding and a provision included in the Covenant (that the restriction would not prevent the Trust from acting in its best interests as determined by the trustees), was that the trustees, in going some way to meeting the forcibly expressed concerns of management, were not prepared to restrict the legal right of the Trust to act in whatever way its best interests required. The company knew of this all along.'

Another point of criticism was that the Trust had not facilitated a higher bid as it was unable to give a counterbidder an absolute irrevocable undertaking (ie, not made subject to a higher bid). This overlooks the fiduciary duty of the trustees: as it could not possibly prevent anyone from making a higher bid, be it either Glaxo or anyone else. It was unquestionably reasonable on the part of the Trust to agree with Glaxo that any counterbidder would be subject to the same degree of irrevocability.

To claim that this was the only, or even the main reason that there was no counterbidder, does not appear to stand up to analysis. Closer to the truth is the fact that Glaxo was offering a good price and that no other bidder was, for whatever reason, either in a position to, or willing to, pay a higher price. The strongest evidence for this is that no alternative suitor actually even contacted the Trust to discuss the situation at any stage. The Trust's adviser received one approach, which consisted of an unattractive and uncertain proposal for the Trust's shareholding.

The price paid by Glaxo

When launched, Glaxo's bid at £10.25 represented a 50 per cent premium on Wellcome plcs share price. Because of the strong performance of Glaxo's share price before closing, the bid was worth £10.60 to the company's shareholders. Before the bid the highest price paid for Wellcome plc's shares since the beginning of 1994 was £7.24, and in March 1994 the share price was as low as £4.90. The numbers are compelling: from the Wellcome Trust's point of view and from that of the Trust's beneficiaries, Sir Roger did the right thing, although, one suspects that, as a gentleman, he will remain uncomfortable about what he had to do for some time to come.

YPF

The privatisation of Argentine state oil company YPF in 1993 was the largest ever in an emerging market and the most politically sensitive of all the country's privatisations. In terms of cash proceeds, the IPO at US$3.04 billion remains the third-largest single company IPO distributed internationally. It has been surpassed only by the ENI IPO in 1995 and the giant Deutsche Telekom offer in 1996.

The IPO of YPF represented the first privatisation of a state oil company in Latin America, a region where national oil companies were regarded as untouchable. 'YPF, created in 1922 as the world's first state-owned oil company, was as symbolic as the national flag,' according to Horacio Liendo, deputy secretary at the Ministry of the Economy. YPF became the first Argentine company to be sold on the basis of international best-practice disclosure and corporate governance standards, the first to be sold by way of bookbuilding, and only the second to be listed on the NYSE.

This IPO allegedly represented the first time that joint global coordinators had adopted a genuine joint books effort in all international tranches of a major global equity offer. CSFB and Merrill Lynch also agreed on joint economics, which meant that at the end of the day, regardless of sales performance, the two banks made exactly the same amount of money from the transaction. This approach meant that each recommendation was based on what was best for the transaction and avoided competition between the two banks.

Numerous interest groups, which apart from YPF itself included pensioners, provinces, trades unions, the federal government, congress, and domestic and international investors, made this a highly complex offer. A structure was found whereby pensioners were offered YPF shares in exchange for Republic of Argentina bonds, with which they had been issued when the government did not have the money to pay their pensions. Resolving pension fund indebtedness was of paramount political importance and it was only by linking this issue to the privatisation that parliamentary approval was given. It also enabled the government to meet its target of selling more than 50 per cent of YPF, thus ensuring that the offer was a true privatisation rather than one in which the state retained majority control. In another deal sparked by the government's lack of cash, Argentina's oil-producing provinces were given 32.5 per cent of YPF in settlement of unpaid royalties. Some two-thirds of these shares were sold as part of the offer.

The YPF transaction undoubtedly deserves to go down in history as the privatisation achievement of the 20th century. There was a great deal of preparation necessary for this issue, as Argentine commercial life had to be revolutionised, the economy radically restructured, the oil and gas sector deregulated and competition introduced. Moreover, YPF itself had to be transformed and restructured in a way that may never again be repeated in a democracy. The fact that all these measures were necessary is a legacy of the Peronists, and the junta which for so many years shaped the destiny of what was once one of the strongest economies in the world.

Exhibit 1
Transaction summary

Issuer name: YPF (Argentina)	*Joint global coordinators and joint bookrunners:* CSFB and Merrill Lynch
Pricing date: 28 June 1993 (Merval: 416.5)	*Pricing/underwriting structure:* Bookbuilding
Vendor: Republic of Argentina	*Primary or secondary:* Secondary
% of company sold: 45% (58% including exchange offer)	*Privatisation or corporate:* Privatisation
	Retail structure: Bonus shares
IPO or non-IPO: IPO	*Industry:* Oil and gas
Type of shares: Ordinary D shares and ADRs representing D shares (1 share = 1 ADR)	*Offer price range:* US$17–20/share and ADR *Offer price:* US$19
Total IPO issue size: US$3,040 million	*US listing/144A :* NYSE listing

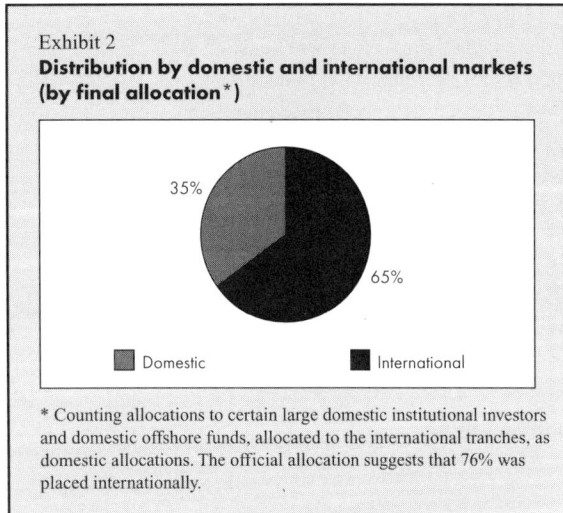

Exhibit 2

Distribution by domestic and international markets (by final allocation*)

35%

65%

■ Domestic   ■ International

* Counting allocations to certain large domestic institutional investors and domestic offshore funds, allocated to the international tranches, as domestic allocations. The official allocation suggests that 76% was placed internationally.

That these preparations were diligently carried out reflects the business culture introduced when Carlos Menem swept to power in May 1989, and the enormous contributions made by the men he chose to push through the widespread reform – notably Domingo Cavallo, who was appointed economy minister in January 1991, and José 'Pepe' Estenssoro who was appointed president and CEO of YPF in August 1989.

It is the work of these men over a period of four years, starting with the passing of the State Reform Law in August 1989, that paved the way for the successful sale of YPF. Menem obtained political support in the country and Congress, Cavallo engineered the revitalisation of the economy, introduced the convertibility plan by pegging the peso to the US dollar and deregulated the Argentine energy sector, while Estenssoro commercialised and restructured YPF. It changed from a trade union-dominated and entirely corrupt organisation that had cost the government over US$6 billion from 1981 to 1991, to a world-class integrated oil and gas company, operating successfully in a competitive domestic sector. In the process he kicked out the trade unions, sold non-strategic assets worth US$2 billion and cut staff by 80 per cent.

The rewards from this transaction were profound on a number of levels and beyond the expectations of any of the parties involved. They will represent for a long time what a highly successful privatisation can bring to an emerging economy. In addition to all the direct and obvious benefits to the company, in a broader national context the impact was felt on three levels:

- On the development of the Argentine capital market;
- On the macroeconomic situation; and
- On Argentine society at large.

Through this privatisation the Argentine stock market acquired its undisputed number-one blue chip, increased domestic market capitalisation by 17 per cent and, perhaps more importantly, doubled the market's public float. The transaction also enhanced the sophistication of local banks and investors, thereby substantially contributing to the increased stability of the local equity market. It also represented an opportunity to upgrade local securities laws and

stock exchange regulations, and harmonise them with international practice. The fact that YPF listed on the NYSE and subjected itself to the most rigorous type of due diligence possible was an unprecedented development in Argentina and set a high standard for other companies.

Fiscally the privatisation contributed US$5 billion of debt reduction for the government (counting the disposal of a 70 per cent stake by the central government) and a US$2 billion direct capital inflow as a result of the participation of foreign investors, a very important figure when measured against the country's total foreign reserves of US$10 billion at the end of 1992. There was also a US$2 billion additional indirect capital inflow between July and October 1993 as many large institutional investors put Argentina on their approved list. These inflows led to reduced interest rates with increased economic activity. According to analysts, convertibility – which together with privatisation is one of the two fundamentals of Cavallo's economic reform programme – may not have been feasible without the proceeds of privatisation and the capital inflow resulting from it, as the country would have crumbled both politically and economically without the stimulus of the privatisation proceeds. YPF began to have a positive effect on the economy as it began to invest more, export more, pay tax rather than deplete the fiscal budget and pay dividends to its shareholders (including the state and the provinces).

In terms of its impact on Argentine society at large, the YPF privatisation helped reduce corruption: 'Clearly privatisation limits the opportunity for corruption' commented Domingo Cavallo. 'In the past everybody practically helped themselves to whatever they wanted and nobody would ask any questions. When the money ran out at YPF, you simply asked the Treasury for more and when its money ran out, it simply printed more. Under private ownership there is control and accountability.' Basic services were also improved as a result of privatisation as Daniel Llambias, general manager of the wholesale division of Banco de Galicia, one of the three book-running joint lead managers of the domestic tranche noted: 'Privatisation represented a cultural revolution in Argentina – today people demand services from the privatised utilities and get them.' The YPF privatisation was also seen as an integral part of the overall programme to transform commercial life in Argentina: 'When a Latin American government privatises its national oil company, typically considered sacred, you know it means business. This sends a very strong signal to the world that there is genuine change in commercial life, from government intervention to a market economy,' explained Guillermo Reca, president of Merrill Lynch Argentina. There was also an important political effect from the 50,000 retail shareholders who subscribed in the IPO and the 90,000 pensioners who took up the pension bond exchange offer only months before the October 1993 congressional elections.

Major challenges

There was a multitude of challenges, the most significant of which were:

- Many analysts and syndicate participants were sceptical of the market's ability to absorb US$3 billion of YPF shares, which was a high number in relation to the US$18 billion market capitalisation of the Argentine equity market. The fact that the public float of the whole market was only US$6–7 billion made the challenge even bigger. Most investment banks recommended an issue size of only US$1–1.5 billion. Given the size of the domestic market it was deemed impossible to sell only to international asset allocators. Additional sources of buyers such as international buyers of oil stocks, growth stocks, etc. therefore needed to be found;

- An ambitious timetable had to be met, as the mandate was awarded on 16 April 1993 with pricing scheduled for 28 June. It was considered important to come to market before the BT3 issue in July and congressional elections in October;

- YPF had just emerged from restructuring and had no visible earnings record. It was also going to be a challenge to compile historic financial statements on a US GAAP basis;

- International investors were unfamiliar with the fact that Argentina was in the process of radically transforming itself, having previously regressed from being a developed country to being a less developed country;

- The Argentine financial community was unfamiliar with bookbuilding as domestic law required a formal auction of state assets. Existing legislation therefore had to be reinterpreted to enable bookbuilding to take place while maintaining public confidence in the transparency of the process;

- Argentine investors were wary of privatisations following a disastrous experience with the Telecom Argentina offer in 1992, and generally participated in equity issues for speculative purposes only. Domestic market reaction to the announcement of the offer was largely negative, as the issue was considered too big and the timetable too ambitious;

- Sceptical pensioners needed convincing of the merits of the proposed offer to exchange pension bonds for YPF shares. Many had sold their bonds (*bocones*) at low prices to financial institutions and speculators, who were also invited to participate in the exchange. Structuring the exchange itself presented a major challenge to the Ministry of the Economy and the domestic banks; and

- Political opposition in Argentina ensured a highly public debate on YPF's valuation, and as the press was against the sale, the president and the economy minister found themselves exposed to criticism. The controversial privatisation law took a year to pass through Congress, and some senior government officials were said to have been reluctant to see YPF privatised.

Rationale and objectives

Reasons for the offer

YPF was a vital part of Argentina's overall privatisation programme, which in turn was one of the most important aspects of the reform strategy.

The driving force behind privatisation in Argentina is fiscal to a certain extent, but more fundamental in a broader sense as it is closely connected to the deregulation, internationalisation and normalisation of Argentine business life. Public companies traditionally served employee interests rather than providing a good service to the wider citizenry, which in turn had become dissatisfied with the quality of such services. One of the main aims of the privatisation process was to improve the quality of these services and remove the burden of subsidies and operating deficits from the country's Treasury.

The vendor's objectives

The government's objectives were comprehensive and ambitious:

- To achieve a successful global public offer;
- To transfer control of YPF to the private sector;
- To realise fair value for YPF and raise cash for the state;
- To promote the development and stability of the domestic capital market, reducing volatility and insider trading;
- To raise cash for the social security system and address the needs of the pensioner holders of *bocones;*
- To promote capital inflow to Argentina; and
- To convince investors of the success of Argentina's economic policies and provide a successful base for future flotations, in the process achieving a re-valuation of the domestic equity market which was undervalued in relation to the bond market.

Use of proceeds

The government earmarked 63 per cent of the proceeds to pay off debt to state pensioners who had received *bocones* in lieu of cash several years earlier. This cash redemption was independent of the bond for equity swap exchange offer. The remaining 37 per cent of proceeds were to be used to pay royalties overdue to the oil-producing provinces which also retained 11.3 per cent of YPF's share capital.

The earlier privatisations

Argentina's state-sector companies were valued at some US$18 billion when Menem assumed power in 1989. There was tremendous fiscal pressure and a strong need to deregulate the relevant industry sectors and restructure companies which had been mismanaged for decades. Early sell-offs included the telephone companies, railways, electricity and gas utilities, water works and the national airline. Telefónica de Argentina in December 1991 and Telecom Argentina in February 1992 had been public share offers – but only after the sale of controlling stakes to foreign operating companies. Telefónica initially was successful, whereas Telecom was a disaster for five main reasons:

1. The timing of the offer coincided with the peak of the Argentine stock market;
2. Disclosure and corporate governance standards (and marketing methods) were highly traditional (most Argentine companies had been controlled by the families in whose interests they were managed);

3. Domestic investors were highly unsophisticated and subscribed at a ridiculously high price, mainly because Telefónica had been a success rather than because of a fundamental view of its value;
4. Local banks, encouraged by the success of Telefónica, aggressively lent as much as 100 per cent of the purchase price to retail investors; and
5. The Dutch auction method was used to price the offer, as required by the legislation then in place. A Dutch auction provides no mechanism to check unrealistically high bids from setting the auction clearing price and all high bidders are fully allocated regardless of investor quality.

Jim Miller, at the time managing director of equity capital markets at Merrill Lynch, pointed out that the problem created by the Dutch auction was not anticipated in 1991 when the methodology for the privatisations was designed. 'The question at that time was if there would be any demand at all,' he explained. 'The swing in sentiment from depression to euphoria was amazing.'

The challenge with YPF was to distance it from the Telecom disaster. In the process, the level of sophistication in the preparation and execution of major equity offers was revolutionised. 'We came to talk about privatisations via the equity market in terms of before and after YPF, referring to the old traditional practices and the new state-of-the-art disclosure, corporate governance and marketing standards,' commented Daniel Marx, at the time under-secretary for finance at the Argentine Ministry of the Economy and now managing director of Darby Overseas Investments in Washington DC.

Transaction components

The offer of (initially) 110 million outstanding shares owned by the Argentine government comprised a US tranche representing 48 per cent of the total offer, an international tranche representing 30 per cent (including the Americas sub-tranche) and a domestic tranche representing 23 per cent. The offer was marketed on an open-priced basis to both international and domestic investors, allowing a book to be built. It was registered with the SEC and the shares were listed on the NYSE. Argentine retail investors were offered bonus shares of 3 per cent and 2 per cent of the total number of shares purchased and held for one and two years respectively. There was a greenshoe initially sized at 15 million shares (see Exhibit 4).

The government also announced an offer to buy from pensioners and other holders of Republic of Argentina debt obligations with a 10-year maturity *(bocones)*, in exchange for YPF shares. These bonds were now trading at less than 50 per cent of face value because of scepticism about government intentions and doubts about its ability to live up to the obligations. The exchange offer was also open to investors who had bought *bocones* in the secondary market. The terms of the exchange would give pensioners, who had priority in the allocation, an effective discount of 15 per cent to the IPO price. The exchange offer closed two months after the IPO pricing, with shares purchased subject to a 12-month lock-up. Whilst it was the overall objective to sell more than 50 per cent of the company, it was also important to maximise the cash proceeds from the offer. In this context the exchange offer provided useful flexibility in so far as it was possible to increase the IPO and reduce the exchange offer should the IPO be well received by the markets – precisely what happened.

How the offer size changed

On 28 June the IPO was increased to 140 million shares and the greenshoe to 20 million. At the same time, the exchange offer, initially sized at up to 80 million shares, was reduced to 45 million (see Exhibit 5).

Exhibit 3

Share capital and ownership

Before offer	
Share capital	353 million shares
Market capitalisation at offer price (1 peso/1US$)	US$6.7 billion
Major shareholder before offer	100% owned by Argentine Government

After offer

Class of shares	Number of shares (million)	Ownership (%)	Holder	Directors	Principal provisions
A	72	20.4	Government	2	Golden share concerning change of control and certain other provisions. A shares must represent at least 20 % of the share capital (unless changed by law)
B	40	11.3	Provinces	1	
C	35	9.9	Employees	1	Should represent up to 10% of the share capital
D	206	58.4	Public	8	Controls the board of directors
Total	**353**	**100.0**			

Exhibit 4
Offer structure

Target markets	*Indicated tranche sizes	Joint bookrunners	Co-lead managers
US	47.7%	CSFB, Merrill Lynch	Goldman, Salomon, Bear Stearns, JP Morgan, Paine Webber
International	25.0%	Merrill Lynch, CSFB	Barings, Cazenove, Deutsche Bank, Kleinwort Benson, Nomura, Paribas
Americas (sub-tranche of international tranche)	4.6%	Merrill Lynch, CSFB	Citibank, RBC Dominion, Santander, Scotia McLeod, Wood Gundy
Argentine	22.7%	Banco Rio de la Plata , Banco de Galicia, Banco de Valores	Banco Roberts, Banco Frances del Rio de la Plata

Total combined offers (shares)   110 million

* Expressed as a percentage of the total indicated offer size at the time of public filing on 28 May 1993 .

Exhibit 5
Development of the offer size

	Indicated (million shares)	Final (million shares)	Final (% of co)
IPO – main offer	110	140	39.7
IPO – greenshoe	15	20	5.7
Shares subject to exchange offer	80	45	12.7
Total number of shares offered	**205**	**205**	**58.1**

Source: Offer circular and CSFB

Exhibit 6
Principal advisers

Financial advisers to YPF	CSFB and Merrill Lynch
Adviser to the joint global coordinators*	Banco General de Negocios
Legal adviser to the Ministry of the Economy	Cleary, Gottlieb, Steen & Hamilton
International legal adviser to YPF	Sullivan & Cromwell
Domestic legal adviser to YPF	Marval, O'Farrell & Mairal
Domestic legal adviser to the managers	Gallo and Bruchou
International legal adviser to the managers	Shearman & Sterling
Auditors	Pistrelli, Diaz y Asociados/Arthur Andersen

* Whereas the Ministry of the Economy did not hire a separate firm to advise on the financial aspects of the transaction, a number of individuals with international experience were employed by the ministry on a temporary basis.

Principal advisers

See Exhibit 6.

The timetable

The initial step towards the privatisation of YPF was taken in August 1989 with the approval in Congress of the president's State Reform Law, which facilitated, by way of decree, the steps necessary to restructure the Argentine oil sector and YPF itself (see Exhibit 7).

Transaction fee distribution

The institutional economics were distributed as shown in Exhibit 8.

CSFB and Merrill Lynch shared a global coordinators'

praecipium of 0.255 per cent, calculated on the gross proceeds of the total transaction. The underwriting fee was split on the basis of underwriting commitment in all tranches, whereby CSFB and Merrill Lynch together underwrote 19.7 per cent of the total transaction of 140 million shares.

Management fee

Outside the US, lead and co-lead managers shared 25 per cent of the total management fee as the lead and co-lead managers' praecipium calculated on the non-US portion of the combined offer. The balance of the management fee was paid to all managers in proportion to their underwriting commitments (see Exhibit 9).

In the US the management fees were allocated among the managers on the basis of underwriting commitment.

Exhibit 7
The timetable

	Preparation of offer
May 1989	• Menem elected president of the Republic of Argentina.
August	• Congress approves State Reform Law.
August 1990	• Menem appoints Estenssoro president and CEO of YPF.
January 1991	• Cavallo appointed Minister of the Economy.
March	• Congress approves Cavallo's convertibility plan linking the peso to the US dollar.
September 1992	• CSFB and Merrill Lynch appointed advisers to YPF.
October	• Congress approves YPF privatisation law after 12 months debate.
End 1992	• The federal government and YPF agree on division of labour in the sale process.
January 1993	CSFB and Merrill advised that: • YPF will be ready to come to market and it could be done in 2Q 1993; and • Equity market outlook is positive.
March	CSFB and Merrill advised that: • Market will value YPF as an IPO at US$6–7 billion; • IPO completion possible before congressional election in October 1993; and • US$2–2.5 billion can be raised if offer well prepared and marketed.
7 April,	• Argentine debt restructuring (Brady Plan) finalised by Cavallo.
	Execution of offer
Early April	• Announcement of intention to sell and timetable of the offer.
16 April	• CSFB and Merrill Lynch appointed joint global coordinators.
10–14 May	• Argentina country roadshow.
12 May	• F-1 registration statement filed with the SEC (on a confidential basis).
28 May	• Filing of price and size range with SEC (public filing).
31 May	• YPF management domestic roadshow.
1–25 June	• YPF management international roadshow.
16 June	• Exchange offer terms announced.
28 June	• Increase of IPO and shrinkage of exchange offer announced; • Pricing of transaction; and • Allotment to institutional and retail shareholders.
29 June	• Trading begins on NYSE and in Buenos Aires.
15 July	• Greenshoe exercised.
31 August	• Closing of exchange offer to pensioners.

Exhibit 8
Distribution of gross spread (%)

Global coordinator praecipium	Management fee	Underwriting fee	Selling concession	Gross spread
0.25*	0.75	0.75	2.25	4.00

* In addition, the joint global coordinators received US$1.8 million in the aggregate for financial advisory services provided in connection with the privatisation of the company.

Exhibit 9
Distribution of management fee outside the US (%)

Total management fee	0.75
Of which: Lead/co-lead managers' praecipium split among all international leads/co-leads	25
Of which: Management fees split among all managers	75

Exhibit 10
Distribution of selling concession in the US (%)

Total selling concession	2.25
Of which: Pre-agreed or fixed portion regardless of sales booked	30
Of which: Paid pro rata according to sales designated by investors	70

Selling concession

The US selling concession had one fixed and one variable component. The fixed component of 30 per cent was calculated on the basis of underwriting commitments. The variable portion was subject to performance and was designated by investors (see Exhibit 10).

In the UK a list was drawn up to coordinate which of the five managers would call which investor. The economics were therefore effectively 100 per cent fixed and shared equally between the five managers. In Europe and the RoW, the selling concession was paid in full to whomever the order was given.

Deal structure

The important decisions taken in devising the structure of the transaction were:

- *To appoint Merrill Lynch and CSFB joint global coordinators.* By appointing two of the top global firms to run this transaction, rather than the domestic houses that had had overall responsibility for Telecom and Telefónica, the government signalled that it was serious about adhering to best international practice;
- *To do a global offer and list the company on the NYSE.* Given the size involved and the lack of domestic institutional capital, this offer would stand or fall with international investor interest and US interest in particular. This fact was reassuring for international investors as the price would not be dictated by inflated domestic interest;
- *To opt for international best practice disclosure and corporate governance standards.* In addition to the SEC registration which would require the highest disclosure standards, the challenge was to construct a set of provisions that reduced the possibility of government intervention in the affairs of the company. Specific decisions in this regard included: size of the board; management participation on the board (unusual in Argentina), inclusion in the golden share of anti-takeover provisions which also apply to hostile action by the state; mandatory bid provisions for minorities; appointment of directors by class of shares; staggered board; and the majority of directors and senior management elected by the public shareholders. Many of these arrangements are not provided for by Argentine law due to the prevailing tradition of family ownership;
- *To price and underwrite by bookbuilding.* Legally, privatisations had to be priced by auction. This legislation was designed to ensure objectivity and fairness, to prevent corruption in the pricing and allocation process and to maximise the offer price. Given the unfortunate experience with Telecom, where demand and issue price were substantially inflated beyond levels sustainable in the secondary market (Singapore Telecom's privatisation was to be a similar case), CSFB and Merrill Lynch worked closely with the Ministry of the Economy to convince the government's legal auditors that bookbuilding was a form of auction and that with full disclosure of the order book to the attorney general's office, this process should be allowed;

- *To do one tranche only, ie, to sell down to below 50 per cent in one step.* Once the global coordinators were confident that the market had the capacity to absorb sufficient volume to take government ownership below 50 per cent it became a political decision. The risks of not selling a majority could be that a new government might seek to renationalise YPF or company management might leave fearing renewed political interference. The Argentine public was highly suspicious that the government would somehow continue to control YPF, and domestic banks were adamant that for the offer to gain momentum locally a majority stake would have to be sold. It was the perception of the transaction that was important, according to Marx: 'The fact of the matter is that we could have sold control even if we had sold less than 50 per cent. If the Argentine government really wanted to exercise influence over the company it probably could';
- *To combine settlement of state pension liabilities with the privatisation of YPF by adding the exchange offer immediately following the IPO.* This substantially increased the likelihood of selling more than 50 per cent of YPF to the public, thereby enhancing the overall credibility of the privatisation. The decision to close the exchange offer at least one month after the IPO was also crucial. It allowed the IPO to be priced and the success of the offer to be established before pensioners decided on whether or not to take up the exchange offer. It also meant that pensioners could be offered an effective discount of approximately 15 per cent, in exchange for which they were compelled to hold the shares for a minimum of one year. It was deemed too complicated for the exchange and the IPO to be carried out simultaneously; and
- *To limit the size of the retail tranche, to include bonus shares and to reject a retail discount and a partly paid structure.* Due to the retail sector's lack of depth, and its speculative nature, this part of the offer was limited to US$400 million. Bonus shares were offered after one and two years and the offer was structured with a dividend yield that would make the return to retail investors competitive with bank certificates of deposit. It was also decided that a retail discount would not be effective as it would encourage immediate selling in the secondary market.

Although many of the underwriters and one of the joint global coordinators initially recommended a partly paid structure, this was ultimately considered too complex and likely to create additional price volatility in the secondary market. Since Argentine investors already had a strong inclination to speculate – encouraged by the historically disappointing performance of the stock market as a vehicle for saving – it was deemed inappropriate to increase leverage through a partly paid structure as this would have added to volatility. Argentina was seen as a highly leveraged country by the international investment community and it was important not to add further leverage in the offer itself. Instead, a decision was taken to structure the shares with an attractive dividend yield.

Two alternative structures were also considered: either to sell YPF to a foreign oil company or to conduct a smaller

IPO. Both were rejected: in the first case – a strategic sale – it was decided that YPF did not need the transfer of technology that might normally follow such a move; that the government's planned timing of the sale would be set back because an extended period of due diligence would be required; that there were a limited number of potential buyers and that the move would be unlikely to yield a higher price. There was also the politically undesirable fact that the company would pass into the control of a foreign oil corporation. The smaller IPO followed by a subsequent share offer was rejected as it did not meet the objective of privatising YPF in one step, it did not provide investors with an assurance that YPF would be run as an independent company, the cash proceeds would be insufficient to retire a substantial amount of the state pension debt and there would be a large overhang of stock.

Marketing

The main points of the marketing strategy were:

Syndication

- There were three coordinated but ring-fenced tranches, tightly managed by CSFB and Merrill Lynch ;
- Syndicate appointments were made by the Ministry of the Economy after consultation with the joint global coordinators to avoid conflicts of interest;
- Co-leads and co-managers were selected mainly on the basis of their research skills in the oil and gas industry, and Latin America. Complementary skills were emphasised in each tranche, meaning that each included managers with respective strengths in oil and gas, Latin America and general stock-picking; and
- Emphasis was placed on cooperation rather than competition among banks. There were no restrictions on access to international investors other than in the UK.

Institutional marketing

- A five-day roadshow by Minister of the Economy Cavallo and under-secretary for finance Marx preceded the company roadshow and was designed to educate key targeted investors about the fast improving Argentine story and to influence asset allocators to put the country on their approved list;
- The company roadshow was an extensive four-week affair with a single team (CEO/CFO) making presentations to 724 institutions in 29 cities, with 69 one-on-one meetings;
- The structure of the offer was designed to appeal to all investment philosophies: oil, Argentina, growth, value and income investors. According to Miller of Merrill Lynch: 'We did the country sale first. This was necessary but not sufficient. We then had to sell the YPF story';
- YPF was promoted as a major international oil and gas corporation. For US investors, it was positioned as an integrated oil company ranking with Elf, Repsol and Total in Europe: the idea was to urge US investors to diversify their foreign portfolios of oil stocks and enhance income by buying a stock with an attractive dividend yield;

- The offer was marketed with a dividend yield range of 4–4.7 per cent and a progressive dividend policy;
- The strategy was to build momentum through 50–60 targeted core accounts and then spread the message to a wider audience; and
- There was also a desire to maximise liquidity and visibility to achieve the greatest possible impact globally, generating important spin-offs for the Argentine capital market as a whole.

Retail marketing

- The Argentine tranche included a dedicated offer of up to US$400 million to Argentine residents;
- The domestic retail strategy focused on high-net-worth individuals, including Argentine flight money and other Latin American offshore money;
- The Argentine mass market was incentivised by the bonus share scheme, whereby retail investors were offered additional shares equivalent to 3 per cent and 2 per cent of the total number of shares purchased and held for one and two years, respectively;
- The strategy in the US was to dedicate a sufficient number of shares to retail investors to encourage a strong response from retail brokers and develop a liquid secondary market on the NYSE. European privatisations usually fail to make an impact with US retail investors because vendors cannot usually commit a minimum amount of stock for offer to US retail investors; and
- Merrill Lynch took 80 retail sales managers and salesmen to Argentina to see and understand the country in order to improve the effectiveness of their retail marketing.

The YPF story

The transformation of YPF from a debt-ridden state enterprise to an efficient company saleable in the international market is little short of remarkable. From 1937 to 1992 the company, founded in 1922, had never paid a dividend to the government and in recent years had cost the state about US$1 billion a year. Investment activities were traditionally driven by capacity expansion rather than by return while there was substantial under-investment in maintenance leading to refineries becoming environmentally hazardous. An almost total absence of investment in YPF's own service stations meant that they maintained market share only because private refineries were allocated insufficient volumes of crude.

The company had historically been run as an instrument of the government's social security policy. There was a YPF station and office in almost every village, often the government's only representative in those communities and the company paid the salaries of thousands of people who never turned up for work, as well as building hospitals, schools and churches. The company was also subjected to numerous regulations dreamt up by corrupt politicians and bureaucrats. Cavallo noted: 'The government decided everything, there was absolutely no room whatsoever for the market mechanism – there were regulations for everything, crazy regulations.'

The unions had a stranglehold on the company, as Cavallo describes: 'The trade union was more important than the president of the company.' All employees except the president and the executive vice president were union members and the union determined the terms of employee contracts, including salaries, promotions and any disciplinary actions. The cost of labour was considered fixed for the short and long term and the company had no control over how many temporary staff it actually employed. Management appointments were a form of patronage – of 32 presidents, 22 lasted less than a year. Federal, provincial and local politicians used YPF as a tool to enrich themselves and buy votes or other favours.

It was into this climate that Peronist Carlos Menem stepped as victor in Argentina's presidential election in May 1989. Although elected on a populist agenda, he promptly unleashed a whirlwind of reformist activity consistent with a market economy. In August 1990 he invited experienced oil industry executive Jose Estenssoro to become the trustee of YPF, which effectively meant that he had complete power over the company. In January 1991 Domingo Cavallo moved from foreign affairs to the Ministry of the Economy. The three men reformed and restructured their respective areas, making important contributions to what would ultimately become the YPF story.

Menem

By August 1989 Menem had obtained congressional approval for the legislation required for one of the world's most ambitious privatisation programmes. Its aims were:

- To reduce the budget deficit by reversing state contributions to state-owned enterprises;
- To incorporate new technology and management techniques to enhance productivity and profitability;
- To encourage capital inflow and domestic investment;
- To reduce the cost and improve the quality of essential services; and
- To reduce the government's domestic and foreign debt through debt-equity swaps.

Although this law did not explicitly single out YPF for privatisation, it made possible by way of decree, the deregulation of the Argentine oil industry and the restructuring of the company that was to proceed rapidly from 1989. A whole series of decrees breaking up the YPF monopoly and deregulating the oil industry followed before the end of 1989. Menem then set to work to break the trade union power that had affected YPF and other state-owned companies for decades. Over the next few years, he would go into battle with the unions on many occasions to secure the commercialisation of YPF.

Menem guided the privatisation law through congress by November 1992. This law, which established the procedures by which the company would be privatised and allowed for a sale of up to 70 per cent of YPF, faced considerable opposition in Congress and was only passed after a year of debate.

Cavallo

While these reforms were in progress, Cavallo was executing his own programme to revitalise Argentina's economy. This required comprehensive measures in five main areas, all of which were crucial for the successful privatisation of YPF:

- Monetary reform;
- Tax reform;
- Trade reform;
- Reorganisation of the public sector; and
- Restructuring of the foreign debt.

Cavallo made monetary reform an immediate priority in order to curb hyperinflation, and the convertibility plan, whereby the peso was pegged to the US dollar in a one-for-one relationship, was introduced in Congress on 20 March 1991 and passed a week later. In 1992 Cavallo made the central bank independent. The convertibility plan and privatisation are the cornerstones of his radical economic reform programme.

Cavallo understood the significance of organising the state-controlled energy sector before privatisation. The policies pursued by Menem since 1989 and subsequently refined by Cavallo allowed for the deregulation of the Argentine oil and gas sector and the transformation of YPF from a politically managed, government-owned monopoly to an efficient and competitive integrated oil and gas company. In line with these policies, the free disposition of hydrocarbons was introduced, price regulation removed, import and export restrictions abolished and exploration and ownership rights fully liberalised.

To open Argentina's oil industry to competition, it was necessary to reduce significantly YPF's control of Argentina's oil and gas reserves. To accomplish this, the government required YPF to sell majority interests in the production rights of four highly productive areas, the so called central areas, as well as other production and exploration rights, the marginal areas.

Estenssoro

On his appointment, Estenssoro immediately set about devising a strategic plan for YPF in conjunction with consultants McKinsey & Co. The plan, the acceptance of which was a pre-condition for him agreeing to take the job at YPF and to which Menem agreed, included three important provisions to sever the strong links between state and company:

- No political interference;
- No government support of the trade unions; and
- YPF to be managed as a private corporation.

To execute the plan, Estenssoro immediately set about renegotiating union contracts and eliminating constraints on productivity. A review of all YPF assets was undertaken, and decisions were taken on whether to retain, sell, close down or put operations into joint ventures. Asset sales realised US$2 billion and YPF's market share was reduced to 50 per cent in production, refining and marketing, which left the company fully balanced between two new business units – upstream and downstream activities. Between January 1991 and March 1993 the number of employees was cut from 51,000 to 10,600. The quality of head-office personnel was upgraded: 80 per cent of the top management team came to comprise industry professionals, many of them recruited by Estenssoro.

The work inspired by these men over a period of four years, beginning with the passing of the State Reform Law in August 1989, paved the way for the successful IPO of YPF.

Exhibit 11
Principal sales points

Dominant market position	• The world's 11th largest publicly traded integrated oil and gas company. Holds about 50% market shares in production, refining and marketing. Represents a unique opportunity to invest in Latin America's oil and gas industry.
Exposure to Argentina	• Participation in the sharply improving Argentine economy. Free-market economics already yielding outstanding results, including: sharply lower inflation and interest rates, currency stability, much better debt service ratios, just under 9% GDP growth, quickly increasing fixed investments.
Impressive restructuring	• Turnaround story – tremendous work already achieved. Much-reduced workforce with more redundancies expected.
High growth potential	• Best cash flow and earnings growth potential of peer group.
Rock-solid balance sheet	• Lowest financial leverage among peers (15% debt/total capital ratio).
Attractive valuation	• Marketed at 7–8.3 x 94 earnings, YPF's P/E ratio represented a substantial discount to its peer group; and • Attractive dividend yield versus peers and overall market (over 4% against only 2.8% for S&P 500).

Exhibit 12
YPF's estimated 1994 price/cashflow against peers (times)

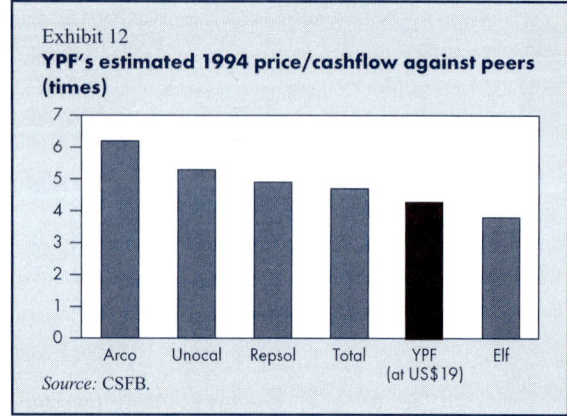

Source: CSFB.

Exhibit 13
YPF's estimated 1994 price/earnings ratio against peers (times)

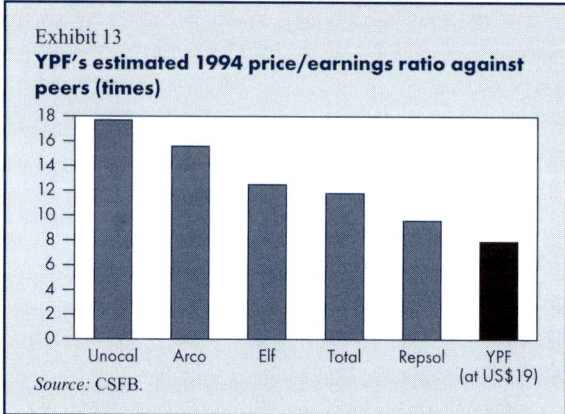

Source: CSFB.

Exhibit 14
Pricing strategy

Objectives	Strategy
1. No restructuring discount 2. No Argentina discount 3. No size discount 4. No government ownership discount	1. Focus on earnings and cash flow from 1994 rather than 1993 2. Focus on growth rather than risk 3. File size of US$1.8–2.2 billion with possibility to increase 4. Independent board of directors and at least 51% privatisation

By the time of the offer Menem, Cavallo and Estenssoro had created a revitalised state oil company operating within a greatly improved domestic economy. YPF, the largest quoted company in Argentina, had become a growth story, a restructuring play and a country story, and represented a unique opportunity to buy a Latin American oil stock at a time when the Argentine government was determined to have a successful transaction.

CSFB and Merrill Lynch sold the offer on the strength of the key sales points shown in Exhibit 11.

YPF was attractively valued on the basis of price/cash flow (see Exhibit 12), and on an earnings basis was more attractive than its US and European peers (see Exhibit 13).

When discussing valuation and pricing with investors, the joint global coordinators argued that none of the typical discounts associated with big privatisations were justified on this occasion (see Exhibit 14).

Reasons for not buying

The following reasons were given by those who decided not to participate:

- Fear of failure of the convertibility plan and a resulting devaluation (which has not happened despite the Mexican crisis);
- Concern about weak after-market performance (based on experience with Telefónica and Telecom);
- Suspicion of continued government influence despite institutional investors' board control;
- Risk of re-nationalisation by a future government; and
- Declining oil prices.

Market conditions

General market conditions were strong, as evidenced by an

increase in the S&P 500 by 3 per cent from 1 January 1993 to 16 April 1993, the date of appointment of the global coordinators. However, between filing of the F-1 registration statement on 12 May and the final day of the YPF management's international roadshow on 25 June, the US market moved only sideways in terms of the S&P 500.

The oil and gas sector was very much in favour with investors. The S&P Integrated Oil Index rose by 13.9 per cent from 1 January 1993 to 16 April on the back of a strong crude oil market. Between 12 May and 25 June, however, oil stocks had fallen by between 1 per cent (Total) and 8.2 per cent (BP) as a result of an 8.8 per cent drop in the price of crude (WTI) from US$20.20/barrel to US$18.42/barrel. While the Argentine market as measured by the Merval Index had traded sideways (off 1.8 per cent) between 1 January and 16 April, it added 15.7 per cent between 12 May and 25 June.

The new-issue environment in general was highly receptive: of the 23 US IPOs launched between 13 January and 4 May, 21 had traded up by 25 June but only six of the dozen launched between 11 May and 23 June had done the same. Sentiment toward emerging market new issuance was probably as strong as it had ever been.

Results

Placement

Based on the initial underwriting amount of 110 million shares, the total offer was six times subscribed (see Exhibit 15).

'The remarkable thing with this transaction was that virtually every high-quality institution world-wide participat-

ed,' commented Bob Cooney, managing director of equity capital markets at CSFB.

The US tranche was almost seven times subscribed. There were 339 institutional orders of which 33 accounted for 50 per cent of total demand. This built gradually, the overwhelming proportion of the US book coming together during the last week. Approximately 35 per cent of institutions that placed orders did not receive stock. Of the institutional pot, 53 per cent was allocated to 16 institutions.

The international tranche was four times subscribed, with good demand coming through during the second week of marketing, and was fully subscribed two weeks before pricing. There were 1,180 institutional orders. The largest markets were the UK and Switzerland, though the UK market was relatively small compared to some other offers: total UK demand was only 41.2 million shares against US institutional demand of 257 million. Forty international institutions accounted for 50 per cent of the total allotment.

The Argentine tranche was more than five times subscribed, with significant demand from high-net-worth individuals and large corporations, though several large orders were allocated to the international tranche. Retail demand concentrated towards the end of the subscription period.

Investor concentration

For such a large offer, placement was concentrated in relatively few hands, with some very large orders being received (see Exhibit 16).

Type of buyer

A very good spread was achieved between oil investors, income funds, value investors, growth investors, Argentina

---

Exhibit 15
Underwriting, demand and allocation (%)

Target markets	Initial underwriting	Final underwriting	Demand	Allocation
US	47.7	46.4	53.0	48.1
International*	29.6	28.6	25.7	27.8
Argentine	22.7	25.0	21.3	24.1
Total combined offer (shares)	**110 million**	**140 million**	**666 million**	**160 million**

* Includes Canadian and Latin American markets as well as certain large Argentine investors and Argentine offshore money.

Sources: CSFB and Merrill Lynch.

Exhibit 16
Investor concentration

	By demand	By allocation
Percentage of total issue accounted for by the 10 largest investors	11%	18%
Number of investors making up 80% of the institutional portion of the issue	170	111
The three largest investors by size	US$342 million US$228 million US$143 million	US$95 million US$77 million US$71 million
Total number of international institutions	984	791

Sources: CSFB and Merrill Lynch.

investors and Latin America buyers. The fact that Fidelity bought shares for 31 separate funds testifies to the broad diversity of interest. The retail/institutional split was fixed one week before pricing and the allocation breakdown per tranche is shown in Exhibit 17.

Exhibit 17
Institutional/retail split (%)

	Institutional	Retail
US tranche	74	26
International tranche	90	10
Argentine tranche	34	66

Sources: CSFB & Merrill Lynch.

Exhibit 18
After-market price performance

Pricing date	28 June 1993
Filing range	US$17–20
Offer price	US$19

First year high/low

High (8 February 1994)	US$29
Low (19 July 1993)	US$19

YPF share price relative to Merval Index (%)

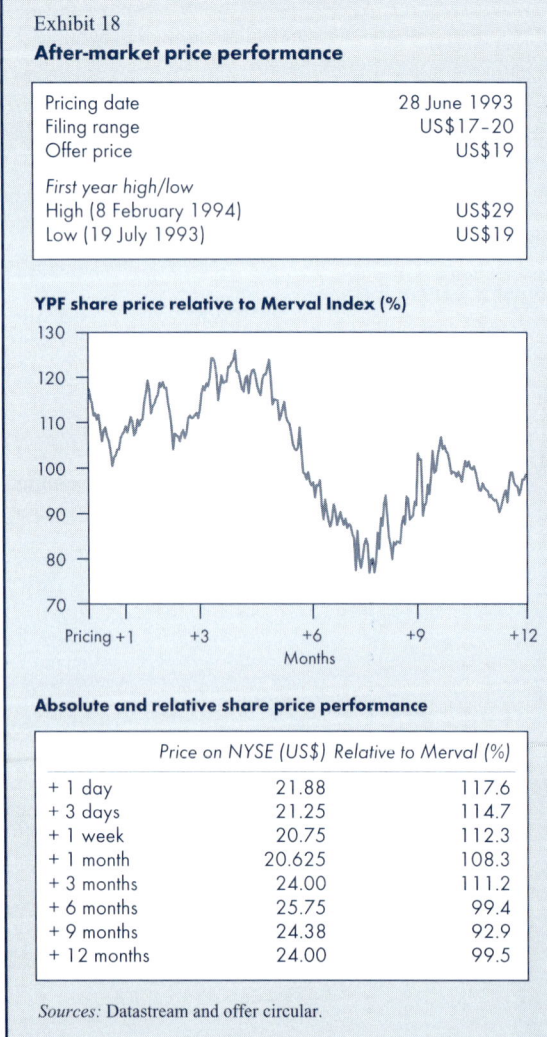

Absolute and relative share price performance

	Price on NYSE (US$)	Relative to Merval (%)
+ 1 day	21.88	117.6
+ 3 days	21.25	114.7
+ 1 week	20.75	112.3
+ 1 month	20.625	108.3
+ 3 months	24.00	111.2
+ 6 months	25.75	99.4
+ 9 months	24.38	92.9
+ 12 months	24.00	99.5

Sources: Datastream and offer circular.

Exhibit 19
Percentage of total issue traded* (%)

	Day 1	Day 2	Day 3	Total Day 1–Day 3
New York	24.5	6.5	4.3	34.1

* Based on the issue of 140 million shares.

In Argentina more than 50,000 retail investors participated and approximately 90,000 pensioners exchanged *bocones* for YPF shares. Of the total US$400 million allocated to US retail, Merrill Lynch alone accounted for 50 per cent through 17,000 orders.

After-market price performance

See Exhibit 18.

YPF has been a strong performer in the secondary market as an oil stock, and has tracked the local market for the most part, staying within a valuation range of its international peer group. It slightly under-performed a strong Argentine market and subsequently outperformed it during a period of weakness.

- On the first day of trading on the NYSE, YPF closed at US$21.875, a premium of 15 per cent over the offer price. Thereafter, the share price fell gradually to a first-year low of US$19 on 19 July 1993 against a flat local market;
- In early August the shares started to perform strongly and after three months had reached US$24, representing an outperformance of 11.2 per cent against the Merval Index. By 28 October the price had risen to a high of US$27.875 and the relative outperformance was 26 per cent;
- Despite holding up reasonably well, the share then began a period of under-performance against a strengthening market and by 28 December YPF at US$25.75 had lost its entire outperfromance against the Merval Index;
- The highest price during the first 12 months of trading was reached on 8 February 1994 when YPF closed at US$29, at which time it had actually under-performed a strong local market by 20 per cent. At this point Merval had risen by 72 per cent since pricing and it would peak a few days later before US monetary tightening began to affect the Argentine market;
- After nine months (by 28 March 1994) YPF had, at US$24.375, under-performed the local market by 8 per cent, but after a year the share price was up US$5 on the offer price, representing performance in line with the market; and
- YPF performed strongly during the Mexican currency and credit crisis in late 1994 and early 1995, though an all-time low of US$14.375 was reached on 8 March 1995. After two years, YPF traded at just over US$19 and had outperformed the market by 3 per cent since the offer.

After-market trading volume

See Exhibit 19.

The NYSE experienced very heavy volume on the first day of trading but this subsided on the next trading day. Argentine volumes were much more modest because those who bought in Argentina were generally longer-term holders. The NYSE has clearly become the home market for YPF: during 1994, 253 million shares traded on the NYSE whereas the equivalent figure for Buenos Aires was just under 16 million.

The performance of the main parties

The vendor

President Menem deserves tremendous credit for his political courage and determination in getting the necessary laws passed to make this privatisation possible. One of the principal reasons for his success with Congress was his strategy of appealing to the people, in a Reagan-like fashion, thereby putting pressure on individual congressmen. According to David Mulford, the man who, as assistant secretary to the US Treasury was responsible for the renegotiation of Argentina's foreign debt, he was 'one of the most effective political leaders in the world today. He has great focus and concentrates on a limited number of key issues.'

Menem also deserves credit for going into battle with the trade unions to secure the commercialisation of YPF. He was friends with Diego Ibanez, the trade union boss for the oil industry, as the two had spent time in prison together during the military governments. Cedric Bridger, YPF's CFO commented: 'Menem at the end told Diego Ibanez that he had gambled to block Pepe's restructuring initiatives at the company and unfortunately had lost and must now lay down his weapons. Ibanez was forced to accept it and from then on, the trade union no longer had a firm grip on the company.'

Although the general direction of economic reform and the political backing came from Menem, there was no overall plan to bring about reform before Cavallo, a brilliant Harvard University-trained economist and technocrat, got involved. His strategy was based on a fundamental view of Argentina's economic system at the time, which he described as 'socialism without a plan and capitalism without a market'.

The successful privatisation of YPF could not have happened without Cavallo's economic reform programme. According to Julio Domingo Barroero, general manager of Banco General de Negocios 'perhaps as much as 75 per cent of the decision to buy YPF was related to the economic reform programme'. Horacio Liendo explained: 'Convertibility forces privatisation as it imposes a fundamental framework of fiscal and monetary soundness. In the past, problems were solved by printing more money.' According to economists, convertibility may not have been feasible without the stimulus provided by the proceeds from privatisation and the capital inflow, as the country would have crumbled both politically and economically without this.

Cavallo, Marx and Liendo deserve credit for the strong leadership of their bankers and for having made many good decisions – some of which were very bold – with respect to the timing and structure of the transaction.

In terms of his more direct contribution towards the sale of the issue, Cavallo, prior to launch, travelled around the world to address senior fund managers and asset allocators. Uniquely for Argentina he was able to present macro-economic graphs which were all pointing in the right direction, after only two years of reform. He had not only successfully reformed the economic policies of the country, he now also sold them to the investment community.

Cavallo has tremendous credibility with the foreign financial community and according to many Argentineans, he is one of the few local politicians who have a reputation for not being corrupt. 'There is no doubt whatsoever,' says David Anderson, managing director of CSFB, 'that YPF could not have been done without Cavallo's successful reform programme.'

The company

Whilst Menem ensured that political interference in the company was stopped, allowing the company to start managing its affairs on a commercial basis, it was Estenssoro who had to break the power of the unions.

Together with a team of hand-picked colleagues and consultants he sold off large parts of the company and rationalised and transformed the business culture of YPF. He was very good both at recognising talent from within the company and attracting the necessary expertise from external sources.

It was to a very large extent these resolute restructuring efforts that created YPF's track record and created the core of the stock story. Investors were attracted not only by the newly acquired competitiveness of YPF itself but also by the management which had achieved this, as investors look forward and expect more of the same. Estenssoro and Cedric Bridger, his CFO, did a fabulous job of selling the YPF story on the roadshow.

Estenssoro had a good track record in the US, the key market for a successful sale, as he knew the industry and sounded American, which was a key advantage when speaking to institutional investors in the US and elsewhere. He was tough and charming, and quickly figured out what he wanted to do at YPF. He knew how to handle politicians, company employees, trade unions, the Argentine public, bankers, consultants and institutional investors. It was these qualities and others which enabled him to do such a good job at YPF, as unlike his successor, Nells León, he was not a nuts and bolts oil man. David Anderson of CSFB explained: 'Everything taken into account, I don't believe that any other man but Pepe would have been able to pull off this transaction.'

The global coordinators

CSFB and Merrill Lynch achieved something that nobody had expected. Their most notable accomplishments included:

- The banks both recognised that an offer of this size could be done. This probably stemmed from CSFB 's intimate knowledge of Argentina and its political situation, and the conviction that YPF could be marketed successfully as a world-class oil company, together with Merrill's reading of investor sentiment toward the country;
- They also recognised the importance of telling the Argentina story before the YPF story. Without the Cavallo/Marx roadshow which convinced international investors of the long-term stability and attractiveness of the country, a transaction of this size would not have been possible. As a result of the roadshow many fund managers upgraded their asset allocation to Argentina;
- David Mulford had credibility with Cavallo and was therefore in a position to make a contribution in driving the execution process forward. This credibility was based on Mulford's knowledge of the macroeconomic situation in

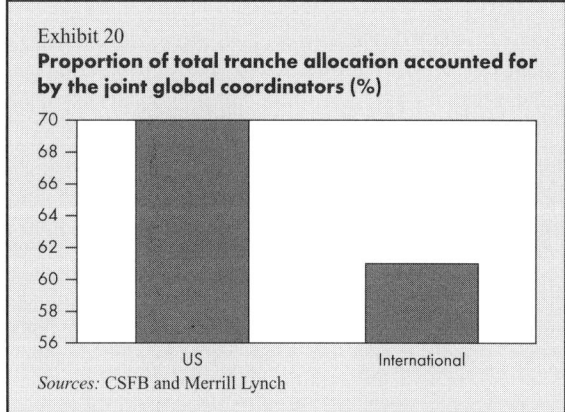

Exhibit 20
Proportion of total tranche allocation accounted for by the joint global coordinators (%)

Sources: CSFB and Merrill Lynch

Argentina and his understanding of the political processes involved in a large privatisation of this kind; and

- The marketing strategy for the issue was of paramount importance. CSFB and Merrill Lynch structured the IPO to appeal to the broadest possible investor audience. They accounted for a large portion of the sales outside Argentina (see Exhibit 20).

In July 1992 YPF initiated the process of interviewing a limited number of investment banks for the role of preparing it for its flotation. Much to YPF's surprise, Goldman Sachs teamed up with NM Rothschild, so other banks also found partners, CSFB joining Merrill Lynch and Salomon joining Morgan Stanley. JP Morgan competed alone. 'This transaction was so big and so important that nobody could afford to lose it and teaming up was perceived as increasing the probability of being able to play an important role,' says Guillermo Reca of Merrill Lynch. The pairings of Goldman Sachs/NM Rothschild and CSFB/Merrill Lynch were considered equally strong. Merrill Lynch's institutional placement power was deemed equivalent to that of Goldman Sachs and it also had the retail strength. Furthermore, Merrill Lynch had maintained an investment banking office in Buenos Aires since the mid 1980s, longer than any other foreign investment bank, and its private banking office had been there for 30 years. CSFB traditionally had the premier oil franchise on Wall Street and several Spanish-speaking individuals, one an Argentine. The bank also had well connected local partners in a former economy minister and the small but reputable merchant bank, Banco General de Negocios. YPF chose CSFB/Merrill Lynch, because of the more personal way they sold themselves. The banks also made an offer YPF could not refuse: the banks would be prepared to take on the advisory work for minimum pay so as to be well positioned for the underwriting job, although Estenssoro very clearly told them that this was not something that YPF could deliver, as the Ministry of the Economy was the owner of the shares. The advisory assignment began in September, before the law allowing for the privatisation of YPF had been passed.

By the end of the advisory phase in early March and following the advice that a global equity issue could be done before the summer, the government urgently needed to appoint global coordinators. Although CSFB/Merrill Lynch had been working on the advisory assignment, Cavallo needed by law

three proposals, and also invited Salomon and Goldman Sachs. Goldman pushed hard, leveraging off its successful experience in selling Telmex and claiming a unique knowledge of key emerging-market buyers. Another factor in its favour was its involvement, together with NM Rothschild, in the multi-billion-dollar privatisation by private sale of Argentine gas utility Gas del Estado, which had earned it widespread praise for professional execution. Merrill Lynch, on the other hand, had been of great service in the Telefónica and Telecom offers, two privatisations totalling over US$2 billion which were fiscally critical to the government. As the only foreign bank involved in these deals, Merrill Lynch gained valuable equity new-issue experience in Argentina. CSFB had advised on the privatisation of Argentina's electricity sector and had in the meantime acquired a further strong card in David Mulford, who had joined the firm after the advisory assignment had started.

After six weeks' deliberation, CSFB and Merrill Lynch were appointed global coordinators on 16 April. Marx commented: 'We felt that CSFB and Merrill Lynch together represented a very strong team in terms of placement power and they knew the company very well, having advised YPF during the preparatory phase. In addition, they offered the lowest overall total commissions. Despite having lost out on the assignment, Goldman Sachs were very helpful in assisting the ministry throughout the execution process when we were interested in a second opinion. This I appreciated very much.'

Key lessons learnt

Preparation

Early preparation and the opportunity to build a track record is crucial to achieve a successful privatisation. 'The key to successful privatisation,' stressed Domingo Cavallo, 'lies in first organising the sector.' This was done with a thoroughness that brought credit to all involved. At the company, the early appointment of first-class management, well ahead of flotation makes all the difference, particularly if the new management can carry out at least part of the required restructuring prior to the sale. The sooner the market's emphasis on this point is realised by privatisation authorities, the more successful they will be in their privatisation sales. It is no longer possible for a newly appointed privatisation team to come into office and hope that within a few months they will be able to compete in the capital markets. Reca noted: 'It is becoming more and more important for governments to pick good managers to run their privatisation candidates, as competition in the global equity market is becoming more and more intense.'

Structure

Philip Mallinckrodt, at the time a managing director of equity capital markets at CSFB, highlighted the significance of the acceptance of market capacity as being more important than price in the YPF privatisation: 'In other words, recognising that the state of the markets was such that it was a unique opportunity to do such a large offer for an oil company.' The ability to read the market made it possible to conduct a near-US$3 billion deal for a once-moribund South American state company.

It is easier to conduct a large sale in connection with an IPO than in a secondary offer because an IPO offers the possibility to segment the market and then structure and price the offer to appeal to each segment. David Mulford says: 'One of the secrets to successful privatisation is to be as bold as you possibly can up front.'

Joint bookrunners can work in favour of the vendor if the latter is sophisticated and prepared to manage its advisers tightly, and if compensation structures are organised to avoid infighting among the advisers. In the case of YPF, the joint global coordinators were threatened with dismissal if infighting was spotted – dramatic but effective.

Timing

In emerging markets, the importance of achieving a successful sale of the country story should not be underestimated. 'It was of key significance that we first concluded the Brady debt plan before Minister Cavallo and myself embarked on the country roadshow, as we needed the maximum possible credibility with regard to the repositioning of the republic,' explained Marx.

The politics

'Privatisation,' commented Mulford, 'is first and foremost a political process. The bigger the issue, the more political it becomes. The particular financial solution has to recognise this reality.'

The degree of success of a particular privatisation is often related to the degree of commitment at the highest political level. However, it is also important for investors to recognise which objective the government is most committed to in any given situation, as this enables a judgment to be made as to the sale's likely success. In the Telefónica and Telecom privatisations, proceeds were the primary concern, but in the case of YPF it was also important that the transaction should be a public success.

Other

Successful privatisations, particularly in controversial industries, require champions, of which YPF had at least three: Menem, Cavallo and Estenssoro. There is a lot of personal and legislative risk involved in what amounts to a war with many battles, and even if the champions emerge victorious they are unlikely to be unscathed.

It was also clear that the more sophisticated the vendor and the more active its involvement, the better the end result of a large offer of this kind. In this case the vendor handled all the syndicate appointments, having consulted with the joint global coordinators. Daniel Marx personally procured the commitment of many of the most senior syndicate members by visiting them in their offices prior to appointment.

Conclusion

The YPF issue was a major challenge met very successfully. Few people initially thought that it would be a triumph but through hard work and boldness the offer was successfully structured, marketed and sold. The vendor, the company and the bankers all did an outstanding job and worked well together.

The joint global coordinators correctly assessed the timing and put the transaction on a fast-track to benefit from a window of opportunity in the market. The oil price had been strong since the fourth quarter of 1992 but had peaked before the end of the marketing period. This, together with the knowledge that second-quarter earnings were not going to be great, was a good reason for not pricing at the top of the range.

The government's objectives were met, as it sold more than 50 per cent of the company and investors were left with the feeling that YPF had indeed passed into private control. The sale also raised enough cash to honour a substantial portion of the government's commitment to pensioners. Some 7 per cent of all pensioners holding *bocones* participated in the exchange offer against an expectation of no more than 2 per cent. Institutions which had not received a full allocation in the IPO bid up the *bocones* to the benefit of the pensioners. Two-thirds of all *bocones* exchanged for YPF shares came from institutions, the remainder coming from pensioners. The issue was seen universally as a success with a strong – but not too strong – after-market performance. Measured against the expectation of an implied IPO discount of at least 10 per cent, the price did well in the immediate after-market. Argentine investors were allocated a meaningful portion of YPF shares and the state benefited through direct external capital inflow of almost US$2 billion.

The global structure of the offer and the absence of restrictions on cross-border portfolio investment meant that the highest standards of transparency, disclosure, corporate governance and avoidance of conflict of interest were imposed upon the Argentine domestic equity market. This substantially enhanced the credibility of the domestic market.

Finally, after all the restructuring and commercialisation, YPF changed from being a major drain on the national budget to become the largest tax payer in Argentina.

Zeneca Group plc

In the spring of 1993 a simultaneous demerger and biggest-ever UK rights offer launched Zeneca Group plc onto the world's equity markets . This raising of US$2.1 billion marked the end of a long road and the beginning of separate routes for one of the stock market's blue-chips, Imperial Chemical Industries and its pharmaceuticals business.

ICI, the UK's largest non-oil manufacturer, was trading in the early 1990s at only half its estimated break-up value despite considerable restructuring during the 1980s. Although there was a strong contribution by the pharmaceuticals oper-ations to group profits, ICI's P/E ratio remained stubbornly in the stock market's chemicals-company range, while pure phar-maceuticals companies were some ten points ahead. ICI there-fore seemed an obvious target for corporate raiders.

Enter Hanson Trust, the highly acquisitive UK group renowned for launching and winning hostile take-overs, which struck with a 2.8 per cent acquisition of ICI stock in May 1991. Clearly chairman Lord Hanson had discovered the grow-ing value of the pharmaceuticals business hidden within an unfocused ICI. This small stake was thought to be the launch pad for a full bid. Although there was nothing in Hanson's criticism that ICI did not already know, the comments were given much publicity and acted as a catalyst on ICI manage-ment, a fact which they would deny.

A strategic review had been initiated by chairman Sir Denys Henderson in September 1990: the group had already looked hard at some form of demerger, but had chosen instead to cut costs and shed a number of smaller businesses. Much

of this was attributable to ICI being hit by the most serious eco-nomic recession in 60 years. With the Hanson take-over threat a real factor in the ICI boardroom, both a mega-merger with another international company and a pharmaceuticals alliance were seriously contemplated to rectify the undervaluation, even though a merger could be highly dilutive for ICI share-holders, given the group's depressed share price.

On 8 May 1992, Hanson sold its ICI stake. ICI had suc-cessfully defended itself by launching a skillful PR campaign, during which it turned the spotlight on Hanson's own weak-nesses. There had also been speculation that with a general election due in April 1992, the Conservative government may have made it clear to Hanson that a hostile bid for, and break-up of, Britain's largest manufacturer would have been inop-portune for the government. Nevertheless, the process of change had been set in motion and on 30 July 1992, after a year of deliberation, Sir Denys announced that ICI was consider-ing a demerger of its bio-science businesses, which included pharmaceuticals. This was Zeneca.

However, if ICI was to give up these cash-generating busi-nesses then it needed to be rewarded for its historical invest-ment in them. Taken together with disappointing operating results and restructuring charges in 1990 and 1992, this required ICI to combine the demerger with a financing. The questions were: how the money should be raised, whether to do so before or after the demerger and which company would be the most attractive vehicle –the old ICI, the new ICI or Zeneca.

While demergers are becoming increasingly frequent as

Exhibit 1

Transaction summary

Issuer name: Zeneca Group plc (UK)	Global coordinator: SG Warburg
Pricing date: 12 May 1993 (FT–SE 100: 2,861)	Pricing/underwriting structure: 'Global SEC registered managed rights issue
Vendor: Company	Primary or secondary: Primary
% of company sold: 23.8% of expanded share capital (5: 16 rights issue)	Privatisation or corporate: Corporate
IPO or non-IPO: IPO/demerger of Zeneca	Industry: Pharmaceuticals, specialty chemicals and agrochemicals
Type of shares: Ordinary shares and ADRs (1ADR= 3 Ordinary Shares)	Offer price: £6/ordinary share
Total issue size: US$2,080 million	US listing/144 A: NYSE listing

Exhibit 2
Distribution by domestic and international markets

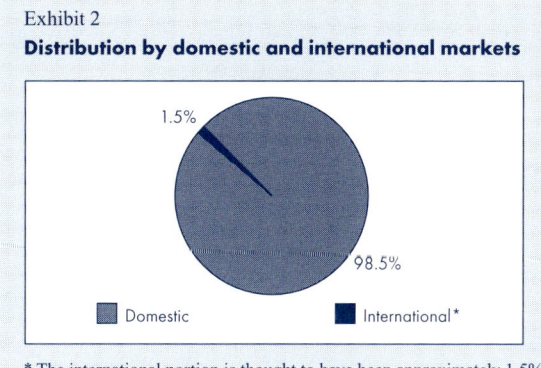

1.5%

98.5%

☐ Domestic   ■ International*

* The international portion is thought to have been approximately 1.5%.
These figures include subscription by existing Zeneca holders (ie, old
ICI shareholders), redistribution of rights not taken up by shareholders
and the placement of the rump.

specialist investors demand pure plays, the combination of a
demerger and a rights issue is highly unusual. The timing was
interesting in that when the demerger was decided upon in
1992 the market for pharmaceutical shares was still relatively strong and the chemicals business was experiencing perhaps
its worst recession ever. However, at the time of the demerger and rights issue in mid-1993, this trend had been reversed
and many investors were expecting an upturn in the chemicals sector.

In order to more effectively reach dedicated pharmaceuticals investors who had not previously invested in ICI, the
company asked the Investor Protection Committee of the
Association of British Insurers and the National Association
of Pension Funds whether a small portion of the total financing, about 10–20 per cent, could be done on a fully market-

Exhibit 3
Developments leading to demerger

September 1989	• Entrepreneur Sir James Goldsmith was rumoured to be looking at ICI as a break-up candidate.
April 1990	• After seven years of wide-scale restructuring and three years of relative consolidation, ICI trad-ed at a 25% discount to the London industrial average despite expenditure of £750 million to buy back 10% of its shares and £10 million on a new image campaign and change of logo. ICI was now only the eighth-largest UK company by market capitalisation, despite being its largest non-oil manufacturer and the fourth-largest chemical company in the world, with 1989 sales of £13.2 billion and pre-tax profits of £1.5 billion. The break-up value was thought to be £15 billion, double the then market capitalisation. At this time, the ICI board thought of its busi-nesses in terms of commodities, consumer and specialty chemicals, and pharmaceuticals. Two principal restructuring alternatives were considered: to sell the commodities business or to demerge the pharmaceuticals operations, as had Dow Chemical and BOC.
September 1990	• Chairman Sir Denys Henderson set up two task forces, one to look at the shape of ICI and the other to consider how to restructure its management. This is thought to have been the critical step leading to eventual demerger. The study analysed the performance of the world chemical industry over the previous 30 years and demonstrated that the seven major companies – Dow, Du Pont and Monsanto in the US; Bayer, BASF and Hoechst in Germany and ICI in the UK – had all performed within 15% of one another in terms of total return to shareholders. At differ-ent times one company or another had been ahead, but the similarity of their performances was striking. Even more striking was that while in current money terms their performances had improved gradually, in real terms there had been a steady decline. A critical assessment of this decline, combined with the prospect of a much less hospitable climate for the industry over the next 25 years caused by greater competition, high costs, lower growth and less invention from research, led ICI management to conclude that the industry would need to be far more focused and effi-cient in the future than it had been in the previous 30 years. Substantial restructuring would be required. Splitting the company was discussed as one option.
February 1991	• ICI revealed a two-year £300 million restructuring plan.
14 May 91	• UK industrial company Hanson bought 2.8% of ICI at £11.94/share, valuing ICI at £8.4 bil-lion. The market expected a full bid. In the past 25 years, ICI had underperformed the London market by 50%, whereas Hanson had risen by 3,000% over the same period. The ICI camp defend-ed itself with the help of SG Warburg, Goldman Sachs and Schroders, painting chairman Lord Hanson as an asset-stripper and questioning who would succeed him at Hanson Trust.
25 July 1991	• ICI announced first-half 1991 pre-tax profits down 31% compared with the first six months of 1990, to a mediocre £507 million. It said it would raise £500 million from disposals and that annual profits would increase by £400 million by 1994. The idea was to sell businesses account-ing for £2–3 billion of group turnover, ie, a reduction in sales terms of some 20%. By 25 July 1991, 4% or 5,000 people had already been cut from ICI's staff. At the time, all ICI's busi-nesses were classified either as 'core' (global and world ranking), 'cash cow' or 'sell candi-dates'. The pharmaceutical business was ranked only 19 in the world in terms of sales and was easily separable from the rest of ICI. Facing a possible full Hanson bid, the ICI board pondered two crucial questions: how did ICI's break-up value compare to its potential value in the long term and had management done enough to secure shareholder loyalty?
December 1991	• Corporate financier John C Mayo of SG Warburg was seconded to ICI to reinforce manage-ment. He formally joined the staff of ICI in September 1992 and became Zeneca's finance direc-tor in December 1992.
8 May 1992	• Hanson Trust sold its ICI stake.
30 July 1992	• ICI announced it was considering a demerger of the bio-science businesses.

ed basis. The intention was to do a bookbuilding simultaneously with the rights issue, with the bookbuilding of the non pre-emptive portion being done at the same time as the bookbuilding of the sub-underwritings of the rights issue. However, the ABI and the NAPF rejected this proposal.

ICI therefore settled for a hybrid structure, a so-called global managed rights issue, the first ever in the UK. This structure recognised shareholders' pre-emptive rights while incorporating a full-blown marketing campaign both to the old ICI shareholders wishing to take up their Zeneca rights and to potential new shareholders who would buy the rights/shares not wanted by the old ICI shareholders. Given that ICI and Zeneca had become two fundamentally different companies operating in different industries, there were much stronger reasons for an elaborate international marketing effort than is usually the case in a traditional rights issue.

Zeneca decided not to seek a listing on any of the numerous overseas stock exchanges on which ICI was already listed other than in New York. Although the demerger was 'grandfathered' by the US Securities and Exchange Commission (SEC), meaning that Zeneca would not have had to register with the SEC to effect the demerger it was considered highly important for the rights issue.

The decision to demerge Zeneca had its roots in the unconvincing attempts of the 1980s and early 1990s to restructure ICI which had been given added impetus by reports of predators at the door. Some of the significant developments leading up to the demerger are shown in Exhibit 3.

Major challenges

Demerger

There were numerous legal, regulatory and tax challenges, the most important of which was the treatment of the minority interests associated with the quoted ICI subsidiaries overseas, for example in Australia and South Africa.

A demerger involving 200 companies in 50 countries also presents a gigantic organisational, logistical and communications challenge.

Rights issue

At the time of the £1.3 billion rights issue, there were major concerns about healthcare reforms in the US and as a result the sector was out of favour with investors.

Two major failures of promising drugs had dented market confidence in ICI Pharmaceuticals. In addition, the patents had recently expired on Zeneca's blockbuster drugs Tenormin for hypertension and Nolvadex for breast cancer, together accounting for 50 per cent of the Pharmaceuticals division's sales, and they were losing market share. The pharmaceuticals side of ICI had been neglected by the equity research community before the demerger and few investors were aware of Zeneca's strengths.

No one knew what the likely demand from existing ICI shareholders would be. In a normal rights issue, a minimum amount of interest from existing shareholders can be taken for granted because they have already taken a conscious decision to own that company. In this case, ICI shareholders had taken a decision to hold ICI (though that included the assets put into Zeneca) but not Zeneca.

Consequently a significant shakeout in the new Zeneca share register could be expected immediately following demerger and the shareholder base in Zeneca would not have time to stabilise before the supply of rights shares. This would potentially create more immediate selling pressure than in a conventional rights issue. The financial advisers therefore faced the challenge of devising an offer structure and marketing strategy designed to maximise demand from both old ICI shareholders and new investors in Zeneca – the best of both worlds.

Connected with this issue was the fact that unlike the case in a bookbuilt offer where the banks have to worry only about selling a certain amount of shares, in a rights issue there is the additional element of not knowing how many rights are going to become available from shareholders not wishing to subscribe. The banks involved with the rights issue therefore do not know upfront how much there is to sell and accordingly have much less control of events. As a result, it is more challenging to motivate the syndicate banks to work hard to generate buy orders from new investors and to motivate busy institutional investors to really study the stock story.

Also, the pricing of the rights offer presented a much bigger challenge than usual, according to a UK-based banker involved in the transaction: 'As there was no market price in Zeneca shares, we had to price the rights offer at a discount to the assumed trading price. Having analysed the value of Zeneca to arrive at a valuation range, the pricing took place following the three-week pre-marketing period, during which time there was a de facto bookbuilding of the sub-underwriting.' The result was a record low 12.4 per cent discount (as per the closing when-issued 'cum price' and subscription rights on 12 May 1993). This was particularly aggressive given that the underwriting period was a record six weeks.

Pricing was not made easier by the fact that Salomon Brothers initiated 'when-issued' trading before the pricing took place. This market was very thin and therefore not representative of an open market price. The London Stock Exchange (LSE) asked Salomon Brothers to put an end to this activity, promising that formal when-issued trading would be allowed after pricing. Following the Zeneca rights offer, the LSE disallowed when-issued trading before the pricing of an issue.

Finally, UK rights issues (and to a slightly lesser extent continental European rights issues) registered with the US SEC are highly complex affairs, due primarily to the many and strict rules imposed by the SEC, most notably in the area of market-making during the subscription and rights trading period.

Rationale and objectives

Demerger

ICI for years had struggled with restructuring in an attempt to reverse the overaggressive and unfocused expansion of the 1970s and 1980s. Institutional investors increasingly demanded pure plays and the arrival of Hanson on the scene added further pressure. A demerger of ICI Pharmaceuticals (Zeneca) seemed to be the answer. This business had been set up in the 1940s but had outgrown the benefit of being part of a larger group. A source familiar with pre-demerger ICI culture commented: 'ICI had not managed to effectively communicate to the stock market the value of its increasingly valuable pharmaceuticals business, a not uncommon phenomenon in huge conglomerates. Those members of staff working within the pharmaceuticals division grew increasingly frustrated at being treated as second-class citizens despite a growing business.' Zeneca needed access to the stock market and a higher stock-market rating to continue this growth. ICI's board of directors expected the demerger to offer the following benefits:

- As creative management energies would be released in both organisations, ICI and Zeneca, operating as independent companies, would be able to fully exploit their respective opportunities and to meet their individual strategic and competitive challenges;
- Financial, management and R&D resources could be concentrated on a smaller number of businesses sharing common features and cost reduction and restructuring measures would be reinforced;
- Healthcare analysts would be able to focus on the phar-maceutical business. ICI traditionally had been covered by chemicals analysts and hence the pharmaceutical operations had received much less attention;
- The underlying values of ICI and Zeneca eventually would be released to the benefit of shareholders.

Rights issue

As a result of the recession which started in 1990, ICI had to take exceptional restructuring charges of £131 million that year and £949 million in 1992. It was felt that if the demerger was combined with a financing of £1.3 billion, this would give the two new companies sufficiently strong balance sheets to enable them to pursue their respective strategies without having to return to the equity market soon after the demerger. Put differently, this represented compensation for ICI giving up its most cash-generative businesses.

The ICI board desired a high level of certainty concerning the targeted amount of proceeds which were intended to be used to repay Zeneca indebtedness to ICI. Zeneca management wanted to market the name and create as wide a shareholder base as possible.

Share capital and ownership

See Exhibit 4.

Exhibit 4
Share capital and ownership

Type of shares offered	Ordinary shares of 25p each or ADRs each representing three ordinary shares.
Ownership restrictions	Not applicable.
Share capital before/after offer	719,763,734/944,689,900 ordinary shares
Listings	ICI had been listed on the London Stock Exchange since 1926 and the NYSE since 1983. Zeneca became listed on these two exchanges in connection with the demerger.
Market capitalisation at offer price(US$1.54/£1)	US$8.8 billion post-rights issue.
Major shareholders before the offer	As at 5 May 1993, the shareholders set out below had an interest larger than 3% in ICI. As ICI shareholders received one Zeneca share for each ICI share held on 1 June, these percentages also equalled the largest initial shareholders of Zeneca: Morgan Guaranty Trust of NY as depositary 7.63%* Schroder Investment Management 3.62% Prudential Corporation Group of Companies 3.09% * This represented only the total holdings of ADRs. Many US institutions held ordinary shares and some European institutions held ADRs. As European ownership of ICI was relatively modest, it is estimated that the total non-UK ownership was no more than 10%–15%.
Number of shareholders before offer	More than 300,000 (as inherited from ICI through the demerger).
Free float before offer	The initial free float was equivalent to that of ICI, ie, 100%.
Liquidity	ICI had for a long time been one of the most important and liquid stocks traded on the LSE. Zeneca inherited the benefits of ICI's broad ownership.
Most relevant stock exchange index/weighting	FT Actuaries All Share Index/Just over 1%. At the time of the original listing in 1993, Zeneca was No. 30 among UK companies in terms of market capitalisation. By October 1996 it had risen to No. 8 based on a strong share price performance.

Exhibit 5
Principal financial advisers and syndicate banks

Parties with overall responsibility for the transaction	
Global coordinator and book-running lead manager	SG Warburg
Financial advisers	SG Warburg and Goldman Sachs
International marketing coordinators	SG Warburg, BZW and Goldman Sachs
Parties to the conventional UK elements of the rights issue	
Sponsor of Zeneca London listing	SG Warburg
UK primary underwriters (commitments in %)	SG Warburg 50% BZW 25% Goldman Sachs 25%
Sub-underwriters	A large number of investment institutions, the outstanding majority of which were from the UK
Brokers	Warburg Securities and BZW (split list)
Rest of the world (excluding the UK and Ireland) marketing and redistribution syndicate	
International bookrunner	SG Warburg
Managers	SG Warburg, BZW, Goldman Sachs ABN AMRO, BNP Capital Markets, Deutsche Bank, Morgan Stanley, Nikko Securities and SBC
US marketing and redistribution syndicate	
US bookrunner	Goldman Sachs
Underwriters (equivalent to managers internationally)	Goldman Sachs, BZW, SG Warburg Donaldson, Lufkin and Jenrette, Merrill Lynch, JP Morgan, NatWest Securities, Paine Webber and Smith Barney
Principal legal advisers	
UK solicitors to Zeneca	Linklaters & Paines
US legal advisers to Zeneca	Davis Polk & Wardwell
UK solicitors to the sponsor and the underwriters	Slaughter & May
US legal advisers to the underwriters	Sullivan & Cromwell

Transaction components

This was a global managed rights issue, meaning that those rights not taken up by existing Zeneca shareholders (who initially were old ICI shareholders) were recirculated and marketed to prospective new investors. John C Mayo, Zeneca's finance director said: 'We wanted to showcase the company and we wanted to be seen by institutions internationally to be making a serious effort to present the company to them. We wanted to be on their radar screens. Although many of these institutions did not buy large numbers of shares, they bought some and were consequently put on the mailing list and over time increased their holdings significantly.'

The rights issue was structured by ICI, assisted by its financial advisers. Except for ICI and Zeneca, the principal parties to the demerger and the rights issue were as shown in Exhibit 5.

The principal structure, terms and process of the demerger and the Zeneca managed rights offer were as shown in Exhibit 6.

Due to the combination of the demerger and the rights issue, the timetable was more drawn out than in a conventional rights issue. (See Exhibit 7.)

Transaction fee distribution

Underwriting fees for primary underwriters, sub-underwrit-ers and brokers totalled 2.25 per cent calculated on the value of shares underwritten at the issue price. These fees were split as follows:

- UK underwriters (ie, primary underwriters) effectively received a net fee of 0.5 per cent, split 50 per cent, 25 per cent and 25 per cent according to commitment.
- The sub-underwriters, who took most of the underwriting risk for six weeks, received 1.5 per cent.
- The two brokers received 0.25 per cent between them for the marketing of the issue, arranging the sub-underwriting and committing to make a market during the subscription period. In addition, commissions of 0.2 per cent split according to sales made were received for placement of the rump, calculated on the value of the rump.

In addition, selling commissions and financial advisory fees were paid as follows:

- Zeneca agreed to pay a selling commission of 2 per cent to the international marketing coordinators (IMCs) on the aggregate prices of all sales of ordinary shares and ADRs, 1 per cent of which was paid to the members of the syndicates on a pre-agreed basis, provided that commissions were paid only on sales to new shareholders to

Exhibit 6
Structure and terms of demerger and rights issue

Terms of demerger and rights issue	• This was an indirect demerger, whereby the newly formed Zeneca Group Plc bought the share capital of the previously existing Zeneca Limited against the issuance of one new Zeneca plc share directly to each holder of one ICI share on the ICI register on 1 June 1993. As there were 719,763,734 ICI shares outstanding, an equal number of Zeneca plc shares were issued and distributed to ICI shareholders. Former holders of one old ICI share therefore retained one share in the streamlined new ICI and became holders of one new share in the newly created Zeneca Group plc; and • This was a 5:16 rights offer – each holder of 16 Zeneca shares had the right to subscribe to five new shares, thereby increasing the total number of Zeneca shares outstanding by 224,926,166 to 944,689,900. The subscription price of £6 implied a 12.4% discount to the valuation of Zeneca at the time of pricing based on the market closing cum price and subscription rights on the first day of trading in Zeneca.

Listings and SEC registration	• The LSE listing was sponsored by SG Warburg. Goldman Sachs advised on the SEC registration process in the US and JP Morgan was the depositary bank;
	• SEC registration and the NYSE listing made it possible for ICI's existing US shareholders (also Zeneca's US shareholders on 1 June 1993) to subscribe in the rights issue. Registration also facilitated subscriptions by new US investors for those shares not subscribed by Zeneca shareholders. The registration process was associated with the customary difficulties related to the stabilisation rules of the SEC. This has to do with the fact these rules conflict with the need of the UK brokers to trade the rights and the ex-rights shares during the subscription period;
	• Initially, the SEC had said that the UK participants did not need to abstain from market-making during the first two weeks but could only stabilise in the third week of the subscription period if the Zeneca share price dropped to below a 5% premium over the issue price (ie, below £6.30). Subsequently, however this restriction for the UK market-makers was also removed for the last week of the subscription period against the undertaking of extensive disclosure to the SEC of all trades carried out by BZW, Goldman Sachs and Warburg Securities during this week (under UK disclosure rules the London market had access to this information anyway). It was unusual for the SEC to have made this exemption, which was important for the transaction; and
	• The SEC registration imposed several further restrictions on the marketing of Zeneca shares, the most important of which were:
	  – A requirement to sell only fully-paid Zeneca shares outside the UK; and
	  – All international buy and sell orders had to be recorded in a separate syndicate book operated by the IMCs and were subject to restrictive pricing rules.

Underwriting/sub-underwriting	• The rights issue was fully underwritten by the three UK primary underwriters at a fixed price of £6 for the six weeks from 12 May until 21 June, the last subscription day. As is customary in the UK, sub-underwriting was arranged on the pricing day by the two brokers to the issue, Warburg Securities and BZW. The amount of primary underwriting risk, if any, retained by the primary underwriters was not disclosed nor was the number of investment institutions participating in the sub-underwriting. However, given the large size of the offer and long underwriting period, at least 200 institutions are estimated to have participated.
Marketing	• To make the international investor community aware of the Zeneca name and maximise demand globally, two separate marketing syndicates were introduced, one for the US under bookrunner Goldman Sachs and one for the Rest of the World (ie, outside the UK and the US) under bookrunner SG Warburg. SG Warburg as global coordinator had overall marketing responsibility. BZW, although not a bookrunner for either of the two syndicates, participated in both of the international marketing syndicates in addition to its responsibilities in the UK as one of the two brokers. There was only one book globally, which was operated from SG Warburg's offices in London and to which all the three IMCs had full and equal access; • UK one-on-ones involving Zeneca management had taken place before the 12 May impact day. The US roadshow and subsequently the RoW roadshow took place between 12 May and 28 May. Investor presentations by Zeneca took place in 19 cities world-wide and management met hundreds of institutions in one-on-one or group meetings. SG Warburg hosted the investor presentations in the UK and the RoW and Goldman Sachs hosted the US presentations. The IMA was signed between Zeneca and the IMCs following the 28 May extraordinary general meeting when the demerger was approved by ICI shareholders; and • Publication of equity research was subject to different restrictions in the US and the UK. In the US, equity research may be published from the day of the first public filing provided the reports do not contain information not already publicly disclosed. In the UK, research must be published some four to five weeks before publication of the pathfinder (red herring), in this case seven to eight weeks before 12 May. As publication of equity research in the US therefore would contravene the UK rules, US research normally is not published in UK/US transactions until after the completion of the issue.
Acquisition of rights	• Subscription rights were acquired by the two brokers and Goldman Sachs directly from the selling shareholders or via any broker or dealer in the market, as is usual in rights issues. Shareholders wishing to sell their rights would deal through their normal contacts with respect to that stock or industry sector of the market. For example, a UK fund manager would deal with his ordinary ICI broker whether or not this broker was included in the syndicate; • To comply with SEC Rule 10B6, which stipulates that underwriters involved in any part of an offer are not allowed to trade during the offer period, so as not to condition the market, there had to

Exhibit 6 *continued*

Structure and terms of demerger and rights issue *continued*

	be a special syndicate book, in which all international purchases and sales of rights on behalf of the whole syndicate were coordinated (ie, in the form of a book of buy and sell orders in Zeneca shares separated from the normal trading activities of the IMCs). This was a joint book, operated from SG Warburg's offices and kept by the three IMCs. Acquisitions of rights were therefore decided on a committee basis. All syndicate buy orders of rights from overseas investors were referred by the US underwriters via Goldman Sachs and by the RoW managers via SG Warburg to this global syndicate book. Nevertheless, the syndicate could not prevent international investors dealing via third parties (ie, not involved in the syndicate) in the UK and who in turn dealt with the market-makers. Thus the global syndicate book could be circumvented; and • However, as old ICI was most probably less than 15% owned from abroad, most of the acquisition of rights was carried out in the UK by Warburg Securities and BZW, the joint brokers, which were not restricted by having to deal through the syndicate book. They were responsible for talking to the institutional shareholders of ICI (the old ICI) and identifying non-subscribers. Having had extensive contact with shareholders during the three-week pre-marketing process and knowing whether institutions had been willing to participate in the sub-underwriting, they also had the best understanding of shareholder intentions. The list of institutions was divided between the two brokers.
Pricing mechanism for sale of fully-paid shares to international investors via the global syndicate book	• Daily purchase orders from investors in the US and the RoW channelled via the syndicate to the IMCs' global syndicate book before the LSE/NYSE close formed the order book for the day and were filled by the acquisition of rights from the market-makers (the two brokers and Goldman Sachs). There was thus a daily market price, subject to extensive restrictions imposed by the SEC. Allocation to investors took place immediately after market closing. The syndicate banks therefore were not exposed to substantial price risk on these rights/shares. However, the sub-underwriters remained exposed to their £6 underwriting until the end of the subscription period. • Daily purchases by UK investors were executed in the normal course of rights trading and were filled directly by the market-makers at the prevailing market price.
Rump placement	• After the end of the subscription period, as is customary in the UK, the brokers placed in the market at the prevailing market price the 14% unsubscribed portion of the rights issue. As the shares were sold at a 12-pence premium to the £6 subscription price, the benefit accrued to those shareholders who failed to subscribe or sell their rights in the market, not to the company or their bankers. This is contrary to practice in continental European rights issues, where the underwriters typically decide how to handle the unsubscribed shares.
Documentation	*Demerger:* 'Super class I document' of ICI: This is a document issued to ICI shareholders requesting them to approve the demerger at the ICI extraordinary general meeting of 28 May 1993. This document was to be read in conjunction with Zeneca's listing particulars; *Listing:* Listing particulars of Zeneca. This prospectus-like document was filed with the LSE and contains a comprehensive Zeneca description. It was issued in draft form three to four weeks before impact day (12 May) to allow for pre-marketing and sub-underwriting in the UK. It was the principal marketing document in the UK; *Rights Issue:* • *Prospectus:* Separate rights issue prospectuses for the UK, US (in the form of F-1), France and the RoW. There was a preliminary prospectus (red herring) published on 21 April and a final prospectus published on 12 May. Those for the US, RoW and UK were all but identical apart from the cover pages. A separate prospectus in French was required because of ICI's listing on the Paris Bourse; • *Underwriting agreement:* Signed by ICI, Zeneca and the three UK underwriters on 12 May, this guaranteed that Zeneca would receive £6 per share for all the shares issued; • *Sub-underwriting letter:* This was sent to the sub-underwriters by the UK brokers on behalf of the primary underwriters on the morning of 12 May. It provided that the sub-underwriters would buy unsubscribed shares at £6 and receive a fee of 1.5% on their total commitment; and • *International marketing agreement (IMA):* This was signed by Zeneca, ICI and the three IMCs on 28 May and set out the terms, conditions and procedures on which the IMCs would coordinate the marketing and sale of rights not bought by the original allottees. The IMA also provided for Zeneca to indemnify the IMCs and give to them certain representations and warranties.

the extent that such sales were covered with ordinary shares or ADRs acquired through the exercise of rights or ADR rights.

• The international marketing agreement (IMA) provided that 50 per cent of dealing profits (net of expenses and not counting the selling commissions) realised by the IMCs through recirculating the rights (buying the rights, subscribing and selling the ordinary shares and ADRs to new investors) should accrue to Zeneca. This was to ensure that the IMCs had an incentive to realise good prices while

reducing the overall expense to Zeneca which in exchange committed to pay selling commissions of 2 per cent on recirculated shares.

• SG Warburg and Goldman Sachs were paid undisclosed financial advisory fees.

Deal structure

When challenged with the task of creating shareholder value

Exhibit 7
Demerger and rights issue timetable

30 July 1992	• ICI announces demerger plan.
1 January 1993	• Zeneca created by separating ICI's bio-science activities from its other chemical operations.
21 April	• Draft listing particulars and prospectuses published; • Pre-marketing begins; • Book-building of sub-underwriting commitments begins.
12 May	*Impact day* • Pricing of rights issue; • Signing of underwriting agreement; • Sub-underwriting arranged by the UK brokers (deadline: 3 pm); • Shares, rights, ADRs and ADR rights start when issued trading on the LSE at 2.30 pm UK time and on the NYSE at 9.30 am New York time.
28 May	• ICI extraordinary general meeting approves demerger in which each holder of one ICI share receives one Zeneca share dividended out of ICI; • Signing of the international marketing agreement.
1 June	• Demerger record date at 7.30 am UK time; • Demerger becomes effective at 8.30 am; • Rights issue record date, immediately after the demerger had become effective; • Official trading of rights and shares begins on the LSE at 8.30 am UK time and of ADR rights and ADRs on the NYSE at 9.30 am New York time.
18 June	• Trading of ADR rights on NYSE ends.
21 June	• Trading of rights on LSE ends and subscription and payment period ends.
22 June	• Result of rights issue announced; • Sale of the rump by the two brokers.

by way of a listing of a separately organised company, ICI was faced with the following main questions:

1. Which businesses were going to be separately listed?
2. How should the demerger be effected?
3. How much, if anything, should ICI retain in this newly created business?
4. To whom were the demerger shares to be sold or distributed, ie, to existing shareholders only or a combination of old shareholders and new investors?
5. Should ICI combine the separate listing with a financing?
6. Should the money be raised from existing shareholders only or from a combination of old shareholders and new investors?
7. When should the financing take place?
8. Through which company should the money be raised?
9. Should Zeneca be listed on the NYSE?
10. How should the rights issue be priced?

This is how ICI answered these questions:

1. Which businesses were going to be separately listed?
John C Mayo, Zeneca finance director, said: 'A demerger was never considered primarily from a financial point of view. When I first came to ICI in late 1991, I started off by reading all the ICI strategy documents since 1980 and at no stage did purely financial considerations dictate the strategic planning.'

Once the immediate Hanson threat had vanished, ICI was able to look at its businesses from the viewpoint of what made the most industrial sense, as against only financial sense. The answer was to organise separately in a new company the bio-sciences businesses (which became Zeneca) from the com-

modity businesses of the old ICI (which became the new ICI). The financial structures of these two companies were going to recognise the differing sensitivities to the business cycle and the differing cash-generating capabilities. The new companies therefore had the following profile pro-forma by the end of 1992, assuming that the £1.3 billion had been raised. (See Exhibit 8.)

2. How should the demerger be effected?
Financially, there were essentially two possible ways to effect the demerger. The first and generally considered the preferable method is by a dividend distribution, which can be direct or indirect. This was an indirect demerger – newly formed Zeneca plc bought the share capital of the previously existing Zeneca Limited against the issuance of shares directly to ICI shareholders. The key to the dividend distribution method is to negotiate with the tax authorities not to levy tax on the distribution as they would in the case of an ordinary dividend. In a successful demerger by way of dividend distribution neither the company nor shareholders are liable to pay tax. This is what ICI managed to do.

The second demerger method is for the old company to liquidate itself and issue to its shareholders shares in a new company. This is far more complicated and employed only when the dividend distribution method does not work.

3. How much would ICI retain in the new business?
There were three realistic alternatives: 70–80 per cent, 30–49 per cent, or 0 per cent.

Retain 70–80 per cent: The purpose of the separate listing would have been to highlight the value of Zeneca to the stock market without ICI giving up a strong majority owner-

Exhibit 8

Profiles of the two new companies

Business and financial characteristics of the new companies

	New ICI	Zeneca
Businesses	Commodity chemicals	Bio-science businesses
	Paints	Prescription drugs
	Materials	Agricultural chemicals
	Explosives	Specialty chemicals
	Industrial chemicals	Seeds
		Biological products
Capital intensity	High – requires high volume production	Low – production small component of total cost
Technology	Large-scale process technology	Medicine, bio-science and organic chemistry
Research intensity	Low	High
Marketing intensity	Low	High
Cost structure	High fixed cost	Low fixed cost
Cash generation	Low	High
Customer base	Building and construction, mining, manufacturing industry	Healthcare providers, farmers

Pro-forma figures for 1992 respectively at 31 December 1992

	New ICI	Zeneca
Sales	£8,383 million	£3,979 million
Operating profit before exceptional charges	£148 million	£587 million
Net profit	(£650 million)	£80 million
Net indebtedness	£1,132 million	£391 million
Shareholders' equity	£4,074 million	£1,522 million
Gearing (net debt/equity)	27.8%	25.7%

ship in this increasingly attractive business. However, studying the example of the trading of UK electronics group Racal's shares after the sale of 20 per cent of mobile-phone subsidiary Vodafone, ICI had reason to believe that it would not gain full credit for the market valuation of its retained stake in Zeneca, ie, ICI would still be trading at a conglomerate discount.

Retain 30–49 per cent: This would mean retaining a significant interest and remaining the largest shareholder while deconsolidating Zeneca.

Retain 0 per cent: This would involve the creation of a completely independent group in recognition of the differences in business and to afford Zeneca maximum management and financial flexibility.

The ICI board opted for the third alternative for the reasons given above and because of the rule that required 75 per cent of Zeneca to be owned by the shareholders of ICI for it to qualify as a tax-free demerger.

4. To whom were the demerger shares to be sold or distributed, ie, to existing shareholders only or a combination of old shareholders and new investors?

There was effectively only one possibility to effect a separate Zeneca listing given that a fully marketed secondary sale of Zeneca shares would have had important capital gains tax implications for Zeneca.

Furthermore, this structure will have defused criticism of selling at too low a price and at a time when pharmaceutical stocks were out of favour – because ICI shareholders were given the shares for free and they retained the flexibility of selling their Zeneca shares when they saw fit.

The major shortcoming of the demerger structure and the principal reason that the financial advisers initially recommended against it was that at the time of the demerger, and starting with when issued trading, there would be selling by ICI holders not wishing to own Zeneca, precisely at the time when the rights issue was to be marketed. The advisers were to a large degree vindicated when, after the 12 May rights issue pricing, the when-issued trading price threatened to fall below the £6 issue price.

5. Should the separate listing be combined with a financing?

According to John Mayo: 'Although ICI did the demerger primarily for industrial reasons, both ICI and Zeneca needed the appropriate financial structure to support the operating activities. The old ICI accounted for such a large proportion of the country's science base and it was crucial to safeguard the long-term viability of both ICI's and Zeneca's independent R&D activities going forward. It was also important that the credit ratings were not eroded. Probably, the ICI board would not have given its approval for the demerger without a financing. It was therefore not a matter of if but only a matter of how.' Then there was the fact that overnight, ICI had given up 80 per cent of its 1992 operating profit by demerging Zeneca and wanted to reassure itself financially.

A financing also would be good for Zeneca because it was an excuse to do a global roadshow and market the new name. A cashless demerger in itself would hardly have justified much more than a London presentation. Also, Zeneca, only a medium-sized pharmaceuticals company, needed the surety of financial resources should a major acquisition be contemplated.

Exhibit 9
The UK equity underwriting system

UK companies usually raise equity through pre-emptive rights issues with a discount. However, UK insurance companies, pension funds and fund managers (the institutions) have agreed to support certain exemptions to this rule. A special resolution in a shareholders' meeting, valid for 15 months, can authorise the board of directors of that company to issue shares to new investors at no more than a 5% total discount to the market price (including commissions and sponsors' fees) by disapplication of pre-emptive rights on the following basis:

- Issuance of shares for cash: The company can issue up to 5% of the issued share capital to new investors in any one year, but it cannot increase its issued capital by more than 7.5% in any single three-year period;
- Vendor placings: In case of an acquisition, the acquiring company can (per transaction) increase its issued capital by 10% by paying the selling shareholders of the acquired company with newly issued shares. The buyer and the seller can arrange for these shares to be placed in the market on behalf of the vendor.

Whereas most institutions are in favour of maintaining the status quo of the present UK underwriting system with pre-emptive rights issues at a discount of 15–20%, fixed commissions and the system of primary and secondary underwriting (sub-underwriting), the reasons are not always understood. Contrary to general belief, the sub-underwriting commissions of 1.25% earned by the institutions for a 2–3 week underwriting period, it is claimed by institutions, is not generally considered to be the most important reason. Rather the main reasons for maintaining the current system are thought to be the following:

- The shareholder's pre-emptive right is a fundamental and sacrosanct right that prevents shareholders from being diluted in voting and economic rights. This and the right to elect and fire the board of directors are the only effective rights enjoyed by today's investment institutions;
- The present system of risk distribution and speed of pricing is extremely efficient and there is the certainty of the company receiving the proceeds;
- Institutions take comfort from the due diligence carried out by the primary underwriter (ie, the investment bank) before signing the prospectus;
- Institutions appreciate the possibility of being able to trade the subscription rights;
- The present system is cheaper for companies than US-style bookbuilding because the fees and issuing expenses usually are lower;
- The fact that there are normally many sub-underwriters which in most cases are also the natural long-term holders of the shares is of substantial comfort to the companies involved when the underwriting has to be called upon.

A more cynical view of why the institutions want to maintain the current system is that fund managers enjoy the status associated with having the power to control whether issuing companies have their new issues underwritten and therefore whether they will succeed in tapping the equity market. This is particularly true of the few (perhaps 20) institutions that together effectively control the London market. In addition, it may give fund managers more flexibility to manage their own performances as they can allocate on a discretionary basis the sub-underwriting commitments and the associated commissions to certain portfolios that have not performed well.

John Mayo and other proponents of change in the UK new issue market argue that the board of directors, in order to exercise the fiduciary duty vested in them by the shareholders, should in each case have the authority to select the most cost efficient of the following four financing options:

1. A normal UK style rights issue with a 15–20% discount;
2. A deep discount rights issue;
3. A 'bought deal' of up to 10% of the equity of the company; and
4. A bookbuilt structure with more flexibility to disapply the pre-emptive rights than currently afforded by the institutions.

Having done the financing, the board of directors should then account for their actions and demonstrate that the course of action chosen was in shareholders' best interests.

The UK underwriting system, whereby UK companies are substantially restricted to raising finance from existing (predominantly UK) shareholders through pre-emptive rights issues may be one of the reasons for the low rate of organic investment by UK companies. The traditional rights issue structure in the UK does not require companies to market their investment case to investors. Instead the UK system lends itself better to the scenario whereby one company takes over another and issues shares to finance the take-over on the basis that the merged company can achieve savings from rationalisation. UK companies would enjoy a lower cost of equity if they had more flexibility to market their shares globally and sell them to those willing to pay the highest price. There are strong signs that this question is taken increasingly seriously by a number of bodies in the UK including: the Hundred Group (a group of 139 UK finance directors) the Confederation of British Industry, the Department of Trade and Industry, the UK Treasury and the government. The Office of Fair Trading has been examining the issue on the grounds that the present system of fixed commissions and inflexible pre-emptive-rights is anti-competitive and leads to an excessive cost of equity. The OFT has threatened a referral to the Monopolies and Merger Commission unless institutional investors and bankers show enough signs that they are prepared to introduce more flexibility – another word for more competition – in the system.

Under this acute threat, institutional shareholders and investment bankers have taken certain steps to introduce more competition into conventional rights issues, most notably an effective bookbuilding of the sub-underwriting on a portion of the total underwriting commitment, with the effect that those institutions which bid at a lower sub-underwriting fee will take on the sub-underwriting commitment. Now that a process of change has been set in motion, it is likely that the UK system will change further with the eventual end-result that the UK underwriting system will allow increasing competition and flexibility, all in the interest of reducing the cost of capital for UK companies. This is also likely to mean that the UK system will gradually become more Americanised and that the bookbuilding system will be increasingly adopted, at first perhaps in combination with rights issues, later in a more pure form and for a larger proportion of the company than the 5% currently allowed in any one year.

6. From whom should the money be raised?

Once it had been decided – primarily for tax and pre-emptive rights reasons – to do the demerger by way of a dividend distribution to existing ICI shareholders, the next step was to decide if it would be a good idea to do at least a proportion of the financing on a non-pre-emptive basis. Zeneca wanted to approach those major domestic and international institutions who were not already shareholders in ICI (and now in Zeneca) with a bookbuilt offer, as such a structure would have allowed Zeneca to offer a certain number of shares to these institutions (subject to a cut-back due to over-subscription) contrary to the rights issue structure where it is highly uncertain what number of shares is available to be marketed to new investors.

To have done a marketed offer to new investors – as a portion, at least, of the entire financing – would, in addition to a higher degree of impact with new investors, have had these major advantages:

- The price and size of the issue would be set only at the end of the marketing period and would reflect the level of investor interest at this time rather than six weeks earlier as in the case of a rights issue;
- Bookbuilding, at least in theory, would have allowed for more flexibility in the timing of pricing, although for a global issue such as this, the pricing date usually is changed by only one or two days – unless a disaster occurs;
- In a bookbuilding, all investors in theory have an equal opportunity to receive shares in the allocation process;
- Shares are allocated according to quality of demand, ensuring that investors with a track-record of long-term investment predominate in the allotment process;
- Given investor scepticism about the pharmaceuticals sector at that time, the bookbuilding approach would have been particularly appropriate to gauge genuine investor interest.

However, as the Association of British Insurers insisted that the entire financing be done on a pre-emptive basis, the idea of a partly bookbuilt offer had to be abandoned.

John Mayo of Zeneca is often referred to as someone who wants to introduce an American style underwriting system (ie, bookbuilding) to the UK, however he emphatically denies this. John Mayo answered:' I am fundamentally a proponent of the UK system but I believe that it has to evolve. It has not changed for 40 years. The present system in the UK whereby the fees are the same for every company and where the rules are biased in favour of funding rationalisation through acquisitions rather than organic investment must change for the good of the companies, shareholders and the country at large.' (See Exhibit 9.)

7. When should the financing take place?

With respect to timing, would it be better to arrange the financing immediately following the demerger (as eventually executed) or sometime later, after the dust had settled and a proper market in Zeneca shares had been established.

The arguments for carrying out the financing immediately after demerger included:

- By carrying out the rights issue simultaneously with the demerger, the market would be given price leadership by the fixing of the subscription price, itself a result of extensive pre-marketing to institutions.
- ICI's board wanted to achieve the certainty of proceeds

from the financing before giving final approval for the demerger. Only an underwritten rights issue executed simultaneously with the demerger would offer this advantage.
- Both the ICI and Zeneca managements needed to get on with the running of their businesses. This structure offered the quickest way of getting back to business. A delayed financing would have extended the period of reorganisation and would have required updated documents – more work and more expense.

The arguments against an immediate financing were:

- The requirement of a six-week underwriting period for a fixed-price offer was demanding, particularly under these circumstances when the discount was small and not transparent to the market. In the event, the when-issued trading price fell to a level uncomfortably close to the issue price. Had it fallen below £6, then the sub-underwriters would have expected to take stock under the sub-underwriting agreement and accordingly would not have subscribed. Some institutions might have sold short. However, Zeneca and SG Warburg were confident about the £6 offer price on the basis of their Zeneca valuation (13.3x 1992 proforma numbers compared to, for example, Wellcome which was trading at 21.3x 1992 earnings on 12 May 1993 when Zeneca was priced), the extensive three-week pre-marketing before pricing and the fact that the sub-underwriting could be arranged at this level. SG Warburg also argued that because the rights issue was flagged well in advance, market capacity was not a major issue;
- The event of the rights issue would coincide with considerable selling pressure as former ICI shareholders not wishing to be invested in a pharmaceutical company sold their Zeneca demerger shares.

The alternative – delaying the financing by three to six months after demerger – also had its pros and cons. In its favour were:

- The market in Zeneca shares would stabilise and become less unpredictable as the shakeout in the share register unfolded and the risk therefore of not achieving a successful financing would be correspondingly smaller;
- The bookrunning lead managers should in theory be in a better position to target the right investors in their marketing as a high proportion of non-pharmaceutical investors will have sold Zeneca during the first weeks and months after the demerger; and
- The Zeneca rights offer could have been priced independently of the new ICI. In the event, Zeneca had to be priced at a higher dividend yield than its growth characteristics warranted as many old ICI shareholders irrationally expected a Zeneca dividend yield as high as that of the new ICI.

Arguments against a delay included:

- There would be additional market risk as seen from the ICI and Zeneca boards' perspectives and thus less certainty about specific proceeds for a given level of dilution. There is always a risk that, regardless of price, the markets would shut down – as happened, for example, following the 1987 stock market crash;

- A lower price (or larger discount) in a later rights issue, given a targeted amount of proceeds, could endanger the tax-free status of the demerger. As the company wanted to raise US$2 billion and as UK demerger tax rules indicate that at least 75 per cent of it had to be demerged to existing shareholders, a higher discount might require a capital increase of more than 25 per cent. This might not have been acceptable to the UK tax authorities, which perhaps could have judged that the demerger and financing together effectively amounted to a disposal, ie, a taxable event;

- It would make it difficult to market the two new companies in connection with the demerger because the pro-forma balance sheets could not have been determined in advance;

- There could be a poor start to the trading of Zeneca shares because the marketing of the demerger without a financing would have been less ambitious than was the case in the simultaneous demerger and financing; and

- There would be duplication in marketing. First, in connection with the demerger itself, both Zeneca and new ICI would require marketing. Then, in connection with the subsequent financing, Zeneca would again need to be marketed, probably with updated documentation.

8. Through which company should the capital be raised?

As in most IPOs, there was flexibility to structure the two new companies' balance sheets according to their respective future business strategies and associated funding needs, and so maximise their combined stock market value. The rights issue proceeds could either be retained in the issuing company or be used to repay inter-company debt to the other vehicle (as happened in this case). The decision on which vehicle to use for the financing could therefore be taken independently. ICI considered three options:

Through old ICI. This would have meant raising the finance shortly before the demerger and stating in the prospectus the degree to which the proceeds would go to the two companies. This would have had the advantage that investors were familiar with old ICI and also that it could have arranged a deeply discounted non-underwritten rights issue just before the demerger became effective and use a shorter underwriting period, thereby reducing the amount of risk and expense. However, there were several problems. The multiple achieved would have been lower than that achieved by Zeneca, although probably higher than that of a financing in new ICI, the pure commodities producer. Moreover, institutional buyers of conglomerates are becoming fewer – many investors would have wanted only one of the stocks and would have waited to buy in the market post-demerger. Investors also had been disillusioned by the lack of performance by old ICI and might for psychological reasons have resisted such a financing (despite the fact that they were to receive shares in the two new companies shortly after the financing giving them the option to

sell the least desired stock). Importantly, raising finance through old ICI would also have meant a lost opportunity to focus attention on either of the two new names with their respective strategies.

Through new ICI. This offered the advantage of instant name recognition together with an opportunity to market the new ICI, which was now a focused commodity chemicals business. US buyers, discouraged by developments in the healthcare sector, would have played a bigger role, particularly since a case could be made that the chemicals industry would emerge soon from recession and that investors ought to get in immediately before prices rose. Nevertheless, ICI's chemicals business was at a cyclical low and trading profits had been falling over the past three years. First-quarter 1993 trading profit was up only 3 per cent on the comparable period of 1992, so the ICI board considered it too early to sell new ICI as a major recovery play. To sell shares of the new ICI also would have been to forego the opportunity to market Zeneca as a new name.

Through Zeneca. This provided an ideal opportunity to market the Zeneca name and explain to investors the strengths of these businesses which hitherto had been hidden within ICI. It is possible that if the Zeneca name had not been as aggressively marketed, then the company would have remained relatively unknown and would have traded at a lower rating. The Zeneca businesses accounted for approximately 80 per cent of the trading profit of the old ICI group during 1992, equivalent to £587 million. This was considered a healthier foundation on which to raise £1.3 billion than either the old or the new ICI. Yet this route also had its drawbacks. The pharmaceuticals business of the old ICI had received setbacks when two promising drugs had failed to make it successfully to market. This had dented confidence. Also, in 1990 the patent had expired on Zeneca's blockbuster drug Tenormin, used to treat hypertension, and Zeneca was perceived as being in a weak position. Generic drugs were expected to catch up in a major way. Few investors were aware of Zeneca's strengths because of the lack of focus by equity analysts on ICI's pharmaceutical activities. Further, the healthcare sector was substantially out of favour with investors, particularly in the US where the Clinton administration had initiated a heated debate on reform of the sector. Wellcome's share price, for example, had fallen by 28 per cent from its 30 November 1992 peak of £10.66.

Nevertheless, Zeneca became the chosen vehicle. John Mayo explained: 'We decided on doing the financing in Zeneca primarily because we felt that we could predict the possible downsides in Zeneca. We did an enormous amount of scenario testing and ultimately arrived at the conclusion that no matter what, the Zeneca financing would succeed.' He added: 'Ultimately, at the time when we had to take the decision, we were of the view that the chemical cycle was too unpredictable. We could not take the risk of a flop'.

9. Should Zeneca have a NYSE listing?

While scepticism about the healthcare sector, especially in the US, had to be taken into account, there were overwhelming arguments in favour of a NYSE listing. ICI was listed on all major stock exchanges around the world. The decision was taken that Zeneca should be listed on the two most important markets of those, ie, London and New York. At the time of that decision, approximately 8 per cent of ICI was owned from the US. This was highly relevant as ICI's US shareholders were also going to become, overnight through the demerger, Zeneca shareholders. Although the demerger was grandfathered and would not have required SEC registration, the latter nevertheless was needed so that Zeneca's US shareholders could subscribe to the rights issue. Without registration and a US listing, there might have been selling pressure on Zeneca shares in London. In the event, irrespective of the registration and listing, such selling pressure did occur though the reasons could hardly have been foreseen at the time the decision was taken.

One other factor had a powerful bearing on the decision to list in New York. The US market was very important commercially for Zeneca, accounting for some 41 per cent of 1992 pro-forma sales. By early 1996, some 8–9 per cent of Zeneca was owned from the US. This would have been unlikely without a full SEC registration and NYSE listing.

10. How should the rights issue be priced?

It was coincidence that after Zeneca was priced at £6 it should share with new ICI an almost identical share price and valuation following the demerger. The two companies were given an identical indicated dividend for 1993. This was regarded as essential to encourage as many as possible of old ICI holders to maintain their Zeneca demerger shares and subscribe to the rights issue. If the financial advisers had not had the old ICI holders to cater for, then perhaps, given its growth characteristics, Zeneca could have been priced at a lower yield. In the event, the identical absolute dividend gave Zeneca a much higher dividend cover than new ICI but the latter had a much higher P/E ratio because of its cyclically depressed earnings level. One of the bankers advising on the transaction noted: 'it became fairly clear early on that we were going to split the old ICI dividend in half.'

If one believes that the size of the discount of a rights issue really does not matter, it might appear an unwarranted risk to set the rights issue subscription price so close to the assumed market price, that even the theoretical cum rights when-issued trading price was close to falling below this level. After all, even if the rights issue had been sub-underwritten and therefore the immediate market risk to Zeneca eliminated, what company would want to start its trading with a failed rights issue. This school of thought would also represent the view that it was unnecessary because a deep discount would have eliminated the need for an expensive underwriting. The counter argument is of course that SG Warburg had done an extensive pre-marketing and book-building of the sub-underwriting and the outcome was that the UK institutions thought the value of Zeneca was at least £6.00 per share. Many institutions questioned by the author, including one of the largest former holders of the old ICI, argued that the size of the discount does not matter. Others argued that the size of the discount in a UK rights issue indeed does matter, primarily for the following reasons:

- If the proceeds from the sale by shareholders of their rights in connection with rights issues are worth more than 5 per cent of the original value of the holding, then these non-subscribing shareholders would be liable to pay capital gains tax on the rights proceeds, whereas if the value is less than 5 per cent, these proceeds are deducted from the acquisition cost base of the holding;
- If the discount is too large, a cut in the absolute dividend may be necessary, which many institutions dislike, although the dividend cover would remain unchanged;
- If a rights issue is done to finance an acquisition, some institutions calculate the pro-forma earnings of the two companies together without taking the bonus element of the rights issue into account with the result that the degree of dilution appears to be larger with a higher discount;
- In a deep discount rights issue, the voting rights dilution can be punitive for non-subscribers;
- In the UK, if the discount is too large, forcing a rights issue larger than 1:3, then shareholder approval is required which creates a significantly longer lead time for the rights issue.

Zeneca's finance director, John C Mayo, who had wanted to do at least a small portion of the total financing by way of a non pre-emptive offer was certainly of the view that the discount ought to be as small as possible. The sub-underwriting method offered him the opportunity ensure this was so. He achieved a highly impressive result because the rights issue was priced at a discount that effectively amounted to only 12.4 per cent. As noted already, Zeneca also had a real constraint, for tax reasons, in that it needed to raise £1.3 billion without expanding the share capital by more than 25 per cent and therefore it was important to keep the discount to a minimum.

(See the feature topic at the end of the Daimler Benz case study for a more detailed discussion of the significance of the discount in a rights issue).

Marketing

Because Zeneca was to become a UK stock, initially 85 to 90 per cent owned by old ICI's UK shareholders, the UK institutional market clearly was the main target market. The strategy adopted was the early publication of research followed by simultaneous company presentations to the UK institutions and bookbuilding of the sub-underwriting with the same institutions. Only after the issue had been priced and sub-underwritten on 12 May, did the roadshow go abroad.

As a consequence, the marketing period became unduly long. (See Exhibit 10.)

Demerger meant a large new audience for Zeneca – the pharmaceuticals equity research analysts who had not bothered to look at old ICI. Previously, ICI had primarily been covered by chemicals analysts who had at best only limited understanding of the pharmaceuticals sector.

The Zeneca story

Zeneca, the world's 15th largest prescription drug company by

Exhibit 10
Marketing timetable

Dates	Marketing phase	Objective
22 April – 11 May	Pre-marketing (by brokers to the issue) including company presentations to UK institutions.	To allow for bookbuilding of the sub-underwriting and the pricing of the rights issue.
12 – 28 May	Marketing continues with US and RoW roadshows.	To minimise selling pressure in the when-issued market of demerger shares and maximise interest in the rights issue.
28 May	Final shareholder approval of the demerger and signature of the IMA.	Formalisation of marketing arrangements for the two international marketing syndicates.
1 – 21 June	Continued marketing by the IMCs and syndicate banks.	To ensure that the market price was kept above the subscription price, otherwise the rights issue would have been tainted as unsuccessful.

Exhibit 11
Zeneca's business mix

	1992 sales (£ millions)	1992 operating profit* (£ millions)
Pharmaceuticals	1,607	488
Agrochemicals	1,288	85
Specialty Chemicals	936	26
Other	148	-12
Total	**3,979**	**587**

* Before exceptional items.

1992 sales, was expected to experience double-digit earnings growth until the end of the decade supported by the existing product portfolio, exciting research developments and tighter cost control. The business mix was as shown in Exhibit 11.

UK institutions and international investors were sold the story through the arguments given in Exhibit 12 and the P/E ratios shown in Exhibit 13.

Reasons for not buying

Those that declined to participate in the Zeneca rights offer gave mainly the following reasons:

- US healthcare reform which was expected to lead to reduced spending on healthcare, both in the US and elsewhere in the world;
- Investors were positioning themselves for recovery from recession by buying cyclical stocks;
- Two major failures of promising drugs at ICI Pharmaceuticals had dented confidence in the company;
- The patents of Zeneca's blockbuster drugs Tenormin and Nolvadex had recently expired and the drugs were losing market share;
- There was a question mark over whether Zeneca as only a medium-sized pharmaceutical company would have sufficient muscle to compete in the key areas of R&D and marketing.

Results

As already mentioned, one of the main challenges in a rights issue is that no party knows in advance how many subscription rights existing shareholders intend to dispose of and therefore how many shares the syndicate has available to be placed with new investors. Furthermore the syndicate does not gain access to all subscription rights for sale because shareholders have the option to sell through any bank or broker in London or elsewhere. In this case, it was only a small consolation that, due to SEC restrictions, all syndicate members were meant to channel all foreign purchases of rights to the syndicate book, globally coordinated by SG Warburg. However, a further challenge is that it is very difficult to work out who has actually subscribed to the issue.

Typically what is announced in a UK rights issue is simply the extent to which the rights has been subscribed at the end of the subscription period. It does not reveal who has subscribed. The second thing that is announced is that the unsubscribed portion of the the rights issue – the rump – has been placed in the market by the brokers and the price at which the rump was placed. In the case of Zeneca, the take-up ratio was 86 per cent – neither remarkably good nor bad. Consequently, the size of the rump was 14 per cent, which was placed by the joint brokers Warburg Securities and BZW immediately after the subscription period at £6.12 per share with the surplus over the £6 issue price remitted to shareholders who did not take up their rights. (See Exhibit 14.)

Further work needs to be done to find out what actually happened in the rights issue and whether or not it can be deemed to have been truly successful.

Based on all customer trades of nil-paid rights on the LSE during the subscription period, it can be estimated that around 70 per cent of old ICI holders subscribed to the Zeneca rights offer. Therefore, of the 225 million nil-paid rights (and therefore new shares), 37 million or 16 per cent were sold by shareholders during the subscription period. These 16 per cent were on the other hand subscribed for by investors who became new Zeneca shareholders during the subscription period.

Total sales by the syndicate book to investors outside the UK, are thought to have amounted to no more than £20 mil-

Exhibit 12
Principal sales points

Pure play	Zeneca was a focused bio-science company. It fitted into a major industrial sector for asset allocation purposes. Management had become free to develop the strengths of its businesses in ways which it judged most appropriate. In addition, demerger benefits are thought to have included: • a less bureaucratic culture; • tighter scientific networking; • more consistent earnings performance; and • greater flexibility in the use of self-generated capital. Zeneca business units were given control over their own balance sheets which increased the emphasis on returns and quality of profits rather than growth for its own sake.
Common technology	There are many similarities between Zeneca's three bio-science businesses: • common discovery skills; • process technology; • products from similar chemistry; and • integrated biological systems. According to an SG Warburg research report of April 1993: 'Zeneca has an attractive portfolio of businesses which are all linked via a common technological thread – bio-science. The great progress which is being made in this area of technology gives Zeneca an extremely large number of longer-term growth opportunities.'
Market position	Zeneca Pharmaceuticals had leading positions within the following therapeutic areas: cardiovascular, anti-cancer and anaesthetics. The three leading new drugs were: • Zestril, the world's third largest ACE inhibitor (against hypertension and congestive heart failure) with 1992 sales of £294m, +32%; • Diprivan, the world's largest intravenous anaesthetic with 1992 sales of £142m, + 49%; and • Zoladex, the world's second largest prostate cancer drug with 1992 sales of £109m, + 58%; In addition: • Agrochemicals was the world's second largest supplier of agricultural chemicals; • Specialty Chemicals ranked third in the world reactive-dyes market, held a world-leading position in the indigo market and was a leader in the world leather-finish market.
Research	• Through strong research, Zeneca's growth was expected to accelerate towards the end of the decade. SG Warburg expected Zeneca to introduce five new chemical entities within five years, a performance unlikely to be matched by other leading players in the industry. Perhaps the most interesting compound was Zeneca's new anti-asthma drug Accolate with potential sales of £700 million per annum by the end of the 1990s.
Growth	• Double-digit earnings growth was expected until the end of the decade. Zeneca's pharmaceuticals division had experienced close to 10% sales growth over the five years to 1992, whereas the Zeneca businesses overall had achieved less than 5%. The fact alone that Zeneca would now be able to use its strong cash flow for R&D should accelerate growth. Previously, much of the cash generated by ICI Pharmaceuticals had been employed elsewhere in the ICI group.
Profitability	• Zeneca's pharmaceuticals businesses had been tightly managed and the company regarded itself as one of the world's leaner operations. This, together with the fact that most of Zeneca's major drugs were self-developed, meant that Zeneca enjoyed among the highest margins in the industry. It was expected to generate incremental earnings growth by tightening management of other Zeneca businesses.
Balance sheet	• Given Zeneca's strong cash flow, the pro-forma gearing of 25.7% at the end of 1992 gave Zeneca a solid balance sheet and a relatively high degree of financial flexibility. (By the end of 1993, gearing had fallen to 11.7%).
Valuation	• The 1993 and 1994 P/E ratios and the sustainable rate of growth in earnings per share were the most important valuation parameters. It also was deemed important that the combined dividend of the new ICI and Zeneca should not be smaller than the former dividend of the Old ICI. Furthermore, it was decided that the two newly created companies would have the same initial dividends. Therefore, Zeneca was priced at a relatively high dividend yield of 4.6% (gross) when compared with the sector.

Sources: Zeneca listing particulars and SG Warburg.

lion (sold as fully-paid shares, equivalent to just over 3 million of the total of 37 million rights traded). The US market supposedly accounted for the largest portion of sales. However, US investors also were the largest sellers of Zeneca shares/rights. According to the global coordinator, total US shareholdings of Zeneca fell by a net 2–3 per cent during the process compared with the ownership of the old ICI shares. US investors had started to buy old ICI shares in the hope of cyclical recovery in the chemicals sector and continued to buy the new ICI shares after the demerger.

The remainder of the 225 million rights, equivalent to 34 million rights were handled by the market-making arms of the IMCs and other banks or brokers. The number of rights handled by the sales and trading operations of the three IMCs were not disclosed between the three parties for competitive reasons. A reasonable assumption might be that between the

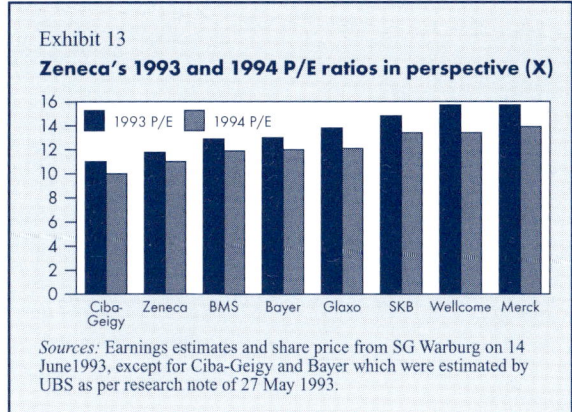

Exhibit 13

Zeneca's 1993 and 1994 P/E ratios in perspective (X)

Sources: Earnings estimates and share price from SG Warburg on 14 June1993, except for Ciba-Geigy and Bayer which were estimated by UBS as per research note of 27 May 1993.

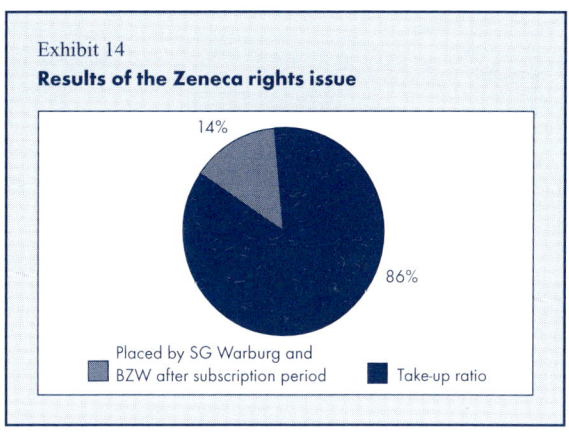

Exhibit 14

Results of the Zeneca rights issue

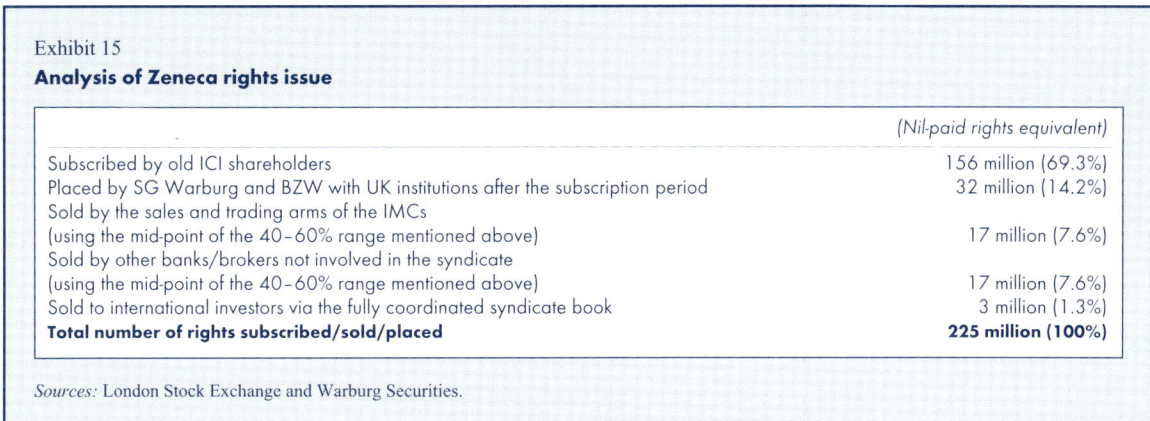

Exhibit 15

Analysis of Zeneca rights issue

	(Nil-paid rights equivalent)
Subscribed by old ICI shareholders	156 million (69.3%)
Placed by SG Warburg and BZW with UK institutions after the subscription period	32 million (14.2%)
Sold by the sales and trading arms of the IMCs (using the mid-point of the 40–60% range mentioned above)	17 million (7.6%)
Sold by other banks/brokers not involved in the syndicate (using the mid-point of the 40–60% range mentioned above)	17 million (7.6%)
Sold to international investors via the fully coordinated syndicate book	3 million (1.3%)
Total number of rights subscribed/sold/placed	**225 million (100%)**

Sources: London Stock Exchange and Warburg Securities.

three houses they accounted for no more than 40–60 per cent of total rights trading. A large portion of all subscription rights changing hands on stock exchanges was thus beyond the control of the three senior syndicate members. If we assume the mid-point of this range we can account for what actually happened in the rights issue as shown in Exhibit 15.

After-market performance

See Exhibit 16.

After-market trading volume

See Exhibit 17.

On the first day of trading (Tuesday 1 June) ICI rose 28p to 636p on volume of 5.5 million shares, one of the strongest performers on the day, and continued on Wednesday to 673p. This rally was partly fuelled by strong US demand. Zeneca (ex-rights) lost 2p to 630p on volume of 10 million shares. The rights lost 3p to close at 34p on LSE turnover of 2.6 million. On Wednesday the price increased to 634p on turnover of 3.1 million shares. By the end of the week they were down to 621p.

In the second week Zeneca traded down to 609p – 'on the edge' of the 600p subscription price – in a major sell-off of pharmaceutical stocks in the US. The price was sometimes 5p to 10p higher in London because selling pressure in the US was so strong. This arbitrage was maintained for some time as all the main arbitrageurs were in the syndicate and therefore not allowed to trade. Twice during the subscription period the price was close to 600p. The shares then traded up to 626p in the last week of the subscription period.

Shortly before the end of the subscription period, barely

any of the Zeneca stock was owned from the US, an ironic situation given that problems with the SEC had almost proved to be a deal-breaker. The SEC initially ruled that the underwriters were allowed to trade only passively in the stock, which meant that they could not bid actively but rather accept offers at the market price. The purpose of this was to maintain a true market. Approximately one week before the end of the subscription period, the SEC modified its ruling and allowed active market-making in the UK on the grounds that the LSE would spot any market manipulation.

Over the first year of trading of Zeneca and new ICI, the latter outperformed the UK market by over 26 per cent whereas the former under-performed by just under 2 per cent.

The performance of the main parties

The decision to carry out the demerger once Hanson's takeover threat had disappeared and to follow through when the pharmaceuticals sector fell out of favour with investors was a brave one by Sir Denys Henderson and the ICI board. It also proved to be a good one industrially, managerially and financially.

Zeneca's management led by David Barnes had lived in relative obscurity under the old ICI structure but now emerged into the limelight to perform well in selling the company to institutions for purposes of the sub-underwriting and the subsequent subscription in the rights issue. Barnes and finance director John Mayo held 93 one-on-one meetings and made group presentations to hundreds of institutions internationally.

At £642 million, Zeneca's pre-tax profit for fiscal 1993 was somewhat below SG Warburg's £654 million forecast made just ahead of the issue in April 1993. But for the six months to June 1994 pre-tax profit rose by 31 per cent, which was better than expected by the market. The chemicals businesses were doing well but pharmaceuticals grew by a modest 6 per cent and fell for the second period running in the US. Though the research pipeline was some years from being realised, with a gearing of only 18 per cent Zeneca was in a position to acquire growth.

SG Warburg and Goldman Sachs as financial advisers deserve considerable credit for the structuring and execution of the the demerger and the rights issue. SG Warburg deserves special credit for its role as global coordinator.

As ICI was very much a UK stock and US investors were sellers of the healthcare sector at the time, the UK brokers, deserve a lot of credit for the sub-underwriting, subscriptions and placement with new shareholders.

Why did ICI hire SG Warburg, Goldman Sachs and BZW? SG Warburg and Goldman Sachs were the best-placed houses to structure this complex equity financing. The former had done SEC-registered rights issues for British Airways and advertising group Saatchi & Saatchi and a rights issue including placement of fully-paid shares with US investors under Rule 144A for Eurotunnel. Goldman Sachs had done managed SEC-registered rights issues for Norsk Hydro of Norway and Novo-Nordisk of Denmark. SG Warburg had been a long-standing merchant bank to ICI and director John Mayo was seconded from the bank to ICI to improve its prospects without limits to his brief. Goldman Sachs had been engaged as defence adviser along with SG Warburg and Schroders, at the time Hanson bought its ICI stake. Schroders had been another long-serving merchant bank to the group. Having been in a position to develop a relationship with ICI, Goldman Sachs was pushing hard for this highly prestigious financing mandate. It was helped by its strong equity franchise, particularly in the US and had considerable experience of managed rights offers. BZW had been an ICI broker for many years and together with SG Warburg was one of the strongest houses in the UK equity market.

Key lessons learnt

Demerger

When a company is faced with as much hostile shareholder pressure as was ICI, it is practically unavoidable for the board of directors of that company not to take drastic action to enhance shareholder value. One senior banker close to the situation noted: 'It was clear that ICI's shareholders wanted

---

Exhibit 16
After-market price performance

Pricing date	12 May 1993
Subscription price	£6
Terms of rights issue	5:16
Rights issue discount	N/A
First year high/low	
High (10 January 1994)	£8.67
Low (22 July 1993)	£5.99

Zeneca share price relative to FTSE-100 (%)

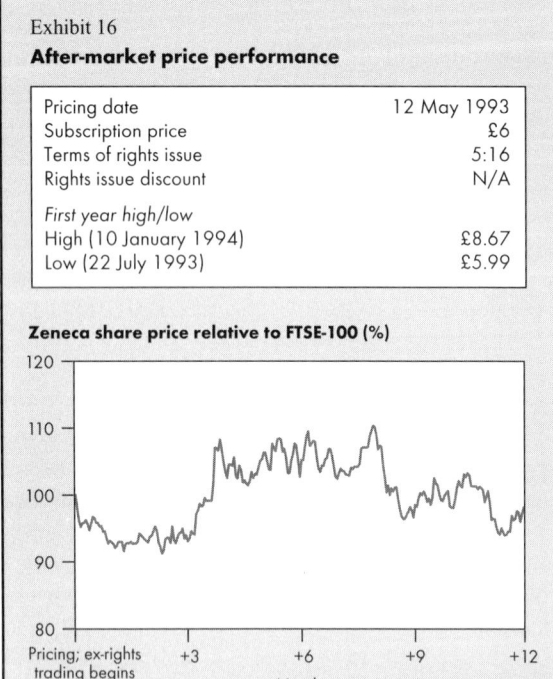

Zeneca and ICI absolute and relative price performance after pricing of Zeneca rights

	Zeneca price (P)	Zeneca relative (FT-SE 100) (%)	Zeneca rights (P)*	ICI Price (P)	ICI relative (FTSE-100) (%)
Pricing date, Zeneca rights (12 May)	664	100.0	66	608	100.0
+ 1 day (13 May)	648	98.0	52	623	102.9
+3 days (17 May)	632	95.3	41	620	102.1
+ 1 week (19 May)	627	95.9	40	619	103.3
+ 2 weeks (26 May)	639	96.7	41	624	103.1
ICI EGM, last day of old ICI trading (28 May)	632	95.9	37	608	100.7
Rights trading and subscription period begin (1 June)	630	95.3	34	636	105.0
8 June (temporary low in Zeneca)	612	92.8	14	697	115.2
15 June (temporary low in Zeneca)	616	92.5	14	705	115.6
Last day of Zeneca rights trading (17 June)	621	93.0	19	696	114.0
28 June	624	92.7	N/A	652	106.0
+ 3 months (12 August)	655	93.5	N/A	695	109.1
+ 6 months (12 November)	754	105.2	N/A	679	103.4
+ 9 months (14 February 1994)	771	98.6	N/A	786	111.7
+12 months (12 May 1994)	716	98.2	N/A	826	126.2

Note: All Zeneca prices are ex rights. All ICI prices are when issued prices. From 12 to 31 May, the prices are when issued prices.
* One Zeneca right entitles the holder to subscribe one new Zeneca share at £6.

Sources: All prices are from Quality of Markets Department, London Stock Exchange. Index information from Datastream.

Exhibit 17

Zeneca ex-rights trading volumes during subscription period, 1–21 June (million)

	Day 1 (1 June)	Day 2 (2 June)	Day 3 (3 June)	Total subscription period
London	10.1	3.1	5.3	84
New York	0.4	0.5	2.4	23

Source: SG Warburg.

a demonstration of action by the ICI board. The ICI board also felt that it was necessary to raise money and the demerger would clearly facilitate a financing'. The ICI board eventually delivered shareholder value by demerging Zeneca and streamlining the new ICI.

A demerger for a huge company such as ICI – in fact this was the largest ever demerger in the UK – can be done but requires a long timetable, the inevitable consequence of which is uncertainty as to what the market will be like at the time of execution. However, because there was time enough to plan and execute the demerger properly, an industrially and financially sound long-term solution was found. If the plan is robust enough, it will work despite pressures from the stock market, the business cycle and adverse analysts and press.

Given that only holdings larger than 3 per cent are disclosed in the UK, the swings in ownership between old ICI and the two new companies between 5 May 1993 and the end of 1993 cannot be determined with precision. Nevertheless, it can be concluded that the largest shareholders had very different views of the prospects of new ICI and Zeneca which is the best proof of the appropriateness of the demerger. It is also noteworthy how the number of shareholders, ADR holdings and total foreign ownership developed differently between the two companies (see Exhibit 18).

Rights issue

The ICI case showed that if a demerger is combined with a financing, then there is a lot of structuring flexibility with respect to the financing. However, because of the long timetable of a demerger, there is limited flexibility with respect to the timing of the associated financing. In this case, the tim-

ing of the sale of shares in a pharmaceuticals company was far from optimal, though this could hardly have been foreseen when the decision was taken to demerge Zeneca in the summer of 1992. Although the financing could have been done in new ICI, it was more logical to do it in Zeneca.

It probably was best to do this financing by way of a rights issue because most of the money was going to come from ICI shareholders and those shareholders wanted it to be a rights issue. Furthermore, due to the depressed state of the pharmaceuticals sector, it would have been a bad time to sell shares of a pharmaceutical company to outside investors. However, if a portion of the total financing had been done through a fully marketed offer, there probably would have been a higher international participation as the rights issue structure is not the best way to reach new investors. Shareholders and tax authorities permitting, instead of just building a book of sub-underwritings of the rights issue before pricing, Zeneca easily could have done a simultaneous offer of a portion of the total financing by way of a fully marketed offer.

The Zeneca rights issue illustrated how important it is in large issues to give ample notice of the issue. This allows institutional investors to earmark funds for the particular issue.

A global managed rights offer is complex and untransparent. Mayo of Zeneca explained: 'It is perhaps true that our issue was in certain respects untransparent. In a rights issue, the market already knows how many shares, at what price and when shares will be sold and consequently rights issues are relatively easy to short. The fact that subscription rights are leveraged pieces of paper makes it even more attractive for shorting purposes. Therefore it can be important for there to be certain elements that are not transparent. In our case, nobody knew how much demand there was going to be from outside the UK and this assisted us in limiting the amount of short-selling. Those that did short the Zeneca rights offer did get burnt.'

The lead banks in a UK rights issue have only limited control over the recirculation of rights because any bank or broker is free to trade the rights. Because of the rigorous SEC restrictions imposed on syndicate members in registered rights issues by UK companies, it was almost an advantage not to be part of the syndicate. Nevertheless, there was in this case considerable control of the offer at the sub-underwriting stage. The broking businesses of SG Warburg and BZW had a natural dia-

Exhibit 18

Ownership breakdown of Zeneca and the new ICI

	Old ICI (31 December 1992)	New ICI (31 December 1993)	Zeneca (31 December 1993)
Mercury Asset Management	4.0%	Less than 3%	10.06% *
Schroder Investment Management	3.1%	Less than 3%	Less than 3%
Prudential Corporation (UK)	4.0%	Less than 3%	Less than 3%
Number of ordinary shareholders	323,589	279,588	283,616
ADRs owned via US depository	3.87%	17.72%*	5.53%
Number of ADR holders	14,500	31,000	16,000
Total foreign ownership	9.4%	24.4%	11.7%

* As per 21 February 1994.

Sources: ICI and Zeneca.

logue with all the significant institutional investors, while marketing and building the book for the sub-underwriting.

In a rights issue, there is often a perception among new investors that they will receive shares only to the extent that existing shareholders do not want to participate. This was particularly true in this case when no large shareholders had declared upfront, for corporate reasons, their intention to sell the whole or a portion of their entitlement. The counter argument on this occasion was that there were no former Zeneca shareholders because all initial shareholders were old ICI shareholders. Thus, potential new investors might accept that old ICI shareholders simply did not want to be exposed to the pharmaceuticals sector, rather than take the position that they had owned Zeneca for a long time and now had decided to sell.

Rights issues are not considered the optimal way of reaching new investors which in this case was an important objective as there was likely to be a shakeout in the share register immediately after the demerger. To counter this, two international marketing syndicates were superimposed on the parties conventionally found in a UK rights issue. 'The managed rights issue structure did two things for us,' said Mayo. 'First, it stabilised the market price during the subscription period, not least for psychological reasons as nobody could tell exactly how much demand there was going to be from abroad; and second, it enabled us to showcase the company with international institutions.'

A global managed rights offer is best suited to situations where one or a few large shareholders declare upfront that they do not wish to subscribe, as it gives the syndicate a minimum number of shares with which to approach new investors.

So long as pre-emptive rights issues remain the predominant way of raising new capital for non-US companies, the US SEC would be well advised to simplify its rules and regulations in connection with rights issues. As it is now, many non-US companies decide not to register their rights issues in the US because of the very high level of complexity. This is not in the interest of US shareholders – in fact the big US institutions get very upset when they do not have an equal opportunity to participate in rights issues.

Conclusion

Demerger

The stock market reacted positively to the formal announcement on 30 July 1992 that Zeneca was to be demerged. ICI's shares rose by 12 per cent on the day, despite the simultaneous announcement of lower-than-expected group profits for the first six months of 1992.

The demerger has worked out well for ICI and Zeneca and the two stocks have traded much better than did old ICI. The two new companies together increased by some 30 per cent in value over the first year compared to the old ICI share price pre-demerger. Largely through US buying, new ICI initially performed strongly on prospects for cyclical recovery in the chemicals sector. It out-performed the sector by 11 per cent over the first year. Zeneca did even better and out-performed the pharmaceuticals sector by 27 per cent over the same period. Zeneca doubled in value from its £6 offer price over the first 30 months of trading. One major London fund manager and long-standing ICI shareholder commented: 'it was a good idea to break up the company and create smaller pure plays with more focused managements'. By late August 1997, Zeneca traded 230 per cent higher than its initial offer price representing an outperformance of 156 per cent against the UK market. Over the same period, the more cyclical ICI traded up by 73 per cent, in line with the performance of the FT–SE 100 index over the same period.

Rights issue

ICI chairman Sir Denys Henderson expressed a high level of confidence in SG Warburg's ability to raise the required amount of money at a price implying a lower-than-usual discount to only an estimated value of the company. This put tremendous pressure on SG Warburg for the six-week underwriting period, the sub-underwriting notwithstanding. The pressure reached all the way up to Sir David Scholey, SG Warburg's then chairman.

In the event, the rights offer was approximately 86 per cent taken up. The subscription price of £6 was more or less in line with market expectations. Zeneca and SG Warburg were confident that at a P/E multiple of 11.4x 1993 earnings (compared to 11x for Ciba-Geigy, 13.8x for Glaxo and 15.7x for Wellcome) represented good value to the investor community. It was estimated that around 70 per cent of old ICI shareholders subscribed to the Zeneca rights offer. This was a considerable achievement given that old ICI and Zeneca were different businesses – chemicals and pharmaceuticals respectively and that the pharmaceuticals sector was out of favour with investors. It was indeed not to be taken for granted that old ICI's shareholders would want to own a pure pharmaceuticals company at this particular time. Based on the trading figures of fully-paid Zeneca shares in London and New York, it can further be estimated that some 6 per cent of the old ICI shareholders sold their Zeneca demerger shares during the three weeks immediately following the demerger.

The global syndicate sold rights to subscribe for approximately £20 million of new Zeneca shares to investors outside the UK. This figure seems very low but is not a fair reflection of the total international demand for Zeneca as many foreign institutions will have traded with UK brokers not involved in the syndicate who then traded with the broking businesses of the three IMCs (these volumes are not included in the £20 million).

'We knew in June 1992 that our plan would work and that gave us tremendous confidence to work towards the demerger and rights issue one year later,' said Zeneca finance director Mayo. Zeneca employed extensive scenario testing to probe its resilience to substantially adverse product price and volume developments over the year from the announcement of the demerger to completion of the financing. This convinced management that Zeneca would be in a position to raise US$2 billion whatever the trading conditions or political decisions concerning the healthcare industry.

Despite the overall success there were still some highly critical voices in the City of London. A fund manager with one of the largest UK investment institutions said: 'Whereas we liked the demerger, we found it completely unnecessary to price the rights issue at such a high price and, as a consequence, having to pay underwriting fees to the banks when a deep discount rights issue is by far the more straightforward solution. We also found the marketing unsuccessful and rather unnecessary.' Critics perceived that the two international marketing syndicates were merely safety nets for placement of unwanted stock. This perhaps is missing the point. Although in total probably no more than 1.5 per cent of the entire rights issue was placed internationally, it is conceivable that the rights issue might have failed without this incremental marketing power. Yet the syndicate was far too large and as expected the IMCs placed most of the stock not subscribed by shareholders.

Sir Denys owes a lot, not least his place in the history books, to SG Warburg, Goldman Sachs and Schroders for successfully defending ICI against Hanson and in turn he and his colleagues at ICI and Zeneca deserve credit for the successful structuring and execution of a complex demerger and financing. The trend of corporate demergers has clearly caught on since Zeneca. Numerous multinational companies, including IT&T, AT&T, British Gas, Hoechst, Ciba-Geigy, Thorn-EMI and Fletcher Challenge have announced demergers. It is perhaps ironic that the company which many people believe was instrumental in bringing about the Zeneca demerger, ie, Hanson Trust, in early 1996 announced that it intended to demerge three of its business areas to create four separate companies.

The top banks

The case studies in Chapter 3 were selected primarily because of their landmark nature, their geographical spread and the nature of the lessons learned. The focus has been on deals that were led by the most active houses during the period under review: consequently, in 17 of the 24 case studies, either of CSFB, Goldman Sachs, Merrill Lynch, Morgan Stanley or SBC Warburg have been the sole or joint global coordinators.

During the four years to 1996 these five banks (the 'top five') accounted for US$209 billion, or 47 per cent, of total cross-border equity issuance (which excludes purely domestic issuance and rights issues without an international marketing syndicate). (See Exhibits 4.1 and 4.12.)

If we look at the principal regions of the world, most of the 'top five' banks rank prominently in most regions, save for SBC Warburg, which does not rank in North America. (See Exhibits 4.2, 4.3, 4.4 and 4.5.) If we then look at global issuance over time, we observe that these houses rank among the top five in most years and there is no

Exhibit 4.1

Domestic and international issuance, 1993–96: global market* (US$ millions)

1	Goldman Sachs	64,172
2	Merrill Lynch	48,246
3	Morgan Stanley	43,612
4	SBC Warburg	29,289
5	CSFB	23,861
6	Dresdner Kleinwort Benson	18,521
7	Lehman Brothers	17,878
8	Paribas	12,886
9	BZW	11,865
10	Salomon Brothers	11,095

* US$ volumes of straight equity only; all credit to the bookrunner(s); domestic and non-domestic portion of cross-border offers.

Source: Capital Data Ltd.

Exhibit 4.3

Domestic and international issuance, 1993–96: American issuers* (US$ millions)

1	Goldman Sachs	42,214
2	Merrill Lynch	31,984
3	Morgan Stanley	27,655
4	CSFB	13,564
5	Lehman Bothers	11,750
6	Donaldson, Lufkin and Jenrette	8,498
7	Salomon Brothers	8,124
8	Smith Barney	7,101
9	Paine Webber	3543
10	JP Morgan	2,214

* US$ volumes of straight equity only; all credit to the bookrunner(s); domestic and non-domestic portion of cross-border offers.

Source: Capital Data Ltd.

Exhibit 4.2

Domestic and international issuance, 1993–96: European issuers* (US$ millions)

1	SBC Warburg	25,786
2	Dresdner Kleinwort Benson	18,258
3	Goldman Sachs	16,455
4	Paribas	12,282
5	Morgan Stanley	12,250
6	ABN AMRO Rothschild	9,832
7	IMI	9,756
8	BZW	9,295
9	BNP	8,297
10	CS First Boston	6,800

* US$ volumes of straight equity only; all credit to the bookrunner(s); domestic and non-domestic portion of cross-border transactions. For the purposes of this chapter, Europe includes the very limited African and Middle Eastern issuance.

Source: Capital Data Ltd.

Exhibit 4.4

Domestic and international issuance, 1993–96: Asia-Pacific (including Japan)* (US$ millions)

1	Merrill Lynch	6,460
2	Goldman Sachs	3,890
3	JB Were	3,844
4	Jardine Fleming/Robert Fleming	3,411
5.	Nomura	3,392
6	Morgan Stanley	2,581
7	Lehman Brothers	2,575
8	ING Barings	2,542
9	BZW	2,469
10	SBC Warburg	2,348

* US$ volumes of straight equity only; all credit to the bookrunner(s); domestic and non-domestic portion of cross-border offers.

Source: Capital Data Ltd.

single year in that period when one of them falls outside the ranks of the top 10. Morgan Stanley took sixth spot in 1993; SBC Warburg was ranked eighth in 1994; and CSFB claimed sixth position in both 1995 and 1996. Otherwise Goldman Sachs, Merrill Lynch, Morgan Stanley, SBC Warburg and CSFB dominated the top five places.

International issuance by region and over time

The same five banks continue to claim a massive market share, particularly if you look at the market over a long period and on a purely international basis, ie, if domestic tranches of cross-border offers are ignored. (See Exhibits 4.6 to 4.10)

Exhibit 4.5

Domestic and international issuance, 1993–96: Latin American issuers* (US$ millions)

1	Merrill Lynch	3,057
2	CSFB	2,095
3	Goldman Sachs	1,601
4	Bear Stearns	1,355
5	Morgan Stanley	1,127
6	JP Morgan	994
7	Lehman Brothers	857
8	Lazards	750
9	SBC Warburg	615
10	ING Barings	541

* US$ volumes of straight equity only; all credit to the bookrunner(s); domestic and non-domestic portion of cross-border offers.

Source: Capital Data Ltd.

Exhibit 4.8

International issuance, 1991–96: North American issuers* (US$ millions)

1	Goldman Sachs	15,401
2	Merrill Lynch	8,548
3	Morgan Stanley	7,743
4	CSFB	4,800
5	Lehman Brothers	4,040
6	Salomon Brothers	3,874
7	Donaldson, Lufkin and Jenrette	2,150
8	JP Morgan	1,788
9	Paine Webber	1,274
10	Smith Barney	1,157

* US$ volumes of straight equity only; all credit to the bookrunner(s); non-domestic portion of cross-border offers only.

Source: Capital Data Ltd.

Exhibit 4.6

International issuance, 1991–96: global market * (US$ millions)

1	Goldman Sachs	42,520
2	Merrill Lynch	26,102
3	Morgan Stanley	25,891
4	SBC Warburg	20,916
5	CSFB	17,204
6	Paribas	12,965
7	Lehman Brothers	12,696
8	BZW	11,256
9	Dresdner Kleinwort Benson	9,252
10	Salomon Brothers	7,679

* US$ volumes of straight equity only; all credit to the bookrunner(s); non-domestic portion of cross-border offers only.

Source: Capital Data Ltd.

Exhibit 4.9

International issuance, 1991–96: Asia-Pacific issuers (including Japan)* (US$ millions)

1	Merrill Lynch	5,491
2	Goldman Sachs	4,385
3	BZW	3,136
4	Jardine Fleming/Robert Fleming	3,086
5	Morgan Stanley	2,945
6	Lehman	2,802
7	ING Barings	2,606
8	SBC Warburg	2,358
9	CSFB	2,238
10	HSBC	1,865

* US$ volumes of straight equity only; all credit to the bookrunner(s); non-domestic portion of cross-border offers only.

Source: Capital Data Ltd.

Exhibit 4.7

International issuance, 1991–96: European issuers* (US$ millions)

1	Goldman Sachs	17,924
2	SBC Warburg	16,808
3	Morgan Stanley	13,423
4	Paribas	12,213
5	Dresdner Kleinwort Benson	8,971
6	Merrill Lynch	8,876
7	BZW	8,058
8	CSFB	7,791
9	Deutsche Morgan Grenfell	5,353
10	UBS	5,166

* US$ volumes of straight equity only; all credit to the bookrunner(s); non-domestic portion of cross-border offers only.

Source: Capital Data Ltd.

Exhibit 4.10

International issuance, 1991–96: Latin American issuers* (US$ millions)

1	Goldman Sachs	4,809
2	Merrill Lynch	3,188
3	CS Fist Boston	2,473
4	Morgan Stanley	1,780
5	JP Morgan	1,705
6	Bear Stearns	1,514
7	SBC Warburg	1,080
8	Lehman Brothers	899
9	Salomon Brothers	806
10	Lazards	750

* US$ volumes of straight equity only; all credit to the bookrunner(s); non-domestic portion of cross-border offers only.

Source: Capital Data Ltd.

The fortunes of these banks have fluctuated over time, but appear to have recovered following some lean years. CSFB was ranked second in 1991, but only eighth in 1995, before recovering to take fifth position in 1996. Morgan Stanley was a relatively distant seventh in 1991, but was ranked second in 1996.

Truly international banks

Not many investment banks can claim to have built a truly international equity new issue business. An indication of this is the extent to which a bank can win and execute significant mandates from companies based outside their respective home markets. Although such statistics are revealing, they should be treated with care, as different banks define their home markets differently. Do you acquire a new home market simply because you acquire a broker, or is it more reasonable to say that you only acquire a new home market if you buy a bank that has previously been active in the new issue market? For the purposes of this book the latter definition has been used, with the implication that Merrill Lynch has not acquired a new home market in the UK through its purchase of Smith New Court, whereas it did acquire one in Australia through the purchase of McIntosh Securities Limited. This way of looking at the market means that all the business that US banks do for US companies, whether domestically or in the international market, is excluded, as is the business that SBC Warburg does for UK and Swiss companies. Using this definition the size of the market in 1996 is reduced from US$143 billion to US$52 billion, and Goldman Sachs, Morgan Stanley, Merrill Lynch, SBC Warburg and CSFB are rated the most 'international' banks in the primary equity market (see Exhibit 4.11).

Market concentration

As a group, these five banks have a strong hold over the market in terms of domestic and international issuance, but the figures from the past four years do not appear to indicate that there is continuing consolidation. (See Exhibit 4.12.) This picture also appears to be reflected in the market share of the 10 most active banks over the same period. (See Exhibit 4.13.)

When taking a more long term view, and considering international issuance in isolation, it appears that in terms of bookrunning volumes, these banks are actually losing market share (see Exhibit 4.14).

The leading houses in each region in 1996

In Europe Goldman Sachs and Morgan Stanley held strong

Exhibit 4.11

Top banks in terms of international business*, 1996 (US$ millions)

1	Goldman Sachs (outside the US)	9,644
2	Morgan Stanley (outside the US)	6,682
3	Merrill Lynch (outside the US/Australia)	3,976
4	SBC Warburg (outside the UK/Switzerland)	3,817
5	CSFB (outside the US/Switzerland)	3,354
6	DMG (outside Germany/UK)	1,992
7	UBS (outside Switzerland)	1,873
8	Salomon Brothers (outside the US)	1,305
9	ING Barings (outside the Netherlands/UK)	1,168
10	JP Morgan (outside the US)	1,103

* US$ volumes of straight equity only; all credit to the bookrunner; domestic and non-domestic portion of cross-border offers reflecting only issuance from issuers outside the banks' home markets.

Source: Capital Data Ltd.

Exhibit 4.12

Development of the market share of the 'top five' banks: domestic and international issuance, 1993–96*

	1993	1994	1995	1996
US$ volumes accounted for by the top five banks	55,596	39,263	48,652	65,556
Top five banks as a % of total market	55%	42%	46%	46%

* US$ volumes of straight equity only; all credit to the bookrunner; domestic and non-domestic portion of cross-border offers.

Source: Capital Data Ltd.

Exhibit 4.13

Development of the market share of the ten most active banks in each year: domestic and international issuance, 1993–96*

	1993	1994	1995	1996
US$ volumes accounted for by the top 10 houses in each individual year	73,761	58,283	68,651	92,588
% of market accounted for by the top 10 houses in each individual year	73%	62%	65%	65%

* US$ volumes of straight equity only; domestic and non-domestic portion of cross-border offers.

Source: Capital Data Ltd.

Exhibit 4.14

Development of the market share of the 'top five' banks: international issuance, 1991–96*

	1991	1992	1993	1994	1995	1996
US$ volumes accounted for by the top five banks	13,117	13,929	20,784	23,949	25,462	35,392
Top five banks as a % of total market	56%	56%	51%	44%	49%	46%

* US$ volumes of straight equity only; non-domestic portion of cross-border offers.

Source: Capital Data Ltd.

Exhibit 4.15

Domestic and international issuance, 1996: European issuers* (US$ millions)

1	Dresdner Kleinwort Benson	9,846
2	Goldman Sachs	7,431
3	SBC Warburg	6,275
4	Morgan Stanley	5,135
5	IMI	4,619
6	BZW	3,969
7	ABN AMRO Rothschild	3,393
8	Paribas	3,108
9	CSFB	2,510
10	Merrill Lynch	2,388

* US$ volumes of straight equity only; all credit to the bookrunner(s); domestic and non-domestic portion of cross-border offers.

Source: Capital Data Ltd.

Exhibit 4.17

Domestic and international issuance, 1996: Asia-Pacific issuers (including Japan)* (US$ millions)

1	JB Were	2,729
2	Nomura	1,994
3	Goldman Sachs	1,302
4	Morgan Stanley	1,158
5	Merrill Lynch	1,089
6	Daiwa	1,000
7	Deutsche Morgan Grenfell	814
8	Jardine Fleming/Robert Fleming	813
9	ING Barings	699
10	Bear Stearns	690

* US$ volumes of straight equity only; all credit to the bookrunner(s); domestic and non-domestic portion of cross-border offers.

Source: Capital Data Ltd.

Exhibit 4.16

Domestic and international issuance, 1996: North American issuers* (US$ millions)

1	Goldman Sachs	12,599
2	Morgan Stanley	12,455
3	Merrill Lynch	7,703
4	Donaldson, Lufkin and Jenrette	3,216
5	CSFB	2,994
6	Smith Barney	2,471
7	Salomon Bothers	2,349
8	Lehman Brothers	1,745
9	RBC Dominion Securities	730
10	Deutsche Morgan Grenfell	539

* US$ volumes of straight equity only; all credit to the bookrunner(s); domestic and non-domestic portion of cross-border offers.

Source: Capital Data Ltd.

Exhibit 4.18

Domestic and international issuance, 1996: Latin American issuers* (US$ millions)

1	Merrill Lynch	694
2	JP Morgan	526
3	Lehman Brothers	517
4	SBC Warburg	315
5	Morgan Stanley	309
6	Paine Webber	290
7	Merinvest Sociedad de Corretaje de Venezuela	240
8	Lazards	222
9	Banco del Credito del Peru	203
10	Bear Stearns	189

* US$ volumes of straight equity only; all credit to the bookrunner(s); domestic and non-domestic portion of cross-border offers.

Source: Capital Data Ltd.

---

market positions against increasing competition from a limited number of European houses which aspire to European 'special bracket' status, such as Dresdner Kleinwort Benson, BZW, ABN AMRO Rothschild, Paribas, UBS and Deutsche Morgan Grenfell. CSFB's ninth position is relatively disappointing, as Europe ought to be one of its strongest markets. Despite the acquisition of Smith New Court, and its overall global strength, Merrill Lynch only achieved tenth place. (See Exhibit 4.15.)

In North America Goldman Sachs and Morgan Stanley were in a league of their own, while Donaldson Lufkin and Jenrette ranked above firms such as CSFB, Lehman Brothers and Salomon Brothers. Of the European firms (other than

CSFB), Deutsche Morgan Grenfell is the only bank which has made an impact in the US. (See Exhibit 4.16.)

In the Asia-Pacific region, which includes Japan, the league table is topped by JB Were and Nomura as a result of a small number of large issues in Australia and Japan. While traditionally strong regional banks such as Jardine Fleming, HSBC and ING Barings have been overtaken by the top three US houses, both CSFB (12th) and SBC Warburg (21st) did not rank as highly as their global positions might have led them to expect. (See Exhibit 4.17.)

Latin America was still a relatively inactive region in 1996 and the league tables were substantially influenced by the two telecom privatisations in Venezuela and Peru. Goldman Sachs' inactivity in the region stands out, while CSFB only managed to take 12th position. (See Exhibit 4.18.)

Global equity research capability

Whereas four of these top five banks rank among the strongest research houses globally, CSFB is ranked only fourteenth in Institutional Investor's All Star Research Team rankings, which are based on surveys conducted in each region. This proves two points: firstly, that research is not the only criteria for success in the global equity new issue market and secondly, that there is a challenge ahead for CSFB in terms of building a serious global equity business supported by an appropriate sales, trading and research infrastructure. As banks which have not previously been awarded global coordinator roles for large transactions outside their home markets gain experience, it will be harder for CSFB to get away with having a weak secondary market presence. Salomon and UBS achieved strong rankings in the global All-Star Team: UBS has long been taken seriously in the global equity business and it appears that Salomon is at last going to shake off its image as a 'bond house'. (See Exhibit 4.19.) Based on its improving equity research capability, it would seem that Salomon has a fair chance, however, the bank is hampered by its image as a trading rather than a corporate finance house.

SBC Warburg is in a commanding position in Europe, with 43 team positions in the 1997 rankings. UBS (33) and Merrill Lynch (31) are close behind. Goldman Sachs and Morgan Stanley took seventh and ninth places, with 19 and 18 team positions respectively. CSFB came thirteenth with only five team positions.

Merrill Lynch, Morgan Stanley and Goldman Sachs dominate US research rankings, with 46, 41 and 35 team posi-

tions respectively. Donaldson, Lufkin and Jenrette and Salomon Brothers take fourth and fifth positions while CSFB was ranked eleventh with 15 team positions. SBC Warburg was not rated.

In Asia (excluding Japan) Jardine Flemings and ING Barings rule the roost, though SBC Warburg (4th), Morgan Stanley (6th) and Merrill Lynch (9th) all managed top ten placings. Goldman Sachs, Morgan Stanley and Merrill Lynch captured second, third and fourth places in Japan, behind Nomura. ING Barings also performed well in Latin America, taking the top spot just ahead of Bear Stearns while Merrill Lynch (3rd), Morgan Stanley (5th) and CSFB (6th) followed close behind.

In the following interviews, representatives of these five banks explain their approaches to and views on the global equity market and their position in it.

CSFB

(represented by James Leigh-Pemberton, managing director and head of European equity capital markets).

What are your goals in the global equity business and why?

We want to offer a superior service in targeted markets and industries around the world and have a leading position both in the US and European markets, while continuing to build our capabilities in Asia and other emerging markets. We are not seeking to be all things to all men in every market. Rather, we want to focus our resources on the markets where we can add value and make a difference.

In addition to these geographic priorities, we want to be a leading player in certain global industry sectors, ie, where the drivers of revenues and profits are determined by global trends. Such industries are, for example, oil and gas; telecommunications; metals and mining; pharmaceuticals; and media. We want to significantly increase our revenues from the equity business, which we think is possible because of an increasing equity culture both from the issuers' and the investors' point of view.

Our strategy is very much driven by the return on capital targets which underpin the activities of the whole Credit Suisse Group. We strive for a reputation of top quality execution in the new issue market and would like to be considered as one of the handful of banks which have a truly global equity business. At the same time, our goals will be very much based on the needs of our clients and the provision of a balanced service to both investors and issuers.

What are your strategies to attain these goals?

Our strategy in the global equity business is developed off the back of the following key strategy drivers:

- Inflation is coming down and staying low, stimulating increased equity investment among both retail and institutional investors;
- World trade volumes are increasing, competitive barriers are coming down and most larger companies are now operating in the global economy;

Exhibit 4.19

Institutional investor, 1997/96 global all star team positions (most recent survey in each region)

Rank 1997	Firm	Total number of positions
1	Merrill Lynch (including McIntosh)	102
2	Morgan Stanley/Dean Witter (pro forma)*	87
3	Goldman Sachs	69
4	SBC Warburg	52
5	Salomon Brothers	47
6	UBS	42
7	ING Barings	38
8	Nomura	34
9	NatWest	34
10	HSBC James Capel	31
10	Donaldson Lufkin and Jenrette	31
11	Bear Stearns	29
12	BZW	27
13	Dresdner Kleinwort Benson	26
14	CSFB	25
15	Smith Barney	24

* Dean Witter earned three Team Positions in the 1996 All America Research Team.

Source: Institutional Investor.

- The global spread of communications technology and an increased sophistication on the part of analysts has led to an increase in cross-border equity capital flows;

- An equity culture is gradually developing around the world. The supply side is driven by increased privatisation volumes and increased sales of shares by private vendors, prompted by a stronger orientation towards shareholder value as a result of increased pressure to perform. The demand side is driven by the fact that an increasing proportion of total savings is held in equities, at the expense of more traditional asset compositions, by the increased internationalisation of the investment strategy of US pension funds and by a dramatic increase in the inflow to US mutual funds; and

- The fund management industry is consolidating worldwide which means not only are institutional investors getting bigger, but they are also getting more international and, as a result of the increased pressure to show a high level of performance, the equity content of portfolios is increasing. Parallel to this development, institutional investors are growing in size and importance as a result of the institutionalisation of 'retail' savings.

CSFB's strategy within this overall framework is:

- To continue to invest in our research, sales and trading capabilities world-wide, keeping pace with the growth in cross-border equity flows;

- To leverage our existing platform by means of this investment, that is to say, to achieve the largest possible marginal contribution from new investment off the back of the already existing infrastructure;

- To strengthen client orientation towards our institutional investor clients in our research and sales service. This has two particular implications; first, that we increasingly develop our equity research product on an industry sector basis to facilitate cross-border comparison and, secondly, that we build global research groups to cover globalised industries. Unlike our competitors, however, we believe that there should be one analyst in overall charge of a particular stock, an 'analyst of record', although that analyst may draw on the expertise of other members of his global industry group. This means, for example, that in the case of ENI, Cathy Arnfield who is based in London, is the analyst of record and the macro assumptions incorporated into her reports are derived from the global oil and gas group run by Jim Clark, our US oil analyst based in New York;

- To differentiate our investor client service strategically through branded research – EVA™-based (economic value added) research – allowing us to determine like-for-like value comparisons across sectors and countries;

- To have a client-driven approach in terms of how institutional investors are covered. Our sales people work with their institutional clients much like our investment bankers work with their corporate clients, basing the service on client requirements;

- To dominate trading in certain stocks and, in so doing, create 'house' stocks where CSFB is the first call; and

---

Exhibit 4.20

Total number of equity professionals employed by CSFB

	Equity research coverage (number of stocks)	Institutional equity professionals*
North America	400	500
Europe/Africa	225	300
Asia-Pacific (including Japan)	200	120
Latin America	75	30
Total	**900**	**950**

* This number includes sales, trading and research personnel as well as ECM professionals at the end of 1996. It does not include any corporate finance staff or support staff.

Source: CSFB.

- To harmonise our investment banking coverage, research and trading activity in key industries and regions to support investment banking advisory and equity capital markets activities. The purpose of this strategy is to allocate scarce resources in the most efficient way possible.

How global are you today? Please describe in as much detail as possible, your sales, trading and research infrastructure.

We currently cover over 900 stocks world-wide and have separate sales forces for European, US, Asian and Latin American stocks, all of which are managed on a global basis and which are represented in London, New York and Hong Kong. In addition to these institutional salesforces, we also have a specialist salesforce dedicated to high net worth individuals in the US.

Exhibit 4.20 illustrates the total number of equity professionals employed, and the way in which research coverage was divided between the four regions. We are planning considerable growth in sales, trading and research and intend to increase the number of equity professionals in the various regions over the next two to three years, as follows: North America 660; Europe/Africa 500; Asia-Pacific (including Japan) 200 and Latin America 40. On a global basis, this amounts to a total percentage increase of over 47 per cent.

The equity capital markets department is managed as a single global entity, whereby the heads in New York, London and Hong Kong report to our global head of ECM. There is a very high level of cross-border cooperation.

How do you distinguish yourself from the other four houses profiled – Goldman Sachs, Merrill Lynch, Morgan Stanley and SBC Warburg?

- Unlike many of our competitors we are not seeking to be all things to all men in every market. We have not established a major UK equities operation, but instead intend to focus our resources on markets in which we can make a difference;

- CSFB's equity business has been created organically, like those of Goldman Sachs and Morgan Stanley, but in contrast to those of SBC Warburg and Merrill Lynch;

- Partly as a result of our growth being organic, we believe that we have established a proper balance between customer and proprietary business; between the cash and derivatives businesses; and between the primary and secondary businesses. This is terribly important, as if any one of these becomes too dominant, it crushes all the others, with all sorts of problems as a consequence;

- CSFB is not a US firm or a European firm. It has a leading presence in both markets, which means that the service we provide to our clients is driven exclusively by the goal of best execution. There is no dominant geographical bias or client franchise bias in our business approach or our execution methods;

- We believe that we have a uniquely powerful profile in terms of the universal banking activities of Credit Suisse and the US bulge bracket status of the former First Boston. Moreover, as a result of the merger between First Boston and Credit Suisse at the end of 1996, we are in a better position to leverage off Credit Suisse's universal banking activities. This is particularly relevant in terms of Credit Suisse's global corporate relationships, institutional fund management and private banking. The former is of value on the corporate finance side and the others are expected, over time, to significantly increase our placement power; and

- Most importantly, we have an exceptional track record in terms of quality of execution. From 1991 to May 1997 our SEC-registered IPOs larger than US$100 million (by US and non-US companies) have, on average, traded up by 10.7 per cent over the first four weeks of trading. This figure is right in the middle of the market, and proves that we have struck a good balance between the interests of the issuers and investors. (See Exhibit 4.21.)

Our strengths and weaknesses can be summarised as follows:

Weaknesses

- In the early days of the international equity market, we had no home market from which to build a franchise. However, although this hampered us in the past, it is now one of the principal reasons for our ability to provide execution which is not defined by regional bias. Today, when cross-border flows dominate our business, lack of identity with a particular region is a strength; and

Exhibit 4.21

After-market price performance of all SEC registered IPOs larger than US$100 million, January 1991–May 1997 (weighted price performance in percentage based on the market price four weeks after pricing)

Donaldson, Lufkin and Jenrette	18.6%
Morgan Stanley	18.5%
Merrill Lynch	15.8%
Goldman Sachs	13.4%
Smith Barney	12.6%
CSFB	10.7%
Lehman Brothers	10.7%
Salomon Brothers	4.2%

Source: Securities Data Corporation and CSFB.

- In the late 1980s and early 1990s when all of the major firms were building the foundations of their international equity franchises, the old CSFB and First Boston were still separate firms. This separation hampered the development of institutional relations until 1992, when the firms merged under a single name and created a single distribution network. As a result, our franchise has had to be developed quickly by comparison with some of our competitors.

Strengths

- Because we are not tied to any regional market, we have not been constrained by the precedent of a single market or product in delivering superior execution to our clients;

- Because of our Swiss parentage and operations, our important London base and our strong US presence, we believe that we have a unique access to the three largest pools of capital available for investment in international equities: US and UK institutions, and Swiss funds;

- We have a culture of attention to our clients' needs which has its origins in our lack of home market. This is a strength but may also be seen as a weakness. We have tended to emphasise first class execution on behalf of our clients at the expense of marketing for new business. Unlike some of our competitors, we never risk sub-optimal execution in pursuit of new mandates; and

- A strong and highly integrated global equity business is at the heart of CSFB's strategic plan and the importance of our equity business has been reflected in the adoption of a major investment programme for the continued development of this business.

What is your philosophy on ad-hoc partnerships/cooperation in deals?

Vendors and issuers typically have a preference for what they want to do, and we try to accommodate their wishes using a flexible and friendly approach. In the case of a privatisation, we feel that it is appropriate for the best qualified domestic bank to be a joint global coordinator, particularly if there is a large retail offer.

The rationale for picking two or more international global coordinators is often less clear-cut, however, at the request of the client we will work together with other houses. We consider ourselves a good partner and have worked well with all four of the institutions featured in this book, as well as many other houses around the world.

How do you see the economics of the equity new business?

Building up the necessary infrastructure to run a global equity business is expensive and we are committing very considerable resources to it. Naturally we require a minimum return on this investment, which is why we are concerned about the compression in spreads.

We believe that the level of fees will self-correct in less bullish market conditions, as governments and companies realise the importance of high quality execution. It is also likely that some of the houses that are now trying to enter the global equity business will realise how expensive it is and will therefore de-emphasise the equity new issue business. This would have a positive effect on spreads.

Institutional investors frequently perceive the equity research analysts of major new issue houses to be as much sophisticated salesmen as independent research analysts and feel that only with great difficulty can they decline to 'cooperate' with IBD/ECM on new issues. What is your strategy for safeguarding the independence of your equity research analysts?

Although the investment banking department pays 50 per cent of the fixed cost of the research department, our analysts' bonuses are the responsibility of the equity department. That does not mean that an analyst is not compensated if he works on a new issue, but it does mean that he has to generate commission income from his ideas through building and maintaining institutional investor client relationships.

Having said that, it would be impossible for an analyst to sell an issue at an inflated price to an institution that did not want to buy it. The firm thinks very carefully about the business it takes on, and we have strict internal procedures both with regard to the valuation of a potential offer and its suitability. Finally, in the case of an IPO, the analyst is usually sceptical about the stock to begin with, and we at ECM have to convince him of the merits of the story before he commits to the project.

In addition to the other four major houses interviewed in this book, who do you consider to be the 'up and coming' global firms?

I believe that of the firms that are aspiring to join the top rank of the global equity new issue market, the following banks are among the ones that stand the best chances of success: ABN AMRO Rothschild, Dresdner Kleinwort Benson, Deutsche Morgan Grenfell and UBS. We have just been appointed to coordinate the Australian telecom privatisation together with ABN AMRO Rothschild and JB Were. In the longer term, I would not discount JP Morgan.

Despite talk of more competition, I believe that the business is still concentrating, principally because new firms need to build a track record of excellence over a three- to five-year period to really break into this market. Along the way many of them are forced to be too aggressive on pricing, which tends to backfire in terms of the franchise development.

It is probably fair to say that you are sometimes forced to undercut on fees and over-represent the likely demand, as telling the 'truth' might lead to somebody else getting the mandate. What are the consequences of this trend and how can it be reversed?

The high quality banks in this business realise how difficult it is to build a track record and how easy it is to lose it. You have, therefore, to decide if you are serious and if you intend to be able to deliver what you promise, or whether you are in the business of back-tracking and not being able to deliver. Even if you only do that once, the whole market will know and I think that you will find that your business will be eroded very quickly indeed.

I feel that it is a myth that investment banks can make a difference to the sustainable price at which investors and issuers meet. If we over-market and sell too expensively, it will always catch up with us. Our job is simply to identify the highest sustainable price at which buyers and sellers will meet. If we can do that consistently, we will be able to build a great business.

An ECM department is situated between two sets of clients – the vendors/issuers via the investment banking department and the investment institutions via the salesforce. What are the particular challenges of this position?

Attention to detail and judgement on the basis of facts are what primarily distinguishes a high quality service from a low quality one. Having said that, judgement is no substitute for knowledge. An ECM professional must be able to balance the interests of the issuing clients and the investors. On the one hand he must be able to identify a fair value for the issuer, and on the other ensure that the investor is left with an investment that will perform in line with, or better than, its peer group over a period of time. This requires him to exercise his duty of care on behalf of both the buyers and the sellers. If he does so consistently, he will help develop the business, which is ultimately what matters. Within his own organisation, an ECM professional stands between the investment bankers and the equity salesforce. In order to have credibility with both sides he must ensure that he is unbiased in his dealings with them.

Conclusion

CSFB has a good name and strong ties to many governments and corporations and has a presence in all the major regions of the world. It has many experienced bankers, good corporate relationships, some of the most experienced ECM professionals in the market and a capacity to manage large transactions. CSFB is a bank that earns high marks for being a good team player in large transactions, regardless of its position. The question is whether, after disruption in the late 1980s and early 1990s caused by the merger between the old Credit Suisse and First Boston, the bank can catch up sufficiently in terms of sales, trading and research to avoid being overtaken by equally capital-strong European banks who are devoting massive resources to the secondary side.

A distinct strategy now appears to be in place: the recently announced merger between CSFB and the institutional banking, sales, trading and research operations of Credit Suisse is evidence of this. The merger appears to have been implemented successfully and some recent major transactions on the corporate side demonstrate the benefits of the merger - one such example is the 100 per cent spin-off of Ciba Specialty Chemicals, the chemicals operations of Novartis, in the spring of 1997. The new CSFB is stronger both in terms of capital and overall resources than its predecessor, and is the only bank which can claim to have both special bracket status in the US and a dominant position in a major European market.

Goldman Sachs

(represented by the members of the ECM department in London and New York)

What are your goals in the global equity business and why?

The global equity business continues to be a core activity for Goldman Sachs' strategic platform and has been a critical part of the firm's development over many years. We want our clients to regard us as the best 'equity house' in the business. This is measured by various polls and does not necessarily mean that we have to be the biggest at all times, but we would certainly have to be among the leaders.

Our targeted client group are the largest capitalisation and emerging growth companies (ie, those that grow fast and are likely to be among the largest companies in the near future) in the Americas, Europe and Asia. Governments also rank very highly on our list of important targeted clients.

What really matters to us is our reputation and the image we have in the market: this is a firm-wide attitude, not limited to our equity business. We believe that we are more conservative than many of our competitors, which is partly a function of our partnership structure, and we think twice about the business we take on.

We aim to be innovative and are prepared to commit significant amounts of capital to support our offers. We wish to be considered by clients and competitors alike as creative, fair, flexible and committed to complete excellence in all aspects of the equity product area.

Goldman Sachs has always taken a long-term approach to success, and this is reflected in the way we hire and train employees as well as by our investments in leading edge technology in terms of hardware and software to support our business.

We are not trying to be all things to all people: we work closely with our clients to understand their needs, and then build businesses to serve them. We try to have the right people in the right places: some firms may have more people, but we believe that we are more effective.

What are your strategies to attain these goals?

We continue to place significant emphasis on our people and culture, and try to develop our business according to the needs of our clients.

We believe in growing organically and are consequently not interested in acquiring local banks or brokerage firms. Instead, we try to hire the best professionals, train them and act as a mentor, while providing them with opportunities and incentives to ensure a successful career within the firm, effectively doing everything internally. This means that we rarely hire senior people from outside, although there are exceptions, such as in equity research where analysts appear to have less loyalty to firms. Secondly, we have cultivated long-term client relationships through emphasis on commitment, loyalty, and the delivery of sound judgement and well-balanced advice. Because of our partnership structure, and our strong culture, heritage and business success, Goldman Sachs has

been able to attract and retain outstanding professionals, resulting in one of the lowest staff turnover rates in the industry. This, in turn, helps support stable, long-term client relationships.

We have found that being able to offer a full range of investment banking services to governmental and corporate clients has been important in identifying new areas of equity business, since many of the most attractive equity transactions emerge from government privatisations, corporate restructurings and/or strategic events.

We want to remain an institutional firm, which also serves high net worth individuals. Consequently, we have no intention of buying a retail distribution network since we believe combining our global institutional distribution system with a network of regional retail firms, specifically selected for each securities offer, provides the custom-tailoring necessary to do a great underwriting job for clients world-wide. We strongly believe retail penetration can best be achieved by the inclusion of selective 'retail houses' in our syndicates. We would only have a problem if all these houses were bought by other banks, so that we were substantially restricted in our choice of the most appropriate bank for a particular offer.

In the equity business, we have two sets of clients – corporate, including governments, who issue or sell the equity securities, and institutional investors who buy them. We have to keep up to date with both sets of clients and make sure that we approach them in a way that makes sense, as requirements vary from market to market and change over time. In Germany, corporate clients have a German focus, whereas fund managers do not want to be covered on a country-specific basis. In the UK the situation is the reverse. Overall, there appears to be a trend towards industry specialisation, especially on the fund management side. This is clearly an advantage for major American houses as we have strong industry expertise in the US.

Unlike certain other houses, we do not have a dedicated privatisation strategy. Yes, we did take a strategic decision to specifically try to cater for the needs of governments, and we consider governments to be among our most important clients, but we don't have a separate department to deal with privatisations. Having had a reasonable amount of success with governments in Europe and Asia, we decided some three years ago to deepen our corporate client penetration, which is a more labour intensive undertaking. That, however, was a natural part of our evolution towards becoming a global investment bank.

How global are you today? Please describe in as much detail as possible your sales, trading and research infrastructure.

Goldman Sachs conducts its equity business on a global basis, although day to day business is managed regionally, with headquarters in New York, London and Hong Kong, with the global head of the equity business residing in New York. Most outside analysts speculate that at least 40 per cent of the firm's revenues comes from the international businesses and that the figure is growing.

As global markets and financing opportunities have developed, Goldman Sachs has consistently made significant investments in sales, trading, research, banking and equity capital

Exhibit 4.22

Goldman Sachs' research coverage (number of stocks

North America	1,102
Europe/Africa/Middle East	368
Asia-Pacific (including Japan)	426
Latin America	41
Total	**1,937**

Source: Goldman Sachs.

markets resources to a point where we now have a highly developed presence as an integrated equity house in all the major financial markets. We take great pride in having achieved a top three position in all the three major regions of the world for the first time in 1996.

This success is to a large extent built on our sales, trading and research organisation. In London for example, we have dedicated teams trading and selling Asian shares, US and Latin American shares, and European shares. Our European sales force is based in London, with one exception – Germany – where pan-European selling to German clients is based in Frankfurt. Similarly, in New York we have teams selling the same three categories of shares while our sales effort to Asian clients is based in Hong Kong. In addition to the general sales-forces, we have a dedicated salesforce for 'high net worth individuals' which is split between Atlanta, Boston, Chicago, London, Memphis, Miami, New York, Philadelphia, San Francisco, Singapore, Tokyo and Zurich.

The equity research analysts for European shares are mainly based in London, although there are many stocks which are covered on a global basis, for which we have analysts in both London and New York. For companies operating in global industries, it makes sense to have dual coverage. The London-based analyst may be more familiar with the European assets of the particular company, the local stock market and European fund managers, whereas the New York-based analyst may be more familiar with the company's US assets and fund managers (at least the so-called 'domestic accounts', which invest primarily in US companies). Which of our analysts covers a particular stock depends on the needs of corporate and fund manager clients and on which of the analysts has the best relationship with the particular client. Our research analysts are organised either on an industry or on a country basis. There is some overlap, but we try to keep duplication to a minimum. We cover almost 2,000 stocks, broken down by region as shown in Exhibit 4.22.

How do you distinguish yourself generally from the other four houses profiled in the book?

Our principal strength is that we have more experience in the equity new issue market than our closest competitors. This is due to the transactions completed and the experience of our senior people. We have two managing directors in the equity capital markets area who have worked in the department for over 20 years and other managing directors each have more than 10 years experience in the area of equity new issuance

both in the US and internationally. It is our understanding that our sales people have a higher average productivity and longevity than those of our competitors and we would not hire anyone who is not a college graduate to join our equity sales force. This expertise and experience together with our track record of successfully completed transactions enables us to call upon first class references. We are relatively conservative and think twice about how we use our capital, so we may not be as aggressive as other houses when it comes to 'bought deals' where the risk to the investment bank can be enormous. On the other hand, with prudent structuring, we are prepared to take on considerable risk. One such example was the US$2 billion spring 1997 sale by way of block trade by the KIO of a three per cent stake in British Petroleum, the largest ever block trade executed by a single investment bank.

We have strong views about how to do things when working with clients and believe in sharing those views. The risks of failure are high and the consequences can be very expensive. In our opinion, the end result of how a transaction is completed is what matters.

As already mentioned, we do not consider the lack of a retail salesforce in the US to be a weakness as we believe that custom-tailoring offers with selected regional retail firms works best. US retail investors are price followers and, therefore, are less important in terms of how transactions are structured and priced compared to institutional investors. It is among the institutions that the success of the majority of transactions is determined.

Just because we are serving an institutional market doesn't mean we are not serving retail investors, as indirectly many of our largest clients are mutual funds. Also, do not forget that we have two unique retail businesses: our private client service, which serves the high net worth individual market; and Goldman Sachs Asset Management, which has a broad range of mutual funds.

Some other houses have a greater presence in certain emerging markets. We, for example, do not own a big brokerage house in Johannesburg as Merrill Lynch does, nor are we as big in Central Europe as CSFB. We have not adopted a 'world strategy' by buying local banks since we believe our system works better for our clients.

We believe that our people pay more attention to detail and have more experience than our competitors. We probably also spend more time on valuing and pricing issues, and in working to stabilise new issues in the after-market.

Sure, there are individual transactions that we have competed for and lost. Perhaps the loss that hurt the most was the Wellcome transaction in 1992, where we lost the US bookrunning role to Morgan Stanley. This was painful, because until that time we had done by far the largest number of the US tranches of international (non-US) transactions. Until then many companies and governments considered that they took a risk by not using Goldman Sachs.

What is your philosophy on ad-hoc partnerships/cooperation in deals?

Goldman Sachs is supportive of ad-hoc partnerships and cooperation with other banks on transactions. Often such partnerships are critical to the success of an offer because either they allow the domestic and international markets to be more closely integrated, or they capitalise on the different strengths and contributions that can be provided by different banks. As transactions have increased in size and complexity, we find ourselves working more often as partners at the global coordinator level. As a result, we have worked jointly with almost all of our principal competitors across the major markets. If it is clearly in the client's best interest to have us partner with another strong bank, then we respect that decision as one that is likely to assist in ensuring a successful transaction.

Having said that, we understand that there is often political pressure, particularly on governments, to appoint a domestic house as joint global coordinator. This is not always optimal, but there is at least a certain rationale for it and the role split is typically reasonably straightforward, particularly when the domestic distribution involves a large retail offer.

If we are the junior partner in a syndicate, we do not mind terribly who the senior partner is, so long as it is one of the top houses who we believe has the necessary global expertise and experience to make a transaction successful. That does not mean that we won't express our views if we disagree with whoever is in charge.

How do you get the best out of Goldman Sachs?

Since we tend to be hands on, we want to have at least a joint bookrunning role of a particular tranche of a transaction, so that the firm is in a senior enough position to leverage its many resources, both geographically and on an industry basis. This means that we are perceived by our clients as an important party to the transaction and that there is a level playing field. This is required to motivate our sales force. There is, therefore, an enormous difference between being a joint lead manager and a joint bookrunner.

All of the above notwithstanding, we believe that it can often be structurally inefficient to have more than one international global coordinator. The greatest value is typically achieved if a single bank is in charge of a transaction, so long as that bank is one of the top houses. The role of a global coordinator is to provide overall leadership of the transaction, be it in terms of providing a consistent research view or to set demand and price signals to the market. The more global coordinators there are, the more that important role is diluted as the market gets many different signals and the various global coordinators try to promote their own tranches. In addition, most global coordinators tend to stress that they are involved in all the regional tranches. If you fill all the tranches with, say three global coordinators, then it is very difficult to motivate the fourth bank in that tranche. Take the IPO of Scania as an example: there were three global coordinators, Morgan Stanley, SBC Warburg and Enskilda. All three wanted to be in the UK tranche, the consequence of which was that UBS, which arguably had the leading analyst, was never going to be particularly motivated, as the UK institutions did not perceive them to be one of the most important managers in that tranche.

If it is determined that it is in the client's best interest to have more than one international global coordinator, then the key to success is to make sure that the amount of overlapping responsibilities are kept to an absolute minimum. It is also essential that at the start of the assignment all fundamental issues and differences are resolved up front so that the result is a harmonious relationship between the underwriters leading the syndicate.

Institutional investors frequently perceive the equity research analysts of major new issue houses to be as much sophisticated salesmen as independent research analysts and feel that only with great difficulty can they decline to 'cooperate' with IBD/ECM on new issues. What is your strategy for safeguarding the independence of your equity research analysts?

This is a sensitive area and it is always essential to tread a fine line between the analytical part of an analyst's job and his selling role in a new issue. Investment banking does pay approximately 50 per cent of the budget of the research department, therefore analysts do take the new issue business seriously and if he gets heavily involved in a new issue, he is likely to be under a certain amount of pressure to assist the sales effort. It is, however, important to recognise that neither the investment banking department nor equity capital markets have any influence over the earnings estimates of the companies covered by equity research. Analysts are very much concerned about their integrity: if they are seen to jeopardise their integrity in the process of working on a new issue, they will soon lose the support of fund managers and, therefore, their overall reputation. This would be a sure way to end a promising career as an equity research analyst.

Our investment research does not stand alone in the market. It is measured daily against a wide variety of research by competitors, boutique research firms and the press.

There are also very strict internal and external legal and procedural guidelines to safeguard the independence of our research analysts. In addition to these internal and external guidelines, all business is reviewed by 'Commitment Committees'. Their responsibility is to analyse and evaluate the appropriateness of each proposed transaction and determine Goldman Sachs' involvement and potential capital commitment.

Who are your competitors?

Depending on the transaction and the market, we compete against many different banks. We view competition from local, regional and international banks as a healthy development, because it exposes the client to the greatest selection of banks capable of providing the highest quality of service. Hopefully, when measured against them, we will continue to win a good portion of the attractive mandates.

There are an increasing number of international competitors. In addition to the five houses that have been the most active in the new issue market on a global basis over the past five years, there is an increasing number of houses knocking on the door to break into that category and becoming highly credible international houses. Furthermore, there are a number of local or regional banks that are making real progress in their home markets, be it in the retail or institutional markets and who have increasing international aspirations.

Most competitors are on the move: some are growing and some are consolidating. The competitive environment is very dynamic: in the US, for example, because Glass-Steagall is effectively dead, commercial banks previously prevented from entering the securities industry are now aggressive competitors, both in the US and globally. US investment banks do have some advantages, ie, selling equities of attractive US companies around the globe while also offer non-US issuers one of the largest markets for non-US securities.

The trend towards consolidation has continued in Europe, Asia and the US. More banks also are growing their equity business. In addition, there has been a trend towards buying resources, rather than growing them in-house. We too, continually consider our internal resources, balancing them with client needs and competitive forces in the marketplace. It is a constant challenge.

It is probably fair to say that you are sometimes forced to undercut on fees and over-represent the likely demand, as telling the 'truth' might lead to somebody else getting the mandate. What are the consequences of this trend and how can it be reversed?

Spread compression is continuing today in Latin America, Western Europe, Eastern Europe, Asia and to a lesser extent in the US. The consequences of this trend are serious, as fees that are too low could affect quality of service by some banks. There also seems to be a discrepancy between the sizes of offers, ie, the bigger the deals, the smaller the spread. Underwriters may end up doing a poor job because of bad economics. In addition, fees that are too low could drive away banks from the syndicate who could help ensure the success of an offer. Fees should be fair so that participating banks are incentivised to do a great job.

We believe fee cutting and the over-representation typically associated with competitive beauty contests are short-term strategies to win business and that over time one's reputation and ability to compete successfully is predicated on consistency in structuring and executing offers successfully. We believe that government, corporations and investor clients are driven principally by performance and reputation. Given that performance is completely transparent, we believe that these pressures will dissipate over time.

An ECM department is situated between two sets of clients – the vendors/issuers via IBD and the investment institutions via the salesforce. What are the particular challenges of this position?

The strength of ECM professionals lies in their ability to make fundamental judgements relating to the structuring and execution of an offer. What separates the best practitioners from the rest is the overall level of experience and its relevant application to new situations, together with the ability to find the on-going delicate balance between the objectives of the issuer and the investor. Additionally, the ability to call upon a wide range of expertise in the firm without regard to department or location gives our professionals a distinct advantage. It may be unusual for some competitors, but it is not unusual for Goldman Sachs ECM professionals to visit two institu-

tions a week and hear how Goldman Sachs is meeting their requirements. This is not hand-holding, it is gaining invaluable market input.

Conclusion

No one will seriously dispute that Goldman Sachs has been the market leader and that it has been the house to emulate and to beat. It has a reputation for winning the mandates that it really wants to win, with the much sought after Singapore Telecom and Deutsche Telekom mandates being the two most notable examples. This is due to an enormous capacity to concentrate and focus on what is important.

Having been the market leader in the US, the bank systematically set about building a European equity franchise, long before the other American houses (although Morgan Stanley had been in Europe at an earlier stage), and over the last few years has focused particular attention on Asia.

The bank, however, appears to be relatively weak in Latin America, despite getting off to a very good start with the Telmex transactions in 1991 and 1992. Goldman Sachs does appear to have a distinctly different strategy to its peers in that it grows only organically, except for on the asset management side. It is also the only house among the top five without a pronounced retail strategy arguing that the retail markets are institutionalising. However, the absence of an ambitious retail strategy is also related to the fact that, as a partnership, the firm is much more careful about how it spends capital on large acquisitions. A major push into the retail markets is perhaps most likely to happen once the firm decides to put into practice what it advises others to do for a living – go public.

Another challenge for the bank is to maintain its high level of professionalism whilst increasingly having to work more with others. The notion of Goldman Sachs as a flexible team player working hard for the benefit of its clients when it is not in complete charge of a transaction is, perhaps, a touch too optimistic. Certainly, it appears to have some further building to do before reaching as strong a position in the secondary market as in the primary market, and the competition is breathing down its neck.

Goldman Sachs may also have to work hard to dispel the widely held belief that its bankers are arrogant and difficult to work with. On the other hand, given its domination of the market, maybe the bank will feel that a little arrogance is merited.

Merrill Lynch

(represented by Michael Ryan, managing director and global co-head of ECM)

What are your goals in the global equity business and why?

We want to build an integrated global equity business and have a global presence in terms not only of new issues, but also of sales, trading and research. We want to have a dominant presence in all the major institutional and retail markets around the world and be in a position to participate in both domestic and cross-border equity business in the major markets. In terms of trading presence, we want to be among the top three houses in all the significant equity markets and to be number one in the major equity markets.

In the equity business, reputation is everything. The successful firm needs an objective research product, the ability to execute trades flawlessly in all market conditions and a high quality research product. We try to safeguard our image and our reputation by upholding the five Merrill Lynch principles, which have remained the same since we started the business, and which were recently codified by our retired Chairman, Dan Tully: client focus, respect for the individual, teamwork, responsible citizenship and integrity. These principles are all-important and they are taken seriously within the organisation and among our clients. I cannot stress the last one – 'integrity' – enough.

What are your strategies to attain these goals?

As competition is increasing in the institutional markets, and as primary and secondary market spreads are eroding, we believe that we need a stronger presence in the local markets around the world. We believe that to ultimately make it in this business, we need to achieve stability in earnings which will support our high debt ratings. In order to achieve that, it is essential to be present in the major geographic markets and to be able to offer domestic and cross-border products to our institutional and private client groups. We are focusing on the penetration of the domestic institutional and retail markets around the world. In the case of Spain, we bought FG Inversiones, the leading Spanish independent securities firm, in 1996, which gives us a major presence in the domestic Spanish institutional markets and a growing private client business. The FG acquisition enabled us to obtain a co-lead role in the Spanish institutional tranche in the 1997 Repsol offer, a 'first' for a non-Spanish bank. This gives Merrill Lynch the opportunity to participate in more tranches of Spanish privatisations and the ability to directly penetrate the Spanish institutional marketplace for domestic offers.

In order to implement this strategy on a world-wide basis, we have recently reorganised our business into four major business groups:

- Asset management;
- Corporate and institutional clients group (including M&A, investment banking, equity and fixed income sales and trading);
- Domestic private clients; and
- International private clients.

Of these four groups, 'International Private Clients' is going to be the subject of the next thrust of our development as we want to develop our local retail presence around the world. Only by being present in the retail markets can we continue to gather assets from individual investors and comprehensively capture the flows of money between fixed-income securities and equities both cross-border and domestically. We will look at the opportunities on a top-down basis and start with the bigger markets. We will also, in each given situation, consider the buy versus build decision. At the end of 1996, approximately 94 per cent of our 13,001 private client officers were working in the US. The only non-US markets where we have a truly domestic private client business are Australia and New Zealand, as a result of the acquisition of McIntosh in 1996. In most other countries, where we have offices, private client financial consultants service the client for offshore investments. Historically, for example, we did not sell 'Spain' to the Spanish. This situation is going to change significantly, either by way of organic growth or as a result of acquisitions, while bearing in mind that we will not, at least in the foreseeable future, expect to be competing with the large commercial banks and their branch networks.

With respect to the equity capital markets department, we emphasise both privatisations and corporate business, recognising that they are both important, but that privatisation is a finite business opportunity. We don't have people who are dedicated to privatisations.

How global are you today? Please describe in as much detail as possible, your sales, trading and research infrastructure?

We firmly believe that our sales, trading and research infrastructure is second to none. We are present in 45 countries around the world, and have 1,591 institutional equity research, sales and trading professionals and 13,001 private client officers covering roughly 4,500 institutional equity investors and 4.4 million individual investors. (See Exhibit 4.23.)

Over the last five years, Merrill Lynch has successfully diversified its sources of revenues and has more closely aligned its human resources with local business opportunities. As a result, revenues from US equities now represent 56 per cent of total equity revenues versus 82 per cent in 1992; and 51 per cent of all equity professionals are now located outside the US versus 82 per cent in 1992.

How do you distinguish yourself generally from the other four houses profiled in this book?

I think we have a bigger commitment to both the institutional and private client markets around the world and I believe that our sales, trading and research infrastructure is the strongest when judged on a global basis.

Furthermore, unlike some of our major competitors, we do not subscribe to the view that the retail business is completely institutionalising. In fact, if you look at the figures,

Exhibit 4.23
Merrill Lynch – Total number of equity professionals

	Research coverage (number of stocks)	Institutional equity professionals*	Private client FCs
North America	1,187	802	12,220
Europe/Africa/ME	990	498	478
Asia-Pacific	416	156	182
Japan	341	98	9
Latin America	107	37	112
Total	**3,041**	**1,591**	**13,001**

Source: Merrill Lynch.

you will see that, for example in the US, the amount of direct retail investment in the equity market is three times bigger than that of mutual funds, at US$4.8 trillion versus approximately US$1.5 trillion. Institutions own approximately US$3 trillion with private pensions making up around half that amount. Only Merrill Lynch is truly organised to service each of those investment constituencies. We were naturally interested to see that Morgan Stanley appeared to have taken the same view when they decided to merge with Dean Witter. We believe that Morgan Stanley's move puts not only the US institutional firms in a new strategic situation, but it also significantly raises the hurdle for many non-US firms which have hitherto believed that they 'only' needed access to US institutional clients in order to make it in the global equity business. Markets outside of the US are changing dramatically as investment trends move towards equity and private pension management. We are moving to position ourselves with those flows. As a result of the Smith New Court acquisition, we can access primary capital for UK companies just like a UK bank and act as a sponsor, broker or both, or execute a cross-border 'bookbuild'. Other than SBC Warburg, our competitors featured in this book can only hope to be able to execute these types of transactions.

Only Merrill Lynch has a leading market share in equities in two major markets – the US and the UK. You could view Merrill Lynch and Morgan Stanley Dean Witter Discovery as the only full line firms with both a retail and institutional presence in their home market and the others as institutional firms. Needless to say, SBC Warburg and CSFB would claim to have access to Swiss local private clients and international private client money managed in Switzerland, but the scale and activity level of those assets do not weigh on the equity capital markets business like private clients in the US.

We believe this knowledge of different distribution channels – private clients/institutional and domestic/cross-border – gives us an advantage. We are structurally and conceptually better organised to be a more effective intermediary between buyers and sellers of shares. This knowledge formalises a direct link between ECM, equity sales and trading, and research.

We don't try to maximise the profits of ECM at the expense of the trading or research business. Let me be specific here. We have a distinct philosophy with respect to trading in the secondary markets. We believe that the net present value of the potential trading profits over a three-year period from a particular stock that we have introduced to the market by far exceeds the initial fees earned at the time of the actual offer. We have dedicated trading staff throughout the world, who are charged with the task of making sure that the market shares in these stocks are maintained. Our senior traders have a particular responsibility in that regard. If, for example, we were to be the fourth-ranked trader in a stock where we did the IPO, something has typically gone substantially wrong. Furthermore, it goes without saying that to win repeat business from that client is going to be a lot more difficult. I do believe that we have a good blend of short and long-term goals that serve both our clients and ourselves.

Our investment in research is unparalleled, with 586 ana-lysts in 22 countries covering over 3,000 stocks. In addition, research is a separate structural entity within the firm and does not report to either Investment Banking or the Sales & Trading Department. This is critical to enable the individuals to maintain an independent view of the companies they cover and the valuation of those stocks.

All of these factors – large client bases (both institutional and private client); big sales network; large market shares and deep research talent – combine to allow us the greatest insight into investors' interests. This represents Merrill Lynch's distinct edge over our closest competitors.

Unfortunately, we haven't communicated the difference to the issuing clients. While we have been busy and successful in integrating many acquisitions, the knowledge of our changed capabilities hasn't gotten around. Our competitors have been quite successful in maintaining our US 'retail' image. Whilst the acquisition of trading and sales skills around the world has been relatively easy, the very difficult part is the building of corporate relationships to leverage those skill sets. We have been behind in building our banking presence to match the sales and trading side of the firm and as a result have come late to both the privatisation and international corporate business. This has held our development as the premier global firm in check – but that is not going to last for long.

What is your philosophy on ad-hoc partnerships/cooperation in deals?

Life is never fair, and although it is sometimes difficult to achieve the necessary level of coordination when two or more of the top houses work together on an equal basis, we are stuck with the trend of joint global coordinators and bookrunners. We have, therefore, to be able to trust each other and work better together. When we are put in a situation of working together with, or for, the other top houses, we prefer to work with those houses that have the highest overall capabilities, which on a global basis, we consider to be Goldman Sachs and Morgan Stanley. We want to achieve a synergy where we can operate as one extended team, in order to leverage off each other. This was achieved in the 1996 offer for Pharmacia & Upjohn, where we worked very well together with Goldman Sachs. This recent example stands in sharp contrast to the situation back in 1991, when, in the case of Telecom Corporation New Zealand, we perhaps didn't trust each other to the same degree. It is a question of trusting both the individuals concerned and the other firms' capabilities.

When we are in a senior role, ie, when we are in overall charge of a transaction, we don't necessarily want Goldman Sachs or Morgan Stanley to work for us, but rather houses that have 'more to prove' as they can be expected to work harder, keeping in mind that in more difficult market conditions, we want to work with banks that have a genuine distribution capability. The challenge lies in properly motivating the banks that you have working for you, such that they help you to distribute the transaction in the best interest of the client. This means that we have to give our partners opportunities to do 'one-on-one' meetings, that we ensure that our partners' marketing expenses (at least at a co-lead manager level) are compensated and that that they are treated fairly in the allocation process. It follows a simple principle that if you work hard you get paid.

In the 1995 Telefónica de España offer, where the market conditions were difficult, those regional lead managers who did a great job got paid accordingly. It is interesting to note that in my fifteen years at Merrill Lynch, no one has ever asked how much money we made in any particular transaction. They are more interested to find out how the deal was executed and how the sellers/buyers felt – not how much we made. We believe this is a long-term business where you invest in every deal to accomplish long-term goals for the issuer, by the distribution of shares to a broad mix of investors and by the encouragement of additional research. This investment, in distributing shares through higher cost channels, pays off over time. We get a high number of referrals from both issuers and other banks.

How do you perceive the development of the economics of the ECM business?

The successful management of a global equity business requires a balance between both the primary and secondary business. It is a costly operation to build a global secondary market capability to support the primary business and you need the commitment of both substantial capital and resources to make it. Merrill Lynch has a corporate objective of a ROE of a minimum of 15 per cent and the equity division runs well in excess of that number.

However, costs continue to increase at a rapid pace, making it critically important that the high margin business of new issues contribute to the overall P/L in a meaningful way. It is against this background that the compression in spreads that we have seen accelerating in the last few years is becoming so concerning. In fact, we find it difficult to believe that, if the pace is maintained, many of the firms that now aspire to compete in the global equity business will have the resources or stamina to succeed.

In 1993, Merrill Lynch and CSFB underwrote the US$3 billion privatisation of the Argentine oil company YPF at a gross spread of four per cent. In the spring of 1997 CSFB won the privatisation of Petrobras at 1.15 per cent which will be approximately 10–15 per cent the size of YPF. It is astounding.

Spreads in Asia continue to fall in line with those in European countries. In addition, we are seeing sub-three per cent spreads throughout the emerging markets in Europe, the Middle East, and Africa. And finally, the impact of international fee erosion will have an impact in the US. It will require great discipline for the banks to maintain fees to pay for their investment in this business. Market conditions over the last two and a half years have not put a premium on distribution capabilities. In recent years, it has been too easy to distribute shares but market conditions will get difficult again and issuers will have to pay more normal fees if they desire high quality execution.

The potential consequences of this development are in my opinion several: issuers should begin to realise that the investment banks are going to be more reluctant to make their capital available to underwrite at high prices. Support in the after-market will not be what it ought to be, as stabilisation is expensive. If you have to buy back shares at issue price (to the extent of the full greenshoe of 15 per cent) that other banks in the syndicate have sold at issue price less selling concession, you effectively lose 7.8 per cent of the total economics of a transaction. As this expense is charged against underwriting fees, and hence shared by the entire syndicate, you can see that people are going to become less committed to underwriting at high prices and to the stabilisation of transactions. Consequently, you are going to get 'agency execution'. In addition, market conditions will deteriorate: we are in a cyclical business and new issue volumes will decline, spreads will remain razor thin because of competition and those banks that are now beginning to make heavy investments to build up the sales, trading and research infrastructure are going to have a very tough time. As margins decline, some of the new entrants and perhaps even some of the more established firms, are going to compromise on standards such as due diligence, quality of equity research etc. At that point there will be some major disasters, which will lead to the trend of fee erosion being reversed and companies again being prepared to pay for high quality execution.

Institutional investors frequently perceive the equity research analysts of major new issue houses to be as much sophisticated salesmen as independent research analysts and feel that only with great difficulty can they decline to 'cooperate' with IBD/ECM on new issues. What is your strategy for safeguarding the independence of your equity research analysts?

We look at this issue in three ways. Firstly, research is an independent structure within our organisation which reports to the EVP, Corporate Strategy and Research, who in fact reports directly to our President. This ensures the ultimate independence of the group and a forum to resolve the potential conflict you mention very efficiently. Secondly, the cost of running the research department is shared equally by investment banking, the equity and private clients divisions. Research analysts provide a service to internal clients on both the buy-side and the sell-side and, in our structure, neither side can overly influence the outcome of any specific situation. In addition, the analysts' compensation is not overly geared towards new issues. Merrill Lynch has a rigorous annual cross evaluation system where the individual analyst performance is reviewed by research management, sales, trading, ECM and the investment banking department. These cross evaluations have a direct impact on compensation, and new issues can therefore only have a small impact. In fact, ECM rates highly analysts who are tough and keeps us out of the 'bad deal'. Fundamentals always win in the after-market.

Finally, we have a rigorous internal process to ensure both the saleability and suitability of the business we take on. The 'Equity Strategy Board', a group of professionals from different disciplines of the bank approve the saleability of a particular potential offer by looking at the valuation and the valuation methodology. In addition, any transaction must be approved by the so called 'Commitment Committee' which is in essence a suitability test. Has the due diligence been done properly and is this a company that we want to have as a client? Is the risk reasonable? The sponsoring investment banker has to present to this committee, which consists of experienced professionals in the areas of credit, legal and compliance, equity research, equity capital markets and at least three peers to the sponsoring managing director. In order to go forward with the transaction, there has to be a unanimous vote in this committee. The philosophy is that there are at least two names that go on the prospectus, that of the issuer, and Merrill Lynch. We live with these deals for ever, particularly if something goes wrong, and it weighs on our reputation for a very long time. The goal is to do good quality business.

Who are your competitors?

In addition to the other houses featured in this book, we certainly believe that UBS, Deutsche Morgan Grenfell and Dresdner Kleinwort Benson stand a very good chance of making a run at the top. They have domestic market new issue distribution capacity, significant market shares in domestic secondary market trading, strong capital bases and the international presence to put all the pieces together. HSBC also has a presence around the world. From the US, JP Morgan has made great strides in the international non-cash equity business and is utilising their historic relationships to build a credible US and international new issue business. It is difficult to really make the call at this moment because of the rapid pace of consolidation currently under way in the market. An unlikely competitor may in fact become a real contender within a short space of time as a result of a well thought-out acquisition programme.

Conclusion

From a position of a relatively modest amount of international equity business in the early 1990s, Merrill Lynch has developed into a formidable global powerhouse, with its sales, trading and research businesses leading the way.

Merrill now has approximately 50 per cent of its equity staff working outside the US. It was the strength of its global placement power that enabled the bank to outclass its competitors during the difficult third quarter of 1996, both in the US and in Latin America. This was widely seen as a contributing factor for the awards by IFR at the end of 1996 for 'US Equity House of the Year' (for the second year running) and 'Latin American Equity House of the Year'.

It is primarily during times of difficult market conditions that distribution strength is most badly needed. Merrill Lynch is the bank with the strongest retail franchise in the US and it also has a clear strategy to conquer the most important retail markets around the world. Merrill is clearly prepared to invest in its equity franchise, as evidenced by several important acquisitions of banks/brokers in recent years (Smith New Court in the UK, FG Inversiones in Spain, McIntosh in Australia and Davis Borkum Hare in South Africa) and by its determined organic growth. Contrary to the case at many of its competitors, Merrill Lynch has stuck to its growth strategy in prioritised markets and has not wavered at times of market disruption. The bank's commitment to Latin America during the Mexican crisis of 1995 is the best example, and has paid handsome dividends as soon as market conditions recovered.

Merrill Lynch is well on its way to establishing itself both as a retail and as an institutional house in several major markets around the world. Competitors can no longer get away with reducing it to the 'retail champion'.

Although Merrill Lynch is a firm with a sound culture and a tremendous track record, one sometimes gets the feeling that its enormous size can be a handicap. However, when the bank fires on all its cylinders, it is difficult to outsell. In future, Merrill Lynch should be able to capitalise on its tremendous distribution strength to take a greater proportion of landmark transactions. In late May, the Spanish government granted Merrill Lynch a global coordinator role in the forthcoming US$6.5 billion Endesa privatisation, one of the most important European mandates of 1997. The bank's clear and consistent strategy will no doubt continue to produce impressive results.

Morgan Stanley

(represented by Jerker Johansson, Managing Director and Head of European ECM)

What are your goals in the global equity business and why?

It is our goal to be the pre-eminent global equity house for our clients. In doing this we seek to find a balance between being the leading house in terms of the number of companies and dollar volume of new issues sponsored, and the quality of new issues we bring to the market. We consider equity new issuance to be an integral part of our investor and investment banking franchise, as the public equity markets grow more accessible year by year to an increasingly large group of issuers from more and more countries. Our primary intention is to compete on the basis of innovation and quality in serving these clients on a global basis in an environment of a dramatically increasing equity culture around the world.

The equity business is expected to continue to be a very important part of Morgan Stanley's overall business. For fiscal 1996 the equity underwriting revenues of US$623 million represented 32 per cent of total global investment banking revenues. The primary equity business is supported by our secondary market equity sales and trading activities, which accounted for US$1,348 million in revenues over the same period (of which US$978 million came from the trading side), equivalent to 47 per cent of our total global sales and trading revenues. In total therefore, our primary and secondary market equity business accounted for approximately 34 per cent of total group-wide net revenues during fiscal 1996.

What are your strategies to attain these goals?

In the last five years, the equity new issue markets have undergone a period of immense change and growth, which has resulted in a set of new challenges and opportunities for the leading securities firms. Historically, our strategy has been to attain these goals through the integrated growth of all relevant parts of our investment banking business. In the future, Morgan Stanley's strategy, as articulated by our senior management, is to grow all the relevant parts of our business –

investment banking advice, research, distribution and capital markets services – both organically and by acquisition.

Accordingly, on 5 February 1997 Morgan Stanley and Dean Witter Discover & Co ('DWD') announced a definitive agreement to merge, forming a new company to be named Morgan Stanley, Dean Witter, Discover & Co with combined revenues and profits of more than double those of Morgan Stanley. In asset management, the combination results in a business that manages more than US$270 billion of assets on a pro forma basis. The new company would have a market capitalisation of approximately US$21 billion.

DWD is one of the top three retail brokerage networks in the US with over 9,000 account executives and 361 branches across the country and manages more than US$100 billion in customer assets. The addition of the Dean Witter retail network will greatly enhance our new issue distribution strength by giving us direct access to the rapidly growing US retail demand for equity new issues. This move is in line with our strategy, as articulated by our senior management, to expand our penetration on the retail side, not only in the high net worth individual market but also in the more traditional retail investor market, initially and primarily in the US, where over half of US retirement assets now reside.

How global are you today?

We have a global infrastructure that supports our services in 65 countries. This gives us coverage which is difficult to match and enables us to take advantage of the rapidly growing capital needs of issuers from developing markets. We are lead managing deals for issuers from a broader range of nationalities than ever before including a number of 'firsts', such as the first international deal by an Indian company (Reliance Industries) and the first truly global offer for a Russian company (Gazprom). We continue to make inroads into other areas of Emerging Europe. In the last five years, we have been involved in deals for issuers from 54 different countries.

This is further illustrated by our international profitability mix. In 1995 over 50 per cent of our investment banking revenues came from outside the US. This number fell substantially in percentage terms in 1996 due to the strength and dominance of the US market in all product areas, though in absolute terms the international business continued to grow. As at the end of FY 1996, 20 per cent of our employees worked in Europe and 13 per cent in Asia.

On the other hand, however, there is no point in pioneering new markets and concepts if you do not have the distribution infrastructure to execute them. We have consistently grown our sales and trading effort, which currently stands at around 290 people on the institutional sales side alone (excluding DWD), distributing product from 50 different countries. Our principal centres for distribution are the US, London, Hong Kong and Tokyo, though we have local distribution in many markets and the number of countries is growing year by year. In addition, we are not just in the international markets but hold local stock exchange licenses giving us the ability to trade as principal in a total of 19 different countries and again, the number is growing

Exhibit 4.24

Morgan Stanley – Research coverage (number of stocks excluding DWD)

North America	1,000
Europe/Africa/Middle East	400
Asia-Pacific (including Australia)	200
Japan	180
Latin America	55
Total	**1,835**

Source: Morgan Stanley.

all the time. We set great store by the strength and quality of our multi-award winning research product and have over 165 analysts in our in-house research department worldwide, excluding any research joint ventures we have in certain local markets.

We cover more than 1800 stocks world-wide, broken down by region (see Exhibit 4.24).

How do you distinguish yourself from the other four houses profiled in this book?

We believe we have the best overall distribution network for international equities, evidenced by the many awards we have won in recent years for our sales, trading and research capabilities. We believe that our new issue franchise is differentiated both in terms of the quality of new issuers we have brought to the market, the innovative structures, such as the Percs security – a convertible bond that mandatorily converts into equity after a certain period – that we have pioneered over the last five years, and in the significance of our large, landmark transactions. We have lead managed the largest ever corporate IPO (Lucent Technologies) and the second largest ever corporate IPO (Scania). In addition, we think we are distinguished by the breadth of business with which we have been involved. In 1996 we lead managed 21 European transactions, more than any other firm.

As a result of the merger with DWD we, together with Merrill Lynch, are the only house among the top global investment banks with a sizeable US retail distribution network. With 9,100 account executives, DWD has the third largest retail distribution network after Merrill Lynch and Smith Barney.

What is your philosophy on ad-hoc partnerships/cooperation in equity transactions?

Cooperation in deals is becoming an increasingly common phenomenon and we actively seek to cooperate with other firms when working jointly with them. We believe that we work well with a broad range of firms, including some which might be identified as being our closest competitors. We seek to be fair and equitable as a bookrunner and to strike a balance in syndication between creating competition, and a reward system for strong marketing efforts. We seek to involve firms on the basis of their local and specialised distribution strengths. We are supportive of the bookrunner's efforts when acting as joint-lead or co-lead manager.

What is your strategy for safeguarding the independence of your equity research analysts?

We attach the highest importance to the independence of our equity research analysts, as the long-term credibility of an analyst, with both investors and issuers, is contingent upon the quality and independence of their judgement. Our equity research department is managed as a fully independent entity and the reporting lines are entirely independent of either the investment banking or the equity divisions. All requests for the use of analysts' time is channelled through senior management of the research department. The first priority of the research analyst is to be the market's primary source of information for the companies that they cover.

Who are your competitors?

In addition to the banks featured in this book, we believe there are an increasing number of domestic houses with international capabilities. We believe strongly in the mutual benefits which accrue from cooperation with such houses. Nonetheless, our philosophy is founded not solely on our pre-eminent global presence, but on an ability, when required, to provide a local investment banking service for our international clients. Our strong local presence in all the major European markets and the ongoing opening of offices around the world bear testament to this objective.

How do you perceive the development of the economics of the ECM business?

We have not observed any trends towards definitively lower fees in the corporate sector, however, the privatisation sector is different. Overall, we have observed greater differentiation between the fees charged for different services. As might be expected, higher fees are charged for more resource-intensive and higher value-added services. For example, the average fee charged in a privatisation secondary offer is significantly lower than the average fee charged in a corporate IPO. It is perhaps worthy of note that this diversity in fees has long been commonplace in the US.

An ECM department situated between two sets of clients. What are the particular challenges of this position?

While we would agree that ultimately Equity Capital Markets does interact with two sets of clients, we believe that the appropriate approach, and one which will reap its own rewards in the long run is the consistent and fair treatment of both parties. We see ourselves as a facilitator, as an arbiter of the conflicting needs of issuers and investors. To regularly favour one set of clients obviously risks alienation of the other and any short-term benefit which it may provide, will be negated by the longer term damage to our reputation which this would engender. To strike an appropriate balance, like so much in this business, is a question of judgement, and good judgement is more likely to come with experience. The accumulation of such experience is obviously a function of the quality and breadth of transactions with which individuals have been associated. Given Morgan Stanley's leading position in new issuance activity and our transaction experience,

we feel that we are in a very strong position when it comes to striking this balance.

Conclusion

Morgan Stanley is undoubtedly the most improved of the top five equity houses, particularly over the past two years. This has been evident both in terms of volumes of new issuance, the number of landmark transactions, and in polls of investors, companies and governments. Morgan Stanley is credited with a strong research, sales and trading operation on a global basis, perhaps only rivalled by that of Merrill Lynch.

Whereas several years ago, Morgan Stanley did not appear to get its fair share of large privatisations, this situation now appears to have changed, most notably in the case of the 1997 Telefónica privatisation in Spain. This progress has also been manifested in a number of high profile large corporate issues in 1995 and 1996, most notably the Lucent Technologies, Scania and Gucci 2 issues.

If Morgan Stanley was already challenging for the top position in 1996, the firm is now in an even better position following the merger with Dean Witter, announced in February 1997. The merger adds considerable retail placement power and overall muscle as, at US$12 billion of common equity capital, the combined capital strength is double that of the old Morgan Stanley.

Although still a few years behind Merrill Lynch in terms of defining and executing a retail strategy, the bank is in a position to challenge both Goldman Sachs as the pre-eminent institutional house and Merrill Lynch as the retail market leader. Morgan Stanley appears to be without any major regional or product weaknesses, though a critical issue for the new firm will be how well it manages to integrate the different corporate cultures of Morgan Stanley and Dean Witter Discover.

SBC Warburg

(represented by Rory Tapner, managing director and global head of ECM)

What are your goals in the global equity business and why?

The equity business remains an integral part of SBC Warburg's world-wide activities, representing (in 1996) 35 per cent of total operating revenues. The firm's objective is to continue to lead many of the significant transactions in the major markets in the world where it has a significant presence and, in so doing, to maintain a consistent position at the top of the global league tables. SBC Warburg also intends to rank consistently in the first tier of geographic and sector league tables; it is the leading research house for European equities, having been voted number one by Institutional Investor for six years in a row (1991–97); it is also the number one ranked firm in many of the sector league tables in terms of country research and individual industry sectors. The firm's reputation for innovation, best advice and total commitment to client needs will continue to underpin our global equity activities and enable us to further enhance our profitability.

SBC Warburg, as a fully integrated organisation, will continue to ensure that its traditional strengths in corporate client coverage, equity research and the distribution of cash equities are optimally combined with Swiss Bank Corporation's pre-eminent position in derivatives, risk management and trading. This will be achieved by emphasising the importance of the linkage of the firm's global sales, research and trading capabilities with an understanding of client funding and risk management requirements in the primary and secondary markets.

What are your strategies to attain these goals?
Some of SBC Warburg's key strategies include:

- Systematically leveraging our leading position in Europe into comparable positions in America and Asia through the merger with Dillon Read and the acquisition of the remaining stake in SBC Warburg Australia;
- To build on the group's two 'world class' strengths – SBC Warburg's fundamental equity research and distribution skills and O'Connor's risk management capability; and
- To build critical mass in core industry sectors, both with respect to equity research and corporate coverage.

The philosophy of SBC Warburg's equity business will continue to be:

- Client-facing;
- Research-driven;
- Committed to excellence in customer execution; and
- Pursuing synergy between the firm's corporate and institutional relationships

How global are you today?
SBC Warburg has a significant world-wide infrastructure:

ECM
- A global equity capital markets group located in London, Zurich, Hong Kong, Melbourne, New York and Tokyo, with a total of 60 ECM professionals in these centres. This will be further enhanced by the addition of the Dillon Read capital markets team.

Research
- Global equity research coverage of over 4,000 companies by 320 research analysts;
- The research department is internationally organised, and most analysts are members of cross-border international sector teams in addition to being local/regional analysts. The firm has the edge over its competitors in cross-border valuation techniques within industries such as banks, mining, telecoms and utilities; and
- The emerging markets research team is comparable to the firm's developed market product. Around 25 per cent of SBC Warburg's analysts are based around the Pacific Rim, where its Asian credit research, application of valuation techniques used by the developed markets team, and newly-formulated methods of valuation especially developed for emerging markets, is felt to be second to none.

Exhibit 4.25
SBC Warburg – Total number of equity professionals

	Institutional equity professionals*
North America	170
Europe/Africa/ ME	780
Asia Pacific (excluding Japan)	320
Japan	90
Latin America	25
Total	**1385**

* Including sales, trading, research and ECM professionals (or otherwise exclusively dedicated to the equity business, however not counting back-office personnel). The above numbers excludes approximately 440 non-permanent staff and support staff, 150 Australian retail sales staff, approximately 400 people employed in Asian joint ventures and the Dillon Read people dedicated to the equity product.

Source: SBC Warburg.

Sales/trading
- Nearly 500 institutional equity sales people world-wide;
- A leading foreign equity market share in the US market, employing 75 sales and trading professionals in the US, all dedicated solely to international equities and equity-linked instruments;
- Global trading skills and risk management technology;
- A leading derivatives broker and trader with a global presence; and
- A member of more than 50 stock exchanges around the world on which cash equity and equity derivatives are being traded.

In summary, SBC Warburg's equity infrastructure is distributed across the world as shown in Exhibit 4.25.

How do you distinguish yourself from the other four houses profiled in this book?
SBC Warburg believes that it is one of only very few truly global investment banks and the only such bank with a European home base. Anchored most strongly in Switzerland and the United Kingdom, the firm has an exceptional local and cross-border investment banking presence in other European countries, as well as in South Africa, Canada, Australia, Asia and Latin America. SBC Warburg's distinguishing characteristics include:

- A truly innovative approach to derivatives using leading edge technology. In the primary markets business, this enables the firm to leverage off its presence in local markets to initiate more cross-border business;
- A higher-ranked, more broadly-based and ultimately more creative research franchise;
- A willingness to leverage capital strength and to use its balance sheet to provide support for client transactions. Since the beginning of 1996, SBC Warburg has been actively involved in over 25 block trades for a total volume of approximately US$4.5 billion in nine countries. In

November 1996 SBC Warburg (jointly with Paribas) bought the French Tresor's residual 4.6 per cent stake in Elf for just over US$1 billion. The block was bought at 11.30pm on 12 November, and entirely sold by 10.15am the next day. SBC Warburg generated nearly 65 per cent of the demand; and

- A leading specialist sales force in the US dedicated to the sales and trading of international equities in the US market.

What is your philosophy on ad-hoc partnerships/cooperation in deals?

Ad-hoc partnerships are becoming a regular feature in the primary markets. Almost 70 per cent of all issues greater than US$500m have, since 1993, had more than one global coordinator. If it is in the issuer's and investing community's interests, SBC Warburg is willing to participate in ad-hoc partnerships and to cooperate with other houses.

Please comment on the trend of falling fees in cross-border equity transactions?

Fees have been shrinking, particularly in the case of privatisations. At the same time, however, underwriting syndicates have been getting smaller, such that the fee pool for the top houses has not necessarily shrunk pro rata. This means that there are fewer fees available for distribution to co-leads and co-managers, which may lead to a shake-out, as only the most successful firms will be able to afford the required commitment to research.

At the same time, the bookrunning lead managers have to do more work in terms of selling directly to end investors. Successful lead managers are going to need a proper distribution network and it is going to need to be global in order to survive. This should also have a stabilising effect on fees, particularly in weaker market conditions.

There is, however, a further threat to the size of the fee pool, as it is estimated that approximately one third of the fees outside the US are derived from privatisations. As European governments are increasingly promoting the use of domestic firms to take on increasing responsibilities in the privatisation programmes, the size of the fee pool is likely to come under threat.

Institutional investors frequently perceive the equity research analysts of major new issue houses to be as much sophisticated salesmen as independent research analysts and feel that only with great difficulty can they decline to 'cooperate' with IBD/ECM on new issues. What is your strategy for safeguarding the independence of your equity research analysts?

SBC Warburg's research department is managed independently from those individuals responsible for the corporate business and it remains independent in its views and opinions. The firm gains comfort from the various independent research surveys which rank its research product very highly and which prove to a large degree that the analysts remain consistently independent.

Because of the way the business works, companies may be forced to undercut on fees and over-represent the likely demand at high prices, as telling the 'truth' might lead to somebody else getting the mandate. What are the consequences of this trend and how can it be reversed?

SBC Warburg does not have a reputation for undercutting firms on fees and it intends to keep that reputation intact. Our aim is to provide the best quality distribution and research and ultimately the fee 'debate' will be determined by the cost of providing quality execution and not by commodity pricing. What typically happens elsewhere, however, is that at least one bank undercuts the general fee level in each privatisation and governments have on several occasions been able to take advantage of that, either by choosing that bank, or by putting pressure on the others to accept those fees. What these governments must realise is that this can mean that banks will not necessarily make their A-team available when it may be needed for a large corporate deal – such as Scania where the fees were 4.5 per cent – where the syndicates are typically much smaller than in privatisations.

An ECM department effectively situated between two sets of clients. What are the particular challenges of this position? How do you manage to strike the balance?

The key is to understand the market and what it can deliver to issuing clients who have a funding requirement which needs servicing.

Conclusion

SBC Warburg belongs firmly at the top of a small group of global equity houses. Based on the foundation of a very strong European business, a local presence in several important equity markets around the world, a first class equity research product, a strong parent with highly regarded top management in SBC and a strong derivatives capability, SBC Warburg can be expected to go from strength to strength in the global equity market.

Prior to the announcement in May 1997 of the acquisition by SBC Warburg of Dillon Read to form SBC Warburg Dillon Read, the question was whether the bank could compete on a world-wide basis without having a strong US presence. Despite its strong secondary market position in terms of selling European and Asian shares to US investors, SBC Warburg did not win many new issue mandates to sell European shares in the US, not due to a lack of ability but because of aggressive marketing by its American competitors. The question now is how much leverage SBC Warburg will be able to draw from the Dillon Read acquisition. Whereas Dillon Read is primarily known as an M&A house and not as an equity house, the firm has excellent US blue chip corporate relationships, which will clearly result in important equity mandates over time.

It will take time for SBC Warburg Dillon Read to build up a sufficiently strong US equity research product to take substantial market share in the US equity new issue market. The strategy of buying Dillon Read, from the equity point of view, was somewhere in between building and acquiring an equity business.

If any bank is able to complete a successful merger, it should be SBC, as it has proven in the past that it is prepared to be bold and acquire the necessary elements to build a strong global business in a given product area (as it did with the acquisition of the derivatives specialist O'Connor Partners in 1992, and that of Brinson Associates, the Chicago based fund management company in 1994). The competition will be tough, as the top US houses are themselves growing aggressively and a number of the European banks are also trying to strengthen their US business.

A further challenge for SBC Warburg is the fact that its investment banking division is considerably smaller than the big US houses. Whereas the new Morgan Stanley Dean Witter will have equity capital of almost US$12 billion, SBC Warburg was allocated around US$3,704 million by its parent during 1996. Is this enough to compete with the biggest houses on a world-wide basis?

The performance in the global equity new issue market of the top five houses

Goldman Sachs has ranked first in terms of volume of international issuance, every year since 1991 except 1992. (See Exhibit 4.26.)

If the domestic portions of cross-border issues are taken into account, Goldman Sachs was the market leader during each of the last four years, while Merrill Lynch's volumes actually decreased over this period, as did those of CSFB and SBC Warburg. Morgan Stanley achieved the biggest increase in new issuance over the same period. (See Exhibit 4.27.)

Over the last four years, Goldman Sachs was ranked first for North American issuers, SBC Warburg first for European issuers and Merrill Lynch led the way in Asia-Pacific/Japan and Latin America. CSFB's strongest relative position was in Latin America where it was second (see Exhibit 4.28).

In terms of the proportion of the total business represented by IPOs, Morgan Stanley led the way and CSFB came in

---

Exhibit 4.26
Consistency over time, 1991–96: international issuance* (US$ millions)

	1991	1992	1993	1994	1995	1996	Total
Goldman Sachs	6,713	3,721	5,452	7,072	7,813	11,749	42,520
Merrill Lynch	2,312	3,282	5,030	5,682	4,597	5,199	26,102
Morgan Stanley	995	3,749	3,163	4,316	5,024	8,644	25,891
SBC Warburg	763	1,341	3,893	3,879	5,321	5,719	20,916
CSFB	2,334	1,836	3,246	3,000	2,707	4,081	17,204

* US$ volumes of straight equity only; all credit to the bookrunner; non-domestic portion of cross-border offers.

Source: Capital Data Ltd.

Exhibit 4.27
Consistency over time, 1993–96: domestic and international issuance* (US$ millions)

	1993	1994	1995	1996	Total
Goldman Sachs	14,685	11,282	16,809	21,391	64,167
Merrill Lynch	14,346	10,938	11,088	11,874	48,246
Morgan Stanley	6,469	8,280	9,805	19,027	43,581
CSFB	7,411	4,978	5,124	6,348	23,861
SBC Warburg	12,685	3,785	5,826	6,993	29,289

* US$ volumes of straight equity only; all credit to the bookrunner; domestic and non-domestic portion of cross-border offers.

Source: Capital Data Ltd.

Exhibit 4.28
Geographic coverage, 1993–96: domestic and international issuance* (US$ millions)

	US/Canada	Europe/Africa/Middle East	Asia-Pacific/Japan	Latin America	Total
Goldman Sachs	42,213	16,455	3,901	1,601	64,170
Merrill Lynch	31,983	6,746	6,458	3,056	48,243
Morgan Stanley	27,654	12,218	2,581	1,128	43,581
CSFB	13,654	6,800	1,312	2,095	23,861
SBC Warburg	494	25,832	2,348	615	29,289

* US$ volumes of straight equity only; all credit to the bookrunner; non-domestic portion of cross-border offers.

Source: Capital Data Ltd.

Exhibit 4.29

Proportion of total business represented by IPOs and non-IPOs, 1993–1996*

	IPOs %	Non-IPOs %	Total US$ billions
Morgan Stanley	50	50	44
Goldman Sachs	48	52	64
SBC Warburg	46	54	29
Merrill Lynch	44	56	48
CSFB	29	71	24
Average for the top five banks	43	57	209

* US$ volumes of straight equity only; all credit to the bookrunner; domestic and non-domestic portion of cross-border offers.

Source: Capital Data Ltd.

Exhibit 4.30

How do the top five houses compare in the two major IPO markets during, 1993–96?* (US$ millions)

	North American IPOs	European IPOs
Goldman Sachs	21,220	7,911
Morgan Stanley	13,788	6,564
Merrill Lynch	12,576	2,659
CSFB	2,630	2,714
SBC Warburg	494	10,863

* US$ volumes of straight equity only; all credit to the bookrunner; domestic and non-domestic portion of cross-border offers.

Source: Capital Data Ltd.

Exhibit 4.31

Proportion of total business represented by privatisations and non-privatisations, 1993–96* (US$ millions)

	Privatisations	Corporate transactions
SBC Warburg	20,308	8,981
Goldman Sachs	7,697	56,474
Merrill Lynch	7,765	40,479
CSFB	5,652	18,209
Morgan Stanley	3,436	40,145

* US$ volumes of straight equity only; all credit to the bookrunner; domestic and non-domestic portion of cross-border offers.

Source: Capital Data Ltd.

Exhibit 4.32

Number of global coordinator mandates in US$1 billion transactions, 1991–96

	Corporate transactions	Privatisations	Total
Goldman Sachs	19	12	31
Morgan Stanley	11	3	14
SBC Warburg	3	9	12
Merrill Lynch	4	7	11
CSFB	4	4	8
Dresdner Kleinwort Benson	4	2	6
Paribas	1	5	6
Lehman Brothers	3	2	5
IMI	1	4	5
Argentaria	0	5	5

Source: Capital Data Ltd.

porate transactions. In these 97 transactions, 157 global coordinator mandates were awarded. Forty-three banks acted as global coordinator in at least one US$1 billion transaction over the period. Only 25 banks received two or more mandates and just 15 banks received three or more (see Exhibit 4.32).

Only nine banks were given at least one global coordinator role for non-domestic issues: Goldman Sachs (19 non-domestic mandates), Morgan Stanley (8), SBC Warburg (7), Merrill Lynch (7), CSFB (5), Lehman Brothers (2), UBS (2) Jardine Fleming (1) and JP Morgan (1).

Awards

A further measure of the overall professionalism of the top firms active in the international equity market is derived from the number of awards received by the leading banks. The awards, made by a number of leading financial magazines are taken very seriously by the banks and are, therefore, meaningful as indicators of the standings of these firms in the international equity new issue market. Taken together with the league tables, they represent the most objective measures as to the overall professionalism of a particular bank as a global coordinator of international equity offers.

International Financing Review

International Financing Review makes annual year-end awards for overall excellence in the equity new issue market. At the beginning of the period under review there was only one award for overall international excellence. In recent years there have been regional awards and a global award. Goldman Sachs and Morgan Stanley have two global and two regional awards each, Merrill Lynch has three regional awards and one global award and CSFB and SBC Warburg each have one European Equity House of the Year Award. (See Exhibit 4.33.)

Euromoney Corporate Finance Magazine

Exhibit 4.34 represents Euromoney *Corporate Finance*'s point of view as to which firms have completed landmark transactions during the period under review.

Global Investor/Euromoney Magazine

This survey is designed to determine those houses which

fifth. The higher this proportion the better, because IPO fees tend to be higher and because it develops a stronger relationship with the companies, which bodes well for future business opportunities (see Exhibit 4.29).

Goldman Sachs is the IPO leader in the US whereas SBC Warburg takes the top slot in Europe (see Exhibit 4.30).

Over the period under review, SBC Warburg was, in terms of new issue volume, the outstanding privatisation bank, whereas Goldman Sachs was supreme in the corporate sector (see Exhibit 4.31).

During the six years to 1996 there were 97 transactions larger than US$1 billion, of which 51 were privatisations and 46 cor-

Exhibit 4.33

International Financing Review: 'Equity House of the Year' Awards, 1991–96*

	Number of nominations
Goldman Sachs	4
Merrill Lynch	4
Morgan Stanley	4
CSFB	1
SBC Warburg	1

* Including regional and global awards from the time when such were awarded but not any awards for individual transactions. Awards are made by a nominated panel of experts.

Exhibit 4.34

Euromoney Corporate Finance Magazine: 'Equity Deals of the Year', 1991–96*

	Number of transactions nominated
Goldman Sachs	9
Morgan Stanley	6
Merrill Lynch	4
SBC Warburg	4
CSFB	1

*Awards are made by a nominated panel of experts.

Exhibit 4.35

Pan-European Equity Research and Pan-European Equity Execution Capability: Global Investor/ Euromoney September poll of European institutional investors, 1992–96*

	Total number of votes*
SBC Warburg	93
Morgan Stanley	92
Goldman Sachs	51
Merrill Lynch	41
CSFB	-

* A number 1 position as best European equity research house earns 10 points. The same applies for number one position as the best equity execution house. Second positions earn 9 points, and so on. The awards are based on a poll of European institutional investors. Points have only been awarded for a top five position or better.

Exhibit 4.36

Euromoney end-users' and equity peers' vote, 1991–96*

	Total number of votes*
Goldman Sachs	87
Morgan Stanley	79
Merrill Lynch	60
SBC Warburg	57
CSFB	37

* A number 1 position as 'best at structuring, pricing and distributing international equity offerings', as voted by the users, and 'the best global coordinator', as voted by the peers, respectively, each earns 10 points. A maximum number of 20 points can be garnered. Second positions earn nine points, and so on. There was no poll in 1992, and in 1991 there was no poll of peers. The maximum number of points that could be earned over the period is 90 points. Points have only been awarded for a top five position or better.

European institutional investors rank highly for their pan-European equity research and execution. SBC Warburg's and Morgan Stanley's strong positions stand out. Goldman Sachs scored well in the beginning of the period, but has slipped substantially in recent years. Merrill Lynch's score reflects Smith New Court's strong position in the European secondary markets while CSFB's failure to show up gives an indication of the firm's traditional lack of secondary market infrastructure in European equities. (See Exhibit 4.35.)

Euromoney Magazine

Both clients and peers of investment banks have been polled for their opinion as to the leading international equity houses since 1991, though no poll was carried out in 1992. The endorsement of Goldman Sachs as the best house in the global equity new issue market is overwhelming: it was only three points away from the maximum score of 90 points. In four out of the five years, Goldman Sachs was voted best international equity house by both its end-users and its peers. (See Exhibit 4.36.)

The investor perspective

The investors

The importance of the international institutional investor market

International institutions – institutional investors based outside the home market of a particular company – account for a very large proportion of most cross-border offers, as illustrated in Exhibit 5.1.

Roche, the Swiss pharmaceutical company and Shandong Huaneng, the Chinese electric utility, both made targeted placements entirely outside their domestic markets. In the cases of Nokia, Mayr-Melnhof and Tele Danmark, operating in small and/or unsophisticated domestic markets, the offers were distributed to a large extent in the international market.

Offers by companies from countries with more developed equity markets such as the US (USX) and the UK (Railtrack) were less reliant on the international market.

US investors play an ever more important role in the financing of non-US corporations around the world, due to the increasing proportion of international equity investment among US pension funds and the dramatic inflow to US equity mutual funds with an international investment horizon (see Exhibit 5.2).

Perhaps somewhat surprisingly, of the 17 offers by non-UK and non-US companies listed in the table below, and for which reliable data is available, 11 were allocated to a higher degree in the US than in the UK, whereas only five were allocated to a higher degree in the UK than in the US.

The power of the large institutions

Though the total number of institutions targeted in large privatisation offers can be high, there is a limited number of institutional investors around the world that can make or break a deal in the new issue market. It is essential for companies and banks to get it right when marketing to these institutions.

Exhibit 5.1

Proportion of selected equity offers sold outside their respective domestic markets

Issuer	Nationality	Pricing date	Total size of offer (US$ millions)	Sold outside the domestic market (% of total offer)
Roche	Switzerland	September 1992	275	100
Shandong Huaneng	China	August 1994	333	100
Nokia	Finland	July 1994	484	89
Mayr-Melnhof	Austria	April 1994	288	83
Tele Danmark	Denmark	April 1994	2,975	82
Akzo	Netherlands	November 1993	745	66
TCNZ	New Zealand	July 1991	818	66
YPF	Argentina	June 1993	3,040	65
KPN	Netherlands	June 1994	3,681	63
Bulgari	Italy	June 1995	138	60
ENI	Italy	November 1995	3,950	46
China Steel	Taiwan	May 1992	782	40
Argentaria	Spain	April 1993	1,008	38
Wellcome	UK	July 1992	4,420	38
Repsol	Spain	April 1995	1,667	37
Deutsche Telekom	Germany	November 1996	11,336	33
Elf Aquitaine	France	February 1994	4,178	32
Pharmacia	Sweden	June 1994	1,156	31
Telefónica	Spain	February 1997	4,400	26
BNP	France	October 1993	3,209	25
USX	US	January 1992	559	20
Railtrack	UK	May 1996	2,948	19
Singapore Telecom	Singapore	October 1993	2,670	11
Zeneca	UK	May 1993	2,080	1.5

Exhibit 5.2
Proportion of selected equity offers allocated to US investors

Issuer	Nationality	Pricing date	Total size of offer (US$ millions)	US listing/ 144 A	Portion of total offer allocated to US/Canadian investors[1]
Roche	Switzerland	September 1992	275	144 A	100%
Nokia	Finland	July 1994	484	NYSE	71%
Shandong Huaneng	China	August 1994	333	NYSE	48%
YPF	Argentina	June 1993	3,040	NYSE	48%
Tele Danmark	Denmark	April 1994	2,975	NYSE	41%
TCNZ	New Zealand	July 1991	818	NYSE	33%[3]
Mayr-Melnhof	Austria	April 1994	288	144A	29%
Wellcome	UK	July 1992	4,420	NYSE	24%
Daimler-Benz	Germany	June 1994	1,789	NYSE	20–25%
ENI	Italy	November 1995	3,950	NYSE	21%
Repsol	Spain	April 1995	1,667	NYSE	18%
Bulgari	Italy	June 1995	138	144A	16%
Pharmacia	Sweden	June 1994	1,156	Nasdaq	16%
Deutsche Telekom	Germany	November 1996	11,336	NYSE	15%
Argentaria	Spain	April 1993	1,008	NYSE	14%
KPN	Netherlands	June 1994	3,681	144A	14%
Telefónica	Spain	February 1997	4,400	NYSE	13%
China Steel	Taiwan	May 1992	782	144A	12%
Railtrack	UK	May 1996	2,948	144A	11%
Elf Aquitaine	France	February 1994	4,178	NYSE	9%
Akzo	Netherlands	November 1993	745	Nasdaq[2]	7%
BNP	France	October 1993	3,209	144A	3%
Zeneca	UK	May 1993	2,080	NYSE	less than 1.5%

[1] Those offers that are registered with the SEC and listed on the NYSE have to a degree been distributed to US retail investors.
[2] Although Akzo was listed on Nasdaq, this was a bought deal and hence this transaction was not registered with the SEC.
[3] This is an estimate.

Exhibit 5.3
Investor concentration

Issuer	Pricing date	Total size of offer (US$ millions)	Number of investors accounting for 80% of institutional allocations	Total number of institutional investors
Roche	September 1992	275	10	29
Shandong Huaneng	August 1994	333	53	92
Nokia	July 1994	484	27	155
Mayr-Melnhof	April 1994	288	41	175
Pharmacia	June 1994	1,156	31	212
USX	January 1992	559	N/A	237
Akzo	November 1993	745	N/A	246
Bulgari	June 1995	138	50	271
Argentaria	April 1993	1,008	45	516[1]
Repsol	April 1995	1,667	244	643
Railtrack	May 1996	2,948	129	719
YPF	June 1993	3,040	111	791
Tele Danmark	April 1994	2,975	466	849
Wellcome	July 1992	4,420	121	1,119
ENI	November 1995	3,950	N/A	1,284
Elf Aquitaine	February 1994	4,178	360	1,858
KPN	June 1994	3,681	100–125	2,500
BNP	October 1993	3,209	3,046	4,088
Deutsche Telekom	November 1996	11,336	N/A	4,796

[1] Does not include domestic institutions.

To give the reader an indication of the number of institutions involved, take the case of the much talked about BT 3 offer of 1993. The global coordinator SG Warburg singled out approximately 500 institutions world-wide to whom only the 11 global managers were allowed to talk and with which the majority of the institutional offer was supposed to be placed. In the US$11.3 billion Deutsche Telekom offer of November 1996, no less than 4,796 insti-

Exhibit 5.4

Twenty of the top fund managers in the US*

Alliance Capital (Equitable group)
Bankers Trust
California Public Employees Retirement System
Capital Group
College Retirement Equities Fund (TIAA – CREF)
Fidelity Investments
Franklin Resources Group (Templeton Worldwide)
GE Investment
Goldman Sachs Asset Management
JP Morgan Investment Management
Mellon Bank Corporation
Merrill Lynch Asset Management
Morgan Stanley Dean Witter Discover
Putnam Investment Management
Scudder Stevens & Clark
State Street Group
T Rowe Price Associates
Travelers Group
Vanguard Group
Wellington Management Company

* Ranked in alphabetical order. Criteria for inclusion is total funds under management. The majority of asset managers in the table manage more than US$100 billion, and up to US$500 billion.

Sources: Georgeson & Company Inc. and Investment Company Institute.

Exhibit 5.6

Twenty of the top fund managers in Continental Europe*

Aachener & Münchener (Germany)
Aegon (Netherlands)
Algemeen Burgerlijk Pensioenfonds (Netherlands)
Allianz Group (Germany)
Allmänna Pensionsfonderna (Sweden)
AXA/UAP (France)
Banque Paribas (France)
Commerzbank (Germany)
Crédit Agricole (France)
Crédit Lyonnais (France)
Credit Suisse Group (Switzerland)
Deutsche Bank Group (Germany)
Dresdner Bank Group (Germany)
Fortis (Belgium)
Groupe Caisse des Dépôts (France)
ING (Netherlands)
Münchener Rückversicherung (Germany)
SBC Group (Switzerland)
UBS Group (Switzerland)
Zürich Insurance (Switzerland)

* Ranked in alphabetical order. Criteria for inclusion is total funds under management. Institutions manage assets of between US$80 billion and US$450 billion.

Source: Euromoney Intersec 250.

Exhibit 5.5

Twenty of the top fund managers in the UK*

Barclays Global Investors
Commercial Union Investment Management
Fleming Investment Management
Foreign & Colonial
Gartmore Investment Management
Hermes Pensions Management
Hill Samuel Asset Management
HSBC Asset Management
Invesco Asset Management
Legal & General Investment Management
Mercury Asset Management
Morgan Grenfell Investment Management
Norwich Union Investment Management
Prudential Portfolio Managers
Royal & Sun Alliance Investment Management
Schroder Investment Management
Scottish Widows Investment Management
Standard Life Investment Management
Sun Alliance
Threadneedle Asset Management

* Ranked in alphabetical order. Criteria for inclusion is total funds under management. Funds under management range between US$35 billion and more than US$350 billion.

Sources: Citywatch and Euromoney Intersec 250.

tutional investors from around the world were allocated shares.

As can be seen from Exhibit 5.3, many very large offers are effectively carried by less than 50 institutions.

The majority of the 50 most active institutional cross-border equity investors are to be found among those listed in Exhibits 5.4, 5.5 and 5.6.

In addition to the institutional investment community in these countries and regions, there are large investment insti-

tutions in Japan, Canada, Australia, the Middle East and Singapore.

According to the head of the European equity capital markets department at one of the major US investment banks, the 20 or so largest institutions world-wide are sufficiently powerful to dictate the terms on which new equity issues are done, particularly in difficult market conditions.

As far as the UK equity market is concerned, it is argued that the five largest domestic institutions control the sub-underwriting business to the extent that they effectively determine the terms on which UK companies can raise new equity.

It is perhaps not surprising that an institution such as Fidelity Investments, with total assets under management of US$498 billion (as at 31 March 1997), an amount larger than the entire cross-border equity new issue market during the four years to 1996, or the Capital Group with total assets of approximately US$300 billion, are in a very strong position to influence the outcome of an offer. Fidelity is known to put in very large orders of several hundred million dollars if the story and valuation are attractive. In some cases, Fidelity has indicated demand larger than the total offer size of the particular offer.

According to Rudolf M. Staehelin, senior vice president at Capital International in Geneva, part of the Capital Group of the US with approximately US$300 billion under management of which more than US$100 billion is invested in international equities: 'If the deal is not going well then the fund managers have a lot of power under the bookbuilding system.' The major institutions wielded their power in the Pechiney privatisation of December 1995. The French government and Pechiney, the aluminium and packaging company, had planned to combine the sale of shares by the government with a huge capital increase for the company. Some of the large institutional holders of Pechiney's investment certificates were unimpressed with the terms of the proposed transactions and disenchanted with the historic performance of the company. They recognised that Pechiney was uncompetitive and were angered that the company now proposed to spend its way out of its difficulties with an ambitious international expansion plan for which more equity was needed. Some of the major shareholding institutions refused to support these expansion plans and asked that the company first achieve a competitive cost structure in its domestic operations before they would support any new equity issue to finance international growth. The transaction, as planned by the French government, the Pechiney management and the financial advisers, had to be restructured such that the issue of new shares was cut in half and the company had to reign in its international ambitions and accept the pressure of a higher level of gearing until tangible results could be shown.

As institutional investors become bigger and more confident, and as their clients put them under increased pressure to perform, so this type of shareholder activism will increase. In the ordinary course of business however, the ability on the part of any one, or even a small group of institutional investors, to influence the structure and pricing of a new issue is relatively limited. This is demonstrated in the way that the market price rises ahead of certain secondary offers, as those institutions who buy are the ones who do not think that they will be allocated as much as they require in the actual offer. But, according to Sandy Nairn, director of global equity research at Templeton Worldwide (a US mutual fund management company with US$80 billion under management, of which more than 70 per cent is invested outside the US): 'Sometimes you must make your views heard, particularly where the rights of shareholders have been infringed. Indeed, we have a fiduciary responsibility to our investors to ensure that this does not happen. We do have some influence given the considerable size of the assets we manage.'

As a result of the overall growth, globalisation and concentration of the fund management industry, the total amount of funds managed by the big institutions is increasing rapidly. Therefore, regarding the new issue process, the buy-side is likely to grow stronger in relative terms and the vendors and the banks are likely to lose power.

According to one fund manager of a small UK fund management organisation, managers of the biggest funds do have enormous influence, as they can demand shares to the value of US$400 million, no more or no less, and tell the companies to take it or leave it. There is no question that these fund managers are privy to better information than the small ones – perhaps even insider information. Confirms Huw Jones, Director of Corporate Finance, Prudential Portfolio Managers, the investment arm of Prudential Corporation, with total assets under management of over £90 billion: 'Yes, we agree that in certain instances, the big institutions have substantial market power'. He continued: 'We believe, however, that normal market processes can be distorted by extremely large shareholdings in listed companies. The spectre of the 'shadow director' then appears.'

The advantages of being a big buyer in the new issue market are numerous: you typically get a one-on-one meeting with the senior management of the company at your convenience and have ready access to quality information on the company; you can have considerable influence on pricing, sizing and other structuring parameters; the investment bank is going to accept your order whenever it comes, regardless of what the general allocation criteria are; and you undoubtedly get better treatment in the allocation process.

What companies should know about the institutions

When marketing in connection with a new issue, as well as subsequently in the secondary market, it is important that companies realise exactly who they are selling to. The more they know about the institutions, the greater the likelihood of a successful presentation and an institutional buy order. Furthermore, the better they know the targeted investors, the more they can assist the investment banks in targeting the right people in the pre-marketing and marketing phases of a new issue. At the same time, professional investment bankers will brief company management well in advance of the roadshow as to the profile and requirements of the targeted investors. However, this briefing is often inadequate.

While it would be wholly unrealistic for a CEO and a CFO embarking on their first roadshow to know much more than the basic information listed in Exhibit 5.7, they would be well advised to build up, over time, a database of investors containing as much of that information as possible.

Institutional investor views on the new issue process

Fund managers have strong views as to how companies go about the new issue process, particularly in the areas of disclosure, the telling of the story and how aggressively they sell the prospects of the company.

Institutional investors also feel strongly about their direct suppliers of raw material – the investment banks. These feelings are stronger in the new issue process than in the secondary market and are particularly strong in the case of IPOs, as there is more room for negotiation on price than in the case of a secondary issue. Institutional investors want to buy at a low price and the vendors want to sell at a high price. Lawrence Banks, deputy chairman of Robert Fleming & Co.: 'You have got to realise that it is a war out there whereby the institutions are trying to drive the price down and the bankers on behalf of the vendor are trying to maximise the price.' Investment banks are seen by most institutional investors as representing the vendors more than the buyers. This is probably a fair perception, as the vendors pay the fees, but it needs to be qualified: the vendors pay the fees, but the banks need the cooperation of the institutions in the allocation and designation processes to realise the expected portion of the total selling concession. The banks themselves claim to represent buyers and sellers equally.

Fund managers are amazed at the number of promises

Exhibit 5.7

Checklist of things companies ought to know about institutional investors

Basic information
- Name and basic contact details of institution;
- Type of organisation (eg, pension fund, mutual fund company, insurance company, bank, private bank, corporation, hedge fund, independent fund/investment manager, etc.);
- History and ownership;
- Corporate structure, principal offices and senior management;
- Total assets under management;
- Number of fund managers and number of research analysts;
- Background on most important fund managers/analysts;
- Attitude towards new issue market; and
- History of investment in your company (if applicable) and in your industry.

Clients and asset classes
If the targeted institution is an independent investment/fund manager:
- Whose money are they managing (pension fund money, mutual funds, corporations, foundations, high-net-worth individuals, etc.);
- How much of the money comes from domestic clients and how much from foreign clients; and
- Of the total assets under management, what proportion is invested in equities? Of the total investment in equities, what proportion is invested in international equities.

Investment philosophy and investment style
- Are they active or passive managers, ie, are they primarily bottom up or top-down investors and what is the attitude to risk in terms of deviating from the given benchmark;
- In terms of the investment decisions that they make, do they invest principally on a country basis, by sector or choose specific companies (see Exhibit 5.71);
- Are they primarily quantitative or primarily qualitative in their investment style;
- What type of funds/portfolios are managed by the fund management company (growth funds, value funds, country funds, regional funds, international funds, global funds, industry funds, income funds, small cap funds, index funds, privatisation funds, recovery funds, special situation funds, etc.);
- Which of these funds are the largest funds and in what funds would your company most logically fit in as an investment? Who is responsible for the funds most relevant to you;
- According to which benchmark(s) do they invest;
- What represents a core holding for this institutional investor;
- What is a typical holding period;
- What is the current asset allocation of the institution or relevant fund/portfolios;
- Does this fund management company have special requirements in the area of due diligence, disclosure, documentation, corporate governance standards, etc; and
- Does this fund management company have strong views on pre-emptive rights.

Investment process
- What is the investment process, ie, what is the decision making process for a particular investment and how long does it take;
- Who are the principal decision maker(s) and where are they based? Is it the analyst or the fund manager who makes the investment decision; and
- How does the fund management company hope to add value to its clients.

Exhibit 5.71

Investment approach (%)

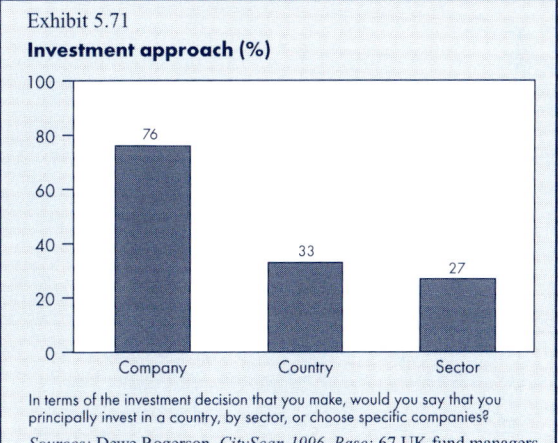

In terms of the investment decision that you make, would you say that you principally invest in a country, by sector, or choose specific companies?

Sources: Dewe Rogerson, *CityScan 1996. Base:* 67 UK fund managers.

---

made by companies and bankers, not least in connection with new issues, which are subsequently broken. Companies and bankers should both recognise that institutional investors have long memories and breaking promises can lose them potential investors for ever. According to fund managers, companies would be better served by following the rule that 'honesty is the best policy'.

What fund managers think of company management

Investors have had different experience in different countries. On one extreme, in countries such as Russia, companies do not understand what equity is, while in more mature markets,

investors complain that company presentations are too stage-managed and polished. There are many specific concerns throughout the spectrum, some of which are general and some country or market specific.

Timing

Fund managers feel that too many companies come to the market before they are ready to do so. One UK fund manager points out that: 'A considerable number of companies are definitely not ready to go public when they do. Two good examples that come to mind are the Austrian packaging company Mayr-Melnhof in 1994, through Morgan Stanley, and the Italian electronics/electricals company Stayer in 1995, through SBC Warburg.' Experience shows that the most successful issues are those where an experienced management team has been in place for some time and has been allowed to restructure the business and properly prepare for the market debut. Two such examples were YPF of Argentina in 1993, and ENI of Italy in 1995.

Another reason that companies come to the market too early is that investment bankers rarely recommend delaying a deal if there is one that can be done in the short-term. Daniel J Barker, vice president-portfolio manager of international equities at GE Investments, with total assets under management of US$60 billion and US$8 billion invested in international equities commented: 'Both governments and corporate vendors are pushed to do many deals too early. Instead, they ought to appoint appropriate management and let them do the necessary restructuring work for two to three years before coming to the market. The Gucci IPO in 1995 was a classic case of a company coming to the market too soon. The vendor would have made several hundred million dollars more by waiting for six months.' Building a good track record before coming to the market can only be to the vendor's advantage.

Because bankers very rarely recommend postponing transactions, companies must bear much of the responsibility for getting the timing right. Jürg Tanner, vice president at Julius Baer, one of the leading private banks in Switzerland, with total assets under management of US$50 billion emphasised the importance of getting the timing of an offer right: 'Even the best bookrunner will struggle to sell a good quality company in a bad market. Equally, even the best managed company will meet with resistance from investors if its business is at the top of the cycle.' Given that lead times are typically long in these transactions, getting the right market conditions is to a large extent a matter of luck. However, selling stock at the right point in the cycle is something that companies can and should control. Tanner added: 'The challenge lies in bringing the right stock at the right time in the right market and at the right price. Argentaria 1 in 1993, for example, was such an issue.' In the case of a cyclical company, it is important that an offer is made at least 12–18 months before the top of the cycle is reached. There is more flexibility with the timing of issues from growth companies.

Disclosure

Jochen Gutbrod, manager of Schroder Investment Management, with £87 billion under management, explained: 'Disclosure is obviously a key area of concern to institutional fund managers such as ourselves. Take, for example, the privatisation of BNP in 1993, which quite clearly was not handled in a way that assisted the overall French privatisation programme. BNP was keen to be the global coordinator of its own privatisation. Although this is understandable, this immediately meant that the disclosure standards were going to be lower than they otherwise would have been, as the tension between issuer and global coordinator was not there to the same extent. Against initial expectations, the issue was actually expensive because the real net asset value was much lower than we were led to believe at the time. Furthermore, because

there had not been proper disclosure at the time of the offer and because it had been handled primarily by BNP and other French banks, the research follow-up in the secondary market was disastrous.'

Robert Davy, director of Schroder Capital Management, which is part of Schroder Investment Management added: 'With respect to disclosure, we find more often than not that companies play down their capital expenditure plans in connection with new issues, which does not add to the credibility of the management. This was the case with YPF of Argentina in connection with its IPO in 1993. We suspect that the bankers often support the decision to play down future capital expenditure as this makes the short term earnings outlook appear better than it is in reality.'

Many companies do not accept shareholders as partners and do not disclose enough information about the business and some fund managers feel that many companies are naive and arrogant about the investment community. Having said that, most institutions agree that the majority of companies, be it in continental Europe or in the emerging markets are getting better in this area. Douglas A Dial, equity portfolio manager at College Retirement Equities Fund with US$190 billion under management, of which US$100 billion is invested in equities noted that: 'Although most non-US issuers have become much more familiar with US investment criteria and more open to discussion, there are still some foreign managements that are arrogant when they come over here to sell themselves. This we find hard to understand. Importantly, for us, the real test of a management's attitude towards disclosure comes when things go badly for the company. At that point we can observe how candid they are about recognising what has gone wrong. Needless to say, how they handle themselves in such situations is crucial for our investment decision.'

Elisabeth Weisenhorn, portfolio manager German equities at DWS, the German mutual funds company owned by Deutsche Bank, with Dm105 billion under management, added: 'Companies going public must learn to understand the basics of the equity market and that being a public company is different from being a private company. They have to learn to appreciate what equity investors look for in terms of information and what their requirements are in terms of meeting with the company. They have to change the approach from only informing the equity market when they want to raise money, to sharing information with it on a regular basis. Managements also have to accept different views and have to learn not to get upset if an equity research analyst changes his recommendation following a period of strong share price performance.' Even the mighty Deutsche Telekom apparently had difficulties with the transition to becoming a publicly owned company. The German telecommunications giant refused to publish its annual results for 1996 earlier than May 1997, as planned, despite substantial weakness in the share price and strong investor demands to do so. It was only when the market in Deutsche Telekom shares was under severe pressure that the Deutsche Telekom management agreed to move its profit announcement forward.

Thomas Madsen, managing director of JP Morgan

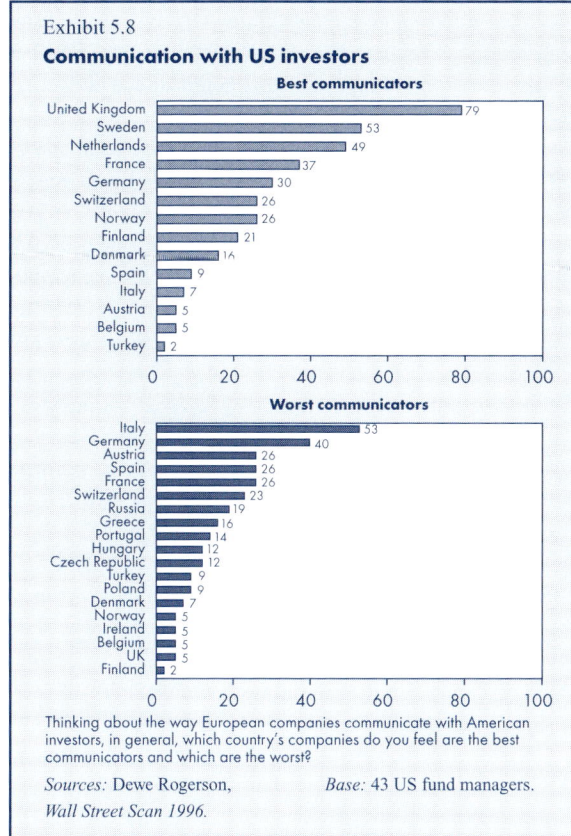

Exhibit 5.8
Communication with US investors

Best communicators

Country	Value
United Kingdom	79
Sweden	53
Netherlands	49
France	37
Germany	30
Switzerland	26
Norway	26
Finland	21
Denmark	16
Spain	9
Italy	7
Austria	5
Belgium	5
Turkey	2

Worst communicators

Country	Value
Italy	53
Germany	40
Austria	26
Spain	26
France	26
Switzerland	23
Russia	19
Greece	16
Portugal	14
Hungary	12
Czech Republic	12
Turkey	9
Poland	9
Denmark	7
Norway	5
Ireland	5
Belgium	5
UK	5
Finland	2

Thinking about the way European companies communicate with American investors, in general, which country's companies do you feel are the best communicators and which are the worst?

Sources: Dewe Rogerson,　*Base:* 43 US fund managers.
Wall Street Scan 1996.

Investment Management (with US$215 billion under management) stressed the importance of having recognisable accounting firms as auditors: 'When companies change their accountants, this is typically a warning signal. Furthermore, we undoubtedly take great comfort from seeing two accounting firms jointly responsible for the audit of a company.'

As can be seen in Exhibit 5.8, managements in Italy, Germany and Austria seem to be the ones that have the worst track record in terms of getting communication with US investors right. According to the same survey, the best communicators with US investors are management teams from the UK, Sweden and the Netherlands. The picture is similar when it comes to the quality of communication with UK investors.

Marketing

Investor presentations, and one-on-one meetings in particular, represent the most important source of information for institutional investors when assessing companies (see Exhibit 5.9). Given the importance of investor presentations, in either a bigger or a smaller forum, it is astonishing that such a high proportion of all presentations is of sub-standard quality.

A clear majority of the fund managers interviewed for this chapter confirmed that the quality of investor presentations is either 'very important' or 'important' for their investment decision.

How important is the quality of the company presentation for your investment decision?

11	Very important
5	Important
6	Not that important

Number of responses: 22.
Total votes add up to the total number of investors polled.

What percentage of company presentations do you consider good, fair or bad (total = 100 per cent)?

32	Good
44	Fair
24	Bad

Number of responses: 22.
Percentages reflect the average of all investors polled.

The most frequent criticisms of company presentations are that they lack interesting content, that management is badly prepared, that delivery is bad, and that the presentations are too rehearsed and oversold. The area in which many presentations appear the most badly prepared is the discussion of the financials.

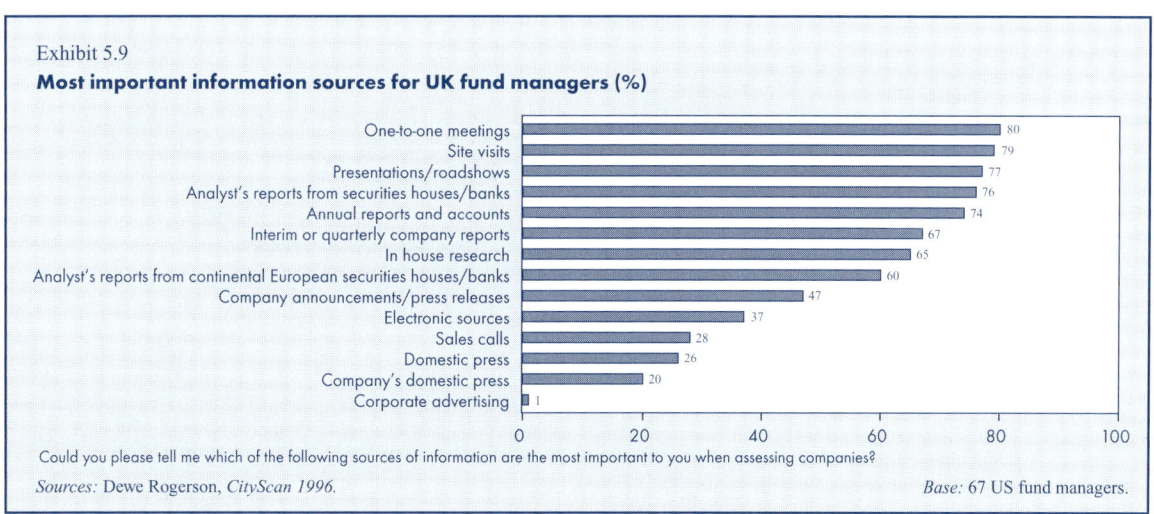

Exhibit 5.9
Most important information sources for UK fund managers (%)

One-to-one meetings	80
Site visits	79
Presentations/roadshows	77
Analyst's reports from securities houses/banks	76
Annual reports and accounts	74
Interim or quarterly company reports	67
In house research	65
Analyst's reports from continental European securities houses/banks	60
Company announcements/press releases	47
Electronic sources	37
Sales calls	28
Domestic press	26
Company's domestic press	20
Corporate advertising	1

Could you please tell me which of the following sources of information are the most important to you when assessing companies?

Sources: Dewe Rogerson, *CityScan 1996.* *Base:* 67 US fund managers.

What are the most common mistakes in connection with company presentations (rank the <u>two</u> most important mistakes)?

8	Management badly prepared
8	Bad delivery
14	Lack of interesting content
3	Too late invitation
7	Too rehearsed and over sold

Number of responses: 20.
Total votes add up to double the number of investors polled.

- *Lack of content:* This is often a problem, particularly for those investors who have read the prospectus and are well prepared. For them, a question and answer session in a one-on-one meeting is the preferred alternative. Some fund managers complain that many managements display a surprising lack of knowledge as to how their competitors are performing. This does not fill investors with a great deal of confidence. Elisabeth Weisenhorn commented: 'We would like to see company managements in investor presentations or in one-on-one meetings doing a better job explaining their business, what the profit drivers are and how they control their business.'

- *Too rehearsed and too oversold:* If the company has all the answers prepared, then the presentation is too rehearsed and too 'packaged'. One fund manager remarked that when he heard a Croatian company talk about 'return on capital employed in the operating divisions', the warning bells started ringing and he was immediately put off because he knew that the manager had simply been advised by his bankers that this was the correct response to any question about key financial criteria. Rudolf Staehelin at Capital International in Geneva recommends company managers to act naturally: 'Don't be too rehearsed and don't oversell, ie, make sure that the story you sell is one that you can deliver – investors won't forgive and they have very long memories. ... The biggest mistake that companies – egged on by their bankers – make is to oversell. That inevitably results in a loss of credibility, which is a precious commodity.'

Successful one-on-one meetings can be of considerable importance. The CEO of Deutsche Telekom, Ron Sommer managed to turn around one major US institution's decision not to buy into the company's IPO during such a meeting. Anthony Regan, chief investment officer for international equities at Putnam Investments, a US investment management company with total funds under management of US$185 billion (of which US$16 billion is invested in international equities) reported: 'We became convinced in the meeting that the company had a viable strategy to pay down its debt and decided to change our minds.' Huw Jones director of corporate finance at Prudential Portfolio Managers says: 'We notice in meetings that those companies which have at least one member of the board with prior experience in running a public company have an advantage on the roadshow. If the operating management does not have public company experience, then at least the chairman should.'

It is important for the managers to know how they are doing while they are on the road. Masden of JP Morgan

---

Exhibit 5.10

What institutions want to know from company presentations

1. What does the business do and what is the vision (including mission statement)?
2. What are the main profit drivers in the business?
3. How is the business doing. What is the recent track record?
4. What is the strategy in terms of technologies, products, markets and the delivery of shareholder value?
5. How will the product and market strategies be realised?
6. What is the financial strategy and according to what financial criteria is the business managed and controlled?
7. What are the key management and reporting structures?
8. How does the company compare against its domestic and international peer groups, in terms of products and market penetration as well as financial structure and performance?
9. What is the outlook and what are the key internal and external factors that might effect the business in the future?
10. Why should an investor buy the company's shares?

All the points listed above cannot be covered in a 20–25 minute presentation. The art lies in touching on the most relevant points for a particular company at a particular point in time.

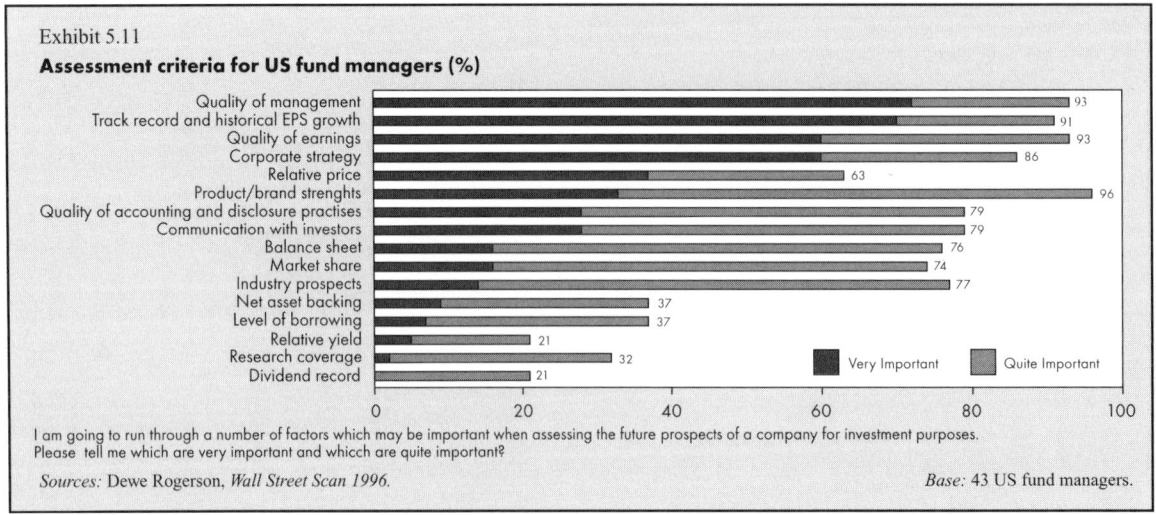

Exhibit 5.11
Assessment criteria for US fund managers (%)

I am going to run through a number of factors which may be important when assessing the future prospects of a company for investment purposes. Please tell me which are very important and whicch are quite important?

Sources: Dewe Rogerson, *Wall Street Scan 1996.*   *Base:* 43 US fund managers.

Investment Management advised: 'Make the one-on-one meeting interactive by asking the investor at the end of the presentation what they think about the story and whether they intend to invest. In this way you would know where you stand. After the roadshow is over, it is too late to make any adjustments.'

Exhibit 5.10 shows what institutional investors typically want to know.

How management presents gives a very good idea of the quality of management, although investors are often put off by overly slick presentations. Some fund managers stress that they want to get to know the management – see how they think and how they answer questions. Others want to see how consistent the strategy has been and whether management can be trusted. Staehelin commented: 'We appreciate companies that have a consistent strategy. We get very nervous when they change their spots.'

So what are the specific assessment criteria that investors look at when taking their investment decisions? US fund managers consider that 'quality of management' and 'track record and historical EPS growth' are the most important criteria followed by 'quality of earnings' and 'corporate strategy' (see Exhibit 5.11).

The main assessment criteria used by UK investors are very similar, however quality of earnings is deemed slightly more important than corporate strategy and the track record and historical EPS growth.

Bluford Putnam, president of CDC Investment Management Corporation, the US subsidiary of the French financial institution with US$184 billion of assets under management explained: 'We consider that half of the value of an equity investment is the quality of management.'

Stephen Lowe, formerly a director responsible for US equities at Gartmore, the UK fund management company owned by NatWest, with £57 billion under management, advised companies of what they ought to be looking at when selling themselves to investors: 'When we look to invest in IPOs, we look in particular at competition, other risk factors and how the ownership changes hand, ie, are the former owners selling out? When, on the other hand, we look at secondary issues, we concentrate on the use of proceeds, the reasons for doing the issue, the pro-forma calculation of earnings per share and cash flow. Is the company growing too strongly to be cash generative, which means that it might be forced into future equity offers which would dilute our ownership interest and perhaps also earnings per share? Finally, having done the analytical part, it comes down to judgment. Is the historic track record such that we should trust this management with our money in connection with a new issue?'

One problem that companies face when roadshowing a new issue is that few serious fund managers want to be seen attending group presentations. Such meetings take more time that one-on-one meetings, and there is less room for direct and personal interaction. Some investors don't want to advertise the fact that they are not big enough to have been granted a one-on-one meeting. So how can companies cater for the smaller institutions that have a serious interest in investing, but are not going to be given a one-on-one meeting, and do not want to be seen at group presentations? One alternative is to organise a smaller dinner or lunch with a limited number of medium-sized or smaller institutions. Another alternative is to distribute a video or CD-ROM of an investor presentation including a question and answer session involving a small number of known, credible equity research analysts.

However good they are, roadshows are not appreciated by all institutions. Indeed, some investors are positively averse to any form of roadshowing. Richard Foulkes, executive vice president of Schroder Capital Management explained: 'It is perhaps ironic, but we do not benefit from very good roadshows. Given that we have a large number of highly competent analysts, we can work out the fundamentals for ourselves. An aggressive and highly 'successful' roadshow simply drives up the price.'

Size of syndicates

There is always an inclination among companies to reward long-standing banking relationships when they bring a new issue. This inclination inevitably leads to the formation of large syndicates, which in turn invariably leads to infighting among the senior syndicate banks and a lack of motivation among the more junior syndicate members. The company's expectations will be unfulfilled, and widespread aggravation is almost a certainty.

When a large syndicate is in place there is contention over the marketing process, the allocation process and designations, all areas of particular concern for investors. Thus, it certainly does not make any sense for companies to include as many as eight or ten banks in a US$100 million offer, when three or four banks would be more than adequate for the job. In any case, investment institutions do not want to talk to more than a couple of investment banks about a particular offer. Any number larger than that is a nuisance for investors and can be off-putting.

Pricing

Institutions believe that companies are usually too greedy for their own good. Richard Watt, director of BEA Associates, which has total equity assets under management of US$31 billion explained: 'It would be very much in their interest to leave a little on the table, particularly when they come to the market for the first time. It is only at times of bad market conditions that companies don't price at the upper end of the range. These companies obviously believe that it is better to be short-term greedy than long-term greedy.'

Shareholder rights

Many companies that are new to the equity market do not accept shareholders as partners because they are insecure or unsophisticated. While most institutional investors do not consider it their business to sit on boards and get involved in the management of a business, preferring the freedom of action of being outside the boardroom, some institutions are getting together to appoint investment advisers and other representatives to sit on the boards of companies in which they have invested. Jean-Marc Fraysse, director of Cazenove Unit Trust Management noted: 'It is becoming increasingly important for shareholder interests to be represented at board level, particularly when things are not going so well for the company. There are many cases throughout Europe where either small or large minority shareholders do get together and elect board representatives. After all, trade unions are represented on the board in many countries, why shouldn't we be as owners?'

Companies should be open to such approaches, as their willingness to observe shareholder rights may affect their future ability to raise equity on favourable terms. They should also be aware of the need to address the issue of pre-emptive rights. Many UK institutions feel very strongly about these and institutions elsewhere can also be expected to take a view as pre-emptive rights are prevalent throughout continental Europe and Latin America.

James Cox, director of Schroder Investment Management responsible for UK equity investment stated: ' I am a strong supporter of pre-emptive rights and seriously disagree with those that try to undermine the system. To me, a pre-emptive right is a very basic right, ie, that it is the owners of the company that should have the first right of refusal on any new shares being issued. Any other structure leads to dilution in voting rights and often in economic rights as well. To those that argue that it is important to market and sell shares to new investors at the prevailing market price, I say that the expense associated with those issues is rarely worth the effort. Once the hype of the new issue process is over, the fundamentals of the business will prevail on the share price and the whole exercise will have led to a loss of value for existing shareholders. I also find it wholly inappropriate for companies to pay underwriting fees in connection with rights issues, when a deeply discounted rights issue can be done without any underwriting fee at all.'

American institutions often feel discriminated against by non-US companies which decide not to register their rights issues with the SEC and instead do only a Rule 144 A placement in the US, meaning that US shareholders are effectively forced to agree that their rights are sold on their behalf on the first day of rights trading. This has two direct negative implications for US shareholders: firstly, they are diluted in terms of ownership and, secondly, the price realised on the first day is typically lower than the average for the rights trading period as a whole.

Anthony Regan commented: 'This is very upsetting for US shareholders. Where this happens, we ask the bank involved which typically tells us that they advised their corporate client to register with the SEC. We then ask the company who says that they followed the advice of their investment bankers, ie, both parties deny responsibility. In some cases it is simply forgotten until it is too late. We want to see the appropriate undertakings in the IPO prospectus and then we want companies to stick to them. It is clearly in their interest to do so if they want to build up a loyal US shareholder base. The US investment community should get together on this one.'

Another area of major concern among US institutional investors is the fact that many non-pre-emptive offers are sold in the US under Rule 144A. Regan continued: 'Many companies and banks are not aware enough about the limitations of 144A securities. The main constraint is that each

and every investment portfolio respectively fund, which is managed by any one single fund manager, cannot have more than a maximum investment of 5 per cent in restricted securities, a category to which 144A securities belong. This means that you are restricted as to the size of a 144A offer that you can buy. We could, for example, not buy more than five stocks of 1 per cent each for any one portfolio. This is a particular area of concern for those US institutions which do not manage money in overseas offices and therefore cannot participate in any of the non-US tranches.'

Investor perceptions of the investment banks

Whereas investors sometimes criticise the way in which management conducts itself in connection with new issues, it is the banks that bear the brunt of their vitriol. Fund managers are typically highly critical of the role of the banks in the new issue process and are sceptical about the value of new issues in general. Bankers are considered too eager to do deals, driven by the attractive economics on offer. Many institutions feel that most new issue houses, even the largest and most reputable ones, have limited credibility and add only limited value to the new issue process. This criticism is only partly fair and institutions often fail to give banks credit for the good work done in issues that perform well. However, with new issue economics being as attractive as they are and with steadily increasing competition, it is unlikely that standards will improve in the foreseeable future.

A highly critical view – but by no means an unrepresentative one – was summed up as follows by a senior London-based fund manager at one of the largest US fund management organisations:

'Investment bankers definitely have a template to sell a story. The first thing that irritates us is that they call us up for a type of pre-screening, whereby they give us some general details without giving us the name of the issuer and then ask us how we would look at the story, how we would value the stock, what we would be prepared to pay and how much we would buy if the issuer indeed decides to come to the market. In short, we are asked to do their work for them, which is a big waste of time for us.

'When the pre-marketing starts, all the salesmen call, anxious to have been the first one to call, as if this would automatically entitle them to get our order. Then they say that they have to get their analyst to see you, without really questioning whether or not such a meeting actually adds value for us.

'When the roadshow starts, the investment banks have a big fight about the one-on-ones and, of course, they all want to be the ones that have brought an important institution such as ourselves to the company. Not too long ago we had a meeting with a company management where there were seven or eight investment banks present just because they all needed to be seen by the company to have arranged a meeting with us.

'The problems continue if you decide to take the deal as you then have to deal with the designations – a nightmare – which we can never get right as far as the bankers are concerned. The lead manager typically tries to exercise a lot of pressure by either saying outright, or by giving us to understand that unless they are designated we will not get a decent allocation. What we would prefer is a system that automatically allocates the economics to the banks involved.

'We are very unhappy about the way the new issue business is handled. I think that the buy-side, ourselves included, should have longer memories and punish the banks for not being professional about the way they conduct themselves and for how their deals perform. Perhaps we should coordinate any punitive action with other institutions.'

Capital International's Staehelin added: 'Whereas there is plenty of competition in both the US and the international new issue markets, in the US market there are typically fewer senior players involved in an offer and the roles are more clearly defined. Due to the large number of parties involved and the loosely defined roles in an international offer, there is a lot of infighting among the managers, which is very silly. It is a big nuisance when up to a dozen of the sell-side analysts involved in the offer try to see us with the sole purpose of getting a higher proportion of our designations. As a consequence, I personally do not want to see, other than on rare occasions, the analysts of the investment banks at the pre-marketing stage, especially since most of what they have to say, you can read in their research reports. This does not mean that Capital's analysts don't sometimes find it useful to see one or two of the sell-side analysts involved in the offer. What really matters to me, in addition to speaking to our own analysts, is to see the company management in a one-on-one meeting.'

Due diligence and documentation

Especially in less developed markets, there is often a problem with due diligence, particularly with respect to corporate governance issues and the issue of legal protection for minority shareholders. Often these issues are not touched upon at all in the prospectus or are misleadingly described. This can be due to eagerness on the part of the bankers and companies to do the deal. When this happens, the large institutions retaliate by paying the banks responsible a smaller proportion of the total selling commissions.

One highly critical US fund manager has the distinct impression that most investment bankers don't really look at the fundamentals in sufficient detail when they do the due diligence. He is often told by salesmen: 'This one is going to go up – you've got to be there.' He replies: 'We have no respect for bankers whose main argument is simply that you have to buy because a particular stock is going into an important index – that is really not to provide any value added at all. We also observe frequently how companies to be sold are positioned against comparable companies in a way that is simply not credible. The Scania IPO was such a case. It was argued that Scania was a non-cyclical engineering company. Whereas Scania might be somewhat less cyclical than other automotive companies, the comparison was highly aggressive and far from credible. We will not easily give the vendor, the company and the bankers involved the benefit of the doubt next time around.'

Most fund managers do not attach a great deal of importance to the lead managers' forecast at the time of issue. They simply do not believe it. Stephen Lowe commented: 'I do not think that it is the job of the lead manager to do an earnings forecast, they should concentrate on due diligence.' However Richard Watt of BEA Associates says: 'In emerging markets it may be more important to have an earnings forecast from the lead manager than it is in a more developed market. We do monitor the lead manager's forecast in great detail after the issue and are, of course, appaled to see the earnings forecast changed shortly after the issue. In the December 1993, US$1 billion transaction for Mexican media and publishing company Grupo Televisa, lead managed by Goldman Sachs, the earnings forecast had to be downgraded twice shortly after the issue.'

Paul Marshall, director responsible for European equity investment at Mercury Asset Management, which has £90 billion under management added: 'We do not attach all that much importance to the earnings forecast of the lead manager but we certainly expect the company to achieve the lead manager's forecast with respect to the first year.'

Most banks have a mixed due diligence record. A bad effort can depend on a particular banker, inadequate work by the legal advisers, or a company that is not being helpful or truthful. Still, the quality of due diligence is a distinguishing feature between the best firms and the second rate ones. Good firms feel confident about putting reluctant management under pressure in the due diligence process while lesser firms are perhaps more easily bullied by recalcitrant companies.

The principal purpose of the prospectus is to let the investment community see that the bank has done the due diligence. Institutions take comfort from the fact that the name of the lead manager is on the front page. Bankers can't afford to make mistakes because their reputations are on the line and the competition would be ruthless in exploiting any due diligence failures.

In the opinion of most investors, the prospectus has lost much of its role as a marketing document and has instead become a legal nightmare and very indigestible. It has become too focused on the past and does not discuss in sufficient detail the risks involved in the business: more should be said about the future. What institutions really need are more user-friendly prospectuses, with more summaries, more information on the state of the business, the industrial environment, estimates of demand and comparative data. What many busy fund managers would appreciate is a good two-page summary on the investment opportunity. Winston Churchill said: 'I didn't have time to write you a short letter so I wrote you a long one.' and bankers should bear in mind that investors prefer concise documentation.

Equity research

As already mentioned, most fund managers rely only to a limited extent on 'sales-side' equity research, which is produced by the lead manager of a new issue. The fact of the matter is that they simply do not trust it and most fund managers say that they consider sell-side research at best to be selectively objective.

Typically, do you consider the equity research of the investment banks to be objective in connection with new issues?

10	Not at all objective
12	Selectively objective
-	Very objective

Number of responses: 22.

Total votes add up to the total number of investors polled.

Investors prefer to rely on their own in-house research and that produced by independent third parties – either banks or brokers which are not involved in a particular issue, or independent research organisations.

To what extent do you rely on the following different sources of research for your investment decision (total = 100 per cent)?

16	lead manager research
45	In house
33	Objective third party

Number of responses: 22.

Percentages reflect the average of all investors polled

Gary Lowe, director responsible for US investment at Mercury Asset Management added: 'The fact of the matter is that the economics of the investment banking business makes it difficult for sell-side equity research analysts to be completely unbiased in their recommendations – this is particularly true in the new issue market. Whereas there are many good analysts out there, it is astonishing how many arrive at their earnings projections by way of extrapolation of a short-term trend, rather than from fundamental analysis including a visit to the company. These were the principal reasons that we decided to commit considerable resources to our own primary research.'

A senior fund manager of a major US fund management company expresses himself in much more direct terms: 'The sale side research in connection with new issues is not worth anything. It is typically contaminated as banks are too driven by new issues. We often laugh when certain research notes come out because it tells us exactly who is competing for a particular mandate. All the investment banks are guilty of this, including the supposedly 'best' firms.'

Sandy Nairn of Templeton Worldwide noted: 'There are a lot of bright analysts out there, but they are not usually taken seriously in the new issue market. The lack of objectivity of new issue research is clearly linked to the fact that the economics of the primary and secondary markets are too skewed, with the economics in the primary market typically being 10 to 20 times more lucrative. Consequently, the analysts are being too heavily influenced by the primary business. The extreme competition for new issue mandates has led to the salaries of sell-side analysts being tremendously inflated and, at the same time, the mobility of these analysts has increased substantially. Perhaps as a consequence of this mobility or

otherwise, we often find that coverage is being dropped within 12 months of an issue, as the analysts are asked to focus on other stocks by their new employers. This causes us to review our relationship with the bank that lead managed a particular issue and who promised an ongoing research commitment. This trend is unfortunately getting worse every year. Consequently, we rely to the extent of at least 50 per cent on our own in-house research. We also increasingly make use of independent third party research. We find that most of the active new issue houses only pay lip service to providing an independent research product.'

Daniel Barker of GE Investments commented: 'We have learnt to treat all equity research from the investment banks with care, both the new issue research and the ongoing research in the secondary market. We know that a buy recommendation is not always what it seems – there are often ulterior motives connected to corporate finance business behind these buy recommendations.' Elisabeth Weisenhorn reflected: 'We typically consider the research view of the sell-side analyst as the best case scenario. Still, it does represent a starting point and a basis for discussion. One should not forget that the analyst on a new issue typically knows the business in much more detail than most fund managers will be able to do. Therefore, so long as we review the research carefully and critically it can be of major help for the understanding of the particular company.' Staehelin recommends a 'buyer beware' approach. He finds however that the research is more valuable in the secondary market than in the primary market. He commented: 'If there is a good relationship between the analyst and the fund manager then there are several ways in which the analyst can say 'watch out' to the fund manager without upsetting the companies.' Staehelin cited an example where the analyst said 'buy the convert' meaning don't buy ordinary shares. He reflected further: 'The fund managers on the other hand can't expect to get everything on a silver plate, they must learn to challenge the analysts to get out of them what they really believe. Fund managers should try to understand the earnings model of the analysts and then make their own assumptions. By the way, contrary to the view of many people, we appreciate the view of many local research analysts. We often find a lot of boilerplate in the pan-European industry research.'

It is a generally held view among fund managers that the US houses are the worst in terms of using equity research aggressively in the new issue market, but the European houses are catching on as they try to compete with the US houses.

If the lack of confidence among fund managers in primary market sell-side research is as fundamental as it appears, then it is important that companies and governments do not pay undue attention to the various published rankings of research analysts when awarding new issue mandates. Instead of relying on the rankings, vendors should themselves do due diligence on the strengths and weaknesses of the analysts of the potential lead manager candidates.

Pricing and underwriting structure

Opinion is divided among fund managers as to the merit of the bookbuilding pricing and underwriting mechanism. Some institutional investors find it fair enough as a pricing mechanism as it establishes a market price. Others are of the opinion that it is clearly to the advantage of the vendor and the banks as they have full transparency whereas the buyers do not. The offer price typically reflects aggressive marketing and maximised demand.

Matthew Beardmore-Gray, director of Prudential Portfolio Managers (part of PPM Worldwide) noted: 'Although the bookbuilding concept appears to be being adopted more widely throughout the world, we do find that there is a lot of gamesmanship involved. Many institutions bid at higher prices than they are willing to pay and for larger quantities of stock than they wish to own, in the full knowledge that they would never have to deal at these levels. In this context, we are therefore much more in favour of the type of auction that has been employed in the demutualisation of the UK building societies, whereby those that bid at higher prices actually have to pay higher prices, unlike the case in bookbuilding where ultimately everyone pays the same price. This concept certainly concentrates the mind. We realise that these transactions are special cases because the sale of shares in the market by former members of building societies received as part of the demutualisation process are deemed to represent secondary market transactions, but we believe this method could be used more widely.'

Most UK and European institutions are favourably disposed towards rights issues. Says Huw Jones of Prudential Portfolio Managers: 'We recognise merit in rights issues as we are very conscious of the higher fee structure associated with bookbuilt offers. Naturally as an existing shareholder we wish to avoid the transfer of value to new shareholders at the expense of the old ones. We support the recent changes to the UK underwriting level such that good companies will be able to have their issues sub-underwritten at a lower cost. We also support deeply discounted rights issues, but emphasise the responsibility of boards who must ensure that their capital raising plans enjoy shareholder support. It may well be in shareholders interests to disapply pre-emptive rights in order to sell shares to new investors who are prepared to pay an appropriate premium to the market price. The problem with many bookbuilt secondary offers is that the market price often falls during the marketing period and that the offer price is often set at a small discount to the market price. We are prepared to look at the merits of each individual case.'

Mercury Asset Management's Paul Marshall commented: 'We do not like pricing by Dutch auction, where all investors ultimately pay one and the same price, as it typically leads to inflated issue prices and bad after-market performance. Although it is slightly better, we also don't like bookbuilding that much and find that it is difficult to make money on bookbuilt issues. In fact, we prefer fixed price offers, as such a pricing method means that as an investor, you can exploit certain market inefficiencies.'

Marketing and sales

Institutions do not appreciate being pursued on an aggressive basis by the investment banks to buy new issues. They are generally approached by too many people and they find the banks far from impartial. One US fund manager noted: 'We are very practical, or perhaps I should say cynical, about the marketing process – that is to say we know how to see through the act.'

There are many specific concerns with regard to the marketing and sales processes:

- *Projections:* Jürg Tanner of Julius Baer commented: 'Whereas the documentation associated with these transactions is generally satisfactory, projections and business plans tend to be euphoric but rather vague. Lead managers tend to present new companies with a touch of over-enthusiasm. If, in a given offer, the lead manager's projections do not come true, as often experienced, the confidence not only in that lead manager, but also in the company concerned is clearly undermined. This can seriously affect the company's long-term relationship with the stock market.'

- *Time considerations:* Elisabeth Weisenhorn commented: 'These one-on-one meetings are typically too short. More often than not, one only spends 45 minutes with the company because they are late from an earlier meeting and there are too many bankers involved. These meetings should be at least two hours long and bankers are no longer invited to join.' Paul Marshall draws attention to two practical problems in connection with new issues: 'First, I find that in many cases we simply do not have enough time to do our homework on new issues, and we would very much appreciate it if companies and bankers could take that into account when designing the timetables for these issues. This concern is more relevant in connection with secondary issues as initial public offers are typically flagged a long time in advance. Ideally, we would like at least five working days between the time when we are first approached, and when we have to decide whether or not to buy the issue. The second concern is that we really do not want to be approached by more than two firms on the same new issue. This causes unnecessary confusion and is highly inefficient for the fund manager.'

- *Syndicate organisation:* Most fund managers consider it a nuisance to be approached by too many houses trying to sell an issue. Salesmen from the syndicate banks rush to be the first bank to call with information on a new issue thinking that that will increase the likelihood of getting an order. Nairn noted: 'We don't want to talk to 15 brokers, all of which are biased to a greater or lesser degree – two is quite enough.' Elisabeth Weisenhorn added: 'The marketing process has become too much. There are too many people involved selling too aggressively.'

- *Information transfer:* One factor often underestimated by new issue bankers is getting the marketing information to investors at the appropriate time – the logistics of the transaction. The logistics do not always work as smoothly as one would have reason to believe. Huw Jones explained: 'We would at least like to have the prospectus in good time before the one-on-one meeting, as we like to do our homework and take advantage of the short time with the management by asking a few important questions. Often, however, this does not appear to be possible and we don't always understand why. Is it because we are right at the beginning of the roadshow, because the lead-manger has simply been disorganised or because they prefer not to give it to us until the transaction has gathered a certain momentum? Ironically, if we have read the prospectus as thoroughly as we would like to and if the management is not prepared to allocate most of the time available to answering questions – sometimes they prefer to stick to the script rather than answering difficult questions – then we get very little out of the one-on-one meetings. It is clear that all fund managers have slightly different ways of doing things and slightly different requirements. Banks and companies are typically not at all good at anticipating this, which makes the information transfer much less efficient than it ought to be. Really, it ought to be the job of the financial adviser to get this right by tailor-making the presentations to a much higher degree.'

- *Information on the progress of transactions:* Many fund managers, even some of the biggest ones, claim that they do not get enough proper information about how certain deals are going. An improved information flow would be appreciated. Whereas syndicate officials to an extent have to keep the institutions guessing about the true level of demand for an issue as they try to create momentum and generate price tension between different investor groups, many fund managers have anecdotes about having been lied to concerning the true subscription levels of various issues, which is to mislead the market. The art lies in maintaining the highest ethical standards whilst still generating the right type of investor psychology.

- *Order-inflation:* One US fund manager comments on order-inflation: 'We only apply for stocks that we really like and in the quantities that we like. In any event, the banks know what our normal holding position is in a particular stock. There are, however, exceptions in the small and hot issues where we are sometimes advised by the banker to inflate our orders.' As far as order-inflation is concerned, it pays to be a good citizen: in the cases of a Repsol or Eni for example, many of those investors who inflated their orders in the first tranche, and then sold in the immediate after-market will have been identified, and will have been penalised in subsequent tranches.

Pricing

Elisabeth Weisenhorn explained: 'Unfortunately, in strong markets, many issues are priced off the back of too much hype. Momentum is built already at the pre-marketing stage, following which the price-range is set. During the roadshow and the bookbuilding further momentum is added and the price is more often than not set at the upper end of the price range. Accordingly, too often issues are being priced at a valuation which is not sustainable in the long term. In less bullish markets, this is less of a problem.'

Allocation and distribution of the selling concession

The allocation of securities to investors, and the designations by investors of the selling concession to banks, is a huge area of contention in the relationship between the fund manager and the banker.

Whereas the allocation process should be based on the aim of achieving the best long-term shareholder structure and after-market performance for a particular company, the reality is different because of its influence on the distribution of the economics of a transaction.

Fund managers often feel that they are treated badly in the allocation process and that the global coordinator effectively blackmails them into giving them their orders. Investors believe that if they give an order to a co-manager rather than to the global coordinator as a reward for good service, they will suffer in the allocation process. Jurg Tanner of Julius Baer commented: 'The fight for the total selling commissions among the managers in an offer is very intense. Whereas we support transparency in these offers and are happy to communicate to the bookrunner how we wish to recognise the contribution of various firms in an offer, it is our experience that bookrunners do not typically appreciate it if we designate a part of the total commissions associated with our order to managers other than themselves'.

One UK fund manager reports that in the case of the Deutsche Telekom IPO, some investors were told by one of the joint global coordinators that if they did not give the order and designations to them, then they would not be given a proper allocation. Another fund manager of a large continental European institution on a different occasion was told by one of the largest American investment banks: 'If you don't do business with us, then we will take you off our most favoured list.'

Most institutional investors feel that the bookrunner has too much say in the allocation process. The large institutions, however, have a significant leverage in the allocation process, particularly during weaker market conditions. Firstly, they are big buyers so they have clout as far as the investment bank is concerned. Secondly, companies want them on their share register and argue for them to get good allocations.

Beardmore-Gray of Prudential Portfolio Managers noted: 'Getting fair allocations is to a significant degree about stating your case. If we think that we have not been treated fairly in the preliminary allocation, then we will complain, but this does highlight the inherent lack of transparency in the allocation procedure.'

Isabel Goiri, director of Schroder Investment Management explained: 'There is a lot of talk about transparency in the new issue business but it is all in favour of the vendor. We have no transparency with regard to the allocation process, whether it works to our advantage as one of the largest investors or not.'

Jean-Marc Fraysse, director of Cazenove Unit Trust Management, underscored the importance of getting the allocation process right from the investor's point of view: ' Given the amount of time required for a fund manager to read the documents, see the bank's analyst and the company, it is essential that we get a decent allocation. If we only get a very small allocation, it may be tempting to sell in the after-market as we, like other fund managers, require a certain minimum holding to justify holding the stock in the long-term.' It is often advisable for bankers to allocate relatively full positions to a few fund managers and very little to others, rather than allocating too little to everyone with the result that no investor has been able to build up a core holding in the stock.

There are two ways to determine who gets the fees associated with a particular order: either they go to whoever gets the order or, as in the US, there is technically a 'pot'. Under the pot system, the order might be processed by the bookrunner, but the economics can be designated to a number of the syndicate members. Stephen Lowe thinks that the pot structure is a nightmare to administer and feels that it is very challenging to keep track of how much Gartmore pays its investment banks in any given year: 'It is sometimes also difficult to keep track of who is actually earning what in a transaction. From the investor's point of view the transparency is low.' Jean-Marc Fraysse added: 'The idea of assigning designations is a good one so long as it happens after the allocation process has been completed. However, in the real world, the allocation and designations are inextricably connected.'

Some investors feel that the pot structure (with designations) is a good one as it can send both positive and negative signals to a number of banks, hence offer a useful bridge into the day-to-day business in the secondary market.

Elisabeth Weisenhorn commented: 'We like designations as it allows us to settle through a single house – a huge advantage – whilst at the same time allowing us to indicate to the banks whether or not we think they are giving us a good service. By the way, it is important to check with the individual banks that the designations are actually handled as decided by ourselves. Needless to say, this is not always the case.'

There are many different views among fund managers about whether or not to look at the economics on a deal-by-deal basis or in terms of the overall business between the bank and the institution. Whereas the smaller fund managers tend to tackle fees on a 'deal by deal' basis, many of the big ones look at the value added by each bank/broker over the year as a whole and try to compensate each bank accordingly. This sometimes means that banks which are not involved in many of the big issues often get disproportionate designations in those issues where they do participate, as it represents a rare opportunity for the institution to pay the bank or a good economy market service. GE Investments' Barker commented: 'We have a points system and an annual budget for each bank/broker based on their performance and general level of service both in the primary and secondary markets seen as a whole. What this means is that if one bank has already made the total annual budget, then they may get no designations in a particular transaction, even if they are the bookrunner. This is in principle a good system because it ought to take away some of the deal pressures, except for the fact that many banks don't understand it – why otherwise would they so desperately try to be the first one to call on a new issue.'

Templeton Worldwide rewards on the basis of the overall group relationship over one year, with bi-annual reviews. The total value added by all the members of staff of a particular bank or broker is the yardstick used for remuneration and this value is determined by all the relevant personnel at Templeton casting votes. The Capital Group looks at the primary business on a deal-by-deal basis and awards points for performance over the year as a whole, whereby its analysts award up to 100 points per country. DWS on the other hand keep the primary and secondary market entirely separate.

Many fund managers – who hold the securities for the long-term – understandably feel that the investment bankers are more interested in getting the deal done than in the performance of the issues in the secondary market. They would therefore welcome performance-related pay. JP Morgan's Madsen says: 'The compensation system should incentivise bankers to do transactions that perform well. Equally, bankers should feel some pain if the issue performs poorly. Such performance-linked compensation needs to be properly structured and perhaps reflect both absolute and relative performance.'

After-market

As far as the investor community is concerned, what happens in the after-market is the decisive factor. Elisabeth Weisenhorn explained: 'We are sometimes given to understand that an issue has been successful because the allocation to end investors was restricted. What transpires after a while is that the issue was actually not at all well placed and that a long period is required to clear the market of the overhang of the unsold shares. If this is not misleading the market I don't know what is. When this happens, we put the bank responsible in the penalty box for a considerable period of time.'

Under normal circumstances, if a company doesn't deliver on the earnings forecast of the lead manager with respect to the first six to twelve months, then the lead-manger will come under substantial pressure from the institutions, as either the due diligence has been poor, or the lead manager has, for whatever reason, been too aggressive on the earnings forecast. Having said that, many experienced investment professionals don't particularly monitor the earnings forecast of the lead manager specifically as they tend not to believe them in the first place – a sad assessment of the role of the banks in these offers. Rather, fund managers first and foremost monitor the overall market consensus forecast and those of the main brokers to the company.

Despite repeated promises to the contrary, equity research coverage is often dropped when analysts move from one bank to another, or when the banks feel that there is no more potential for new issue business. Investors often get the impression that they have been subjected to a 'one night stand' as analysts drop coverage and bankers move on to the next deal. It is important to investors that the information flow keeps up after the deal has been done. Investment banks don't always provide secondary market liquidity as they promise either: beware of a bank that says 'we will make a market for our clients'.

Reputation of the investment bank

To many fund managers, the reputation of the lead manager does not appear to make a significant difference to their decision as to whether or not to buy a new issue. Most fund managers interviewed for this chapter felt that the reputation of the lead manager was only 'reasonably important'. Some of those who answered 'not important' qualified the statement by suggesting that it was important that the lead manager was one of the top firms. However, the relative indifference as to the choice of lead manager appears to correlate with the fact that many fund managers don't trust the bankers and the equity research analysts of the investment banks.

How important is the reputation of the lead manager/ global coordinator for your investment decision?

4	Very important
12	Reasonably important
4	Not important

Number of responses: 20.

Total votes add up to the total number of investors polled

Few fund managers actually notice a marked difference in the after-market price performance of issues lead managed by the different houses, a fact which contradicts a substantial part of the marketing myth of the top equity houses. A senior US fund manager noted: 'It really doesn't matter who the lead manager is – there actually is no franchise – it is more a question of personalities, but then again bankers move around so fast that it is difficult to build a lasting relationship with any one firm. We try to keep track of some good individuals that we can trust. There are very few exceptions to this negative picture. JP Morgan is one such bank. They have an excellent reputation and do things the proper way.' Nairn added 'After all we are buying the issue not the lead manager, aren't we?'

Certain fund managers have 'A' lists and 'B' lists, whereby the 'A' list consists of a top tier of banks which they trust more than the others. Some fund managers simply won't deal with certain houses, while other experienced fund managers deal only with certain individuals that they trust and are less interested in the firm itself.

Madsen reported: 'We do consider it important who the lead manager is. The bigger the firm the better for us because we have more leverage with the bigger firms, given the amount of business that we do in a number of areas. The reputational risk is too high for the big firms to have anything go wrong.'

When asked what distinguishes a good investment bank from a bad one in terms of the new issue market, the response typically involves at least one of the following answers:

- The honesty and integrity the key people involved; the thoroughness of the due diligence process and how upfront they are with the risks at every level; how tough the particular bank is on corporate governance, fiduciary and accounting issues; how well they explain the main profit drivers of the business and how they anticipate investor questions at the roadshow;
- A good investment bank is one with a sensible flow of high-quality offers: the result of intense competition between banks in the new issue market means that a number of issues come to the market that should not do so, as they do not meet the minimum quality criteria; and
- How the banks act in the market prior to the pricing of the issue: some fund managers claim to notice that certain banks, in particular American banks, drive up the share price in advance of new issues for egotistical reasons and to earn higher fees. Sometimes this starts during the solicitation phase whereby banks put out strong buy recommendations and push the price in order to demonstrate their market clout in the particular stock.

How banks price and allocate issues and how they handle the after-market are also critically important factors to establishing a 'good' reputation.

'What matters most as far as we are concerned', commented one UK fund manager: 'is that bankers are honest – that they do not lie about how a particular issue is doing, as is not infrequent – that they do a proper due diligence and that they conduct themselves professionally overall. There really ought to be an opportunity for a bank, which wanted to stand out in terms of honesty, integrity and overall level of professionalism. As it is now, everybody is sinking down and nobody is rising up. I guess there are too many young people in the business. Qualities such as trust and consistency are rare.'

Anthony Regan added: 'The large institutions, I am sure, would finance a serious firm who wanted to get into the market by offer an excellent service with a credible sales and research effort. There is definitely room for a firm like that and it is most likely to be one outside the group of the top five banks. '

The role of the new issue market in institutional investment

Despite the fact that investors have strong views on the new issue market, the fact is that the primary market is not that important to most fund managers. Investment performance is only dependent to a limited extent on the new issue market. However, the US IPO market is important due to the supply of exciting new companies coming to the market, particularly in the technology, media and pharmaceuticals sectors.

How important is the equity new issue business for the way you run your business?

2	Very important
4	Rather important
14	Not that important
2	Not at all important

Number of responses: 22.

Total votes add up to the total number of investors polled.

The principal reasons that institutions participate in the new issue market are:

- In order to buy size, to get one time liquidity in a stock they want to own, ie, to build a core holding without driving up the price;
- To gain exposure to a new company in a sector, or to an entirely new sector. This approach is particularly relevant in emerging-market investment;
- Country funds come under pressure to buy stocks such as Deutsche Telekom or Telefónica due to their heavy weighting in the local index. Per Ström, head of equity investment with Swedish insurance company Trygg-Hansa remarked: 'The new issue market is neither more nor less

important than the secondary market as we review each investment opportunity according to our investment criteria; If it is an index stock, we would buy it automatically for our index portfolios. Half of the equity portfolio of Trygg-Hansa Life is indexed.';

- Many fund managers regard participation in the primary market as a means of paying banks and brokers who provide them with good secondary market service throughout the year;

- Investors also participate on an opportunistic basis: fund managers buy when a stock seems undervalued or otherwise appears to be a good opportunity to make some quick money. For instance, according to Staehelin: 'The primary market is no more or no less important to us than the secondary market. As a bottom-up driven investor, we always try to find undervalued companies for our clients, and investment bankers try to achieve at least fair, if not top, value for their clients. Still, we often find good opportunities in the primary market.'

Richard Foulkes reported: 'In our business, the new issue business really is not that important, despite our considerable size. In the case of IPOs, we often find that we do not have enough information, and there is often not much of a track record, so that in the end we cannot really take a view on some of these companies. As long-term, bottom-up investors concerned with the quality of the companies we invest in, we have found that we can afford to wait until the company has established a certain track record.'

Pierre Daviron, president of Oppenheimer Capital International with US$50 billion under management added: 'It is hard to find value in new issues, as they are by definition heavily marketed. Furthermore, in terms of our core list, we research on a fundamental basis a total of 240 companies globally, not more and not less. Any new issue, if not already on our list, would have to replace an existing name and this is kind of difficult. In total, there are only 25–30 new names added to our list each year.'

Robert LaFleur, senior vice president and chief investment strategist of Northern Trust in Chicago with US$35 billion of equities under management reported: 'For several reasons, the international new issue market is not that significant for us. We are relatively small as far as international equity investment is concerned and our investment style reflects our client base, which is conservative. We typically only invest in listed ADRs of big capitalisation stocks that are high-quality growth companies. We would very rarely invest in companies with a market capitalisation of less than US$500 million. The bad issues nobody wants to have, and of the good ones, we typically get too small an allocation to make it worthwhile. How do you allocate 50,000 shares over 8,000 individual portfolios? Furthermore, we believe that the privatisation game is nearly over and we find that the big new issue houses, with only few exceptions, publish too much of what I would refer to as new issue research.'

Lessons for company executives

Many seasoned investment professionals only deal with certain people in the banking community, who they feel they can

trust. Some fund managers blacklist certain banks, even some of the top ones while other investors blame themselves for not punishing companies and bankers sufficiently for bad performances and broken promises. Instead of boycotting those companies and banks, they are sucked into buying the next issue.

Most fund managers consider that the banks work primarily for the vendors and point out that the banks have to be very careful not to lose their credibility with the investment community. Given that most fund managers are sceptical about the new issue market, companies either considering becoming a publicly owned company, or having already made an IPO would be well advised to note the following:

- Ensure that you understand the institutional investor perspective and recognise that there is considerable tension between the investment banks and investors. Bear in mind that the institutions are your potential long-term shareholders;

- Having made an issue, take control of the secondary market: develop a direct relationship with as many of your large shareholders as possible, listen to them to see how they regard your business generally and what their needs are in terms of information, dialogue, etc. As you cannot typically cater for all of these institutions yourself, you must reach many of the smaller and medium-sized institutions through the analyst community. Consequently, it is also important to develop strong personal relationships with a significant number of analysts. Remember that the credibility of the analyst community is much higher in the secondary market than in the primary market;

- Remain proactive in your investor relations effort, in terms of mailings, one-on-one meetings, conference calls, investor conferences, etc. Make sure that investors and analysts have good access to the company and, if appropriate, obtain the help of investor relations consultants. Work on your disclosure standards, in terms of your annual report and your interim reports: try to report quarterly, or at least as often as your peers. The market continues to demand improved disclosure so you will gain credibility for being at the forefront of the trend: provide investors with the information that they require but don't bury them under an avalanche of unwanted paper; and

- Adopt a conservative attitude which will enable you to deliver on your promises. Nothing creates a stronger share price than if you can gain a reputation for being conservative. Try to match or beat the market's expectations: if you foresee problems meeting the market's expectations, advise the market immediately. Companies can build more credibility during times of a crisis than when things go well as Richard Watt, a fund manager with BEA Associates pointed out: 'We consider this a *quid pro quo* for giving our money to people to employ in their business.' Huw Jones added: 'The best advice that I can give to companies coming to the market for the first time is not to over-egg expectations. If you do, you will find it virtually impossible to sustain your credibility in the equity market. Company directors who lose credibility in the equity market often find that their jobs can be lost as well.'

Getting the offering process right – the Art of the Deal

Drawing extensively from the experience gained by hundreds of people in the 24 financings analysed in the case studies, this chapter attempts to summarise the key lessons and examine them in the context of the offer process. This chapter is therefore a guide for vendors, be they companies, governments or other private vendors how to conduct an offer and pitfalls to avoid. It is also intended to give the other parties involved in an equity transaction, ie, bankers, investors and other professional advisers, an insight into how these deals should best be done. The focus of the book is on getting the offer process right, and this chapter sets out to make the essentials available to the reader.

Preparation of assets for sale and appointment of parties

Fund managers often feel that companies come to the market before they are ready. This is the case with many privatisations where politicians dictate the timetable and where banks feel compelled for competitive reasons to recommend that the company do a deal as soon as possible.

Experience shows that the most successful issues are those where a good management has been in place for some time and has been allowed to restructure the business and prepare for the market debut. Not only will the business be in better shape but the management will have a track record to demonstrate on the roadshow. Quality of management is one of the most important criteria by which fund managers assess investment opportunities, so the importance of appointing a high-quality management at an early stage cannot be too strongly emphasised.

The process of preparing for and executing an international equity offer is frequently underestimated. Global equity transactions are much more complex than most people initially assume, and by the time they appreciate this fact, it is often too late. Inexperienced people should realise that this is a technical and highly specialised field and be prepared to listen to advice, even if it sometimes comes from overly aggressive bankers. The difference between a well prepared offer and a badly prepared one can be reflected in a significant difference in the share price and the valuation of the company. Although highly competitive and for the most part professional, this market is in many ways also unsophisticated, and

human egos and errors play a large part. Large equity offers are gigantic logistical challenges and many things can and do go wrong. The vendor needs to stay on top of the entire process and recognise that it is only possible to have a successful issue if there is absolute commitment from the top of the company and from the vendor. The success of international equity offers comes down to planning, organisation and hard work.

Key decisions

The first decisions are the most important, when the foundations are laid for success or failure. They include: what to sell, how much to sell, who is going to run the sale, how (not just how much) the bankers are going to be compensated and what the overall rules of engagement for the key bankers and advisers are. Furthermore, it must be decided what type of pricing/underwriting structure will be employed: whether it will be a US public issue or private placement and what the key timing and timetable considerations are. Once the process is underway, other considerations take over: how much will be available to sell in each region; how the company's strategy should be articulated; how the offer will be marketed; what the dividend policy should be; what level of disclosure is acceptable; what anti-takeover provisions are to be put in place and what is the best conservative estimate of future earnings. The final decisions include exact sizing, pricing and allocation.

For privatisations, the regulatory regime and the industry structure must also be decided on, and the degree and nature of continued government involvement settled. Specific decisions include: state board representation; proportion of issue to be sold to retail investors; the type and price of retail incentives, and additional anti-takeover provisions such as a golden share or core shareholders.

Appointment of parties

Hiring, managing and incentivising an investment banking team is often more difficult than most inexperienced vendors assume. Lawyers, accountants and marketing advisers must also be found.

The global coordinator

Selecting the appropriate bankers is one of the most important decisions. There are at least six basic criteria worth applying when selecting the global coordinator:

- *Track record:* The bank's overall market position, its credibility in the local market, in a particular industry sector and with regard to the particular type of equity financing are all good indications of its track record;

- *Commitment:* The bank's commitment to the vendor and offer itself is vital. The vendor must therefore know how important the deal will be to the bank, and it may help if there is an established relationship between the vendor and the bank. The length of time that the bank has been pursuing the mandate and how professional the solicitation process has been is a good indicator of how serious they are about the deal. The bank's supportiveness in a crisis must be gauged, and commitments should be given in writing as to how they would react in such a situation so that there can be no misunderstanding;

- *Secondary market presence:* Any global coordinator should be active in the secondary market, ie, in sales, trading and research. In an IPO it is important that the global coordinator has a strong trading presence in the relevant industry sector and country, as both of these are important in establishing credibility with institutional investors. In a secondary offer the global coordinator should be one of the largest traders in the stock and investors must be regularly updated with research;

- *Quality of the working team:* The quality of the working team fielded by the bank is vital. The team leader and his team must be trustworthy: individuals are often more important than the institution itself. The fact that the team leader is respected within the bank means that he can fight (and win) battles on behalf of the vendor. It is important to be allocated the A-team and to know that those individuals will stay until completion. The members of the working team should interact well with the vendors, the domestic bankers, and other advisers as well as with one another. The equity research analyst is a crucial member of the team in two respects: he is the person to whom the team will turn to find out how investors judge the story and how they value the company. He is also the chief salesman for the entire syndicate. The success or failure of a potential global coordinator's recent deals can be a significant influence on the investor view of an offer. In addition it is important that the firm is doing well overall and is free of undue turbulence and staff turnover. The vendor would like to be assured that the working team members will be employed for the duration of the offer and preferably be available for some time after its completion;

- *After-sales service:* After-sales service can be of enormous importance if something goes wrong in the after-market: the global coordinator should continue to pay careful attention to the company once trading has started. It is important to know that they are not going to move onto the next deal immediately, leaving the offer unsupported; and

- *Reputation as effective partners:* Bankers should also be selected according to their reputation as effective partners in transactions. While the way banks work together is fairly standardised in the US, this is not so elsewhere. Banks are often put in uncomfortable and confusing positions by inexperienced vendors who appoint too many parties without telling them exactly what to do. This can lead to considerable infighting among banks, which is both time-consuming and unconstructive. Bankers who have a good reputation for finding constructive ways of cooperation are of great value. The domestic banks must be involved, and the global coordinators must earn their respect and work closely with them, as without the full support of the domestic lead manager, the after-market will suffer. Foreign and domestic banks should discuss valuation, sizing of the total offer and tranches, timing, pricing and all the other crucial decisions. This requires a certain type of individual at the foreign bank who is knowledgeable and competent, yet humble and flexible. It is always helpful if the global coordinator is in a position to indicate who they want to work with as domestic and foreign lead managers. Effective communication between all parties is crucial. Only those who are good communicators should be asked to play leading roles in complex processes of this kind.

In order to select the most appropriate global coordinator it helps to talk to other vendors who have used these firms, and have personal experience of working with key members of the proposed teams. Multiple meetings with the whole working team, including the equity research analyst, may be useful before making the final decision. The analysts' track record in research calls on other companies in the industry sector should be examined, as well as whether they have experience conducting successful new issues, and whether this success has carried through to the secondary market. Whilst doing corporate finance work, analysts should remain independent in their recommendations. This due diligence on the research analysts will prove more valuable in establishing their credibility with institutional investors than their rankings in polls. It is better to interview fewer banks and research them thoroughly than to examine many banks superficially. A meeting with the senior management of the bank or banks under consideration should also be proposed.

Unless an offer is very large or prestigious, the level of fees being considered should not be too low. Paying a little more than other vendors may prompt a move further up the priority list, resulting in a better team and better execution. The difference in the quality of the execution team can easily make a more significant difference on the issue price net of fees than the reduction that might be achieved through tough fee negotiations. The question of what is paid relative to the rest of the market should be considered independently of the fees in absolute terms, as anyone going to the market will pay more or less the market rate. It should be recognised that it is what you receive in net proceeds rather than what you pay in fees that matters for the long-term cost of capital. It is crucial to have a complete understanding of the structure and dynamics of the economics in order to get maximum leverage out of every dollar of fees paid. The compensation should be structured in such a way as to avoid excessive competition and constant infighting among the senior banks in the transaction. Ideally, the structure of the economics should promote cooperation within the syndicate. One way to do this is to structure the transaction with equal economics between the global coordinators.

Appointment of an independent adviser

The increasing popularity of the bookbuilding process has brought with it a corresponding increase in transparency, which in turn has meant that the global coordinator has become more powerful. Furthermore, an increasing amount of work is required to meet ever more demanding disclosure requirements and to maintain credibility with investors. Only the global coordinator is really capable of achieving this through the due diligence process, and the other senior banks therefore tend to focus more on their own transactions. The major reason for engaging an independent adviser is to offset the huge power vested in the global coordinator.

An independent adviser should assist the management in picking a global coordinator, in negotiations with the global coordinator concerning the structure of the syndicate, in drawing up the terms of reference for the global coordinator and the entire syndicate, and in helping the management understand and cater for the many conflicts of interest that arise throughout the preparation and execution process. It is important that the entire syndicate is motivated and fairly compensated for effort and achievement: the global coordinator must be able to justify the commitment of all its relevant resources to the transactions, and syndicate banks should be fairly compensated for effort and achievement. The adviser should work out in advance the amount of money that the different levels of syndicate banks will stand to make, given different allocation assumptions. If the sums are too small in comparison to the value that they are asked to add to the transaction, then there may be too many banks in the syndicate. The adviser must take into account the fact that most global coordinators, once they have a mandate, will pay only lip-service to the idea of fair economics, particularly once they are confident that the offer will be successful.

It is not in the interest of either the issuer or the vendor for the global coordinator to take too large a proportion of the total economics (the combination of underwriting fee, management fee and selling concession). Full value for money is unlikely to be achieved if as much as 80 or 90 per cent of the total fees ends up with the global coordinator. Although privatisations are different, it is not a coincidence that the global coordinators do not usually take more than 20–40 per cent of the total economics in a large privatisation. In a large issue with multiple regional lead managers, it is important that the regional and co-leads can also make a decent amount of money, otherwise they will not allocate enough resources to the offer.

Investment bankers are motivated by two things: by doing a good deal, which becomes an important reference for further business, and by maximising their fees. Therefore, when vendors work with advisers they should not always assume that the bankers will be looking for the easiest way out (for example on pricing). Investment banks risk their reputations in every transaction, and in most cases will try hard to get it right: a possible exception to this is if the bank has been working too long on a mandate and is keen to be paid. However,

since the sums at stake are huge and the personal compensation of the individual banker may depend to a large extent on the economic success of the offer, once success is assured, the banks will quickly focus on how to maximise their own economic take. This is not in the interest of the vendor, or of the other syndicate banks. Neither is it in the interest of institutional investors who often want to use the allocation and designation processes to reward banks other than the global coordinator for a good overall service.

There are several ways in which the global coordinator can optimise its economics and vendors should be aware of the most important ones. The most significant conflicts of interest surround the way in which the three components of total commissions are distributed between the global coordinator and the rest of the syndicate. The global coordinator and the other senior syndicate banks should not take too high a proportion of the total underwriting at the expense of the other syndicate members, as this will not only have an impact on the underwriting fee but also on the management fee. In the case of a pot structure this will also affect the fixed portion of the selling concession. As far as the management fee is concerned, the praecipia paid to the global coordinator and the lead managers (including the global coordinator) for their management roles should not be too high. With regard to the selling concession, the global coordinator should not be allowed to monopolise the entire marketing effort and in the process decide unilaterally on the allocation to end investors.

Syndicate

There should be a specific reason for the inclusion of each and every bank in the syndicate. They are usually included because of their regional, country or industry strengths; they may have a highly respected industry analyst, particular placement power and overall credibility in a region. To ensure the maximum success of the offer, it is vital to resist the temptation to appoint banks purely for relationship reasons. These banks may be of value to the company overall but are unlikely to add value to the offer. It is important to have a small syndicate with a high degree of motivation, as large syndicates with many free-loaders create frustration and disappointment on all sides. A small syndicate facilitates communication and coordination within the syndicate and to the market at large.

Motivation of syndicate

Given the conflicts of interest referred to above, consideration must be given to how bankers can be incentivised and motivated. This can be done by ensuring up front that all banks will be able to earn a minimum fee, that the regional lead managers and the co-lead managers know that they have a say and that their work is appreciated by the vendor. There should be some direct dialogue with these banks, although too much vendor communication with banks below the level of global coordinator can undermine the global coordinator's authority: conversely, if the regional leads and co-leads are approached only through the global coordinator, valuable information and motivation may be lost. In addition to the remarks on economics above, capping the global coordinator's portion of the selling concession should be considered. There should be no more than two global coordinators, as the more there are, the longer the preparations take. The market spots vendor weakness and normally demands a price, meaning that market opportunities are often missed. The best example is the 1995 offer for Indonesian company PTT Telekom which had four domestic and four international global coordinators and which was an altogether messy affair until the eventual successful execution.

Lawyers and accountants

The decision as to which lawyers to use can be almost as important as picking the right bankers. The lawyers do a lot of the work including the due diligence, part of the structuring work and all the documents, including the prospectus. Ultimately it is the company's counsel that protects it against liability and looks after its best interests. Many of the criteria for selecting a legal counsel are similar to those applied to the selection of bankers.

It is crucial that the particular partner with whom ultimate responsibility for the offer lies has experience representing companies in the relevant industry and with the particular type of offer, that he is a strong personality who can lead large meetings in an efficient and pragmatic way, and that he has good inter-personal skills. He should also have the necessary resources, and it is vital that he does not have too many other commitments.

The right accounting firm is also important, particularly if the offer requires the inclusion of a reconciliation with a second set of accounting standards such as IAS or US GAAP, or if there are significant corporate developments with complex accounting implications. Many institutional investors are happier if there are two accounting firms, not just in the case of the offer, but on an ongoing basis.

After the solicitation process is over it is important to forget everything the bankers have said: those that have been solicited, in particular company management, the government if applicable, and other vendors, have been told how great they are, how good the company story is and how relatively straightforward it will be to execute the particular issue. Only after the mandate is awarded, will the true challenges be discussed in a more objective fashion, as banks have learnt through bitter experience that mandates are not won by stressing the difficulties. The whole truth is therefore not revealed until after the mandate is awarded.

Preparation of the offer

Rationale and objectives

In order to communicate effectively with the investment bank and with the market it is important to be able to articulate clearly the objectives of the offer and the rationale behind it. The long-term international equity strategy should also be considered, including future equity financing needs and the related requirement to build up certain shareholder bases.

Timing and timetable issues

Timing and timetable issues are often underestimated and should receive full attention at an early stage. Some aspects can be influenced, but others are beyond the control of the vendor. In most cases the timing can be influenced only in terms of which year or half year the offer comes to the market. This is of crucial importance in relation to the business cycle, operating results, corporate developments and share price. The company or vendor will be judged on how this aspect is handled. Then there is the issue of fixing the timetable, including the roadshow and pricing: although this can be influenced, there is less flexibility than is often assumed, and the importance of having adequate time to prepare should never be underestimated. The question of whether or not the timing is likely to be good is to a large a extent a question of luck. It depends on general market conditions, the new issue calendar, specific developments in the industry sector (eg, legislative or regulatory changes) and corporate developments (eg, positive or negative geological discoveries for a mining company). Once the timetable for a major offer is fixed it is very difficult to fine-tune it, although it is somewhat easier in an open-priced bookbuilt offer than in a fixed-price issue.

Primary or secondary IPOs

The dynamics of a primary sale are very different from those prevailing in a secondary sale. If the proceeds go to the company, the management is likely to be motivated to try its hardest in terms of the quality of the due diligence, the prospectus and the investor presentation. It will therefore achieve the highest possible price. On the other hand the vendor of a large shareholding in a publicly traded company is dependent on the cooperation of the company. The relationship between vendor and company is not usually straightforward, and the success of a secondary IPO therefore depends on delicate negotiation involving give and take on both parts, legal rights notwithstanding. It is important to define up front the relationship between the vendor and the company, and to reflect the division of labour in a memorandum of understanding between the vendor and the company. In most secondary IPOs the reward system has traditionally been designed so that the management will benefit if the stock price rises from the flotation price. Consequently the management will, from the outset, be more cautious about the prospects of the business and will attempt to avoid a high offer price. In a secondary sale, whether or not it is a privatisation, there need to be special incentives to motivate the management to maximise proceeds. These incentives, provided by the vendor, should encourage a higher offer price to link the interests of the vendor and the management more closely. Such an approach should be balanced with long term incentives so as not to encourage the management to oversell. A wholly different approach to the motivation of management is to restructure what is naturally a secondary sale to a primary sale by declaring an extraordinary dividend in advance of the sale, or to load the company with debt repayable to the vendor and then let the company be the issuer. All steps would close simultaneously and be contingent upon the successful closing of the equity offer in order not to weaken the credit quality of the company. This approach is likely to have substantial motivational advantages, although the vendor will lose some control over the process.

Pricing and underwriting methods

Traditional domestic ways of issuing equity are being challenged and gradually replaced by global issuing methods and techniques. American techniques are increasingly being adopted as US investment banks, US institutional investors and US stock exchanges are becoming ever-more important for non-US companies. The fact that the global equity market is Americanising will challenge cosy relationships and vested interests in the domestic markets around the world, and require dramatic and painful change. Those countries whose financial establishments resist this trend are likely to be less successful in the quest for long-term low-cost international equity capital.

Bookbuilt offer

The open-priced, best efforts pricing and underwriting structure (bookbuilding) is now increasingly widely recognised as the preferred way of selling equity. The sooner companies, investors, investment banks, legislators, stock exchanges and securities regulators around the world recognise this, the sooner local market practices can be harmonised with international standards and companies in those jurisdictions can access low-cost international capital. There are critics of bookbuilding – corporate and state vendors are of the view that all the risks stay with the seller, while many investment institutions maintain that the balance of power is skewed in favour of the investment bank and the vendor. The employment of bookbuilding across the globe does not mean that vendors cannot and should not, when circumstances so require, ask their banks to provide hard underwriting at a suitable discount to the proposed offer price (or market price) in order to guarantee a minimum level of proceeds.

Rights offers

Pre-emptive rights are fundamental rights that will remain in many markets. However it is important that companies are given enough flexibility to waive these rights when the situation so warrants. This quest for flexibility has meant that the power of pre-emptive rights have been eroded in countries such as Switzerland and Germany in recent years. Even in the UK there have been some changes in the way that rights offers are sub-underwritten and more changes are likely to come. The major drawback of the rights issue structure is that it is less effective at targeting new shareholders than is a bookbuilt offer. It may however be the most efficient way of reaching existing shareholders, although this does not stimulate an expansion of the shareholder base and, one could argue, the maximisation of the value of the company.

Managed rights offers

This hybrid structure combines elements of a traditional rights issue and a bookbuilt (or marketed) offer. It is complex and opaque but should lead to increased demand tension and a better end result for the company. It is most suitable in situations where one or a few large shareholders declare upfront that they do not intend to take up their rights, making a specified quantity of rights available for the marketing syndicate to sell to new investors.

Dutch auction

This structure is likely to become less and less frequent in cross-border offers, as it carries a high risk of hype with resulting over-pricing and the inevitable consequence of a disappointing after-market performance. This is particularly likely at the time of a strong market where investors buy securities for reasons other than fundamental ones. The main difference between a bookbuilt offer and a Dutch auction is that in the latter, allocation of shares is based solely on price and not on investor quality.

Bought deals/accelerated global tender

In recent years, bought deals and other structures that combine elements of bought deals and open-priced bookbuilding – such as accelerated global tenders, have become increasingly popular with vendors. The main advantage of these structures are the speed of execution and the lack of need for time-consuming due diligence and documentation: even governments have jumped on the band-wagon. These structures have been promoted by capital-strong universal banks which have bought investment banks and want to take market share: they are capital intensive, carry low returns, are risky for the banks and can have substantial negative consequences for the companies. Although their emergence is to an extent a reflection of a bull-market environment, for the right companies and right situations they will represent a valid alternative way of issuing equity.

Selecting pricing and underwriting methods

When selecting the pricing and underwriting method and the offer structure (ie, the syndicate and tranches) a few important principles are of particular importance. The first is that you cannot bypass the domestic market in a global equity offer, especially not when there is also a domestic offer: the domestic and international offers of a global transaction must either be completely separate or completely integrated. Furthermore, for simultaneous domestic and international offers, particularly for companies that are unknown, untried and untested in the international market, it should be the domestic market that sets the pace. The second important principle is to create competitive tension between the different investor bases in the offer: ideally a sense of scarcity should develop. By bringing competing pools of capital into play, you deprive a single constituency of investors of dominant pricing power. This principle works between institutional investor bases and between institutions and retail investors alike. Another key principle is to maintain the flexibility to take decisions on sizing (total offer and tranche sizes), timing and pricing as much as possible and as late as possible in an offer.

All the latest structural innovations are employed in privatisations, and often result from the presence of several global coordinators, at least one independent adviser and perhaps most importantly, an experienced and strong vendor. Corporate vendors should therefore study the structure of privatisations to help bridge a portion of the informational disadvantage vis-à-vis the global coordinator, and create a stronger position in negotiations with bankers.

Other preparatory steps

Due diligence

The due diligence process, particularly if done according to best practice, typically represents the single biggest challenge for first time issuers. The process is most often underestimated, or even resisted, by company management, which can be extremely counterproductive as the quality of the due diligence has a decisive impact on the quality of the execution of the offer. If the corporate finance team of the investment bank, together with the underwriters' counsel, have performed a high quality due diligence, this soon becomes apparent to all concerned and substantial incremental confidence will be transmitted to the ECM department, the salesforce and investors. The responsible ECM professional(s) will feel more confident about pricing at a higher level and investors will, if they trust the bankers, take a more positive view with regard to the proposed investment. In selecting bankers, it is important to look at the reputation of the bank, in particular in relation to its track record in due diligence.

For a company doing US style due diligence for the first time a lot of questions will come up that the management may never have had to think about in such detail before. All processes, procedures and systems are challenged and often compared to those of the issuing company's competitors. The issuer has to explain why it is doing certain things and not others. Companies who have gone through the process stress the absolute importance of getting organised in advance. It is important to have a definite strategy and to have broad horizons, for example focusing more on the external environment in terms of what is happening in the industry, what the business opportunities are and what competitors are doing. In most cases it is advisable to field a team of people dedicated to the project so as not to disrupt the operating management of the company. In the end, most professional managements find the due diligence work productive and most rewarding for the future.

SEC registration/US listing

A US listing can – but not always does – make a big difference for non-US companies. Although all investment banks claim to offer only truly objective advice, this very often is not the case. Recommendations are frequently tainted by the overriding consideration of getting the mandate and maximising the economics of the transaction. A US bank is therefore likely to recommend SEC registration and a US listing where a UK bank would not. If the vendor decides on a US listing, then it makes more sense to give the global coordinator mandate to a US bank. Furthermore, a US listing means that the US tranche is likely to be larger than it otherwise would be, hence making it possible for the US bank to earn more from the transaction. Whether or not to register with the SEC and to list on a US stock exchange is undoubtedly one of the most crucial decisions to take in connection with an international equity offer.

Although there is often no absolute right or wrong with respect to the US listing decision, if many or all of the following 10 criteria apply, then in the majority of cases a US listing should make sense:

- if the company has a large financing need or is subject to a large sale;
- if the company is in an industry that is well understood in the US and if there are sophisticated US based equity research analysts covering the industry sector;
- if the company is obviously undervalued against a truly representative peer group;
- if the traditional investor bases are fully weighted in the company's shares;
- if the company has a substantial and growing US business presence;
- if the company management is sophisticated and in a position to make the necessary commitment to a new and demanding investor base;
- if the company can offer enough US liquidity in its equity securities;
- if there is a need to change the management culture internally and the pressure from US investors in terms of disclosure and dialogue is thought to provide useful leverage for this change; and
- if the company's basic accounting is in good shape.

Documentation

Even if the legal and regulatory constraints associated with a prospectus – supposedly a marketing document – are fully appreciated by investors, prospectuses are increasingly perceived as a legal nightmare for all but the lawyers who write them. Most investors find them difficult to read – in fact the majority of investors probably do not read much more than the cover page and the very beginning of the prospectus. The investor view is that there is limited useful content for the investment decision, the profit drivers are not easily found and the risks very often not highlighted. Given that investors rarely find the research reports provided by the syndicate banks objective and credible in terms of how the future is portrayed, this is quite a problem. What is clearly called for is a more user-friendly summary, more description of the business and the competitive environment, and more about the company's prospects.

Valuation and development of the story

It is during this phase that companies should pay particular attention to not becoming too much part of an obviously packaged story. Investment banks are great sales organisations and sometimes get too carried away with the task of describing the business and its prospects. Companies are portrayed in a favourable light relative to their peers in terms of the positioning of the story. The forecast based on discussions with the management is often more optimistic than the company can realistically be expected to deliver. A cyclical paper company may for example be positioned by the banker as a high-value added non-cyclical packaging company; a cyclical automotive company may be sold as a non cyclical engineering company.

Aggressive positioning can be achieved in several ways: first, the selection of the right comparables, second an unrealistic earnings forecast which will make the company look attractively valued against its peer group and third the unreasonable emphasis on certain valuation parameters, for example the use of price/cash flow instead of P/E when in fact the market values the company on the basis of the latter. Companies must try to fend off attempts by their bankers to oversell, which can be difficult for managements without stock market experience, particularly since, during the solicitation process, the banks have heaped compliments on them in order to get the mandate in the first place. This type of overselling, which most investment banks are accused of, can do very substantial long term damage to managements and cause them in some cases an irreparable loss of credibility.

Execution of the offer

Pre-marketing

As competition between banks intensifies not only in terms of getting the big mandates but also in terms of earning selling commissions in every transaction, fund managers are becoming increasingly frustrated with the pre-marketing process. The purpose of the pre-marketing process is for the bookrunner(s) to gain investor feed-back for the preliminary sizing and pricing decisions and to prepare the ground for the company roadshow by identifying suitable candidates for one-on-one meetings. However, this part of the execution process has increasingly become a battlefield for the banks, where the name of the game is to be the first house among many to contact important investors in the hope of receiving the highest possible share of the selling commissions. This is very disturbing for investors who do not want to talk to more than two or three banks about the same offer. What many investors fail to comprehend is that the equity sales community does not understand that this approach does not provide value to institutions, and that institutions typically remunerate banks in terms of overall performance in the primary and secondary markets. The global coordinator should therefore discipline the syndicate in such a way that not too many banks call on a single investor. Failure to do so can have a significant negative impact on the offer, possibly even an outright investor boycott. Some fund managers have become so fed up with aggressive pre-marketing calls that they have completely refrained from participating at the pre-marketing stage.

Marketing

Selling shares is not so different from selling other goods or services – it doesn't happen simply because the product is available on the shelf – it has to be actively promoted by persuading investors to consider the merits of buying or not buying. This may be sad news for those who argue that the market is perfect and efficient, but in reality, because the choice of investment is so broad, each name in the market has to compete for the attention of fund managers. In the case of retail investment, a high advertising budget and generous retail incentives in the 1996 Deutsche Telekom offer is an excellent example of the fact that a concentrated marketing effort can mobilise pools of capital which have hitherto remained dormant. On the institutional side, a powerful investment bank can, within a relatively short period of time, use intensive and skillful marketing to generate very substantial demand for a completely unknown name.

Notwithstanding the efforts of the bankers, it is the management that sells the shares through the company roadshow. The one-one-one meetings with the big institutions can be decisive in the success or failure of an offer. Institutional investors who meet the management in one-on-one meetings typically account for 50–75 per cent of the total institutional demand of an offer. Given that the management presentation is what really counts in selling equity new issues, it is striking that institutional investors only consider a small proportion of presentations to be good. The most common reasons for this include a lack of interesting content, bad preparation, bad delivery and overselling. Managers can be the best operators in the world, but if they are unable to explain their business to institutional investors they will not easily be able to sell equity. Companies wishing to build and sustain their credibility in the market should try to be honest in these meetings and resist the temptation to oversell. Whereas it is crucial to have done all the homework and have anticipated all the questions, experienced investors see through the act if the management is not genuine. Since most managements, egged on by their bankers, appear over-optimistic in these meetings, it can be highly constructive to be seen to be conservative. If investors get the impression that the company and the bankers are being conservative they are likely to pay more for the shares because they are more likely to trust the management.

Managements, assisted by their bankers, would be well advised to try to tailor-make the one-on-one meetings – at least for the largest investors – by attempting to ascertain what they know about the sector and the company and whether they are likely to have read the prospectus. Some fund managers are completely unprepared, others are highly prepared and only want to ask questions.

To give a good investor presentation requires tremendous preparation and modern management skills. Corporate executives should be prepared to accept help in this area, in whatever form suitable to the specific situation. To deny the need for help can be very costly for the company and all its shareholders. If the CEO has to take a course in effective public speaking, then so be it.

It is important to recognise that for most large institutional investors the new issue market is not a very important part of their business, not least because of their many negative experiences of buying hyped new issues. They approach the market with a great deal of scepticism, and if investment banks do not clean up their act, particularly in terms of the pre-marketing and marketing, there is an increasing risk that some of the large institutional investors will get together to coordinate sanctions against the new issue community. Whereas this is not likely to happen in bull markets, when the vendors and the banks have the upper hand, it may well happen when the market conditions are tougher and the institutions have more leverage over the banks. Such sanctions may be temporary, or in some cases may be of a more permanent nature. It is entirely possible that individual banks and certain offers, including privatisations, can be substantially affected by such measures. By way of an example, one major US institution is known to have reacted to poor due diligence and overaggressive marketing by requiring the lead-manger to buy back all the securities at issue price, against a threat that the failure to do so would mean that the investor would cease to do any further business with that bank. Investment banks may want to get together to coordinate the introduction of improved standards in the new issue market before they lose the investment community on a more permanent basis. Despite tough competition, it would be in their best interest to come up with something like a code of best practice. Investment banks have opinions about companies adhering to the highest corporate governance standards. Why then should the corporate and investment communities not require the same of the banks? Critics among institutional investors of the way that many banks handle the new issue business are of the view that one way to bring back soundness to this market is for vendors to pay a portion of the fees based on the after-market price performance of issues. This will force higher due diligence standards, more careful timing, a higher degree of cooperation among the syndicate banks, higher coverage of the stock in the after-market in terms of research and trading support etc. It would also force higher standards of company management as the bankers would be more cautious before backing a particular management for a particular fund raising.

Bookbuilding/pricing

During the roadshow the banks will take indications of interest from institutional investors at different prices within a defined price range, such that at the end of the marketing and bookbuilding period there is a proper demand curve. This demand includes orders from investors of varying quality. In most cases the serious long-term institutional investors dominate the book but there are also the so-called 'flippers', who only buy new issues with the objective of selling them the same day. However, in many cases, even the orders from allegedly serious institutions do not reflect the real demand to hold securities long term. As a result of this mixture of low- and high-quality demand, it is not uncommon for 20–30 per cent of the new issue to trade on the first day, sometimes more. Therefore it is essential that vendors are not overly impressed if the issue is two to three times subscribed at the upper end of the indicated price range as even if they are, it is by no means infrequent that such apparently oversubscribed issues trade down in the after-market. Vendors should therefore, in certain cases, resist the temptation to insist on pricing at the top of the pricing range. It is important to rely on the experience of the investment banks to judge the quality of each individual order and for each given increment in the proposed offer price, the extent to which potential after-market orders may be lost. It is not possible to negotiate with the capital market, ie, it does not pay to play hardball with the investment bank if a successful issue is required. Successful and powerful entrepreneurs are particularly guilty of this mistake as they are used to having their way and have difficulty in accepting that they are in fact dependent on a bunch of young and often relatively inexperienced traders. Once the offer has been priced and trading has begun, the market gives its verdict, by which time it is too late to do anything except for a certain amount of stabilisation in case of price weakness, which may or may not be sufficient to restore confidence in the issue. The effects of too aggressive pricing can snowball and haunt the company for years to come. Being modest on pricing – being long-term greedy instead of short-term greedy – pays unless it is the company's very last transaction. Investors will give the company credit for it and they have very long memories. When and if there is a problem in the future, the company will enjoy more credibility and trust. It is hardly a coincidence that it is often the least experienced managers who try to achieve the most aggressive pricing. When an issue is successful, the level of over-subscription becomes relatively meaningless, as people expect an excess of demand, and so swell the size of their applications, as the final allocation is related to the level of applications. Even substantially over-subscribed offers can trade poorly in the immediate after-market.

Allocation

This is one of the most contentious areas of the new issue process, for two primary reasons. First, in order for the investment bank to do a good job, sophisticated bookbuilding and allocation models notwithstanding, qualitative judgments on the part of a few people are what really matter. This is therefore not an objective process – it is really an art rather than a science. Second, and related to this, is the fact that the process is susceptible to abuse and manipulation. The global coordinator has tremendous power to decide which orders are good and which are not: it may, for example, be perfectly true that in some cases different orders from the same institution may not be of the same high quality. This does not mean, however (as global coordinators often argue) that the global coordinator's orders are always the best ones. Due to the way that the global coordinator tries to maximise its own economics by arm-twisting institutions in the allocation and designation processes, the other managers and institutional investors often feel hurt at the end of the process. The lack of clear and objective allocation criteria is one of the biggest frustrations for fund managers. The way in which different banks handle the allocation process is one of the main criteria by which global coordinators are judged by both their peers and investors. It is worth the company finding out in advance what reputation the proposed global coordinator has in this respect. Furthermore, the allocation process is an excellent opportunity for the company to get to know more about its future shareholders. Investment banks will often resist company participation in this process, but it is very much in the company's best interest to get involved.

Immediate after-market/ongoing secondary market

There is a considerable skill associated with the pricing, allocation and management of the immediate after-market. This is one of the areas where the extensive experience of the highest quality investment banks really matters. The art lies in ensuring that there are enough after-market orders from high-quality institutions to offset the inevitable sales orders. How the global coordinator handles the after-market during the first one to three days can be vital for the success of the ongoing trading. The global coordinator has to be seen to be in firm control, in order to create confidence that the issue will trade well in the short and medium term. At this stage there is little that the company can do, although its input is required when it comes to deciding whether or not the greenshoe should be exercised. In every offer structured with a greenshoe, there has typically been a degree of over-allocation amounting to at least the size of the greenshoe (usually 15 per cent). If the market is weak, the global coordinator simply buys shares in the market to stabilise the offer and the greenshoe is not exercised. If the after-market is strong and the market price is trading up from the issue price, then the global coordinator is not going to want to buy further shares in the market. Since the global coordinator has already sold short to the extent of 15 per cent, he needs the greenshoe to be exercised, with the issuer selling further shares (typically at issue price less full commissions or at issue price less selling commissions). Companies should be cautioned against deciding to exercise the greenshoe before it is absolutely clear that the after-market is strong enough to warrant this step. Investors are not amused by the extra supply if the consequence is a falling share price because the greenshoe has been exercised prematurely. Bankers are of course eager to cash the extra fees.

Once investors have passed judgment in the immediate after-market on quality of placement and pricing, the focus slowly switches back to the company. Having marketed the company's story, the management now has to begin the process of delivering on promises made during the roadshow. While many bankers are inclined to move on to the next deal, the management is now left to cope with the day-to-day pressures of the stock market. Good bankers will however stay in close contact with the company to provide support until the company management and the IR team have become familiar with their briefs.

As bankers and research analysts often fail to provide the appropriate leadership in the secondary market, companies are well advised to take charge of the secondary market by getting to know their largest shareholders and establishing direct contacts with them. Treating large shareholders with the same care as large suppliers and end-customers means that the company is more likely to enjoy trust and credibility in the equity market and ultimately a lower cost of capital. Sensitivity to investor requirements in terms of the information they need and the form in which they need it is also important.

The bankers to the issue feel particularly responsible for the share price performance in absolute and relative terms for at least the first 6–12 months. Good bankers also feel responsible for the company delivering at least on the first year profit forecast made in connection with the issue, as if that is not achieved, the quality of the due diligence will usually be questioned. Investors equally expect the company to deliver at least on the forecast for year one. Rather than simply looking at the global coordinator's forecast, which they in any event treat with caution, they will look at consensus earnings. For the company, it is therefore essential to match or beat the bookrunner's forecast made at the time of the offer (which should have been approved by the company). The importance of this notwithstanding, fund managers are amazed how many promises are made and broken by companies and bankers. Investors have long memories and by breaking promises, a company may lose important potential investors for ever. In the case of a company coming to the market for the first time, if investors buy they do so because they are giving an untested management team the benefit of the doubt. Credibility can only be built over time. The challenge lies not only in building credibility but also in sustaining it. Companies wishing to build up a good name in the equity market should do everything in their power to avoid embarrassing bankers, analysts and salesmen by producing lower than expected profits on the first reporting occasion following an offer. While this is always important, it is particularly so over the first 6–12 months following an offer. Analysts and equity sales people will try to avoid repeat embarrassment by one and the same company. They may stop recommending the purchase of certain shares, which may result in these shares trading at a considerable discount to its peers.

How do you maintain successful investor relations in the secondary market? In addition to delivering profits and dividends, the company must maintain the initiative vis-à-vis the stock market by communicating all adverse information immediately. It should be focused, and report only information that is of value to the recipient. Information should be reported consistently, and at regular intervals, and investors should have access to knowledgeable people who are authorised to talk, such that the company can respond to any queries within 24 hours. In order to build up trust, it is essential to report good and bad news on a completely honest basis. Only by being open and by adhering to a high level of disclosure standards will true confidence be established among investors. Those companies that tell investors what is going on should ultimately trade better than highly secretive companies.

Conclusion

The global equity new issue market is a dynamic and intensely competitive area of banking. Whether the market is measured by the ownership of national equity markets, by the distribution of global equity offers or by the operations of the major banks, it is truly global. It is also one of the most important areas of investment banking, with the top investment banks deriving from 25 to 40 per cent of their revenues from the equity product, of which probably more than 50 per cent comes from new issues. The margin earned in the equity new issue business is between 2.5 and 5 per cent, whereas M&A generates between 0.5 and 1 per cent, and the bond business scarcely more than 20 or 30 bp.

Supply and demand factors in market development

The annual volume in the cross-border equity new issue market has increased by over 200 per cent in the past five years. Behind this headline figure lie new geographic sectors, new industries and new issue structures. In 1991, issuers in the cross-border market came from 34 countries; 64 countries were represented in 1996.

A thriving continental European corporate IPO market is beginning to emerge, and has grown much faster during the 1990s than in the US. In 1996, the European IPO market was worth US$34 billion, 70 per cent more than the US IPO market.

The growth in European IPOs was fuelled by privatisations in the early nineties, but latterly corporate IPOs have

made a more important contribution to overall market growth.(see Exhibit 7.1).

The potential for further growth in the European IPO market is evident from the fact that the ratio of equity market capitalisation to GDP is still very low in countries such as Germany, Italy, France and Spain, ranging from 20 to 40 per cent. This compares with over 130 per cent for the UK, where the equity market is better developed.

Supply side

On the supply side, growth is driven by a number of forces, and their diversity should underpin the stability and further growth of the market. The most important drivers are:

Privatisations

Although the programmes are coming to an end in some countries – most notably the UK – there is more to come in western and central Europe, Latin America, Australasia and Africa. Privatisation appears to be an accepted policy, although there are temporary setbacks for political reasons. Privatisations have also contributed indirectly to an expanded supply by developing the sophistication and liquidity of emerging markets.

Restructuring and concentration on core activities

As institutional investors come under increased pressure to perform, they – as shareholders – demand more professional management of all corporate units and more transparency to measure performance. These demands have led to increased concentration on core activities and emphasis on shareholder value. Companies are selling stakes in subsidiaries or are demerging whole companies.

Globalisation

Together with the pressure from the investment community comes pressure on companies to compete globally. This trend forces the sale or demerger of non-core activities and the acquisition of companies within core businesses. Increased globalisation of business, and coverage by buy- and sell-side equity research analysts have also meant greater access by a larger number of companies to large pools of capital, further adding to supply.

Generation shift

Family-owned companies in need of capital to grow and com-

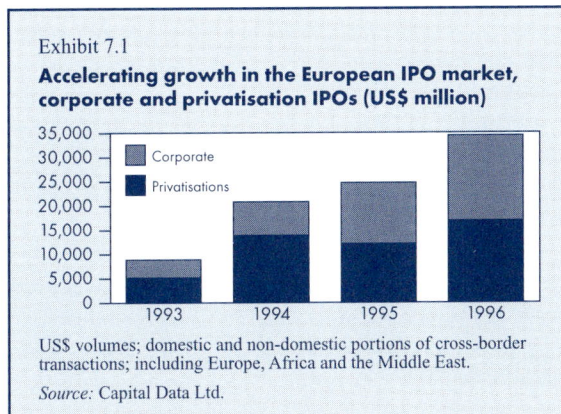

Exhibit 7.1

Accelerating growth in the European IPO market, corporate and privatisation IPOs (US$ million)

US$ volumes; domestic and non-domestic portions of cross-border transactions; including Europe, Africa and the Middle East.

Source: Capital Data Ltd.

pete internationally have fuelled market growth. In some cases, children of entrepreneurs are not interested in or not capable of running the business and therefore sell out via the stock market. A generation well versed in the equity culture is replacing a generation that was more inclined to rely on bank financing than the capital markets.

Competition and deregulation

As a result of increased competition and deregulation in key industry sectors, the harmonisation of cross-border legislation and improvements in technology, an increasing number of companies need to have better access to the main pools of liquid institutional capital.

Demutualisation

There is an increasing trend among mutual companies, notably among UK insurance companies and building societies, to convert to publicly quoted joint stock companies to gain access to the equity capital markets.

More efficient allocation of capital

As the takeover game continues to gather momentum, as companies in an increasing number of countries are allowed to buy back their own shares and as shareholder pressure demands that excess capital is distributed to shareholders, so the leverage of corporations will increase. Further along the economic cycle, this additional risk will be redistributed to the equity market by selling shares either in the parent company or in subsidiaries or associated companies. In the US, this trend is already firmly established. The US auto industry has seen a continuation of equity capital raising and buy-back programmes over recent years.

Lower fees

Increased competition among banks has led to lower fees in international equity transactions. This translates into a reduction in the cost of capital and an increased supply of shares.

Demand side

On the demand side, growth has been driven by responsible macroeconomic policies leading to non-inflationary economic growth and the impetus of demographically inspired savings flows.

Sound economic policies

As a result of sound economic policies leading to lower interest rates, there has been a considerable shift from bank deposits to equity investment. In the US, corporate equities as a percentage of total 'US Household Financial Assets' increased from 12 per cent in 1985 to 20 per cent in 1995 (source: Investment Company Institute). The equity culture in key European countries remains underdeveloped: of total mutual funds at the end of 1996, equity mutual funds accounted for only 2.8 per cent in Spain, 10.9 per cent in France, 26.7 per cent in Germany and 16.7 per cent in Italy, whereas the equivalent figures were 88.4 per cent in the UK, 74.6 per cent in Sweden and 53.8 per cent in the Netherlands (source: FEFSI). Sound macroeconomic management leading to a

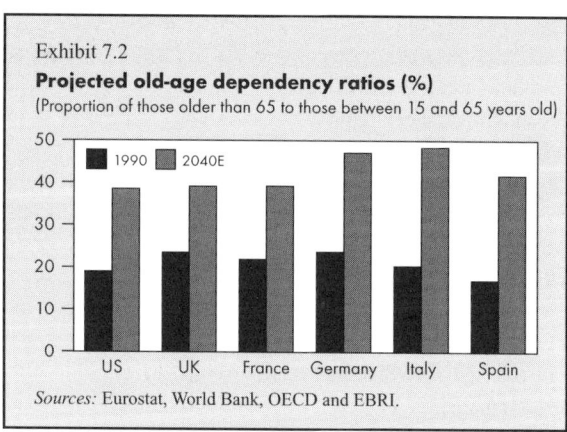

Exhibit 7.2
Projected old-age dependency ratios (%)
(Proportion of those older than 65 to those between 15 and 65 years old)

Sources: Eurostat, World Bank, OECD and EBRI.

lower interest rate environment and a better equity market performance has in recent years led to a substantial increase in the number of retail investors buying shares in major European privatisations. Two million Germans participated in the 1996 issue for Deutsche Telekom, 1.4 million Spaniards participated in the 1997 Telefónica offer and 800,000 Italians participated in ENI 3. Although these numbers are a far cry from those achieved in some UK and French privatisations during the 1980s, they are unprecedented in these countries.

Doubling of dependency ratios and the need for private pension funds

It is generally expected that dependency ratios in the US and in the EU will double between 1990 and 2040 in terms of the number of retired people as a percentage of those of working age (see Exhibit 7.2).

This trend will require a massive shift from government sponsored pay-as-you-earn pension payments funded out of annual government budgets, to funded corporate and state-employee pension schemes managed by professional fund management companies. A study by EFRP estimates that in order to meet the future pensions demand in the EU, funded pension schemes would have to cover 60 per cent of the population by the year 2020 (against only 22.6 per cent in 1993) and pay out 25 per cent of total pensions (against only 7 per cent in 1993. Assets in European pension funds would have to increase tenfold to Ecu10.2 trillion by the year 2020 in current money terms.

Liberalisation of asset allocation

In recognition of the changing demographic outlook, a much higher equity content in pension funds will be needed to generate the necessary growth. Accordingly, pension systems around the world are in the process of being liberalised, albeit slowly, in terms of how they can invest. The privatisation of pension funds to reduce dependency on the state is a further significant trend. In Asia, development is much faster than in Europe: in Singapore for example, the asset allocation of the US$50 billion state pension fund CPF is evolving. Prior to 1996, CPF funds had to be invested entirely in government bonds and advance deposits with the Monetary Authority of Singapore: from 1996 Singaporeans have been able to invest 20 per cent of their CPF funds in Singapore-listed stocks and bonds. In 1998 it is expected that 40 per cent will be allowed to be invested in other Asian markets and, as of 1999, US and other western stock markets will become open to pension funds and unit trusts. Other Asian countries are likely to follow the Singaporean model.

Competition and liberalisation in manager selection

Increasing emphasis on defined contribution – where pension income is determined by the scale of the individual's contributions – rather than defined benefit – where the future benefit is pre-determined by salary – has led to more emphasis on performance, more products and more competition among fund managers. With defined benefit, employees did not care who managed the pension fund, but with defined contribution, the employee has become the client of the fund manager. In order for pension trustees around the world to deliver the required performance, domestic pensions markets will open up to sophisticated third-party fund management organisations, whose major expertise lies in equity investment. The liberalisation now gathering pace in the Japanese pension market is widely expected to lead to an increase in the pension assets managed by investment advisers from 7 per cent in 1997 to 30 per cent by 2001, with the inevitable implication of a radically increased equity content. UK and US organisations are likely to be the main beneficiaries of this trend.

The emergence of a global pension consultancy industry

The spread of US and UK techniques and investment management philosophies is being further reinforced by the internationalisation of investment management consultancies. This has resulted in a number of very powerful global pensions consulting firms, such as William Mercer, Bacon Woodrow and Frank Russell, advising multinational corporations in major financial centres. These consultants act as catalysts in exporting the US pension model to overseas markets. Their increasingly global infrastructure will make it possible for them to tailor the US model to local economic and cultural considerations.

European economic and monetary union

With the strong possibility of EMU in Europe, the key currency risk element of cross-border investment may be removed. The performance of national economies would be harmonised and interest rates in many European countries would be likely to fall. This would lead to a higher proportion of total funds under management invested in equity and to significantly higher cross-border equity investment. One of the fundamental driving forces behind EMU – reducing the currency risk for European companies – would reduce the overall risk level of equities and further underpin the trend towards more equity investment.

Corporate governance

Improvement and standardisation of corporate governance standards, recognition among corporate executives of the need to deliver shareholder value, companies' growing dedication to more sophisticated investor relations, a globalisation of accounting standards and generally more transparent equity markets will all lead to increased equity investment. Market liquidity will improve, further underpinning market growth.

The core considerations: a word to the vendor

As a result of all these dynamics of supply, demand and environment, companies will come to the equity market in ever greater numbers for an increasing variety of reasons. Corporate and state vendors need to prepare themselves for an ever more sophisticated market.

In order for these vendors, their advisers and the investors who buy their stock to thrive in this innovative and competitive market, trust and credibility on all levels are paramount. The company and its investment bank must trust each other for the preparation and execution of the offer to succeed. Investors must trust the investment bank's due diligence, its research, pricing and after-market support. The bank must also build credibility with the investor community. The issuing company has to live up to the investors' expectations and operate with full and immediate disclosure of all price-sensitive information. This also applies to public-sector vendors who need to retain credibility for a continuing privatisation programme, as well as to owner-managers.

The quality of management in the offer company is crucial to engendering this confidence. How well the management understands the whole offer process, its degree of involvement in it, and how well it sells on the roadshow are at the heart of the deal. If the management lives up to the market's expectations afterwards, it will be proof that the deal was worth doing. If the team has a track record prior to the issue, that will always help the sales case, but it is how it performs later that provides shareholder value. Of course, as managements can rarely be reinvented, shareholders may have to replace or complement the management. For this the shareholders need the help of trusted financial advisers: thus the circle of credibility is complete.

One sure way to lose credibility is over-aggressive pricing. Aggressive pricing should be adopted by the participants in a deal only when they want it to be their last transaction. Typically it is the least experienced vendors who are tempted to price themselves too high, and do not realise that sometimes no deal is better than a bad deal. A successful transaction is one where both vendor and shareholders win. If the industrial cycle is wrong, if the company is not ready to come to market or if due diligence throws up something untoward, then it is better to postpone the issue. Here of course is where the relationship of trust between bank and issuer is most strained, as for competitive reasons bankers are reluctant to postpone: as much as a bank may be in the business for the long term, when the timing is not right then the vendors must usually take responsibility themselves.

To become a publicly quoted company is a fundamental process – it is very challenging but at the same time can be very rewarding. If you want to have success in the international equity markets you have not only to accept that challenge, but to embrace it and invite your shareholders to become partners in your business. You can learn a lot from them and substantially improve the efficiency of your organisation. If you do not wish to accept that challenge, you should either sell your business or accept the inevitable constraint on growth of not being part of the equity capital market. To be a publicly quoted company stimulates efficiency and value creation. The constant and pervasive relationship with investors and financial markets becomes a permanent measure of the company's health. A major difference between being a private company and a public one is that in a public company management typically focuses more on value creation for shareholders than simply creating the best industrial strategy. In order to be successful as a quoted company, you have to have a clear strategy, you have to match and preferably exceed the market's expectations and you constantly need to explain what you are doing. Public companies must operate with a much higher level of transparency than private companies are used to.

When you run a private company you are pessimistic and keep a low profile in order to maintain good relations with employees, trade unions and the tax authorities. When you are a public company, you constantly need to talk about how successful you are and in so doing you obviously raise the expectations of employees and you get problems with the trade unions.

Ultimately, the more credibility you can build and the greater the number of investors that trust you, the higher the stock market rating you will enjoy. While the bankers move on to the next deal, you hope your shareholders stay with you: treat them as your customers and learn from them. It is the best free advice you are likely to get.

Glossary

Accelerated global tender. A pricing and underwriting structure which combines elements of a bought deal and a bookbuilding. A non-underwritten offer launched with a price range and without a prospectus where the pricing of the transaction takes place within a couple of days of the announcement. This structure was used by SG Warburg in the 1993 transaction for Akzo after it had bought the shares from the company (see Akzo case study). Other names include express bookbuilding and crash bookbuilding.

Accredited investors. Certain institutional investors and high-net-worth individuals satisfying SEC rules for traditional US private placements.

Adjusted market value (AMV). AMV (enterprise value) is the sum of the market value of the debt (net debt) and the market value of the equity. Together they represent the market value of the total assets. AMV is frequently set in relation to sales, operating income or operating cash flow generated by the assets of the company, to compute a ratio for purposes of comparison with similar companies. These ratios are used together with P/E, price/cash flow and dividend yield and are particularly relevant for the valuation of companies in certain industries. In the private market, AMV is also referred to as aggregate value. AMV can be seen as the total financial commitment on the part of the investor, who is responsible not only for buying the rights to dividends but also for the servicing of the debt.

ADRs. Certificates of deposit representing foreign shares, issued by a depository bank which holds the foreign shares in custody. ADRs are generally denominated and traded in US dollars and are seen as US securities. For many US investors they are a more accessible, liquid, cheaper and easier way to trade than the shares that they represent.

Most depository receipts are referred to as ADRs; however they may also be referred to as global depository receipts (GDRs), European depository receipts (EDRs) or international depository receipts (IDRs). All depository receipts are the same from a legal and administrative point of view.

After-market. The trading market in a particular stock following the pricing and allocation of a new issue. Market participants talk about the immediate after-market, ie, the first

few days of trading. Some people define the after-market as the stabilisation period, ie, the first 30 days of trading following the closing of the offer. Others consider the after-market to represent trading beyond the stabilisation period as well; however this period is more commonly referred to as the secondary market.

Agreement among managers. See *Documentation.*

Allocable demand. Of the total demand indicated by institutions in the bookbuilding process, the allocable demand is a more accurate reflection of what those institutions wish to hold for the long term. Allocable demand is the total demand less order-inflation. Allocable demand is the demand from investors that, if allocated, should ensure a stable after-market.

Allocation. The process of accepting investor bids in full or in part and confirming the number of shares sold to each investor. Under the bookbuilding system, allocations are entirely discretionary, such that the lead manager or global coordinator will choose to allocate in such a way as to ensure the most stable after-market, although at times the bookrunner will allocate in a way that will tend to favour its own economic interest. Typically the vendor and the lead manager or global coordinator will have developed certain allocation criteria. In most cases, institutional investors are divided into different quality categories in advance of the bookbuilding period, ranking them according to their different propensity to hold shares for the long term. Allocation is sometimes referred to as allotment.

Allocation criteria. Allocation criteria are typically defined up front by the vendor and its advisers, to make the allocation process more objective and fair. In the case of an IPO such criteria might include:

- *Price leadership:* Bids at specified prices are preferred to bids at strike (ie, good at any price);
- *Timeliness:* The prompt submission (say within 48 hours) of a bid following any contact with management on the roadshow;
- *Investor quality:* The vendor's independent assessment, based on the recommendation by the lead manager/global coordinator, of an investor's likely short- and long-term after-market behaviour;

- *Involvement:* Interest in the offer expressed by participation in pre-marketing, company group presentation or one-on-one meetings with the management.

Blow-out. Investment banking jargon for a highly successful issue.

Blue sky. All securities offers in the US are subject to both federal and state securities laws: the latter are generally referred to as blue sky laws.

Bonus shares. Incentive to encourage retail (or individual) investors to participate in privatisations, whereby the state undertakes to deliver free of charge a set number of extra shares for every block of a specified number of shares held for a minimum period, typically 12–18 months (also referred to as loyalty shares).

Book. A book kept by equity syndicate or ECM, which contains the shares to be sold in a new issue and the orders received. (See *Bookbuilding, Bookrunner* and *Shadow book.*)

Bookbuilding. A pricing and underwriting method whereby the offer price is fixed and the offer underwritten after a book of preliminary orders has been built at the end of the marketing period.

Bookbuilding allows the bookrunner to compile a comprehensive picture of the strength of institutional demand for the shares over a range of prices by obtaining non-binding expressions of interest from potential investors. The aim is to ensure that the shares are spread across a wide range of high-quality investors and that price tension and an impression of scarcity is created among different investor groups. At the end of the bookbuilding period the price is fixed, the prospectus is finalised, the shares are allotted to investors and dealings in the shares begin.

The advantages of open-price bookbuilding over a fixed-price underwritten offer include: the price matches demand; competition and price tension between different investor bases; flexibility regarding issue size until the end of the process; shorter underwriting period; improved access to international markets and higher degree of investor transparency.

Bookrunner. The bank responsible for keeping the books for an offer, ie, the bank responsible for the syndication, tranche-sizing, marketing, bookbuilding, pricing, allocation and stabilisation of an offer. In a small corporate issue, there is usually only one bookrunner – the bookrunning lead manager. In a larger offer with several regional tranches, there may be regional bookrunning lead managers, which report to a global coordinator. In such cases there are several books which are ultimately merged into one global book. In some offers there are joint bookrunners and the responsibility for the bookrunning function (in each tranche or for the offer as a whole) is divided among two (or more) banks. To run the books in an offer is associated with considerable power to determine how the economics of a transaction are distributed.

Bottom-up approach. In a new-issue context, the employment of a bottom-up approach means that only tangible evidence from institutions is used to determine tranche-sizing, underwriting commitments and allocation. This principle leads to a high degree of transparency and fairness. This approach is distinctly different from the top-down approach where the lead manager estimates investor interest based on previous offers, general market conditions and the particular investment case.

Bought deal. Bought deals are usually substantial secondary sales of shares, whereby one company is selling already outstanding and publicly traded shares in another company.

They are by definition underwritten transactions, whereby the lead bank(s) underwrite a fixed number of shares at a fixed price before the deal is announced to the market. More precisely, the lead bank(s) actually buy(s) the shares from the vendor, hence the name. The bought deal structure implies that the shares are sold to a large number of investors. There are generally no fees in a bought deal, instead, the relevant 'issue price' is usually the prevailing market price less a discount of typically 3–5 per cent. As a rule, no due diligence is carried out in connection with a bought deal, nor is a prospectus published.

Buy-side analysts. Equity research analysts working for institutional investors.

Chinese wall. The practice in an investment bank which separates the advisory side from the trading or investment side of the bank such that price-sensitive information held by the advisory side and not yet publicly disclosed (insider information) is not made available to those that buy and sell securities or publish research on them. If a research analyst or sales person is 'brought over the wall', that person becomes restricted and can no longer recommend or sell that stock. Matters relating to the Chinese Wall and the treatment of non-public and price- sensitive information are the subject of strict legal and compliance rules and regulations.

Clawback. A mechanism in privatisations involving substantial retail offers, whereby shares provisionally allocated to institutional investors are reallocated to retail investors in case of strong retail demand. The extent and basis on which this reallocation (or clawback) can take place is typically set out in the prospectus. The clawback mechanism serves the political purpose of giving more shares to retail investors in case of over-subscribed offers and helps create a sense of scarcity among institutional investors. The announcement of the exercise of the clawback option usually adds momentum to the institutional offer.

Co-lead manager. In an international syndicate (as opposed to a US syndicate), this typically represents the second tier of the syndicate in terms of underwriting commitment, after the lead managers but before the co-managers. This tier does not exist in a US syndicate as the second tier in a US syndicate is the co-manager.

Co-manager. In an international syndicate (as opposed to a US syndicate), this represents the third tier of the syndicate in terms of underwriting commitment, after the lead manager(s) and the co-lead managers. In a US syndicate, co-managers represent the second tier of banks. In the US, they are typically more involved in the preparation of an offer than the co-lead managers in an international syndicate.

Comparable companies. Companies with similar operating and financial characteristics as the issuer. It is important to find good comparables when valuing the shares of an issuer for purposes of an IPO. No two companies are truly comparable but the best yardsticks for comparability are operational characteristics such as industry, markets, customers, seasonality, cyclicality and geographic spread, and financial characteristics, such as size and leverage.

Conference call. In connection with equity new issues, there are typically two types of conference calls: those between research analysts and investors and those between the company management and investors.

Confidential filing. To facilitate the registration process, the SEC will allow non-US companies to conduct a non-public filing with them and receive confidential feed back on that filing prior to the public filing.

Corporate governance. The way that the company is governed, in particular with respect to the rights and influence of minority shareholders. High corporate governance standards mean that the board of directors is independent of the management and that it carries out its fiduciary duties in the best interest not only of the company but also of all shareholders. It implies a high level of transparency and accountability and, for publicly quoted companies, that there are sufficient board seats occupied by non-executive directors.

Corporatisation. The process of incorporating departments of the government (or organisations with a similar status) to limited liability companies with a dedicated balance sheet and board of directors. This is the step that is taken before a company can be privatised.

Cum-trading. The period between the announcement of the terms of a rights issue and the beginning of the subscription period, when the rights begin to trade separately. (See also *Ex-rights trading*.)

Demerger. See *Spin-off.*

Depository agreement. Used to establish an ADR programme. The agreement is entered into by the issuer and the depository bank. It describes the terms of the ADRs, including issuing and cancellation procedures.

Designations. See *Institutional pot* and *Jump-ball.*

Dilution. There are two basic types of dilution: economic and voting. Economic dilution takes place when, as a result of an issue of new shares, the prospective earnings per share are reduced as a result of the fact that the incremental earnings from the proceeds of the issue are not sufficient to compensate for the increased number of shares. Voting dilution takes place when as a result of a new issue, the voting interests of those investors who do not participate in the issue are reduced.

Documentation. In addition to the prospectus (or offer circular), the principal documents entered into in connection with an international offer include:

- *Subscription agreement:* The contract between the issuer and/or selling shareholders, and all the subscribing banks in a syndicate (the managers) setting forth the terms and conditions of the sale of the securities to the managers (equivalent to underwriting agreement in the US).

   The subscription agreement also includes the representations and warranties and indemnities, pursuant to which the parties provide each other with certain guarantees and an agreement to which the other party is held in case such guarantees prove not to be true and accurate. Typically the issuer's representations and warranties include company-specific and transaction-related guarantees.
- *Agreement among managers:* Agreement between the managers of an offer providing for the manner in which shares are to be marketed in the various jurisdictions. It defines the roles and responsibilities of the various managers and records the commercial arrangements between the banks.
- *Agreement for warranties and indemnities:* In the case of a secondary sale where a third party sells shares in a company (such as most privatisations), liability issues relating to the contents of the offer circular are typically regulated by a separate contractual agreement (Agreement for warranties and indemnities). Under this agreement, the vendor gives certain warranties to the company and its directors relating to the various offer documents and indemnifies the company and its directors in relation to certain liabilities under the offer. The company, for its part, gives the vendor certain warranties with regard to the information relating to the description of the company, its business and its prospects contained in the offer documents.

Dual-track strategy. The simultaneous pursuit of private and public sales of a company. (See New Zealand Telecom case study.)

Due diligence. A comprehensive investigation of a company's business, financial position and prospects, including major risks, for the purpose of underwriting a securities issue. There are two types of due diligence: business and legal.

   The business due diligence typically includes overview meetings with senior management, presentations by operating division heads, plant tours, a review of historical financial statements and projections, and discussions with accountants.

   The legal due diligence is a thorough review of the company's legal situation and typically includes a review of board minutes, key company contracts, licences, trademarks and any litigation that the company might be involved in.

As a result of the legal due diligence and the work with the prospectus, if securities are to be sold in the US, it is usual for both the issuer's and underwriters' US counsel to provide the underwriters with a so-called 10-b-5 opinion, which provides that in the course of the preparation of the prospectus, such counsel have not discovered any material mis-statement or omission in the prospectus. In addition, the company's auditor provides a so-called comfort letter certifying all figures derived from the company's accounting records.

Outside the US, due diligence is typically followed by the verification process.

ECM. The Equity Capital Markets department of an investment bank typically stands in between the corporate finance and equity sales departments. ECM, in cooperation with corporate finance, structures, prices and allocates equity new issues. Following pricing, ECM also coordinates the trading and, if necessary, the stabilisation of new issues.

Elephant order. Large orders from high-quality investors, which can serve as a foundation of the book in a particular issue. Other investors are often attracted if the big names are thought likely to participate. Also known as a leadership order.

Equal economics. If a new issue is structured with equal economics, it means that the most senior parties to the transaction will earn exactly the same amount of money from the transaction, regardless of sales performance. This approach can facilitate better cooperation among the senior managers in an offer as it leads to less bias with respect to tranche sizing, underwriting commitments and allocations.

Equity story. Investment banking jargon for the 'investment case' of a particular company. A good equity story can typically be summarised in only a few words, such as growth story (a company that has excellent prospects in terms of earnings per share growth); a value story (a company that is attractively valued in relation to its adjusted net asset value); restructuring story (a company that has undergone substantial restructuring which is expected to lead to an improvement in earnings); a country story (a company that is located in a country, typically an emerging country, with good economic prospects), etc.

Ex-rights trading. When the shares and the rights entitling shareholders to buy new shares at a certain ratio to the number of shares held trade separately in the market. See also Cum-trading.

Exempt list. A list of investment institutions that can only be contacted by certain banks in the syndicate but not by others. The principal purpose of the exempt list is to ensure a coordinated marketing approach vis-à-vis the investment institutions.

fixed-price offer. An offer structure where the price is fixed at the beginning of the marketing period. These are typically underwritten at a sizeable discount to the market price depending on the quality of the company, market conditions and length of the offer period. This offer structure is used less and less as it is not thought to maximise proceeds.

Flowback. Flowback from the international market to the home market can take one of three forms:

- Immediate resale of the shares by foreign investors wishing to make a quick profit;
- Sale of any unplaced shares by syndicate members; and
- Orderly profit taking by long-term international investors.

Free float. The percentage of the total number of shares outstanding in a company which is held by institutional investors and the public.

Fungibility. Two securities are 'fungible' when they have the same terms and conditions and are interchangeable, and can therefore be freely traded across borders. The question of fungibility typically arises in emerging markets. Securities traded internationally, eg, GDRs are typically not fungible with domestically traded securities, at least not for some time after the new issue, either because they cannot be bought by domestic investors or because domestic investors cannot buy the currency to buy them. Foreigners are not usually allowed to buy domestic shares either because they are prohibited from doing so or because they cannot, for foreign exchange control reasons, acquire the necessary currency. The result is two separate markets, one domestic and one international, with the international price typically trading at a premium to the domestic one.

GAAP. General Accepted Accounting Principles. Typically this means either US or UK GAAP but it could also apply to other countries. In Europe there is now a drive to introduce IAS (International Accounting Standards) in all countries. There is also a strong lobby attempting to press the SEC to accept IAS for purposes of listing in the US (see Roche case study).

GAS. The concept of the Groupe d'Actionnaires Stables was introduced in French privatisations in order to ensure initial stability in the ownership structure (ie, anti-takeover). The market offers have generally been supplemented by placements of 10–20 per cent with investors wishing to invest large sums of money in privatised companies for a period of at least 18–24 months. The GAS provides visible, ongoing sponsorship and governance oversight, and is put in place in advance of the market offer. Proponents argue that the GAS may reduce possible investor misgivings if less than 51 per cent of a state-owned company is sold. Critics argue that it may tie the hands of the board of directors to actions benefiting certain investors rather than all shareholders. This concept was previously known as Noyaux Durs and referred to in English as core shareholders. (See BNP case study and feature topic.)

GDRs. Global depository receipts are similar to ADRs and are usually issued by companies in emerging markets because of foreign exchange regulations in the country of the issuer, foreign ownership restrictions or sub-standard settlement practices in the issuer's home market. GDRs are typically listed in London or Luxembourg, more for disclosure and reporting purposes than in order to maintain liquidity. (See also *ADRs.*)

Global coordinator. The global coordinator has overall responsibility for the success of a multi-market offer in all its parts and during all phases of the offer, from the preparation, through execution, to the post-execution phases. It designs the offer structure and marketing strategy, coordinates the appointment of parties, oversees the preparation of the documentation and coordinates the marketing. It maintains a global book working closely with the regional lead managers (the GC is typically responsible for at least one regional tranche) evaluates global demand by account and by region. Together with the vendor and the regional lead managers, the GC prices the offer and allocates to end-investors. It also manages after-market activity, including, if necessary, stabilisation.

Global underwriting structure. See *Regional underwriting structure.*

Golden share. A special share issued by the company and typically held by the government in connection with a privatisation. The purpose of a golden share is to enable a full privatisation whilst at the same time safeguarding certain interests which are of strategic importance to the state by making the company take over-proof. A golden share usually includes one or several of the following provisions: the prior approval by the state of acquisition of shares above certain thresholds; the veto on certain strategic transactions, such as mergers, acquisitions and divestitures of principal businesses; board representation by the state; consent by the state for the change of the articles of association for issuance of shares and disapplication of pre-emptive rights and capital expenditure above a certain size and under certain conditions.

Greenshoe (or over-allotment option). The over-allotment is a crucial ingredient in any offer, especially when using the bookbuilding method. The success of underwritten offers is attributable largely to the generation of investor demand in excess of the amount offered. This unsatisfied demand leads to after-market orders, strong price performance and secondary market liquidity. To enable the underwriters to over-allocate and then have the flexibility to buy back shares in the market with a view of stabilising the price in after-market trading, issuers grant a greenshoe, typically of 15 per cent of the offer size, thus giving the underwriters the option to purchase additional shares from the issuer at the offer price within a period of 30 days following pricing (the stabilisation period). The additional shares may only be used to cover sales made to investors in excess of the amount offered. The over-allotment option is usually only exercised if the shares increase in price in the secondary market, otherwise excess sales are covered by purchases in the secondary market.

Whereas the principal purpose of the greenshoe is to facilitate stabilisation of the after-market price, in some cases it is used as a disguised way of increasing the offer size.

Grey market trading. Unofficial over-the-counter trading of shares to be issued, before the offer price has been set (ie, before official trading has begun). This practice is also referred to as when-issued or conditional trading. Grey market trading can be very thin and is therefore not representative of an open market price: it can be misleading and make it more difficult to set a fair offer price. In some cases this is prohibited.

Gross spread. Also referred to as total commissions or total fees. The gross spread consists of three components; the underwriting fee (typically 20 per cent), the management fee (typically 20 per cent) and the selling concession (typically 60 per cent).

Hard underwriting. The underwriting of a fixed number of shares at a fixed price for a fixed period. This is different from underwriting in a bookbuilding sense or the underwriting of a pricing formula.

IAS. International Accounting Standards.

Impact day. The day on which the price is fixed, listing particulars are issued, the offer is underwritten and the offer period starts in a traditional UK offer for sale.

Index weighting. In the context of the primary and secondary equity markets, a stock's weighting in a particular index is of significant importance, in that investors who use the particular index in which the stock is included as a benchmark typically need to own that stock, particularly if it has a large weighting. Failure to buy the particular share can lead to under-performance of that index. Different national or international indices have different rules as to how much the minimum free float must be for inclusion in the index and how much of the company's share capital is included in the particular index. For large offers in big markets, index considerations can have a major impact on the structure of the offer.

Initial public offering (IPO). An offer whereby the shares of a company first start trading in the public market (on a stock exchange or in an over-the-counter market). An IPO can be a sale of new shares by a company or already outstanding shares by a third party. IPOs are either corporate transactions (ie, the vendor is a private entity) or privatisations. In some jurisdictions IPOs are referred to as flotations.

Insider trading. The trading of price-sensitive corporate information which has not yet been publicly disclosed and which would seriously affect the company's share price if it was widely known. Insider trading typically occurs prior to unannounced mergers and acquisitions but can also occur prior to important profit announcements and other corporate developments. It is a punishable offence in most major jurisdictions.

Institutional pot. Under this system, originating from the US, a portion of the selling concession (typically 30 per cent) is guaranteed among the managers, pro rata to their underwriting commitments and irrespective of actual sales made. The remainder (70 per cent) is earned according to actual designations received from investors. The idea behind designations is for the institutions to reward those houses involved in an offer in proportion to the amount of value added to that client in connection with the new issue or otherwise. This system does remove some of the discretionary power enjoyed by the global coordinator/bookrunning lead manager although an institutional investor will only designate the selling concession on the amount of stock that it has been allocated. In practice, a global coordinator/bookrunning lead manager may try to give higher allocations to those investors from whom it is likely to get a high portion of the designations.

Under this system, if handled correctly, the allocation is carried out independently of the subsequent designations which makes the process more fair and the quality of the allocation better. The idea is that the global coordinator should not have access to the designations when carrying out the allocation, as this would enable it to maximise its own economics whilst compromising the quality of the placement.

Investor targeting. An internal process whereby prior to the pre-marketing phase, the lead manager draws up a list of the most likely investors in a particular company. Confidential discussions with in-house research and sales professionals are used to identify the most logical group of investors on a global basis.

Issuer. The company issuing shares.

Joint books. Where two (or more) bookrunners share the responsibility of the bookrunning function. The rationale behind this approach is to have two strong investment banks working closely together in a spirit whereby each recommendation is based upon what is best for the transaction. However the joint books method is rarely employed as it can hamper the efficiency of the execution process and as the big investment banks prefer to have a clear division of labour and responsibilities. To be successful, this approach requires a very strong vendor.

Jump-ball. In an institutional pot system where the selling concession consists of one fixed and one variable component, the jumpball portion refers to the variable component. The jumpball is paid on the basis of investor designations.

Lead manager. The lead manager is responsible for managing the offer process from the initial decision to proceed, through the pricing, after-market trading and public market sponsorship. The LM's responsibilities include advice on structure and timing; valuation; marketing strategy and pricing; and running of the book, including the taking of orders, controlling the process and allocating stock to the other syndicate members and end investors. The lead manager is usually also the bookrunner, however there may be joint lead managers, in which case some of the LM's responsibilities may be divided between the two parties, although this does not usually happen with the bookrunning role; the LM's responsibilities also include the provision of support in the after-market; managing the short position; trading support and research support. If the particular issue is a large global issue, a single lead manager role is usually replaced by a global coordinator and several regional lead managers.

Level I, II and III ADRs. Non-listed ADRs sponsored by the company by way of it being party to a depository agreement. Level II ADRs are SEC registered and US listed ADRs. Level III ADRs are SEC registered and US listed ADRs issued in connection with a US public offer.

Level playing field. A state of affairs whereby syndicate banks who work hard in an offer have a fair chance of making decent money. This means that the more junior syndicate members (below the global coordinator and the regional lead managers) have at least a minimum of access to the management and key investors during the marketing phase and that they are treated fairly in the allocation process.

Listing particulars. This is a prospectus-like document filed with the London Stock Exchange and contains a full and comprehensive description of the issuer. It is required for a London listing and serves as the principal marketing document in the UK, whether or not there is a new issue in connection with the listing.

Lock-up. Undertaking on the part of the company and, if applicable, a third party vendor not to sell further shares without the prior written consent of the managers (underwriters). The lock-up period is typically 180 days, but can be considerably longer.

Managed rights issue. A rights issue which includes a significant international marketing programme and active re-circulation, through the underwriting syndicate, of rights not taken up by existing shareholders, to new shareholders.

Management fee. The management fee, typically representing 20 per cent of the gross spread, is paid to compensate the banks for the work involved in managing the preparation and execution of an offer, including the structuring of the offer, the syndication, the preparation of documentation and marketing materials, etc. The basic way of splitting the management fee is to pay according to underwriting commitment, recognising that the higher the underwriting commitment, the more work is generally carried out by a particular institution. In addition, to further reward the senior parties to the offer, there is the praecipium.

Managers. All members of a non-US syndicate with an underwriting responsibility, regardless of seniority and underwriting commitment, are together referred to as the managers (the international equivalent of underwriters in a US syndicate).

Marketing. The marketing phase of an offer includes the company roadshow, where the management presents the company story to investors, and the bookbuilding, whereby the bookrunner takes orders from investors. During this phase, there is also a regular dialogue between sales and research representatives of the bank and the investors. The marketing follows the pre-marketing and ends with the end of the book-building process and the pricing of the offer.

MD&A. An important part of a US-style prospectus: management's discussion & analysis of financial condition and results of operations is a review of the company's recent financial performance.

Money-back guarantee. A type of retail incentive whereby the vendor reimburses retail investors who hold the shares for a certain period, say 12 months, from the offer date if at that time the company's share price is lower than the retail offer price, subject to a maximum reimbursement of about 10 per cent of the retail offer price. This structure was first employed in the 1995 Repsol offer and subsequently employed in the 1995 IPO of ENI in Italy.

Naked short. In connection with international equity offers, the bookrunner (or global coordinator), may allocate a larger number of shares than are being sold by the company. In so doing, the bookrunner incurs a short position. This short position may be negated partly by the company selling more shares to the bookrunner (under the greenshoe) and partly by the bookrunner (subject to stabilisation restrictions) buying more shares in the market. The portion of the total short position not accounted for by the greenshoe is typically referred to as the naked short.

Nasdaq quotation. Some of the advantages of a Nasdaq quotation when compared to an NYSE listing include: more companies listed than any other US exchange; maximum entry fee US$50,000; independent market makers provide trading, research and sales sponsorship. Some of the disadvantages compared to a NYSE listing include: it is a dealer-driven system which allows for trading inefficiency and wider bid/ask spreads; and dealers may sell long or short without restrictions.

New issues. A new issue is an offer in the primary market of new or already outstanding shares which is typically syndicated and documented. It can be either an IPO or a secondary offer, where the shares are already trading in the market. In an investment bank, new issues are typically handled jointly by the corporate finance, ECM and equity sales departments. The antithesis of a new issue is a sale of shares as part of the ongoing sales and trading activity in the secondary market. The fees in the secondary market are a fraction of those in the new issue market.

Noyaux durs. See *GAS*.

NYSE listing. Some of the advantages of a NYSE listing when compared to a Nasdaq quotation (see *Nasdaq quotation*) include: largest dollar trading volume of any US exchange; auction-based system provides greater liquidity as investors directly make a market in shares resulting in tighter bid/ask spreads; specialists are mandated at the NYSE to support shares and step in when there is a trading imbalance; selling restrictions limit speculative trading. Some of the disadvantages compared to Nasdaq include: minimum entry fee of US$100,000; a newly quoted small issue might not always receive the best specialist sponsorship upon listing; and specialists do not provide research or sponsorship. (See Nokia case study.)

Offer for sale. Traditional UK-style fixed-price public offer.

Offer price. The price paid by investors in a new issue. In privatisations, there are often different offer prices for institutional and retail investors. For political reasons, retail investors often receive a discount to the institutional offer price.

Offer circular. See *Prospectus*.

One-on-one. A meeting where an issuer meets with a single institutional investor. One-on-ones are typically afforded only to the big institutions which are most likely to buy in considerable size and which have expressed an interest in seeing the management.

Open-price offer. Generally the equivalent of a book-building.

OPV. *Offre Publique de Vente* – a public offer in France.

Order-inflation. The process whereby institutional investors exaggerate their demand in the hope of receiving better allocations.

Over-allotment option. See *Greenshoe*.

Over-subscription. An issue is considered over-subscribed when demand for the issue, in terms of number of shares, is larger than the number of shares on offer. The degree of over-subscription is often used as a measure of success of an offer. By way of an example, if the demand for an issue of one million shares is three million shares, then it is three times subscribed (or twice over-subscribed).

Overhang. An expectation in the market that a large holder will some time in the near future announce further sales of shares of a company. An overhang tends to depress the company's share price.

Partly paid offer structure. A type of offer structure whereby investors pay in two or three instalments. Historically used primarily in UK privatisations, this structure has been considered, but typically rejected, in many jumbo offers around the world. Partly paid structures are designed to facilitate the execution of large transactions by providing investors with essentially three incentives to purchase the issue:

- A time-value-of-money discount for the deferred portion of the purchase price;
- A leveraged capital gain on the partial payment stock; and
- A leveraged dividend yield (partially paid shares typically are entitled to the full dividend payment).

Due to the scope for larger issues, the overhang in a company's shares is significantly reduced.

The partly paid structure makes share valuation more complex for the investor. After benefiting from higher leveraged returns, partly paid shares tend to flow back to the home market as the instalment payment approaches and the leverage disappears. If partly and fully paid shares are offered, liquidity in each type is correspondingly reduced. The added leverage increases the volatility of the partly paid share, which can have significant implications for the ongoing valuation.

Peer group. Other companies in the same business as the issuer. An issuer is compared to and valued against its peer group (or comparable companies) in order to give the market initial direction on value.

PEPs. Personal equity plans are a form of tax-effective investment for UK retail investors.

Pink herring. See *Prospectus.*

Pink sheets. A form of over-the-counter quotation off the US exchanges and Nasdaq for ADRs of non-US companies (Level 1 ADRs). So called because of the colour of paper on which the quotation is printed. Published and circulated daily by the National Quotation Bureau, Inc., Pink Sheets contain the previous day's price quotations along with the name and telephone number of those market makers willing, but not obligated, to quote prices. Applications for Pink Sheet listings are subject to NASD review.

Placing agent. Banks or brokers who are not formally part of a syndicate but who get paid a fee by the vendor for selling a particular offer. The participation of placing agents will help broaden the placement of shares, particularly with respect to the retail market.

PORTAL. The Private Offer, Re-sales and Trading through Automated Linkages (PORTAL) market is a real-time electronic network offered by NASD in the US to help in negotiating the trading of primary and secondary private placement issues under Rule 144A among QIBs.

Positioning. This is an exercise in portraying a company as a certain type of equity story in absolute terms and in relation to its comparable companies.

Praecipium. A certain portion carved out of the management fee (itself a portion of the total commissions, total fees or gross spread) to reward the global coordinator (global coordinator's praecipium) and in the case of non-US offers the lead and co-lead managers (lead managers' praecipium) for their extra work in preparing and executing an issue, further to the underwriting risk and sales effort. Of the total management fees paid, the global coordinator's praecipium typically amounts to 25 per cent and the lead managers' praecipium also to 25 per cent. The remaining 50 per cent is paid to all managers and underwriters according to their underwriting commitments. (See Argentaria feature topic.)

Pre-marketing. The process by which equity research analysts contact the investor base to present the investment case. The purpose is to prepare the ground for the company roadshow by collecting investor feedback on the equity story, including investor concerns, and the valuation. In a classic bookbuilding, indicative price and size ranges are set at the end of the pre-marketing process. (Also referred to as warm-ups). The object of the exercise is to receive high-quality feed back from high-quality institutions concerning investor intentions. The second major purpose is to determine where efforts should be concentrated during marketing.

Pre-registration. A process whereby retail investors effectively register their interest prior to the beginning of the retail offer to buy during the offer period against the promise of priority in the allocation process. This gives the lead managers and institutional investors a reading of the likely retail interest before the beginning of the bookbuilding period (see Argentaria and Railtrack case studies).

Preferential allocation. A mechanism in a non-pre-emptive offer whereby existing shareholders receive preferential treatment in the allocation if they wish to subscribe. This can take the form of higher allocation or a discount to the subscription price. It applies mainly to existing institutional shareholders. It could be structured to be pre-committed pro rata by some existing major shareholders.

Price leadership. Price leadership is displayed by those investors who in the bookbuilding process are specific about the price they are prepared to pay as opposed to those investors that simply indicate demand at the offer price. In an IPO it is typically sophisticated institutional investors in the UK and the US who have the clearest idea of value. Price leadership can sometimes mean those investors who are prepared to pay the highest price in a given offer.

Price talk. Early discussions on price between banks and investors before price range has been set. This is part of the pre-marketing.

Price tension. Price tension – an important feature of a global bookbuilding – is created by competition between different investor bases around the world for a finite number of shares in a single offer, whereby the price is one of the principal allocation criteria. Those investors prepared to pay the highest price deemed to be sustainable in the secondary market are going to get the highest allocation.

Pricing date. The date on which the offer price is fixed. In an open-price offer (bookbuilding), the pricing date is at the end of the marketing period. In a fixed-price offer (pre-emptive or non-pre-emptive offer) the pricing date is at the beginning of the marketing period and typically coincides with the announcement of the offer. In some large offers involving both retail and institutional investors, there are separate pricing dates for the retail and institutional tranches.

Primary offer. An offer where the company issues new shares, thereby enlarging the share capital, as opposed to a secondary sale whereby outstanding shares are sold by a third party. (See *Secondary offer.*)

Priority allocation. Priority allocation occurs particularly in privatisations where retail investors who have registered their interest to buy or given purchase mandates are treated more favourably in the allocation process. Priority allocation can also mean that existing shareholders receive preferential treatment in non-pre-emptive offers.

Private placement. A sale of shares that does not comply with regulatory requirements for conducting a public offer. Typically such offers are made to a limited number of sophisticated institutional investors.

Private sale. A private sale or a strategic sale is one which is negotiated between two parties in the private market (M&A market), as opposed to a public sale, which is a sale via the stock market to a broad group of investors.

Privatisation. In this book, privatisation, unless otherwise specifically defined, means the sale by the government of shares in a company or the dilution of a state holding as a result of the sale of new shares by the company.

Pro rata allocation. An allocation system where all investors get a proportion of their total orders. This system is typically employed in most retail offers. It is a distinctly different approach from the discretionary allocation system employed in bookbuilding or the allocation system in an auction (see *Tender*), where all those investors who bid above a certain price get their total demand satisfied.

Profit warning. A formal announcement by a company outside the scheduled reporting occasions that the profit in the current year is likely to be lower than previously expected. A profit warning should be issued as soon as the board of directors decides that the company is unlikely to meet the market's expectations.

Prospectus. The prospectus (offer circular or offer memorandum) is the name of the offer or disclosure document provided to presumptive investors prior to their making an investment decision. It contains information pertaining to the securities being offered and the issuer's business, operations, prospects, capital structure and financial performance. Information provided typically also includes information on the issuer's business environment; the market for the securities; market regulation and taxation; the arrangements for the purchase and sale of the offered securities; and other matters that would be relevant to an investment decision.

Typically a preliminary version of the prospectus – referred to as preliminary prospectus or red herring – without specific information about issue size and issue price, is issued for marketing and bookbuilding purposes, and a final version is issued following pricing of the offer. In some cases, a so-called pink herring is issued in advance of the red herring to facilitate pre-marketing.

Protection. A traditional practice whereby syndicate members are protected, or guaranteed a certain number of shares in the allocation by the lead manager to make it worthwhile for the syndicate member to commit to writing equity research, lend their name to the transaction, etc. This practice is less relevant in an environment of full transparency, where each individual order is considered on its merits.

Public offer. See *Private placement.*

Public sale. See *Private sale.*

Purchase mandates. Also referred to as mandates or early orders. In the case of ENI this structure was confusingly referred to as pre-registration.

Under this structure retail investors could, during the pre-marketing period, give any receiving bank a mandate to spend a certain amount of money on the purchase of shares in the offer on his behalf. This mandate could be withdrawn at any time until some time during the OPV period, failing which the mandates would be automatically converted into orders. This structure was originally developed by BNP in connection with its 1993 privatisation, because it was deemed impossible for the bank branches to process the huge number of orders during an OPV period of only six or seven days. A further reason was the fact that French OPV legislation stipulates that the price must be known to retail investors when they subscribe. This legal challenge was elegantly overcome as the purchase mandate structure was deemed legal, because retail investors were not obligated to buy but could cancel the orders during the actual OPV period when they did know the price. A further advantage of this structure is that it gives the lead manager an important early reading on the likely success of the OPV.

Pure play. A company with activities focused in one particular business area: the antithesis of a conglomerate. Pure plays are created either by organic growth in only one business or by selling or demerging non-core activities.

QIBs. A qualified institutional buyer is an institution that, in the aggregate owns and invests on a discretionary basis at least US$100 million in securities. For a banking institution, a US$25 million minimum net-worth test must also be satisfied.

Quality of investor. Perceived propensity of an investor to hold the shares of a particular company long term.

Reallowance. A form of discount applicable to intermediaries. Managers in a syndicate are typically prevented from selling shares to any person at a price below the offer price, other than to persons whose business it is to buy and sell securities, in which case the minimum price permissible is the offer price less a maximum permissible reallowance.

Red herring. Typically this would be part of the first filing with the SEC, the equivalent of the preliminary offer circular in an international context (pathfinder in the UK). The red herring is usually issued immediately prior to the marketing period.

Regional underwriting structure. A syndicate organised along regional lines with regional underwriting and selling responsibilities. This structure is considered by some market participants to be more suited to achieving maximum breadth of placement, often required in an IPO, rather than a global underwriting structure which is often considered more suited to achieving maximum depth of placement in a secondary offer.

Regulation S. Exemption from the registration requirement under the Securities Act for an offer conducted offshore, ie, outside of the US.

Representations and warranties. See *Documentation.*

Restrictions on circulation of research. Equity research by members of the syndicate may not be published within certain time periods before and after an offer. The exact time constraints depend on whether or not there is a US distribution, and if so, whether it is a public or a private transaction, as well as on the internal guidelines of the bank lead-managing the transaction.

Retention. Retention refers to a block of shares given directly to underwriters to place with their retail investors, as opposed to the institutional pot whereby institutional orders over, say, 10,000 shares in a US-style offer are kept on record by the bookrunners and where the bookrunners decide on the allocation to each institutional client. Retail retention fees are only paid to the extent that actual demand is deemed to exist by the US lead manager.

Reverse investor relations. Contrary to conventional investor relations where the company communicates to investors, reverse investor relations means that the IR department provides feed back from existing or potential future institutional shareholders to the management of the company. Such feed back might include comments on the strategy and performance of the company as well as general industry developments.

Rights issue. A type of fixed-price offer where the issuing company offers its shareholders the pre-emptive right to purchase a sufficient number of shares to maintain their existing ownership percentages. In most jurisdictions, the rights issue is set at a substantial discount to the market price. Most rights issues priced at discounts of up to 25–30 per cent are underwritten. In some countries (eg, Sweden) deeply discounted non-underwritten rights issues are the norm.

Ring-fencing. A type of selling restriction agreed among all the syndicate banks participating in an issue, whereby these banks agree to restrict the sale of shares to designated regions. In a structure with several regional syndicates, this means that you can only sell in the region covered by the particular syndicate of which you are a part. The global coordinator/overall lead manager may reallocate shares underwritten in one region, to another, in order to optimise global allotment.

RLMs. Regional lead managers are responsible for running the books of the regional tranches in a global offer.

Roadshow. The process by which the management of the company selling shares goes on the road to market the company to investors. In connection with a sizeable new issue, the roadshow typically takes the management to a significant number of cities in the UK, the US, continental Europe and the RoW. The roadshow consists of different types of meetings, most notably bigger investor presentations and one-on-one meetings however there are occasionally also meetings with small groups of investors. It includes breakfast meetings, lunch meetings, meetings for cocktails and dinner meetings. A roadshow typically takes place over one or two weeks. In a jumbo privatisation it can require three or four.

RPI-X formula. Cornerstone of the UK system of utility regulation, whereby the regulated company is obligated to reduce prices by a certain amount in real terms each year. This formula provides a strong incentive for management to rationalise the business as it does not cap returns to shareholders emanating from cost cutting. This is radically different from cost plus or explicit rate of return regulations, both of which cap the return to investor.

Rule 144A. Rule 144A provides an exemption from the registration requirement under the Securities Act of 1933 for resales of certain securities to QIBs. By providing an exemption from registration, Rule 144A has significantly increased the opportunities for US institutional investors to acquire the securities of foreign companies. There are more than 3,500 QIBs in the US. Securities of the same class as those listed on a US securities exchange are not eligible for resale under Rule 144A. US institutional investors are subject to significant restrictions with regard to Rule 144A ADRs and in most cases have a strong preference for listed ADRs. (See Roche case study.)

Rump. The portion of a UK rights issue not subscribed by the end of the subscription period, which is typically placed by the brokers to the rights issue, during the morning after the end of the subscription period.

Sales points. The key reasons why an investor should buy the securities of a particular offer.

SEAQ International. A UK-based over-the-counter trading market, on which non-UK companies trade. That a stock is traded on Seaq International is by no means the same thing as being listed on the LSE.

SEC. Securities & Exchange Commission. The SEC is the principal securities regulatory authority in the US. It was created by the 1934 Exchange Act and is charged with the responsibility for administering the provisions of both the 1933 and 1934 acts. It is an independent regulatory agency of the US government, which has broad powers to issue regulations, institute administrative proceedings and bring suits in the federal courts to enforce securities provisions.

SEC filing forms for non-US companies.
*   *F-1:* This form, essentially a prospectus, would typically be used by non-US companies offering securities in the US for the first time.
*   *F-2 and F-3:* A non-US company may be eligible to use the abbreviated Form F-2 or Form F-3 if it has filed periodic reports with the SEC for at least 12 months.
*   *F-6:* When ADRs are to be traded publicly on a US exchange or over the counter, they must be registered on Form F-6. F-6 requires only a description of the ADRs and the securities to be deposited.
*   *20-F:* the form on which annual filings for all non-US companies are made with the SEC on an ongoing basis.
*   *6-K:* Forms on which non-US companies must publish promptly after relevant interim information is made public to non-US investors. The information filed on Form 6-K is not subject to SEC requirements, it merely consists of copies of information filed or made public in the foreign private issuer's country.

Secondary offer. This term is confusing because it means one of two different things depending on to whom you talk. On the one hand it means the opposite of a primary offer, ie, the sale of already outstanding shares by a third party. On the other hand, however, market participants refer to a secondary offer as the opposite of an IPO, that is, a sale of either new or outstanding shares so long as the company has for some time been a publicly traded company. To avoid possible confusion, in this book secondary offer means the opposite of an IPO and a secondary sale means the opposite of a primary offer.

Secondary sale. The opposite of a primary offer, ie, the sale of already outstanding shares by a third party.

Securities Act of 1933. The 1933 act requires the registration of securities with the SEC prior to their sale to the public. It is a disclosure statute designed to protect prospective investors from misrepresentation, manipulation and other fraudulent practices in connection with the public offer of a company's securities.

Securities Exchange Act of 1934. The 1934 act created the SEC. In contrast to the 1933 act which is essentially concerned with the initial distribution of securities, the 1934 act is concerned principally with trading in existing securities. Under this act companies listed on NYSE and AMEX or traded over the counter on Nasdaq must register those securities.

The 1934 act prohibits insider trading and securities market manipulations (which give a false or misleading appearance of active trading) by any deceptive device or fraudulent practice and it restricts certain activities that have been used to manipulate the securities market in the past.

Sell-side analysts. Equity research analysts working for investment banks or brokers.

Selling concession. A portion (typically 60 per cent) of the gross spread paid to syndicate members on the basis of either shares sold or designations by investors. The selling concession is a type of sales incentive. (For a detailed analysis see Argentaria feature topic.)

Shadow book. Due to the fact that many, if not most, institutions inflate their orders in the hope of getting higher allocations, it is important to determine the extent to which indicated demand reflects true long-term demand. For this purpose, a so-called shadow book is kept of institutions' real demand. See also *Allocable demand*.

Share information office. In the early UK privatisations, UK retail investors were encouraged to register their preliminary interest with specially constituted government-run share information offices (SIOs). The SIOs provided information on the offers and took pre-registrations and applications but they were not equipped to handle secondary market sales orders.

Share shops. Share shops – a distinct feature of UK privatisations and the result of a further development of the SIO – are mainly high street banks that take registrations and applications and provide cheap and accessible buying and selling services for privatisation shares. Those who register with and apply through a share shop receive preferential allocation and, if applicable, certain other retail incentives. All share shops are required to be members of a self-regulatory organisation and authorised to carry out investment business, enabling them to market the public offer. The reason that there has been a need for share shops in UK privatisations is that traditionally, UK high street banks acted only as receiving banks. Although the stockbroking arms of these high street banks have become more active as share shops in some recent UK offers, they have not historically been sufficiently equipped to handle share dealing services for retail clients.

Shareholder value. If a company's management is managing it for maximum shareholder value, it takes actions that will increase the value of the shares as traded in the market including the payment of higher dividends, the buy-back of shares, the sale or demerger of non-core activities, the rationalisation of the business, etc.

Short selling. Short selling is the sale of securities by a party which does not own them, in the hope that the share price will fall so that they can buy the shares needed to settle the sale at a lower price. Ideally, no delivery of the underlying shares ever takes place. If the original selling position is carried beyond the due settlement date without being closed, then the stock is either borrowed to effect settlement, rolled-over, or the vendor simply fails to settle. Short selling can occur in the ordinary course of secondary market trading or specifically at the time of a new issue. In connection with an equity offer certain market participants might sell shares during the marketing period in the hope of being allocated shares in the offer at a lower price than the price at which they executed the short sale. Other market participants may just believe that they can close out their short positions by buying at a lower price in the secondary market once official trading has begun.

Solicitation process. In the context of the new-issue market, this is the process whereby investment bankers try to get hired to handle the new issue on behalf of the vendor. For big issues, the solicitation process typically involves several written submissions and oral presentations including so-called beauty parades where the principal candidates get an opportunity to explain why they are best qualified to do the job.

Spin-off. In a spin-off (or demerger), parent company stockholders receive a new share in an independent and separately quoted subsidiary. The spun-off company will have a separate and dedicated board of directors. If the spin-off is done for a valid business purpose and structured properly, it is typically not a taxable event – either at the company or at the shareholder level (see Zeneca and USX case studies).

Stabilisation. Market activities conducted by the lead manager and possibly other syndicate members to ensure an orderly after-market. Stabilisation activities are highly regulated to ensure that they do not amount to market manipulation.

Stags. People who apply for shares in an offer with the aim of selling them immediately afterwards at a higher market price.

Strike price. The equivalent of the offer price in a tender or auction. In a typical equity new-issue auction, the strike price is the lowest successful bid price in a system where allocations are filled starting with the highest bidder. In the most conventional type of auction, all bidders pay the strike price; however there are exceptions to this rule.

Sub-underwriting. The process of laying off, wholly or partly, primary underwriting risk with a large number of sub-underwriters. This practice is primarily a British practice where new issues have generally been underwritten by only one or two primary underwriters and then laid off with a large number of UK institutional investors.

Subscription. See *Over-subscription.*

Subscription agreement. See *Documentation.*

Syndicate. In the context of the equity new-issue market, a syndicate is a group of banks assembled to sell the shares in a particular company. A syndicate has a leader, the lead manager (or if it is a large global issue, a global coordinator), and a whole variety of banks and brokers which are more or less senior in the syndicate.

Syndicate member. In the US, banks below the level of co-managers are typically referred to as syndicate members. Syndicate members have a small underwriting commitment and don't receive any management fee. In the international market, the equivalent status is co-manager.

Targeted stock. Targeted stocks of a company are classes of parent company stock that track the performance of the business groups of that company. There is only one corporate entity which owns all the company's assets and is responsible for all the company's liabilities, one board of directors and one consolidated federal income tax return. The business groups are therefore not subsidiaries and the shareholders have no claim on the underlying assets of the targeted businesses. Other names for what is largely the same thing include letter stock; alphabet stock and tracking stock. (See USX case study.)

Teach-in. Presentation to the managers' salesforces by research analysts to explain the equity story.

Tender offer. The most common type of tender in the international capital markets is an auction such as the one used in the 1993 privatisation of Singapore Telecom (see SingTel case study). With this structure, demand and therefore the offer price tend to be inflated, particularly in a bullish market. The vendor has no control over the quality of investors, as bidders above the strike price are allocated in full. The after-market performance is typically weak.

Term also used in the US for an offer to purchase outstanding, publicly held stock.

Transparency. In connection with equity new issues, the degree of transparency is a measure of the extent to which the vendor and the lead manager can identify the origin of individual orders. The degree of transparency has increased dramatically with the introduction of bookbuilding as this method requires the identification of each individual institutional order above a certain size, say US$100,000, regardless of which member of the syndicate generated the order. The purpose of this transparency is that the bookrunner can identify the quality of each bid in order to ensure that the allocation of shares to end-investors is based on a genuine interest to hold the shares for the long term. The introduction of transparency has reduced the power of the more junior members of a syndicate and increased the power of the most senior syndicate member. Before the introduction of bookbuilding and a high level of transparency, a co-manager only disclosed a consolidated figure for the total demand generated from its client base and it was difficult for the bookrunner to determine the quality of those orders. Accordingly, banks were either allocated the same number of shares as the number of shares underwritten or an overall assessment was made by the bookrunner as to the quality of the orders of a particular syndicate member. Banks unfamiliar with bookbuilding typically resist divulging the identity of their best clients.

The rules of engagement agreed upon by all managers accepting an invitation to participate in an offer, typically stipulate that each manager shall name each client bidding in the offer (over a certain size).

Treasury stock. Outstanding shares which are owned by the company or a subsidiary of the company. These shares have either resulted from a strategic transaction or have been purchased in the open market. Different jurisdictions have different laws and regulations as to how shares can be bought from the open market and how long they can be held in treasury before they have to be cancelled.

Underwriters. The US equivalent of managers.

Underwriting. In a traditional sense, the process whereby one or several banks guarantee for a certain number of days the purchase of a certain number of shares at a fixed price. This type of underwriting is nowadays typically referred to as hard underwriting as opposed to the underwriting in a bookbuilding sense, which in fact represents a best efforts structure other than at the end of the bookbuilding process. The underwriters commit themselves to take up any shares that are not taken up under the offer.

Underwriting fee. The underwriting fee, typically representing 20 per cent of the gross spread, is shared between all syndicate members, calculated on notional underwriting amounts. The underwriting fee is paid to compensate the syndicate members for the underwriting risk associated with an equity offer. In addition, the underwriting fee is used to absorb stabilisation expenses and any expense overruns which are not covered by underwriters' expense reimbursement.

US GAAP reconciliation. The process whereby major accounting differences between the domestic accounting standards and US GAAP are identified and quantified. Major items are typically the treatment of goodwill, other non-tangible assets, provisions, pension liabilities, derivatives, etc. Issues that are registered with the SEC, require as a minimum

a US GAAP reconciliation of the net earnings, total assets and shareholders equity.

Variable commissions. Progressive commissions to incentivise placement with retail investors. The progression might have two dimensions: higher remuneration for earliness of orders and higher remuneration for achieving more than the original commitment. (See Repsol case study.)

Vendor. The seller of securities. In this book, vendor is used interchangeably for both an issuing company and a selling third party.

Vendor placing. In connection with an acquisition, the acquiring company increases its issued capital by paying the selling shareholders of the acquired company with newly issued shares. The buyer and the seller can arrange for these shares to be placed in the market on behalf of the seller (or vendor).

Verification. The process in non-US markets of confirming that the information obtained during the due diligence and the contents of the prospectus are true and not misleading. In the US the underwriters acquire the equivalent comfort from the so-called 10-b-5 opinion. (See also *Due diligence*).

Appendices

Appendix 1

Common stocks or ADRs representing common stocks of non-US companies listed on the New York Stock Exchange (as of 15 August 1997)

Company	Industry	Listed	ADR	IPO
Argentina (11 ADR companies)				
BAESA-Buenos Aires Embotelladora, SA	Bottling/distribution	5-May-93	X	
Banco Frances del Rio de la Plata, S.A.	Banking	24-Nov-93	X	X
DISCO S.A.	Food retail	3-Apr-96	X	X
IRSA-Inversiones y Representaciones, S.A.	Real estate	20-Dec-94	X†	X
MetroGas, S.A.	Gas distribution	17-Nov-94	X	X
NORTEL INVERSORA S.A.	Telecommunications	17-Jun-97	X	X
Quilmes Industrial (QUINSA), Societe Anonyme	Beer production	28-Mar-96	X	X
TELECOM ARGENTINA STET-France Telecom, S.A.	Telecommunications	9-Dec-94	X	
Telefónica de Argentina, S.A.	Telecommunications	8-Mar-94	X	
Transportadora de Gas del Sur, S.A.	Gas transportation	17-Nov-94	X	
YPF Sociedad Anonima	Oil/gas exploration	29-Jun-93	X	X
Australia (9 ADR companies)				
Australia and New Zealand Banking Group Limited	Banking/financial services	6-Dec-94	X	
Australia and New Zealand Banking Group Limited (PFD)	Banking/financial services	2-Mar-93		
Broken Hill Proprietary Company Limited (The)	Mining/exploration/prod.	28-May-87	X	X
Coles Myer Ltd.	Retail operations	31-Oct-88	X	
FAI Insurances Limited	Property/casualty insurance	28-Sep-88	X	
National Australia Bank Limited	Banking	24-Jun-88	X	
News Corporation Limited (The)	International media	20-May-86	X	
News Corporation Limited (The) (PFD)	International media	3-Nov-94	X	
Orbital Engine Corporation Limited	Engine technology dev./mfg.	4-Dec-91	X	
Westpac Banking Corporation	Banking	17-Mar-89	X	X
WMC Limited	Mining	2-Jan-90	X	
Bahamas (2 non-ADR companies)				
Sun International Hotels Limited	International resort dev.	27-Feb-96		
Teekay Shipping Corporation	Crude oil/petroleum transp.	20-Jul-95		X
Bermuda (8 non-ADR companies)				
ACE Limited	Insurance	25-Mar-93		X
LaSalle Re Holdings Limited	Holding co./reinsurance	11-Apr-97		
Mid Ocean Limited	Reinsurance	30-May-96		
PartnerRe Ltd.	Reinsurance	7-Nov-96		
RenaissanceRe Holdings Ltd.	Reinsurance	24-Jul-96		
Sea Containers Ltd. (Class A)	Transportation/real estate	1-Jul-94		
Sea Containers Ltd. (Class B)	Transportation/real estate	15-Mar-84		
Sphere Drake Holdings Limited	Insurance	22-Sep-93		X
Terra Nova (Bermuda) Holdings Ltd.	Insurance	17-Apr-96		X
Brazil (6 ADR companies)				
Aracruz Celulose S.A.	Wood pulp/paper	27-May-92	X	X
Companhia Companhia Brasileira de Distribui cao	Food retail	29-May-97	X	X
Companhia Cervejaria Brahma	Holding co./beer prod./fist.	4-Jun-97	X	
Companhia Paranaense de Energia - COPEL	Electricity generation	30-Jul-97	X	X
Telecomunicações Brasileiras S.A.-Telebrás	Telecommunications	1-Nov-95	X	
Unibanco	Banking	22-May-97	X	X
Canada (63 non-ADR companies)				
Abitibi-Price Inc.	Paper mfg./newsprint	1-Jul-87		
Agnico-Eagle Mines Limited	Gold exploration/prod.	22-Nov-94		
Agrium Inc.	Fertilizer production/mktg.	4-Oct-96		
Alberta Energy Company Ltd.	Oil/gas	21-Sep-95		
Alcan Aluminium Limited	Aluminum mfg./prod.	31-May-50		

Appendix 1 *continued*

Common stocks or ADRs representing common stocks of non-US companies listed on the New York Stock Exchange (as of 15 August 1997) *continued*

Company	Industry	Listed	ADR	IPO
Avenor Inc.	Integrated forest products	19-Mar-97		
Bank of Montreal	Banking	27-Oct-94		
Barrick Gold Corporation	Gold mining	25-Feb-87		
BCE Inc.	Telecommunications	18-Aug-76		
BCE Mobile Communications Inc.	Telecommunications	10-Sep-96		
Biovail Corporation International	Broadcasting	12-Dec-96		
Cameco Corporation	Uranium/gold production	14-Mar-96		
Campbell Resources Inc.	Gold/minerals rxploration	13-Jun-83		
Canadian National Railway Company	Railroad dystems operation	17-Nov-95		X
Canadian Pacific Limited	Transportation/energy/real estate	1/24/1883		
CanWest Global Communications Corporation	Television broadcasting	4-Jun-96		X
Cineplex Odeon Corporation	Movie theatre operation	14-May-87		X
Domtar Inc.	Pulp/paper production	22-Sep-87		
Encal Energy Ltd.	Oil/gas exploration/production	6-Jun-97		
Extendicare Inc.	Health care facilities	16-May-96		
Fahnestock Viner Holdings, Inc.	Brokerage services	28-Aug-96		
Four Seasons Hotels Inc.	Luxury hotels management	7-Feb-97		X
Glamis Gold Ltd.	Gold mining	20-Jan-93		
Goldcorp Inc. (Class A)	Gold mining	16-Jun-95		
Goldcorp Inc. (Class B)	Gold mining	16-Jun-95		
Gulf Canada Resources Limited	Crude oil/natural gas production	2-Feb-96		
INCO Limited	Nickel/copper mining	20-Dec-28		
INCO Limited (VBN Shares)	Nickel/copper mining	22-Aug-96		
Intrawest Corporation	Real estate development	25-Mar-97		X
IPSCO Inc.	Steel manufacture	31-Dec-96		
Kinross Gold Corporation	Gold production	17-Oct-94		
Laidlaw Inc. (Class A)	Transportation/waste services	10-Dec-90		
Laidlaw Inc. (Class B)	Transportation/waste services	10-Dec-90		
Loewen Group Inc. (The)	Funeral services	2-Oct-96		
Magna International Inc.	Automotive part mfg.	9-Oct-92		
Meridian Gold Inc.	Mining	31-Jul-96		
Mitel Corporation	Telecomm. equip./sys. mfg.	18-May-81		
Moore Corporation Limited	Business forms/sys./svcs.	13-Nov-80		
Newbridge Networks Corporation	Digital telecomm. networks	14-Sep-94		
Newcourt Credit Group Inc.	Finance	30-Apr-97		
Northern Telecom Limited	Telecomm. equip. mfg.	10-Nov-75		
Northgate Exploration Limited	Exploration/mining	3-Feb-70		
NOVA Corporation	Gas pipelines/petrochemicals	13-Jun-88		
Petro-Canada	Oil/gas production/refining	13-Sep-95		X
Philip Environmental, Inc.	Industrial services	30-Apr-96		
Placer Dome Inc	Gold/silver mining	13-Aug-87		
Potash Corporation of Saskatchewan Inc.	Mining	2-Nov-89		X
Precision Drilling Corporation	Oilfield/industrial services	15-Nov-96		X
Premdor Inc.	Door manufacture	2-Apr-93		
Quebecor Printing Inc.	Commercial printing	7-Dec-95		X
Ranger Oil Limited	Oil/gas exploration/prod.	28-Jan-83		
Rogers Cantel Mobile Communications Inc.	Wireless telecommunications	11-Jan-96		
Rogers Communications Inc.	Communications services	11-Jan-96		
Royal Bank of Canada	Financial services	16-Oct-95		
Royal Group Technologies Limited (Formerly Royal Plastics)	Plastic building products	2-Apr-96		
Seagram Company Ltd. (The)	Distilleries	2-Dec-35		
Stampeder Exploration Ltd.	Oil/gas exploration	11-Oct-96		
Suncor Energy Inc.	Oil/gas production	18-Apr-97		
Teleglobe Inc	Holding co. telecomm. services	12-Jun-97		
Toronto-Dominion Bank (The)	Banking	30-Aug-96		
TransCanada Pipelines Limited	Natural gas pipelines	30-May-85		
Trizec Hahn Corporation	Holding co./oil ref./real es.	15-Jan-90		
TVX Gold Inc.	Exploration/mining	10-Aug-94		
United Dominion Industries Limited	Industrial engineering	6-Dec-83		
Westcoast Energy Inc.	Natural gas transmission	15-Aug-64		
Zemex Corporation (Corp. Headqtrs. moved f/NY to Ontario 1994)	Minerals production/operation	24-Apr-86		
Cayman Islands				
Santa Fe International Corporation	Offshore/land contract drilling	10-Jun-97		X
Chile (20 ADR companies)				
Administradora de Fondos de Pensiónes-Provida, S.A.	Pension fund administration	16-Nov-94	X	X
Banco BHIF	Banking	19-Jun-96	X	X

Appendix 1 *continued*

Common stocks or ADRs representing common stocks of non-US companies listed on the New York Stock Exchange (as of 15 August 1997) *continued*

Company	Industry	Listed	ADR	IPO
Banco de A. Edwards	Banking	3-Nov-95	X	X
Banco de Santiago (Merged w/Banco O'Higgins, OHG)	Banking	13-Jan-97	X	
Banco Santander-Chile	Banking	4-Nov-94	X	X
Chilgener S.A.	Electricity generation	19-Jul-94	X	X
Compañia de Telecomunicaciones de Chile, S.A.	Telecommunications	20-Jul-90	X	
Cristalerías de Chile, S.A.	Glass manufacture	25-Jan-94	X	X
Embotelladora Andina, S.A. (Series A)	Coca-Cola production/distribution	6-Jul-94	X	X
Embotelladora Andina, S.A. (Series B)	Coca-Cola production/distribution	6-Jul-94	X	X
Empresa Nacional de Electricidad, S.A. (Chile)	Electricity generation	27-Jul-94	X	X
Empresas Télex-Chile, S.A.	Telecommunications	14-Oct-94	X	X
Enersis, S.A.	Holding co./eectricity gen.	20-Oct-93	X	X
Laboratorio Chile, S.A.	Pharmaceutical ganufacture	29-Jun-94	X	X
Madeco, S.A.	Telecom./industrial prod. mfg.	28-May-93	X	X
MASISA-Maderas y Sintéticos Sociedad Anónima	Wood products	17-Jun-93	X	X
Quinenco S.A.	Diversified industrial/fin services	25-Jun-97	X	X
Santa Isabel S.A.	Supermarket chain	27-Jul-95	X	X
SQM-Sociedad Química y Minera de Chile, S.A.	Chemical	21-Sep-93	X	X
Supermercados Unimare S.A.	Retail/supermarkets/food store	9-May-97	X	X
Viña Concha y Toro, S.A.	Wine production/export	14-Oct-94	X	X
Colombia (2 ADR companies)				
Banco Ganadero, S.A.	Banking	15-Nov-94	X	
Banco Industrial Colombiano S.A.	Banking	26-Jul-95	X	X
Denmark (3 ADR companies)				
ISS-International Service System A/S	Cleaning/maintenance service	27-Oct-94	X	
Novo-Nordisk A/S	Pharmaceutical manufacture	9-Jul-81	X	
Tele Danmark A/S	Telecommunication services	28-Apr-94	X	X
Finland (3 ADR companies)				
Nokia Corporation	Telecommunication/electronics	1-Jul-94	X	X
Rauma Oy	Industrial machinery mfg.	22-Jun-95	X	X
Valmet Oy	Ind. group/paper/pulp machinery	31-May-96	X	X
France (9 ADR /1 non-ADR company)				
Alcatel Alsthom Compagnie Générale d'Electricité	Telcommunications/energy	20-May-92	X	X
AXA	Insurance/financial services	25-Jun-96	X	X
Bouygues Offshore S.A.	Oil/gas contracting/services.	7-Nov-96	X	X
compagnie Générale de Géophysigue	Oil/gas exploration	7-May-97	X	X
Elf Aquitaine	Oil/gas exploration	14-Jun-91	X	X
Groupe AB SA	Television programming prod.	12-Dec-96	X	X
Pechiney	Aluminum production	18-Dec-95	X	X
Rhône-Poulenc, S.A.	Pharmaceuticals/chemicals	26-Jan-93	X	
SCOR	Holding Co./reinsurance	10-Oct-96	X	X
SGS-THOMSON Microelectronics N.V.	Integrated circuits Mfg.	8-Dec-94		X
TOTAL	Oil/gas exploration/chemicals	25-Oct-91	X	X
Germany (6 ADR companies)				
Daimler-Benz AG	Automobile mfg./aerospace	5-Oct-93	X	
Deutsche Telekom AG	Telecommunications services	18-Nov-96	X	X
Fresenius Medical Care AG	Health care facilities	17-Sep-96	X	
Fresenius Medical Care AG (PFD)	Health care facilities	25-Nov-96	X	
Pfeiffer Vacuum Technology AG	Turbomolecular vacuum pumps	16-Jul-96	X	X
SGL CARBON Aktiengesellschaft	Carbon/graphite products mfg.	5-Jun-96	X	X
Sulzer Medica	Health care equipm. design/manuf.	14-Jul-97	X	X
Ghana (1 ADR co)				
Ashanti Goldfields Company Limited	Gold mining/production	21-Feb-96	X†	
Hong Kong (3 ADR /5 non-ADR companies)				
Amway Asia Pacific Ltd.	Amway distribution	15-Dec-93		X
APT Satellite Holdings Limited	Holding co./satellite services	17-Dec-96	X	X
Asia Satellite Telecommunications Holdings Ltd.	Satellite transponder	18-Jun-96	X	X
Brilliance China Automotive Holdings Limited	Holding co./automotive mfg.	9-Oct-92		X
China Tire Holdings Limited	Holding co./tire manufacture	15-Jul-93		X
Ek Chor China Motorcycle Co., Ltd.	Holding co./motorcycle mfg.	29-Jun-93		X
Hong Kong Telecommunications Limited	Telecommunications	8-Dec-88	X	X
Tommy Hilfiger Corporation	Sportswear design/marketing	23-Sep-92		X
Indonesia (3 ADR companies)				
Indonesian Satellite Corporation	Telecommunication services	18-Oct-94	X	X
P.T. Telekomunikasi Indonesia	Telecommunication services	14-Nov-95	X	X
P.T. Tri Polyta Indonesia	Polypropylene resin prod.	14-Mar-96	X	
Ireland (4 ADR companies)				
Allied Irish Banks, P.L.C.	Banking	28-Nov-90	X	X

Appendix 1 *continued*

Common stocks or ADRs representing common stocks of non-US companies listed on the New York Stock Exchange (as of 15 August 1997) *continued*

Company	Industry	Listed	ADR	IPO
Elan Corporation, plc	Pharmaceutical mfg./dist.	3-Jan-95	X	
Governor and Company of the Bank of Ireland (The)	Banking	17-Sep-96	X	
Jefferson Smurfit Group plc	Paper/packaging manufacture	13-Jul-95	X	
Israel (3 ADR /1 non-ADR company)				
Blue Square-Israel Ltd.	Retail/supermarkets/dept. stores	1-Aug-96	X	X
Elscint Limited	Medical technology sys. mfg.	20-Sep-84		
Koor Industries Limited	Telecommunications mfg.	13-Nov-95	X	X
Tadiran Limited	Telecommunications mfg.	6-Aug-92	X	X
Italy (11 ADR companies)				
Benetton Group, S.p.A.	Clothing manufacture/mktg.	9-Jun-89	X	X
De Rigo S.p.A.	Sunglasses manufacture	20-Oct-95	X	X
ENI S.p.A.	Oil/gas tefining/marketing	28-Nov-95	X	X
Fiat, S.p.A.	Automotive manufacture	14-Feb-89	X	
Fila Holdings, S.p.A.	Sportswear design/mfg.	27-May-93	X	X
Industrie Natuzzi, S.p.A.	Furniture design/mfg.	13-May-93	X	X
Instituto Mobiliare Italiano, S.p.A.	Banking	9-Feb-94	X	X
Instituto Nazionale delle Assicurazioni, S.p.A.	Insurance	6-Jul-94	X	X
Luxottica Group, S.p.A.	Eye wear design/mfg.	24-Jan-90	X	X
Montedison, S.p.A.	Chemical/energy production	16-Jul-87	X	
STET-Società Finanziaria Telefonica p.a. (Ord.)	Telecommunication	27-Jul-95	X	
STET-Società Finanziaria Telefonica p.a. (Svgs.)	Telecommunication	27-Jul-95	X	
Japan (11 ADR companies)				
Amway Japan Limited	Amway Products Distribution	29-Jun-94	X	X
Hitachi, Ltd.	Diversified elec. machinery mfg.	14-Apr-82	X	
Honda Motor Co., Ltd.	Auto/motorcycles mfg.	11-Feb-77	X	
Kubota Corporation	Agricultural machinery	9-Nov-76	X	
Kyocera Corporation	Ceramic products	23-May-80	X	
Matsushita Electric Industrial Co., Ltd.	Electronic products	13-Dec-71	X	
Bank of Tokyo-Mitsubishi, Limited	Banking	19-Sep-89	X	
Nippon Telegraph and Telephone Corporation	Telecommunications	29-Sep-94	X	
Pioneer Electronic Corporation	Consumer electronics	13-Dec-76	X	
Sony Corporation	Electronics/entertainment	10-Sep-70	X	
TDK Corporation	Electronic components mfg.	15-Jun-82	X	
Korea (3 ADR companies)				
Korea Electric Power Corporation	Utility	27-Oct-94	X	X
SK Telecom Co., Ltd. (Formerly Korea Mobile Telecomm.)	Telecommunications	27-Jun-96	X	X
Pohang Iron & Steel Co., Ltd.	Steel production	14-Oct-94	X	X
Liberia (1 non-ADR company)				
Royal Caribbean Cruises Ltd.	Cruise lines	28-Apr-93		X
Luxembourg (1 ADR company)				
Espírito Santo Financial Holding, S.A.	Holding co./financial Sservices	30-Jun-93	X	X
Mexico (25 ADR companies)				
Altos Hornos de Mexico, S.A. de C.V. (AHMSA)	Steel manufacture/distribution	11-Dec-96	X	
Bufete Industrial, S.A.	Engineering/construction	4-Nov-93	X	X
Coca-Cola FEMSA, S.A. de C.V.	Bottling/soft drinks prod.	14-Sep-93	X	X
Consorcio G Grupo Dina, S.A. de C.V.	Truck/bus manufacturing	31-Mar-93	X	X
Consorcio G Grupo Dina, S.A. de C.V. (Ser. L)	Truck/bus manufacturing	8-Aug-94	X	
Controladora Comercial Mexicana, S.A. de C.V.	Holding co./retail/restaurant	11-Oct-96	X†	X
Desc, S.A. de C.V.	Holding co./prod. mfg./fin. services	14-Jul-94	X	X
Empresas ICA-Sociedad Controladora, S.A. de C.V.	Construction	9-Apr-92	X	X
Empresas la Moderna, S.A. de C.V.	Cigarette production	2-Feb-94	X	X
Grupo Casa Autrey, S.A. de C.V.	Pharmaceutical/food prod. dist.	7-Dec-93	X	X
Grupo Elektra, S.A. de C.V.	Electronics	5-Dec-94	X†	
Grupo Financiero Serfin, S.A.	Holding co./financial services	1-Dec-93	X	X
Grupo Imsa, S.A. de C.V. (IMSA)	Steel processing/auto. batteries	11-Dec-96	X	X
Grupo Industrial Durango, S.A. de C.V.	Forest products	15-Jul-94	X	X
Grupo Industrial Maseca, S.A. de C.V.	Corn flour production	17-May-94	X	
Grupo Iusacell, S.A. de C.V. (Series L)	Wireless telecommunication	15-Jun-94	X	X
Grupo Iusacell, S.A. de C.V. (Series D)	Wireless telecommunication	15-Jun-94	X	
Grupo Mexicano de Desarrollo, S.A. de C.V. (Ser. L)	Construction	14-Dec-93	X	X
Grupo Mexicano de Desarrollo, S.A. de C.V. (Ser. B)	Construction	14-Dec-93	X	
Grupo Radio Centro, S.A. de C.V.	Radio broadcasting	1-Jul-93	X	X
Grupo Televisa, S.A.	Media	14-Dec-93	X†	X
Grupo Tribasa, S.A. de C.V.	Construction	22-Sep-93	X	X
Internacional de Ceramica, S.A. de C.V.	Ceramic tile mfg./dist.	8-Dec-94	X	X
Pepsi-Gemex, S.A. de C.V. (Formerly Grupo Embotellador)	Bottling	29-Mar-94	X†	X
Telefonos de Mexico, S.A. de C.V.	Telecommunication services	14-May-91	X	

Appendix 1 *continued*

Common stocks or ADRs representing common stocks of non-US companies listed on the New York Stock Exchange (as of 15 August 1997) *continued*

Company	Industry	Listed	ADR	IPO
Transportacion Maritima Mexicana, S.A. de C.V. (Ser. L)	Cargo shipping	10-Jun-92	X	X
Transportacion Maritima Mexicana, S.A. de C.V. (Ord.)	Cargo shipping	10-Jun-92	X	
TV Azteca, S.A.	Television broadcasting	15-Aug-97	X	X
Vitro, S.A.	Glass products mfg./mktg.	19-Nov-91	X	X
Netherlands (12 ADR /3 non-ADR companies)				
ABN AMRO Holding N.V.	Holding co./universal banking	21-May-97	X	X
AEGON N.V.	Insurance	5-Nov-91	X*	
Elsag Bailey Process Automation N.V.	Industrial technology	19-Nov-93		X
Elsevier NV	Publishing	6-Oct-94	X	
Gucci Group N.V.	Luxury apparel	24-Oct-95		X
ING Group N.V.	Holding co/diversified fin. services	13-Jun-97	X	X
Ispat International N.V.	Holding co./steel production	7-Aug-97	X	X
KLM Royal Dutch Airlines	Airline services	22-May-57	X*	
Koninklijke Ahold NV	Supermarket chains oper.	15-Nov-93	X	
New Holland N.V.	Argicultural equip. mfg./Mmktg.	1-Nov-96		X
Philips Electronics N.V.	Consumer electronics	14-Apr-87	X*	
PolyGram N.V.	Entertainment	14-Dec-89	X*	X
Royal Dutch Petroleum Company	Oil/gas poduction	20-Jul-54	X*	
Royal PTT Nederland NV	Telecommunications/postal	23-Oct-95	X	X
Unilever N.V.	Foods/commodities	12-Dec-61	X*	
New Zealand (2 ADR companies)				
Fletcher Challenge Limited (Forest Division Shares)	Forestry	13-Dec-93	X	
Fletcher Challenge Building	Construction/building materials	14-Mar-96	X	
Fletcher Challenge Energy	Oil/gas production	14-Mar-96	X	
Fletcher Challenge Paper	Pulp/paper production	14-Mar-96	X	
Telecom Corporation of New Zealand Limited	Telecommunications	17-Jul-91	X	X
Norway (5 ADR companies)				
Norsk Hydro A.S.	Natural sources product mfg.	25-Jun-86	X	
Nycomed ASA	Pharmaceuticals	14-May-96	X	X††
Petroleum Geo-Services ASA	Holding co./oil-field services	16-Apr-97	X	
Saga Petroleum a.s. (Series A)	Oil/gas exploration	28-Apr-95	X	
Saga Petroleum a.s. (Series B)	Oil/gas exploration	28-Apr-95	X	
Smedvig asa (Class A)	Offshore drilling/oil services	8-Nov-96	X	X
Smedvig asa (Class B)	Offshore drilling/oil services	8-Nov-96	X	
People's Republic of China (8 ADR companies)				
Beijing Yanhua Petrochemical Company Limited	Petrochemicals production	24-Jun-97	X	X
China Eastern Airlines Corporation Limited	Passenger airline	4-Feb-97	X	X
China Eastern Airlines Company Limited	Commercial airline services	30-Jul-97	X	X
Guangshen Railway Company Limited	Rail transportation	13-May-96	X	X
Huaneng Power International, Inc.	Holding co./power plants	6-Oct-94	X	X
Jilin Chemical Industrial Company Limited	Chemical products mfg.	22-May-95	X	X
Shandong Huaneng Power Development Co. Ltd.	Electricity generation	4-Aug-94	X	X
Shanghai Petrochemical Company Limited	Petrochemical production	26-Jul-93	X	X
Peru (3 ADR /1 non-ADR company)				
Banco Wiese Limitado	Banking	21-Sep-94	X	X
Compañía de Minas Buenaventura S.A.	Mining	15-May-96	X	X
Credicorp Ltd.	Financial services	25-Oct-95		
Telefonica del Peru S.A.	Telecommunications	2-Jul-96	X	X
Philippines (1 ADR /1 non-ADR company)				
Benguet Corporation	Mining	27-Jun-49		
Philippine Long Distance Telephone Company	Telecommunication	19-Oct-94	X	
Portugal (3 ADR companies)				
Banco Comercial Portugues, S.A.	Banking	12-Jun-92	X	X
Electricidade de Portugal, S.A.	Electricity production/distribution	17-Jun-97	X	X
Portugal Telecom, S.A.	Telecommunication	2-Jun-95	X	X
Russian Federation (1 ADR company)				
Vimpel-Communications	Telecommunications	15-Nov-96	X	X
Singapore (1 ADR /3 non-ADR companies)				
Asia Pacific Resources International Holdings Ltd.	Holding co./pulp/paper prod.	6-Apr-95		X
Asia Pacific Wire & Cable Corporation Limited	Telecommunications prods. mgf.	26-Mar-97		X
Asia Pulp & Paper Company Ltd	Pulp/paper production	7-Apr-95	X	X
China Yuchai International Limited	Holding co./diesel engines mfg.	16-Dec-94		X
Spain (7 common ADR companies)				
Argentaria-Corporacion Bancaria de España, S.A.	Banking	12-May-93	X	X
Banco Bilbao Vizcaya, S.A.	Banking	14-Dec-88	X	X
Banco Central Hispanoamericano, S.A.	Banking	20-Jul-83	X	
Banco de Santander, S.A.	Banking	30-Jul-87	X	X

Appendix 1 *continued*

Common stocks or ADRs representing common stocks of non-US companies listed on the New York Stock Exchange (as of 15 August 1997) *continued*

Company	Industry	Listed	ADR	IPO
Empresa Nacional de Electricidad, S.A.	Electric utility	1-Jun-88	X	X
Repsol, S.A.	Oil/gas refining/marketing	11-May-89	X	X
Telefónica de España, S.A.	Telecommunications	12-Jun-87	X	X
Sweden (2 ADR companies)				
Astra AB (Class A)	Pharmaceutical mfg./mktg.	23-May-96	X	
Astra AB (Class B)	Pharmaceutical mfg./mktg.	23-May-96	X	
Scania AB (Series A)	Heavy vehicle production	1-Apr-96	X	X
Scania AB (Series B)	Heavy vehicle production	1-Apr-96	X	
Switzerland (1 ADR company)				
TAG Heuer International SA	Sports watch design/mgf./mktg.	27-Sep-96	X	X
United Kingdom (43 common ADR companies)				
AMVESCO PLC (Formerly INVESCO PLC, IVC)	Investment management	25-Aug-95	X	X
Barclays Bank PLC	Banking	9-Sep-86	X	
Bass Public Limited Company	Brewing/hotel operation	8-Feb-90	X	
BG plc (Formerly British Gas Public Limited Company)	Natural gas distribution	8-Dec-86	X	
BOC Group plc (The)	Diversified chemicals	18-Sep-96	X	
British Airways Plc	Airline services	11-Feb-87	X	X
British Petroleum Company P.L.C. (The)	Petroleum refining/mktg.	23-Mar-70	X	
British Sky Broadcasting Group Plc	Broadcasting services	8-Dec-94	X	X
British Steel Plc	Steel mfg./dist.	5-Dec-88	X	X
British Telecommunications Plc	Telecommunications	3-Dec-84	X	
Cable & Wireless Telecommunications plc	Telecommunications	28-Apr-97	X	
Cable and Wireless Plc	Telecommunications	27-Sep-89	X	X
Cadbury Schweppes plc	Beverage/confectionary prod.	2-May-96	X	
Central Transport Rental Group plc	Transport equipment leasing	1-Oct-91	X	
Cordiant PLC	Advertising services	8-Dec-87	X	
DONCASTERS plc	Aerospace equipment mfg.	30-Jan-97	X	X
Energy Group PLC (The)	Energy and related services	24-Feb-97	X	
Enterprise Oil Plc	Oil/gas exploration/prod.	16-Oct-92	X	
Gallaher Group Plc	Tobacco manufacture/marketing	30-May-97	X	
Glaxo Wellcome plc	Pharmaceuticals	10-Jun-87	X	
Grand Metropolitan Public Limited Company	Food/beverage	13-Mar-91	X	
Hanson Plc	Industrial management	3-Nov-86	X	
Huntingdon Life Sciences Group Plc (formerly Huntingdon International.)	Bio./eng./chemical services	16-Feb-89	X	
Imperial Chemical Industries PLC	Industrial chemicals mfg.	1-Nov-83	X	
LASMO plc	Oil/gas exploration/prod.	8-Jun-93	X	
LucasVarity plc	Electronics	6-Sep-96	X	
Medeva plc	Pharmaceuticals	5-Mar-97	X	
National Power PLC	Electricity generation	6-Mar-95	X	X
National Westminster Bank Plc	Banking	22-Oct-86	X	
PowerGen plc	Electricity generation	6-Mar-95	X	X
Premier Farnell plc	Electronic components distribution	12-Apr-96	X	
Reed International P.L.C.	Holding co./publishing/info. services	6-Oct-94	X	
RTZ Corporation Plc (The)	Mining	28-Jun-90	X	
Sedgwick Group Plc	Insurance	2-Jun-97	X	
Shell Transport and Trading Company, P.L.C. (The)	Oil/gas exploration/dist.	13-Mar-57	X	
SmithKline Beecham plc	Pharmaceuticals	21-Jun-89	X	
Tomkins PLC	Industrial management	21-Feb-95	X	
Unilever PLC	Food/commodities	12-Dec-61	X	
Unionamerica Holdings plc	Casualty/property reinsurer	6-Dec-95	X	X
Vodafone Group Public Limited Company	Mobile telecommunications	26-Oct-88	X	
Waste Management International plc	Environmental service	7-Apr-92	X	X
Willis Corroon Plc	Insurance	9-Oct-90	X	
Zeneca Group PLC	Pharmaceuticals	12-May-93	X	
Venezuela (2 ADR companies)				
Compania Anonima Nacional Telefonos de Venezuela (CANTV)	Telecommunications services	22-Nov-96	X	X
Mavesa, S.A.	Food/household items mfg./mktg	7-Jan-97	X	

†† Predecessor Parent, Hafslund Nycomed, list date: 24 June 1992.
* Series A, list date 16 October 1989, removed 16 October 1996.

Source: New York Stock Exchange

Appendix 2
List of interviewees

I would like to acknowledge the contribution of the people listed below. Whilst the majority have been interviewed on a one-one-basis, some have been informally consulted and others have made important contributions by supplying information or reading and correcting consecutive drafts of the manuscript. I also want to express my sincere appreciation to those people who have assisted off the record and who have expressly asked not to be included in this list.

The interviews were conducted during 1995, 1996 and 1997. The titles reflect in the first instance the positions and titles held at the time of interview. In most cases, where people have moved on, the positions most relevant to the book have been reflected rather than the position held at the time of the interview or the most recent position. This list is consequently not an attempt to reflect the current (as per October, 1997) positions held by all the interviewees. In the text itself, however, the current positions of people interviewed are reflected where this seems particularly relevant.

Name	Christian name	Title	Company/organisation
Adami	Dr. Manfred	Member of the Executive Board, responsible for Asset Management	Credit Suisse, Zürich
Ahlers	Sabine	Senior Manager, Investor Relations	Daimler Benz
Aitken-Davies	Richard	Privatisation Director	Railtrack Plc
Albertini	William O.	Executive Vice President and Chief Financial Officer	Bell Atlantic Corporation
Allouche	Philippe	Adjoint Chef du Bureau	Ministère de l'Economie, Direction du Trésor, Paris
Alonso Rivas	Andres	Adviser	National Energy Commission, Santiago
Alt	Anthony	Director	N.M. Rothschild & Co, London
Amethier	Jan	Special Adviser	Ministry of Industry and Commerce, Stockholm
Anderson	David	Managing Director, Investment Banking	CSFB, New York
Ang	Eric	Senior Vice President, Investment Banking	DBS Bank, Singapore
Anserini	Giorgio	Head of Investor Relations	ENI
Asprem	Mads	Executive Director, Equity Research	Morgan Stanley, London
Atkinson	Simon	Vice President, Senior Credit Officer	Moody's Investors Service, London
Austin	Jeremy	Analyst, Programmer	Datastream
Azzimondi	Andrea	Vice President, Equity Research	CSFB, London
Bailey	Jeremy W.	Director, Corporate Finance	S.G. Warburg & Co, London
Banks	Lawrence	Vice Chairman	Robert Fleming, London
Barker	Daniel J.	Vice President – Portfolio Manager – International Equities	GE Investments, London
Barnasconi	Simon	Vice President, Equity Syndicate	ABN AMRO, Amsterdam
Barroero	Julio Domingo	Head of Asset Management	Banco General de Negocios, Buenos Aires
Bayless	Robert	Chief Accountant, Division of Corporation Finance	Securities & Exchange Commission, Washington D.C.
Beardmore-Gray	Matthew	Director	PPM Worldwide (Prudential Portfolio Managers), London
Bènèzit	Christian	Director	Lazard Capital Markets, Paris
Benson	Lennart	Head of International Sales	Carnegie Asset Management, Stockholm
Berchtold	Walter	Member of Senior Management, Head of Security Trading and Sales	Credit Suisse, Zürich
Bergendahl	Johan	Managing Director, Investment Banking	JP Morgan, London
Bergengren	Tore	Partner	Bank Lips AG, Zürich
Bergsma	Dr. Syb	Executive Vice President, Financial Affairs	Akzo Nobel
Bernabè	Franco	Chief Executive Officer	ENI
Bernard	Bruno	Executive, European Equity Capital Markets	Paribas Capital Markets, London
Berryer	Nicolas	Corporate Finance Executive	BNP, London
Betting	Andre	Project coordinator, Flotation	Ministry of Transport, the Netherlands
Birdt	Stuart J.	Executive Director, International Equity Research,	Goldman Sachs, London
Blaschke	Dr. Andreas	Group Treasurer	Mayr-Melnhof Karton
Blomberg	Jan	Chief Financial Officer	Pharmacia
Bogle	Harold	Managing Director, Former Head of European Equity Capital Markets	CSFB, London
Bolwell	Farley	Managing Director, Equity Capital Markets	Merrill Lynch, London
Bott	Richard H.	Managing Director, Investment Banking	CSFB, New York
Bourne	Tony	Global Head of Equity	Paribas Capital Markets, London
Brabers	Jeroen	Secretary KPN Steering Group Floatation	KPN
Bradley	Philip	Director, Investment Banking	Robert Fleming, London
Braisey	Andrew	Associate Director	Swiss Bank Corporation, London

Brandt	Martin	Associate Director	Enskilda Corporate Finance, Stockholm
Brau	Kevin	Director, Equity Research	CSFB, London
Bridger	Cedric	Vice President Finance and Corporate Development	YPF
Broadhurst	Norman	Finance Director	Railtrack
Broadley	Mark	Director	HSBC Corporate Finance, Hong-Kong
Brodin	Thomas	Director, Equity Research	Salomon Brothers, London
Brooks	Anthony	Managing Director, Head of European Equities	Lehman Brothers, London
Brown	Stephen	Group Head of Research	Hoare Govett Asia, Hong-Kong
Bruns	Dr. Hans-Georg	Senior Vice President, Financial Disclosure and Reporting, Investor Relations and Accounting	Daimler Benz
Bucalossi	Annalisa	-	Bank of Italy, London
Bunting	Tim	Executive Director, Equity Capital Markets	Goldman Sachs, London
Bush	Harry	Head of Privatisation	H.M. Treasury, United Kingdom
Caillaux	Rémy	Head of French Investment Banking,	Banque Paribas, Paris
Campbell	Ross	Chief Financial Officer	Telecom Corporation of New Zealand
Capo	Thomas P.	Vice President -Treasurer	Chrysler Corporation
Carney	Sean	Director, Investment Banking	Merrill Lynch, London
Carter	Christopher	Managing Director, Head of Global Equity Capital Markets	CSFB, New York
Cavallo	Domingo	Minister of the Economy	Republic of Argentina
Chandler	Edward	Director, Corporate Finance	SG Warburg & Co, London
Chen	Sunny	Managing Director	W.I Carr (Far East) Limited, Taipei
Christie	Denis	Director, Equity Research	Dresdner Kleinwort Benson, London
Chu	Cherry	Associate, Corporate Finance	Goldman Sachs, Hong-Kong
Chui-Zon	Hon	Chief Manager	Securities & Exchange Commission, Ministry of Finance, Taipei
Chung	L.M	Chief Financial Officer	China Steel Corporation
Cicchetti	Claude C.	Director, Institutional Asset Management	Swiss Bank Corporation, Basle
Clark	James F.	Managing Director, Equity Research	CSFB, New York
Clark	Peter	-	International Accounting Standards Board
Clarke	Alvaro	Adviser to the Minister of Finance	Ministry of Finance, Santiago
Clausson	Olof	Counsel	Rogers & Wells, London
Colas	Nicholas J.	Director, Equity Research	CSFB, New York
Colin	Harry	Company Secretary	Nokia
Cooney	Robert	Managing Director, Equity Capital Markets	CSFB, New York
Corbett, CBE	Graham	Chief Financial Officer	Eurotunnel
Cotton	Annabel	Investor Relations Manager	Telecom Corporation of New Zealand
Couch	Andrew	Fund manager	Guiness Flight Hambro Asset Management, London
Cox	James M.	Director	Schroder Investment Management, London
Crawford	Peter D	Executive Director, Investor Relations	Bell Atlantic Corporation
Crawford	Andrew	Partner	Cameron Markby Hewitt
Crichton	Bob	Assistant Treasurer, Director of Corporate Finance	Ameritech
Cruz	Ernesto	Managing Director, Head of US Equity Capital Markets	CSFB, New York
Cruz Zabala	Ignacio	Managing Director	Excel Chile
Czepliewicz	Matthew	Director, Equity Research	Salomon Brothers, London
Daly	Larissa	Latin American Strategist	ING Barings, London
Dan	Lu	Director	Shandong Huaneng Power Development Corporation
Daviron	Pierre	President	Oppenheimer Capital International, New York
Davy	Robert G.	Director	Schroder Capital Management International, London
de Jager	Menno	Senior Vice President, Equity Capital Markets	ABN AMRO, Amsterdam
de las Morenas López	Carmelo	Finance Director	Repsol
De Nevares	Rodolfo	Vice President, Capital Markets	Banco General de Negocios, Buenos Aires
de Veer	Robert K.	Managing Director, Investment Banking	CSFB, New York
de Verdier	Jonas	Director	Maizels, Westerberg & Co, London
Dellsperger	Peter	Head of Investment Research	Credit Suisse, Zürich
Dempsey	Joe	Executive Director, Investment Banking	Goldman Sachs, New York
Dennert	Jürgen	Head of Equity Capital Markets	IMI Sigeco Sim, Rome
Denoon Duncan	Russel	Senior Partner	Cameron Markby Hewitt
Dial	Douglas A.	Equity Portfolio Manager	College Retirement Equities Fund, New York
Dixon	David	Executive, European Equity Capital Markets	Paribas Capital Markets, London
Dobie	Clare	Director	BZW Investment Management, London
Dobkin	Eric	Partner, Global Head of Equity Capital Markets	Goldman Sachs, New York
Doft	Michael	Financial Analyst, Investor Relations Department	General Motors
Downing	John	Partner, Equity Capital Markets	Goldman Sachs, New York
Draghi	Prof. Mario	Director General	Ministry of the Treasury, Rome
Dulá	Sonia L.	Vice President, Investment Banking	Goldman Sachs, New York
Ekman	Jan	Member of the Board of Directors	Waste Management International, London
Elwing	Fredrik	Senior Vice President, Private Client Services	Lehman Brothers, London

Erbe	Henry H.	Senior Vice President, Equity Capital Markets	Lehman Brothers, New York
Estela	Jorge A.	Investor Relations Manager	YPF
Evans	Mark	Partner, Head of Non-Japan Asia	Goldman Sachs, Hong-Kong
Evans	J. Michael	Partner, Head of European Equity Capital Markets	Goldman Sachs, London
Evans	Michelle	Equity Research Analyst	James Capel, London
Ewerlöf	Johan	Executive Director, Head of Pan – European Equity Distribution	SBC Warburg Dillon Read, London
Falgas	José	Vice President, Investment Banking	Merrill Lynch, New York
Fanjul	Oscar	Chairman and Chief Executive	Repsol
Fermoso	Inés	Adviser to Under-Secretary for Banking and Insurance	Ministry of the Economy, Buenos Aires
Finn	Brian	Managing Director, Head of Mergers & Acquisitions	CSFB, New York
Fleuriet	Michel	President	Merrill Lynch France
Foulkes	Richard R.	Executive Vice President	Schroder Capital Management International, London
Franceschi	Jean-Marc	Secretariat Financier	BNP-BFI, Paris
Frank	Frederick	Vice Chairman	Lehman Brothers, New York
Frauenfelder	Dr. Eduard	Vizedirektor, Finanzstudien International	Bank Julius Bär, Zürich
Fraysse	Jean-Marc	Director	Cazenove Unit Trust Management, London
Fremont-Smith	Matthew T.	Vice President, Investment Banking	Goldman Sachs, Singapore
French	Christopher G.	Managing Director, Investment Banking	Goldman Sachs, London
Freud	David	Managing Director, Corporate Finance	SBC Warburg Dillon Read, London
Garcia	Anthony T.	Senior Vice President, Strategic Advisory	Lehman Brothers, New York
Garett	Greg	Vice President	Scudder Stevens Clark, New York
Garrud	Pamela	Investment Consultant	William M. Mercer, London
Gerraden	Maria Isabel	Under-Secretary	Ministry of Energy, Santiago
Giacopazzi	Mark	Head of Research	Carnegie Espana, Madrid
Giavazzi	Prof. Francesco	Former Head of Italian Privatisation	Ministry of the Treasury, Rome
Gibbs	Sir Roger	Chairman	The Wellcome Trust
Gilfond	Santiago	Associate, Equity Capital Markets	CSFB, New York
Ginman-Jones	Charlotta	Associate, Corporate Finance	SBC Warburg, London
Giorgianni	Francesco	Solicitor	Ministry of the Treasury, Rome
Goess – Sarau	Carl Anton	Chairman of the Supervisory Board	Mayr-Melnhof Karton
Goess – Sarau	Clemens	Member of the Supervisory Board	Mayr-Melnhof Karton
Goiri	Isabel	Director	Schroder Investment Management, London
Gómez Roldán	Francisco	Chief Executive Officer	Argentaria, Madrid
Graham	Stephen H.	Vice President, Equity Research	CSFB, New York
Grant	Michael	Treasurer	Eurotunnel
Grantham	Jeremy	Partner	Grantham, Mayo, van Otterloo & Co., Boston
Greaves	Mark	Managing Director	NM Rothschild, Singapore
Greco	Ernesto	Chief Financial Officer	Bulgari
Griffioen	Cees	Chief Financial Officer	KPN
Grilli	Prof. Vittorio	Head of Privatisation and Debt Management	Ministry of the Treasury, Rome
Grinstead	Verne	Executive Director	Lazard Capital Markets, London
Gröller	Michael	Chief Executive Officer	Mayr-Melnhof Karton
Gu	Sam X.	Vice President, Investment Banking	CSFB, Beijing
Guillaume	Jean-Marie	Co-head, Equity Capital Markets	BNP, Paris
Gurtner	Max	Head of Investor Relations	F. Hoffman – La Roche AG
Gutbrod	Dr. Jochen	Manager	Schroder Investment Management, London
Haggerty	Gretchen R.	Vice President – Treasurer	USX Corporation
Hahn	John C.	Executive Director, Investment Banking	Morgan Stanley, New York
Hammar	Bengt	Managing Director, Investment Banking	BZW, London
Hampel	Sir Ronald	Chairman	ICI
Hannam	Ian	Director, Capital Markets	Robert Fleming, London
Heald	Richard	Managing Director	ABN AMRO Rothschild, London
Hehir	Brian	Managing Director, Global Co-head of Equity Capital Markets	Merrill Lynch, New York
Heider	Dr. Manfred	General Secretary	Vienna Stock Exchange
Heinesen	Knud	Chairman	Tele Danmark
Henderson	Sir Denys	Former Chairman	ICI
Hermon	Colin	Director, Head of Capital Markets Asia	Jardine Fleming Securities, Hong-Kong
Hernandez	Robert M.	Vice Chairman and Chief Financial Officer	USX Corporation
Hiaojing	Fu	Corporate Secretary	Huaneng Power Generation Corporation, Beijing
Higgs	Derek	Vice Chairman	SG Warburg Group, London
Ho Siew Wah	William	Director, Head of Project Finance, Capital Markets Group	Standard Chartered Markets, Singapore
Hodgson	Michael	-	Citywatch, London
Hörmanseder	Dr. Wilhelm	Chief Financial Officer	Mayr-Melnhof Karton
Howard	Alan H.	Managing Director, Investment Banking	CSFB, New York
Howland	Doug	Executive Director, Equity Capital Markets	Goldman Sachs, London
Hu	L.R.	Assistant Vice President	China Steel Corporation
Hultin	Anders	Head of Corporate Finance	Carnegie & Co, Stockholm
Hurd	David P.	Senior Analyst, Chile	Smith New Court, Santiago

Hurst-Brown	Nigel	Chairman	Warburg Asset Management, London
Hyman	John	Executive Director, Equity Capital Markets	Morgan Stanley, London
Iarezza	Juan C.	Head of Investment Banking	Banco General de Negocios, Buenos Aires
Inselbuch	Adam	Director, Investment Banking	CSFB, New York
Isoz	Jan	Vice President, Investor Relations	Pharmacia
James	Ulla	Assistant Vice President, Investor Relations	Nokia
Jaubert	Pascal	Director and Head of Primary Market	Crédit Lyonnais, Paris
Jennings	Robert	Executive Director, Corporate Finance	SBC Warburg Dillon Read, London
Jensen	John	Managing Director, Equity Capital Markets	Merrill Lynch, London
Jiang	Quek How	Press Officer	Monetary Authority of Singapore
Johansen	Lars	Financial Consultant	Johansen & Co, Copenhagen
Johansson	Jerker	Managing Director, Head of European Equity Capital Markets	Morgan Stanley, London
Jones	Garri W.	Associate, UK Equity Sales	Goldman Sachs, London
Jones	Howard	Co-head European Equity Capital Markets	Paribas Capital Markets, London
Jones	Huw	Director, Corporate Finance	Prudential Portfolio Managers, London
Joshua	John	Privatisation Team	H.M. Treasury, United Kingdom
Kahn	David	Manager	ABN AMRO Rothschild, London
Kallasvuo	Olli-Pekka	Chief Financial Officer	Nokia
Kao	Anne	Equity Research Analyst	CSFB, Hong-Kong
Kay	Lawrence Y.	Director, Investor Relations	IMI, Rome
Keelan	Brian	Managing Director, Corporate Finance	Swiss Bank Corporation, London
Kent	Claire A.	Executive Director, Equity Research	Morgan Stanley, London
Killer	Réne J.	Member of Senior Management, Asset Management	Credit Suisse, Zürich
King	Peter	Partner	Linklaters & Paines, London
Kingzett	Jan	Director	Schroder Investment Management, London
Kirwan-Taylor	Charles P.	Managing Director, Corporate Finance	BZW, London
Kjerulf	Dan	Vice President, Investment Banking	Den Danske Bank, Copenhagen
Klaus	Erich	Senior Manager, Financial Reporting and Disclosure	Daimler Benz
Kneisel	William	Managing Director, Head of Global Equity Capital Markets	Morgan Stanley, New York
Koenig	James E.	Finance Director	Waste Management International, London
Korff	Phyllis	Partner	Skadden, Arps, Slate, Meagher & Flom, New York
Korhonen	Johanna	Market Information Department	Helsinki Stock Exchange
Krähenmann	Annette	Investor Relations Officer	F. Hoffman – La Roche AG
Kunz	Heidi	Treasurer	General Motors
Kurz	Peter	Director of North Asia Research	Baring Securities, Taipei
Laffitte	Michel	Chef Du Bureau	Ministère de l'Economie, Direction du Trésor, Paris
LaFleur	Robert A	Senior Vice President and Chief Investment Strategist	Northern Trust
Lauer	Friedrich	Vice President, Financial Reporting and Disclosure	Daimler Benz
Le Gouvello	Tanguy	Partner	Lazard Freres & Cie
Le Pan de Ligny	Bertrand	Investment Manager & Founder partner	Silchester International Investors, London
Lee	Paul J.D.	Section Chief	Securities & Exchange Commission, Ministry of Finance, Taipei
Lei	Ph.D., Chung-Dar Paul	Senior Economist, Department of Foreign Exchange	Central Bank of China, Taipei
Leigh-Pemberton	James	Managing Director, Head of European Equity Capital Markets	CSFB, London
Lemonius	Lars	Associate, International Equities	Morgan Stanley, London
Leroy	Françoise	Head of Capital Markets and Financing Division	Elf Acquitaine
Lesser	Jorge	Chief Financial Officer	Endesa
Lewin	Walter M.	Associate Director, Equity Capital Markets	Swiss Bank Corporation, London
Lewis	Charles A.	Vice Chairman, Investment Banking	Merrill Lynch, Chicago
Li	Dr. Simon F. S.	Vice Chairman, Hong-Kong Special Administrative Region Preparatory Committee	Hong-Kong
Liendo	Dr. Horacio Tomas	Deputy Secretary	Ministry of the Economy, Buenos Aires
Liener	Dr. Gerhard	Chief Financial Officer	Daimler Benz
Lilienfeld	Alejandro	Director of Companies	Buenos Aires
Lilja	Mari	Manager, Nordic Equities	Dresdner Kleinwort Benson, London
Lim	Quek Pek	Director	PrimeEast Capital Group, Singapore
Lin	Allen J	Senior Manager, Underwriting Department	Chinatrust Commercial Bank, Taipei
Lindholm	Sten	Senior Vice President, Corporate Communications	SCA, Stockholm
Llambias	Daniel	General Manager, Wholesale Division	Banco de Galicia, Buenos Aires
Lönnberg	Anne-Maj	Executive Assistant, Investor Relations	Nokia
Lowe	Stephen W.	Director, US equities	Gartmore, London
Lowe	Gary	Director, US Equity Investment	Mercury Asset Management, London
Lu	James	Assistant Vice President, Research Department	Peregrine Securities, Taipei
Lukas	Edmund	Vice President, International Business Development	New York Stock Exchange
Lundgren	Hans	Under-secretary for Planning	Ministry of Industry and Commerce, Stockholm
Machin	Mark G.A.	Executive Director, Equity Capital Markets	Goldman Sachs, Hong-Kong

Macnamara	Rory P.	Director	Morgan Grenfell, London
Madsen	Thomas P.	Managing Director	JP Morgan Investment Management, London
Mallinckrodt	Philip	Managing Director, Equity Capital Markets	CSFB, London
Mallinson	Peter G. C.	Partner, Equity Capital Markets	Goldman Sachs, Hong-Kong
Mañas Antón	Luis	Deputy Chief Financial Officer	Repsol
Marbacher	Josef	Chief Economist and Chief Strategist	Bank Julius Bär, Zürich
Marshall	Jorge	Vice President	Central Bank of Chile
Marshall	Paul	Director, European Equity Investment	Mercury Asset Management, London
Martin	Cary	Chief Executive Officer	Dewe Rogerson, London
Marx	Daniel	Under-Secretary for Finance	Ministry of the Economy, Buenos Aires
Mathieu	Beau	Managing Director, Investment Banking	CSFB, London
Maugeri	Leonardo	Assistant to the Chief Executive Officer and Managing Director	ENI
Maxwell-Arnot	Patricia	Managing Director and Head of European Equities	Credit Suisse Asset Management, London
Mayo	John	Finance Director	Zeneca
Mazzacurati	Chantal	Head of Global Equities	BNP, Paris
Mc Elroy	John	Director, Corporate Finance	SBC Warburg Dillon Read, New York
Mc Nish	Michael	Executive Director, Corporate Finance	SBC Warburg, London
Meier	Dr. Henri B.	Chief Financial Officer and Member of the Executive Committee	F. Hoffman – La Roche AG
Meissner	Christian	Associate, Equity Capital Markets	Goldman Sachs, London
Melliger	Eugen	Member of the Senior Management, Asset Management	Credit Suisse, Zürich
Merriam	Jill	Analyst, Equity Capital Markets	CSFB, London
Middleton	Lindsay	Solicitor	Linklaters & Paines, London
Miller	Sandy	Privatisation Team	H.M. Treasury, United Kingdom
Miller	James F.	Managing Director, Equity Capital Markets	Merrill Lynch, New York
Millman	Stewart	Managing Director, Investment Banking	Natwest Markets, London
Mitra	Robin	First Vice President, Equity Research	Merrill Lynch, London
Molinar	Cees	Investment Manager	Delta Lloyd Investments, Amsterdam
Molkhou	Brigitte	Chef du Bureau	Ministère de l'Economie, Direction du Trésor
Molnár	Dr. Attila	Director, Head Portfolio Management, Private Clients Switzerland	Swiss Bank Corporation, Basle
Molson	Ian	Managing Director, Head of Capital Markets	CSFB, London
Montero V.	Jaime	Investor Relations Director	Endesa
Morante	Andrea	Managing Director, Investment Banking	CSFB, London
Moreno	Jacobo	Director of Financial Analysis	Argentaria, Madrid
Morgan	Philip	European Equity Research	Paribas Capital Markets, London
Morris III	Robert	Partner, International Equity Research	Goldman Sachs, London
Morse	Richard	Director, Corporate Finance	Dresdner Kleinwort Benson, London
Mosler	Matthias R.	Executive Director, Equity Capital Markets	Goldman Sachs, London
Mulford	David	Chairman, CSFB Europe	CSFB, London
Munk Nielsen	Hans	Group Managing Director, Chief Financial Officer	Tele Danmark
Murphy	Robert	Associate	JP Morgan Investment Management, London
Musulin	Dr. Marko	Director, Capital Markets & Investment Banking	Creditanstalt – Bankverein, Vienna
Nairn	Dr. Sandy	Director, Global Equity Research	Templeton Worldwide, Edinburgh
Nathan	Saul	Executive Director, Equity Capital Markets	Morgan Stanley, New York
Neyens	Frank	Managing Director, Equity Capital Markets	CSFB, London
Ng	Siew Mun	Managing Director, Investment Banking	CSFB, Singapore
Nicelli	Gian Marco	Manager, Equity Capital Markets	IMI Sigeco Sim, Milan
Niederer	Ulrich	Executive Director, Head of Institutional Asset Management	Swiss Bank Corporation, Basle
Northrop	Anthony	Managing Director	Lazard Brothers, London
Nyrén	Anders	Chief Financial Officer	Securum, Stockholm
O'Brien	H.	-	PPI This Week, Brussels
Olgiati	Susana	Alternate Financial Representative	Office of the Financial Representative of the Argentina Republic for Europe, London
Orrgard	Michael	Director	Enskilda Corporate Finance, Stockholm
Ousbäck	Lars	Investor Relations Officer	Pharmacia
Palmeri	Chiara	Analyst, Equity Capital Markets	Morgan Stanley, London
Panikar	Mathew	Managing Director	Reliance Europe, London
Pawel	Elizabeth T.	Director, Technology Investment Banking	Cowen & Company, New York
Pehlke	Richard	Treasurer	Ameritech
Pendock	Julian	Analyst	BZW, London
Persson	Ulf	Statistics Officer	Stockholm Stock Exchange
Peyrouse	Jane V.	Vice President	Wellington Management Company, Boston
Phillips	Alexander	Associate, Equity Capital Markets	CSFB, London
Pickford	Emma	-	Dewe Rogerson
Pillonel	Philip	Vice President, Investment Banking	Merrill Lynch, London
Plaxton	John	Director, Investment Banking	Merrill Lynch, London
Plou	Jean-Michel	First Vice President, Equity New Issues	Banque Indosuez, Paris
Porter	John	Associate, Equity Capital Markets	Morgan Stanley, London
Putnam	Bluford H.	President	CDC Investment Management Corporation
Ravery	Pascal J.F.	Managing Director, Investment Banking	JP Morgan, Paris
Reca	Guillermo	President	Merrill Lynch Argentina

Regan	Anthony W.	Chief Investment Officer, International Equities	Putnam Investments, London
Regli	Philip	Chargè de Mission	BNP, Paris
Richards	Dr. Albert	Managing Director & Head of European Equity Research	Salomon Brothers, London
Ritsholm	Mogens	Senior Engineer	Ministry of Research, Copenhagen
Robb	John	Chairman and Chief Executive Officer	Wellcome Plc
Robson	Steve	Director, Finance, Regulation and Industry	H.M. Treasury, United Kingdom
Romeri	Gabriela	Research Director	Baring Securities, Buenos Aires
Roscini	Dante	Managing Director, Equity Capital Markets	Goldman Sachs, London
Rostung	Henning	Senior Vice President, Head of Investor Relations	Tele Danmark
Ruigómez Sánchez	Luis	Deputy General Manager	BBV Interactivos, Madrid
Ruiz	Roberto M.	Vice Chairman	CCI Capital Investors, Buenos Aires
Russell	Nigel J	Principal	NJR Research, Edinburgh
Ryan	Philip K.	Managing Director, Investment Banking	CSFB, New York
Ryan	Michael P	Managing Director, Co-Head Global Equity Capital Markets	Merrill Lynch, London
Sainz	Jose	Chief Executive Officer	Argentaria Banco de Negocios, Madrid
Sandelin	Martin	Vice President, Investor Relations	Nokia
Sassoon	James M.	Managing Director, Global Head of Privatisation	SBC Warburg Dillon Read, London
Schortemeier	Raymond G.	Managing Director, Investment Banking Services	New York Stock Exchange
Seligman	Mark	Director , Corporate Finance	S.G. Warburg & Co, London
Shale	Tony	Freelance Journalist	Hong-Kong
Shallcrass	Richard	Director, Commercial Relations	New Zealand Treasury
Shapera	Todd D.	Vice President	Scudder Stevens Clark, New York
Shelton	Robert A.	Analyst, Equity Capital Markets	CSFB, London
Sheridan	Dan	Head of Market Regulation	London Stock Exchange
Siddiqi	Saleem	Analyst, Equity Capital Markets	Merrill Lynch, London
Silverman	Aaron	–	Investment Company Institute, Washington D.C.
Simpson	Julie	–	Georgeson & Company Inc, London
Sock Koong	Chua	Senior Vice President, Corporate Affairs and Finance	Singapore Telecom
Sormunen	Kirsi	Treasurer	Nokia
Spingardi	Tomaso	Executive Director, Investment Banking	Morgan Stanley, London
Sposito	Claudio	Managing Director, Investment Banking	Morgan Stanley, Milan
Staehelin	Rudolf M.	Senior Vice President	Capital International, Geneva
Steinmüller	Werner	Head of Corporate and Institutional Banking	Deutsche Bank, Frankfurt
Stig Andersen	Jorgen	Deputy Permanent Secretary	Ministry of Research, Copenhagen
Stoessel	Didier	Director, Investment Banking	Merrill Lynch, London
Stonberg	Peter	Chief Investment Officer	State Street Global Advisors, Boston
Strängh	Håkan	Executive Director, German Equity Sales	Goldman Sachs, Frankfurt
Ström	Per	Head of Equity Investment	Trygg-Hansa, Stockholm
Sundling	Krister L.	Associate, Equity Capital Markets	Goldman Sachs, London
Sung	Hsueh J	Executive Director & Taiwan Representative	Goldman Sachs, Taipei
Suominen	Arja	Information Manager	Nokia
Tanner	Jürg	Vice President	Bank Julius Bär, Zürich
Tapner	Rory	Managing Director, Global Head of Equity Capital Markets	SBC Warburg Dillon Read, London
Tegnér	Per	Under Secretary	Ministry of Industry and Commerce, Stockholm
Tepper	David	Director, Investment Banking	Merrill Lynch, London
Tercek	Mark	Executive Director, Equity Capital Markets	Goldman Sachs, New York
The Rt Hon Lord Lawson	Nigel	Chairman	Central Europe Trust, London
Thompson	Maurice	Director, Head of Equity Syndication	S.G. Warburg & Co, London
Tijssen	José	Investor Relations Manager	KPN
Tobin	Jean	International & Research Department	New York Stock Exchange
Toft	Jens Peter	Executive Vice President, Investment Banking	Den Danske Bank, Copenhagen
Topper	David J.	Managing Director, Investment Banking	Morgan Stanley, New York
Trapani	Francesco	Chief Executive Officer	Bulgari
Tuft	Tom	Partner, Equity Capital Markets	Goldman Sachs, New York
Turowski	Dieter	Vice President, Investment Banking	Morgan Stanley, London
Usano Crespo	Dionisio	Head of Privatisation	SEPPA
Valcarce Durán	Mario	Deputy Finance Director	Endesa
Valdivia Bernstein	Mario	Executive Director	Excel Chile
van Heugten	Henri	Head of State Participations	Ministry of Finance, the Netherlands
van Schelle	Charles	Director of Corporate Finance	ABN AMRO Hoare Govett Corporate Finance
Villanueva	Ricardo	Investor Relations Officer	Singapore Telecom
Waldron	Julian	Executive Director, Equity Capital Markets	SBC Warburg Dillon Read, London
Walker	James A.	General Manager	Baring Securities, Santiago
Walter	Carl	Director and Chief Representative	CSFB, Beijing
Wang	Jessy	Chief Accountant and Director of International Operations	China Securities Regulatory Commission, Beijing
Wang	C.Y	Chairman	China Steel Corporation
Watt	Richard	Managing Director, International Department	BEA Associates, New York
Weisenhorn	Elisabeth	Director and Portfolio Manager, German Equities	DWS, Frankfurt

Werdelin	Ulrika	Associate, Investment Banking	Goldman Sachs, London
Werner	Jan	Executive Director, Investment Banking	Goldman Sachs, London
West	Colin	Executive Director, Equity Capital Markets	Union Bank of Switzerland, Singapore
Westerman	Matthew	Managing Director	ABN AMRO Rothschild, London
Wich	Frederick P.	Vice President, Investment Banking	Goldman Sachs, Chicago
Wiener	Ori	Director, Corporate Finance	SBC Warburg Dillon Read, London
Wijngaard	Barbara	UK Investor Relations Manager	ICI
Williams	Jenny	Director of Railways	Department of Transport, London
Wilmot – Sitwell	Peter S.	Chairman	Warburg Securities, London
Winther Nielsen	Henrik	Vice President, Investment Banking	Den Danske Bank, Copenhagen
Wisch	Steven J.	Partner, Head of Asian Equity Capital Markets	Goldman Sachs, Hong-Kong
Wong	Lucien YK	Partner	Allen & Gledhill, Singapore
Woodyatt	Miguel	Director	Galicia Capital Markets, Buenos Aires
Woolland	John L.	Executive Director, Corporate Broking	SBC Warburg Dillon Read, London
Wright	Tammy	Senior Financial Representative	USX Corporation
Wu	Chun-Huei	Stocks & Fixed Assets Section, Finance Department	China Steel Corporation
Wu	Tang-Chieh	Director, Division 1	Securities & Exchange Commission, Ministry of Finance, Taipei
Yu	M.N.	Assistant General Manager, Foreign Exchange Department	The Central Bank of China, Taipei
Yuan	Christopher	Research Manager	Peregrine Securities, Taipei
Zehnder	Hans-Ruedi	Head of Capital Markets	Credit Suisse, Zürich
Zellenrath	Mark	Media Department	KPN